Toyota Corolla Owners Workshop Manual

IM Coomber

Models covered
Toyota Corolla Sedan, Wagon, Hardtop and Liftback variants
All models with 108 cu in (1.8 liter) engine

Covers manual and automatic transmission
Does not cover front-wheel-drive models

ISBN 1 85010 239 2

Printed in England *(961-4M2)*

ABCDE
FGHI

Haynes Publishing Group
Sparkford Nr Yeovil
Somerset BA22 7JJ England

Haynes Publications, Inc
861 Lawrence Drive
Newbury Park
California 91320 USA

Library of Congress
Catalog card number
85-82096

Acknowledgements

Our thanks are due to the Toyota Motor Sales Company Limited (USA) and Toyota (GB) Limited for their assistance with technical information and the supply of certain illustrations. Castrol Limited supplied lubrication data, and the Champion Sparking Plug Company supplied the illustrations showing the various spark plug conditions.

Lastly, thanks are due to all of those people at Sparkford who helped in the production of this manual.

About this manual

Its aim

The aim of this manual is to help you get the best value from your vehicle. It can do so in several ways. It can help you decide what work must be done (even should you choose to get it done by a garage), provide information on routine maintenance and servicing, and give a logical course of action and diagnosis when random faults occur. However, it is hoped that you will use the manual by tackling the work yourself. On simpler jobs it may even be quicker than booking the car into a garage and going there twice, to leave and collect it. Perhaps most important, a lot of money can be saved by avoiding the costs a garage must charge to cover its labour and overheads.

The manual has drawings and descriptions to show the function of the various components so that their layout can be understood. Then the tasks are described and photographed in a step-by-step sequence so that even a novice can do the work.

Its arrangement

The manual is divided into twelve Chapters, each covering a logical sub-division of the vehicle. The Chapters are each divided into Sections, numbered with single figures, eg 5; and the Sections into paragraphs (or sub-sections), with decimal numbers following on from the Section they are in, eg 5.1, 5.2, 5.3 etc.

It is freely illustrated, especially in those parts where there is a detailed sequence of operations to be carried out. There are two forms of illustration: figures and photographs. The figures are numbered in sequence with decimal numbers, according to their position in the Chapter – eg Fig. 6.4 is the fourth drawing/illustration in Chapter 6. Photographs carry the same number (either individually or in related groups) as the Section or sub-section to which they relate.

There is an alphabetical index at the back of the manual as well as a contents list at the front. Each Chapter is also preceded by its own individual contents list.

References to the 'left' or 'right' of the vehicle are in the sense of a person in the driver's seat facing forwards.

Unless otherwise stated, nuts and bolts are removed by turning anti-clockwise, and tightened by turning clockwise.

Vehicle manufacturers continually make changes to specifications and recommendations, and these, when notified, are incorporated into our manuals at the earliest opportunity.

Whilst every care is taken to ensure that the information in this manual is correct, no liability can be accepted by the authors or publishers for loss, damage or injury caused by any errors in, or omissions from, the information given.

Introduction to the Toyota Corolla

A best seller in the 1970's, the Toyota Corolla continues into the 1980's with various improvements made to both body styling and mechanics.

The Corolla model range is quite comprehensive, as are the fittings and equipment on all models. There are four basic body styles available these being the two-door and four-door Saloon variants, the Estate, Liftback and Coupe variants. All models are fitted with an in-line, four cylinder, water cooled OHV engine of 1290 cc or 1588 cc, dependent on model. USA models are fitted with the 3T engine of 108 cu in (1770 cc).

A range of gearbox types is also fitted dependent on model and year. The manual gearbox types fitted are the K40 (4-speed), K50 (5-speed), the T40 (4-speed) or T50 (5-speed).

Two automatic transmission types have been fitted, the earlier UK models being fitted with the 2-speed Toyoglide transmission (type A20), whilst later UK models and all USA models are fitted with the Toyota A40 type 3-speed automatic transmission.

The front suspension is independent with MacPherson struts, coil springs and an anti-roll bar on all models. The rear suspension consists of a live axle with four-link location in conjunction with coil springs. The Estate differs at the rear in having leaf springs.

Contents

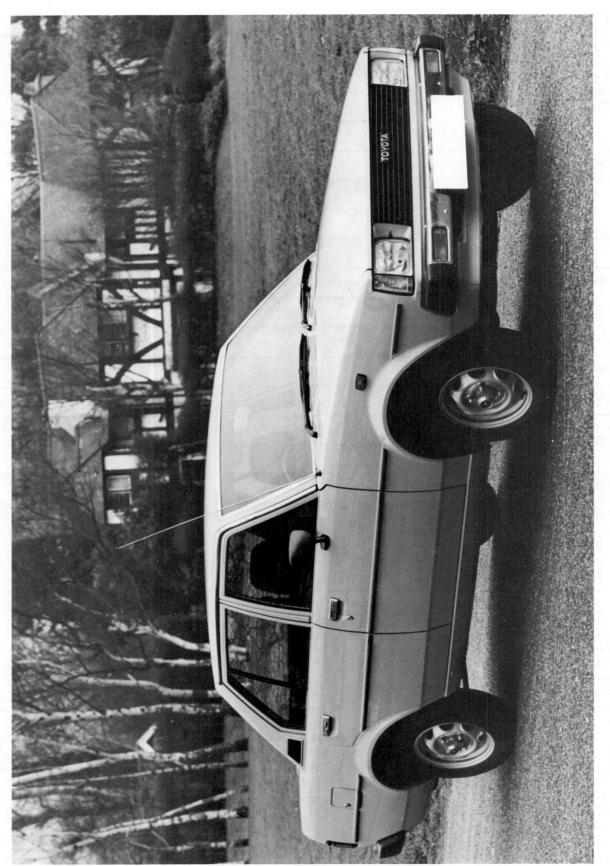

Toyota Corolla 1300 four-door Saloon

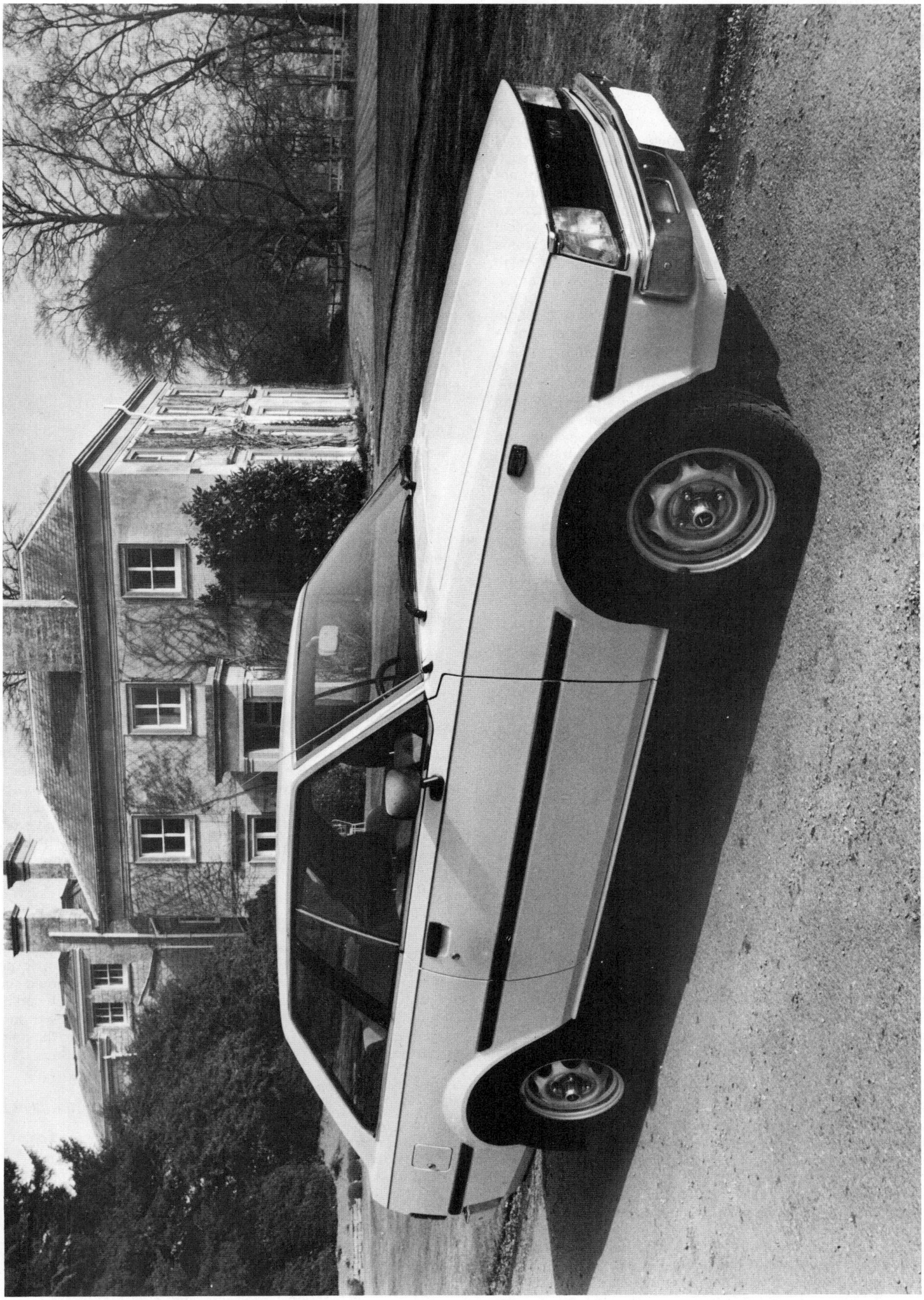

Toyota Corolla 1600 Liftback

Fault diagnosis

Introduction

The vehicle owner who does his or her own maintenance according to the recommended schedules should not have to use this section of the manual very often. Modern component reliability is such that, provided those items subject to wear or deterioration are inspected or renewed at the specified intervals, sudden failure is comparatively rare. Faults do not usually just happen as a result of sudden failure, but develop over a period of time. Major mechanical failures in particular are usually preceded by characteristic symptoms over hundreds or even thousands of miles. Those components which do occasionally fail without warning are often small and easily carried in the vehicle.

With any fault finding, the first step is to decide where to begin investigations. Sometimes this is obvious, but on other occasions a little detective work will be necessary. The owner who makes half a dozen haphazard adjustments or replacements may be successful in curing a fault (or its symptoms), but he will be none the wiser if the fault recurs and he may well have spent more time and money than was necessary. A calm and logical approach will be found to be more satisfactory in the long run. Always take into account any warning signs or abnormalities that may have been noticed in the period preceding the fault – power loss, high or low gauge readings, unusual noises or smells, etc – and remember that failure of components such as fuses or spark plugs may only be pointers to some underlying fault.

The pages which follow here are intended to help in cases of failure to start or breakdown on the road. There is also a Fault Diagnosis Section at the end of each Chapter which should be consulted if the preliminary checks prove unfruitful. Whatever the fault, certain basic principles apply. These are as follows:

Verify the fault. This is simply a matter of being sure that you know what the symptoms are before starting work. This is particularly important if you are investigating a fault for someone else who may not have described it very accurately.

Don't overlook the obvious. For example, if the vehicle won't start, is there petrol in the tank? (Don't take anyone else's word on this particular point, and don't trust the fuel gauge either!) If an electrical fault is indicated, look for loose or broken wires before digging out the test gear.

Cure the disease, not the symptom. Substituting a flat battery with a fully charged one will get you off the hard shoulder, but if the underlying cause is not attended to, the new battery will go the same way. Similarly, changing oil-fouled spark plugs for a new set will get you moving again, but remember that the reason for the fouling (if it wasn't simply an incorrect grade of plug) will have to be established and corrected.

Don't take anything for granted. Particularly, don't forget that a 'new' component may itself be defective (especially if it's been rattling round in the boot for months), and don't leave components out of a fault diagnosis sequence just because they are new or recently fitted. When you do finally diagnose a difficult fault, you'll probably realise that all the evidence was there from the start.

Electrical faults

Electrical faults can be more puzzling than straightforward mechanical failures, but they are no less susceptible to logical analysis if the basic principles of operation are understood. Vehicle electrical wiring exists in extremely unfavourable conditions – heat, vibration and chemical attack – and the first things to look for are loose or corroded connections and broken or chafed wires, especially where the wires pass through holes in the bodywork or are subject to vibration.

All metal-bodied vehicles in current production have one pole of the battery 'earthed', ie connected to the vehicle bodywork, and in nearly all modern vehicles it is the negative (–) terminal. The various electrical components – motors, bulb holders etc – are also connected to earth, either by means of a lead or directly by their mountings. Electric current flows through the component and then back to the battery via the bodywork. If the component mounting is loose or corroded, or if a good path back to the battery is not available, the circuit will be incomplete and malfunction will result. The engine and/or gearbox are also earthed by means of flexible metal straps to the body or subframe; if these straps are loose or missing, starter motor, generator and ignition trouble may result.

Assuming the earth return to be satisfactory, electrical faults will be due either to component malfunction or to defects in the current supply. Individual components are dealt with in Chapter 10. If supply wires are broken or cracked internally this results in an open-circuit, and the easiest way to check for this is to bypass the suspect wire temporarily with a length of wire having a crocodile clip or suitable connector at each end. Alternatively, a 12V test lamp can be used to verify the presence of supply voltage at various points along the wire and the break can be thus isolated.

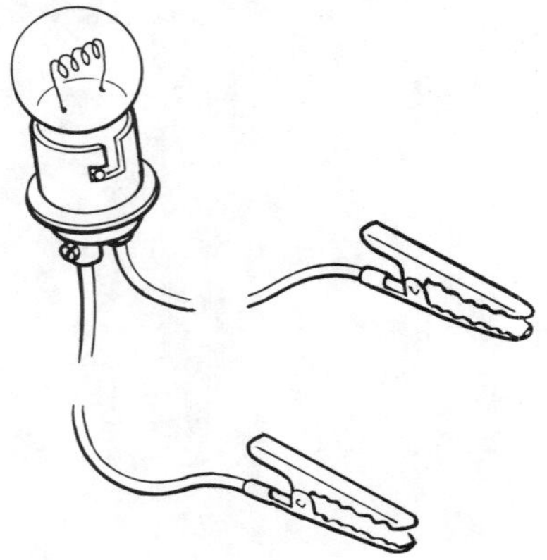

A simple test lamp is useful for checking electrical faults

If a bare portion of a live wire touches the bodywork or other earthed metal part, the electricity will take the low-resistance path thus formed back to the battery: this is known as a short-circuit. Hopefully a short-circuit will blow a fuse, but otherwise it may cause burning of the insulation (and possibly further short-circuits) or even a fire. This is why it is inadvisable to bypass persistently blowing fuses with silver foil or wire.

Spares and tool kit

Most vehicles are supplied only with sufficient tools for wheel changing; the *Maintenance and minor repair* tool kit detailed in *Tools and working facilities,* with the addition of a hammer, is probably sufficient for those repairs that most motorists would consider attempting at the roadside. In addition a few items which can be fitted without too much trouble in the event of a breakdown should be carried. Experience and available space will modify the list below, but the following may save having to call on professional assistance:

Spark plugs, clean and correctly gapped
HT lead and plug cap – long enough to reach the plug furthest from the distributor
Distributor rotor, condenser and contact breaker points
Drivebelt(s) – emergency type may suffice
Spare fuses
Set of principal light bulbs
Tin of radiator sealer and hose bandage
Exhaust bandage
Roll of insulating tape
Length of soft iron wire
Length of electrical flex
Torch or inspection lamp (can double as test lamp)
Battery jump leads
Tow-rope

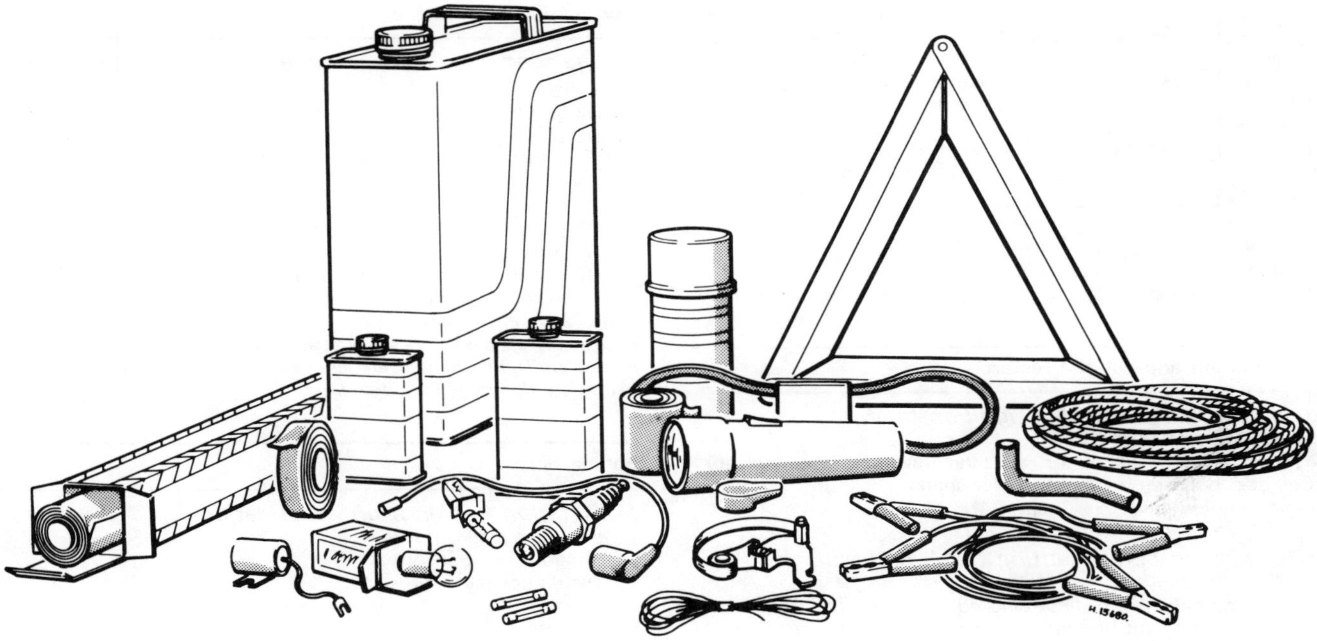

Carrying a few spares can save a long walk!

Ignition waterproofing aerosol
Litre of engine oil
Sealed can of hydraulic fluid
Emergency windscreen
'Jubilee' clips
Tube of filler paste

If spare fuel is carried, a can designed for the purpose should be used to minimise risks of leakage and collision damage. A first aid kit and a warning triangle, whilst not at present compulsory in the UK, are obviously sensible items to carry in addition to the above.

When touring abroad it may be advisable to carry additional spares which, even if you cannot fit them yourself, could save having to wait while parts are obtained. The items below may be worth considering:

Clutch and throttle cables
Cylinder head gasket
Alternator brushes
Fuel pump repair kit
Tyre valve core

One of the motoring organisations will be able to advise on availability of fuel etc in foreign countries.

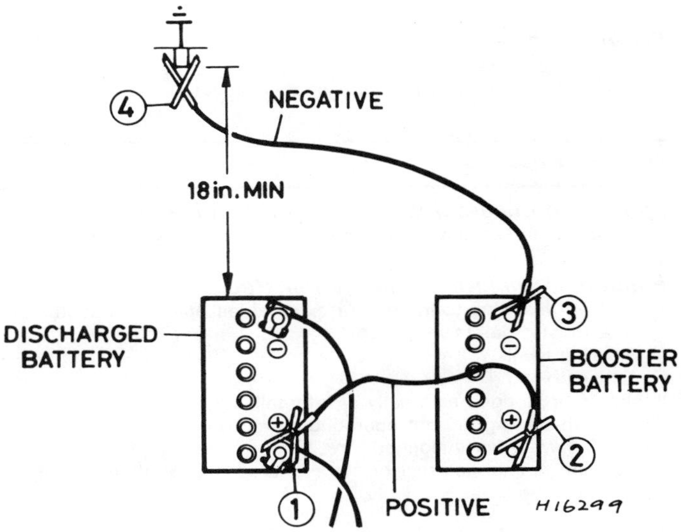

Jump start lead connections for negative earth – connect leads in order shown

Engine will not start

Engine fails to turn when starter operated
Flat battery (recharge, use jump leads, or push start)
Battery terminals loose or corroded
Battery earth to body defective
Engine earth strap loose or broken
Starter motor (or solenoid) wiring loose or broken
Automatic transmission selector in wrong position, or inhibitor switch faulty
Ignition/starter switch faulty
Major mechanical failure (seizure)
Starter or solenoid internal fault (see Chapter 10)

Starter motor turns engine slowly
Partially discharged battery (recharge, use jump leads, or push start)
Battery terminals loose or corroded
Battery earth to body defective
Engine earth strap loose
Starter motor (or solenoid) wiring loose
Starter motor internal fault (see Chapter 10)

Starter motor spins without turning engine
Flat battery
Starter motor pinion sticking on sleeve
Flywheel gear teeth damaged or worn
Starter motor mounting bolts loose

Engine turns normally but fails to start
Damp or dirty HT leads and distributor cap (crank engine and check for spark)
Dirty or incorrectly gapped distributor points (if applicable)

No fuel in tank (check for delivery at carburettor)
Excessive choke (hot engine) or insufficient choke (cold engine)
Fouled or incorrectly gapped spark plugs (remove, clean and regap)
Other ignition system fault (see Chapter 4)
Other fuel system fault (see Chapter 3)
Poor compression (see Chapter 1)
Major mechanical failure (eg camshaft drive)

Engine fires but will not run

Insufficient choke (cold engine)
Air leaks at carburettor or inlet manifold
Fuel starvation (see Chapter 3)
Ballast resistor defective, or other ignition fault (see Chapter 4)

Engine cuts out and will not restart

Engine cuts out suddenly – ignition fault

Loose or disconnected LT wires
Wet HT leads or distributor cap (after traversing water splash)
Coil or condenser failure (check for spark)
Other ignition fault (see Chapter 4)

Engine misfires before cutting out – fuel fault

Fuel tank empty
Fuel pump defective or filter blocked (check for delivery)
Fuel tank filler vent blocked (suction will be evident on releasing cap)
Carburettor needle valve sticking
Carburettor jets blocked (fuel contaminated)
Other fuel system fault (see Chapter 3)

Engine cuts out – other causes

Serious overheating
Major mechanical failure (eg camshaft drive)

Engine overheats

Ignition (no-charge) warning light illuminated

Slack or broken drivebelt – retension or renew (Chapter 2)

Ignition warning light not illuminated

Coolant loss due to internal or external leakage (see Chapter 2)
Thermostat defective
Low oil level
Brakes binding
Radiator clogged externally or internally
Electric cooling fan not operating correctly
Engine waterways clogged
Ignition timing incorrect or automatic advance malfunctioning
Mixture too weak

Note: *Do not add cold water to an overheated engine or damage may result*

Low engine oil pressure

Gauge reads low or warning light illuminated with engine running

Oil level low or incorrect grade
Defective gauge or sender unit
Wire to sender unit earthed
Engine overheating
Oil filter clogged or bypass valve defective
Oil pressure relief valve defective
Oil pick-up strainer clogged
Oil pump worn or mountings loose
Worn main or big-end bearings

Note: *Low oil pressure in a high-mileage engine at tickover is not necessarily a cause for concern. Sudden pressure loss at speed is far more significant. In any event, check the gauge or warning light sender before condemning the engine.*

Engine noises

Pre-ignition (pinking) on acceleration

Incorrect grade of fuel
Ignition timing incorrect
Distributor faulty or worn
Worn or maladjusted carburettor
Excessive carbon build-up in engine

Whistling or wheezing noises

Leaking vacuum hose
Leaking carburettor or manifold gasket
Blowing head gasket

Tapping or rattling

Incorrect valve clearances
Worn valve gear
Worn timing chain or belt
Broken piston ring (ticking noise)

Knocking or thumping

Unintentional mechanical contact (eg fan blades)
Worn fanbelt
Peripheral component fault (generator, water pump etc)
Worn big-end bearings (regular heavy knocking, perhaps less under load)
Worn main bearings (rumbling and knocking, perhaps worsening under load)
Piston slap (most noticeable when cold)

Safety first!

Professional motor mechanics are trained in safe working procedures. However enthusiastic you may be about getting on with the job in hand, do take the time to ensure that your safety is not put at risk. A moment's lack of attention can result in an accident, as can failure to observe certain elementary precautions.

There will always be new ways of having accidents, and the following points do not pretend to be a comprehensive list of all dangers; they are intended rather to make you aware of the risks and to encourage a safety-conscious approach to all work you carry out on your vehicle.

Essential DOs and DON'Ts

DON'T rely on a single jack when working underneath the vehicle. Always use reliable additional means of support, such as axle stands, securely placed under a part of the vehicle that you know will not give way.
DON'T attempt to loosen or tighten high-torque nuts (e.g. wheel hub nuts) while the vehicle is on a jack; it may be pulled off.
DON'T start the engine without first ascertaining that the transmission is in neutral (or 'Park' where applicable) and the parking brake applied.
DON'T suddenly remove the filler cap from a hot cooling system – cover it with a cloth and release the pressure gradually first, or you may get scalded by escaping coolant.
DON'T attempt to drain oil until you are sure it has cooled sufficiently to avoid scalding you.
DON'T grasp any part of the engine, exhaust or catalytic converter without first ascertaining that it is sufficiently cool to avoid burning you.
DON'T allow brake fluid or antifreeze to contact vehicle paintwork.
DON'T syphon toxic liquids such as fuel, brake fluid or antifreeze by mouth, or allow them to remain on your skin.
DON'T inhale dust – it may be injurious to health (see *Asbestos* below).
DON'T allow any spilt oil or grease to remain on the floor – wipe it up straight away, before someone slips on it.
DON'T use ill-fitting spanners or other tools which may slip and cause injury.
DON'T attempt to lift a heavy component which may be beyond your capability – get assistance.
DON'T rush to finish a job, or take unverified short cuts.
DON'T allow children or animals in or around an unattended vehicle.
DO wear eye protection when using power tools such as drill, sander, bench grinder etc, and when working under the vehicle.
DO use a barrier cream on your hands prior to undertaking dirty jobs – it will protect your skin from infection as well as making the dirt easier to remove afterwards; but make sure your hands aren't left slippery.
DO keep loose clothing (cuffs, tie etc) and long hair well out of the way of moving mechanical parts.
DO remove rings, wristwatch etc, before working on the vehicle – especially the electrical system.
DO ensure that any lifting tackle used has a safe working load rating adequate for the job.
DO keep your work area tidy – it is only too easy to fall over articles left lying around.
DO get someone to check periodically that all is well, when working alone on the vehicle.
DO carry out work in a logical sequence and check that everything is correctly assembled and tightened afterwards.
DO remember that your vehicle's safety affects that of yourself and others. If in doubt on any point, get specialist advice.
IF, in spite of following these precautions, you are unfortunate enough to injure yourself, seek medical attention as soon as possible.

Asbestos

Certain friction, insulating, sealing, and other products – such as brake linings, brake bands, clutch linings, torque converters, gaskets, etc – contain asbestos. *Extreme care must be taken to avoid inhalation of dust from such products since it is hazardous to health.* If in doubt, assume that they *do* contain asbestos.

Fire

Remember at all times that petrol (gasoline) is highly flammable. Never smoke, or have any kind of naked flame around, when working on the vehicle. But the risk does not end there – a spark caused by an electrical short-circuit, by two metal surfaces contacting each other, by careless use of tools, or even by static electricity built up in your body under certain conditions, can ignite petrol vapour, which in a confined space is highly explosive.

Always disconnect the battery earth (ground) terminal before working on any part of the fuel or electrical system, and never risk spilling fuel on to a hot engine or exhaust.

It is recommended that a fire extinguisher of a type suitable for fuel and electrical fires is kept handy in the garage or workplace at all times. Never try to extinguish a fuel or electrical fire with water.

Fumes

Certain fumes are highly toxic and can quickly cause unconsciousness and even death if inhaled to any extent. Petrol (gasoline) vapour comes into this category, as do the vapours from certain solvents such as trichloroethylene. Any draining or pouring of such volatile fluids should be done in a well ventilated area.

When using cleaning fluids and solvents, read the instructions carefully. Never use materials from unmarked containers – they may give off poisonous vapours.

Never run the engine of a motor vehicle in an enclosed space such as a garage. Exhaust fumes contain carbon monoxide which is extremely poisonous; if you need to run the engine, always do so in the open air or at least have the rear of the vehicle outside the workplace.

If you are fortunate enough to have the use of an inspection pit, never drain or pour petrol, and never run the engine, while the vehicle is standing over it; the fumes, being heavier than air, will concentrate in the pit with possibly lethal results.

The battery

Never cause a spark, or allow a naked light, near the vehicle's battery. It will normally be giving off a certain amount of hydrogen gas, which is highly explosive.

Always disconnect the battery earth (ground) terminal before working on the fuel or electrical systems.

If possible, loosen the filler plugs or cover when charging the battery from an external source. Do not charge at an excessive rate or the battery may burst.

Take care when topping up and when carrying the battery. The acid electrolyte, even when diluted, is very corrosive and should not be allowed to contact the eyes or skin.

If you ever need to prepare electrolyte yourself, always add the acid slowly to the water, and never the other way round. Protect against splashes by wearing rubber gloves and goggles.

When jump starting a car using a booster battery, for negative earth (ground) vehicles, connect the jump leads in the following sequence: First connect one jump lead between the positive (+) terminals of the two batteries. Then connect the other jump lead first to the negative (–) terminal of the booster battery, and then to a good earthing (ground) point on the vehicle to be started, at least 18 in (45 cm) from the battery if possible. Ensure that hands and jump leads are clear of any moving parts, and that the two vehicles do not touch. Disconnect the leads in the reverse order.

Mains electricity

When using an electric power tool, inspection light etc, which works from the mains, always ensure that the appliance is correctly connected to its plug and that, where necessary, it is properly earthed (grounded). Do not use such appliances in damp conditions and, again, beware of creating a spark or applying excessive heat in the vicinity of fuel or fuel vapour.

Ignition HT voltage

A severe electric shock can result from touching certain parts of the ignition system, such as the HT leads, when the engine is running or being cranked, particularly if components are damp or the insulation is defective. Where an electronic ignition system is fitted, the HT voltage is much higher and could prove fatal.

General dimensions, weights and capacities

Dimensions (overall)

	Saloon	Estate	Liftback	Coupe
Wheelbase	94.5 in (2400 mm)	94.5 in (2400 mm)	94.5 in (2400 mm)	94.5 in (2400 mm)
Length	161.6 in (4105 mm)	163. 2 in (4145 mm)	163.8 in (4160 mm)	164.4 in (4176 mm)
Height	54.9 in (1394 mm)	54.7 in (1389 mm)	52.8 in (1341 mm)	52.6 in (1336 mm)
Width	63.4 in (1610 mm)	63.4 in (1610 mm)	64.0 in (1626 mm)	64.0 in (1626 mm)
Track:				
Front	52.0 in (1321 mm)	52.0 in (1321 mm)	52.0 in (1321 mm)	52.0 in (1321 mm)
Rear	52.6 in (1336 mm)	52.6 in (1336 mm)	52.6 in (1336 mm)	52.6 in (1336 mm)
Ground clearance	5.3 in (135 mm)	5.3 in (135 mm)	4.5 in (114 mm)	4.5 in (114 mm)
Turning circle between kerbs (all models)	368 in (9347 mm)			

Weights

Kerb weights:	
2-door Saloon	1852 lb (840 kg)
4-door Saloon	1885 lb (855 kg)
Estate	1951 lb (885 kg)
Liftback	2070 lb (941 kg)
Coupe	2094 lb (950 kg)
Towing capacity (with brake) – all models	2205 lbs (1000 kg)
Towing capacity (without brake) – all models	882 lbs (400 kg)

Capacities

Fuel tank:	
All models except Estate	11.0 Imp gal (50 litre; 13.2 US gal)
Estate models	10.3 Imp gal (47 litre; 12.4 US gal)
Cooling system:	
4K engine models	10.2 Imp pt (5.8 litre; 12.2 US pt)
2T and 2T–B engine models	13.5 Imp pt (7.7 litre; 16.2 US pt)
3T–C engine models:	
Manual transmission	14.0 Imp pt (8.0 litre; 16.9 US pt)
Automatic transmission	13.9 Imp pt (7.9 litre; 16.7 US pt)
Engine oil (drain and refill including filter change):	
4K engine models	6.1 Imp pt (3.5 litre; 7.4 US pt)
2T, 2T–B and 3T–C engine models	6.6 Imp pt (3.8 litre; 8.0 US pt)
Manual transmission:	
K40, T40 and T50 type gearboxes	3.0 Imp pt (1.7 litre; 3.6 US pt)
K50 type gearbox	4.4 Imp pt (2.5 litre; 5.3 US pt)
Automatic transmission:	
A20 type:	
Total capacity	9.3 Imp pt (5.3 litre; 5.6 US pt)
Drain and refill	4.1 Imp pt (2.3 litre; 4.8 US pt)
A40 type:	
Total capacity	11.1 Imp pt (6.3 litre; 13.3 US pt)
Drain and refill	4.2 Imp pt (2.4 litre; 5.1 US pt)
Rear axle	1.7 Imp pt (1.0 litre; 2.1 US pt)

Use of English

As this book has been written in England, it uses the appropriate English component names, phrases, and spelling. Some of these differ from those used in America. Normally, these cause no difficulty, but to make sure, a glossary is printed below. In ordering spare parts remember the parts list may use some of these words:

English	American	English	American
Accelerator	Gas pedal	Leading shoe (of brake)	Primary shoe
Aerial	Antenna	Locks	Latches
Anti-roll bar	Stabiliser or sway bar	Methylated spirit	Denatured alcohol
Big-end bearing	Rod bearing	Motorway	Freeway, turnpike etc
Bonnet (engine cover)	Hood	Number plate	License plate
Boot (luggage compartment)	Trunk	Paraffin	Kerosene
Bulkhead	Firewall	Petrol	Gasoline (gas)
Bush	Bushing	Petrol tank	Gas tank
Cam follower or tappet	Valve lifter or tappet	'Pinking'	'Pinging'
Carburettor	Carburetor	Prise (force apart)	Pry
Catch	Latch	Propeller shaft	Driveshaft
Choke/venturi	Barrel	Quarterlight	Quarter window
Circlip	Snap-ring	Retread	Recap
Clearance	Lash	Reverse	Back-up
Crownwheel	Ring gear (of differential)	Rocker cover	Valve cover
Damper	Shock absorber, shock	Saloon	Sedan
Disc (brake)	Rotor/disk	Seized	Frozen
Distance piece	Spacer	Sidelight	Parking light
Drop arm	Pitman arm	Silencer	Muffler
Drop head coupe	Convertible	Sill panel (beneath doors)	Rocker panel
Dynamo	Generator (DC)	Small end, little end	Piston pin or wrist pin
Earth (electrical)	Ground	Spanner	Wrench
Engineer's blue	Prussian blue	Split cotter (for valve spring cap)	Lock (for valve spring retainer)
Estate car	Station wagon	Split pin	Cotter pin
Exhaust manifold	Header	Steering arm	Spindle arm
Fault finding/diagnosis	Troubleshooting	Sump	Oil pan
Float chamber	Float bowl	Swarf	Metal chips or debris
Free-play	Lash	Tab washer	Tang or lock
Freewheel	Coast	Tappet	Valve lifter
Gearbox	Transmission	Thrust bearing	Throw-out bearing
Gearchange	Shift	Top gear	High
Grub screw	Setscrew, Allen screw	Trackrod (of steering)	Tie-rod (or connecting rod)
Gudgeon pin	Piston pin or wrist pin	Trailing shoe (of brake)	Secondary shoe
Halfshaft	Axleshaft	Transmission	Whole drive line
Handbrake	Parking brake	Tyre	Tire
Hood	Soft top	Van	Panel wagon/van
Hot spot	Heat riser	Vice	Vise
Indicator	Turn signal	Wheel nut	Lug nut
Interior light	Dome lamp	Windscreen	Windshield
Layshaft (of gearbox)	Countershaft	Wing/mudguard	Fender

Buying spare parts and vehicle identification numbers

Buying spare parts

Spare parts are available from many sources, for example: Toyota garages, other garages and accessory shops, and motor factors. Our advice regarding spare part sources is as follows:

Officially appointed Toyota garages – This is the best source of parts which are peculiar to your car and are otherwise not generally available (eg complete cylinder heads, internal gearbox components, badges, interior trim etc). It is also the only place at which you should buy parts if your car is still under warranty – non-Toyota components may invalidate the warranty. To be sure of obtaining the correct parts it will always be necessary to give the storeman your car's engine and chassis number, and if possible, to take the old part along for positive identification. Remember that some parts may be available on a factory exchange basis – any parts returned should always be clean! It obviously makes good sense to go to the specialists on your car for this type of part for they are best equipped to supply you.

Other garages and accessory shops: These are often very good places to buy materials and components needed for the maintenance of your car (eg oil filters, spark plugs, bulbs, fan belts, oils and grease, touch-up paint, filler paste etc). They also sell general accessories, usually have convenient opening hours, charge lower prices and can often be found not far from home.

Motor factors: Good factors will stock all of the more important components which wear out relatively quickly (eg clutch components, pistons, valves, exhaust systems, brake cylinders/pipes/hoses/seals/shoes and pads etc). Motor factors will often provide new or reconditioned components on a part exchange basis – this can save a considerable amount of money.

Vehicle identification numbers

Modifications are a continuing and unpublicised process carried out by the vehicle manufacturer quite apart from major model changes. Spare parts manuals and lists are compiled upon a numerical basis, the invidual vehicle number being essential to correct identification of the component required.

The vehicle identification number is shown on a plate attached to the engine compartment bulkhead on UK models or on the upper surface of the instrument panel just inside the windscreen on USA and Canada models. The prefix KE indicates 4K (1290 cc) engine, while the prefix TE indicates 2T or 2T–B engine (1588 cc UK models) or 3T–C engine (1770 cc USA and Canada models).

The engine number is stamped on a machined surface on the side of the cylinder block (photo).

Vehicle identification plate location on bulkhead

Engine identification number – 2T type shown

Tools and working facilities

Introduction

A selection of good tools is a fundamental requirement for anyone contemplating the maintenance and repair of a motor vehicle. For the owner who does not possess any, their purchase will prove a considerable expense, offsetting some of the savings made by doing-it-yourself. However, provided that the tools purchased are of good quality, they will last for many years and prove an extremely worthwhile investment.

To help the average owner to decide which tools are needed to carry out the various tasks detailed in this manual, we have compiled three lists of tools under the following headings: *Maintenance and minor repair, Repair and overhaul,* and *Special.* The newcomer to practical mechanics should start off with the *Maintenance and minor repair* tool kit and confine himself to the simpler jobs around the vehicle. Then, as his confidence and experience grow, he can undertake more difficult tasks, buying extra tools as, and when, they are needed. In this way, a *Maintenance and minor repair* tool kit can be built-up into a *Repair and overhaul* tool kit over a considerable period of time without any major cash outlays. The experienced do-it-yourselfer will have a tool kit good enough for most repair and overhaul procedures and will add tools from the *Special* category when he feels the expense is justified by the amount of use to which these tools will be put.

It is obviously not possible to cover the subject of tools fully here. For those who wish to learn more about tools and their use there is a book entitled *How to Choose and Use Car Tools* available from the publishers of this manual.

Maintenance and minor repair tool kit

The tools given in this list should be considered as a minimum requirement if routine maintenance, servicing and minor repair operations are to be undertaken. We recommend the purchase of combination spanners (ring one end, open-ended the other); although more expensive than open-ended ones, they do give the advantages of both types of spanner.

Combination spanners - 10, 11, 12, 13, 14 & 17 mm
Adjustable spanner - 9 inch
Spark plug spanner (with rubber insert)
Spark plug gap adjustment tool
Set of feeler gauges
Brake bleed nipple spanner
Screwdriver - 4 in long x $\frac{1}{4}$ in dia (flat blade)
Screwdriver - 4 in long x $\frac{1}{4}$ in dia (cross blade)
Combination pliers - 6 inch
Hacksaw (junior)
Tyre pump
Tyre pressure gauge
Grease gun
Oil can
Fine emery cloth (1 sheet)
Wire brush (small)
Funnel (medium size)

Repair and overhaul tool kit

These tools are virtually essential for anyone undertaking any major repairs to a motor vehicle, and are additional to those given in the *Maintenance and minor repair* list. Included in this list is a comprehensive set of sockets. Although these are expensive they will be found invaluable as they are so versatile - particularly if various drives are included in the set. We recommend the $\frac{1}{2}$ in square-drive type, as this can be used with most proprietary torque wrenches. If you cannot afford a socket set, even bought piecemeal, then inexpensive tubular box spanners are a useful alternative.

The tools in this list will occasionally need to be supplemented by tools from the *Special* list.

Sockets (or box spanners) to cover range in previous list
Reversible ratchet drive (for use with sockets)
Extension piece, 10 inch (for use with sockets)
Universal joint (for use with sockets)
Torque wrench (for use with sockets)
'Mole' wrench - 8 inch
Ball pein hammer
Soft-faced hammer, plastic or rubber
Screwdriver - 6 in long x $\frac{5}{16}$ in dia (flat blade)
Screwdriver - 2 in long x $\frac{5}{16}$ in square (flat blade)
Screwdriver - $1\frac{1}{2}$ in long x $\frac{1}{4}$ in dia (cross blade)
Screwdriver - 3 in long x $\frac{1}{8}$ in dia (electricians)
Pliers - electricians side cutters
Pliers - needle nosed
Pliers - circlip (internal and external)
Cold chisel - $\frac{1}{2}$ inch
Scriber
Scraper
Centre punch
Pin punch
Hacksaw
Valve grinding tool
Steel rule/straight-edge
Allen keys
Selection of files
Wire brush (large)
Axle-stands
Jack (strong scissor or hydraulic type)

Special tools

The tools in this list are those which are not used regularly, are expensive to buy, or which need to be used in accordance with their manufacturers' instructions. Unless relatively difficult mechanical jobs are undertaken frequently, it will not be economic to buy many of these tools. Where this is the case, you could consider clubbing together with friends (or joining a motorists' club) to make a joint purchase, or borrowing the tools against a deposit from a local garage or tool hire specialist.

The following list contains only those tools and instruments freely available to the public, and not those special tools produced by the vehicle manufacturer specifically for its dealer network. You will find occasional references to these manufacturers' special tools in the text of this manual. Generally, an alternative method of doing the job without the vehicle manufacturers' special tool is given. However, sometimes, there is no alternative to using them. Where this is the case and the relevant tool cannot be bought or borrowed, you will have to entrust the work to a franchised garage.

Valve spring compressor
Piston ring compressor
Balljoint separator
Universal hub/bearing puller
Impact screwdriver
Micrometer and/or vernier gauge
Dial gauge
Stroboscopic timing light
Dwell angle meter/tachometer
Universal electrical multi-meter
Cylinder compression gauge
Lifting tackle
Trolley jack
Light with extension lead

The term SST (special Service Tool) appears in some of the illustrations and denotes the use of a Toyota tool designed for a specific purpose. We have, however, whenever possible described procedures using conventional workshop tools.

Buying tools

For practically all tools, a tool factor is the best source since he will have a very comprehensive range compared with the average garage or accessory shop. Having said that, accessory shops often offer excellent quality tools at discount prices, so it pays to shop around.

Remember, you don't have to buy the most expensive items on the shelf, but it is always advisable to steer clear of the very cheap tools. There are plenty of good tools around at reasonable prices, so ask the proprietor or manager of the shop for advice before making a purchase.

Care and maintenance of tools

Having purchased a reasonable tool kit, it is necessary to keep the tools in a clean serviceable condition. After use, always wipe off any dirt, grease and metal particles using a clean, dry cloth, before putting the tools away. Never leave them lying around after they have been used. A simple tool rack on the garage or workshop wall, for items such as screwdrivers and pliers is a good idea. Store all normal wrenches and sockets in a metal box. Any measuring instruments, gauges, meters, etc, must be carefully stored where they cannot be damaged or become rusty.

Take a little care when tools are used. Hammer heads inevitably become marked and screwdrivers lose the keen edge on their blades from time to time. A little timely attention with emery cloth or a file will soon restore items like this to a good serviceable finish.

Working facilities

Not to be forgotten when discussing tools, is the workshop itself. If anything more than routine maintenance is to be carried out, some form of suitable working area becomes essential.

It is appreciated that many an owner mechanic is forced by circumstances to remove an engine or similar item, without the benefit of a garage or workshop. Having done this, any repairs should always be done under the cover of a roof.

Wherever possible, any dismantling should be done on a clean, flat workbench or table at a suitable working height.

Any workbench needs a vice: one with a jaw opening of 4 in (100 mm) is suitable for most jobs. As mentioned previously, some clean dry storage space is also required for tools, as well as for lubricants, cleaning fluids, touch-up paints and so on, which become necessary.

Another item which may be required, and which has a much more general usage, is an electric drill with a chuck capacity of at least $\frac{5}{16}$ in (8 mm). This, together with a good range of twist drills, is virtually essential for fitting accessories such as mirrors and reversing lights.

Last, but not least, always keep a supply of old newspapers and clean, lint-free rags available, and try to keep any working area as clean as possible.

Spanner jaw gap comparison table

Jaw gap (in)	Spanner size
0.250	$\frac{1}{4}$ in AF
0.276	7 mm
0.313	$\frac{5}{16}$ in AF
0.315	8 mm
0.344	$\frac{11}{32}$ in AF; $\frac{1}{8}$ in Whitworth
0.354	9 mm
0.375	$\frac{3}{8}$ in AF
0.394	10 mm
0.433	11 mm
0.438	$\frac{7}{16}$ in AF
0.445	$\frac{3}{16}$ in Whitworth; $\frac{1}{4}$ in BSF
0.472	12 mm
0.500	$\frac{1}{2}$ in AF
0.512	13 mm
0.525	$\frac{1}{4}$ in Whitworth; $\frac{5}{16}$ in BSF
0.551	14 mm
0.563	$\frac{9}{16}$ in AF
0.591	15 mm
0.600	$\frac{5}{16}$ in Whitworth; $\frac{3}{8}$ in BSF
0.625	$\frac{5}{8}$ in AF
0.630	16 mm
0.669	17 mm
0.686	$\frac{11}{16}$ in AF
0.709	18 mm
0.710	$\frac{3}{8}$ in Whitworth; $\frac{7}{16}$ in BSF
0.748	19 mm
0.750	$\frac{3}{4}$ in AF
0.813	$\frac{13}{16}$ in AF
0.820	$\frac{7}{16}$ in Whitworth; $\frac{1}{2}$ in BSF
0.866	22 mm
0.875	$\frac{7}{8}$ in AF
0.920	$\frac{1}{2}$ in Whitworth; $\frac{9}{16}$ in BSF
0.938	$\frac{15}{16}$ in AF
0.945	24 mm
1.000	1 in AF
1.010	$\frac{9}{16}$ in Whitworth; $\frac{5}{8}$ in BSF
1.024	26 mm
1.063	$1\frac{1}{16}$ in AF; 27 mm
1.100	$\frac{5}{8}$ in Whitworth; $\frac{11}{16}$ in BSF
1.125	$1\frac{1}{8}$ in AF
1.181	30 mm
1.200	$\frac{11}{16}$ in Whitworth; $\frac{3}{4}$ in BSF
1.250	$1\frac{1}{4}$ in AF
1.260	32 mm
1.300	$\frac{3}{4}$ in Whitworth; $\frac{7}{8}$ in BSF
1.313	$1\frac{5}{16}$ in AF
1.390	$\frac{13}{16}$ in Whitworth; $\frac{15}{16}$ in BSF
1.417	36 mm
1.438	$1\frac{7}{16}$ in AF
1.480	$\frac{7}{8}$ in Whitworth; 1 in BSF
1.500	$1\frac{1}{2}$ in AF
1.575	40 mm; $\frac{15}{16}$ in Whitworth
1.614	41 mm
1.625	$1\frac{5}{8}$ in AF
1.670	1 in Whitworth; $1\frac{1}{8}$ in BSF
1.688	$1\frac{11}{16}$ in AF
1.811	46 mm
1.813	$1\frac{13}{16}$ in AF
1.860	$1\frac{1}{8}$ in Whitworth; $1\frac{1}{4}$ in BSF
1.875	$1\frac{7}{8}$ in AF
1.969	50 mm
2.000	2 in AF
2.050	$1\frac{1}{4}$ in Whitworth; $1\frac{3}{8}$ in BSF
2.165	55 mm
2.362	60 mm

Jacking and towing

Jacking points

For emergency roadwheel changing, use the jack supplied with the vehicle tool kit. Always engage the jack with the jacking points located under the side body sills. The Corolla tool kit also includes a pair of wheel chocks (blocks) and these should be positioned fore and aft of the wheel diagonally opposite the one to be changed before raising the vehicle.

To remove a roadwheel, apply the handbrake fully and loosen the roadwheel nuts **before** raising the vehicle. Once the vehicle is jacked up, remove the nuts completely and remove the wheel.

When carrying out repairs or adjustments jack up and support the vehicle under the support points shown in the illustrations. Always make sure the vehicle is securely supported before working underneath it!

Towing

In an emergency your vehicle may be towed or you may tow another vehicle by attaching the tow line to the transportation lash down hooks or by passing the tow line round the rear roadspring shackle, (Estate only).

If a vehicle is equipped with automatic transmission, it should not be towed further than 50 miles (80 km) or in excess of 30 mph (45 km/h) otherwise disconnect and remove the propeller shaft.

Before towing the vehicle ensure that the ignition key is not set in the locked position! Turn the key to the position marked ACC and have it in this position for the duration of the journey. Check that the handbrake is released.

When being towed with the engine OFF, the brake servo unit will not be operating so allow for a greater braking effort.

On models with power-assisted steering, the steering pump unit will not be operating when the engine is OFF so allow for extra steering effort.

Do not tow or attempt to drive the vehicle if any part of the steering, suspension or brakes are damaged or faulty.

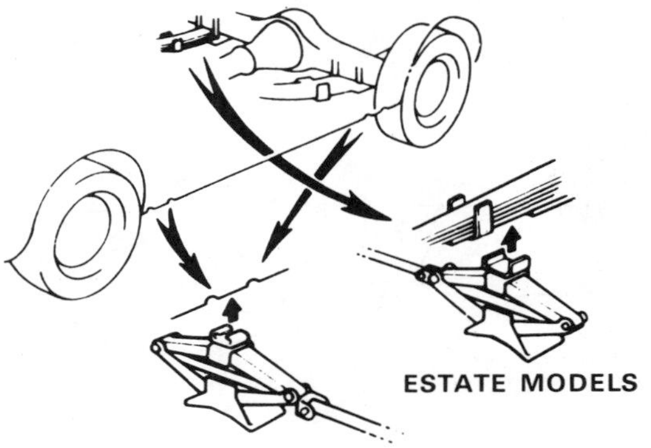

Jack location points

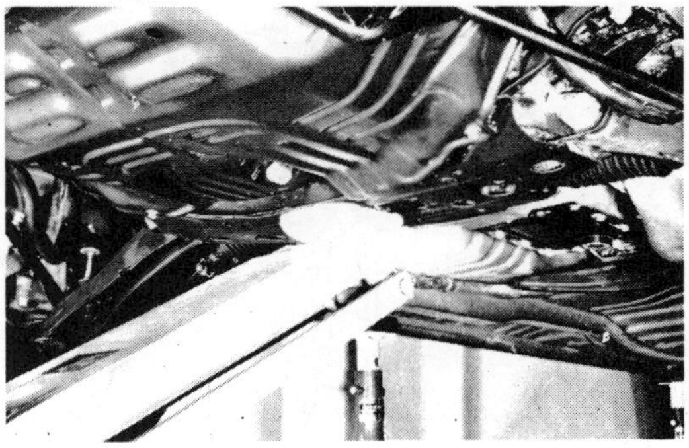

Central jack point at front, under crossmember

Chock the wheels before jacking up

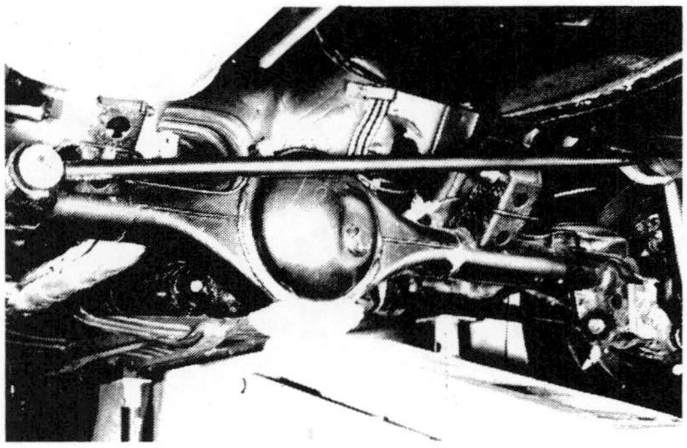

Central jack point at rear, under differential housing

The Toyota jack in position

Vehicle lash down hook

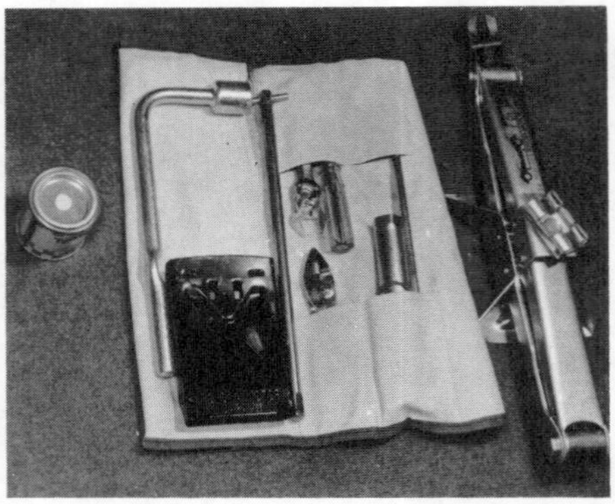

Toyota tool kit, jack and touch-up paint supplied with vehicle when new

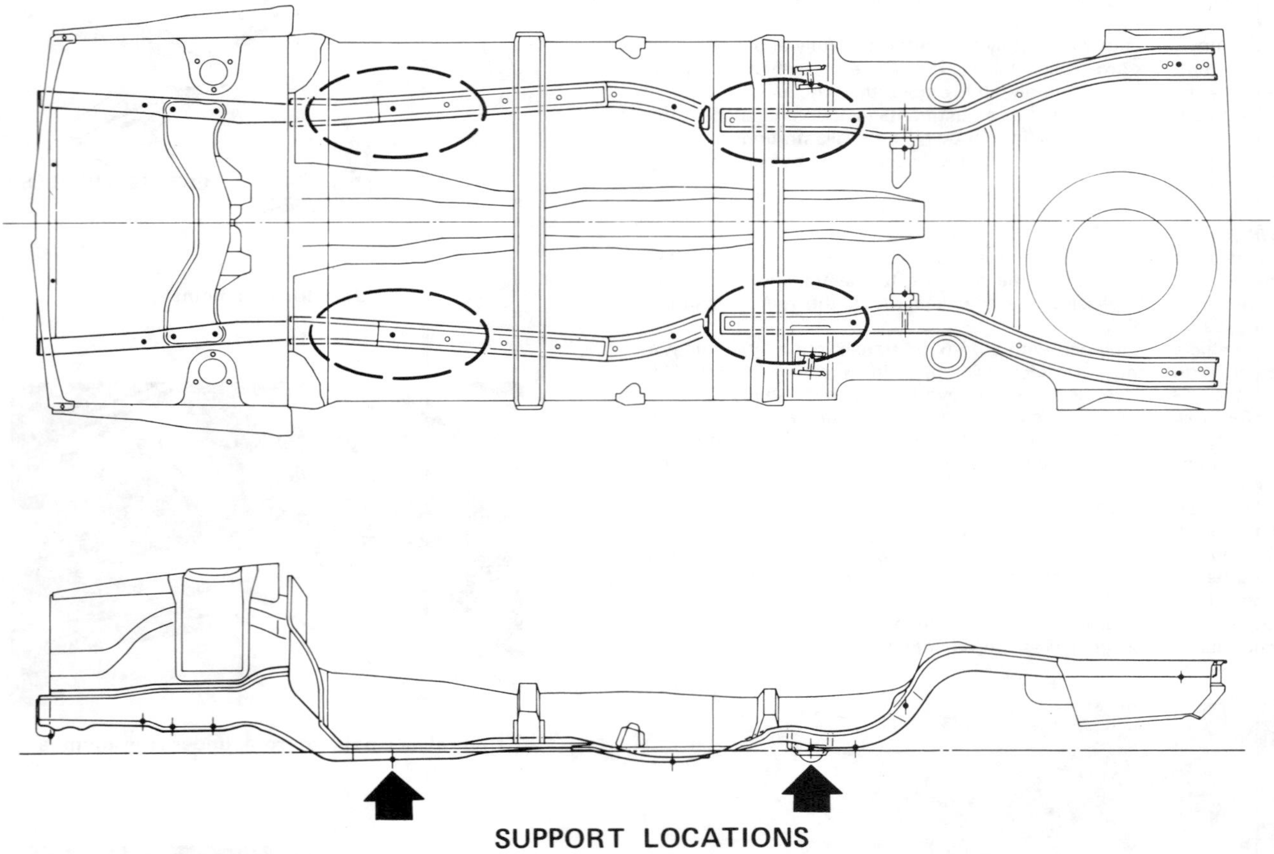

Support location positions on underframe

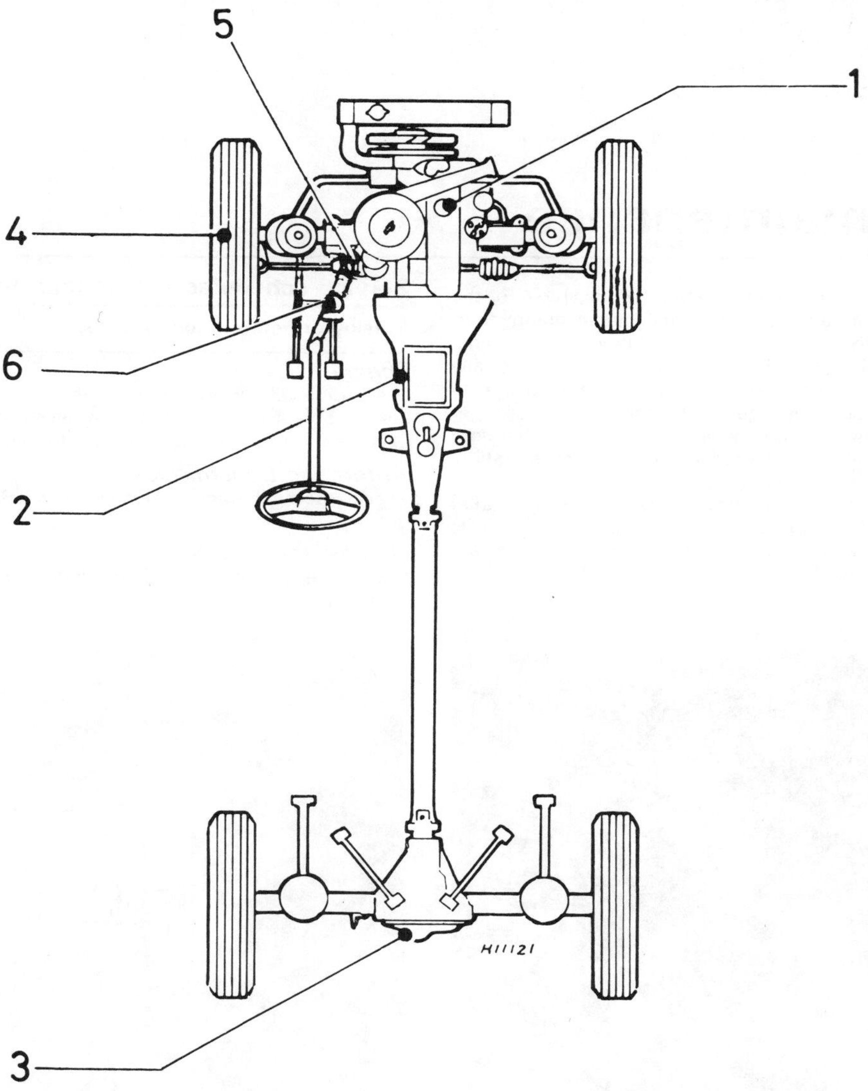

Recommended lubricants and fluids

Component or system		Lubricant type or specification
1	Engine	SAE 15W/50 multigrade engine oil*
2	Manual gearbox Automatic gearbox	Gear oil SAE 80 EP ATF Type F
3	Differential	SAE 90 EP**
4	Wheel bearings	Multipurpose grease
5	Steering gearbox oil (recirculating ball type) Power steering	API GL-4, SAE 90 ATF type Dexron®
6	Brake and clutch master cylinder	DOT 3 SAE J1703 C

**Alternatively, use an equivalent multigrade engine oil having a viscosity rating compatible with temperatures in the vehicle operating area – see manufacturer's handbook.*
***Use SAE 80 EP for temperatures below –10°F (–23°C)*

Routine maintenance

Maintenance is essential for ensuring safety and desirable for the purpose of getting the best in terms of performance and economy from the car. Over the years the need for periodic lubrication – oiling, greasing and so on – has been drastically reduced if not totally eliminated. This has unfortunately tended to lead some owners to think that because no such action is required the items either no longer exist or will last for ever. This is a serious delusion. It follows therefore that the largest initial element of maintenance is visual examination. This may lead to repairs or renewals.

The following maintenance schedules are for European market models and are sub-divided into service intervals. The service intervals and requirements for USA and Canada market models differ and are therefore listed separately.

Service schedules – European models

Weekly or before a long journey

Engine
Check oil level and top up if necessary (photo).
Check coolant level and top up if necessary (photo).
Check battery electrolyte level and top up if necessary (photo).

Automatic transmission
Check automatic transmission fluid level. Refer to Chapter 6, Part B for details.

Brakes and clutch
Check master cylinder reservoir fluid level (photo).

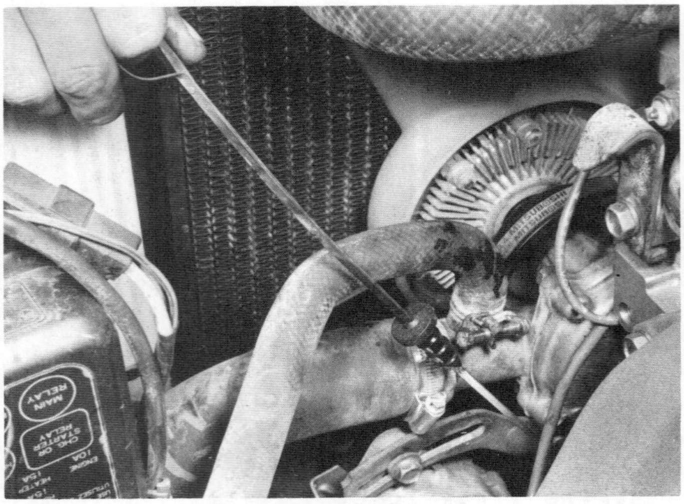

Check the engine oil level

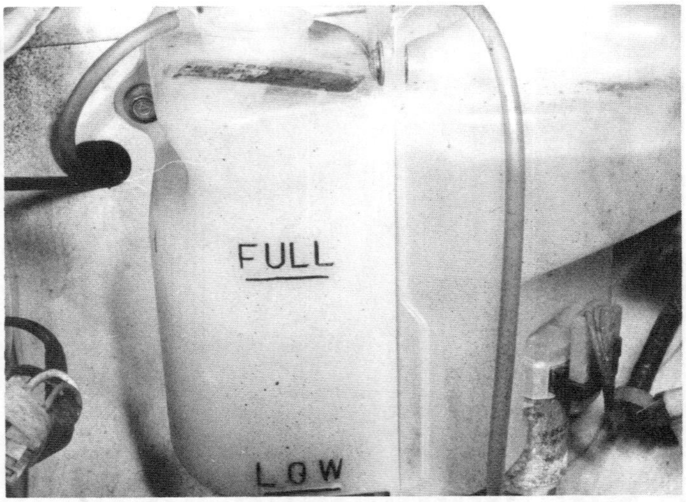

Check the engine coolant and washer fluid levels

Check and if necessary top up the battery electrolyte level

Check the brake and clutch master cylinder reservoir levels

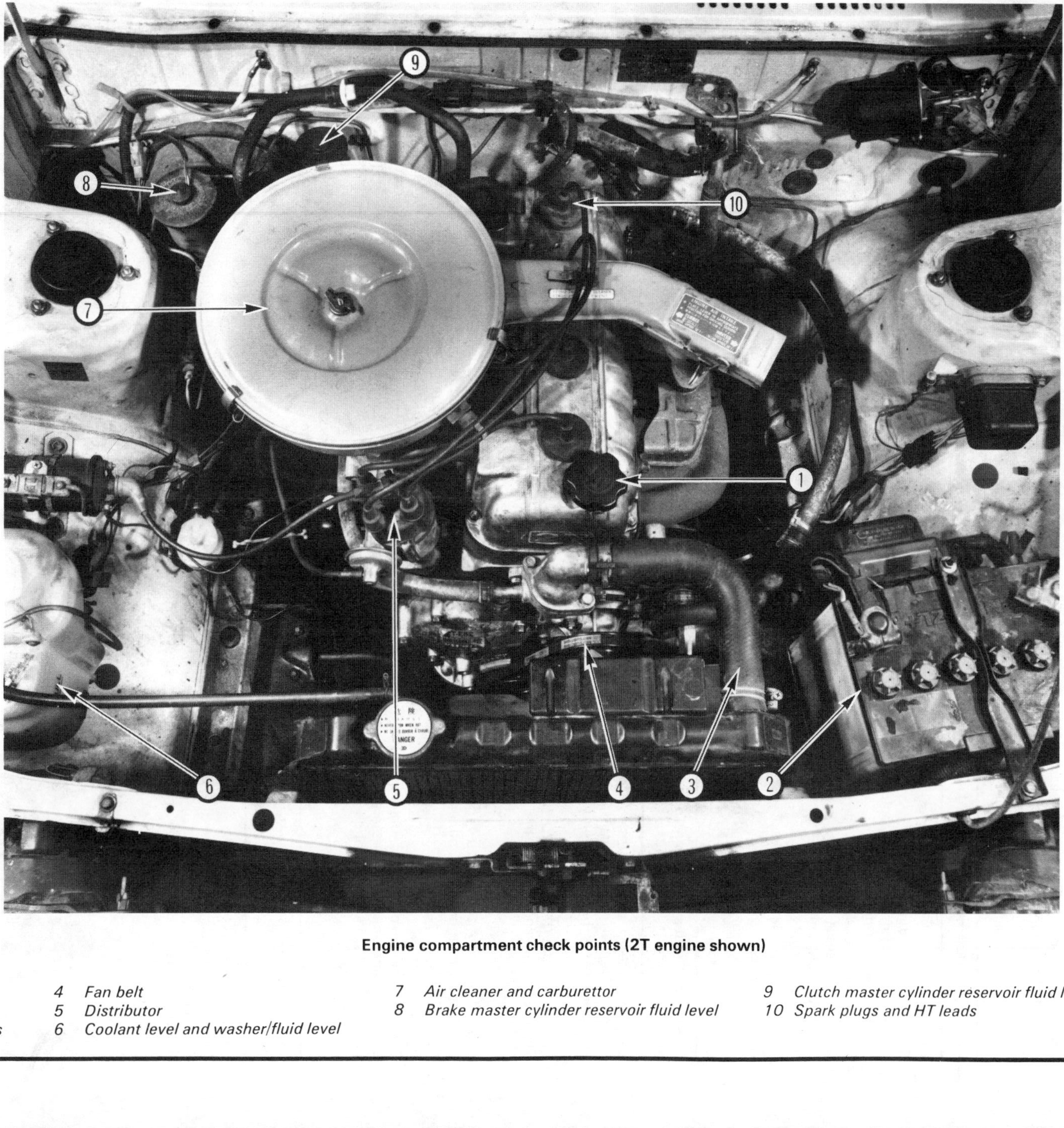

Engine compartment check points (2T engine shown)

1 *Engine oil*
2 *Battery*
3 *Coolant hoses*
4 *Fan belt*
5 *Distributor*
6 *Coolant level and washer/fluid level*
7 *Air cleaner and carburettor*
8 *Brake master cylinder reservoir fluid level*
9 *Clutch master cylinder reservoir fluid level (where fitted)*
10 *Spark plugs and HT leads*

Steering and suspension
Check tyre pressures. Pressure requirements according to model are given in Chapter 11.
Check tyres visually for wear or damage.

Lights, wipers and horns
Check operation of all lights front and rear.
Check operation of windscreen wipers and horns.
Check and top up windscreen washer reservoir fluid.

Remove spark plugs for inspection and cleaning

After first 1000 miles (1600 km) – new vehicle

Engine
Check valve clearances.
Check torque of cylinder head bolts.
Check tension of drivebelts.
Check idling speed.
Check dwell angle.
Check ignition timing.
Renew engine oil.

Body and underframe
Check tightness of all nuts and bolts.

Every 4500 miles (7500 km) or six months – which ever comes first

Engine – refer to Chapter 1 for details
Drain the engine oil (when warm) and refill with the correct quantity and grade of oil. Renew the oil filter.

Ignition system – refer to Chapter 4 for details
Remove, clean and inspect the spark plugs. Clean and adjust the electrode gap.

Clutch – refer to Chapter 5 for details
Check the clutch pedal adjustment.

Brakes
Check the brake pedal adjustments and clearances as described in Chapter 9 and adjust if necessary.
Check the operation of the handbrake and check cable for wear. Adjust as necessary.

Every 9000 miles (15 000 km) or 12 months – whichever comes first

Engine
Check and if necessary adjust the valve clearances as described in Chapter 1 (photo).
Check drivebelt(s) for condition and tension and adjust if necessary.
Check the exhaust pipes and connections for security and condition.

Fuel system – refer to Chapter 3 for details
Remove and inspect the air filter element as given in Chapter 3.
Wipe clean the element container and renew element if necessary.
Check the carburettor and fuel hoses for condition and security.
Check the carburettor idle speed settings and choke according to model.
Check the emission control system hoses and components for condition and security.

Ignition system – refer to Chapter 4 for details
Check the spark plug leads and the distributor to coil lead.
Also check the ignition low tension leads for condition and security.
Remove and renew the spark plugs.
Remove the distributor cap and check its condition and also that of the rotor arm. Check the action of the advance mechanism.
Clean and adjust the distributor contact breaker points.
Check the ignition timing and adjust if necessary.

Transmission – refer to Chapter 6 for details
Check the oil level (manual transmission) and top up if necessary (photo).

Propeller shaft and rear axle – refer to Chapters 7 and 8 for details
Check the condition and security of the propeller shaft universal joints and where applicable the centre support assembly.
Check the differential unit oil level and top up if necessary (photo).

Check/adjust the valve clearances – T series engine shown

Check and if necessary top up manual transmission oil level

Check rear axle oil level

Brakes – refer to Chapter 9 for details

Check the disc brake pads for excessive wear and renew if necessary.
Check discs for excessive wear or scoring.
Check the drum brakes for excessive shoe lining wear and renew if necessary. Also check the drums for condition and excessive wear. Renew or have friction surfaces reground if/as necessary.
Check the brake servo unit hose for condition and security.
Check the brake hydraulic lines for condition and security (photo). Renew as and if necessary.

Steering and suspension – refer to Chapter 11 for details

Examine all steering and front suspension joints and fixings for signs of excessive wear and security. Renew any worn or damaged components. Lubricate the lower steering balljoint.
On power steering models check the pump reservoir oil level and top up if necessary.
On manual steering models check the steering box oil level (recirculating ball type) and top up if necessary.
Check all steering and suspension balljoints and dustcovers for condition and renew if necessary. Check wheel alignment after renewing any joints (photo).
On rack and pinion steering models check the condition of the rack bellows and renew if necessary.
Check the shock absorbers (front and rear) for condition and security. Renew if worn or defective (photo).
Check the rear suspension components for signs of excessive wear or damage, in particular the link arm bushes or leaf spring bushes (as applicable). Renew if necessary (photo).

General checks

Check the windscreen and rear window wiper blades for wear and deterioration and renew if necessary.
Detach the battery leads, clean terminals and connectors and apply petroleum jelly when reconnecting.

Every 18 000 miles (30 000 km) or 24 months – whichever comes first

Check the condition of the various cooling system and emission control hoses and their connections for security.
Remove and renew the distributor contact breaker points (as described in Chapter 4).
Check the operation of the inlet air temperature control system (Chapter 3).
Check condition of fuel tank filler cap and all fuel lines and connections for condition and security.
Check the PCV system and connections for condition and security (Chapter 3).
Where fitted, check the spark control system (Chapter 3).

Check brake lines and hoses

Check steering and suspension components

Check shock absorbers and mountings

Check link arm bushes

Check the steering geometry and front wheel alignment as described in Chapter 11.
Drain and renew the manual transmission oil.
Drain and renew the rear axle oil.
Drain off and renew the brake system hydraulic fluid (Chapter 9).

Every 27 000 miles (45 000 km) or 36 months – whichever comes first

Remove and renew the drivebelt(s). Readjust their tension after an initial run-in period.
Check all vacuum hoses, fittings and connections and renew any that are defective.
Remove and renew the air filter (Chapter 3).
Drain and renew the automatic transmission fluid (Chapter 6 Part B).
Clean, repack and adjust the front wheel bearings as described in Chapter 11 (photo).

Every 36 000 miles (60 000 km) or every 48 months – whichever comes first

Drain the coolant from the cooling and heating circuit and renew it using the correct anti-freeze ratio for your climatic conditions. Refer to Chapter 2.
Remove and renew the in-line fuel filter unit. Refer to Chapter 3.

Service schedules – USA and Canada models

Every 250 miles (400 km) or weekly – whichever comes first

Carry out those items listed in the weekly service checks for European models.

Every 7500 miles (12 000 km) or 6 months – whichever comes first

Remove and clean the spark plugs. Reset the electrode gap adjustment before refitting (Chapter 4).

Every 10 000 miles (16 000 km) or 8 months – whichever comes first

Drain and renew the engine oil. At the same time renew the oil filter (Chapter 1).

Every 15 000 miles (24 000 km) or 12 months – whichever comes first

Engine
Check and if necessary adjust the valve clearances as described in Chapter 1.
Check the exhaust system pipes and connections for condition and security. Repair or renew if necessary (Chapter 3).

Ignition system – refer to Chapter 4 for details
Remove and renew the spark plugs.
Remove distributor cap and check its condition, also check the HT leads and connections.

Fuel system – refer to Chapter 3 for details
Check the idle and fast idle speed settings and adjust if necessary.
On Canadian models, check the idle mixture setting adjustment.
Check the choke operating system.
Check the throttle positioner system (USA models only).

Clutch – refer to Chapter 5 for details
Check the clutch pedal setting and the clutch adjustment.

Clean and check the front wheel bearing assemblies

Manual transmission
Check the transmission oil level and top up if necessary.

Automatic transmission – refer to Chapter 6 Part B for details
Check the automatic transmission fluid level and top up if necessary.

Propeller shaft and rear axle – refer to Chapters 7 and 8 for details
Check the condition of the propeller shaft universal joints and the security of the central support assembly (where applicable).
Check the oil level in the rear axle and top up if necessary.

Brakes – refer to Chapter 9 for details
Check the disc brake pads and discs for excessive wear and renew if necessary.
Check the drum brakes for excessive shoe lining wear and renew if necessary. Also check the condition of the drums. Renew the drums or have the friction surfaces reground if/as necessary.
Check the brake servo unit hose for condition and security.
Check the brake hydraulic lines and hoses for condition and security. Renew if/as necessary.
Check the handbrake for satisfactory operation.
Check the brake pedal adjustment.

Steering and suspension – refer to Chapter 11 for details
Examine all steering and suspension joints and fixings for condition and security. Renew any excessively worn or damaged components.
Check the condition of the steering balljoints and their dust covers for damage.
Check the steering box oil level and on power steering models check the power steering pump oil level in the reservoir.
Check the shock absorbers front and rear for condition and security. Renew if worn or defective.
Check the rear suspension components for wear or damage, in particular the link arm bushes or leaf spring bushes (as applicable). Renew as necessary.

General checks
Make general checks as given for the 9000 mile 'General checks' given for European models.

Every 30 000 miles (48 000 km) or 24 months – whichever comes first

Engine
Remove and renew the drivebelts.
Drain and renew the engine coolant adding the correct ratio of anti-freeze solution for the climatic conditions.

Inspect the various vacuum hoses and fittings for condition and security and renew any defective hoses.

Fuel system – refer to Chapter 3 for details
Remove and renew the air filter.
Check the inlet air temperature control valve for satisfactory operation. The cold air inlet should open when the engine is hot. Renew the valve unit if found to be defective.
Check all fuel pipes and connections for signs of leaks or damage, renew as necessary. Also check the fuel tank filler cap, its check valve operation and also that the gasket is in good condition. Renew as necessary.

Ignition system – refer to Chapter 4 for details
Check and if necessary adjust the ignition timing.
On Canadian models check the spark control system (where fitted).

Emission control system – refer to Chapter 3 for details
Check the PCV system hoses and connections for condition and security. The hoses should also be checked for blockage, particularly on worn engines. Renew the PCV valve on non-California models.
On USA models check the air injection system and the oxygen sensor in the exhaust emission control (where fitted).
On Canadian models check the air suction system.
In the fuel evaporative emission control system, check the charcoal canister for internal clogging or possibly damage. Clean it through with compressed air or renew if necessary. Check the hoses and connections for condition and security elsewhere in this system.

Steering – refer to Chapter 11 for details
Remove, clean and relubricate the front wheel bearing assemblies.

Every 60 000 miles (96 000 km) or every 48 months – whichever comes first

Check the cooling system hoses and connections, also those of the heater unit. Renew any which are perished or suspect.
Renew the in-line fuel filter – see Chapter 3 for details.
Renew the fuel tank filler cap gasket.
On California models remove and renew the PCV valve as well as checking the system hoses for condition and security.

Blow dirt from air cleaner element

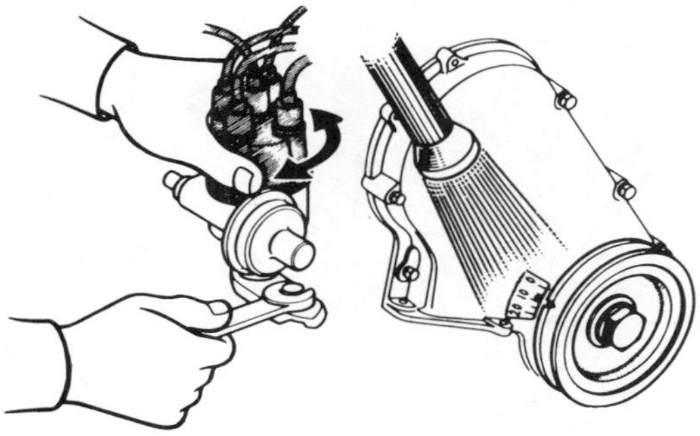

Check/adjust ignition timing

Lubricate steering lower joint – use only molybdenum disulphide lithium based grease. Refit plugs on completion

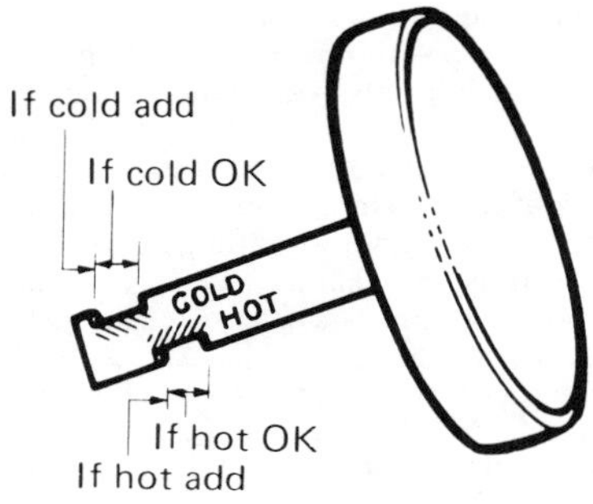

Check power steering reservoir oil level

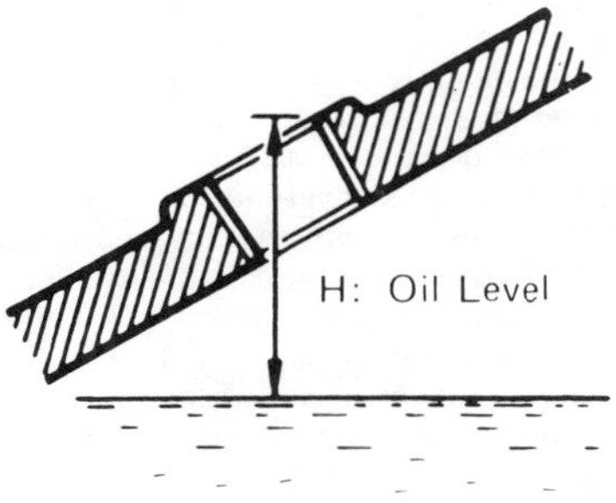

Check steering box oil level

Chapter 1 Engine

Contents

Specifications

UK models

General

Type	Four cylinder in-line, overhead valve	
Designation:		
Saloon and Estate	4K	
Liftback	2T	
Coupe	2T–B	
Bore:		
4K engines	3.0 in (75.0 mm)	
2T and 2T–B engines	3.3 in (85.0 mm)	
Stroke:		
4K engines	2.9 in (73.0 mm)	
2T and 2T-B engines	2.8 in (70.0 mm)	
Capacity:		
4K engine	1290 cc	
2T and 2T-B engines	1588 cc	
Compression ratio:		
4K engine:		
Up to August 1981	9.0:1	
From August 1981 on	9.5:1	
2T engine	9.0:1	
2T–B engine	9.4:1	
Compression pressures (engine cranking):		
4K engine:		
Standard	156 lbf/in^2 (11.0 kgf/cm^2)	
Minimum	128 lbf/in^2 (9.0 kgf/cm^2)	
2T engine:		
Standard	163 lbf/in^2 (11.5 kgf/cm^2)	
Minimim	128 lbf/in^2 (9.0 kgf/cm^2)	
2T–B engine:		
Standard	170 lbf/in^2 (12.0 kgf/cm^2)	
Minimum	142 lbf/in^2 (10.0 kgf/cm^2)	
Maximum allowable pressure difference between cylinders	14.0 lbf/in^2 (1.0 kgf/cm^2)	

Cylinder block	4K engine	2T and 2T–B engine
Bore diameter:		
Standard	2.955 to 2.956 in (75.00 to 75.05 mm)	3.349 to 3.350 in (85.00 to 85.05 mm)
Wear limit	0.008 in (0.2 mm)	0.008 in (0.2 mm)
Maximum allowable distortion of cylinder block face	0.002 in (0.05 mm)	0.002 in (0.05 mm)
Crankshaft		
Main bearing journal diameter	1.9690 to 1.9700 in (49.976 to 50.00 mm)	2.2842 to 2.2852 in (57.976 to 58.0 mm)
Main bearing journal minimum regrind diameter	1.9496 to 1.9500 in (49.483 to 49.493 mm)	2.2651 to 2.2655 in (57.490 to 57.50 mm)
Main bearing journal running clearance:		
Standard	0.0006 to 0.0016 in (0.016 to 0.040 mm)	0.0012 to 0.0022 in (0.032 to 0.056 mm)

Wear limit	0.004 in (0.10 mm)	0.004 in (0.10 mm)
Maximum allowable main bearing journal taper or ovality	0.0004 in (0.01 mm)	0.0004 in (0.01 mm)
Crankpin journal diameter	1.6538 to 1.6548 in (41.976 to 42.00 mm)	1.8902 to 1.8912 in (47.976 to 48.00 mm)
Crankpin journal minimum regrind diameter	1.6241 to 1.6245 in (41.223 to 41.233 mm)	1.8711 to 1.8715 in (47.490 to 47.50 mm)
Crankpin journal running clearance:		
Standard	0.0006 to 0.0016 in (0.016 to 0.040 mm)	0.0009 to 0.002 in (0.024 to 0.048 mm)
Wear limit	0.004 in (0.10 mm)	0.003 in (0.08 mm)
Maximum allowable crankpin journal taper or ovality	0.0004 in (0.01 mm)	0.0004 in (0.01 mm)
Crankpin endfloat:		
Standard	0.0016 to 0.0095 in (0.040 to 0.242 mm)	0.0007 to 0.008 in (0.020 to 0.220 mm)
Wear limit	0.012 in (0.3 mm)	0.012 in (0.3 mm)

Connecting rods

Endfloat on crankpin journal:		
Standard	0.008 to 0.012 in (0.20 to 0.304 mm)	0.006 to 0.010 in (0.16 to 0.26 mm)
Wear limit	0.014 in (0.35 mm)	0.012 in (0.30 mm)
Small-end bearing running clearance:		
Standard	0.0001 to 0.0003 in (0.004 to 0.008 mm)	Interference fit
Wear limit	0.002 in (0.05 mm)	

Pistons and piston rings

Piston diameter	2.9534 to 2.9553 in (74.96 to 75.01 mm)	3.3466 to 3.3486 in (84.94 to 84.99 mm)
Piston oversizes available	0.020 in, 0.030 in, 0.040 in (0.050 mm, 0.75 mm, 1.0 mm)	0.020 in, 0.030 in 0.040 in (0.50 mm, 0.75 mm, 1.0 mm)
Piston-to-cylinder bore clearance	0.0012 to 0.0020 in (0.03 to 0.05 mm)	0.0020 to 0.0027 in (0.05 to 0.07 mm)
Piston ring-to-groove clearance:		
Top compression ring	0.0012 to 0.0027 in (0.03 to 0.07 mm)	0.0007 to 0.0023 in (0.02 to 0.06 mm)
2nd compression ring	0.0007 to 0.0023 in (0.02 to 0.06 mm)	0.0006 to 0.0021 in (0.015 to 0.055 mm)
Oil control ring	0.0006 to 0.0023 in (0.015 to 0.06 mm)	0.0006 to 0.0023 in (0.015 to 0.06 mm)
Piston ring end gap:		
Top compression ring	0.086 to 0.0153 in (0.22 to 0.39 mm)	0.0098 to 0.0220 in (0.25 to 0.56 mm)
2nd compression ring	0.0006 to 0.0189 in (0.15 to 0.48 mm)	0.0078 to 0.0201 in (0.20 to 0.51 mm)
Oil control ring	0.0118 to 0.0401 in (0.30 to 1.02 mm)	0.0006 to 0.0023 in (0.015 to 0.060 mm)

Camshaft

Journal diameter:		
No 1	1.7024 to 1.7030 in (43.209 to 43.225 mm)	1.8304 to 1.8311 in (46.459 to 46.475 mm)
No 2	1.6923 to 1.6930 in (42.954 to 42.970 mm)	1.8206 to 1.8212 in (46.209 to 46.225 mm)
No 3	1.6825 to 1.6831 in (42.704 to 42.720 mm)	1.8107 to 1.8114 in (45.959 to 45.975 mm)
No 4	1.6728 to 1.6735 in (42.459 to 42.475 mm)	1.8009 to 1.8015 in (45.709 to 45.725 mm
No 5	–	1.7910 to 1.7917 in (45.459 to 45.475 mm)
Bearing running clearance:		
Standard:		
Journal No 1 and No 4	0.0009 to 0.0026 in (0.025 to 0.066 mm)	0.0009 to 0.0026 in (0.025 to 0.066 mm)
Journal No 2 and No 3	0.0011 to 0.0027 in (0.030 to 0.071 mm)	0.009 to 0.0026 in (0.025 to 0.066 mm)
Journal No 5	–	0.0009 to 0.0026 in (0.025 to 0.066 mm)
Wear limit	0.0039 in (0.10 mm)	0.0039 in (0.10 mm)

Camshaft endfloat:		
Standard	0.0027 to 0.0543 in (0.070 to 0.138 mm)	0.0027 to 0.0059 in (0.070 to 0.15 mm)
Wear limit	0.012 in (0.3 mm)	0.012 in (0.3 mm)
Cam lobe height:		
Standard:		
Inlet	1.4368 to 1.4408 in (36.469 to 36.569 mm)	1.5113 to 1.5153 in (38.36 to 38.46 mm)
Exhaust	1.4329 to 1.4368 in (36.369 to 36.469 mm)	1.5070 to 1.5109 in (38.25 to 38.35 mm)
Wear limit:		
Inlet	1.4250 in (36.17 mm)	1.5086 in (38.29 mm)
Exhaust	1.4211 in (36.07 mm)	1.5046 in (38.19 mm)

Timing chain, tensioner and damper

Maximum allowable chain elongation under 11 lbf (5 kgf) load	10.74 in (272.7 mm)	11.48 in (291.4 mm)
Minimum allowable tensioner plunger head thickness	0.472 in (12.0 mm)	0.492 in (12.5 mm)
Minimum allowable vibration damper thickness	0.275 in (7.0 mm)	0.197 in (5.0 mm)

Cylinder head

Maximum allowable distortion of cylinder head face	0.002 in (0.05 mm)	0.002 in (0.05 mm)
Maximum allowable refacing cut	0.008 in (0.2 mm)	0.008 in (0.2 mm)
Valve seat angle	45°	45°
Valve seat contact width:		
Inlet	0.043 to 0.071 in (1.1 to 1.8 mm)	0.047 to 0.063 in (1.2 to 1.6 mm)
Exhaust	0.047 to 0.071 in (1.2 to 1.8 mm)	0.047 to 0.063 in (1.2 to 1.6 mm)

Valves

Face angle	44.5°	44.5°
Overall length:		
Standard:		
Inlet	3.936 in (99.9 mm)	4.294 in (109.0 mm)
Exhaust	3.943 in (100.1 mm)	4.294 in (109.0 mm)
Wear limit:		
Inlet	3.916 in (99.4 mm)	4.274 in (108.5 mm)
Exhaust	3.924 in (99.6 mm)	4.274 in (108.5 mm)
Stem diameter:		
Inlet	0.3138 to 0.3144 in (7.965 to 7.980 mm)	0.3140 to 0.3146 in (7.970 to 7.985 mm)
Exhaust	0.3136 to 0.3142 in (7.960 to 7.975 mm)	0.3138 to 0.3144 in (7.965 to 7.980 mm)
Stem-to-guide clearance:		
Standard:		
Inlet	0.0012 to 0.0025 in (0.030 to 0.065 mm)	0.0010 to 0.0023 in (0.025 to 0.060 mm)
Exhaust	0.0014 to 0.0027 in (0.035 to 0.070 mm)	0.0012 to 0.0025 in (0.030 to 0.065 mm)
Wear limit:		
Inlet	0.0031 in (0.08 mm)	0.0031 in (0.08 mm)
Exhaust	0.0039 in (0.10 mm)	0.0039 in (0.10 mm)
Minimum allowable valve head edge thickness:		
Inlet	0.031 in (0.08 mm)	0.020 in (0.5 mm)
Exhaust	0.035 in (0.9 mm)	0.027 in (0.7 mm)
Valve clearances:		
Hot:		
Inlet	0.008 in (0.20 mm)	0.008 in (0.20 mm)
Exhaust	0.012 in (0.30 mm)	0.013 in (0.33 mm)
Cold:		
Inlet	0.005 in (0.13 mm)	0.007 in (0.18 mm)
Exhaust	0.009 in (0.23 mm)	0.012 in (0.30 mm)
Valve spring free length	1.832 in (46.5 mm)	1.658 in (42.1 mm)
Valve spring installed length	1.512 in (38.4 mm)	1.485 in (37.7 mm)
Valve guide outer diameter	0.5137 to 0.5142 in (13.040 to 13.051 mm)	0.5137 to 0.5142 in (13.040 to 13.051 mm)
Valve guide inner diameter	0.3155 to 0.3163 in (8.01 to 8.03 mm)	0.3155 to 0.3163 in (8.01 to 8.03 mm)
Cam follower outer diameter	0.7871 to 0.7879 in (19.978 to 19.999 mm)	0.8738 to 0.8746 in (22.178 to 22.199 mm)
Cam follower running clearance:		
Standard	0.0006 to 0.0011 in (0.015 to 0.029 mm)	0.0008 to 0.0012 in (0.02 to 0.03 mm)

Wear limit	0.0039 in (0.1 mm)	0.0039 in (0.1 mm)
Rocker arm-to-shaft clearance:		
Standard	0.0008 to 0.0015 in (0.02 to 0.04 mm)	0.0004 to 0.0020 in (0.01 to 0.05 mm)
Wear limit	0.0023 in (0.06 mm)	0.0023 in (0.06 mm)

Flywheel

Maximum allowable flywheel run-out	0.0039 in (0.1 mm)	0.0039 in (0.1 mm)

Oil pump

Rotor lobe clearance:		
Standard	0.0015 to 0.0063 in (0.04 to 0.16 mm)	0.0015 to 0.0063 in (0.04 to 0.16 mm)
Wear limit	0.0078 in (0.2 mm)	0.0098 in (0.25 mm)
Rotor endfloat:		
Standard	0.0012 to 0.0035 in (0.03 to 0.09 mm)	0.0012 to 0.0035 in (0.03 to 0.09 mm)
Wear limit	0.0059 in (0.15 mm)	0.0059 in (0.15 mm)
Outer rotor-to-body clearance:		
Standard	0.0039 to 0.0063 in (0.10 to 0.16 mm)	0.0039 to 0.0063 in (0.10 to 0.16 mm)
Wear limit	0.0078 in (0.2 mm)	0.0098 in (0.25 mm)
Oil pressure:		
At idle speed	4.3 lbf/in^2 (0.3 kgf/cm^2)	4.3 lbf/in^2 (0.3 kgf/cm^2)
At 3000 rpm	35.5 to 71 lbf/in^2 (2.5 to 5.0 kgf/cm^2)	35.5 to 71 lbf/in^2 (2.5 to 5.0 kgf/cm^2)

Torque wrench settings

	lbf ft	kgf m
4K engine		
Cylinder head bolts	40 to 47	5.4 to 6.6
Rocker arm support to cylinder head	14 to 17	1.8 to 2.4
Manifold to cylinder head	15 to 21	2.0 to 3.0
Main bearing cap bolts	40 to 47	5.4 to 6.6
Connecting rod bolts	29 to 37	4.0 to 5.2
Crankshaft pulley bolt	55 to 75	7.5 to 10.5
Flywheel bolts	40 to 47	5.4 to 6.6
Camshaft sprocket	40 to 47	5.4 to 6.6
Sump:		
Standard bolt	1.5 to 3.0	0.2 to 0.4
Step bolt	2.2 to 5.0	0.3 to 0.7
Exhaust manifold to pipe	22 to 32	3.0 to 4.5

2T, 2T–B and 3T–C engines		
Cylinder head/rocker pedestal	66 to 68	9.0 to 9.5
Inlet manifold	13 to 18	1.8 to 2.5
Exhaust manifold	22 to 32	3.0 to 4.5
Main bearing caps	53 to 63	7.2 to 8.8
Connecting rod bolts	29 to 36	4.0 to 5.0
Crankshaft pulley	29 to 43	4.0 to 6.0
Flywheel	42 to 47	5.8 to 6.6
Camshaft sprocket	51 to 79	7 to 11
Sump	4.0 to 5.7	0.5 to 0.8
Exhaust manifold to pipe	29 to 36	4.0 to 5.0

USA and Canada models

The engine specification is identical to the 2T and 2T–B units for UK models except for the following differences

General

Designation	3T–C
Bore	3.3 in (85.0 mm)
Stroke	3.1 in (78.0 mm)
Capacity	1770 cc (108.0 cu in)
Compression ratio	9.0:1
Compression pressures (engine cranking):	
Standard	163.5 lbf/in^2 (11.5 kgf/cm^2)
Minumum	129.4 lbf/in^2 (9.0 kgf/cm^2)

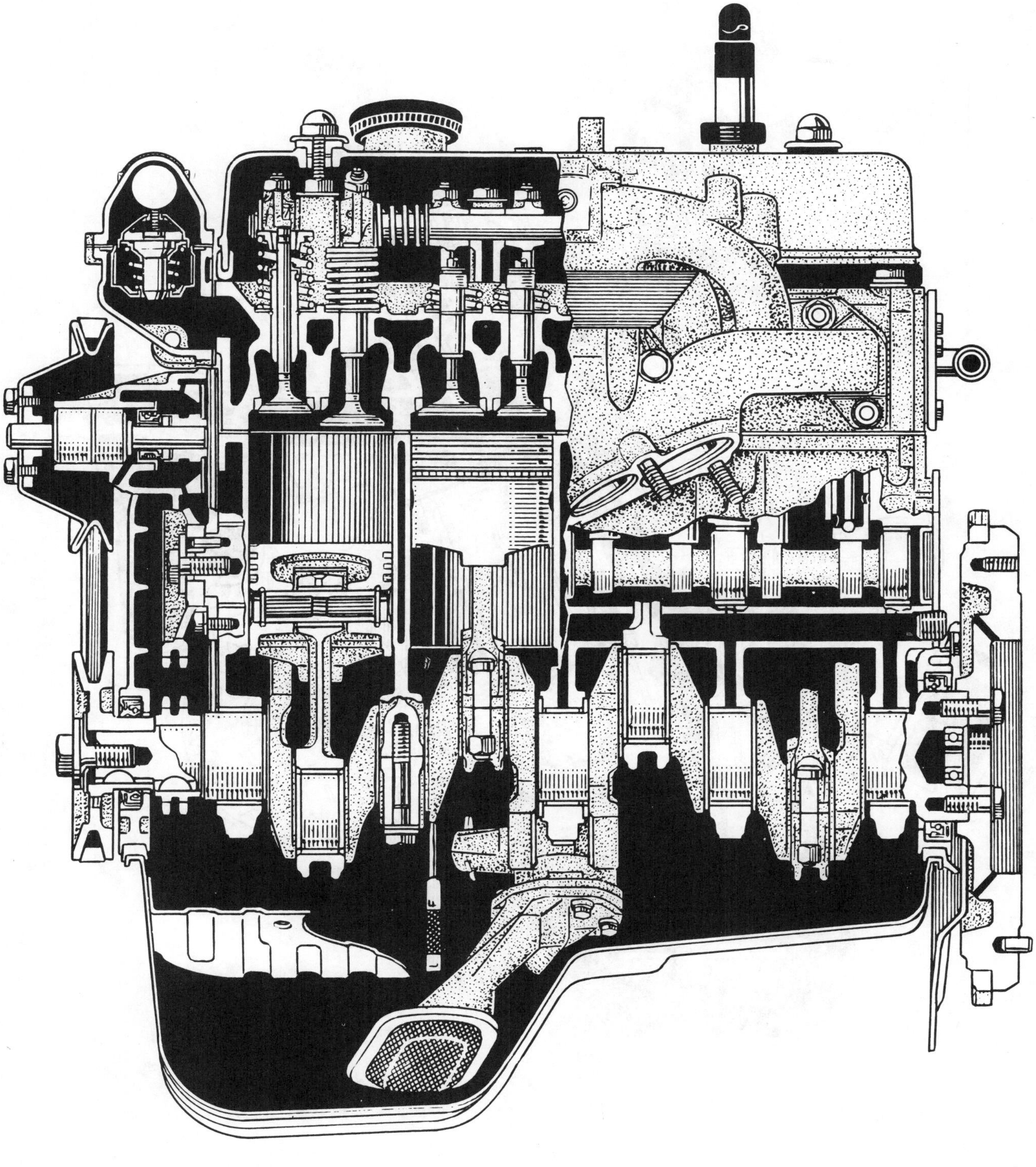

Fig. 1.1 4K engine – side sectioned view (Sec 1)

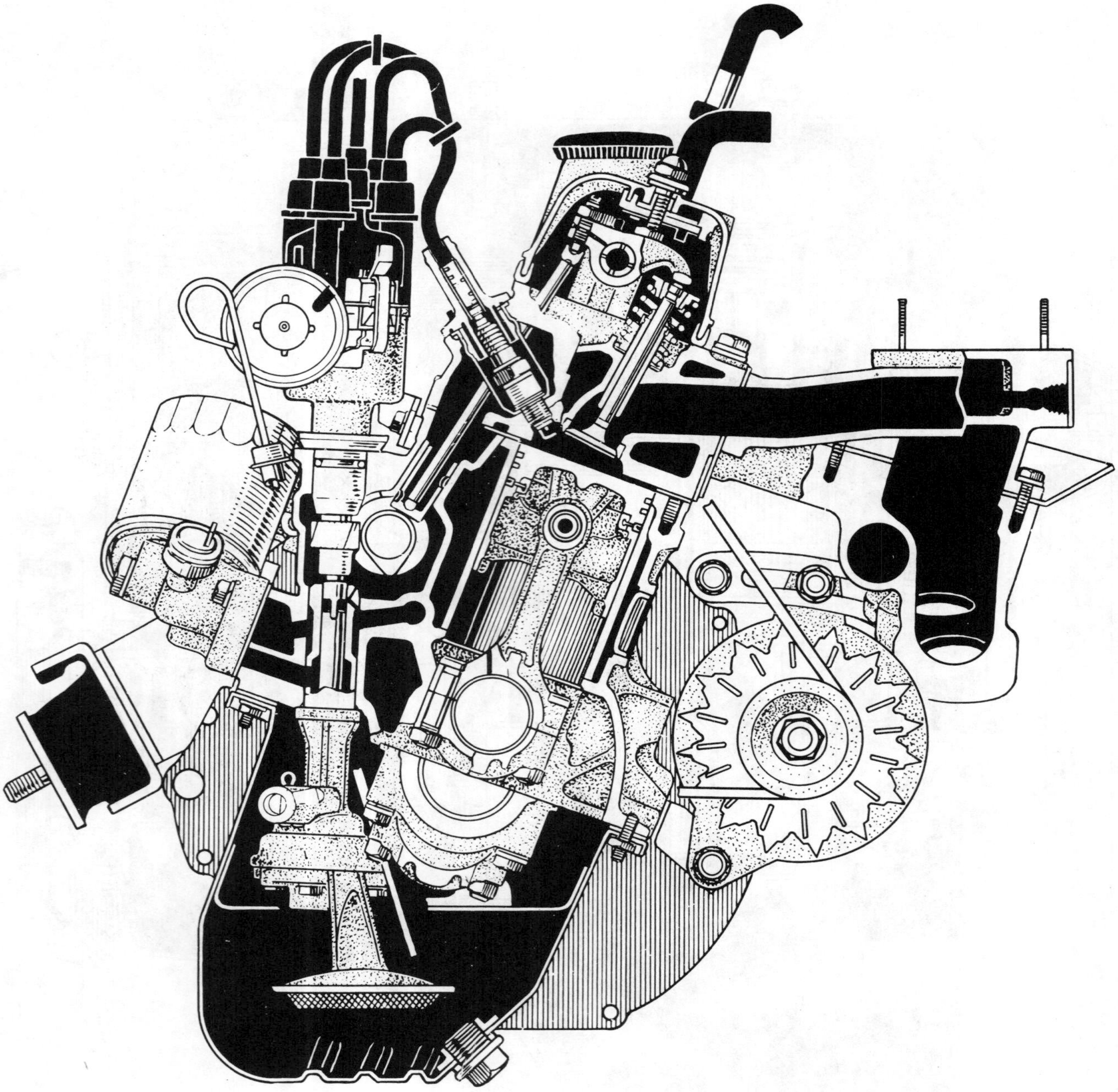

Fig. 1.2 4K engine – front sectioned view (Sec 1)

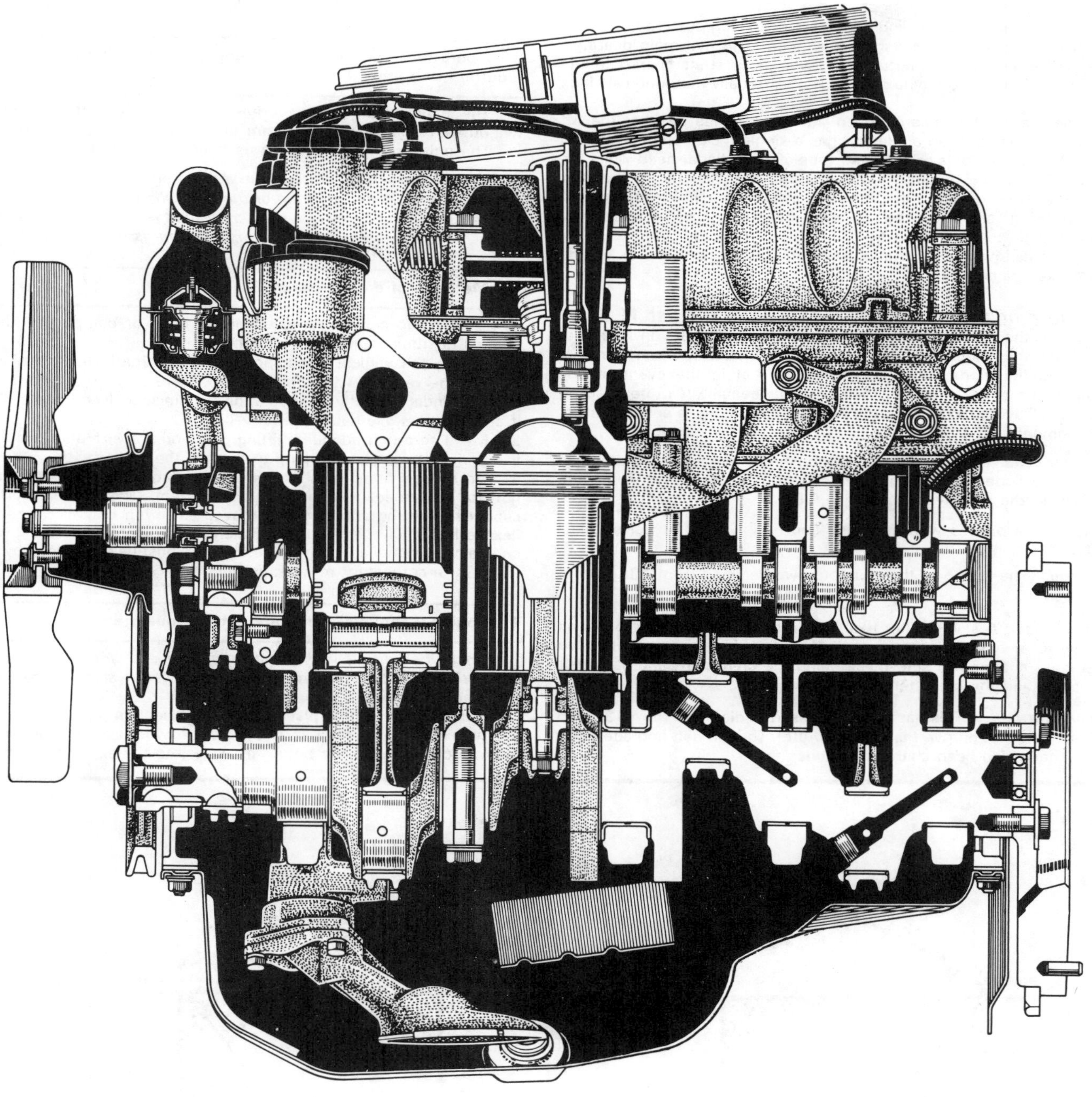

Fig. 1.3 2T, 2TB and 3T-C engines – side sectioned view (Sec 1)

1 General description

The engines used in the vehicles covered by this manual will be the 1290 cc (4K), the 1588 cc (2T and 2T-B) or the 1770 cc (108.0 cu in) (3T-C) according to model and market.

All units are of four cylinder in-line type having push rod operated overhead valves. The crankshaft is supported in five main bearings. The oil pump and distributor are driven by a shaft geared to the camshaft. The full-flow type oil filter is of externally mounted cartridge design.

The main differences between the two engines are that the 4K engine is inclined at an angle and has a single rocker shaft with inlet and exhaust manifolds on the same side of the cylinder head while the 2T, 2T-B and 3T-C engines have separate rocker shafts for the inlet and exhaust valves and the intake and exhaust manifolds are located on opposing sides of the cylinder head, to give a crossflow characteristic to the engine.

Since its introduction the following modifications to the 4K engine have taken place.

Engine modifications – 4K engine from August 1981

Since the introduction of the 'New Toyota Corolla' in March of 1980, the following modifications have been made to the 4K engine. These modifications should be noted so that in the event of any components being renewed, their interchangeability can be checked with your Toyota dealer prior to purchase and fitting to ensure correct replacement.

Cylinder head: The shape of the combustion chambers were modified and the cylinder head height reduced from 82.3 mm to 76.5 mm, increasing the compression ratio to 9.5:1.

Pistons: The pistons were modified and new type compression rings fitted.

Pushrods: The length of the pushrods was reduced from 186 mm to 179 mm.

Timing chain: A single roller type was fitted in place of the previous double roller type. In consequence, the associated components have also been changed to suit, these being the crankshaft and camshaft sprockets and the chain tensioner and damper.

Crankshaft pulley: This has been increased in diameter from 130 mm to 142 mm (to improve the charging rate). The fan belt and alternator pulley have also been changed to suit.

Flywheel: The profile was changed to improve balance.

Note: *All original photographs used in this Chapter depict an operation being carried out on the 1588 cc 2T engine unless otherwise stated. Where the procedure or operation described differs significantly on 2T-B or 3T-C engines, this will be stated in the text.*

2 Operations possible with engine in position and those requiring its removal

1 The majority of major overhaul operations can be carried out without removing the engine from the vehicle.
2 The only exception requiring its removal are the following:

- (a) *Removal and refitting of the main bearing shells*
- (b) *Removal and refitting of the crankshaft*
- (c) *Attention to the flywheel, crankshaft rear oil seal can be given if the gearbox (or auto. transmission) is first removed*

3 Methods of engine removal

1 The engine can be removed on its own, or complete with the manual gearbox for later separation.
2 Where the vehicle is equipped with automatic transmission, in view of the weight of the transmission, the engine should always be removed independently as should the transmission (see Chapter 6B) if it also requires overhaul or repair.
3 Make sure that adequate lifting gear and if possible a trolley jack, are available before attemping to remove the engine.
4 On models fitted with air conditioning equipment it is important not to disconnect any part of the system. The compressor and condenser can be unbolted and moved aside but only as far as their flexible hoses will permit. If insufficient room is provided to allow the engine to be removed, then the refrigerant must be discharged by your dealer or a competent refrigeration engineer.

4 Engine – removal complete with manual gearbox

On models fitted with air conditioning equipment, refer to the precautionary notes in the previous Section before starting any engine removal procedures.

1 If the vehicle can be placed over an inspection pit or raised three or four inches on ramps or blocks of wood placed under the roadwheels so much the better, as access to the exhaust mountings

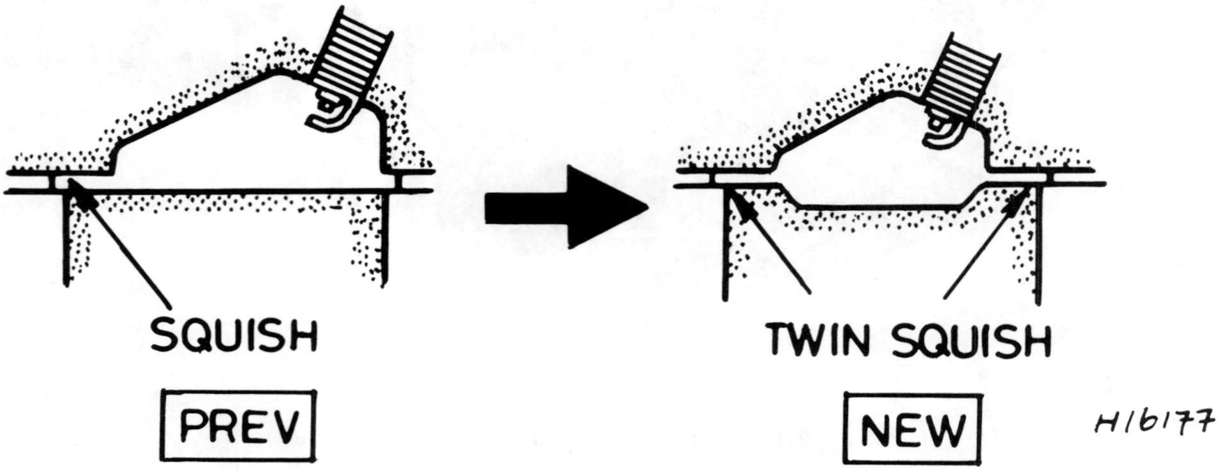

Fig. 1.4 4K engine modification showing the early and late type combustion chamber/piston profile (Sec 1)

and rear engine mounting will be that much easier.
2 Unbolt and withdraw the engine undertray.
3 Remove the bonnet as described in Chapter 12 and store it where it will not get damaged.
4 Disconnect the negative lead from the battery.
5 Drain the coolant from the engine cooling system as described in Chapter 2. Retain the coolant for further use if it contains fairly fresh anti-freeze (photo).
6 Drain all the engine oil into a suitable container. Refit the drain plug.
7 Drain the gearbox oil by unscrewing the filler/level plug and then the drain plug. Refit the drain plug and fully tighten it but the filler plug need only be tightened finger tight at this stage.
8 Disconnect the hoses and remove the radiator as described in Chapter 2.
9 If power steering is fitted remove the drivebelt and detach the vane pump. Leave the pump hoses connected and position the pump back out of the way.
10 Remove the air cleaner assembly according to type and by reference to Chapter 3.
11 Disconnect the HT lead (from the coil) and the LT lead from the distributor.
12 Disconnect the heater hoses and their supporting clips and tie them back out of the way.
13 Detach the accelerator linkage/cable from the carburettor. On models fitted with a manual choke, disconnect the choke cable. On models fitted with an electric choke, detach the lead connections.
14 Disconnect the fuel supply and return hoses between the pump and carburettor(s). Plug the hoses to prevent fuel leakage (photo).
15 Detach the following wires according to model and equipment:

(a) *Alternator wires (photo)*
(b) *Fuel cut solenoid wire*
(c) *Water temperature sender unit wire*
(d) *Oil pressure switch wire/or sender unit wire (as applicable)*
(e) *Thermo-switch wire*
(f) *Vacuum switch wire*
(g) *Vacuum switching valve wire(s)*
(h) *Oxygen sensor wire*
(i) *Engine/transmission to body earth straps (photos)*

Where confusion could possibly arise during reassembly, mark the wires for correct identity.
16 Disconnect and where necessary remove any emission control hoses which affect engine removal. Identify each hose as it is detached and mark it accordingly to avoid confusion during reassembly. The extent of emission control equipment fitted is varied depending on

4.5 Cylinder block drain plug

4.8 Detach cooling system hoses

4.14 Disconnect the fuel hoses at the carburettor

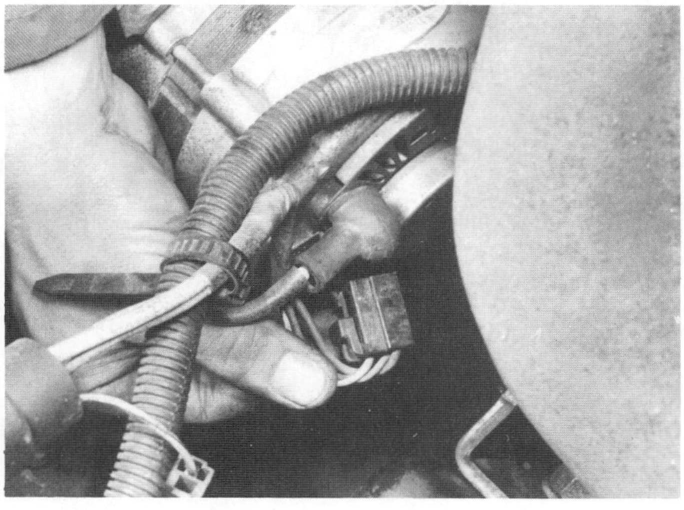
4.15a Disconnect the alternator wires

4.15b disconnect the earth straps located on the right-hand side of cylinder head at rear and ...

4.15c ... lower right-hand side of cylinder block

4.25a Detach the engine mounting each side ...

4.25b ... and where fitted, the stabiliser rod

4.25c Disconnect the cable location clip from the left-hand engine mounting bracket

4.28 Lifting out the engine and gearbox

model and operating territory. For details and system diagrams refer to Chapter 3.
17 Working underneath the vehicle disconnect the clutch operating mechanism according to type (cable or hydraulic). Refer to Chapter 5 for details.
18 Unbolt and detach the exhaust downpipe from the manifold. Where applicable disconnect the downpipe from the steady bracket attached to the bellhousing.
19 Disconnect the starter motor leads.
20 Disconnect the leads from the reverse lamp switch on the side of the gearbox.
21 Remove the gearshift lever as described in Chapter 6A.
22 Remove the propeller shaft as described in Chapter 7.
23 Disconnect the speedometer drive cable from the side of the gearbox. To do this, simply unscrew the knurled ring and withdraw the cable assembly.
24 Attach a suitable hoist to slings or chains attached to the engine lifting hooks and just take the weight of the engine.
25 Disconnect the front engine mountings from their brackets on the crossmember by unscrewing the nuts (photo). When dismantling the engine mounting on the left-hand side on some models it will, where fitted, be necessary to detach the engine stabiliser rod at the bottom (photo) and the cable clip.
26 Place a jack under the gearbox and with its weight supported, unbolt and remove the rear mounting and crossmember.
27 With the engine and gearbox now free and ready for removal, make a final check to see that no wires, cables or controls have been overlooked and are still attached to the engine or gearbox.
28 With the help of an assistant, simultaneously raise the hoist and lower the gearbox jack until the combined assembly can be raised and lifted out of the engine compartment at an inclined angle (photo).

5 Engine – removal, leaving manual gearbox in vehicle

1 Carry out the operations described in paragraphs 1 to 19 of the previous Section with the exception of paragraphs 8 and 17.
2 Unbolt and remove the starter motor.
3 Unbolt and remove the bolts which secure the clutch bellhousing to the engine. *Note that two of the bolts pass through reinforcement brackets on some engines.*
4 Proceed as given in paragraphs 24 and 25 in the last Section.
5 Place a jack under the gearbox and support its weight.
6 Using the hoist, raise the engine until the rear face of the cylinder head is almost touching the engine compartment bulkhead. Raise the jack to support the gearbox. *Two changes should now have occurred, (i) the engine front mountings should be clear of the crossmember brackets and (ii) the engine sump should be just clear of the crossmember.*
7 Now pull the engine forward to clear the input shaft of the gearbox and lift the engine out of the vehicle.

6 Engine – removal, leaving automatic transmission in vehicle

1 Carry out the operations described in paragraphs 1 to 19 of Section 4 with the exception of paragraph 7, but drain the transmission fluid and disconnect the fluid cooler pipes from the base of the radiator. Plug the pipes after removal.
2 Detach the fluid cooler pipes from the engine brackets.
3 Disconnect the transmission kickdown cable.
4 Unbolt and remove the starter motor.
5 Unbolt and remove the engine to transmission support brackets.
6 Prise out the two rubber plugs from the semi-circular plate at the lower part of the torque converter housing. Using a spanner on the crankshaft pulley bolt, turn the crankshaft until one of the torque converter to driveplate retaining bolts becomes accessible through the opening. Undo the bolt then remove the remaining five bolts in the same way.
7 As the engine is removed it is essential that the torque converter remains in place on the transmission. To assist with this, as the engine is initially pulled clear, a guide pin to act as a fulcrum when easing the engine away should be made up and used as described in Chapter 6, Section 31.
8 Attach a suitable hoist to slings or chains attached to the engine lifting hooks and just take the weight of the engine.
9 Undo all the bolts securing the engine to the transmission.
10 Disconnect the front engine mountings from their brackets on the crossmember noting that on certain models the engine stabiliser rod bottom mounting must also be disconnected.
11 Place a jack with an interposed block of wood under the transmission.
12 Make a final check that all wires, cables, hoses and other connections are all removed and positioned well clear.
13 Raise the engine hoist and transmission jack and free the engine from the transmission with the help of the guide pin. With the engine free from the transmission lift it straight up and out of the engine compartment.
14 Make up a small plate suitably cranked which can be bolted to the transmission face to retain the torque converter while the engine is removed.

7 Engine/manual gearbox – separation

1 Where the engine was removed complete with the gearbox, lower the assembly to the ground and remove the starter motor.
2 Unscrew and remove the bolts which secure the clutch bellhousing to the engine.
3 Support the weight of the gearbox and withdraw it in a straight line from the engine. On no account let the weight of the gearbox hang upon the input shaft while the latter is still engaged in the splines of the clutch driven plate (photo).

7.3 Withdrawing the gearbox from the engine

8 Engine – dismantling general

1 Keen home mechanics with previous engine dismantling experience may well have a stand on which to put the engine components, but most will make do with a work bench which should be large enough to spread around the inevitable bits and pieces and tools, and strong enough to support the engine weight. If the floor is the only place, try and ensure that the engine rests on a hard wood platform or similar rather than on concrete.
2 Spend some time on cleaning the unit. If you have been wise this will have been done before the engine was removed at a service bay. Good water soluble solvents will help to 'float off' caked dirt/grease under a water jet. Once the exterior is clean dismantling may begin. As parts are removed clean them in petrol/paraffin (do not immerse parts with oilways in paraffin – clean them with a petrol soaked cloth and clean oilways with wire). If an air line is available use it for final cleaning off. Paraffin, which could possibly remain in oilways and would dilute the oil for initial lubrication after reassembly, must be blown out.
3 Always fit new gaskets and seals – but do not throw the old ones away until you have the new one to hand. A pattern is then available if they have to be made specially. Hang them up on a nail.
4 In general it is best to work from the top of the engine downwards.

In all cases support the engine firmly so that it does not topple over when you are undoing stubborn nuts and bolts.
5 Always place nuts and bolts back with their components or place of attachment, if possible – it saves much confusion later. Otherwise put them in small, separate pots or jars so that their groups are easily identified.
6 If you have an area where parts can be laid out on sheets of paper, do so – putting the nuts and bolts with them. If you are able to look at all the components in this way it helps to avoid missing something on reassembly.

9 Engine ancillaries – removal

1 If you are stripping the engine completely or preparing to install a reconditioned unit, all the ancillaries must be removed first. If you are going to obain a reconditioned 'short' motor (block, crankshaft, pistons and connecting rods) then obviously the cylinder head and associated parts will need retention for fitting to the new engine. It is advisable to check just what you will get with a reconditioned unit as changes are made from time to time.
2 The removal of all those items connected with fuel, ignition and charging systems are detailed in the respective Chapters but for clarity they are listed here:

Distributor
Carburettor(s) can be removed together with inlet manifold
Alternator (photo)
Fuel pump
Water pump
Starter motor
Thermostat (photo)
Exhaust manifold (photo)
Emission control equipment including, air pump, vacuum valves, connecting pipes etc
The clutch assembly

10 Cylinder head – removal

1 If the engine is in the car carry out the following operations. If the engine is on the bench, proceed to paragraph 11 or 16 according to engine type.
2 Disconnect the battery negative terminal.
3 Drain the cooling system as described in Chapter 2.
4 Remove the air cleaner as described in Chapter 3.
5 Disconnect all cooling system hoses from the cylinder head.
6 Make a note of their locations then disconnect all electrical leads and wiring from the cylinder head and cylinder head ancillary components (emission control, carburettor etc).
7 Refer to Chapter 3 if necessary and disconnect the accelerator and choke controls from the carburettor.
8 Undo the nuts and separate the exhaust downpipe from the manifold at the flange joint.
9 Disconnect the fuel inlet pipe and distributor vacuum pipe from the carburettor.
10 Disconnect the crankcase breather hose then remove the rocker cover and gasket.

4K engines

11 Unbolt the inlet/exhaust manifold assembly and lift it, complete with carburettor, from the cylinder head.
12 Referring to Fig. 1.5, unbolt the rocker shaft assembly in the sequence shown and remove it from the cylinder head.
13 Extract the pushrods and keep them in order by inserting them in a strip of cardboard having eight numbered holes punched in it.
14 Undo each cylinder head bolt half a turn at a time, in the sequence shown in Fig. 1.9. When all the bolts are slack, remove them from their locations.
15 Lift the cylinder head from the engine and remove the gasket. If the head is stuck, tap it free using a soft-faced mallet.

9.2a Removing the alternator

9.2b Detach the connecting hose to the water pump and remove the thermostat unit complete

9.2c Unbolt and withdraw the exhaust manifold

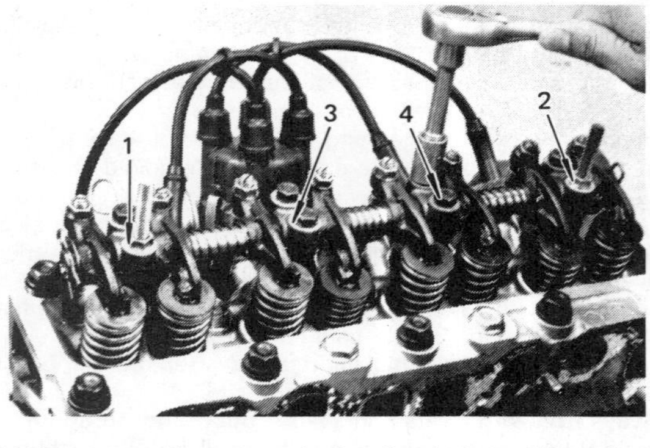

Fig. 1.5 Sequence for removal of rocker bolts – 4K engine (Sec 10)

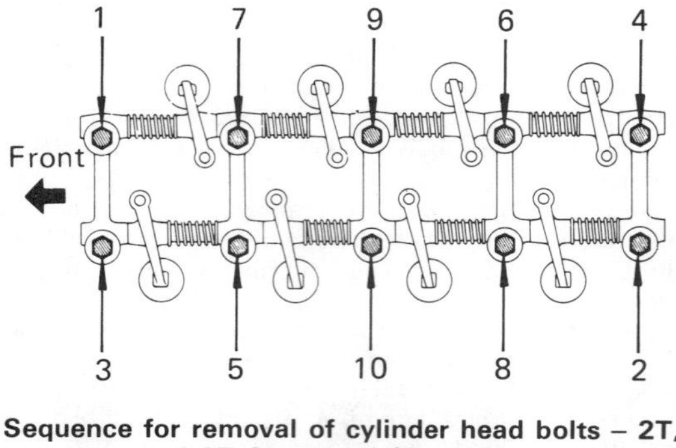

Fig. 1.6 Sequence for removal of cylinder head bolts – 2T, 2T-B and 3T-C engines (Sec 10)

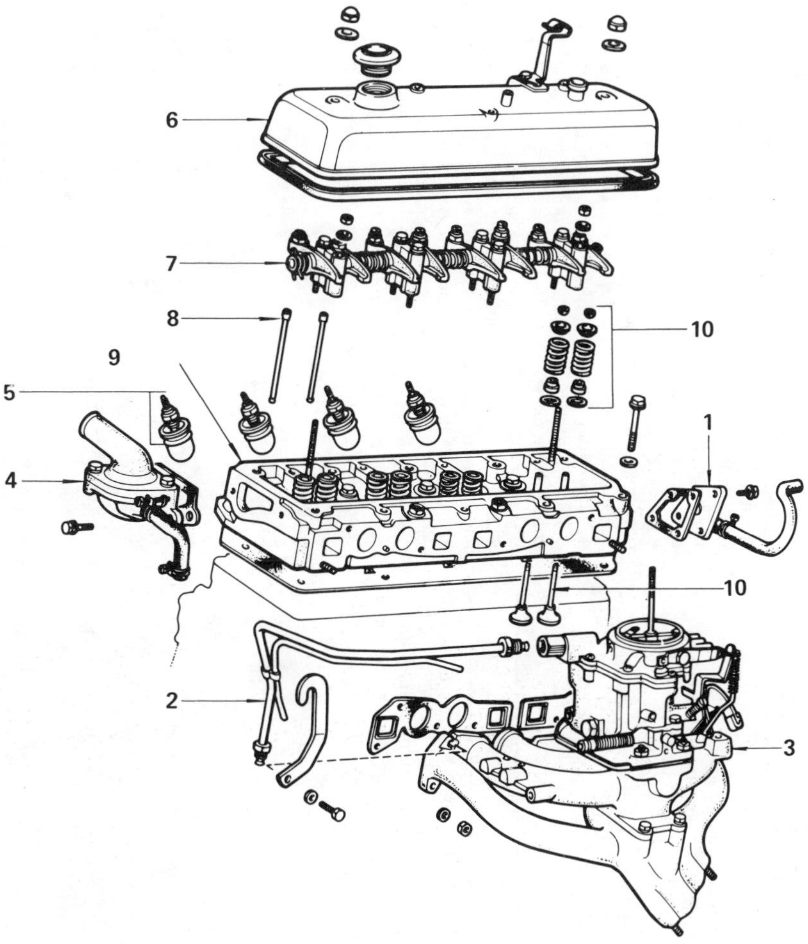

Fig. 1.7 Cylinder head components – 4K engine (Sec 10)

1 *Head rear plate*
2 *Fuel pipe & vacuum hose*
3 *IN & EX manifold*
4 *Thermostat housing*
5 *Spark plug & tube*
6 *Rocker cover*
7 *Rocker shaft assembly*
8 *Pushrod*
9 *Cylinder head*
10 *Valve, spring & oil seal*

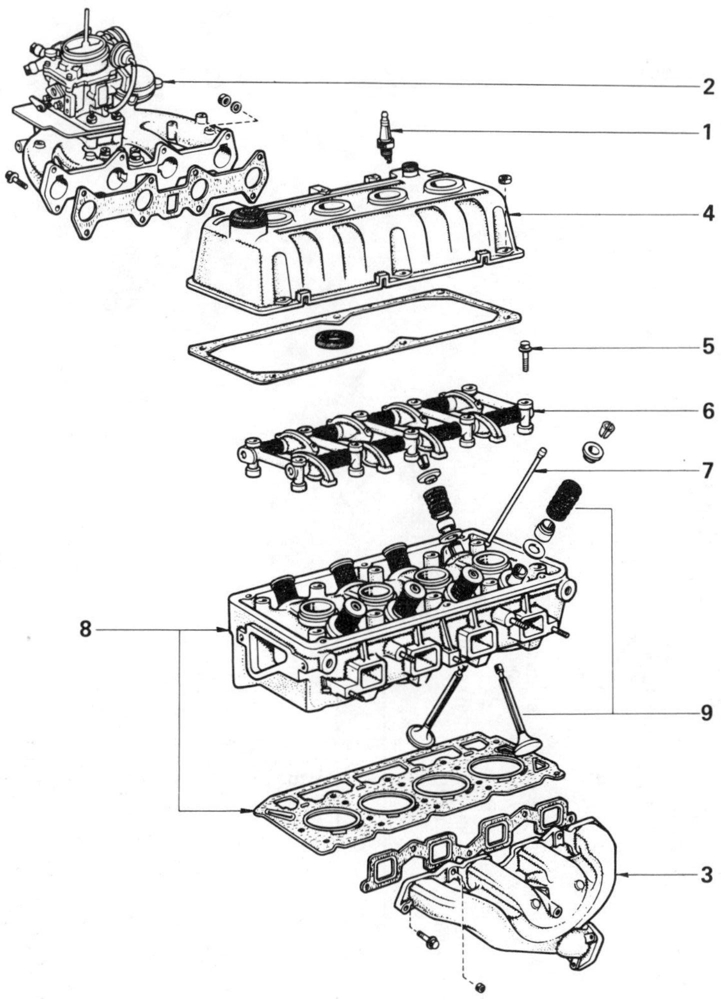

Fig. 1.8 Cylinder head components – 2T, 2T-B and 3T-C engines (Sec 10)

1 *Spark plug*
2 *Inlet manifold and carburettor assembly*
3 *Exhaust manifold*
4 *Rocker cover*
5 *Cylinder head bolt*
6 *Rocker shaft assembly*
7 *Pushrod*
8 *Cylinder head & cylinder head gasket*
9 *Valve & valve spring*

2T, 2T-B and 3T-C engines

16 Ensure that all pipes and hoses attached to the carburettor that are likely to impede removal are disconnected and moved well clear.
17 Unbolt and remove the inlet manifold complete with carburettor from one side of the cylinder head and then unbolt and remove the exhaust manifold from the other side.
18 Working in the sequence shown in Fig. 1.6, undo each cylinder head bolt half a turn at a time. When all the bolts are slack, remove them from their locations.
19 Lift off the rocker shaft assembly then extract the pushrods one at a time keeping them in order. A strip of cardboard having eight numbered holes punched in it is useful for this purpose.
20 Lift the cylinder head from the engine and remove the gasket. If the head is stuck, tap it free using a soft-faced mallet.

11 Tappets (cam followers) – removal

1 Once the cylinder head has been removed, the tappets can be extracted by pushing a finger into each one in turn and drawing them from the cylinder block (photo).
2 Keep the tappets in order so that they can be returned to their original positions. The best way of doing this is to mark each one with a piece of masking tape and number them 1 to 8, starting with 1 nearest the front of the engine. Do not punch or scratch marks on the tappets.

12 Cylinder head – dismantling

1 With the cylinder head removed, it should be dismantled if the valve components are to be inspected and renovated or decarbonising carried out as described in Sections 28 or 30.
2 To remove a valve, a valve spring compressor will be required. Fit the compressor to the valve nearest the front of the cylinder head and compress the valve spring until the split collets which secure the spring retainer can be removed (photo).
3 Slowly release the compressor and then remove it. Extract the spring retainer, the valve spring, the valve stem oil seal and the plate washer.
4 Withdraw the valve from its cylinder head guide.
5 It it essential that all components of this and the other valves are kept together with their valves so that they will all be returned to their original locations. One method of doing this is to have a box with internal divisions numbered 1 to 8, ready before dismantling commences.
6 Repeat the foregoing operations on the remaining seven valves.

13 Sump and oil pump – removal

1 If the engine is out of the vehicle, drain the engine oil (if not already done), unbolt and remove the sump. If it is stuck tight, cut round the upper and lower surfaces of the gasket with a sharp knife. If this operation is carried out carefully, then the gasket can be used again after coating both of its sides with jointing compound (photo).

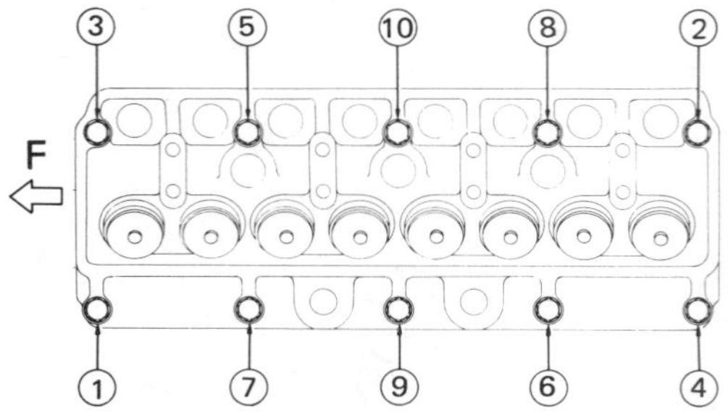

Fig. 1.9 Sequence for removal of cylinder head/rocker assembly retaining bolts – 4K engine (Sec 10)

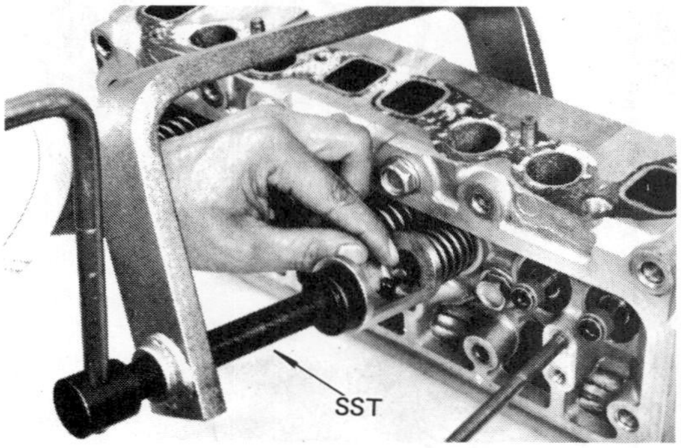

Fig. 1.10 Valve removal using a spring compressor – 4K engine (Sec 12)

2 If the engine is still in the vehicle, then dependent upon the vehicle type and engine, some or all of the following operations must be carried out before the sump can be removed. Inspection will determine the extent to which dismantling must be carried out on your particular vehicle. It is emphasised that removal of the sump without first lifting the engine out of the vehicle is a very difficult and complicated task and no advantage is to be obtained compared with first removing the engine. However, to remove the sump from an 'in-situ' engine, proceed in the following way.
3 Unbolt and remove the engine undershield.
4 Unbolt and remove the reinforcement plates which are located at the rear corners of the sump and connect between the clutch or torque converter housing.
5 Unbolt and remove the front suspension stabiliser bar.
6 As the sump will not clear the internally mounted oil pump, the engine front mounting bolts must be released and the engine raised just enough to enable the sump to be unbolted and dropped about two inches (50 mm). Two precautions must be observed during this operation, *(i) jack up under the gearbox or automatic transmission, (ii) only raise the engine the minimum necessary, otherwise the radiator hoses and possibly other leads and controls will be strained.*

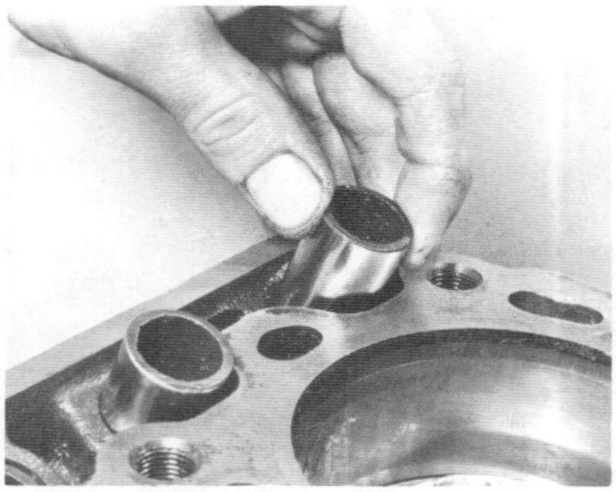

11.1 Extract the tappets

12.2 Compress the valve springs to release tension and enable the collets to be extracted

13.1 Sump removal, engine out of car

7 With the sump dropped as previously explained, the oil pump mounting bolts will now be visible. Insert a spanner through the space between the sump and the crankcase and unscrew the bolts. Lever the oil pump downwards and once the oil pump is released, the sump and oil pump can be removed.
8 Normally, once the sump has been removed, the oil pump is unbolted and withdrawn independently. If it is tight in the crankcase, tap it out gently from the distributor side.

14 Timing cover – removal

1 If the engine is in the vehicle, remove the radiator grille, drain the cooling system and remove the radiator. Release and remove the drivebelts from the alternator, water pump, air pump and compressor as applicable then move the relevant ancillary components aside to give access to the timing cover. Having done this, remove the sump as described in the previous Section.
2 Unscrew and remove the crankshaft pulley bolt. To do this a ring spanner should be used which is of sufficient length to give a good leverage. The crankshaft can be prevented from turning while the bolt is removed using a block of wood between the crankcase and one of the crankshaft webs.
3 With the bolt removed, withdraw the crankshaft pulley. This can usually be done by using two large screwdrivers as levers. If this fails, then a suitable two or three legged puller must be used.
4 Unbolt and remove the water pump from the front face of the timing cover. This is only necessary on 2T, 2T-B and 3T-C engines or where complete engine dismantling is necessary.
5 Unscrew and remove all the timing cover securing bolts. It is advisable to draw the position of the bolt holes on a sheet of paper and then push the bolts through the paper in their original positions as each one is removed. This will facilitate refitting as the lengths of the bolts differ and screwing them into the wrong holes could fracture the casting of the engine.
6 Remove the timing cover and the gasket.
7 Unbolt and remove the chain tensioner.

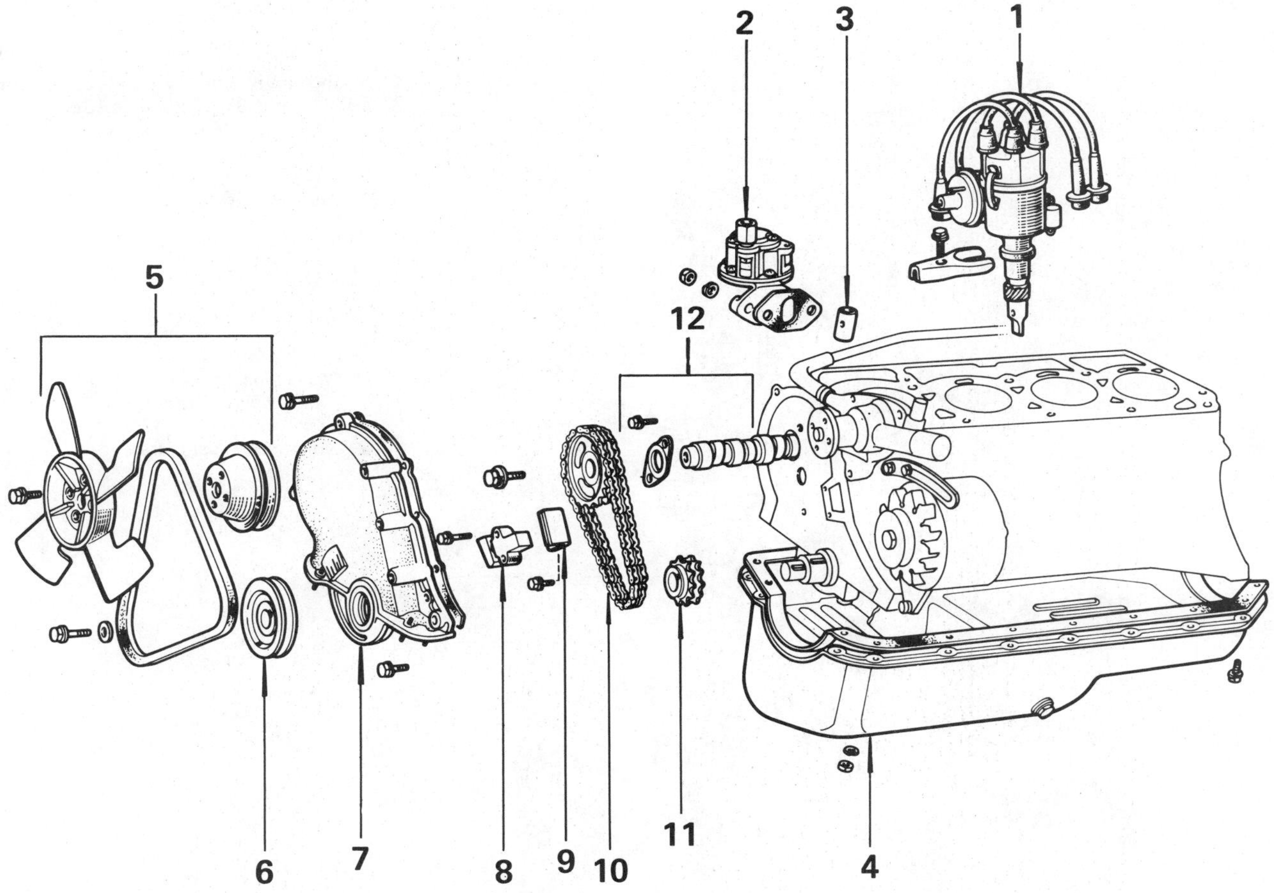

Fig. 1.11 Timing cover and associated components – 4K engine (Sec 14)

1 Distributor
2 Fuel pump
3 Tappet
4 Oil pan (sump)
5 V belt & fan pulley
6 Crankshaft pulley
7 Timing cover
8 Chain tensioner
9 Chain vibration damper
10 Timing chain & camshaft sprocket
11 Crankshaft sprocket
12 Camshaft and thrust plate

8 Unscrew and remove the camshaft sprocket bolt. The sprocket can be held still either by placing a block of wood between one of the crankshaft webs and the inside of the crankcase or inserting a rod through one of the holes in the camshaft sprocket and using the rod to lever against the cylinder block.
9 The camshaft sprocket complete with chain should now be pulled away and the chain unlooped from the crankshaft sprocket.

15 Camshaft – removal

1 If the engine is in the vehicle, then the radiator grille and radiator must be removed. Disconnect the exhaust downpipe and its retaining bracket and support the transmission on a jack, remove the rear mounting crossmember and carefully lower the rear end of the transmission, taking care that none of the engine controls and leads are strained, and that the front universal joint of the propeller shaft is bent at such an acute angle that no further movement is available. The purpose of lowering the rear end of the transmission is to enable the camshaft to be extracted at an inclined angle, otherwise it would be obstructed by the front body panel and reinforcement crossmember. Before lowering the transmission, disconnect the gearshift (or selector) lever and the leads from the reversing light switch – see Chapter 6 for details.
2 The distributor, cylinder head, sump, oil pump and tappets will have to be removed as described in earlier Sections.
3 Unscrew and remove the two bolts which secure the camshaft thrust plate.
4 Remove the thrust plate and withdraw the camshaft, taking great care that the cam lobes do not damage the camshaft bearings as they pass through them.

16 Oil filter – renewal

1 The disposable type cartridge oil filter should be unscrewed from the engine using a strap or chain wrench. If such a tool is not available, drive a large screwdriver through the filter about 1 in (25 mm) from its outer end and use this to unscrew it (photo).
2 If the filter is being removed at a regular service interval and the vehicle has just come in from the road, be prepared for some loss of oil as the filter is unscrewed. Also the oil may be very hot.

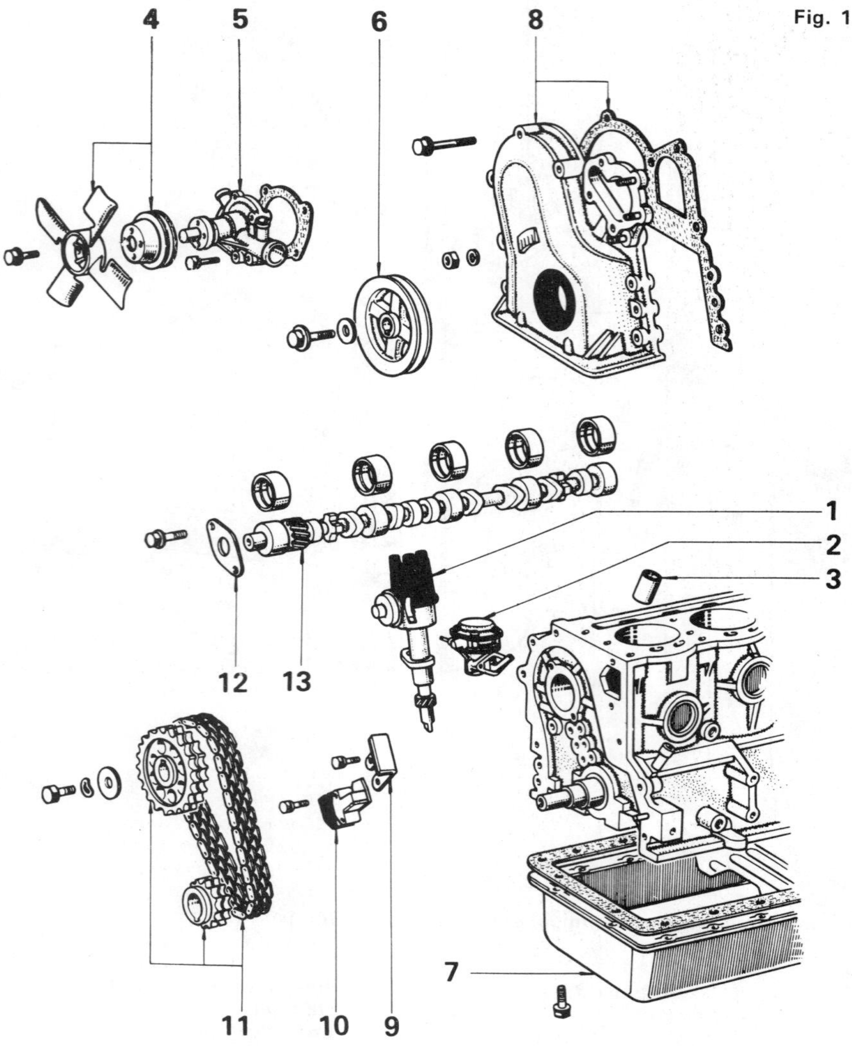

Fig. 1.12 Timing cover and associated components – 2T, 2T-B and 3T-C engines (Sec 14)

1 Distributor
2 Fuel pump & insulator
3 Tappet
4 Fan & fan pulley
5 Water pump
6 Crankshaft pulley
7 Oil pan (sump)
8 Timing cover & gasket
9 Chain damper
10 Chain tensioner
11 Timing chain & timing gear
12 Camshaft thrust plate
13 Camshaft

16.1 Oil filter removal

3 The replacement filter should be of Toyota manufacture if possible since they are fitted with an integral valve which prevents oil loss from the filter when the engine is standing for long periods. This ensures that when the engine is restarted, a supply of filtered oil is instantly supplied to the bearings and journals, thus preventing the rattle sometimes heard when an engine is initially restarted.

4 When installing the oil filter during a routine service, smear the rubber seal ring of the filter with oil or grease and screw the filter home using only hand pressure. Do not use a wrench or tool to tighten the filter. Overtightening of the filter can not only distort the seal, but will, as many people find out, cause problems the next time the filter has to be removed.

5 When the engine is restarted check the filter joint for any signs of leaks.

17 Pistons and connecting rods – removal and dismantling

1 If the engine is still in the vehicle, remove the cylinder head and sump as described in previous Sections.

2 Undo and remove the big-end cap retaining nuts using a socket and remove the big-end caps one at a time, taking care to keep them in the right order and the correct way round.

3 Ensure that the shell bearings are also kept with their correct

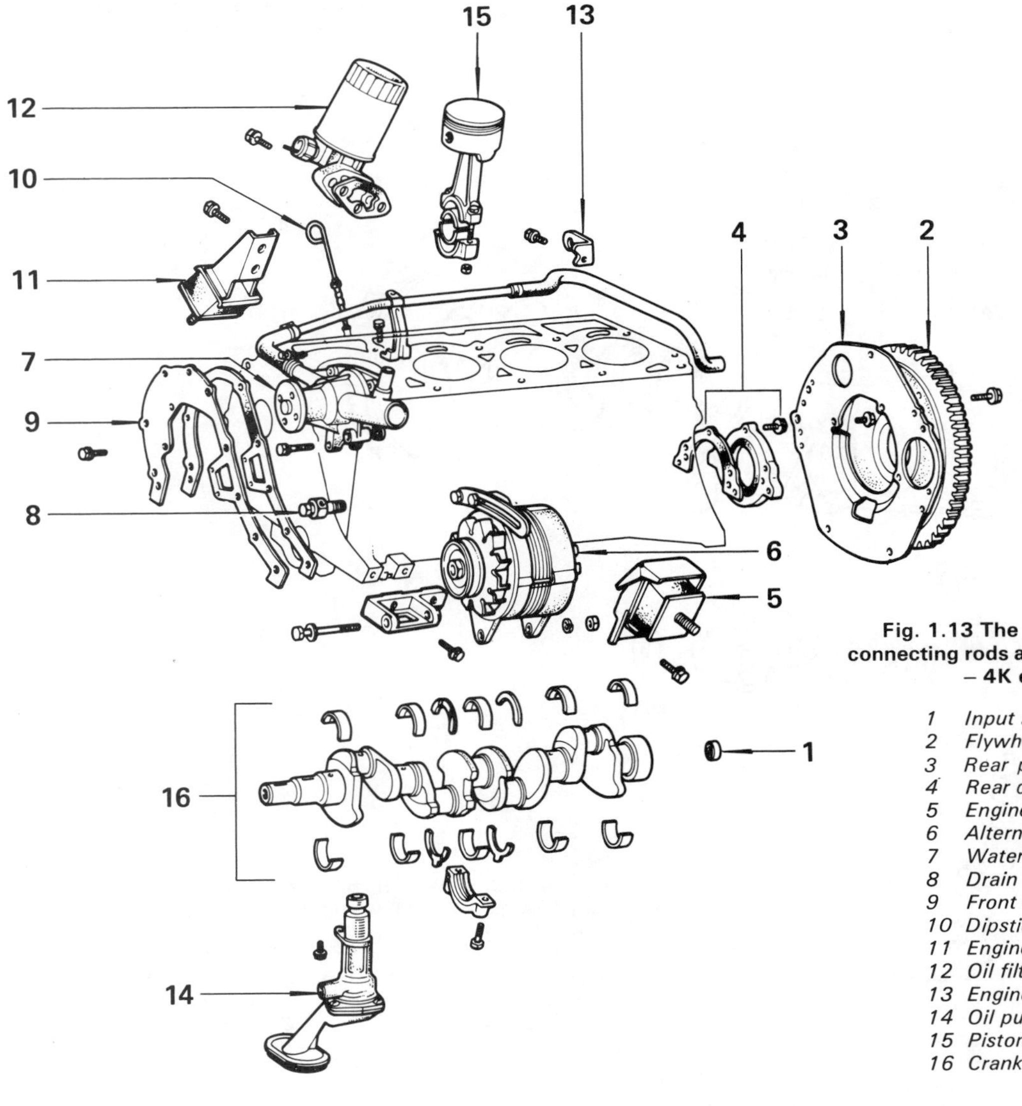

Fig. 1.13 The crankshaft, pistons and connecting rods and associated components – 4K engine (Sec 17)

1 Input shaft bearing
2 Flywheel
3 Rear plate
4 Rear oil seal
5 Engine front mounting, LH
6 Alternator & bracket
7 Water pump & heater hose
8 Drain cock
9 Front end plate
10 Dipstick
11 Engine front mounting, RH
12 Oil filter
13 Engine rear hanger
14 Oil pump
15 Piston & connecting rod
16 Crankshaft & bearing

connecting rods and caps unless they are to be renewed. Normally the numbers 1 to 4 are stamped on adjacent sides of the big-end caps and connecting rods, indicating which cap fits on which rod and which way round the cap fits. If no numbers or lines can be found then scratch mating marks across the joint from the rod to the cap with a sharp screwdriver. One line for connecting rod number 1, two for connecting rod number 2 and so on. This will ensure there is no confusion later as it is most important that the caps go back in the position on the connecting rods from which they were removed.

4 If the big-end caps are difficult to remove they may be gently tapped with a soft hammer.

5 To remove the shell bearings press the bearing opposite the groove in both connecting rod and the connecting rod cap, and the bearing shell will slide out easily.

6 Withdraw the pistons and connecting rods upwards and out of the top of the cylinder block. Ensure they are kept in the correct order for refitting to the same bore. Refit the connecting rod caps and bearings to the rods (if the bearings do not require renewal) to minimise the risk of getting the caps and rods muddled.

7 On engines which have covered a high mileage, it is possible for a severe wear ridge to have worn at the top of the cylinder bores. These ridges should be carefully scraped away to enable the piston rings to pass out of the tops of the bores. Use a deridging tool if available but do not allow swarf to drop down into the engine.

8 *On 4K engines,* the piston can be dismantled by extracting one of the circlips from the ends of the gudgeon pin. Heat the piston in boiling water and push the gudgeon pin out.

9 *On 2T, 2T-B and 3T-C engines,* the gudgeon pins are a press fit in the connecting rod small end and in view of the need for pressing facilities and guide tools, it is recommended that this work is left to your Toyota dealer.

10 The piston rings may be removed by opening each of them in turn, just enough to enable them to ride over the lands of the piston body. In order to prevent the lower rings dropping into an empty groove higher up the piston as they are removed, it is helpful to use two or three narrow strips of tin or old feeler blades inserted behind the ring at equidistant points and then to employ a twisting motion to slide the ring from the piston.

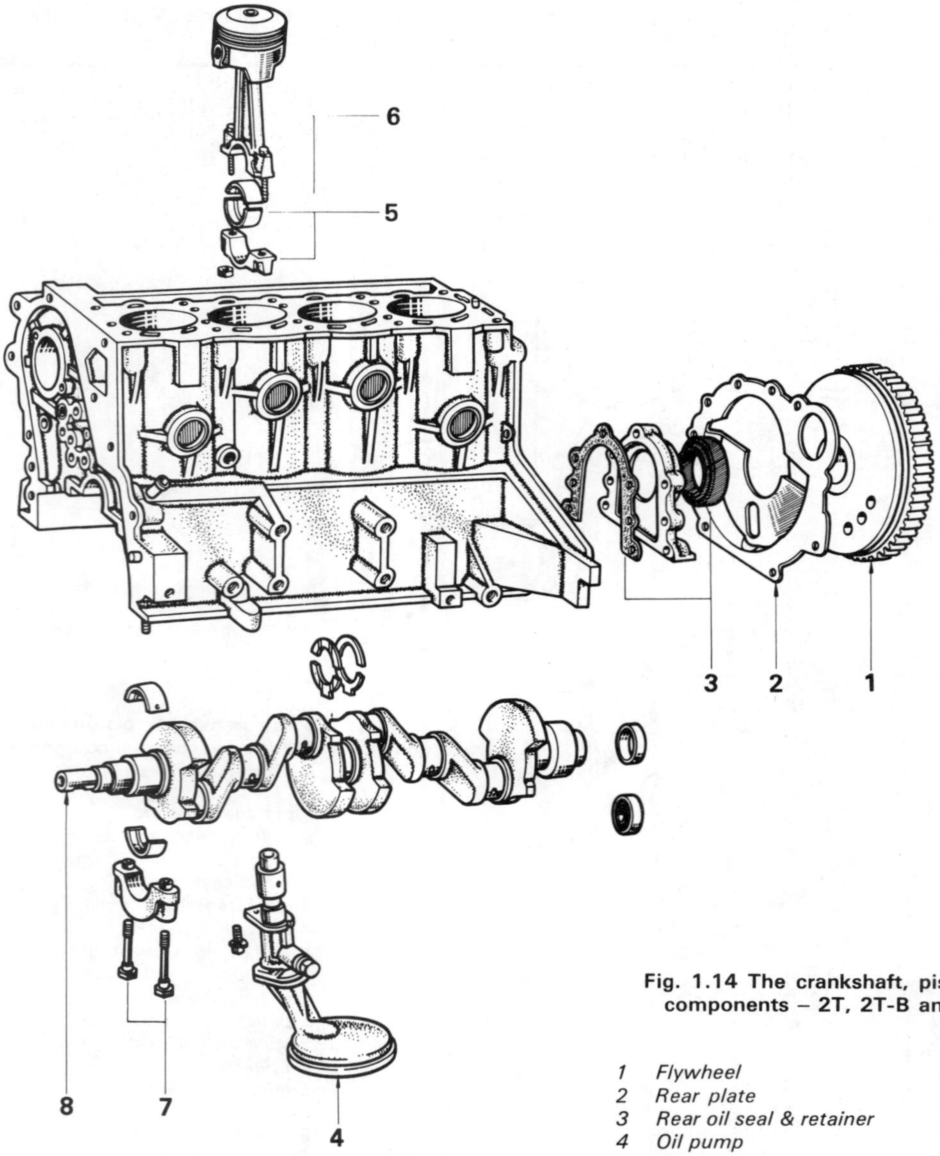

Fig. 1.14 The crankshaft, pistons, rods and associated components – 2T, 2T-B and 3T-C engines (Sec 17)

1 *Flywheel*
2 *Rear plate*
3 *Rear oil seal & retainer*
4 *Oil pump*
5 *Connecting rod bearing cap*
6 *Connecting rod & piston*
7 *Crankshaft bearing cap*
8 *Crankshaft*

18 Flywheel (or driveplate – auto. transmission) crankshaft and main bearings – removal

1 With the clutch assembly already removed, the bolts which secure the flywheel (or driveplate) should be unscrewed and removed. On some models, the flywheel bolts are secured with lockplates and these should be bent back first (photo).
2 In order to prevent the flywheel (or driveplate) turning when attempting to unscrew the securing bolts, either place a block of wood between one of the webs of the crankshaft and the inside wall of the crankcase or jam the starter ring gear with a cold chisel or something similar.
3 Remove the flywheel (or driveplate) and then unbolt and remove the engine rear plate (photo).
4 Unbolt and remove the crankshaft rear oil seal retainer.
5 Undo and remove the ten bolts securing the main bearing caps to the cylinder block.
6 Make sure that the main bearing caps are numbered 1 to 5 on the front faces and also show an arrow towards the front of the engine.
7 Remove the main bearing caps and the bottom half of each bearing shell, taking care to keep the bearing shells in the right caps.
8 When removing the centre bearing cap, note the bottom semi-circular halves of the thrust washers, one half lying on either side of the main bearing. Lay them with the centre bearing along the correct side.
9 Slightly rotate the crankshaft to free the upper halves of the bearing shells and thrust washers which can be lifted away and placed over the correct bearing cap when the crankshaft has been lifted out.
10 Remove the crankshaft by lifting it away from the crankcase.
11 Lift away the bearing shells.

19 Lubrication system – description

The lubrication system is similar in both types of engine. Oil is drawn from the sump through a strainer by an oil pump which is driven by a gear on the camshaft. The pump and strainer assembly is mounted within the sump.

Pressurised oil is first passed through the externally mounted full-flow oil filter and then to the main gallery. From there, it passes through various passages and drilling to all the friction surfaces of the engine.

An oil pressure switch is screwed into the cylinder block which is connected to the oil pressure warning light on the instrument panel.

On some models, an oil pressure gauge is fitted instead of a warning light and even an oil temperature gauge and a low oil pressure warning light (refer to Chapter 10).

18.1 Flywheel retaining bolts

18.3 Remove the engine rear plate – note locating dowels

Fig. 1.15 Engine lubrication system – 4K engine (Sec 19)

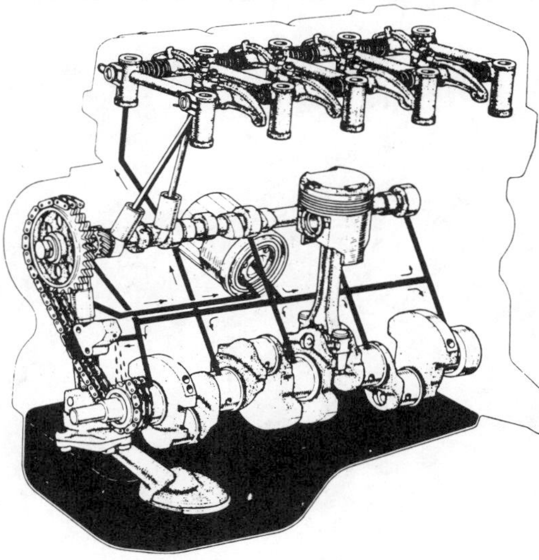

Fig. 1.16 Engine lubrication system – 2T, 2T-B and 3T-C engines (Sec 19)

20 Engine components – examination and renovation general

When the engine has been stripped down and all parts properly cleaned decisions have to be made as to what needs renewal and the following Sections tell the examiner what to look for. In any border line case it is always best to decide in favour of a new part; even if a part may still be serviceable its life will have been reduced by wear and the degree of trouble needed to replace it in future must be taken into consideration.

21 Crankshaft, bearings and flywheel – examination and renovation

1 Look at the main bearing journals and the crankpins and if there are any scratches or score marks then the shaft will need regrinding. Such conditions will nearly always be accompanied by similar deterioration in the matching bearing shells.
2 Each bearing journal should also be round and can be checked with a micrometer or caliper gauge around the periphery at several points. If there is more than 0.0004 in (0.01 mm) of ovality or taper regrinding is necessary (photo).
3 Your main Toyota dealer or motor engineering specialist will be able to decide to what extent regrinding is necessary and also supply the special under-size shell bearings to match whatever may need grinding off the journals. On later 4K engines a modified type of main bearing cap shell is fitted which has no oil groove in it. For details see Section 35.
4 Before taking the crankshaft for regrinding check also the cylinder bores and pistons as it may be more convenient to have the engineering operations performed at the same time by the same engineer.
5 With careful servicing and regular oil and filter changes bearings will last for a very long time but they can still fail for unforeseen reasons. With big-end bearings the indications are regular rhthymic loud knocking from the crankcase, the frequency depending on engine speed. It is particularly noticeable when the engine is under load. This symptom is accompanied by a fall in oil pressure although this is not normally noticeable unless an oil pressure gauge is fitted. Main bearing failure is usually indicated by serious vibration, particularly at higher engine revolutions, accompanied by a more significant drop in oil pressure and a rumbling noise.
6 Bearing shells in good condition have bearing surfaces with a smooth even, matt silver/grey colour all over. Worn bearings will show patches of a different colour where the bearing metal has worn away and exposed the underlay. Damaged bearings will be pitted or scored. It is nearly always well worthwhile fitting new shells as their cost is relatively low. If the crankshaft is in good condition it is merely a question of obtaining another set of standard size. A reground crankshaft will need new bearing shells as a matter of course.
7 Connecting rods are not normally subject to wear but in extreme cases such as engine seizure, they could be distorted. Such conditions may be visually apparent but where doubt exists their alignment must be checked and straightened if possible. If not they will have to be renewed. The bearing caps should also be examined for indications of filing down which may have been attempted in a mistaken idea that bearing slackness could be remedied in this way. If there are such signs then the connecting rods should be renewed.
8 While the flywheel is out of the vehicle, take the opportunity to examine the spigot bearing in the centre of the crankshaft rear flange. If it is worn or noisy when rotated, renew it (photo).
9 The old bearing must be extracted using a suitable puller or alternatively, apply heat to the bearing recess when it is usually possible to lever out the bearing.
10 Drive in the new bearing applying pressure to the outer bearing track only.
11 Examine the flywheel itself. If the clutch surface is scored or grooved, or there are lots of small cracks visible (caused by overheating) then the flywheel must either be refinished or a new one obtained. Refinishing must be left to your dealer as the overall thickness of the flywheel must not be reduced beyond a specified limit.
12 If the flywheel starter ring gear teeth are worn or chipped, a new ring gear should be fitted. In the case of a driveplate, renew the driveplate complete.
13 Although a starter ring gear can be removed with a cold chisel and a new one fitted after heating it in an oven or oil bath (392°F – 200°C), it is recommended that this work is left to your dealer or specialist engineering works.

22 Cylinder bores – examination and renovation

1 A new cylinder bore is perfectly round and the walls parallel throughout its length. The action of the piston tends to wear the walls at right angles to the gudgeon pin due to side thrust. This wear takes place principally on that section of the cylinder swept by the piston rings.
2 It is possible to get an indication of bore wear by removing the cylinder head with the engine still in the car. With the piston down in the bore first signs of wear can be seen and felt just below the top of the bore where the piston ring reaches, and there will be a noticeable lip. If there is no lip it is fairly reasonable to expect that bore wear is low and any lack of compression or excessive oil consumption is due to worn or broken piston rings or pistons or valves not seating correctly.
3 If it is possible to obtain a bore measuring micrometer, measure the bore in the thrust plane just below the lip and again at the bottom of the cylinder in the same plane. If the difference is more than 0.008 in (0.2 mm), then a rebore is necessary. Similarly a difference of 0.008 in (0.2 mm) or more across the bore diameter is a sign of ovality calling for a rebore.

21.2 Checking crankshaft journals for excessive wear with a micrometer

21.8 Check the crankshaft spigot bearing for excessive wear

4 Any bore which is significantly scratched or scored will need reboring. This sympton usually indicates that the piston or rings are damaged in that cylinder. In the event of only one cylinder being in need of reboring it will still be necessary for all four to be bored and fitted with new oversize pistons and rings.

5 Your Toyota dealer or local engineering specialist will be able to rebore and obtain the necessary matched pistons. If the crankshaft is undergoing regrinding it is a good idea to let the same firm renovate and reassemble the crankshaft and pistons to the block. A reputable firm normally gives a guarantee for such work.

23 Pistons, rings and connecting rods – examination and renovation

1 Worn pistons and rings can usually be diagnosed when the symptoms of excessive oil consumption and low compression occur and are sometimes, though not always, associated with worn cylinder bores. Compression testers that fit into the spark plug holes are available and these can indicate where low compression is occurring. Wear usually accelerates the more it is left so when the symptoms occur, early action can possibly save the expense of a rebore.

2 Another symptom of piston wear is piston slap – a knocking noise from the crankcase not to be confused with big-end bearing failure. It can be heard clearly at low engine speed, when there is no load (idling for example) and the engine is cold, and is much less audible when the engine speed increases. Piston wear usually occurs in the skirt or lower end of the piston and is indicated by vertical streaks in the worn area which is always on the thrust side. It can be seen when the skirt thickness is different.

3 Piston ring wear can be checked by first removing the rings from the pistons as described in Section 17. Then place the rings in the cylinder bores from the top, pushing them down about 1.5 in (38.1 mm) with the head of a piston (from which the rings have been removed) so that they rest squarely in the cylinder. Then measure the gap at the ends of the ring with a feeler gauge. If it exceeds the limits specified at the beginning of this Chapter then they will need renewal.

4 The grooves in which the rings locate in the piston can also become enlarged in use. The clearance between ring and piston, in the groove should not exceed the limits specified at the beginning of this Chapter.

5 However, it is rare that a piston is only worn in the ring grooves and the need to replace them for this fault alone is hardly ever encountered. Whenever the pistons are renewed, the weight of the four piston/connecting rod assemblies should be kept within the limit variation of 8 gms to maintain engine balance. Note that a new design of piston was fitted to the 4K engine in August of 1981 and the new piston type is not interchangeable with the earlier type.

6 The connecting rod and the gudgeon pin do not normally require renewal. If the pistons are being changed then the new pistons are usually supplied complete with gudgeon pins.

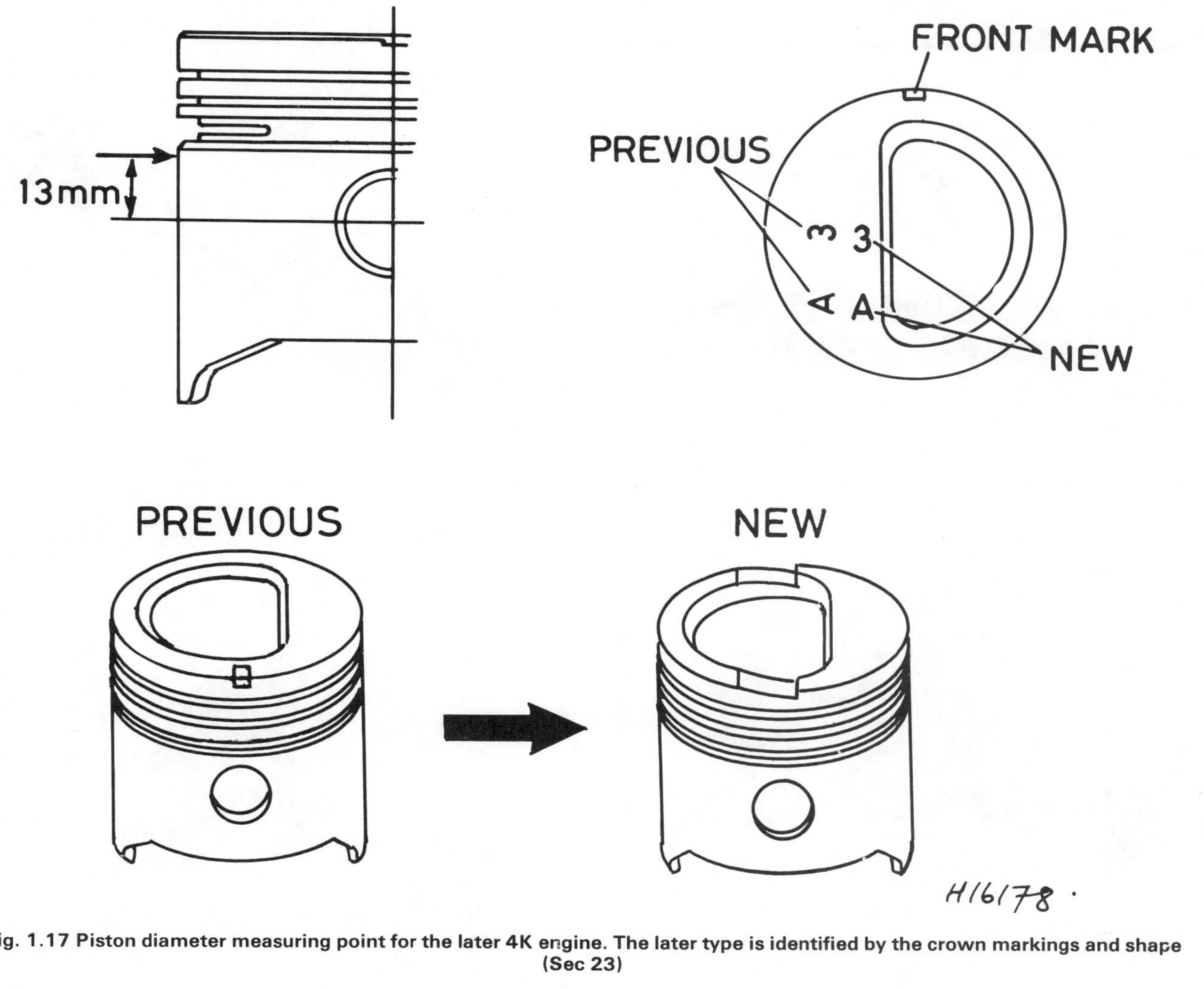

Fig. 1.17 Piston diameter measuring point for the later 4K engine. The later type is identified by the crown markings and shape (Sec 23)

24 Camshaft and bearings – examination and renovation

1 Renewal of the camshaft bearings is normally only required if the camshaft itself is reground, in which case undersize bearings will be supplied by the regrinder.

2 The old bearings can be drawn out if the blanking plug is first removed from the rear end of the camshaft and a length of studding with distance pieces and nuts used to withdraw them one by one.

3 Draw the new bearings into position in the same way but make quite sure that the oil hole in the bearing is in exact alignment with the hole in the crankcase bearing seat. Also ensure that the bearing location groove faces forwards. It should be noted that later 4K engines (from June 1982), have bearings which have just two oil holes drilled in them instead of the four on earlier models. This modification was made in the interests of reducing noise, but otherwise the two types are similar and are interchangeable. When the bearings have been renewed insert a new blanking plug into the rear bearing having first smeared it with a suitable sealant.

4 The camshaft itself may show signs of wear on the bearing journals, cam lobes or the skew gear. The main decision to take is what degree of wear justifies replacement, which is costly. Any signs of scoring or damage to the bearing journals must be rectified and as undersize bearing bushes are available the journals may be reground. If there is excessive wear on the skew gear which can be seen by close inspection of the contact pattern the whole camshaft will have to be renewed.

5 The cam lobes themselves may show signs of ridging or pitting at the high points. If the ridging is light then it may be possible to smooth it out with fine emery. The cam lobes, however, are surface hardened and once this is penetrated wear will be very rapid thereafter. The cams are also offset and tapered to cause the tappets to rotate – thus ensuring that wear is even – so do not mistake this condition for wear.

6 The camshaft run-out should be checked by supporting the camshaft by its forward and rear bearing on a pair or V-blocks and the shaft rotated a complete turn whilst the run-out is measured on the central bearing with a clock gauge as shown (Fig. 1.20). The maximum reading of the tolerance given is then divided by two to assess the run-out which must not exceed 0.002 in (0.06 mm). If it does exceed this figure then the camshaft must be renewed.

7 Finally check the camshaft end float. To do this, temporarily refit the thrust plate and sprocket and tighten the securing bolt to the specified torque wrench setting.

8 Using a feeler gauge, measure the clearance between the rear face of the thrust plate and the camshaft front bearing. Where this exceeds 0.012 in (0.3 mm), the camshaft will have to be renewed.

25 Rocker gear – examination and renovation

1 Examine the rocker arms and shafts for wear (photo).

2 If the assembly must be dismantled to renew a component, keep each part in its original sequence for correct refitting.

3 On 2T, 2T-B and 3T-C engines do not mix up the two rocker shafts. The rocker arms and springs can be removed from the shafts after first extracting the spring clips. When reassembling these rocker shafts, note the location of the differing pedestals and the location of the shaft groove to accommodate the cylinder head bolts (photos).

4 On later 2T, 2T-B and 3T-C engines, the rocker support is located

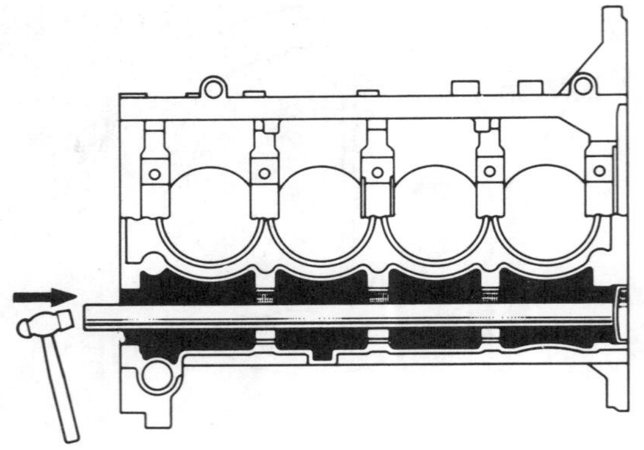

Fig. 1.18 Camshaft rear bearing plug removal method (Sec 24)

Fig. 1.19 Check the camshaft lobes and skew gear for excessive wear (Sec 24)

Fig. 1.20 Camshaft run-out check method (Sec 24)

Fig. 1.21 Camshaft endfloat check method (Sec 24)

25.1 Check rocker arms at points indicated for excessive wear

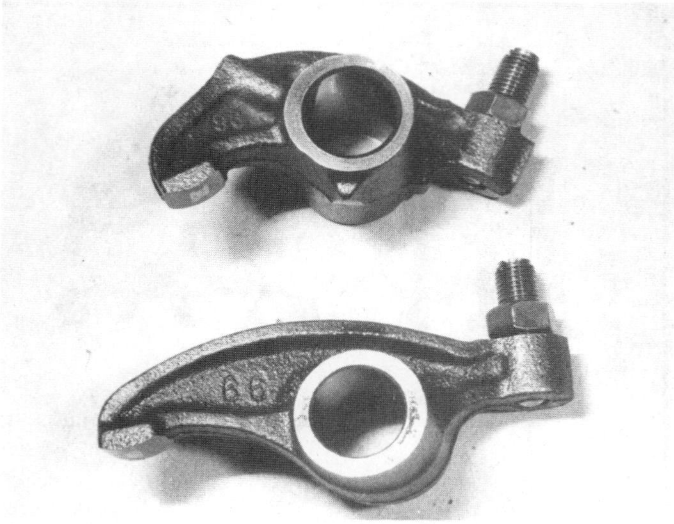

25.3a Rocker arms on the 2T engine: Top is inlet, bottom is exhaust

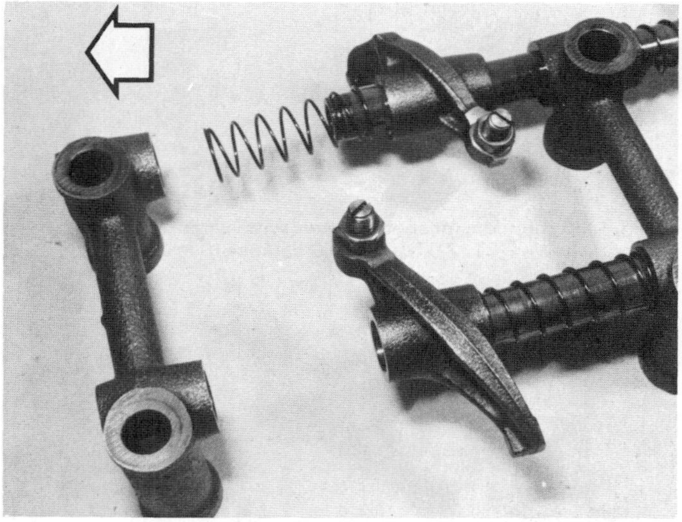

25.3b Reassembly order of rocker components – arrow indicates front

25.3c Locate retaining clips into shaft grooves to secure

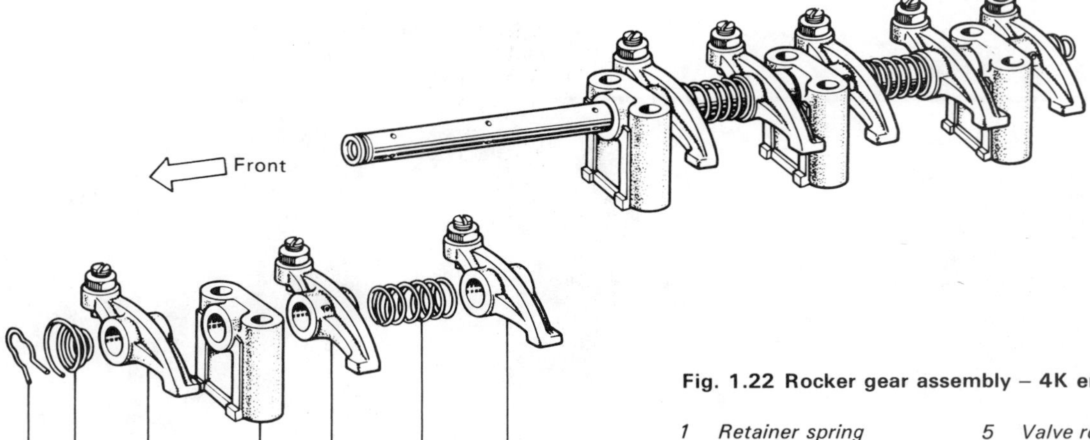

Fig. 1.22 Rocker gear assembly – 4K engine (Sec 25)

1 Retainer spring
2 Conical spring
3 Valve rocker arm, No 1
4 Valve rocker support
5 Valve rocker arm, No 2
6 Compression spring
7 Valve rocker arm, No 3

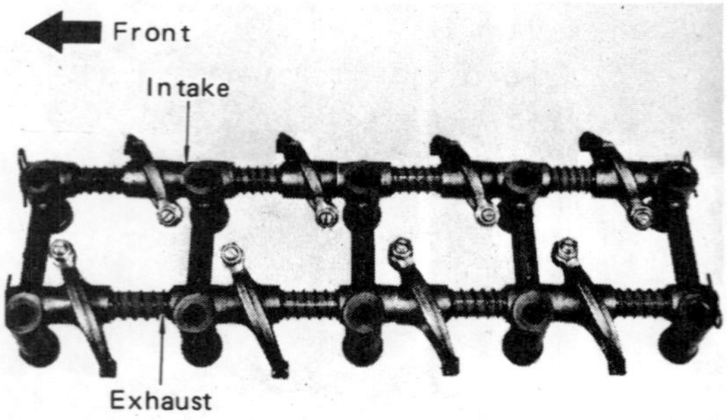

Fig. 1.23 Rocker gear assembly – 2T, 2T-B and 3T-C engines (Sec 25)

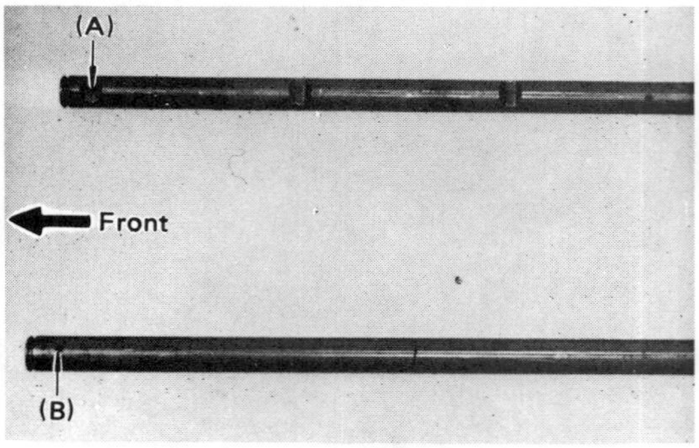

Fig. 1.24 Inlet (A) and exhaust (B) rocker shaft oil holes must be to front – 2T, 2T-B and 3T-C engines (Sec 25)

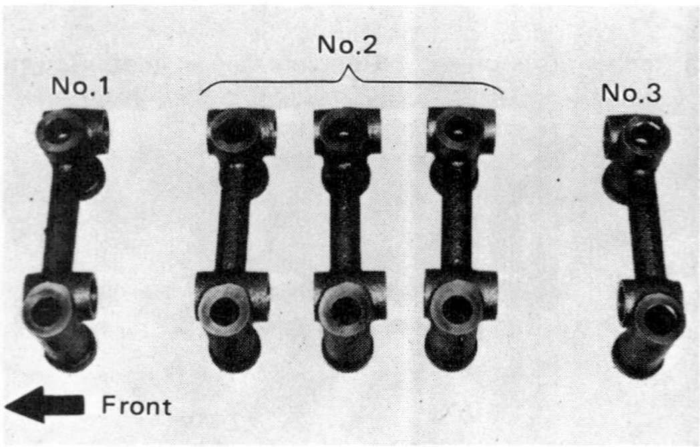

Fig. 1.25 Rocker supports identification – 2T, 2T-B and 3T-C engines (Sec 25)

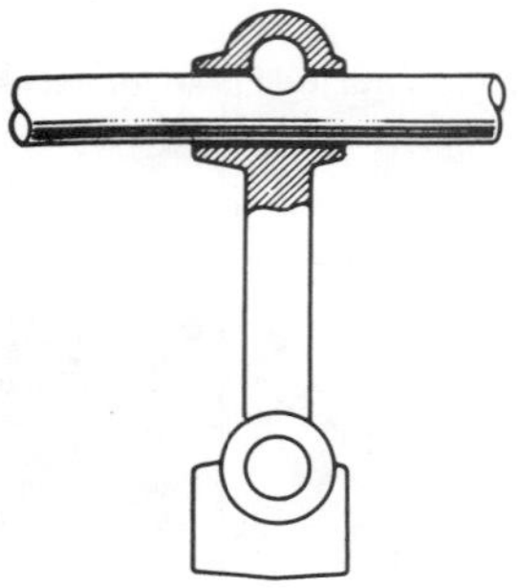

Fig. 1.26 Align rocker shaft grooves with support holes as shown – 2T, 2T-B and 3T-C engines (Sec 25)

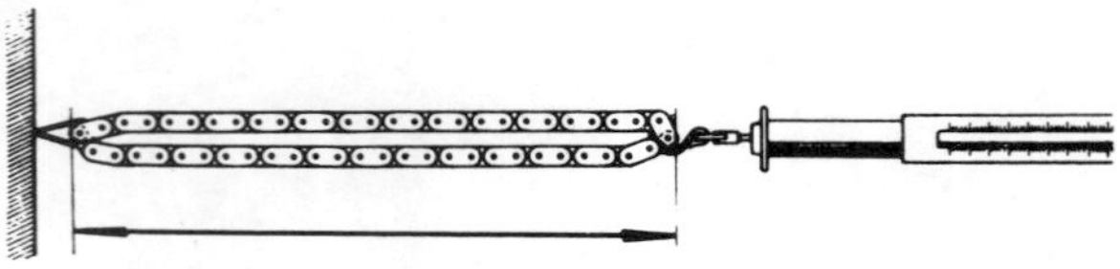

Fig. 1.27 Timing chain wear check method using spring gauge (Sec 26)

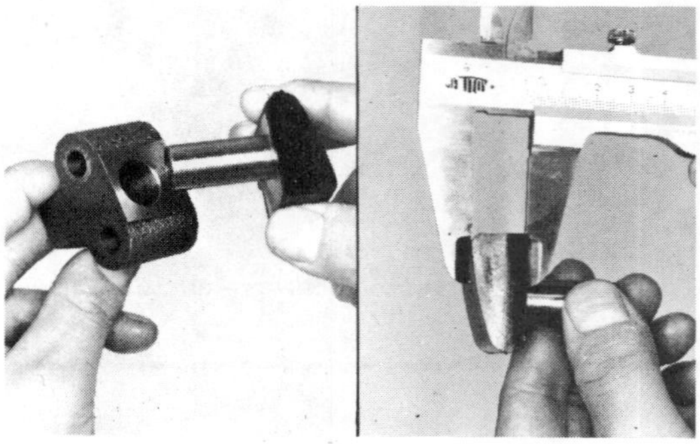

Fig. 1.28 Chain tensioner body and plunger wear check method – 2T, 2T-B and 3T-C engines (Sec 26)

26.3 Examine the chain tensioner components

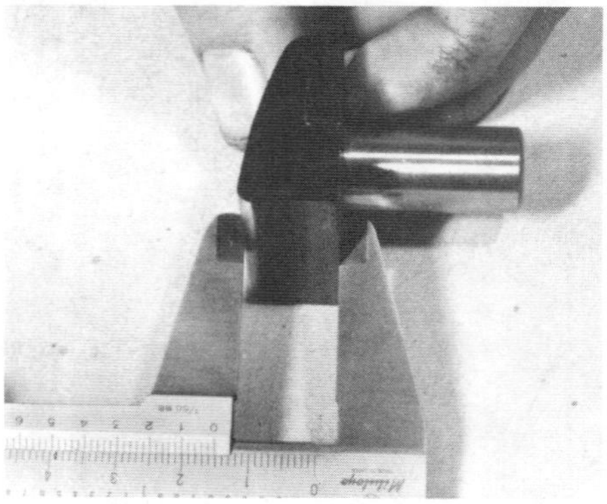

26.4 Check the tensioner slipper thickness for excessive wear

26.5 Check the chain damper for excessive wear

on the cylinder head by a guide pin. If it is necessary to fit an earlier type support to a later cylinder head then the guide pin must be extracted to allow fitting.

26 Timing sprockets, chain and tensioner – examination and renovation

1 Examine the teeth on both the crankshaft gearwheel and the camshaft gearwheel for wear. Each tooth forms an inverted V with the gearwheel periphery, and if worn the side of each tooth under tension will be slightly concave in shape when compared with the other side of the tooth ie; one side of the inverted V will be concave when compared with the other. If any sign of wear is present the gearwheels must be renewed.
2 Examine the links of the chain for side slackness and renew the chain if any slackness is noticeable when compared with a new chain. It is a sensible precaution to renew the chain at about 30 000 miles (48 000 km) and at a lesser mileage if the engine is stripped down for major overhaul. The actual rollers on a very badly worn chain may be slightly grooved. The correct method for checking the chain for wear is shown in Fig. 1.27. A spring gauge tensioner will be necessary for this test.
3 The chain tensioner should be checked by applying oil to the plunger and then placing two fingers over the oil passages in the tensioner body. Now pull the plunger and the suction should be strong enough to return the plunger as soon as the hand is removed. If this is not the case, then the tensioner assembly must be renewed (photo).
4 Now measure the thickness of the slipper which rests against the chain. If it is less than the minimum dimension given in the Specifications, then the plunger must be renewed (Fig. 1.28) (photo).
5 Check the chain damper for wear or grooves. If the thickness of the section which bears against the chain is less than the specified amount then the damper must be renewed (Fig. 1.29) (photo).

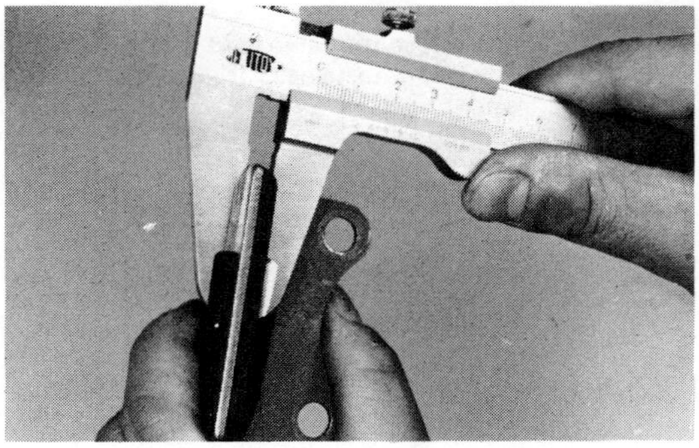

Fig. 1.29 Chain damper wear check method – T series shown (Sec 26)

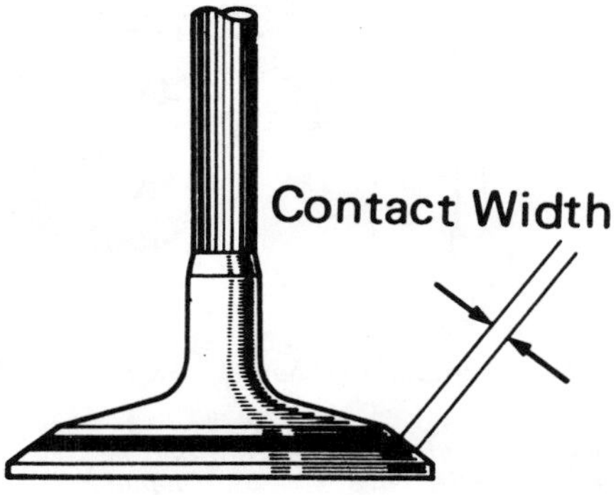

Fig. 1.30 Check valve head contact width and condition. Regrind face against valve seat as described to renovate (Sec 30)

27 Pushrods and tappets – examination and renovation

1 The pushrods should be examined visually for straightness, any that are bent should be renewed.
2 The faces of the tappets which bear on the camshaft should show no signs of pitting, scoring or other form or wear. They should also not be a loose fit in their housing. Wear is only normally encountered at very high mileage or in cases of neglected engine lubrication – renew if necessary.

28 Cylinder head – decarbonising and examination

1 When the cylinder head is removed either in the course of an overhaul, or inspection of the bores or valve condition when the engine is in the car, it is normal to remove all carbon deposits from the piston crowns and head.
2 This is best done with a cup shaped wire brush and an electric drill and is fairly straightforward when the engine is dismantled and the pistons removed. Sometimes hard spots of carbon are not easily removed except by a scraper. When cleaning the pistons with a scraper take care not to damage the surface of the piston in any way.
3 When the engine is in the car certain precautions must be taken when decarbonising the piston crowns in order to prevent dislodged pieces of carbon falling into the interior of the engine which could cause damage to the cylinder bores, piston and rings – or if allowed into the water passages – damage to the water pump. Turn the engine, therefore so that the piston being worked on is at the top of its stroke and then mask off the adjacent cylinder bore and all surrounding water jacket orifices with paper and adhesive tape. Press grease into the gap all round the piston to keep particles out and then scrape all carbon away by hand, carefully.
4 When completed, carefully clean out the grease round the rim of the piston – bringing any carbon particles with it. Repeat the process on the other three piston crowns. It is not recommended that a ring of carbon is left round the edge of the piston on the theory that it will aid oil consumption control. This was valid in the earlier days of long stroke low revving engines but modern engines, fuels and lubricants cause less carbon deposits anyway and any left behind tends merely to cause hot spots.

29 Valve guides and springs – examination and renovation

1 Measure the internal diameter of the valve guides or alternatively test for wear by checking the fit of a new valve in each guide.
2 Any valve guides which are excessively worn will have to be renewed and then reamed to a standard size. Owing to the need for special tools this work should be entrusted to a Toyota dealer or engineering works.
3 Compare the free length of the valve springs with the figure given in the Specifications. If the springs are not of the specified length, renewal is necessary.

30 Valves and valve seats – examination and renovation

1 With the valves removed from the cylinder head as described in Section 12, examine the head for signs of cracking, burning away and pitting of the edge where it seats in the port. The seats of the valve in the cylinder head should also be examined for the same signs. Usually it is the valve that deteriorates first but if a bad valve is not rectified the seat will suffer and this is more difficult to repair.
2 If pitting on the valve and seat is very slight the marks can be removed by grinding the seats and valves together with coarse and then fine valve grinding paste.
3 Where bad pitting has occurred to the valve seats it will be necessary either to re-cut the seats or in severe cases, to fit new valve seats. Grinding can be done if pitting on the valve and seat is only very light or if as is usually the case, the valves only are badly burned then a new set of valves can be ground into the seats.

4 Valve grinding is carried out as follows. Smear a trace of coarse carborundum paste on the seat face and apply a suction grinder tool to the valve head. With a semi-rotary motion, grind the valve head to its seat, lifting the valve occasionally to redistribute the grinding paste. When a dull matt even surface finish is produced on both the valve seat and the valve, wipe off the paste and repeat the process with fine carborundum paste, lifting and turning the valve to redistribute the paste as before. A light spring placed under the valve head will greatly ease this operation. When a smooth unbroken ring of light grey matt finish is produced, on both valve and valve seat faces, the grinding operation is completed.
5 Scrape away all carbon from the valve head and the valve stem. Carefully clean away every trace of grinding compound, taking care to leave none in the ports or in the valve guides. Clean the valves and valve seats with a paraffin soaked rag, with a clean rag and finally, if an air line is available blow the valves, valve guides and valve ports clean.
6 If it is found necessary to recut the valve seat faces then this is really a task best entrusted to an automotive engine workshop or your Toyota dealer. When completed the respective seat widths should comply with those given for the engine concerned in the Specifications. When the seats have been recut, the valves should be lapped in with grinding paste as previously described.
7 If new valve seat inserts are needed, then this is definitely a job for your Toyota dealer who will have the necessary equipment for doing the work or will contract the job to a specialist engineering company.
8 On completion, wash the cylinder head and valve assembly components thoroughly with a suitable solution to remove all traces of carbon, swarf and grinding paste. Blow dry with compressed air to complete prior to reassembly of the valve assembly components (see Section 40).
9 As from May 1982, the exhaust valves of the 4K engine have the carbon relief and not the guides as on previous models. Both the valves and guides of the new type are interchangeable with the earlier type but only as a set (Fig. 1.32).

Fig. 1.31 Valve seat recutting (Sec 30)

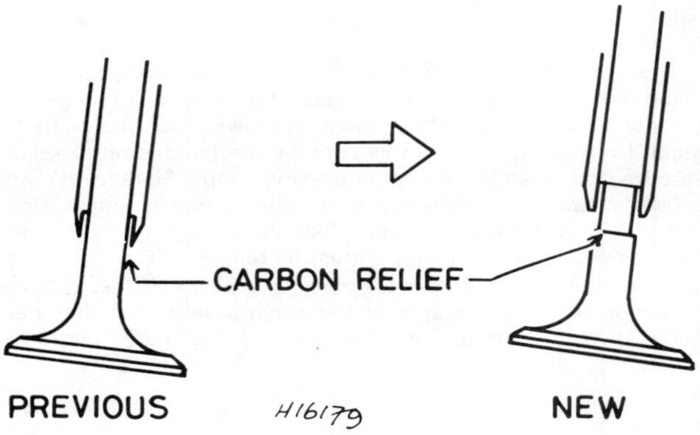

Fig. 1.32 Early and late type valve and guide profiles – 4K engine (Sec 30)

31 Oil pump – overhaul

1 If the oil pump is worn it is best to purchase an exchange reconditioned unit as a good oil pump is at the very heart of long engine life. Generally speaking an exchange or overhauled pump should be fitted at a major engine reconditioning.
2 If it is wished to check the oil pump for wear undo and remove the three bolts securing the oil pump body to the lower body and pick-up assembly. Separate the two parts.
3 Undo and remove the relief valve plug or extract the split pin then withdraw the washer, spring and valve plunger (photo).
4 Check the clearance between the lobes of the inner and outer rotors using feeler gauges. The clearance should not exceed the figures given in the Specifications (photo).
5 Replacement rotors are supplied only as a matched pair so that, if the clearance is excessive, a new rotor assembly must be fitted.
6 Lay a straight edge across the face of the pump in order to check the clearance between the faces of the rotors and the bottom of the straight edge. This clearance should not exceed the rotor endfloat figures specified. If the clearance is excessive the face of the pump body can be carefully lapped on a flat surface (photo).
7 Using feeler gauges measure the clearance between the rotor and the body and this should not exceed the rotor-to-body clearance specified. If wear is evident a new pump will be required (photo).
8 Inspect the relief valve for pitting and the oil passages and sliding surfaces for damage in the form of score marks. Check that the spring is not damaged and finally the pick-up gauze for blockage or tearing.
9 Reassembly of the pump is the reverse sequence to dismantling. On some models the drive and driven rotors are provided with punch marks and these must be aligned during reassembly.

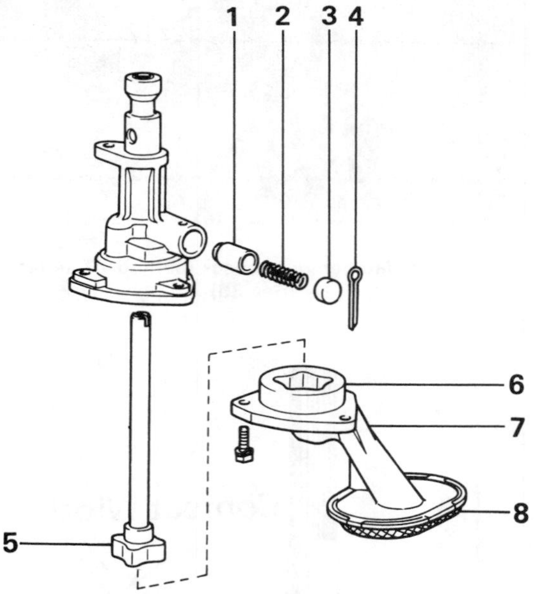

Fig. 1.33 Oil pump components – 4K engine (Sec 31)

1 Oil pump relief valve
2 Oil pump relief valve spring
3 Oil pump relief valve retainer
4 Split pin
5 Oil pump drive rotor
6 Oil pump driven rotor
7 Oil pump cover
8 Oil strainer

32 Oil seals – renewal

1 At the time of major overhaul, always renew the oil seals as a matter of routine even though they may appear to be satisfactory.

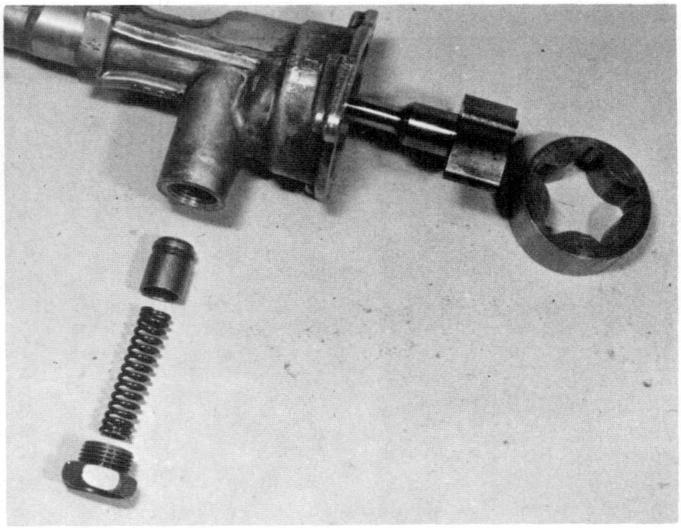

31.3 Oil pump components

31.4 Check inner to outer lobe clearance

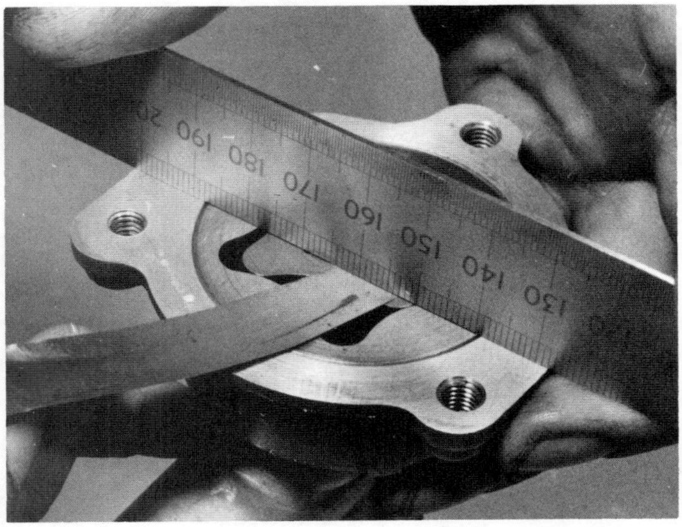

31.6 Check rotor endfloat

31.7 Check rotor-to-body clearance

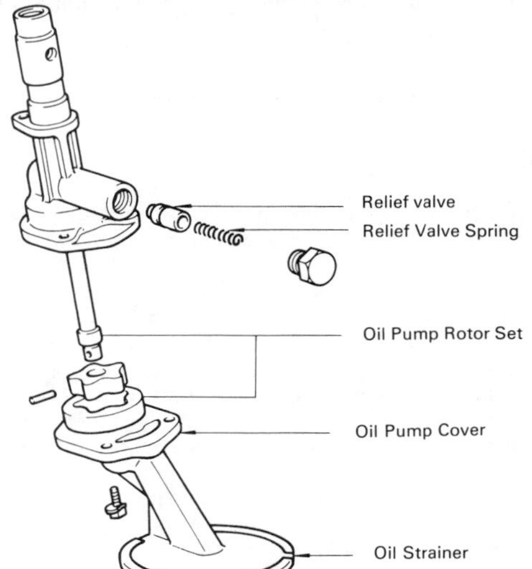

Fig. 1.34 Oil pump components – 2T, 2T-B and 3T-C engines (Sec 31)

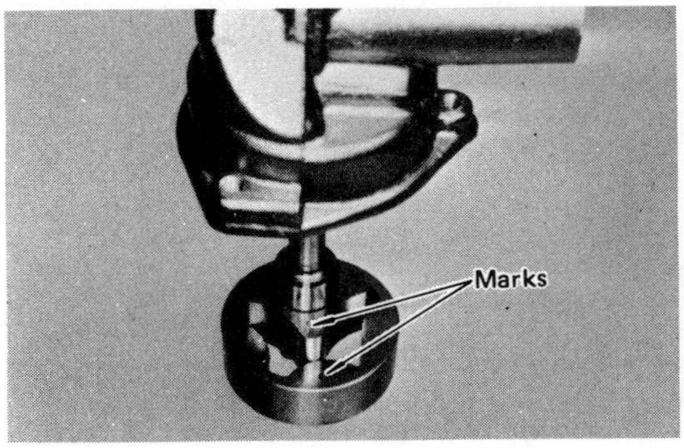

Fig. 1.35 Align rotor punch marks when reassembling the pump (Sec 31)

2 The crankshaft front and rear seals are renewed simply by driving the old ones from the timing cover or rear oil seal retainer and tapping in the new ones, taking care to have the lips of the seals facing the correct way.
3 The timing cover oil seal can be renewed while the engine is still in the vehicle provided that the radiator and crankshaft pulley are removed first.
4 Draw out the old seal using a small claw type puller. Clean the oil seal recess and tap in the new seal using a piece of tubing of suitable diameter.
5 The crankshaft rear oil seal and its retainer are only accessible after removal of either the engine or if the engine is left in the vehicle, then the gearbox must be withdrawn followed by the clutch and flywheel (or driveplate) (photo).

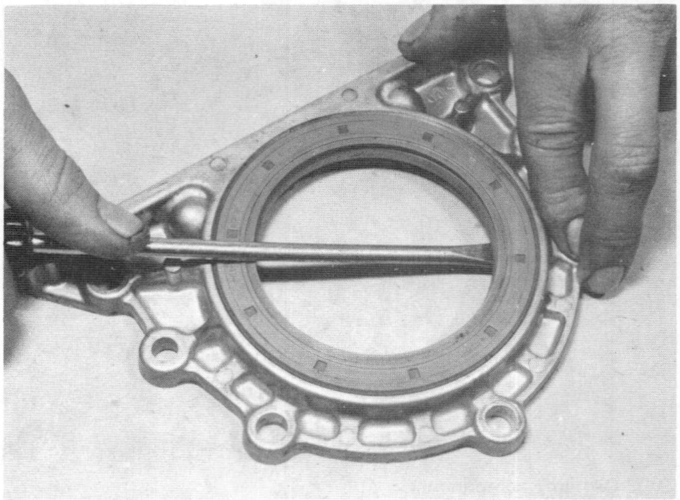

32.5 Crankshaft rear oil seal removal

33 Crankcase and cylinder block – examination

1 With the engine completely stripped, this is a good time to check for cracks, stripped threads and other faults in the engine castings.
2 Leaking core plugs should be renewed. Old plugs can be extracted by drilling a hole in their centres and either levering them out or tapping a thread in them and then screwing in bolts with a distance piece to draw them out. If the engine coolant has frozen at some time, the core plugs may have become partially displaced. Always clean the core plug recess and do not use more force than is necessary to ensure a tight fit when installing the new one.
3 If the camshaft bearings have been renewed, remember to install a new blanking plug at the rear end (Fig. 1.36).
4 Finally probe all the oilways and galleries with wire and blow them out with compressed air, if available.

Fig. 1.36 Camshaft rear bearing blanking plug installation – 4K engine (Sec 33)

34 Engine reassembly – general

1 Prior to reassembling the engine, make sure that you have all the necessary gaskets ready, also a torque wrench and the correct range of socket and other spanners.
2 Always lubricate each component with fresh engine oil before reassembling or installing it.

35 Crankshaft and main bearings – refitting

1 Fit the five upper halves of the main bearing shells to their location in the crankcase, after wiping the recess clean (photo).
2 Note that on the back of each bearing is a tab which engages in the locating grooves in either the crankcase or the main bearing cap housings.
3 If new bearings are being fitted, carefully clean away all traces of the protective grease with which they are coated. The 1982 4K engine differs from the previous type in that the crankshaft bearing shells which fit into the main bearing caps now have no oil groove cut in them but have an additional location tab (see Fig. 1.37). During assembly of this type it is most important that the non-grooved bearing shell is fitted to the lower (cap) only. If fitted to the upper (crankcase) side, the crankshaft journals will suffer from lubrication problems. These later bearing types also differ in that they are supplied in pairs for each journal according to the size of each journal. The following bearing thicknesses are available for fitment:

No	Bearing thickness
3	0.0783 to 0.0785 in (1.990 to 1.994 mm)
4	0.0785 to 0.0786 in (1.994 to 1.998 mm)
5	0.0786 to 0.0788 in (1.998 to 2.002 mm)
6	0.0788 to 0.0789 in (2.002 to 2.006 mm)
7	0.0789 to 0.0791 in (2.006 to 2.010 mm)

The bearings are selected in the following manner. First check the cap size 'location' number, stamped on the underside of the cylinder block as shown in Figure 1.38. The number will be 6, 7 or 8. Now look for the journal size. This will be marked on the crankshaft, see Figure 1.39. Subtract the crankshaft journal size marking number from the cap size number on the cylinder block to give the code number of the crankshaft bearing to be used, e.g.:

Cap size 7, minus journal size 3, equals bearing number 4 required.

The bearing cap size code number will be marked as shown on the rear face (see Figure 1.40).
4 With the five upper bearing shells securely in place, wipe the lower bearing cap housings and fit the five lower bearing shells to their caps ensuring that the right shell goes into the right cap if the old bearings are being refitted.
5 Wipe the recesses either side of the centre main bearing which locate the upper halves of the thrust washers.
6 Smear a little grease onto the thrust washers and slip into position (photo).
7 Generously lubricate the crankshaft journals and the upper and lower main bearing shells and carefully lower the crankshaft into position. Make sure it is the right way round (photo).
8 Fit the main bearing caps in position ensuring that they locate properly. The mating surfaces must be spotlessly clean or the caps will not seat correctly (photo). The arrow marking on each cap must point to the front of the engine when fitted.
9 When locating the centre main bearing cap, ensure that the thrust washers, generously lubricated, are fitted with their oil grooves facing outwards and the locating tab of each washer is in the slot in the bearing cap (photo).

35.1 Locate the main bearing shells into position with location tabs in groove

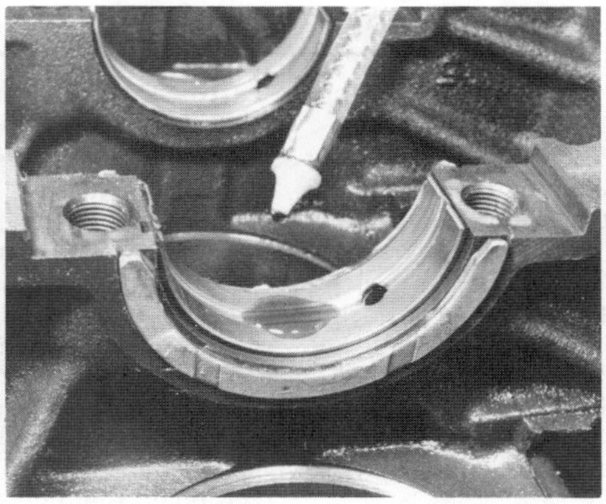

35.6 Locate the thrust washers and lubricate bearings ...

35.7 ... then lower crankshaft into position

35.8a Fit respective main bearing caps ensuring ...

35.8b ... correct positioning. This as indicated is the No. 2 cap

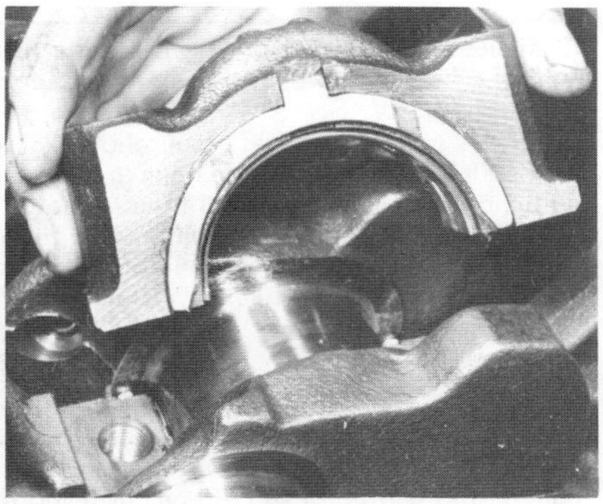

35.9 Centre main bearing cap is fitted with thrust washer

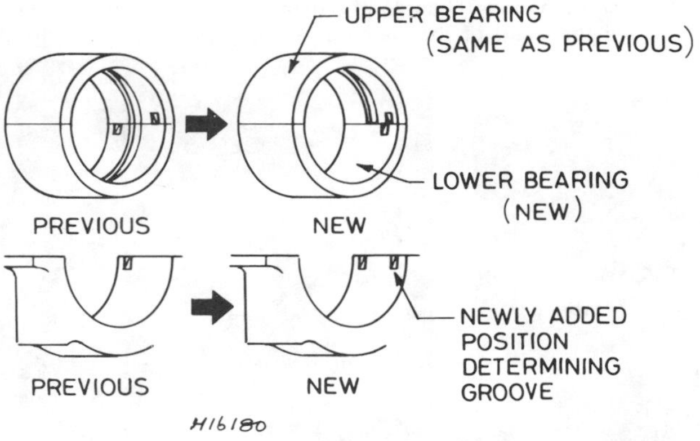

Fig. 1.37 Early and later type crankshaft bearings and caps identification on the 4K engine (Sec 35)

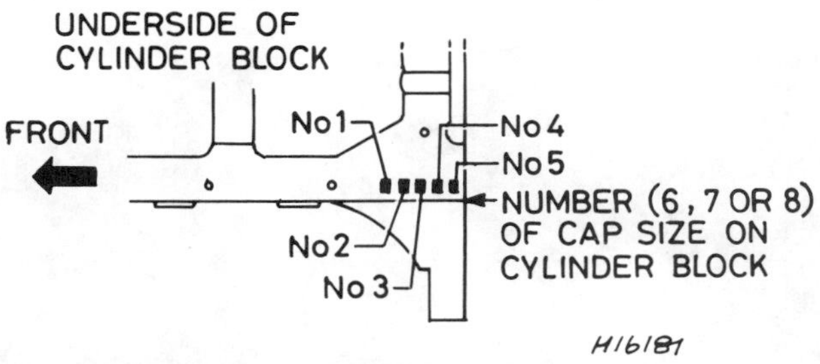

Fig. 1.38 Bearing designation marking location on later type 4K engine (Sec 35)

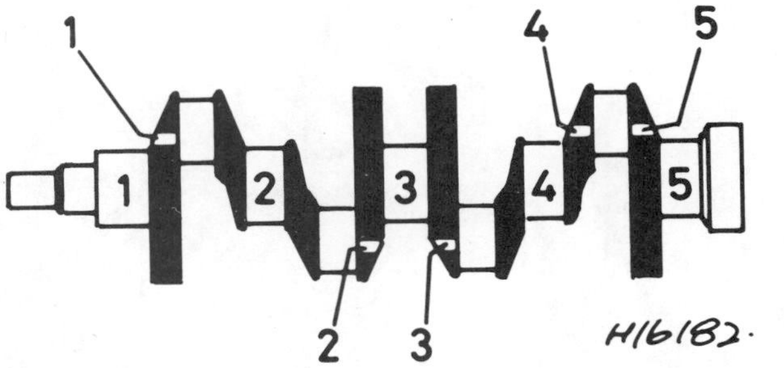

Fig. 1.39 Journal size mark positions on crankshaft – later type 4K engine (Sec 35)

Fig. 1.40 Bearing cap size code number location – later type 4K engine (Sec 35)

10 Insert the main bearing cap bolts and screw them up finger tight (photo).
11 Test the crankshaft for freedom of rotation. Should it be very stiff to turn, or possess high spots a most careful inspection must be made, preferably by a skilled mechanic with a micrometer to trace the cause of the trouble. It is very seldom that any trouble of this nature will be experienced when fitting the crankshaft.
12 Tighten the main bearing cap bolts to the specified torque wrench setting (photo) then again check the crankshaft for freedom of rotation.
13 Using a screwdriver between one crankshaft web and main bearing cap, lever the crankshaft forwards and check the endfloat using feeler gauges. This should be as given in the Specifications according to engine type. If excessive, new thrust washers or slightly oversize ones must be fitted (photo).

36 Crankshaft rear oil seal, flywheel (or driveplate) – refitting

1 Place a new gasket on the rear face of the crankcase and then install the crankshaft rear oil seal retainer complete with new oil seal (see Section 32).
2 Fit the engine rear plate (see photo 18.3).
3 Install the flywheel, fit the bolts and tighten to the specified torque and bend up the lock plates (if fitted) (photo). Smear the bolt threads under the heads with engine oil prior to fitting.
4 On vehicles equipped with automatic transmission, installation of the driveplate is very similar to installing the flywheel.

37 Pistons/connecting rods – reassembly and refitting

1 *On 4K engines,* immerse the piston in hot water so that the gudgeon pin can be pushed in or out using finger pressure only.
2 Assemble the piston to the connecting rod so that the notch in the piston crown is on the same side as the 'Front' mark on the connecting rod (Fig. 1.41) (photo).
3 Install one gudgeon pin circlip, push in the gudgeon pin and fit the second circlip making sure that it is well seated in its groove (Fig. 1.42).

On 2T, 2T-B and 3T-C engines, the gudgeon pins require special equipment for removal and installation and as previously explained, the pistons will have been reassembled to the rods by your dealer. If the same pistons are being used, then they must be mated to the same connecting rod with the same gudgeon pin. If new pistons are being fitted it does not matter which connecting rod is used, but the gudgeon pins are not to be interchanged.
4 If new piston rings have been supplied, it is best to check the compression rings in the piston grooves for side clearance and then insert them into the cylinder bores to check the end gaps. Although the clearances and gaps should be correct, it could be disastrous if the rings are tight when compared with the clearances in the Specifications. Slight easing of the rings in their grooves can be done by rubbing them on emery cloth held on a flat surface. Ring end gaps can be increased by grinding them squarely and carefully (photo).
5 Fit the rings to the pistons over the crown of the piston by reversing the removal operations described in Section 17. The two upper piston rings are compression type while the lower one is an oil control ring.
6 Fit the oil control ring first. This requires a special technique for installation. First fit the bottom rail of the oil control ring to the piston and position it below the bottom groove. Refit the oil control expander into the bottom groove and move the bottom oil control ring rail up into the bottom groove. Fit the top oil control rail into the bottom groove.
7 Fit the second compression ring and then the top compression ring noting that the markings on the rings should face upwards (Fig. 1.43).
8 When all the rings are fitted, stagger their end gaps at equidistant points of a circle to prevent gas blow-by (Fig. 1.44).
9 Wipe the first cylinder bore clean and smear it with clean engine oil.
10 Install a piston ring compressor to the piston rings, first having lubricated the rings liberally. Compress the rings.
11 Lower the big-end of the connecting rod into the bore from above until the piston ring compressor is standing squarely on the top of the cylinder block and the piston crown notch is facing the front (timing cover) end of the engine (photo).
12 Place the wooden handle of a hammer on the crown of the piston and give the head of the hammer a sharp blow to drive the piston

35.10 Fit main bearing cap bolts ...

35.12 ... and tighten to specified torque setting

35.13 Check crankshaft endfloat

36.3 Fit and tighten flywheel retaining bolts to specified torque

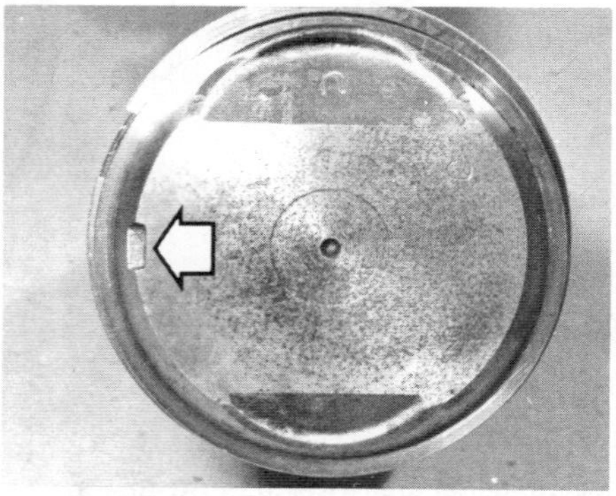
37.2 Piston front mark notch (arrowed)

37.4 Piston ring to groove side wall clearance check

37.11a Insert connecting rod and piston into cylinder bore ...

37.11b ... then compress rings with ring compressor as shown

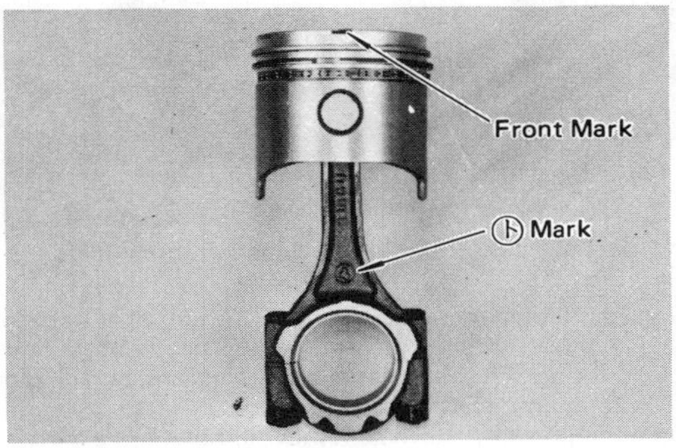

Fig. 1.41 Align front marks of rods and pistons when assembling – 4K engine (Sec 37)

Fig. 1.42 Insert the gudgeon pin circlips – make sure they are fully engaged in their grooves (Sec 37)

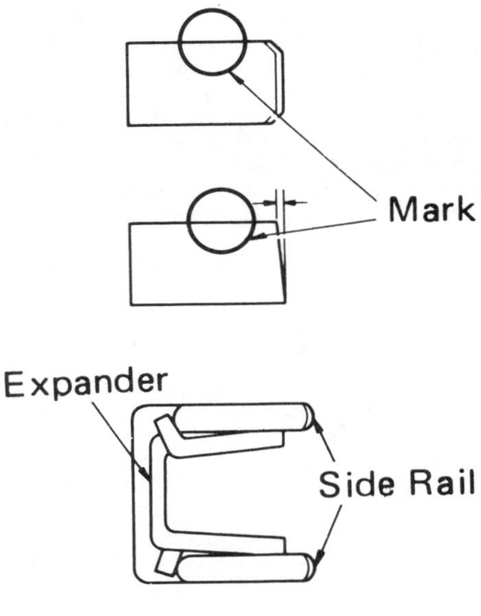

Fig. 1.43 Ring markings to face upwards when fitted (Sec 37)

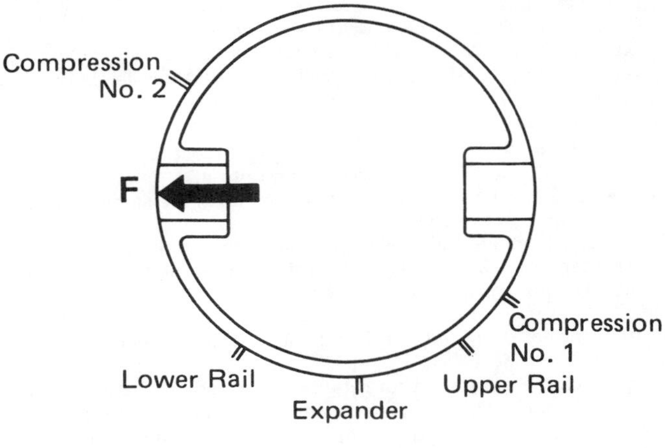

Fig. 1.44 Position piston ring gaps as shown before assembly into bores (Sec 37)

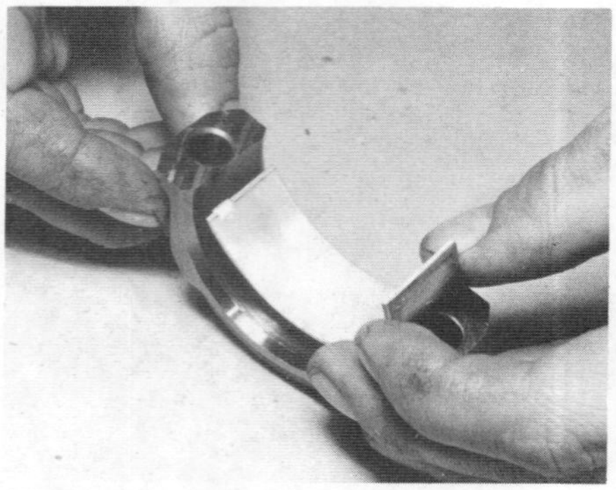
37.13 Locate the bearing shells to connecting rods and caps

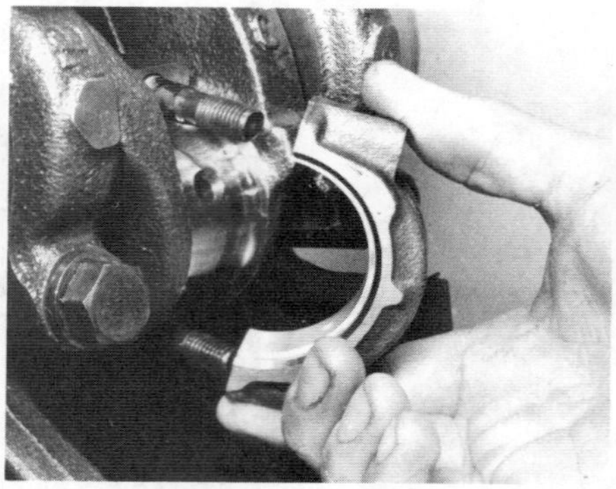
37.16a Locate the rod onto journal and fit cap

37.16b Check that rod and cap alignment marks correspond

37.17 Tighten big end caps nuts to the specified torque setting

38.1 Carefully insert the camshaft

38.2 Fit the camshaft thrust plate

assembly into its bore. As this happens, the ring compressor will fly off.

13 Wipe the connecting rod half of the big-end bearing location and the underside of the shell bearing clean, (as for the main bearing shells) and fit the shell bearing in position with its locating tongue engaged with the corresponding groove in the connecting rod. Always fit new shells (photo). Note that on 2T, 2T-B and 3T-C engines from September 1982 on the method of selecting the correct size of big-end bearing shells is the same as for the later type 4K engine main bearings described in Section 35. The cap size 'location' number is stamped on the side of the connecting rod cap, eg, 6, 7 or 8, and the journal size number will be found on the edge of the large counter-balance weights at each end of the crankshaft, eg, 1, 2 or 3. Having determined the bearing number required the bearing thicknesses are as follows:

No	**Bearing thickness**
3	*0.0584 to 0.0586 in (1.484 to 1.488 mm)*
4	*0.0586 to 0.0587 in (1.488 to 1.492 mm)*
5	*0.0587 to 0.5892 in (1.492 to 1.496 mm)*
6	*0.05892 to 0.0591 in (1.496 to 1.500 mm)*
7	*0.0591 to 0.0592 in (1.500 to 1.504 mm)*

14 Generously lubricate the crankpin journals with engine oil and turn the crankshaft so that the crankpin is in the most advantageous position for the connecting rod to be drawn onto it.

15 Fit the bearing shell to the connecting rod cap in the same way as with the connecting rod itself.

16 Generously lubricate the shell bearing and offer up the connecting rod bearing cap to the connecting rod. Fit the connecting rod retaining nuts (photos) and ensure that the rod and cap match marks are aligned.

17 Tighten the retaining nuts to the specified torque wrench setting (photo).

18 Now check the crankshaft for rotation. There should be a certain amount of resistance, as the pistons and connecting rods are now fitted, but any severe effort required to rotate the crankshaft should be treated with suspicion and an inspection made to find the cause.

38 Camshaft and timing gear – refitting

1 Lubricate the camshaft bearings and install the camshaft taking great care not to damage the bearings with the lobes (photo).

2 Fit the camshaft thrust plate and tighten the two securing bolts to the specified torque. Fit the plate with its marked side facing outwards on the 2T, 2T-B and 3T-C engines (photo).

3 If the engine front plate was removed, now is the time to refit it using a new gasket (4K engine only)

4 Fit the timing chain damper (not the tensioner).

5 If the crankshaft sprocket was removed during overhaul, refit it now with its Woodruff key. Drive the sprocket onto the front end of the crankshaft with a suitable piece of tubing.

6 Turn the crankshaft (by means of the flywheel or driveplate) in the normal direction of rotation until No. 1 piston is at TDC. The Woodruff key in the crankshaft sprocket should be at the top and perpendicular.

7 *On 4K engines,* turn the camshaft until its sprocket mounting dowel pin is in alignment with the timing mark on the camshaft thrust plate (Fig. 1.45).

8 *On 2T, 2T-B and 3T-C engines,* turn the camshaft until its sprocket mounting Woodruff key is in alignment with the timing mark on the camshaft thrust plate (Fig. 1.46).

9 Engage the timing chain round the camshaft sprocket so that the 'bright' link on the chain is in alignment with the timing mark on the sprocket (photo).

10 Engage the other loop of the chain round the crankshaft sprocket

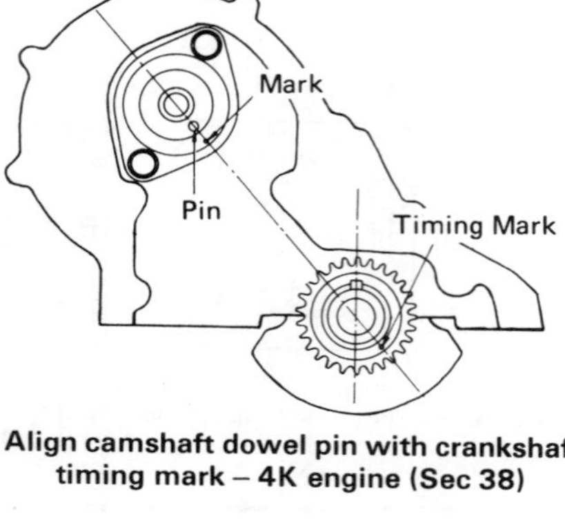

Fig. 1.45 Align camshaft dowel pin with crankshaft sprocket timing mark – 4K engine (Sec 38)

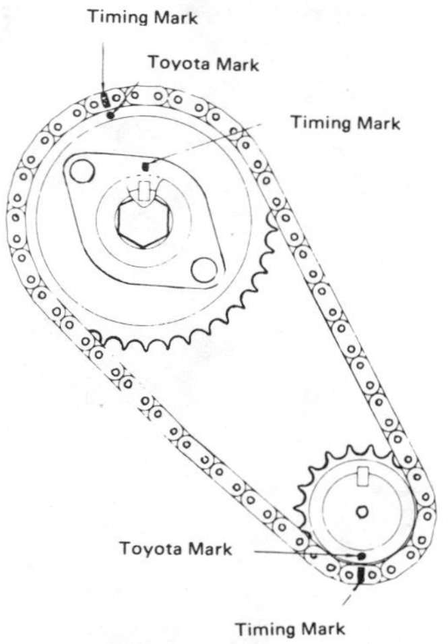

Fig. 1.46 Alignment of timing marks – 2T, 2T-B and 3T-C engines (Sec 38)

Fig. 1.47 Timing chain and sprockets assembly – 4K engine (Sec 38)

38.9 Align bright chain links with timing marks on sprockets

38.10a Timing chain and sprockets assembled and at TDC position

38.10b Fit camshaft sprocket retaining bolt and washers then ...

38.10c ... tighten to specified torque wrench setting

38.11a Fit the chain tensioner and damper unit ...

38.11b ... then check chain clearance as shown

38.12a Locating the timing cover (with new gasket)

38.12b Refit the crankshaft pulley ...

38.13a ... the retaining bolt and washer

38.13b ... and tighten to specified torque setting

so that the second 'bright' link is in alignment with the timing mark on the sprocket. Push the camshaft sprocket onto the camshaft mounting flange without moving any of the settings, screw in and tighten the sprocket securing bolt (Fig. 1.47). Give the bolt threads and the underside of the bolt head a light coating of engine oil before fitting (photo).

11 Lubricate then refit the chain tensioner and damper. When fitted check the damper to chain clearance as shown in the photos.

12 Fit a new timing cover gasket, bolt on the timing cover (complete with new oil seal) and fit the crankshaft pulley (photos). Ensure that the timing cover bolts are correctly positioned (regarding length) before fully tightening them.

13 Screw in and tighten the pulley bolt to the specified torque wrench setting. Hold the pulley against rotation by jamming the starter ring gear on the flywheel or by placing a block of wood between a crankshaft web and the inside of the crankcase (photos).

Fig. 1.48 Apply liquid sealant to points indicated before fitting sump – 4K engine (Sec 39)

39 Oil pump and sump – refitting

1 Offer up the oil pump complete with strainer to its crankcase location. Install the securing bolts and tighten to the specified torque wrench setting (photo).

2 *On 4K engines,* apply jointing compound to the areas shown on the sump gasket (Fig. 1.48).

3 *On 2T, 2T-B and 3T-C engines,* the gasket is flat and jointing compound should only be applied to the four corners.

4 Offer up the sump and bolt it into place.

5 Check that the oil drain plug is tight.

6 If the sump and oil pump were removed with the engine still in position in the vehicle, the oil pump will have to be placed inside the sump and both components offered up together. Once the oil pump is located onto its mounting reach through the gap between the sump and crankcase and screw in the mounting bolts.

40 Cylinder head – reassembly and refitting

1 Refit the valves to their guides in their original sequence, or if new valves are being fitted, in their 'ground in' sequence. Start by inserting No. 1 valve (nearest the front of the cylinder head) (photo).

2 Over the valve stem fit the plate washer, the valve stem oil seal, the valve spring, and the spring retainer (photos).

3 Compress the valve spring and drop in the split retaining collets (photo).

4 Gently release the compressor making sure that the collets are secure in their valve stem cut outs.

5 Repeat the procedure on the remaining seven valves, then tap each valve in turn to ensure satisfactory assembly and valve movement (photo).

6 At this stage it is recommended that the tappets (cam followers) are fitted in their original position (see photo 11.1).

7 After checking that both the cylinder block and head mating faces are perfectly clean, generously lubricate each cylinder bore with engine oil.

8 Always use a new cylinder head gasket. The old gasket will be compressed and incapable of giving a good seal as well as probably being damaged during removal (photo).

39.1 Refit the oil pump

40.1 Fit the valve into the guide

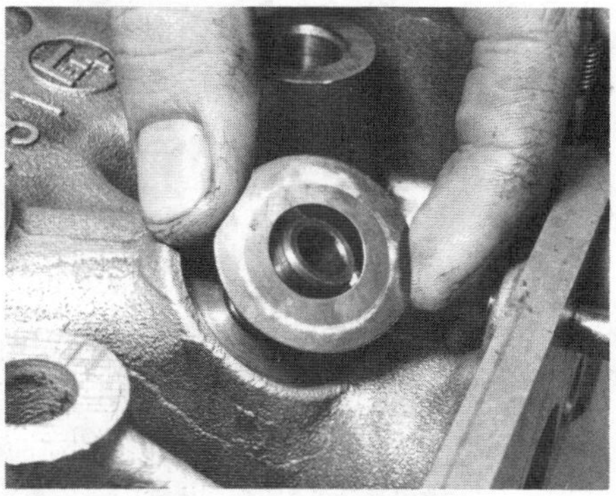

40.2a Locate the washer over the guide ...

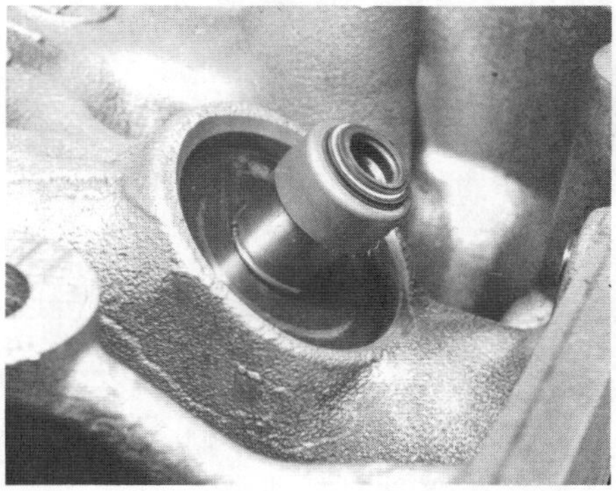

40.2b ... followed by the stem oil seal ...

40.2c ... the spring ...

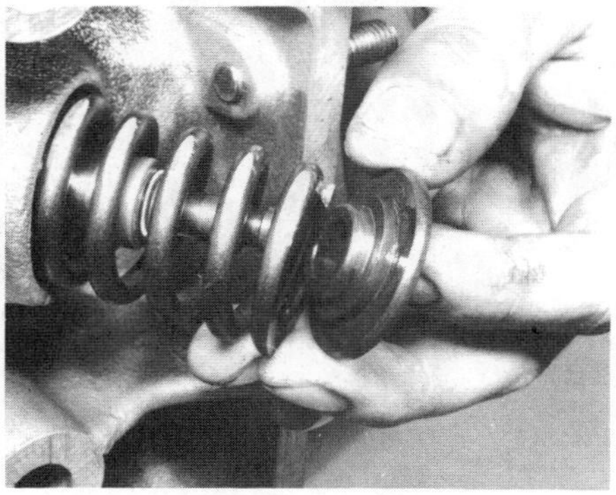

40.2d ... and spring retainer

40.3 Compress the spring and locate the collets

40.5 Tap the end of the valves to ensure satisfactory assembly

40.8 Locate the new head gasket

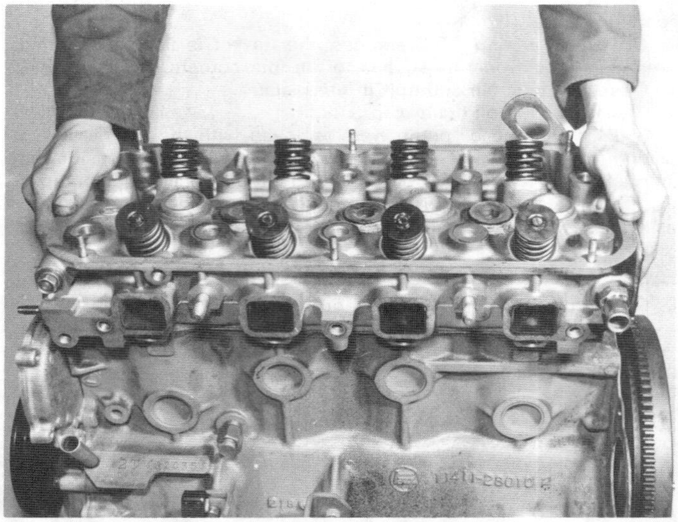

40.11 Refit the cylinder head

40.14 Insert the pushrods ...

40.15 ... then locate the rocker assembly with F mark to front (arrowed)

9 Never smear grease or gasket cement either side of the gasket for pressure leaks may blow through it.
10 The cylinder head gasket is usually marked 'Front' and should be fitted in position according to the markings. Ensure that all holes line up.
11 Carefully lower the cylinder head onto the block so that it is correctly located on its dowels (photo).
12 *On 4K engines,* insert all the cylinder head bolts finger tight and then tighten them to the specified torque in the sequence shown. To refit the rocker shaft assembly refer to the next Section (Fig. 1.49).
13 *On 2T, 2T-B and 3T-C engines,* as the cylinder head bolts also retain the rocker shaft support pedestals, the following procedure must be followed.
14 Install the pushrods into their original positions (photo).
15 Locate the rocker shaft assembly onto the cylinder head so that the F mark on the end support pedestal is nearest the front (timing cover end) of the engine. The rocker arm adjuster screws should be fully unscrewed and the ends of the pushrods not trapped under the rocker arms as the rocker assembly is lowered (photo).
16 Screw in the cylinder head bolts finger tight and then fully tighten them to the specified torque wrench setting and in the sequence shown (Fig. 1.50).
17 Engage the pushrods under the rocker arms and tighten the adjuster screws finger tight. The crankshaft will have to be rotated in order to be able to engage all the pushrods under the rocker arms.

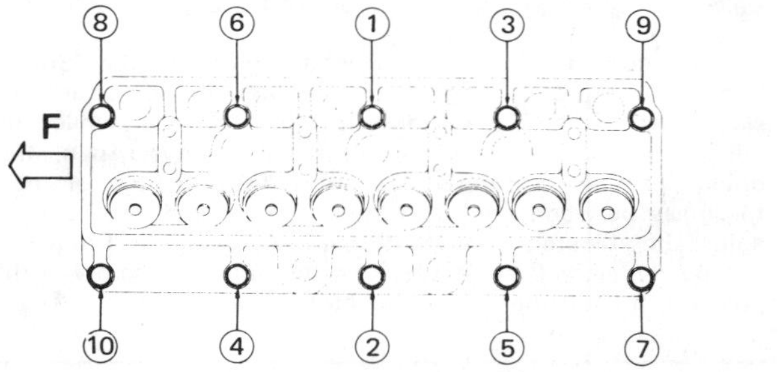

Fig. 1.49 Cylinder head bolt tightening sequence – 4K engine (Sec 40)

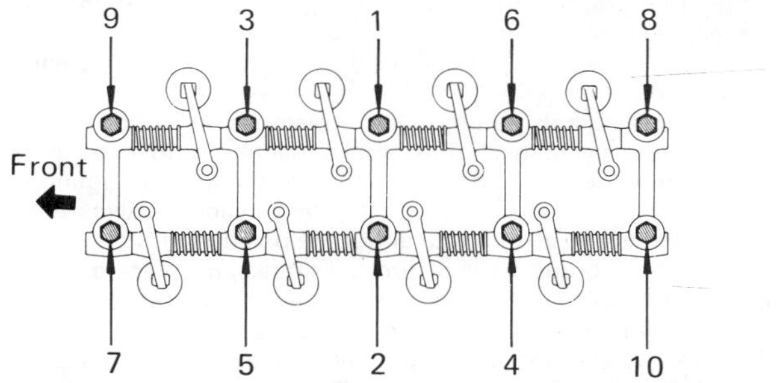

Fig. 1.50 Cylinder head bolt tightening sequence – 2T, 2T-B and 3T-C engines (Sec 40)

41 Rocker shaft assembly (4K engine) – refitting

1 Install the pushrods into their original locations (photo).
2 Release all the rocker arm adjuster screws and unscrew them as far as possible.
3 Install the rocker shaft assembly, engaging the pushrods with the rocker arms (photo).
4 Insert the rocker support pedestal bolts and tighten them evenly a turn at a time to the specified torque wrench setting working from the centre bolts towards the ends.

42 Valve clearances (4K engine) – adjustment

1 The valve clearances should normally be adjusted with the engine temporarily COLD. The importance of correct rocker arm valve stem clearances cannot be overstressed as they vitally affect the performance.
2 If the clearances are set too wide, the efficiency of the engine is reduced as the valves open late and close earlier than was intended. If the clearances are set too close there is a danger that the stem and pushrods upon expansion when hot will not allow the valves to close properly which will cause burning of the valve head and possible warping.
3 If the engine is in the car, to get at the rockers, it is merely necessary to remove the rocker cover. Once the cable support bracket and hose bracket have been detached undo and remove the two securing nuts and sealing washers then lift off the rocker cover and gasket.
4 It is important that the clearance is set when the tappet of the valve being adjusted is on the heel of the cam (ie; opposite the peak). This can be done by carrying out the adjustments in the following order, which also avoids turning the crankshaft more than necessary:

Valve fully open	*Check and adjust*
Valve number 8 Ex	Valve number 1 Ex
Valve number 6 In	Valve number 3 In
Valve number 4 Ex	Valve number 5 Ex
Valve number 7 In	Valve number 2 In
Valve number 1 Ex	Valve number 8 Ex
Valve number 3 In	Valve number 6 In
Valve number 5 Ex	Valve number 4 Ex
Valve number 2 In	Valve number 7 In

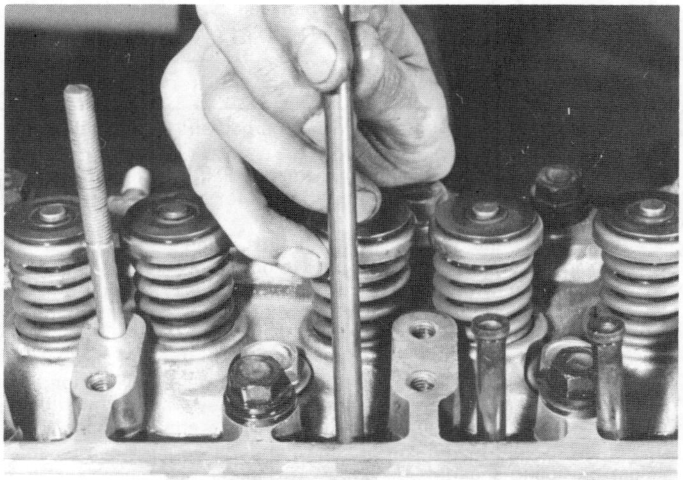

41.1 Installing pushrods into the 4K engine

41.3 Refitting the rocker shaft assembly (4K engine)

Valves are numbered from the front of the engine – inlet 2 – 3 – 6 – 7; exhaust 1 – 4 – 5 – 8.

5 The correct valve clearances are given in the 'Specifications' Section at the beginning of this Chapter. Clearance is obtained by slackening the hexagonal locknut with a spanner while holding the adjusting screw against rotation with a screwdriver. Then, still pressing down with the screwdriver, insert a feeler gauge of the required thickness between the valve stem and head of the rocker arm and adjust the adjusting screw until the feeler gauge will move in and out without nipping. Then still holding the adjusting screw in the correct position, tighten the locknut (photo).

43 Valve clearances (2T, 2T-B and 3T-C engines) – adjustment

1 The valve clearances should normally be adjusted with the engine at operating temperature. During engine reassembly, they will have to be adjusted temporarily COLD and re-checked later.

2 If the engine is in the vehicle, first remove the air cleaner and the rocker cover.

3 Turn the crankshaft until No. 1 piston is at TDC on its compression stroke. Turn the crankshaft by applying a ring spanner to the pulley nut. TDC can be determined by reference to the ignition timing marks (see Chapter 4). Also check that both No. 1 cylinder valves are closed.

4 If you are at all doubtful about the position of No. 1 piston, remove the spark plug and as you turn the crankshaft place a finger over the plug hole and feel the compression being generated. As soon as this is felt, refer to the ignition timing marks.

5 Now check and adjust the valve clearances 1 and 2 on the inlet side and 1 and 3 on the exhaust side.

6 The appropriate feeler blade should be a stiff sliding fit between the end of the valve stem and the rocker arm. If it is not, release the adjuster screw locknut and turn the adjuster screw in or out as necessary to achieve the gaps specified in the Specifications. Re-tighten the locknut (photo).

7 Now turn the crankshaft through one complete turn (360°) and check and adjust valve clearances 3 and 4 on the inlet side and 2 and 4 on the exhaust.

8 Refit the rocker cover on completion (and air cleaner unit where applicable) (photo).

44 Engine ancillaries – refitting

1 Detailed fitting instructions for the ancillary components are given in the Chapters indicated but the following sequence should be followed.

Distributor (Chapter 4)
Carburettor and inlet manifold (Chapter 3) (photos)
Alternator (Chapter 10)
Fuel pump (Chapter 3)
Water pump (Chapter 2)
Starter motor (Chapter 10)
Thermostat (Chapter 2)
Exhaust manifold (Chapter 3)
Clutch assembly (Chapter 5)
Emission control equipment (Chapter 3)
Air conditioning equipment (where applicable)

45 Engine/transmission – refitting

1 The operations are reversals of removal and reference should be made to the appropriate Section at the front of this Chapter.

2 When reconnecting the engine and manual gearbox, make sure that the clutch driven plate has been centralised as described in Chapter 6.

3 When assembling the engine to the transmission ensure that the crankcase support brackets and the exhaust location bracket are fitted as shown (photos).

4 Once the engine (and transmission) have been installed and there is no longer any danger of damaging it, fit a new oil filter cartridge. Smear the rubber sealing ring of the filter with grease and screw it on using hand pressure only. On no account use any sort of wrench or tool to tighten it. The engine, transmission and cooling system should now be filled.

42.5 Checking a valve clearance (4K engine)

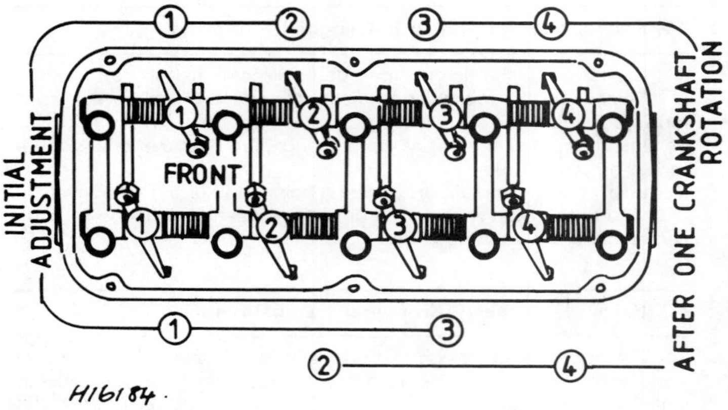

Fig. 1.51 Valve clearance check/adjustment diagram – 2T, 2T-B and 3T-C engines (Sec 43)

5 Remember to connect the battery and then double check for loose connections, hoses and controls and make sure that all tools have been removed from the engine compartment.

46 Engine – initial start up after overhaul or repair

1 Make sure that the battery is fully charged and that all lubricants, coolant and fuel are replenished.

2 If the fuel system has been dismantled, it will require several revolutions of the engine on the starter motor to pump petrol to the carburettor.

3 As soon as the engine fires and runs, keep it going at a fast tickover only (no faster) and bring it up to normal working temperature.

4 As the engine warms up, there will be odd smells and some smoke from parts getting hot and burning off oil deposits. Look for water or oil leaks which will be obvious if serious. Check also the clamp connection of the exhaust pipe to the manifold as these do not always 'find' their exact gas tight position until the warmth and vibration have acted on them, and it is almost certain that they will need tightening further. This should be done of course with the engine stationary.

5 When the normal engine running temperature has been reached, adjust the idling speed as described in Chapter 3.

6 Stop the engine and wait a few minutes to see if any lubricant or coolant leaks.

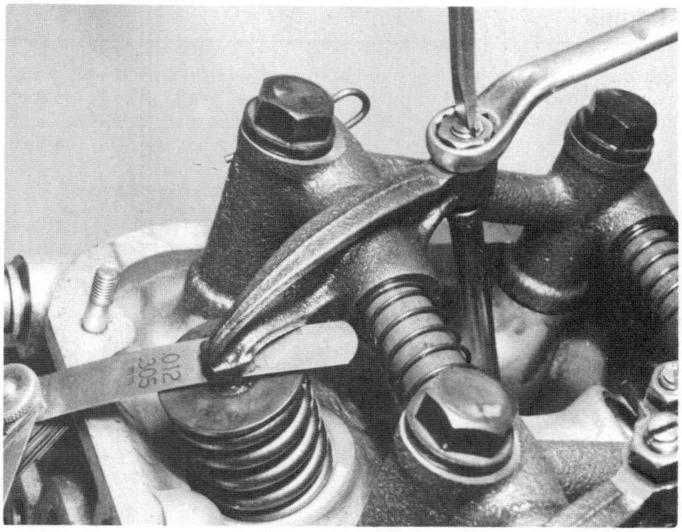

43.6 Valve clearance adjustment

43.8 Refit the rocker cover

44.1a Always use new gasket ...

44.1b ... when refitting the inlet manifold and carburettor

45.3a Crankcase support bracket on right-hand side

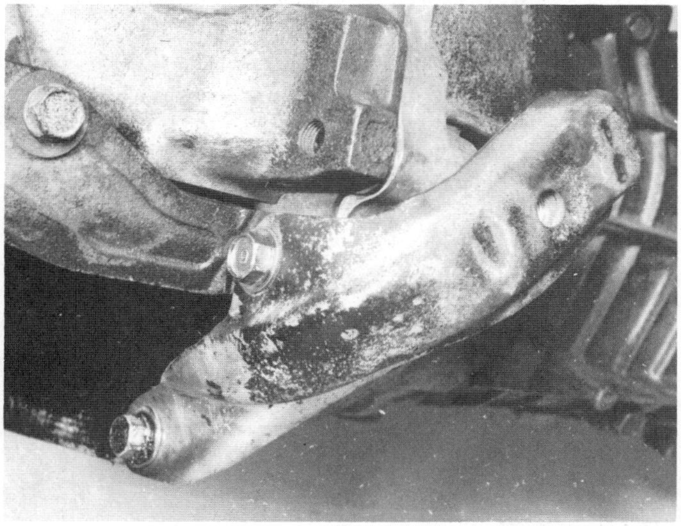
45.3b Crankcase support bracket and exhaust location bracket on left-hand side

7 Road test the car to check that the timing is correct and giving the necessary smoothness and power. Do not race the engine. If new bearings and/or pistons and rings have been fitted, it should be treated as a new engine and run in at reduced revolutions for 500 miles (800 km).

8 At the end of the first 1000 miles (1600 km) renew the engine oil and filter if a number of new components were installed at time of overhaul, also check the torque of the cylinder head bolts. To do this, unscrew each bolt (one at a time) in the specified sequence one quarter of a turn and then retighten it to torque. Follow with the next bolt in sequence and so on.

9 Finally check and adjust if necessary, the valve clearances.

47 Fault diagnosis – engine

Symptom	Reason(s)
Engine fails to turn over when starter operated	Discharged or defective battery Dirty or loose battery leads Defective starter solenoid or switch Engine earth strap disconnected Jammed starter motor drive pinion Defective starter motor
Engine turns over but will not start	Ignition damp or wet Ignition leads to spark plugs loose Shorted or disconnected low tension leads Dirty, incorrectly set or pitted contact breaker points Faulty condenser Defective ignition switch Ignition LT leads connected wrong way round Faulty coil Contact breaker point spring earthed or broken No petrol in petrol tank Vapour lock in fuel line (in hot conditions or at high altitude) Blocked float chamber needle valve Fuel pump filter blocked Choked or blocked carburettor jets Faulty fuel pump Too much choke allowing too rich a mixture to wet plugs Float damaged or leaking or needle not seating Float lever incorrectly adjusted
Engine stalls and will not start	Ignition failure – sudden (see Chapter 4) Ignition failure – misfiring precludes total stoppage (see Chapter 4) No petrol in petrol tank Petrol tank breather choked Obstruction in carburettor Water in fuel system
Engines misfires or idles unevenly	Ignition leads loose Battery leads loose on terminals Battery earth strap loose on body attachment point Engine earth lead loose Low tension leads to '+' and '–' terminals on coil loose Low tension lead from coil '–' terminal to distributor loose Dirty or incorrectly gapped spark plugs Dirty, incorrectly set or pitted contact breaker points Tracking across distributor cap Ignition too retarded Faulty coil Mixture too weak Air leak in carburettor Air leak at inlet manifold to cylinder head, or inlet manifold to carburettor Incorrect valve clearances

Chapter 2 Cooling system

Contents

Specifications

System type	Pressurized, pump-assisted, thermo-syphon
Thermostat	
Type	Wax
Identification:	
Low temperature type	Stamped '82' or blue paint mark
High temperature type	Stamped '88' or red paint mark
Opening temperature:	
Low temperature type	180°F (82°C)
High temperature type	190°F (88°C)
Fully open temperature:	
Low temperature type	203°F (95°C)
High temperature type	212°F (100°C)
Minimum valve opening travel	0.31 in (8.0 mm)
Radiator	
Cap relief valve opening pressure	10.7 to 15 lbf/in^2 (0.75 to 1.05 kgf/cm^2)
Drivebelt adjustment	
Approximate deflection under 22 lbf (10 kgf) load – all belts	0.3 to 0.5 in (8.0 to 12.0 mm)
Approximate deflection using Burroughs tension gauge BT – 33 – 73F – all belts	60 to 100 lbf (27 to 45 kgf)

1 General description

The cooling system is of pressurised type and the main components of the system are a front mounted radiator, a belt driven water pump and a thermostat.

The cooling fan fitted will be either a thermostatically controlled electric type mounted in a frame and attached to the radiator, or a viscous coupled type fan attached to the water pump spindle flange.

The electric type cooling fan is actuated in accordance with the temperature of the coolant in the radiator by means of a radiator mounted thermo-switch.

The viscous coupled fan is a variable speed type having a fluid coupling incorporated into its central hub. This allows the fan to operate at a reduced speed at higher engine speeds and thus reduces fan noise and power dissipation from the engine. Some models may have a 'tempered' cooling fan which additionally incorporates a bi-metallic control. This opens and closes a valve in the fluid coupling according to the engine compartment temperature, and provides varying amounts of fan 'slip' to maintain optimum cooling efficiency.

Water temperature is measured by a thermo-electric capsule located below the thermostat housing, and the reading is shown on a gauge mounted on the car instrument panel.

Drain plugs are provided on the bottom of the radiator and on the cylinder block.

The system functions as follows. With the engine running, cold water from the bottom of the radiator is drawn through the bottom radiator hose to the water pump. The water pump then forces the water through the cylinder block and water jackets to the cylinder head.

When the engine is cold and the thermostat is closed, the water passes through the by-pass hose and is drawn into the water pump again; the water circulation is thus confined to the cylinder block and head. This assists rapid warming up.

The wax type thermostat is located in an outlet housing on the front of the cylinder head.

When the temperature of the coolant reaches the predetermined level, the thermostat opens and the water is forced through the top radiator hose to the radiator. The water is air cooled as it passes down through the radiator matrix and the cycle is then repeated.

The heater unit is supplied with hot water from the engine cooling system, but the coolant flow through the heater is controlled by a valve manually operated by means of a cable connected to the heater control panel within the vehicle driving compartment. When the heater is off the valve is closed.

Maintenance of the system consists of periodic checks on the coolant level in the reservoir, checking the cooling fan/water pump drivebelt tension and condition, and inspecting the various system hoses for security and signs of leaks or deterioration. These checks should be made as described in the 'Routine Maintenance' Section.

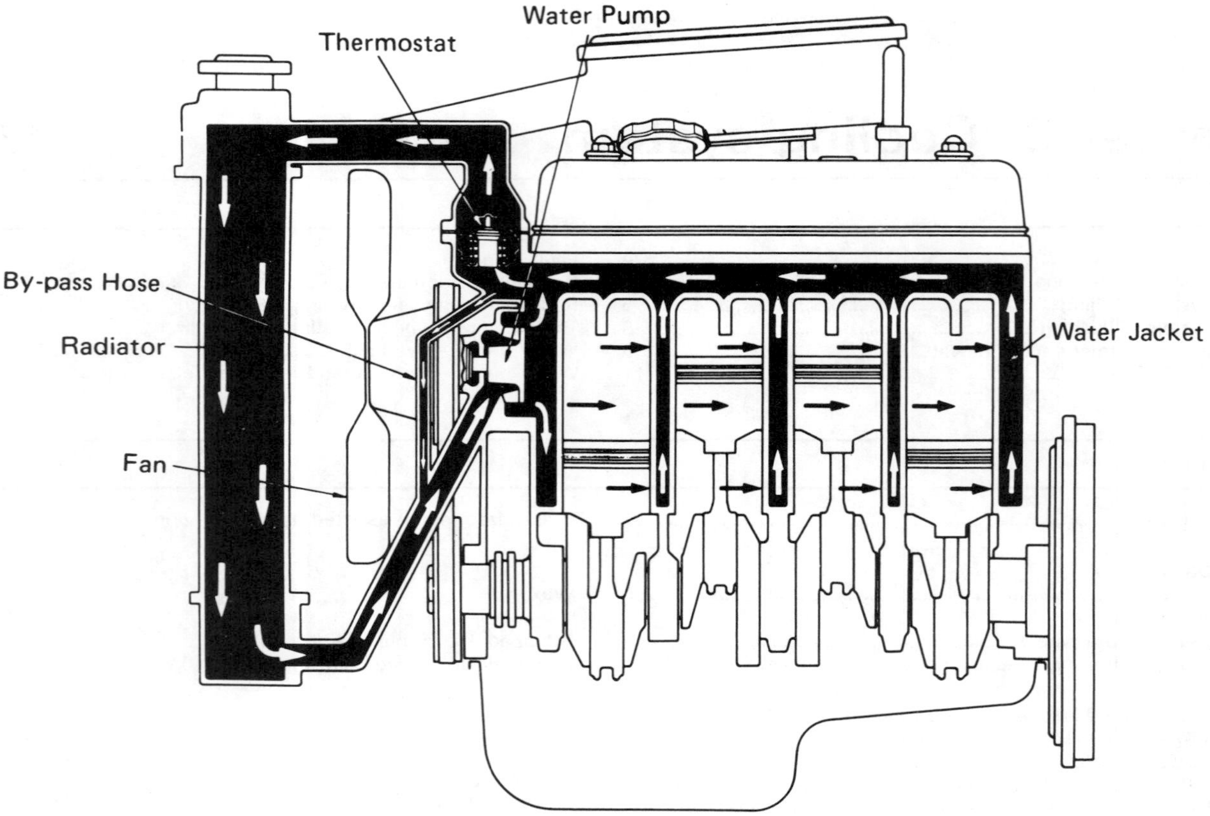

Fig. 2.1 Sectional view of the cooling system on the 4K engine (Sec 1)

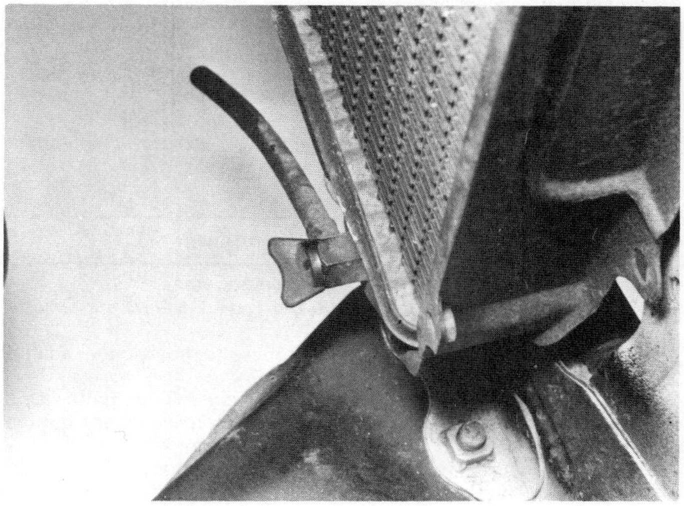

2.3a Radiator drain plug

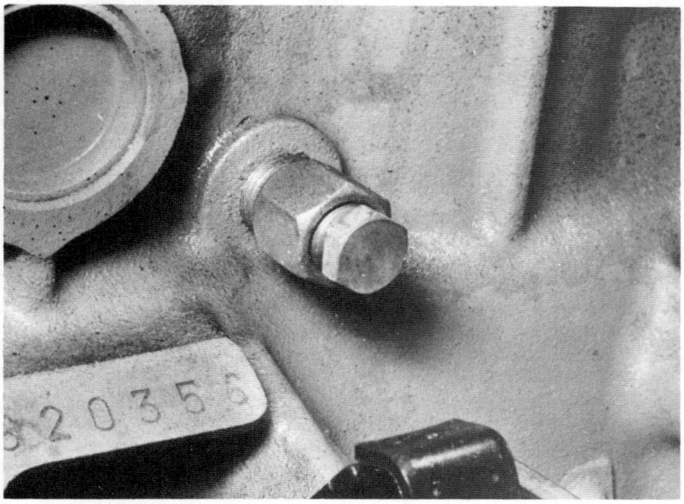

2.3b Engine cylinder block drain plug

2 Cooling system – draining

1 With the car on level ground drain the system as follows. If the engine is cold, remove the filler cap from the radiator by turning it anti-clockwise. If the engine is hot, then turn the filler cap very slightly until the pressure in the system has had time to disperse. Use a rag over the cap to protect your hand from escaping steam. If, with the engine very hot, the cap is released suddenly, the drop in pressure can cause the water to boil. With the pressure released the cap can be removed.
2 If anti-freeze is in the cooling system drain it into a clean bowl for re-use. A wide bowl will be necessary to catch all the coolant.
3 Open the radiator and cylinder block drain plugs. When the water has finished running, probe the plug holes with a piece of wire to dislodge any particles of rust or sediment which may be causing a blockage and preventing all the coolant draining out (photo).

3 Cooling system – flushing

1 With time the cooling system will gradually lose its efficiency as the radiator becomes choked with rust scale, deposits from the water and other sediment. To clean the system out, first drain it – leaving the drain plugs open. Then remove the radiator cap and leave a hose running in the radiator cap orifice for ten to fifteen minutes.
2 In very bad cases the radiator should be reverse flushed. This can be done with the radiator in position. A hose must be arranged to feed water into the lower radiator outlet pipe. Water, under pressure, is then forced up through the radiator and out of the header tank filler orifice. *Take care not to allow water spray to splash onto the ignition leads and associated components and do not flush a hot engine with cold water!*
3 On completion, remove the hose and then flush through again in the normal manner inserting it through the radiator filler orifice.

4 Anti-freeze solution

1 Apart from climatic considerations, anti-freeze mixture should always be used in the engine cooling system to help combat rust and corrosion.
2 Standard solutions should be renewed every year while 'long life' products usually give protection for periods of two years. Renew the coolant just before the winter season commences.
3 Before refilling the cooling system with anti-freeze solution it is best to drain and flush the system as described in Section 2 and 3 of this Chapter.
4 Because anti-freeze has a greater searching effect than water make sure that all hoses and joints are in good condition.

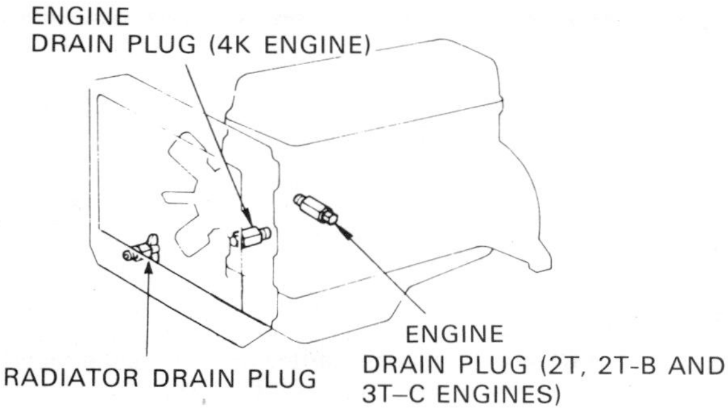

Fig. 2.2 Radiator and engine drain plug positions (Sec 2)

5 Ideally, a 50% solution of anti-freeze with 50% soft water should be used but where financial considerations dictate weaker mixtures, the table gives the protection to be expected from smaller percentages.

%	*Complete protection*	
25	–11°C	12.2°F
30	–14°C	6.8°F
35	–19°C	–2.2°F
40	–23°C	–9.4°F
45	–29°C	–20.2°F
50	–35°C	–31.0°F

6 Where the cooling system contains an anti-freeze solution any subsequent topping up should be done with a solution of similar proportions to avoid dilution.

5 Cooling system – filling

1 Refit and tighten the radiator and cylinder block drain plugs.
2 Move the heater control lever to HOT.
3 Remove the radiator cap and pour anti-freeze mixture slowly into the radiator until it is full to the brim.
4 Start the engine and let it run at a fast idle. The coolant level in the radiator will drop; make this up by adding more coolant until the level no longer falls.
5 Switch off the engine, refit the radiator cap and then fill the expansion tank to the level mark halfway up its side.
6 When the engine is restarted and reaches its normal operating temperature, make a further check to ensure that the coolant level in the reservoir is correct and that the drain plugs and hoses show no signs of leaking.

6 Drivebelts – adjustment and renewal

1 The number of drivebelts fitted and their arrangement will depend upon the equipment fitted (water pump, emission control air pump, alternator, air conditioning compressor, power steering pump).

2 The respective drivebelt arrangements and their tension check-points are shown in the accompanying illustrations (Fig. 2.3). Refer to the Specifications for details on the belt adjustments.

3 Adjustment is carried out by slackening the mounting and adjustment link bolts of the driven component and pushing it in towards or pulling it away from the engine. The exception to this is that the air conditioner compressor has an idler pulley and the pulley should be moved to alter the belt tension.

4 If a drivebelt requires renewal because of wear, cuts, fraying or breakage, always release the mountings of the driven components and push it in towards the engine as far as possible so that the belt can be slipped over the pulley rims with the least strain.

5 With multiple belt arrangements, if a rear belt requires renewal then the ones nearer the front will of course have to be removed first.

6 With a new belt check the tension 250 miles (400 km) after fitting.

7 Periodic checking of the belt tension is necessary and there is no hard and fast rule as to the most suitable interval, because a fan belt does not necessarily stretch or wear at a predetermined rate. Assuming most owners check their own oil and water levels regularly it is suggested as a good habit to check the fan belt tension every time the bonnet is opened (photo).

8 Where an air pump drivebelt is being removed do not apply abnormal pressure to the pump casing which, being manufactured in aluminium, is likely to be damaged.

9 For removal, renewal and adjustment of the power steering pump (where fitted) refer to Chapter 11.

7 Radiator – removal, servicing and refitting

1 Refer to Section 2 and drain the cooling system.

2 Slacken the clip which holds the top water hose to the radiator and carefully pull off the hose.

3 Slacken the clip which holds the bottom water hose to the radiator bottom tank and carefully pull off the hose.

4 On models fitted with the automatic transmission wipe the area round the oil cooler pipe unions and then detach these pipes from the radiator. Plug the end to prevent dirt entering the pipes.

5 If a fan shroud is fitted this should be detached from the radiator and placed over the fan.

6 Undo and remove the radiator securing bolts and lift the radiator upwards and away from the front of the car. The shroud (if fitted) may next be lifted away (photos).

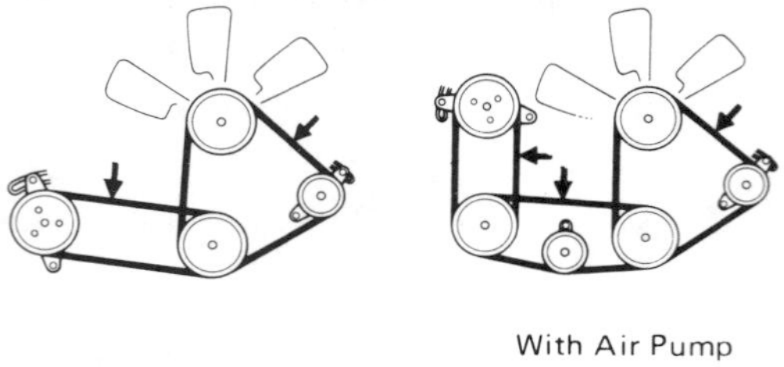

Fig. 2.3 Drivebelt arrangements and their respective tension check points (Sec 6)

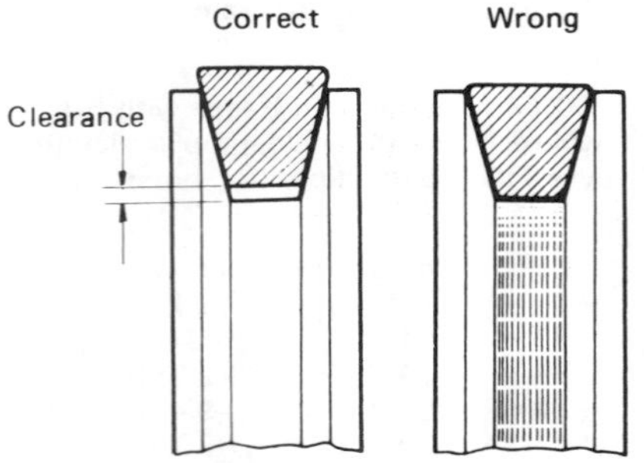

Fig. 2.4 Sectional view to show correct drivebelt tension to pulley fitting (Sec 6)

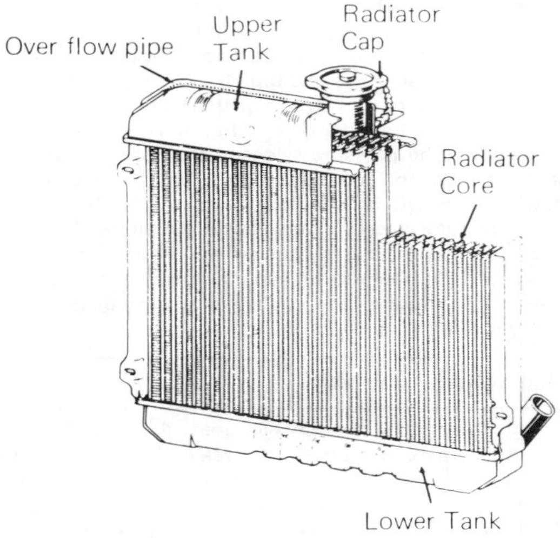

Fig. 2.5 Construction of radiator (Sec 7)

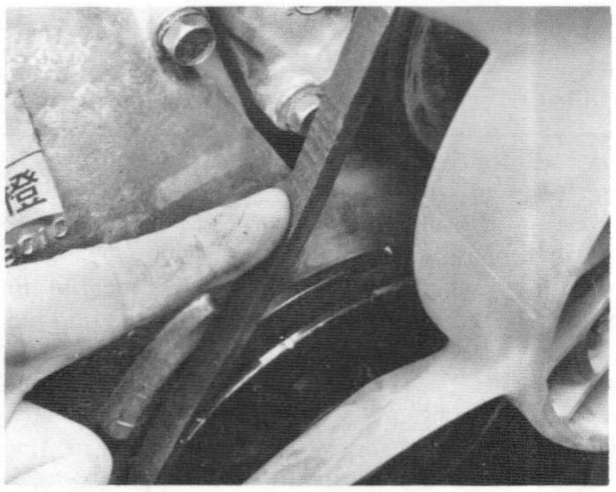

6.7 Check condition and tension of drivebelts during the Routine Maintenance procedures

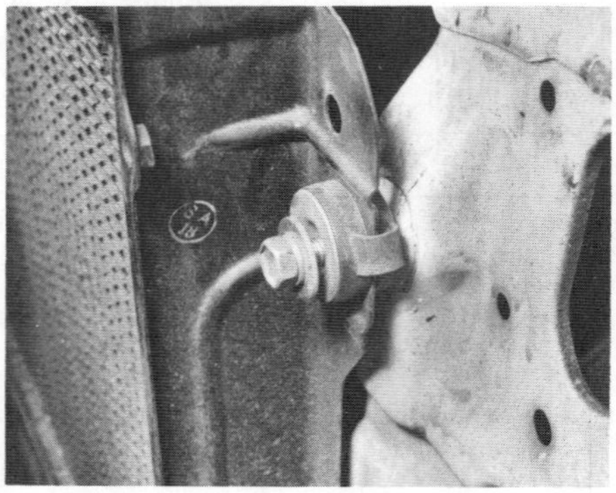

7.6a Remove the radiator securing bolts ...

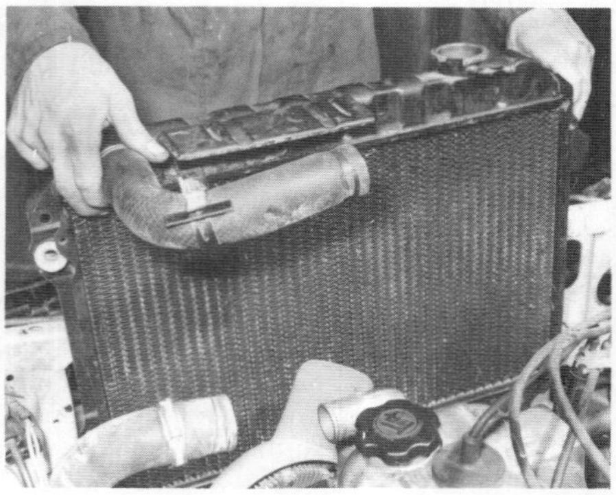

7.6b ... then lift it carefully upwards and clear of the engine compartment

7 On engines having an electrically-operated cooling fan, detach the electrical leads from the fan motor and the themostatic switch in the radiator. The radiator is removed complete with fan which is unbolted afterwards together with its supporting frame.
8 Clean out the inside of the radiator by flushing as described in Section 3. When the radiator is out of the car it is well worthwhile to invert it for reverse flushing. Clean the exterior of the radiator by hosing down the matrix with a strong water jet to clean away embedded dirt and debris, which will impede the air flow. When an oil cooler is fitted (automatic transmission) make sure no water is allowed to enter.
9 If it is thought that the radiator is partially blocked, a good proprietary chemical product should be used to clean it.
10 If the radiator is leaking, a temporary repair may be made by plugging with a fibreglass type filler or by using a leak sealing product in the coolant. Permanent repairs should be left to your dealer or a radiator repair specialist. Localised heat has to be used to repair a radiator, obviously experience is necessary otherwise the problem could be made worse.
11 Inspect the radiator hoses for cracks, internal or external perishing and damage caused by the securing clips. Renew the hoses as necessary. Examine the radiator hose securing clips and renew them if they are rusted or distorted.
12 Refitting the radiator is the reverse sequence to removal. If automatic transmission is fitted check and top-up its fluid level.
13 On electric cooling fan models check that the fan cuts-in when the coolant temperature reaches 194°F (90°C).
14 On completion check the radiator and its hose connections for any signs of leaks.

8 Thermostat – removal, testing and refitting

1 To remove the thermostat, partially drain the cooling system as described in Section 2. The removal of 4 pints (2.27 litres) is usually enough.
2 Slacken the radiator top hose at the thermostat housing elbow and carefully draw it off the elbow (photo).
3 Unscrew the two bolts and spring washers securing the thermostat housing elbow (photo), and lift the housing and gasket away. If it has stuck because a sealing compound has been previously used, tap with a soft faced hammer to break the seal.
4 Lift out the thermostat and observe if it is stuck open. If this is the case discard it (photo).
5 Suspend it by a piece of string together with a thermometer in a saucepan of cold water. Neither the thermostat nor the thermometer should touch the sides or bottom of the saucepan or a false reading could be obtained.
6 Heat the water, stirring it gently with the thermometer to ensure temperature uniformity, and note when the thermostat begins to open. Note the temperature and this should be comparable with the figure given in the 'Specifications' Section at the beginning of this Chapter.
7 Continue heating the water until the thermostat is fully open. Now let it cool down naturally and check that it closes fully. If the thermostat does not fully open or close then it must be discarded and a new one obtained (Fig. 2.7).

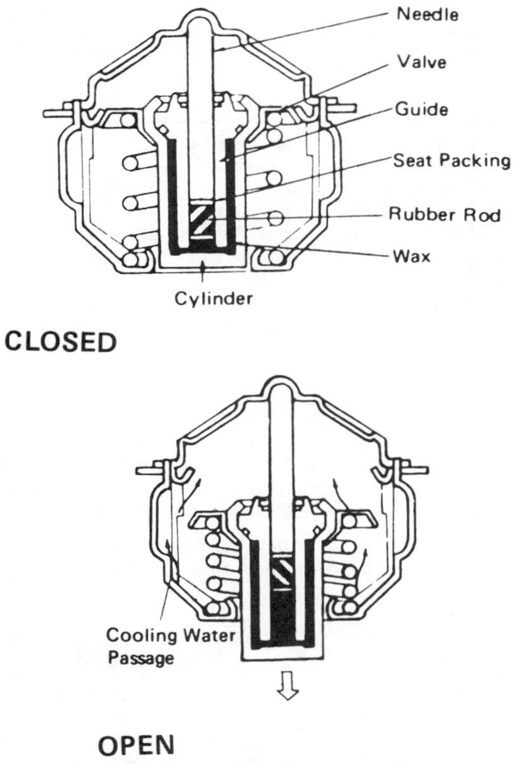

Fig. 2.6 Diagram of thermostat showing closed and open positions of valve (Sec 8)

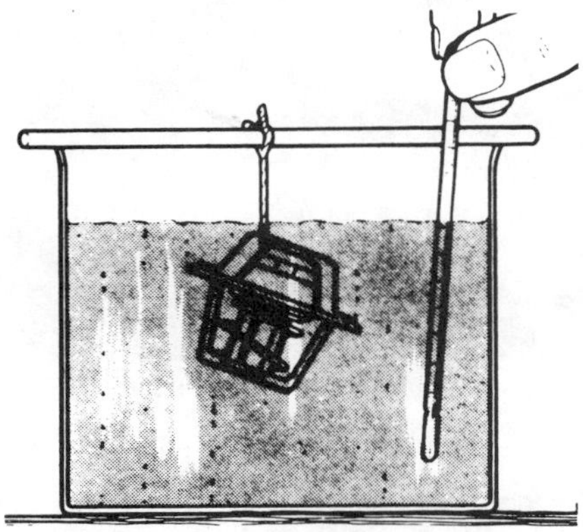

Fig. 2.7 Thermostat test method (Sec 8)

8.2 Detach top elbow hose from thermostat

8.3 Unscrew bolts and remove housing ...

8.4 ... then lift out the thermostat

8 Refitting the thermostat is the reverse of the removal procedure. Always clean the mating faces thoroughly and use a new flange gasket.

9 Water pump – removal and refitting

1 Refer to Section 2 and drain the cooling system.
2 Refer to Section 7 and remove the radiator.
3 Refer to Section 6 and remove the fan belt.
4 Slacken the bottom hose clip and carefully detach the radiator hose from the water pump.
5 Slacken the water bypass hose clip and carefully detach the bypass hose from the water pump. Disconnect the heater hose from the water pump (photo).
6 Undo and remove the four bolts securing the fan and hub assembly (hub only where an electronic cooling fan is fitted), from the water pump spindle flange and lift away the fan assembly (photo).
7 Undo and remove the bolts securing the water pump body to the cylinder block. Lift away the water pump and recover the old gasket.
8 Refitting the water pump is the reverse sequence to removal, but the following additional points should be noted (photos).

- (a) *Make sure the mating faces of the pump body and cylinder block are clean. Always use a new gasket*
- (b) *Refer to Section 6 and adjust the fan belt tension. If the belt is too tight undue strain will be placed on the water pump and alternator bearings. If the belt is too loose, it will slip and wear rapidly as well as giving rise to possible engine overheating and low alternator output*
- (c) *On completion top up the cooling system, run the engine and check for leaks around the water pump and hoses*

10 Water pump – overhaul

1 If the water pump has been removed for inspection owing to noisy operation or possibly because it has developed a leak, overhaul is possible, but is not recommended. In the first place spare parts for the pump may not be readily available and secondly the cost of a factory reconditioned unit should not prove that expensive.
2 The various pump types fitted according to engine type are shown in the accompanying illustrations.
3 Where spare parts are available and it is preferred to overhaul the original pump unit, first clean away all external dirt.
4 Support the underside of the pulley seat and, supporting the pump unit so that it does not fall and damage the housing, drive the shaft down through the pulley seat. Alternatively use a puller to withdraw the pulley seat from the shaft (Fig. 2.10).
5 Heat up the pump unit in a bowl of hot water to a temperature of

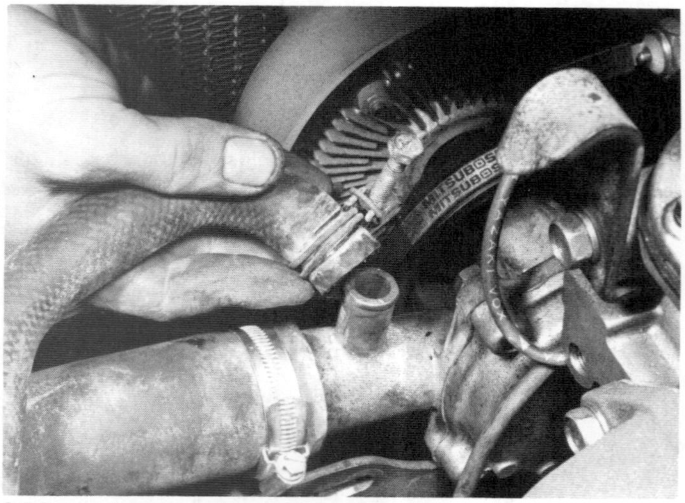
9.5 Detach bypass and heater hoses from the pump

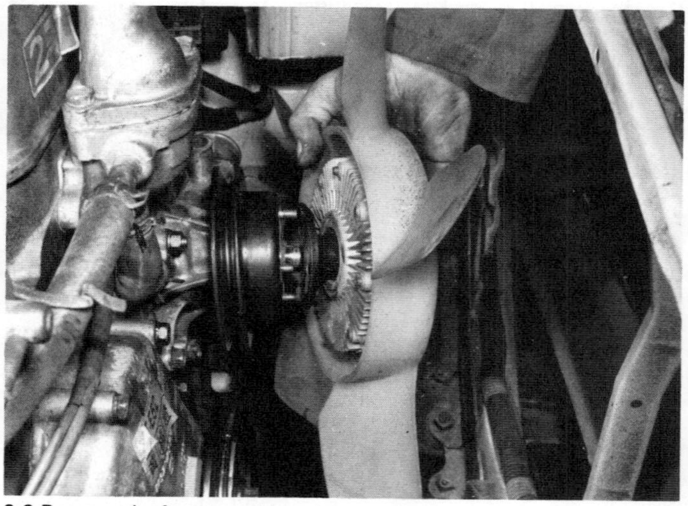
9.6 Remove the fan assembly

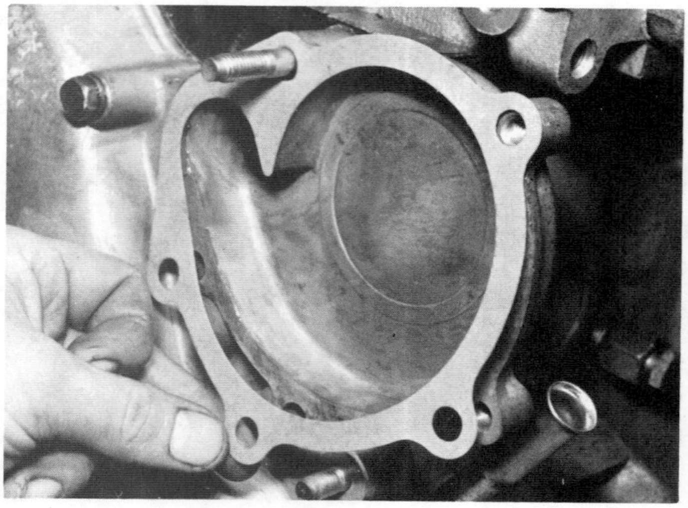
9.8a Use a new water pump gasket

9.8b Refitting the water pump

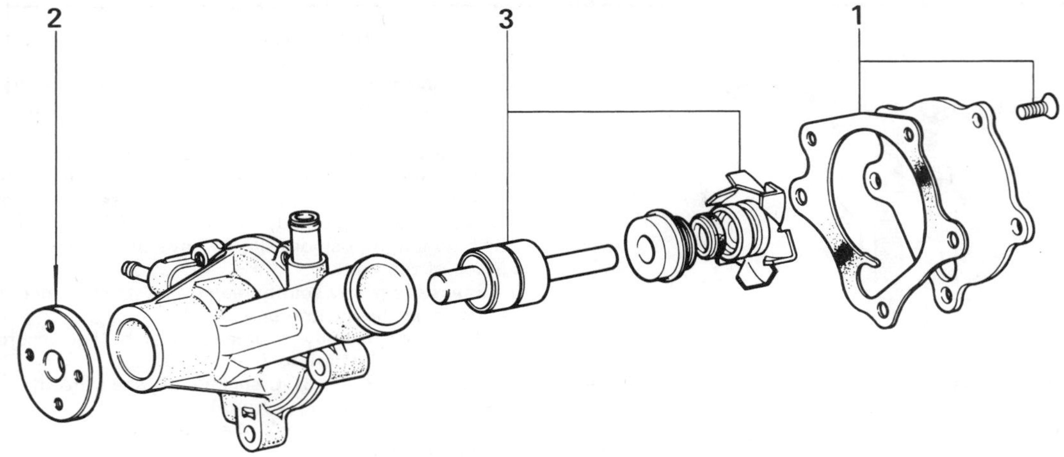

Fig. 2.8 Water pump components – 4K engine (Sec 10)

1 Plate and gasket *2 Pulley seat* *3 Bearing, seal set and rotor*

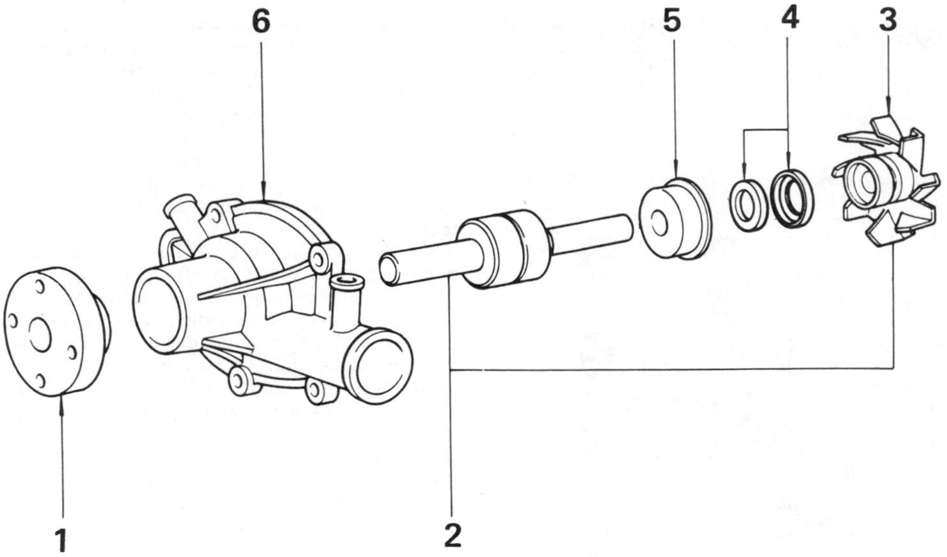

Fig. 2.9 Water pump components – 2T, 2T-B and 3T-C engines (Sec 10)

1 Pulley seat
2 Shaft, bearing & rotor
3 Rotor
4 Seal
5 Seal
6 Pump body

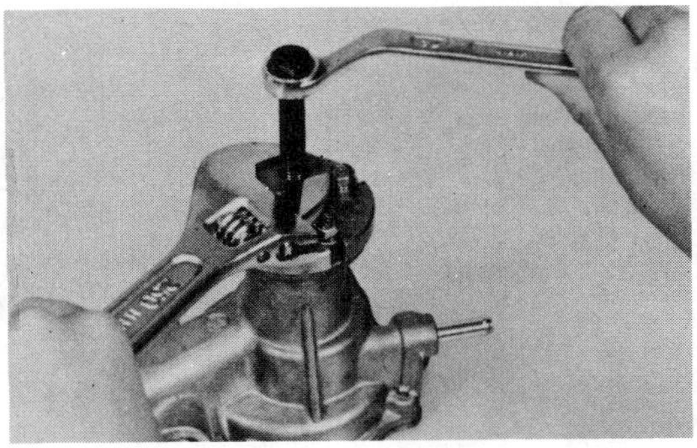

Fig. 2.10 Using a puller to remove the water pump pulley seat – 4K engine (Sec 10)

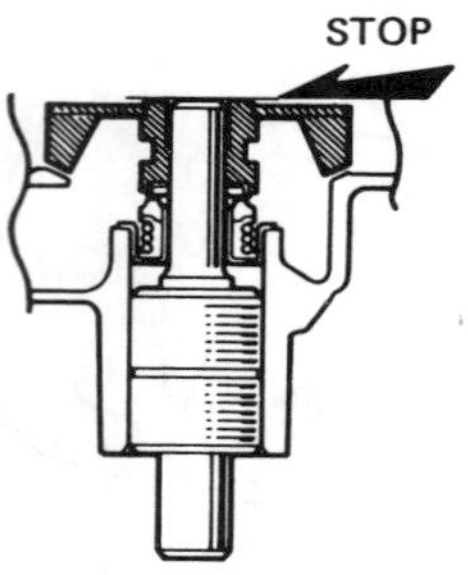

Fig. 2.11 Rotor to shaft position when fitted on the 4K engine water pump (Sec 10)

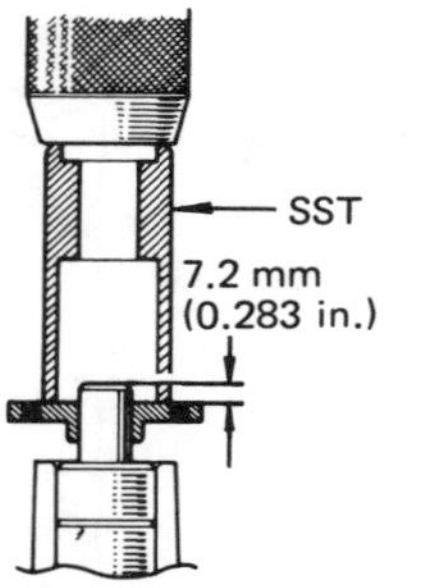

Fig. 2.12 Pulley seat depth to be as shown on the 4K type (Sec 10)

Fig. 2.13 Pulley seat depth to be as shown on 2T, 2T-B and 3T-C type (Sec 10)

A = 0.079 in (2.0 mm)

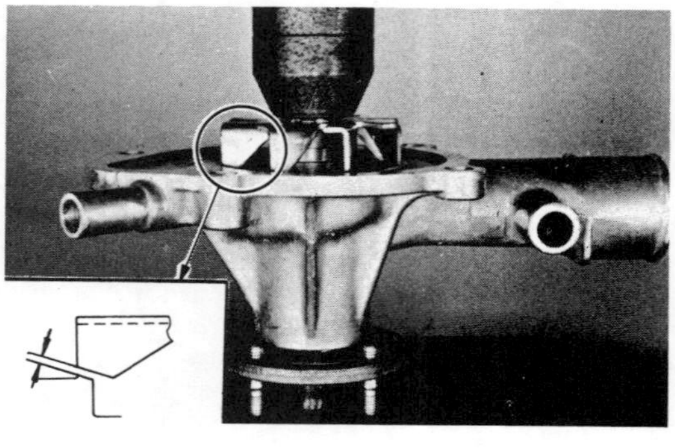

Fig. 2.14 Check rotor to body clearance on 2T, 2T-B and 3T-C type which must be 0.039 in (1.0 mm) (Sec 10)

80°C (176°F) then press or drift out the bearing and rotor assembly from the body.

6 Support the rotor on the underside of its inner flange (not on the blades) and press or drift the shaft from it to enable the seal assembly to be removed.

7 Renew any damaged or defective components.

8 Reassembly is the reversal of the dismantling procedure. Smear the seal surface in the pump body with sealant before inserting the new seal. Reheat the body to 80°C (176°F) before fitting the bearing which, when in position, should have its end face flush with the top surface of the body.

9 Press the pulley seat home so that its clearance from the body is as shown in the illustrations.

10 The rotor to body clearance must be set according to type as shown in the illustrations.

11 On 2T, 2T-B and 3T-C engines the shaft protrusion from the rotor must be set at 0.51 in (13 mm).

12 On completion check that the rotor turns smoothly without binding or tight spots.

13 Where fitted, the viscous fan unit is not repairable and therefore if known to be defective this must be renewed during reassembly.

11 Electric cooling fan

1 This type of fan was introduced in order to improve fuel consumption and to reduce noise (Fig. 2.15).

2 The system incorporates the fan/motor assembly, a relay and a thermostatically operated switch together with the necessary circuitry.

3 The fan thermostat is pre-set to turn the fan on and off at pre-set temperature levels. This prevents over cool running when the ram effect of the cooling air provided by the forward motion of the vehicle is adequate.

4 **Take great care to keep away from the fan blades when working on an engine with the ignition switched on as the fan could cut in at any time due to the rise in coolant temperature level.**

5 If the fan fails to operate, first check the fuse in the main fuse block and then switch on the ignition and listen for a distinct 'click' from the relay which is located under the instrument panel.

6 If these tests prove satisfactory, again turn on the ignition switch (engine cold) and disconnect the lead from the thermo-switch on the radiator header tank. As soon as the lead is disconnected, the fan should turn. It should stop when the lead is reconnected.

7 Now check high temperature operation by letting the engine run until the coolant temperature reaches about 194°F (90°C) when the fan should cut in.

8 If these tests prove satisfactory then there must be a fault in the fan motor itself.

9 Renewal of the thermo-switch will of course necessitate partial draining of the cooling system.

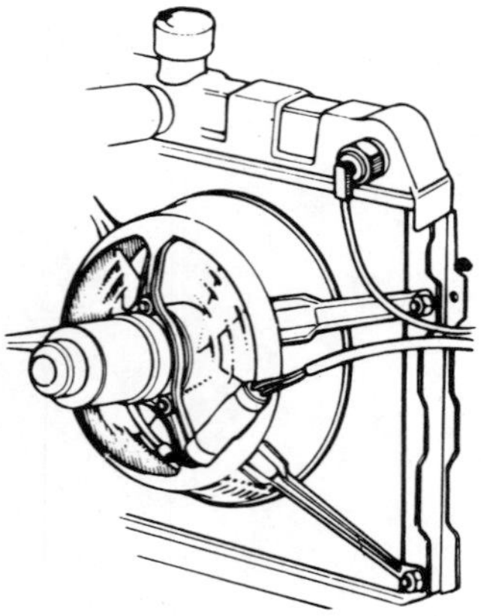

Fig. 2.15 Electrically-operated thermostatically controlled radiator fan fitted to some models (Sec 11)

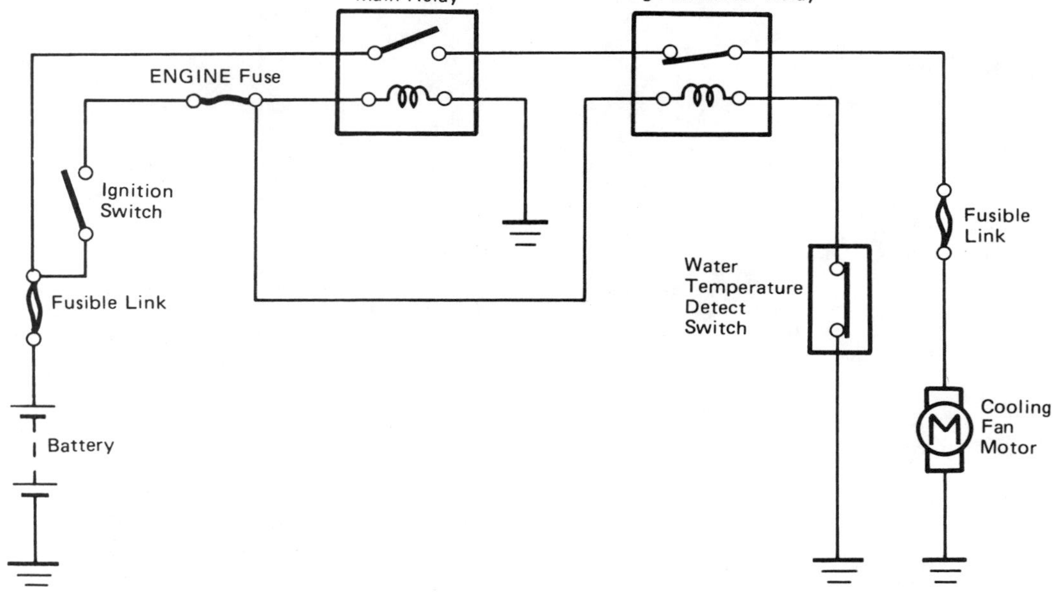

Fig. 2.16 Electrically operated cooling fan circuit fitted to the 4K engine (Sec 11)

12 Fault diagnosis – cooling system

Symptom	Reason(s)
Engine overheats	Insufficient water in cooling system. Fan belt slipping (accompanied by a shrieking noise on rapid engine acceleration). Radiator core blocked or radiator grille restricted. Bottom water hose collapsed, impeding flow. Thermostat not opening properly. Ignition advance and retard incorrectly set (accompanied by loss of power and perhaps, misfiring). Carburettor incorrectly adjusted (mixture too weak). Exhaust system partially blocked. Oil level in sump too low. Blown cylinder head gasket (water/steam being forced down the radiator overflow pipe under pressure). Viscous coupled fan defective. Electronic cooling fan not operating. Faulty electronic cooling fan thermo-switch. Engine not yet run-in. Brakes binding.
Engine being overcooled	Thermostat jammed open. Incorrect grade of thermostat fitted allowing premature opening of valve. Thermostat missing.
Leaks in system	Loose clips on water hoses. Top or bottom water hoses perished and leaking. Radiator core leaking. Thermostat gasket leaking. Pressure cap spring worn or seal ineffective. Blown cylinder head gasket (pressure in system forcing water/steam down overflow pipe). Cylinder wall or head cracked.

Chapter 3
Fuel, exhaust and emission control systems

Contents

Specifications

System type	Rear mounted fuel tank, mechanical fuel pump and single or twin downdraught carburettórs according to model
Fuel octane rating	
4K, 2T and 3T–C engines	90 RON
2T–B engine	98 RON
Carburettor	
4K engine – UK models	
Carburettor type	Single Aisin twin choke downdraught
Idling speed:	
Manual transmission models	750 rpm
Automatic transmission models	850 rpm
CO mixture	0.5 to 1.5%
Accelerator pump stroke	0.191 in (4.85 mm)
Float level:	
Raised position	0.295 in (7.5 mm)
Lowered position	0.023 in (0.6 mm)
Throttle valve angles (from horizontal):	
Primary valve closed	9°
Secondary valve closed	20°
Primary valve open	90°
Secondary valve open	90°
Primary valve fast idle angle (choke valve closed)	26°
Choke breaker clearance (automatic transmission models)	0.087 to 0.091 in (2.22 to 2.32 mm)
2T and 2T–B engines – UK models	
Carburettor type	
2T engine	Single Aisin twin choke downdraught
2T–B engine	Twin Aisin twin choke downdraught
Idling speed:	
2T engine	650 rpm
2T–B engine	800 rpm
Fast idle speed:	
2T engine	2700 rpm
2T–B engine	2500 rpm
CO mixture	1.0 to 2.0%
Fast idle clearance:	
Automatic choke	0.032 in (0.81 mm)
Manual choke	0.040 in (1.01 mm)
Accelerator pump stroke:	
2T engine	0.2 in (5.0 mm)
2T–B engine	0.12 in (3.0 mm)
Float level:	
Raised position	0.16 in (4.0 mm)
Lowered position	0.05 in (1.2 mm)
Throttle valve closed angle:	
Primary	7°
Secondary	20°
Throttle valve open angle:	
Primary	90°
Secondary:	
2T engine	80°
2T–B engine	90°
Secondary touch angle	50 to 57°
Kick-up:	
Secondary throttle valve to body clearance (primary valve fully open)	0.008 in (0.2 mm)
Fast idle angle:	
2T engine	15 to 22°
2T–B engine	8.5 to 15.5°

Unloader angle:	
2T engine only	27 to 47°
Choke valve fully closed angle	20°
Throttle positioner setting angle:	
2T engine	9 to 16°
2T–B engine	5.5 to 12.5°
Choke breaker angle:	
2T engine only	19 to 39°

3T–C engines (USA and Canada models)

Carburettor type	Single Aisin twin choke downdraught
Idling speed:	
Manual transmission without power steering:	
USA models	650 rpm
Canada models	700 rpm (cooling fan off)
Automatic transmission without power steering:	
USA models	750 rpm
Canada models	750 rpm (cooling fan off)
Manual or automatic transmission with power steering:	
USA models	850 rpm
Canada models	850 rpm (cooling fan off)
Fast idle speed:	
Manual transmission without power steering:	
USA models	3400 rpm
Canada models	3000 rpm (cooling fan off and choke opener system off)
Automatic transmission without power steering:	
USA models	3200 rpm
Canada models	3000 rpm (cooling fan off and choke opener system off)
Manual transmission with power steering:	
USA models	3200 rpm (choke opener and choke breaker 2nd stage systems off)
Canada models	2800 rpm
Automatic transmission with power steering:	
USA models	3000 rpm (choke opener and choke breaker 2nd stage systems off)
Canada models	2800 rpm
Float level:	
Raised position	0.36 in (9.2 mm)
Lowered position	0.06 in (1.6 mm)
Throttle valve closed angle:	
Primary	7°
Secondary	20°
Throttle valve open angle:	
Primary	90°
Secondary	80°
Secondary touch angle	57°
Kick-up	0.006 in (0.15 mm)
Fast idle angle:	
USA models	25°
Canada models	24°
Unloader angle	47°
Choke breaker angle:	
USA models:	
1st	38°
2nd	55°
Canada models	40°
Choke valve fully closed angle	20°
Choke opener angle:	
USA models	85°
Canada models	77°
Accelerator pump stroke	0.2 in (5.0 mm)
Throttle positioner setting angle:	
USA models only	16°

1 General description

All models are fitted with a rear mounted fuel tank, a mechanically operated fuel pump and an Aisin downdraught carburettor of twin choke design.

The carburettor model fitted is dependent on the engine and market to which it has been supplied. The 2T-B engine models are fitted with twin Aisin.

The air cleaner type and the complexity of the emission control system depends upon the operating territory for which the vehicle is destined.

The type of cold start device may be a manual choke, or an electrically-heated automatic choke depending upon the date of production and operating territory for which the vehicle is destined.

Numerous emission control system components are used in conjunction with the fuel and exhaust system. The extent of emission control equipment used is dependent on model and operating territory but is dealt with from Section 20 onwards.

2 Air cleaner element – renewal

1 Access to the air cleaner element is obtained in the same way for all types. Unscrew and remove the wing nut and release the toggle clips and remove the lid. Extract the element (photo).

2 If the element is only discoloured in one spot move its position round to present a new surface to the air intake flow.

3 If the element is dirty all round and oil stained or it has been in use for the specified mileage, extract it and discard it.
4 Wipe out the air cleaner casing and fit a new element, making sure that the rubber sealing rings are in good condition and are in position, (photo).
5 Refit the lid, wing nut and toggle clips ensuring that the arrow markings on the filter lid and intake spout are aligned (Fig. 3.2).
6 On some models it will also be necessary to remove and clean the pre-air cleaner dust cup at the same time as the filter is serviced. Unclip the dust cup cover, remove the cup for cleaning, then refit in reverse order, (Fig. 3.3).
7 If the air cleaner is being removed completely from the engine, after unscrewing the securing bolts, do not pull the body away from the engine without having released the flexible pipes which are clipped to its underside (photo).
8 To verify that an automatic temperature control type air cleaner is functioning correctly, hold a mirror at the end of the air intake spout with the engine cold and running, check that the valve plate is closed against cold air. Allow the engine to warm up and again check to see that it is open to cold air.
9 On twin carburettor models the air filter body houses two filter elements and the cover is secured by two wing nuts. In all other respects the element removal and renewal details are the same as that given for the single carburettor types (Fig. 3.4).

2.1 Single carburettor air filter element – cover removal

2.4 Check rubber seal rings in cover are in good condition

2.7 Detach hose(s) from underside of filter body when removing

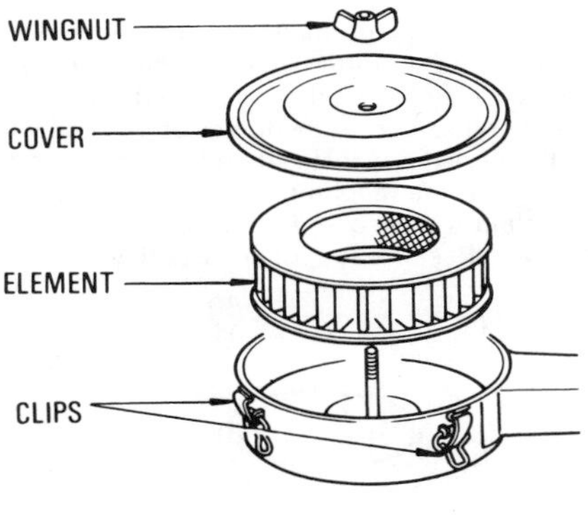

Fig. 3.1 Air filter unit components – single carburettor models (Sec 2)

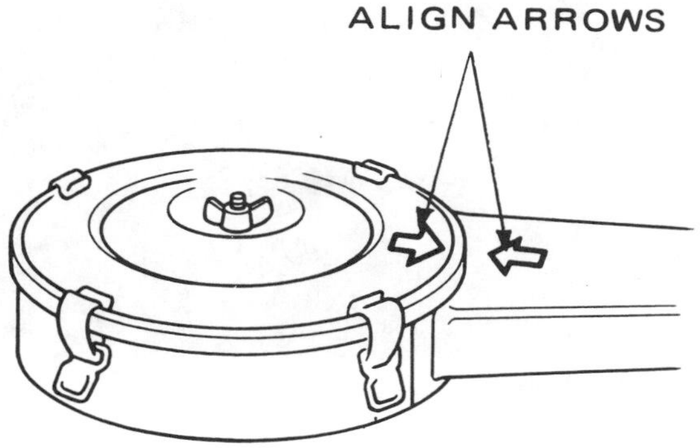

Fig. 3.2 Air filter cover arrow mark must align with arrow mark on spout (Sec 2)

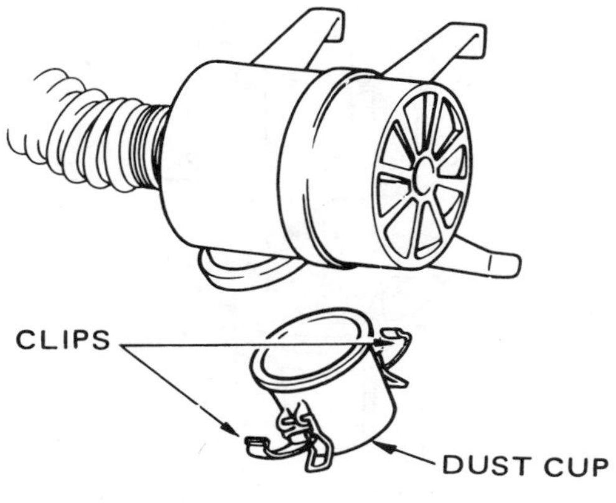

Fig. 3.3 Pre-air cleaner dust cap fitted to some models (Sec 2)

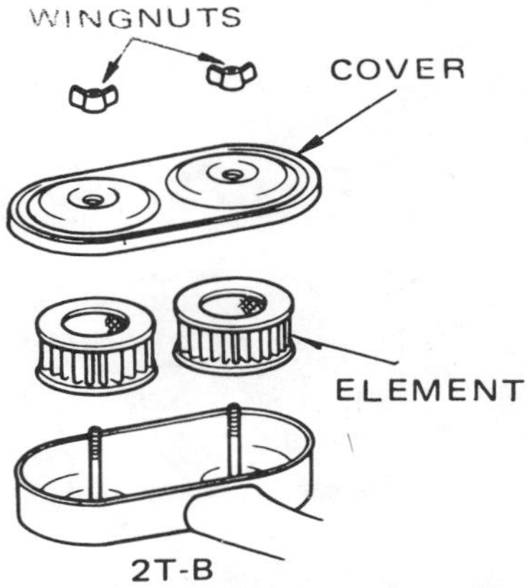

Fig. 3.4 Twin carburettor air cleaner assembly (Sec 2)

3 Fuel filter – renewal

1 A disposable type fuel filter is fitted in the line to the fuel pump (photo).
2 At the specified intervals, disconnect the fuel lines from the filter and discard the filter.
3 Fit the new filter making sure that the directional arrow on the outside of the unit is pointing in the direction of fuel flow to the pump.
4 Check that the hose connections are secure and on changing the filter recheck for any sign of fuel leaks when the engine is restarted.

4 Fuel pump – testing in vehicle

1 Where lack of fuel is evident at the carburettor, (level visible through float chamber sight glass) first check that there is fuel in the tank and that the in-line filter is not choked through not being renewed at the specified mileage.
2 Disconnect the fuel inlet pipe from the carburettor and place its open end in a container.
3 Disconnect the HT lead from the coil to prevent the engine firing and turn the ignition switch to 'start'. Let the starter motor turn the engine over for several revolutions when regular spurts of fuel should be seen being ejected from the open end of the fuel pipe.

3.1 Fuel line fuel filter

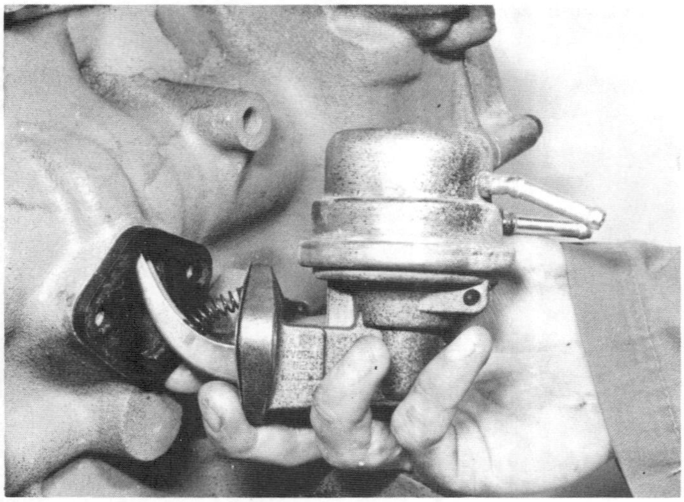

5.2 Removing the fuel pump

4 If no fuel is observed then the pump must be faulty, there is a break in the fuel line or tank union is allowing air instead of fuel to be drawn in.

5 Fuel pump – removal, overhaul and refitting

1 Disconnect the flexible inlet hose and outlet pipe from the fuel pump. Tape over the ends to stop dirt entering.
2 Undo and remove the nuts and spring washers or bolts securing the fuel pump to the engine. Lift away the fuel pump. Recover the gasket, (photo).
3 Before dismantling, clean the exterior of the pump and wipe dry with a clean non-fluffy rag.
4 The pump type fitted is dependent on model, year of manufacture and market, but basically there are two types. The first types shown (Fig. 3.5 & 3.6) can be dismantled for inspection and overhaul but the second type (shown in Fig. 3.7, 3.8 & 3.9) is a sealed unit and therefore if found to be defective must be renewed. To dismantle the first type proceed as follows.
5 Undo and remove the top cover securing screws and spring washers. Before lifting off the top cover and its gasket, make an alignment mark across the cover, the upper body and lower body so that they can be reassembled in their correct original positions.
6 Undo and remove the screws and spring washers securing the two body halves together.
7 Carefully lift off the upper body. It is possible for the diaphragm to stick to the mating flanges. If this is the case free with a sharp knife, (Fig. 3.10 & 3.11).
8 Using a parallel pin punch carefully tap out the rocker arm pin.
9 Lift out the rocker arm and recover the spring.
10 Depress the centre of the diaphragm and detach the rocker arm link. Lift away the rocker arm link.
11 Carefully lift the diaphragm and spring up and away from the lower body.
12 The valves should not normally require renewal but in extreme cases this may be done. Carefully remove the peening and lift out the valves. Note which way round they are fitted.
13 To remove the oil seal from the lower body, note which way round it is fitted and then prise out the seal and retainer using a screwdriver.
14 Carefully examine the diaphragm for signs of splitting, cracking or deterioration. Obtain a new one if suspect.
15 Obtain a new oil seal ready for reassembly.

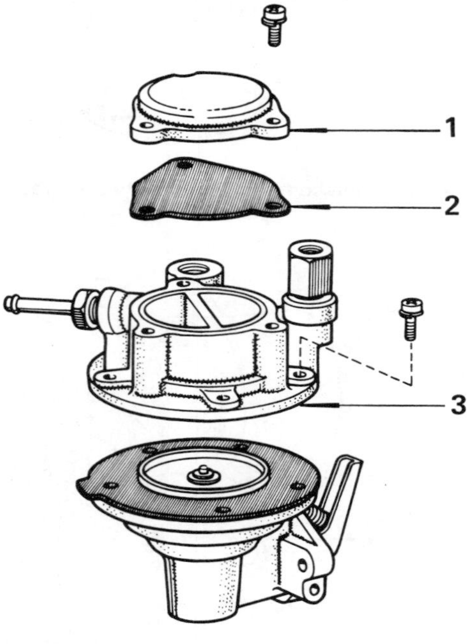

Fig. 3.5 Fuel pump as fitted to 4K engine models – serviceable type (Sec 5)

1 Cover
2 Gasket
3 Upper body

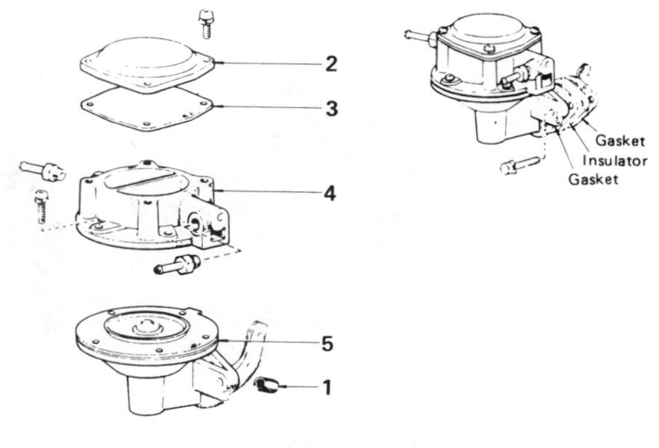

Fig. 3.6 Fuel pump as fitted to 2T and 2T-B engine models – serviceable type (Sec 5)

1 *Return spring*
2 *Cover*
3 *Gasket*
4 *Upper body and check valve*
5 *Lower body, lever and diaphragm*

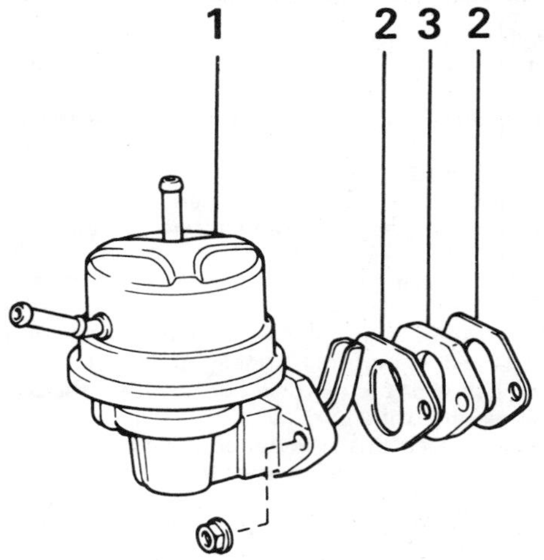

Fig. 3.7 Non-serviceable fuel pump – 4K engine (Sec 5)

1 *Pump unit*
2 *Gaskets*
3 *Spacer insulator*

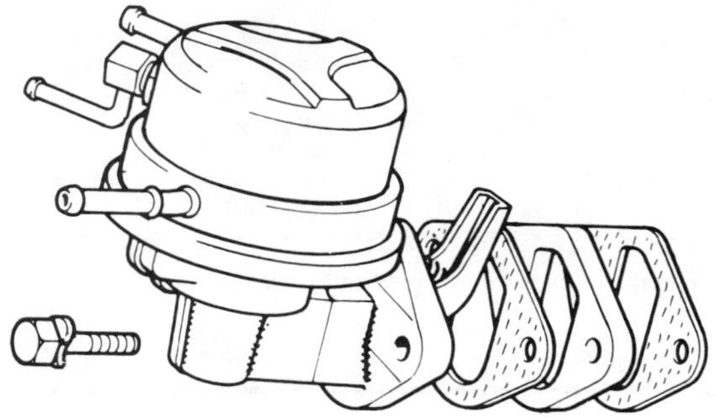

Fig. 3.8 Non-serviceable fuel pump – 3T-C engine – USA models (Sec 5)

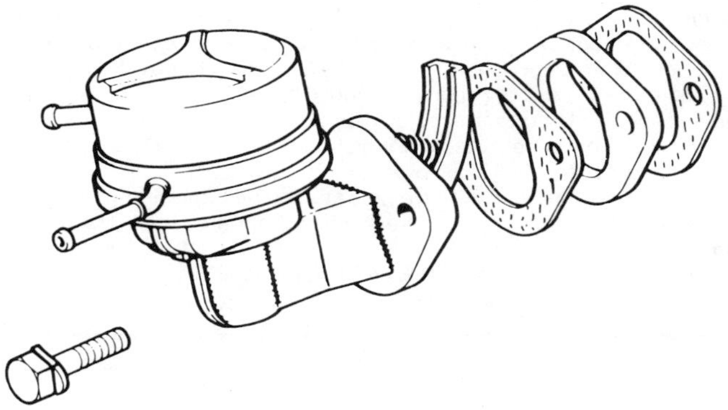

Fig. 3.9 Non-serviceable fuel pump – 3T-C engine – Canada models (Sec 5)

Fig. 3.10 Fuel pump shown with upper body removed – 4K engine (Sec 5)

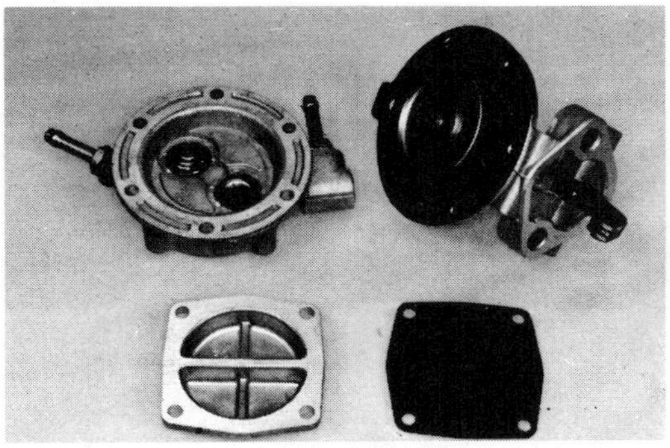

Fig. 3.11 Dismantled fuel pump – 2T and 2T-B engines (Sec 5)

16 Inspect the pump bodies for signs of cracks or stripped threads. Also inspect the rocker arm, link and pin for wear. Obtain new parts as necessary.
17 Clean the recesses for the two valves and refit the valves making sure they are the correct way round. Use a sharp centre punch to peen the edges of the casting.
18 Carefully refit the oil seal and retainer.
19 Refit the diaphragm spring and insert the diaphragm pull rod through the oil seal.
20 Insert and hook the end of the rocker arm link onto the end of the pullrod.
21 Refit the rocker arm into the lower body and locate the spring.
22 Insert the rocker arm pin, lining up the hole with a small screwdriver. Peen over the pin hole edges with a sharp centre punch to retain the pin in position.
23 Fit the upper body to the lower body and line up the previously made marks. Where retaining screws are used these should next be refitted (Fig. 3.12).
24 Refit the cover and gasket to the upper body and secure with the screws and spring washers.
25 The fuel pump is now ready for refitting to the engine. Refitting is a reversal of removal.

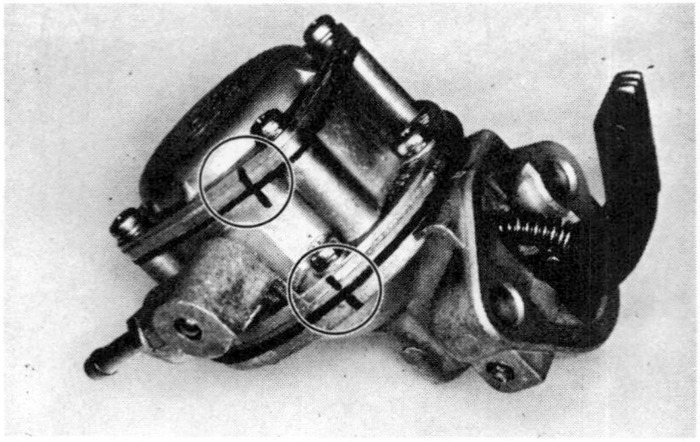

Fig. 3.12 Realign the body marks on reassembly (Sec 5)

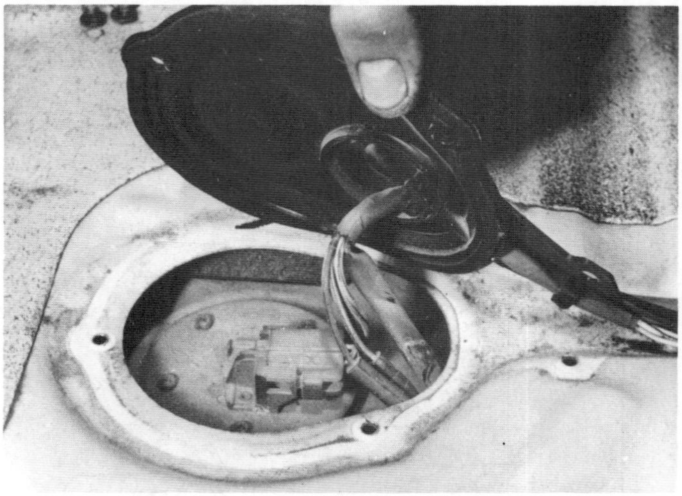

6.7 Remove cover for access to fuel tank sender unit (Liftback shown)

6 Fuel tank – removal, inspection and refitting

1 On all models the fuel tank is rear mounted to the floor panels. Two types of tank are fitted depending on model and these are shown in the accompanying illustrations (Fig. 3.13 & 3.14).
2 If the fuel tank is to be removed for any reason, it is not a difficult job, but the tank should first be drained of fuel into a suitable container. A tank drain plug is fitted. *At all times during tank draining, removal and refitting, exercise extreme caution with regard to fire risk.* Disconnect the battery earth lead before starting removal.
3 To improve access when working underneath the vehicle, raise and support it at the rear end (or use ramps if available).
4 Remove the panel or shield which covers the tank.
5 Disconnect the fuel filler pipe.
6 Disconnect the fuel outlet pipe, return pipe, emission, and where applicable the expansion tank pipes, noting their respective connections.
7 Disconnect the leads to the fuel level sender unit (photo).

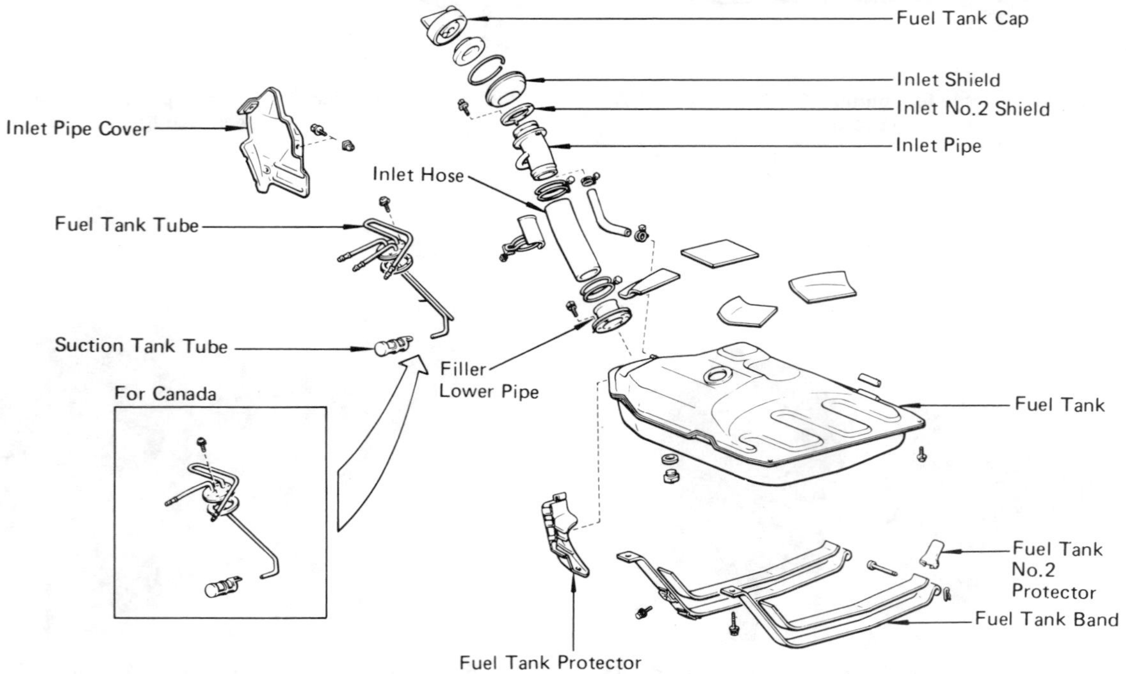

Fig. 3.13 Fuel tank and associated components – Saloon, Liftback and Coupe models (Sec 6)

8 Disconnect all breather or fuel evaporative system hoses according to type.
9 Disconnect the tank mounting straps or withdraw the mounting bolts and withdraw the tank from the vehicle (Fig. 3.15).
10 If a leak is detected in a fuel tank, a temporary repair may be made with fibreglass or similar material but never attempt to weld or solder a leak. Renew the tank complete or take it for professional repair.
11 The fuel contents sender unit can be unscrewed using a suitable pin wrench.
12 Water and sediment often collect at the base of the tank, this can be removed using two or three changes of clean paraffin with a final rinse of fuel. Shake the tank and tip out the flushing solvent but having removed the sender unit.
13 Refitting is a reversal of removal but always use a new sealing gasket for the sender unit.

7 Fuel contents gauge and sender unit – testing

1 Should a fault develop in the fuel gauge reading, first check the security of the electrical leads to the gauge and to the sender unit in the fuel tank.
2 Disconnect the lead which runs from the fuel gauge to the sender unit, from the back of the fuel gauge.
3 From this terminal on the gauge run a lead to a good earth incorporating a 3.4W bulb in the lead. Turn the ignition switch on

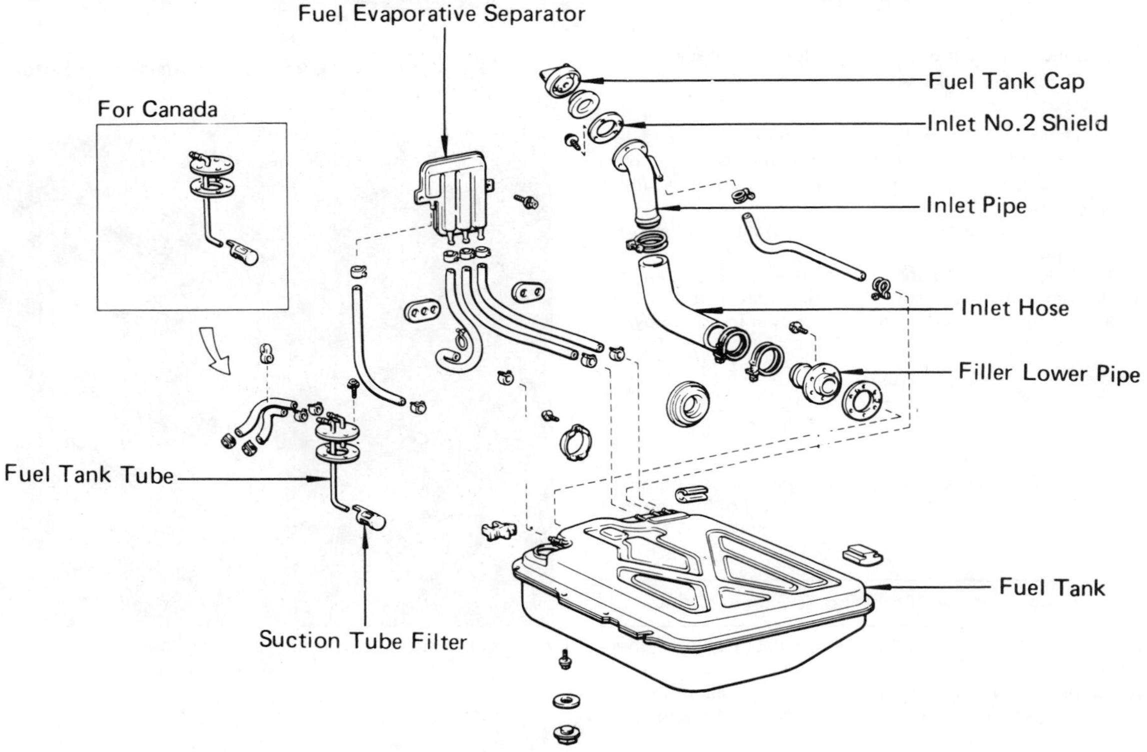

Fig. 3.14 Fuel tank and associated components – Estate (Sec 6)

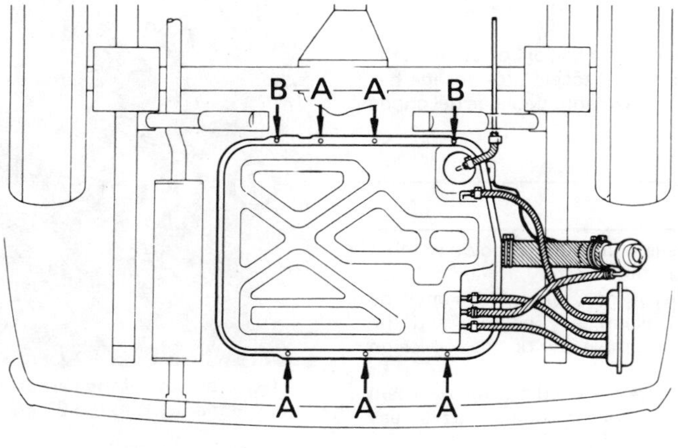

Fig. 3.15 Fuel tank securing bolt positions. Remove bolts B then A (Sec 6)

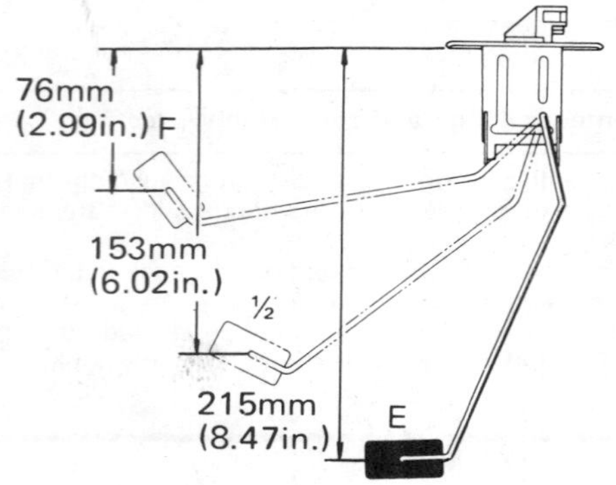

Fig. 3.16 Fuel tank float arm positions (Saloon, Liftback and Coupe) (Sec 7)

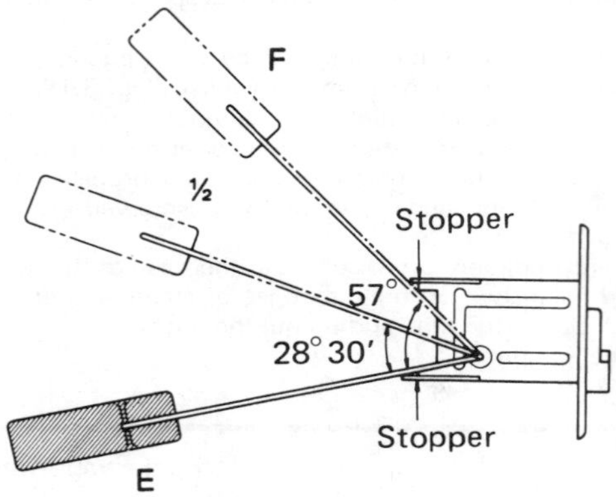

Fig. 3.17 Fuel tank float arm positions (Estate) (Sec 7)

when the test bulb should light and then start to flash after a few seconds. The gauge needle should also deflect. If this test proves satisfactory then the gauge is in good condition and the sender unit is probably at fault.

4 To check the sender unit, remove it from the fuel tank as described in the preceding Section.

5 Using a circuit tester, measure the resistance between the terminal on the sender unit and earth. Move the float arm smoothly and compare the readings obtained with those shown in the following table (Fig 3.16 & 3.17).

Float position	Resistance
FULL	*3 ± 2.1 ohms*
½ FULL	*32.5 ± 4.8 ohms*
EMPTY	*110 ± 7.7 ohms*

6 The fuel level warning light is actuated by a level switch mounted on the sender unit. When just over 1 Imp. gal. (5.0 litre) of fuel remains in the tank the light comes on as a reminder to re-fuel.

8 Accelerator linkage – removal, refitting and adjustment

1 Some models are fitted with an accelerator cable whilst others have a rod and balljoint linkage system.

2 To remove either type, disconnect the ends of the cable or rods from the lever on the carburettor and from the accelerator pedal.

3 Release the cable grommets and support bracket (photo).

4 With the rod systems, unbolt the trunnions which support the iron rods.

5 Refitting is a reversal of removal. Adjust the cable outer conduit or the effective length of the control rods so that when the accelerator pedal is depressed to within 0.5 in (12.7 mm) of the floor, the throttle valve plate in the carburettor is fully open.

6 On vehicles equipped with automatic transmission, disconnect the downshift cable from the carburettor until the accelerator linkage has been set and then connect and adjust the downshift cable as described in Part B of Chapter 6.

9 Carburettors – description

1 The carburettors fitted to all models is of dual barrel down draught type. According to engine type and operating territory, the differences between the units used includes the type of choke, which may be manual or automatic (exhaust gas or electrically heated) and the various modifications dictated by the complexity of the emission control system fitted (photo).

2 On "B" suffix engines twin carburettors are used but the overhaul and adjustment procedures are the same as for single units unless described otherwise.

3 The carburettor design gives correct and efficient performance under all operating conditions so giving a good engine performance whilst maintaining an acceptable fuel economy. It is similar to two single barrel carburettors but built into one body.

4 The primary system incorporates a double type venturi whilst the

8.3 Accelerator cable to carburettor support bracket connection

9.1 General view of the carburettor, manifold and emission control components fitted to the 2T engine model

1 Choke opener
2 Electric choke
3 Choke breaker
4 2nd throttle valve diaphragm
5 Thermostatic vacuum switching valve
6 Vacuum restrictor
7 Throttle positioner
8 Vacuum control valve

secondary system is provided with a triple type venturi. Each system consists of an air horn, main nozzle and throttle valve. One set forms the primary circuit whilst the other set forms the secondary circuit. The primary circuit consists of the low speed, high speed, power valve, accelerating and choke systems and is able to supply the correct air/fuel ratio for normal operation.

5 When the throttle valve is fully open as for fast motoring or acceleration, or a fully laden car, the secondary system also operates to supply an additional air/fuel mixture together with the primary circuit. The throttle valves of both the primary and secondary circuits are operated by a linkage which is interlocked so enabling both the throttle valves to open fully simultaneously. The high speed valve is located in the secondary circuit together with the power valve and enable the performance range to be extremely smooth.

10 Idle speed and mixture adjustment – 4K and 2T engines

Note: *Carburettor adjustments should only be made with the aid of a tachometer and vacuum gauge as detailed in this Section. On some models a plastic cap is fitted on the idle mixture screw; this must be removed for any adjustment, but note that it may be necessary to use the Toyota tool No. 09243-00010 to turn the screw.*

1 Initially check that the fuel level is up to the centre of the window in the float chamber.

2 Ensure that the valve clearances are correctly set, that the air cleaner element is clean and that the ignition system is correctly adjusted (eg, spark plugs, points gap/dwell angle, ignition timing, etc.).

3 Run the engine up to the normal operating temperature, then connect a tachometer and vacuum gauge in accordance with the manufacturer's instructions. The vacuum gauge is connected into the distributor/carburettor vacuum line.

4 Check that all accessories are switched off. On automatic transmission models the selector should be in the N position. If an electric cooling fan is fitted wait until it stops running before making any adjustment.

10.7 2T engine carburettor showing the idle speed (1) and mixture (2) adjustment screws

5 Where fitted disconnect the HIC (hot idle compensation) hose and plug the hose (Fig. 3.18).

6 If an idle limiter cap is fitted on the idle speed screw break it free using a suitable pair of pliers (Fig. 3.19).

7 With the engine running, turn the idle speed screw to obtain the idle speed given for your model (see Specifications at the beginning of this Chapter) (photo).

8 The idle mixture adjustment screw must now be turned to obtain

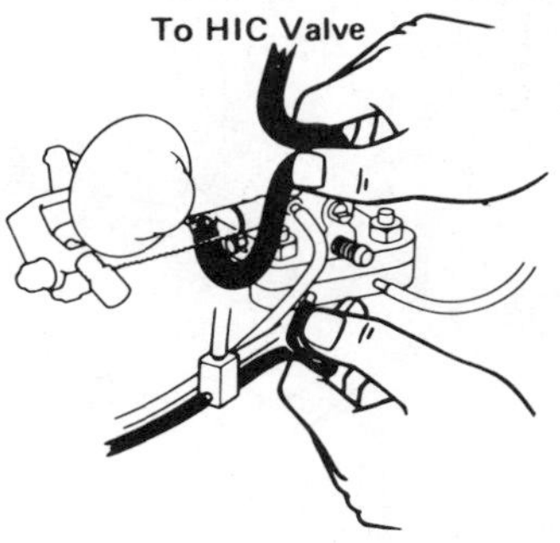

Fig. 3.18 Detach and plug the HIC valve hose (Sec 10)

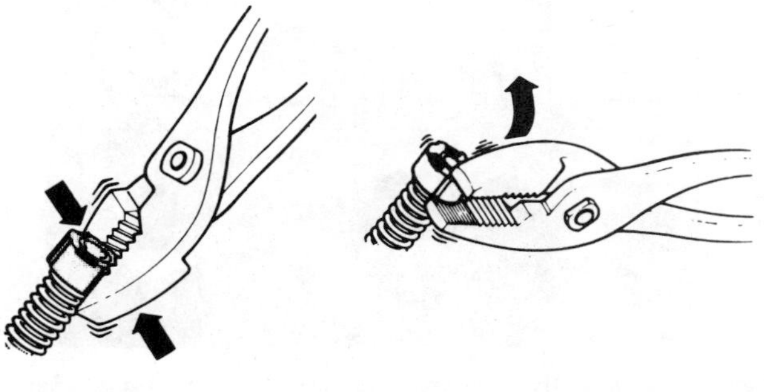
Fig. 3.19 Limiter cap removal method (Sec 10)

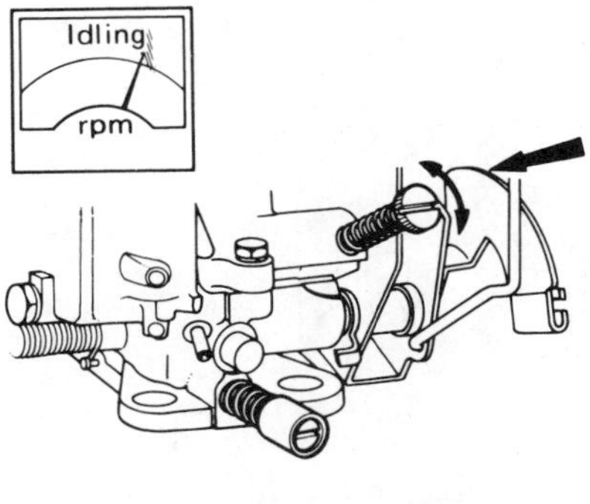

Fig. 3.20 Adjust idle speed screw as necessary – 4K engine (Sec 10)

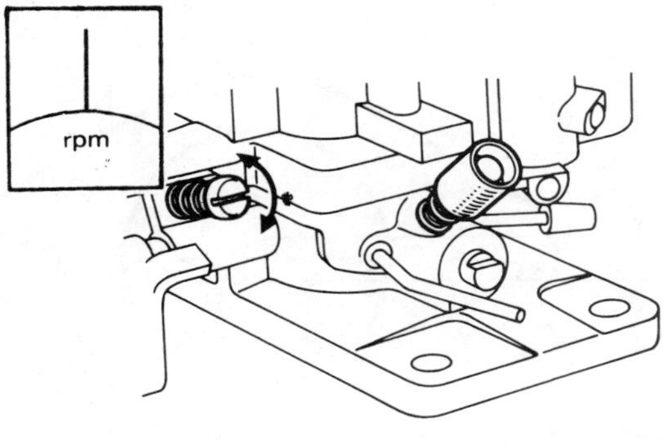

Fig. 3.21 Adjust idle speed screw as necessary – 2T engine (Sec 10)

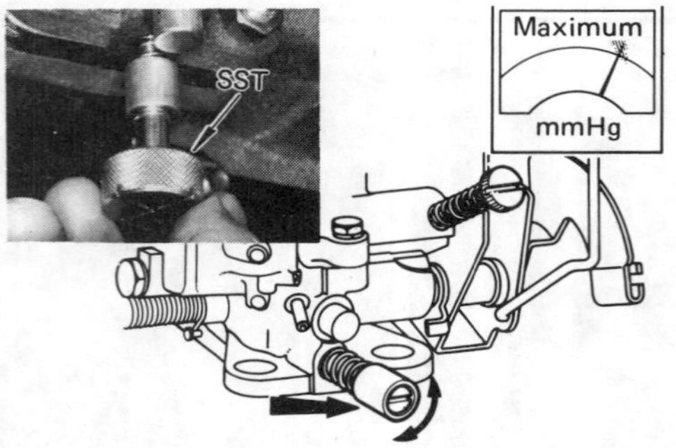

Fig. 3.22 Idle mixture screw adjustment – 4K engine (Sec 10)

Fig. 3.23 Disconnect the linkage rods – 2T-B engine (Sec 11)

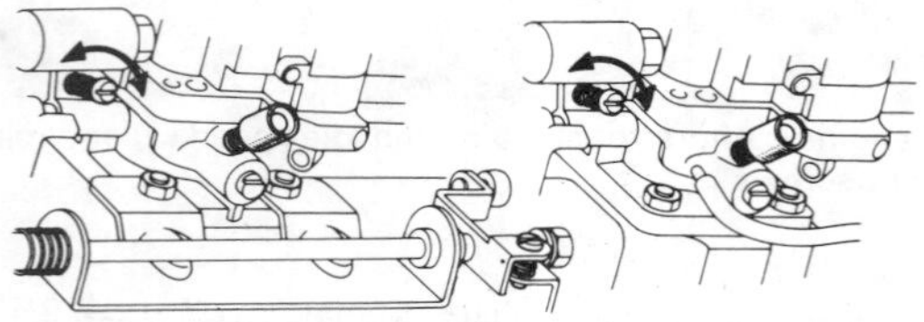
Fig. 3.24 Idle speed adjuster screws – 2 T-B engine (Sec 11)

Fig. 3.25 Idle mixture adjuster screws – 2T-B engine (Sec 11)

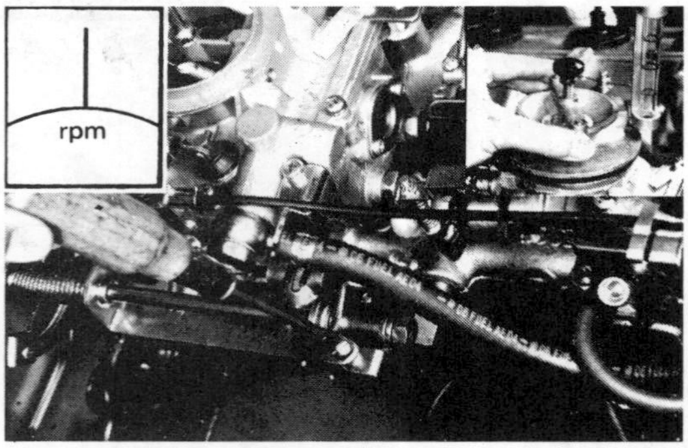

Fig. 3.26 Adjust the synchroniser screw – 2T-B engine (Sec 11)

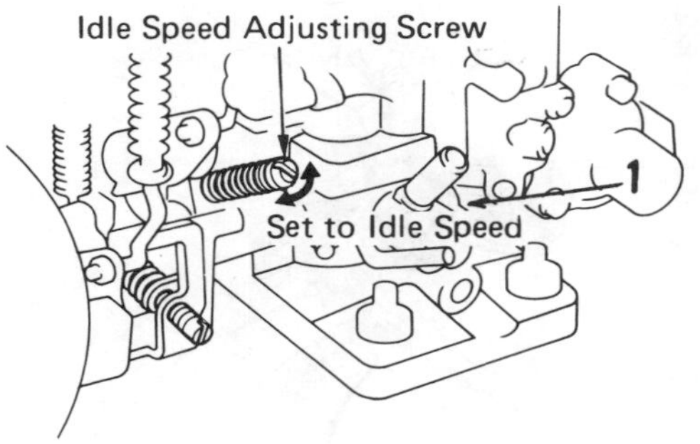

Fig. 3.27 Idle speed and mixture adjuster screws – 3T-C engine (Sec 12)

1 Idle mixture screw position

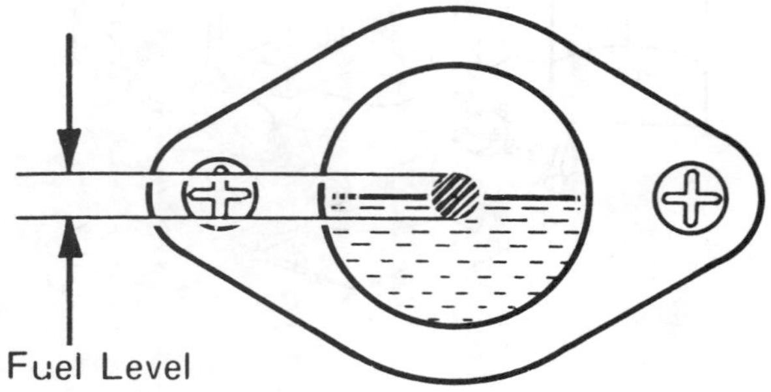

Fig. 3.28 Fuel level to be as shown – 3T-C engine (Sec 12)

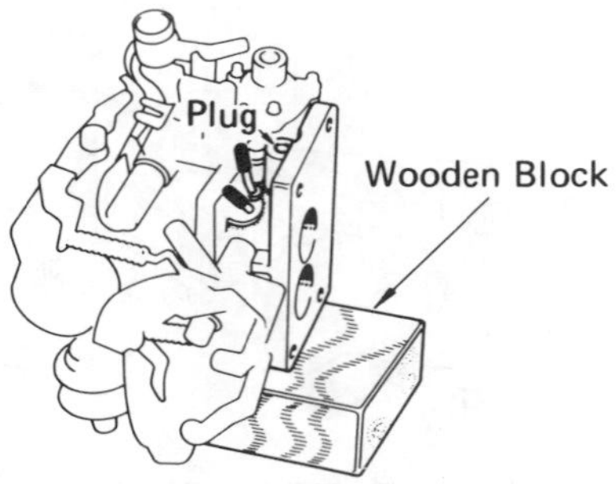

Fig. 3.29 Support carburettor as shown and plug hose connection pipes – 3T-C engine (Sec 12)

the highest possible vacuum reading, then readjust the idle speed setting as necessary to readjust the idle speed to that specified. It should be noted that when making an adjustment to the idle mixture screw and it is tightened to the point where the engine speed suddenly drops by an appreciable amount, the screw must not be tightened any further. When adjusted the idle speed setting should be within 50 rpm of that specified (Fig. 3.22).

9 On achieving the specified engine idle speed, accelerate the engine for a moment and then check that the idle speed is correct when the throttle is released.

10 Reconnect the HIC hose and detach the tachometer and vacuum gauge. Fit a new idle limiter cap to complete.

11 Idle speed and mixture adjustment – 2T-B engine

1 Proceed as given in the previous Section in paragraphs 1 to 4 inclusive, but remove the air cleaner assembly from the carburettors. Note also that in addition to those items mentioned you will also need a dual carburettor balancer device in order to check that an equal volume of air is drawn into each carburettor.

2 Disengage the two carburettors by detaching the linkage rods between the front and rear units (Fig. 3.23).

3 Connect a vacuum gauge to the inlet manifold and a tachometer to the engine (if not already so equipped) in accordance with the manufacturer's instructions.

4 Using a carburettor balancer (flow meter) turn each idle speed screw until the air intake flow is equal, when the balancer is used, on first one carburettor and then the other, checking that at the same time the idling speed is as specified (Fig. 3.24).

5 Now turn each of the idle mixture screws until the maximum vacuum reading is obtainable on the gauge, (Fig. 3.25).

6 If as a result of the last adjustment, the engine idling speed has altered, repeat all of the adjustments again to bring it to specified level.

7 Now turn each idle mixture screw in to the point where any further movement of the screw would cause the speed and vacuum to drop.

8 Reconnect the carburettor link rod ensuring that as it is attached, the idle speed remains as set. Should it change, then the rod length can be adjusted as necessary to return the idle speed to that specified.

9 With the carburettors reconnected, adjust the synchronizer screw to provide an equal volume of air to enter each carburettor at an engine speed of about 1200 rpm. Again use the carburettor balancer for this check and adjustment, (Fig. 3.26).

10 Open the throttle momentarily and allow it to return to normal idle position, then ensure that the idle speed is correct. On completion switch off the ignition, remove the tachometer and vacuum gauge and refit the air cleaner.

11 It is further recommended that a CO emission test be carried out by your Toyota dealer or local garage, where an exhaust gas analizer is available, to ensure that the mixture settings are correct.

12 Idle speed and mixture adjustment – 3T-C engine (USA and Canada)

1 The idle speed and mixture adjustment procedures for the carburettor fitted to the 3T-C engine models are, in general, the same as those described for the 4K and 2T engine in Section 10.

2 Reference to Fig. 3.27 shows the idle and mixture adjustment screw positions for the USA and Canadian carburettor types.

3 When making this adjustment on Canadian models ensure that the fuel level in the float bowl is at the correct level (Fig. 3.28) and also make the adjustment with the cooling fan off.

4 On USA models the idle mixture adjusting screw is fitted with a tamperproof plug, the screw position being set during manufacture and the plug fitted to prevent the setting from being altered. It is not necessary to remove the plug to make an adjustment however, but you will need to drill away its top face as shown, using a 0.2559 in (6.5 mm) diameter drill to make an access hole (Fig. 3.30).

5 It is recommended that the carburettor is removed for this operation and the vacuum ports plugged to prevent the entry of swarf and dirt.

6 Mark the plug with a centre punch, before drilling through, to prevent the drill wandering. When drilling, support the carburettor firmly and note that there is only 0.04 in (1 mm) clearance between the screw head and the plug so do not put any more pressure on the drill than necessary (Fig. 3.29 and 3.30).

7 If you wish to remove the plug completely use a 0.2953 in (7.5 mm) diameter drill to force the plug off (Fig. 3.31).

8 When the plug is drilled through or removed, the carburettor can

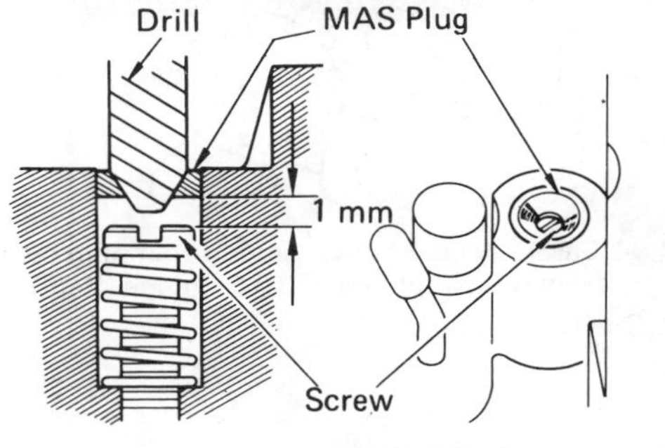

Fig. 3.30 Mixture adjusting screw (MAS) plug removal. Note shallow depth beneath the plug so extra care is needed – 3T-C engine (Sec 12)

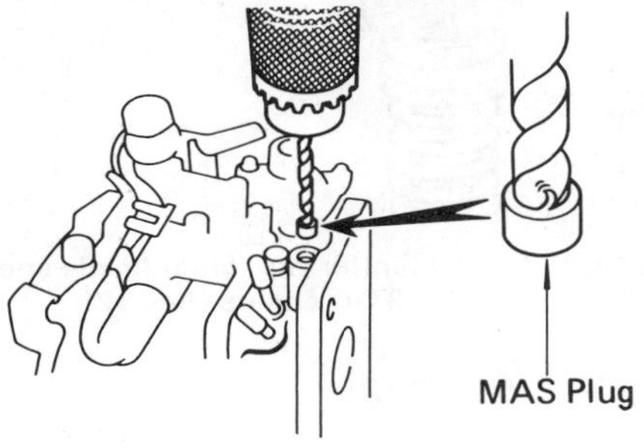

Fig. 3.31 For mixture adjuster screw tamperproof plug removal use a 7.5 mm diameter drill – 3T-C engine (Sec 12)

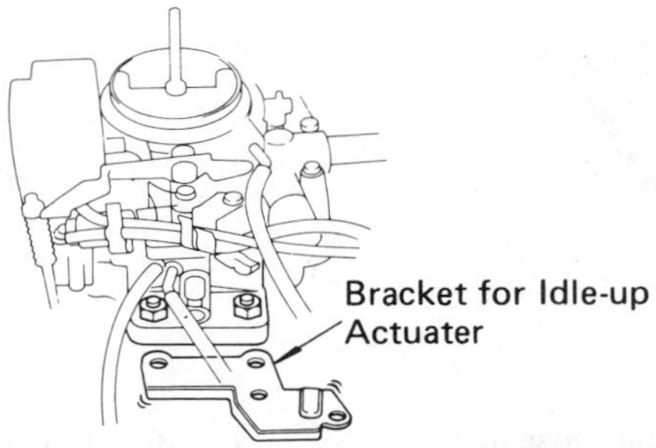

Fig. 3.32 Idle-up actuator bracket fitted to some USA models should be removed during idle speed and mixture adjustment and refitted on completion – 3T-C engine (Sec 12)

be refitted and the various vacuum lines and controls reconnected so that the idle speed and mixture settings can be made.

9 On completion a new tamperproof limiter cap (Blue) should be fitted into position over the idle speed adjusting screw (if previously fitted) and a new tamperproof limiter cap tapped into position over the idle mixture adjusting screw (Fig. 3.33 & 3.34).

13 Fast idle speed adjustment

4K engine

1 On the 4K engine the fast idle speed is determined by the primary throttle valve angle and this operation is carried out with the carburettor removed from the engine. Full details will be found in Section 16.

2T engine

2 With the engine at normal operating temperature remove the air cleaner then disconnect and plug the vacuum hose at the choke opener diaphragm (Fig. 3.35).

3 With the throttle valve slightly open, shut the choke valve switch with your finger and then shut the throttle valve.

4 Start the engine without depressing the accelerator pedal.

5 Hold the throttle valve slightly open, shut the choke valve once more with your finger and hold it shut as you release the throttle valve (Fig. 3.36).

6 Check that the engine is running at the specified fast idle speed and if necessary turn the fast idle adjustment screw until the correct speed is obtained (Fig. 3.37).

7 On completion reconnect the vacuum hose and refit the air cleaner. Check that the engine returns to idle when the accelerator pedal is pressed then released.

2T–B engine

8 With the engine at normal operating temperature, remove the air cleaner and check that both carburettor choke valves open together and at the same time. If not, adjust at the linkage adjusting screw (Fig. 3.38).

9 Pull the choke knob fully out and hold the choke valves open with the blade of a screwdriver (Fig. 3.39).

10 Start the engine and adjust the fast idle speed at the adjusting screw as necessary (Fig. 3.40).

11 On completion remove the screwdriver, push in the choke control and check that the engine returns to idle. Refit the air cleaner.

3T–C engine (USA and Canada)

12 With the engine at normal operating temperature remove the air cleaner then disconnect and plug the HIC system hose (Fig. 3.41).

13 Disconnect the hose between the choke opener diaphragm and the BVSV at the choke opener diaphragm end, and plug the hose (Fig. 3.42). Additionally on USA models disconnect the hose between the choke breaker diaphragm 2nd stage and the restrictor at the choke breaker diaphragm end, and plug the hose (Fig. 3.43).

14 Hold the throttle valve slightly open, shut the choke valve with your finger and hold it shut as you release the throttle (Fig. 3.44).

15 Start the engine without touching the accelerator pedal.

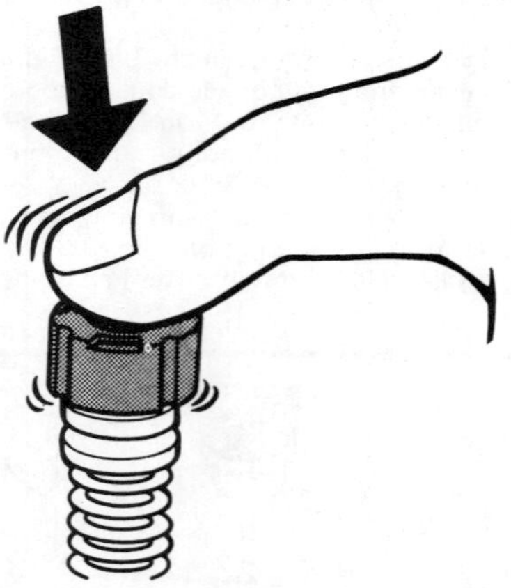

Fig. 3.33 Refit the idle limiter cap (blue) to idle speed screw if fitted – 3T-C engine (Sec 12)

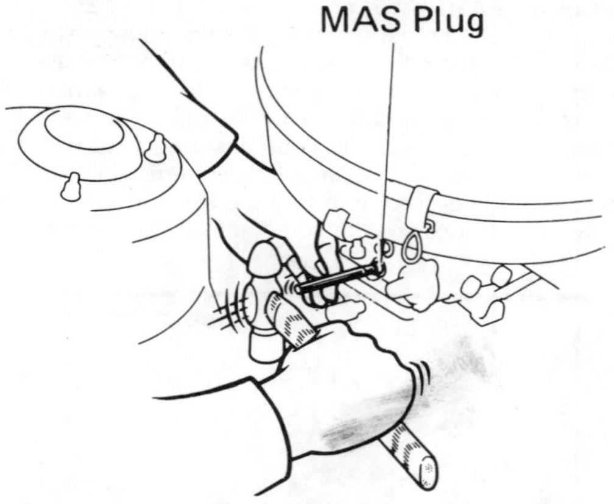

Fig. 3.34 Carefully insert new tamperproof plug over mixture screw on completion – 3T-C engine (Sec 12)

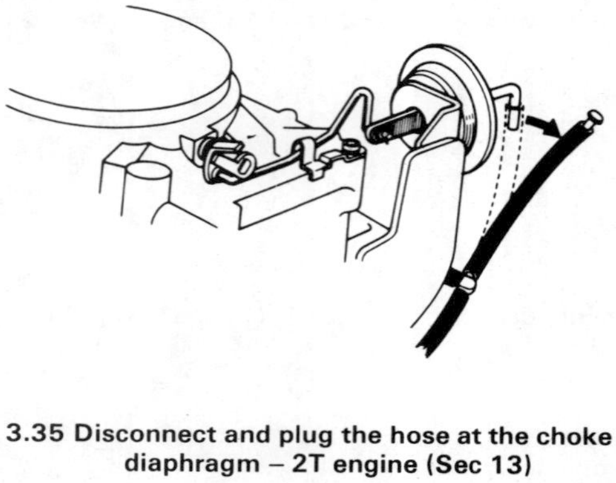

Fig. 3.35 Disconnect and plug the hose at the choke opener diaphragm – 2T engine (Sec 13)

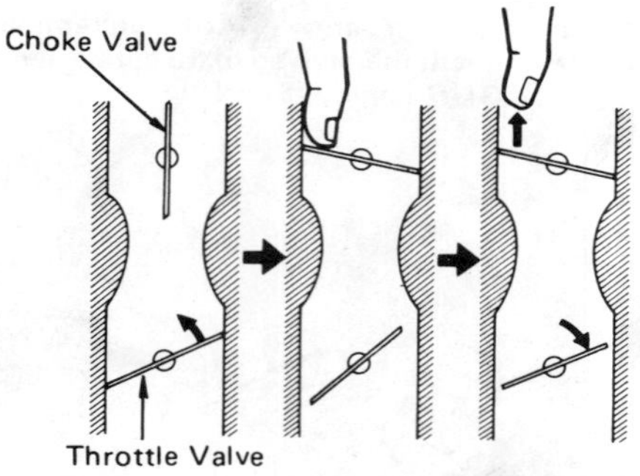

Fig. 3.36 Choke valve shut with throttle valve slightly open – 2T engine (Sec 13)

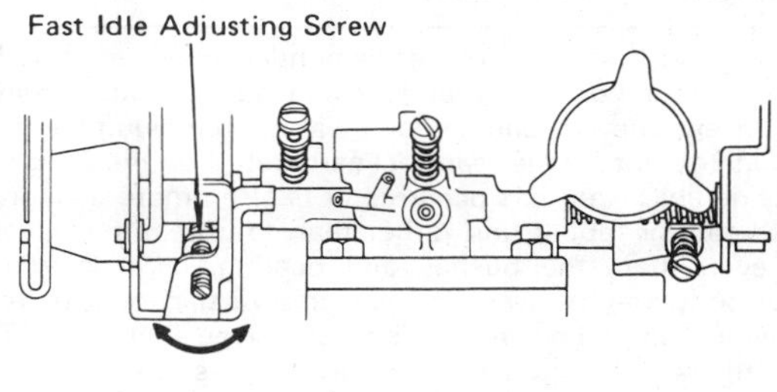

Fig. 3.37 Fast idle adjustment screw – 2T engine (Sec 13)

Fig. 3.38 Front and rear choke valve opening adjustment on the 2T-B engine (Sec 13)

Fig. 3.39 Hold the choke valves open with a screwdriver – 2T-B engine (Sec 13)

Fig. 3.40 Fast idle speed adjustment – 2T-B engine (Sec 13)

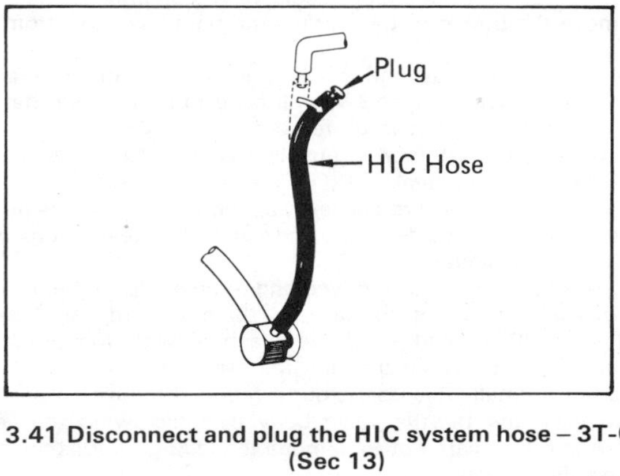

Fig. 3.41 Disconnect and plug the HIC system hose – 3T-C engine (Sec 13)

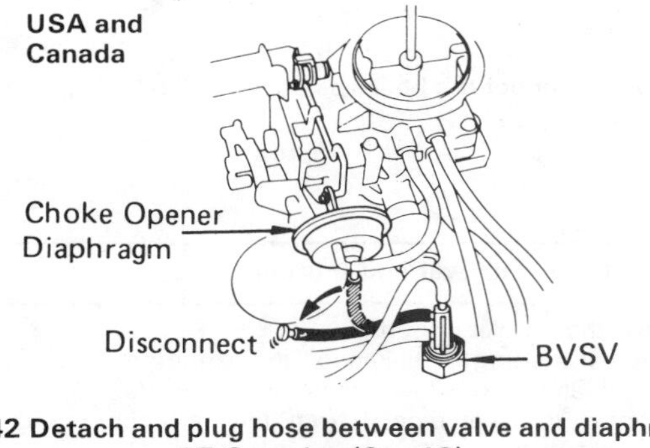

Fig. 3.42 Detach and plug hose between valve and diaphragm – 3T-C engine (Sec 13)

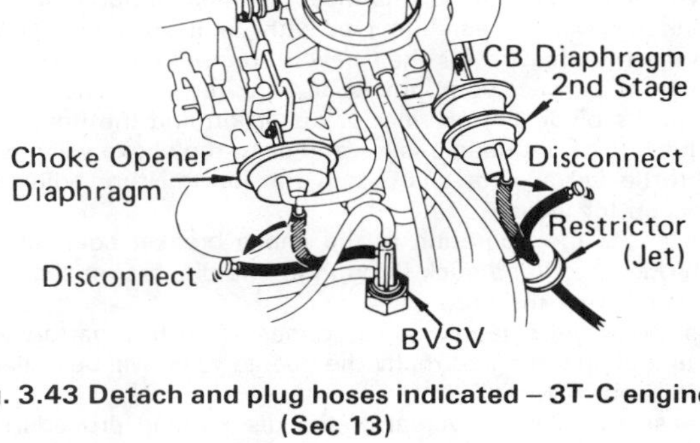

Fig. 3.43 Detach and plug hoses indicated – 3T-C engine (Sec 13)

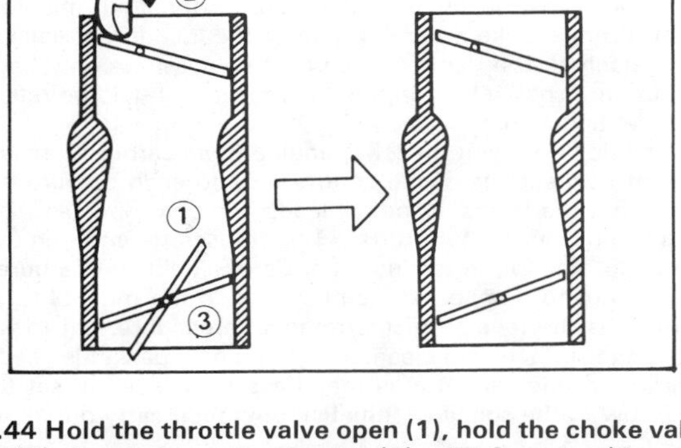

Fig. 3.44 Hold the throttle valve open (1), hold the choke valve closed (2), then release the throttle (3) – 3T-C engine (Sec 13)

16 Turn the fast idle adjusting screw as necessary to obtain the specified fast idle speed (Fig. 3.45). On Canada models make sure that the cooling fan is off when making the adjustments.
17 On completion reconnect the hoses (Fig. 3.46) and refit the air cleaner.

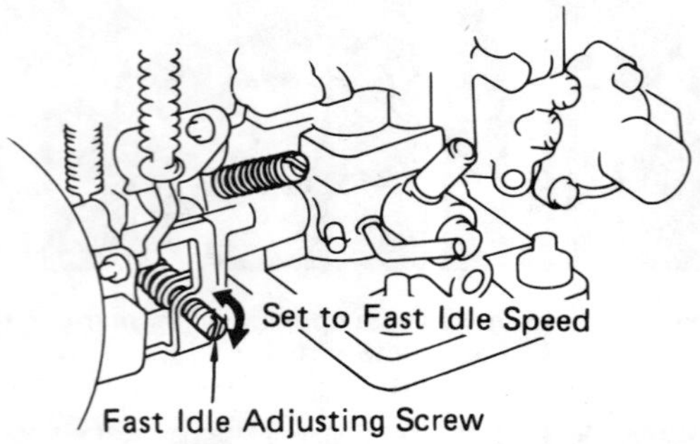

Fig. 3.45 Fast idle adjuster screw – 3T-C engine (Sec 13)

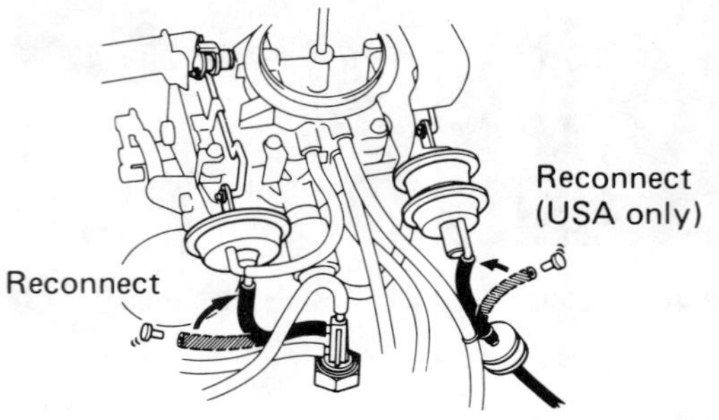

Fig. 3.46 Reconnect the hoses as shown – 3T-C engine (Sec 13)

14 Carburettor – removal and refitting

1 Remove the air cleaner unit.
2 Disconnect the throttle linkage at the carburettor and where fitted the choke cable(s) or kickdown cable as applicable.
3 Disconnect the fuel pipe(s) from the carburettor and plug the hose(s) to prevent leakage.
4 On models fitted with the electrically heated automatic choke disconnect the leads.
5 Disconnect the distributor vacuum hose and the various emission control device hoses between the carburettor and manifolds or associated fittings. Take a careful note of the location of each before they are detached. Diagrams of the various emission control systems and circuitry are shown later in this Chapter and should be referred to for hose identification.
6 On models fitted with the 2T-B engine (twin carburettors), detach the balljoint connections of the control rods to each carburettor.
7 Check that the hoses, electrical leads and control cables/rods are detached from the carburettor(s). Then unscrew and remove the carburettor to manifold retaining nuts. Carefully lift the carburettor(s) clear, trying not to damage the joint gasket to the manifold.
8 Refitting is the reverse of the removal procedure, but make sure that the flange surfaces are clean, and that a new gasket is used. After refitting, where original settings may have been altered, set the idle mixture screw to the specified initial setting, then carry out all the idle adjustments.
9 When reconnecting the choke linkage connections, note that the rod is secured by a screw whilst the rear carburettor choke control rod is retained by a split pin, (use a new one).

15 Carburettor overhaul – general

1 The carburettor should not be dismantled unnecessarily. In fact, removal of the air horn in order to clean out the float chamber is usually sufficient and this can be done without removing the unit from the manifold, (except for the rearmost carburettor on the 2T-B engine).
2 If considerable wear has occurred, it is often more economical to purchase a new or rebuilt unit rather than to obtain individual spare parts as even then, the bushes and bearing surfaces within the carburettor body may be worn out and this wear cannot be rectified.
3 Complete dismantling instructions are given, but only carry out those operations which are needed to give access to a particular worn component or to correct a fault.
4 There are detail differences between the carburettors used on the different engines but these will be apparent from the exploded drawings.
5 If complete dismantling is being carried out, always purchase a repair kit in advance. This will contain all the necessary gaskets and other renewable items required.
6 Remove the carburettor from the inlet manifold as previously described and clean away all external dirt.

16 Carburettor overhaul – 4K engine

1 Refer to Figure 3.47 and then remove the hose and thermostat valve shown from the carburettor.
2 Unscrew and remove the pump arm setscrew, detach the pump connecting link and the fast idle linkage noting how they are assembled.
3 On automatic transmission models detach and remove the choke breaker unit.
4 The air horn (upper body) is now ready for removal from the carburettor main body. Remove the retaining screws and carefully lift the air horn free. Try not to break the air horn to body gasket as it is withdrawn.
5 If the air horn is to be dismantled, push out the float pivot pin, remove the float and fuel inlet needle valve components (Fig. 3.48).
6 Remove the power piston, spring and boot assembly from the air horn.
7 Do not dismantle beyond this unless essential, in which case the peened choke valve plate screws will have to be filed flat before the choke valve and spindle can be removed.
8 Turn the carburettor body upside down and remove the pump discharge weight and steel ball (Fig. 3.49).
9 Use a pair of tweezers and extract the check ball retainer. Then turn the carburettor upside down and catch the steel ball as it drops from the pump cylinder.
10 The jets can now be unscrewed and removed from the main body. Take particular care not to damage them in removal. Note their respective positions and keep the washers with the primary and secondary main jets when they are removed.
11 It is not normally necessary, but if required the main body can be removed from the throttle valve body by unscrewing the securing screws. Again take care not to damage the joint gasket as the two are separated (Fig. 3.50).
12 The idle mixture screw and spring can be removed from the throttle valve body, but further dismantling of this section is not recommended.
13 With the carburettor dismantled, clean all components in fuel and examine for wear. Clean out jets with air from a tyre pump, never probe them with wire for their calibration will be ruined. Renew any defective or suspect components as required. In particular check the float and its pivot pin for wear or distortion and the float for leaks.
14 Check the float needle valve and seat, the choke valve pivot shaft, the throttle valve pivot shafts and the idle mixture adjusting screw tapered tip for wear.
15 To check the operation of the choke breaker connect a hose as shown (Fig. 3.51) and suck through it. The diaphragm should move, if it doesn't renew the unit.
16 To check the solenoid valve connect it up to a battery as shown. If the unit is operating correctly the needle valve will be pulled into the solenoid body (Fig. 3.52).
17 Reassembly is a reversal of the dismantling procedure, but the following special points and adjustments should be made.

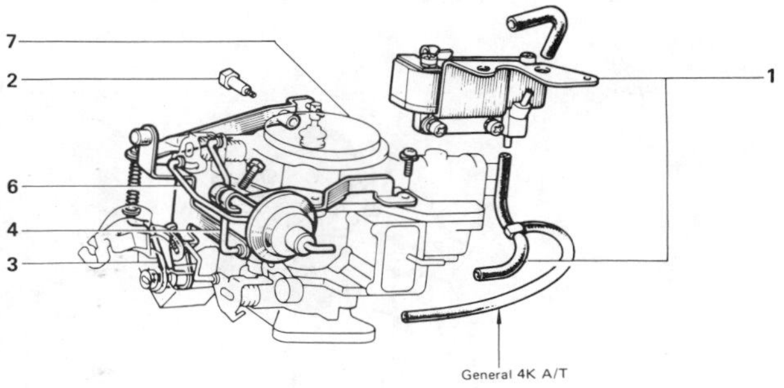

Fig. 3.47 Carburettor as fitted to the 4K engine (Sec 16)

1 Hose and thermostat valve
2 Pump arm setscrew
3 Pump connecting link
4 Fast idle connector rod
6 Choke breaker (automatic transmission)
7 Air horn

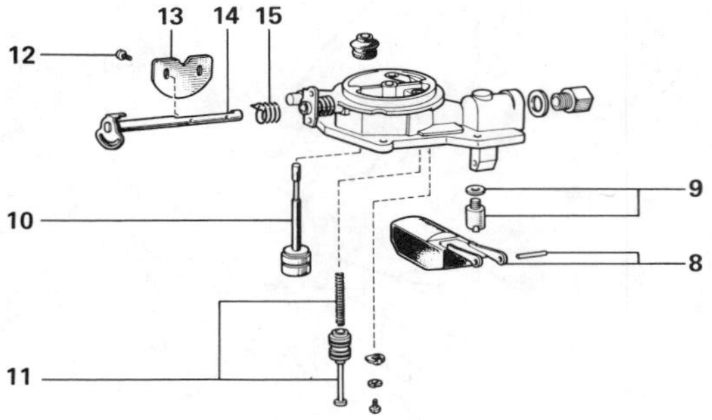

Fig. 3.48 Air horn assembly components – 4K engine (Sec 16)

8 Float and pivot pin
9 Needle valve
10 Pump plunger
11 Power piston and spring
12 Valve setscrew
13 Choke valve
14 Choke valve shaft
15 Relief spring

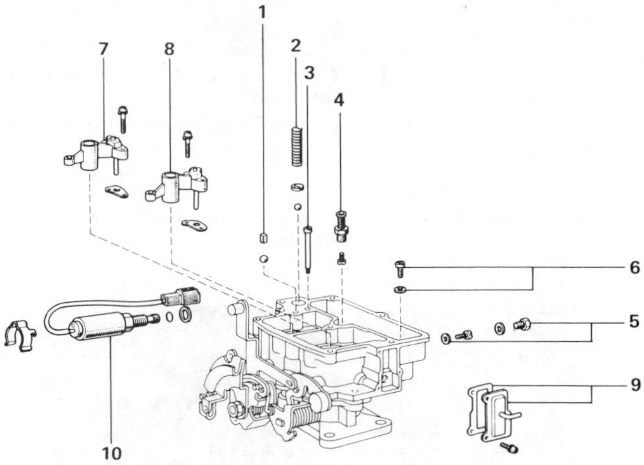

Fig. 3.49 Carburettor body components – 4K engine (Sec 16)

1 Pump discharge weight & steel ball
2 Pump damping spring & steel ball
3 Slow jet
4 Power valve & power jet
5 Primary main jet (brass)
6 Secondary main jet (chrome)
7 Primary small venturi
8 Secondary small venturi
9 Thermostatic valve cover (where fitted)
10 Solenoid valve

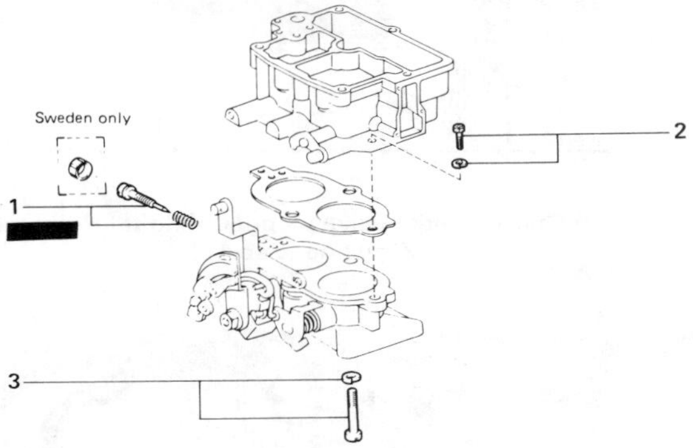

Fig. 3.50 Carburettor main body and throttle valve body separation on the 4K engine (Sec 16)

1 Idle mixture adjusting screw
2 Bolt
3 Vacuum passage bolt

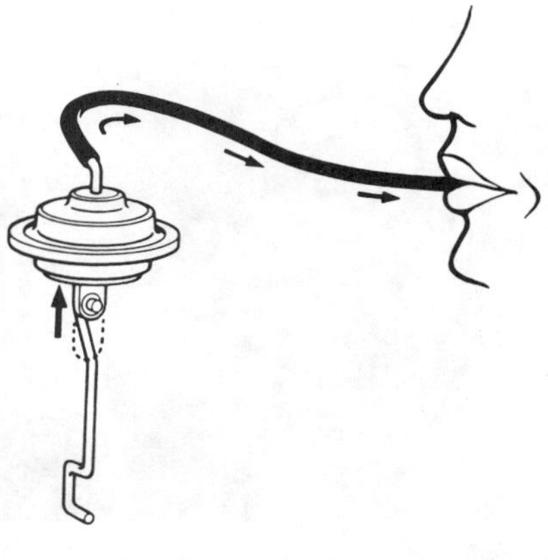

Fig. 3.51 Testing the choke breather – 4K engine (Sec 16)

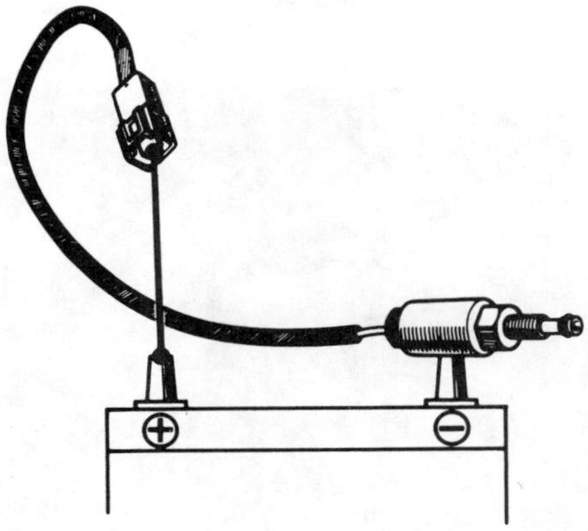

Fig. 3.52 Solenoid valve test – 4K engine (Sec 16)

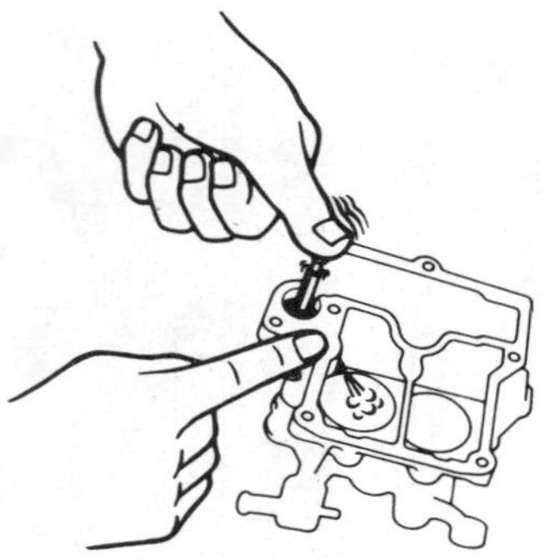

Fig. 3.53 Accelerator pump test method – 4K engine (Sec 16)

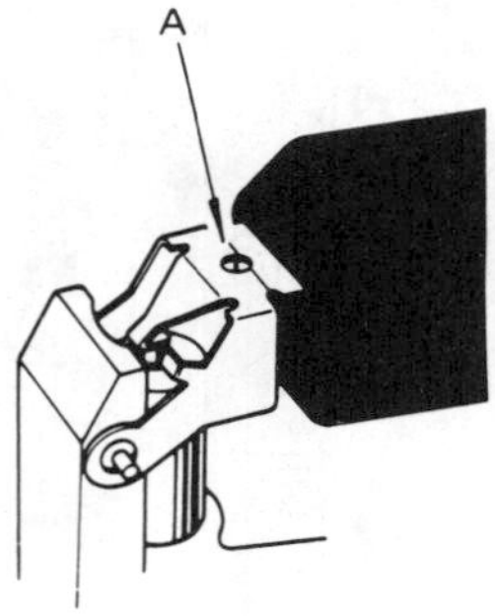

Fig. 3.54 Float adjustment point A – 4K engine (Sec 16)

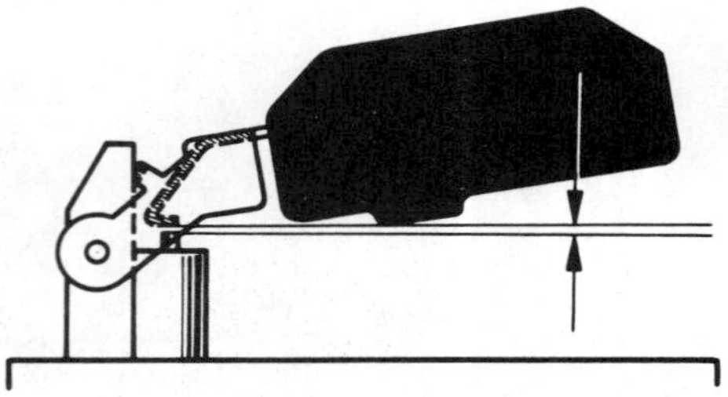

Fig. 3.55 Check needle valve plunger to float lip clearance – 4K engine (Sec 16)

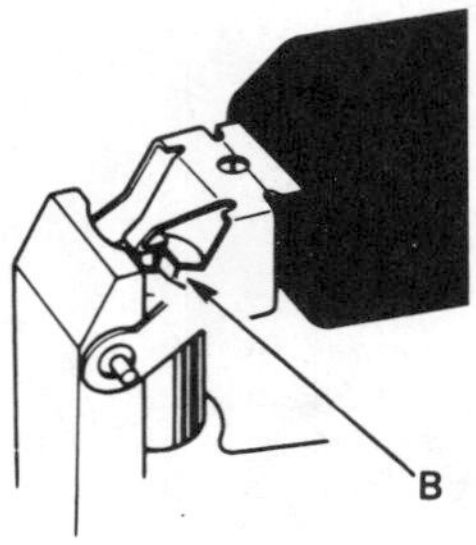

Fig. 3.56 Bend float tab B to adjust clearance – 4K engine (Sec 16)

Fig. 3.57 Check throttle opening angle (primary) – 4K engine (Sec 16)

Fig. 3.58 Adjust primary throttle valve opening angle by bending stopper – 4K engine (Sec 16)

Fig. 3.59 Secondary throttle valve opening angle adjustment. Bend throttle shaft rod (1) – 4K engine (Sec 16)

Fig. 3.60 Fast idle adjustment screw (A). Ensure that clearance remains after adjustment – 4K engine (Sec 16)

18 When inserting the pump inlet ball, outlet ball and weight, the larger ball is fitted into the pump outlet, the small ball to the inlet.
19 Seal off the discharge weight with a finger as shown. Put some petrol into the float chamber and then press the accelerator pump to ensure that fuel spurts from the nozzle.
20 Before refitting the air horn check and if necessary adjust the float level. Allow the float to hang by its own weight and check the clearance between the surface of the air horn and the float. This should be as given in the Specifications. The gasket should not be fitted when making this check. Should adjustment be necessary bend at point indicated (A) in Fig. 3.54.
21 The clearance between the needle valve plunger and the float, when the float is lowered, should also be checked as shown in Figure 3.55. Check this clearance against that given in the Specifications and if necessary adjust by bending the tab (B) (Fig. 3.56).
22 Always use a new gasket between the main body and the air horn and when assembling the two ensure that the pump jet is correctly positioned.
23 With the carburettor reassembled the following initial checks and if necessary adjustments should be made.
24 Fully open the primary throttle valve and check that its opening angle is 90°. If necessary adjust by bending the throttle lever stopper with a suitable pair of pliers (Fig. 3.57 & 3.58).
25 Fully open the secondary throttle valve and check that its opening angle is 90°. If necessary adjust by bending the throttle valve shaft link rod (Fig. 3.59).
26 Check the fast idle setting by fully closing the choke valve and then with the choke valve held closed see if the primary throttle valve is at the specified fast idle angle of 26°. Unless you have a special angle checking service tool you will need to fabricate a tool to assess the angle of the valve. If adjustment is necessary turn the fast idle adjustment screw accordingly, but ensure that when set there is a clearance at the end of the screw (Fig. 3.60).
27 Initial setting of the idle mixture adjustment screw is made by screwing it fully in then unscrewing it $2\frac{1}{2}$ turns. *Do not overtighten the screw when screwing it in.*
28 On automatic transmission models, the choke breaker clearance should also be checked. To do this you will need to apply a vacuum to the choke breaker and simultaneously measure the choke valve to bridge clearance as shown. If this clearance is not as given in the Specifications adjust as necessary by bending the connection link rod as shown in Fig. 3.62.
29 Check the accelerator pump stroke against the specified figure and if necessary bend the cranked link rod (A) to adjust. On completion actuate the pump to ensure that the linkage operates smoothly (Fig. 3.63).
30 When the carburettor is refitted to the engine check and adjust as necessary the idle and mixture settings (Section 10).

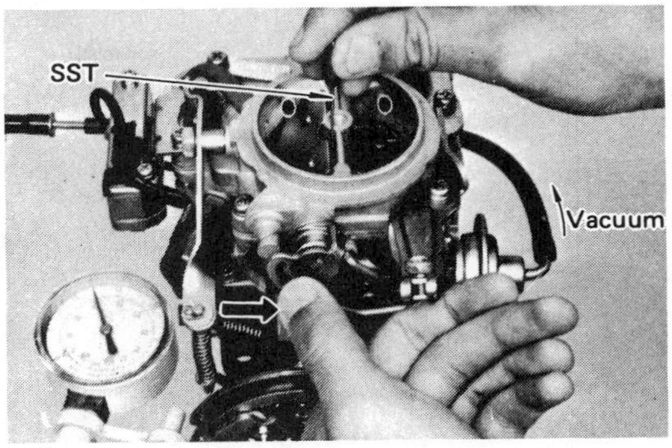

Fig. 3.61 Choke breaker clearance check (4K engine with automatic transmission) (Sec 16)

Fig. 3.62 Choke breaker clearance adjustment. Bend link rod A – 4K engine (Sec 16)

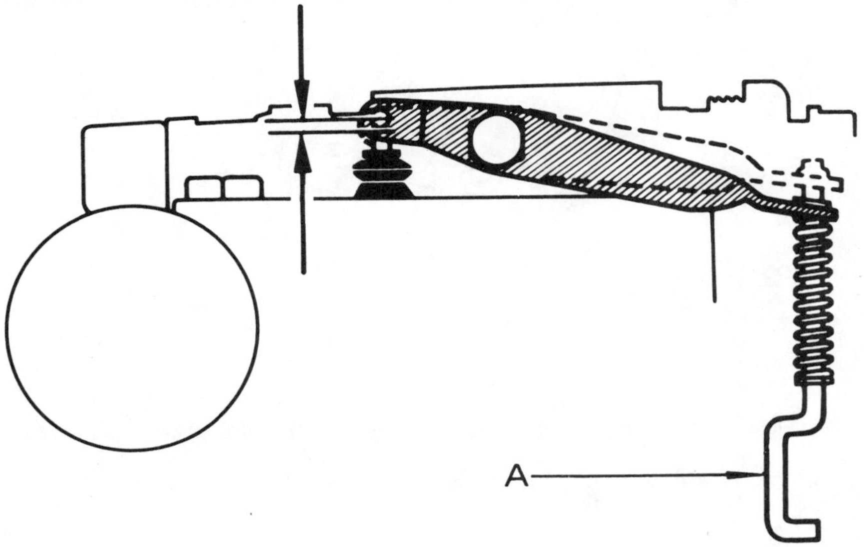

Fig. 3.63 Check accelerator pump stroke and measure at points indicated – 4K engine (Sec 16)

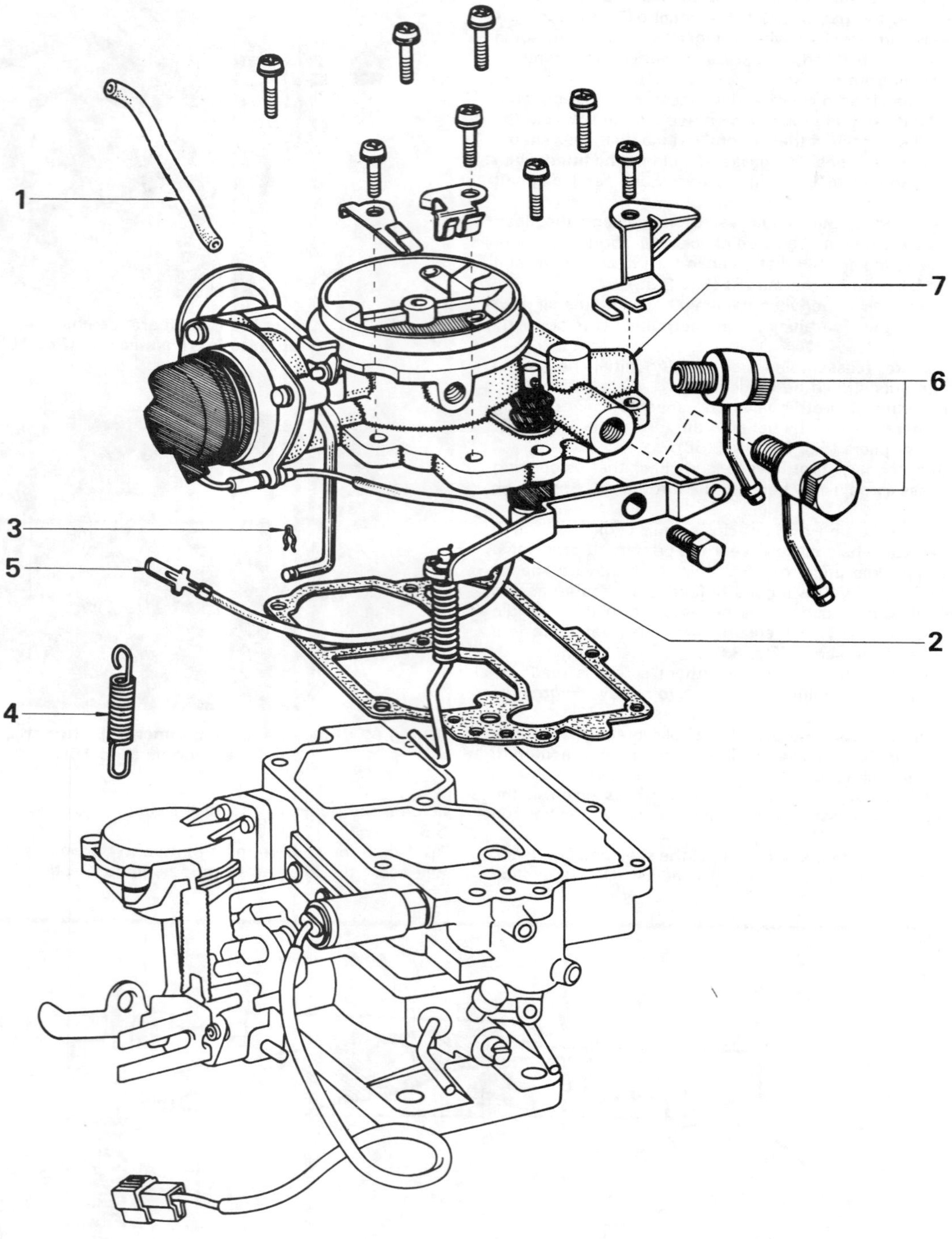

Fig. 3.64 Air horn and associated components – 2T and 2T-B engines (Sec 17)

1 Choke breaker hose
2 Pump lever & connecting link
3 Fast idle cam link
4 Throttle valve return spring
5 Terminal
6 Union
7 Air horn

17 Carburettor overhaul – 2T and 2T-B engines

1 Refer to Figures 3.64 and dismantle the air horn ancillary components in the numerical order shown. Start by detaching the choke breaker hose. It should be noted that the twin carburettors fitted to the 2T-B engine are basically the same as the single carburettor fitted to the 2T engine, except that a manual choke is fitted. Where applicable therefore, ignore references regarding the automatic choke components.

2 Unscrew and remove the pump arm lever pivot bolt, then extract the retaining clip from the connecting link at the bottom end and remove the arm and link.

3 Extract the retaining clip and detach the fast idle cam link.

4 Detach the throttle valve spring.

5 To remove the terminal block of the electric choke unit, insert a thin screwdriver blade as shown to compress the securing lug within the block and withdraw the block from the lead (Fig. 3.65).

6 Remove the fuel pipe unions.

7 Remove the air horn retaining screws noting accessory attachments and lift the horn and gasket from the main body. Try not to damage the gasket.

8 To dismantle the air horn, extract the float pivot pin and remove the float. Now remove the needle valve unit, noting order and orientation of the parts as they are withdrawn (Fig. 3.66). The needle valve seat and filter are screwed into position. As it is removed check the power piston movement by pressing it down and releasing it.

9 To remove the electrical choke unit, unscrew the three retaining

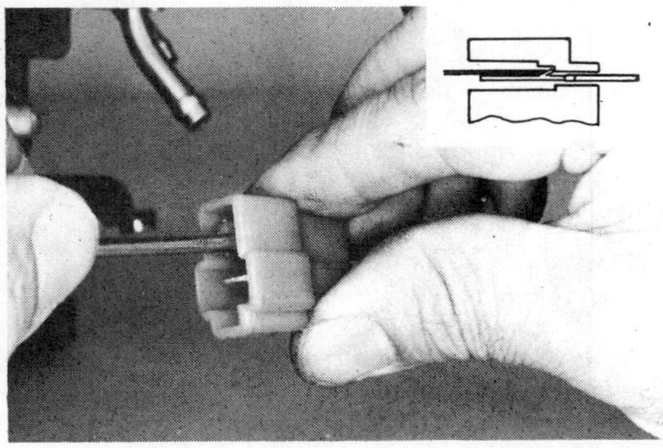

Fig. 3.65 Electric choke lead connector detachment – 2T engine (Sec 17)

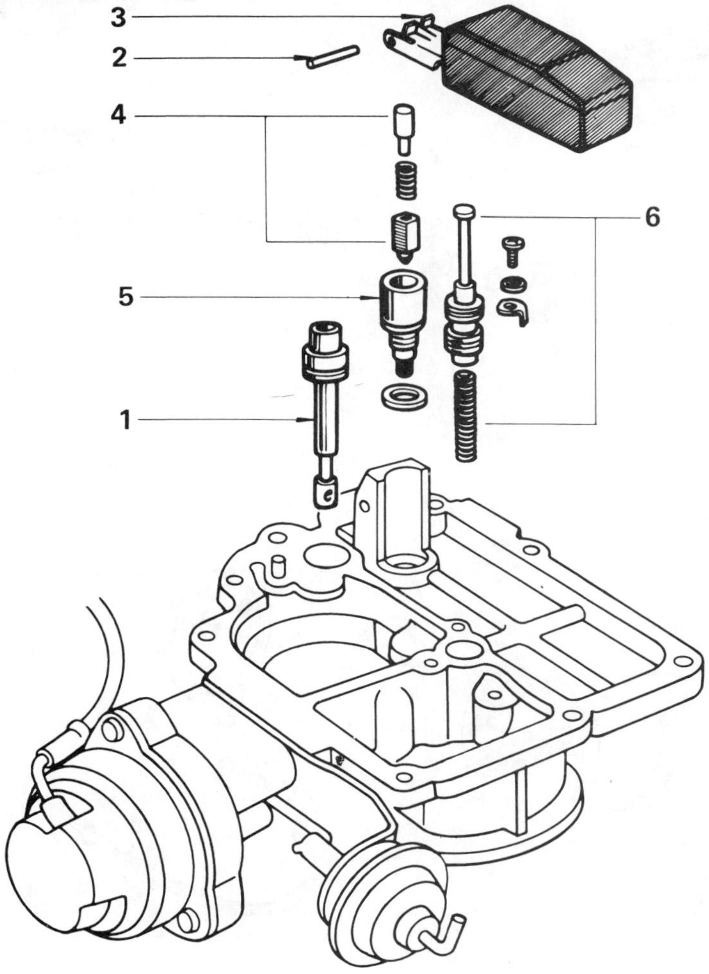

Fig. 3.66 Float and associated components – 2T and 2T-B engines (Sec 17)

1 Pump plunger
2 Pin
3 Float
4 Needle valve pin, spring & valve
5 Needle valve seat & filter
6 Power piston & spring

plate screws then remove the plate, coil unit and O-ring.

10 The choke breaker unit can be removed by disconnecting the link rod, then the unit bracket screws (Fig. 3.67).

11 The carburettor main body can now be dismantled. As the parts are removed it is essential to keep them in order to avoid confusion when reassembling. Figure 3.68 shows the various components and suggested numerical order of dismantling.

12 Disconnect and remove the throttle positioner unit and connecting links.

13 Remove the three retaining screws and carefully withdraw the AAP diaphragm unit (auxiliary acceleration pump).

14 Unscrew and remove the fuel cut solenoid(s).

15 Carefully unscrew and extract the power valve, the slow jet, the AAP inlet and outlet valves, also the pump inlet valve. Take care not to lose the balls as they are removed.

16 Unscrew and remove the 1st and 2nd main jets.

17 Remove the securing screws and lift out the venturis with gaskets.

18 Remove the securing screws and withdraw the second throttle valve diaphragm and recover the gasket.

19 Unscrew and remove the screws securing the HIC valve unit in position and remove the valve assembly.

20 To separate the main body from the throttle valve body remove the securing screws. As the two are separated try not to damage the gasket.

21 Unscrew and remove the idle mixture adjusting screw.

22 Clean and inspect the various components as described in Section 16 paragraphs 13 to 16 inclusive. In addition inspect the choke coil housing for cracks and its thermostatic bimetal coil for signs of deformity (Fig. 3.69).

23 Check the AAP diaphragm and secondary diaphragm for signs of cracks or damage.

24 Do not dismantle the throttle valve plates or spindles from the flange unless absolutely essential as the valve plate securing screws are peened and they must be filed off to extract them.

25 Renew any worn or suspect components and obtain a repair kit which will contain all of the necessary gaskets.

26 Reassembly is a reversal of the dismantling procedure. As the carburettor is reassembled ensure that the following special points and adjustments are observed.

27 When assembling the main body to the throttle valve body fit the vacuum passage screws as shown in Figure 3.70. Fit them both finger tight then screw them firmly (but don't overtighten) to secure.

28 When fitting the main jets, the 1st jet is brass, the 2nd is chrome. Both are fitted with washers.

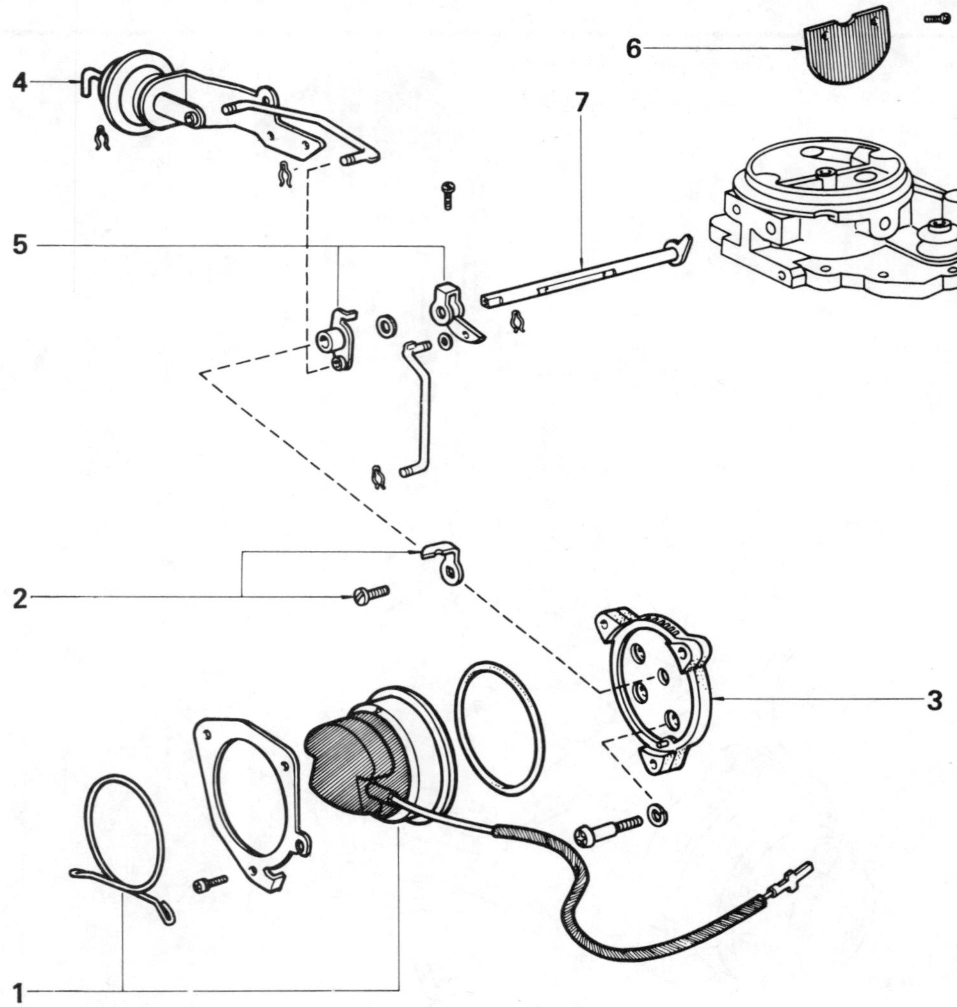

Fig. 3.67 Automatic choke components – 2T engine (Sec 17)

1 Coil housing	*5 Relief lever*
2 Choke lever	*6 Choke valve*
3 Thermostat case & gasket	*7 Choke valve shaft*
4 Choke breaker	

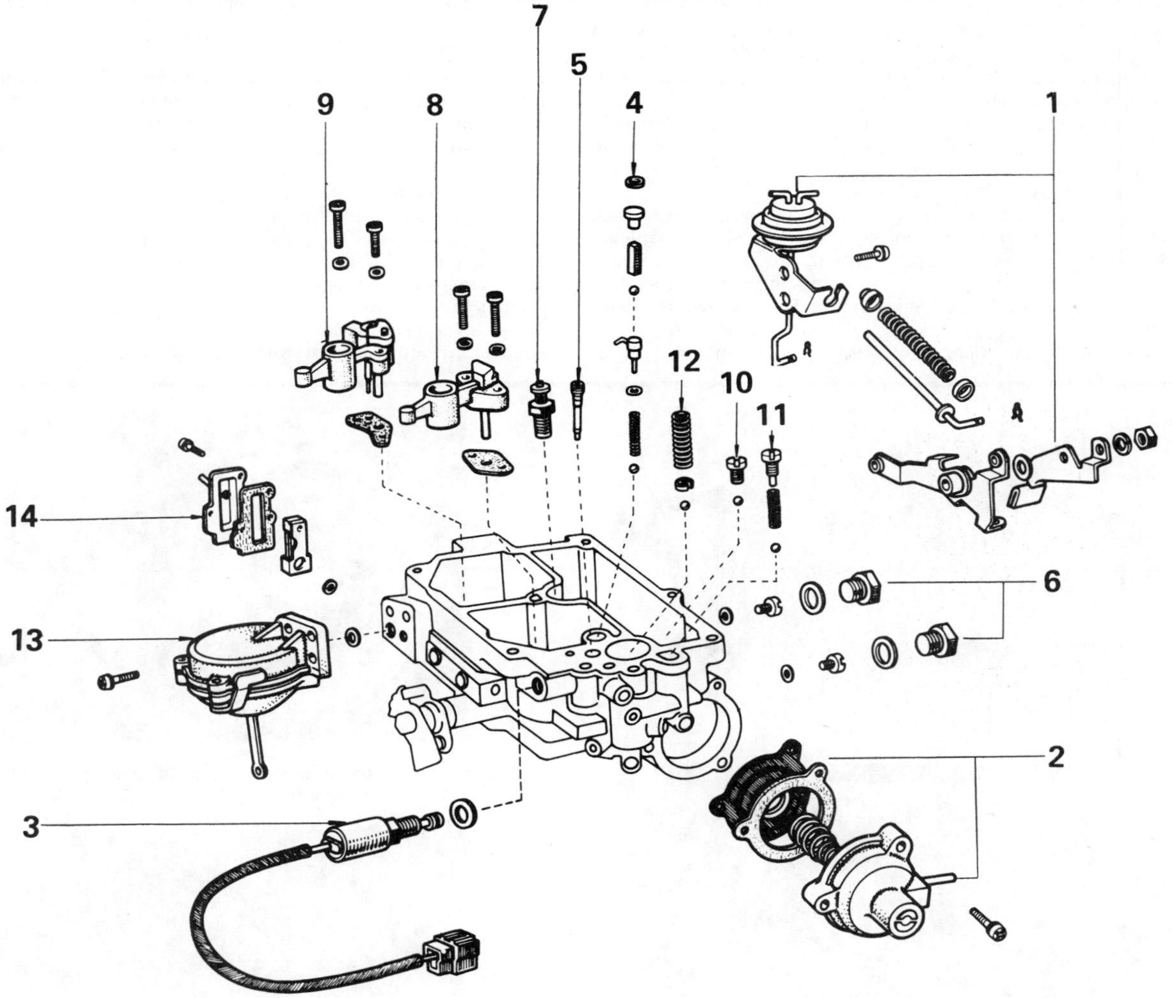

Fig. 3.68 The carburettor main body components – 2T and 2T-B engines (Sec 17)

1 *Throttle positioner*
2 *AAP diaphragm*
3 *Fuel cut solenoid valve*
4 *Pump discharge weight & outlet valve*
5 *Slow jet*
6 *First & second main jet*
7 *Power valve*
8 *First small venturi*
9 *Second small venturi*
10 *AAP inlet valve*
11 *AAP outlet valve*
12 *Pump inlet valve*
13 *Second throttle valve diaphragm*
14 *HIC valve*

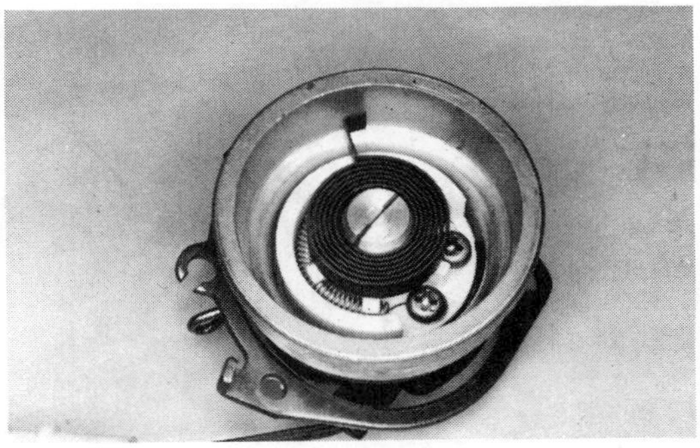

Fig. 3.69 Check the coil housing and bi-metal coil – 2T engine (Sec 17)

Fig. 3.70 Vacuum passage screw locations – 2T and 2T-B engines (Sec 17)

29 The locations for the jets, air bleed, valve and plugs are shown in Figure 3.71.
30 Do not forget to locate the small gasket washer into position when fitting the diaphragm housing.
31 When assembling the electronic choke coil unit, locate the choke lever onto the bimetal spring (Fig. 3.72). When in position align the case marking with the central adjuster scale line. Then check the choke valve action by depressing it with a finger.
32 When the float and needle valve assembly is reassembled check that the power piston movement is smooth, then check the float level adjustment (without the air horn gasket fitted). Check the float upper setting level as shown in Figure 3.73 and compare with the specified setting. Adjust if necessary by bending the float lip as shown in Figure 3.74.
33 Check the float lower adjustment position between the float lip and needle valve plunger (Fig. 3.75). Adjust if required by bending the float lip (Fig. 3.76).
34 Before refitting the air horn to the main body check that the pump plunger movement is smooth by pressing it with a finger.
35 When tightening down the air horn to main body retaining screws, tighten them progressively and in a diagonal sequence. The clamps should be in position under the screw heads as shown (Fig. 3.77). Tighten air horn screws in diagonal order shown (Fig. 3.78).
36 Check that with the primary throttle valve held full open, its opening angle is 90°. Bend the throttle lever stopper to adjust if necessary (Fig. 3.79).
37 Check the secondary throttle valve opening by holding open the primary throttle valve and then fully opening the secondary throttle valve lever. The secondary throttle valve opening should be as specified. Bend the throttle lever stopper to adjust if necessary.

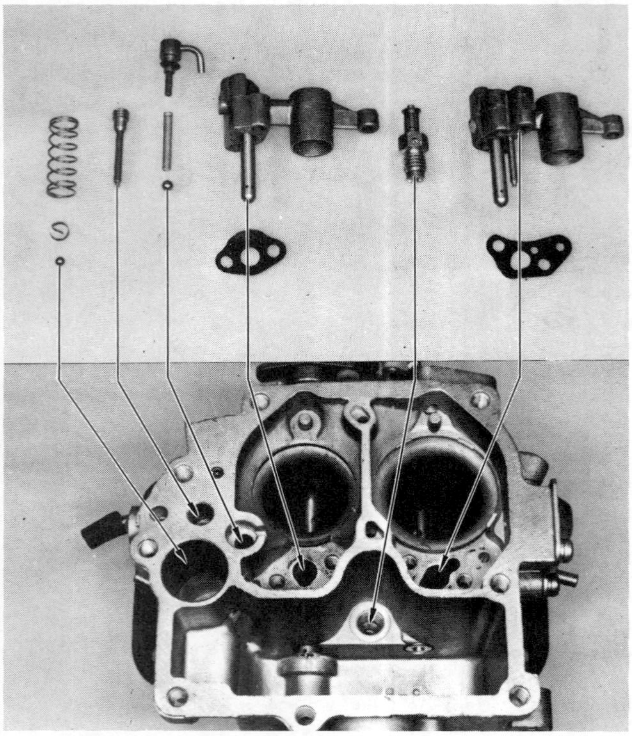

Fig. 3.71 Locations for the jets, air bleed, valve and plugs in the carburettor main body – 2T and 2T-B engines (Sec 17)

Fig. 3.72 Engage lever with bi-metal spring when refitting the choke unit – 2T engine (Sec 17)

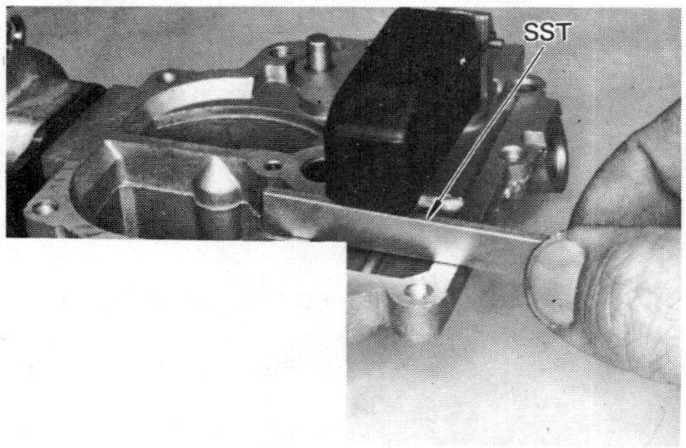

Fig. 3.73 Float level setting check, air horn inverted. A special Toyota service tool is being used in this instance – 2T and 2T-B engines (Sec 17)

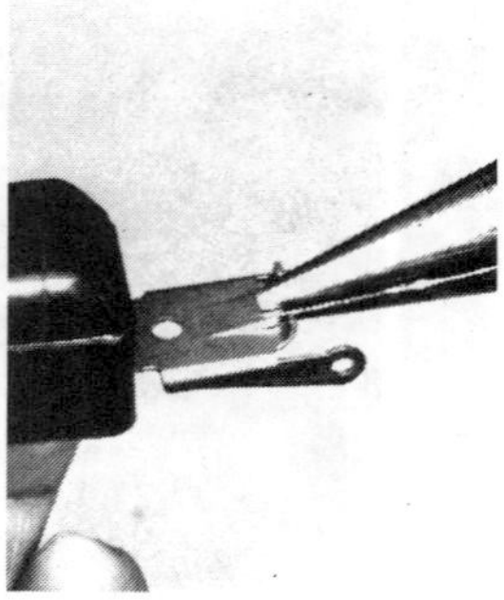

Fig. 3.74 Bend float lip as necessary to adjust level setting – 2T and 2T-B engines (Sec 17)

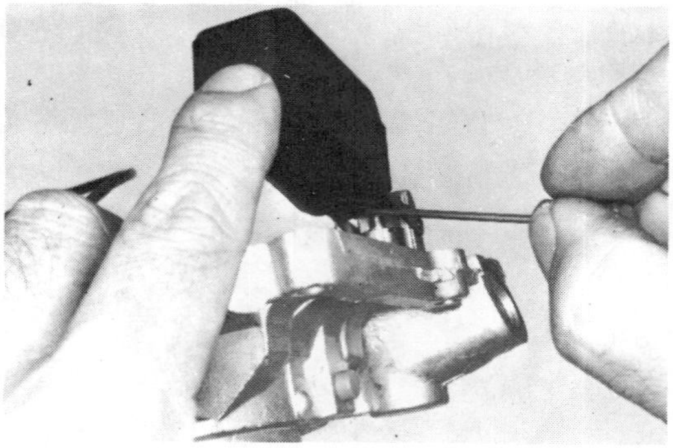

Fig. 3.75 Float lower adjustment piston check – 2T and 2T-B engines (Sec 17)

38 Check the secondary touch angle by opening the primary throttle valve so that its lever (A) just touches part (B), see Figure 3.81. Now check the primary throttle valve opening which should be as specified. If required, adjust the tag (A) as shown to adjust this angle (Fig. 3.82).
39 Check the kick-up by opening the primary valve so that the kick up arm just opens the secondary throttle valve, then check the secondary throttle valve to body clearance. Compare this with the specified kick-up clearance and if necessary adjust by bending tag (A). (Fig. 3.83).
40 Check the fast idle setting on automatic choke models by loosening and then rotating the choke housing anti-clockwise. Open the primary throttle valve a fraction then shut it. Check that the throttle lever mechanism and fast idle cam are engaged (Fig. 3.84). Then measure the primary throttle valve to bore clearance. Compare this with the fast idle clearance given in the Specifications and if necessary adjust by resetting the fast idle adjuster screw setting.
41 Check the fast idle setting on manual choke models by shutting off the choke valve (pivot operating lever anti-clockwise) and then measuring the clearance between the primary throttle valve and the bore. Compare this with the fast idle setting given in the Specifications and if necessary adjust by turning the fast idle adjusting screw accordingly.
42 On automatic choke valve models check the unloader. Close off the choke valve by rotating the coil (anti-choke) housing anti-clockwise, then fully opening the primary throttle valve measure the choke valve opening angle which should be as specified. Bend tag (A) shown in Figure 3.85 to adjust.
43 To check the choke breaker on auto-choke models, close off the choke valve as described in the previous paragraph. Connect a hose up to the diaphragm unit and suck through the hose with your mouth whilst simultaneously checking the choke valve to bore clearance. If

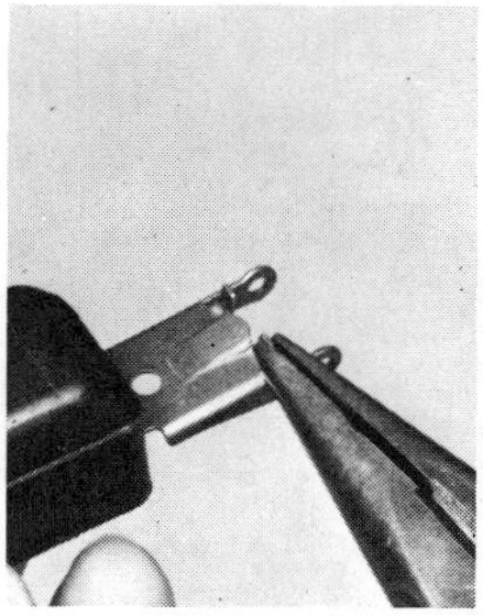

Fig. 3.76 Bend float lip as shown to adjust level setting – 2T and 2T-B engines (Sec 17)

Fig. 3.77 Locate the clamps (encircled) under screw heads when reassembling – 2T and 2T-B engines (Sec 17)

Fig. 3.78 Tighten screws in sequence shown – 2T and 2T-B engines (Sec 17)

Fig. 3.79 Bend throttle lever stopper to adjust throttle valve opening angle – 2T and 2T-B engines (Sec 17)

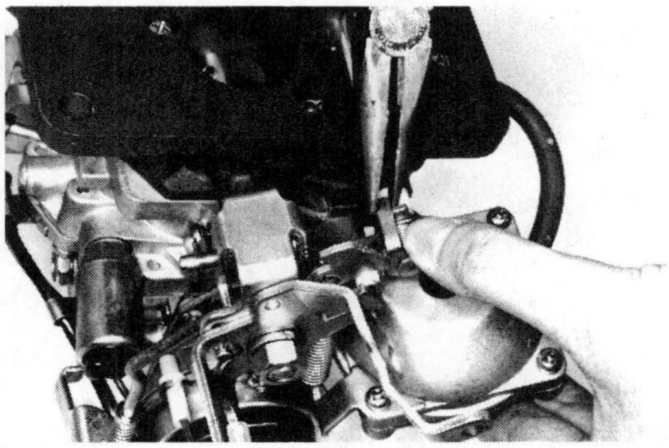

Fig. 3.80 Secondary throttle valve opening adjustment – 2T and 2T-B engines (Sec 17)

Fig. 3.81 Secondary touch angle check – 2T and 2T-B engines (Sec 17)

required bend the tag (A) shown in Figure 3.86 to adjust.
44 Set the auto-choke adjustment by first moving the coil housing so that its scale marking aligns with the central marking on the body. In this position the choke valve becomes fully shut when the atmospheric temperature reaches 77°F (25°C). If, depending on vehicle operating conditions, you wish to adjust the choke otherwise, turn it clockwise to weaken the choke mixture, or anti-clockwise to richen the choke mixture.
45 Set the idle mixture adjuster screw by first screwing it fully in (do not overtighten though). Then unscrew it out three full turns.
46 Finally check the setting of the accelerator pump stroke at points shown (Fig. 3.87). Bend the linkage if adjustment is necessary, but check the linkage movement on completion to ensure that it operates in a satisfactory manner.
47 When the carburettor is refitted to the engine and fully reconnected you will need to run the engine and make further checks and adjustments as necessary to the idle speed and mixture settings as described in Section 10 or 11. The fast idle speed setting should also be checked as described in Section 13. The reassembled carburettor and associated components and hoses are shown in the accompanying photos.

18 Carburettor overhaul – 3T-C engine (USA and Canada)

1 The dismantling, inspection and reassembly details for the 3T-C engine carburettor are basically the same as those given for the 2T engine unit in the previous Section. On USA models the automatic choke unit differs and this can be seen in Fig. 3.88.

Fig. 3.82 Secondary touch angle adjustment – 2T and 2T-B engines (Sec 17)

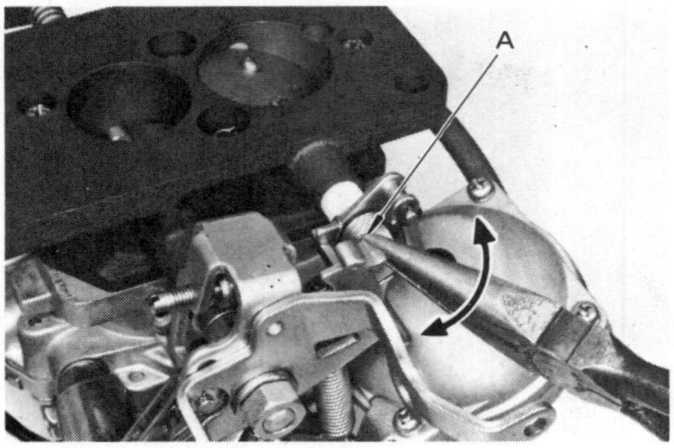

Fig. 3.83 Adjust secondary throttle valve to body clearance at point A – 2T and 2T-B engines (Sec 17)

Fig. 3.84 Throttle lever A mechanism and fast idle cam – 2T engine (Sec 17)

Fig. 3.85 Bend tag A to adjust choke valve opening angle – 2T engine (Sec 17)

Fig. 3.86 Bend tag A to adjust the choke breaker – 2T engine (Sec 17)

Fig. 3.87 Check accelerator pump stroke between points indicated and adjust if necessary – 2T and 2T-B engines (Sec 17)

17.47a 2T engine carburettor and associated components viewed from above

17.47b 2T engine carburettor and associated components – right-hand side view

17.47c 2T engine carburettor and manifold showing the hose connections of the throttle positioner (1), the vacuum control valve (2) and the gas filter (3)

17.47d 2T engine carburettor top front view showing the choke opener and linkage assembly. Note also the positions of the air horn screw brackets and the identity tag

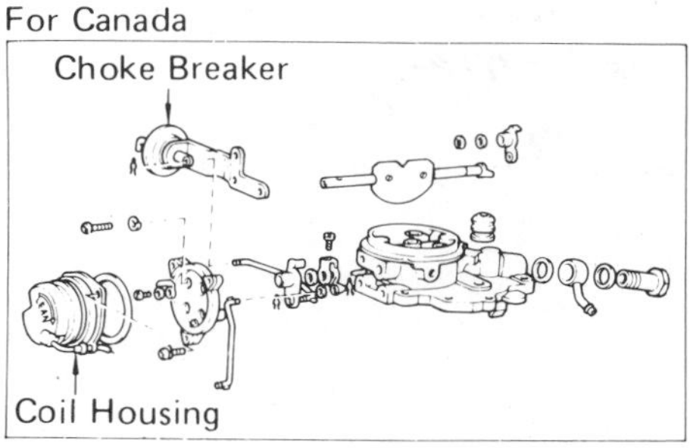

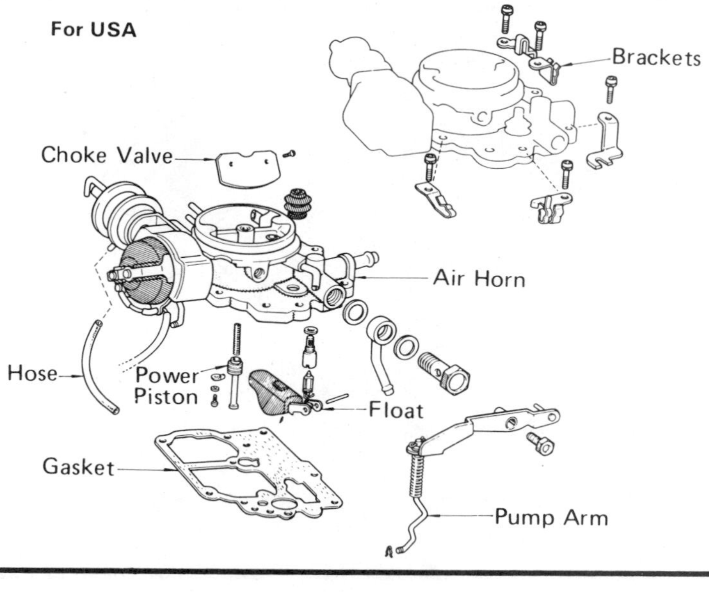

Fig. 3.88 Air horn and associated components – 3T-C engine (Sec 18)

2 The main body of both carburettor types is also much the same although some differences do occur. For example the 3T-C model has a primary and secondary solenoid cut off valve. Exploded diagrams showing the components are shown in Figures 3.89 and 3.90.
3 When making the initial adjustments and checks during reassembly, refer to the Specifications for the 3T-C engine carburettor. The following checks and adjustments differ.
4 *Fast idle setting adjustment.* Position the throttle shaft lever on the 1st step on the fast idle cam (see Fig. 3.91) then with the choke valve fully closed check that the primary throttle valve angle is as given in the Specifications. If adjustment is necessary turn the fast idle adjustment screw in the required direction.
5 *Check and if necessary adjust the unloader:* Open the primary throttle valve fully and check the choke valve angle. Compare with that given in the Specifications and if adjustment is necessary bend the fast idle lever with a suitable pair of pliers as shown (Fig. 3.92).
6 *Check the choke opener:* Apply a vacuum to the opener unit and simultaneously check the choke valve opening. If adjustment is necessary bend part (A) shown in Figure 3.93.
7 *Check the choke breaker setting:* To carry out this check you will need to apply a vacuum to both vacuum diaphragms simultaneously and then whilst they are under vacuum, check the choke valve angle and compare it with that specified. On Canadian models adjustment is possible by bending the tag as shown in Figure 3.86. On USA models, no adjustment is possible and the air horn unit must be renewed.
8 Adjust the throttle positioner as described in Section 23 and the accelerator pump stroke as described in Section 17, (paragraph 46).

19 Manifolds and exhaust systems

1 On the 4K engine the inlet and exhaust manifolds are located on the left-hand side of the engine.
2 On 2T, 2T-B and 3T-C engines the inlet manifold is located on the right-hand side of the engine while the exhaust manifold is on the left-hand side providing a crossflow characteristic to the engine.

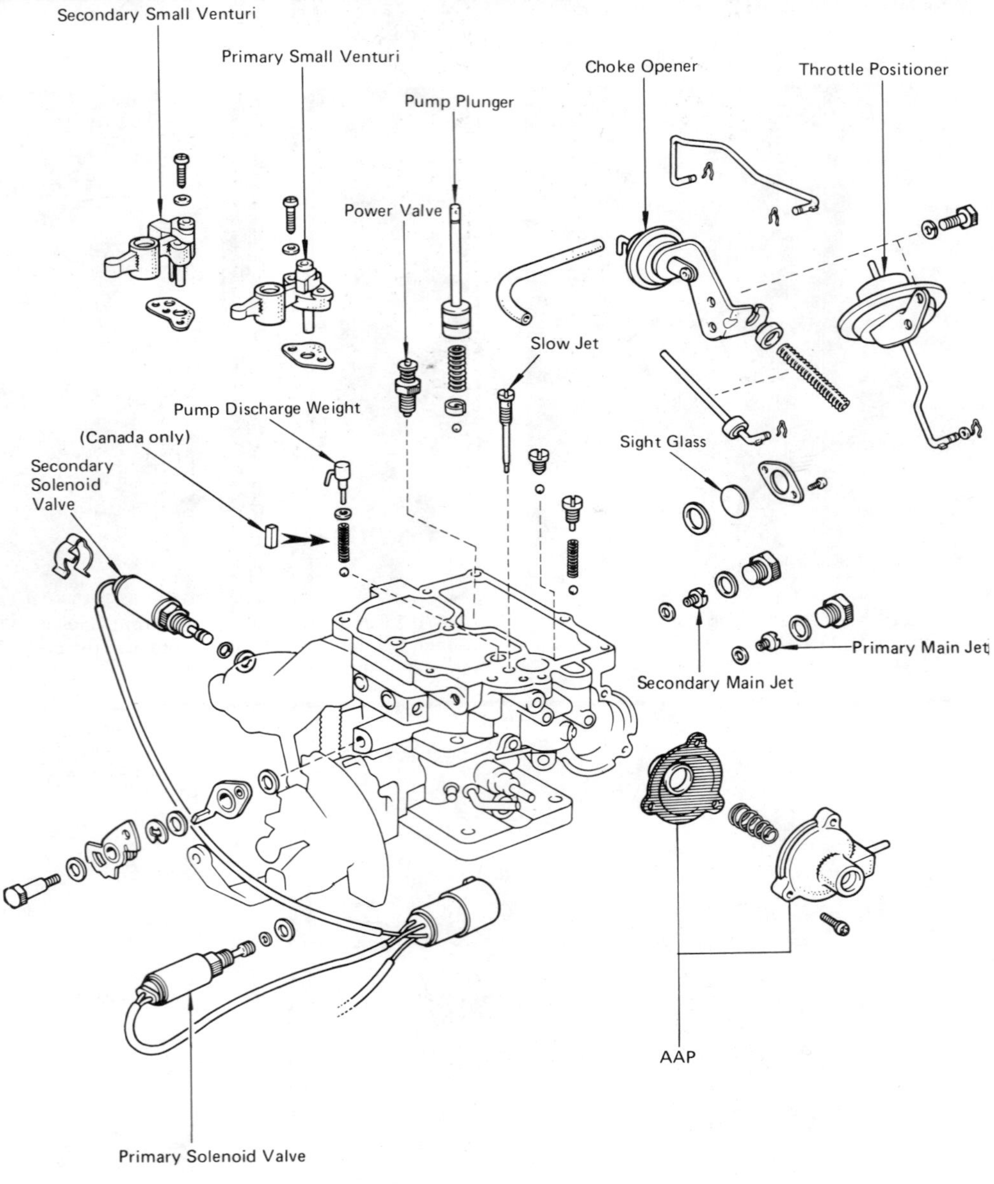

Fig. 3.89 Carburettor main body and associated components – 3T-C engine (Sec 18)

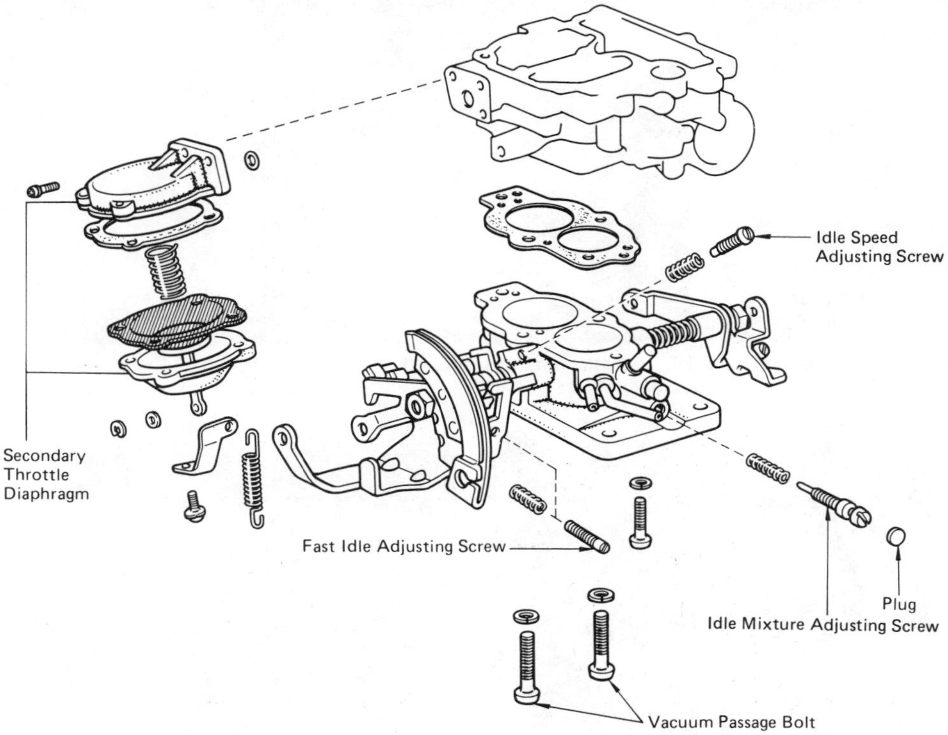

Fig. 3.90 Throttle valve body components – 3T-C engine (Sec 18)

Fig. 3.91 Throttle shaft lever set on 1st step of fast idle cam – 3T-C engine (Sec 18)

Fig. 3.92 Bend fast idle lever to adjust the choke valve angle – 3T-C engine (Sec 18)

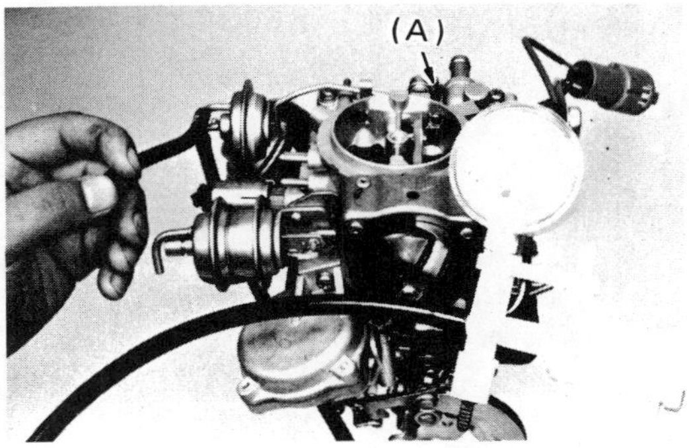

Fig. 3.93 Checking the choke opener. Adjust by bending part A – 3T-C engine (Sec 18)

19.5 Typical exhaust system flexible mounting assembly

19.7 Exhaust pipe to silencer flange connection

19.8 Exhaust manifold to downpipe connection viewed from underneath

19.12 Manifold to downpipe – top view. Use a new gasket

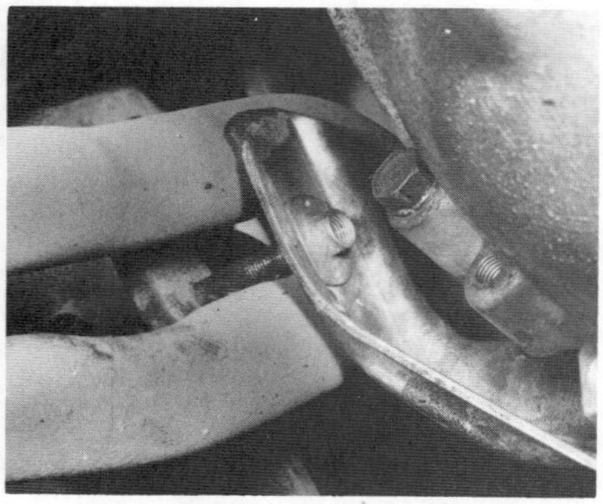

19.14 Downpipe to gearbox bellhousing location clamp

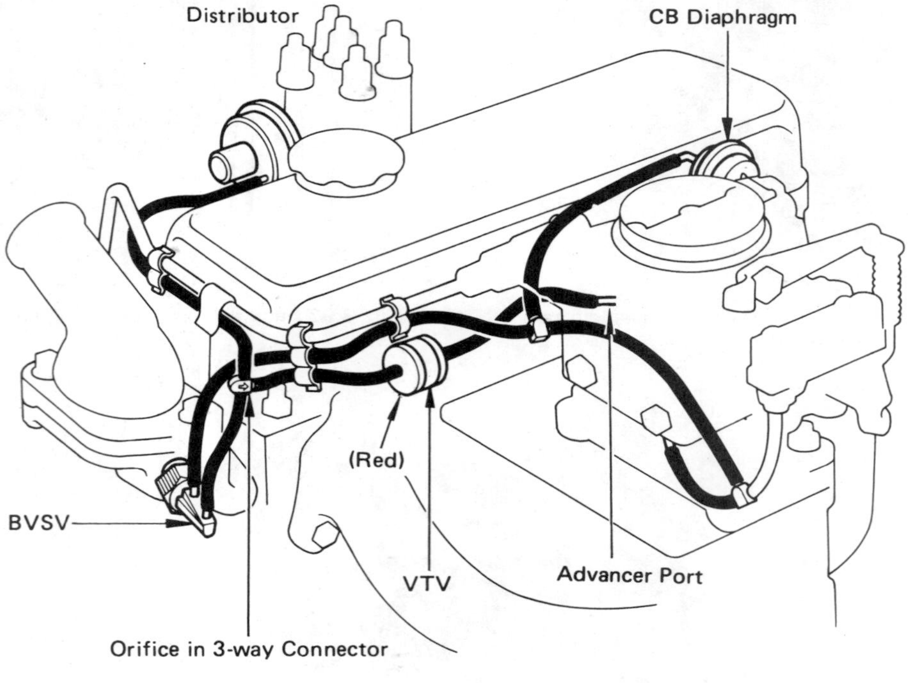

Fig. 3.94 Emission control system component layout – 4K engine models with automatic transmission (Sec 20)

BVSV – Bi-metal vacuum switching valve
CB – Choke breaker
VTV – Vacuum transmitting valve

3 On all engine types the inlet and exhaust manifolds can be removed and refitted individually, the inlet manifold together with the carburettor(s) if required (see photo 9.1).
4 The layout of the exhaust system is similar on all models although the individual components may vary in detail design. Some 3T-C engine variants have a catalytic converter incorporated into the exhaust system which is part of the emission control system, the description of which is given in Section 39.
5 The exhaust system is supported on flexible mountings and incorporates a main silencer and expansion box (photo).
6 Examination of the exhaust pipe and silencers at regular intervals is worthwhile as small defects may be repairable. If left, they will almost certainly require renewal of one of the sections of the system. Also, any leaks, apart from the noise factor, may cause poisonous exhaust gases to get inside the car which can be unpleasant, to say the least, even in mild concentrations. Prolonged inhalation could cause sickness and giddiness.
7 As the sleeve connections and clamps are usually very difficult to separate it is quicker and easier in the long run to remove the complete system from the car when renewing a section. It can be expensive if another section is damaged when trying to separate a bad section from it (photo).
8 To remove the system, jack-up the car at front and rear and then disconnect the front downpipe from the exhaust manifold (photo).
9 Disconnect all the flexible mountings and withdraw the complete system from the rear of the vehicle. In most instances it will be found necessary to disconnect the rear shock absorber at its lower mounting on the exhaust side and the body raised at the rear to allow sufficient clearance for removal of the exhaust system between the axle and underbody at the rear.
10 Cut away the bad sections, taking care not to damage the good sections which are to be retained.
11 File off any burrs at the ends of the new sections of pipe and smear them with grease. Slip the clamps over the pipes and connect the sockets but do not tighten the clamps at this stage.
12 Push the complete system under the vehicle and jack it up so that the front pipe can be bolted to the manifold and the rear tail pipe mounting connected. Use a new gasket between the manifold and downpipe (photo).
13 Now turn the silencer sections to obtain their correct attitudes so that they will not touch or knock against any adjacent parts when the system is deflected to one side or the other.
14 Tighten all clamps and flexible mountings, (photo).
15 Lower the vehicle, reconnect the shock absorber and tighten its fastening to the specified torque wrench setting (see Chapter 11).
16 On completion start the engine and check the system joints for any signs of leaks.

20 Emission control – general description

To prevent pollution of the atmosphere, a number of (fume) emission control systems are fitted to all vehicles. Their complexity depends upon the operating territory but as a general rule vehicles with the larger capacity engine and destined for North America have the most comprehensive and sophisticated systems. All vehicles have a Positive Crankcase Ventilation (PCV) System. Many models have a Fuel Evaporative Emission Control System. Some vehicles have one or more of the following in order to reduce the emission of noxious gases from the exhaust system.

Throttle Positioner (TP) see Section 23
Spark Control (SC) system, see Section 34
Air injection (AI) system, see Section 37
Air suction system, see Section 37
Mixture Control (MC) system, see Section 24
Catalytic Converter – see Section 39
Exhaust Gas Recirculation (EGR) system, see Section 25
Choke Opener system, see Section 26
Choke Breaker (CB) system, see Section 27
Auxiliary Acceleration Pump (AAP) system, see Section 28
Deceleration fuel cut system, see Section 29
High Altitude Compensation (HAC) system, see Section 30
Double vacuum advance distributor, see Section 40
Fuel system feedback, see Section 31
Automatic Hot Air Intake (HAI), see Section 32
Hot Idle Compensation (HIC), see Section 33
Automatic choke system, see Section 35

The respective emission control systems and layouts are shown in the accompanying illustrations. It must be emphasised that correct tuning and adjustment of the fuel and ignition systems are extremely important for the maintenance of low levels of fume emission from the exhaust.

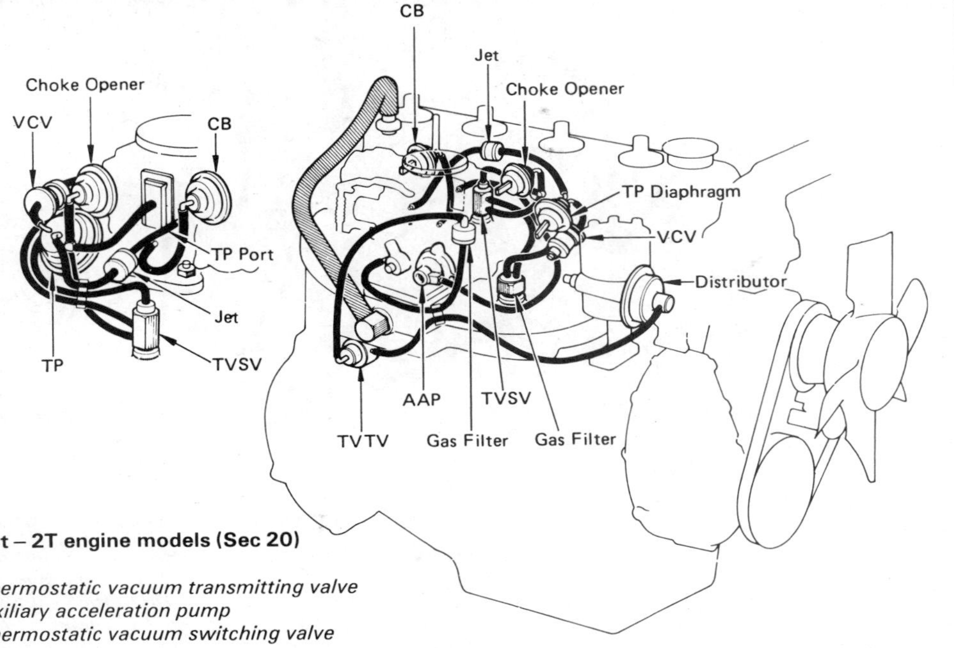

Fig. 3.95 Emission control system layout – 2T engine models (Sec 20)

VCV – Vacuum control valve
CB – Choke breaker
TP – Throttle positioner
TVTV – Thermostatic vacuum transmitting valve
AAP – Auxiliary acceleration pump
TVSV – Thermostatic vacuum switching valve

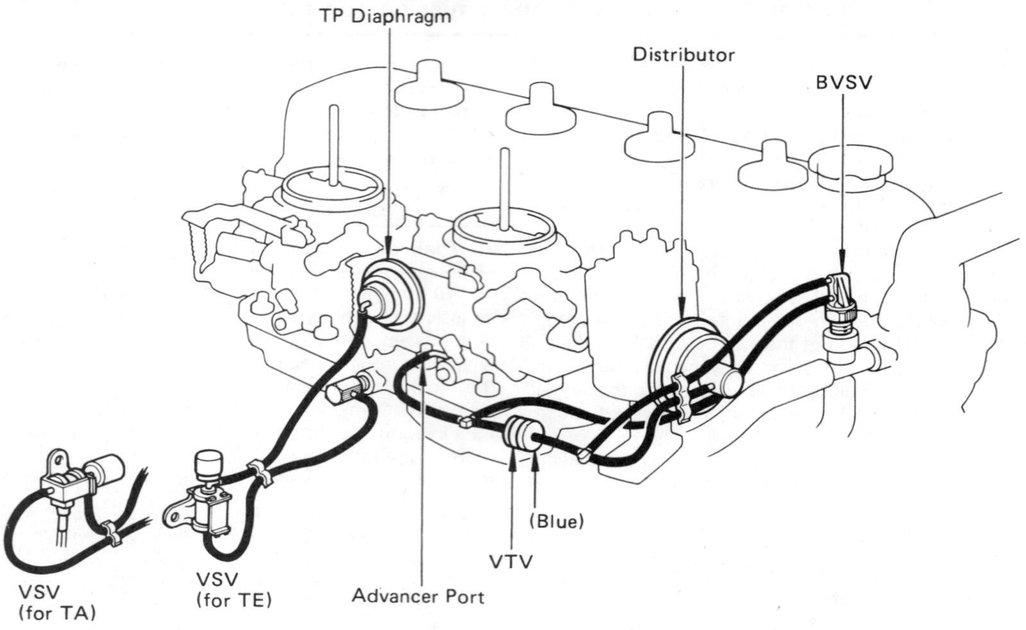

Fig. 3.96 Emission control system layout – 2T-B engine (Sec 20)

TP – Throttle positioner BVSV – Bi-metal vacuum switching valve VTV – Vacuum transmitting valve VSV – Vacuum switching valve

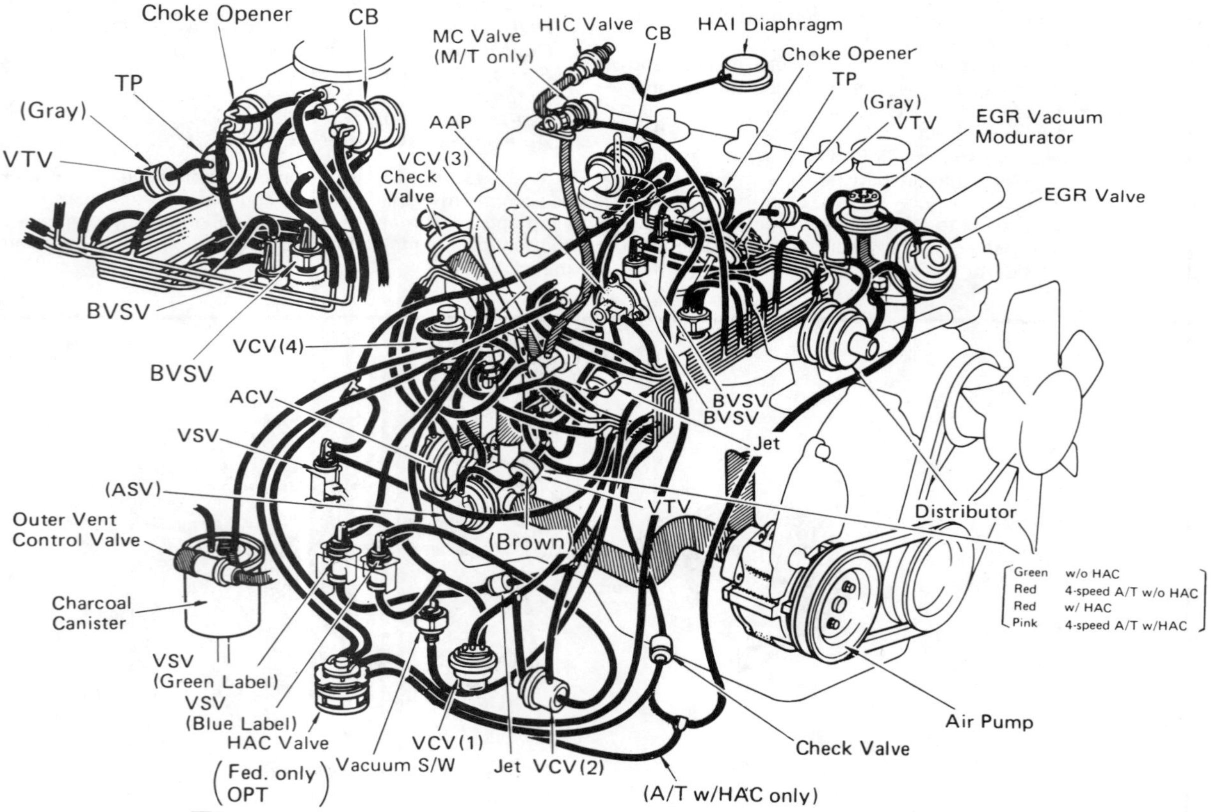

Fig. 3.97 Emission control system layout – 3T-C engine (USA) (Sec 20)

VTV – Vacuum transmitting valve
TP – Throttle positioner
CB – Choke breaker
BVSV – Bi-metal vacuum switching valve
VCV – Vacuum control valve
AAP – Auxiliary acceleration pump
HIC – Hot idle compensation
HAI – Hot air intake
EGR – Exhaust gas recirculation
HAC – High altitude compensation
A/T – Automatic transmission
VSV – Vacuum switching valve
ASV – Air suction valve
ACV – Air control valve

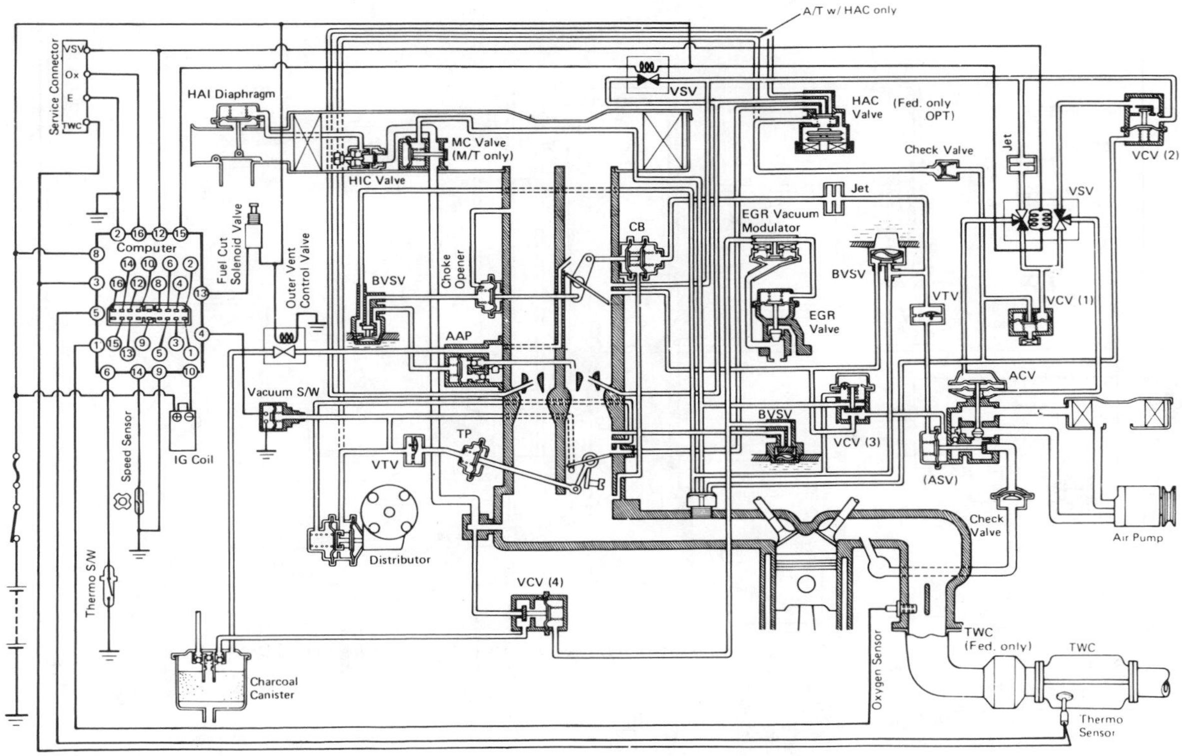

Fig. 3.98 Emission control system and circuits – 3T-C engine (USA) (Sec 20)

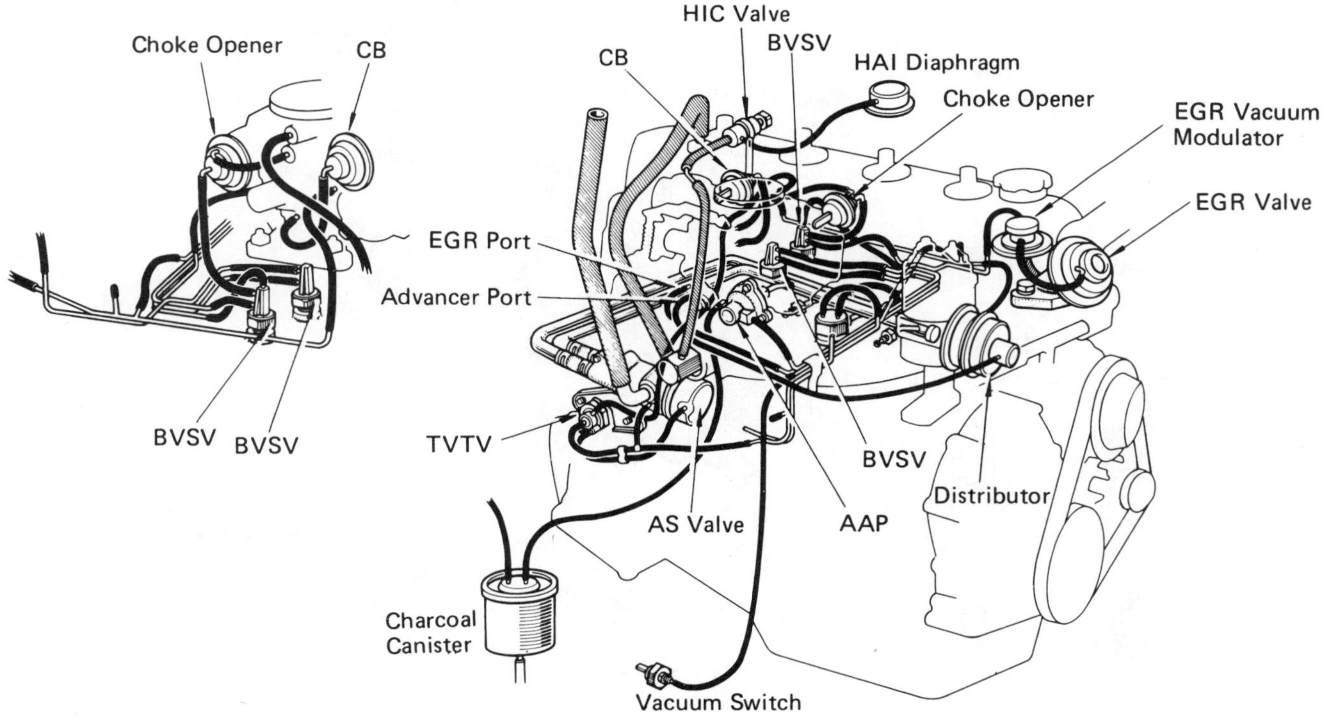

Fig. 3.99 Emission control system – 3T-C engine (Canada) (Sec 20)
For caption abbreviations, descriptions see Fig. 3.97

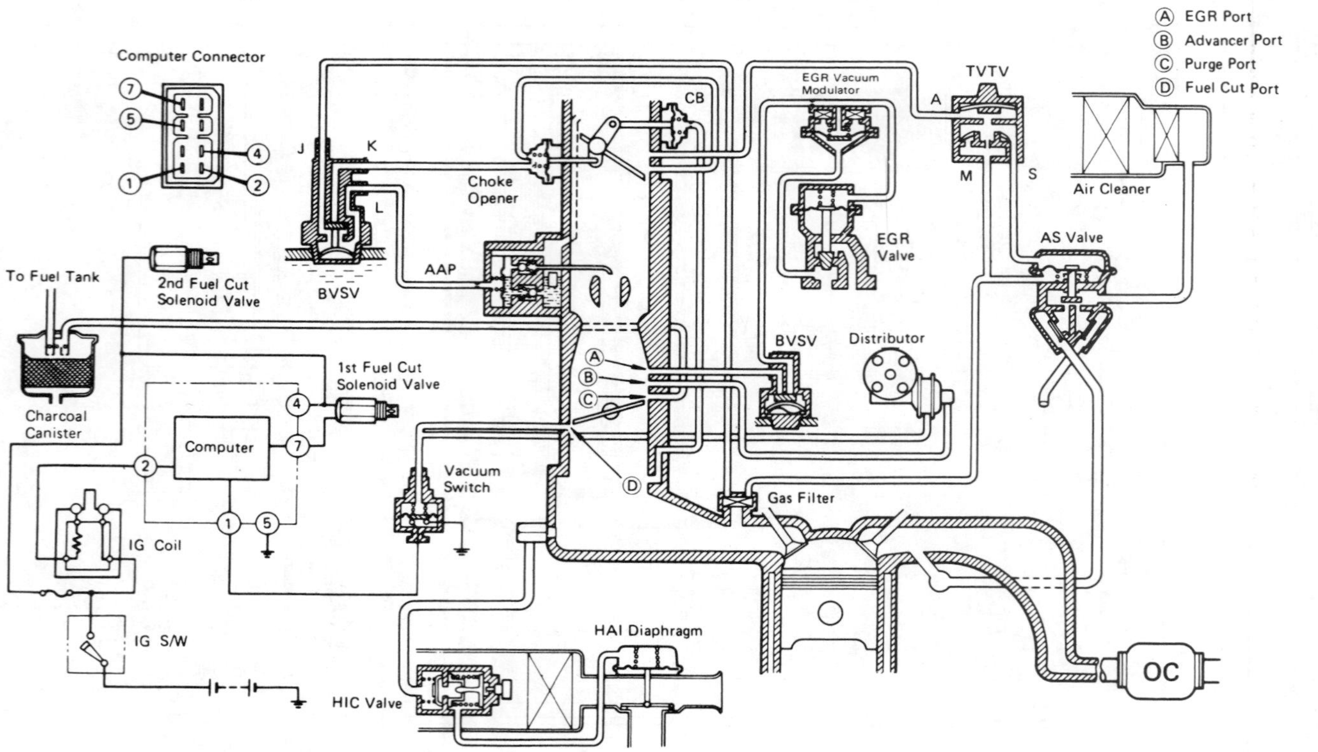

Fig. 3.100 Emission control system and circuits – 3T-C engine (Canada) (Sec 20)

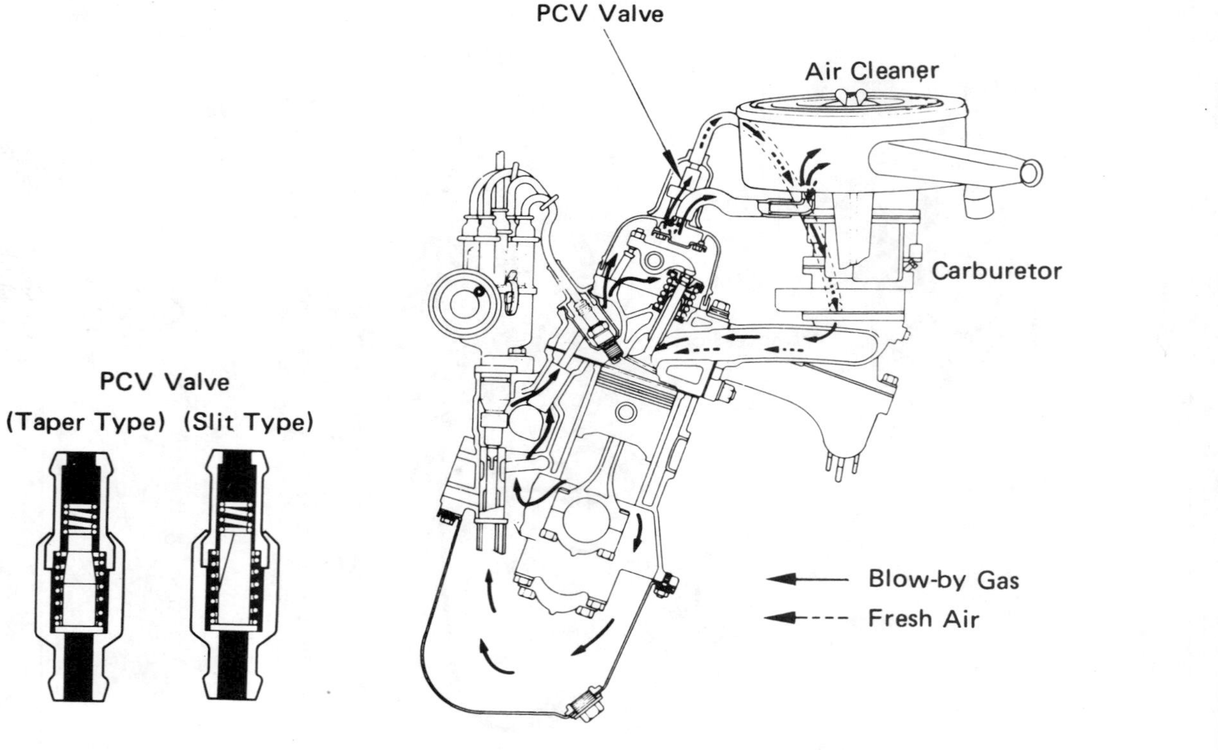

Fig. 3.101 Positive crankcase ventilation system – 4K engine (Sec 21)

21 Positive crankcase ventilation (PCV) system – description and maintenance

1 The system is designed to draw blow-by gas from the crankcase and rocker chamber into the air cleaner where it is led into the intake manifold and is then burned during the normal combustion cycle.
2 A ventilation valve is incorporated in the connecting hoses.
3 Periodically inspect the hoses for security of connections and for splits or deterioration.
4 Check the operation of the valve by having the engine running at idling speed and then pinch the valve connecting hose several times and listen for the valve seating. If this can be heard, the valve is operating satisfactorily. If it cannot be heard seating, renew the valve. Renewal should be carried out in any event at the specified intervals.

22 Fuel evaporative emission control systems – description and maintenance

1 The system is designed to reduce the emission of fuel vapour to the atmosphere by directing the vapour from the fuel tank through a non-return valve into an absorbent charcoal-filler canister.
2 Some layouts have a fuel/vapour separator and all models are fitted with a special filler cap which although normally sealed, does include a valve to admit air when partial vacuum conditions are created within the system or fuel tank.
3 At certain road speeds, a vacuum switching valve is actuated and the vapour stored in the canister is then drawn into the intake manifold where it is burned as a controlled fuel/air mixture within the engine combustion chambers.

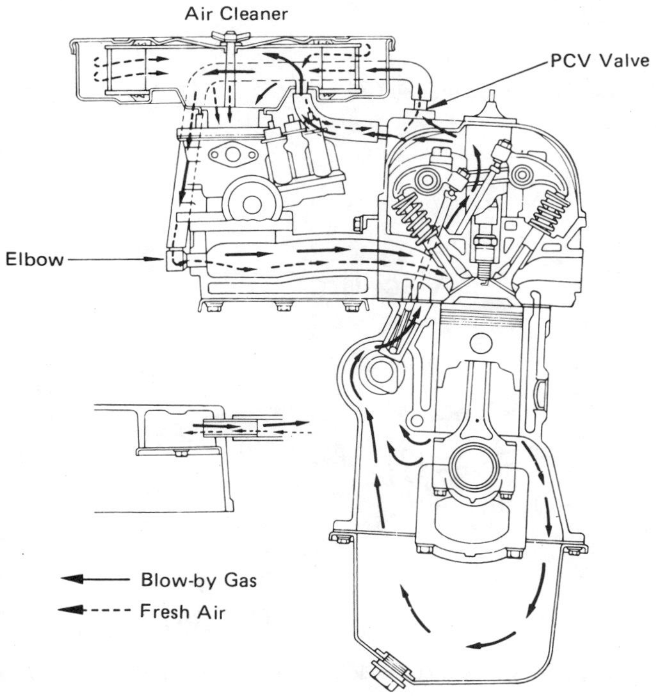

Fig. 3.102 Positive crankcase ventilation system – 2T, 2T-B and 3T-C engines (Sec 21)

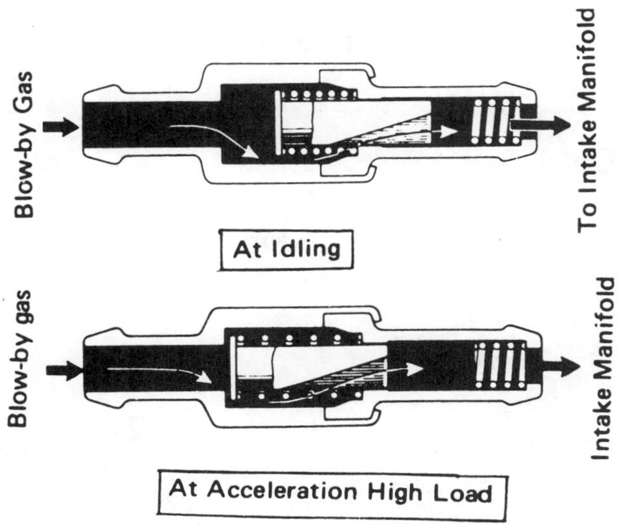

Fig. 3.103 Crankcase ventilation valve diagram (Sec 21)

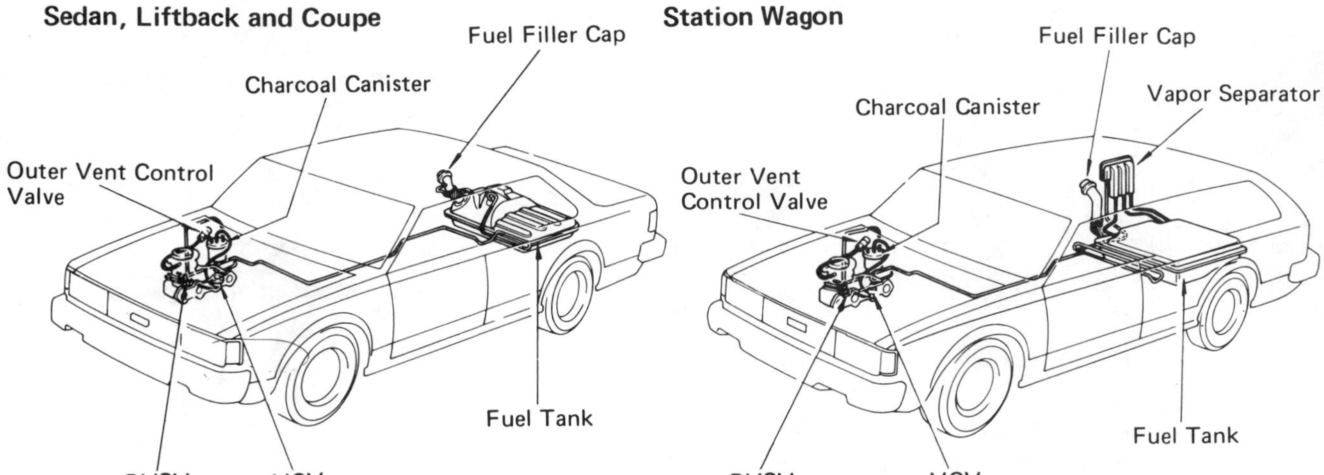

Fig. 3.104 Fuel evaporative emission control system (USA models) (Sec 22)

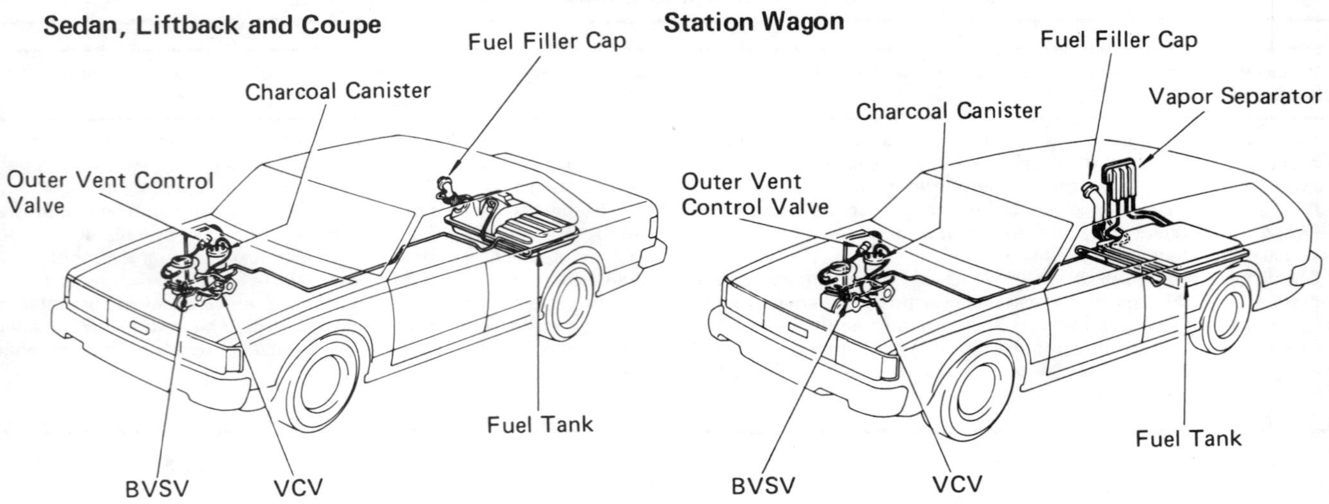

Fig. 3.105 Fuel evaporative emission control system (Canada models) (Sec 22)

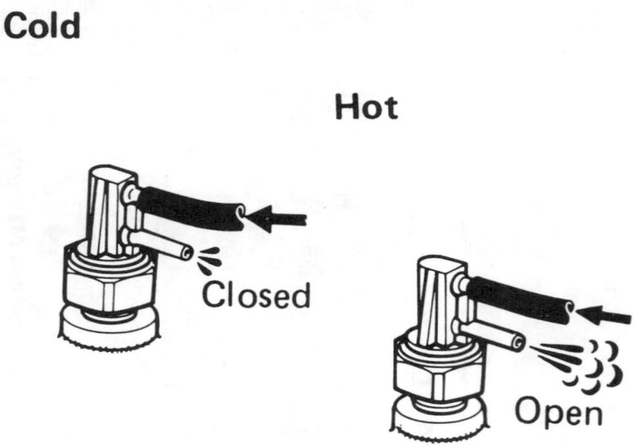

Fig. 3.106 BVSV valve check method – USA models (Sec 22)

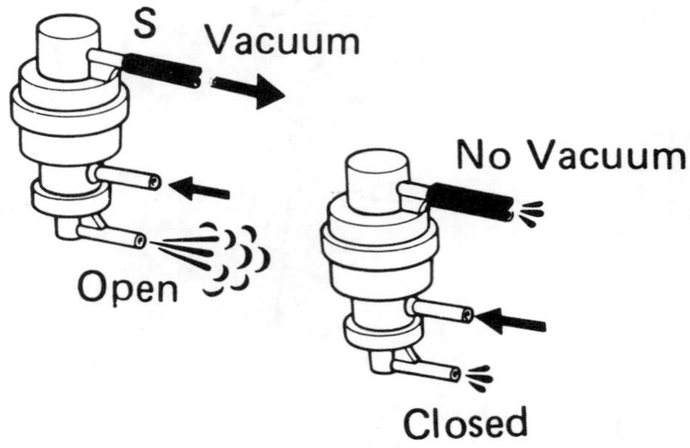

Fig. 3.107 VCV valve check method – USA models (Sec 22)

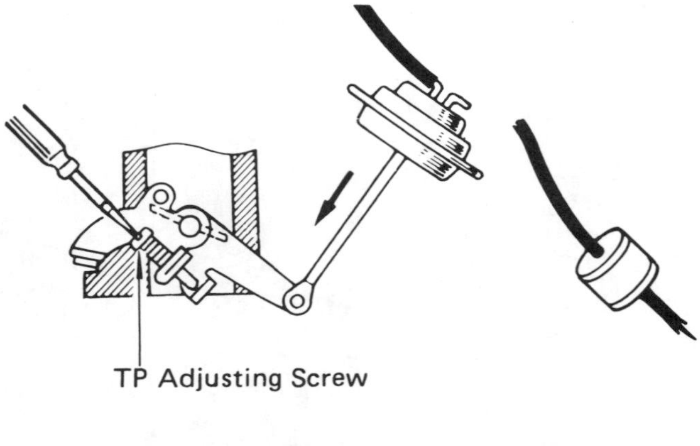

Fig 3.108 Throttle positioner adjustment for correct setting according to engine type (Sec 23)

2T engine – 1300 rpm
2T-B engine – 1200 rpm
3T-C engine – 1400 rpm

Fig. 3.109 VTV unit check method (Sec 23)

4 Check the system hoses at the specified intervals (see Routine Maintenance) also the condition of the filler cap seal.
5 Renew the non-return valve as specified.
6 Renew the charcoal canister at the specified intervals.
7 When checking the system on USA models check that the bi-metal vacuum switching valve (BVSV) is operational by blowing air into the pipe shown (Fig. 3.106) with the coolant temperature under 104°F (40°C). The valve should close. Warm up the engine and apply the same test. The valve should then open. Renew the BVSV if found to be defective.
8 The vacuum control valve (VCV) on USA models should also be checked at the same time. Referring to Figure 3.107 blow air into the pipe connection indicated and apply a vacuum of 2.95 in Hg (75 mm Hg) to the top pipe shown (S). The valve should open.
9 To check that the valve closes, stop the vacuum previously applied and continue blowing into the middle pipe of the valve. If the valve is found to be defective, renew it.

23 Throttle positioner – description and adjustment

1 This device is fitted to the carburettor on 2T and 3T-C engines and it is designed to hold the throttle valve plate slightly open during deceleration when the accelerator is released. Without this, the throttle valve plate would close to the idle position and in consequence compression pressure would drop. The mixture would become rich and would then not burn completely so causing increased emission of noxious fumes.
2 To adjust the throttle positioner, first run the engine to normal operating temperature and then check the idle speed is as specified.
3 Disconnect the vacuum hose from the diaphragm unit of the throttle positioner. The engine speed should increase to the throttle positioner setting speed as specified. If it does not, turn the adjustment screw to achieve the specified engine speed (Fig. 3.108)
4 Reconnect the hose to the throttle positioner diaphragm unit and check that the engine speed slows to the specified idle speed within 1 to 3 seconds of the hose being attached. Should this not be the case a check must be made on the linkage, the vacuum transmitting valve (VTV) and the throttle positioner diaphragm to find which is at fault.
5 To check the VTV unit disconnect it and apply air to the hose connector on side (B) (Fig. 3.109). The airflow through the unit should be unimpeded, application of air from A to B however should be felt to be restricted. Renew the unit if it is found to be defective.
6 To check the TP diaphragm detach the vacuum hose then reattach it and pinch the hose. The TP linkage should move in accordance with the vacuum being supplied. Renew the unit if found to be defective (Fig. 3.110).

24 Mixture control (MC) system – description and maintenance

1 Fitted to 3T-C engines with manual transmission only.
2 Its purpose is to permit fresh air to enter the inlet manifold at time of sudden deceleration in order to improve combustion and reduce the emission of hydrocarbons.
3 Maintenance consists of checking the hoses and connections.
4 In the event of a suspected fault, start the engine, disconnect the vacuum sensing hose from the valve and block the hose. Now place the hand over the air intake of the valve, no vacuum should be felt.
5 Reconnect the hose and as it is connected, vacuum should be felt momentarily, together with rough idle condition.
6 If the valve does not operate as described, renew it as a sealed unit.

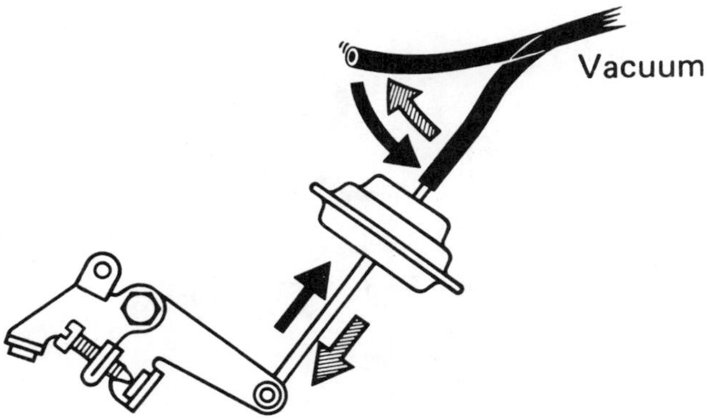

Fig. 3.110 TP linkage movement check (Sec 23)

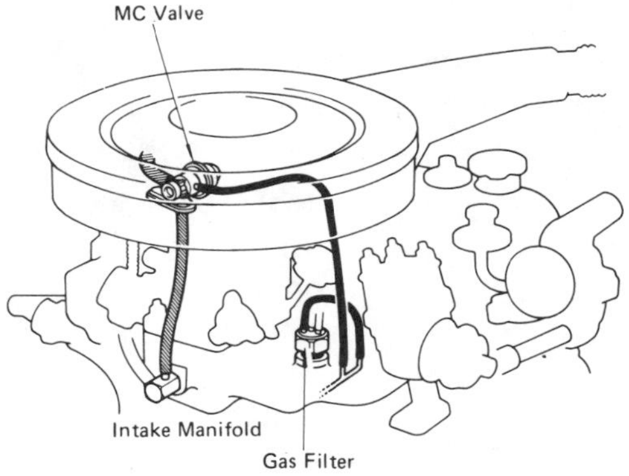

Fig. 3.111 Mixture control (MC) system (Sec 24)

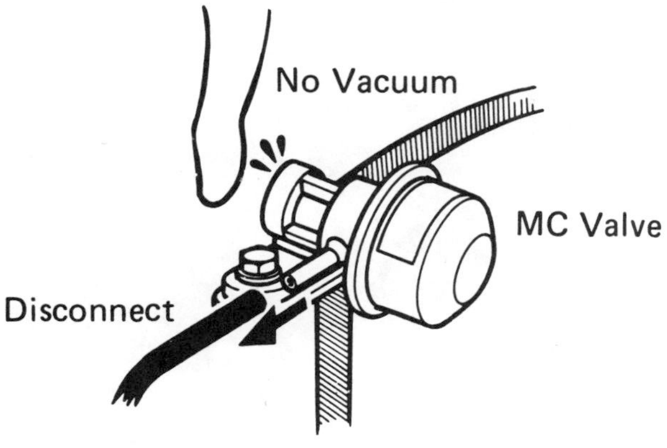

Fig. 3.112 Mixture control valve check method, hose disconnected (Sec 24)

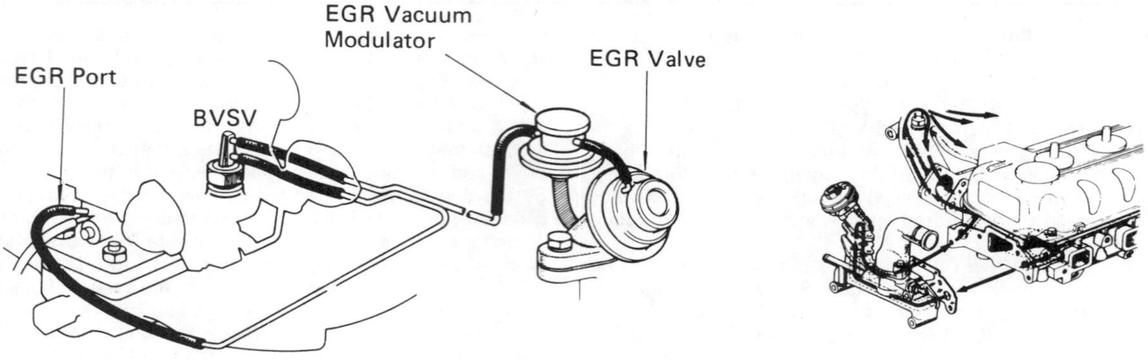

Fig. 3.113 Exhaust gas recirculation (EGR) system layout and components (Sec 25)

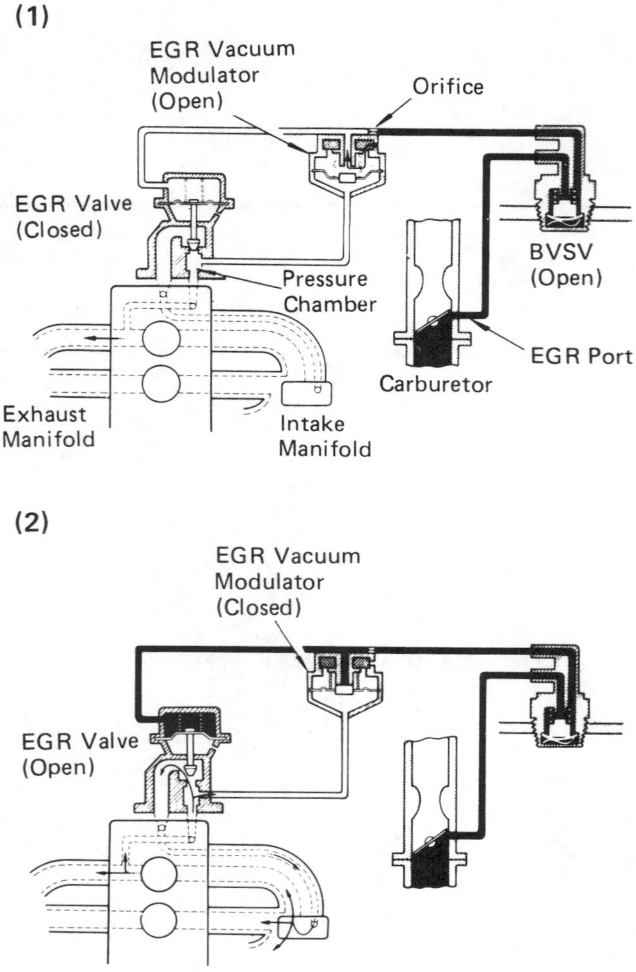

Fig. 3.114 EGR system operation diagrams (Sec 25)

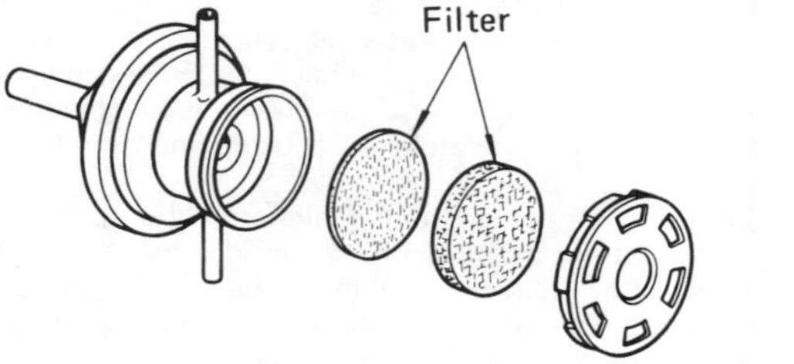

Fig. 3.115 EGR system vacuum modulator filters (Sec 25)

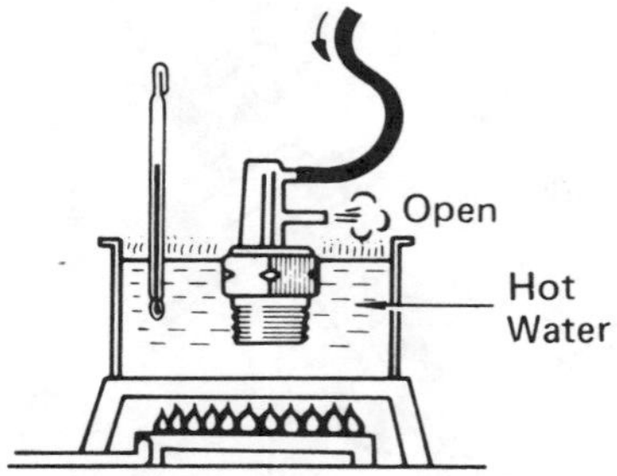

Fig. 3.116 BVSV unit test (Sec 25)

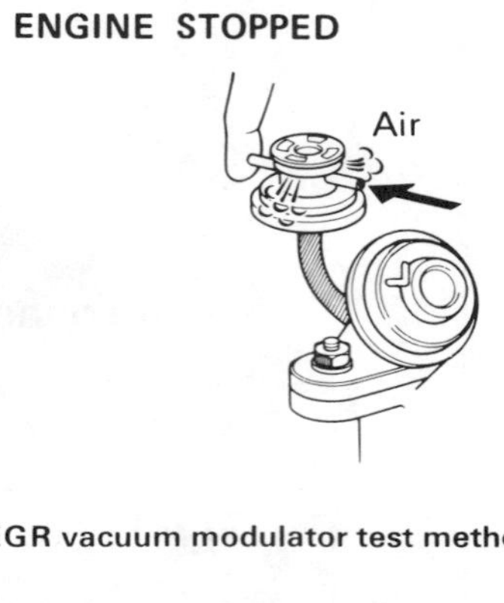

Fig. 3.117 EGR vacuum modulator test method (Sec 25)

25 Exhaust gas recirculation (EGR) system – description and maintenance

1 This system is designed to re-introduce small amounts of exhaust gas into the combustion cycle to reduce the generation of oxides of nitrogen (NOx) by the reduction of combustion temperatures. The amount of gas re-introduced is governed by engine vacuum and temperature.

2 The EGR valve is connected to the inlet and exhaust manifold; the internal spring-tensioned diaphragm is operated by inlet manifold vacuum and is controlled by a thermal valve (BVSV).

3 When the engine coolant temperature is below 40°C (104°F) on USA models, 60°C (140°F) Canadian models, the thermal valve is open and atmospheric pressure from the inlet manifold allows the EGR valve to be closed, thus restricting any exhaust gas recirculation (Fig. 3.114).

4 When the engine coolant temperature exceeds those temperatures given above, thermal valve closes and prevents atmsopheric pressure reaching the EGR valve. Vacuum from the inlet manifold opens the EGR valve and exhaust gas is thus recirculated.

5 On vehicles operating in California or at high altitude, a vacuum modulator is included in the EGR system which effectively increases the amount of gas recirculated when the engine is under high load. The vacuum modulator is controlled by the amount of exhaust pressure present in a constant pressure chamber.

6 Maintenance of the EGR system consists of cleaning the EGR port orifice when it becomes restricted and, on vehicles operating in California and at high altitudes, periodically cleaning the filter in the vacuum modulator. Should any component fail to function correctly it must be renewed in accordance with local regulations.

7 To check the operation of the EGR valve, run the engine at idle speed and apply a direct vacuum to the valve having detached the modulator hose. The engine should run roughly or even stop. Reconnect the correct vacuum hose. If defective, renew the EGR valve unit.

8 On removal of the EGR valve it may well be found to have heavy carbon deposits on inspection and this is what causes the valve to stick. Do not try to clean the valve, it must be renewed.

9 When refitting the valve be sure to use a new gasket.

10 The BVSV can be checked for satisfactory operation by first draining the cooling system (Chapter 2) then removing the valve. To test the valve first partially immerse it as shown in cool water, then in hot water above the specified valve opening temperature (Fig. 3.116). During each test blow through a tube connected to the upper port connection to ensure that the valve is only open when the water temperature rises above the specified opening temperature.

11 Renew the valve if it is found to be defective. When refitting it apply a liquid sealant to its threads.

12 Reconnect the hoses and top up the engine coolant. Check for signs of leaks around the valve on completion.

13 To test the EGR vacuum modulator, disconnect the vacuum hoses each side of it, plug one pipe connector with a finger and blow through the other connector (inlet side), (Fig. 3.117). The applied air flow should be felt to pass freely through the modulator unit to the air filter side.

14 Now start the engine and run it at 3000 rpm. Repeat the above test – an air flow resistance should be felt.

15 If the EGR vacuum modulator is found to be defective it must be removed and renewed.

26 Choke opener system – description and maintenance

1 This system reduces unnecessary emission of noxious gases when the automatic choke is in operation by forcibly holding the choke valve open. The choke opener system layout is shown in Fig. 3.118.

2 The choke valve is actuated in accordance with the engine temperature and is actuated by the TVSV (thermostatic vacuum switching valve) on the 2T engine or the BVSV (bi-metal vacuum switching valve) on the 3T-C engine.

3 When the engine coolant temperature is cool the TVSV or BVSV (as applicable) is closed, the choke opener diaphragm is released under spring tension, the choke valve closed by the automatic choke and the fast idle cam will be set at the 1st or 2nd cam position giving a high idle speed.

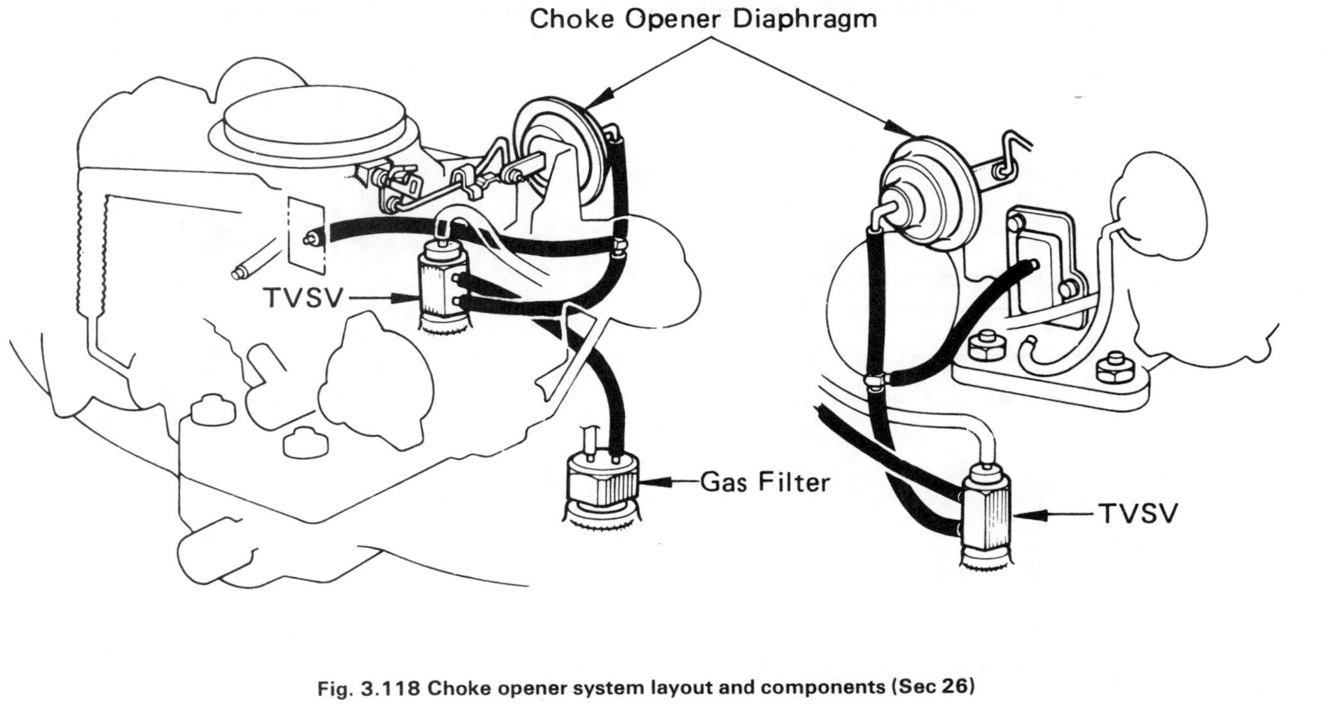

Fig. 3.118 Choke opener system layout and components (Sec 26)

Note: TVSV unit referred to a BVSV unit on some models

4 When the engine temperature rises the TVSV (or BVSV) opens, the choke opener diaphragm is actuated under manifold vacuum, the choke valve opened and the fast idle cam set at the 3rd position which reduces the engine idle speed. Figure 3.119 illustrates the actuation of the system under the cold and hot operating conditions.
5 Maintenance of the choke opener system consists of periodically checking the vacuum hoses for signs of deterioration and ensuring that their connections are secure.
6 To check that the system is functioning correctly, first test the operation of the TVSV or BVSV as applicable, with the engine cold. Detach the vacuum hose at the choke opener (from the TVSV/BVSV), then depress the accelerator pedal once and release it. Start the engine and then reattach the vacuum hose. The choke linkage should not move.
7 Start the engine and run it up to its normal operating temperature, then stop the engine. Again detach the vacuum hose at the choke opener (from the TVSV/BVSV). Hold the throttle slightly open and push down on the choke valve to shut it and retain it in this position as you simultaneously release the throttle valve. Restart the engine but do not depress the accelerator. Now reconnect the vacuum hose. The choke linkage should be seen to move and the fast idle cam released to the 3rd step or more.
8 If each test was satisfactory, then the system is fully operational. If the tests proved the existence of a defect, then the cause must be found by checking the TVSV/BVSV unit and/or the choke opener diaphragm unit and the culprit renewed.
9 To check the TVSV/BVSV unit, first drain the cooling system and then remove the valve from the inlet manifold. Partially immerse the valve in cold water and apply an air flow through the upper connector (J). It should exit through connection (L), (Fig 3.120 and 3.121).
10 To check the valve when hot, heat up the water to or above the temperatures indicated in Figures 3.122 and 3.123 as applicable and then inject air through the same connector (J) and note if this time the air exits through the third connector (K).

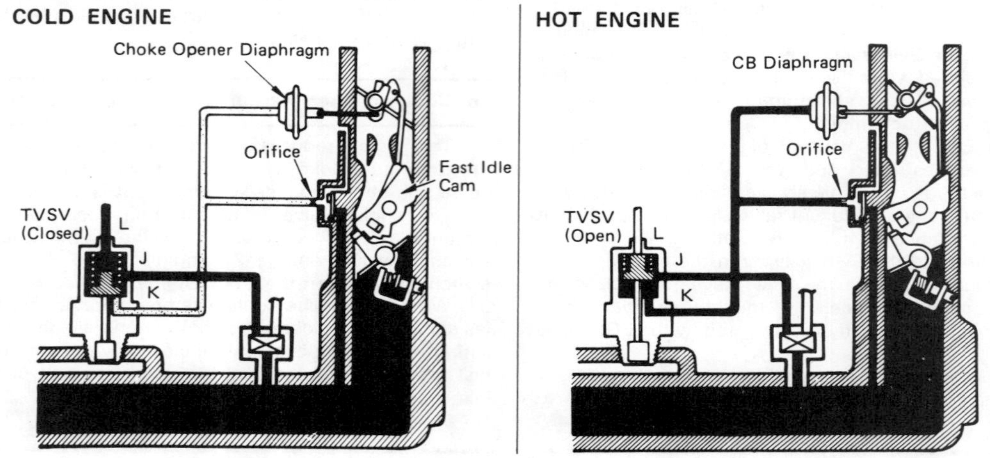

Fig. 3.119 Choke opener system operating diagrams for cold and hot engine (Sec 26)

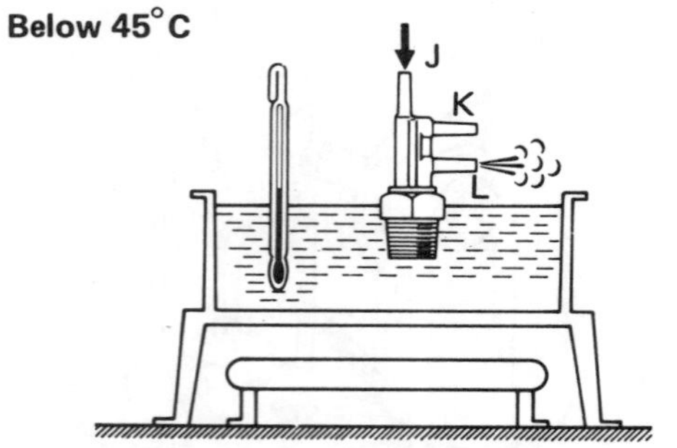

Fig. 3.120 BVSV unit test – 3T-C engine (Sec 26)

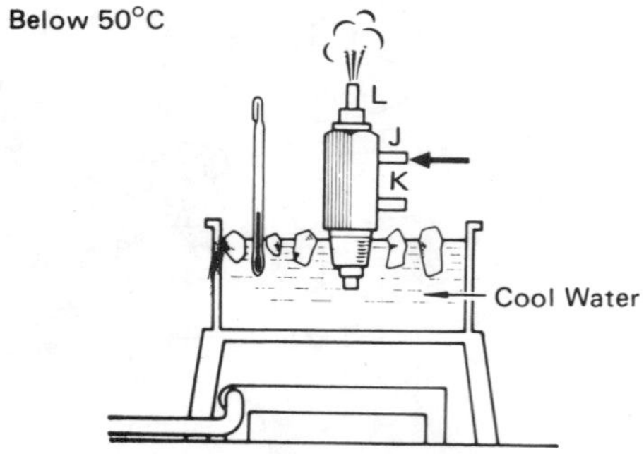

Fig. 3.121 BVSV unit test – 2T engine (Sec 26)

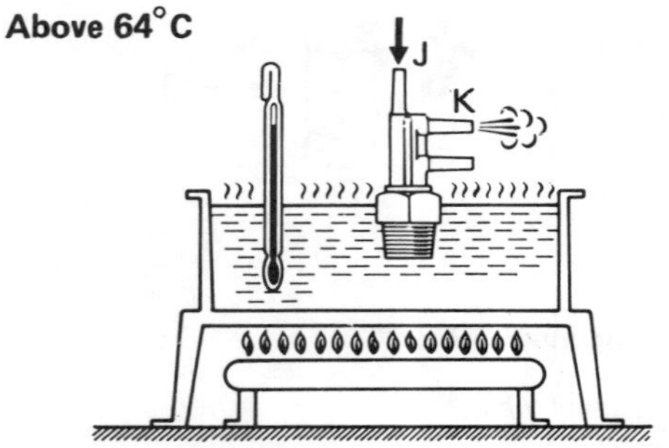

Fig. 3.122 BVSV unit (hot) test – 3T-C engine (Sec 26)

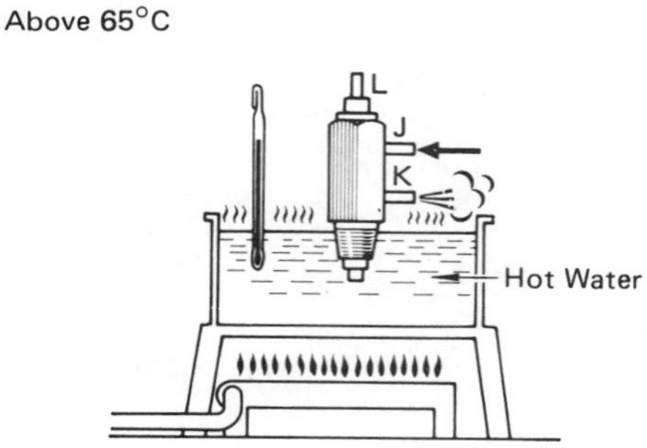

Fig. 3.123 BVSV unit (hot) test – 2T engine (Sec 26)

11 If the valve unit is found to be defective it must be renewed. When refitting the valve, smear the threads with a suitable liquid sealant. Top up the cooling system and check for leaks on completion.
12 The choke opener diaphragm can be checked by observing if its linkage moves according to vacuum. If it does not then it must be renewed.

27 Choke breaker (CB) system – description and maintenance

1 This system operates in an identical manner to the choke opener system in that it holds the choke valve open.
2 When the engine is started and idles with the throttle valve closed, vacuum from the engine side of the throttle valve operates a diaphragm which in turn opens the choke valve.
3 When the throttle valve is opened the vacuum to the diaphragm is reduced and the choke valve closes to enrich the fuel/air mixture.
4 Maintenance is confined to checking the hoses for deterioration.
5 The CB diaphragm can be checked for satisfactory operation by starting the engine and detaching the vacuum hose at the CB diaphragm unit. The choke linkage should return but when the hose is reconnected then the linkage should be pulled by vacuum from the diaphragm. The CB diaphragm unit must be renewed if defective.
6 On USA models the CB system differs and the system layout is shown in Fig. 3.126. The main difference on this system is that a double diaphragm unit is used and a restrictor jet is fitted into the vacuum line.
7 To check the actuation of the double diaphragm unit, start with the engine cold, disconnect each hose in turn (engine idling). When the hose is removed from diaphragm (A) the choke linkage should not move but when the hose to diaphragm (B) is detached (hose to diaphragm (A) reconnected) the linkage should be seen to move (Fig. 3.27). Reconnect this hose.
8 Run the engine and warm it up to its normal operating

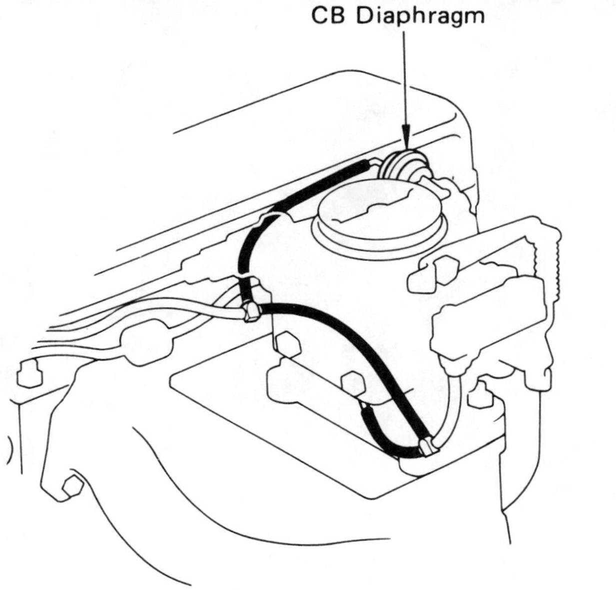

Fig. 3.124 Choke breaker diaphragm and hoses – 4K engine with automatic transmission only (Sec 27)

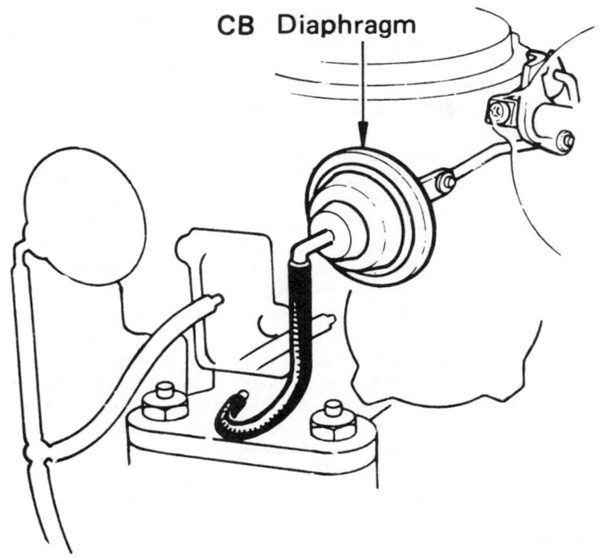

Fig. 3.125 Choke breaker diaphragm unit location – 2T engine (Sec 27)

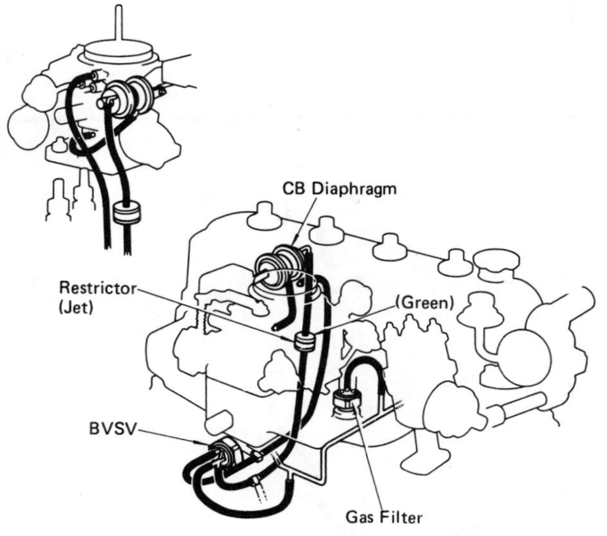

Fig. 3.126 Choke breaker diaphragm and associated system components – 3T-C engine (USA) (Sec 27)

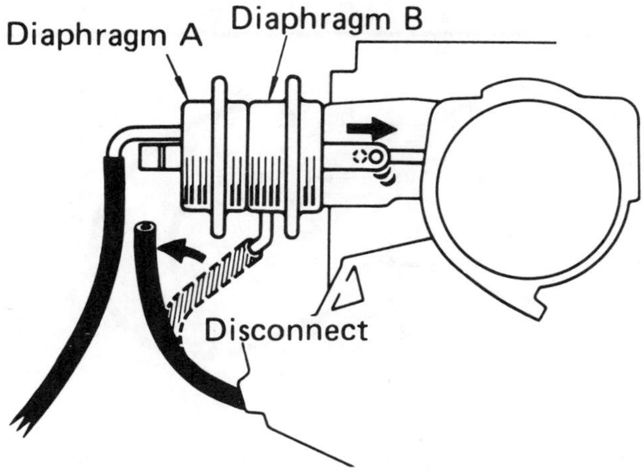

Fig. 3.127 CB diaphragm check (engine cold) – 3T-C engine (Sec 27)

temperature then detach the vacuum hose from diaphragm (A). The choke linkage should return. Refit the vacuum hose to diaphragm (A) and note if the choke linkage moves within 4 to 10 seconds of the hose being connected. If so the diaphragm is operational.

9 Before assuming that the diaphragm is at fault check the BVSV valve. Drain the cooling system (Chapter 2) then remove the valve. Partially immerse it in cold water. Plug the top connector, blow through the side connector and ensure that air exits from the third connector (Fig. 3.128). Now heat the water to a minimum temperature of 19°C (66°F) and apply the same test. The valve should close.

10 If either the diaphragm unit or BVSV unit are faulty they must be renewed. Smear the threads of the BVSV unit with sealant prior to refitting. When fitted top up the coolant and check for signs of leaks.

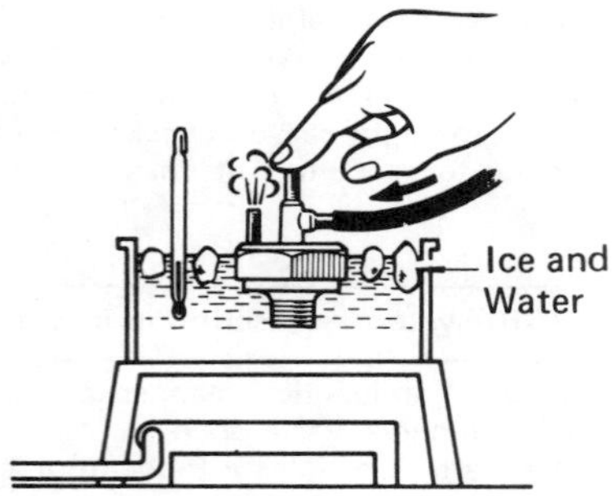

Fig. 3.128 BVSV unit check (choke breaker system – USA) (Sec 27)

28 Auxiliary acceleration pump (AAP) system – description and maintenance

1 This system supplements the main accelerating pump when the engine coolant is cold and thus the quantity of fuel required for acceleration is increased.

2 A thermal valve is employed to connect the inlet manifold depression to a diaphragm on the acceleration chamber and, when the throttle valve is closed, the high vacuum acts on the diaphragm to draw fuel into the chamber.

3 When the throttle valve is opened for acceleration, the inlet manifold depression drops and spring pressure acts on the diaphragm to inject additional fuel into the carburettor venturi.

4 The system only operates when the engine is cold and maintenance is confined to checking the hoses for deterioration.

5 The AAP system can be checked for satisfactory operation in the following manner. The engine must be cold (coolant temperature under 45°C [113°F]) and the air cleaner unit cover removed.

6 Start the engine then pinch the AAP hose and stop the engine. When the hose is released fuel should eject from the acceleration nozzle (photo).

7 Repeat this test with the engine at its normal operating temperature. This time no fuel should be ejected from the nozzle.

8 If the above tests prove a defect in the system check the AAP diaphragm unit by detaching the AAP hose from the TVSV/BVSV unit (as applicable) and then apply and release vacuum to the diaphragm unit while the engine is idling. The engine speed should be observed to change as the vacuum is released. Renew the unit if found to be defective.

9 To check the TVSV/BVSV unit proceed as described in paragraph 9 in the previous Section

28.6 The AAP unit location on the 2T engine carburettor

29 Deceleration fuel cut system – description and maintenance

1 This system effectively controls the idle circuit of the carburettor.

2 When the engine speed is lower than 2100 rpm, or the carburettor vacuum below 14.17 in Hg, a solenoid valve is energised and the idle circuit is opened.

3 In addition to providing the normal idle function, the system reduces overheating and afterburn in the exhaust system during periods of protracted deceleration.

4 Maintenance consists of checking the security and condition of the vacuum hoses and electrical wiring.

5 Should the system be suspected of being defective it is recommended that it be checked by your local Toyota dealer.

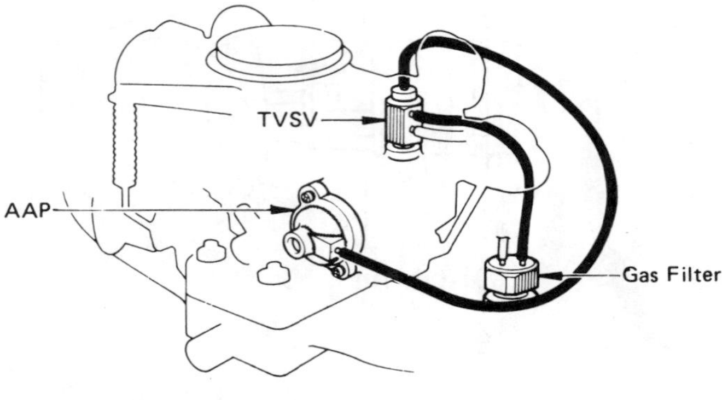

Fig. 3.129 Auxiliary acceleration pump (AAP) system (Sec 28)

Note: TVSV unit referred to as BVSV on some models

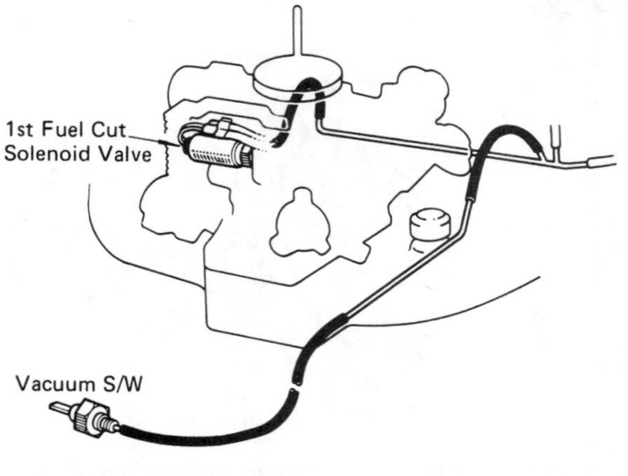

Fig. 3.130 Deceleration fuel cut system – 3T-C engine (Sec 29)

30 High altitude compensation (HAC) system – description and maintenance

1 This system supplies additional air to the carburettor when the vehicle is being operated at high altitudes (above 2570 feet/783 m). The ignition timing is also advanced in order to improve engine control. The system circuit and components are shown in Figure 3.131.
2 The only maintenance normally required is to check the system hoses and their connections periodically to ensure that they are satisfactory.
3 The HAC valve can be checked for position by blowing into any one of the three valve connector ports on the top of the valve when the engine is idling (Fig. 3.132). If in its normal setting position no air flow should be felt underneath the unit. If an air flow can be felt then the passage is open and in the high altitude position (Fig. 3.133).
4 To test the check valve, disconnect it and apply an air flow through the white pipe (orange on automatic transmission models). The air should flow freely through the valve and be felt to exit on the black side. When air is applied through the black side it should not flow freely to the white side (Fig. 3.134). Renew the valve if found to be defective.
5 It should be noted that the HAC valve can be open or closed between the altitude levels of 2570 to 3930 feet (783 to 1198 m) depending on the atmospheric pressure.
6 On 1982 models fitted with automatic transmission the system is designed to advance the ignition timing at high altitude by means of a vacuum hose connected to the sub-diaphragm on the distributor. On such models, if a malfunction is suspected, have the system checked by your Toyota dealer.

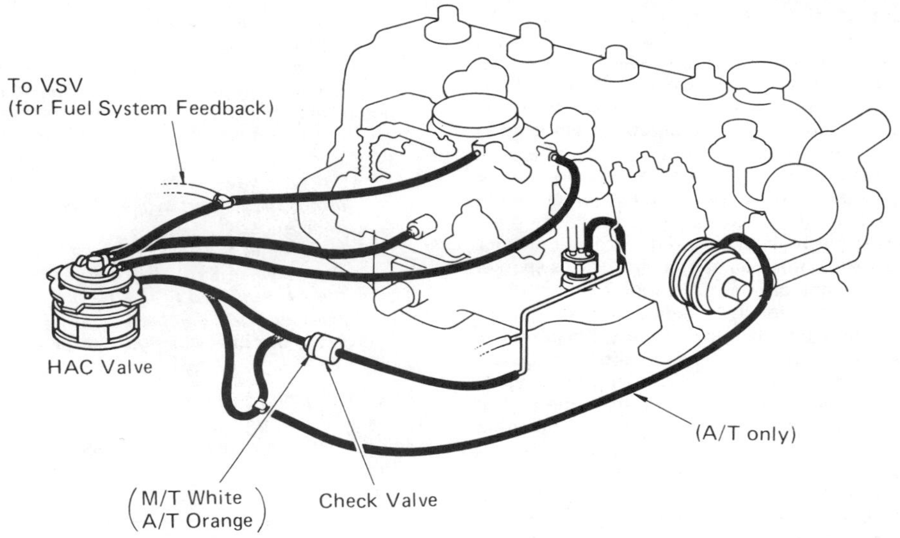

Fig. 3.131 High altitude compensation (HAC) system layout (Sec 30)

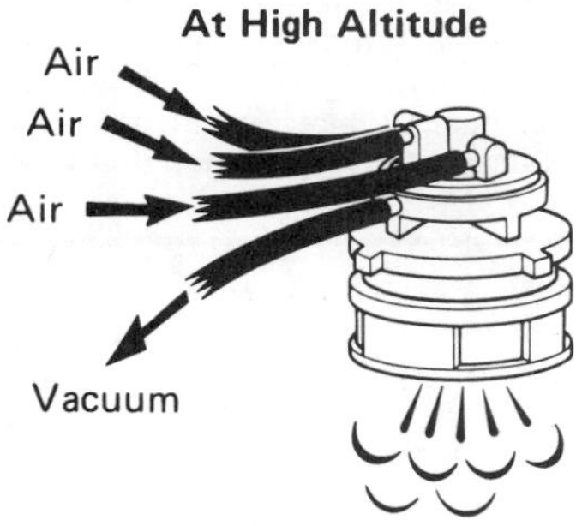

Fig. 3.132 HAC valve check for low altitude operation (Sec 30)

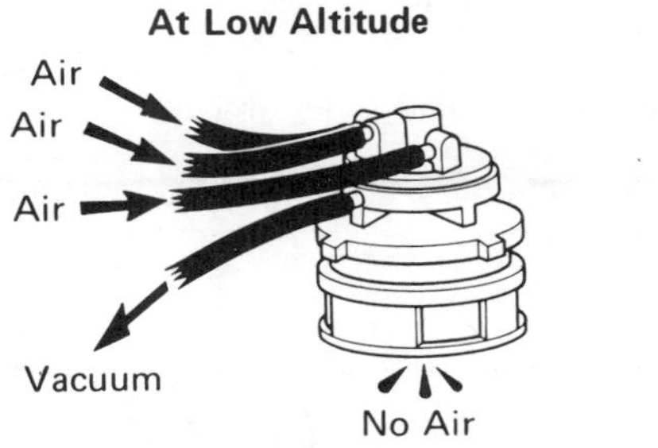

Fig. 3.133 HAC valve check for high altitude operation (Sec 30)

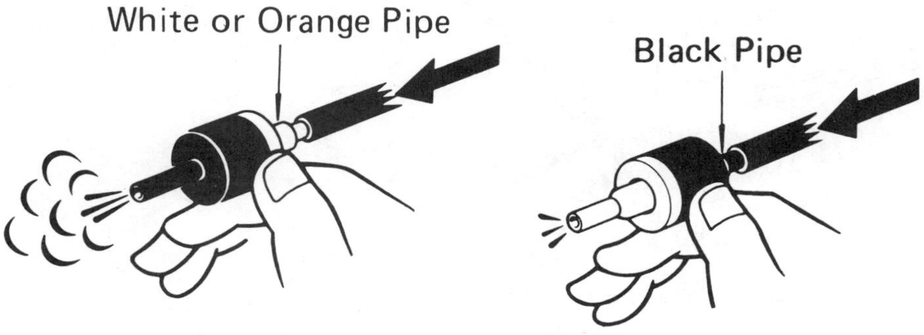

Fig. 3.134 Check valve operation test (Sec 30)

31 Fuel system feedback – description and maintenance

1 This system is designed to reduce the harmful emissions by maintaining the correct ratio of fuel/air mixture passing through the three-way catalyst (TWC).
2 Only fitted to some USA models, the system circuit is shown in Figure 3.135.
3 Routine maintenance of this system consists of checking the hoses and their connections for security, also the lead connections at the vacuum switching valve (VSV).
4 An in-line fuse is fitted into the electrical circuit and should a malfunction occur or be suspected this can be easily checked.
5 Any problems or repairs concerning this system should be entrusted to your Toyota dealer.

32 Automatic hot air intake (HAI) system – description and maintenance

1 This system is designed to improve cold weather driveability. It does this by leading warmed air directly to the carburettor. This helps the carburettor to warm up and prevent the carburettor from icing in extremely cold weather.
2 The components which make up this system do not require routine maintenance and require only a periodic check normally performed at the same time a tune-up is done, (Fig. 3.136).
3 Locate the HAI diaphragm on the intake snorkel of the air cleaner assembly. Now position yourself so that you can see inside this snorkel assembly to watch the movement of the HAI diaphragm valve. A mirror and flashlight may be needed for this visual check.
4 Allow the vehicle to sit overnight so it is completely cold during this first check of the system. Look through the snorkel tube of the air cleaner and have an assistant start the engine. The air control valve inside the diaphragm should close off all air coming from the end of the snorkel and allow only warmed air from the exhaust manifold flexible tube.
5 As the engine warms to normal operating temperature, this air control valve inside the snorkel should slowly open up to allow cool fresh air through the end of the snorkel. This may take some time depending upon the outside temperature. You may want to actually drive the car around and then check the air control valve once the engine is at normal temperature.
6 If the above tests prove that the system is not functioning properly, you should first inspect all hoses and their connections. Then, if no faults are found, the HIC valve which monitors temperature and controls the snorkel diaphragm, should be renewed. The HAI diaphragm will normally not be a problem; however, if the system still does not function properly, the HAI diaphragm should be renewed as a last resort.
7 If the HIC valve is to be renewed ensure that the replacement has the same operating temperature as the original one.

33 Hot idle compensation (HIC) system, – description and maintenance

1 This system functions during high engine temperatures by allowing the air controlled by the HIC valve to enter the inlet manifold. This maintains the proper air fuel-mixture within the carburettor (see Fig. 3.137).
2 The only component in this system is the HIC valve and its related vacuum hoses. Failure rarely occurs in this valve but it can be checked as follows:-

(a) *Remove the HIC valve from inside the air cleaner assembly.*
(b) *Use your finger to close off the small atmospheric port near the bottom of the valve and then check that air flows from the HAI diaphragm side to the inlet manifold side, (Fig. 3.138).*
(c) *Check that air does not flow from the inlet manifold side to the HAI side when the atmospheric port is open.*
(d) *With the valves below 32° Centigrade (89°F), make sure that air will now flow from the HAI diaphragm side to the armospheric port while closing the inlet manifold side with your finger.*
(e) *Now heat the valve in water to 39° Centigrade (101°F).* **Note:** *Make sure that water does not enter the valve. With the valve heated to this temperature check that air does flow from the HAI diaphragm port to the small atmospheric port while the inlet manifold port is blocked with your finger (Fig. 3.139).*

3 As mentioned previously, the only parts within this system are the HIC valve inside the air cleaner assembly and the vacuum lead hoses leading away from this valve. These components are renewed in a straightforward manner.

34 Spark control (SC) system – description and maintenance

1 This system is fitted to the 4K, 2T and 2T-B engine models.
2 This arrangement delays the distributor vacuum advance of the ignition timing for a predetermined period in order to reduce the formation of noxious gases which would normally be produced by shortening the combustion time as the ignition is advanced.

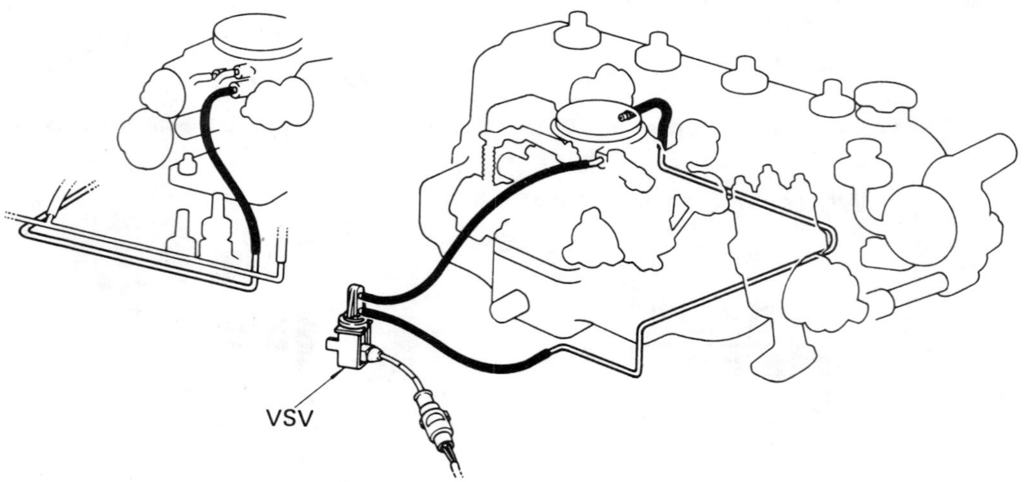

Fig. 3.135 Fuel system feedback system layout (Sec 31)

VSV = Vacuum switching valve

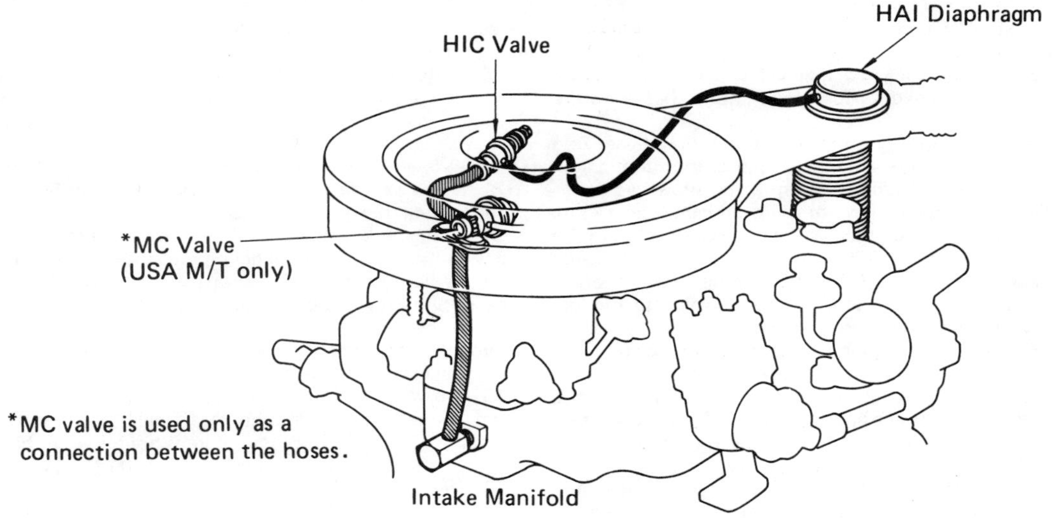

Fig. 3.136 Automatic hot air intake (HAI) system (Sec 32)

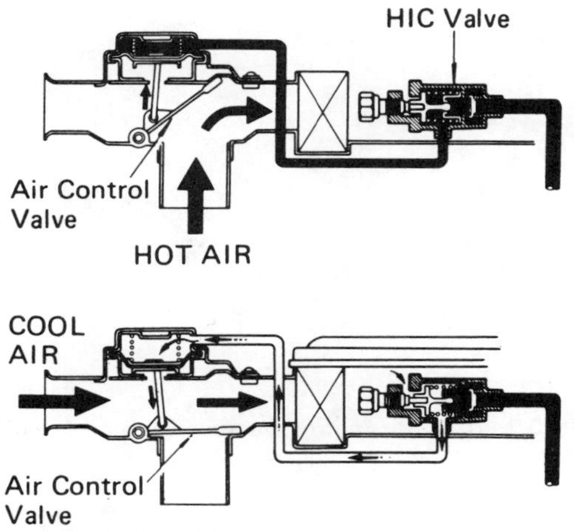

Fig. 3.137 Air intake passage under hot and cold conditions (Sec 32)

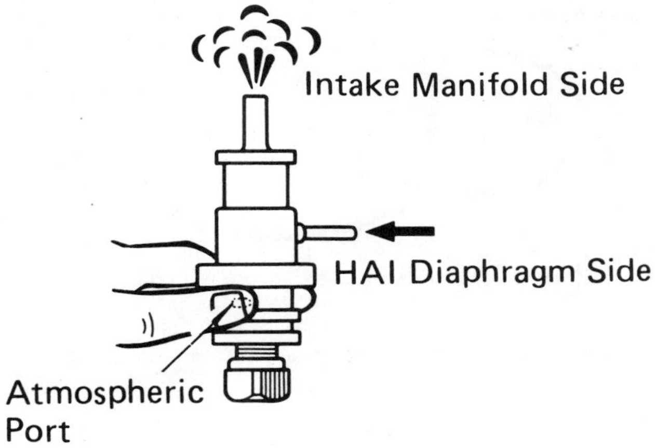

Fig. 3.138 HIC valve air flow check (to manifold) (Sec 33)

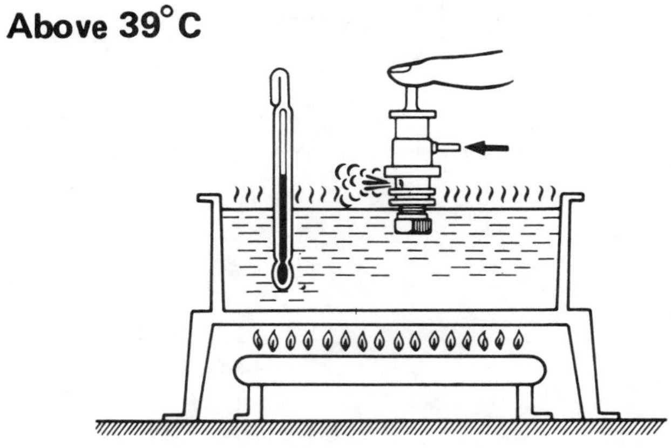

Fig. 3.139 HIC valve airflow check (from HAI diaphragm to atmosphere) Do not allow water to enter the valve (Sec 33)

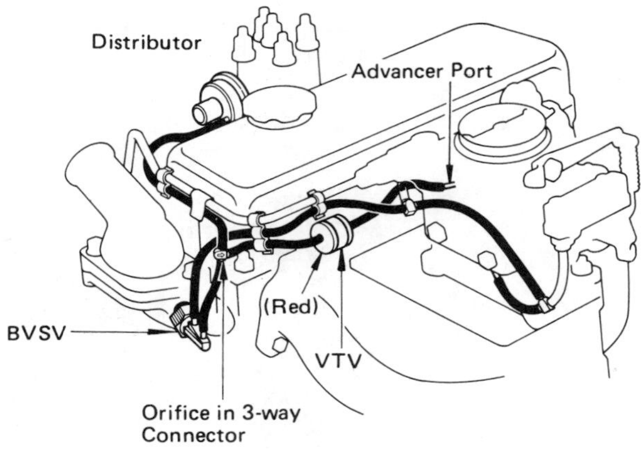

Fig. 3.140 Spark control system – 4K engine – automatic transmission model (Sec 34)

3 Maintenance consists of periodically inspecting the condition of the connecting hoses.
4 Tests on this system can only be made if you have a vacuum gauge and a tachometer. Proceed as follows to make checks on the various components.
5 Detach the distributor diaphragm unit vacuum supply hose. Run the engine at idle speed (engine cold) and check that the gauge registers the amount of inlet manifold vacuum being produced.
6 Continue running the engine to warm it up and then check the gauge reading, again at idle speed, it should read zero. Accelerate the engine speed to 2000 rpm (4K) or 3000 rpm (2T) and check that the vacuum reading changes from 0 to 100 mm Hg within a period of 10 to 35 seconds (4K) or 1 to 3 seconds (2T). On returning to the idle speed the vacuum should revert to zero instantly.
7 Disconnect the gauge and reconnect the vacuum hose to the distributor diaphragm.
8 Now check the distributor vacuum advancer by first removing the distributor cap followed by the rotor and dust cover. Apply vacuum to the diaphragm and check that the vacuum advancer is seen to operate in accordance with the applied vacuum (Fig. 3.142).
9 If these tests are satisfactory refit the dust cover, rotor and distributor cap and then check the BVSV unit (bi-metal vacuum switching valve) on 4K engines or the TVTV unit (thermostatic vacuum transmitting valve) on 2T engines. It will have to be removed for this test and therefore you will first have to drain the cooling system (Chapter 2).
10 With the BVSV/TVTV removed, partially immerse it in cold water (under 30°C), blow through the top hose connector and check that the applied air exits from the lower connector. On the 2T TVTV unit it should be possible to blow through either connector and feel an unrestricted flow exit from the other connector (Fig. 3.143).
11 Now heat the water to a temperature over 54°C (4K) or 44°C (2T) and repeat the test. On the 4K engine the BVSV should be closed whilst on the 2T engine TVTV a large amount of air should be able to flow from the upper (plastic) pipe to the lower (metal) pipe. But when the air flow is reversed only a small amount of air should be able to pass through and out of the upper plastic pipe.
12 If the BVSV/TVTV is in order refit it to the engine. Smear the threads with sealant when fitting the valve and top up the cooling system to complete.
13 The vacuum transmitting valve (VTV) unit on the 4K engine can be checked by blowing through it from each side in turn to ensure that the airflow is without any restriction although when blowing from side A to B a slight resistance should be felt (Fig. 3.144).
14 The only other item to check on the 4K engine is the three-way connector and this should be inspected carefully for any signs of blockage or damage. When refitting the three-way connector fit the orifice as shown in Figure 3.145.

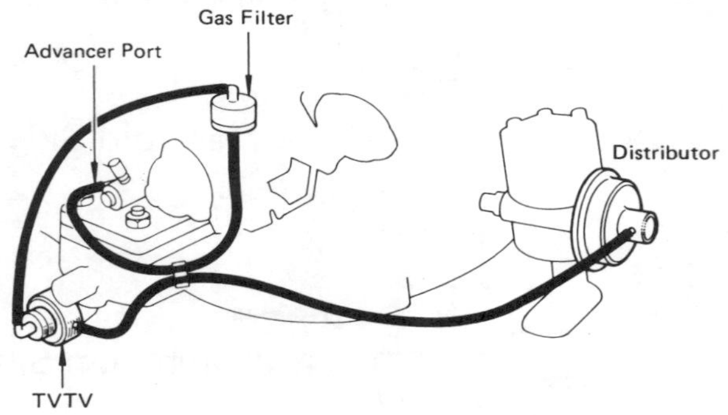

Fig. 3.141a Spark control system – 2T engine (Sec 34)

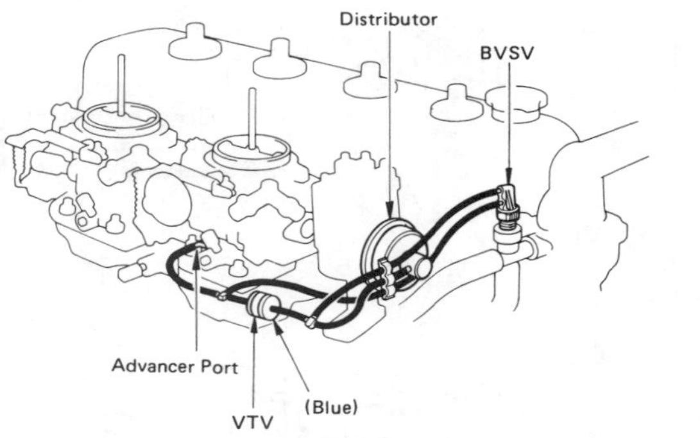

Fig. 3.141b Spark control system – 2T-B engine (Sec 34)

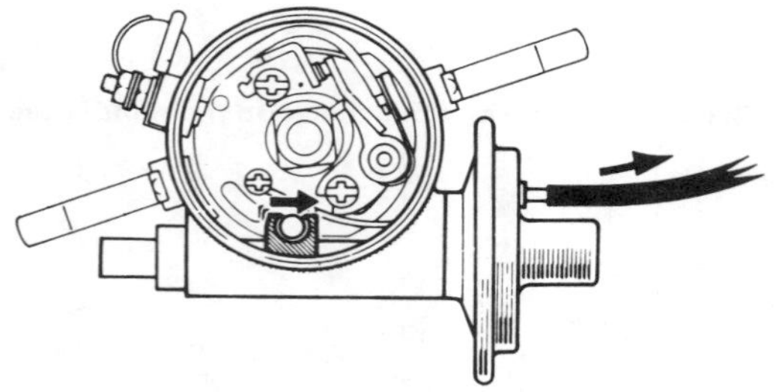
Fig. 3.142 Distributor vacuum advancer check (Sec 34)

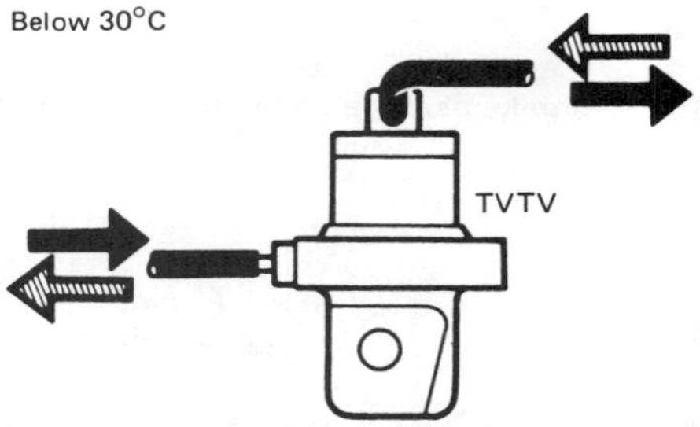

Fig. 3.143 Check for unrestricted air flow through the TVTV unit in both directions – 2T engine (Sec 34)

Fig. 3.144 VTV unit check – 4K engine (Sec 34)

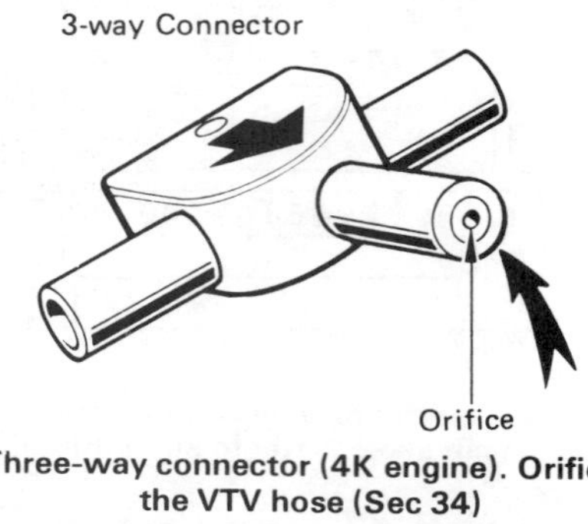

Fig. 3.145 Three-way connector (4K engine). Orifice connects to the VTV hose (Sec 34)

35 Automatic choke system

1 An automatic choke system is fitted to the carburettor on 2T engines and 3T-C engines. This device is mounted on the side of the carburettor and combines an electrically heated bi-metal coil which expands and contracts to close and open the choke in a progressive manner according to the engine temperature.
2 The system circuit is shown in Fig. 3.146.
3 On the 2T engine and 3T-C engine fitted to Canadian models, the choke is adjustable by loosening off the three retainer plate screws and rotating the choke coil housing in the desired direction, clockwise to weaken, anti-clockwise to richen the choke mixture. This should not normally be necessary and the single marking on the coil housing should align with the central graduation on the choke body.
4 On the 3T-C engine fitted to USA models the choke differs and is not adjustable.
5 To check the choke for operation, start the engine (cold) and after a few moments feel the choke housing for warmth. With the air cleaner cover removed the choke valve should be seen to start to open. If the choke is malfunctioning have it checked by your Toyota dealer as the heating coil in the unit is most probably defective.

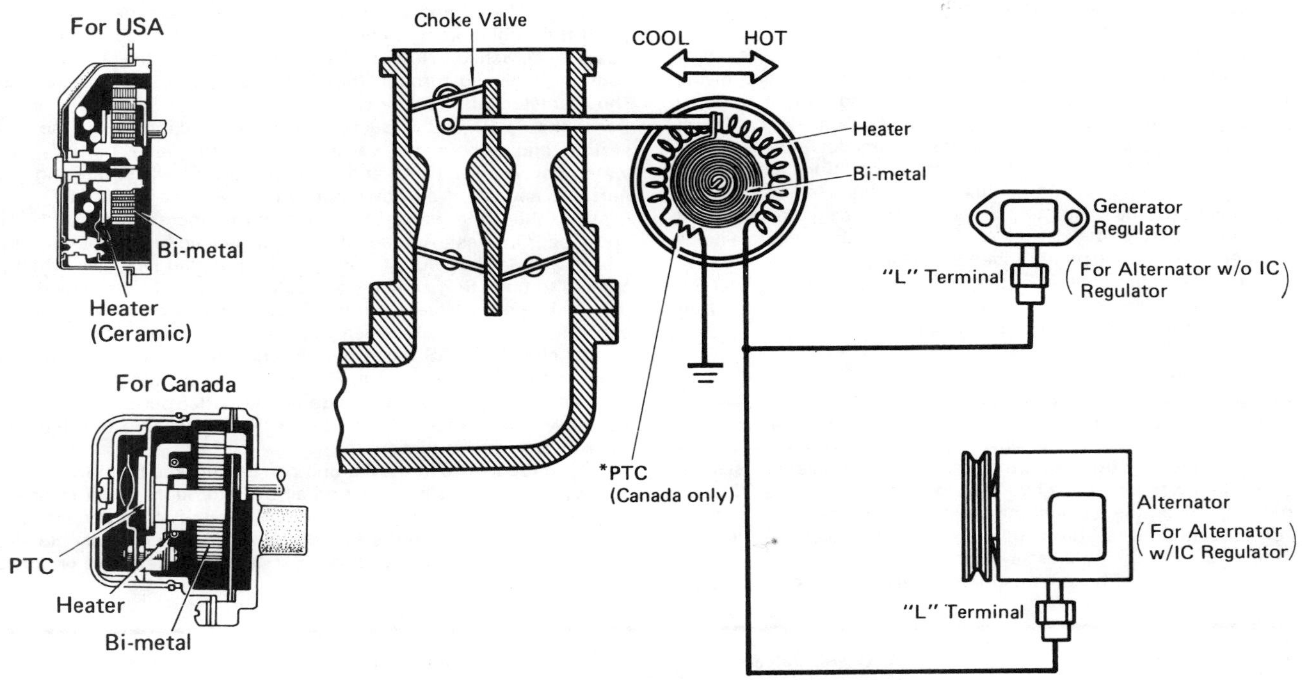

Fig. 3.146 Automatic choke system (Sec 35)

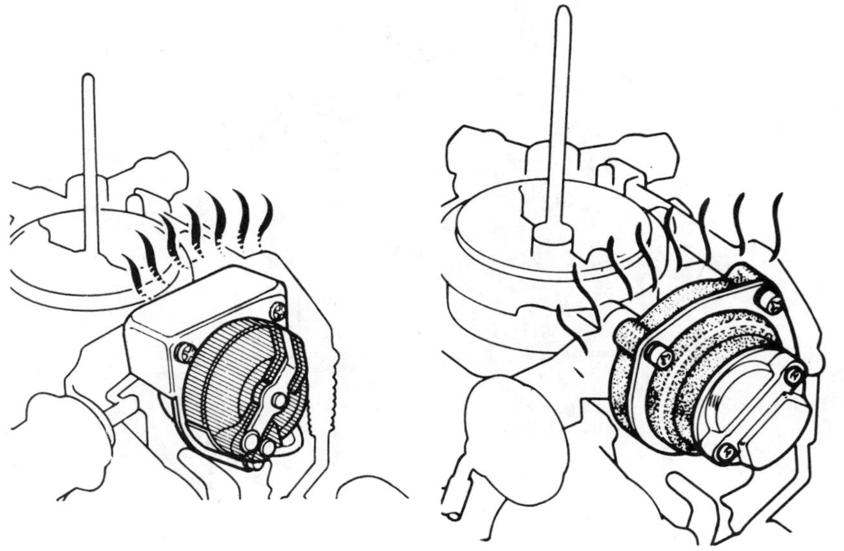

Fig. 3.147 Automatic choke housing types, USA (left), UK and Canada type (right). Check their operation by feeling them for warmth (Sec 35)

36 Air injection (AI) with feedback system – description and maintenance

1 This relatively complex system is fitted to USA models only and the system layout is shown in Figure 3.148.
2 Briefly described, the system injects air, by means of a belt-driven air pump into an air injection manifold mounted above the exhaust manifold. The air in the air injection manifold is then fed under pressure into the respective exhaust manifold ports through check valves (one for each port). The injected air then mixes with the hot exhaust gases to promote burning of the unburned hydrocarbons and carbon monoxide.
3 The air supply from the air pump is regulated by an oxygen sensor fitted to the exhaust manifold. When air is not required from the air pump it is diverted into the air cleaner unit.
4 The oxygen sensor relays information to the computer unit which in turn is also receiving information fed from a thermo-switch giving the engine coolant temperature, the ignition coil and a thermo-sensor for the three-way catalyst (TWC) in the exhaust system. The computer then actuates the respective vacuum control and switching valves according to engine temperature and operating conditions to open and close the air supply and vacuum circuits within the system.
5 Maintenance of the system consists of periodically checking the conditon and security of the air and vacuum hoses, the electrical leads of the system and the air pump drivebelt tension.
6 Should a malfunction occur in the system, apart from making the above mentioned checks, the system should be checked by your Toyota dealer to find the cause of the problem.

37 Air suction (AS) system – description and maintenance

1 This system is only fitted to Canadian market models. The system is designed to lower emissions by drawing air through the air filter to be burned directly in the exhaust manifold. This fresh air helps to burn some of the unburned hydrocarbons before being released to the atmosphere through the exhaust system (Fig. 3.149).
2 The system only becomes operational above a crankcase temperature of 66°F (19°C). It is then dependent on the throttle movement and consequent vacuum.
3 Maintenance consists of checking the hoses for signs of deterioration and security. The system components can be checked as follows.
4 The TVTV (thermostatic vacuum transmitting valve) can be checked when the engine is cold, coolant temperature under the 46°F (8°C), by disconnecting the AS (air suction) hose from the air cleaner unit. With the engine idling listen through the hose for a bubbling sound coming from the AS hose. If you can hear a bubbling sound then the TVTV or AS valve is defective and should be renewed.
5 Warm up the engine and make the above check again. This time the bubbling from the valve should be heard when the engine is idling (Fig. 3.150).
6 To check the TVTV valve, detach the AS valve to TVTV unit hose (at the TVTV end) and, listening through the air cleaner hose as before (with the engine idling), check that the bubbling sound stops as the hose is detached. Now reattach the hose to the TVTV unit and continue listening through the air cleaner hose. The bubbling sound should restart after a few seconds.
7 If the TVTV unit is suspected of malfunction, drain the cooling system and remove the valve. Immerse the valve partially in cold water, below 46°F (8°C) and close off port (S) whilst blowing though port (M) and see if air flows out of port (A) (see Fig. 3.152).
8 Now heat the water to a minimum temperature of 66°F (19°C) and repeat the test. Air should not now be able to flow out of port (A), but air should flow out of port (S) when unplugged. Also when air is applied to port (S) it should exit freely from port (M). Renew the TVTV unit if defective. When refitting it apply sealant to the threads and check for signs of leaks when the cooling system is topped up.
9 To check the AS valve detach and remove it and then apply a vacuum to the chamber B in Fig. 3.153. Air should not flow through the unit from the air cleaner side to the outlet ports.
10 Now blow through the air cleaner port to ensure that the applied air exits from the outlet ports.
11 The reed valve in the AS unit can be checked by blowing into the outlet pipes and ensuring that no air exits through the air cleaner port (Fig. 3.154). Renew the AS valve unit if found to be defective.
12 The AS air filter on the side of the air cleaner case should also be periodically checked and cleaned (Fig. 3.155). If defective or damaged then this must be renewed.

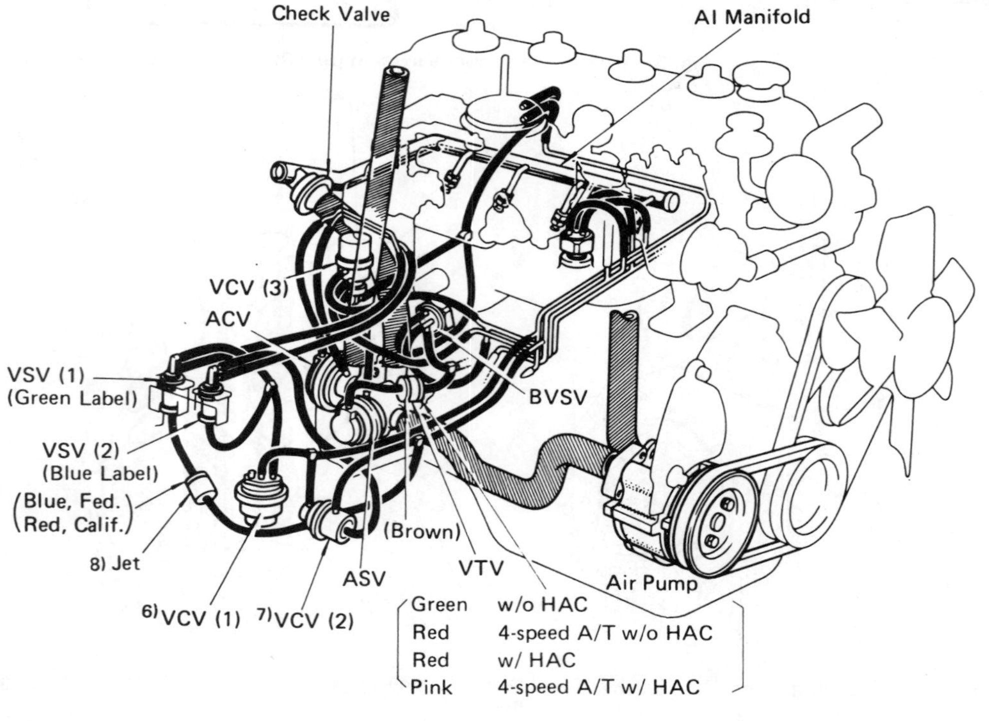

Fig. 3.148 Air injector with feedback system (USA models) (Sec 36)

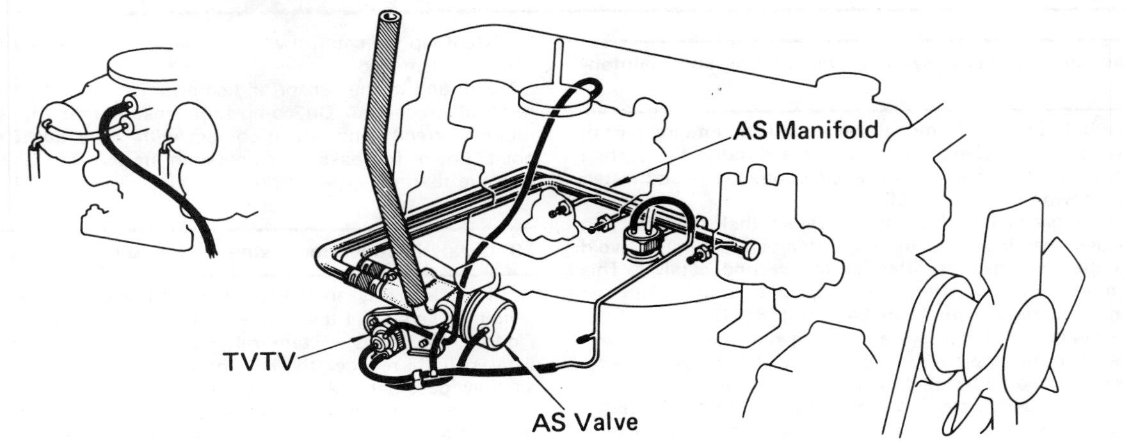

Fig. 3.149 Air suction (AS) system (Canada models) (Sec 37)

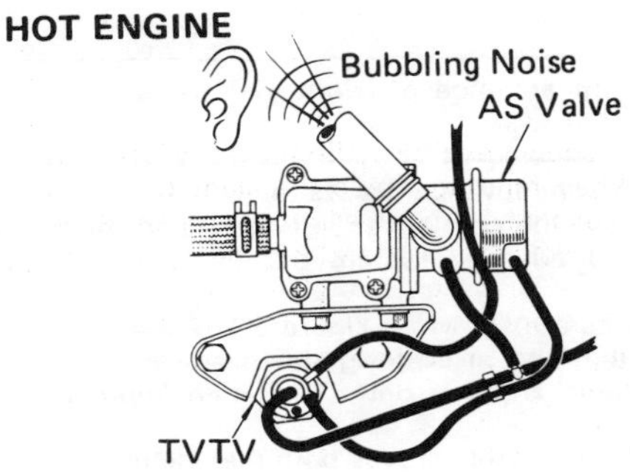

Fig. 3.150 TVTV and AS valve check with warm engine (Sec 37)

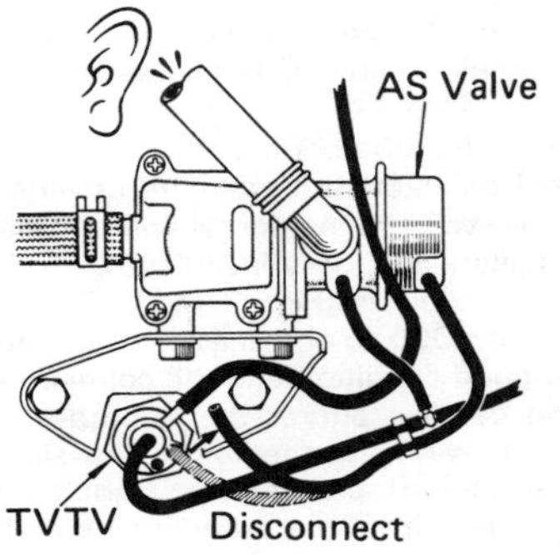

Fig. 3.151 Detach hose indicated to test TVTV unit (Sec 37)

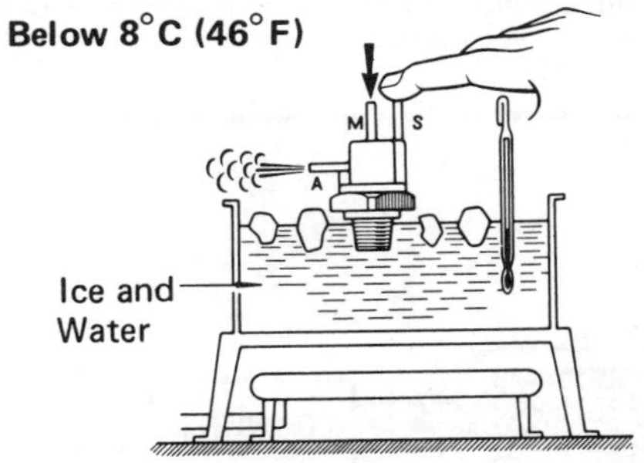

Fig. 3.152 TVTV valve airflow check in cold water (Sec 37)

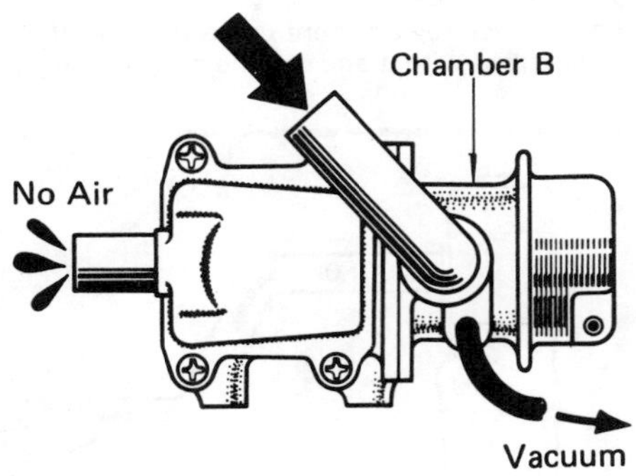

Fig. 3.153 AS valve check (Sec 37)

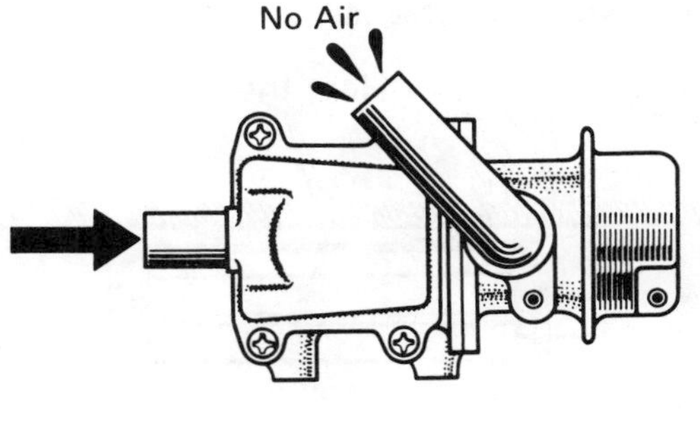

Fig. 3.154 AS reed valve check (Sec 37)

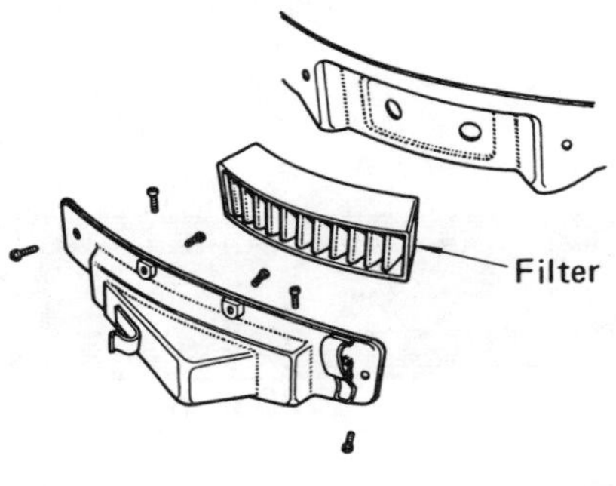

Fig. 3.155 AS air filter location on side of air cleaner case (Sec 37)

38 Three-way catalyst (TWC) system – description and maintenance

1 This device is fitted to USA models only and is an integral part of the exhaust system. As the exhaust gases pass through the system they are oxidized and converted to nitrogen, carbon dioxide and water. The system is shown in Figure 3.156.
2 As the exhaust gases pass through the system, their oxidation and reduction causes an increase in their temperature. To avoid overheating a thermo-sensor is fitted to the second catalyst. This switches off the air induction into the exhaust system should the temperature in the catalyst rise above 1445°F (785°C).
3 When checking the exhaust system during the routine maintenance at the specified mileage intervals the following additional checks on the TWC system should be made when the system is cool.
4 Check the respective system connections and components for signs of damage or excessive deterioration. Make a careful inspection of the number two catalyst for damage or dents. Any dent beyond a depth of 0.79 in (20 mm) necessitates renewal of the catalyst. The catalyst should also be shaken to see if it rattles. If it does rattle then it must be renewed (Fig. 3.157).
5 Check that the heat insulator above the catalyst is in good condition and that a suitable clearance exists between the catalyst and the insulator.
6 The thermo-sensor should be periodically checked by unplugging the thermo-sensor lead connection (under the driver's seat) and the resistance between the two connector terminals tested using an ohmmeter with the engine idling. Only insert the ohmmeter probes on the rear side of the connector (Fig. 3.159). There should be a resistance reading of 2 to 200 kilo ohms. At the same time check that the sensor wiring is in good condition and the connections are secure.
7 If the number two catalyst and/or the thermo-sensor are to be removed, disconnect the wiring connector to the sensor within the vehicle then raise and support the vehicle. Unbolt and detach the catalyst at the front and rear from the exhaust pipe and withdraw the catalyst and gaskets from the joint flanges. Only remove the catalyst when it is cool.
8 To remove the thermo-sensor, support the catalyst so that the sensor is uppermost then unbolt and withdraw the sensor from the catalyst. Remove the joint gasket.
9 When fitting a service replacement catalyst, insert the sensor into the plastic guide supplied with it and use the new gasket supplied (Fig. 3.160). Keep the catalyst with the sensor aperture upwards whilst the sensor is removed.
10 Refitting of the sensor and catalyst is otherwise a reversal of the removal procedure. On completion ensure that the sensor wire is routed correctly and not in contact with the exhaust system at any point. Check for leaks on completion around the catalyst joints and also the thermo-sensor joints.

39 Catalytic converter system – (Canadian market models)

This device is an integral part of the exhaust system and is a simplified version of the TWC system fitted to USA models. Shown in Figure 3.161, this system referred to by Toyota as the oxidation catalyst (OC), reduces the HC and CO contents of the exhaust gases as they pass through the system. No thermo-sensor is fitted and therefore the routine maintenance checks and when necessary the removal and refitting of the catalyst is simplified.

Refer to the previous Section, paragraphs 4 and 5 for the maintenance check procedures which are the same. The removal of the catalyst is also as given in the previous Section but ignore references to the thermo-sensor.

40 Double diaphragm advance distributor (USA and Canada) – description

1 The double diaphragm advance distributor is fitted to (a) USA and Canada models without the cold advance system and (b) to Canada models with the cold advance system but fitted with automatic transmission.
2 The system circuits are shown in Figure 3.162 and 3.163.
3 In instance (a) the system is designed to advance the ignition timing when the engine is idling only. This is to improve the fuel economy.
4 In instance (b) the system improves both the engine performance when cold and also the fuel economy by advancing the ignition timing when the engine is cold and idling.
5 With each system type the two diaphragms have differing vacuum advance characteristics.
6 Double diaphragm distributors are also used in conjunction with the high altitude control system (HAC) the details of which are given in Section 30 of this Chapter.

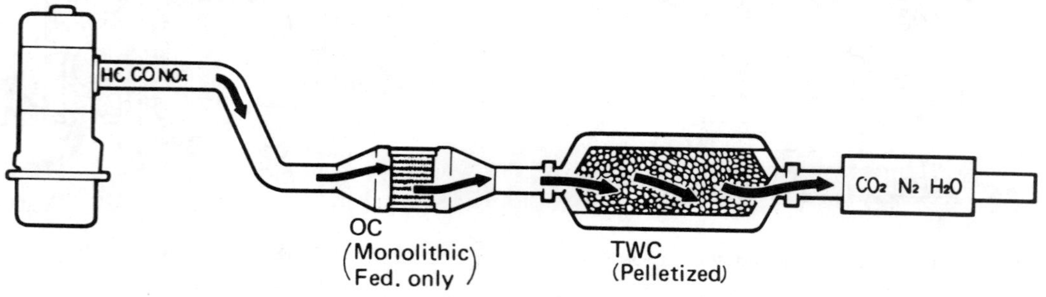

Fig. 3.156 Three-way catalyst system diagram (USA models) (Sec 38)

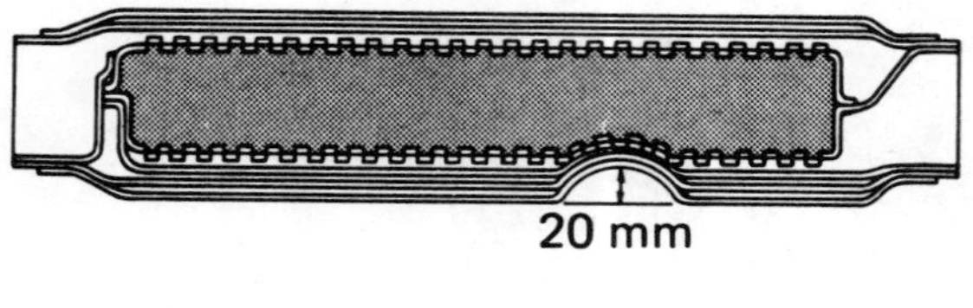

Fig. 3.157 Dents in catalyst must not exceed that shown (Sec 38)

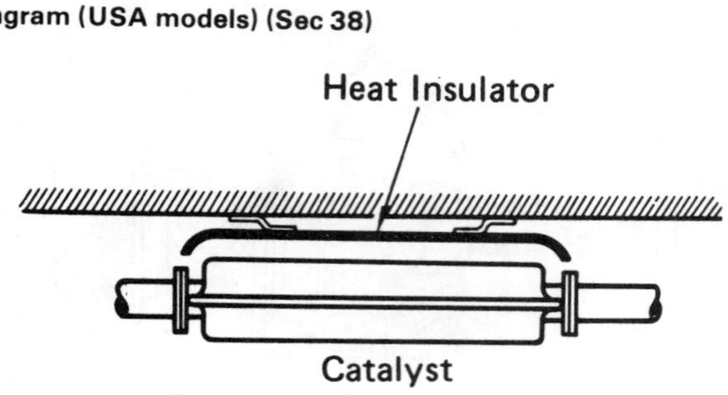

Fig. 3.158 Check insulator clearance and condition (Sec 38)

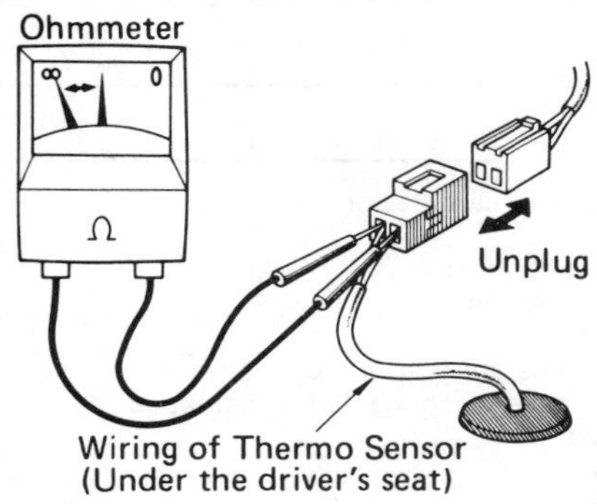

Fig. 3.159 Thermo-sensor check (Sec 38)

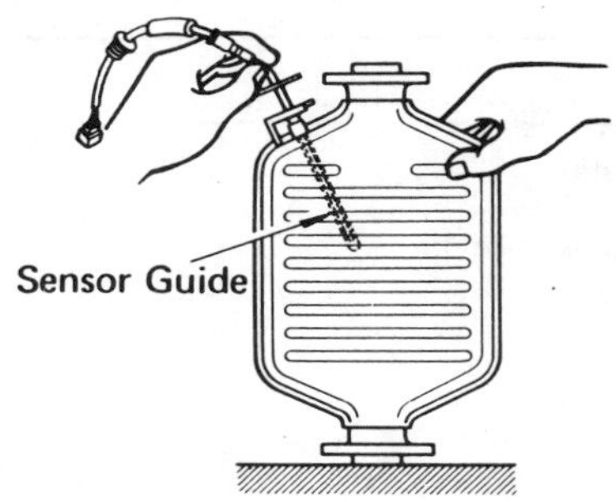

Fig. 3.160 Inserting sensor into plastic guide (Sec 38)

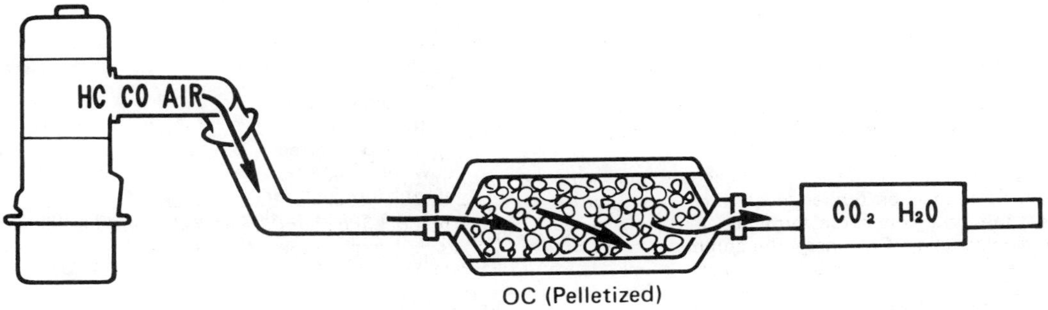

Fig. 3.161 Catalytic converter system – Canadian models (Sec 39)

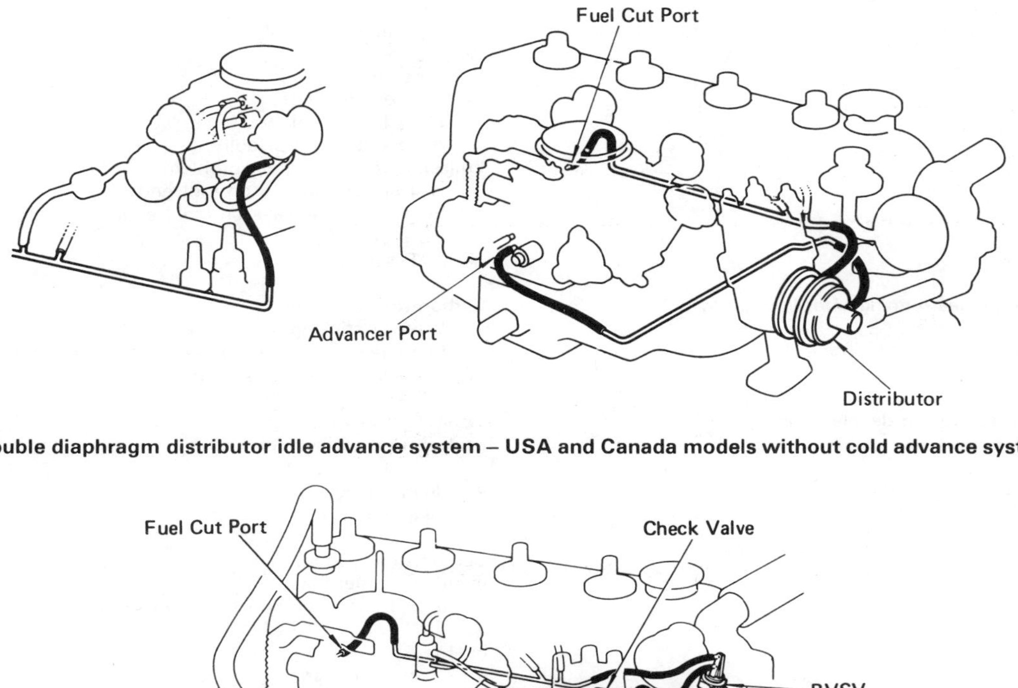

Fig. 3.162 Double diaphragm distributor idle advance system – USA and Canada models without cold advance system (Sec 40)

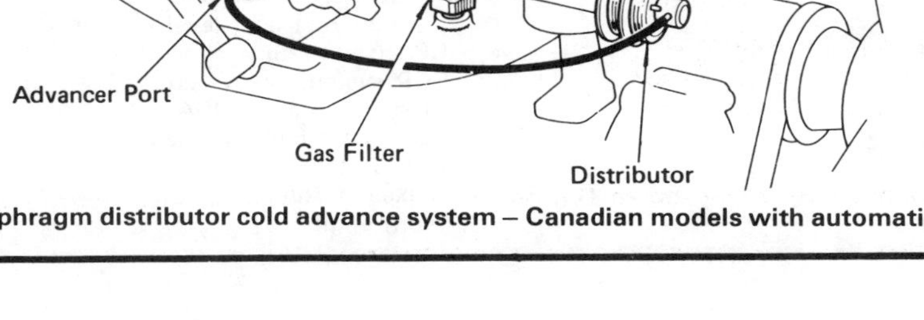

Fig. 3.163 Double diaphragm distributor cold advance system – Canadian models with automatic transmission (Sec 40)

41 Fault diagnosis – Fuel, exhaust and emission control systems

Symptom	Reason(s)
Engine will not start	No fuel supply to carburettor

Hard to start (cranks okay)	Carburettor problems:
	    Choke operation
	    Flooding
	    Needle valve sticking or clogged
	    Vacuum hose disconnected or damaged
	Vacuum leaks:
	    PCV line
	    EGR line
	    Inlet manifold

Rough idle or stalls	Vacuum leaks:
	    PCV line
	    EGR line
	    HIC line
	    HAC line
	    Inlet manifold leak
	Carburettor problems:
	    Idle speed incorrect
	    Slow jet clogged
	    Idle mixture incorrect
	    Fast idle speed setting incorrect (cold engine)
	HAI system fault
	EGR valve faulty

Engine hesitates/poor acceleration	Vacuum leaks:
	    PCV line
	    EGR line
	    HAC line
	    HIC line
	    Inlet manifold leak
	Air cleaner clogged
	Fuel line clogged
	Carburettor problems:
	    Float level too low
	    Accelerator pump faulty
	Emission control system problem:
	    HAI system always on (hot engine)
	    EGR system always on (cold engine)
	    SC system faulty
	    AAP system fault

Engine dieseling (continues running after ignition switch is turned off)	Carburettor problems:
	    Linkage sticking
	    Idle speed or fast idle speed out of adjustment
	TP (Throttle-positioner) system faulty

Muffler explosion (after fire) on deceleration only	TP system always off Leak in exhaust system
Muffler explosion (after fire) all the time	Air cleaner clogged Exhaust system leak
Engine backfires	Carburettor vacuum leak Insufficient fuel flow Valve clearances/ignition timing incorrect

Poor petrol mileage	Fuel leak
	Air cleaner clogged
	Carburettor problems:
	    Choke faulty
	    Idle speed too high
	    Incorrect float level setting
	SC system faulty
	EGR system always on
	AI system faulty (USA only)
	AS system faulty (Canada)
	AAP system stuck on
	Brakes sticking
	Worn engine

Note: *The efficiency of the fume emission control system is also dependent upon the correct setting and adjustment of all other engine components. These include the ignition, cooling and lubrication systems, the valve clearances and the condition generally of the engine. Refer to the appropriate Sections and Chapters of this manual for servicing procedures.*

Chapter 4 Ignition system

Contents

Specifications

General

System type:	
4K, 2T and 2T–B engines (UK models)	Conventional contact breaker and coil ignition
3T–C engines (USA and Canada models)	Electronic breakerless ignition
Firing order	1 – 3 – 4 – 2

Distributor

4K, 2T and 2T–B engines:	
Rubbing block gap	0.018 in (0.45 mm)
Dwell angle	52°
Damping spring gap (2T and 2T–B engines)	0.004 to 0.016 in (0.1 to 0.4 mm)
Governor shaft thrust clearance	0.006 to 0.020 in (0.15 to 0.50 mm)
3T–C engine:	
Air gap	0.008 to 0.016 in (0.2 to 0.4 mm)
Governor shaft thrust clearance	0.006 to 0.020 in (0.15 to 0.50 mm)

Ignition timing (at idling speed, vacuum advance hose disconnected):

4K engine	8° BTDC
2T and 2T–B engines	10° BTDC
3T–C engine:	
USA models	7° BTDC
Canada models	10° BTDC

Spark plugs

Type:	
4K engine	Nippon-Denso W16EPR or W16EXR-U NGK BPR5EY or BPR5EA-L
2T and 2T–B engines	Nippon-Denso W16EPR or W16EXR-U NGK BP5ES-L, BPR5ES or BPR5EA-L
3T–C engine:	
USA (except California)	Nippon-Denso W16EXR-U11 or W14EXR-U11 NGK BPR5EA-L11, BPR5EY11, BPR5EA11 or BPR4EY11
USA (California)	Nippon-Denso W16EXR-U11 NGK BPR5EA-L11 or BPR5EA11
Canada	Nippon-Denso W16EPR, W16EXR-U or W14EXR-U NGK BPR5ES, BPR5EA-L, BPR5EA, BPR4EY or BPR5EY

Electrode gap:	
4K, 2T and 2T–B engines	0.031 in (0.8 mm)
3T–C engine:	
USA models	0.043 in (1.1 mm)
Canada models	0.031 in (0.8 mm)

Ignition coil

4K engine:	
Primary resistance	1.2 to 1.5 ohms
Secondary resistance	8 to 12 k ohms
External ballast resistance	1.3 to 1.5 ohms
2T and 2T–B engines:	
Primary resistance	1.3 to 1.5 ohms
Secondary resistance	7.2 to 9.8 k ohms
External ballast resistance	1.3 to 1.7 ohms
3T–C engine:	
Primary resistance	0.8 to 1.1 ohms
Secondary resistance	11.5 to 15.5 ohms

Torque wrench settings

	lbf ft	kgf m
Spark plugs	11 to 15	1.5 to 2.1
Distributor clamp bolt	11 to 15	1.5 to 2.1

1 General description

Toyota Corolla models covered by this manual are equipped with either a conventional contact breaker ignition system (UK models) or an electronic breakerless system (USA and Canada models). A description of the operation of the two types is given below.

Conventional ignition

The ignition system consists of several components, the battery, the ignition/starter switch, the coil, the distributor and the spark plugs. Low and high tension wires connect the various components.

The coil acts as a transformer to step up the 12 volt battery voltage to many thousands of volts, sufficient to jump the spark plug gaps.

The distributor consists of a contact breaker, condenser, rotor arm, distributor cap with brush, and centrifugal and vacuum advance and retard mechanism, and is driven by the oil pump driveshaft or camshaft at half crankshaft speed.

The spark plugs ignite the compressed mixture in the combustion chambers.

When the ignition is switched on, a current flows from the battery to the ignition switch, through the coil primary winding to the moving contact breaker inside the distributor cap and to earth when the contact breaker points are in the closed position. During this period of points closure, the current flows through the primary winding of the coil and magnetises the laminated iron core which in turn creates a magnetic field through the coil primary and secondary windings.

Each time the points open due to the rotation of the distributor cam, the current flow through the primary winding of the coil is interrupted. This causes the induction of a very high voltage (25,000 volts) in the coil secondary winding. This HT (high tension) current is distributed to the spark plugs in correct firing order sequence by the

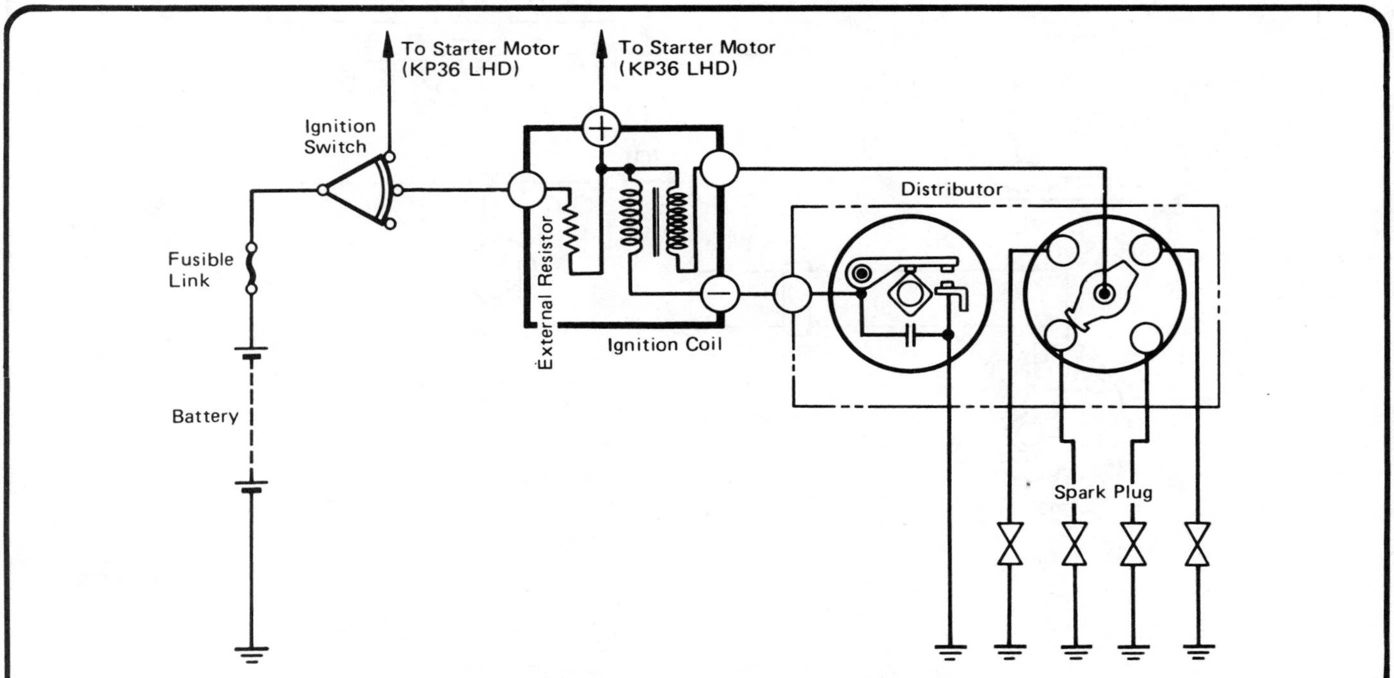

Fig. 4.1 Ignition system circuit – 4K engine (Sec 1)

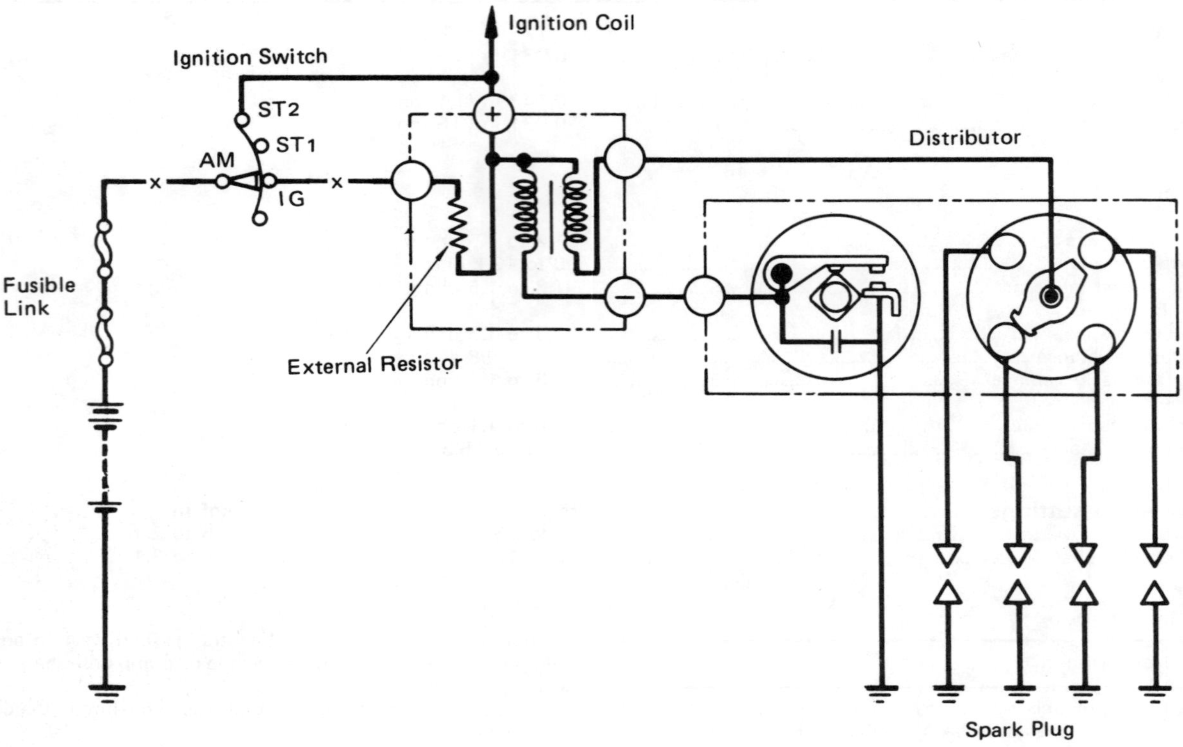

Fig. 4.2 Ignition system circuit – 2T and 2T-B engines (Sec 1)

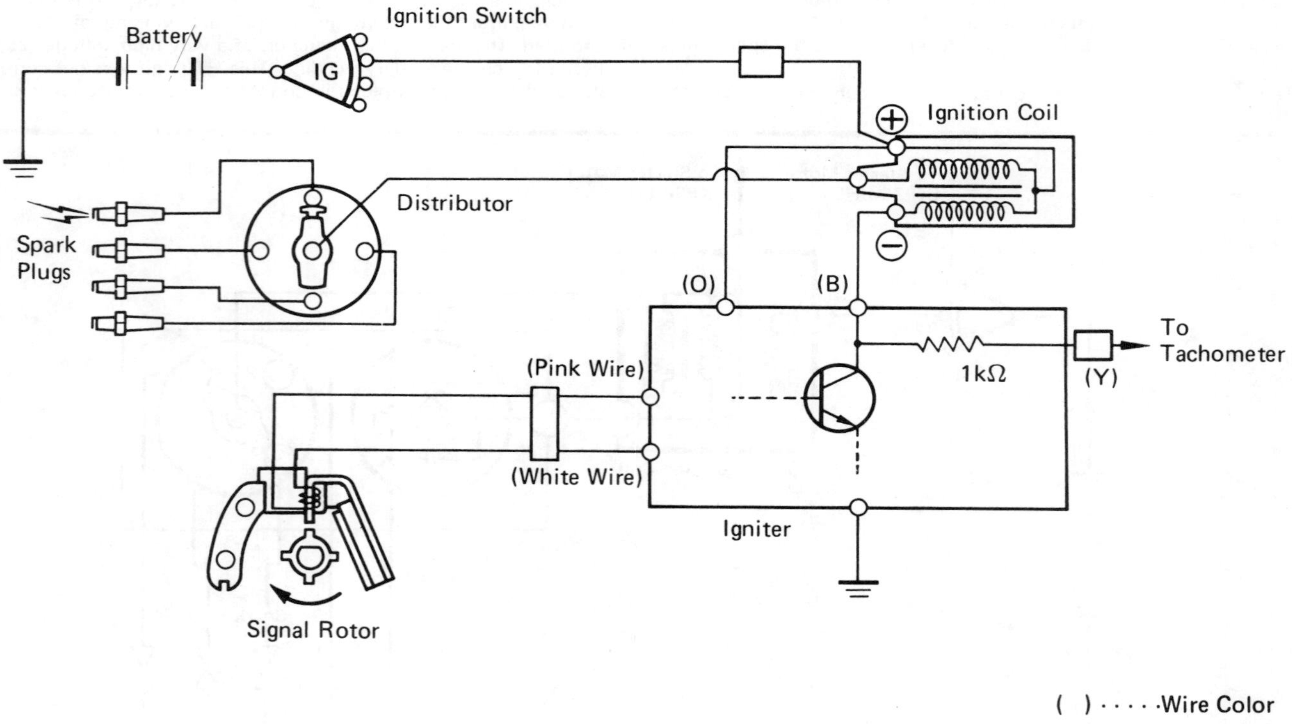

Fig. 4.3 Ignition system circuit – 3T-C engine (Sec 1)

rotor arm and by means of the cap brush and HT leads.

A condenser is fitted to the distributor, and is connected between the moving contact breaker and earth. It prevents excessive arcing and pitting of the contact breaker points, and also assists in the rapid breakdown of the coil magnetic field.

The actual point of ignition of the fuel/air mixture which occurs a few degrees before TDC is determined by correct static setting of the ignition timing as described in Section 8. The ignition is advanced to meet varying operating conditions by the centrifugal counterweights fitted in the base of the distributor body and by vacuum from the inlet manifold operating through a capsule linked to the movable distributor baseplate.

Electronic ignition

The electronic ignition system functions in a similar manner to that of the conventional type previously described, but instead of having contact breaker points fitted to the distributor, a signal generator is used and this operates in conjunction with a device known as an igniter. The system operates as follows.

The low tension (primary) circuit consists of the battery, lead to the ignition switch, lead from the ignition switch to the low tension or primary coil windings (terminal +), and the lead from the low tension coil windings (coil terminal –), to the igniter, through the signal generator (pick-up coil), through a resistor and back to the igniter.

The high tension circuit consists of the high tension or secondary coil windings, the heavy ignition lead from the centre of the coil to the centre of the distributor cap, the rotor arm, and the spark plug leads and spark plugs.

The system functions in the following manner. Low tension voltage is changed in the coil into high tension voltage breaking a magnetic field in the low tension circuit. High tension voltage is then fed via the carbon brush in the centre of the distributor cap to the rotor arm of the distributor. Each time the rotor arm comes in line with one of the four metal segments in the cap, which are connected to the spark plug leads, breaking a magnetic field causes the high tension voltage to build up, jump the gap from the rotor arm to the appropriate metal segment and so via the spark plug lead to the spark plug where it finally jumps the spark plug gap before going to earth.

The advantages of the electronic system are that there is no contact breaker to adjust or maintain, low speed performance is improved and cold starting under adverse weather conditions is less likely to be affected.

Certain precautions must be observed with an electronic ignition system.

(a) Do not disconnect the battery leads when the engine is running
(b) Make sure that the igniter is always well grounded (earthed)
(c) Keep water away from the igniter and distributor
(d) If a tachometer is to be connected to the engine, always connect the tachometer (+) terminal to the ignition coil (–) terminal; never to the distributor
(e) Do not allow the coil terminals to be earthed (grounded) – the igniter and/or coil could be damaged
(f) Do not leave the ignition switch on for more than ten minutes if the engine isn't running

As with conventional ignition distributors a mechanical and vacuum advance system is used, but on some models a dual diaphragm vacuum unit is used. These are known as the main diaphragm which operates in a normal manner and a sub-diaphragm unit. Their purpose is to advance the ignition timing on models fitted with an Idle Advance System (to increase the fuel economy when the engine is idling) and for a High Altitude Control System (to improve performance at high altitude).

2 Contact breaker points – adjustment

1 To adjust the contact breaker points to the correct gap first release the two clips securing the distributor cap to the distributor body, and lift away the cap. Clean the cap inside, and out, with a dry cloth. It is unlikely that the four segments will be badly burned or scored, but if they are the cap will have to be renewed. On some distributors, a moisture proof cover is fitted which must be released before the distributor cap can be removed (photo).

2 Inspect the contact located in the centre of the cap and make sure it is serviceable.

3 Lift off the rotor arm and dust proof cover. Gently prise the contact breaker points open and examine the condition of their faces. If they are rough, pitted or dirty it will be necessary to remove them for refacing or a replacement set to be fitted.

4 Presuming that the points are satisfactory, or that they have been cleaned and refitted, check the breaker points clearance and if necessary adjust as follows.

5 Turn the engine over by hand until the points are closed and the rubbing block of the moving point arm is midway between two of the distributor cam peaks.

6 Using a feeler gauge equal to the specified rubbing block gap, measure the clearance between the rubbing block and the flat of the cam (Figs. 4.4 and 4.5).

7 If adjustment is necessary, slacken the adjuster/securing screws and move the points as necessary until the feeler gauge is a sliding fit

2.1 Distributor cap removal – 2T engine

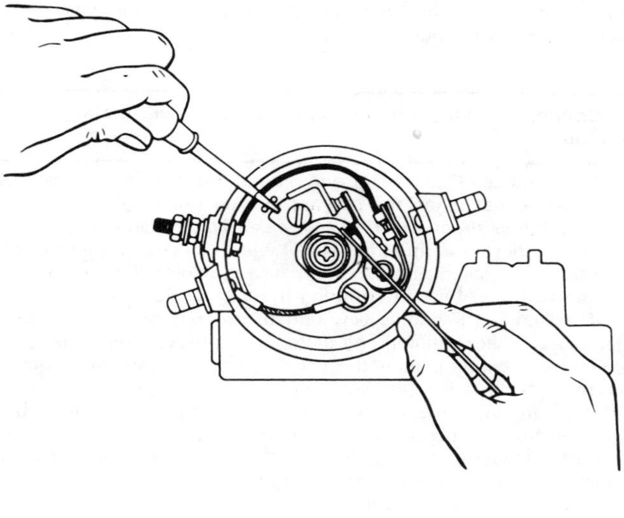

Fig. 4.4 Check the rubbing block gap clearance – 4K engine (Sec 2)

between the cam and rubbing block. Hold the points in this position and tighten the screws.
8 On 2T and 2T–B engine models the damping spring gap should also be checked and if necessary adjusted as follows.
9 Turn the engine over by hand until the rubbing block of the damping spring is midway between two of the cam peaks.
10 Using the same procedure as for the contact breaker points, check and if necessary adjust the clearance between the cam and damping spring rubbing block (Fig. 4.6).
11 On completion refit the dust cover, rotor arm and distributor cap.

3 Contact breaker points – renewal

1 If the contact breaker points are burned, pitted or badly worn they must be removed and renewed.
2 With the distributor cap removed lift off the rotor arm by pulling it straight up from the spindle. Also remove the dust cover.
3 Detach the contact breaker points lead from the LT terminal on the side of the distributor body. Release the terminal nuts to do this.
4 Extract the two securing screws which hold the contact breaker arm to the distributor baseplate. Note that an earth lead is retained by one of these screws.
5 Lift the contact breaker set from the distributor.
6 If the contact points are only lightly pitted or burred they can be cleaned up using fine abrasive paper and used again. Severe burning or pitting will mean renewal of the contact breaker assembly.
7 Consistent severe burning or pitting of the points may mean that the condenser is faulty (see Section 5) or that one of the engine earth bonds is loose or that one of the distributor baseplate or earth lead screws requires tightening.
8 Refitting is a reversal of removal, set the points gap and check the dwell angle as described in Section 4.

4 Dwell angle – checking

1 On modern engines, setting the distributor contact breaker gap with feeler blades must only be considered an initial step to get the engine running. For optimum engine performance, the dwell angle must always be checked as soon as possible.
2 The dwell angle is the number of degrees through which the distributor cam turns between the closure and opening of the contact breaker points. It can only be checked using a dwell meter.
3 Connect the dwell meter in accordance with the maker's instructions (usually between the negative LT terminal on the coil and a good earth) and with the engine running at the specified idling speed, check the dwell angle on the meter.
4 If the dwell angle is larger than that specified, switch off the engine and increase the points gap, if it is too much, decrease the gap. Recheck the dwell angle.

5 Condenser (conventional ignition) – removal, testing and refitting

1 The purpose of the condenser, (sometimes known as a capacitor) is to ensure that when the contact breaker points open there is no sparking across them which would waste voltage and cause wear.
2 The condenser is fitted in parallel with the contact breaker points. If it develops a short circuit, it will cause ignition failure as the points will be prevented from interrupting the low tension circuit.
3 If the engine becomes very difficult to start or begins to misfire after several miles running and the contact breaker points show signs of excessive burning, then the condition of the condenser must be suspect. A further test can be made by separating the points by hand with the ignition switched on. If this is accompanied by a flash it is indicative that the condenser has failed.
4 Without special test equipment the only sure way to diagnose condenser trouble is to replace a suspected unit with a new one and note if there is any improvement.
5 To remove a condenser from the distributor take off the distributor cap to give better access.
6 Detach the condenser lead from the terminal block.
7 Undo and remove the screw and washer securing the condenser to the distributor body. Lift away the condenser and lead (photo).
8 Refitting the condenser is the reverse sequence to removal.

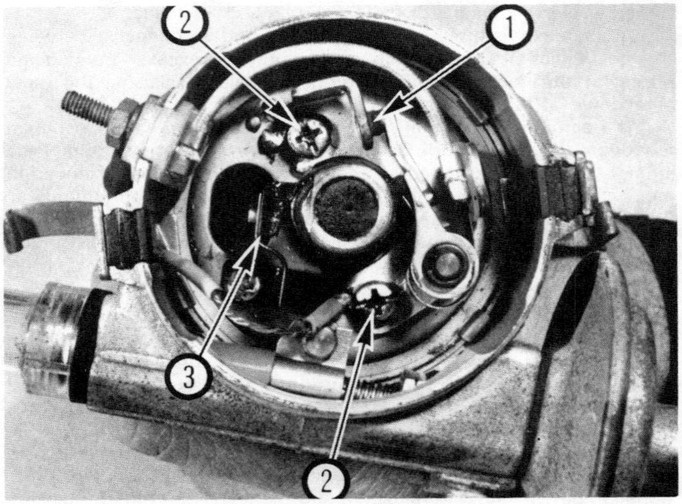

2.7 Distributor contact breaker points (1), adjuster/securing screws (2) and damper spring unit (3) – 2T engine

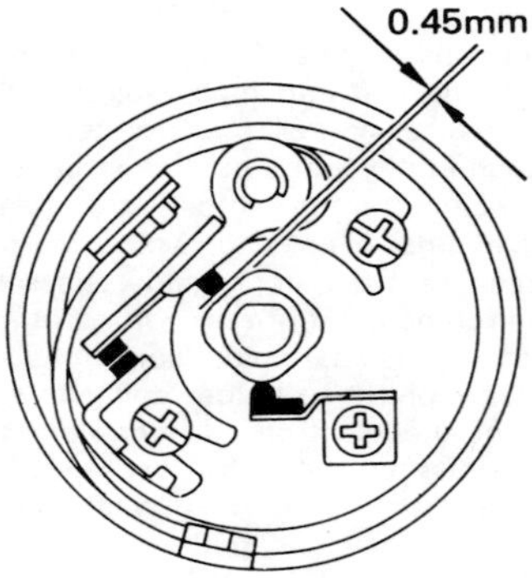

Fig. 4.5 Check the rubbing block gap clearance – 2T and 2T-B engines (Sec 2)

Fig. 4.6 Damper spring adjustment – 2T and 2T-B engines (Sec 2)

5.7 Condenser location – 2T engine

6 Signal generator adjustment (electronic ignition)

1 To adjust the air gap to the correct distance first release the two screws or clips securing the distributor cap to the distributor body, and lift away the cap. Clean the cap inside, and out, with a dry cloth. It is unlikely that the four segments will be badly burned or scored, but if they are the cap will have to be renewed.
2 Inspect the contact located in the centre of the cap and make sure it is serviceable.
3 Lift off the rotor arm and dust proof cover.
4 Turn the engine over by hand until one of the signal rotor limbs is directly in line with the head of the signal generator.
5 Using feeler gauges check that the air gap between the signal rotor limb and signal generator is as given in the Specifications (Fig. 4.7).
6 If adjustment is necessary, slacken the signal generator retaining screws and move the unit as necessary until the specified clearance is obtained. Tighten the retaining screws.
7 After adjustment refit the dust cover, rotor and distributor cap.

7 Distributor – removal and refitting

1 Release the distributor cap retaining springs or on later 3T-C engine models, remove the two cap securing screws, then lift the distributor cap clear complete with leads and place to one side out of the way.
2 Disconnect the LT lead from the terminal on the side of the distributor body.
3 Disconnect the vacuum pipe(s) from the distributor diaphragm capsule (photo).
4 Unscrew and remove the bolt which holds the distributor clamp to the cylinder block and then withdraw the distributor from the engine (photos).
5 When refitting the distributor it is essential that it is accurately repositioned to ensure the correct timing adjustment. To do this on the 4K engine models, remove the No 1 spark plug and turn the engine over until the No 1 piston is felt to be rising on its compression stroke. This can be felt by pressing your thumb over the exposed plug hole and the compression will be felt on the correct stroke.
6 On 2T, 2T–B and 3T–C engine models the spark plugs are too deeply recessed to check the No 1 compression stroke in this manner and unless you can improvise with a suitable compression tester or possibly a plastic tube or similar, you will need to remove the rocker cover to check the No 1 cylinder valve actions. The No 1 valves (inlet and exhaust) will be fully closed when the No 1 piston is on its compression stroke.
7 When the No 1 piston is on its compression stroke, continue turning the crankshaft until the timing mark notch on the crankshaft pulley is aligned with the appropriate BTDC timing mark on the timing cover for your particular model as given in the Specifications, (Fig. 4.8).
8 The oil pump driveshaft must now be correctly positioned. On the 4K engine the slot in the top of the oil pump driveshaft must be

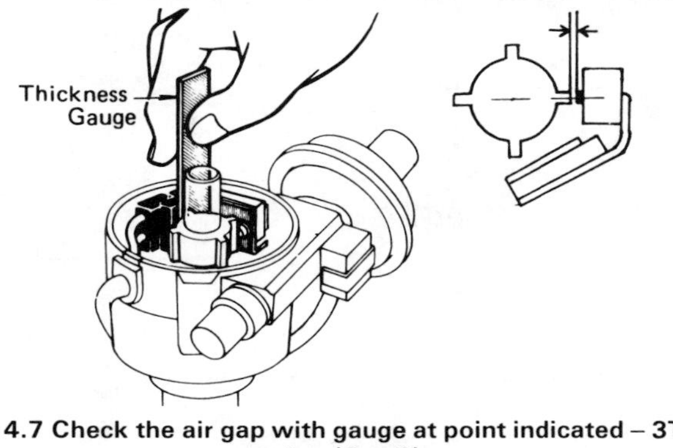

Fig. 4.7 Check the air gap with gauge at point indicated – 3T-C engine (Sec 6)

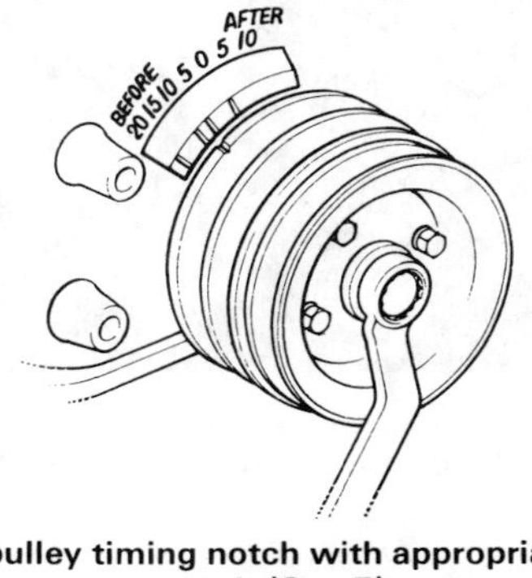

Fig. 4.8 Align pulley timing notch with appropriate BTDC timing mark (Sec 7)

7.3 Disconnect the diaphragm unit vacuum pipe – 2T engine

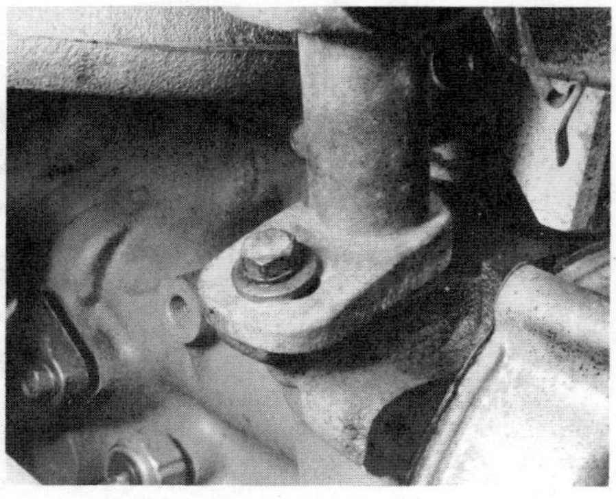

7.4a Unscrew the retaining bolt ...

7.4b ... then withdraw the distributor – 2T engine

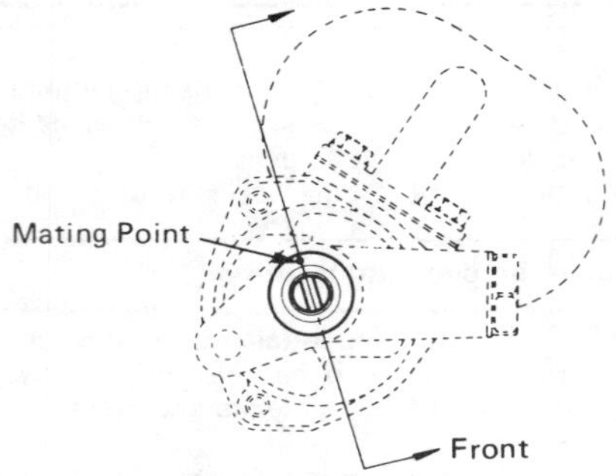

Fig. 4.9 4K engine distributor installation – align the oil pump driveshaft slot as shown (Sec 7)

Fig. 4.10 2T, 2T-B and 3T-C engine distributor installation – align the oil pump driveshaft slot as shown (Sec 7)

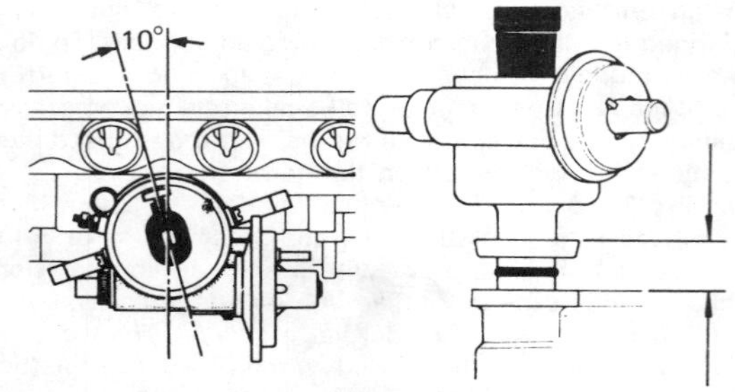

Fig. 4.11 Distributor pre-fitting position showing rotor alignment – 4K engine (Sec 7)

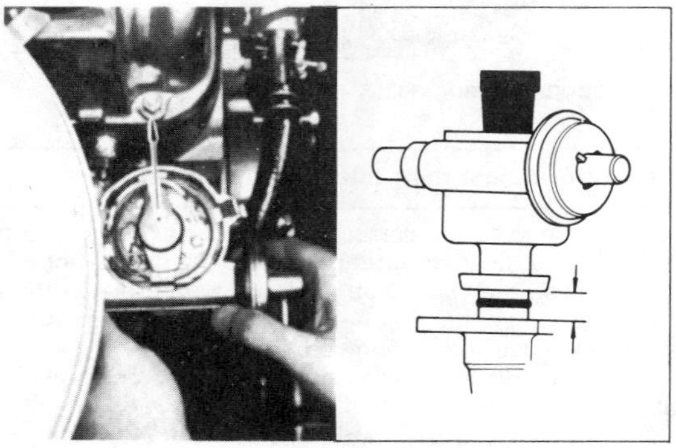

Fig. 4.12 Distributor pre-fitting position showing rotor alignment – 2T and 2T-B engines (Sec 7)

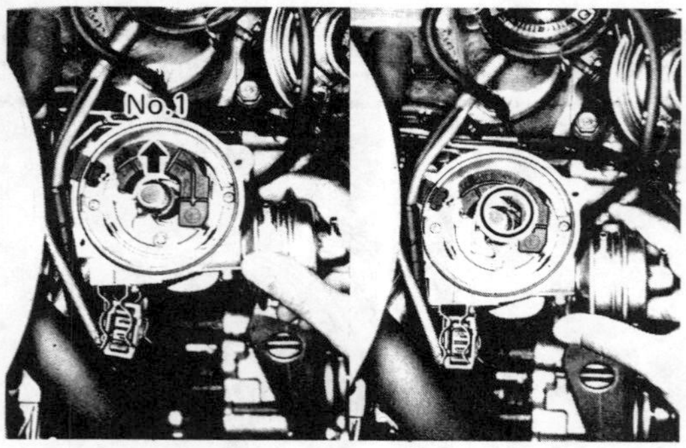

Fig. 4.13 Distributor pre-fitting and fitted position showing rotor alignment – 3T-C engine (Sec 7)

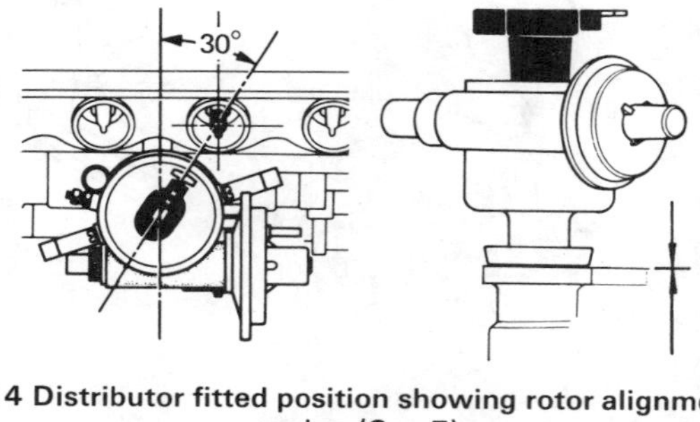

Fig. 4.14 Distributor fitted position showing rotor alignment – 4K engine (Sec 7)

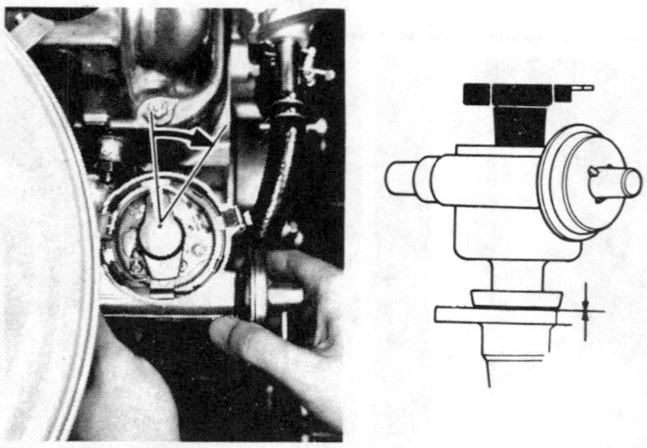

Fig. 4.15 Distributor fitted position showing rotor alignment – 2T and 2T-B engines (Sec 7)

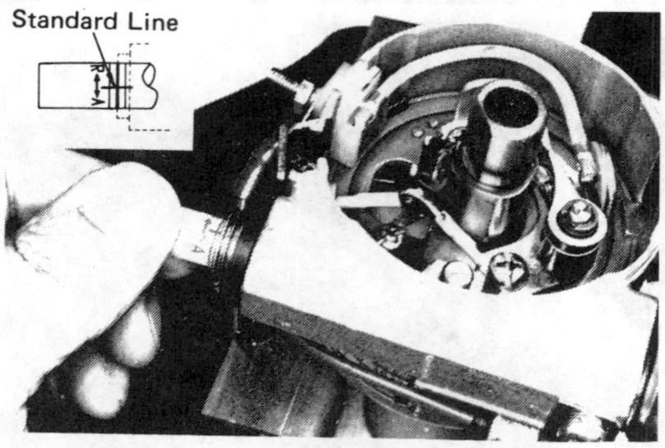

Fig. 4.16 Octane selector to be neutralized – 4K, 2T and 2T-B engines (Sec 7)

as shown in Fig. 4.9, with the slot centre line against the oil hole mark on top of the pump body. On 2T, 2T-B and 3T-C engine models the oil pump driveshaft slot must be positioned as shown in Fig. 4.10.
9 Before fitting the distributor into position, align the rotor according to engine type as shown in the accompanying diagrams, (Figs. 4.11, 4.12 & 4.13). Lower the distributor into position and engage with the slot in the oil gauge shaft.
10 When the distributor is fully fitted check that the rotor arm now points to the position shown for your engine type (Figs 4.13, 4.14 & 4.15). As the distributor is pushed down into position the rotor will turn to the positions shown.
11 With the distributor correctly repositioned, semi-tighten the retaining bolt, refit the distributor cap and connect the LT lead and vacuum hose(s), then make an accurate timing check and adjustment as described in Section 8. Refit the rocker cover (if removed) and/or the No 1 sparking plug and reconnect its lead before making the check.
12 Check that the octane selector is set at the standard line setting position (Fig. 4.16).

8 Ignition timing – checking and adjustment

4K, 2T and 2T-B engine models

1 Setting of the static (BTDC) advance angle should only be regarded as an initial setting. A stroboscope should then be used to check and adjust the timing more precisely.
2 Check that the dwell angle is correct, the vernier adjuster (octane selector) is in the standard position and that the contact breaker points are just about to open when the notch on the crankshaft pulley is opposite the specified static timing mark on the engine timing cover scale.
3 Run the engine to normal operating temperature and check that the idling speed is as specified.
4 Pull off the vacuum pipe from the distributor diaphragm and plug the pipe.
5 Connect a stroboscope in accordance with the manufacturer's instructions (usually between No. 1 spark plug and the end of No. 1 spark plug lead).
6 Point the stroboscope at the timing cover scale when the notch in the crankshaft pulley and the appropriate (BTDC) mark on the scale will appear stationary. Any difficulty in observing these marks clearly can be overcome by painting them with quick drying white paint.
7 If the timing is correct, the notch should appear to be in alignment with the specified BTDC mark on the scale. If it is out of alignment then loosen the distributor clamp bolt and turn the distributor body one way or the other. Retighten the clamp bolt when adjustment is correct. Gross errors in ignition timing will be due to incorrect installation of the distributor. Refer to Section 7. Note that the ignition timing adjustment must only be made turning the distributor body as described above and not by adjusting the octane selector.
8 While the stroboscope is connected, it is useful to check the efficiency of the centrifugal and vacuum advance mechanisms of the distributor.
9 With the vacuum pipe still disconnected and plugged, speed up the engine. The timing marks which were in alignment at idling will move apart, proving that the centrifugal advance mechanism is operating.
10 Now reconnect the vacuum pipe to the distributor and again speed up the engine. The timing marks will move apart a much greater distance for the same relative engine speed. This proves that both the centrifugal and vacuum advance mechanisms of the distributor are functioning.

3T–C engine models

11 The timing check and adjustment procedure is similar to that described for other engine types given above except for the following differences.
12 Disconnect the distributor sub-diaphragm hose as well as the main diaphragm hose and plug them both to prevent the ingress of dirt (Fig. 4.18). With reference to paragraph 8 above, reconnect the sub-diaphragm hose and then carry out the check on the centrifugal and vacuum advance mechanisms. Then connect the main diaphragm hose and repeat the check.
13 If the diaphragms are suspect these can be checked by removing the distributor cap, the rotor and dust cover and detaching both diaphragm vacuum hoses. Apply a vacuum to the units and check to see that the advancer mechanism moves accordingly (Fig. 4.18).
14 On all 3T–C engine models, except those fitted with an HAC valve

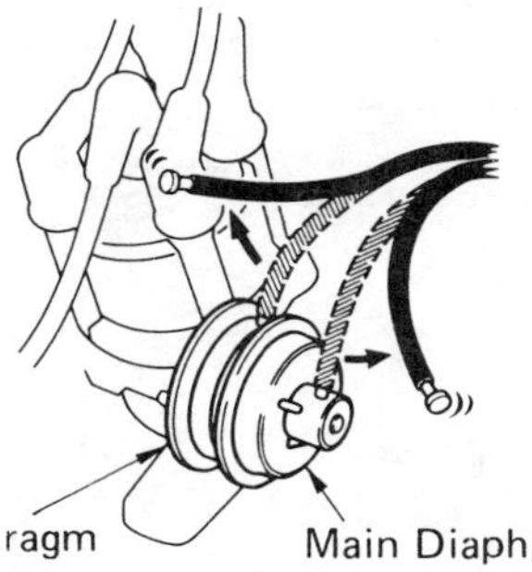

Fig. 4.17 Detach the main and sub-diaphragm hoses – 3T-C engine (Sec 8)

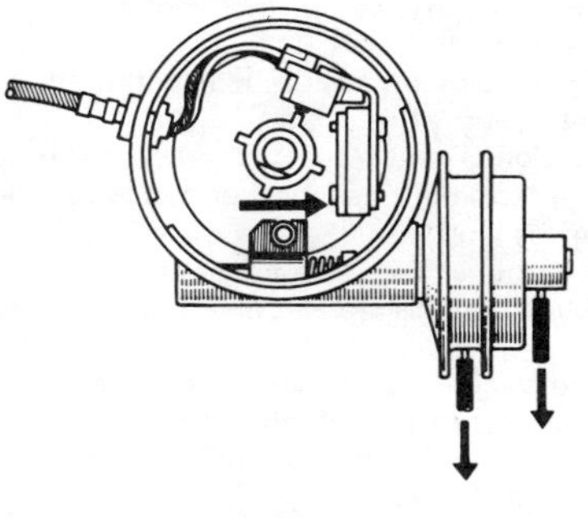
Fig. 4.18 Distributor advancer mechanism check – 3T-C engine (Sec 8)

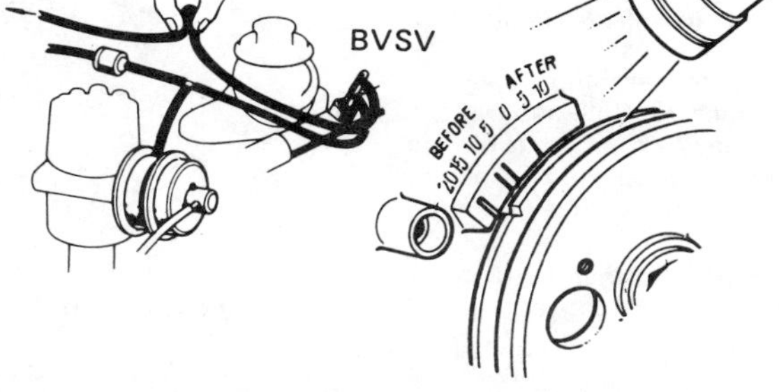

Fig. 4.19 Pinch the BVSV hose and check timing advance – 3T-C engine without HAC valve (Sec 8)

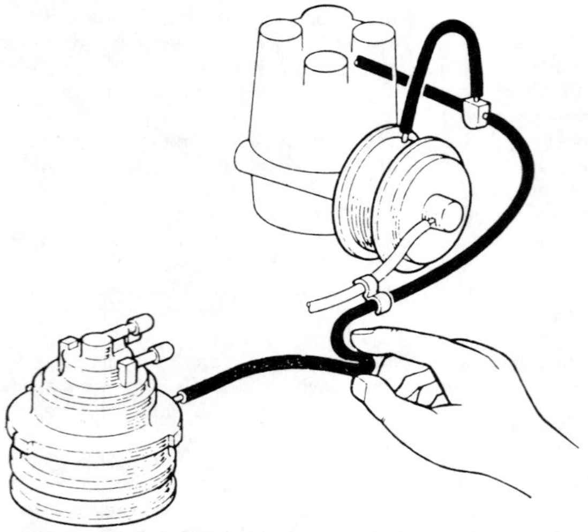

Fig. 4.20 Pinch the HAC valve to 3-way connector hose and observe timing advance – 3T-C engine (Sec 8)

9.2 Remove rotor, arm and dust cover (arrowed) – 2T engine

(see Chapter 3), with the engine running pinch together the BVSV hose to the carburettor and check that the ignition timing simultaneously advances to about 20° BTDC, (Fig. 4.19).

15 On 3T engine models fitted with an HAC valve, detach the HAC valve hose to distributor (at the distributor) and plug the hose. With the engine idling at 900 rpm loosen off the distributor clamp bolt and turn the distributor to give the ignition timing of 10° BTDC then retighten the clamp bolt. Refit the vacuum hose to the sub-diaphragm on the distributor and check that the timing is then 20° BTDC. Should the timing remain at 10° BTDC, pinch together the HAC valve to three-way connector hose which should change the timing to 20° BTDC (Fig. 4.20).

9 Distributor (conventional ignition) – dismantling and overhaul

1 There are detail differences between the distributors used on the 4K and 2T/2T-B engine types but the dismantling operations for both are similar (Figs. 4.21 to 4.29).

2 With the distributor on the bench, withdraw the rotor arm and remove the dust cover (photo).

3 Refer to Section 3 and remove the contact breaker points.

4 Unscrew the terminal post through bolt securing nut and disconnect the condenser lead.

5 Undo and remove the screw securing the condenser to the distributor body. Lift the condenser and lead away from the distributor body.

6 Unscrew the vacuum unit vernier adjuster (octane selector) and draw the assembly from the distributor body.

7 Undo and remove the two screws securing the distributor cap spring clips to the distributor body. Lift away the two clips noting that the earth wire is retained by one of the clips securing screws on some models.

8 The contact breaker plate assembly may now be lifted from the distributor body. To assist refitting note which way round it is fitted.

9 Undo and remove the screw located at the top of the cam spindle and lift away the cam.

10 Using a pair of pliers carefully disconnect and lift away the two centrifugal weight springs noting their respective positions.

11 Carefully remove the circlips and lift away the centrifugal weights.

12 Using a suitable diameter parallel pin punch carefully tap out the pin securing the spiral gear to the spindle. It may be found that the pin ends are peened over. If so it will be necessary to file flat before attempting to drift out the pin. The gear may now be removed from the spindle.

13 The spindle may now be drawn upwards from the distributor body. Take care to recover the washer(s) fitted between the centrifugal weight plate and distributor body (Fig. 4.25).

14 Wash all parts and wipe dry with a clean non-fluffy rag. Check the contact breaker points for wear. Inspect the distributor cap for signs of tracking (indicated by a thin black line between the segments). Also look at the segments for signs of excessive corrosion. Renew the cap if necessary.

15 If the metal portion of the rotor arm is badly burned or loose renew the arm. If only slightly burned, clean the end with a fine abrasive paper.

16 Check that the contact in the centre of the distributor cap is in good order (Fig. 4.26).

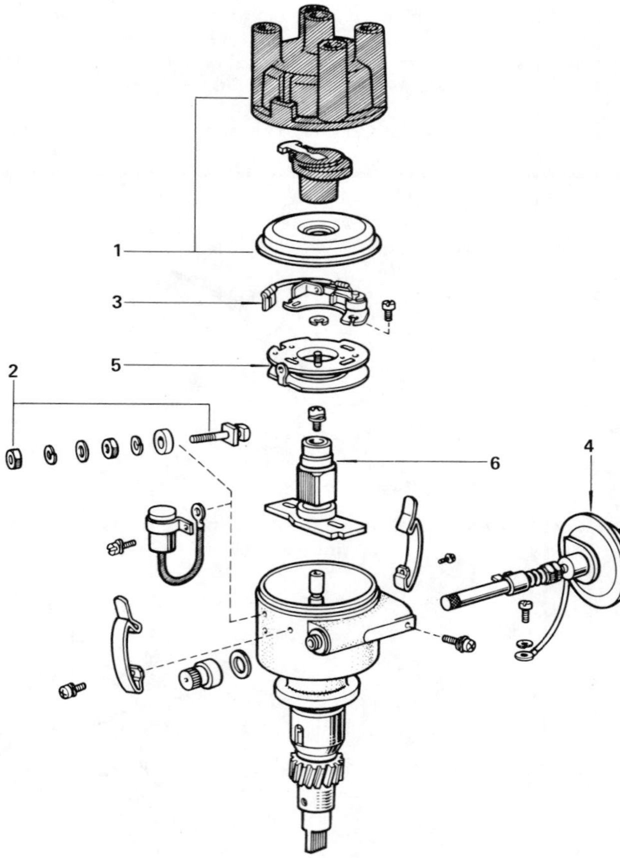

Fig. 4.21 Distributor components – 4K engine (Sec 9)

1 Cap, rotor & cover
2 Terminal
3 Breaker point
4 Vacuum advancer
5 Breaker plate
6 Cam

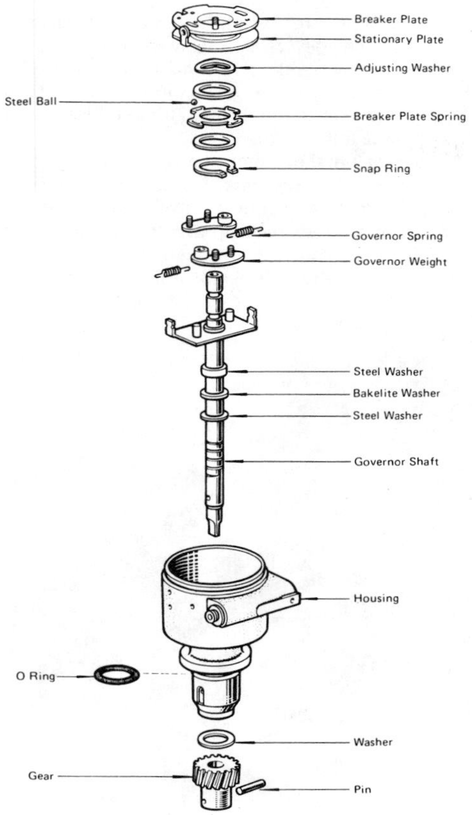

Fig. 4.22 Distributor shaft components – 4K engine (Sec 9)

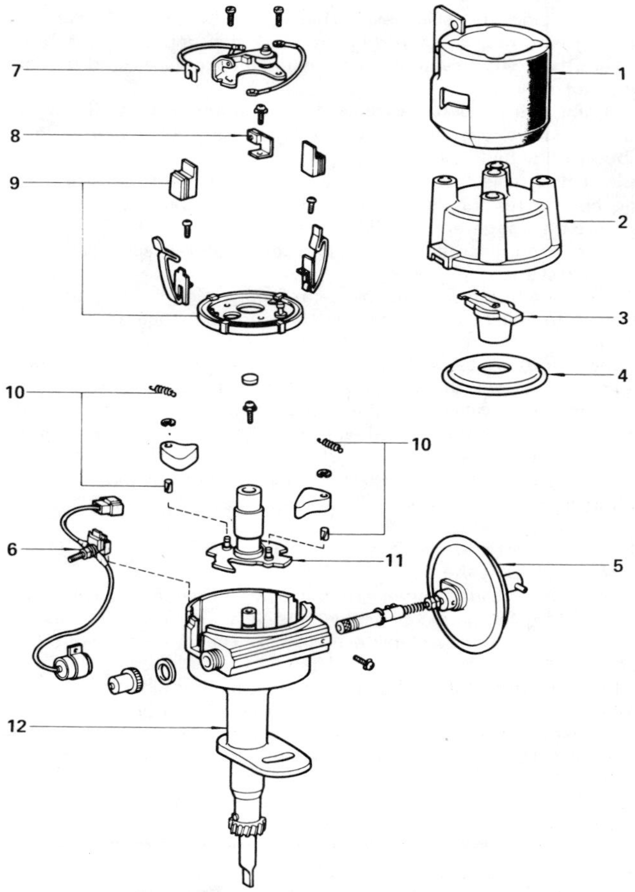

Fig. 4.23 Distributor components – 2T and 2T-B engines (Sec 9)

1	*Dust cover*	8	*Damping spring*
2	*Cap*	9	*Breaker plate*
3	*Rotor*	10	*E Ring, governor spring & governor weight*
4	*Dustproof cover*	11	*Cam*
5	*Vacuum advancer*	12	*Housing*
6	*Terminal*		
7	*Point*		

Fig. 4.24 Note positions and detach the springs – 2T and 2T-B engines (Sec 9)

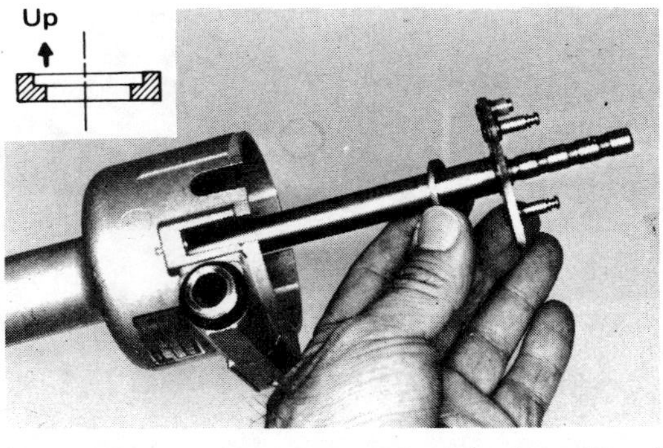

Fig. 4.25 Remove spindle and note washer(s) orientation – 2T and 2T-B engines (Sec 9)

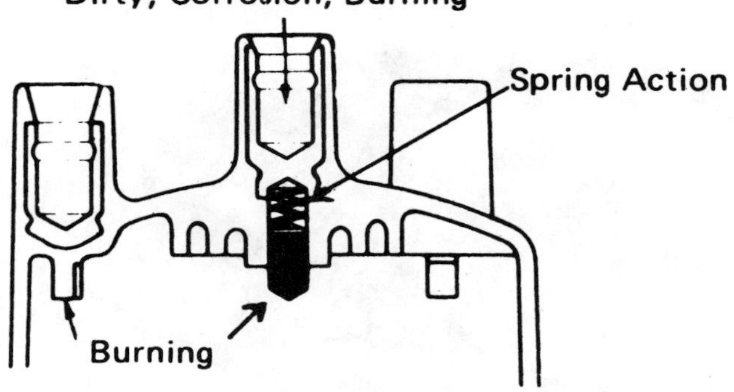

Fig. 4.26 Check distributor cap body, centre contact and segments – 4K, 2T and 2T-B engines (Sec 9)

17 Examine the centrifugal weights and pivots for wear and the advance springs for slackness. These can be best checked by comparing with new parts. If they are slack they must be renewed.
18 Check the points assembly for fit on the breaker plate, and the cam follower for wear.
19 Examine the fit of the spindle in the distributor body. If there is excessive side movement it will be necessary to obtain a new distributor body and spindle.
20 Check the resistance of the breaker plate sliding part. Ideally it should have a resistance of 2.2 lb (1 kg). If it appears to be tight lubricate with a little engine oil.
21 Check the fit between the cam and spindle. If it is slack new parts will be necessary.
22 To reassemble, first, refit the centrifugal weights into place and retain with the circlips, ensuring that they are fully located (Fig. 4.27 & 4.28).
23 Lubricate the outer surface of the spindle and slide the cam over the spindle and hook the springs onto the posts.
24 Fit the steel washer onto the shaft and lubricate with a little engine oil. Ensure that the steel washer is fitted with its recess facing upwards. On the 4K engine distributor, the washers must be fitted in the following order of thicknesses: (1) top washer - 2 mm thick, (2) 2nd washer - 0.2 mm thick, (3) Bakelite washer, (4) 4th and 5th washers - 0.2 mm (Fig. 4.29).
25 Slide the shaft into the body and locate the spiral gear. Line up the pin holes and insert the pin.
26 Using feeler gauges measure the shaft thrust clearance which should be as given in the Specifications. If adjustment is necessary select a steel washer of suitable thickness. These are available in a range of thicknesses.
27 Peen over the ends of the spiral gear retaining pin.
28 Refit the breaker plate assembly to the distributor body and locate the two distributor cap spring clips. Secure the clips with the screws and washers. Do not forget the earth wire is secured by the screw on the terminal side.
29 Note that the four breaker plate clips must be in position in the distributor body. Also the cap spring without the cap position locator must be on the terminal side of the distributor body.
30 Refit the terminal insulator and through bolt. Position the condenser cable terminal onto the through bolt and retain with the nut. Do not tighten the nut fully at this stage.
31 Fit the contact breaker points onto the breaker plate and secure with the two screws and washers. Do not forget the earth wire to be attached to the arm side securing screw on some models.
32 Insert the vacuum advance unit to the housing, engaging it with the breaker plate and screw on the vernier adjuster (octane selector) until it is set at the standard position (photo).

9.32 Remove cap and neutralise the octane adjuster – 2T engine

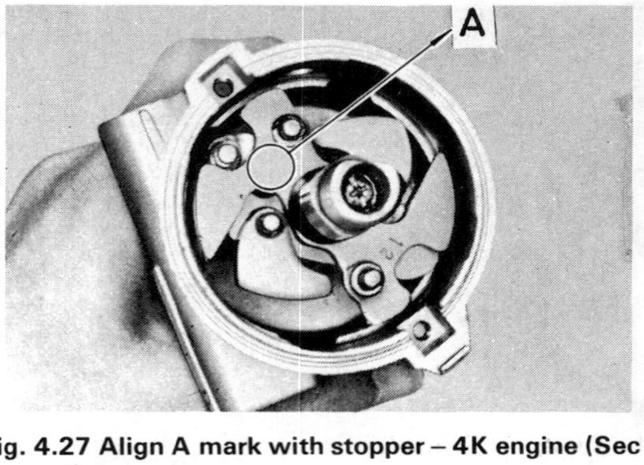

Fig. 4.27 Align A mark with stopper – 4K engine (Sec 9)

Fig. 4.28 Align mark with stopper – 2T and 2T-B engines (Sec 9)

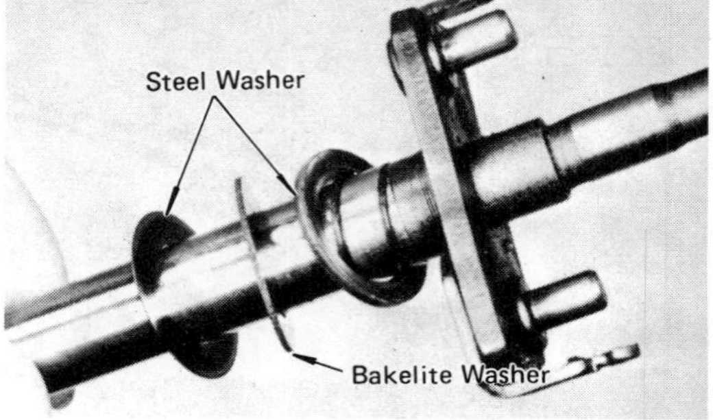

Fig. 4.29 Locate washers as shown – 4K engine (Sec 9)

33 Secure the condenser to the side of the distributor body with the screw and washer.

34 Refer to Section 2 and adjust the contact breaker points. Connect the wire to the terminal block and tighten the nut.

35 Before refitting the rotor arm and dust cover, the distributor should be lubricated as follows:

(a) Lubricate the distributor cam by smearing liberally with petroleum jelly

(b) Apply two drops of engine oil into the recess in the top of the cam spindle (rotor removed). This then runs down the spindle when the engine is hot and lubricates the bearings

(c) To lubricate the automatic timing control allow a few drops of engine oil to pass through the hole in the contact breaker baseplate through which the four sided cam emerges. Apply not more than one drop of oil to the moving contact pivot post and remove any excess

(d) Wipe clean any excess oil or petroleum jelly so that when operating none may be dispersed onto the contact breaker points to cause burning and/or misfiring

(e) Check that the shaft rotates freely (photo)

9.35e Check that shaft rotates freely

10 Distributor (electronic ignition) – dismantling and overhaul

1 With the distributor removed as previously described in Section 7, withdraw the rotor arm and dust cover (with gasket if fitted).

2 Remove the screws securing the signal generator in position and withdraw it.

3 Remove the vacuum advancer unit according to type by removing the E-ring and screw (late models with double diaphragm) or two screws (earlier models) – see Figs. 4.30 and 4.31.

4 Extract the screws and lift out the base plate, noting its fitted position.

5 If the distributor must be further dismantled, carefully grind the drivegear as shown in (Fig. 4.32) and then knock out the securing pin. Discard the gear. Remove the thrust washer from the shaft.

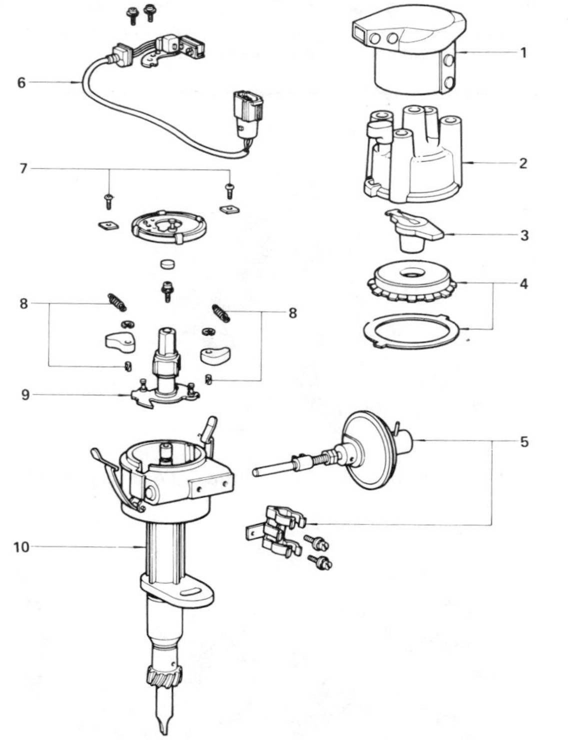

Fig. 4.30 Distributor components – earlier 3T-C engine (Sec 10)

1 *Dust cover*
2 *Cap*
3 *Rotor*
4 *Dustproof cover & gasket*
5 *Vacuum advancer*
6 *Signal generator*
7 *Breaker plate*
8 *E Ring, governor spring & governor weight*
9 *Cam*
10 *Housing*

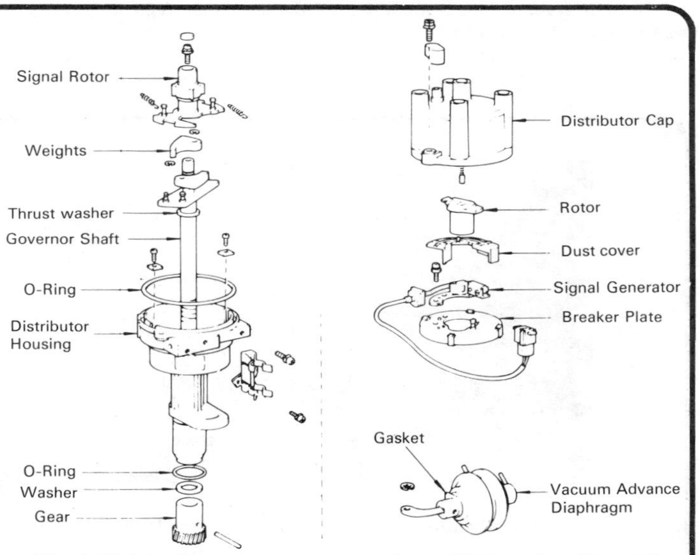

Fig. 4.31 Distributor components – later 3T-C engine (Sec 10)

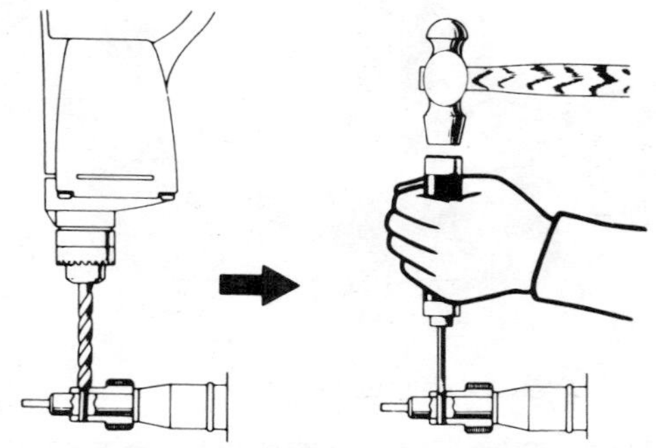

Fig. 4.32 Carefully grind or drill drivegear then knock out securing pin – 3T-C engine (Sec 10)

6 Tap the shaft upwards through the body to remove it using a plastic-faced hammer.
7 Use a suitable pair of long nose pliers and detach the governor springs noting their positions and orientation.
8 Prise free the grease stopper from the recess in the top end of the cam (signal rotor) housing. Then unscrew and remove the cam to shaft securing screw. Pull free the cam housing.
9 To dismantle the governor weights assembly, first note their fitted positions and orientation, then release the circlips from the pivot posts and remove the governor weights.
10 Inspect all components and renew any which are worn, cracked or deformed. Renew the O-ring on the distributor lower body (Fig. 4.33).
11 Commence reassembly by applying a little grease to the distributor shaft and inner surface of the cam. Install the cam assembly to the shaft so that the timing mark is adjacent to the counterweight stop (Fig. 4.34).
12 Fit the counterweights and their circlips, reconnect the springs, making sure that they go back in their original positions and the correct way round. Fit the cam housing.
13 Fit the screw at the top of the shaft, press in some grease and fit the grease retainer.
14 Slide the thrust washer upwards onto the shaft with its recessed side up (in same manner as that shown in Fig. 4.25).
15 Now slide the distributor body up the shaft followed by the washer and new drivegear which fit onto the lower end of the shaft. Align the gear and shaft pin holes and insert the retaining pin by driving it home. Before stake punching it to secure, check the shaft thrust clearance which should be as given in the Specifications. Adjust if necessary by changing the thrust washer.
16 Fit the base plate into position in the housing and locate the four clips into the housing slots. Fit the hold down clips and retaining screws (Fig. 4.35).
17 Refit the vacuum advancer unit. On the earlier type distributor, insert the vacuum unit so that its groove engages with the pin and then screw in the wiring connector clamp screw. On later models insert the vacuum unit into position together with a new gasket and locate the lever hole over the plate pin. Fit a new E-ring to secure, then locate and tighten the securing screw from the outside (Fig. 4.36).
18 Refit the signal generator unit and adjust the air gap as described in Section 6. The dust cover can then be refitted together with the new gasket, O-ring seal and rotor arm.
19 The distributor is now reassembled and ready for refitting into the car.

11 Coil polarity and testing

1 High tension current should be negative at the spark plug terminals. If the HT current is positive at the spark plug terminals then the LT leads to the coil primary terminals have been incorrectly connected. A wrong connection can cause as much as 60% loss of spark efficiency and can cause rough idling and misfiring at speed.
2 With a negative earth electrical system, the LT lead from the distributor connects with the negative (primary) terminal on the coil.
3 The simplest way to test a coil is by substitution with another coil. It is, however, recommended that the primary and secondary resistances be checked by your Toyota dealer. He can also check for an insulation breakdown between the coil casing and the primary terminals using a megohmmeter. The specified resistance readings vary according to model.

12 Spark plugs and HT leads

1 The correct functioning of the spark plugs is vital for the correct running and efficiency of the engine. The plugs fitted as standard are listed in the Specifications page.
2 At specified intervals, the plugs should be removed, examined, cleaned and, if worn excessively, renewed. The condition of the spark plug will also tell much about the overall condition of the engine.
3 When detaching the spark plug leads grip and pull on the rubber

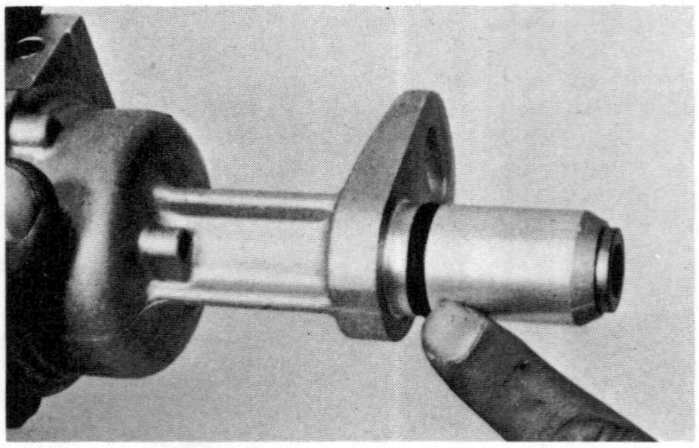

Fig. 4.33 Renew the O-ring – 3T-C engine (Sec 10)

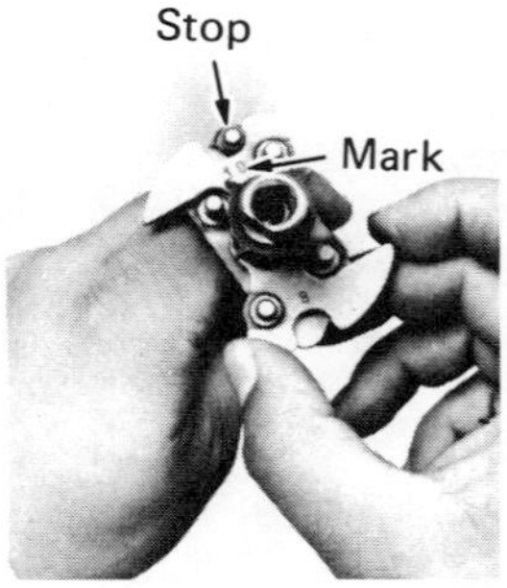

Fig. 4.34 Align timing mark with stop – 3T-C engine (Sec 10)

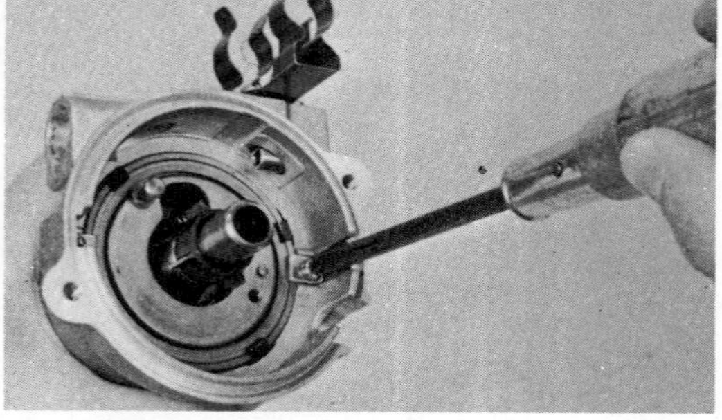

Fig. 4.35 Tightening the baseplate retaining screws – 3T-C engine (Sec 10)

Fig. 4.36 Fit circlip, then tighten vacuum unit securing screw – 3T-C engine (Sec 10)

Measuring plug gap. A feeler gauge of the correct size (see ignition system specifications) should have a slight 'drag' when slid between the electrodes. Adjust gap if necessary

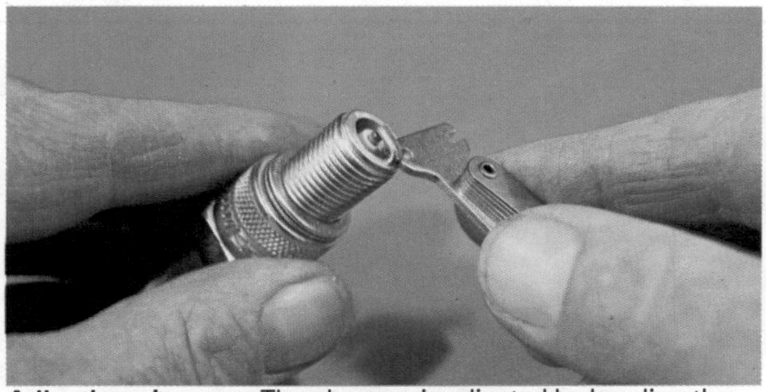

Adjusting plug gap. The plug gap is adjusted by bending the earth electrode inwards, or outwards, as necessary until the correct clearance is obtained. Note the use of the correct tool

Normal. Grey-brown deposits, lightly coated core nose. Gap increasing by around 0.001 in (0.025 mm) per 1000 miles (1600 km). Plugs ideally suited to engine, and engine in good condition

Carbon fouling. Dry, black, sooty deposits. Will cause weak spark and eventually misfire. Fault: over-rich fuel mixture. Check: carburettor mixture settings, float level and jet sizes; choke operation and cleanliness of air filter. Plugs can be re-used after cleaning

Oil fouling. Wet, oily deposits. Will cause weak spark and eventually misfire. Fault: worn bores/piston rings or valve guides; sometimes occurs (temporarily) during running-in period. Plugs can be re-used after thorough cleaning

Overheating. Electrodes have glazed appearance, core nose very white – few deposits. Fault: plug overheating. Check: plug value, ignition timing, fuel octane rating (too low) and fuel mixture (too weak). Discard plugs and cure fault immediately

Electrode damage. Electrodes burned away; core nose has burned, glazed appearance. Fault: pre-ignition. Check: as for 'Overheating' but may be more severe. Discard plugs and remedy fault before piston or valve damage occurs

Split core nose (may appear initially as a crack). Damage is self-evident, but cracks will only show after cleaning. Fault: pre-ignition or wrong gap-setting technique. Check: ignition timing, cooling system, fuel octane rating (too low) and fuel mixture (too weak). Discard plugs, rectify fault immediately

12.3a Spark plug lead/connector removal method – 2T engine

12.3b Spark plug removal using Toyota plug spanner – 2T engine

seal as shown and not on the lead (photo). You will need a suitable extension socket to reach the plug body hexagon section which is recessed within the cylinder head. Take care not to tilt the socket during plug removal and refitting or you may break the ceramic insulator. On removal of a plug inspect the insulator nose of the plug before cleaning it since it is this which is the guide to the efficiency of combustion.

4 If the insulator nose of the spark plug is clean and white, with no deposits, this is indicative of a weak mixture, or too hot a plug.

5 If the top and insulator nose is covered with hard black looking deposits, then this is indicative that the mixture is too rich. Should the plug be black and oily, then it is likely that the engine is fairly worn, as well as the mixture being too rich.

6 If the insulator nose is covered with light tan to greyish brown deposits, then the mixture is correct and it is likely that the engine is in good condition.

7 If there are any traces of long brown tapering stains on the outside of the white portion of the plug, then the plug will have to be renewed, as this shows that there is a faulty joint between the plug body and the insulator, and compression is being allowed to leak away.

8 Plugs should be cleaned by a sand blasting machine, which will free them from carbon more thoroughly than cleaning by hand. The machine will also test the condition of the plugs under compression. Any plug that fails to spark at the recommended pressure should be renewed.

9 The spark plug gap is of considerable importance, as, if it is too large or too small the size of the spark and its efficiency will be seriously impaired. The spark plug gap should be set to the specified clearance.

10 To set it, measure the gap with a feeler gauge, and then bend open, or close the outer plug electrode until the correct gap is achieved. The centre electrode should never be bent as this may crack the insulation and cause plug failure.

11 The HT leads to the coil and spark plugs are of internal resistance, carbon core type. They are used in the interest of eliminating interference caused by the ignition system. They are much more easily damaged than copper cored cable and they should be pulled from the spark plug terminals by gripping the metal end fitting at the end of the cable. Occasionally wipe the external surfaces of the leads free from oil and dirt using a fuel moistened cloth.

12 Always check the connection of the HT leads to the spark plugs (and distributor cap) is in correct firing order sequence 1-3-4-2.

13 If it is necessary to detach the HT leads from the distributor cap at any time, do not pull on the leads, but grip the rubber insulators and pull on them. Note the sequence of the leads for correct refitting.

13 Spark control (SC) system

For a description of this system and its maintenance requirements refer to Chapter 3, Section 34.

14 Fault diagnosis – ignition system

Symptom	Reason(s)
Engine turns over normally on starter but will not fire	Damp HT leads or moisture inside distributor cap. Faulty condenser/igniter (as applicable). Oil on contact breaker points/signal generator (as applicable). Disconnected lead at distributor, ignition switch or coil.
Engine runs but misfires	Faulty spark plug. Faulty HT lead. Contact breaker gap too close, too wide or pitted points. Signal generator air gap too close or too wide. Crack in rotor arm. Crack in distributor cap. Faulty coil.
Engine overheats or lacks power	Faulty distributor condenser/or igniter (as applicable). Seized centrifugal advance weights or cam on shaft. Perforated vacuum pipe from vacuum diaphragm unit. Incorrectly timed ignition.
Engine 'pinks' (pre-detonation) under load	Ignition timing too advanced. Centrifugal advance mechanism stuck in advance position. Broken centrifugal advance spring. Octane rating of fuel too low.

Chapter 5 Clutch

Contents

Specifications

Type	Single dry plate diaphragm spring with cable actuation on 4K engine models and hydraulic actuation on 2T, 2T-B and 3T-C engine models	
Clutch pedal		
Pedal height:		
4K, 2T and 2T-B engine models	6.5 to 6.9 in (165 to 175 mm)	
3T-C engine models	6.9 to 7.3 in (175 to 185 mm)	
Pedal free play:		
4K engine models	0.79 to 1.38 in (20 to 35 mm)	
2T, 2T-B and 3T-C engine models	0.5 to 0.91 in (13 to 23 mm)	
Clutch disc		
Maximum allowable disc run-out	0.031 in (0.8 mm)	
Minimum allowable rivet head depth	0.012 in (0.3 mm)	
Torque wrench settings	**lbf ft**	**kgf m**
Clutch housing to engine bolts	37 to 57	5.0 to 8.0
Clutch cover bolts to flywheel	11 to 15	1.5 to 2.2
Master cylinder set bolt	15 to 22	2.0 to 3.0
Release fork support to transmission	22 to 32	3.0 to 4.5
Master cylinder reservoir tank	15 to 21	2.0 to 3.0
Bleed plug	7 to 9	0.9 to 1.3
Master cylinder reservoir set bolt	15 to 22	2.0 to 3.0
Steering column retaining bolts	22 to 32	3.0 to 4.5

1 General description

The models covered by this manual are fitted with a diaphragm spring clutch operated mechanically (by cable) on 4K engine models and hydraulically on 2T, 2T-B and 3T-C engine models.

The clutch consists of a steel cover which is bolted and dowelled to the rear face of the flywheel and contains the pressure plate and clutch disc (driven plate).

The pressure plate and diaphragm spring are attached to the clutch assembly cover.

The clutch disc is free to slide along the splined gearbox input shaft and is held in position between the flywheel and pressure plate by the pressure of the diaphragm spring.

Friction lining material is riveted to the clutch disc which has a cushioned hub to absorb transmission shocks and to help ensure a smooth take off.

The mechanically operated clutch system utilises a pendant pedal which is attached to a heavy duty cable. The other end of the cable is attached to the clutch release arm.

With the hydraulically operated clutch system the pendant clutch pedal is connected to the clutch master cylinder and hydraulic fluid reservoir by a short pushrod. The master cylinder and fluid reservoir are mounted on the engine side of the bulkhead in front of the driver.

Depressing the clutch pedal moves the piston in the master cylinder forwards so forcing hydraulic fluid through to the slave cylinder.

The piston in the slave cylinder moves rearwards on the entry of

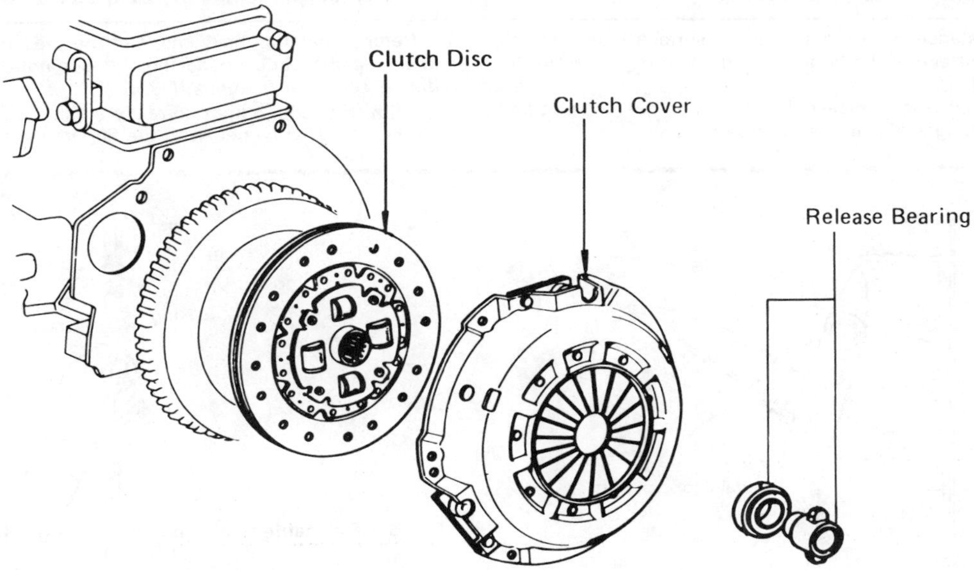

Fig. 5.1 Clutch assembly components (Sec 1)

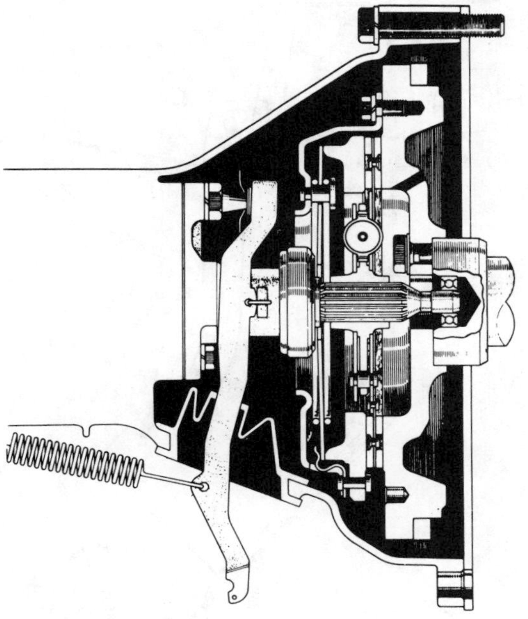

Fig. 5.2 Sectional view of clutch unit as fitted to 4K engine models (Sec 1)

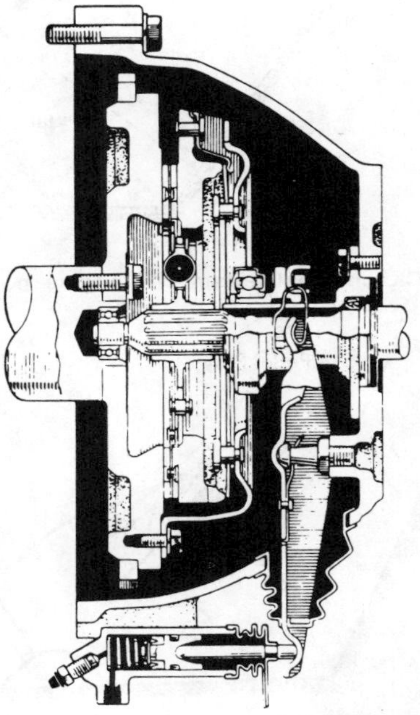

Fig. 5.3 Sectional view of clutch unit as fitted to 2T, 2T-B and 3T-C engine models (Sec 1)

the fluid and actuates the clutch release arm, via a short pushrod. The opposite end of the release arm is forked and carries the release bearing assembly.

As the pivoted clutch release arm moves rearwards it pushes the release bearing forwards to bear against the diaphragm spring and pushes forwards so moving the pressure plate backwards and disengaging the pressure plate from the clutch disc.

When the clutch pedal is released the pressure plate is forced into contact with the high friction linings on the clutch disc and at the same time pushes the clutch disc a fraction of an inch forwards on its splines so engaging the clutch disc with the flywheel. The clutch disc is now firmly sandwiched between the pressure plate and the flywheel so the drive is taken up.

2 Clutch adjustment – 4K engine models

1 Measure the distance between the upper surface of the clutch pedal pad and the surface of the floor. This should be as given in the Specifications (Fig. 5.4).

2 If adjustment is necessary, release the locknut on the stop bolt and adjust the effective length of the stop bolt as required.

3 Working within the engine compartment, grip the clutch outer cable conduit and pull it until a resistance is felt. A total of 5 or 6 grooves and ridges should now be able to be counted between the E-clip and the end face of the conduit support (Fig. 5.5).

4 If necessary, move the position of the E-clip to achieve this.

5 Let the clutch cable resume its normal position and then depress the clutch pedal several times and measure the free movement at the pedal pad. The free movement is the distance through which the pedal can be depressed with the fingers until firm resistance is met with. The free movement should be between the free play tolerances given in the Specifications (Fig. 5.6).

6 Recheck the clutch pedal height and retighten the stop bolt locknut.

3 Clutch adjustment – 2T, 2T-B and 3T-C engine models

1 Refer to paragraphs 1 and 2 of the preceding Section and check and adjust the clutch pedal height, but note that the pedal height differs – see Specifications (Fig. 5.7).

2 With the pedal height correctly adjusted check the pedal play by depressing the pedal pad with the fingers until firm resistance is met.

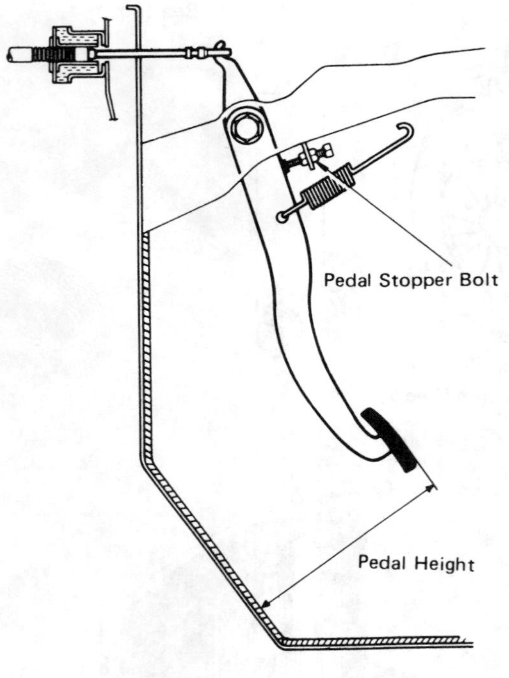

Fig. 5.4 Clutch pedal setting – 4K engine models (Sec 2)

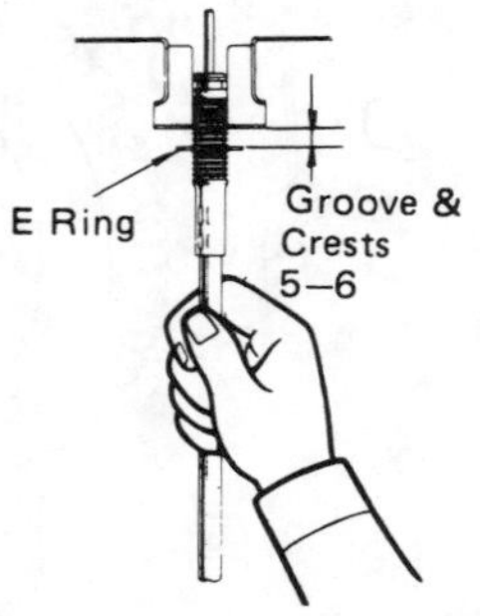

Fig. 5.5 Pull cable to give correct setting – 4K engine models (Sec 2)

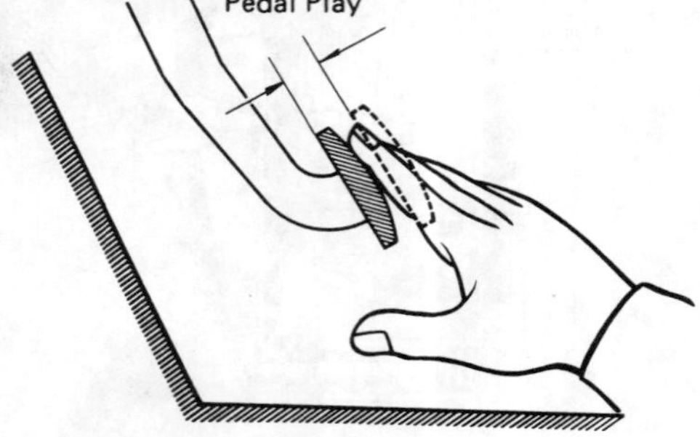

Fig. 5.6 Pedal play – check distance indicated – 4K engine models (Sec 2)

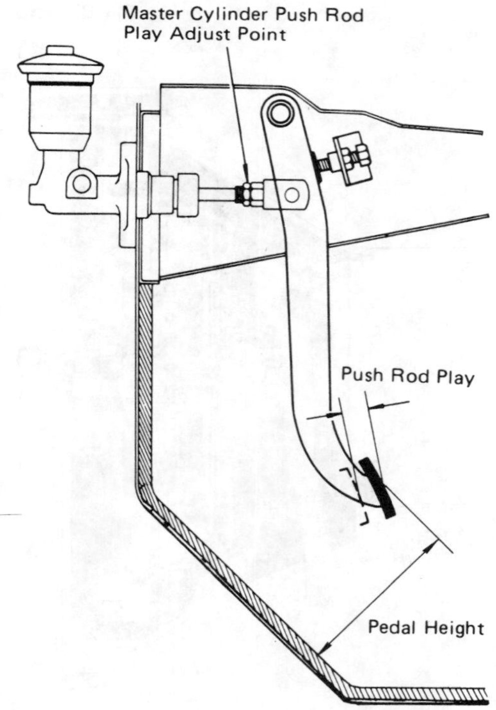

Fig. 5.7 Clutch pedal adjustment check points – 2T, 2T-B and 3T-C engine models (Sec 3)

If the pedal play is outside the tolerance given in the Specifications adjust the master cylinder pushrod length as necessary.

4 Clutch cable – renewal

1 Remove the E-ring from the top end of the clutch outer cable. cable.
2 Remove the split pin and then disconnect the lower end of the inner cable from the clutch release fork (Fig. 5.8).
3 Detach the cable from the transmission case.
4 Disconnect the top end of the cable from the clutch pedal and withdraw the cable assembly.
5 Inspect the hooks at both ends of the inner cable for signs of wear or damage. If evident a new cable assembly will be required.
6 Inspect the outer cable, O-ring and rubber boot for damage.
7 Refitting the clutch cable is the reverse sequence to removal. Smear some grease onto the end fittings and ensure that the rubber dust boot is correctly located (Fig. 5.9). Carry out the adjustments in Section 2 after fitting.

5 Clutch hydraulic system – bleeding

1 Gather together a clean glass jar, a length of rubber/plastic tubing which fits tightly over the bleed nipple on the slave cylinder, and a tin of hydraulic brake fluid. You will also need the help of an assistant.
2 Check that the master cylinder reservoir is full. If it is not, fill it and also fill the bottom two inches of the jar with hydraulic fluid.
3 Remove the rubber dust cap from the bleed nipple on the slave cylinder, and with a suitable spanner open the bleed nipple approximately three-quarters of a turn.
4 Place one end of the tube over the nipple and insert the other end in the jar so that the tube orifice is below the level of the fluid.
5 The assistant should now depress the pedal and hold it down at the end of its stroke. Allow the pedal to return to its normal position.
6 Continue this series of operations until clean hydraulic fluid without any traces of air bubbles emerges from the end of the tubing. Be sure that the reservoir is checked frequently to ensure that the hydraulic fluid does not drop too far, thus letting air into the system.
7 When no more air bubbles appear tighten the bleed nipple during a downstroke.
8 Refit the rubber dust cap over the bleed nipple.
9 Wipe away any hydraulic fluid that may have spilt onto the bodywork of the vehicle as the fluid is harmful to paintwork.

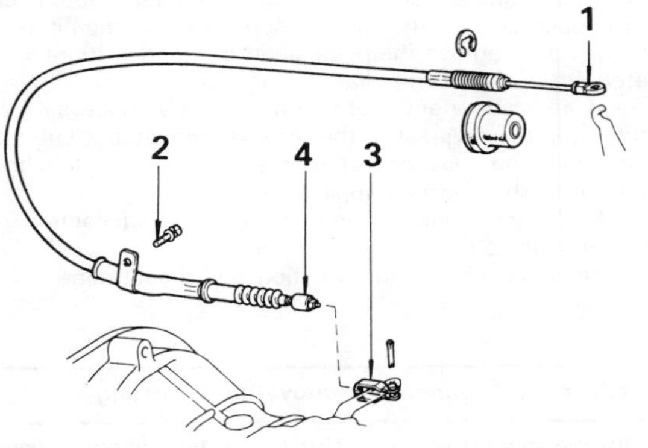

Fig. 5.8 Clutch cable and associated components – 4K engine models (Sec 4)

1 Cable end (clutch pedal side)
2 Cable clamp
3 Clevis
4 Cable end (fork lever side)

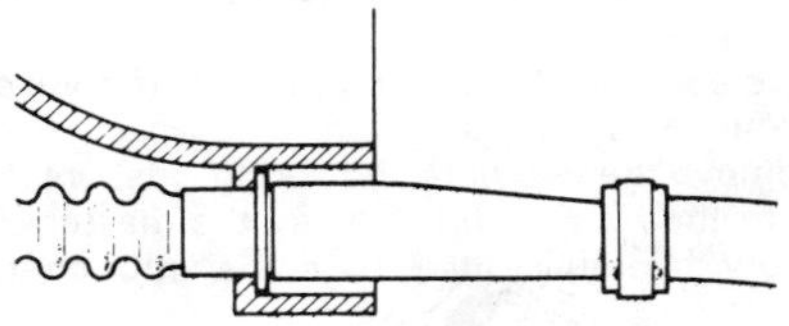

Fig. 5.9 Cable dust boot location – 4K engine models (Sec 4)

6 Clutch pedal – removal and refitting

1 On 4K engine models (with cable clutch actuation), detach and remove the cover from the underside of the steering column, then unscrew the two column tube to dashboard retaining bolts and lower the column. Now refer to Section 4 and disconnect the clutch cable from the pedal (Fig. 5.10).
2 On all models detach the clutch pedal return spring.

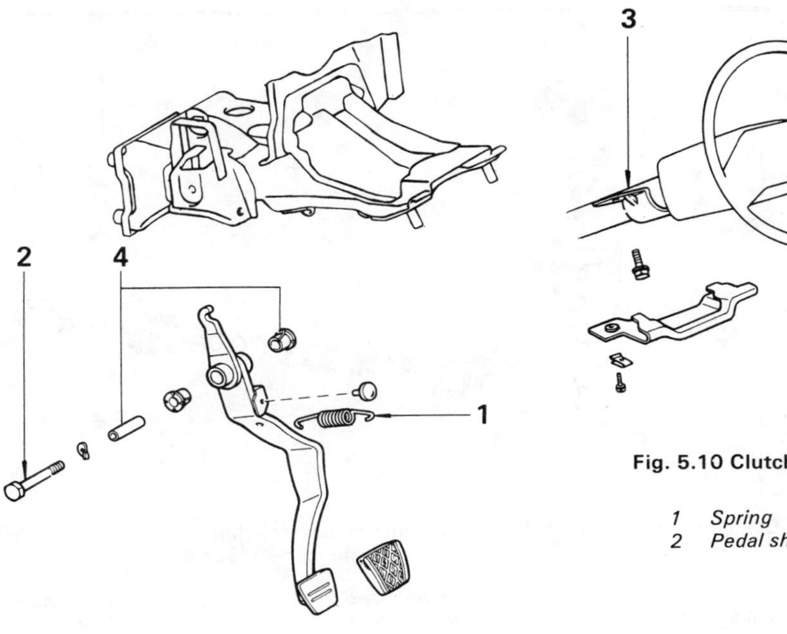

Fig. 5.10 Clutch pedal and associated components – 4K engine models (Sec 6)

1 Spring
2 Pedal shaft
3 Steering column tube
4 Bushing, collar & pedal

3 On 2T, 2T-B and 3T-C engine models (hydraulic clutch actuation), extract the pushrod pin retaining clip and withdraw the pin (Fig. 5.11).
4 Unscrew and remove the pedal shaft bolt and withdraw the pedal complete with bushes and collar.
5 Inspect and renew any worn components as necessary.
6 Refitting is the reversal of the removal procedure. Lubricate with grease the collar and bushes as they are assembled. Also lubricate the cable end or pushrod pin as applicable.
7 On 4K engine models retighten the steering column retaining bolts to the specified torque wrench setting.
8 On completion check clutch action and adjustments as given in Section 2 or 3.

7 Clutch master cylinder – removal and refitting

1 Drain the fluid from the clutch master cylinder reservoir by attaching a rubber or plastic tube to the slave cylinder bleed nipple. Undo the nipple by approximately three-quarters of a turn and then pump the fluid out into a suitable container by operating the clutch pedal repeatedly until the fluid reservoir is empty.
2 Place a rag under the master cylinder to catch any hydraulic fluid that may be spilt. Unscrew the union nut from the end of the metal pipe where it enters the clutch master cylinder and gently pull the pipe clear.
3 Withdraw the split pin that retains the pushrod yoke to the pedal clevis pin and remove the clevis pin.
4 Undo and remove the two nuts and spring washers that secure the master cylinder to the bulkhead. Lift away the master cylinder taking care not to allow hydraulic fluid to come into contact with the paintwork.
5 Refitting the master cylinder is the reverse sequence to removal. Bleed the system as described in Section 5 and finally carry out the adjustments described in Section 3.

8 Clutch master cylinder – overhaul

1 Peel back the flexible boot from the end of the master cylinder to expose the circlip. Extract the circlip so that the pushrod and piston stop plate can be withdrawn (Fig. 5.13).
2 Remove the piston/seal assembly by either tapping the end of the master cylinder on a block of hardwood or by applying air pressure at the fluid outlet port.
3 Examine the bore of the cylinder carefully for any signs of scores or ridges and, if this is found to be smooth all over, new seals can be

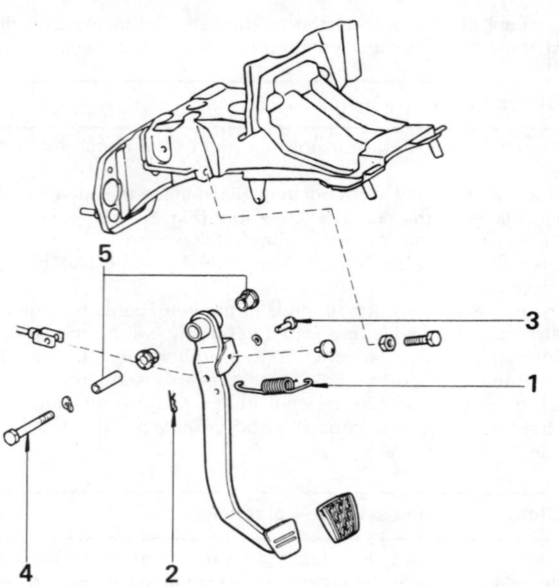

Fig. 5.11 Clutch pedal and associated components – 2T, 2T-B and 3T-C engine models (Sec 6)

1 Spring
2 Push rod pin
3 Pin
4 Pedal shaft
5 Bushing, collar & pedal

fitted. If there is any doubt of the condition of the bore then a new cylinder must be fitted complete.
4 If examination of the seals shows them to be apparently oversize or swollen, or very loose on the piston suspect oil contamination in the system. Ordinary lubricating oil will swell these rubber seals, and if one is found to be swollen it is reasonable to assume that all seals in the clutch hydraulic system will need attention. Fit them using the fingers only to manipulate them into position.
5 Thoroughly clean all parts in either fresh hydraulic fluid or methylated spirit. Ensure that the bypass ports are clear.
6 All components should be assembled wetted with clean hydraulic fluid.
7 Check that the master cylinder bore is clean and smear with clean hydraulic fluid. With the piston suitably wetted with hydraulic fluid,

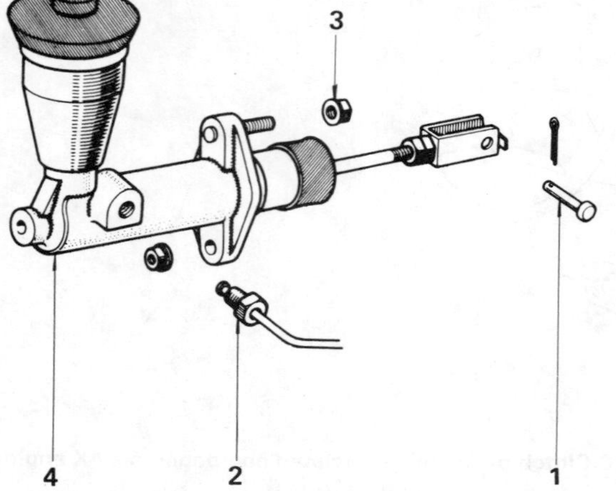

Fig. 5.12 Clutch master cylinder – 2T, 2T-B and 3T-C engine models (Sec 7)

1 Pushrod clevis pin and split pin
2 Hydraulic line nut union
3 Nut
4 Master cylinder

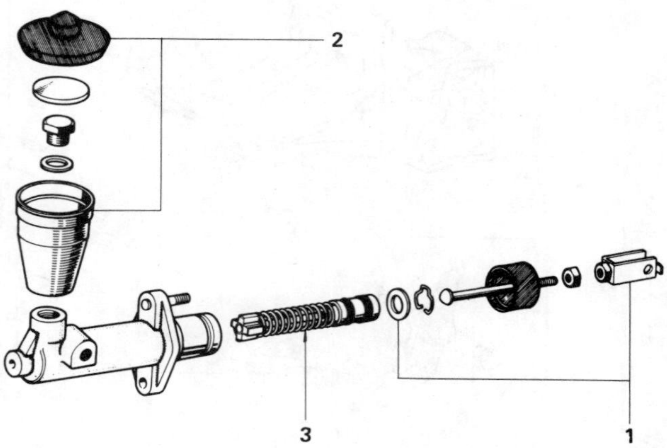

Fig. 5.13 Components of master cylinder – 2T, 2T-B and 3T-C engine models (Sec 8)

1 Pushrod, boot and circlip
2 Reservoir assembly
3 Piston assembly

carefully insert the assembly into the bore – valve end first. Ease the lip of the piston seal carefully into the bore.
8 Refit the pushrod and refit the snap ring into the groove in the cylinder bore. Smear the sealing areas of the dust cover with a little rubber grease and pack the cover with the rubber grease so as to act as a dust trap. Fit the cover to the master cylinder body. The master cylinder is now ready for refitting to the car.

9 Clutch slave cylinder – removal and refitting

1 Wipe the top of the clutch master cylinder, unscrew the cap and place a piece of polythene sheet over the top to create a partial vacuum and to stop hydraulic fluid syphoning out when the slave cylinder is removed. Refit the cap.
2 Wipe the area around the union on the slave cylinder and unscrew the union. Tape the end of the pipe to stop dirt entering (photo).
3 Undo and remove the two cylinder retaining bolts and then withdraw the cylinder from the clutch housing simultaneously disengaging the pushrod from the release arm.
4 Refitting the clutch slave cylinder is the reverse sequence to removal. It will be necessary to bleed the hydraulic system as described in Section 5.

10 Clutch slave cylinder – overhaul

1 Clean the exterior of the slave cylinder using a dry non-fluffy rag.
2 Carefully ease back the dust cover from the end of the slave cylinder and lift away.
3 The piston and seal assembly should now be shaken out. If a low pressure air jet is available, the piston and seal may be ejected using this method. Place a rag over the open end so that when the piston is ejected it does not fly out onto the floor.
4 Carefully prise free the piston seals noting their orientation. Do not

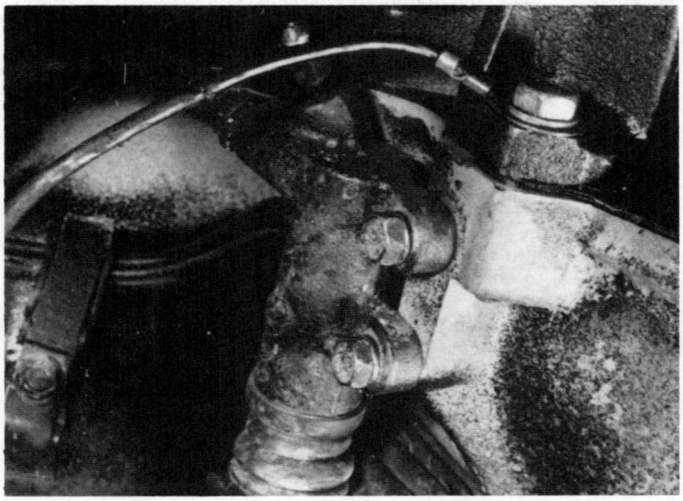

9.2 Clutch slave cylinder

scratch the piston surfaces during removal of the seals.
5 Inspect the inside of the cylinder for score marks caused by any impurities in the hydraulic fluid. If any are found then the slave cylinder unit complete must be renewed.
6 If the cylinder is found to be in good condition, thoroughly clean it with clean hydraulic fluid.
7 The old rubber seals must be renewed irrespective of condition.
8 Smear the new seals with hydraulic fluid and fit into position on the piston. Use only the fingers to manipulate the seals into position.
9 To reassemble first insert the spring into the cylinder with its wide taper leading (Fig. 5.17). Lubricate the piston and seals in hydraulic

Fig. 5.14 Piston assembly – take care when renewing the seals – 2T, 2T-B and 3T-C engine models (Sec 8)

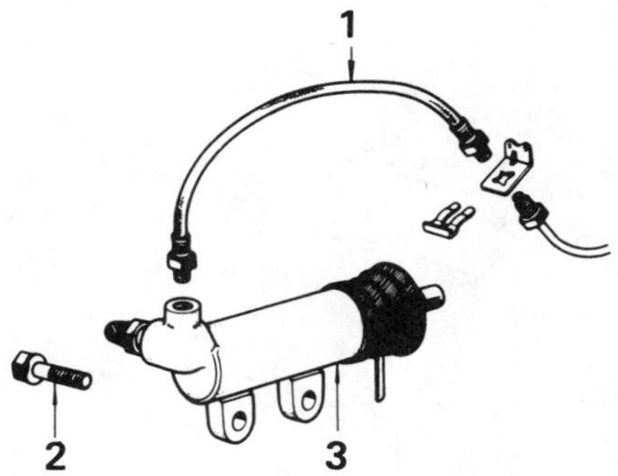

Fig. 5.15 Clutch slave cylinder showing the hydraulic hose (1), retaining bolts (2) and cylinder (3) – 2T, 2T-B and 3T-C engine models (Sec 9)

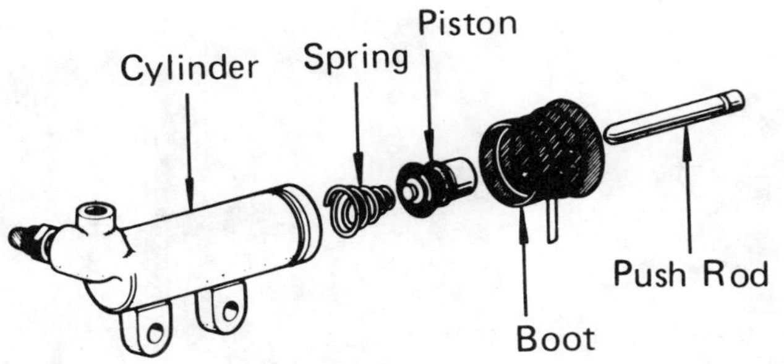

Fig. 5.16 Clutch slave cylinder components – 2T, 2T-B and 3T-C engine models (Sec 10)

Fig. 5.17 Piston and spring orientation – 2T, 2T-B and 3T-C engine models (Sec 10)

fluid and then carefully refit into the cylinder. Gently ease the edge of the seal into the bore so that it does not distort.
10 Smear the sealing areas of the dust cover with rubber grease and pack the cover with rubber grease to act as a dust trap. Fit the cover to the slave cylinder body. The slave cylinder is now ready for refitting to the car.

11 Clutch – removal and inspection

1 Remove the gearbox as described in Chapter 6.
2 With a centre punch, mark the relative position of the clutch cover and flywheel to ensure correct refitting if the original parts are to be reused.
3 Remove the clutch assembly by unscrewing the six bolts holding the cover to the rear face of the flywheel. Unscrew the bolts diagonally half a turn at a time to prevent distortion of the cover flange, also to prevent an accident caused by the cover flange binding on the dowels and suddenly flying off.

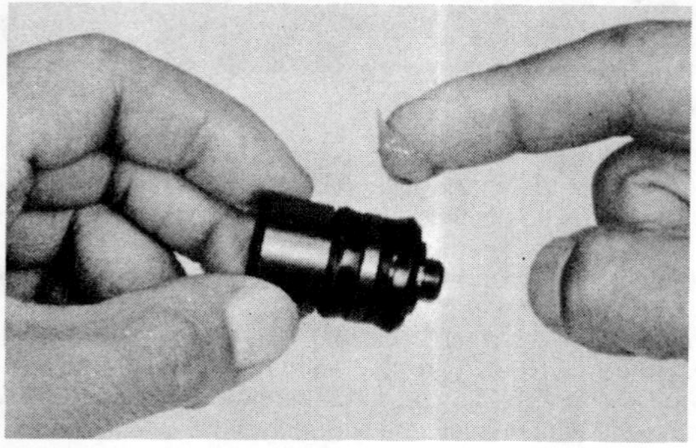

Fig. 5.18 Fit the seals to the piston and coat them with rubber grease or clean hydraulic fluid – 2T, 2T-B and 3T-C engine models (Sec 10)

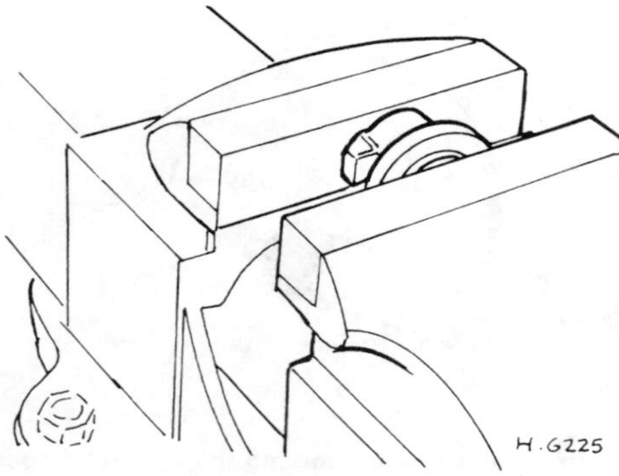

Fig. 5.19 Pressing a new clutch release bearing into hub (Sec 12)

4 With the bolts removed, lift the assembly off the locating dowels. The driven plate or clutch disc will fall out at this stage, as it is not attached to either the clutch cover assembly or flywheel. Carefully note which way round the driven plate is fitted (greater projecting side away from flywheel).
5 It is important that no oil or grease gets on the clutch disc friction linings, or the pressure plate and flywheel faces. It is advisable to handle the parts with clean hands and to wipe down the pressure plate and flywheel faces with a clean dry rag before inspection or refitting commences.
6 In the normal course of events clutch dismantling and reassembly is the term for simply fitting a new clutch pressure plate and friction disc. Under no circumstances should the pressure plate assembly be dismantled. If a fault develops in the assembly an exchange replacement must be fitted.
7 If a new clutch disc is being fitted it is false economy not to renew the release bearing at the same time. This will preclude having to replace it at a later time when wear on the clutch linings is very slight, see Section 12.
8 Examine the clutch disc friction linings for wear or loose rivets and the disc for rim distortion, cracks and worn splines.
9 Renew the driven plate complete, do not attempt to reline this component yourself.
10 Check the machine faces of the flywheel and the pressure plate. If either is badly grooved it should be machined until smooth, or replaced with a new item. If the pressure plate is cracked or split it must be renewed.
11 Examine the hub splines for wear and make sure that the centre hub is not loose.
12 Check the spigot bearing in the crankshaft rear face and renew it if it shows any signs of advanced wear (see Chapter 1, photo 21.8).

12 Clutch release bearing – removal and refitting

1 To gain access it is necessary to remove the gearbox as described in Chapter 6.
2 Detach the spring clips from the release bearing carrier and release fork. Draw the release bearing carrier from the flat bearing retainer (photos).
3 Check the bearing for signs of overheating, wear or roughness, and, if evident, the old bearing should be drawn off the carrier using a universal two or three leg puller. Note which way round the bearing is fitted.
4 Using a bench vice and suitable packing, press a new bearing onto the carrier (Fig. 5.19).
5 Apply some high melting point grease to the contact surfaces of the release lever and pivot assembly, and bearing carrier. Pack some grease into the inner recess of the bearing carrier (photo).
6 Refitting the bearing and carrier is the reverse sequence to removal.

13 Clutch – centralising and refitting

1 To refit the clutch plate, place the clutch disc against the flywheel with the larger end of the hub away from the flywheel. On no account

12.2a Prise free the retaining clips ...

12.2b ... and withdraw the bearing

12.2c The release arm can be extracted through the housing aperture

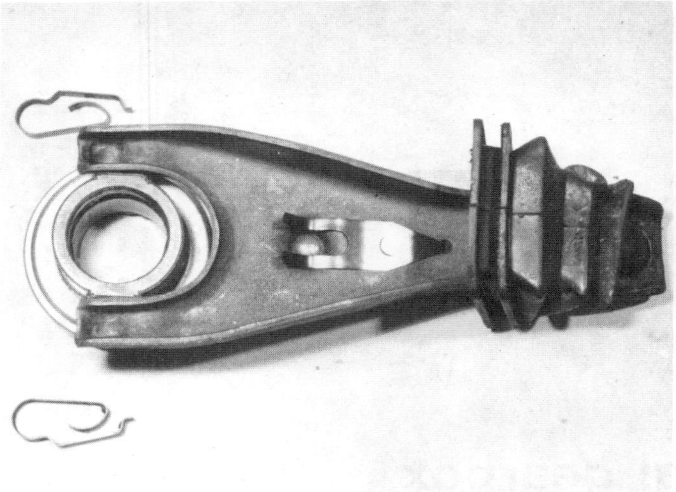

12.5 The clutch release arm, bearing assembly and securing clips

13.1 Locate clutch disc as shown, then fit cover assembly into position

should the clutch disc be refitted the wrong way round as it will be found impossible to operate the clutch (photo).

2 Refit the clutch cover assembly loosely on the dowels. Locate the six bolts and tighten them finger tight so that the clutch disc is gripped but can still be moved, sideways but stiffly.

3 The clutch disc must now be centralised so that when the engine and gearbox are mated, the gearbox input shaft splines will pass through the splines in the centre of the hub.

4 Centralisation can be carried out quite easily by inserting a round bar or long screwdriver through the hole in the centre of the clutch, so that the end of the bar rests in the small hole in the crankshaft containing the input shaft bearing bush. Moving the bar sideways or up and down will move the clutch disc in whichever direction is necessary to achieve centralisation.

5 Centralisation is easily judged by removing the bar or screwdriver and viewing the driveplate hub in relation to the hole in the centre of the diaphragm spring. When the hub is exactly in the centre of the release bearing hole, all is correct. Alternatively, if an old input shaft can be borrowed this will eliminate all the guesswork as it will fit the bearing and centre of the clutch hub exactly, obviating the need for visual alignment.

6 Tighten the clutch bolts firmly in a diagonal sequence to ensure that the cover plate is pulled down evenly and without distortion of the flange.

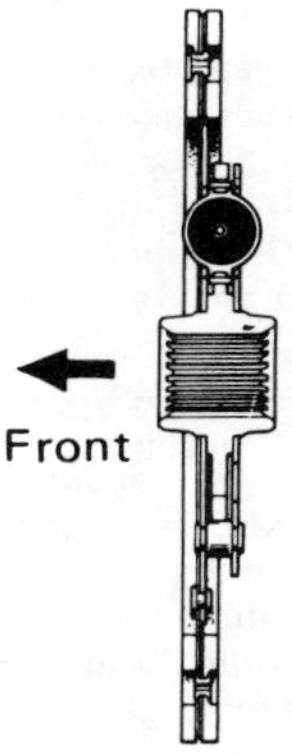

Fig. 5.20 Clutch disc fitting direction (Sec 13)

7 Check that the bolts are tightened to specified torque wrench setting.

8 Install the gearbox (see Chapter 6).

9 Adjust the clutch free movement.

14 Fault diagnosis – clutch

Symptom	Reason(s)
Judder when taking up drive	Loose engine or gearbox mountings. Driven plate linings worn or contaminated with oil. Worn splines in driven plate hub or on input shaft of gearbox. Worn flywheel centre spigot bearing.
Clutch spin (failure to disengage completely so that gears cannot be meshed)	Incorrect clutch pedal free movement. Air in clutch hydraulic system. Damaged or misaligned pressure plate assembly.
Clutch slip (increase in engine speed does not result in vehicle speed increasing – particularly on uphill gradients)	Incorrect pedal free movement. Driven plate friction linings worn out or oil contaminated.
Noise evident on depressing clutch pedal	Faulty or worn release bearing. Insufficient pedal free movement.
Noise evident as clutch pedal released	Distorted driven plate. Weak driven plate torsion shock absorbers in hub. Insufficient pedal free movement. Weak or broken pedal or release lever return spring. Distorted or worn input shaft. Release bearing loose on retainer hub.

Chapter 6 Part A Manual gearbox

Contents

Specifications

Type
Four or five forward speeds (all synchromesh) and reverse

Application

4K engine models	K40 (4-speed) or K50 (5-speed)
2T, 2T-B and 3T-C engine models	T40 (4-speed) or T50 (5-speed)

Ratios

	K40	K50	T40	T50
1st	3.789 : 1	3.789 : 1	3.587 : 1	3.587 : 1
2nd	2.220 : 1	2.220 : 1	2.022 : 1	2.022 : 1
3rd	1.435 : 1	1.435 : 1	1.384 : 1	1.384 : 1
4th	1.000 : 1	1.000 : 1	1.000 : 1	1.000 : 1
5th	–	0.865 : 1	–	0.861 : 1
Reverse	4.316 : 1	4.316 : 1	3.484 : 1	3.484 : 1

Tolerances (K40 and K50 gearboxes)

Countershaft endfloat:	
K40	0.0020 to 0.0098 in (0.05 to 0.25 mm)
K50	0.0031 to 0.0157 in (0.08 to 0.40 mm)
Mainshaft gear endfloat:	
1st gear	0.0071 to 0.0110 in (0.18 to 0.28 mm)
2nd gear	0.0039 to 0.0078 in (0.10 to 0.25 mm)
3rd	0.0020 to 0.0059 in (0.05 to 0.15 mm)
5th gear	0.0079 to 0.0118 in (0.20 to 0.30 mm)
Maximum endfloat all gears	0.012 in (0.3 mm)
1st, 2nd, 3rd gear running clearance on mainshaft	0.0020 to 0.0039 in (0.05 to 0.10 mm)
Shift fork to synchro sleeve groove clearance (maximum)	0.0032 in (0.8 mm)
Synchro ring clearance when pressed onto cone of gear (maximum)	0.032 in (0.8 mm)

Circlip thicknesses

Input shaft bearing to shaft circlip (snap-ring)	0.0925 to 0.0945 in (2.35 to 2.40 mm)
	0.0965 to 0.0984 in (2.45 to 2.50 mm)

Mainshaft front synchro hub to shaft circlip (snap-ring)	0.0807 to 0.0827 in (2.05 to 2.10 mm)
	0.0827 to 0.0845 in (2.10 to 2.15 mm)
	0.0845 to 0.0866 in (2.15 to 2.20 mm)
	0.0866 to 0.0886 in (2.20 to 2.25 mm)
	0.0886 to 0.0906 in (2.25 to 2.30 mm)
	0.0906 to 0.0925 in (2.30 to 2.35 mm)
	0.0925 to 0.0945 in (2.35 to 2.40 mm)
	0.0945 to 0.0965 in (2.40 to 2.45 mm)
Mainshaft rear bearing (K50) circlip (snap-ring)	0.0807 to 0.0827 in (2.05 to 2.10 mm)
	0.0827 to 0.0846 in (2.10 to 2.15 mm)
	0.0846 to 0.0866 in (2.15 to 2.20 mm)
	0.0866 to 0.0886 in (2.20 to 2.25 mm)
	0.0886 to 0.0906 in (2.25 to 2.30 mm)
	0.0906 to 0.0925 in (2.30 to 2.35 mm)
	0.0925 to 0.0945 in (2.35 to 2.40 mm)
	0.0945 to 0.0965 in (2.40 to 2.45 mm)
	0.0965 to 0.0984 in (2.45 to 2.50 mm)
	0.0984 to 0.1004 in (2.50 to 2.55 mm)
Countershaft rear (K50) circlip (snap-ring)	0.0886 to 0.0925 in (2.25 to 2.35 mm)
	0.0925 to 0.0965 in (2.35 to 2.45 mm)
	0.0965 to 0.1004 in (2.45 to 2.55 mm)
Fifth gear (K50) circlip thickness (snap-ring)	0.0807 to 0.0827 in (2.05 to 2.10 mm)
	0.0827 to 0.0846 in (2.10 to 2.15 mm)
	0.0846 to 0.0866 in (2.15 to 2.20 mm)
	0.0866 to 0.0886 in (2.20 to 2.25 mm)
	0.0886 to 0.0906 in (2.25 to 2.30 mm)
	0.0906 to 0.0925 in (2.30 to 2.35 mm)
	0.0925 to 0.0945 in (2.35 to 2.40 mm)
	0.0945 to 0.0965 in (2.40 to 2.45 mm)
	0.0965 to 0.0984 in (2.45 to 2.50 mm)
	0.0984 to 0.1004 in (2.50 to 2.55 mm)
	0.1004 to 0.1024 in (2.55 to 2.60 mm)
	0.1024 to 0.1043 in (2.60 to 2.65 mm)
	0.1043 to 0.1063 in (2.65 to 2.70 mm)
	0.1063 to 0.1083 in (2.70 to 2.75 mm)
	0.1083 to 1.1102 in (2.75 to 2.80 mm)

Thrust washers and spacers

Mainshaft 3rd gear to synchro hub spacer thickness	0.1693 to 0.1713 in (4.30 to 4.35 mm)
	0.1713 to 0.1732 in (4.35 to 4.40 mm)
	0.1732 to 0.1753 in (4.40 to 4.45 mm)
Front bearing retainer gasket thickness	0.020 in (0.5 mm)
	0.012 in (0.3 mm)
Countergear thrust washer thickness (K40)	0.0512 to 0.0532 in (1.30 to 1.35 mm)
	0.0551 to 0.0561 in (1.40 to 1.45 mm)
	0.0591 to 0.0610 in (1.50 to 1.55 mm)
	0.0630 to 0.0650 in (1.60 to 1.65 mm)
Countergear case thrust washer thickness (K50)	0.0673 to 0.0713 in (1.71 to 1.81 mm)
	0.0720 to 0.0760 in (1.83 to 1.93 mm)
	0.0768 to 0.0807 in (1.95 to 2.05 mm)
Output shaft journal diameter (limit)	1.252 in (31.8 mm)
Output shaft flange thickness	0.138 in (3.5 mm)
Output shaft deflection	0.0024 in (0.06 mm)
1st gear bushing flange thickness limit	0.1319 in (3.35 mm)
Gear inside diameter limits:	
1st	1.4626 in (37.15 mm)
2nd and 3rd	1.2657 in (32.15 mm)
5th (K50)	1.1083 in (28.15 mm)
Extension housing bush:	
Oil clearance	0.0004 to 0.0023 in (0.009 to 0.059 mm)
Inside diameter	1.2598 to 1.2608 in (32.00 to 32.025 mm)
Reverse idler gear inside diameter limit	0.717 in (18.2 mm)
Reverse idler shaft outer diameter limit	0.705 in (17.9 mm)

Tolerances (T40 and T50 gearboxes)

Reverse idler gear endfloat:	
Standard	0.0020 to 0.0197 in (0.05 to 0.50 mm)
Maximum	0.04 in (1.0 mm)
Mainshaft gear endfloat:	
1st	0.0059 to 0.0108 in (0.15 to 0.275 mm)
2nd	0.0059 to 0.0098 in (0.15 to 0.25 mm)
3rd	0.0059 to 0.0118 in (0.15 to 0.30 mm)
Reverse	0.0079 to 0.0127 in (0.20 to 0.325 mm)
5th (up to June 1981)	0.0059 to 0.0108 in (0.15 to 0.275 mm)
5th (from June 1981)	0.0039 to 0.0366 in (0.100 to 0.930 mm)

Maximum 1st, 2nd, 5th gears	0.020 in (0.5 mm)
Maximum 3rd, reverse gears	0.024 in (0.6 mm)
Shift fork to synchro sleeve groove clearance	0.039 in (1.0 mm)
Synchro ring to gear clearance when ring pressed against cone of gear	0.04 to 0.08 in (1.0 to 2.0 mm)
Maximum	0.032 in (0.8 mm)
Input shaft bearing to shaft circlip thickness	0.0925 to 0.0945 in (2.35 to 2.40 mm)
	0.0945 to 0.0965 in (2.40 to 2.45 mm)
	0.0965 to 0.0984 in (2.45 to 2.50 mm)
	0.0984 to 0.1004 in (2.50 to 2.55 mm)
	0.1004 to 0.1417 in (2.55 to 2.60 mm)
Input shaft bearing spacer thickness	0.0719 to 0.0738 in (1.825 to 1.875 mm)
	0.0762 to 0.0781 in (1.935 to 1.985 mm)
	0.0805 to 0.0825 in (2.045 to 2.095 mm)
	0.0848 to 0.0868 in (2.155 to 2.205 mm)
	0.0892 to 0.0911 in (2.265 to 2.315 mm)
	0.0935 to 0.0955 in (2.375 to 2.425 mm)
Mainshaft front synchro hub to shaft circlip thickness	0.0768 to 0.0787 in (1.95 to 2.00 mm)
	0.0787 to 0.0807 in (2.00 to 2.05 mm)
	0.0807 to 0.0827 in (2.05 to 2.10 mm)
	0.0827 to 0.0847 in (2.10 to 2.15 mm)
	0.0847 to 0.0866 in (2.15 to 2.20 mm)
Mainshaft rear (No. 1) circlip thickness	0.1024 to 0.1043 in (2.60 to 2.65 mm)
	0.1043 to 0.1063 in (2.65 to 2.70 mm)
	0.1063 to 0.1083 in (2.70 to 2.75 mm)
	0.1083 to 0.1102 in (2.75 to 2.80 mm)
	0.1102 to 0.1122 in (2.80 to 2.85 mm)
	0.1122 to 0.1142 in (2.85 to 2.90 mm)
	0.1142 to 0.1161 in (2.90 to 2.95 mm)
	0.1162 to 0.1181 in (2.95 to 3.00 mm)
	0.1181 to 0.1201 in (3.00 to 3.05 mm)
	0.1201 to 0.1220 in (3.05 to 3.10 mm)
	0.1220 to 0.1240 in (3.10 to 3.15 mm)
	0.1240 to 0.1260 in (3.15 to 3.20 mm)
	0.1260 to 0.1280 in (3.20 to 3.25 mm)
	0.1280 to 0.1299 in (3.25 to 3.30 mm)
	0.1299 to 0.1319 in (3.30 to 3.35 mm)
Mainshaft rear (No. 2) circlip thickness	0.0925 to 0.0945 in (2.35 to 2.40 mm)
	0.0945 to 0.0965 in (2.40 to 2.45 mm)
	0.0965 to 0.0984 in (2.45 to 2.50 mm)
	0.0984 to 0.1004 in (2.50 to 2.55 mm)
	0.1004 to 0.1024 in (2.55 to 2.60 mm)
	0.1024 to 0.1043 in (2.60 to 2.65 mm)
	0.1043 to 0.1063 in (2.65 to 2.70 mm)
Journal clearance of gears (limit):	
1st, 5th, Reverse	0.0025 in (0.064 mm)
2nd and 3rd	0.0039 in (0.100 mm)
Reverse idle	0.008 in (0.2 mm)
Mainshaft 2nd and 3rd gear journal diameter limit	1.488 in (37.8 mm)
Mainshaft run-out limit	0.0024 in (0.06 mm)
Mainshaft bush flange thickness limit	0.157 in (4.0 mm)
Countergear circlip thickness:	
T40 gearbox	0.0709 to 0.0728 in (1.80 to 1.85 mm)
	0.0748 to 0.0768 in (1.90 to 1.95 mm)
T50 gearbox	0.0787 in (2.0 mm)
	0.0709 in (1.8 mm)
	0.0630 in (1.6 mm)

Torque wrench settings

K40 and K50 type gearboxes

	lbf ft	kgf m
Clutch bellhousing to engine bolts	37 to 50	5.0 to 7.0
Extension housing to gearbox bolts	22 to 32	3.0 to 4.5
Front bearing retainer bolts	11 to 15	1.5 to 2.2
Mainshaft nut	33 to 72	4.5 to 10.0
Reverse idler gear shaft retainer bolt	10 to 13	1.3 to 1.8
Restrict pin	27 to 31	3.7 to 4.3
Oil pan	4.0 to 5.0	0.55 to 0.70

T40 and T50 type gearboxes

	lbf ft	kgf m
Clutch housing to gearbox bolts	22 to 32	3.0 to 4.5
Transmission to engine bolts	37 to 57	5.0 to 8.0
Extension housing bolts	22 to 32	3.0 to 4.5
Gearbox case cover RH and LH	14 to 15	1.8 to 2.2
Mainshaft nut	33 to 72	4.5 to 10.0
Reverse idler gear shaft bolt	10 to 13	1.3 to 1.8
Restrict pin	27 to 31	3.7 to 4.3

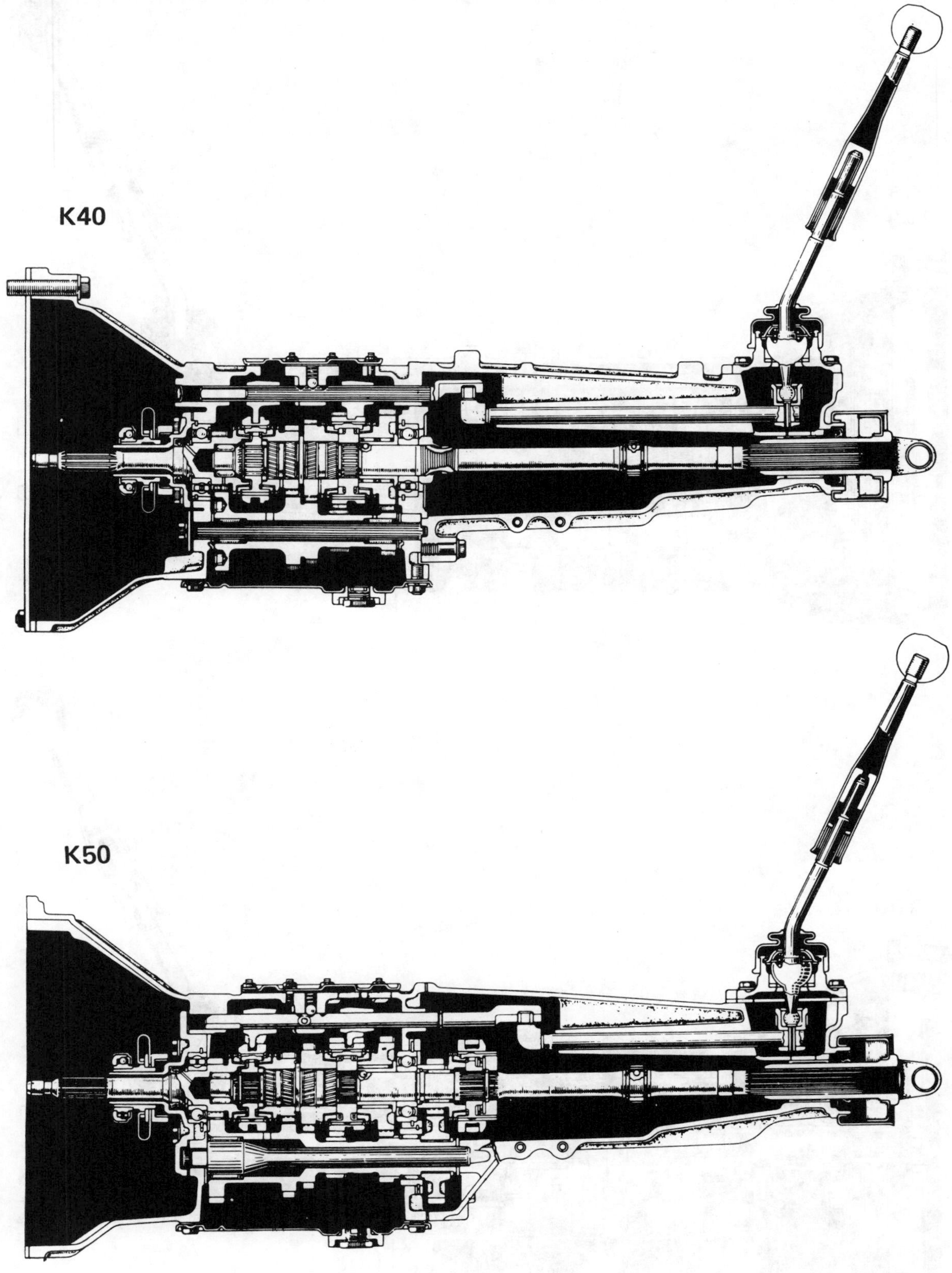

Fig. 6.1 Sectional views of the K40 (4-speed) and K50 (5-speed) gearboxes (Sec 1)

T40

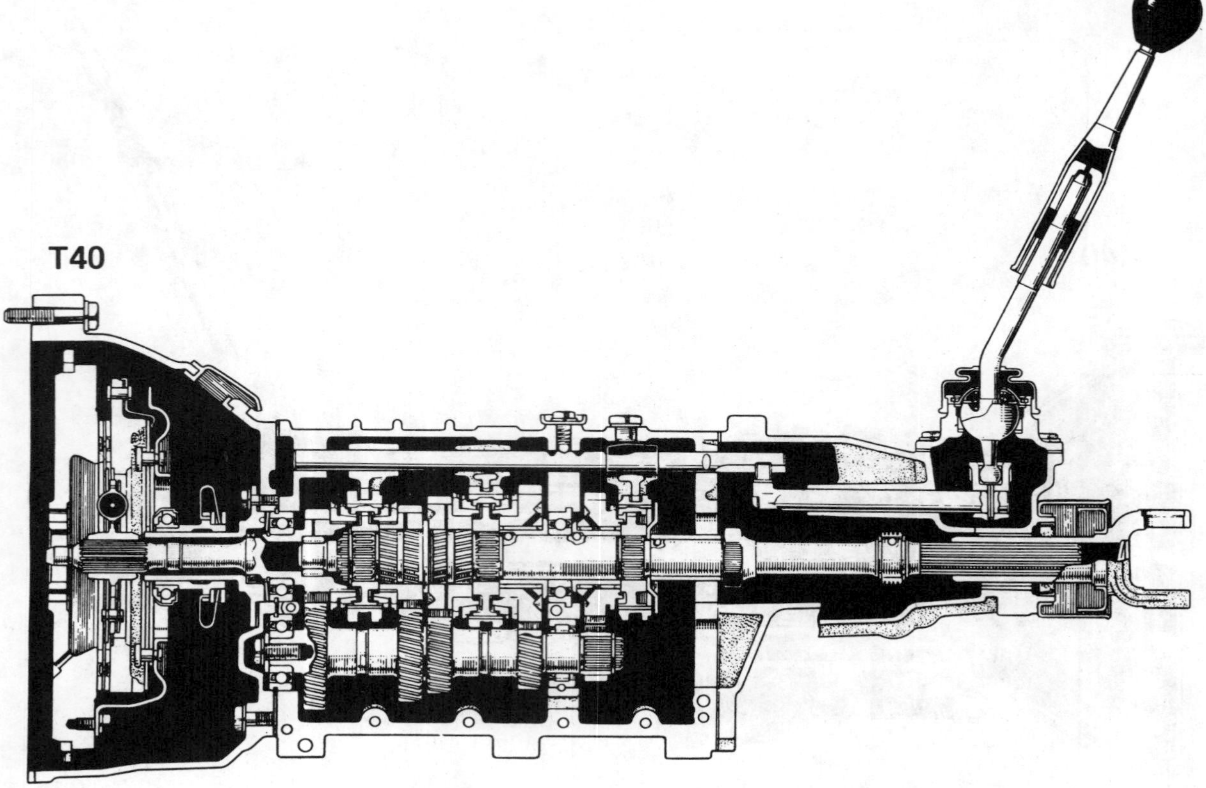

T50

Fig. 6.2 Sectional views of the T40 (4-speed) and T50 (5-speed) gearboxes (Sec 1)

1 General description

Four different manual gearbox types are fitted to Toyota Corolla models covered by this manual. The K40 (4-speed) and K50 (5-speed) are used on 4K engine models and both have casings of externally similar one-piece construction. The T40 (4-speed) and T50 (5-speed) units used on 2T, 2T-B and 3T-C engine models are virtually identical in internal and external construction apart from the additional 5th gear on the T50 type.

All gearboxes feature synchromesh engagement on all forward gears actuated by a centrally mounted gearshift lever.

2 Gearbox – removal and refitting

1 If the engine is being removed at the same time, refer to Chapter 1 for removal procedure.
2 If the gearbox is to be removed on its own, carry out the following operations, having first drained the gearbox oil.
3 If an inspection pit is not available, run the rear roadwheels up on ramps or jack-up the rear of the vehicle and secure on axle stands so that there is a clearance below the gearbox at least equal to the diameter of the clutch bellhousing to enable the gearbox to be removed from below, and to the rear of, the vehicle.
4 Disconnect the lead from the battery negative terminal.
5 If a centre console is fitted inside the vehicle, extract its securing screws and remove it.
6 Peel back the floor carpet to give access to the base of the gearshift lever.
7 The gearshift control lever is held in its retainer by means of a circlip and this is accessible after removing the rubber dust cover upwards over the lever. Remove the circlip using a pair of suitable narrow nosed pliers, then withdraw the gearshift lever (photo).
8 Partially drain the cooling system so that the coolant level drops below the line of the radiator header tank. Refer to Chapter 2 if necessary.
9 Disconnect the top hose between the radiator and the thermostat housing (at one end only).
10 Now working underneath the vehicle, disconnect the leads from the reversing lamp switch on the gearbox.
11 Remove the propeller shaft as described in Chapter 7.
12 Disconnect the speedometer cable from the gearbox by unscrewing the knurled ring. Take care not to lose the felt seals (photo).
13 Disconnect the exhaust downpipe from the manifold and disconnect the exhaust pipe support bracket from the gearbox.
14 Disconnect the earth bonding strap at the rear of the engine cylinder block.
15 Unbolt and remove the starter motor from the bellhousing. If removing the starter motor completely you will also need to detach the lead connections so make a note of their positions to ensure correct refitting (photo).
16 *On vehicles with hydraulic clutch actuation,* unbolt the clutch slave cylinder from the clutch bellhousing and tie it up and out of the way. There is no need to disconnect the hydraulic system, but whilst the slave cylinder is detached take care not to depress the clutch pedal.
17 On vehicles fitted with a cable operated clutch mechanism, extract the C-washer from the clutch cable at the engine compartment rear bulkhead. Then detach the cable from the release lever. When removing the C-washer note which groove it is removed from to assist adjustment on reassembly.
18 Place a jack under the engine sump using a block of wood as an insulator and support the weight of the engine.
19 Unbolt the rear mounting crossmember from the bodyframe (photo).
20 Unbolt the crossmember from the gearbox extension housing and remove it.
21 Lower the engine support jack enough to give access to the upper bolts which secure the clutch bellhousing to the engine. Remove the remaining bolts (photo).
22 Support the gearbox on a trolley jack and then lower both jacks

2.7 Remove the gear lever assembly

2.12 Detach the speedometer drive cable

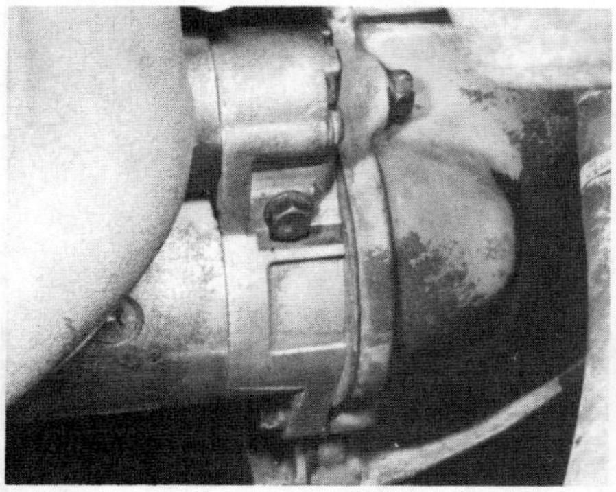
2.15 Unbolt and remove the starter motor

2.19 Rear mounting crossmember

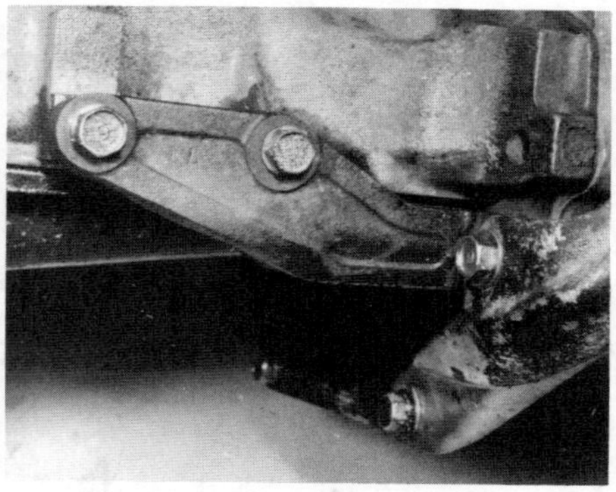
2.21 Lower housing bolts also secure exhaust support bracket and crankcase support bracket on left-hand side (where fitted)

together until the gearbox can be withdrawn rearwards and removed from below the vehicle. If the vehicle is over an inspection pit then the help of two assistants should be obtained to withdraw the gearbox. On no account let the weight of the gearbox hang upon the input shaft while the latter is still engaged in the splines of the clutch driven plate.
23 Refitting is a reversal of removal but if the clutch mechanism has been disturbed, make sure that the clutch driven plate has been centralised as described in Chapter 5.
24 If the gearbox has been dismantled and reassembled, make sure that it is refilled with the correct grade and quantity of lubricant.
25 On models fitted with a cable operated clutch reconnect the cable and check adjustment as given in Chapter 5 before lowering the vehicle.

3 Gearbox (Type K40) – dismantling into major assemblies

1 Drain the lubricant and clean the outside of the unit with paraffin and a stiff brush or use a water soluble solvent.
2 Refer to Chapter 5 and remove the clutch release lever and bearing assembly.
3 Unscrew the bolts which secure the front bearing retainer to the inside of the clutch bellhousing. Slide the retainer from the input shaft (Fig. 6.3).
4 Remove the nuts and withdraw the cover and gasket from the top of the gearcase. As the cover is withdrawn, carefully recover the three detent balls and their springs. Unscrew and remove the reversing lamp switch.
5 Unbolt and remove the bottom cover and its gasket from the gearcasing.
6 Unbolt and remove the speedometer driven gear from the extension housing.
7 Unbolt and remove the restrict pins from each side of the extension housing then remove the nuts which secure the extension housing to the main gearcase. Withdraw the extension housing moving it towards the bottom cover side. Be careful not to damage the rear seal in the housing on the mainshaft splines as it is removed. Remove the housing gasket.
8 Remove the locking bolt and its washer which secures the reverse idler gear shaft to the main gear case (photo).

3.8 Remove reverse idler shaft lock bolt (K40 gearbox)

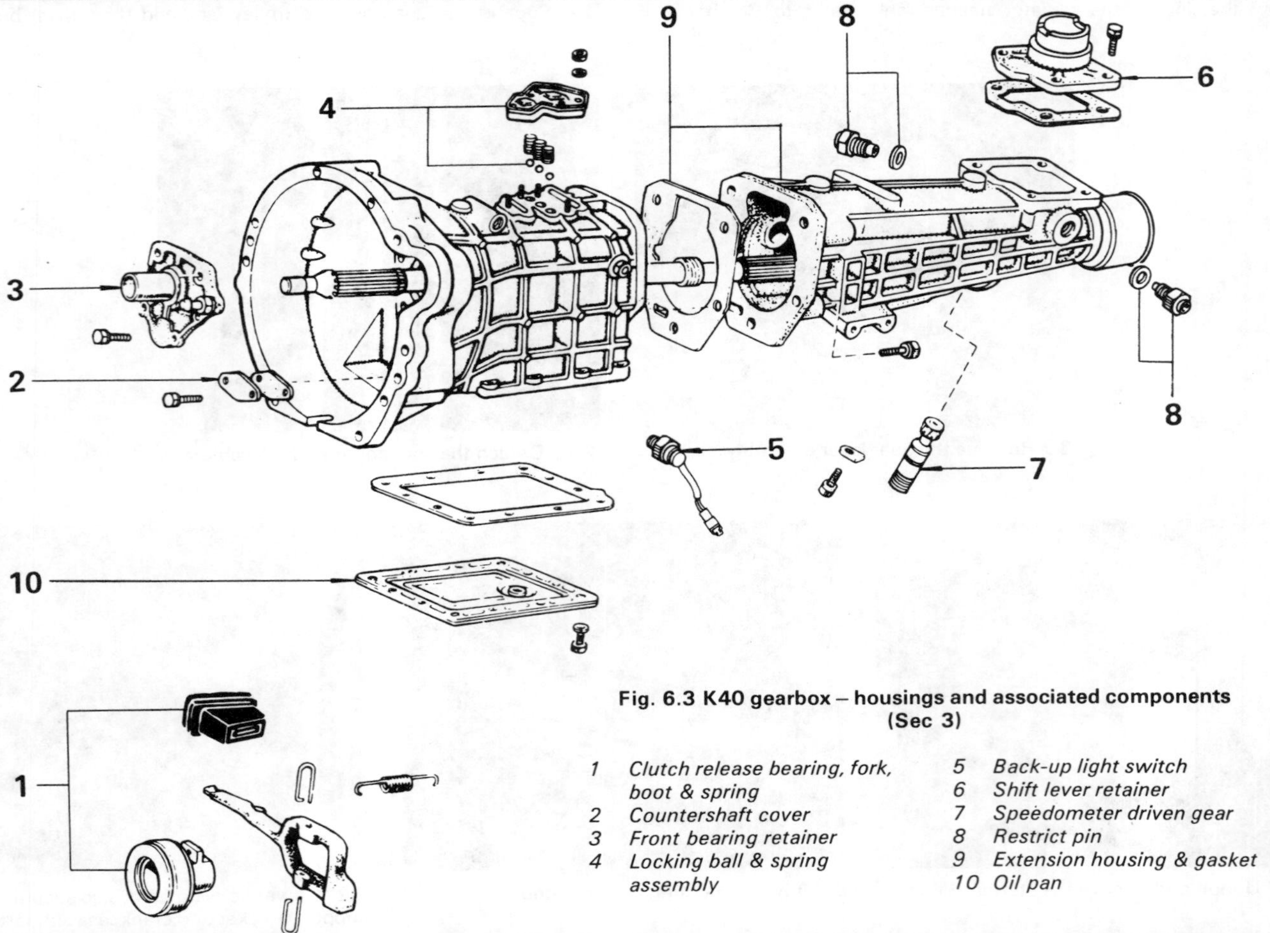

Fig. 6.3 K40 gearbox – housings and associated components (Sec 3)

1 Clutch release bearing, fork, boot & spring
2 Countershaft cover
3 Front bearing retainer
4 Locking ball & spring assembly
5 Back-up light switch
6 Shift lever retainer
7 Speedometer driven gear
8 Restrict pin
9 Extension housing & gasket
10 Oil pan

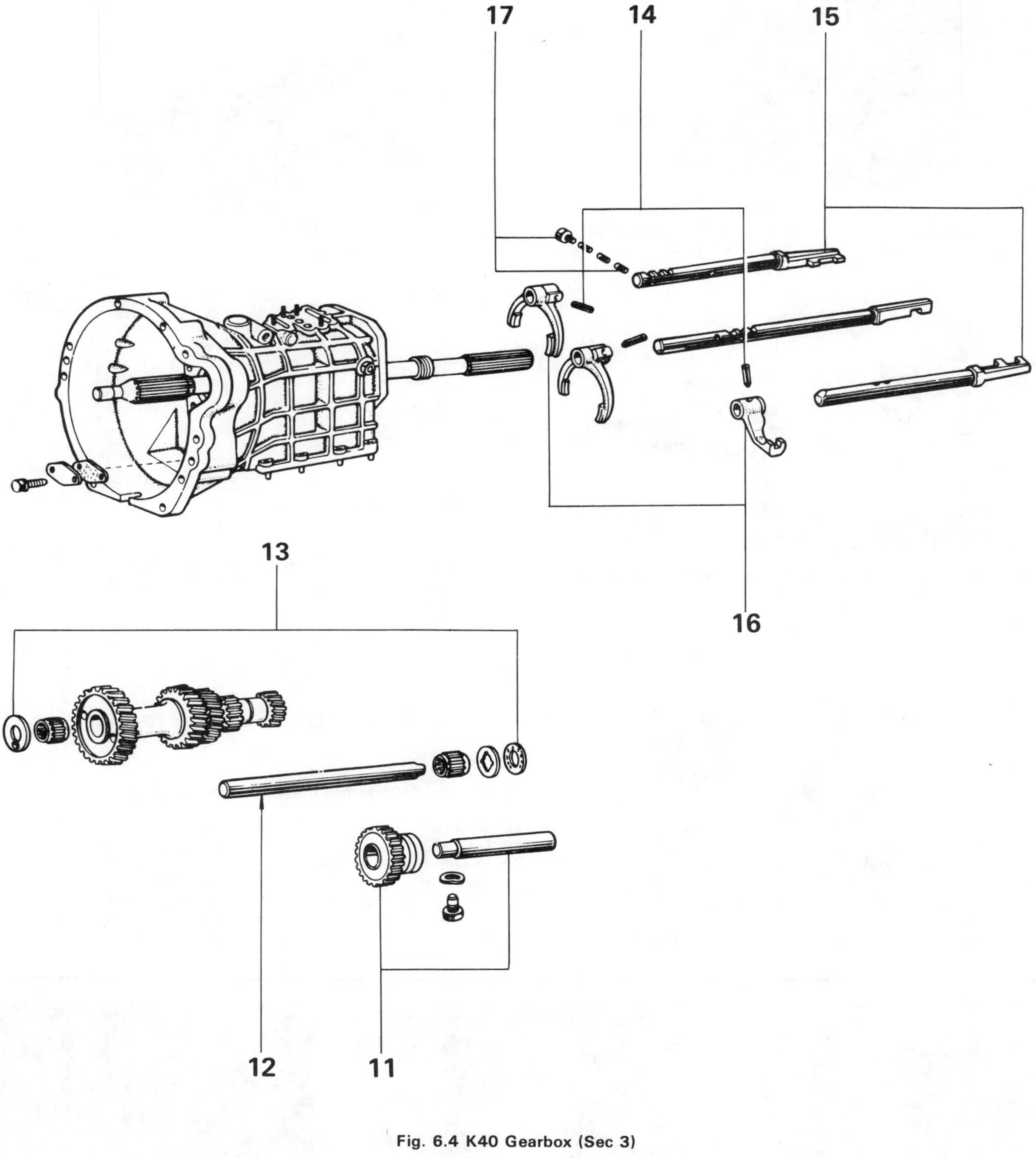

Fig. 6.4 K40 Gearbox (Sec 3)

11 Reverse idle gear & shaft
12 Counter gear shaft
13 Counter gear bearing & washer
14 Slotted spring pin
15 Shift fork shaft
16 Shift fork
17 Shift interlock pin

Fig. 6.5 Check countershaft thrust clearance before removal – K40 gearbox (Sec 3)

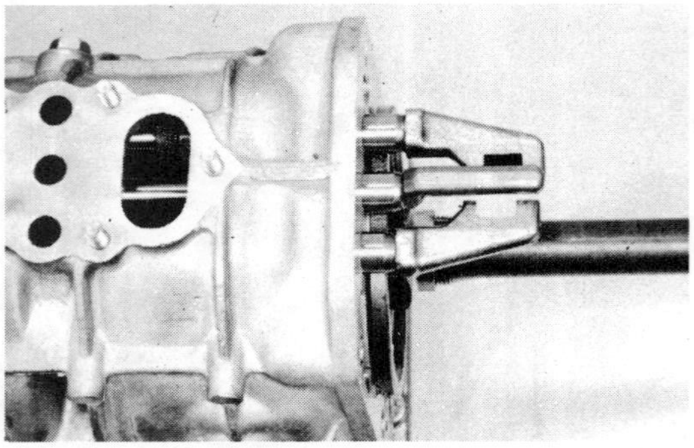

Fig. 6.6 K40 gearbox – move No 1 shift fork to neutral (Sec 3)

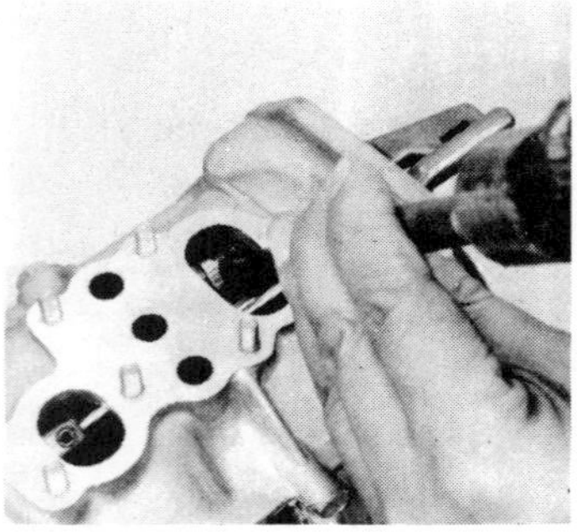

Fig. 6.7 Drive out the roll pin – K40 gearbox (Sec 3)

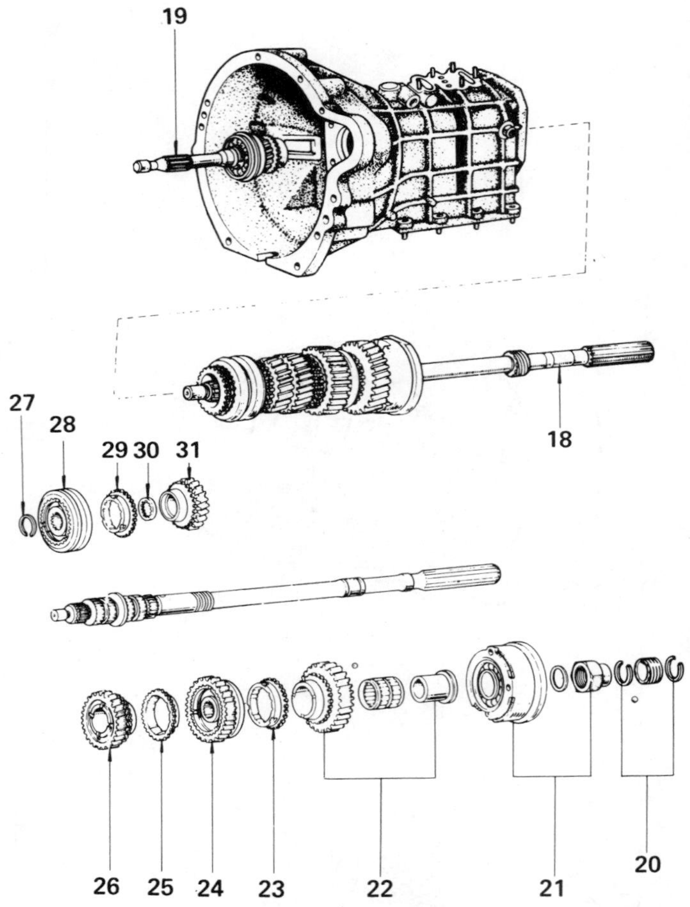

Fig. 6.8 The K40 gearbox mainshaft assembly components (Sec 3)

18 Mainshaft
19 Input shaft
20 Speedometer drive gear
21 Rear bearing
22 1st gear, bushing, needle roller bearing & locking ball
23 Synchronizer ring
24 No.1 clutch hub & sleeve
25 Synchronizer ring
26 2nd gear
27 Circlip
28 No.2 clutch hub & sleeve
29 Synchronizer ring
30 Spacer
31 3rd gear

3.9 Withdraw the reverse idler shaft and gear (K40 gearbox)

3.10 Countershaft front retaining plate (K40 gearbox)

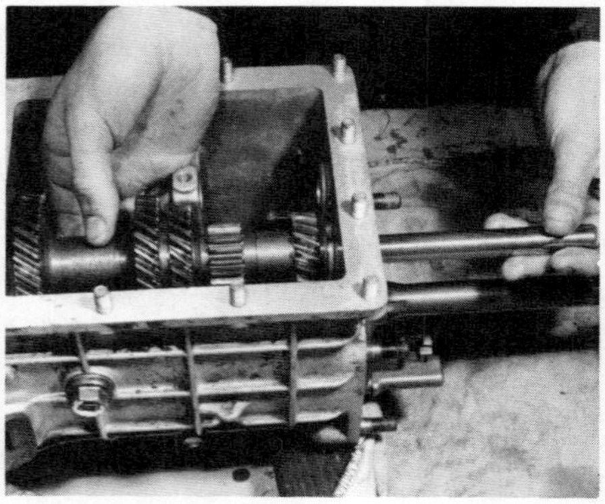

3.11 Withdrawing the countershaft (K40 gearbox)

3.12 Countergear and thrust washers (K40 gearbox)

3.13a Dislodging input shaft bearing (K40 gearbox)

3.13b Withdrawing the input shaft (K40 gearbox)

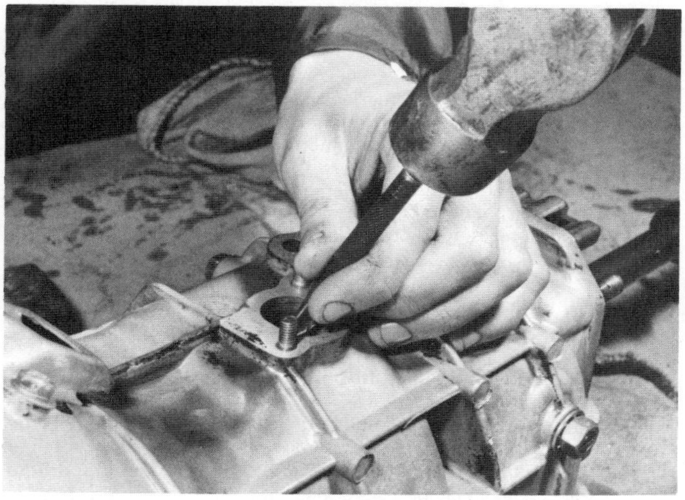

3.15 Driving out a shift fork roll pin (K40 gearbox)

9 Withdraw the reverse idler shaft and lift off the idler gear (photo).
10 The countershaft is next to be removed, but before doing so check the thrust clearance with a feeler gauge and note the clearance for reference during inspection and assembly (Fig. 6.5). Remove the countershaft by first unscrewing the two bolts which secure the retaining plate to the front face of the gear case (photo).
11 Hold the countergear assembly steady and withdraw the countershaft rearwards (photo), drifting it out from the front.
12 Lift the countergear assembly from the gearbox and recover the thrust washers (photo).
13 Remove the input shaft by tapping its bearing track towards the front of the gearcase (photos).
14 The shift forks are secured to the selector shafts by roll (tension) pins which are accessible through the top cover aperture.
15 Drive out the roll pins using a suitable drift (photo).
16 First move the No. 1 shifter fork shaft to neutral (Fig. 6.6) then drive out the roll pin (Fig. 6.7).
17 Position the respective fork shafts to neutral and then pull them free. When withdrawing a shaft, hold its shift fork steady and once it is removed, recover the interlock plungers. Move No. 1 clutch hub into 2nd gear to remove its shift fork.
18 Remove the centre (3rd/4th) selector shaft last.
19 Extract the 1st/2nd shift fork from the groove in the synchro unit sleeve.
20 Extract the 3rd/4th shift fork from the groove in the synchro unit sleeve.
21 Extract reverse shift fork.
22 Withdraw the mainshaft assembly from the rear of the gear casing. If it is tight, tap it gently with a plastic faced mallet.
23 The reverse selector arm can be removed if it is worn or damaged but this is not normally required.

4 Gearbox components (Type K40) – inspection

1 It is assumed that the gearbox has been dismantled for reasons of excessive noise, lack of synchromesh action on certain gears or for failure to stay in gear. If anything more drastic than this (total failure, seizure or main casing cracked) it would be better to leave well alone and look for a replacement, either secondhand or an exchange unit.
2 Examine all gears for excessively worn, chipped or damaged teeth. Any such gears should be renewed.
3 Check all synchromesh rings for wear on the bearing surfaces, which normally have clear machined oil reservoir lines in them. If these are smooth or obviously uneven, replacement is essential. Also when the rings are fitted to their gears – as they would be in operation – there should be no rock. This would signify ovality or lack of concentricity. One of the most satisfactory ways of checking is by comparing the fit of a new ring with an old one in the gearwheel cone. The teeth and cut outs in the synchro rings also wear and for this reason also it is unwise not to fit new ones when the opportunity avails.
4 All ball race bearings should be checked for chatter and roughness

Fig. 6.9 Check the mainshaft gear thrust clearances and their general condition – K40 gearbox (Sec 4)

after they have been washed out. It is advisable to renew these any way even though they may not appear too badly worn.

5 Circlips which are all important in locating bearings, gears and hubs should be checked to ensure that they are undamaged and not distorted. In any case a selection of new circlips of varying thicknesses should be obtained to compensate for variations in new components fitted, and wear in old ones. The Specifications indicate what is available.

6 The thrust washers at the end of the countergear should be renewed as they will most certainly have worn if the gearbox is of any age. Compare the thrust clearance noted during gearbox dismantling with that given in the Specifications. If the specified thrust clearance limit is exceeded, new thrust washers must be fitted during assembly.

7 Needle roller bearings between the input shaft and mainshaft are usually found to be in good order, but if in any doubt renew the needle roller bearings.

8 Before finally going ahead with dismantling first ascertain the availability of spare parts – particularly shims, which could be difficult.

5 Extension housing (Type K40 gearbox) – servicing

1 It is rarely necessary to dismantle the extension housing but if, due to wear or damage, this is essential, remove the gearshift lever retainer and then drive out the roll pin to release the selector control rod from the gearshift lever housing.

2 The oil seal in the end of the housing can be renewed by levering out the old one.

3 To remove the extension housing bush, heat the housing to 100°C (212°F) then drive the bush out using a drift of suitable diameter. When driving the new bush into position ensure that the oil hole is at the top (Fig. 6.10).

4 Tap the new oil seal into position using a suitable drift (Fig. 6.11). Lubricate the seal lip with grease.

5 When refitting the selector control rod, use a new roll pin to retain it.

6 The speedometer gear unit oil seal can be extracted for renewal by prising out using a hooked implement (Fig. 6.12). When inserting the new seal, its fitted depth should be as shown (Fig. 6.13).

6 Input shaft (Type K40 gearbox) – servicing

1 The shaft and bearing are located in the front of the main casing by a large circlip in the outer track of the bearing.

2 To renew the bearing first remove the circlip from the front end of the bearing (Fig. 6.14).

3 Place the outer track of the race on the top of a firm bench vice and drive the input shaft through the bearing. Note that the bearing is fitted with the circlip groove towards the former end of the input shaft. Lift away the bearing.

4 The spigot bearing needle roller assembly may be slid out of the inner end of the input shaft.

5 Using a suitable diameter tubular drift carefully drive the ball race into position. The circlip in the outer track must be towards the front of the input shaft.

6 Retain the bearing in position with a circlip. This is a selective circlip which is available in two thicknesses to provide the closest fit (Fig. 6.15).

7 Work some grease into the needle bearing assembly and insert into the end of the input shaft (photo).

7 Mainshaft (Type K40 gearbox) – servicing

1 Before dismantling the mainshaft components for inspection, measure the thrust clearances of each gear using a feeler gauge and compare with the respective thrust limits given in the Specifications for the K40 gearbox. Note the thrust clearances of the 1st, 2nd and 3rd gear in turn for assessment during inspection.

2 Remove the circlip from the rearmost end of the mainshaft (photo).

3 Slide off the speedometer drive gear and recover the key (photo).

4 Remove the second circlip from the rear end of the mainshaft.

5 Hold the mainshaft firmly in the vice, straighten the staking locking the large nut and then remove the nut (photo).

6 Slide the shim(s) from the end of the mainshaft (photo).

7 Remove the rear bearing retainer from the end of the mainshaft (photo).

8 Slide off the first speed gear noting which way round it is fitted.

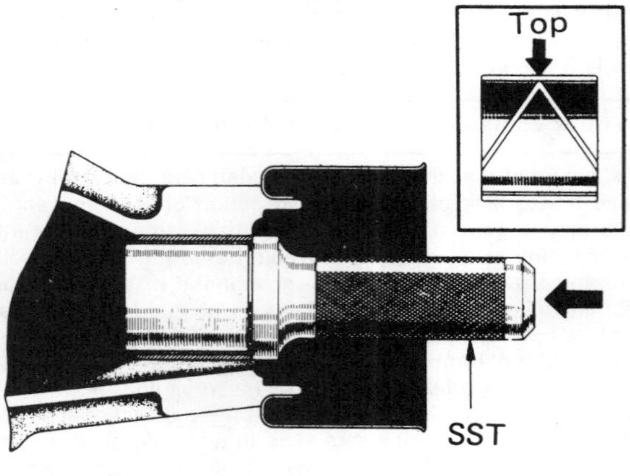

Fig. 6.10 Extension housing bush must have oil hole at top – K40 gearbox (Sec 5)

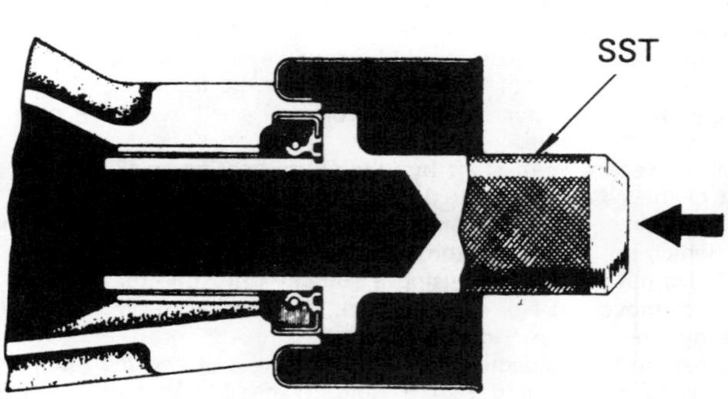

Fig. 6.11 Drive new extension housing oil seal into position as shown – K40 gearbox (Sec 5)

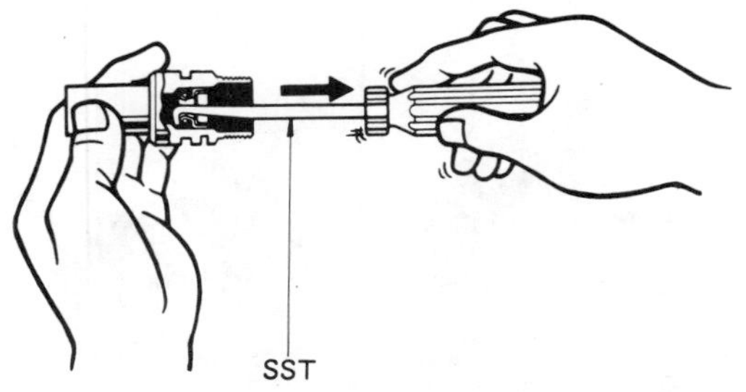

Fig. 6.12 Speedometer gear oil seal removal using a hooked tool – K40 gearbox (Sec 5)

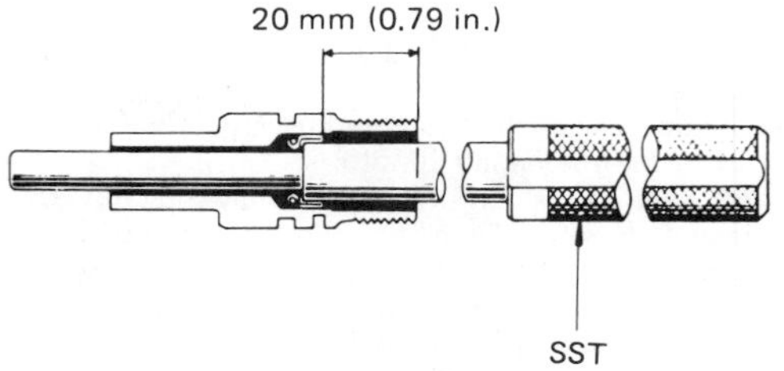

Fig. 6.13 Insert new speedometer oil seal to depth shown – K40 gearbox (Sec 5)

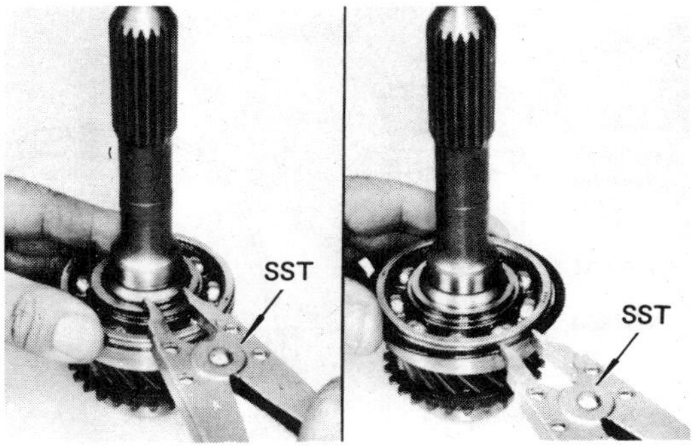

Fig. 6.14 Removal of input shaft bearing circlips – K40 gearbox (Sec 6)

Fig. 6.15 Select circlip of suitable thickness to take up play – K40 gearbox (Sec 6)

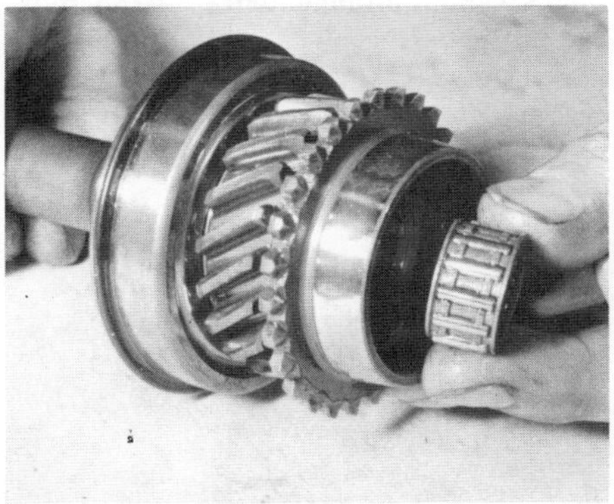

6.7 Input shaft needle roller bearing (K40 gearbox)

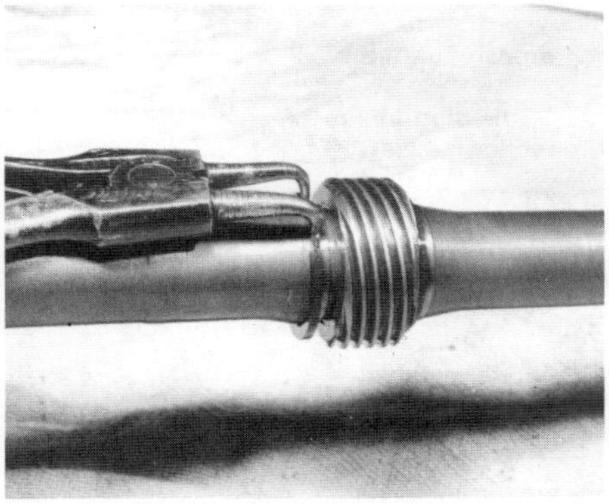

7.2 Extract the speedo drivegear circlip from mainshaft (K40 gearbox)

7.3 ... then withdraw the drivegear and key (K40 gearbox)

7.5 Unscrewing the mainshaft locknut (K40 gearbox)

7.6 Recover the mainshaft shims (K40 gearbox)

7.7 Removing mainshaft rear bearing retainer (K40 gearbox)

Then remove the synchroniser ring (photo). Keep the ring with the gear.
9 The first speed gear bush and needle roller bearing are next removed from the mainshaft (photo).
10 The first speed gear bush is retained by a ball bearing that should be lifted out from the mainshaft (photo).
11 The reverse gear and synchroniser assembly may next be removed from the mainshaft (photo). Then remove the synchroniser ring.
12 Slide off the second speed gear (photo).
13 Turning to the front end of the mainshaft, remove the shaft snap ring located at the end of the splines (photo).
14 Slide off the top/third synchroniser unit, noting which way round it is fitted (photo). Remove the synchroniser ring.
15 Finally slide off the third speed gear and splined thrust washer (photo).
16 Dismantling of the mainshaft is now complete.
17 The synchro hubs are only too easy to dismantle – just push the centre out and the whole assembly flies apart. The point is to prevent this happening, before you are ready. Do not dismantle the hub without reason and do not mix up parts of the hubs.
18 It is most important to check backlash in the splines between the outer sleeve and inner hub. If any is noticeable the whole assembly must be renewed.
19 Mark the hub and sleeve so that you may reassemble them on the same splines. With the hub and sleeve separated, the teeth at the end of the splines which engage with corresponding teeth of the gearwheels, must be checked for damage or wear.
20 Do not confuse the keystone shape at the ends of the teeth. This shape matches the gear teeth shape and it is a design characteristic to minimise jump-out tendencies.
21 If the synchronising cones are being renewed it is sensible also to renew the sliding keys and springs which hold them in position. Check rings for wear as shown (Fig. 6.16).
22 The hub assemblies are not interchangeable so they must be reassembled with their original or identical new parts.
23 The pips on the keys are symmetrical so may be refitted either way round into the hub.
24 One slotted key is assembled to each hub for locating the turned out end of the key spring.
25 It should be noted that the keys for each synchromesh unit are of different lengths.
26 The turned out end of each spring must locate in the slotted key and be assembled to the hub in an anticlockwise direction as viewed from either side of the hub (Fig. 6.17, 6.18).
27 Commence reassembly of the mainshaft by sliding 3rd speed gear and the splined thrust washer onto the front end of the mainshaft.
28 Fit the third speed gear synchroniser ring onto the synchromesh unit and slide the synchromesh unit onto the end of the mainshaft. Ensure the ring grooves are aligned with the keys.
29 Refit the shaft snap ring located at the end of the mainshaft splines. Measure the thrust clearance between the circlip and synchromesh unit hub. A range of 8 circlips is available to obtain the correct clearance (see Specifications Section).
30 Slide the second speed gear onto the rear end of the mainshaft.
31 Fit the second speed gear synchroniser ring onto the second speed synchromesh unit and slide the reverse gear and synchromesh unit onto the mainshaft. Ensure the ring grooves are aligned with the keys (Fig. 6.19).

Fig. 6.16 Check synchroniser rings for wear – ring to gear clearance (left) and braking action (right) – K40 gearbox (Sec 7)

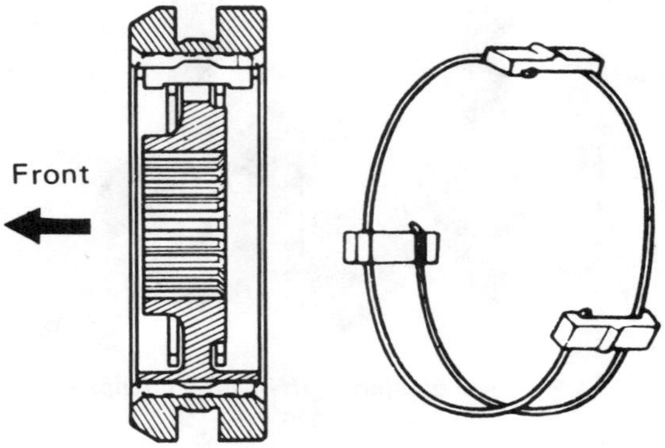

Fig. 6.17 The No 2 clutch hub – sectional view showing orientation and key spring assembly arrangement – K40 gearbox (Sec 7)

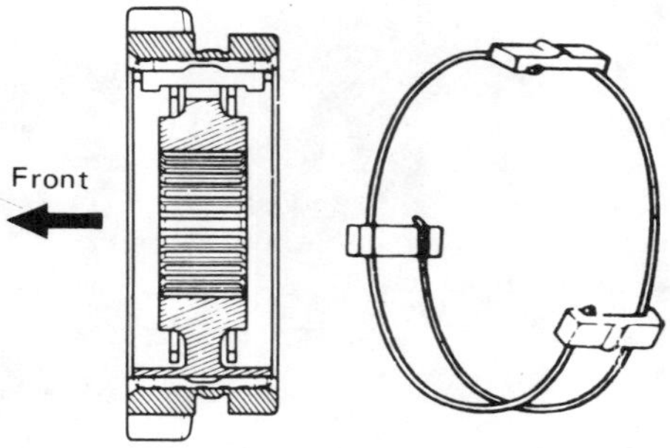

Fig. 6.18 The No 1 clutch hub – sectional view showing orientation and key spring arrangement – K40 gearbox (Sec 7)

7.8 1st gear removal from mainshaft (K40 gearbox)

7.9 1st gear bearing and bush (K40 gearbox)

7.10 1st gear bush and lock ball (K40 gearbox)

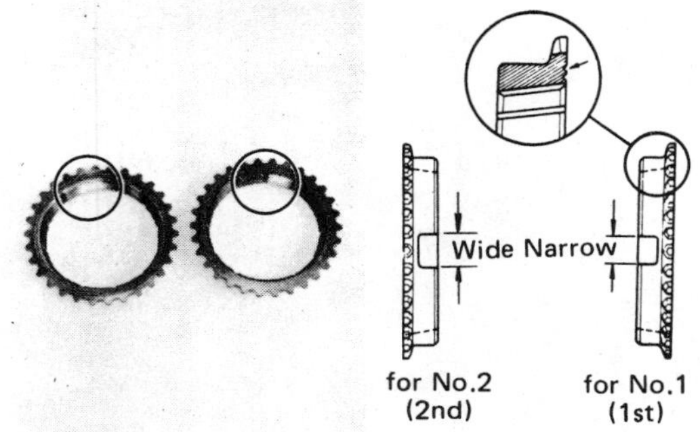

Fig. 6.19 1st and 2nd synchroniser rings identification – K40 gearbox (Sec 7)

Fig. 6.20 Locate lock ball (left) then slide gear and bush assembly into position – K40 gearbox (Sec 7)

32 Fit the first speed gear synchroniser ring onto the synchromesh unit ensuring the ring grooves are aligned with the keys.
33 Insert the locking ball onto the mainshaft and assemble the first speed gear bush, needle roller bearing and first speed gear onto the mainshaft (Fig. 6.20).
34 Refit the rear bearing retainer onto the end of the mainshaft and follow this with the shim(s) previously removed (photo).
35 Hold the mainshaft firmly in a vice and refit the large nut. Do not stake over yet.
36 Using feeler gauges measure the thrust clearance between the 3rd gear and hub. This should be as specified and is adjustable by a range of 3 different thicknesses of hub spacers (see Specifications Section) (Fig. 6.21).
37 The following thrust clearances should also be checked using feeler gauges as follows:

(a) 2nd gear to mainshaft flange
(b) 1st gear to 1st gear bush flange

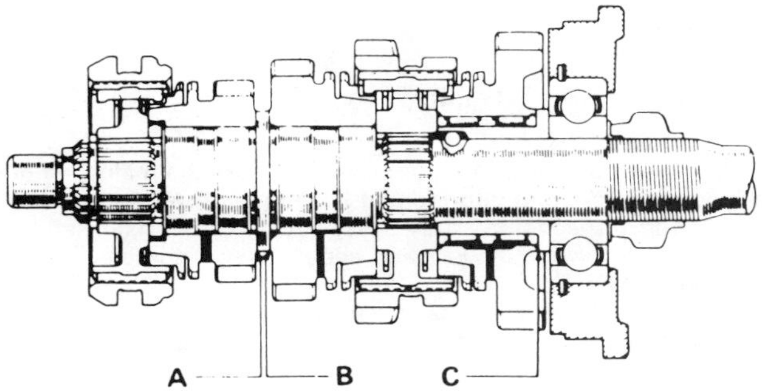

Fig. 6.21 Mainshaft gear thrust clearance (end-float) measurement diagram (K40 gearbox) (Sec 7)

7.11 Reverse gear and synchro unit removal (K40 gearbox)

7.12 2nd gear removal from mainshaft (K40 gearbox)

7.13 Mainshaft front circlip (K40 gearbox)

7.14 Remove 3rd/4th synchro unit from mainshaft (K40 gearbox)

7.15 Remove 3rd gear and thrust washer from mainshaft (K40 gearbox)

7.34 Refitting the mainshaft rear bearing retainer (K40 gearbox)

7.41 Assembled mainshaft (K40 gearbox)

8.1 Countergear needle roller bearing (K40 gearbox)

38 When all thrust clearances are correct ensure the mainshaft nut is tight and stake the end into the slot in the mainshaft.
39 Fit the first speedometer drivegear circlip to the mainshaft.
40 Replace the Woodruff key and slide the speedometer drivegear onto the mainshaft.
41 The mainshaft is now assembled and ready for refitting to the gearbox (photo).

8 Countergear (Type K40 gearbox) – servicing

1 Dismantling of the countergear assembly simply entails the removal of the needle roller bearing assemblies located at either end of the bore. This is a straightforward operation and will present no problems (photo).
2 Refitting the needle roller bearings is the reverse sequence to removal.
3 As mentioned previously, the thrust washers will probably be well worn and new washers should therefore be obtained. Various washer thicknesses are available and you should therefore obtain washers of thickness to provide the necessary countershaft thrust clearance when fitted (see Specifications).

9 Gearbox (Type K40) – reassembly

1 With all parts clean reassembly can be begun.
2 First insert the mainshaft assembly into the gearbox casing (photo).
3 Make sure that the bearing retainer peg correctly engages in the cut out in the casing (photo).
4 Place a large washer and nut onto one of the extension housing securing studs to hold the mainshaft in position (photo).
5 Refit the 3rd/4th speed shift fork making sure it is the correct way round (Fig. 6.22).
6 Refit the 1st/2nd speed fork making sure it is the correct way round.
7 Apply a little grease to the interlock pins and insert them into the selector shafts.
8 Insert the 1st/2nd speed selector shaft engaging it in the shift fork.
9 Insert the 3rd/4th speed selector shaft engaging it in the shift fork.
10 Hold the reverse selector fork in position and insert the reverse selector shaft (photo).
11 Line up the selector shafts and insert plunger (Fig. 6.3).
12 The shift fork securing roll pins should next be refitted. Make sure the hole in the fork and shaft line up and carefully drift the pins into position.
13 Insert the three selector shaft detent balls and springs into the three holes (photo).
14 Refit the cover and gasket and secure with the five securing nuts and washers (photo).

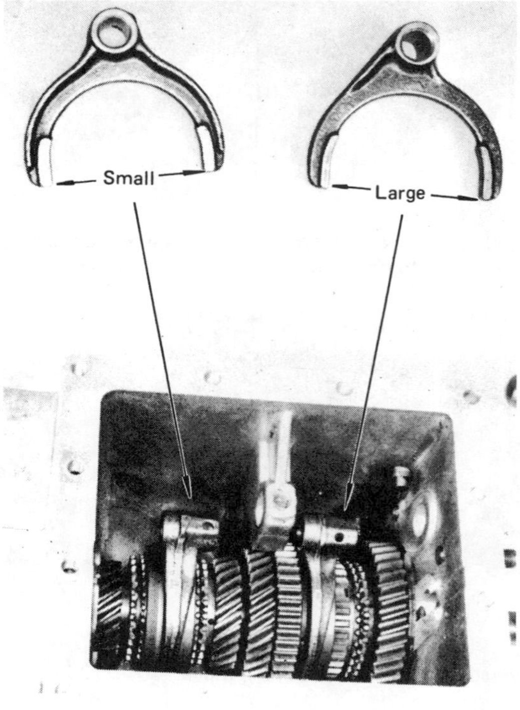

Fig. 6.22 Shift fork positions – K40 gearbox (Sec 9)

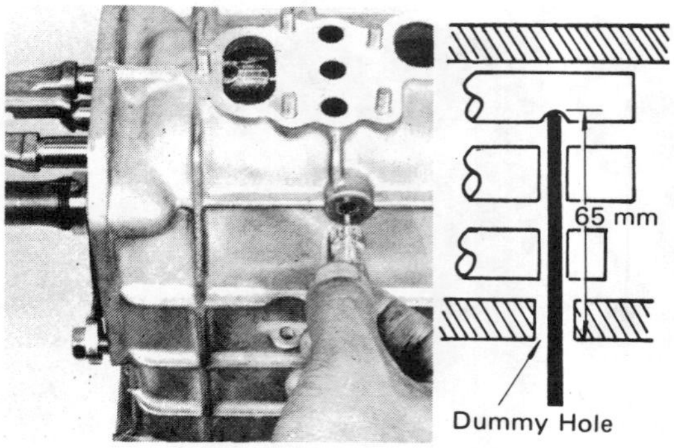

Fig. 6.23 Insert screwdriver shaft through dummy hole to ensure that the shafts are positioned as shown before inserting plunger – K40 gearbox (Sec 9)

9.2 Refit the mainshaft assembly (K40 gearbox)

9.3 Mainshaft rear bearing retainer peg (K40 gearbox)

9.4 Method of temporarily securing mainshaft (K40 gearbox)

9.10 Holding reverse shift fork ready for insertion of selector shaft (K40 gearbox)

9.13 Locate the selector shaft detent springs (K40 gearbox)

9.14 Refit the cover with gasket (K40 gearbox)

9.15 Refitting the input shaft (K40 gearbox)

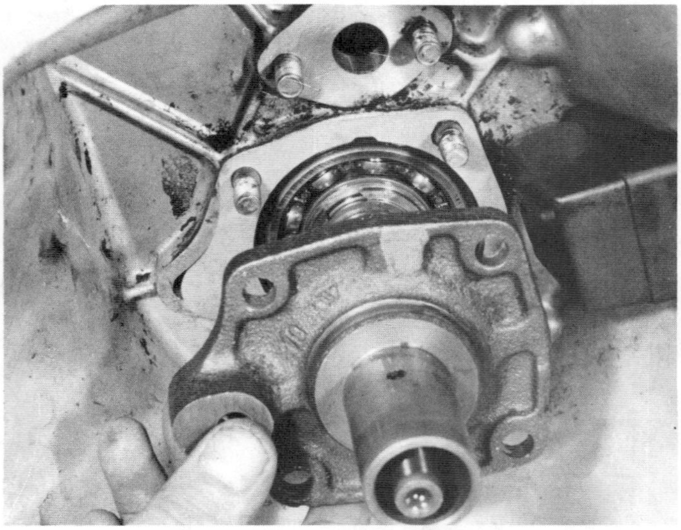

9.16 Fitting the input shaft retainer (K40 gearbox)

9.17 Fitting reverse idler shaft and gear (K40 gearbox)

9.19 Locate the countergear thrust washers (K40 gearbox)

9.20 Lower countershaft into gearbox (K40 gearbox)

9.21 Insert the countershaft (K40 gearbox)

15 Make sure the fourth speed synchroniser ring is in position and fit the input shaft into the front face of the main casing (photo).

16 Fit a new gasket and then the input shaft bearing retainer. Secure with the four nuts and washers (photo). Select gasket thickness according to bearing to gearcase protrusions as shown (Fig. 6.24, 6.25).

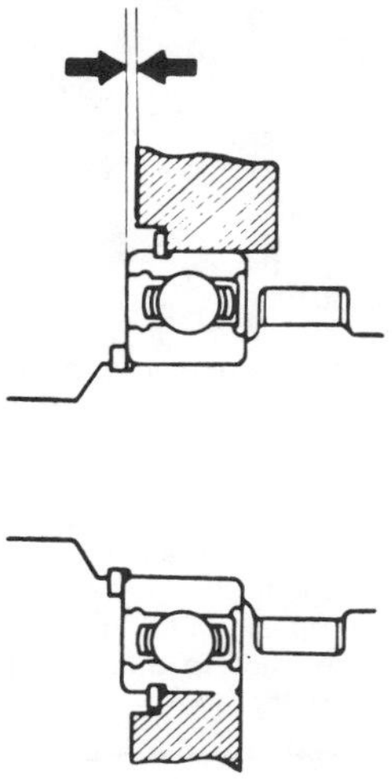

Fig. 6.24 Input shaft bearing protrudes – use gasket No 1 (0.020 in thick) – K40 gearbox (Sec 9)

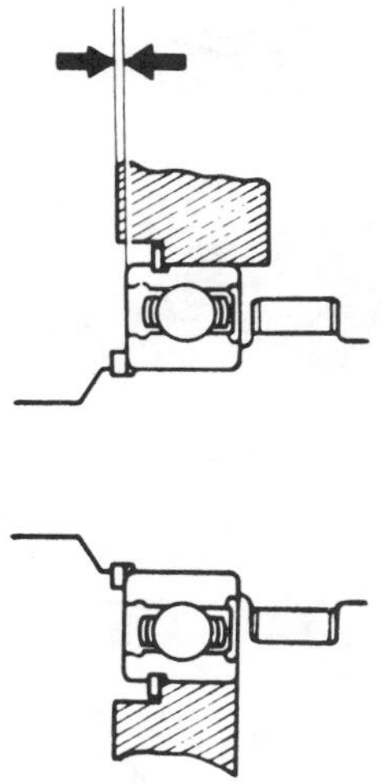

Fig. 6.25 Input shaft bearing recessed – use gasket No 2 (0.012 in thick) – K40 gearbox (Sec 9)

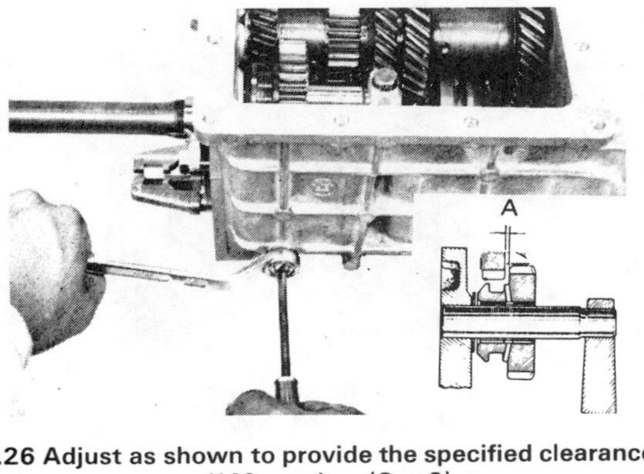

Fig. 6.26 Adjust as shown to provide the specified clearance at A – K40 gearbox (Sec 9)

17 The reverse idler is next to be refitted. Hold the gear in position (and the correct way round) and slide in the shaft making sure the dowel bolt hole lines up with the hole in the web (photo).

18 Refit the reverse idler shaft locking dowel bolt and washer. Check that when the reverse idler gear is against the case end face, that distance A (Fig. 6.26) has a minimum clearance of 0.020 in (0.5 mm). If it doesn't then you will have to fit a spacer between the case end face and the reverse idler gear. A certain amount of adjustment is available by loosening the locknut and turning the pivot screw accordingly as shown in Fig. 6.26. The ideal clearance at A is between 0.039 and 0.079 in (1.0 to 2.0 mm).

19 Smear some grease onto the faces of the countergear thrust washers and position them on the inside faces of the main casing (photo).

20 Carefully lower the countergear into position so as not to dislodge the thrust washers (photo).

21 Slide the countershaft into position from the rear (photo).

22 The raised portion on the end of the countershaft must be positioned as shown (photo) so as to engage in the cut out in the front face of the extension housing.

23 Place the gearbox on end and fit a new gasket to the extension housing mating face. Do not forget to remove the nut and large washer retaining the mainshaft (photo).

24 Carefully lower the extension housing into position ensuring that

9.22 Position the countershaft as shown (K40 gearbox)

9.23 Fit the extension housing gasket (K40 gearbox)

the gear selector lever shaft engages with the selector fork shafts.
25 Secure the extension housing with the nuts and washers, then refit the restrict pins (Fig. 6.27).
26 Fit a new bottom cover gasket and refit the oil pan. Secure with the twelve nuts and washers, tightening in a progressive and diagonal manner.
27 Fit a new countergear shaft retaining plate gasket and refit the plate. Secure with the two nuts and washers.
28 Refit the clutch release arm and bearing assembly as described in Chaper 5.
29 The gearbox is now ready for refitting to the car. Do not forget to refill the gearbox with the recommended grade of oil.

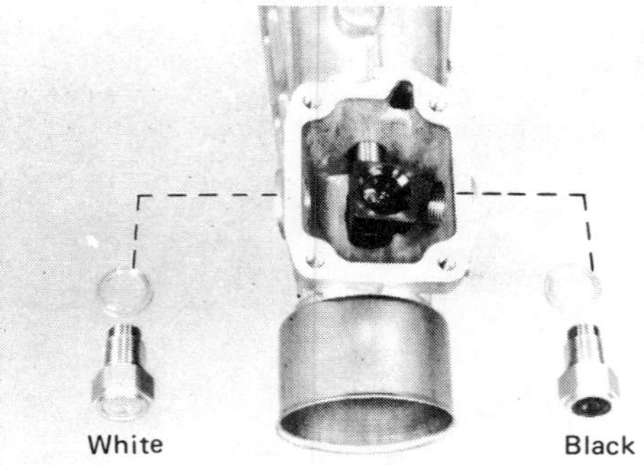

Fig. 6.27 Refit respective restrict pins into correct side of extension housing – K40 gearbox (Sec 9)

10 Gearbox (Type K50) – dismantling into major assemblies

1 Drain the lubricant and clean the outside of the unit with paraffin and a stiff brush or use a water soluble solvent.
2 Remove the clutch release lever and bearing assembly (see Chapter 5).
3 Remove the reversing light switch by unscrewing it from the gearcase.
4 Unbolt and remove the speedometer driven gear unit.
5 Unscrew and remove the restrictor pins from the extension housing, see Figure 6.28. Unbolt and remove the retainer and gaskets.
6 Unbolt and remove the bottom cover and gasket.
7 Prior to removal of the extension housing, use feeler gauges and check the end thrust clearance of the countershaft and make a note of it for reference during inspection and reassembly.
8 Unbolt the extension housing and, moving it to the bottom cover side, remove it taking care not to damage the rear oil seal on the mainshaft splines as it is withdrawn.

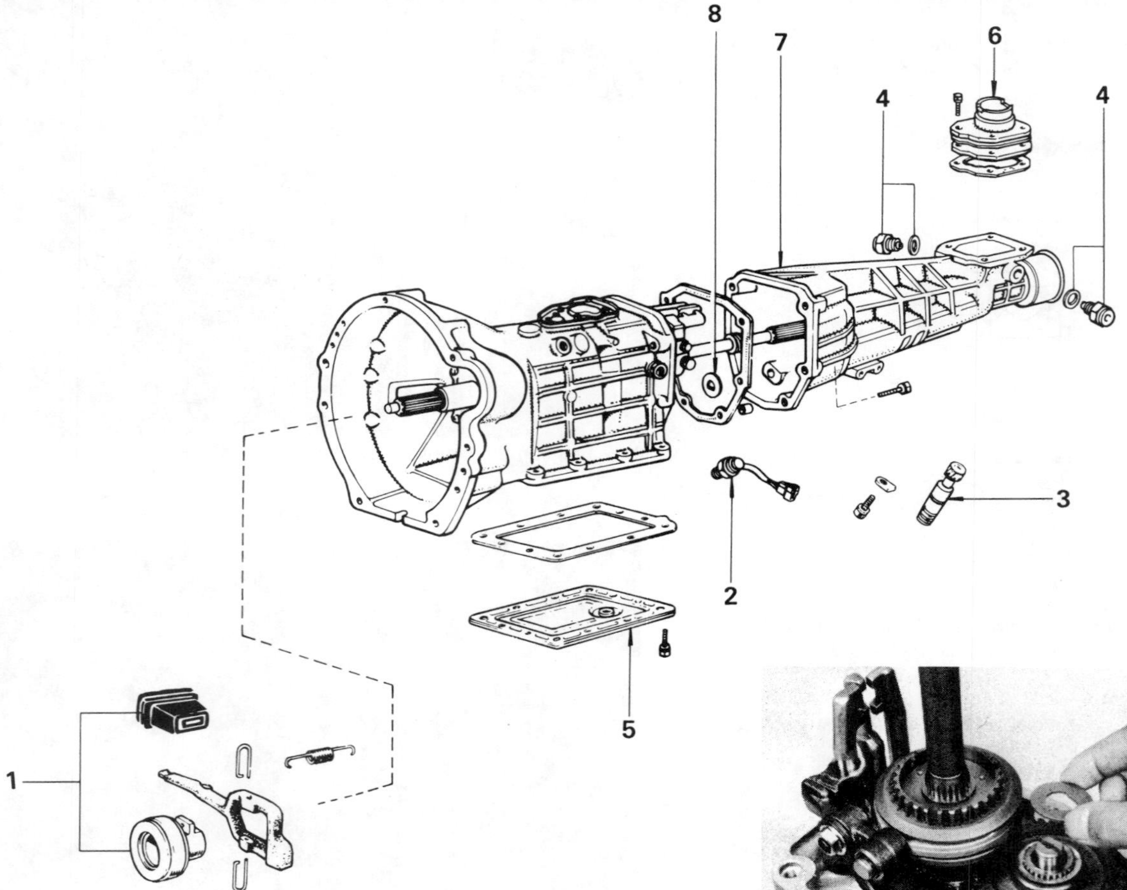

Fig. 6.28 K50 gearbox housing, extension housing and associated components (Sec 10)

1 Clutch release bearing, fork, boot & spring
2 Back-up light switch
3 Speedometer driven gear
4 Restrict pin
5 Oil pan
6 Shift lever retainer
7 Extension housing
8 Counter gear thrust washer

Fig. 6.29 Withdraw and retain the countergear thrust washer – K50 gearbox (Sec 10)

9 Remove the thrust washer from the countergear and keep it in a safe place (Fig. 6.29).
10 Remove the speedometer drivegear. This is secured on the mainshaft by circlips which must be prised free to allow the gear to be removed complete with its location ball (Fig. 6.30).
11 Unscrew and remove the 5th gear shift arm bracket and fork unit.
12 Using a suitable screwdriver, prise up 5th gear and check the thrust clearance as shown (Fig. 6.31) with feeler gauges. Having noted the thrust clearance, prise free the circlip and remove the number three clutch hub and synchroniser ring. When removed, keep the respective clutch hubs and synchronisers together in sets.
13 Now prise free the circlip securing the countershaft 5th gear in place and lever free the gear with a pair of suitable screwdrivers as shown (Fig. 6.32), taking care not to damage the rear face of the gearcase.
14 Prise open the countershaft rear bearing retainer circlip (Fig. 6.33) and then drift or lever out the bearing. The countershaft and its thrust washer and front bearing can then be removed from the gearcase (Fig. 6.34).
15 Remove the selector forks and shafts as given in Section 3, paragraphs 13 to 21 inclusive.
16 Unbolt and remove the input shaft and front bearing retainer

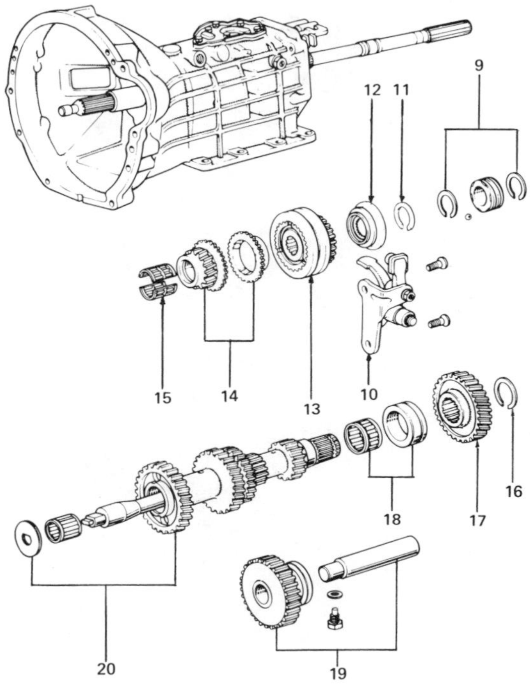

Fig. 6.30 K50 gearbox countershaft, 5th gear and reverse idler gear and associated components (Sec 10)

9 Speedometer drivegear
10 5th gear shift arm bracket arm, and No. 3 shift fork
11 Snap ring
12 Shifting key retainer
13 No.3 clutch hub & sleeve
14 Synchronizer ring & 5th gear
15 Needle roller bearing
16 Circlip
17 Counter 5th gear
18 Counter gear rear bearing
19 Reverse idle gear & shaft
20 Counter gear shaft, needle roller bearing & washer

Fig. 6.31 Check 5th gear thrust clearance – K50 gearbox (Sec 10)

Fig. 6.32 Lever free the countershaft 5th gear – K50 gearbox (Sec 10)

Fig. 6.33 Prise open bearing circlip whilst levering on the bearing from inside the gearbox – K50 gearbox (Sec 10)

Fig. 6.34 Withdraw the countergear from the gearbox – K50 gearbox (Sec 10)

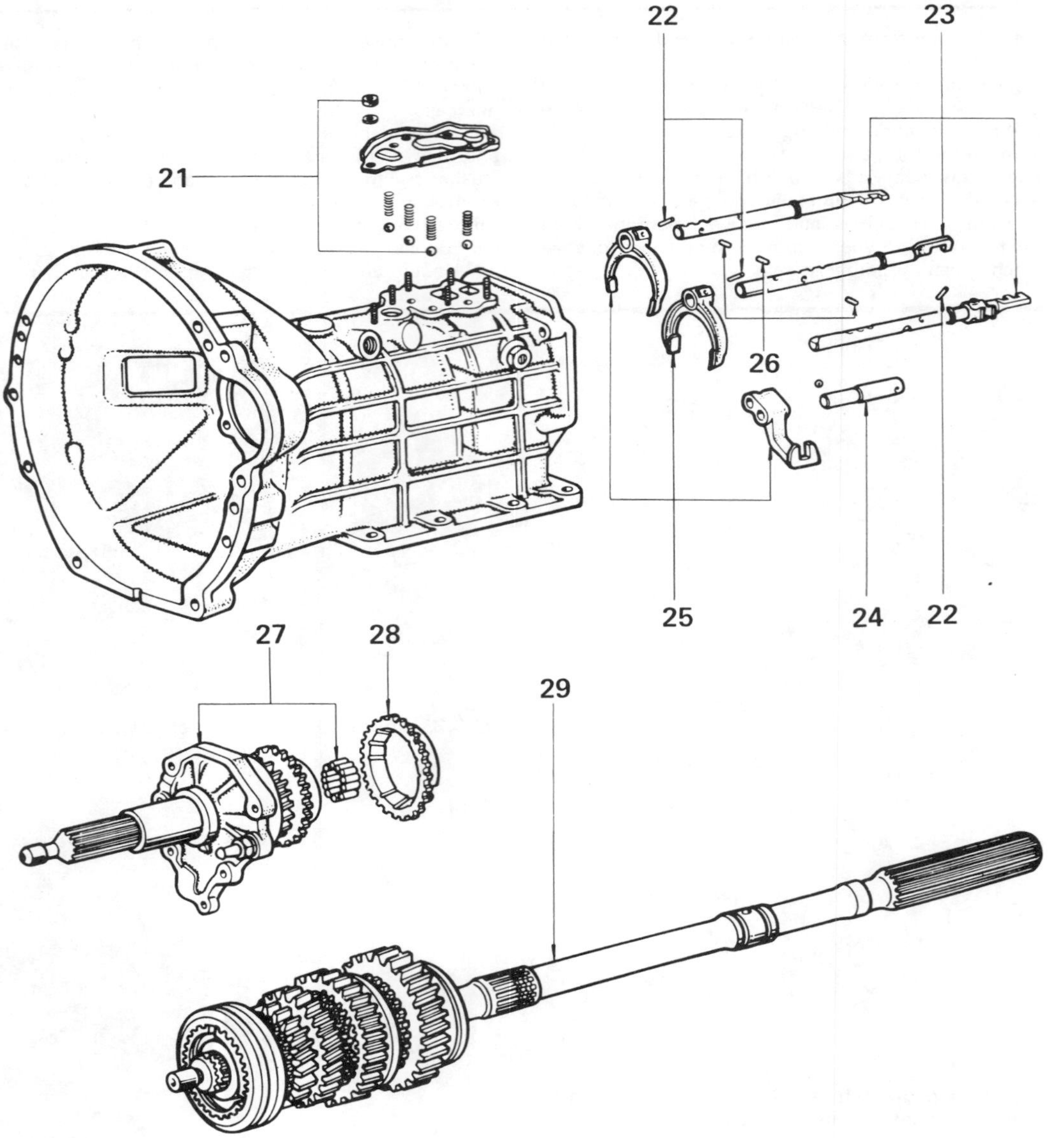

Fig. 6.35 K50 gearbox showing the shift (selector) fork assemblies, the input shaft assembly and the mainshaft unit (Sec 10)

21 Locking ball & spring
22 Slotted spring pin
23 Shift fork shaft
24 Reverse shift fork shaft
25 Shift fork
26 Interlock pin
27 Input shaft & front bearing retainer
28 Synchronizer ring
29 Mainshaft

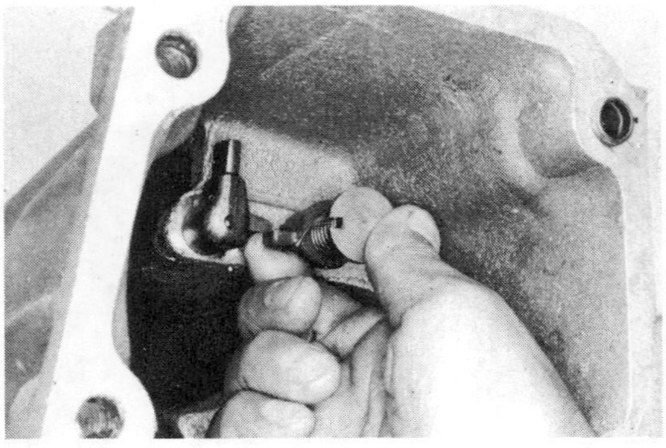

Fig. 6.36 Check the reverse restrict pin action – K50 gearbox (Sec 12)

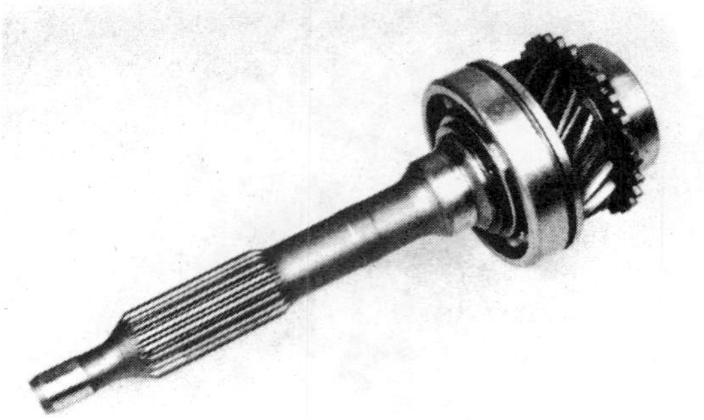

Fig. 6.37 Input shaft unit showing bearing outer race groove orientation – K50 gearbox (Sec 13)

assembly. As it is withdrawn from the mainshaft, collect the needle roller bearings and the synchroniser ring (Fig. 6.35).

17 Using suitable circlip pliers expand the mainshaft rear bearing locating circlip and withdraw the mainshaft assembly forwards from the gearcase.

11 Gearbox components (Type K50) – inspection

Refer to Section 4 in this Chapter for general inspection notes concerning the gearbox.

12 Extension housing (Type K50 gearbox) – servicing

1 Proceed as given in Section 5 of this Chapter but note the following additional point.

2 Inspect the reverse restrict pin for signs of wear or damage and if necessary renew it (Fig. 6.36).

3 The sliding action of the pin should be satisfactory. If it isn't, remove it by unscrewing the Allen screw on the outside and drifting out the roll pin with a punch of suitable diameter.

4 Use a new roll pin on reassembly and when in position smear the threads of the Allen screw with a liquid sealant before refitting.

13 Input shaft (Type K50 gearbox) – servicing

1 To separate the input shaft from the bearing housing, open the circlip and press or tap, with a soft head mallet, the input shaft from the bearing retainer.

2 Check the teeth of the gear and shaft splines for wear. If wear is evident, renew the shaft.

3 If the oil seal contact surface of the shaft is grooved then the shaft will have to be renewed.

4 The shaft bearing should be renewed if it is worn or noisy when spun with the fingers. Press the old one from the shaft and press the new one on until it is in full contact with the face of the gear. Make sure that the bearing outer track circlip groove is nearest the rear of the shaft (Fig. 6.37).

5 Select a bearing retaining circlip from the thicknesses listed in the Specifications which will eliminate any bearing endfloat on the shaft (Fig. 6.15).

6 Renew the oil seal in the bearing retainer.

14 Mainshaft (Type K50 gearbox) – servicing

1 Prior to dismantling the mainshaft assembly use feeler gauges to check the thrust clearances of the gears. Make a note of the thrust clearance for the 1st, 2nd and 3rd gears in turn and compare them with the tolerances and limits given in the Specifications for the K50 gearbox to assess excessive wear (see Fig. 6.9).

2 To dismantle the mainshaft, extract the circlip from the front end of the shaft, withdraw the 3rd/4th synchro assembly, the synchro hub spacer, the synchro ring and 3rd gear. Note carefully the location of each synchro ring; they are not interchangeable.

3 From the rear end of the mainshaft extract the circlip, and the bearing. To remove the latter, a press or puller will be required.

4 Now withdraw 1st gear bush, the needle roller bearing, 1st gear, the locking ball, synchro ring, 1st/2nd synchro unit, synchro ring and 2nd gear.

5 Servicing of the synchro units is as described in Section 7, paragraphs 17 to 26.

6 Commence reassembly of the mainshaft by installing onto the rear end the following components; 2nd gear and synchro ring, the 1st/2nd synchro unit and lockball, then the 1st gear synchro ring, 1st gear bush, needle roller bearing and 1st gear. Note that the synchroniser

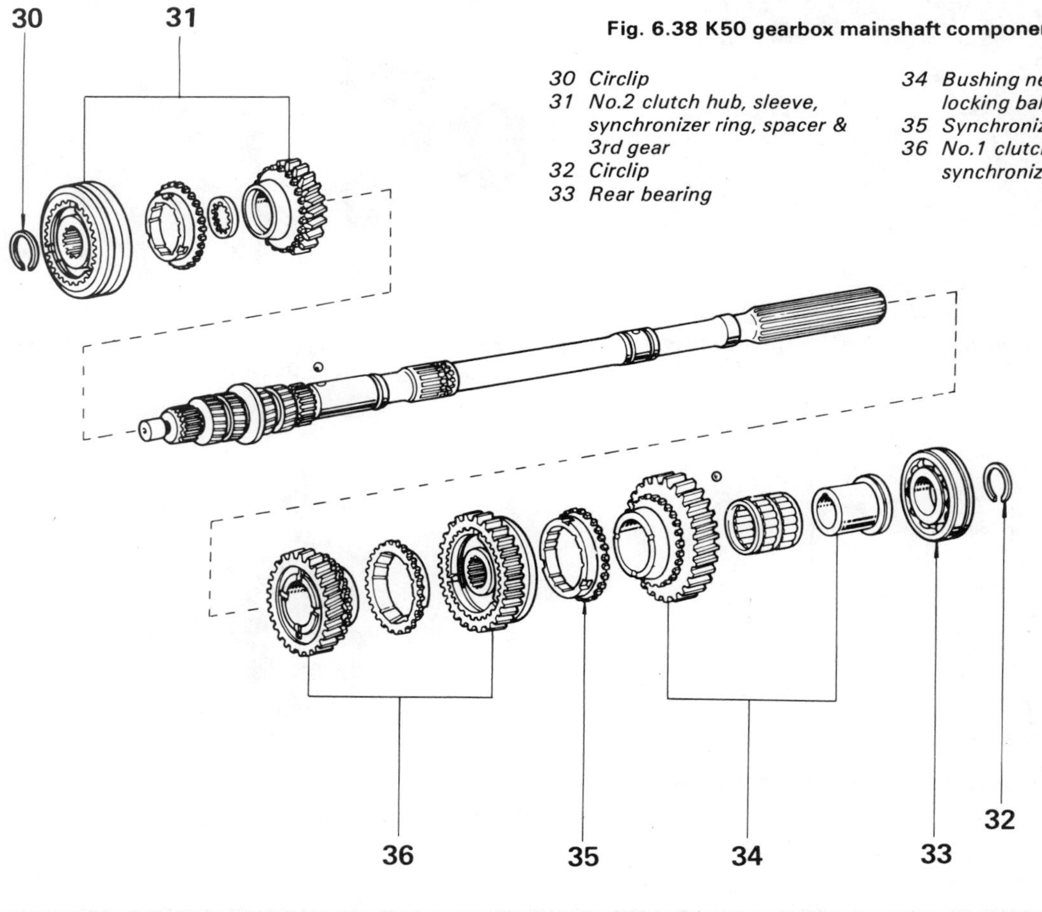

Fig. 6.38 K50 gearbox mainshaft components (Sec 14)

30 Circlip
31 No.2 clutch hub, sleeve, synchronizer ring, spacer & 3rd gear
32 Circlip
33 Rear bearing
34 Bushing needle roller bearing, locking ball & 1st gear
35 Synchronizer ring
36 No.1 clutch hub, sleeeve, synchronizer ring & 2nd gear

Fig. 6.39 Align shift keys with key slots of synchro ring (K50 gearbox) (Sec 14)

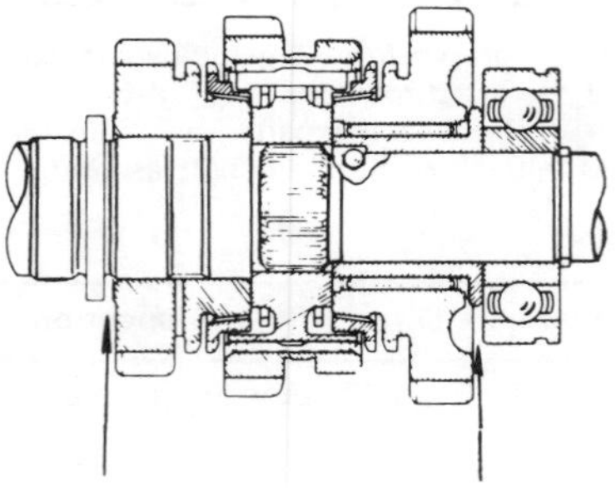

Fig. 6.40 Check 1st and 2nd gear thrust clearances at points indicated – K50 gearbox (Sec 14)

Fig. 6.41 Check 3rd gear thrust clearance as shown – K50 gearbox (Sec 14)

Fig. 6.42 Select and fit spacer to provide correct 3rd gear thrust clearance as necessary – K50 gearbox (Sec 14)

Fig. 6.43 Select and fit a circlip of suitable thickness to take up synchro hub endfloat – K50 gearbox (Sec 14)

Fig. 6.44 The countergear and roller bearings – K50 gearbox (Sec 15)

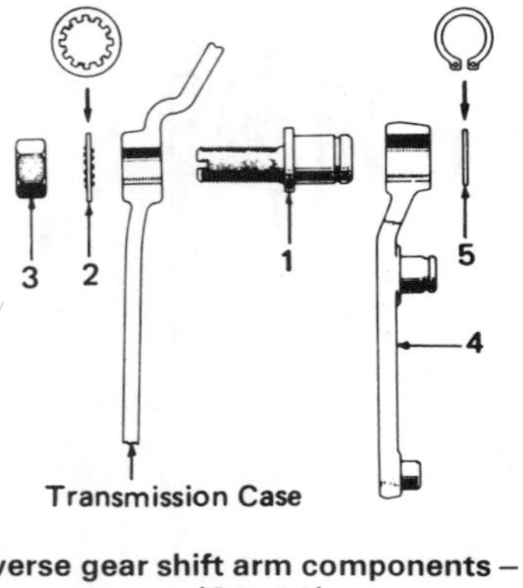

Fig. 6.45 Reverse gear shift arm components – K50 gearbox (Sec 16)

1 Pivot
2 Lockwasher
3 Nut
4 Shift arm
5 Circlip

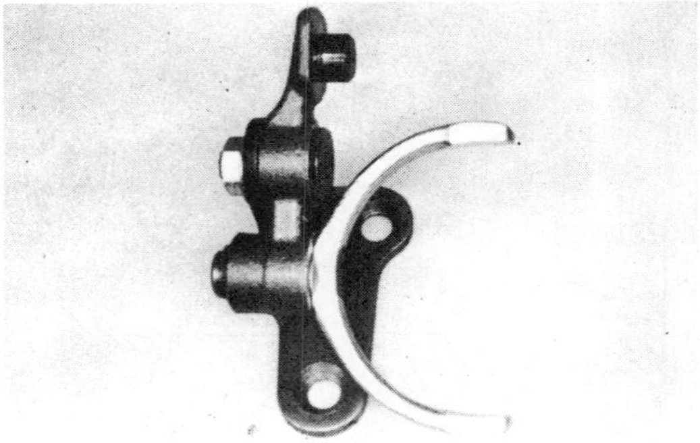

Fig. 6.46 Shift arm and fork for 5th gear – K50 gearbox (Sec 16)

Fig. 6.47 Insert the mainshaft assembly from the front – K50 gearbox (Sec 17)

Fig. 6.48 Align the keys with the slots of the synchro ring – K50 gearbox (Sec 17)

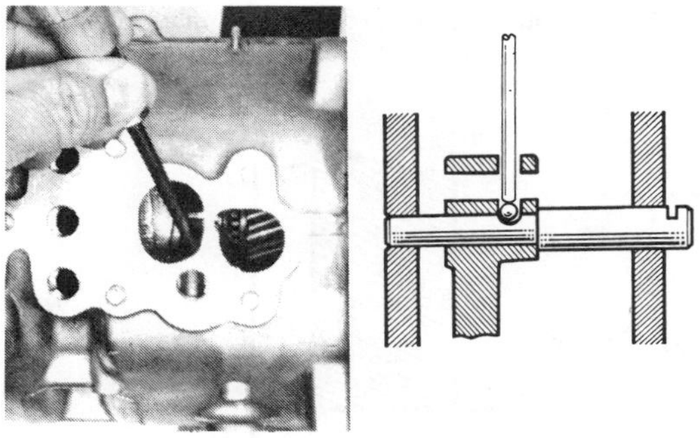

Fig. 6.49 Reverse fork interlock ball fitting – K50 gearbox (Sec 17)

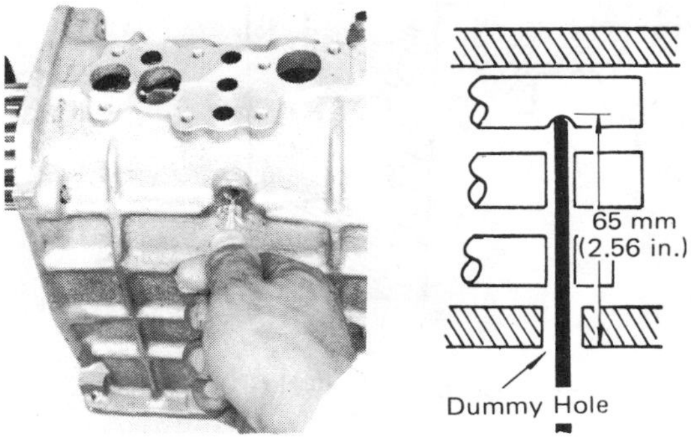

Fig. 6.50 Align selector shafts as shown before fitting the interlock pins into position – K50 gearbox (Sec 17)

rings are different and must be correctly fitted – for identification refer to Fig. 6.19. During assembly, align the shift keys with the key slots of the synchroniser ring (Fig. 6.39).

7 Press on the mainshaft rear bearing so that the bearing outer track circlip groove is nearer the rear of the shaft.

8 Select a circlip which is the closest fit in the shaft groove from the thicknesses available (see the Specifications).

9 Using feeler blades check the 1st and 2nd gear endfloat (thrust) is in accordance with that given in the Specifications (Fig. 6.40).

10 To the front of the mainshaft fit 3rd gear and the synchro hub spacer. With 3rd gear pressed against the mainshaft flange, the selection of the correct spacer from those listed in Specifications can be determined by measuring as shown with a feeler gauge. A spacer should be selected which provides the smallest increment in thickness above the dimension measured (Fig. 6.41 and 6.42).

11 Fit the synchro ring and 3rd/4th synchro unit and then install a circlip from the range of thicknesses available (see the Specifications) which will eliminate any endfloat of the synchro hub (Fig. 6.43).

12 Check 3rd gear endfloat (thrust clearance) is as specified using a feeler blade.

15 Countergear (Type K50 gearbox) – servicing

1 Provided the gear teeth are not worn or chipped and the shaft is not grooved, the only items which can be renewed independently are the bearing at the rear end, the two sets of needle rollers and 5th gear (Fig. 6.44).

2 The remainder of the assembly is only renewable complete.

3 If the endthrust of the countergears was beyond the specified limit when checked during dismantling, then the thrust washers must be renewed.

16 Reverse shift and fifth gear shift arms (Type K50 gearbox) – servicing

1 Wear in these components can be rectified by dismantling and renewing the parts as necessary.

2 Dismantle the reverse shift arm by unscrewing the nut and extracting the circlip (Fig. 6.45).

3 Dismantle the fifth gear shift arm in similar manner (Fig. 6.46).

17 Gearbox (Type K50) – reassembly

1 Install the mainshaft assembly into the gearcase, entering it from the front end (Fig. 6.47).

2 Secure it in position with a circlip.

3 If not already in position, locate the needle roller bearings into position in the input shaft, smearing them with grease to retain them. Place a new gasket into position on the bearing retainer to gearcase face. Locate the synchroniser and then refit the input shaft assembly carefully into position so that as it slides over the mainshaft the needle roller bearings are not dislodged. Align the shift keys with the synchroniser ring key slots (Fig. 6.48). If the input shaft fails to slide fully into position, withdraw it and check that the bearings are in position.

4 Smear the threads of the retainer bolts with a jointing compound and fit and tighten to the specified torque wrench setting.

5 The shift forks and shafts are fitted next. First move the No 1 hub sleeve into 2nd gear engaged position.

6 Locate 1st/2nd shift fork in the synchro unit sleeve groove.

7 Move reverse gear so that 3rd/4th shift fork can be engaged in its synchro sleeve groove.

8 Install reverse shift fork then align the groove in the fork tip with the pin on the reverse shift arm and insert the reverse shift fork shaft and ball. The ball is easily installed by coating it with grease and dropping it into position (Fig. 6.49). Push the ball fully home into the shaft groove with a screwdriver.

9 Install the selector shafts, making sure that they pass through the holes in their respective shift forks and check that the ball is correctly located in its recess in the reverse selector shaft.

10 Align the holes in the selector shafts using a thin screwdriver and then insert the interlock pins. Apply jointing compound to the hole and fit the plug (Fig. 6.50).

11 Secure the shift forks to their selector rods by driving in the tension pins. To do this, select 2nd gear and drive in the 1st/2nd fork pin. Shift the gears to neutral to drive in the remaining pins. When driving in the reverse fork roll pin, drive it in until it is quite flush with the upper surface of the shift fork (Fig. 6.51).

12 Stick the needle rollers into the recess in each end of the countergear and the thrust washers to the end faces of the countergear using thick grease. Note that the dimpled sides (with oil grooves) of the thrust washers are against the countergear.

13 Hold the countergear in position and pass the countershaft through it without displacing the needle rollers or thrust washers making sure that the key on the shaft is aligned with the cut-out on the front bearing retainer.

14 When correctly installed, the rear end of the countershaft should project by 0.374 in (9.5 mm) as shown in Fig. 6.52.

15 Engage the reverse shift arm with the groove of the reverse idler gear and install the reverse idler shaft and gear assembly. Lock with the bolt, if necessary turn the idler shaft with a screwdriver engaged in the slot in the end of the shaft (Fig. 6.53).

16 To the rear end of the countershaft, fit the outer bearing track and retaining circlip.

17 Fit the needle roller bearing and the counter fifth gear. Make sure that the components are fitted the correct way round and then fit a circlip selecting a thickness to give the closest fit in its groove (Fig. 6.54 and 6.55).

18 The countergear thrust washer must now be selected and fitted. To do this, temporarily install the extension housing and a new gasket, tighten the securing bolts to specified torque. The thrust washer should be selected from the thicknesses available (see the Specifications) which will give a clearance (A) of between 0.0032 and 0.0016 in (0.08 and 0.04 mm) (Fig. 6.56 and 6.57).

19 To the rear end of the mainshaft now fit 5th gear, synchro ring, 5th gear synchro unit and the shift key retaining plate.

20 Select and fit a securing circlip. To do this, tap the mainshaft towards the front of the gearbox and press the shift key retainer hard against the synchro hub. From the circlip thicknesses available (see the Specifications) select one which will give a 5th gear endfloat (A in Fig. 6.58), of between 0.008 and 0.012 in (0.2 and 0.3 mm).

21 Assemble the shift arm by first lifting up the reverse idler gear so that the fork shaft protrudes from the gearcase rear face as shown (Fig. 6.59). When fitting the shift arm assembly check that the fork claw engages in the hub sleeve, the shift arm shaft engages in the shift head No 1 groove and the bracket with the reverse fork shaft groove (Fig. 6.60). Fit and fully tighten the retaining screws (Fig. 6.61).

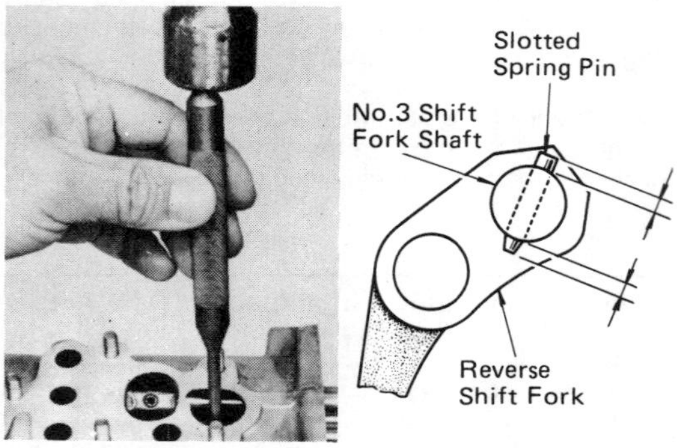

Fig. 6.51 Roll pin (spring pin) fitted position in reverse shift fork – K50 gearbox (Sec 17)

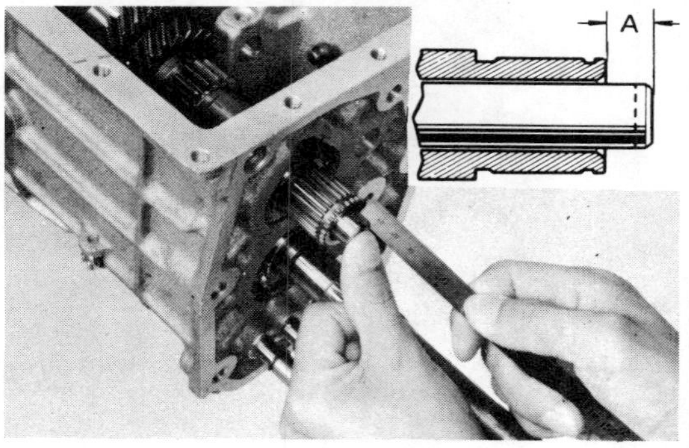

Fig. 6.52 Check countershaft protrusion A is as specified – K50 gearbox (Sec 17)

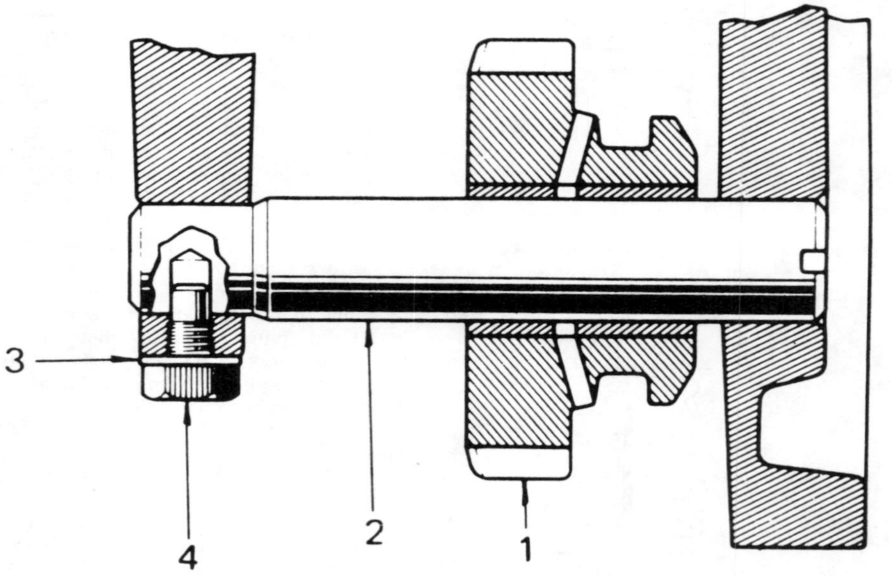

Fig. 6.53 Correct installation of reverse idler components – K50 gearbox (Sec 17)

1 Idler gear
2 Idler shaft
3 Washer
4 Lockbolt

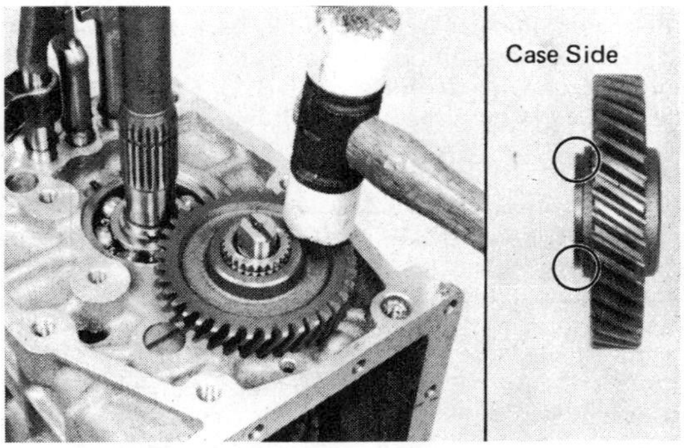

Fig. 6.54 Countershaft with gear to be fitted as shown – K50 gearbox (Sec 17)

Fig. 6.55 Select circlip of suitable thickness to take up play – K50 gearbox (Sec 17)

Fig. 6.56 Fit selected thrust washer to countershaft – K50 gearbox (Sec 17)

Fig. 6.57 Check countershaft thrust clearance – K50 gearbox (Sec 17)

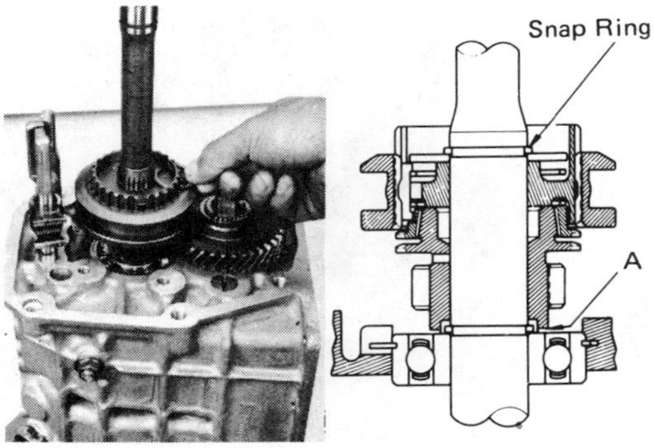

Fig. 6.58 Select circlip to give specified thrust clearance at A for 5th gear – K50 gearbox (Sec 17)

Fig. 6.59 Shift arm fitting method – K50 gearbox (Sec 17)

Fig. 6.60 Engage fork claw with sleeve and shaft with shift head No 1 groove – K50 gearbox (Sec 17)

Fig. 6.61 Shift arm retaining screws tightening method – K50 gearbox (Sec 17)

22 With the reverse idler gear in neutral, slacken the pivot locknut and turn the pivot until dimension A is between 0.039 and 0.079 in (1.0 to 2.0 mm) when viewed through the bottom of the gearcase (Fig. 6.62).
23 Next to be adjusted is the No 3 clutch hub sleeve position. To do this move the sleeve to engage 5th gear (Fig. 6.63), loosen off the locknut and turn its pivot to provide the specified clearance at A which should be 0.039 to 0.059 in (1.0 to 1.5 mm), see Fig. 6.64. Retighten the locknut when set.
24 To the rear end of the mainshaft fit a circlip, the locking ball, the speedometer drivegear and the second circlip.
25 Into the top face of the gearcase fit the four detent balls, the sleeves, the springs, gasket and the cover plate.
26 Position the previously selected countershaft thrust washer with the pitted oil groove side towards the gear into position.
27 Refit the extension housing to the main gearcase having already positioned a new flange gasket both sides coated with jointing compound. As it is fitted engage the selector lever with the slots of the fork shafts and take care not to damage the extension housing oil seal during this operation.
28 Install the extension housing and then coat the threads of the securing bolts with jointing compound and screw them into position and tighten to specified torque.
29 Refit the restrict pins ensuring that they are located in the respective positions in the extension housing as shown in Fig. 6.27. Tighten them to the specified torque wrench setting.
30 Fit the speedometer driven gear into the extension housing.
31 Fit the gearshift lever retainer and gasket.
32 Move the gear lever through its respective selection positions to ensure that movements can be made smoothly.
33 Fit the bottom cover using a new gasket.
34 Fit the drain plug.
35 Install the reversing lamp switch
36 Fit the clutch release bearing and lever as described in Chapter 5.
37 Fill the transmission with the correct quantity and grade of lubricant and screw in the filler plug.
38 The gearbox is now ready for refitting.

18 Gearbox (Type T40 and Type T50) – dismantling into major assemblies

1 Drain the lubricant and clean the outside of the unit with paraffin and a stiff brush or use a water-soluble solvent.
2 Refer to Chapter 5 and remove the clutch release lever and bearing assembly.
3 Undo and remove the four bolts and spring washers securing the front bearing retainer to the inner face of the clutch bellhousing. Slide the retainer from the input shaft.
4 Recover the paper gasket from the retainer or bellhousing face.
5 Undo and remove the bolts and spring washers that secure the clutch bellhousing to the front face of the main casing. Lift away the bellhousing. Recover the gasket.
6 Note the location of the cone washers which will be exposed when the clutch bellhousing is removed (photo).
7 Undo and remove the four bolts and spring washers securing the gearchange lever to the upper face of the extension housing. Lift away the retainer and recover the gasket.
8 Undo and remove the bolt, spring washer and clip retaining the speedometer driven gear assembly to the extension housing.
9 Using a screwdriver carefully ease the assembly from its location in the extension housing (photo).
10 Unscrew and remove the restrict pins from the extension housing. Unless they are colour coded, mark each pin to ensure correct refitting (photo).

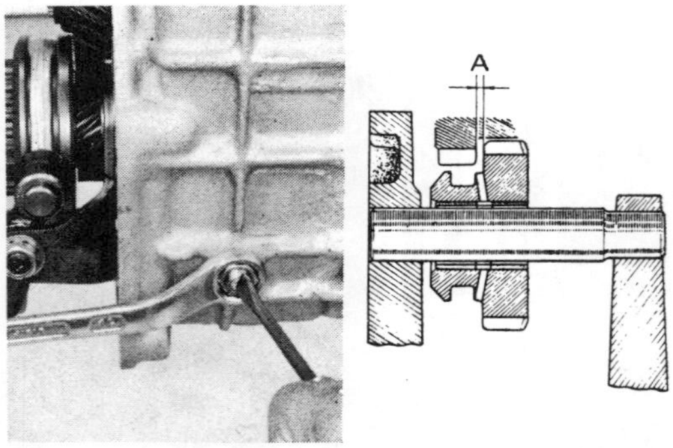

Fig. 6.62 Adjust reverse idler gear position and check at A – K50 gearbox (Sec 17)

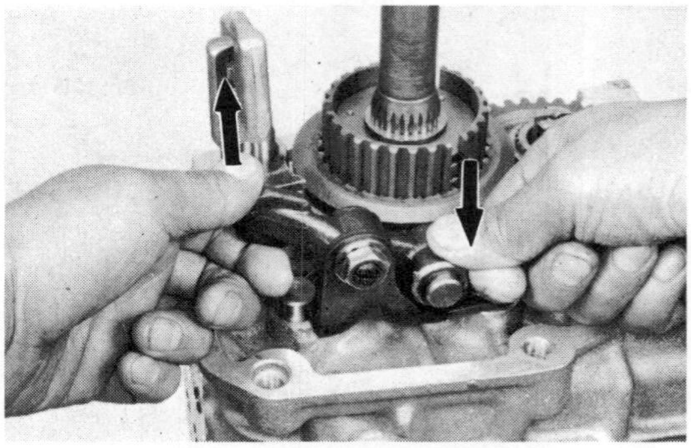

Fig. 6.63 Move No 3 clutch hub into 3rd gear position – K50 gearbox (Sec 17)

Fig. 6.64 Adjust the No 3 clutch hub to give specified clearance at A – K50 gearbox (Sec 17)

18.6 Note location of washers when bellhousing is withdrawn (T40 gearbox shown)

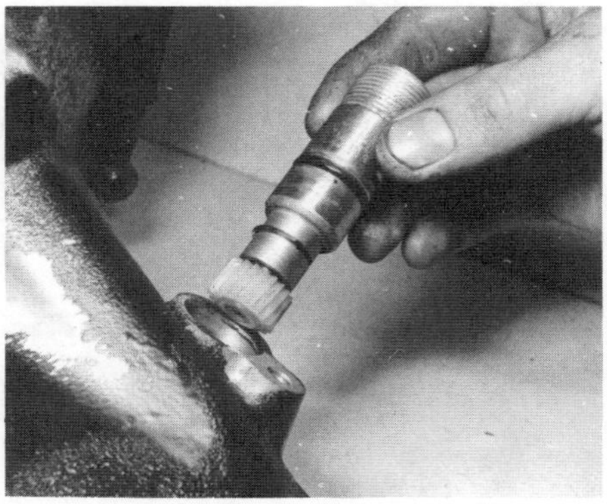

18.9 Withdrawing the speedometer driven gear unit (T40 gearbox shown)

18.10 Remove the restrict pins from the extension housing (T40 gearbox shown)

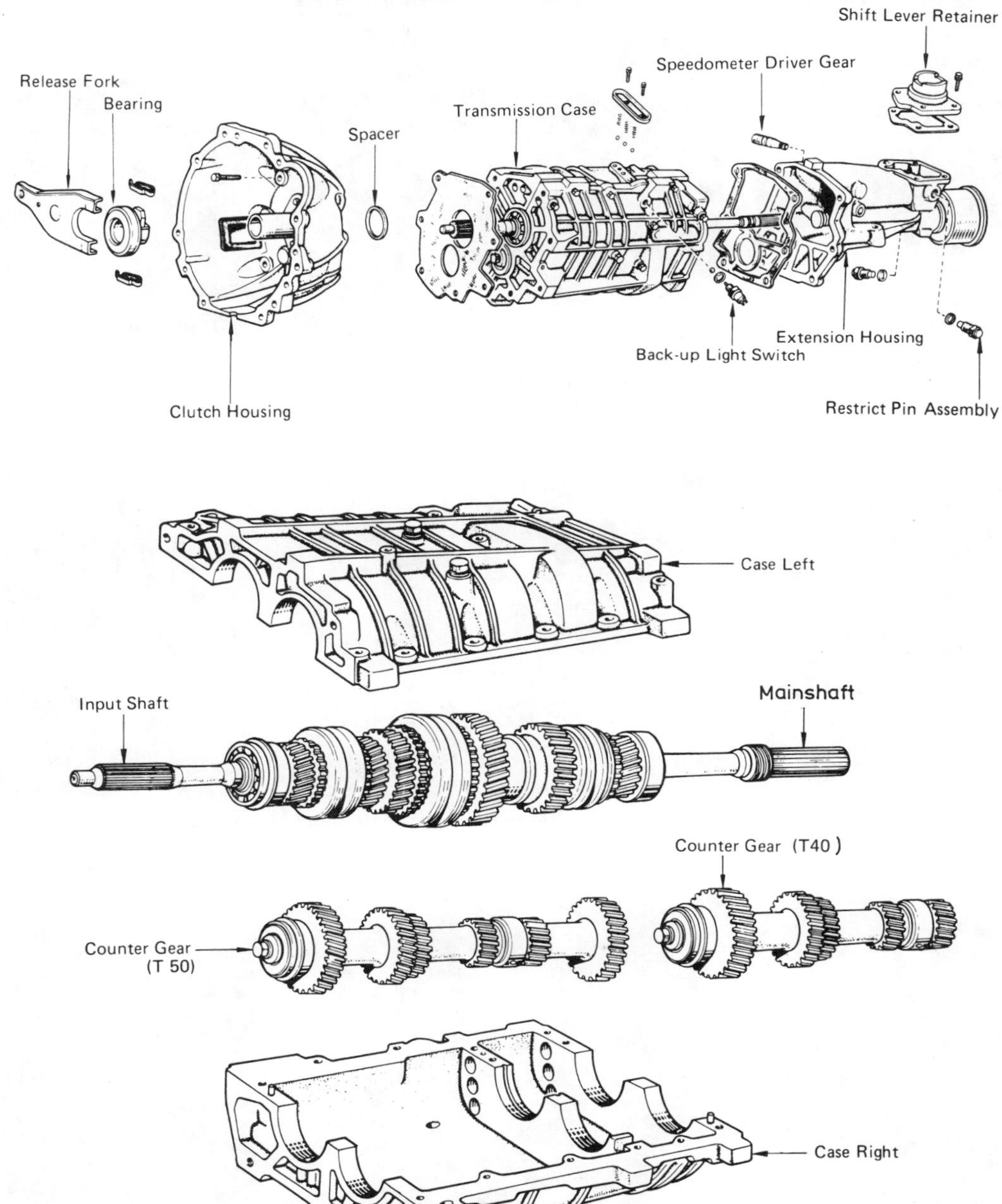

Fig. 6.65 T40 and T50 gearbox and associated components (Sec 18)

18.11 Withdraw the extension housing (T40/T50 gearbox)

18.13 Separate the gearbox casing halves (T40 gearbox shown)

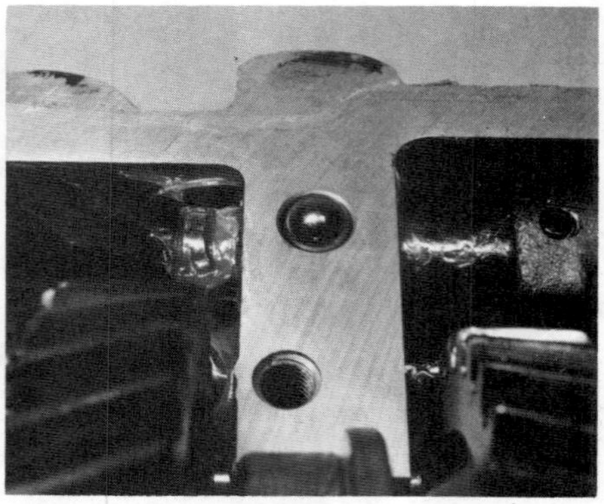

18.14 Remove lock ball from gearbox central web (T40 gearbox shown)

18.19 Reverse idler gear and shaft in T40 gearbox showing lock bolt

18.21a General view showing the T40 gearbox selector rods and forks and their relative locations in the gearcase

18.21b Use suitable punch to drive out roll pins securing shift forks to shafts (T40 gearbox shown)

18.21c Remove plug from casing to allow roll pin removal (T40 gearbox shown)

19.3a Remove the synchro ring from the input shaft (T40 gearbox shown)

19.3b Extract the roller bearings from the input shaft (T40 gearbox shown)

19.5 Spread and remove the input bearing retaining circlip (T40 gearbox shown)

20.2 Remove the circlip from the front end of the mainshaft (T40 gearbox shown)

20.3a Remove the synchro unit ...

11 Undo and remove the bolts and spring washers securing the extension housing to the main casing. Draw the extension housing rearwards moving the selector rod to the left and right to disengage it from the shift selectors. Remove the housing to gearbox gasket (photo).
12 On the T50 gearbox, the reverse restrict pin can be removed by removing the plug and driving out the retaining roll pin.
13 Unbolt and remove the lock ball and spring cover and extract the balls and springs. Undo and remove the bolts and spring washers securing the two halves of the gearbox main casing. Note their respective lengths and locations. Tap the joint to release and lift away the upper main casing half. No gasket is used between these two mating faces (photo).
14 Carefully recover the locking ball located in the central web (photo).
15 Gently tap the countershaft assembly with a soft faced hammer and lift up from the main casing half.
16 Carefully remove the locking ball from the countershaft bearing outer track.
17 Lift away the countershaft assembly.
18 The mainshaft and input shaft may now be lifted away from the main casing half.
19 If necessary undo and remove the bolt and spring washer securing the reverse idler gearshaft (photo).
20 Carefully tap out the idler gearshaft and recover the gear and thrust washers.
21 The gearbox may now be considered to be dismantled into major assemblies. Normally it will not be necessary to remove the selector forks and rods. Should it be desirable to remove these parts mark the relative positions of the selector forks and rods and tap out the fork retaining roll pins using a suitable diameter parallel pin punch (photos). Where necessary remove plug from gearcase to allow roll pin to be driven through.
22 Withdraw the selector shafts and recover the interlock pins, detent balls, spring and spring seat.
23 Clean out the casing and place it to one side ready for reassembly.
24 Inspect the gearbox components as described in Section 4.

19 Input shaft (Type T40 and Type T50 gearbox) – servicing

1 Take care not to let the synchromesh hub assemblies come apart before you want them to. It accelerates wear if the splines of the hub and sleeve are changed in relation to each other. As a precaution it is advisable to make a line up mark with a dab of paint.
2 Draw the input shaft from the front of the mainshaft.
3 Remove the synchro ring (photo) and extract the needle roller bearings from the input shaft (photo).
4 The shaft and bearing are located in the front of the main casing by a large circlip in the outer track of the bearing.
5 To renew the bearing, first remove the circlip from the front end of the bearing (photo).
6 Place the outer track of the race on top of a firm bench vice and drive the input shaft through the bearing. Note that the bearing is fitted with the circlip groove towards the forward end of the input shaft. Lift away the bearing.
7 If the bearing is found to be worn or damaged on removal it must be renewed. Drive the new bearing onto the shaft using a suitable diameter tubular drift. Ensure that the bearing outer circlip groove is offset to the front. Fit a new outer circlip into position.
8 A new bearing retaining circlip must also be fitted. This is a selective circlip which is available in a range of different thicknesses as given in Specifications. Select a circlip to provide the minimum of axial play in the groove. When fitted, check that the selected bearing is fully engaged in the groove.
9 It is always advisable to renew the needle roller bearings as a matter of course. When fitting them into position smear them with grease to retain them against the walls of the housing. The application of grease to the rollers will hold them in position when the input shaft is eventually refitted to the mainshaft.
10 If the synchro ring is worn this must be renewed.

20 Mainshaft (Type T40 and Type T50 gearbox) – servicing

1 Before dismantling the mainshaft assembly, check each gear thrust clearance using a set of feeler gauges. Make a note of the clearances so that they can be compared with the recommended thrust clearances given in the Specifications when assessing component wear (Fig. 6.66).

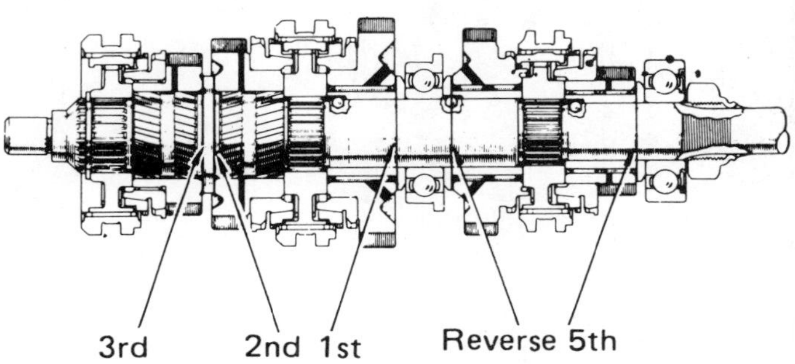

Fig. 6.66 Check thrust clearances at points indicated before dismantling the mainshaft – T40 and T50 gearbox (Sec 20)

2 Remove the circlip from the front end of the mainshaft (photo).
3 Withdraw 3rd gear synchroniser unit (photo) and then the gear (photo) from the front end of the mainshaft.
4 Using circlip pliers, remove the circlip retaining the speedometer drivegear in position on the rear end of the mainshaft (photo).
5 Withdraw the speedometer from the mainshaft, tapping it lightly with a soft head mallet to initially release it (photo).
6 Recover the speedometer gear lock ball from the shaft and then remove the second circlip from the shaft groove.
7 Hold the mainshaft firmly in a vice and on models produced up to

20.3b ... and 3rd gear from front of mainshaft (T40 gearbox shown)

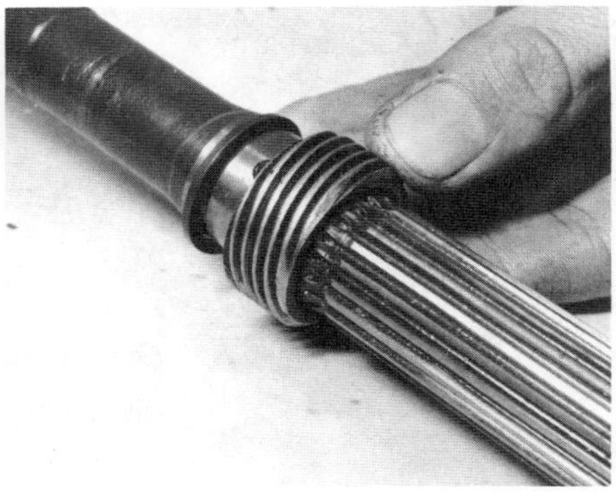

20.4 Remove the speedometer drivegear ...

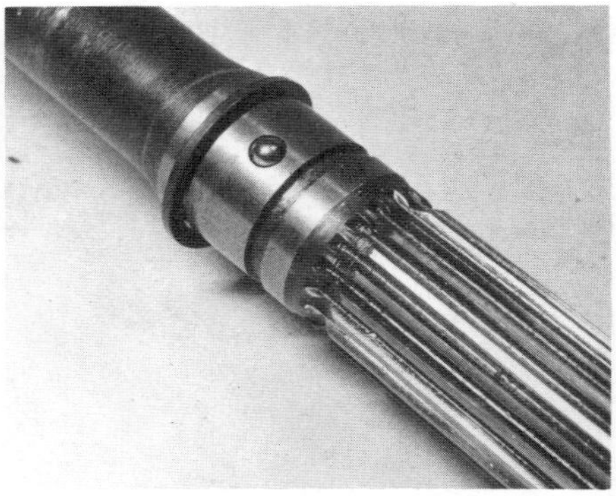

20.5 ... extract the lock ball and remove the second circlip (T40 gearbox shown)

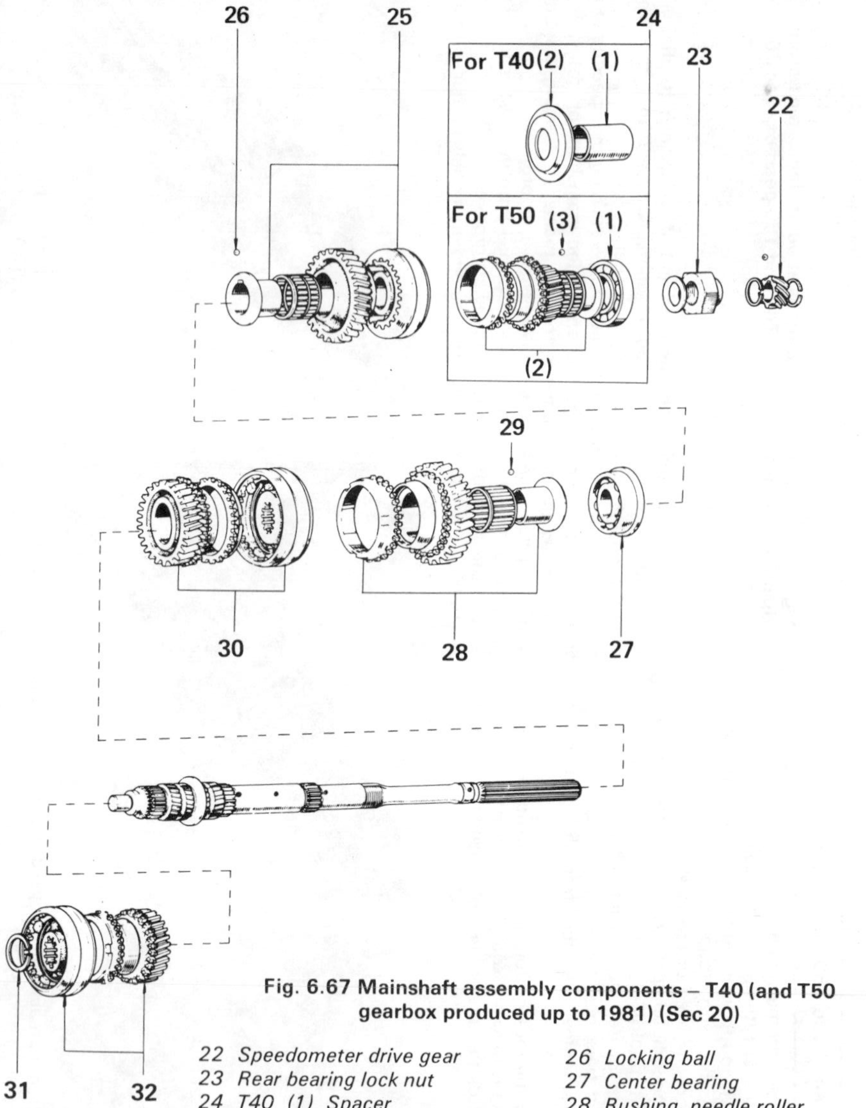

Fig. 6.67 Mainshaft assembly components – T40 (and T50 gearbox produced up to 1981) (Sec 20)

22 *Speedometer drive gear*
23 *Rear bearing lock nut*
24 *T40 (1) Spacer*
(2) Shift stop plate
T50 (1) Rear bearing
(2) Bushing, needle roller bearing, 5th gear & synchronizer ring
(3) Locking ball
25 *No.3 clutch hub & sleeve, reverse gear, needle roller bearing & bushing*
26 *Locking ball*
27 *Center bearing*
28 *Bushing, needle roller bearing, 1st gear & synchronizer ring*
29 *Locking ball*
30 *No.1 clutch hub & sleeve synchronizer ring & 2nd gear*
31 *Circlip*
32 *No.2 clutch hub & sleeve, synchronizer ring & 3rd gear*

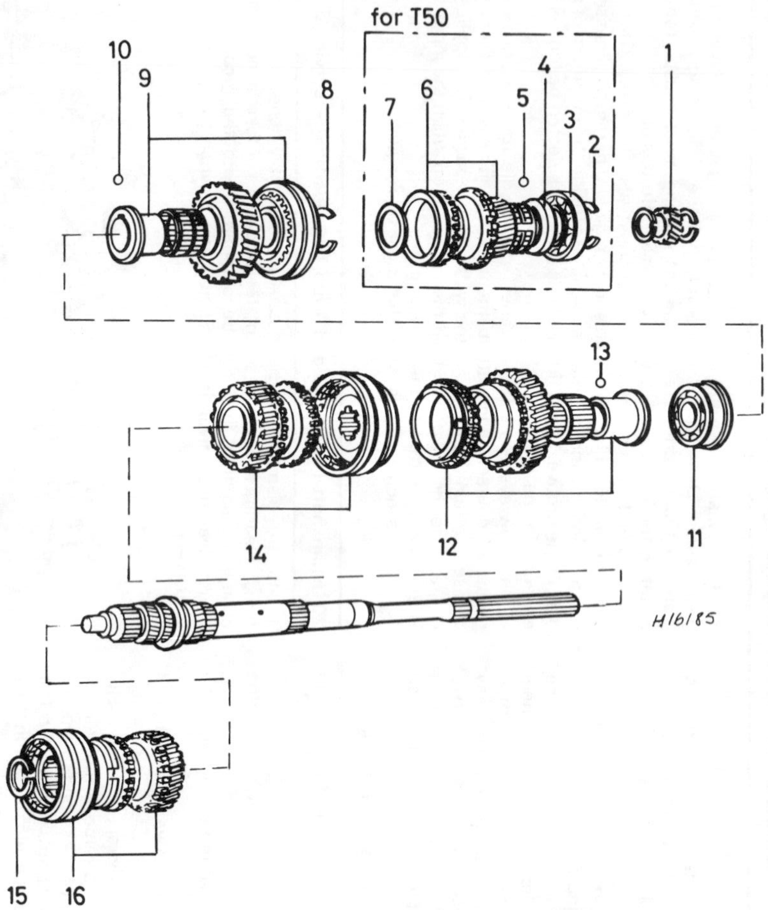

Fig. 6.68 Mainshaft assembly components – T50 gearbox produced from 1981 (Sec 20)

1 *Speedometer drivegear*
2 *Snap ring*
3 *Rear bearing*
4 *Spacer (for rear bearing)*
5 *Locking ball*
6 *Needle roller bearing, 5th gear & synchronizer ring*
7 *Spacer (for needle roller bearing)*
8 *Circlip*
9 *No.3 clutch hub & sleeve, reverse gear, needle roller bearing & bushing*
10 *Locking ball*
11 *Center bearing*
12 *Bushing, needle roller bearing, 1st gear & synchronizer ring*
13 *Locking ball*
14 *No.1 clutch hub & sleeve, synchronizer ring and 2nd gear*
15 *Circlip*
16 *No.2 clutch hub & sleeve, synchronizer ring & 3rd gear*

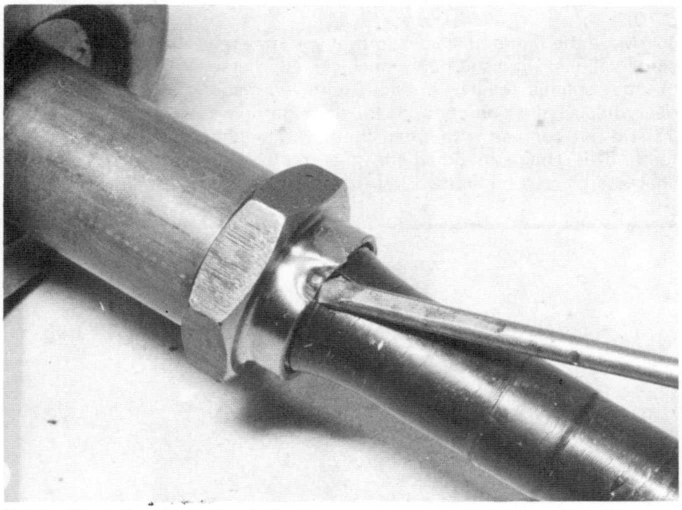

20.7a Unstake the locknut then ...

20.7b ... unscrew and remove it (T40 gearbox shown)

20.8a Remove the spacer collar ...

20.8b ... and shift stop plate (T40 gearbox shown)

August of 1981, unstake the locking nut as shown (photo) and then unscrew and remove the nut (photo). On gearboxes produced from this date, the gear and bearing retainer was changed from a nut to a circlip. Therefore on later models remove the circlip.

8 With the nut or circlip (as applicable) removed proceed as follows according to gearbox type:

T40 gearbox – withdraw the spacer collar and the shift stop plate from the rear end of the mainshaft (photos)
T50 gearbox – withdraw the rear bearing, the bush or spacer (as applicable) needle roller bearing, 5th gear and the synchroniser ring and lock ball

Refer to Fig. 6.67 and 6.68 as applicable.

9 On later T50 gearboxes remove the circlip then on all types, support the mainshaft as shown in Fig. 6.69 and tap the end with a soft faced hammer to release the reverse gear assembly from the mainshaft.

10 Lift away the reverse gear assembly, needle roller race, bush and lock ball.

11 Remove the rear bearing ball race retaining ball bearing and slide off the rear bearing assembly, first gear assembly, needle roller race and bush.

12 Slide off the thrust washer.

13 The second gear assembly can now be removed from the mainshaft.

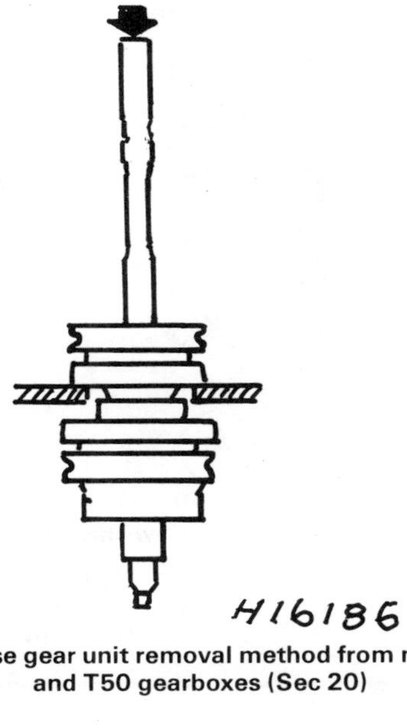

Fig. 6.69 Reverse gear unit removal method from mainshaft – T40 and T50 gearboxes (Sec 20)

14 With the mainshaft components removed they can be laid out in order of fitting for further dismantling and inspection.
15 The synchro hubs are only too easy to dismantle – just push the centre out and the whole assembly flies apart. The point is to prevent this happening before you are ready. Do not dismantle the hubs without reason and do not mix up the parts of the hubs.
16 It is most important to check backlash in the splines between the outer sleeve and inner hub. If any is noticeable the whole assembly must be renewed. Check the clearance between synchro ring and gear does not exceed the specified limit using feeler gauges as shown (Fig. 6.70).
17 Mark the hub and sleeve so that you may reassemble them on the same splines. With the hub and sleeve separated, the teeth at the end of the splines which engage with corresponding teeth of the gearwheels, must be checked for damage or wear.
18 Do not confuse with wear, the keystone shape at the ends of the teeth. This shape matches the gear teeth shape and it is a design characteristic to minimise jump-out tendencies.

Fig. 6.70 Check the synchro ring to gear clearances – T40 and T50 gearboxes (Sec 20)

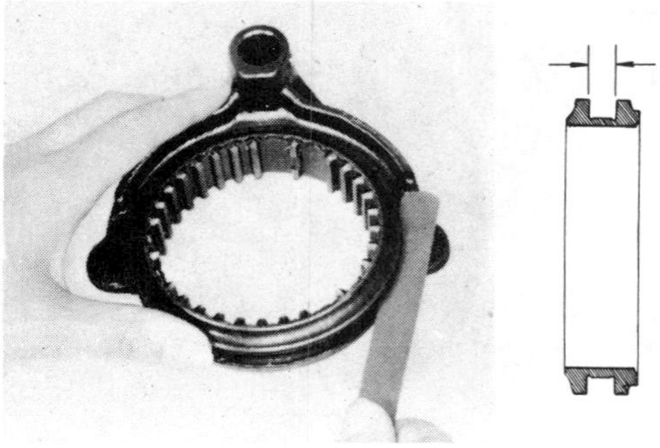

Fig. 6.71 Check the sleeve to shift fork clearances – T40 and T50 gearboxes (Sec 20)

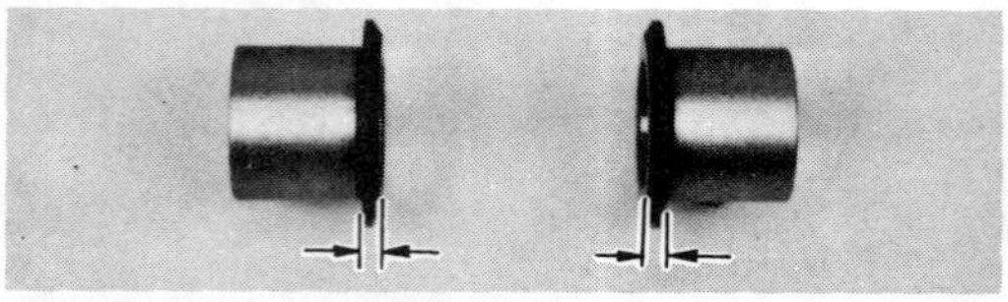

Fig. 6.72 Check the bush flange thicknesses – T40 and T50 gearboxes (Sec 20)

Fig. 6.73 Check the bushes for excessive wear in their gears – T40 and T50 gearboxes (Sec 20)

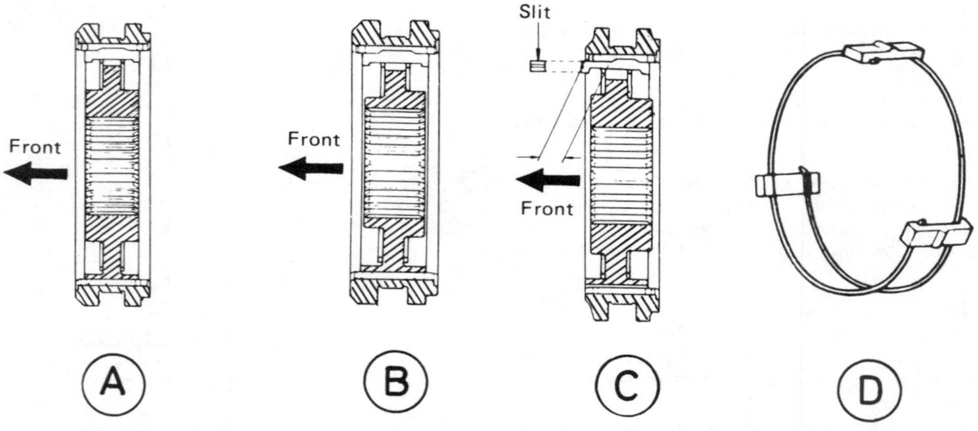

Fig. 6.74 Synchro unit identification and orientation – T40 and T50 gearboxes (Sec 20)

A 3rd/4th (No 1)
B 1st/2nd (No 2)
C Reverse (No 3)
D Key spring assembly to be as shown for all synchro units

19 If the synchronising cones are being renewed it is sensible also to renew the sliding keys and springs which hold them in position.
20 The hub assemblies are not interchangeable so they must be reassembled with their original or identical new parts.
21 Check the sleeve to shift fork clearances as shown (Fig. 6.71). If beyond the specified limit they must be renewed.
22 Check the respective bush flange thicknesses using a vernier gauge or a micrometer. The minimum allowable flange thickness permissible is 0.150 in (3.8 mm), see Fig. 6.72.
23 Check the respective oil clearances between the gears and their corresponding races and compare them against the specified limits allowable. Renew as necessary (Fig. 6.73).
24 Inspect and renew any suspect or worn bearings.
25 When reassembling the synchromesh hubs, the ridges on the sliding keys are symmetrical and can therefore be refitted either way round in the hub during assembly. Assemble the keys and springs in a staggered manner as shown in Fig. 6.74. Identification profiles and orientation for fitting of hubs are as shown. It should be noted that the keys for each synchromesh unit are of different lengths. The turned out end of each spring must locate in the slotted key and be assembled to the hub in an anticlockwise direction as viewed from either side of the hub.
26 Slide the third speed gear assembly and synchromesh assembly onto the front end of the mainshaft.
27 Refit the circlip and check the endfloat which should be as specified. If the reading obtained is outside the limit a new circlip will be required (photo 20.2 refers).
28 Slide the second gear assembly onto the mainshaft from the rear end (photo).
29 Follow this with the synchromesh unit and needle roller bearing (photos).
30 Slide on the first gear assembly and bush. A locking ball must be fitted in the hole in the mainshaft between the synchromesh unit and first gear assembly (photos).
31 Slide on the ball race and push up to the back of the first gear assembly (photo). The bearing must be fitted with its flanged face

20.28 Refit 2nd gear to mainshaft (T40 gearbox shown)

20.29a Locate the synchro ring into its hub ...

20.29b ... then slide the hub into position along the shaft (T40 gearbox shown)

20.30a Locate opposing synchro ring into hub ...

20.30b ... and lock ball into position in shaft (T40 gearbox shown)

20.30c Fit 1st gear and ...

20.30d ... the needle roller bearing assembly ...

20.30e ... and bush into position on shaft (T40 gearbox shown)

20.31a Fit mainshaft ball bearing ...

Fig. 6.75 Fit 5th gear and synchro ring, aligning the key slots with the shift keys – T50 gearbox (early type) (Sec 20)

Fig. 6.76 Fit ball bearing with shielded face to rear – T50 gearbox (early type) (Sec 20)

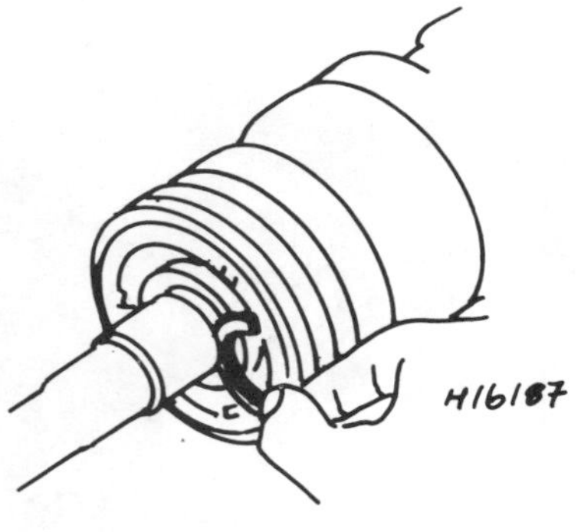

Fig. 6.77 Select a circlip to allow specified axial play – T50 gearbox (late type) (Sec 20)

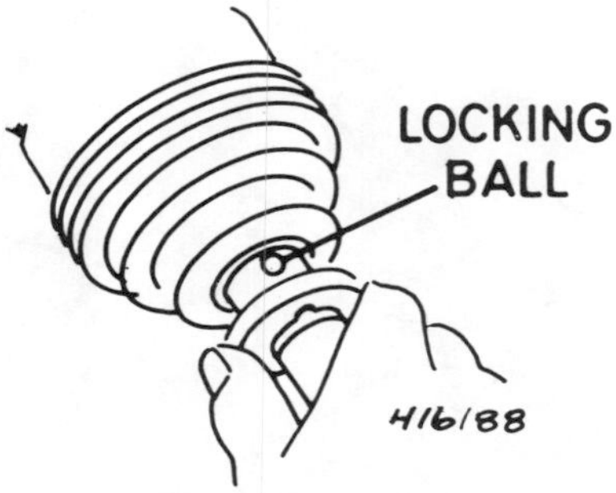

Fig. 6.78 Locate bearing spacer ring with slot over lock ball in mainshaft – T50 gearbox (late type) (Sec 20)

20.31b ... and insert lock ball into shaft (T40 gearbox shown)

20.32a Slide bush into position on mainshaft ...

20.32b ... fit roller bearings over bush ...

20.32c ... then locate reverse gear ...

20.32d ... and the synchro hub (T40 gearbox shown)

20.33 Stake lock the retaining nut (T40 gearbox)

rearwards. Lock the ball race with a ball bearing in the exposed hole in the mainshaft (photo).
32 Refit the reverse gear and synchromesh unit together with bush and needle roller bearing in order shown in the photos.
33 On the T40 gearbox, refit the shift stop plate facing it as shown in photo (20.8b), spacer, shim (if fitted) and nut. Tighten the nut to the specified torque wrench setting whilst supporting the mainshaft in a vice fitted with soft jaws and stake lock nut (photo).
34 On the early T50 gearbox, reassemble the synchroniser ring, 5th gear, the needle roller bearing, bush and ball bearing (Fig. 6.75 and 6.76). Fit the shim and locknut and tighten it to the specified torque wrench setting.
35 On the later T50 gearbox (from August 1981) locate the circlip as shown in Fig. 6.77. Select a circlip allowing an axial play of up to 0.004 in (0.1 mm). Having fitted the selected circlip into position in its groove on the mainshaft, locate the needle roller bearing spacer ring. Then refit 5th gear with its synchroniser and needle bearing assembly. Ensure that the synchroniser ring slots align with the shift keys when assembling. Now locate the rear bearing spacer and lock ball, engaging the spacer groove over the ball (Fig. 6.78). Support the front end of the mainshaft and press or drift the rear bearing into position whilst simultaneously retaining the 5th gear and spacer. With the bearing fully in position, select a circlip to provide an axial play of up to 0.004 in (0.1 mm), then fit the circlip into position to secure the bearing.

All models

36 Fit the first circlip to the end of the mainshaft. Insert the locking ball and slide on the speedometer drivegear.
37 Retain the speedometer drivegear with the second circlip.
38 With the mainshaft now reassembled use feeler gauges or a dial gauge and measure each gear thrust clearance to ensure that they are within the manufacturer's recommended limits. If there is a significant difference the cause must be found and rectified (Fig. 6.66).

21 Countershaft (Type T40 and Type T50 gearbox) – servicing

1 Undo and remove the bolt, spring washer and plain washer holding the ball race onto the end of the countershaft (photo).
2 Using a universal puller and suitable thrust block draw the bearing from the end of the countershaft. Note which way round the bearing is fitted.
3 On the T40 gearbox, use a pair of circlip pliers and remove the circlip retaining the reverse gear on the end of the countershaft (photo).
4 On the T50 gearbox support the front face of the 5th gear and press or drive out the countershaft forwards through it (Fig. 6.79).
5 Remove the reverse gear and central bearing rearwards from the countershaft. Note that the bearing roller cage is fitted with its larger diameter facing forwards (photos).
6 Examine the various components and renew as necessary.
7 Reassembly of the countershaft is a reversal of the removal procedure on both gearbox types. Be sure to refit the bearings the correct way round.
8 Select circlips as required to provide the minimum clearance possible where they are fitted. The respective circlip thicknesses available are given in the Specifications.
9 On the T40 gearboxes complete the countershaft servicing by securing the ball bearing to the spigot end of the countershaft with the bolt, spring and plain washer and tighten the bolt to the specified torque wrench setting.

21.1 Countershaft ball bearing and retaining bolt and washer (T40 gearbox shown)

Fig. 6.79 5th gear removal method from the countershaft – T50 gearbox (Sec 21)

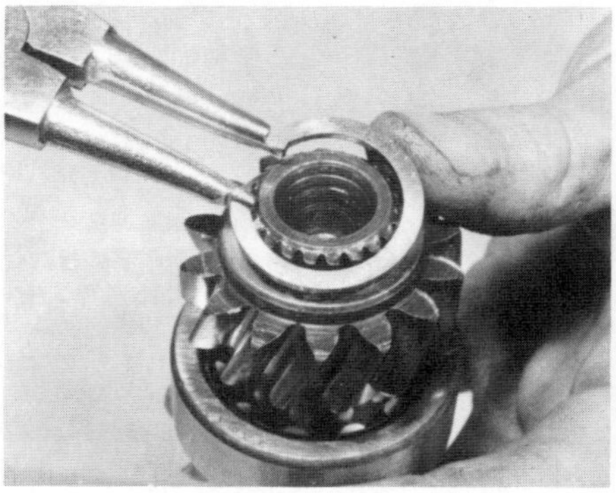

21.3 Removing the reverse gear circlip (T40 gearbox shown)

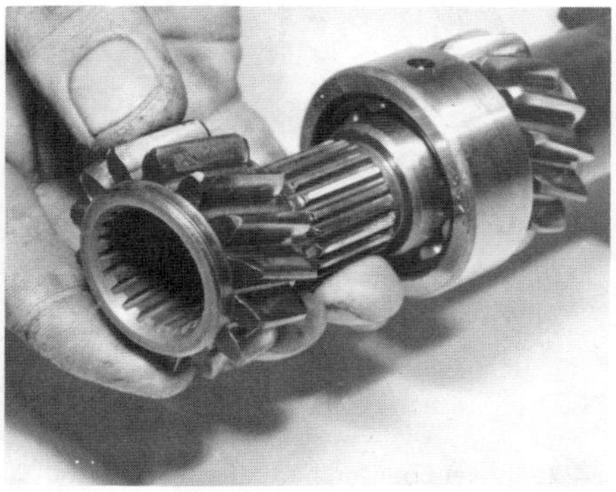

21.5a Withdraw the reverse gear from the countershaft ...

21.5b ... then the bearing (T40 gearbox shown)

22 Reverse idler gear and shaft (Type T40 and Type T50 gearbox) – servicing

1 If the reverse idler gear is still in position in the gearbox use a feeler gauge to check its endthrust clearance which should not exceed 0.039 in (1.0 mm).
2 The gear can be removed by unscrewing the shaft retaining bolt, the shaft extracted and the gear and thrust washers lifted out. Note which way round the gear is fitted (photo 18.19).
3 Check the shaft for wear on its outside diameter. This should not be less than 0.626 in (15.9 mm). Renew the shaft if necessary.
4 Measure the inside diameter of the gear bush for excessive wear. Renew the bush if worn beyond 0.634 in (16.1 mm). The bush will have to be pressed out of the gear. When pressing the new bush into position ensure that the oil holes in the gear and bush align.
5 When refitting the gear back into position in the gearbox engage the projecting part of the thrust washer into the slot in the casing. Tighten the securing bolt to the specified torque wrench setting.

23 Extension housing (Type T40 and T50 gearbox) – servicing

1 Refer to Section 5, the operations being similar, but refer to Fig. 6.80 which applies to the T40 and T50 gearbox (photo).

24 Gearbox (Type T40 and Type T50) – reassembly

1 if the selector forks and rods have been removed they should be refitted. This is a direct reversal of the removal procedure (Fig. 6.8). It should be noted that models produced from August 1981 differ slightly in that the detent is located on the reverse shift fork shaft instead of the No 3 hub sleeve as on previous models. This is to prevent the T40 (4-speed) gearbox overselecting into the 5th gear position.
2 Check that the main casing halves are clean and then carefully lower the assembled countershaft into position. Locate the lock ball into the bearing central web (photos).
3 Lower the combined mainshaft and input shaft assembly into position engaging with the selector forks as it is fitted (photo).
4 Locate the detent ball into the hole in the central web (photo 18.14) then smear the mounting face of the gearcase with sealant.
5 Carefully reassemble the two halves of the casing. Smear the securing bolt threads with sealant and insert the bolts. Tighten them in a progressive manner in the sequence shown to the specified torque wrench setting (Fig. 6.82) (photo).
6 Now check the input shaft vertical movement as shown to ensure there is about 0.012 in (0.3 mm) play (Fig. 6.83).
7 Insert the selector detent balls and springs then locate the gasket and plate cover and secure with the two bolts (photo).
8 Operate the selector shafts to ensure that their movement is smooth and positive.
9 Smear the gearbox rear face with sealant then locate the gasket into position on it (photo). Smear the mating face of the extension housing with sealant and then refit the extension housing onto the end of the gearbox engaging the lug of the selector lever rod into the engagement slot of the No. 2 selector fork shaft. Fit and tighten the securing bolts to the specified torque wrench setting. Take care when fitting the extension housing not to damage the oil seal on the splines of the mainshaft.
10 Before inserting the speedometer driven gear unit check that the oil seal is in good condition and correctly located. If fitting a new seal it must be fitted to the depth shown (Fig. 6.13).
11 Refit the speedometer driven assembly to the extension housing and retain with the bolt, spring washer and clip. Tighten the bolt to specified torque wrench setting.
12 Refit the restrict pins to the extension housing using a new washer for each pin. Ensure that the pins are correctly fitted as marked during removal or with the white pin on the left side and black pin to the right, if colour coded. Tighten the pins to the specified torque wrench setting.
13 Fit a new gasket to the gearchange lever retainer mating face and

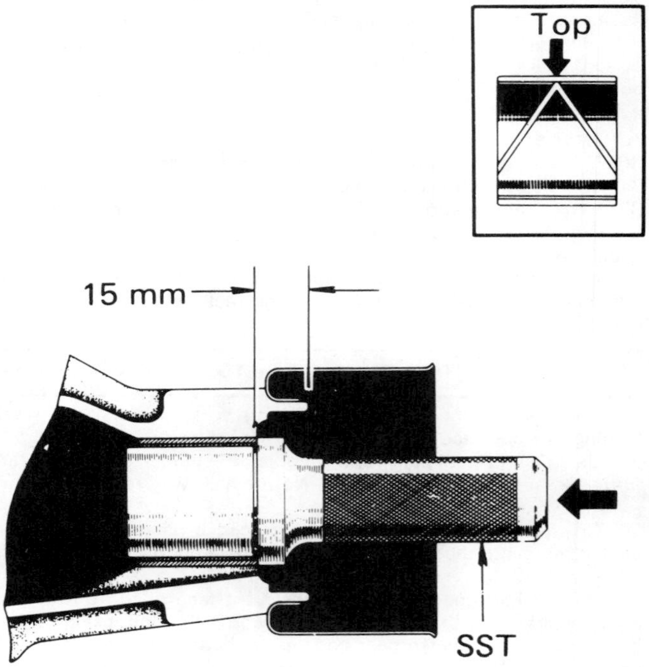

Fig. 6.80 Extension housing bush insertion depth and orientation – T40 and T50 gearbox (Sec 23)

23.1 Rear extension oil seal location (T40 gearbox shown)

24.2a Lower countershaft into position and ...

24.2b ... insert lockball as shown (T40 gearbox shown)

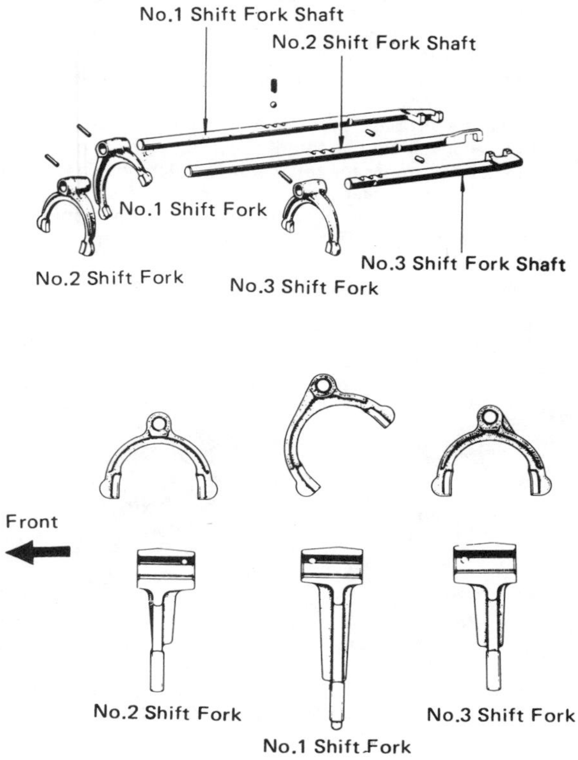

Fig. 6.81 Shift fork and shaft assembly components – T40 and T50 gearbox (Sec 24)

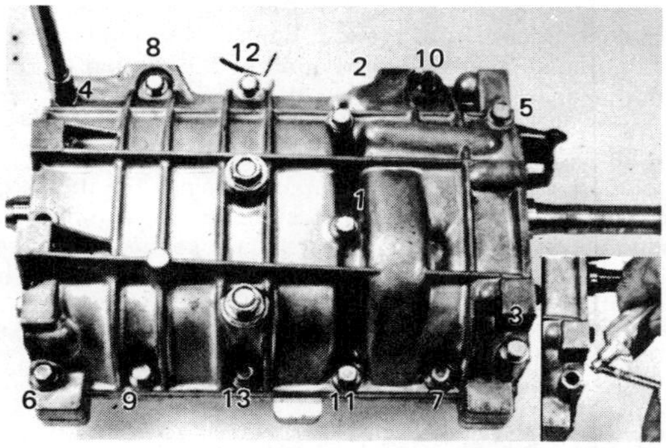

Fig. 6.82 Tighten gearcase bolts to specified torque in sequence shown – T40 and T50 gearboxes (Sec 24)

Fig. 6.83 Check input shaft play – T40 and T50 gearbox (Sec 24)

24.3 Lower the combined mainshaft and input shaft assemblies into the gearcase (T40 gearbox shown)

24.5 Locate cable clip under gearcase bolt head (T40 gearbox shown)

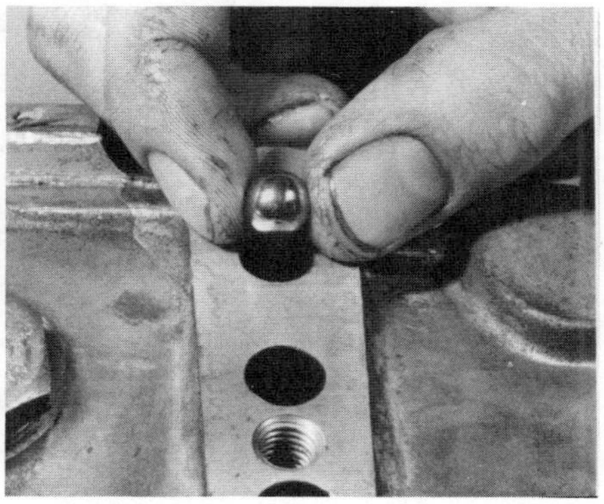

24.7a Insert selector balls ...

24.7b ... then the springs ...

24.7c ... and fit the cover and gasket (T40 gearbox shown)

24.9 Locate gasket onto gearbox rear face (T40 gearbox shown)

refit the retainer. Secure with the four bolts and spring washers which should be tightened to specified torque wrench setting (photo).
14 Smear the gearbox front face with sealant and then locate the gearbox onto it.
15 Fit the flat washer then the small coned washer into the recess in the countershaft aperture in the clutch housing. Fit the large cone washer into the recess in the input shaft aperture (photos). These coned washers are fitted so that their concave section faces rearwards (towards the gearbox) when in position. Grease the washers to retain them when fitting the clutch housing.
16 Smear the clutch housing to gearbox mating face with sealant and then fit it into position on the front end of the gearbox, taking care not to damage the front oil seal in the input shaft bearing retainer, if fitted, at this stage (photo).
17 Tighten the clutch housing retaining bolts to the specified torque wrench setting (photo).
18 If the input shaft bearing retainer is still to be fitted check that the oil seal (a new one should be fitted) is correctly positioned. Grease the lips of the seal and smear the retainer and clutch housing mating faces with sealant. Fit the gasket into position on one face and then locate the bearing retainer. Secure it with the four bolts and spring washers and tighten it to the specified torque wrench setting.
19 Refit the clutch release arm and bearing carrier (see Chapter 5).
20 The gearbox is now ready for refitting to the car.

24.13 Refit the gearchange lever retainer (T40 gearbox shown)

24.15a Fitting the coned washer into the countershaft recess (T40 gearbox shown)

24.15b Large coned washer fits into the input shaft aperture (T40 gearbox shown)

24.16 Refit clutch housing to gearbox (T40 gearbox shown)

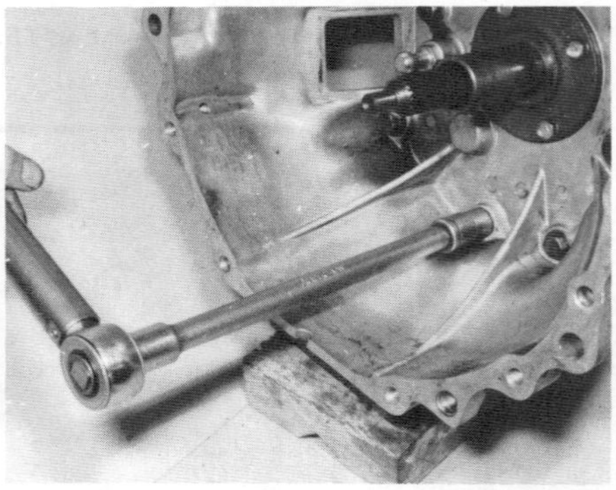
24.17 Tighten the clutch housing bolts to the specified torque (T40 gearbox shown)

25 Fault diagnosis – manual gearbox

Symptom	Reason(s)
Ineffective synchromesh on one or more gears	Worn synchro rings. Worn shift keys
Jumps out of one or more gears	Weak detent springs Worn shift forks Worn engagement dogs Worn synchro hubs
Whining, roughness, vibration allied to other faults	Bearing failure and/or overall wear
Noisy and difficult gear engagement	Clutch not operating correctly
Sloppy and impositive gear selection	Overall wear throughout the selector mechanism

Chapter 6 Part B Automatic transmission

Contents

Specifications

Type	Hydraulically operated with two or three forward speeds and reverse	
Application		
4K engine:		
Early models	Type A20 two-speed	
Later models	Type A40 three-speed	
3T-C engine	Type A40 three-speed	
Transmission ratios	**Type A20**	**Type A40**
1st	1.82 : 1	2.45 : 1
2nd	1.00 : 1	1.45 : 1
3rd	–	1.00 : 1
Reverse	1.82 : 1	2.20 : 1
Torque converter		
Fitted depth (front face to transmission housing face)	1.02 in (26.0 mm)	
Maximum allowable drive plate run-out:		
Type A20	0.005 in (0.12 mm)	
Type A40	0.008 in (0.20 mm)	
Torque wrench settings	**lbf ft**	**kgf m**
Type A20 transmission		
Driveplate to crankshaft	33 to 43	4.5 to 6.0
Driveplate to torque converter	8 to 11	1.0 to 1.6
Transmission housing to engine	37 to 50	5.0 to 7.0
Transmission oil pan bolts	4 to 6	0.5 to 0.8
Oil pan drain plug	20 to 23	2.7 to 3.3
Oil cooler tube to hose	1 to 2	0.15 to 0.25
Type A40 transmission		
Driveplate to crankshaft	51 to 57	7.0 to 8.0
Torque converter	11 to 15	1.5 to 2.2
Rear support	26 to 36	3.5 to 5.0
Transmission housing to engine	37 to 57	5.0 to 8.0
Transmission oil pan bolts	3.0 to 3.6	0.4 to 0.5
Oil cooler pipe union nut	15 to 21	2.0 to 3.0

26 General description

On earlier UK market models the optional automatic transmission was the Toyoglide A20 two-speed transmission. All USA models and all later UK market models have the three-speed A40 transmission unit fitted as an option to the manual gearbox types.

A sectional view of the A20 two-speed transmission is shown in Fig. 6.84, the main components and their locations being indicated. The torque converter, which is a fluid type, transfers the engine torque in accordance with the tractive resistance of the vehicle. The planetry gears are centrally situated and are controlled hydraulically in accordance with the selector lever position and the engine loading.

A sectional view of the A40 three-speed transmission is shown in Fig. 6.85. This transmission has a three-element torque converter, two clutches and three multi-disc brakes which actuate the planetry gears. An integral oil pump supplies the pressure for actuation of the clutches and brakes.

On both transmission types, only periodic maintenance tasks can be undertaken by the home mechanic owing to the specialised knowledge and equipment required to dismantle, overhaul and reassemble these transmissions. The operations described in the following Sections are therefore restricted to the basic maintenance and adjustment procedures possible by the home mechanic.

Towing precautions

Should it be necessary at any time to have your vehicle towed with the rear wheels on the ground, it is most important that the selector lever is in the N position. In addition, the vehicle must not be towed in excess of 30 mph (48 km/h) or further than 50 miles (80 km)

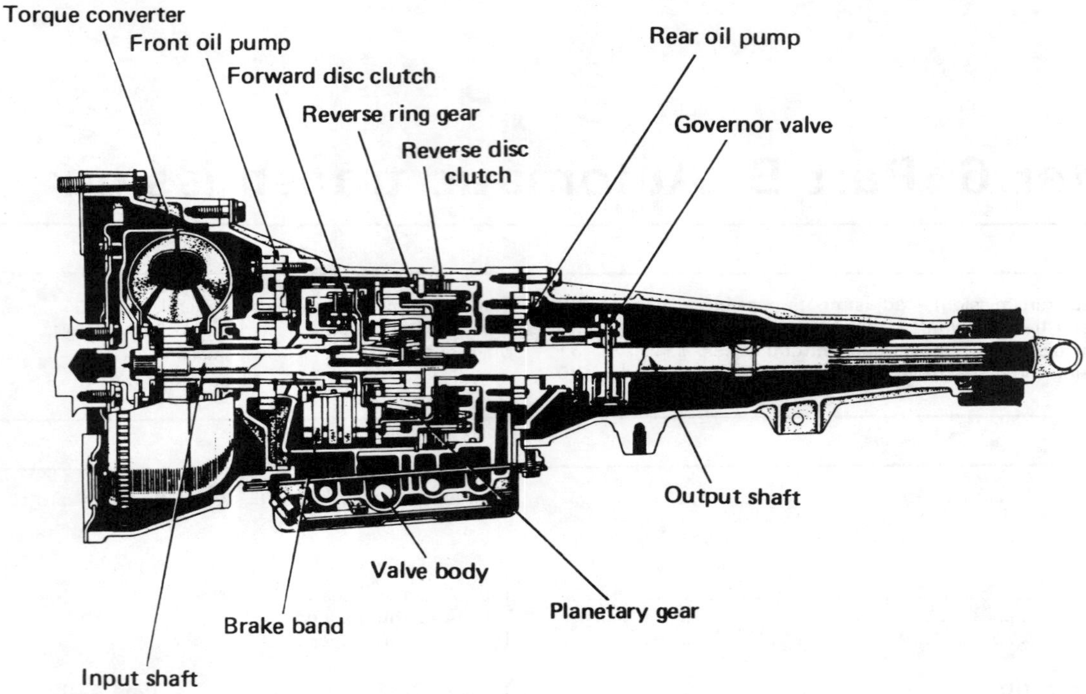

Fig. 6.84 Sectional view of the A20 automatic transmission (Sec 26)

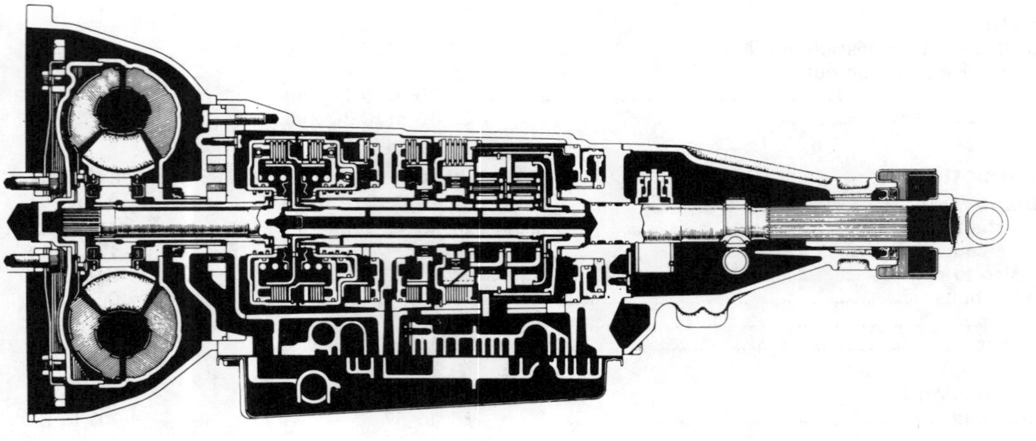

Fig. 6.85 Sectional view of the A40 automatic transmission (Sec 26)

unless the propeller shaft is disconnected. Failure to observe this requirement may cause damage to the transmission due to lack of lubrication.

27 Maintenance

1 If the transmission fluid is cold, withdraw the dipstick, wipe it, re-insert it and withdraw it again. The fluid level should be within the cold range. If the vehicle has travelled at least 5 miles (8 km) the fluid level should be within the hot range of the dipstick when the same checking procedure is followed. Top-up with fluid of the specified grade only when necessary. Do not overfill. If the engine is idling when making the fluid check, ensure that P is selected and take care to keep hands and clothing away from the fan, drivebelts and the exhaust system.
2 It should be noted that a fluid level check should not be made directly after driving the vehicle for an extended period at high speed, after pulling a trailer, in hot weather or after driving in congested traffic conditions, since under these circumstances an accurate fluid level check cannot be made. Therefore allow vehicle to stand for about thirty minutes before checking the level.
3 Keep the external surfaces of the transmission unit clean and free from mud and grease to prevent overheating. An oil cooler is fitted, make sure that the connecting pipes are secure and in good condition (see Fig. 6.87).
4 The automatic transmission fluid normally only requires changing at the specified intervals (see Routine Maintenance), but if the oil on the dipstick appears burned or discolored or if particularly arduous or dusty operating conditions prevail, the fluid should be drained by removing the plug, at more frequent intervals.

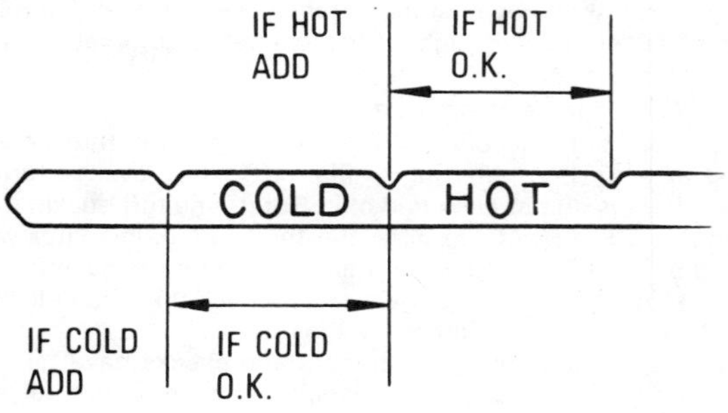

Fig. 6.86 Dipstick fluid level markings (Sec 27)

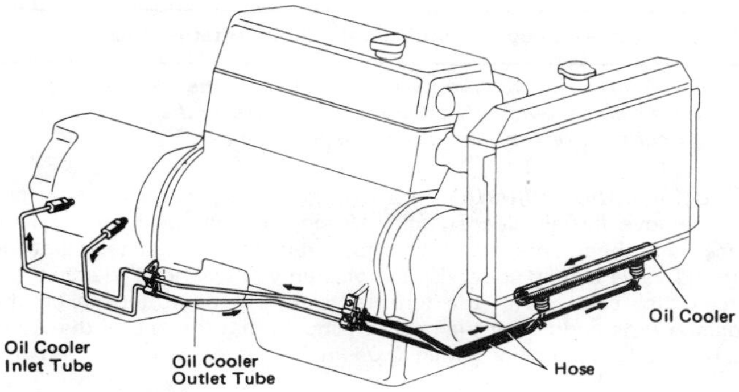

Fig. 6.87 Oil cooling system circuit layout (Sec 27)

28 A20 (two-speed transmission) – adjustments possible

The following adjustments are not part of the routine servicing procedures and should only be made when wear in the components or faulty operation of the transmission is experienced.

Selector lever adjustment

1 Refer to Fig. 6.88. Move the manual valve control lever (1) to the N position and then locate the shift lever pin to the N position on the detent plate stopper. To do this loosen off the control rod swivel locknut and adjust the control rod length. Then retighten the locknut. Check the operation of the selector lever through each position to ensure that the manual lever engages fully with the detent in all gear positions. Slight readjustment may be necessary to achieve this.

Control and adjustment

2 Position the manual control outer lever in neutral, then loosen the connecting rod swivel locknut and adjust the rod length to set the selector pointer in the N position. The relative positions of the control shaft lever and lever retainer must be so adjusted to provide a clearance equal to the gap between the lever pin and the lower stopper in the L range. Adjustment to this effect is made by loosening

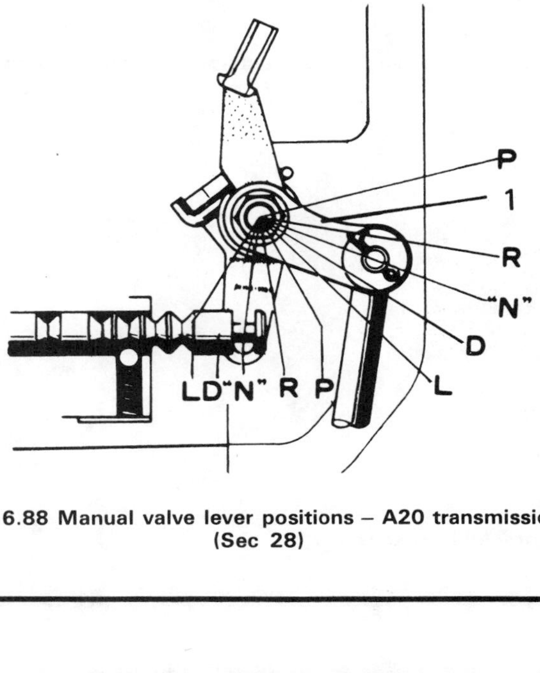

Fig. 6.88 Manual valve lever positions – A20 transmission (Sec 28)

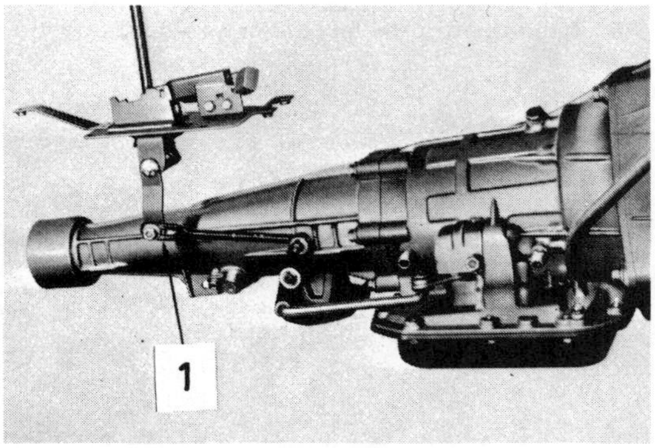

Fig. 6.89 Shift lever adjustment showing control rod swivel locknut 1 – A20 transmission (Sec 28)

off the control shaft lever stopper pin locking nut and turning the stopper pin accordingly. Retighten the locknut to complete (Fig. 6.90).

Throttle link connecting rod

3 Fully depress the accelerator linkage to open the throttle valve to its fullest extent. Then, referring to Fig. 6.91, unscrew the turnbuckle locknuts. There is one at each end of it. Rotate the turnbuckle to adjust the connecting rod length to align the throttle link indicator with the mark on the gearbox casing. Retighten the turnbuckle locknuts, release the throttle, then fully open it again and recheck that the indicator and gearcase mark are in alignment as shown.

4 After any of the above adjustments and checks have taken place road test the vehicle. If a fault persists, have your Toyota dealer carry out a more thorough examination at the earliest opportunity.

Neutral start switch adjustment

5 To adjust the neutral start switch refer to Chapter 10 for details.

29 A40 (three-speed transmission) – adjustments possible

The following adjustments are not part of the routine servicing procedures and should only be made when wear in the components or faulty operation of the transmission is experienced.

Throttle cable adjustment

1 Remove the air cleaner unit, referring to Chapter 3 for details if necessary, then depress the accelerator pedal fully and check that the throttle valve is fully open. If it is not then you will need to adjust the accelerator cable. With the throttle valve fully open, loosen off the adjuster nuts and adjust the cable casing so that the end of the 'boot' to the cable stopper is within 0.04 in (1.0 mm). On achieving this retighten the locknuts and recheck the adjustment (Fig. 6.92) then refit the air cleaner.

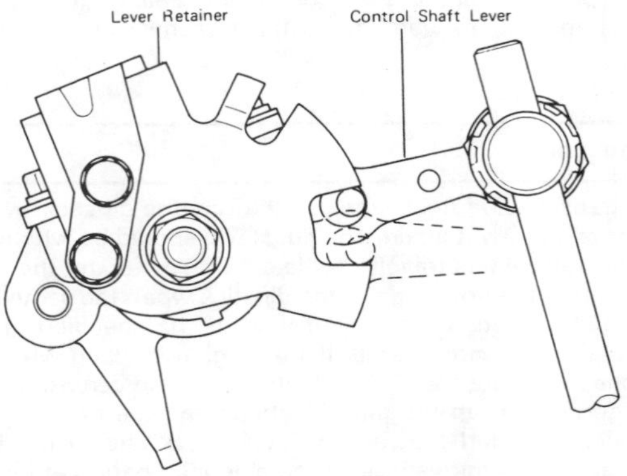

Fig. 6.90 Control rod adjustment showing the adjusting stopper position – A20 transmission (Sec 28)

Floor shift linkage adjustment

2 Loosen off the connecting rod nut and adjust the shift linkage by first pushing the manual lever fully to the front then pulling it back three notches (to neutral position). Move the shift selector to N and then whilst holding the selectors lightly towards the R side, retighten the connecting rod nut.

Neutral start switch adjustment

3 To check and adjust this switch refer to Chapter 10.

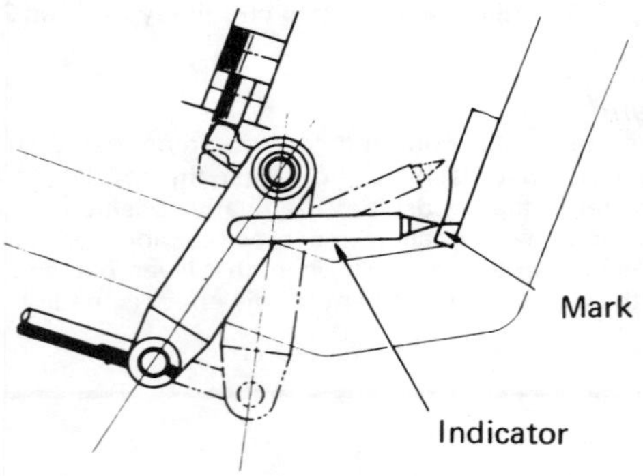

Fig. 6.91 Align the throttle link indicator – A20 transmission (Sec 28)

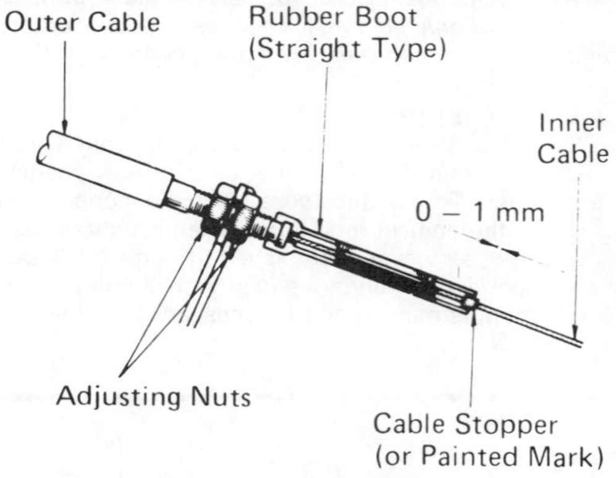

Fig. 6.92 Throttle cable adjustment – A40 transmission (Sec 29)

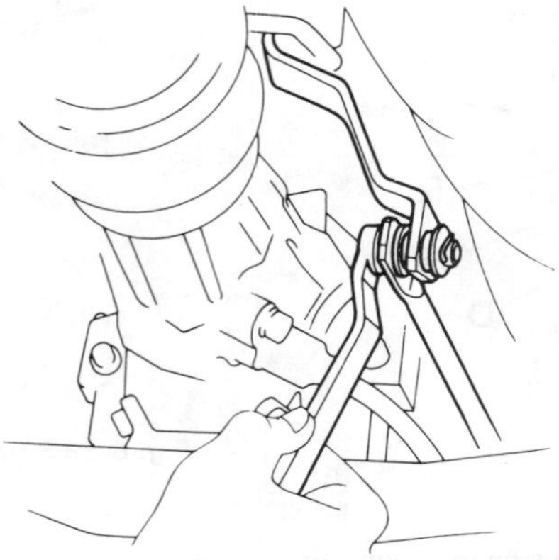

Fig. 6.93 Floor shift linkage adjustment – A40 transmission (Sec 29)

30 Extension housing oil seal – renewal

1 Renewal of the oil seal may be carried out with the transmission unit in position in the vehicle.
2 Remove the propeller shaft as described in Chapter 7.
3 Knock off the dust deflector towards the rear and prise out the dust seal. Using a suitable extractor and levering against the end face of the mainshaft, extract the oil seal (Fig. 6.95).
4 Drive in the new oil seal with a tubular drift, fit a new dust seal and refit the dust deflector.
5 Refit the propeller shaft after first greasing the front sliding sleeve both internally and externally. Make sure that the propeller shaft and pinion driving flanges have their mating marks aligned.
6 On completion check and top up the transmission fluid level as necessary as described in Section 2.

31 Automatic transmission – removal and refitting

1 It must be realised that the automatic transmission unit is of considerable weight and adequate assistance or the use of a trolley jack will be required for the following operations.
2 Disconnect the lead from the battery negative terminal.
3 Drain the cooling system and disconnect the radiator top hose.
4 Remove the air cleaner and disconnect the throttle control at the carburettor.
5 On two-speed transmission (A20) models, disconnect the heater hose clamp to the rocker cover (adjacent to the carburettor).
6 Unless the vehicle is over a pit or raised on a hoist, jack-up the front and rear so that there is an adequate working clearance between the underside of the body floor and the ground to permit the torque converter housing to be withdrawn. When raised, remove the engine undertray (where fitted).
7 Drain the fluid from the transmission unit.
8 Remove the starter motor.
9 Disconnect the propeller shaft from the rear axle (see Chapter 7) and withdraw it from the transmission rear extension housing.
10 Disconnect the exhaust downpipe from the manifold and detach the support bracket from the transmission unit.
11 Disconnect the fluid cooler pipes from the transmission and plug them. Remove the pipe supports from the transmission (Fig. 6.87).
12 Disconnect the speedometer drive cable from the extension housing (Fig. 6.96).
13 Unbolt the two reinforcement brackets from the torque converter housing. Pull the fluid filler tube from the transmission and retain the O-ring seals.
14 Detach the wiring connectors from the neutral start switch and the reverse light switch.
15 On the two-speed transmission, detach the transmission control rod from the control shaft, then disconnect the throttle link rod at its connection to the throttle valve lever.
16 On the three-speed transmission, detach the shift linkage at the rear as shown (Fig. 6.96) and the downshift cable at the engine.
17 Position a jack (preferably trolley type) under the transmission and raise the jack to support the weight of the transmission. A suitable piece of wood should be used between the transmission and jack to prevent distortion of the transmission oil pan.

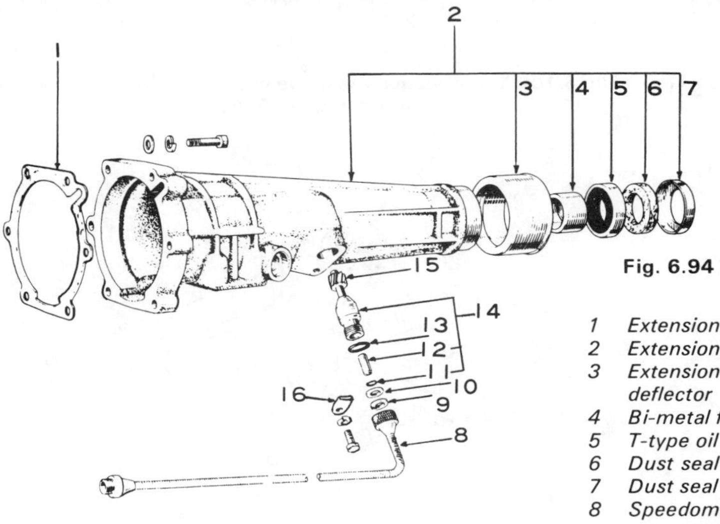

Fig. 6.94 Extension housing components – A20 transmission shown (Sec 30)

1 Extension housing gasket
2 Extension housing
3 Extension housing dust deflector
4 Bi-metal formed bushing
5 T-type oil seal
6 Dust seal
7 Dust seal retainer
8 Speedometer drive cable assembly
9 Gasket
10 Collar
11 O-ring
12 Bushing
13 O-ring
14 Speedometer shaft sleeve
15 Speedometer driven gear
16 Speedometer sleeve lock plate

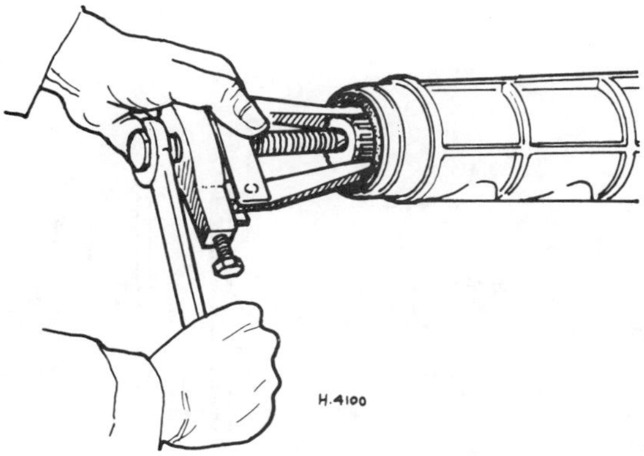

Fig. 6.95 Extension housing oil seal removal using puller (Sec 30)

Fig. 6.96 Disconnect the shift linkage (left) and the speedometer cable connection to the transmission (Sec 31)

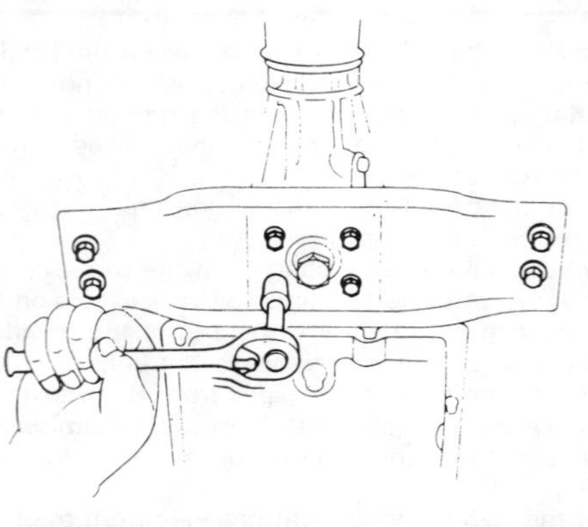

Fig. 6.97 Unbolt and remove the rear mounting/crossmember (Sec 31)

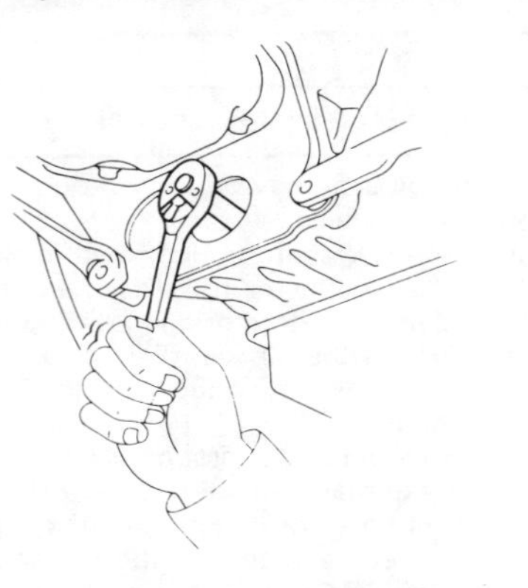

Fig. 6.98 Torque converter bolt removal (Sec 31)

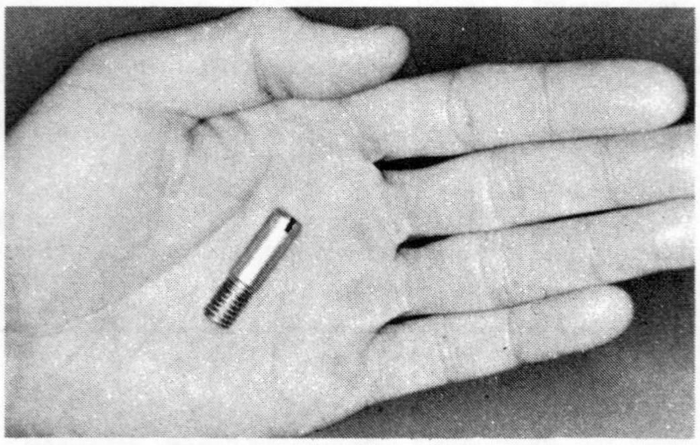

Fig. 6.99 Guide pin to assist removal of transmission (Sec 31)

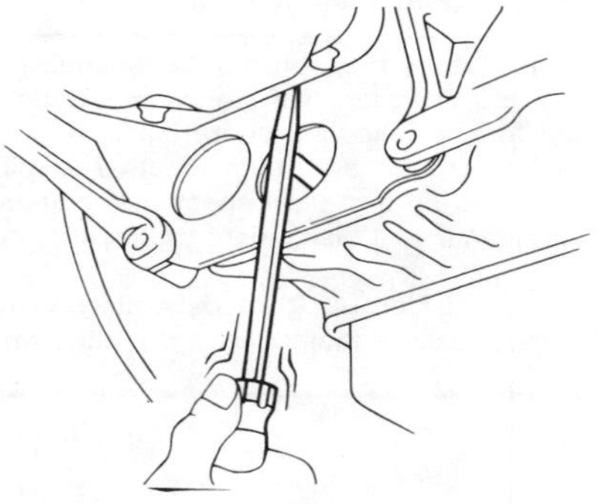

Fig. 6.100 Lever against the guide pin to withdraw transmission from engine (Sec 31)

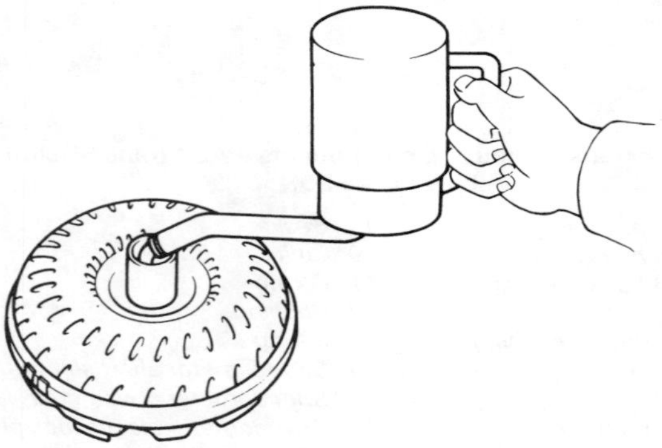

Fig. 6.101 Refilling the torque converter with fluid (Sec 31)

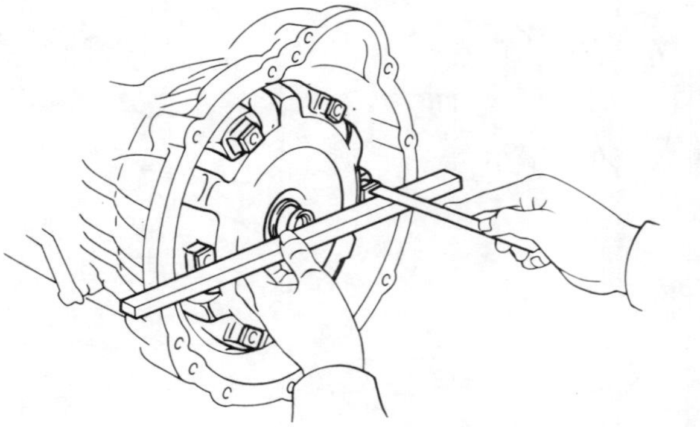

Fig. 6.102 Check converter fitted depth from transmission housing (Sec 31)

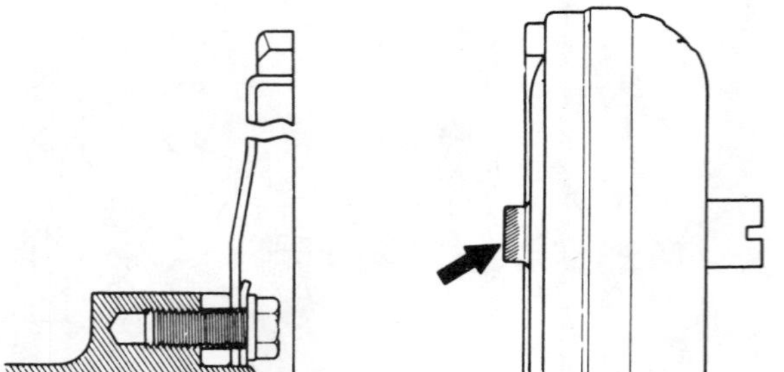

Fig. 6.103 Grease points indicated on converter hub and driveplate (Sec 31)

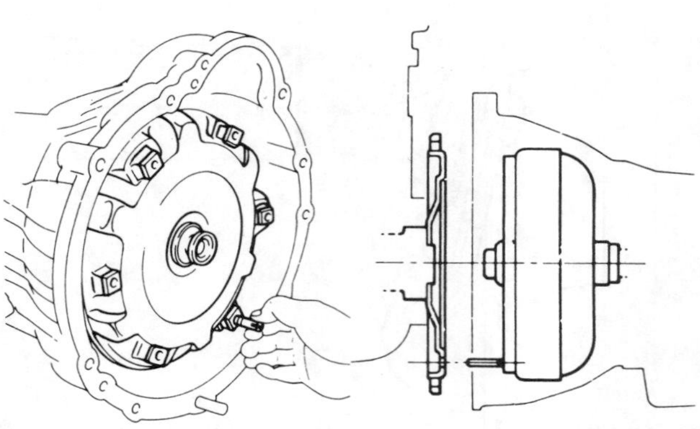

Fig. 6.104 Locate guide pin at bottom of converter (Sec 31)

18 With the jack in position, unbolt and remove the rear mounting and crossmember (Fig. 6.97).

19 Prise free the rubber plug from the inspection hole in the rear engine plate, then using a socket and extension inserted through the hole, unscrew the bolts which hold the driveplate and torque converter together. The bolts can be brought into view one at a time by rotating the crankshaft with a ring spanner applied to the crankshaft pulley bolt (Fig. 6.98).

20 When all of the bolts are removed, screw a guide pin (which can be fabricated from an old bolt with the head cut off – see Fig. 6.99), into a torque converter bolt hole. The guide pin should be of suitable length so that when fitted, its front end will protrude beyond the rear plate inspection hole and will provide a leverage point when separating the transmission from the engine and driveplate.

21 Place a jack under the engine sump (use a block of wood to protect it) and remove the bolts which secure the torque converter housing to the engine.

22 Lower both jacks progressively until the transmission unit will clear that lower edge of the engine rear bulkhead.

23 The aid of an assistant will be needed at this point to steady the transmission as it is withdrawn. Use a suitable lever and prise against the end of the guide pin as shown (Fig. 6.100), and simultaneously withdraw the transmission unit, complete wth the torque converter, away from the engine. Catch the fluid which will run from the torque converter during this operation. **On no account should levers be placed between the driveplate and the torque converter as damage or distortion will result.** As the transmission moves away from the engine, the driveplate will remain bolted to the rear flange of the crankshaft. On the A20 two-speed transmission care must be taken to avoid damaging the oil seal of the front oil pump.

24 The torque converter should be kept in position in its housing whilst the transmission is removed. To do this bolt a temporary plate and spacer across the front face of the housing with a suitable spacer to retain the converter unit.

25 If the converter unit is removed for any reason on the A40 (three-speed) transmission, it will have to be refilled with the specified fluid (ATF) before refitting, its capacity being 3.6 Imp pts (2.0 litres/2.1 US qts). Refill as shown in Fig. 6.101. In addition, check that the fitted depth from the converter front face to the transmission housing surface is 1.02 in (26 mm), (see Fig. 6.102), and take care when fitting the converter not to damage the oil pump oil seal with the converter oil seal.

26 Lubricate the converter hub and its location shoulder in the driveplate with grease before fitting (Fig. 6.103). It is also advisable to check that the driveplate run-out is within the specified limit before starting reassembly.

27 Refitting of the transmission is a reversal of the removal procedure, but the following points should be noted.

28 When the transmission is being manoeuvred into position take care that the torque converter does not slip forward. Align the driveplate hole with the guide pin in the torque converter for ease of engagement. Locate the guide pin at the bottom of the converter for convenience (Fig. 6.104).

29 The upper converter housing bolts are the longest on the A40 transmission (Fig. 6.105).

30 Retighten all bolts and fastenings to their specified torque settings in a progressive manner.

31 When the transmission is refitted, top it up with transmission fluid and adjust as necessary the selector lever setting, the control rod adjustment, throttle link connecting rod (A20 transmission) and the throttle cable, and floor shift linkage (A40 transmission).

32 Road test the vehicle and then check for any signs of fluid leaks, especially from the oil cooler pipes on the A20 transmission. Recheck the fluid level of the transmission when the oil is hot and top up as necessary. On the A20 transmission extra fluid will probably be required to top up the level owing to some of the fluid being circulated through the oil cooler and pipes and the converter.

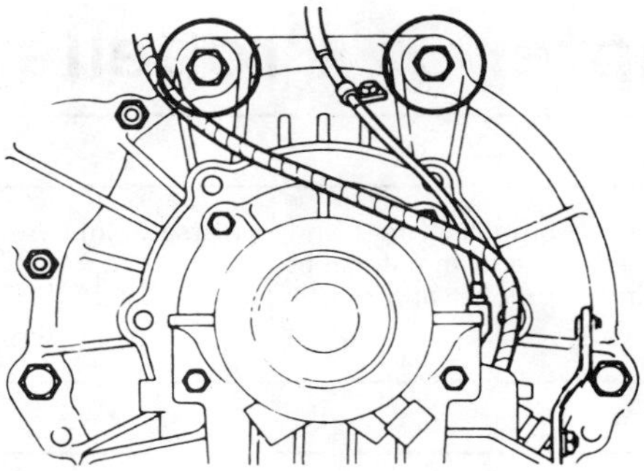

Fig. 6.105 Longer mounting bolt positions on the A40 transmission (Sec 31)

32 Fault diagnosis – automatic transmission

Symptom	**Reason(s)**
Oil on dipstick appears burned or discoloured	Transmission misused by towing overweight loads or by wheel spinning in mud or snow.
Water on dipstick	Leak in fluid cooler tube within radiator.
No vehicle movement in forward range, or reverse	Incorrectly adjusted selector linkage.
Harsh engagement when any drive range selected	Incorrectly adjusted downshift cable.
Screech or whine increasing with engine speed	Cracked driveplate. Oil pump screen (within oil pan) clogged.
Delayed upshifts or downshifts	Incorrectly adjusted downshift cable.
Slip on upshifts, downshifts squawk or shudder on take off	Incorrectly adjusted speed selector linkage or downshift cable.
Vehicle will not hold parked in 'P'	Incorrectly adjusted selector linkage.

Before carrying out any of the foregoing diagnosis checks always verify that the transmission fluid is at its correct level.

Chapter 7 Propeller shaft and universal joints

Contents

Specifications

Type	Tubular with two or three universal joints according to model. Centre bearing with three-joint type. Front sliding sleeve	
Universal joints	Greased, sealed for life, needle roller bearing	
Bearing cup circlip thicknesses available		
External circlip type joint	0.0512 in (1.30 mm) – Blue colour code	
	0.0492 in (1.25 mm) – Brown colour code	
	0.0472 in (1.20 mm) – No colour code	
Enclosed circlip type joint	0.0935 to 0.0955 in (2.37 to 2.42 mm) – No colour code	
	0.0955 to 0.0974 in (2.42 to 2.47 mm) – Brown colour code	
	0.0974 to 0.0994 in (2.47 to 2.52 mm) – Blue colour code	
	0.0994 to 0.1014 in (2.52 to 2.57 mm) – No colour code	
Spider axial play allowance limit		
Types A, B and E	0.002 in (0.05 mm)	
Types C and D	Zero	
Propeller and intermediate shaft run-out limit	0.031 in (0.8 mm)	
Torque wrench settings	**lbf ft**	**kgf m**
Central flange nut to splined end of intermediate shaft:		
1st tightening	123 to 144	17.0 to 20.0
2nd tightening	19 to 25	2.5 to 3.5
Propeller shaft to pinion flange	15 to 28	2.0 to 4.0
Propeller shaft to intermediate flange	15 to 28	2.0 to 4.0
Centre bearing attachment bolts	22 to 32	3.0 to 4.5

1 General description and maintenance

The drive from the gearbox to the rear axle is transmitted by the tubular propeller shaft. Due to the variety of angles caused by the up and down motion of the rear axle in relation to the gearbox, universal joints are fitted to each end of the shaft to convey the drive through the constantly varying angles. As the movement also increases and decreases the distance between the rear axle and the gearbox, the forward end of the propeller shaft is a splined sleeve which is a sliding fit over the rear of the gearbox splined mainshaft.

Five types of propeller shaft have been fitted to the Corolla range and the type fitted to your particular model will depend on its year and market. The five types are illustrated in Fig. 7.1.

[TYPE] [A]

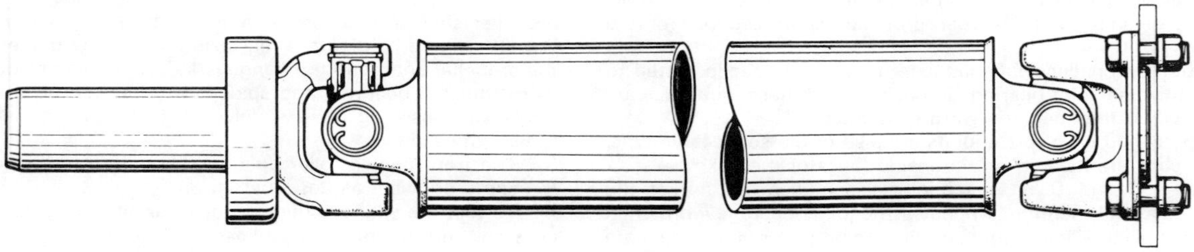

[TYPE] [B]

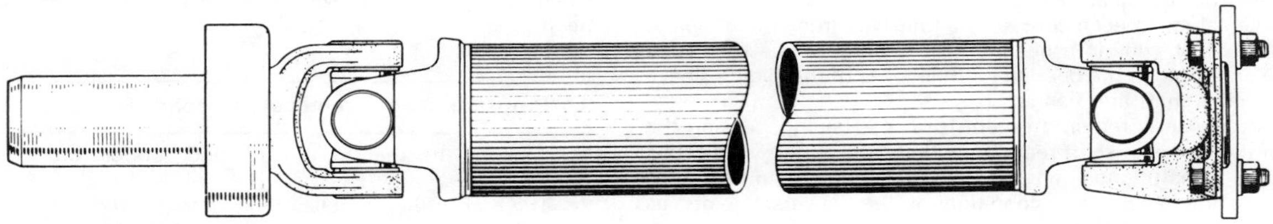

[TYPE] [C]

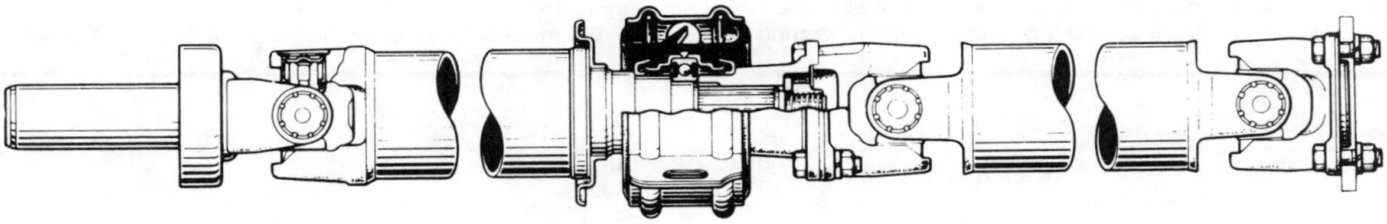

[TYPE] [D]

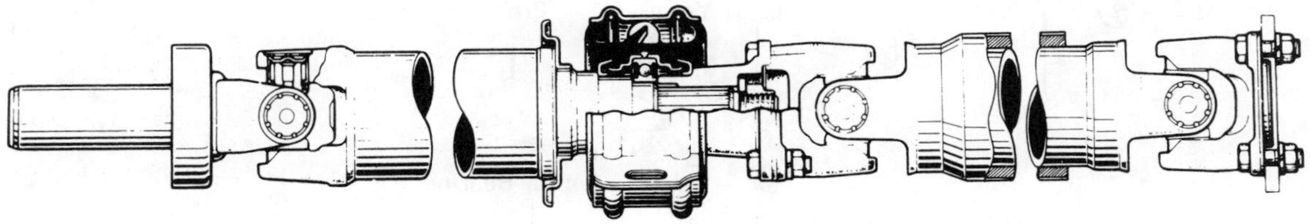

[TYPE] [E]

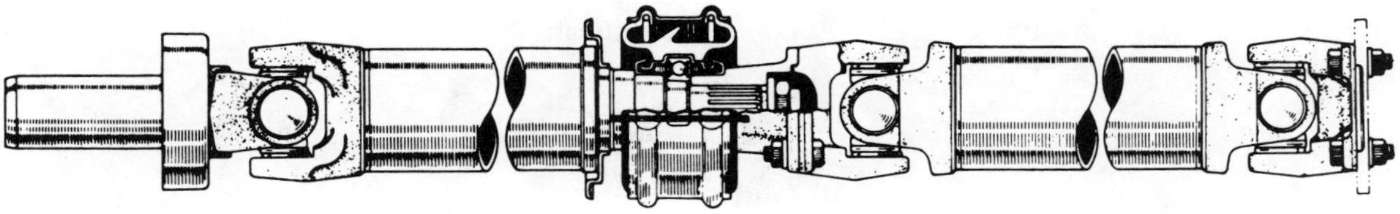

Fig. 7.1 The various propeller shaft assemblies fitted (Sec 1)

The propeller shaft fitted will either be of single or two piece type, the latter having a central steady bearing fitted between the intermediate (front) shaft and the rear propeller shaft sections of the assembly.

The type A propeller shaft has externally visible circlips fitted to secure the universal joint bearings in position and these joint units are serviceable when they become worn or damaged.

The type B and E universal joints are also of the serviceable type, but their circlips are located on the inside faces of the yokes.

The types C and D universal joint assemblies are not of the serviceable type and therefore whenever the joints become worn, then the complete universal joint together with the propeller or intermediate shaft assembly must be renewed.

The splined sleeve runs in an oil seal in the gearbox rear extension housing and is supported with the mainshaft on the gearbox rear bearing. The splines are lubricated by oil in the rear extension housing which comes from the gearbox.

The universal joints each consist of a four-way trunnion, or spider – each leg of which runs in a needle roller bearing race – preloaded with grease and fitted in the bearing journal yokes of the sliding sleeve and the propeller shaft and flange.

No maintenance is required except for occasionally checking the tightness of the propeller shaft rear flange bolts and, where applicable, the intermediate shaft flange bolts and central bearing mounting bolts. At the same time check the condition of the universal joints as described in the next Section.

2 Universal joints – inspection

1 Wear in the needle roller bearings is characterised by vibration in the transmission, 'clonks' on taking up the drive and in extreme cases of lack of lubrication, metallic squeaking, and ultimately grating and shrieking sounds as the bearings break up.

2 It is easy to check if the needle roller bearings are worn, with the propeller shaft in position, by trying to turn the shaft with one hand, the other hand holding the rear axle flange. Any movement between the propeller shaft and the flange is indicative of considerable wear. If worn, the old bearings and spiders will have to be discarded and a repair kit consisting of new universal joint spiders, bearings and oil seals purchased.

3 The front needle roller bearings should be tested for wear using the same principle as described in paragraph 2.

4 To test the splined coupling for wear, lift the end of the shaft and note any movement in the splines.

5 Check the splined coupling dust cover for signs of damage or looseness on the shaft.

6 If renewal or repairs are necessary to any part(s) of the propeller shaft and/or intermediate shaft then the propeller shaft assembly, complete, must be removed from the vehicle as described in the next Section.

3 Propeller shaft – removal and refitting

1 Jack-up the rear of the car and support on firmly based axle stands.

2 The rear of the propeller shaft is connected to the rear axle pinion by a flange held by four nuts and bolts. Mark the position of both flanges relative to each other, and then undo and remove the nuts and bolts.

3 On models fitted with the two-joint type propeller shaft, draw the other end of the propeller shaft, that is the splined sleeve, out of the rear of the gearbox. The shaft is then clear for removal from the underside of the car (photo).

4 On models fitted with the three-joint type propeller shaft, remove

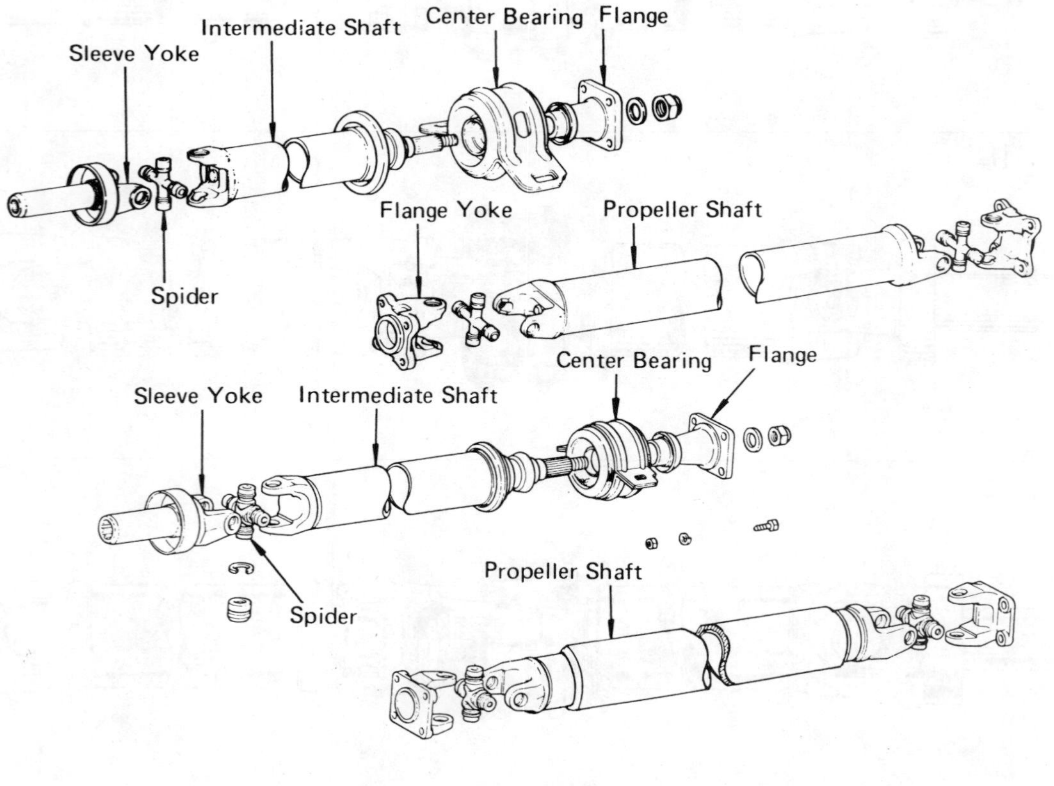

Fig. 7.2 Component parts of the two-piece type propeller shaft assembly types (Sec 1)

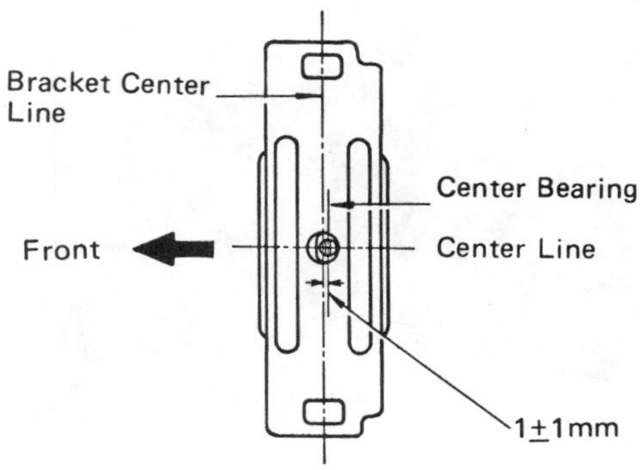

Fig. 7.3 Centre bearing orientation (two-piece type) (Sec 3)

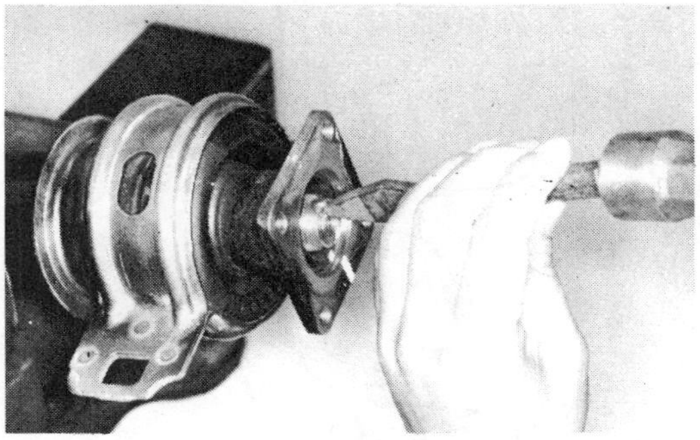

Fig. 7.4 Relieve the nut retainer staking using suitable chisel (Sec 4)

the centre bearing securing strap bolts, lower the strap and centre bearing assembly and note the position of the strap bolt washers (photo).

5 Support the propeller shaft and withdraw it from the rear of the gearbox, then lower and remove the shaft assembly complete from underneath the car.

6 Place a container under the gearbox rear extension housing to catch any oil which will certainly come out. Refitting the propeller shaft is the reverse sequence to removal but the following additional points should be noted:

(a) Ensure that the mating marks on the propeller shaft and differential pinion flanges are lined up (photo)

(b) On the three-joint type propeller shaft, hand tighten only the central bearing support bolts. Then when the pinion joint is reconnected, check to make sure that the bearing support bracket is at right-angles to the propeller shaft. When the central bearing is secure the bearing should be positioned as shown (Fig. 7.3), 0.04 in (1 mm) to the rear under a no load condition

(c) Tighten all bolts to the specified torque wrench setting

(d) Don't forget to check the gearbox oil level and top-up if necessary

4 Three-joint propeller shaft – dismantling and assembly

1 Scribe or paint an alignment mark across the joint faces of the propeller shaft and intermediate shaft flanges (photo).

2 Unscrew and remove the four attachment bolts and nuts, then separate the two assemblies (photo).

3 To remove the centre bearing unit from the intermediate shaft, support the shaft securely in a vice as shown (Fig. 7.4), then using a suitable chisel relieve the staking on the nut. Unscrew the nut and remove it. The intermediate shaft can then be withdrawn through the bearing, but should it prove tight, support the flange in a vice and use a soft metal drift to drive the shaft through.

4 Inspect the centre bearing for wear or damage and renew it as a

3.3 Propeller shaft withdrawal from gearbox

3.4 Centre bearing assembly and support bolts – (two piece – three joint type propeller shaft)

3.6a Propeller shaft to differential pinion flange joint – align markings made on removal

4.1 Make alignment mark across flanges before separating the central universal joint

4.2 Intermediate shaft separation from the propeller shaft

unit if necessary. The central bearing should turn freely (Fig. 7.5).
5 Check the universal joints of each shaft for wear and if necessary renew the shaft(s) and joints complete or overhaul the joint units where they are of the repairable type as described in Section 5.
6 If the propeller shaft run-out is checked and is found to be beyond the specified maximum limit, then the shaft will have to be renewed.
7 Reassembly is a reversal of the dismantling procedure but note the following points:

(a) Lubricate the intermediate shaft splines with a medium grease before fitting
(b) Tighten the intermediate shaft flange retaining nut to the initial specified torque setting. Then having pressed the bearing into position, loosen off the nut and retighten it to its final torque wrench setting (see Specifications), then stake lock the nut (photo)
(c) Align the flange marks made during dismantling and fit and tighten the four attachment nuts and bolts to the specified torque wrench setting

Fig. 7.5 Check centre support bearing for wear or damage (Sec 4)

5 Repairable universal joints – dismantling and overhaul

Refer to the accompanying photos for a typical universal joint dismantling and overhaul sequence.
1 Clean away all traces of dirt and grease from the universal joint yoke. Match mark the yoke, shaft and spider.
2 Using a pair of pliers compress the circlips and lift away. If the circlips are tight in their grooves tap the ends to shock move the bearing cups slightly.
3 Note that on the type A propeller shaft assembly, the circlips are visible and removable from the outer end faces of the bearing cups, but the types B and E shafts have their universal joint retaining clips located on the inside of the yoke (Fig. 7.6).
4 With the circlips removed, hold the propeller shaft and using a suitable socket and soft-faced hammer, tap the yoke to jar the bearing cups from the yoke (photo).
5 When a bearing cup has emerged, it can be gripped in the jaws of a wrench or vice and twisted out. As the cups are to be discarded, it does not matter if they are damaged (photo).
6 Remove all four bearing cups as described and then separate the yoke from the shaft *but not before marking their relationship.*
7 Clean all the parts and thoroughly inspect them for wear and damage (photo).
8 If wear or damage is obvious in the joint assemblies, they must be renewed as a unit, or repaired using a kit which consists of the spider and bearing assemblies. Components are not available individually.
9 When renewing the universal joint assemblies it should be noted that on the external location circlip type joints there are three thicknesses of circlip available to provide the correct spider endplay requirement. This must not exceed 0.002 in (0.05 mm). These circlips are identified as follows:

Colour code	Thickness
Blue	*0.0512 in (1.30 mm)*
Brown	*0.0492 in (1.25 mm)*
None	*0.0472 in (1.20 mm)*

See Figure 7.7.

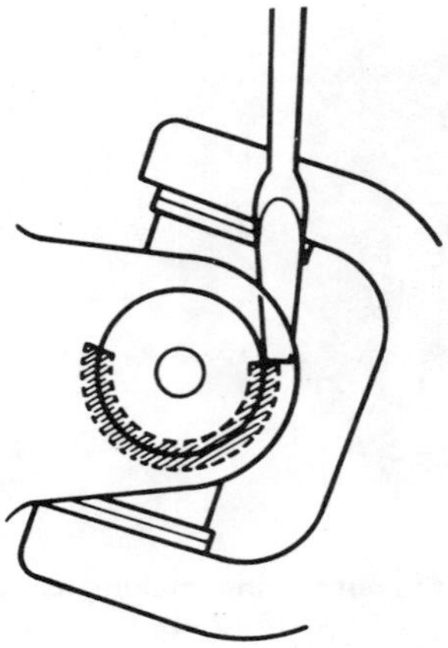

Fig. 7.6 Circlip removal method – joint types B and E (Sec 5)

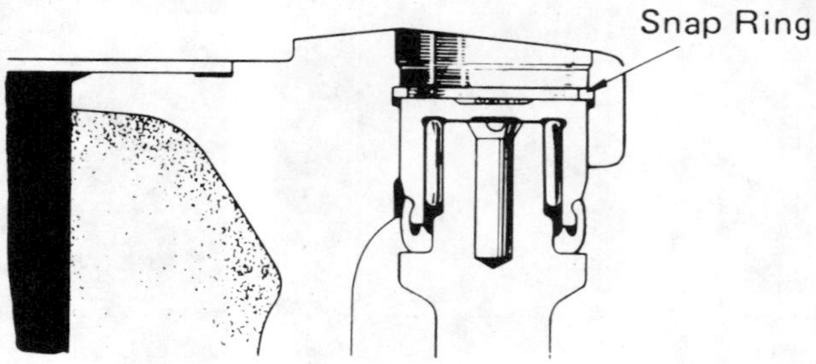

Fig. 7.7 Assemble selected circlips (types B and E). Always use new circlips (Sec 5)

4.7b Stake lock the intermediate flange retaining nut to secure

5.4 Tap yoke to jar the bearing cups from the yoke ...

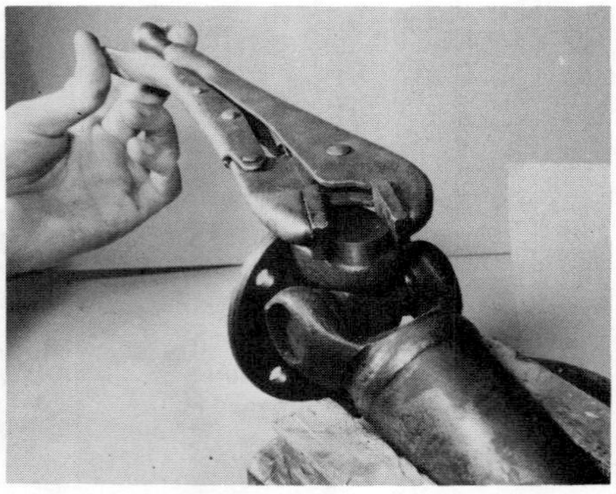

5.5 ... then grip cup exposed section and twist it free

10 On the enclosed circlip joint type there are four circlip thicknesses available to provide the above mentioned endplay of the spider. These are as follows:

Colour code	Thickness
No colour	*0.0935 to 0.0955 in (2.37 to 2.42 mm)*
Brown	*0.0955 to 0.0974 in (2.42 to 2.47 mm)*
Blue	*0.0974 to 0.0994 in (2.47 to 2.52 mm)*
No colour	*0.0994 to 0.1014 in (2.52 to 2.57 mm)*

11 Before starting reassembly ensure that the yokes and spiders are clean. Check that the oil seals are correctly located.

12 Place the spider on the propeller shaft yoke and assemble the needle rollers into the bearing cups retaining them with some thick grease. Align the yoke and shaft mating marks before dismantling.
13 Fill each bearing cup about $\frac{1}{2}$ full with grease. Also fill the grease holes on the spider with grease taking care that all air bubbles are eliminated.
14 Press the bearing cups squarely into the yokes so that the needles are not displaced as the ends of the spiders pass into them. Use a suitable size socket in the jaws of a vice to do this (photos).
15 The cups should be pressed in until the axial movement of the spider is eliminated or is less than 0.0020 in (0.05 mm) then select suitable circlips and install them.

5.7 Clean and inspect the universal joint components for wear or damage

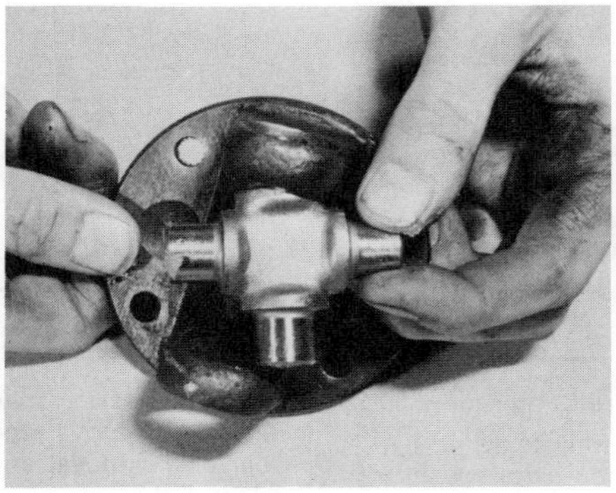
5.14a Insert spider into yoke ...

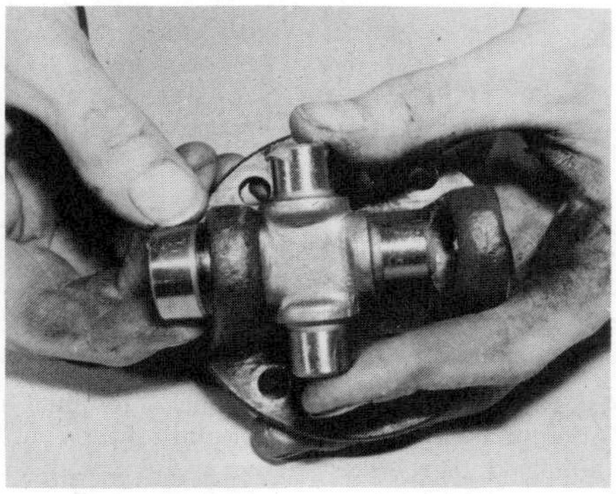
5.14b ... locate bearing ...

5.14c ... and press it home ...

5.14d ... then insert new circlip

5.14e Repeat procedure assembling the yoke and joint to the shaft yoke

6 Fault diagnosis – propeller shaft and universal joints

Symptom	Reason(s)
Propeller shaft vibration	Universal joint spider bearing worn or damaged. Incorrect bearing cup circlip thickness. Bent propeller shaft. Propeller shaft out of balance. Worn gearbox extension housing bush. Universal joint mounting loose. Worn central bearing (where applicable).
Noisy starting or while coasting	Universal joint spider bearing worn or damaged. Incorrect bearing cup circlip thickness. Slackness in the spider bearings. Universal joint mounting loose. No preload of the differential drive pinion bearing. Worn splines of drive pinion companion flange. Worn splines of universal joint sleeve yoke. Incorrect installation of splined coupling dust cover.

Chapter 8 Rear axle

Contents

Specifications

Type	Rigid, semi-floating hypoid
Ratios	
UK models:	
Saloon, Estate and Liftback (with manual transmission)	3.909 to 1
Saloon and Estate (with automatic transmission)	4.100 to 1
Coupe SR	4.100 to 1
USA and Canadian models:	
1980 models	2.72 to 1
1981 models	3.58 to 1 or 3.73 to 1
1982 models	3.31 to 1
Pinion oil seal fitting depth	
6.0 in differential	0.039 in (1 mm)
6.38 in differential	0 to 0.020 in (0 to 0.5 mm)
6.7 in differential	0.157 in (4.0 mm)
Pinion starting preload (old bearing)	
6.0 in differential	3.5 to 6.1 lbf in (4 to 7 kgf cm)
6.7 in and 6.38 in differential	4.3 to 6.9 lbf in (5 to 8 kgf cm)
Pinion starting preload (new bearing)	
6.0 in differential	5.6 to 10.9 lbf in (6.5 to 12.5 kgf cm)
6.7 in and 6.38 in differential	8.7 to 13.9 lbf in (10.0 to 16.0 kgf cm)
Crownwheel (ring gear) run-out limit	0.0028 in (0.07 mm)
Crownwheel/pinion backlash	
6.0 in differential	0.0039 in to 0.0059 in (0.10 to 0.15 mm)
6.7 in and 6.38 in differential	0.0051 to 0.0071 in (0.13 to 0.18 mm)
Side gear backlash (standard)	
6.0 in differential	0.0008 to 0.0059 in (0.02 to 0.15 mm)
6.38 in differential	0.0008 to 0.0079 in (0.02 to 0.20 mm)
6.7 in differential	0.0020 to 0.0079 in (0.05 to 0.20 mm)
Axleshaft oil seal fitting depth	
6.0 in differential	0.221 in (5.6 mm)
6.3 in differential	0.232 in (5.9 mm)
6.3 in (Estate) differential	0.197 in (4.9 mm)
6.7 in differential	0.236 in (6.0 mm)

Torque wrench settings

	lbf ft	kgf m
Drive pinion flange nut:		
6 in differential	70 to 144	9.5 to 20.0
6.7 in and 6.38 in differential	80 to 173	11.0 to 24.0
Differential carrier to axle casing nuts	19 to 27	2.5 to 3.8
Axleshaft bearing retainer nuts	44 to 53	6.0 to 7.4
Propeller shaft to pinion flange nuts	15 to 28	2.0 to 4.0

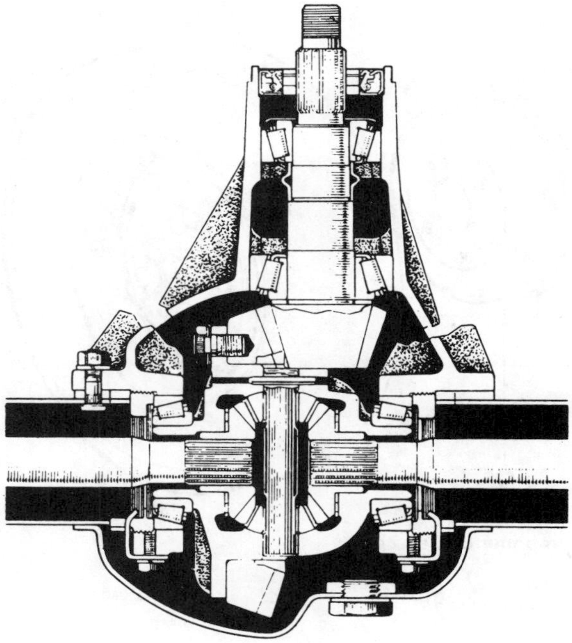

Fig. 8.1 Sectional view showing the differential unit and axle casing – 2 pinion/6 in axle type (Sec 1)

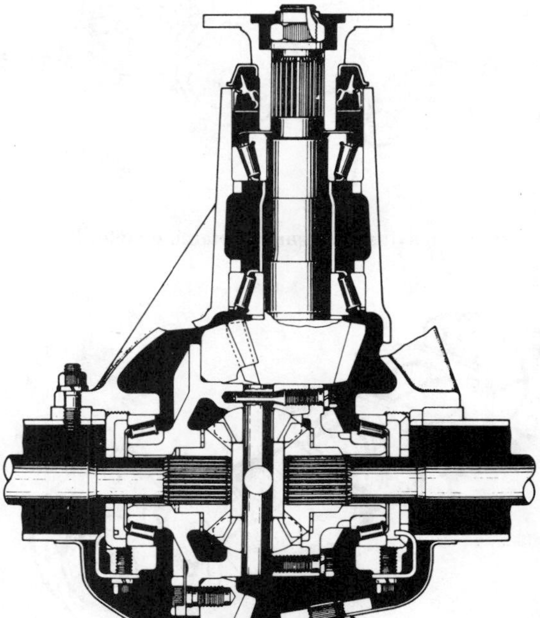

Fig. 8.2 Sectional view showing the differential unit and axle casing – 4 pinion/6.38 in axle type (Sec 1)

1 General description

The rear axle is of hypoid semi-floating type. The differential and hypoid gear pinion are carried on taper roller bearings, and are housed in a differential casing which is bolted to the banjo type axle tube.

The axle casing is located in one of two ways according to suspension type. On rear leaf spring type suspension models the axle casing is located by the semi-elliptic roadsprings by U-bolts. On other models fitted with the four-link type suspension, the axle casing is located both laterally and longitudinally by two upper and two lower control arms attached to the body underframe. Two coil springs support the weight of the body. Gas-filled telescopic shock absorbers dampen the up and down movement of the axle assembly on both types.

The axleshafts (or halfshafts) are splined into the differential side gears and are supported at the ends of the axle tubes by ball bearings held by bearing retainer plates.

Various sizes of differential unit have been used according to vehicle model.

It is not recommended that the differential unit is dismantled or rebuilt by the home mechanic due to the need for special gauges and setting tools. The differential casing being mounted on the front face of the banjo axle housing is so easy to remove that it is recommended that the unit is removed and taken to your Toyota dealer, leaving the axle in position in the vehicle.

Restrict operations on the rear axle to those described in this Chapter.

2 Axleshafts, bearing and oil seals – removal and refitting

1 Jack up the rear axle and support it securely on axle stands.
2 Remove the rear roadwheel.
3 Remove the brake drum, (referring to Chapter 9 if necessary).
4 Insert a socket and extension through one of the holes in the axleshaft flange and unscrew the four nuts which secure the brake backing plate to the axle casing (photo).
5 A slide hammer will now be required to extract the axleshaft from the axle casing. A slide hammer can easily be made up or if this is not possible, try bolting an old roadwheel onto the axle flange studs and striking two opposite points on the inner rim simultaneously to drive the axleshaft out of the axle casing. It is pointless to just try and pull

2.4 Unscrew backing plate to axle casing nuts

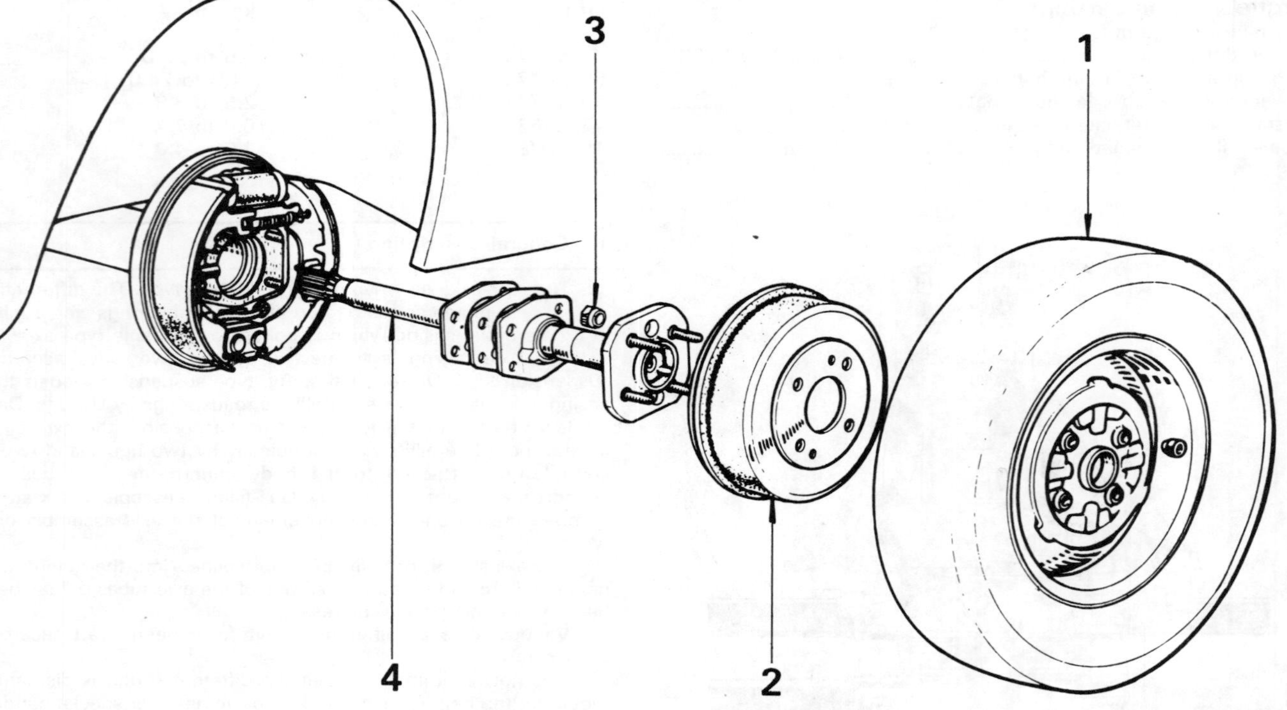

Fig. 8.3 Axleshaft and associated components (Sec 2)

1 *Wheel*
2 *Brake drum*
3 *Nut*
4 *Rear axle shaft*

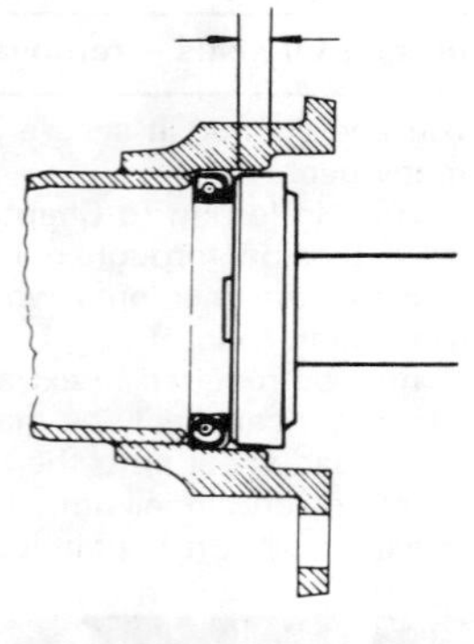

Fig. 8.4 Insert new oil seal to appropriate depth (Sec 2)

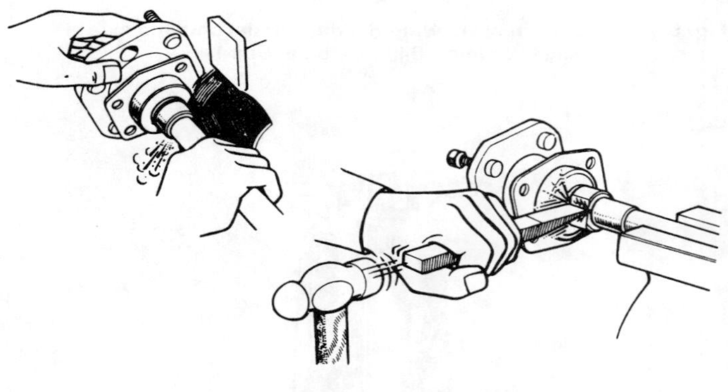

Fig. 8.5 Removing axleshaft bearing retaining collar (Sec 2)

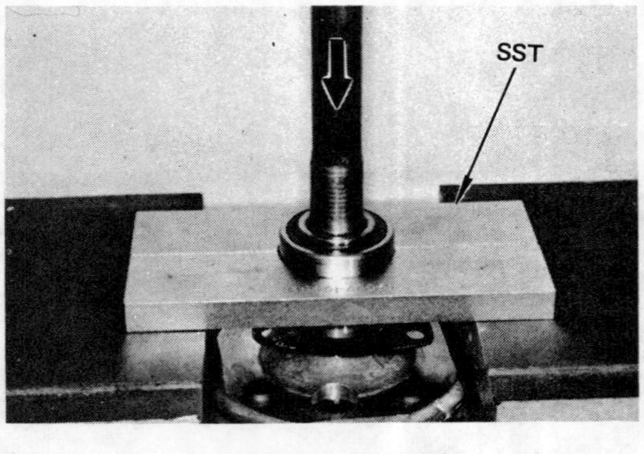

Fig. 8.6 Push axleshaft through bearing (Sec 2)

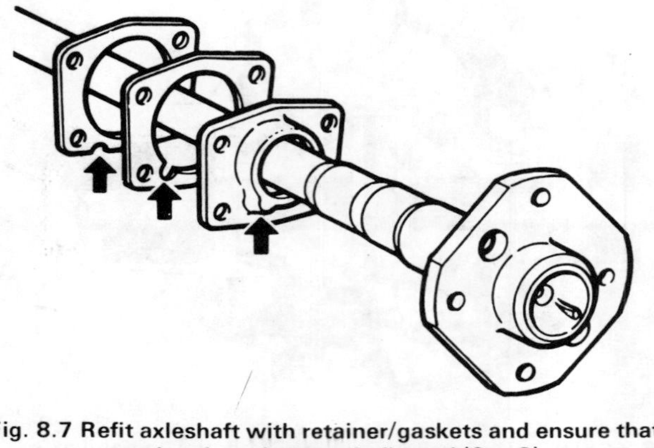

Fig. 8.7 Refit axleshaft with retainer/gaskets and ensure that notches face down as indicated (Sec 2)

the shaft out, you will only succeed in pulling the vehicle off the axle stands.
6 With the axleshaft removed, if it is only the oil seal that is leaking, lever the old one from the axle casing and drive a new one in using a distance piece of tubing as a drift. Make sure that the lips of the seal are facing inwards and that the end-face of the oil seal is the specified distance below the end of the axle casing flange.
7 Refer to Figure 8-4 and the Specifications for axleshaft oil seal fitting depth.
8 If the axleshaft bearing is rough or noisy when turned, it must be renewed.
9 To remove the old bearing, first grind a flat on one side of the bearing retaining collar and then split it with a sharp cold chisel. Take care not to damage the axleshaft (Fig. 8.5).
10 Remove the bearing from the shaft either by supporting the bearing and pressing the axleshaft from it or by drawing it off if a suitable extending leg extractor can be obtained (Fig. 8.6).
11 The new bearing should be pressed onto the shaft but don't forget to apply pressure to the bearing centre track only and make sure that the spacer bearing retainer plate and gaskets are in position on the shaft first.
12 With the bearing fitted, the bearing retaining collar must be pressed onto the shaft. Before pressing the collar onto the shaft it should be heated in an oven to between 284 and 320°F (140 to 160°C).
13 Before refitting the axleshaft, smear the oil seal lip with a medium grade grease. Allow the collar to fully cool off before inserting the axleshaft.
14 Pass the assembled axleshaft into the casing taking care not to damage the oil seal. Hold the shaft quite level and turn it gently until the splines on its inner end can be felt to pick up those in the differential side gears then push the shaft fully home (Fig. 8.7).
15 Refit the backplate bolts, the brake drum and the roadwheel. Check that the roadwheel rotates freely and the brakes are operational.
16 Lower the vehicle to the ground.

3 Pinion oil seal – renewal

1 The pinion oil seal may be renewed with the differential carrier still in position on the rear axle casing and the casing still attached to the rear suspension.
2 Jack up the rear of the vehicle and mark the edges of the propeller shaft rear flange and the pinion driving flange. Then disconnect the flanges and tie the propeller shaft up out of the way.
3 Ensure that the handbrake is fully off and then attach a spring balance to a length of cord wound round the pinion driving flange. Give an even pull and read off the bearing preload on the spring balance. Note the figure for later comparison (Fig. 8.9).
4 Mark the pinion coupling in relation to the pinion splines and knock back the staking on the pinion nut with a drift or narrow chisel.
5 Hold the pinion coupling quite still by bolting a length of flat steel to two of the coupling flange holes and then unscrew the pinion nut. A ring spanner of good length will be required for this.
6 Remove the lever from the coupling flange and withdraw the coupling. If it is tight, use a two or three legged puller but on no account attempt to knock it from the splined pinion.
7 Measure the inserted depth of the oil seal, then remove the defective oil seal using a two legged extractor.
8 Refit the new oil seal first having greased the mating surfaces of

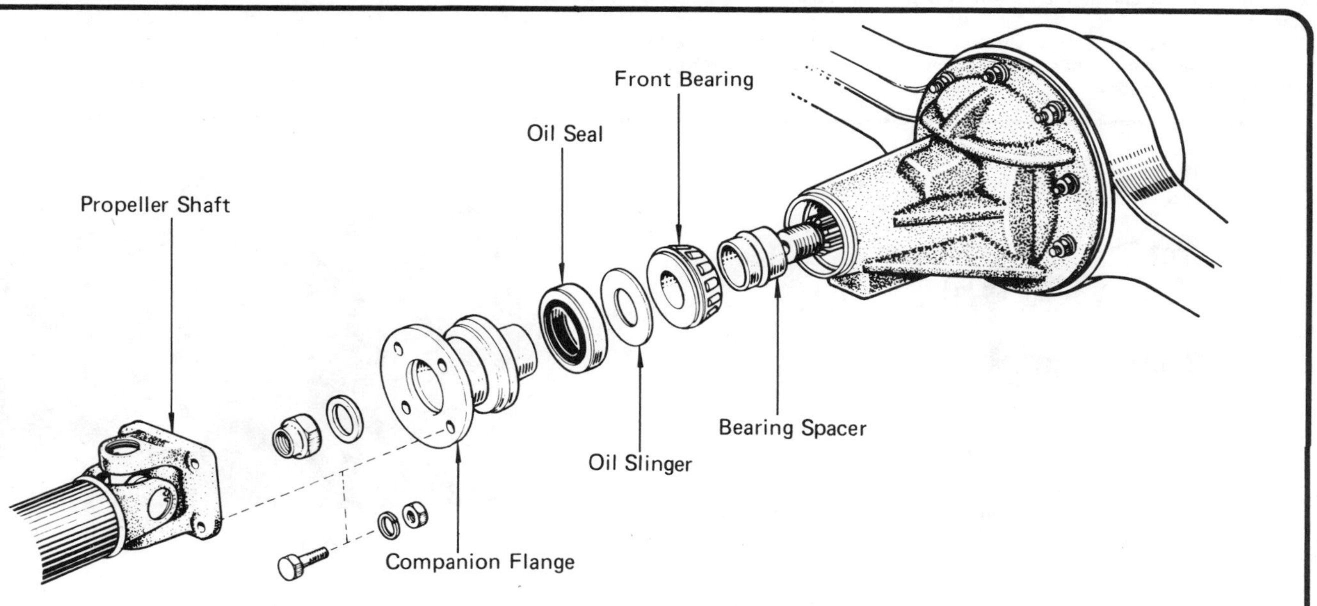

Fig. 8.8 Pinion oil seal and associated components (Sec 3)

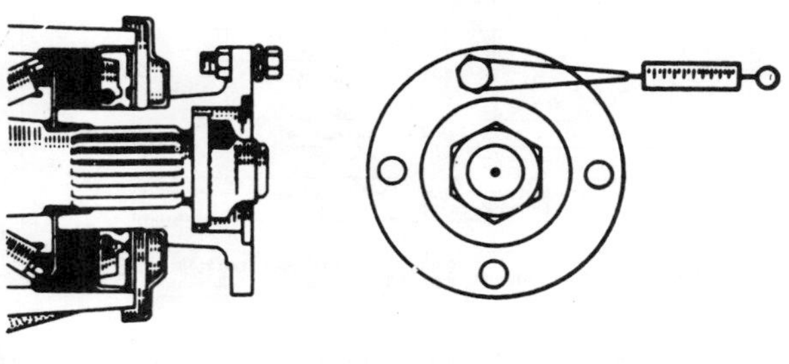

Fig. 8.9 Axle pinion bearing preload test method using spring balance (Sec 3)

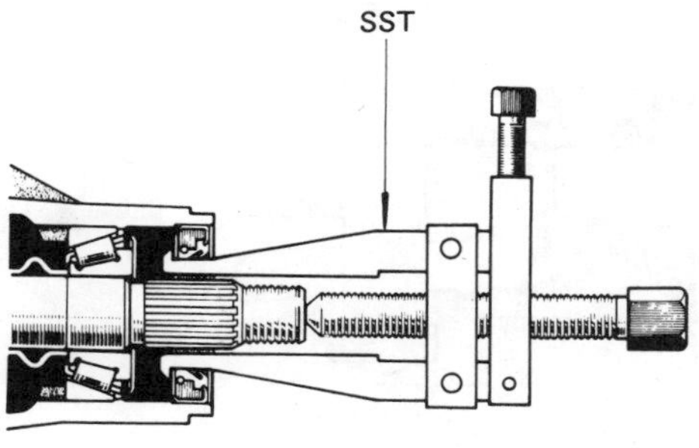

Fig. 8.10 Oil seal removal using extractor (Sec 3)

the seal and the axle housing. The lips of the oil seal must face inwards. Using a piece of brass or copper tubing of suitable diameter, carefully drive the new oil seal into the axle housing recess until the face of the seal is at the specified insertion depth (drive-in depth) according to axle type. Take particular care not to knock the end of the pinion during this operation. The seal fitting depths are to be found in the Specifications.

9 Refit the coupling to its original position on the pinion splines.

10 Fit a new pinion nut and holding the coupling still with the lever, tighten the nut until the pinion endfloat only just disappears. Do not overtighten. The torque wrench setting should not exceed the specified limit.

11 Rotate the pinion to settle the bearings and then check the preload using the cord and spring balance method previously described and by slight adjustment of the nut and rotation of the pinion, obtain a spring preload figure to match that which applied before dismantling. Do not overtighten the nut as it cannot be backed off without having to renew the internal compressible spacer. Access to the spacer, if it has to be removed, is gained by removing the oil seal and the taper roller bearing located behind it. You will need a suitable puller for bearing removal as shown in Figure 8-12.

12 When preload tightening the nut, refer to Fig. 8.13 for a sequence table, then on completion, stake the nut, refit the propeller shaft, making sure to align the mating marks (photo).

13 Lower the vehicle and check the oil level in the axle.

3.12 Stake back the pinion nut into shaft slot

4 Differential carrier – removal and refitting

1 Drain the oil from the differential by removing the drain plug..

2 Jack up the car at the rear and support it each side on safety stands.

3 Refer to Section 2 and withdraw the axleshaft on each side far enough to allow the inner end of each shaft to disengage from the differential side gears.

4 Make an alignment mark across the faces of the propeller shaft and pinion coupling flanges and then unbolt and separate the two. If it is not necessary to remove the propeller shaft completely, rest it to one side out of the way.

5 Undo the ten nuts and washers holding the differential carrier to the casing. The whole unit can be drawn forward off the studs and taken out.

6 The differential unit can now be cleaned and inspected for signs of excessive wear or damage, which if evident, will necessitate a complete or at least partial dismantling and overhaul of the unit. This

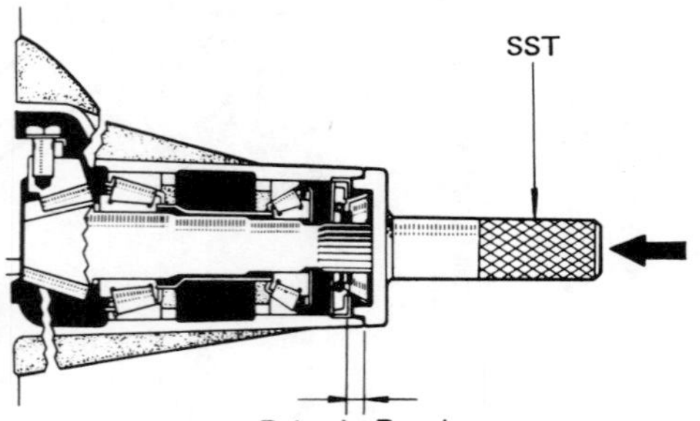

Fig. 8.11 Insert new oil seal to its 'drive-in depth' (Sec 3)

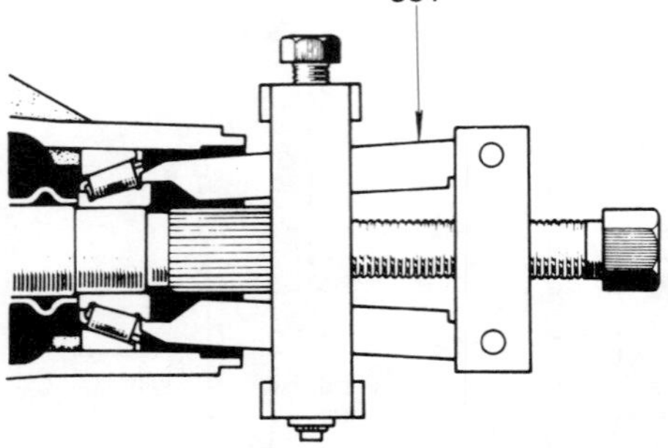

Fig. 8.12 Bearing removal using puller (Sec 3)

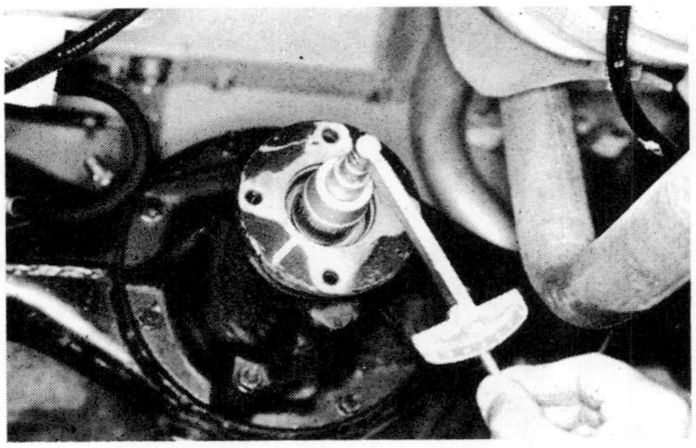

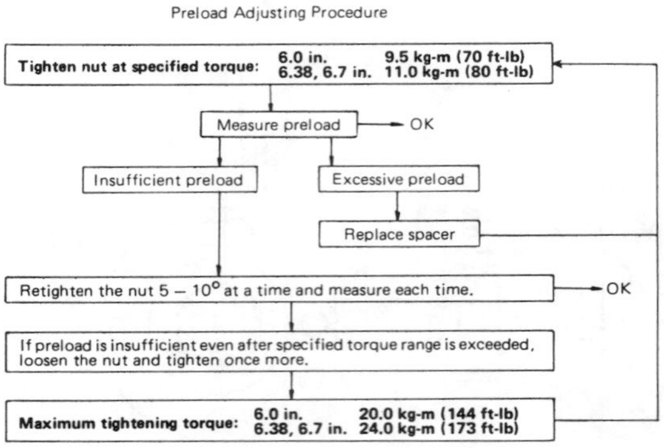

Fig. 8.13 Tighten pinion nut according to axle type to provide correct bearing pre-loading (Sec 3)

is a task to be entrusted to your Toyota dealer or a qualified automotive engineer since special tools and setting procedures are required during reassembly.
7 When refitting the differential carrier assembly, ensure that the mating faces are perfectly clean and free from burrs. A new gasket coated with sealing compound should also be used. Otherwise refitting is a reversal of the removal operation. Tighten the nuts to the specified torque.
8 Refill the unit with the correct grade and quantity of oil.

5 Rear axle removal and refitting – leaf spring rear suspension

1 Jack-up the rear of the vehicle, place axle stands under the rear body frame members and securely chock the front wheels. Place the jack under the differential and take its weight.
2 Remove the road wheels and disconnect the propeller shaft at the rear axle pinion coupling flange. Remember to mark the edges of the flange before disconnecting them so that they will be refitted in their original positions. Move the rear end of the propellor shaft to one side and support it.
3 Remove the brake drums and disconnect the handbrake cables from the actuating levers and then detach them from the brake backplate. Refit the drums to protect the brake shoe assemblies. Refer to Chapter 9 for further details and illustrations.
4 Disconnect the brake hydraulic line at the union on top of the axle casing. Plug both ends of the line to prevent loss of fluid or ingress of dirt.
5 Disconnect the rear shock absorber lower mountings from the road leaf spring support plates. Refer to Chapter 11 for further details and illustrations.
6 Unscrew and remove the four road spring U-bolts.
7 Remove each of the lower rear spring shackle bolts and lower the rear ends of the road springs to the ground.
8 Lower the jack previously placed under the differential until the rear axle assembly can be drawn out sideways from under the vehicle. Refitting is a reversal of removal but refer to Chapter 11, for details of loading/tightening conditions for the suspension components and to Chapter 9, for a description of bleeding the brake hydraulic system.

6 Rear axle removal and refitting – four-link rear suspension

1 Proceed as given in paragraphs 1 to 5 inclusive in the previous Section.
2 Remove the retaining nut and disconnect the lateral control rod from the axle casing. Refer to Chapter 11 for suspension details and illustrations.
3 Unbolt and detach the stabilizer bar from the brackets on the underside of the axle casing and then pivot the bar downwards out of the way.
4 Disconnect the upper and lower control arms from their axle or body mountings (as required). Check that the jack is securely positioned under the axle before disconnecting the arms.
5 As the axle is now only supported by the jack, get a couple of assistants to support and steady the axle each side at the wheel hubs, then slowly lower the jack under the differential.
6 When the tension of each coil spring is fully released they can be removed together with their respective seatings.
7 The axle unit can now be withdrawn from under the car.
8 Refitting is a reversal of the removal process, but when attaching the various associated suspension components refer to the refitting details given in the appropriate Sections in Chapter 11. Tighten the respective fastenings to the specified torque wrench settings, as given in that Chapter, only when they are fully connected and with the jack raised under the axle so that the body is clear of the safety stands.
9 Reconnect the brake components and bleed the hydraulic system as given in Chapter 9 to complete.

7 Fault diagnosis – rear axle

Symptom	Reason(s)
Noisy differential	
(a) During normal running	Lack of oil, damaged or worn gears, incorrect adjustment.
(b) During deceleration	Incorrect adjustment or damage to drive pinion bearings.
(c) During turning of vehicle	Worn or damaged axleshaft bearing, worn differential gears.
Noisy rear hub	Worn axleshaft bearings, buckled roadwheel, defective tyre, bent axleshaft.
Oil leakage at hub and pinion oil seals	May be caused by blocked breather plug on axle casing or over-filled unit.

Chapter 9 Braking system

Contents

Specifications

System type	Servo assisted dual circuit hydraulic with cable operated handbrake acting on rear wheels
Front brakes	
Type	Disc with AD type or PS type single piston sliding calipers
Disc thickness:	
Standard:	
AD type	0.394 in (10.0 mm)
PS type	0.492 in (12.5 mm)
Wear limit:	
AD type	0.354 in (9.0 mm)
PS type	0.453 in (11.5 mm)
Maximum allowable disc run-out	0.006 in (0.15 mm)
Minimum allowable pad thickness	0.039 in (1.0 mm)

Rear brakes

Type	Self-adjusting single leading shoe drum
Drum diameter:	
Standard:	
8 in drum	7.874 in (200.00 mm)
9 in drum	9.0 in (228.6 mm)
Wear limit:	
8 in drum	7.953 in (202.0 mm)
9 in drum	9.079 in (230.6 mm)
Minimum allowable lining thickness	0.039 in (1.0 mm)

Brake pedal

Pedal height from asphalt sheet:	
Right-hand drive with manual transmission	6.50 to 6.89 in (165 to 175 mm)
Right-hand drive with automatic transmission	6.65 to 7.05 in (169 to 179 mm)
Left-hand drive (all models)	6.89 to 7.28 in (175 to 185 mm)
Pedal free play	0.12 to 0.24 in (3.0 to 6.0 mm)
Pedal reserve distance (under 110 lbf/50 kgf force)	3.15 in (80 mm) minimum

Vacuum servo unit

Pushrod to piston clearance:	
With no vacuum	0.0024 to 0.0026 in (0.60 to 0.65 mm)
With idling vacuum	0.004 to 0.020 in (0.1 to 0.5 mm)

Handbrake

Lever travel under moderate pressure	3 to 7 clicks
Adjuster lever to shoe web clearance	0 to 0.014 in (0 to 0.35 mm)

Torque wrench settings

	lbf ft	kgf m
Pedal shaft bolt	22 to 33	3.0 to 4.5
Piston stopper bolt to master cylinder	6 to 10	0.8 to 1.5
Master cylinder outlet plug	25 to 40	3.5 to 5.5
Front disc to axle hub	29 to 40	4.0 to 5.5
Disc caliper retaining bolt (AD type)	12 to 17	1.6 to 2.4
Disc caliper bridge bolt (PS type)	58 to 69	8.0 to 9.5
Caliper bracket to steering knuckle (PS type)	40 to 54	5.5 to 7.5
Rear drum brake backplate to axle	43 to 53	6.0 to 7.4
Bleed screw	5 to 7	0.7 to 1.0
Servo unit to pedal bracket	7 to 12	1.0 to 1.6
Master cylinder to servo unit	7 to 12	1.0 to 1.6
Rear wheel cylinder to backplate	6 to 9	0.8 to 1.2

1 General description

All vehicles have a four wheel hydraulically operated braking system with a mechanically operated handbrake on the rear wheels only.

All models are fitted with front disc brakes and rear drum brakes, a dual circuit hydraulic system and a vacuum servo booster.

A fluid level warning switch is fitted to the master cylinder reservoir and in the event of the fluid dropping below the minimum level, the switch actuates a warning light to advise the driver.

2 Disc pads – inspection and renewal

1 No adjustment is required to the front disc brakes, the pads being kept in contact with the disc through the flexible characteristic of the cylinder boot and piston seal.

2 Jack up and support the front of the vehicle with safety stands, then remove the roadwheels.

3 One of two types of brake caliper will be fitted, being either the AD type or PS type. Identify which type you have fitted by the profile of the caliper unit and then proceed as follows for the AD type or from paragraph 12 for the PS type.

AD type

4 With the wheel(s) removed, the brake pad thicknesses can be checked through the inspection aperture in the caliper unit. If the pads are worn down to or beyond the specified wear limit they must be removed and renewed as a set, (renew the pads of both front brake caliper units).

5 To remove the pads, use a pair of spanners as shown to retain the bushing head and unscrew and remove the cylinder unit retaining bolt. The cylinder can then be pivoted upwards and retained in this position to allow pad removal by inserting the retainer bolt into the torque plate hole (Fig. 9.3 and 9.4). It is not necessary to disconnect the brake hose or the cylinder from the torque plate, but do not strain the flexible hose.

6 Withdraw the inner pad and then the outer pad with its anti-squeal shim.

7 Prise free the anti-rattle springs and guides from the housing noting how they are located. Keep them in order of fitting.

8 Remove the inner pad support spring from the caliper mounting.

9 Brush any dust or dirt from the caliper recesses, the housing, and springs. Do not inhale the dust as it is harmful. Using a piece of wood, press the piston into the caliper to accommodate the new linings. Keep an eye on the brake fluid level in the reservoir during this operation and, if necessary, syphon some out to prevent it overflowing.

10 Whilst the pads are removed, the brake disc should be checked for condition, wear and run-out to ensure that the specified wear limits are not exceeded. Removal and refitting of the brake disc is given in Section 6.

11 Fitting of the new pads is a reversal of the removal procedure but the following points must be observed.

(a) Locate the anti-squeal shim onto the outer pad and insert them into position whilst pushing in the anti-squeal spring.
(b) When fitting the inner pad, push up on the anti-squeal spring.
(c) When lowering the cylinder back into position take care not to wedge or damage the rubber protection boot.
(d) Hold the bush hexagons stationary while tightening the caliper retaining bolts to the specified torque. If this precaution is not taken, uneven pad wear may occur.
(e) With the disc pads fitted, depress the footbrake pedal several times, and if necessary top-up the master cylinder fluid level.

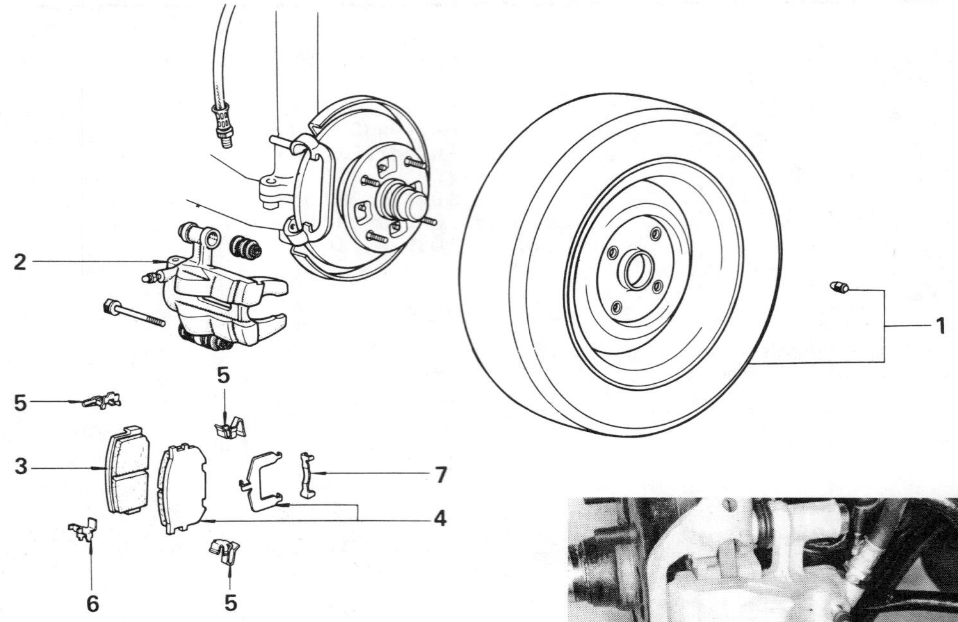

Fig. 9.1 AD type disc brake assembly components (Sec 2)

1 *Wheel*
2 *Disc brake cylinder*
3 *Inner pad*
4 *Outer pad & anti-squeal shim*
5 *Anti-rattle spring*
6 *Pad guide plate*
7 *Pad support plate*

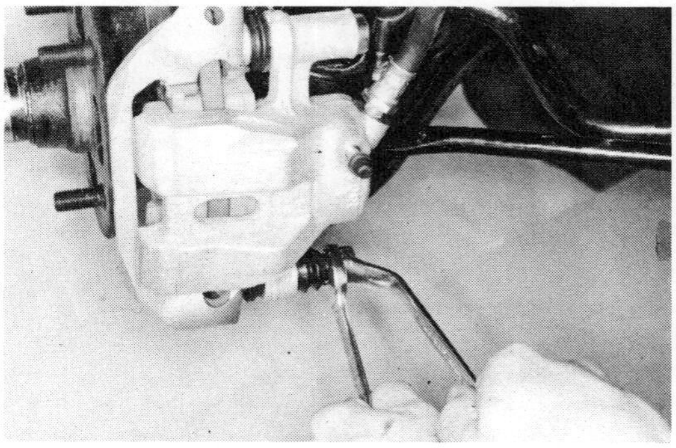

Fig. 9.3 Cylinder unit retaining bolt removal method – AD type (Sec 2)

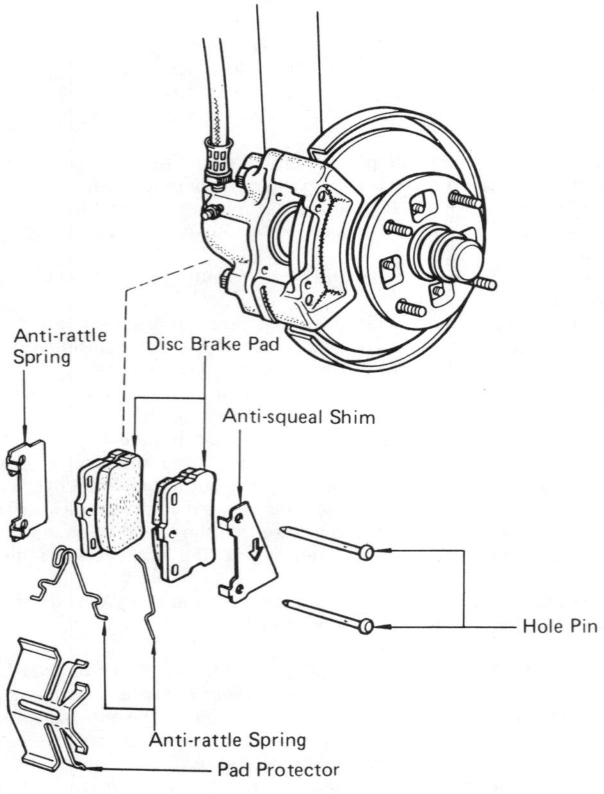

Fig. 9.2 PS type disc brake assembly components (Sec 2)

Fig. 9.4 Insert retainer bolt as shown to retain cylinder in raised position – AD type (Sec 2)

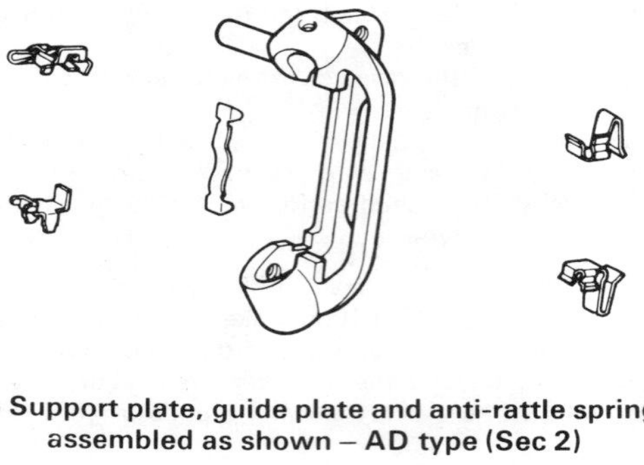

Fig. 9.5 Support plate, guide plate and anti-rattle spring to be assembled as shown – AD type (Sec 2)

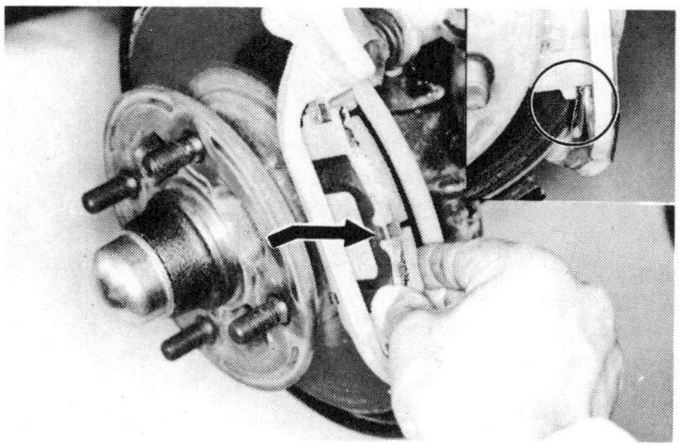

Fig. 9.6 Outer pad installation. Push anti-squeal spring inwards – AD type (Sec 2)

Fig. 9.7 Do not wedge rubber boot when fitting cylinder – AD type (Sec 2)

PS type

12 With the wheel(s) removed, the brake pad thickness can be checked through the inspection aperture in the caliper unit after removal of the pad protector. If the pads are worn down to or beyond the specified wear limit they must be renewed as a set (renew the pads of both front brake caliper units).

13 To remove the pads use a pair of thin nose pliers to grip and extract the anti-rattle spring (outermost) noting how it is located in the pad retainer pins (photo).

14 Now withdraw the pad retainer pins and disengage and remove the innermost anti-rattle spring. The pads can now be extracted together with the anti-squeal and rattle shims (photos).

15 With the pads removed, proceed as described in paragraphs 9 and 10 in this Section.

16 Fitting of the new pads is a reversal of the removal procedure. Check that the pad linings are free of grease before fitting and ensure that the retainer pins, anti-squeal shims and anti-rattle springs are correctly and securely located before refitting the pad protector (photos).

Fig. 9.8 Measure pad thickness with protector removed – PS type (Sec 2)

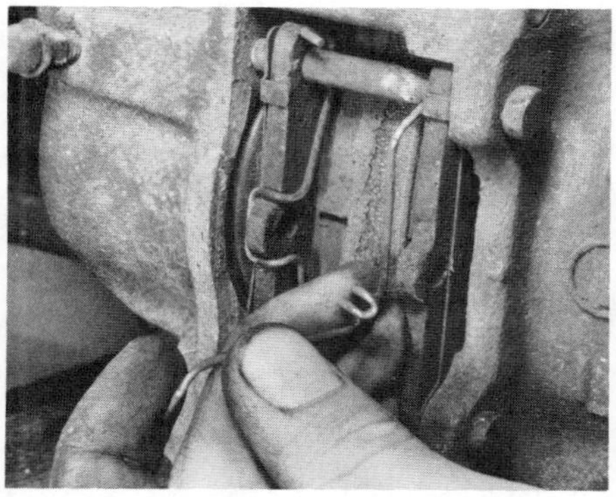

2.13 Anti-rattle spring removal – PS type caliper

2.14a Withdraw the retainer pins ...

2.14b ... remove the anti-squeal shim and pad ...

2.14c ... and the anti-rattle shim and pad – PS type

2.16a With pads, shims and springs reassembled ...

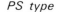

2.16b ... refit the pad protector – PS type

17 On completion, top up the fluid level as necessary in the fluid reservoir and check the brakes for satisfactory operation.

3 Rear drum brake shoes – inspection and renewal

1 Securely chock the front wheel, jack-up the rear of the car and remove the roadwheels. Fully release the handbrake lever. Support the car with axle stands placed beneath the axle tube.

2 Withdraw the brake drum from the wheel studs. If this proves difficult, extract the rubber plug from the brake backplate and use two screwdrivers to lift the automatic adjuster lever and back off the toothed wheel on the adjuster strut.

3 Brush away any accumulated dust, taking care not to inhale it, and inspect the linings. If the friction material is worn below the specified limit, renew the shoes as a complete axle set. If the linings are in good condition, clean and refit the drum (photo).

4 To renew the shoes, first depress the shoe steady springs with a pair of pliers and turn them through 90° to release them from the pins (photo).

5 Disconnect the upper shoe return spring and expand the shoes over the lower anchor. Disconnect the lower shoe return spring (photo).

6 Remove the leading shoe and strut, then disconnect the spring and remove the strut.

7 Disconnect the handbrake cable from the lever and withdraw the trailing shoe.

8 Disconnect the short spring and extract the C-washer. The handbrake lever and automatic adjuster lever can now be transferred to the new shoe. If necessary, separate the two levers after extracting the retaining C-washer. Turn the toothed wheel on the adjuster strut so that the strut is fully retracted.

9 After high mileages the brake drums should also be examined for deterioration and wear. If excessive scoring is evident, the drum must either be renewed or ground by an engineering works. If the drum is to be ground, the specified maximum internal diameter must not be exceeded.

10 Inspect the springs, levers and strut for wear, and renew them as necessary (photos).

11 Using a feeler gauge, check the clearance between the trailing shoe web and the automatic adjuster lever. If necessary, fit a shim between the C-washer and the shoe web to obtain the specified clearance (Fig. 9.11).

12 Clean the brake backplate and check for oil leakage (see Chapter 8 for axle shaft seal renewal), or a leaking wheel cylinder. If evident, the fault should be rectified before proceeding.

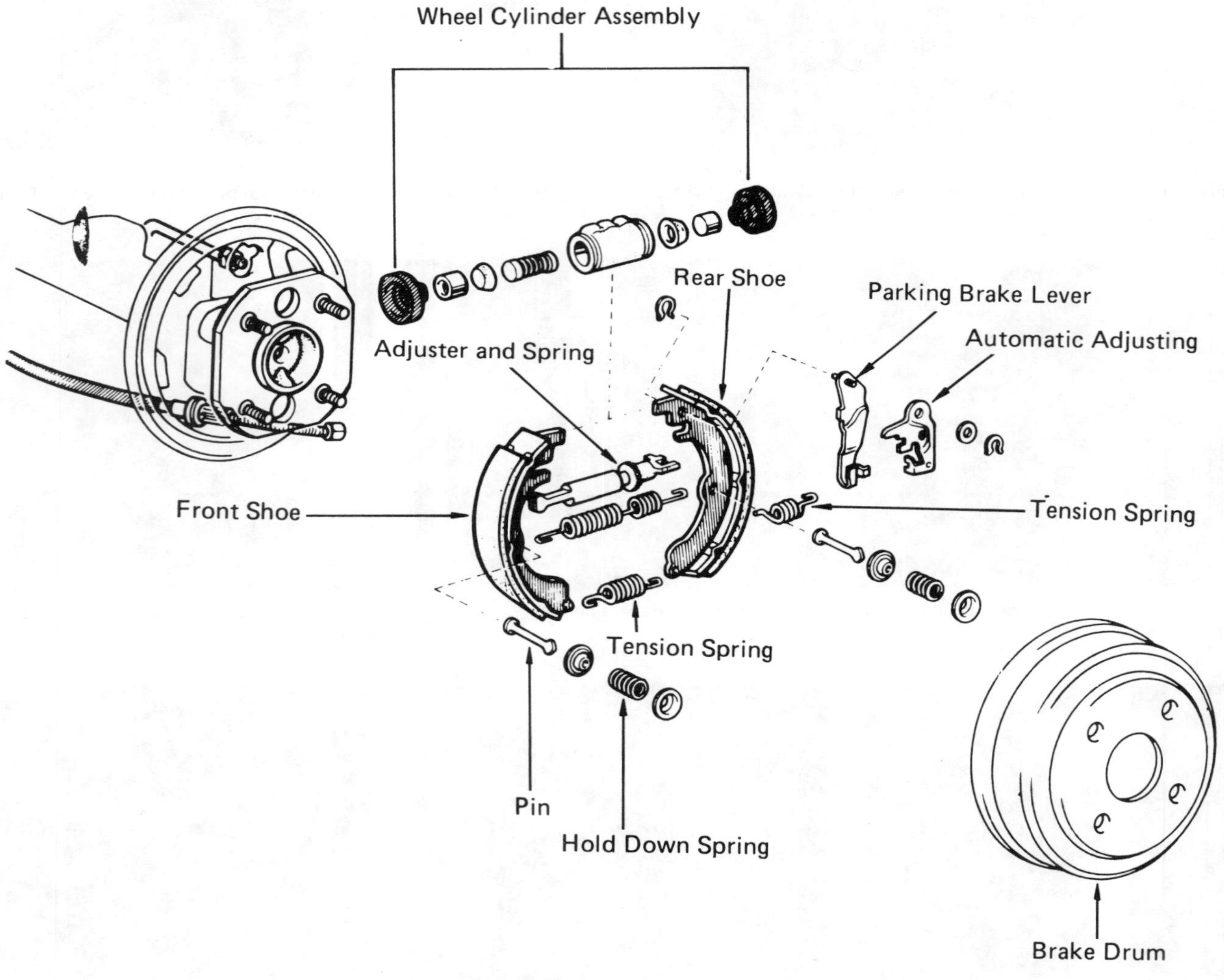

Fig. 9.9 Rear brake drum and associated components (Sec 3)

3.3 General view of rear brake assembly with drum removed

3.4 Depress and rotate shoe steady spring and retainer to remove

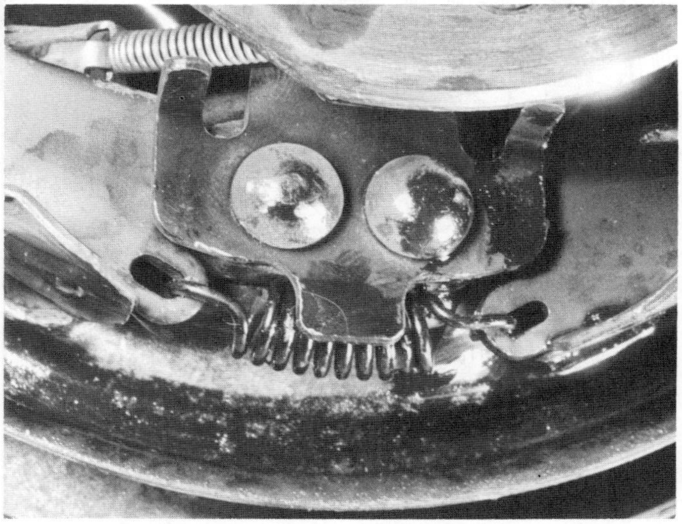

3.5 Lower shoe return spring

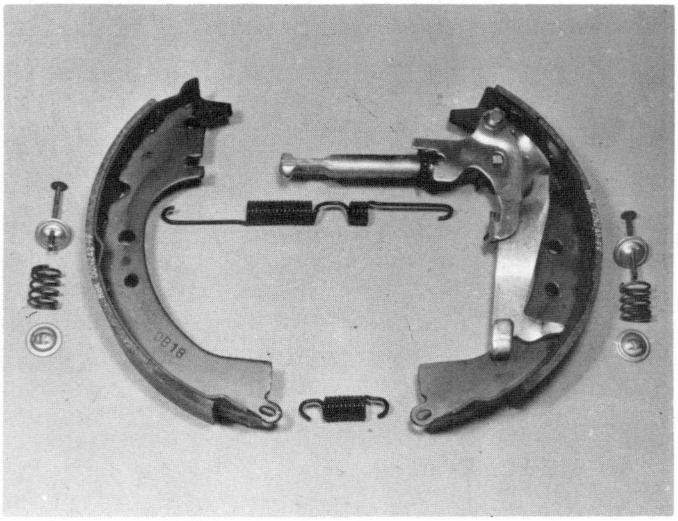

3.10 Brake shoes and associated components cleaned and laid out for inspection

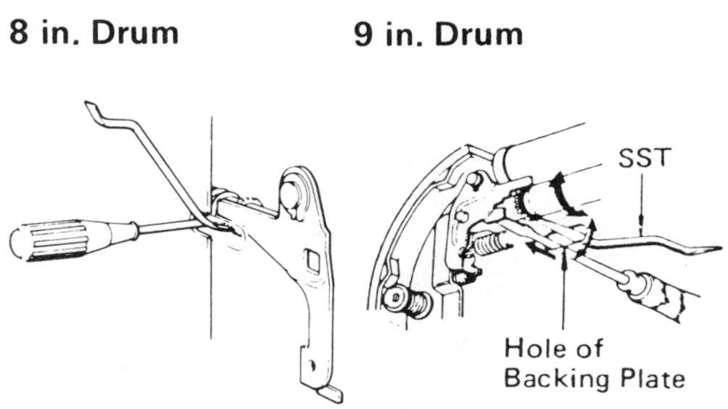

Fig. 9.10 Slacken off brake adjuster according to type to enable drum to be removed (Sec 3)

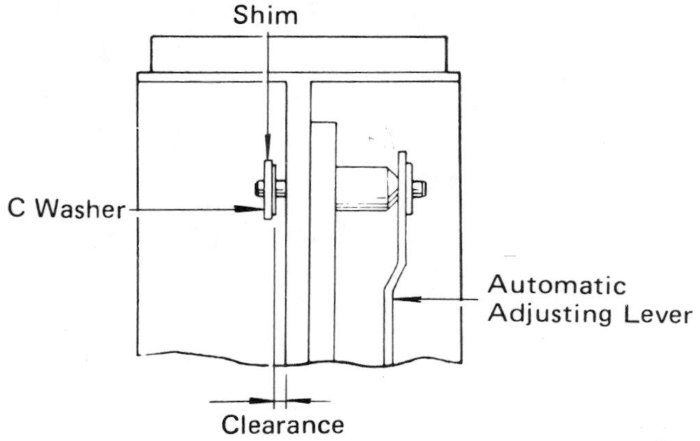

Fig. 9.11 Check automatic adjuster lever to trailing shoe web clearance and adjust with shim if necessary. Use new C-washer when reassembling (Sec 3)

13 Refer to Fig. 9.12 and note the position of the brake shoes in relation to the front of the car. The shoes must be assembled as shown.
14 Smear a little brake grease on the rubbing surfaces of the backplate and on the shoe web ends (Fig. 9.13).
15 Connect the handbrake cable to the lever on the trailing shoe with the short return spring disconnected, then fit the spring.
16 Fit the strut and spring to the leading shoe, locate it on the backplate, then locate the trailing shoe on the backplate and refit the lower return spring. Make sure that both shoes are engaged correctly on the lower anchor.
17 Fit the upper return spring to the trailing shoe, making sure that the strut is located correctly and the shoe webs are engaged in the wheel cylinder piston grooves.
18 Fit the two shoe steady springs to the pins with the open ends facing upwards.
19 Centralise the brake shoes so that the timing contour matches that of the backplate. Now expand the shoes by turning the toothed adjuster wheel until the point is reached where the brake drum will just slide over them and any further rotation of the adjuster wheel would obstruct the fitting of the drum.
20 Fit the brake drum, roadwheel, and backplate plug.
21 Repeat the procedure on the remaining rear brake, then operate the handbrake lever several times. With the lever applied, both rear

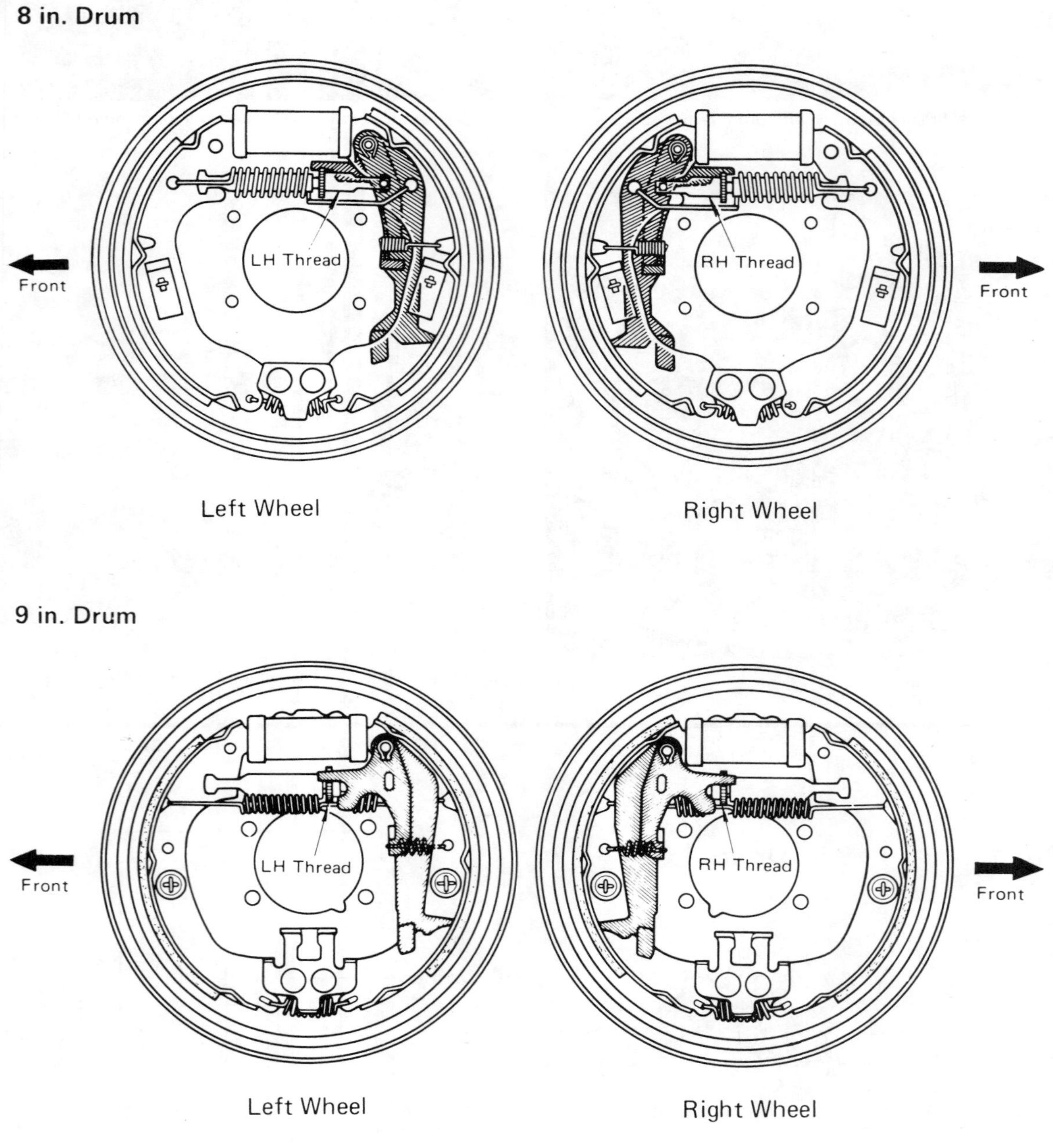

Fig. 9.12 Assemble brake shoes and associated components according to type and side as shown (Sec 3)

Fig. 9.13 Using non melting brake application grease, lubricate the points indicated prior to reassembly (Sec 3)

wheels should be locked, and with it fully released both wheels should be free. If necessary adjust the handbrake as described in Section 19.
22 Lower the car to the ground.

4 Disc caliper (AD type) – removal, servicing and refitting

1 Jack up the front of the vehicle and support it on safety stands. Remove the roadwheel.
2 To prevent loss of hydraulic fluid during subsequent operations, either seal the master cylinder at the vent hole and round the rim of the cap with adhesive tape, or clamp the flexible hose with a suitable clamp, being careful not to damage the hose.
3 Unscrew the cylinder retaining bolt and withdraw it. Secure the bushing with a spanner when undoing the bolt to prevent it from turning.
4 Withdraw the cylinder unit from the pivot pin and support it to prevent straining the hose then loosen the flexible hose union at the caliper and unscrew the caliper from the hose. Retain the sealing washer, and plug the end of the hose to prevent entry of foreign matter.
5 The cylinder unit can now be removed for external cleaning.
6 With a suitable screwdriver, prise out the main pin boot (Fig. 9.14).
7 Prise free the protector boot set ring and remove the boot from the cylinder bore.
8 Remove the piston from the caliper leg applying air pressure to the inlet port with a foot pump. Take care not to damage the piston.
9 Extract the piston seal from the cylinder bore with a small screwdriver taking care not to damage or scratch the bore surface (Fig. 9.15).
10 Wash all components in clean brake fluid or methylated spirits and wipe them dry with a lint-free cloth (Fig. 9.16).
11 All seals and dust covers must be renewed so a service repair kit must be obtained containing these items.
12 Carefully inspect the cylinder bore and piston surfaces. If they show signs of advanced wear or damage then a new caliper cylinder unit must be fitted.
13 To reassemble first lubricate the piston seal with a rubber grease

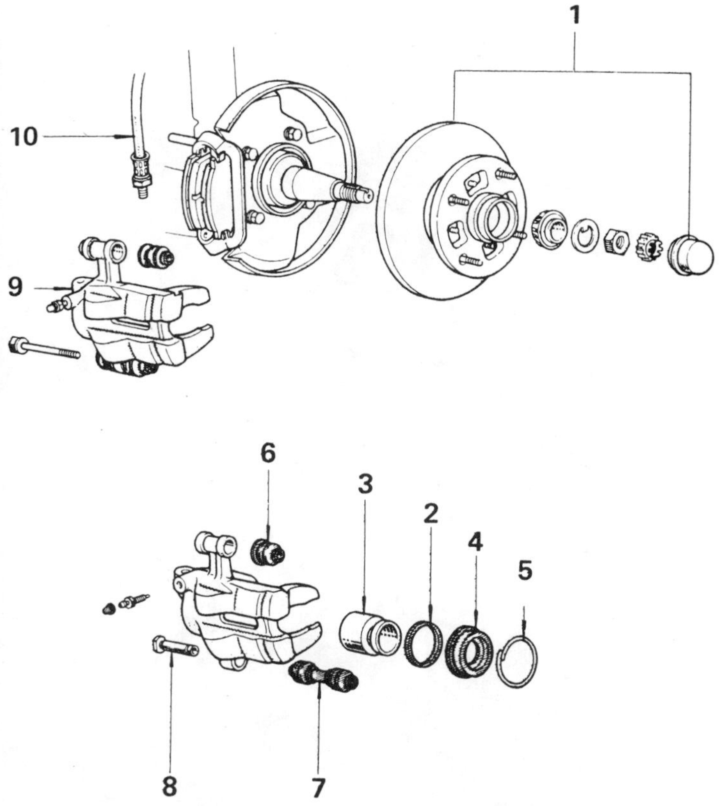

Fig. 9.14 Front brake and caliper components – AD type (Sec 4)

1 Axle hub with disc
2 Piston seal
3 Piston
4 Cylinder boot
5 Cylinder boot set ring
6 Main pin boot
7 Dust boot
8 Cylinder slide bushing
9 Disc brake cylinder
10 Flexible hose

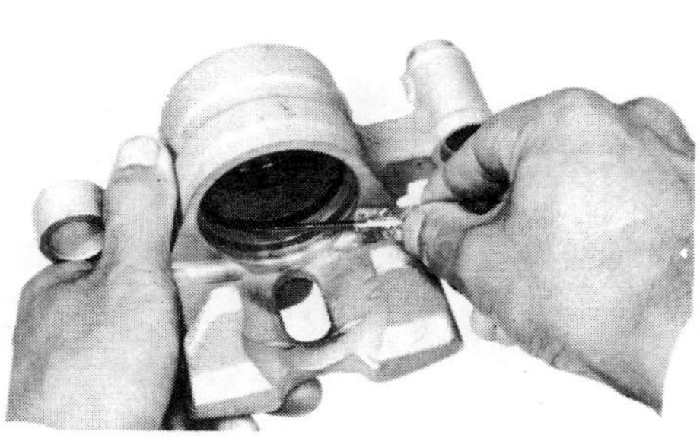

Fig. 9.15 Extract the piston seal – AD type (Sec 4)

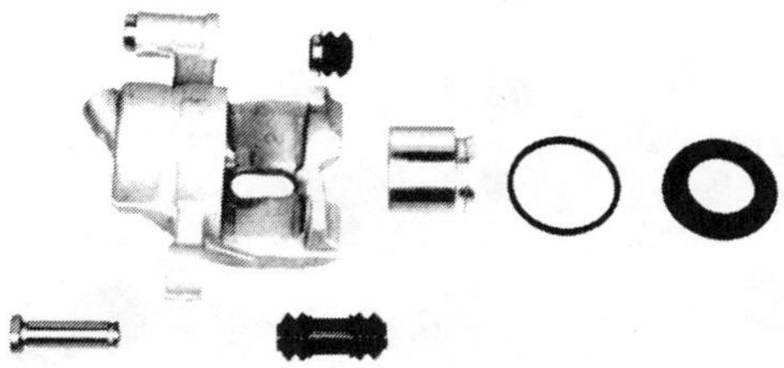

Fig. 9.16 Caliper piston and seal components – AD type (Sec 4)

and manipulate it into its groove in the cylinder using fingers only. Check that it is correctly seated and not distorted.
14 Smear the piston with rubber grease and then insert it into position in the cylinder bore (Fig. 9.18).
15 Smear the rubber boot with rubber grease and locate it into position as shown and secure with the set ring (Fig. 9.19, 9.20).
16 Lubricate the main pin boot and press it into position using a 21 mm socket and vice as shown in Fig. 9.21. Do not reuse the old boot. Press it in to point A to prevent distortion or snaring.
17 Lubricate the dust boot and slide bush with rubber grease and locate them, but ensure that the seal is not distorted (Fig. 9.22).
18 Fit the cylinder unit onto the main pin taking care not to wedge the boot as it is pivoted down to align with the securing bolt hole and bushing.
19 Insert the retaining bolt, and tighten to the specified torque wrench setting whilst simultaneously preventing the bush head from rotating.
20 Reattach the flexible hydraulic hose then top up the fluid level in the master cylinder reservoir and bleed the system as given in Section 23.
21 Check that the brake operation is satisfactory, then refit the roadwheel and lower the vehicle.

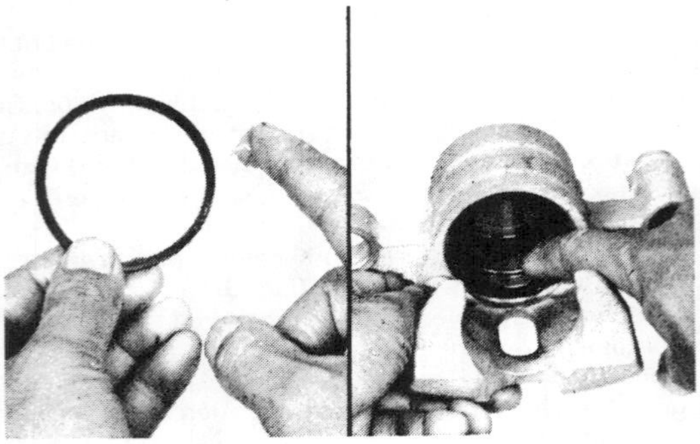

Fig. 9.17 Lubricate the seal then fit it into the cylinder groove – AD type (Sec 4)

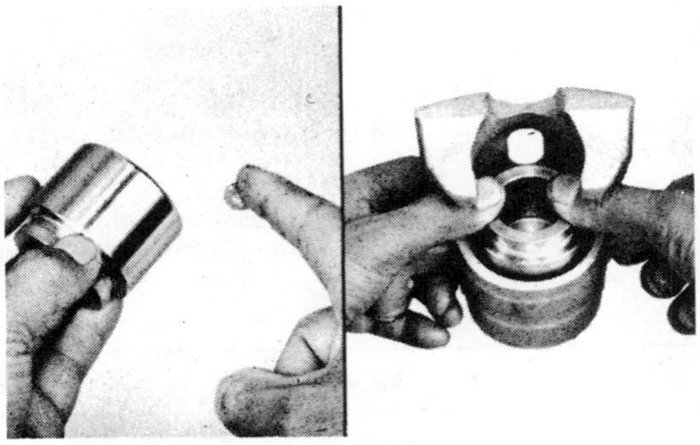

Fig. 9.18 Lubricate the piston and fit it into the cylinder – AD type (Sec 4)

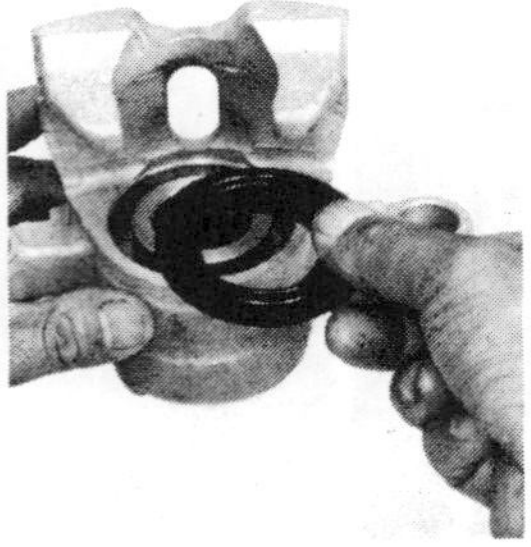

Fig. 9.19 Fit cylinder boot as shown – AD type (Sec 4)

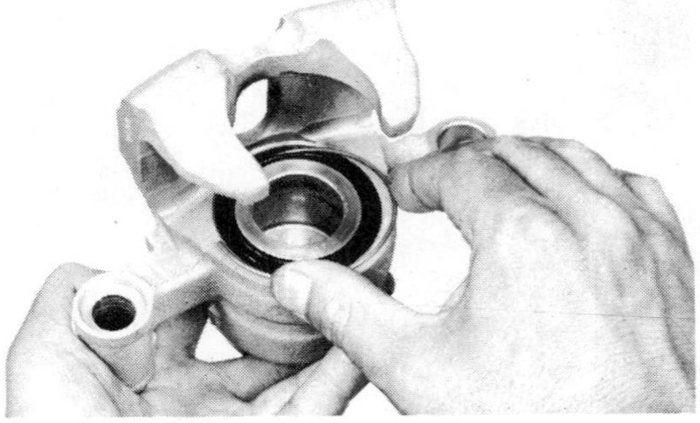

Fig. 9.20 Secure cylinder boot with set ring – AD type (Sec 4)

Fig. 9.21 Press main pin rubber boot into position up to point A – AD type (Sec 4)

Fig. 9.22 Fit dust boot and sliding bush – AD type (Sec 4)

5 Disc caliper (PS type) – removal, servicing and refitting

1 Jack-up the front of the car and support it on axle stands. Remove the roadwheel.
2 Remove the disc pads as described in Section 2.
3 To prevent loss of hydraulic fluid during subsequent operations, either seal the master cylinder at the vent hole and round the rim of the cap with adhesive tape, or clamp the flexible hose with a suitable clamp, being careful not to damage the hose.
4 Loosen the flexible hose union at the caliper and unscrew the hose. Retain the sealing washer, and plug the end of the hose to prevent entry of foreign matter (photo).
5 Unbolt and remove the caliper unit from the car. Before dismantling it, clean off its external surfaces.
6 Unscrew and remove the two bridge bolts whilst supporting the caliper torque plate in a vice with soft jaws. When the bolts are removed the caliper, torque plate and outer body can be separated, but keep them together so that they are not mixed up with other components.
7 Remove the piston from the caliper by applying air pressure to the union inlet with a footpump. Take care not to damage the piston.
8 Extract the piston seal from the caliper bore with a small screwdriver, being careful not to scratch the bore surface.
9 Press the mounting bushes from the caliper and remove the rubber boots and collars.
10 Clean all components in fresh brake fluid or methylated spirit and wipe dry with a lint-free cloth.

5.4 Detach the hydraulic hose at the caliper (PS type shown)

11 Discard the piston seal and dust excluder and obtain a repair kit. Inspect the surfaces of the piston and caliper bore; if any scratches or bright wear areas are evident, the complete caliper must be renewed.

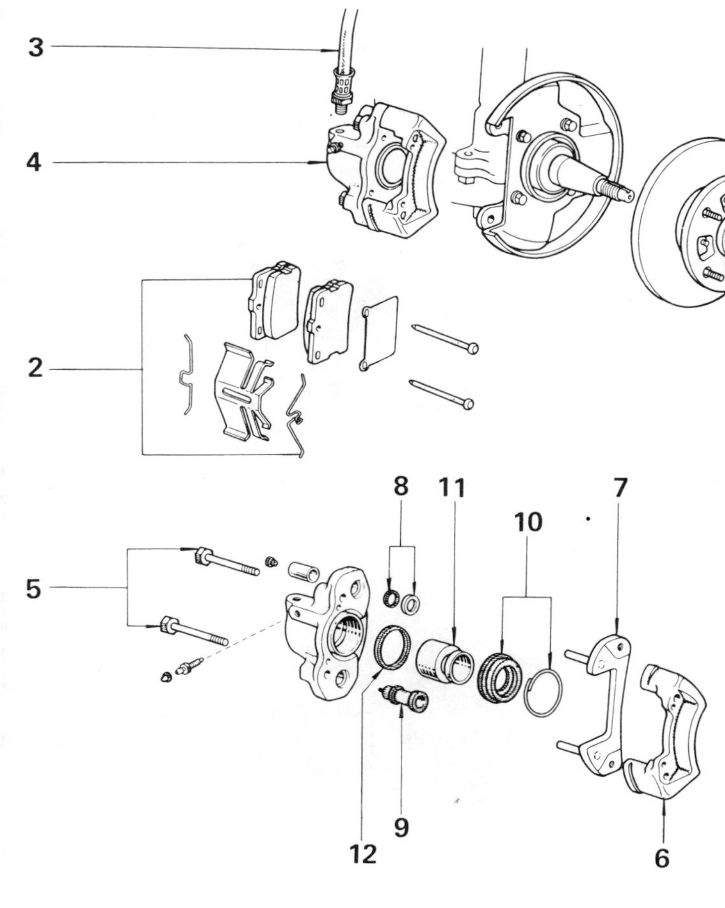

Fig. 9.23 Caliper and disc components – PS type (Sec 5)

2 Pad
3 Flexible hose
4 Caliper
5 Bridge bolt
6 Outer body
7 Torque plate
8 Dust seal & retainer
9 Torque plate bin bushing
10 Set ring & cylinder boot
11 Piston
12 Piston seal
13 Axle hub with disc

12 Smear some rubber grease or brake fluid on the piston seal and locate it in the caliper bore groove using the fingers only (Fig. 9.24).
13 Smear the piston with rubber grease or brake fluid and press it fully into the caliper through the seal (Fig. 9.25).
14 Smear the dust excluder with rubber grease or brake fluid, locate it over the piston, and refit the retaining ring (Fig. 9.26).
15 Fit the collars, rubber boots, and mounting bushes to the caliper. At the same time smear the components with rubber grease to ensure a free sliding action of the caliper.
16 Refit the torque plate, smear the bridge bolts with brake fluid and tighten them to the specified torque wrench setting. *This is most important and it is also imperative that only the special bridge bolts are used.*
17 Refit the caliper to the axle unit and tighten the securing bolts to the specified torque wrench setting.
18 Reconnect the flexible hydraulic fluid hose (having removed the seal plug).
19 Refit the disc pads as described in Section 2.
20 Remove the adhesive tape from the fluid reservoir or the clamp from the flexible hose, and bleed the hydraulic system as described in Section 23 and check the brake action.
21 Refit the roadwheel and lower the car to the ground.

6 Brake disc – examination, removal and refitting

1 Jack up the front of the vehicle, remove the roadwheel and caliper.
2 Inspect the disc surfaces for deep scoring or grooves. Light scoring is normal.
3 Using a dial gauge or similar instrument, check for run-out (buckle). This should not exceed that given in the Specifications; if it does the disc should be renewed.
4 The disc thickness should not be reduced below the minimum specified, either by normal wear or by grinding to remove scoring.

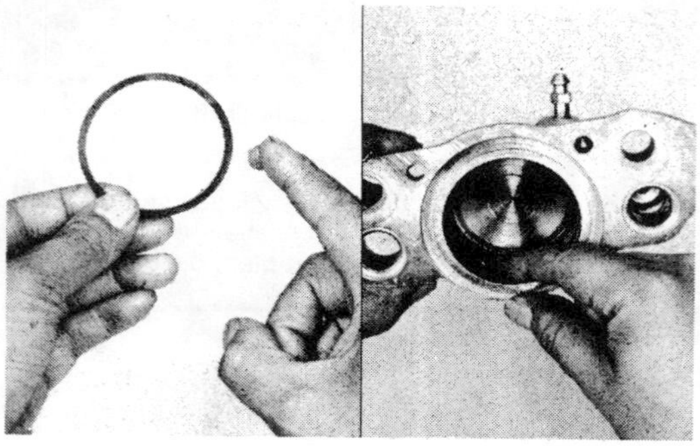

Fig. 9.24 Lubricate and insert rubber seal into cylinder groove – PS type (Sec 5)

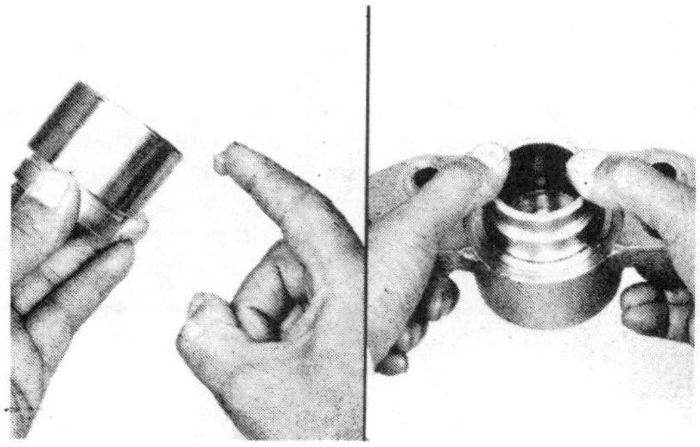

Fig. 9.25 Lubricate and insert the caliper piston – PS type (Sec 5)

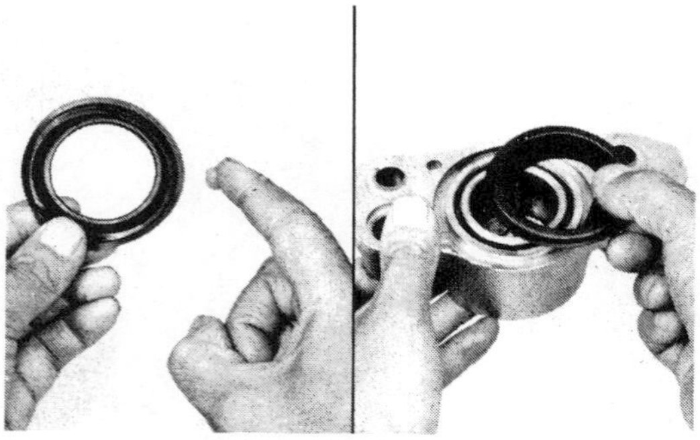

Fig. 9.26 Lubricate and locate the cylinder dust boot – PS type (Sec 5)

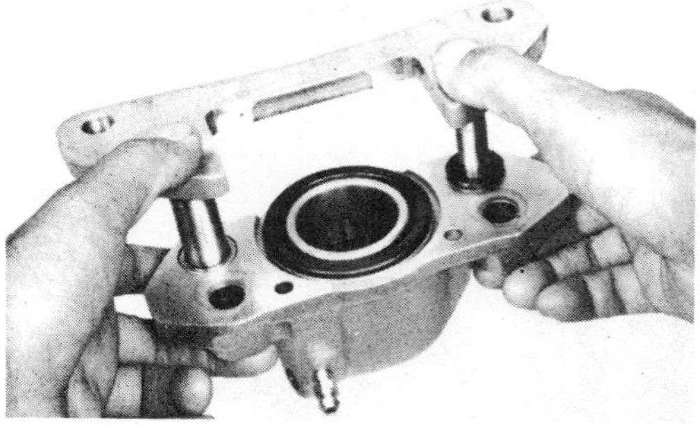

Fig. 9.27 Refit the torque plate – PS type (Sec 5)

Fig. 9.28 Disc run out check method using clock gauge (Sec 6)

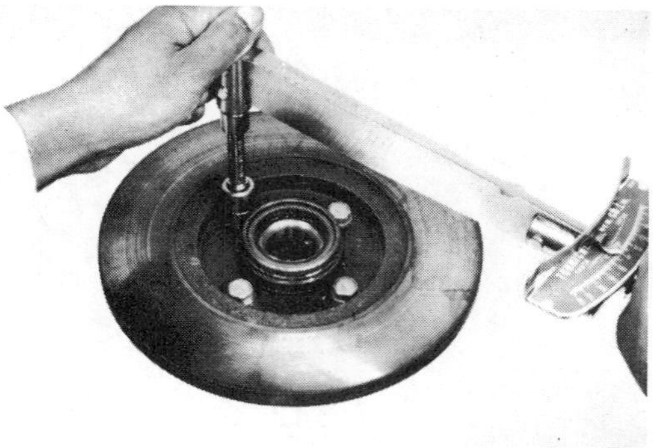

Fig. 9.29 Unscrew retaining bolts to separate disc from hub (Sec 6)

5 To remove the disc/hub assembly, refer to the procedure given in Chapter 11.
6 Unscrew the disc-to-hub bolts, and separate the two parts.
7 Refitting is the reverse of the removal procedure. Adjust the disc/hub as described in Chapter 11.

7 Brake drums – examination, removal and refitting

1 Whenever the rear brake drums are removed they should be examined for cracks, damage or grooving of the friction surface.
2 After a high mileage the drums may also become out of round.
3 To remove scoring or to correct out of round, the drums must either be ground or renewed. If the drums are ground then their internal diameter must not exceed the maximum specified.

8 Rear wheel cylinder – removal, servicing and refitting

1 Chock the front wheels, jack up the rear of the car and support it on axle stands. Remove the roadwheel.
2 Remove the rear brake shoes as described in Section 3.
3 To prevent loss of hydraulic fluid in subsequent operations either seal the master cylinder reservoir cap vent with adhesive tape to create a vacuum or clamp the rear flexible hose with a suitable clamp.
4 Wipe clean the area around the rear of the cylinder and unscrew the hydraulic line, bleed screw and cylinder retaining bolts. Remove the wheel cylinder from the backplate.
5 Prise the rubber boots from each end of the cylinder then withdraw the two pistons, rubber seals and spring. On the cylinder fitted to the 8 in brake assembly, remove the rubber seals from the pistons.
6 Clean all the components in clean hydraulic fluid or methylated spirit and dry with a lint-free cloth. Inspect the surfaces of the pistons and cylinder bore. If any scoring or bright wear areas are evident, renew the complete wheel cylinder. If the components are satisfactory obtain a new set of seals in the form of a repair kit.
7 Lubricate all the internal surfaces with hydraulic fluid and apply rubber grease to the new seals. On the 8 in brake assembly fit the new seals to the pistons so that their larger diameter is towards the spring when fitted.
8 Insert the spring into the cylinder bore followed by the two seals on 8 in assemblies (larger diameter towards the spring).
9 Carefully insert the two pistons followed by the rubber boots.
10 Refitting the wheel cylinder is the reverse sequence of removal bearing in mind the following:

(a) Take care not to cross thread the hydraulic line when reconnecting to the cylinder
(b) Refit the brake shoes as described in Section 3
(c) Remove the adhesive tape from the master cylinder or the flexible hose clamp and bleed the hydraulic system as described in Section 23

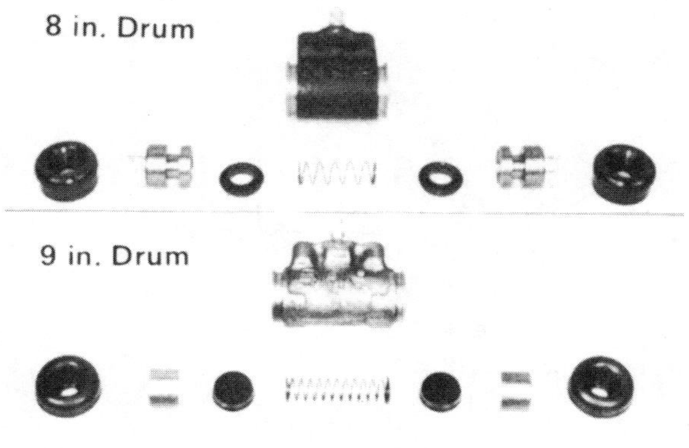

Fig. 9.30 Exploded view of the wheel cylinder components (Sec 8)

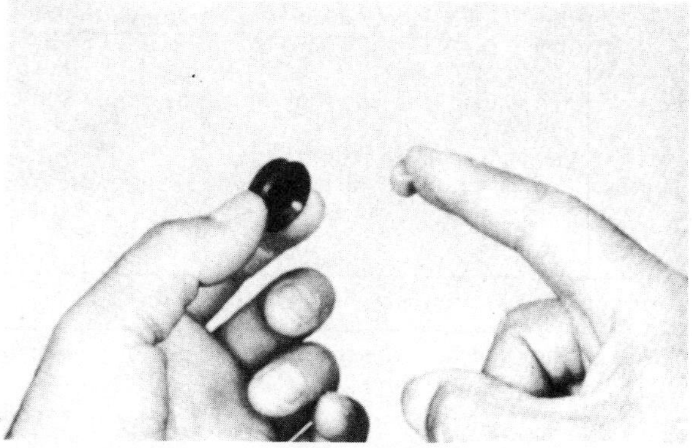

Fig. 9.31 Apply rubber grease to the piston rubber seals (Sec 8)

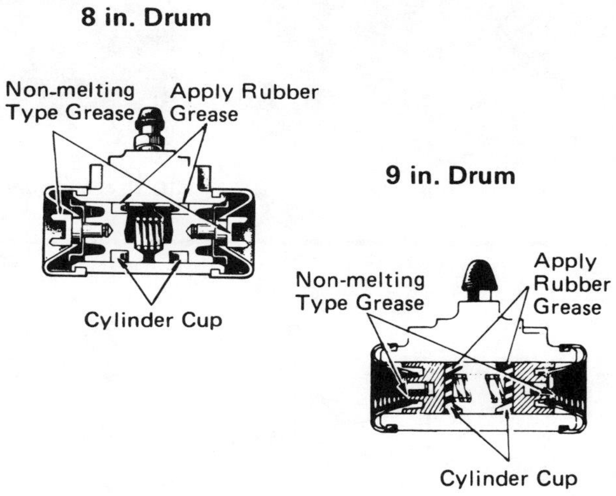

Fig. 9.32 Assemble cylinders according to type and lubricate where shown (Sec 8)

9 Rear brake backplate – removal and refitting

1 Chock the front wheels, jack-up the rear of the car and support it on axle stands. Remove the roadwheel.
2 Remove the brake shoes as described in Section 3.
3 Remove the wheel cylinder as described in Section 8.
4 Remove the axleshaft (halfshaft) as described in Chapter 8.
5 Prise out the handbrake cable and withdraw the backplate and gasket from the axle tube.
6 Clean the mating surfaces of the axle tube and backplate.
7 Refitting is a reversal of removal, but the following points must be observed:

(a) Apply a liquid sealant to the backplate gasket
(b) Follow the refitting procedures given in Chapter 8 and in Sections 8 and 3 of this Chapter

10 Handbrake – adjustment

1 The handbrake is normally adjusted automatically by the action of the self-adjusting rear brake mechanism. However, due to cable stretch or when fitting a new cable, adjustment will be required to make sure that the handbrake is fully applied with the lever within the specified number of notches from the released position.

2 To adjust the handbrake cable you will need to remove the trim cover from the handbrake lever. Unscrew and remove the side and front cover retaining screws and then lift the cover over the lever (photos).
3 Loosen off the adjuster cap and turn the nut as required to adjust the handbrake (photo).
4 Tighten the adjuster cap by hand.
5 If necessary adjust the handbrake warning switch position before refitting the trim cover.

11 Handbrake lever – removal and refitting

1 Chock the front and rear wheels and fully release the handbrake lever.
2 Remove the handbrake lever trim cover which is secured by screws.
3 Unscrew and remove the adjusting knob and locknut from the end of the cable.
4 Unscrew the mounting bolts and withdraw the handbrake lever. Note the location of the handbrake warning switch.
5 Refitting is a reversal of removal, but it will be necessary to adjust the handbrake as described in Section 10.

12 Handbrake cable – renewal

1 The handbrake cable is in three sections, any of which can if necessary be removed separately.
2 Remove the handbrake lever as described in Section 11.

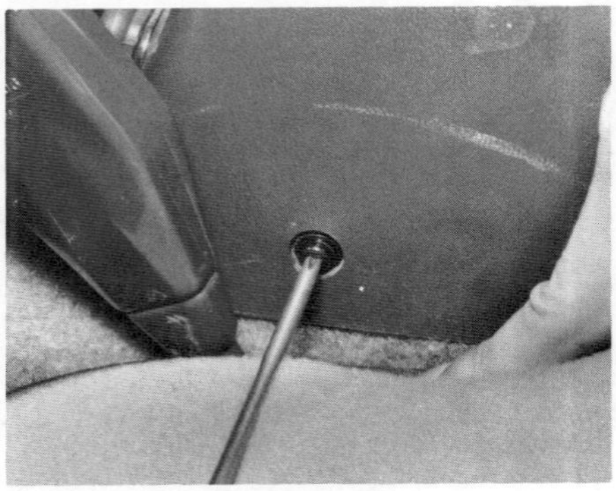

10.2a Remove cover side screws ...

10.2b ... and front screw to remove it

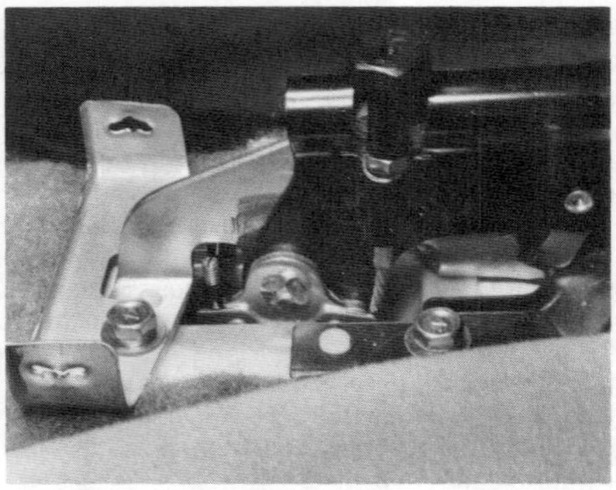

10.3 Handbrake adjuster cap and nut (cover removed)

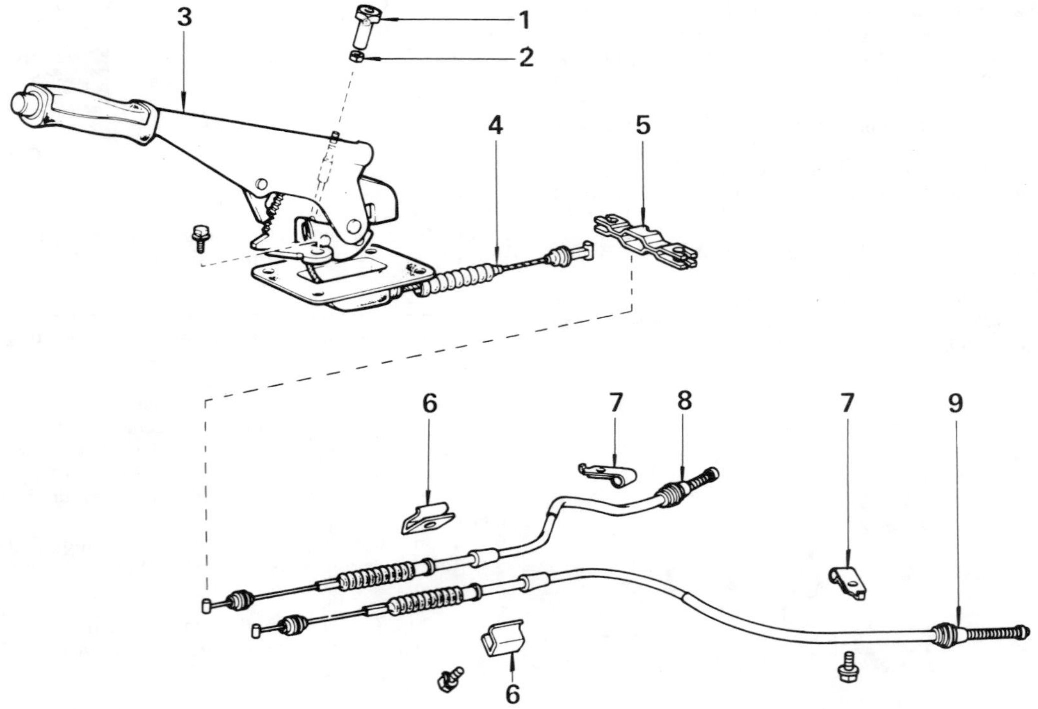

Fig. 9.33 Handbrake lever and cable assembly components (Sec 11)

1 Wire adjusting cap
2 Cable lock nut
3 Parking brake lever
4 No. 1 cable
5 Equalizer
6 Cable retainer
7 Cable clamp
8 No. 2 cable
9 No. 3 cable

3 With the front wheels chocked, jack-up the rear of the car and support it on axle stands.
4 Reach over the propeller shaft and disconnect the front cable from the equaliser by turning the cable stop plate through 90° (photo). Withdraw the cable through the handbrake lever baseplate.
5 Prise the guide grommets at the front of the rear cables from the underframe brackets, then disconnect the equaliser (photo).
6 Remove the rear brake shoes as described in Section 3.
7 Unbolt the rear cable from the suspension lower control arm and prise the cable out of the rear brake backplate.
8 Unscrew the bolts from the retainer mountings and withdraw the cable from beneath the car.
9 Refitting is a reversal of removal, but it will be necessary to refit the brake shoes as described in Section 3 and also to adjust the handbrake as described in Section 10.

13 Brake pedal – height adjustment

1 Refer to Fig. 9.34 and measure the height from the brake pedal rubber to the floor (with the carpet folded back). Check the measured height against the specified height.
2 If pedal height adjustment is necessary loosen off the stop (brake)-light switch securing nut and then detach the stop-light switch leads.
3 Loosen off the pushrod locknut and then adjust the pushrod to give the correct pedal height. You may need to unscrew the stop-light switch assembly to allow an increase in the height.
4 With the correct pedal height adjustment made, tighten the pushrod locknut and then adjust the stop-light switch unit so that it is lightly touching the pedal stopper. Retighten the locknut to secure the switch in this position and then reconnect the switch wires. Check the stop-light switch operation is satisfactory.
5 The pedal free play should now be checked. The engine must be switched off for this check and vacuum remaining in the servo booster expelled by pressing down on the pedal a few times.
6 To make the check, press the pedal down by hand until the initial increase in pressure is felt. This is the total of the pedal free play travel and when measured it should be within the pedal free play tolerance limits given in the Specifications.
7 If the free play measured is not within the specified limits then

12.4 Handbrake cable equalizer location

12.5 Cable to underframe brackets location

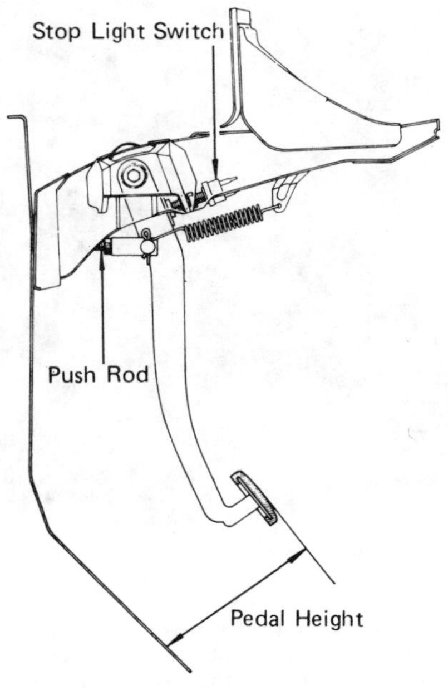

Fig. 9.34 Footbrake pedal height measurement (Sec 13)

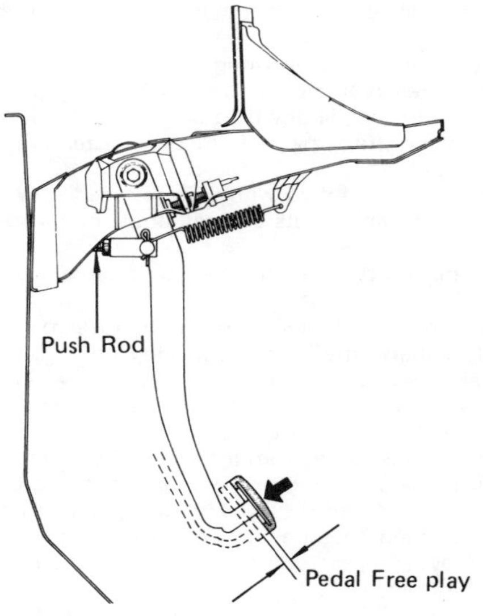

Fig. 9.35 Footbrake pedal height freeplay check (Sec 13)

further adjustment of the pushrod is necessary. Adjustment should be made so that the pedal height specified is also complied with as given previously.
8 Finally recheck the pedal with the engine running and with the servo boost vacuum applied, but note that the pedal free play during this check is not measured from the time that the servo booster piston is actuated. Check that the pedal reserve travel distance is as specified.

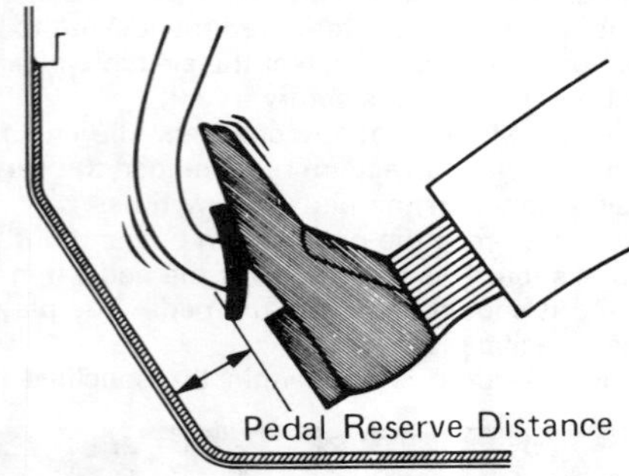

Fig. 9.36 Footbrake pedal reserve distance (Sec 13)

14 Brake pedal – removal and refitting

1 Disconnect the pedal return spring.
2 Extract the retaining clip and withdraw the clevis pin.
3 Unscrew and remove the pedal pivot bolt retaining nut, withdraw the bolt (shaft) and remove the pedal.
4 Clean and inspect the bush and collars and renew if worn or damaged.
5 Refit in the reverse order to removal coating the bush with grease. Tighten the pedal shaft bolt to the specified torque wrench setting.
6 On completion the pedal action should be checked. The pedal action should be smooth and return fully when released.
7 Finally check the brake pedal height and adjust if necessary as described in the previous Section.
8 Finally check the brake pedal height and adjust if necessary as described in the previous Section.

15 Master cylinder – removal, servicing and refitting

1 The master cylinder is of tandem type and is mounted on the front face of the servo unit (photo).
2 Disconnect the fluid level wiring at the plug.
3 Remove the reservoir cap and float and syphon out the hydraulic fluid. Take care not to spill any fluid onto the paintwork.
4 Disconnect the brake pipes from the master cylinder and wipe away any surplus fluid.
5 Wash off any spilled fluid with water immediately.
6 Unscrew the retaining nuts and withdraw the master cylinder and gasket.
7 Clean the master cylinder and reservoir externally before dismantling.
8 Disconnect the elbow pipe between the reservoir and the master cylinder body (where fitted), then reaching down into the reservoir with a suitable socket and extension, unscrew and remove the reservoir retaining union. Extract the union and washer and lift the reservoir clear of the cylinder body.
9 Prise free the dust cover from the rear end of the cylinder then use a pair of circlip pliers to compress and extract the circlip (Fig. 9.38).
10 Press the pistons into the cylinder and remove the stopper bolt. The pistons can then be extracted from the cylinder bore by shaking them out or by applying compressed air into the cylinder outlet aperture at the front.
11 Clean the pistons, springs and cylinder bore for inspection by washing them in hydraulic fluid or methylated spirits.
12 Examine the pistons and cylinder bore surfaces for scoring or bright wear areas. Where these are evident, renew the complete master cylinder. If the surfaces are good discard the seals and obtain a master cylinder repair kit. Dip all components in fresh hydraulic fluid before reassembling to lubricate them.
13 Fit the new seals to the pistons with reference to Fig. 9.39 using the fingers only to manipulate them into position.
14 Refit the pistons to the master cylinder body by reversing the removal procedure and similarly reassemble the remaining components. As the pistons are inserted, ensure that the seals seat correctly in the bore and do not distort.
15 When the pistons and springs are all in position, press them fully into the cylinder and then insert the stop bolt in the side of the cylinder.
16 Insert the circlip into the end of the cylinder bore to secure the piston assemblies and then fit the new rubber dust boot.
17 Fit the outlet check valve into the forwardmost aperture then locate the elbow and secure with snap ring in the aperture that is second from the front.
18 Relocate and secure the master cylinder reservoir. The MAX level marking must face to the front.

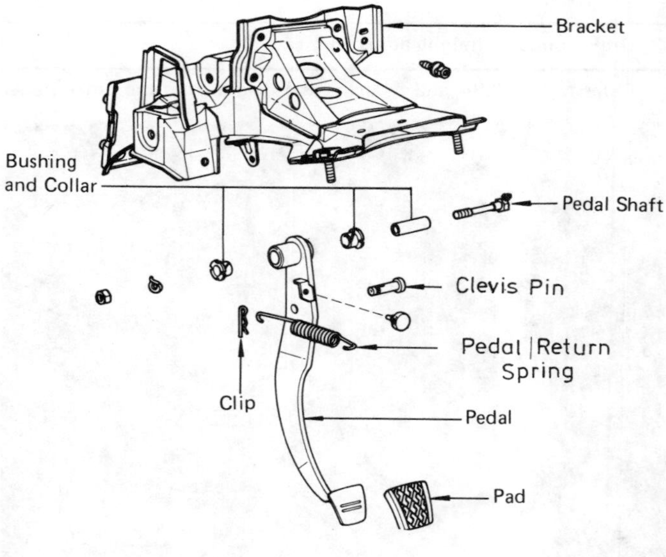

Fig. 9.37 Footbrake pedal components (Sec 14)

15.1 Master cylinder and servo unit

19 Reconnect the elbow pipe between the reservoir and the cylinder (where fitted).
20 The master cylinder can now be refitted to the car and the hydraulic lines reconnected. You will need to check the adjustment of the servo pushrod once the master cylinder is refitted.
21 The servo pushrod must be adjusted to achieve the specified fitted clearance. A special tool can be obtained from Toyota for this purpose, but if this is not available, proceed as follows. Unscrew the adjustment bolt until it can be felt to touch the primary piston when the master cylinder is mounted on the servo together with the gasket. Screw in the bolt until it just contacts the primary piston, then screw it in a further small amount to achieve the specified clearance. Vernier calipers may be of use to measure the movement of the bolt. Refit and tighten the retaining nuts to the specified torque. The remaining refitting procedure is a reversal of removal, but it will be necessary to bleed the hydraulic system as described in Section 23.

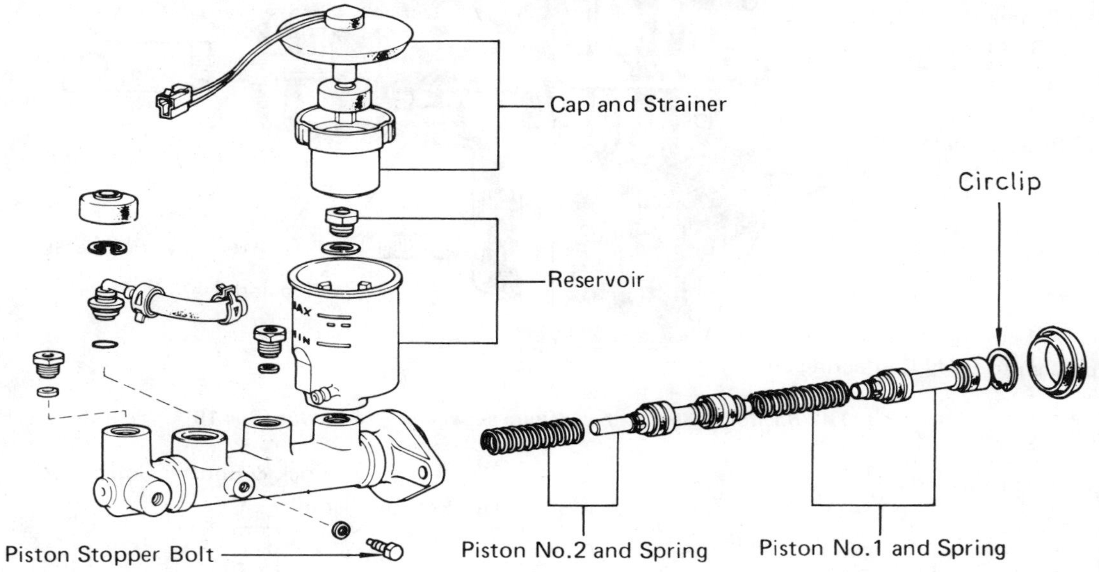

Fig. 9.38 Exploded view showing the master cylinder components (Sec 15)

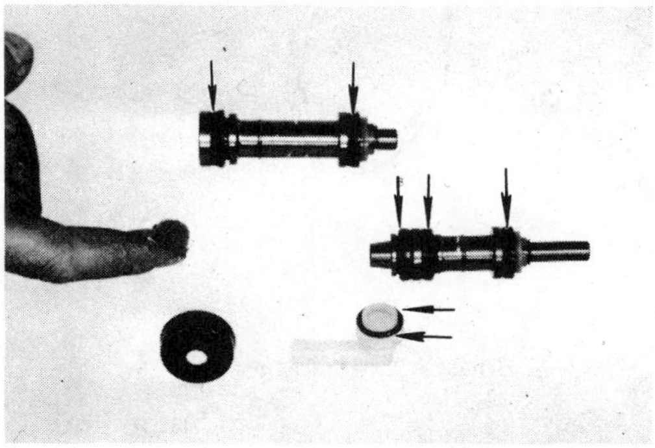

Fig. 9.39 Lubricate the piston and seals before assembling (Sec 15)

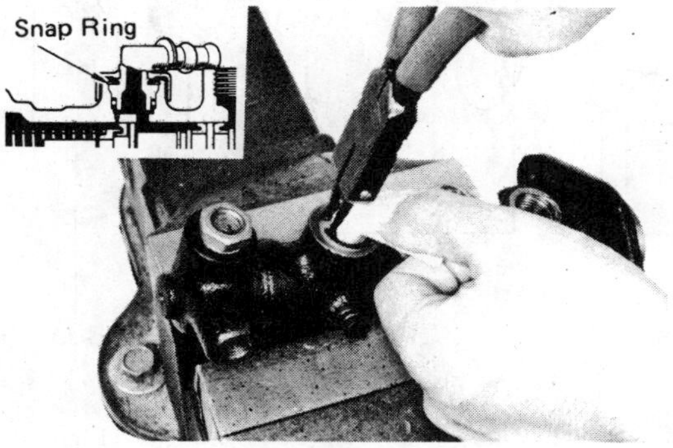

Fig. 9.40 Locate the elbow and secure it with snap ring (Sec 15)

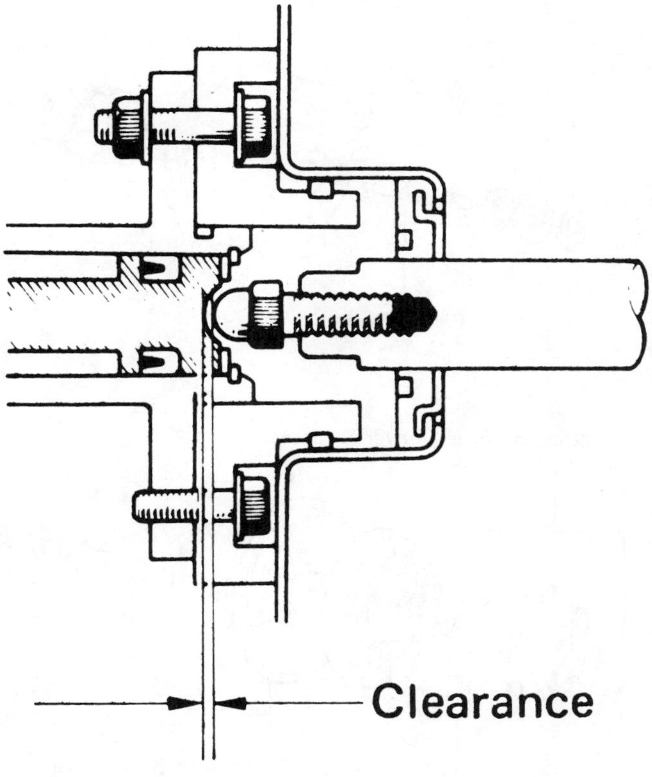

Fig. 9.41 Adjust the servo pushrod to piston clearance (Sec 15)

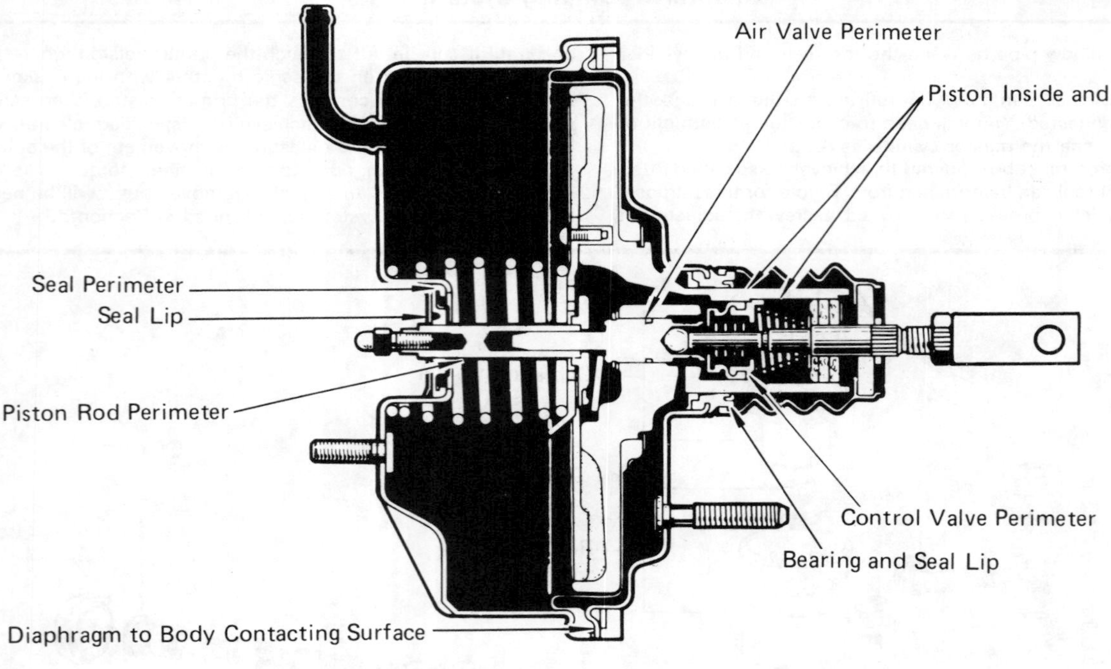

Fig. 9.42 Sectional view of the vacuum servo unit – Aisin type (Sec 16)

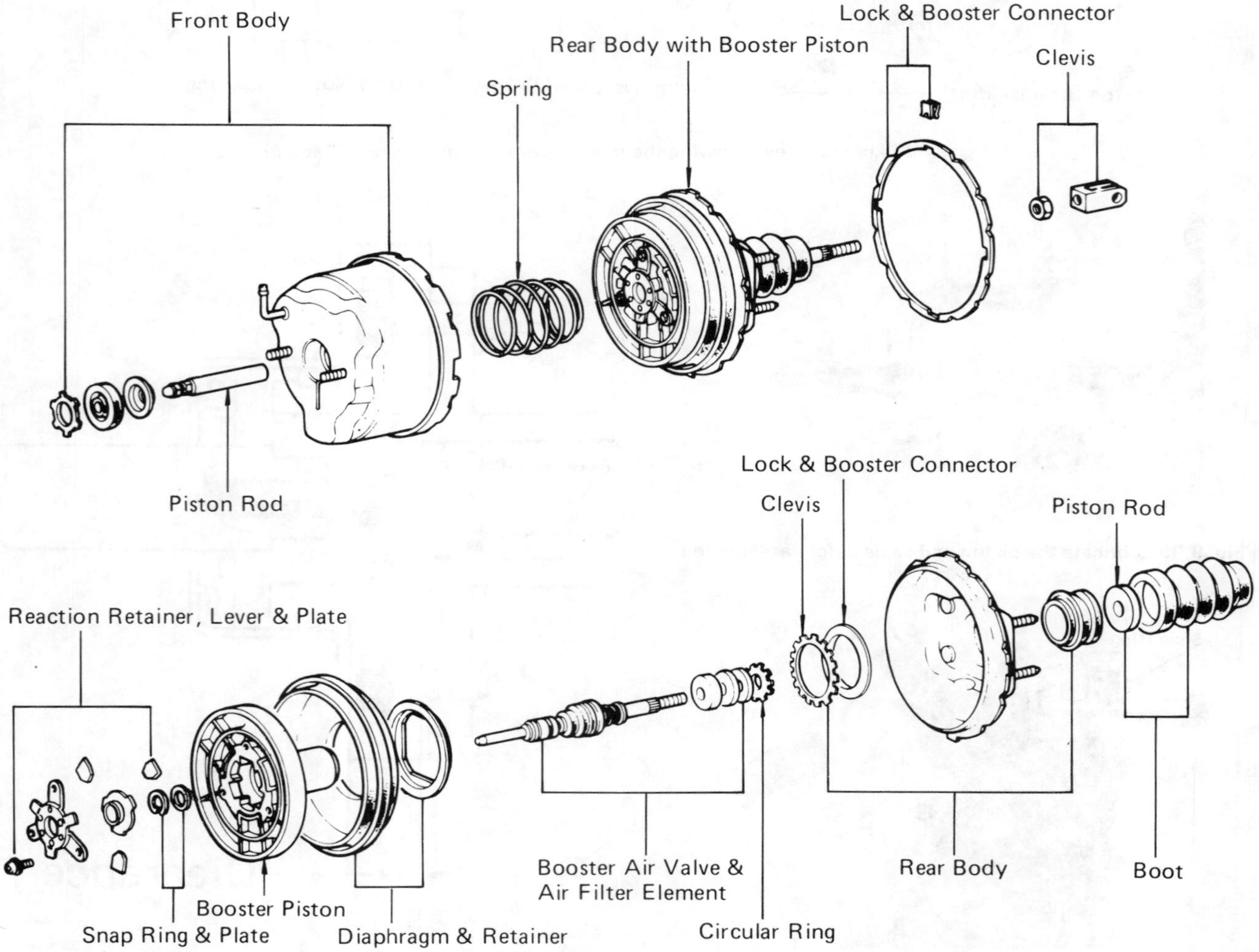

Fig. 9.43 Exploded view of the Aisin servo unit (Sec 17)

16 Vacuum servo (brake booster) unit – description

1 The vacuum servo unit is designed to supplement the effort applied by the driver's foot to the brake pedal.
2 The unit is an independent mechanism so that in the event of its failure the normal braking effort of the master cylinder is retained. A vacuum is created in the servo unit by its connection to the engine inlet manifold and with this condition applying on one side of the diaphragm, atmospheric pressure applied on the other side of the diaphragm is harnessed to assist the foot pressure on the master cylinder. With the brake pedal released, the diaphragm is fully recuperated and held against the rear shell by the return spring. The operating rod assembly is also fully recuperated and a condition of vacuum exists each side of the diaphragm.
3 When the brake pedal is applied, the valve rod assembly moves forward until the control valve closes the vacuum port. Atmospheric pressure then enters the chamber to the rear of the diaphragm and forces the diaphragm plate forward to actuate the master cylinder pistons through the medium of the vacuum servo unit pushrod.
4 When pressure on the brake pedal is released, the vacuum port is opened and the atmospheric pressure in the rear chamber is extracted through the non-return valve. The atmospheric pressure inlet port remains closed as the operating rod assembly returns to its original position by action of the coil return spring.
5 The diaphragm then remains in its position with vacuum conditions on both sides until the next depression of the brake pedal when the cycle is repeated.
6 *It should be remembered that in the event of a malfunction in the servo unit or when the vehicle is being towed with the engine off, the servo vacuum will not be operational and a greater pedal pressure will therefore be required to operate the brakes.*

17 Vacuum servo (brake booster) air filter – renewal

1 At the specified intervals (see Routine Maintenance) the air filter disc which surrounds the pushrod should be renewed.
2 To do this, disconnect the pushrod from the brake pedal.
3 Pull back the dust excluding flexible boot.
4 Withdraw the silencer and retainer (AISIN type) or the retainer (JKC) to give access to the air filter element. To avoid dismantling the pushrod and the need for subsequent readjustment and pedal height setting, cut the air filter element from the pushrod hole to its edge, remove and discard it.
5 Cut the new element in a similar way and refit it together with retainer and silencer.

18 Vacuum servo (brake booster) – removal and refitting

1 Destroy the vacuum in the unit by making repeated applications of the brake pedal.
2 Disconnect the vacuum hose from the servo unit.
3 On right-hand drive models, removal of the air cleaner unit will provide improved accessibility.

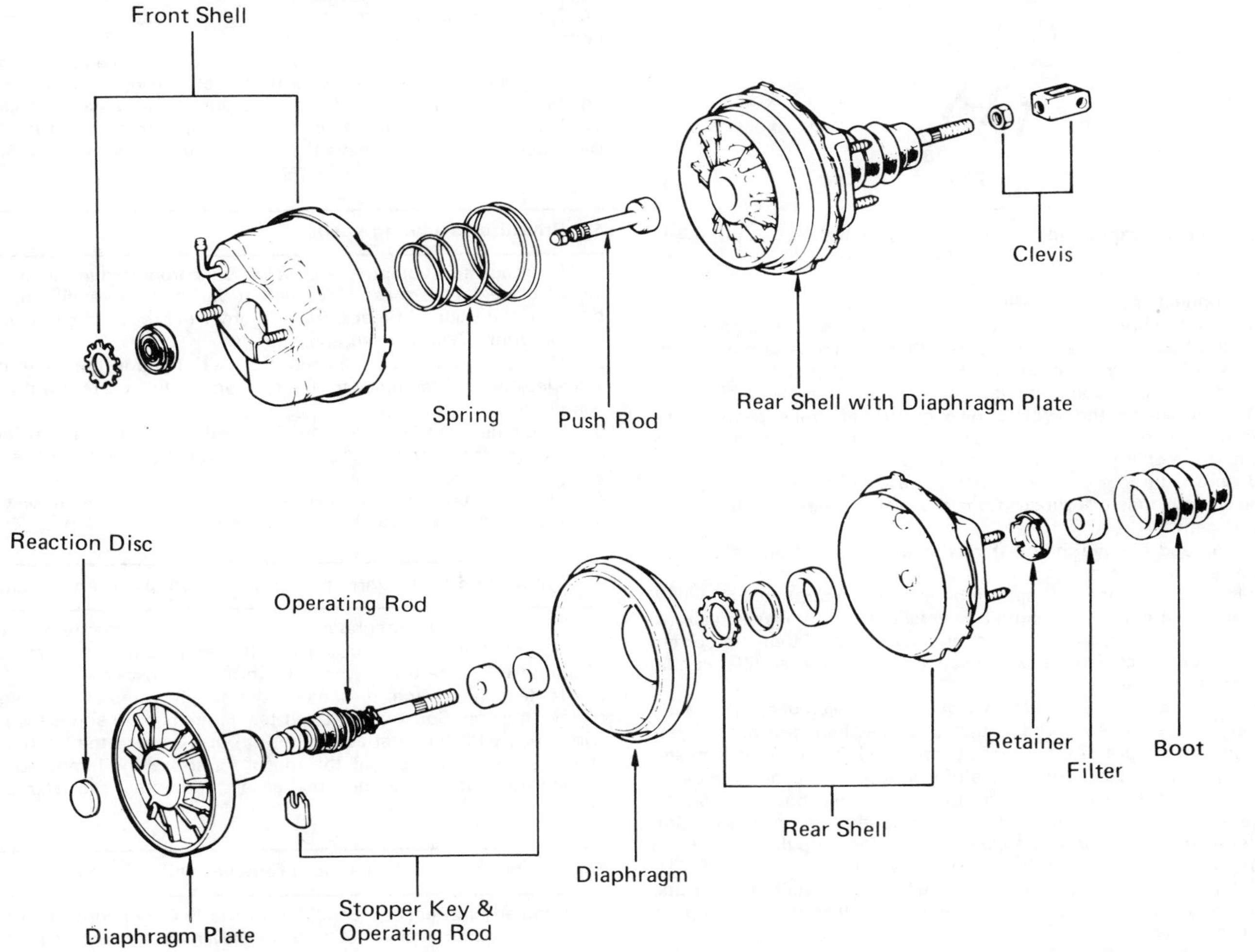

Fig. 9.44 Exploded view of the JKC servo unit (Sec 17)

18.6 View showing brake pedal, return spring and pushrod clevis connection

21.1 Check flexible and rigid brake hoses, lines and their support brackets for condition and security

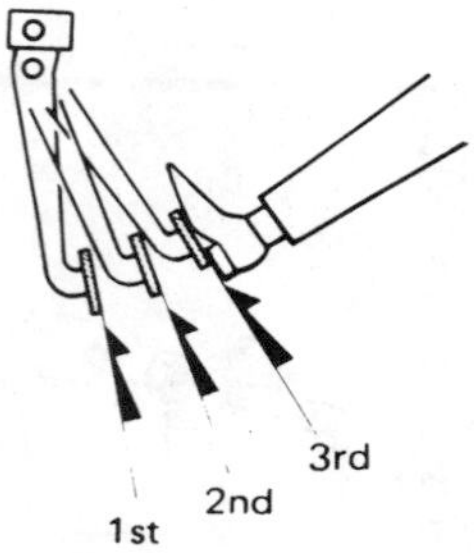

Fig. 9.45 Check that pedal pressure rises each time it is pumped (Sec 18)

4 Disconnect the master cylinder switch leads.
5 Syphon the brake fluid from the master cylinder reservoir and then detach the hydraulic hose brake pipes. Plug the pipes to prevent the ingress of dirt and wipe clean any hydraulic fluid that has spilt onto bodywork or engine components.
6 Working inside the vehicle, disconnect the brake pedal return spring and then disconnect the pushrod from the pedal arm by extracting the split pin and clevis pin (photo).
7 Unscrew the four booster mounting nuts and then lift the booster complete with master cylinder from the rear bulkhead of the engine compartment.
8 Unbolt and remove the master cylinder from the front face of the vacuum servo booster.
9 It is not recommended that the booster is dismantled but if faulty, renew it with a new or rebuilt unit. Several different makes and size of booster are used according to model so make sure that the correct type for your vehicle is ordered. Renewal of the servo air filter can be carried out (see Section 17).
10 Refitting is a reversal of removal but before assembling the master cylinder to the booster, check that the specified clearance exists between the end of the servo unit pushrod and the end of the master cylinder piston. Check by using the official tool or making up a depth gauge so that the projection of the servo unit pushrod can be compared with the depth of the recess to the end of the master cylinder piston. Carry out any adjustment by loosening the locknut and rotating the front section of the vacuum servo nut pushrod (Fig. 9.41).
11 When installation is complete, bleed the hydraulic system and check and adjust the brake pedal height and free play settings as described in Section 13.
12 On completion check the vacuum unit operation by first running the engine for a couple of minutes and then stopping it. Now press the brake pedal down three times in succession and check that the pedal rises each time. If it doesn't then an air leak exists, so check the booster unit and vacuum lines for signs of a leak.
13 To further check the booster operation, pump the brake pedal several times applying an even pressure and check that with the engine off, the pedal height does not change.
14 Now apply a pressure on the pedal and restart the engine. The pedal should be felt to go down slightly.
15 With the engine running, press down on the brake pedal and then stop the engine whilst the pedal pressure remains for a further half minute, during which time the pedal height should remain unchanged.
16 If any of these tests prove that a malfunction exists in the brake servo booster operation, have the system checked out by your Toyota dealer.

19 Pressure regulating valve

1 On models so equipped, this valve is incorporated in the hydraulic circuit close to the master cylinder. It varies the hydraulic pressure between the front and rear circuits in order to prevent the rear wheels locking during heavy brake applications.
2 The valve cannot be adjusted or repaired and in the event of the valve leaking or a tendency for the rear wheels to lock, renew the valve complete.
3 Disconnect the fluid pipes from the valve body by unscrewing the unions and then remove the valve securing bolts and lift the valve away.
4 Installation of the new valve is a reversal of removal but bleed the hydraulic system as described in Section 23.

20 Brake fluid level warning switch – description and testing

1 The switch is an integral part of the master cylinder reservoir cap. Should the fluid level drop below the minimum limit, the switch contacts will operate the warning light on the instrument panel.
2 To test the switch, disconnect the supply wires at the plug and remove the cap. Connect a 12 volt test lamp, battery and leads to the two wires; with the float at the bottom of its stroke the lamp should glow, but with the float at the top of its stroke the lamp should be extinguished. If this is not the case, renew the cap and switch assembly.

21 Flexible hoses – inspection, removal and refitting

1 Regularly inspect the condition of the flexible hydraulic hoses. If they are perished, chafed, or swollen they must be renewed (photo).
2 To remove a flexible hose, first disconnect the rigid brake line unions while holding the hose stationary.
3 Extract the retaining clip(s) from the bracket(s) and withdraw the flexible hose.

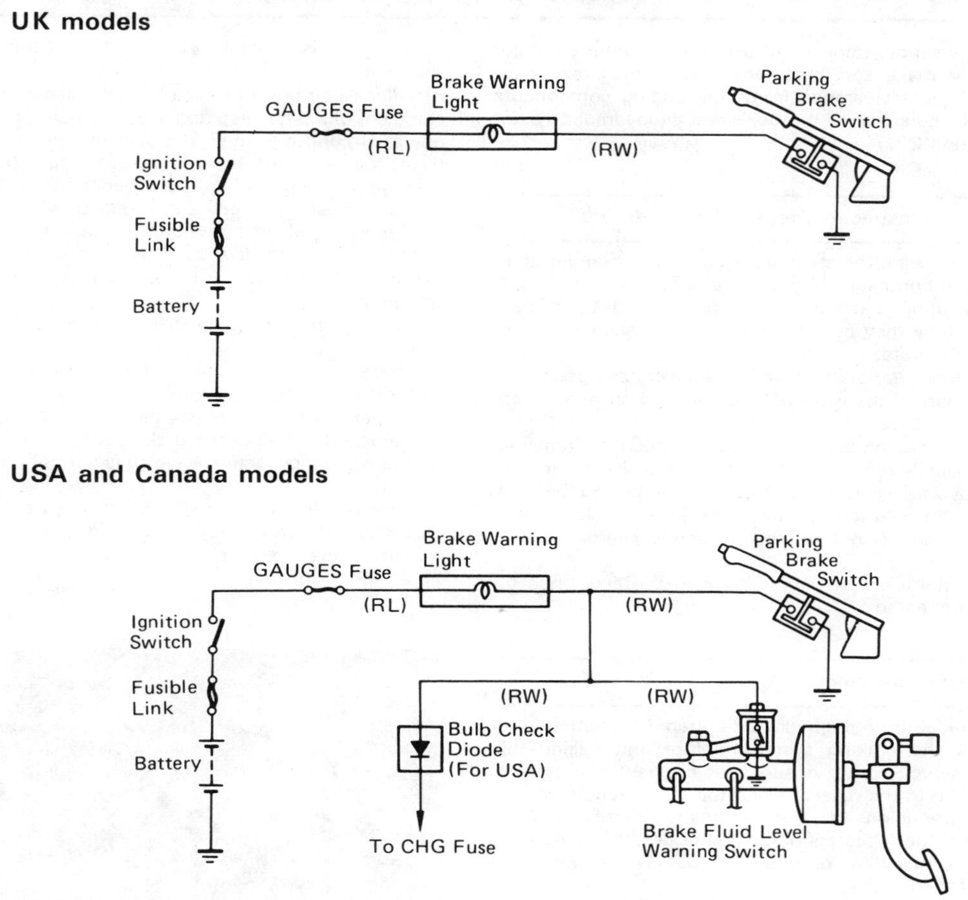

Fig. 9.46 Brake warning circuit diagrams (Sec 20)

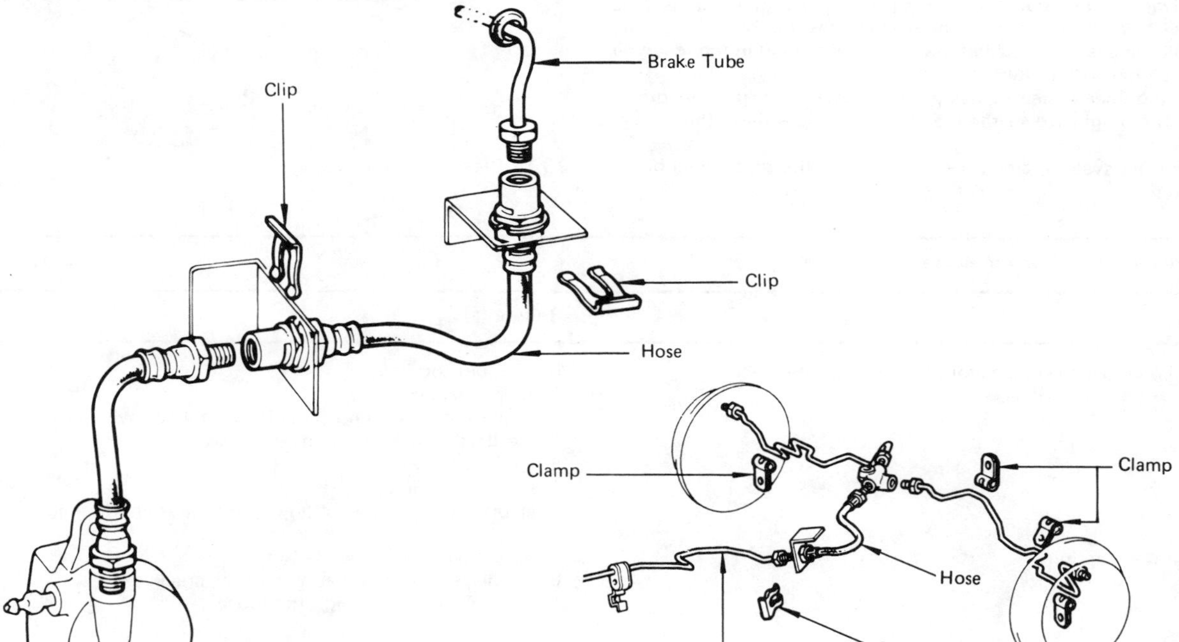

Fig. 9.47 Typical flexible hose to rigid hose connections (Sec 21)

4 Refitting is a reversal of removal, but take care to enter the union threads correctly and make sure that when fitted, the hose is not twisted and has sufficient clearance from surrounding components. Tighten the unions to the specified torque. Bleed the hydraulic system as described in Section 23.

22 Rigid brake lines – inspection, removal and refitting

1 At regular intervals wipe the steel pipes clean and examine them for signs of rust or denting caused by flying stones.
2 Examine the securing clips. Bend the tongues of the clips if necessary to ensure thay they hold the brake pipes securely without letting them rattle or vibrate.
3 Check that the pipes are not touching any adjacent components or rubbing against any part of the vehicle. Where this is observed, bend the pipe gently away to clear.
4 Any section of pipe which is rusty or chafed should be renewed. Brake pipes are available to the correct length and fitted with end unions from most Toyota dealers and can be made to pattern by many accessory suppliers. When fitting the new pipes use the old pipes as a guide to bending and do not make any bends sharper than is necessary.
5 The hydraulic system will of course have to be bled when the circuit has been reconnected.

23 Hydraulic system – bleeding

1 Removal of all the air from the hydraulic system is essential to the correct operation of the braking system. Before undertaking this, examine the fluid reservoir cap to ensure that the vent hole is clear. Check the level of fluid in the reservoir and top-up as required.
2 Check all brake line unions and connections for possible leakage, and at the same time check the condition of the flexible hoses.
3 If the condition of the caliper or wheel cylinders is in doubt, check for possible signs of fluid leakage.
4 If there is any possibility that incorrect fluid has been used in the system, drain all the fluid out and flush through with hydraulic fluid. Renew all piston seals and cups since they will be contaminated and could possibly fail under pressure.
5 One advantage of a dual line braking system is that if work is done to either the front or rear part of the system it will only be necessary to bleed half the system provided that the level of fluid in the reservoir has not fallen below half full.
6 Gather together a clean glass jar, a 12 inch (305 mm) length of tubing which fits tightly over the bleed screws and a tin of the correct brake fluid.
7 To bleed the system, clean the area around the rear wheel bleed screw which is furthest away from the master cylinder and remove the dust cap.
8 Place one end of the tube in the clean jar, which should contain sufficient fluid to keep the end of the tube underneath during the operation, and the other end over the bleed nipple.
9 Open the bleed screw $\frac{1}{4}$-turn with the right sized spanner and have an assistant depress the brake pedal. When the brake pedal reaches the floor close the bleed screw and slowly return the pedal.
10 Open the bleed screw and continue the sequence in paragraph 9 until air ceases to flow from the end of the pipe. At intervals make certain that the reservoir is kept topped-up, otherwise air will enter at this point.
11 Finally press the pedal down fully and hold it there whilst the bleed screw is tightened.
12 Repeat this operation on the other rear brake, and then the right and left front wheels (photo).
13 When completed, check the level of the fluid in the reservoir and then check the feel of the brake pedal, which should be firm and free from any 'spongy' action – which is normally associated with air in the system.
14 Always discard fluid which has been expelled from the hydraulic system, and always top-up the level with fresh fluid which has remained unshaken for the previous 24 hours and has been stored in an airtight container.

23.12 Bleeding the brakes

24 Fault diagnosis – braking system

Symptom	Reason(s)
Pedal travels almost to floor before brakes operate	Brake fluid too low Caliper leaking Master cylinder leaking (bubbles in master cylinder fluid) Brake flexible hose leaking Brake line fractured Brake system unions loose Rear brakes badly out of adjustment (automatic adjusters seized)
Brake pedal feels springy	New linings not yet bedded-in Brake discs or drums badly worn or cracked Master cylinder securing nuts loose

Symptom	Reason(s)
Brake pedal feels 'spongy' and 'soggy'	Caliper or wheel cylinder leaking Master cylinder leaking (bubbles in master cylinder fluid) Brake pipe line or flexible hose leaking Unions in brake system loose
Excessive effort required to brake car	Faulty vacuum servo unit Pad or shoe linings badly worn New pads or shoes recently fitted – not yet bedded-in Harder linings fitted than standard causing increase in pedal pressure Linings and brake drums contaminated with oil, grease or hydraulic fluid
Brake uneven and pulling to one side	Linings and discs or drums contaminated with oil, grease or hydraulic fluid Tyre pressures unequal Brake caliper loose or seized Brake pad or shoes fitted incorrectly Different type of linings fitted at each wheel Anchorage for front suspension or rear suspension loose Brake discs or drums badly worn, cracked or distorted
Brakes tend to bind, drag or lock-on	Faulty pressure regulating valve (where applicable) Air in system Handbrake cable over-tightened Wheel cylinder or caliper pistons seized
Brake warning light stays on	Leak in front or rear hydraulic circuits Faulty handbrake switch Faulty master cylinder fluid level switch

Chapter 10 Electrical system

Contents

Specifications

System type	12 volt negative earth (ground)
Battery capacity	40 or 60 amp hours depending on vehicle model and operating territory

Alternator

Output current (maximum)	40A, 45A, 50A or 55A
Rotor coil resistance	4.0 to 4.2 ohms (2.8 to 3.0 ohms - 55A alternator)
Brushes:	
Exposed length (standard)	0.49 in (12.5 mm)
Exposed length (limit)	0.22 in (5.5 mm)
Regulating voltage:	
Tirrill type	13.8 to 14.8 volt (50A alternator)
IC type	13.8 to 14.4 volt (55A alternator)

Starter motor – UK models

Type	Series wound, pre-engaged with solenoid
Rating and output power	12 volt, 0.8 kW or 12 volt, 1.0 kW
No load characteristic at 11 volts	50 amp maximum at minimum of 5000 rpm
Armature shaft:	
Outside diameter	0.489 to 0.490 in (12.45 to 12.44 mm)
Bush bore	0.4937 to 0.4945 in (12.54 to 12.56 mm)
Bush to shaft clearance:	
Standard	0.004 to 0.006 in (0.10 to 0.14 mm)
Limit	0.01 in (0.2 mm)
Thrust clearance limit	0.03 in (0.8 mm)
Commutator:	
Outer diameter, standard	1.29 in (32.7 mm)
Outer diameter, limit	1.21 in (30.7 mm)
Run-out limit	0.012 in (0.3 mm)
Mica depth:	
Standard	0.02 to 0.03 in (0.5 to 0.8 mm)
Limit	0.01 in (0.2 mm)

Brush length:	
Standard	0.7 in (19 mm)
Limit	0.5 in (12 mm)
Pinion end stop collar clearance	0.04 to 0.16 in (1 to 4 mm)
Moving stud length	1.3 in (34 mm)
Centre bearing clearance limit	0.01 in (0.2 mm)

Starter motor – USA and Canada models

Type	Reduction gear, pre-engaged
Rating and output power	12 volt, 1.0 kW or 12 volt, 1.4 kW
No load characteristic at 11.5 volts	90 amp maximum at minimum of 3000 rpm (1.0 kW) or 3500 rpm (1.4 kW)
Commutator:	
Outside diameter, standard	1.18 in (30 mm)
Outside diameter, limit	1.14 in (29 mm)
Run-out limit	0.008 in (0.2 mm)
Mica depth:	
Standard	0.0177 to 0.0295 in (0.45 to 0.75 mm)
Limit	0.008 in (0.2 mm)
Brushes:	
Standard length – 1.0 kW model	0.531 in (13.5 mm)
1.4 kW model	0.571 in (14.5 mm)
Brush length limit (1.0 and 1.4 kW)	0.39 in (10 mm)

Fuses – UK models

Fuse holder	Rating	Protected circuits
1	20A	Heater main relay coil, rear screen wiper/washer, windscreen wipers/washers, rear wiper indicator light
2	7.5A	Radio, cassette player
3	7.5A	Spare fuse
4	7.5A	Reverse lights, brake system warning light, choke button warning light, engine temperature gauge, fuel gauge, low level warning light, oil pressure warning light and gauge, handbrake reminder light, tachometer, voltmeter
5	15A	Cigarette lighter, clock (digital)
6	7.5A	Signal indicator lights and indicator lights
7	7.5A	Discharge warning light and relay coil, ignition main relay coil, engine cooling fan relay
Drivers side kick panel fuses:		
10	10A x 2*	Rear screen defogger/indicator light
11	15A	Auto-transmission shift indicator light, panel lights, number plate lights, park (side) lights, rear foglight(s) and indicator light, rear lights and relay
12	7.5A	Clock (digital), interior light, luggage compartment light, door open warning light
13	10A	Stop (brake) lights
14	10A	Auto-transmission shift indicator light, instrument panel lights
Engine compartment fuses:		
15	15A	Left-side headlight, rear foglight relay
16	15A	Right-side headlight, rear foglight relay
17	15A	Emergency flashers and flasher indicator lights, horn
18	7.5A	Carburettor choke heater coil
19	15A x 2*	Air conditioner heater blower motor
20	15A	Alternator voltage regulator (IG terminal), emission control system, fuel cut solenoid

***If either fuse blows, renew both**

Fuses – USA and Canada models

Fuse holder	Rating	Protected circuits
1	20A	Windscreen wiper/washer, rear window wiper/washer and rear wiper indicator light
2	5A	Radio and stereo tape player
3	10A	Spare fuse
4	10A	Oil pressure warning light, brake warning light, back-up light, tachometer, voltmeter, oil pressure gauge, seat belt warning light
5	10A	Cigarette lighter, clock (digital)
6	7.5A	Turn signal (indicator) light and indicator light
7	10A	Discharge warning light, main relay, charcoal canister control valve (USA), emission control computer (USA), cooling fan relay (Canada), secondary fuel cut solenoid, vacuum switching valve

Left-side kick panel fuses:		Protected circuits
8	15A x 2*	Rear window defogger panel indicator light
9	10A	Tail light relay, clearance light, licence plate light(s), instrument panel light, transmission indicator light, side marker light
10	5A	Interior lights, clock (3-hand), door open warning light
11	10A	Stop lights
Engine compartment fuses:		
12	15A	Headlight – left-side
13	15A	Headlight – right-side
14	10A	Hazard warning light, horn
15	10A	Discharge warning light, charge light relay
16	15A x 2*	Heater relay, heater blower motor, air conditioner
17	10A	Voltage regulator (IG terminal), charge light relay (point)

***If either fuse blows, renew both**

Bulbs

	Wattage (UK)	Wattage (USA/Canada)
Parking (side) lights	5	7.5
Front indicator lights	–	27
Steel bumper	21	–
Urethene bumper	23	–
Side turn signal lights (side marker)	5	3.8
Rear indicator lights	–	27
Estate	21	–
Other models	23	–
Stop and tail lights	21/5	27/8
Rear foglight	21	–
Reverse (back-up) lights	21	27
Licence plate lights	–	7.5
Steel bumper	10	–
Urethene bumper	5	–
Interior light	10	10
Luggage compartment light	5	5
Rear side marker lights	–	3.8
Headlights	–	65/55
Semi-sealed beam	45/40	–
Halogen	60/55	–

Torque wrench setting

	lbf ft	kgf m
Alternator pulley nut	37 to 47	5.0 to 6.5

1 General description

A 12 volt negative earth system is used on all models. The main components of the electrical system consists of a battery, an alternator with voltage regulator and a pre-engaged starter motor.

The battery supplies a steady amount of current for the ignition, lighting, and other electrical circuits and provides a reserve of electricity when the current consumed by the electrical equipment exceeds that being produced by the alternator.

All electrical circuits are protected by fuses and the main power cable from the battery incorporates a fusible link.

2 Battery – maintenance

1 Once a week, check the level of electrolyte in the battery cells and top up if necessary with distilled or purified water.

2 Various types of battery may be encountered but of the two most popular types, one has a translucent case where the electrolyte level should be maintained between the two marks on the casing (Fig. 10.1).

3 Where a non-translucent battery case is used, the electrolyte level should be maintained at the bottom of the filler tubes.

4 The acid in a battery does not evaporate, it is only the water which requires replenishment. Acid is used in the electrolyte when the battery is first filled and charged and no acid should be needed throughout the life of the unit.

5 Periodically clean the top of the battery, check the tightness of the battery leads and apply petroleum jelly to the terminals to prevent corrosion.

6 If corrosion is evident (white fluffy deposits) on the battery tray or clamp, the battery should be removed as described in the next Section and the corrosion removed by wire brushing and by applying household ammonia. Paint the cleaned components with anti-corrosive paint.

7 To check the state of charge of the battery, use a hydrometer to draw up electrolyte from each of the cells in turn. The specific reading on the hydrometer should be in accordance with the following at an ambient temperature of 68°F (20°C).

Fully charged	*1.260*
Half charged	*1.160*
Discharged	*1.060*

8 Any variation in reading in excess of 0.025 between the cells will indicate an internal failure and battery renewal should be anticipated.

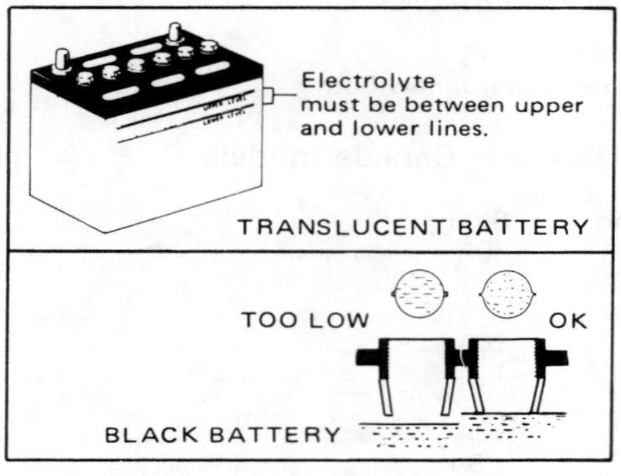

Fig. 10.1 Battery refill levels to be as shown according to type (Sec 2)

3 Battery charging

1 In winter time when heavy demand is placed upon the battery, such as when starting from cold, and much electrical equipment is continually in use, it is a good idea to occasionally have the battery fully charged from an external source at the rate of 3.5 or 4 amps.
2 Continue to charge the battery at this rate until no further rise in specific gravity is noted over a four hour period.
3 Alternatively, a trickle charger charging at the rate of 1.5 amps can be safely used overnight.
4 Specially rapid 'boost' charges which are claimed to restore the power of the battery in 1 to 2 hours are not recommended as they can cause serious damage to the battery plates.
5 Before charging the battery from an external source always disconnect the battery leads to prevent damage to the alternator.

4 Battery – removal and refitting

1 The battery is located at the front left-hand corner within the engine compartment.
2 Disconnect the leads from the battery terminals.
3 Unbolt the battery hold down clamp and lift the battery from the battery support tray.
4 Refitting is a reversal of removal. If any corrosive deposits have been noticed on the battery terminals and connectors, they must be cleaned using hot water or ammonia and then smeared with petroleum jelly before reconnection.

5 Alternator – general description, maintenance and precautions

1 The alternator generates three-phase alternating current which is rectified into direct current by three positive and three negative silicone diode rectifiers installed within the end frame of the alternator. The in-built characteristics of the unit obviate the need for a cut-out or current stabiliser.
2 A voltage regulator unit is incorporated in the charging circuit to control the exciting current and the current applied to the voltage coil.
3 Check the drivebelt tension at the intervals specified in 'Routine Maintenance' and adjust, as described in Chapter 2, by loosening the mounting bolts. Pull the alternator body away from the engine block; do not use a lever as it will distort the alternator casing.
4 No lubrication is required as the bearings are grease sealed for life.
5 Take extreme care when making circuit connections to a vehicle fitted with an alternator and observe the following.

When making connections to the alternator from a battery always match correct polarity.
Before using electric-arc welding equipment to repair any part of the vehicle, disconnect the connector from the alternator and disconnect the positive battery terminal.
Never start the car with a battery charger connected.
Always disconnect the battery leads before using a mains charger.
If boosting from another battery, always connect in parallel using heavy cable.

6 Alternator – testing in vehicle

1 In the event of failure of the normal performance of the alternator, carry out the following test procedure paying particular attention to the possibility of damaging the charging and electrical system unless the notes (a) to (c) are observed.

(a) *The alternator output B terminal must be connected to the battery at all times. When the ignition switch is operated, the F terminal is also at battery voltage*
(b) *Never connect the battery leads incorrectly or the rectifiers and flasher unit will be damaged*
(c) *Never run the engine with the alternator B terminal disconnected otherwise the voltage at the N terminal will rise abnormally and damage to the voltage relay will result*

2 Check the security of the alternator mountings, the terminal leads and the drivebelt tension (Chapter 2).
3 Check the ignition fuse, the charge fuse and the engine fuse and renew them if they are blown.
4 Check that all of the alternator and charge circuit wiring

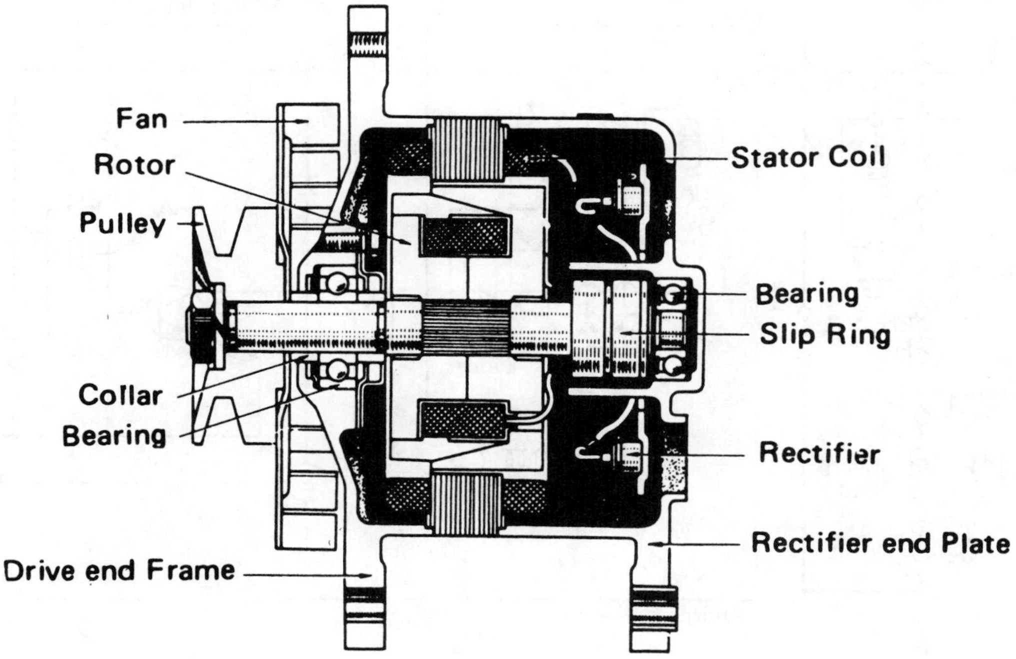

Fig. 10.2 Sectional view of the alternator (Sec 5)

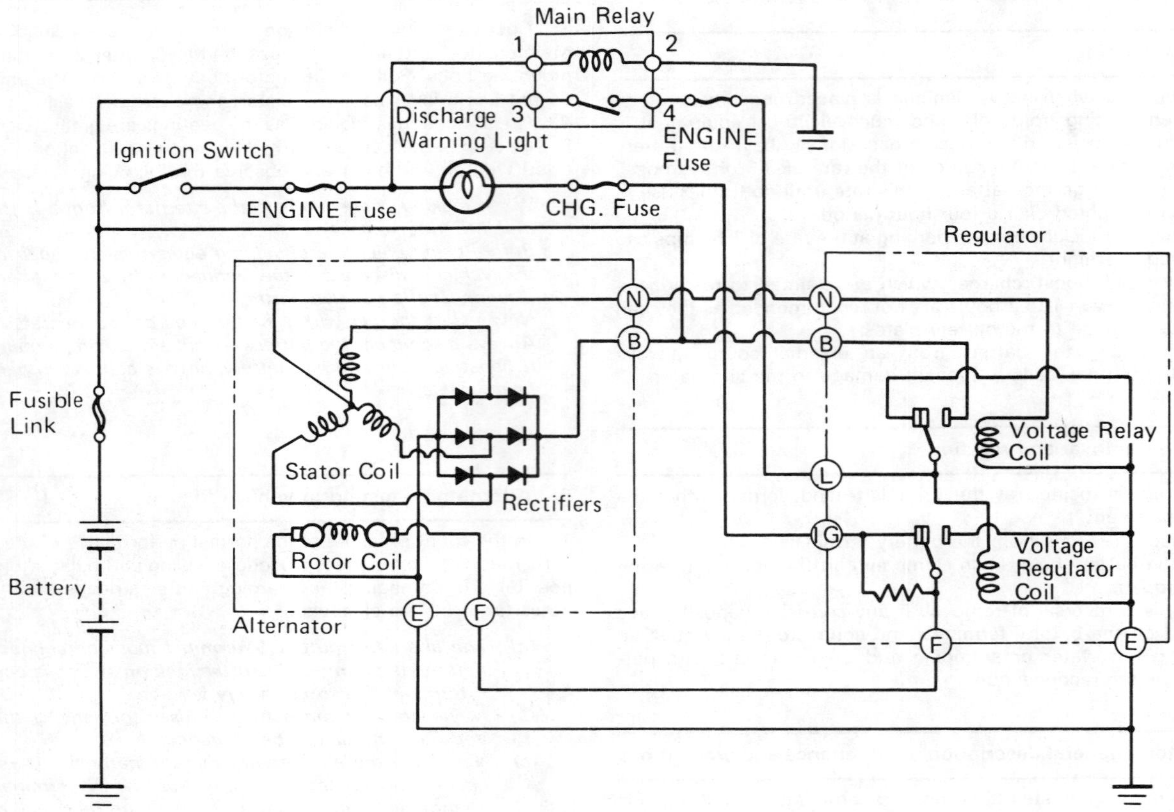

Fig. 10.3 Charging system circuit with external regulator (Sec 6)

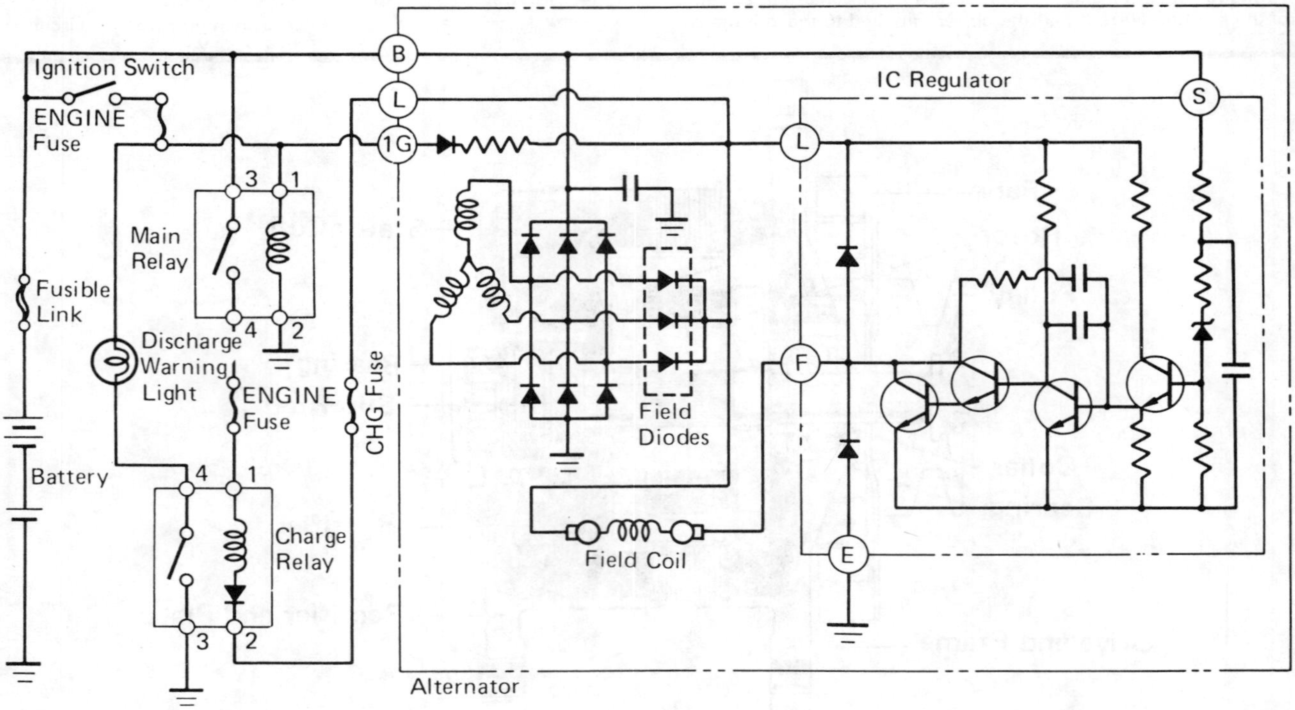

Fig. 10.4 Charging system circuit with integrated circuit (IC) regulator (Sec 6)

connectors are secure and that the wiring is in good condition (Fig. 10.3 & 10.4).
5 If the alternator is making abnormal noises when the engine is running then an internal malfunction is indicated. It should be removed as described in the following Section and dismantled for inspection as described in Section 8.
6 To check the charge circuit you will need a voltmeter and an ammeter. Connect them as follows referring to the figure.
7 Disconnect the terminal B wire from the alternator and connect it to the ammeter negative terminal. The ammeter positive lead is then connected to the terminal B on the alternator as is the positive voltmeter test lead. The negative lead of the voltmeter must be earthed (grounded). To test the circuits proceed as follows.
8 Run the engine at a speed of 2000 rpm and check the readings of the ammeter and voltmeter. Compare them with the following specified amperage readings according to type.

Separate regulator types

Under 10 amps, between 13.8 and 14.8 volts. If readings are not as specified the voltage regulator will need adjusting or renewing. Adjustment of the regulator is dealt with in Section 9.

55A (IC type)

Under 10 amps, between 13.8 and 14.4 volts. If the reading is outside the specified range check the unit in the following way. Earth (ground) terminal F and then start the engine and check the terminal B voltage. A voltage reading above that specified necessitates renewal of the IC regulator whilst a lower reading indicates an alternator fault.
9 The charge circuits should also be checked under load conditions. Start the engine and run it at 2000 rpm, then turn on the headlight main beams and the heater fan to the HI position. The minimum ammeter reading should be 30 amps although if the battery is in a fully charged state, it may cause the reading to drop below the specified minimum figure. The test should therefore be rechecked with the battery in a semi-charged state. A lower reading than specified indicates a malfunction of the alternator.

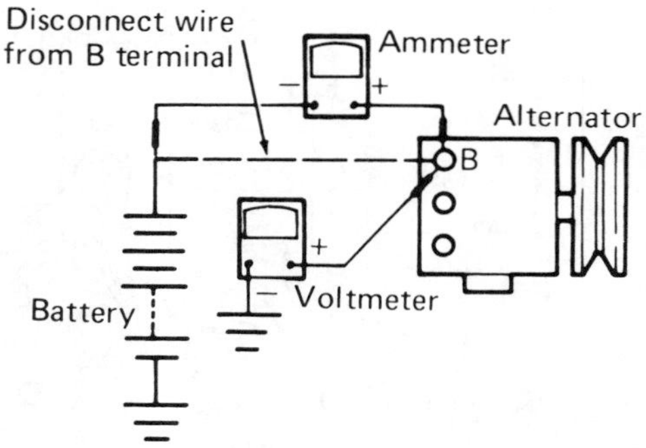

Fig. 10.5 Alternator check – connect voltmeter and ammeter as shown (Sec 6)

7.3 Alternator showing mounting/adjustment strap

7 Alternator – removal and refitting

1 Disconnect the cable from the battery negative terminal.
2 On USA models remove the air cleaner ducting. Disconnect and remove the battery and its carrier.
3 Loosen the alternator mounting bracket bolts and the adjustment strap bolts and then push the alternator in towards the engine block so that the driving belt can be removed from the pulley (photo).
4 Disconnect the electrical plug from the alternator terminals, remove the mounting bolts and lift the unit from its location.
5 Refitting is a reversal of removal but adjust the driving belt tension, as described in Chapter 2.

8 Alternator – dismantling, servicing and reassembly

1 Remove the three tie bolts which secure the two end frames together (Fig. 10.6 & 10.7).
2 Insert screwdrivers in the notches in the drive end frame and separate it from the stator.
3 Hold the front end of the rotor shaft still with an Allen key and remove the securing nut, pulley, fan and spacer. If an Allen key and socket is not provided, grip the rotor between wooden blocks in a vice fitted with soft jaws to support it.
4 Press the rotor shaft from the drive end frame.
5 Withdraw the bearing retainer and front bearing assembly (Fig. 10.9).
6 The rear end frame is now removed from the stator and rectifier holder in the following manner according to type.

55A (IC type)

Unscrew and remove the four nuts, the suppression condenser and two terminal insulators. Withdraw the rear frame from the stator and then remove the insulator from the rectifier holder stud.

Other types

Unscrew and remove the four nuts, detach the two terminal insulators and withdraw the end cover. The rear end frame can now be removed from the stator and the insulators from the rectifier holder studs.
7 The stator leads are detached from the rectifier holder by holding the terminal with a pair of long nose pliers whilst the leads are unsoldered (Fig. 10.10).
8 On the 55A type, unsolder the IC leads of the regulator from the rectifier holder, but protect the diode from heat damage during this operation (Fig. 10.11).
9 Test the rotor coil for an open circuit by connecting a circuit tester between the two slip rings located at the rear of the rotor. The indicated resistance should be:

50A type – 4.0 to 4.2 ohms
55A type – 2.8 to 3.0 ohms
Other types – 4.1 to 4.3 ohms

10 Test the rotor for earthing (grounding) by connecting a circuit tester as shown between the slip ring and rotor. If continuity exists the rotor must be renewed.
11 Inspect the slip ring surfaces for signs of excessive wear, roughness or scoring and if defective renew the rotor.
12 Test the insulation of the stator coil by connecting the tester between the stator coil and the stator core. If the tester needle moves then the coil is earthed through a breakdown in the insulator and must be renewed.
13 Check the four stator coil leads for conductance. If the tester needle does not flicker then the coil has an open circuit and it must be renewed.
14 The testing of the rectifiers requires the use of specialised equipment and should therefore be entrusted to an auto electrician.
15 If more than one of the preceding tests proves negative then it will be economically sound to exchange the alternator complete for a factory reconditioned unit rather than renew more than one individual component.

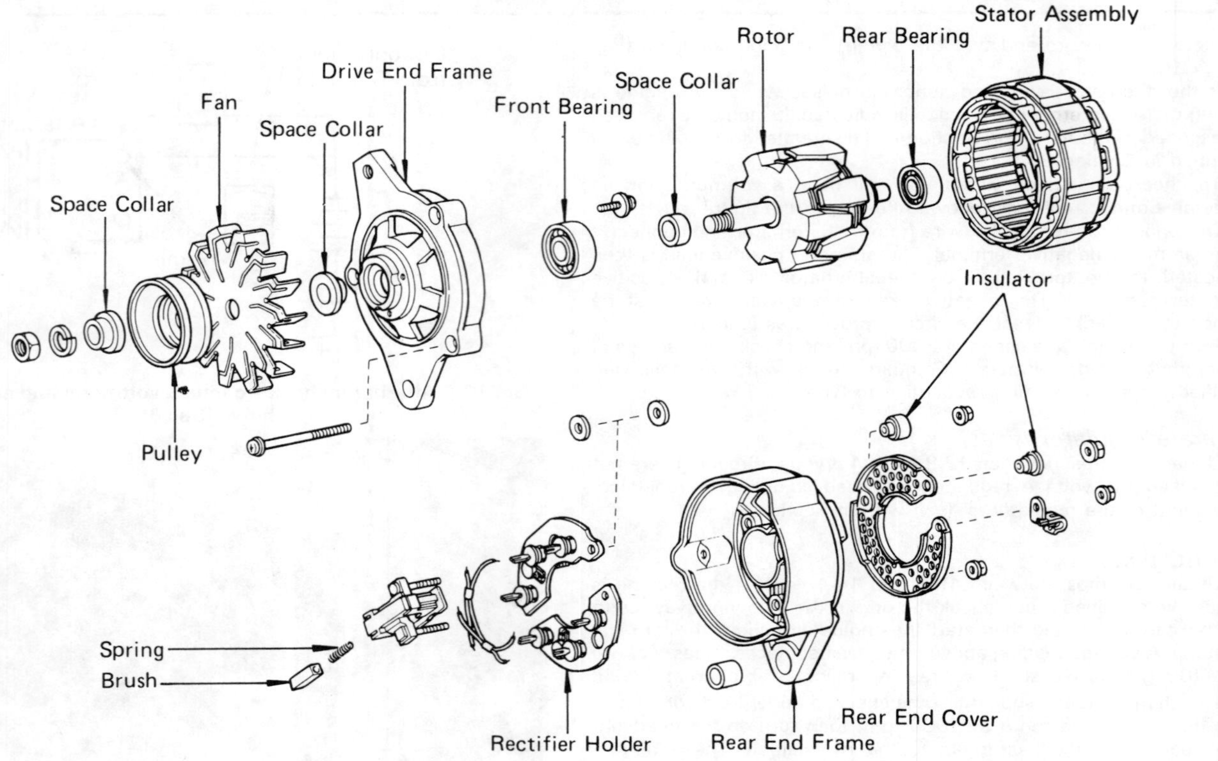

Fig. 10.6 Alternator components – external regulator type (Sec 8)

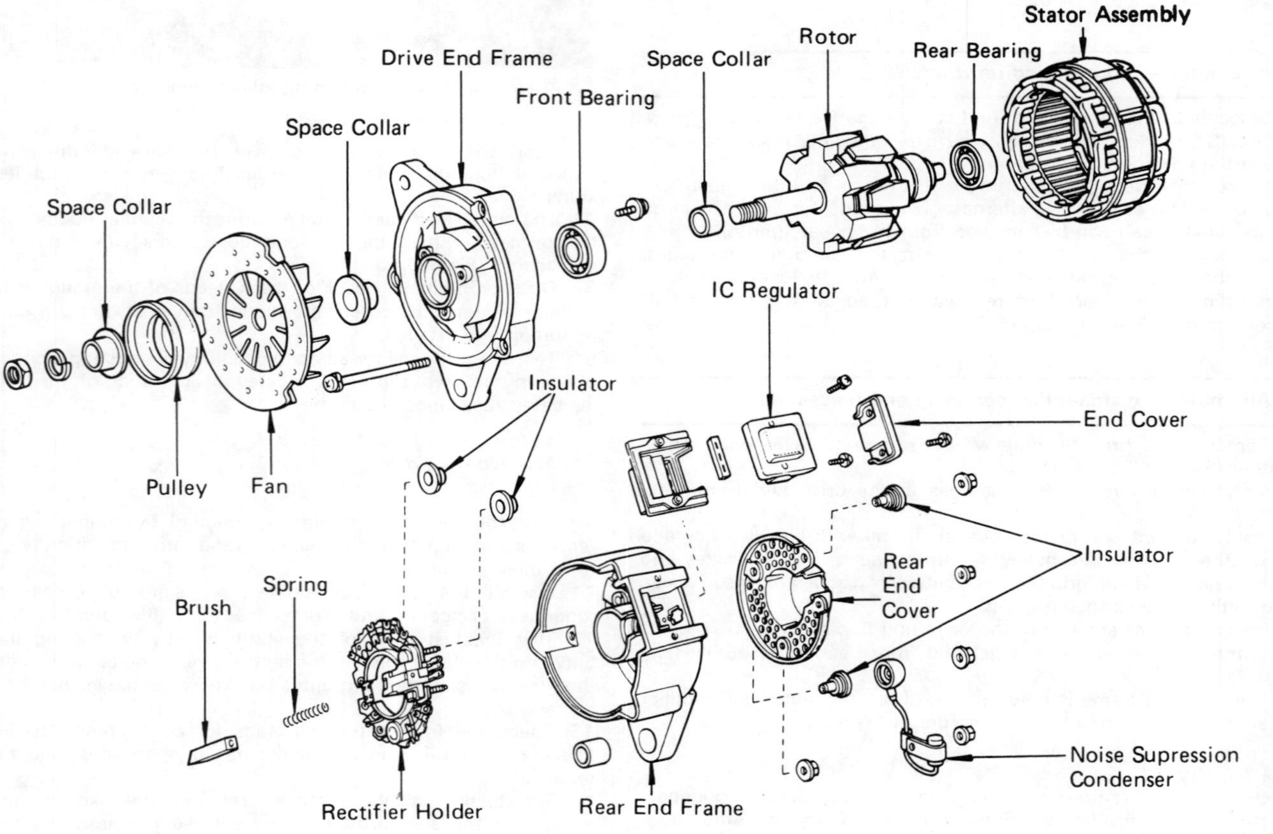

Fig. 10.7 Alternator components – IC regulator type (Sec 8)

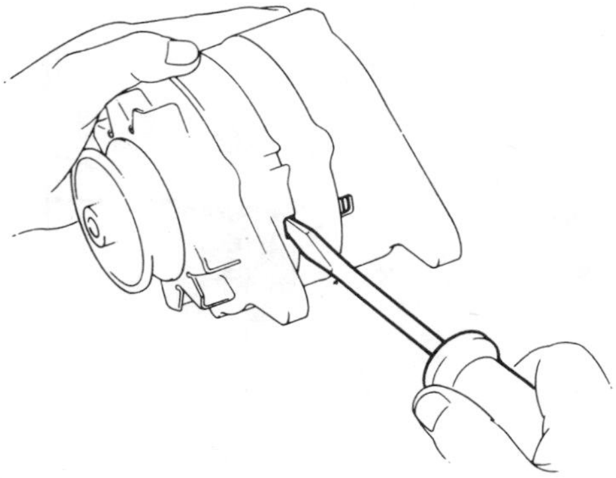

Fig. 10.8 Separate the end frame from the stator (Sec 8)

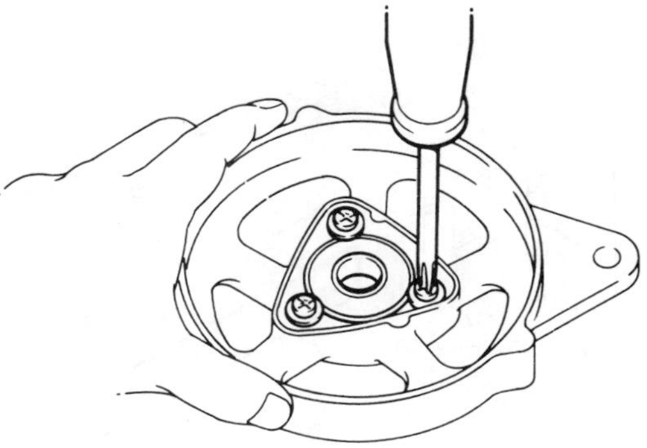

Fig. 10.9 Removing the front bearing retaining screws (Sec 8)

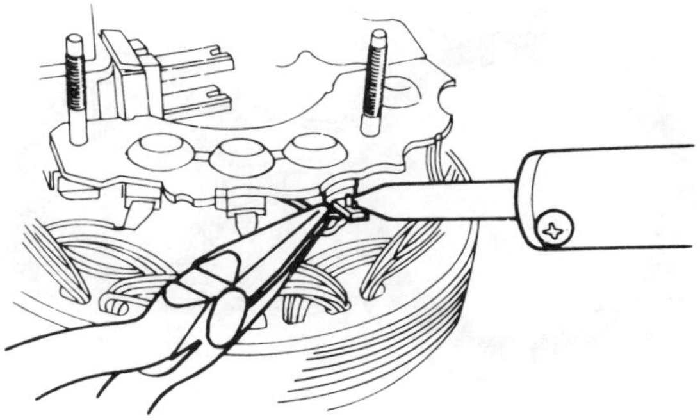

Fig. 10.10 Stator leads detachment method (Sec 8)

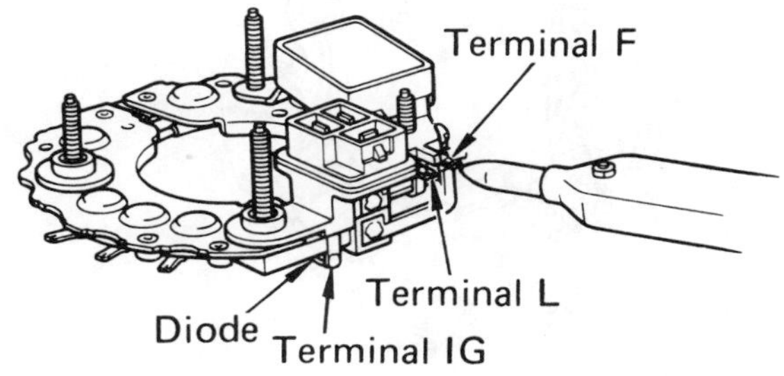

Fig. 10.11 Regulator leads detachment from rectifier (IC type) (Sec 8)

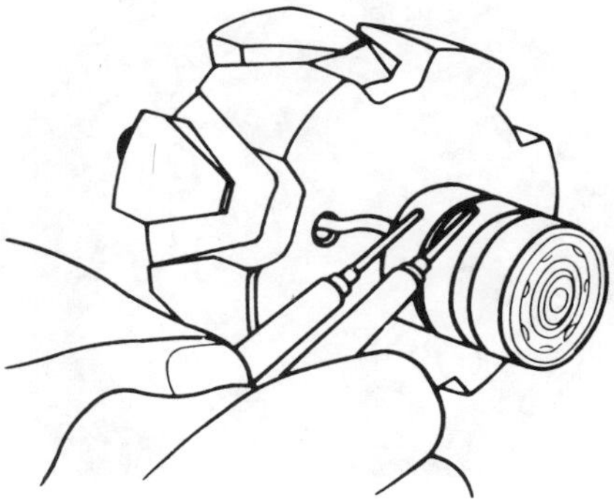

Fig. 10.12 Rotor coil test method for open circuits (Sec 8)

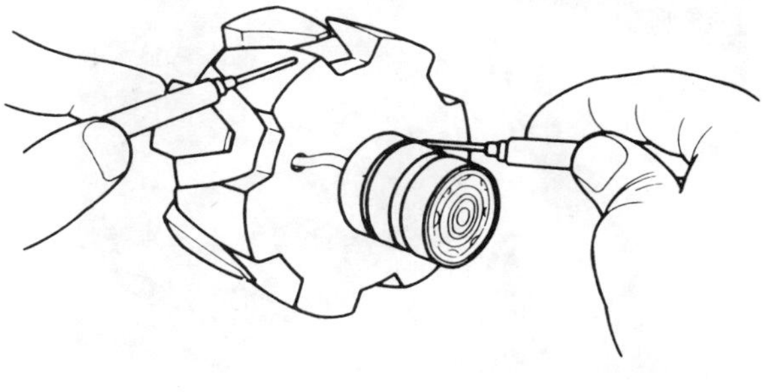

Fig. 10.13 Rotor coil test method for earthing (grounding) (Sec 8)

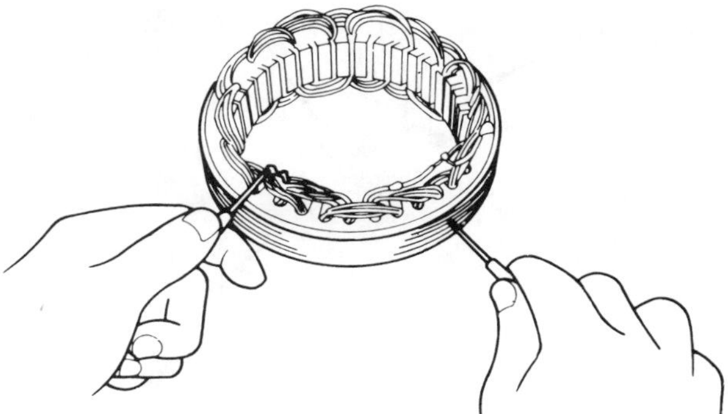

Fig. 10.14 Stator coil insulation test method (Sec 8)

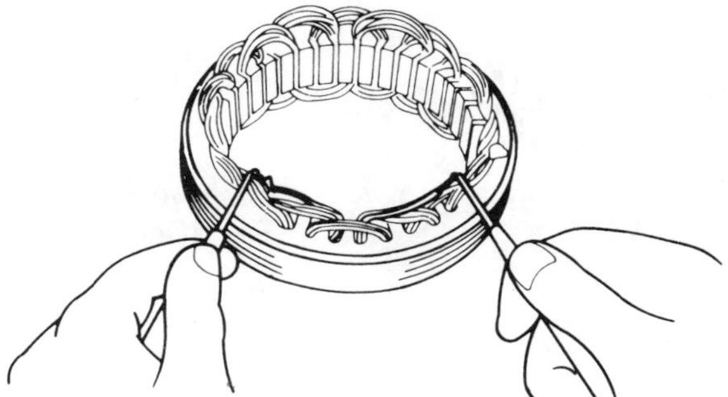

Fig. 10.15 Stator coil continuity check method (Sec 8)

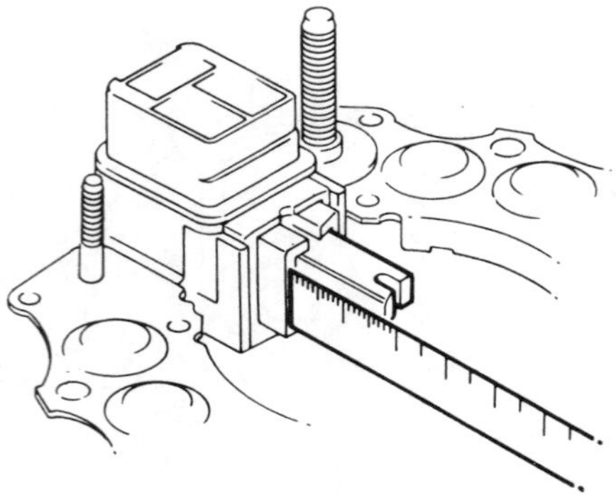

Fig. 10.16 Check the brushes for excessive wear (Sec 8)

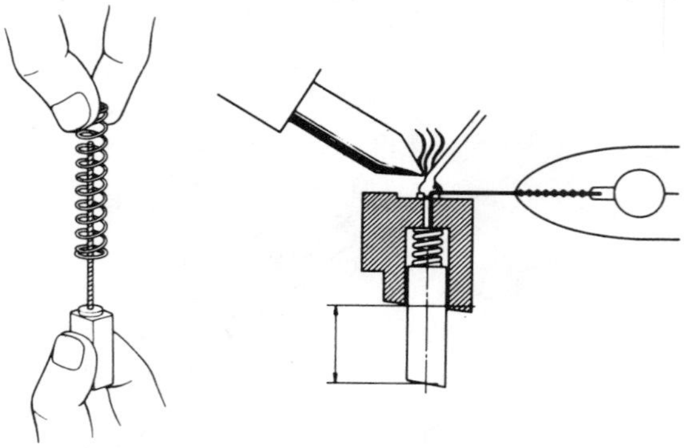

Fig. 10.17 Insert wire through spring, brush in holder and solder wire to the brush holder (Sec 8)

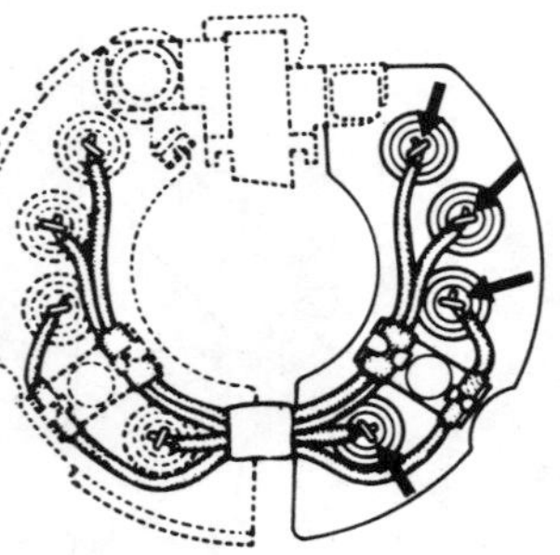

Fig. 10.18 Negative side rectifier lead connections (8 rectifier type) (Sec 8)

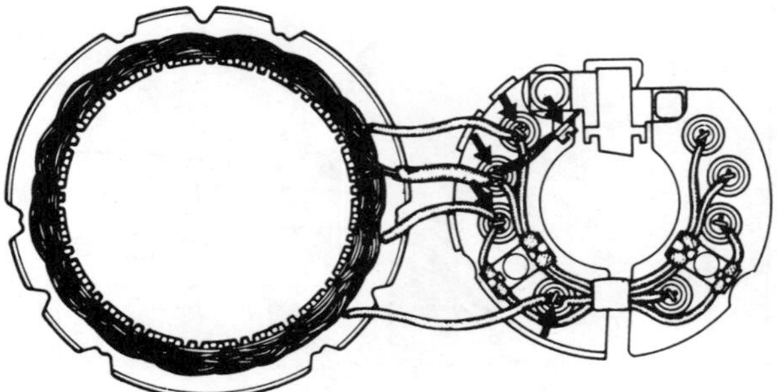

Fig. 10.19 Stator coil N lead connection to + rectifier terminal and brush holder (8 rectifier type) (Sec 8)

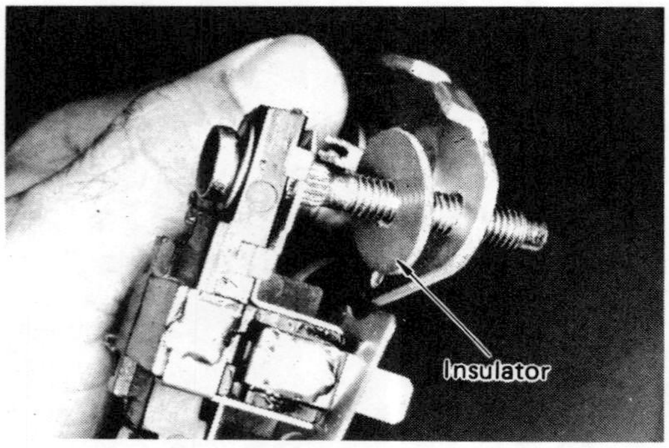

Fig. 10.20 Insulating washer location (Sec 8)

Fig. 10.21 Lead wires to rectifier/terminal soldered connections – on the 6 rectifier type (Sec 8)

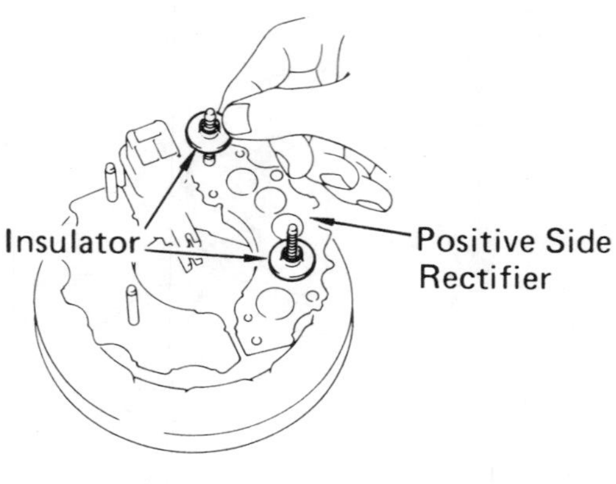

Fig. 10.22 Insulating washers to be fitted as shown (Sec 8)

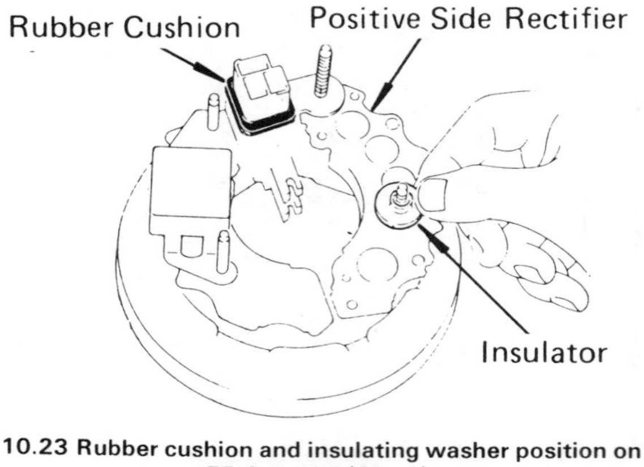

Fig. 10.23 Rubber cushion and insulating washer position on the 55 A model (Sec 8)

16 Examine the brushes for wear. If worn down to or beyond the specified limit then they must be renewed. The old brushes will have to be unsoldered for removal. With the old brushes removed, insert the new brush wires through their springs, slide the brushes down into their holders and resolder the wire to the brush holder. Check that the brush exposed length is as specified as each one is fitted. Also check that the brushes can slide smoothly in their holders. Cut off any excess wire (Fig. 10.17).

17 Finally check the front and rear bearings for excessive wear and renew if necessary. The rear bearing will have to be withdrawn from the rotor shaft using a suitable puller. Press or drift the new bearing into position on the rotor shaft. Refit the front bearing and tighten the retainer screws.

18 Reassembly of the alternator is basically a reversal of the dismantling procedure, but the following special points should be noted.

19 On models fitted with 8 rectifiers reconnect the leads as shown in Fig. 10.18 and 10.19. If the brush holder was removed, locate the insulating washer between the rectifier and brush holder, before pressing the brush holder onto the rectifier stud.

20 On 6 rectifier types solder the leads as shown in Fig. 10.21.

21 Locate the insulating washers onto the rectifier studs before refitting the end frame. The rubber cushion must also be fitted over the brush holder. On the 55A type there is only one positive side stud over which the single insulating washer is fitted.

22 Two further insulating washers are fitted to each type when the rear end frame is in position.

23 When reassembling the fan and pulley onto the rotor shaft refit the spacer collar, followed by the drive end frame then the thin spacer. Locate the fan, pulley, thick spacer and spring washer and nut which must be tightened to the specified torque wrench setting.

24 When assembling the drive end frame to the rectifier end frame the rectifier lead wires must clear the rotor and may need to be bent back to achieve this. The brushes must be pushed back into their holders and held in this position temporarily by inserting a stiff wire through the access aperture in the frame (Fig. 10.24). When the drive end and rectifier end frames are assembled together, refit the three through bolts and then withdraw the temporary brush retaining wire (Fig. 10.25).

25 On reassembly check that the rotor turns smoothly and then seal off the brush access hole to complete.

9 Alternator regulator (Tirrill external type) – testing and adjustment

1 Testing of the relay operating voltage and the regulator output voltage and amperage levels should be left to an auto-electrician as special equipment is needed. However, circuit testing and mechanical adjustments may be carried out in the following manner:

2 Disconnect the regulator connector plug. Remove the cover from the regulator unit and inspect the condition of the points. If they are pitted, clean with very fine emery cloth otherwise clean them with methylated spirt.

3 Connect a circuit tester between the IG and F terminals of the connector plug when no resistance should be indicated. If a resistance is shown, then the regulator points assembly P1 is making poor contact. Now press down the regulator armature and check the resistance which should be about 11 ohms. If it is much higher, the control resistance is defective and must be renewed.

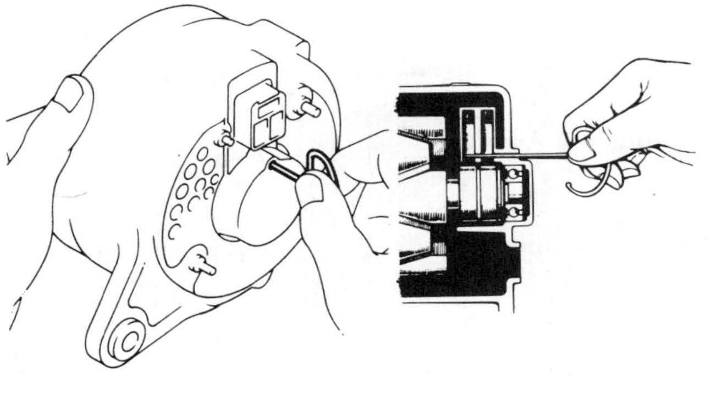

Fig. 10.24 Insert wire as shown to support brushes when assembling the end frames (Sec 8)

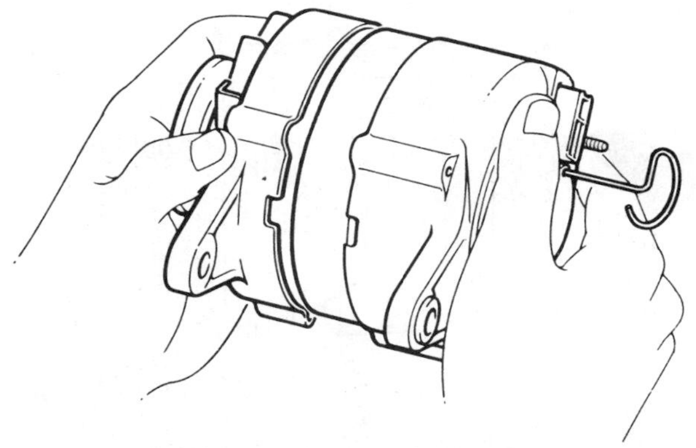

Fig. 10.25 When end frames are assembled remove brush support wire (Sec 8)

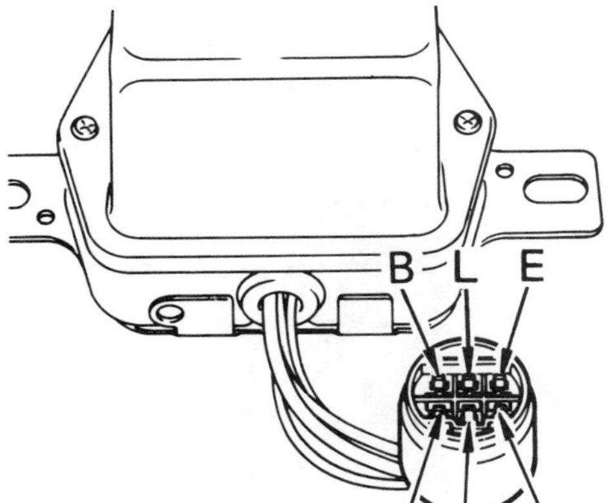

Fig. 10.26 Regulator connector plug terminal positions (Sec 9)

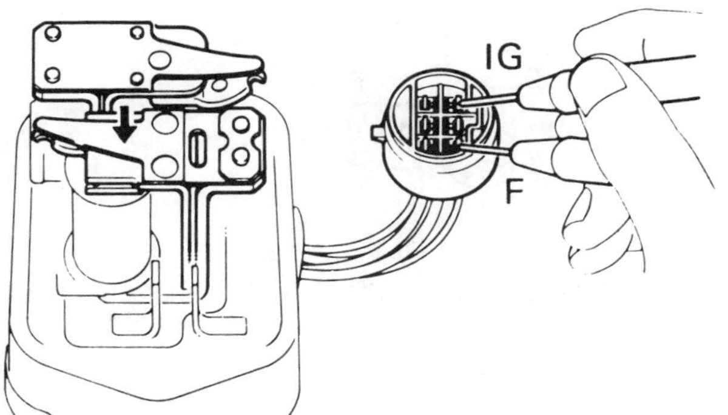

Fig. 10.27 Regulator control resistance check (Sec 9)

4 Connect the circuit tester between the connector plug L and E terminals when no resistance should be indicated. If a resistance is shown then the contact point P4 is making poor contact. Press down the relay armature and check the resistance which should be about 100 ohms. If it is higher, the voltage coil has an open circuit or if lower, the points P4 are fused together or the coil is shortened.

5 Connect the circuit tester between the N and E terminals when a resistance of 23 ohms should be indicated. If the resistance is much higher, the pressure coil has an open circuit, if lower then it is short circuited.

6 Connect the circuit tester between the B and L terminals and depress the voltage relay armature. There should be no indicated resistance but if there is this will show that the contact of the points assembly P6 is poor.

7 Connect the circuit tester between the B and E terminals when the indicated resistance should be infinity. Where this is not so the points assembly P6 are fused together. Depress the relay armature and check the resistance which should be about 100 ohms. If the resistance is higher then the voltage coil has an open circuit and if lower it has a short circuit.

8 With the connector plug still disconnected carry out the following mechanical checks. Refer to illustration and depress the voltage relay armature. Using a feeler gauge check the deflection gap between the contact spring and its supporting arm. This should be between 0.008 and 0.024 in (0.20 and 0.60 mm) if not, bend the contact point holder (P6). Release the armature and check the point gap which should be between 0.016 and 0.047 in (0.4 to 1.2 mm) if not bend the contact point holder (P4).

9 Check the armature gap on the voltage regulator which should be in excess of 0.012 in (0.30 mm) otherwise bend the contact point holder P1 to adjust the gap. Check the voltage regulator point gap which should be between 0.012 and 0.018 in (0.30 and 0.45 mm) otherwise bend the contact point holder P3 to adjust. Depress the voltage regulator armature and check the deflection gap between the contact spring and its supporting arm. This should be between 0.008 and 0.014 in (0.2 and 0.6 mm). If not renew the regulator as an assembly. Finally depress the voltage regulator armature and check

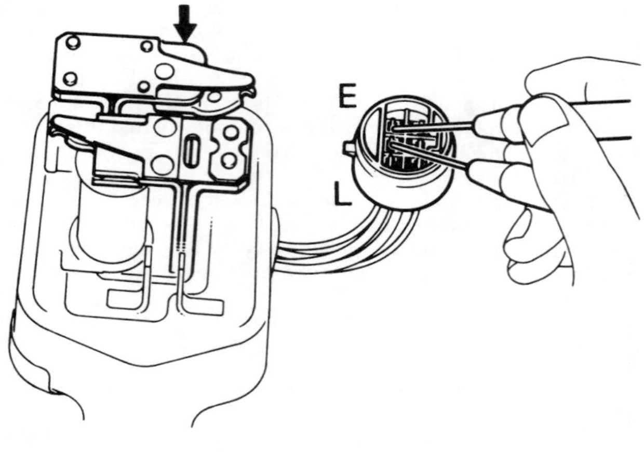

Fig. 10.28 Relay armature resistance check (Sec 9)

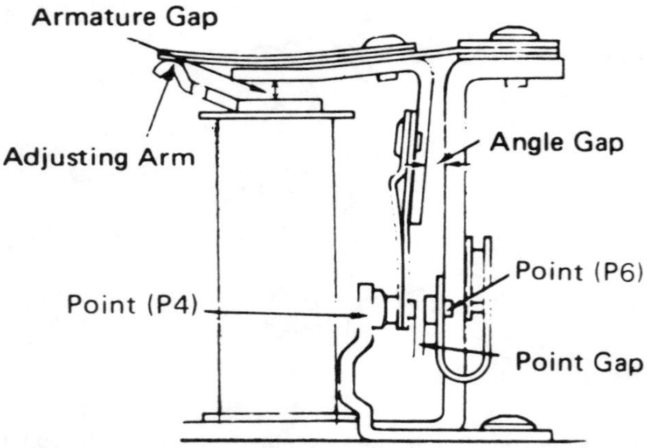

Fig. 10.29 Alternator voltage relay components (Sec 9)

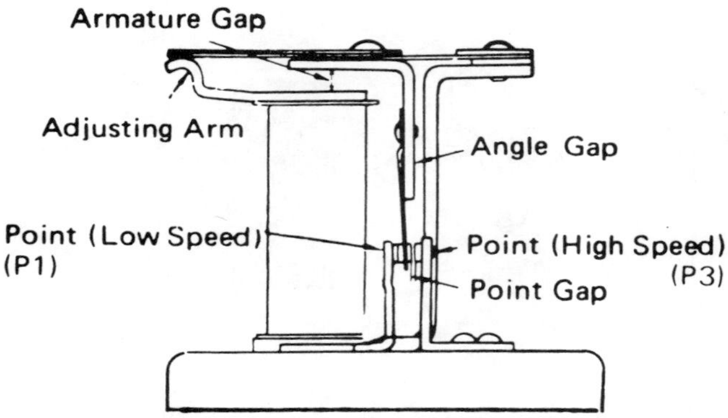

Fig. 10.30 Alternator voltage regulator components (Sec 9)

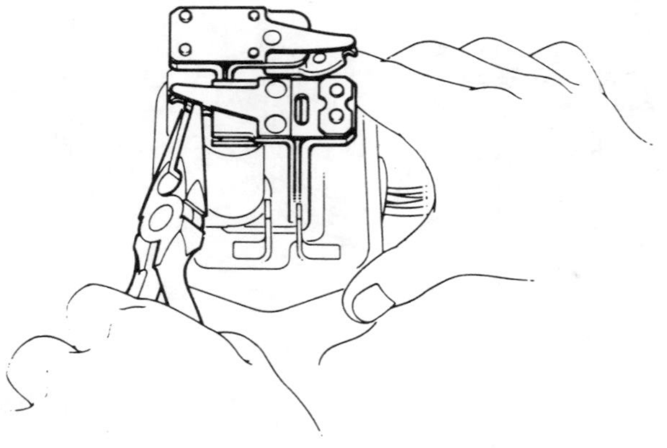

Fig. 10.31 Voltage regulator adjustment (Sec 9)

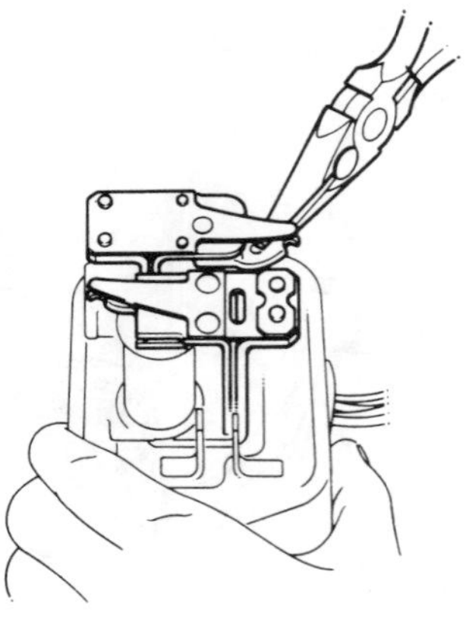

Fig. 10.32 Voltage relay adjustment (Sec 9)

the angle gap at its narrowest point. This gap should not exceed 0.008 in (0.2 mm) otherwise renew the unit as an assembly.

10 Starter motor – general description

The starter operates on the principle of pre-engagement which, through the medium of a solenoid switch, meshes the starter drivegear with the ring gear on the flywheel (or torque converter – automatic transmission) fractionally in advance of the closure of the main starter motor contacts. This slight delay in energising the starter motor does much to extend the life of the starter drive and ring gear components. As soon as the engine fires and its speed or rotation exceeds that of the armature shaft of the starter motor, a built-in clutch mechanism prevents excessive rotation of the shaft and the release of the starter switch key causes the solenoid and drive engagement fork to return to their de-energised positions. The armature shaft is fitted with rear and central rotational speed retarding mechanisms to stop its rotational movement rapidly after the starter has been de-energised (Fig. 10.33).

One of three starter motor types will be fitted depending on year and model and will be of reduction gear or non reduction gear design.

Wiring layouts and circuit diagrams for the starting system are shown in the accompanying figures.

10.1 Removing the starter motor

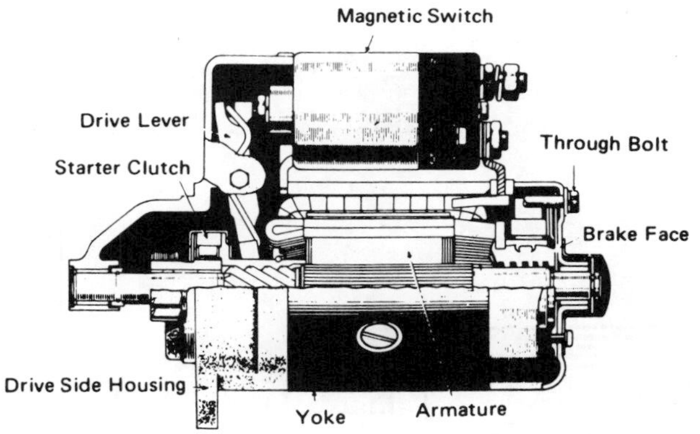

Fig. 10.33 Sectional view of the starter motor – conventional type (Sec 10)

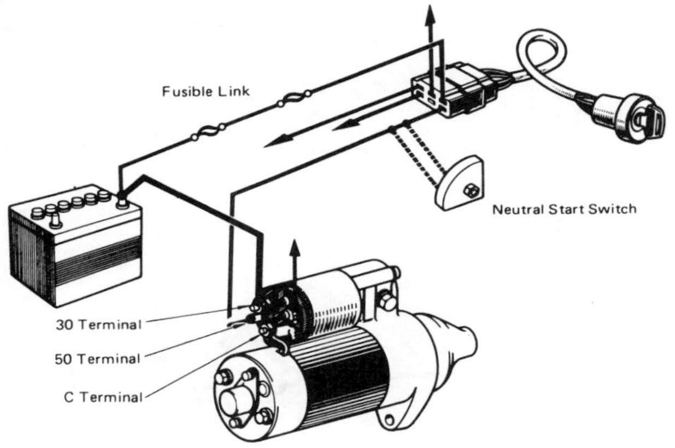

Fig. 10.34 Starter motor circuit layout – conventional type (Sec 10)

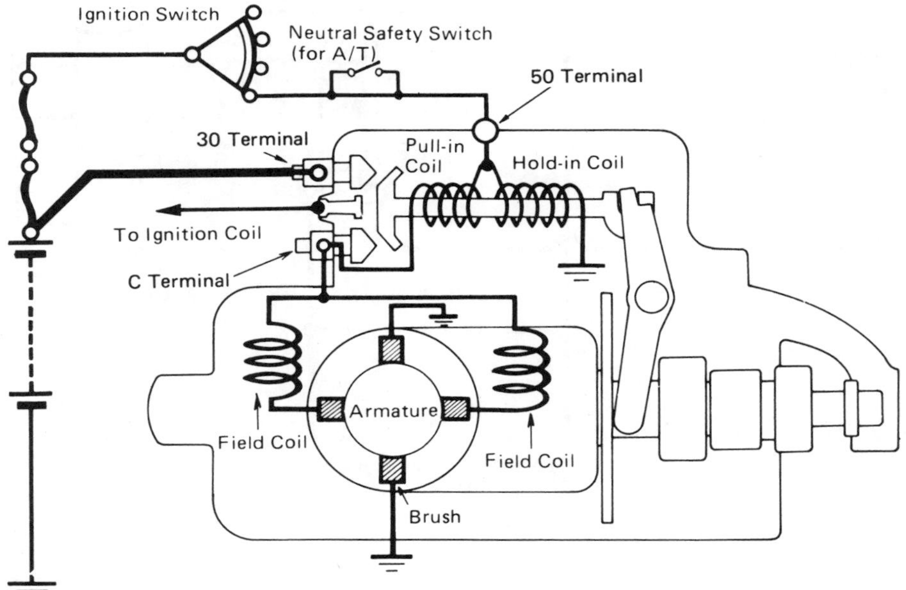

Fig. 10.35 Starter motor wiring diagram – conventional type (Sec 10)

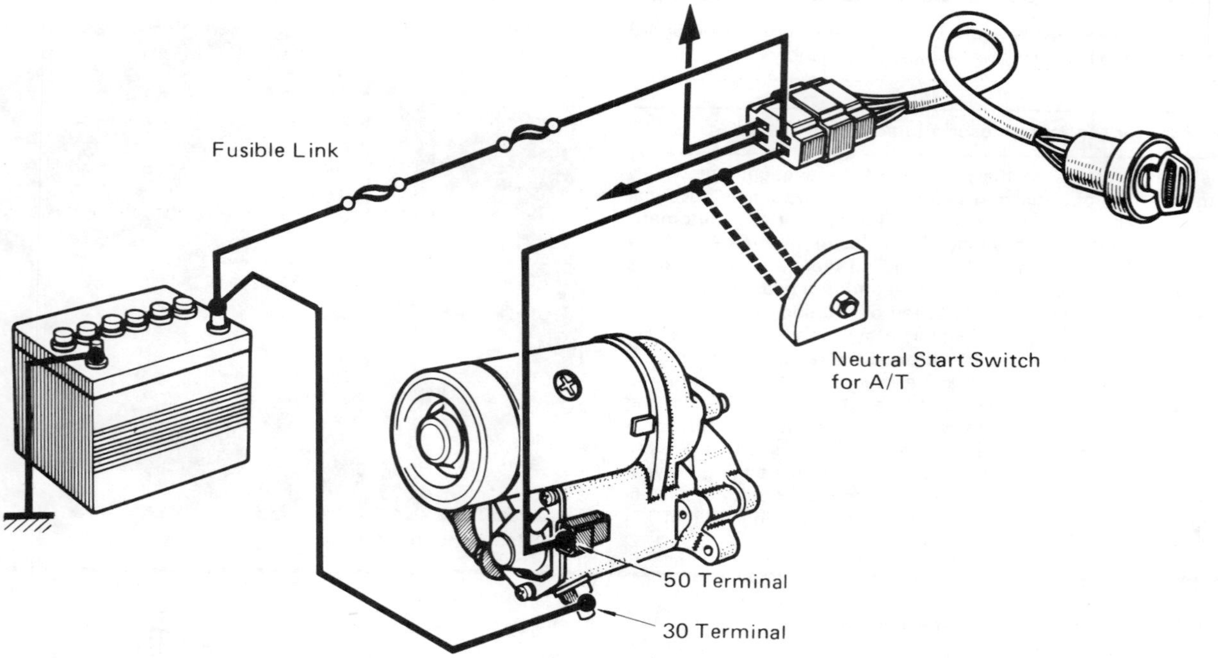

Fig. 10.36 Starter motor circuit layout – reduction gear type (Sec 10)

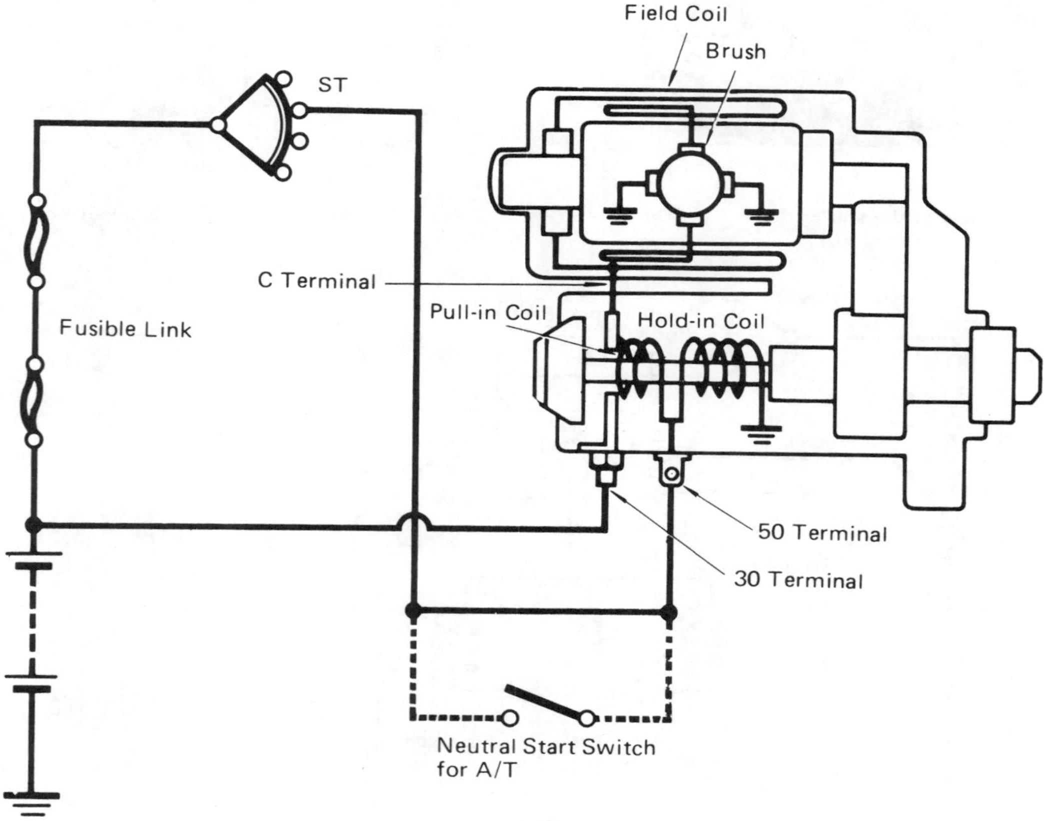

Fig. 10.37 Starter motor wiring diagram – reduction gear type (Sec 10)

11 Starter motor – testing in vehicle

1 If the starter motor fails to operate, test the state of charge of the battery by checking the specific gravity with a hydrometer or switching on the headlamps. If they glow brightly for several seconds and then gradually dim, then the battery is in an uncharged state.
2 If the test proves the battery to be fully charged, check the security of the battery leads at the battery terminals, scraping away any deposits which are preventing a good contact between the cable clamps and the terminal posts.
3 Check the battery negative lead at its body frame terminal, scraping the mating faces clean if necessary.
4 Check the security of the cables at the starter motor and solenoid switch terminals.
5 Check the wiring with a voltmeter for breaks or short circuits.
6 Check the wiring connections at the ignition/starter switch terminals.
7 If everything is in order, remove the starter motor as described in the next Section and dismantle, test and service according to type.

12 Starter motor – removal and refitting

1 Disconnect the lead from the battery negative terminal.
2 Disconnect the cables from the starter solenoid terminals.
3 Unscrew and remove the starter motor securing bolts and withdraw the unit from the clutch bellhousing (or torque converter housing – automatic transmission).
4 Refitting is a reversal of removal.

13 Starter motor (conventional type) – dismantling, overhaul and reassembly

1 Disconnect the field coil wire from the starter motor solenoid terminal.
2 Remove the two end cover screws and remove the cover (photo).
3 Prise free the lockplate (photo) and withdraw the washer, spring and seal (photos).
4 Remove the two securing screws from the solenoid and withdraw the solenoid far enough to enable it to be unhooked from the drive engagement lever fork (photo).
5 Unscrew and remove the two tie bolts and withdraw the commutator end frame (photo).
6 Pull out the brushes from their holders and remove the brush holder assembly.
7 Pull the yoke from the drive end frame.
8 Remove the engagement lever pivot bolt from the drive end frame and detach the rubber buffer and its backing plate. Remove the armature, complete with drive engagement lever from the drive end frame.
9 With a piece of tubing, drive the pinion stop collar up the armature shaft far enough to enable the circlip to be removed and then pull the stop collar from the shaft together with the pinion and clutch assembly.
10 Clean the respective components and lay them out for inspection.
11 The armature shaft bearings must be checked for wear. The shaft to bearing clearance must not exceed the specified limit.
12 Normally the bearings will require renewal by pressing out the old ones from the end frames and pressing in the new, but before doing this check the diameter of the armature shaft which should be within the limits specified. If this is worn then a new armature will be required and it will be more economical to exchange the starter complete for a reconditioned unit.
13 Armature shaft bearings are available in standard sizes and undersizes where it is decided to have the original shaft turned down as the method of renovation.
14 Check the armature shaft for bend or ovality and renew if evident.
15 Check the commutator segments and undercut the mica insulators if necessary, using a hacksaw blade ground to correct thickness. If the commutator is burned or discoloured, clean it with a piece of fine glass paper (not emery or carborundum) and finally wipe it with a solvent moistened cloth.

13.2 Remove the end cover screws

13.3a Remove the lockplate ...

13.3b ... washer and spring ...

13.3c ... and seal

13.4 Remove solenoid screws

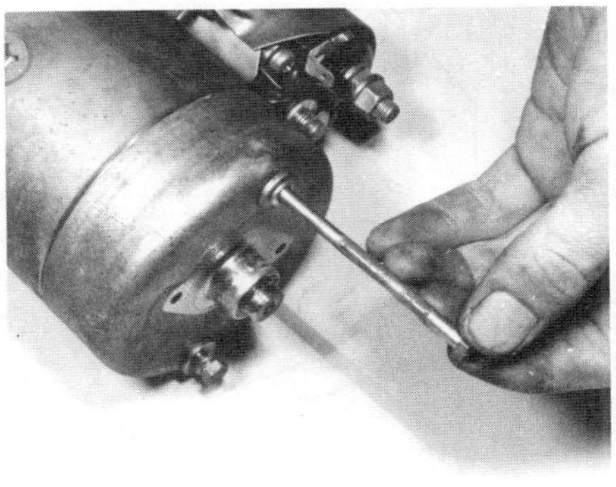

13.5 Unscrew and withdraw the tee (through) bolts

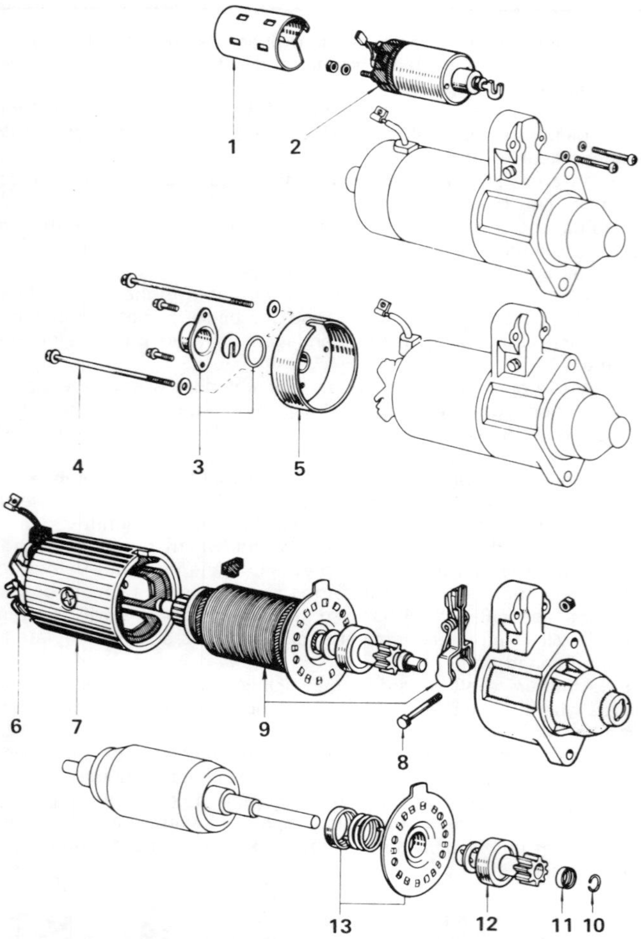

Fig. 10.38 Conventional starter motor components (Sec 13)

1 Insulator
2 Magnetic switch (solenoid)
3 Bearing cover & lock plate
4 Bolt
5 Commutator end frame
6 Brush holder
7 Yoke
8 Drive lever bolt
9 Armature & drive lever
10 Snap ring
11 Stop collar
12 Clutch with pinion gear
13 Center bearing

Fig. 10.39 Drift the stop collar towards the pinion far enough to allow circlip removal – conventional type starter (Sec 13)

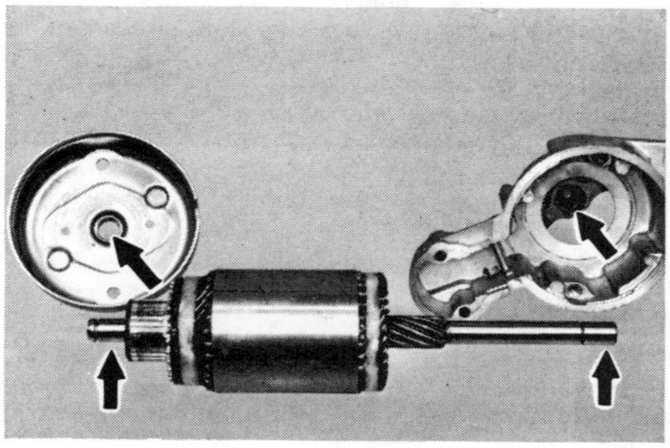

Fig. 10.40 Check the bearing surfaces for wear – conventional type starter (Sec 13)

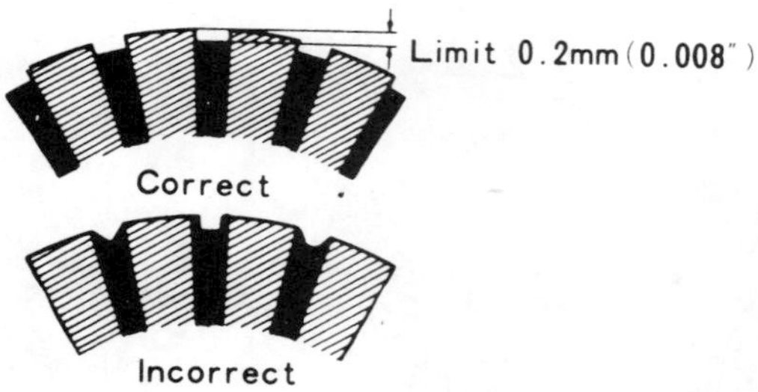

Fig. 10.41 Starter commutator mica segment undercutting diagram – conventional type starter (Sec 13)

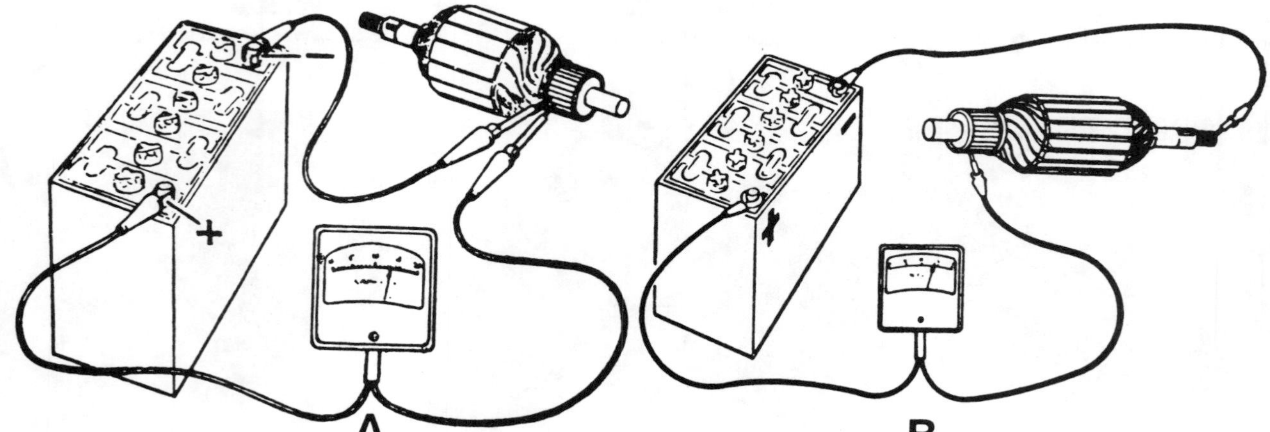

Fig. 10.42 Testing the starter motor armature (A) for open circuit and (B) for breakdown of wiring insulation – conventional type starter (Sec 13)

16 To test the armature is not difficult but a voltmeter or bulb and 12 volt battery are required. The two tests determine whether there may be a break in any circuit winding or if any wiring insulation is broken down. The illustration shows how the battery, voltmeter and probe connectors are used to test whether (a) any wire in the windings is broken or (b) whether there is an insulation breakdown. In the first test the probes are placed on adjacent segments of clean commutator. All voltmeter readings should be similar. If a bulb is used instead it will glow very dimly or not at all if there is a fault. For the second test any reading or bulb lighting indicates a fault. Test each segment in turn with one probe and keep the other on the shaft. Should either test indicate a faulty armature the wisest action in the long run is to obtain a new starter. The field coils may be tested if an ohmmeter or ammeter can be obtained. With an ohmmeter the resistance (measured between the terminal and the yoke) should be 6 ohms. With an ammeter, connect it in series with a 12 volt battery again from the field terminal to the yoke. A reading of 12 amps, is normal. Zero amps or infinity ohms indicate an open circuit. More than 2 amps or less than 6 ohms indicates a breakdown of the insulation. If a fault in the field coils is diagnosed than a reconditioned starter should be obtained as the coils can only be removed and refitted with special equipment.,

17 Check the insulation of the brush holders and the length of the brushes. If these have worn to below the specified limit, renew them. Before fitting them to their holders, dress them to the correct contour by wrapping a piece of emery cloth round the commutator and rotating the commutator back and forth (photo).

18 Check the starter clutch assembly for wear or sticky action, or chipped pinion teeth and renew the assembly if necessary.

19 Check the centre bearing for excessive wear or damage and renew if necesary (Fig. 10.44).

20 Check the solenoid (magnetic switch) by pushing the plunger as shown. When released the plunger should instantly return to its original position (Fig. 10.45).

21 Commence reassembly by refitting the centre bearing, clutch unit and new pinion stop collar and snap ring. With the snap ring engaged in its groove use a drift and tap the stop collar into position over the snap ring.

22 Locate the drive engagement lever to the armature shaft as shown in Fig. 10.46 with the spring towards the armature and the steel washer up against the clutch.

13.17 Check the brushes for wear

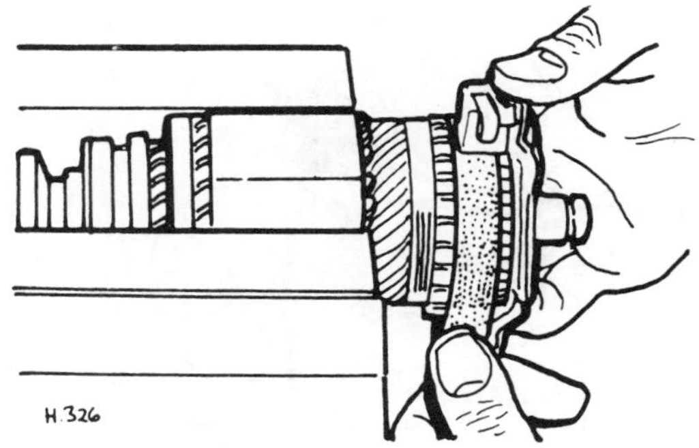

Fig. 10.43 Dressing starter motor brushes to correct shape – conventional type starter (Sec 13)

Fig. 10.44 Check centre bearings for wear – conventional type starter (Sec 13)

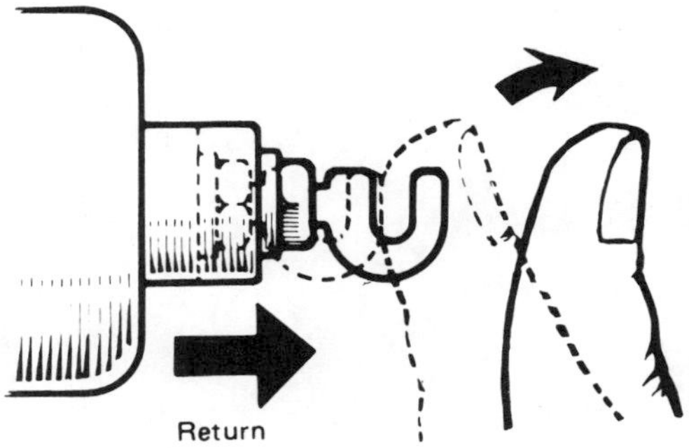

Fig. 10.45 Check that solenoid plunger returns after compression – conventional type starter (Sec 13)

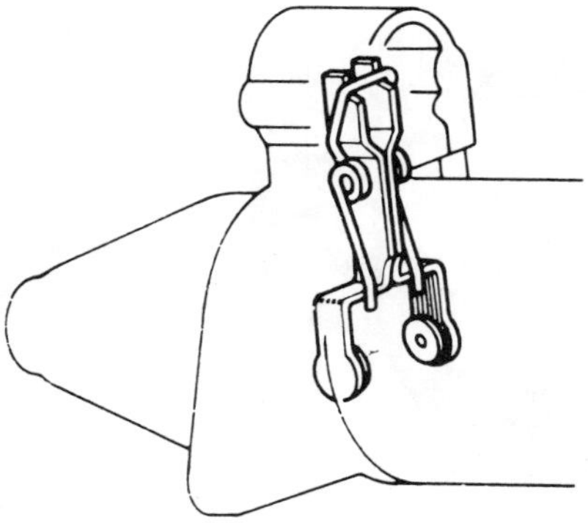

Fig. 10.46 Drive engagement lever fitted position – conventional type starter (Sec 13)

23 Apply grease to all sliding surfaces and locate the armature assembly in the drive end frame. Insert the drive engagement lever pivot pin, well greased (photo).
24 Fit the rubber buffer aligning the yoke notch with the rubber plate tab. Then align and offer into position the yoke to the drive end frame.
25 Fit the brush holder to the armature and then insert the brushes.
26 Grease the commutator end frame bearing and then fit the end frame into position. Insert and tighten the two tie bolts.
27 Fit the washer, spring and lockplate and then measure the thrust clearance of the armature. If the endfloat exceeds 0.03 in (0.8 mm) an additional thrust washer must be fitted. Half pack the end cover with a multi-purpose grease and refit it securing with the two screws.
28 Install the solenoid switch making sure that its hook engages under the spring of the engagement lever fork.
29 Set up a test circuit similar to the one shown.
30 To check the pinion clearance move the pinion towards the armature to take up any slack and measure the pinion end to stop collar clearance. If the clearance is not as specified, remove the solenoid switch and adjust the length of the switch mounting surface to stud end to give a stud length of 1.3 in (34 mm) (photo).

13.23 Refit the armature into the drive end frame

13.30 Measure the pinion end to stop collar clearance

Fig. 10.47 Locate holder as shown – conventional type starter (Sec 13)

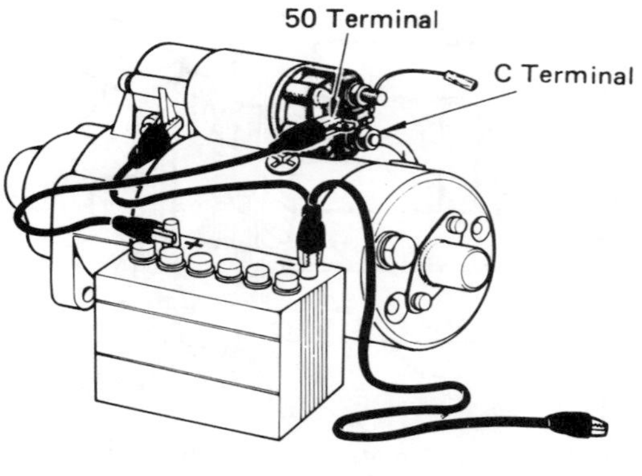

Fig. 10.48 Connect as shown for testing – conventional type starter (Sec 13)

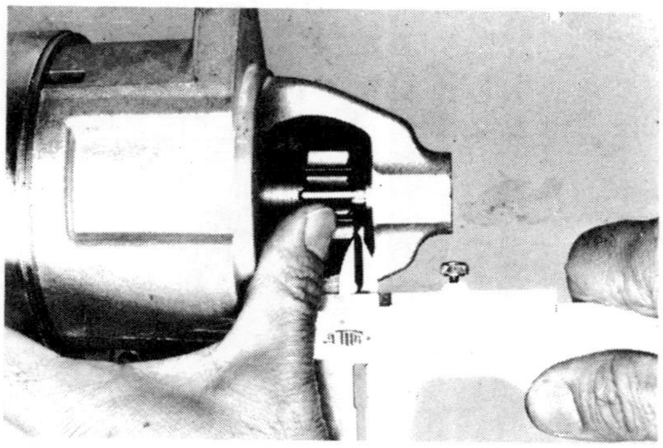

Fig. 10.49 Check the pinion end to stop collar clearance – conventional type starter (Sec 13)

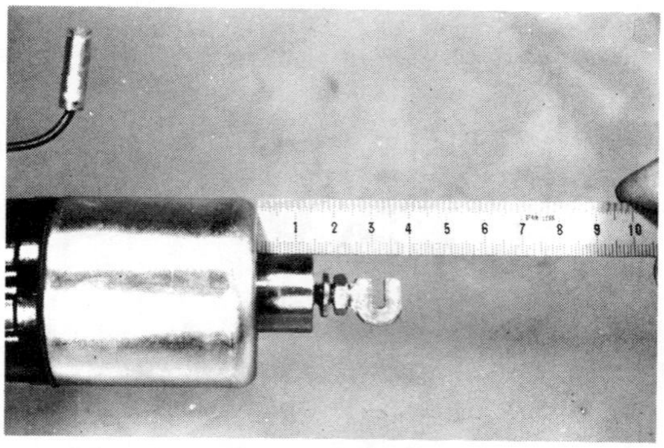

Fig. 10.50 Check switch mounting surface to stud end and adjust if necessary by screwing stud in or out – conventional type starter (Sec 13)

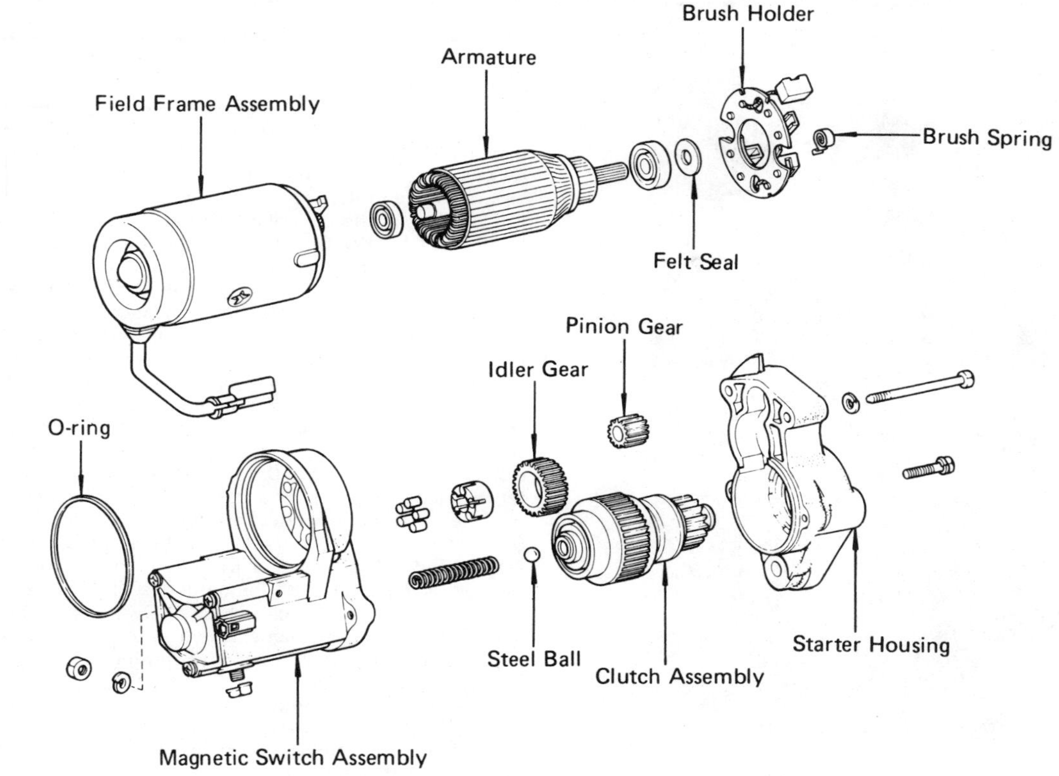

Fig. 10.51 Reduction starter motor components – 1.4 kW type (Sec 14)

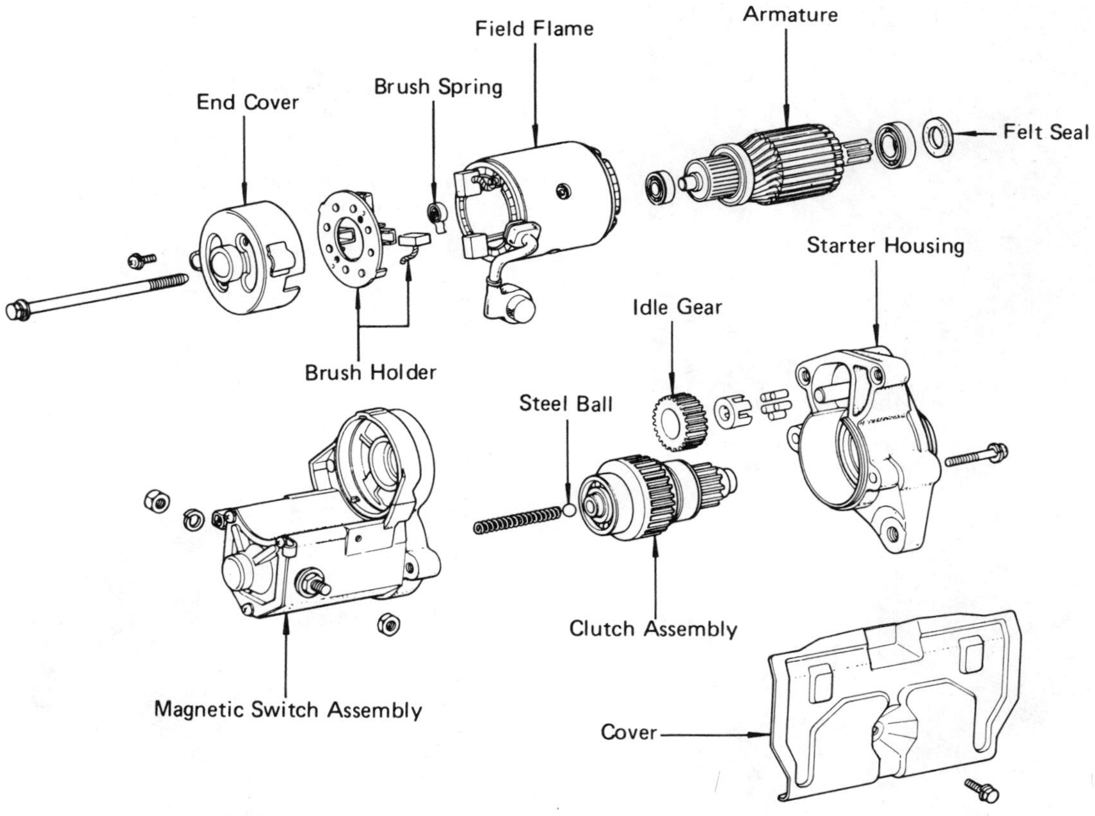

Fig. 10.52 Reduction starter motor components – 1.0 kW type (Sec 14)

Fig. 10.53 Separating the starter housing assembly – 1.4 kW reduction gear type (Sec 14)

Fig. 10.54 Separating the starter housing assembly – 1.0 kW reduction gear type (Sec 14)

Fig. 10.55 Hook back springs and withdraw brushes – reduction gear type (Sec 14)

14 Starter motor (reduction gear type) – dismantling, overhaul and reassembly

1 One of two types of reduction starter motor may be fitted, the main components of each being shown in Figs. 10.51 and 10.52. The two types are similar in design, but where differences occur they will be mentioned in the following operations.
2 Disconnect the main lead wire at the solenoid switch.
3 On the 1.4 kW type, unscrew the through bolts and separate the starter housing complete with the reduction gears and clutch.
4 On the 1.0 kW type, unscrew the through bolts and separate the starter housing complete with idler gear and clutch.
5 Withdraw the felt seal from the bearing and on the 1.4 kW type remove the O-ring from the clutch holder periphery.
6 Unscrew and remove the setscrew and separate the housing from the clutch/reduction gear(s) assembly. Collect the ball and return spring, the ball being located in the clutch shaft bore.
7 Hook back the brush springs and extract the brushes from their respective holders (Fig. 10.55). On the 1.0 kW type you will have to remove the end cover for access to the brushes.
8 The armature can now be removed from the field frame.
9 Clean the components and lay them out for inspection.
10 In general, the inspection procedures closely follow those given for the non reduction type starter motor described in the previous Section, paragraphs 10 to 17 inclusive, but refer to the reduction gear type starter motor specifications where applicable. The following items should also be checked when checking the 1.4 and 1.0 kW reduction starter motors.
11 Check the reduction gears for signs of excessive wear or damage. Also check the roller bearings and cage. Renew as necessary.
12 Before reassembling, ensure that all components are clean. During reassembly lubricate those items indicated in Fig. 10.58 with a high temperature grease. Do not get grease onto any other components.
13 To reassemble, insert the armature into the field frame and then locate the brush holder so that its tab aligns with the field frame notch. Hook back the brush springs and slide the brushes into their holders, then check that the positive leads are not earthed (grounded).
14 On the 1.4 kW type locate a new O-ring over the brush holder, then refit the end cover.
15 Relocate the field washer, smeared with grease, against the bearing on the armature shaft.
16 Refit the armature/field frame unit to the solenoid switch housing assembly. On the 1.4 kW type assemble so that the bolt anchors align with the mark on the solenoid switch housing as shown (Fig. 10.60). On the 1.0 kW type align the yoke core and housing notches (Fig. 10.61).
17 Lubricate the ball bearing with grease and insert it into the clutch shaft bore followed by the spring, then reassemble the idler gear/reduction gear unit (Fig. 10.62).
18 Reconnect the solenoid switch wire.
19 Before refitting to the car you will find it beneficial to test the motor for satisfactory operation. To do this mount it securely in a vice

Fig. 10.56 Check pinion teeth for excessive wear – reduction gear type (Sec 14)

Fig. 10.57 Check reduction gears and bearings for excessive wear – reduction gear type (Sec 14)

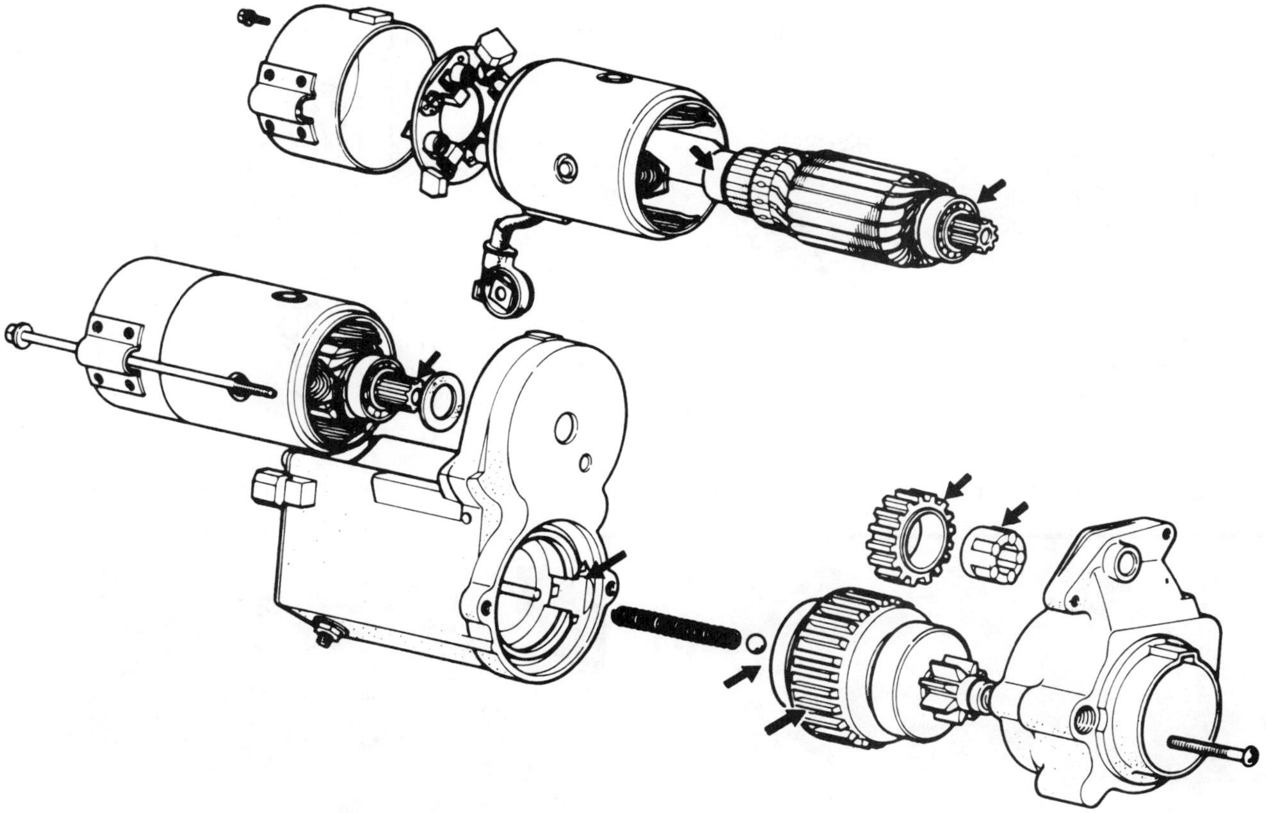

Fig. 10.58 Lubricate items indicated by arrows with a high temperature grease – reduction gear type (Sec 14)

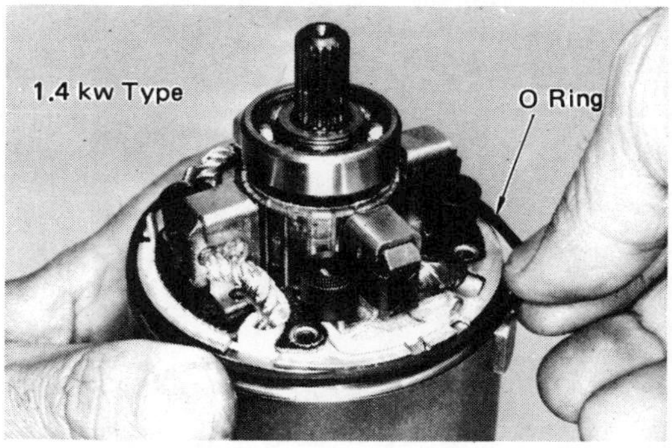

Fig. 10.59 Locate the O-ring – 1.4 kW reduction gear type (Sec 14)

Fig. 10.60 Align the bolt anchors with mark on housing – 1.4 kW reduction gear type (Sec 14)

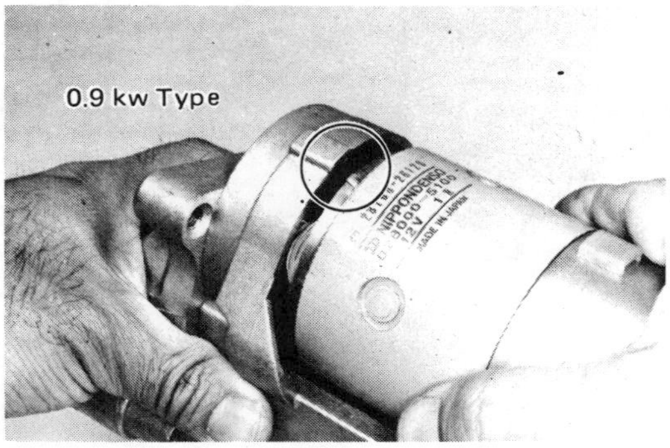

Fig. 10.61 Align yoke and housing marks as shown – 1.0 kW reduction gear type (Sec 14)

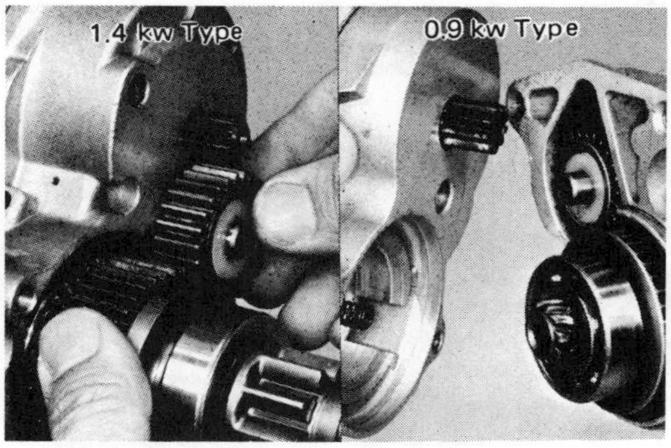

Fig. 10.62 Assemble the idler and reduction gear units accordingly – reduction gear type (Sec 14)

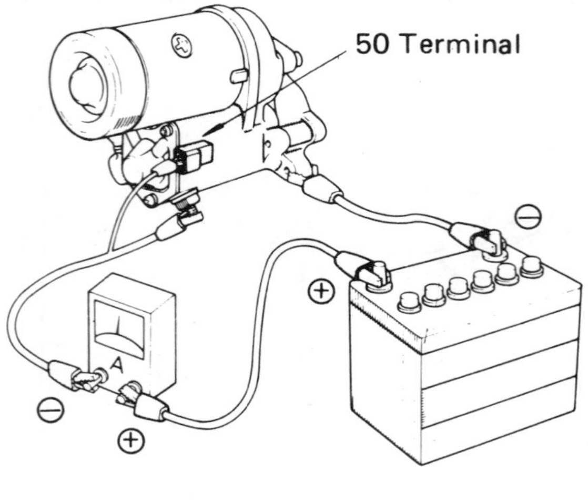

Fig. 10.63 Starter motor test connections (Sec 14)

Fig. 10.64 The fuse panel in the driver's side kick panel (Sec 15)

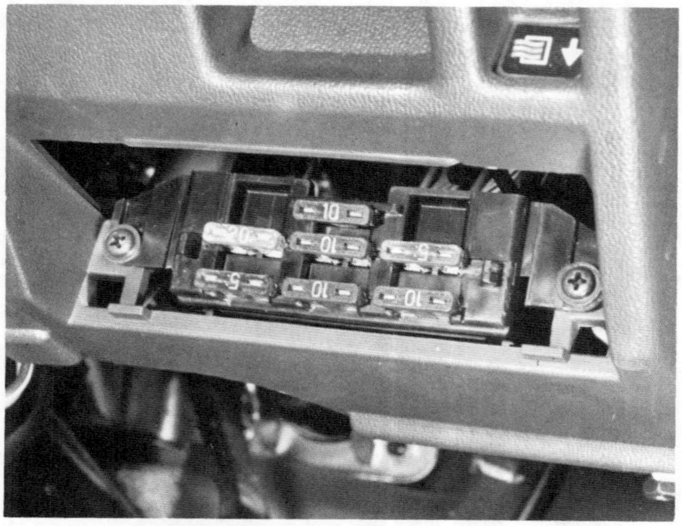

15.1 Remove panel cover for access to fuses

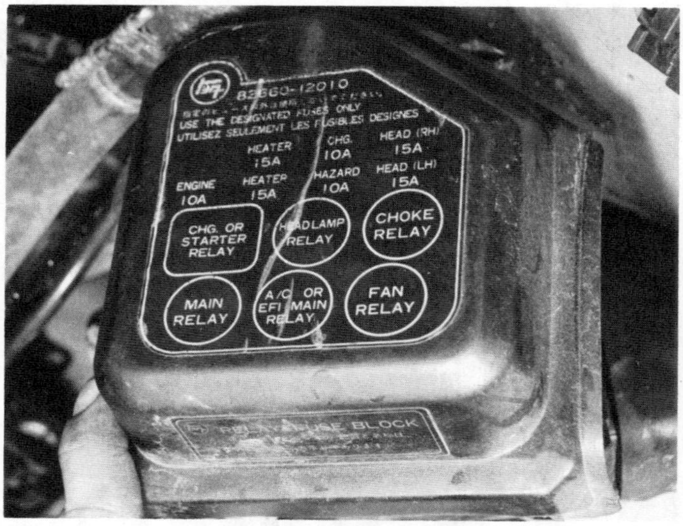

15.5a The engine compartment fuse/relay block (shown inverted for identification) – Liftback model

15.5b Engine compartment fuses and relays shown with cover removed on the Liftback model

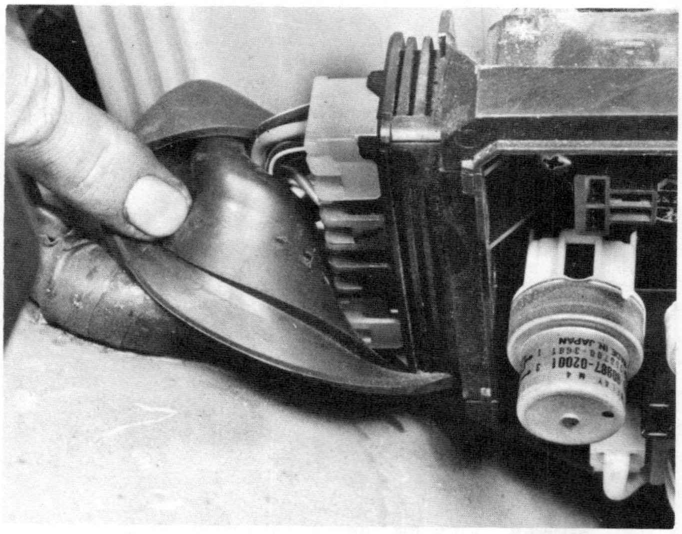

15.5c Prise free rubber boot for access to engine compartment fuse/relay block side wiring connections

and connect it up to a battery and ammeter as shown in Fig. 10.63, with the ammeter negative wire connected to the 30 terminal and the positive to the 50 terminal as indicated (arrow). The starter should rotate smoothly, the pinion disengage and a maximum of 180 amps be drawn.

15 Fuses and fusible link

1 The main fuse block is located under the instrument panel. The fuse ratings and circuits protected vary acccording to model, but the fuse block is clearly marked (photo).
2 A fuse 'pull out' removal tool is located on the inner face of the fusebox lid.
3 In the event of a fuse blowing, always find the reason and rectify the trouble before fitting the new one. Always renew a fuse with one of the same amperage rating as the original. For this reason it is a good idea to carry a spare set of fuses in the car at all times. A spare 7.5 or 10.5 amp fuse is supplied as standard with all models.
4 In addition to the main fuse block, you will also find additional blocks in the engine compartment and in the driver's side-kick panel. Again in both cases the respective fuse positions are marked on the lids.
5 A double protection is provided for the electrical harness by fusible links installed in the lead running from the battery positive terminal. The fusible links must never be by-passed and should either melt, the cause of the circuit overload must be established before renewing the link with one of similar type and rating (photos).

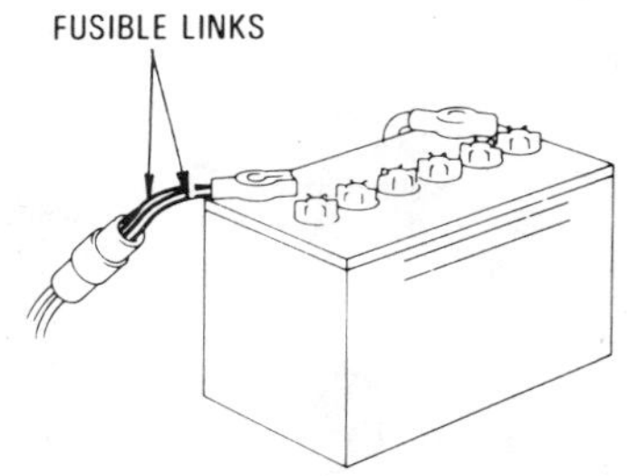

Fig. 10.65 The fusible link locations (Sec 15)

16 Relays

1 The number of relays fitted to individual vehicles depends upon the equipment and the operating territory.
2 Examples of relay locations are shown and they may be positioned under the instrument panel or within the engine compartment (Figs. 10.67, 10.68, 10.69 & 10.70).
3 In the event of failure of an electrical component, first check the fuse and then the bulb (where applicable).
4 Check the security of all connecting wires and terminals.
5 If all these are in order then the relay is probably faulty and as they are all sealed units, it must be renewed as a unit.

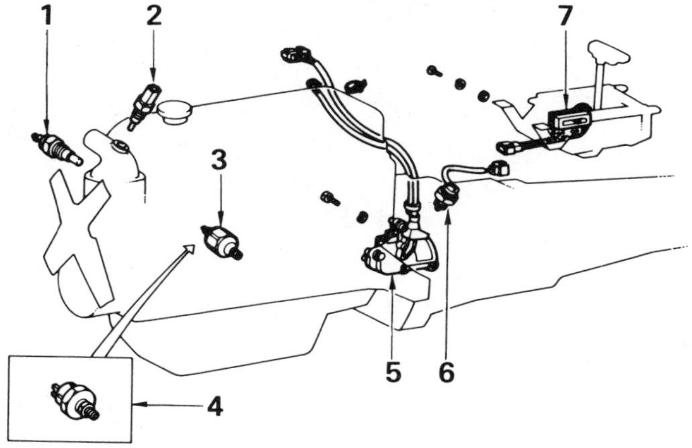

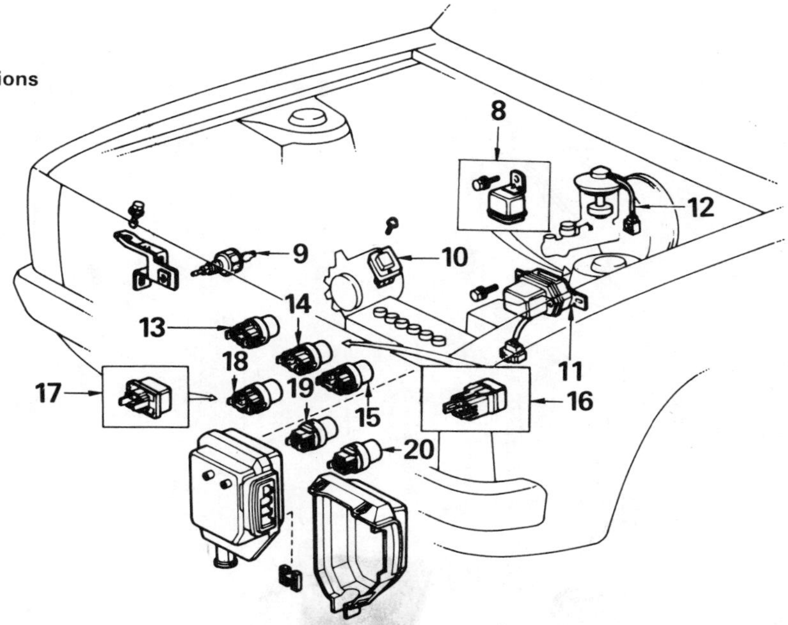

Fig. 10.66 Engine compartment switch and relay positions (Sec 16)

1 *Water temperature detect switch*
2 *Water temperature sender gauge*
3 *Oil pressure switch*
4 *Oil pressure sender gauge*
5 *Neutral start switch (A-40 type transmission)*
6 *Back-up light switch*
7 *Neutral start switch (A-20 type transmission)*
8 *Headlight dimmer relay (for W. Germany only)*
9 *Vacuum switch*
10 *Charging I.C. regulator (for Canada only)*
11 *Charging regulator (except Canada)*
12 *Brake fluid level warning switch*
13 *Main relay*
14 *Air conditioner relay (USA optional)*
15 *Cooling fan relay*
16 *Headlight fuse holder (for W. Germany only)*
17 *Starter relay*
18 *Charging light relay*
19 *Headlight relay (except W. Germany)*
20 *Choke relay (except Canada & Frigid Zone USA)*

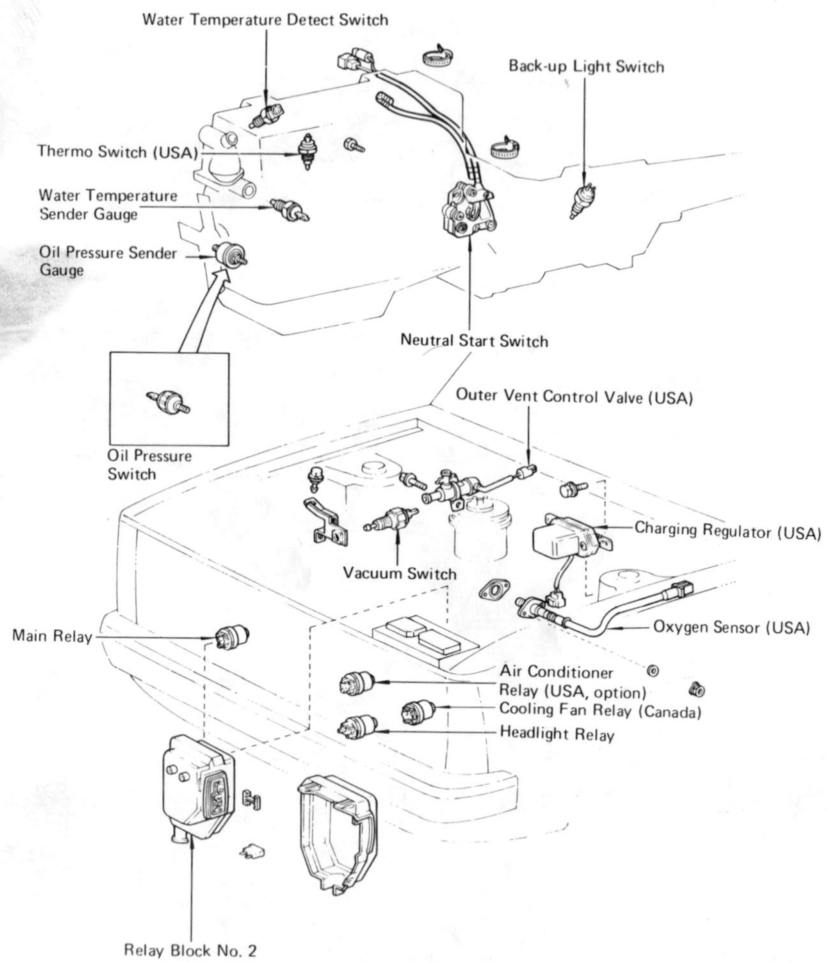

Fig. 10.67 Engine compartment switch and relay positions – USA/Canada models for 1981/82 (Sec 16)

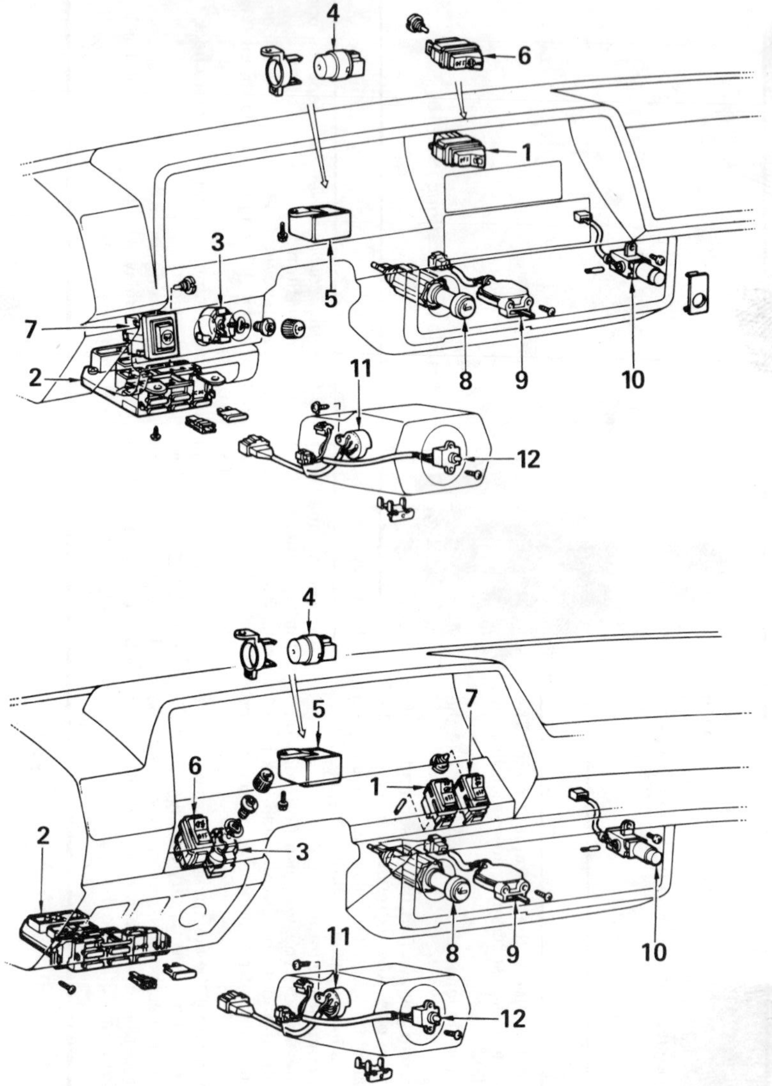

Fig. 10.68 Switches and relay locations in interior of vehicle – Saloon and Estate (top) Coupe and Liftback (bottom) (Sec 16)

1 *Defogger switch*
2 *Fuse block*
3 *Light control rheostat*
4 *Hazard relay (for W. Germany & France only)*
5 *Seat belt warning relay & buzzer (for USA and Canada models)*
6 *Rear fog light switch (UK models)*
7 *Rear wiper switch*
8 *Cigarette lighter*
9 *Heater blower switch*
10 *Air conditioner switch*
11 *Ignition switch*
12 *Unlock warning switch*

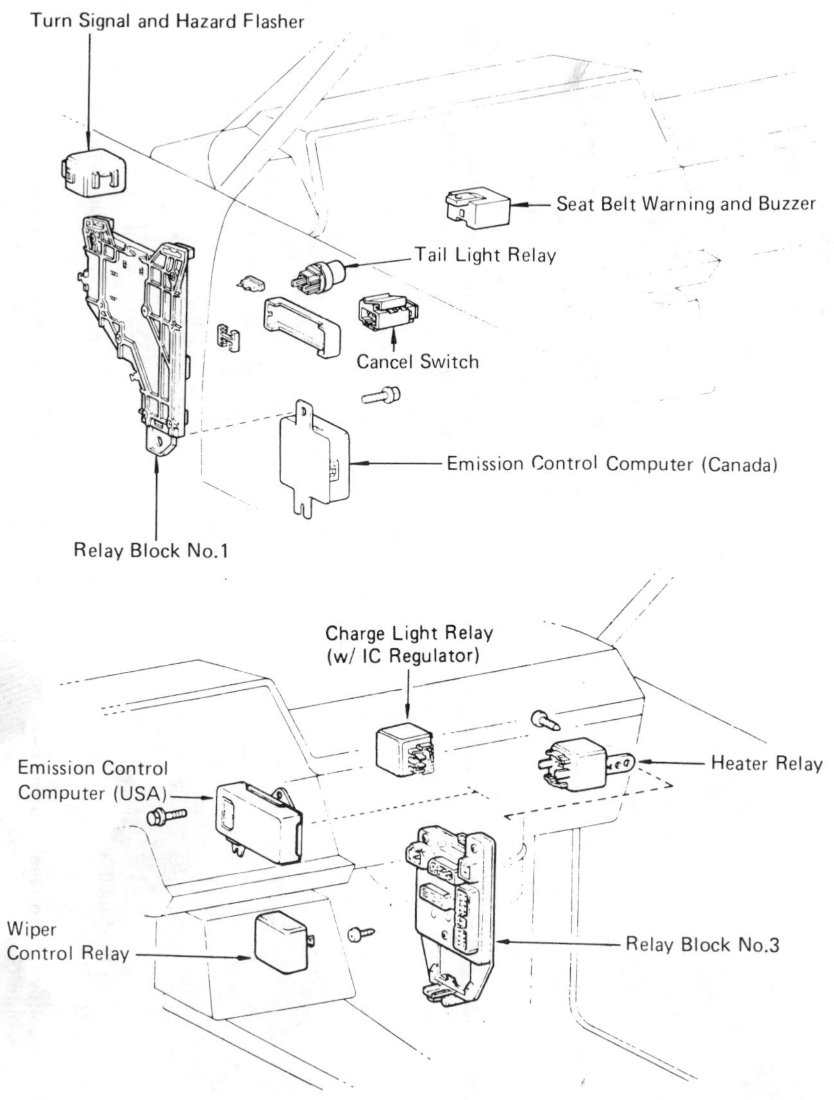

Fig. 10.69 Switch and relay positions (interior) – USA and Canada 1981/82 models (Sec 16)

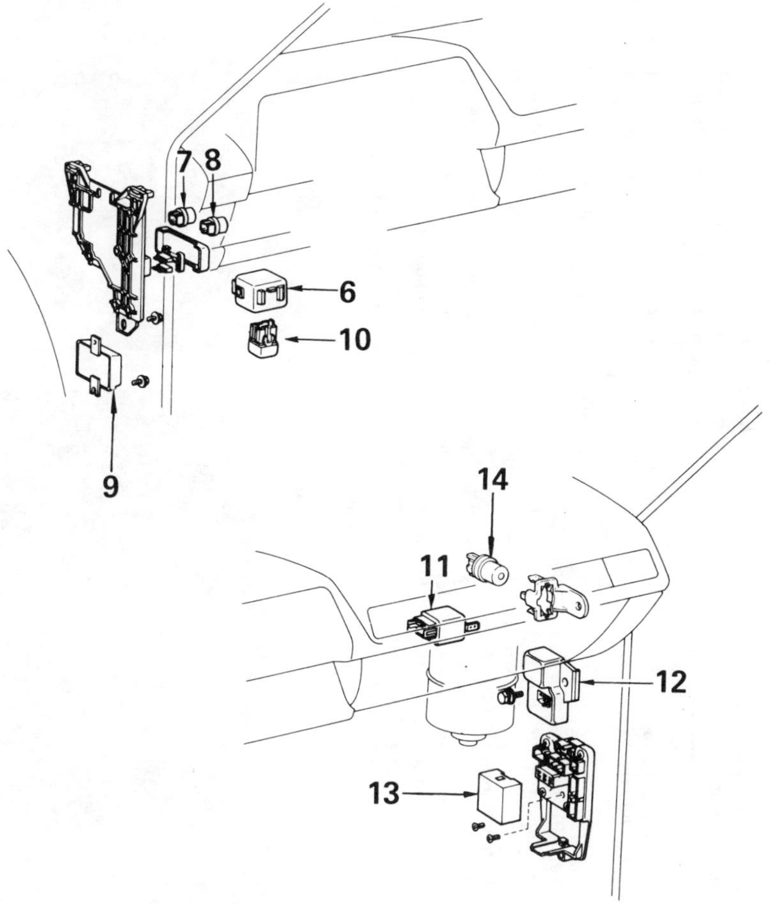

Fig. 10.70 Switch and relay positions (interior) (Sec 16)

6 *Turn signal & hazard flasher*
7 *Rear fog light relay (UK models) or bulb check relay (Australia)*
8 *Tail light relay*
9 *Emission control computer*
10 *Tail light fuse holder (W. Germany)*
11 *Heater relay*
12 *Headlight cleaner relay (ECE & Sweden: optional)*
13 *Wiper control relay*
14 *Choke relay (Canada & Frigid Zone USA)*

17 Headlight sealed beam units and bulbs – renewal

The headlights fitted will be of sealed beam or semi-sealed beam type (with removable bulb), according to model and operating territory. For access on either type, raise and support the bonnet.

Sealed beam unit

1 Remove the front sidelight unit (Section 19), then remove the headlight surround panel by levering and twisting free the retaining clips (Fig. 10.71).

2 Now unscrew and remove the four headlight unit retaining screws, withdraw the unit and detach the wiring connector.

3 Refit in the reverse order to removal ensuring that the protrusion on the glass face is at the top (Fig. 10.72). Make sure that the wiring connection is secure. The headlight aim adjusting screws should not be touched during this operation. On reassembly check the headlights for satisfactory operation and adjustment.

Semi-sealed beam unit

4 Access to the bulb(s) can be made by reaching down behind the unit from the engine compartment, but the battery will have to be removed on the left-hand side.

5 First compress and release the wiring connector. Withdraw the protector rubber, then unclip the bulb retaining spring. The bulb can then be withdrawn (photos).

6 If the headlight unit is to be removed, proceed as described for the sealed beam unit.

7 Do not handle the bulb with fingers if it is of halogen type. If you do then the glass must be cleaned with methylated spirit and a clean rag.

8 Refit in the reverse order of removal. Align the bulb according to type when refitting as shown in Figs. 10.73 and 10.74. When refitting the rubber protector boot ensure that the TOP marking is fitted uppermost. Make sure that the wiring connection is secure.

9 On completion check the headlight for satisfactory operation and adjustment.

17.5a Remove rubber protector boot from back of bulbholder (semi-sealed beam unit)

17.5b Turn bulb holder anti-clockwise ...

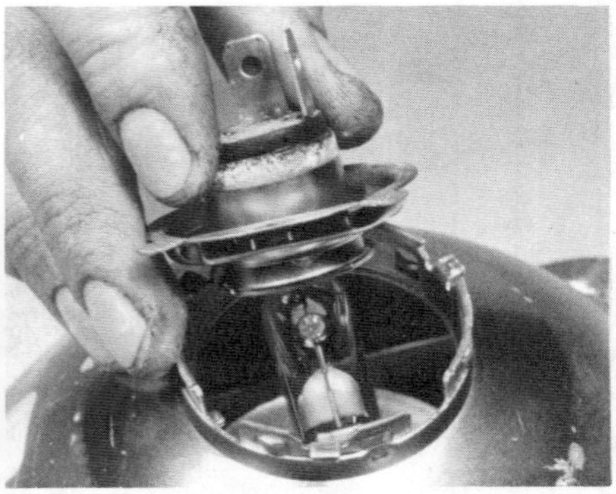

17.5c ... and withdraw the holder and bulb (Halogen type shown)

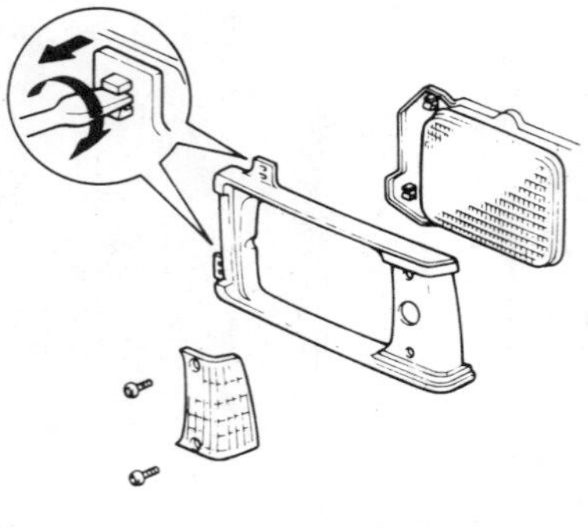

Fig. 10.71 Headlight surround and retaining clips (inset) (Sec 17)

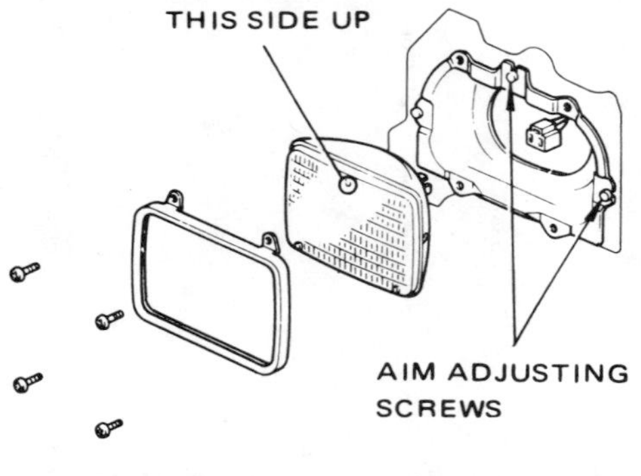

Fig. 10.72 Headlight unit orientation and beam adjustment screw positions (sealed beam) (Sec 17)

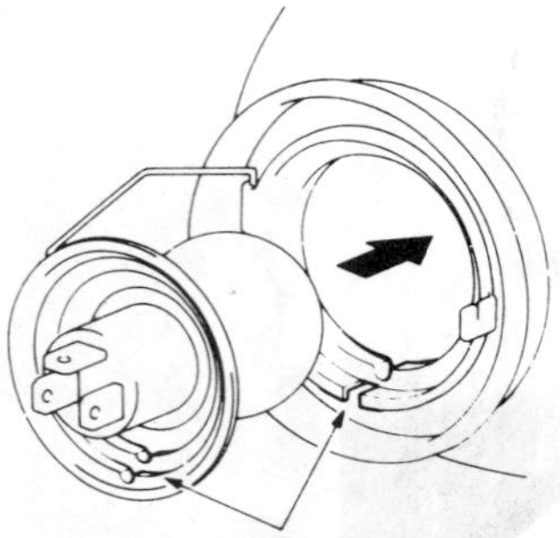

Fig. 10.73 Align bulb as shown (semi-sealed beam) – standard bulb (Sec 17)

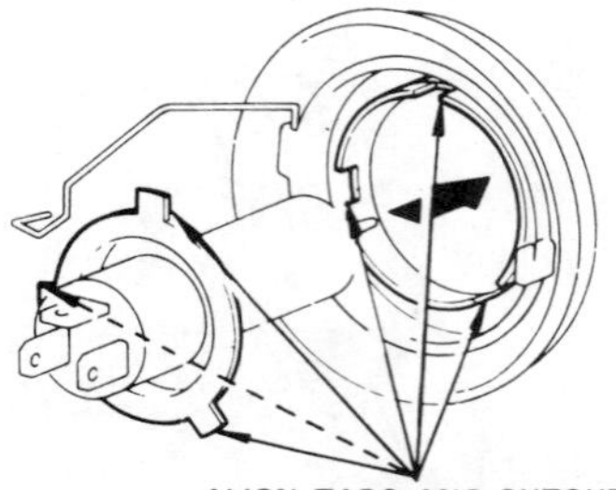

Fig. 10.74 Align bulb as shown (semi-sealed beam) – Halogen bulb (Sec 17)

18 Headlight beam – adjustment

1 Headlight beam adjustment is made by means of the arrowed screws shown in Fig. 10.72. However in view of the variation in regulations in different operating territories, specific adjustment details cannot be provided.
2 A temporary adjustment can be made by turning the screws as necessary, top screw for vertical adjustment, side screw for horizontal adjustment. A more accurate beam alignment check must be made at the earliest opportunity by your local garage or Toyota dealer using optical alignment equipment.
3 Later models with rectangular semi-sealed headlights have adjuster screws at the top of the headlight units which are accessible when the bonnet is raised.

19 Light bulbs – renewal

1 Access to most bulbs is obtained simply by extracting the lens securing screws and removing the lens (photos).
2 Bulbs for most lights are of bayonet fixing type or wedge type and they should always be renewed with ones of similar type.
3 On Coupe and Liftback versions, the rear light bulbs are accessible from within the luggage boot or luggage compartment (photos). On these models detach and remove the rear interior panel then withdraw

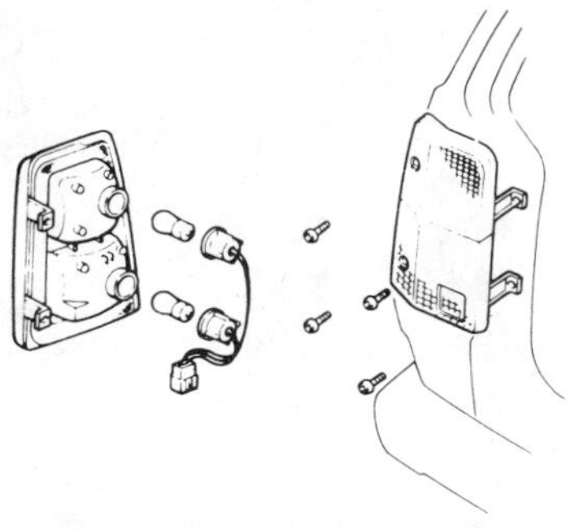

Fig. 10.75 Rear indicator/tail/stop light assembly – Estate (Sec 19)

the bulb and holder from the back of the light (photo).
4 For removal of the licence plate light refer to photos 19.4a, b and c.
5 Fog light bulb removal is shown in photo 19.5 (where fitted).
6 The interior light bulb is of festoon type and can be reached by pinching the sides of the lens inwards and withdrawing it. On Liftback versions, the luggage compartment light lens is held by two screws (photos).

19.1a Removing lens on front indicator for ...

19.1b ... bulb removal

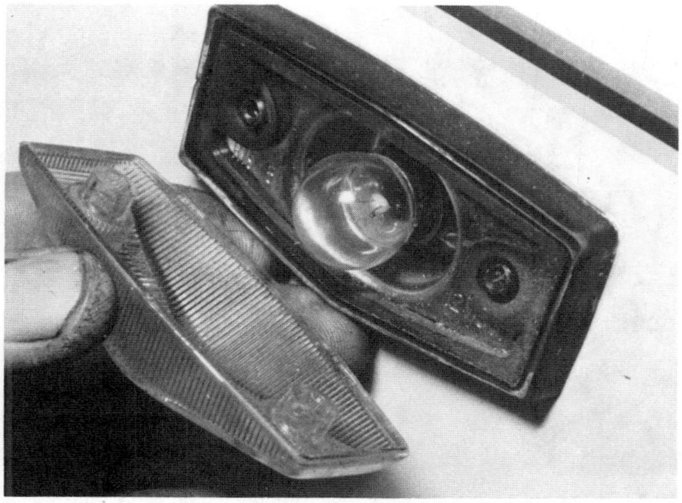

19.1c Side marker light lens removed for bulb renewal

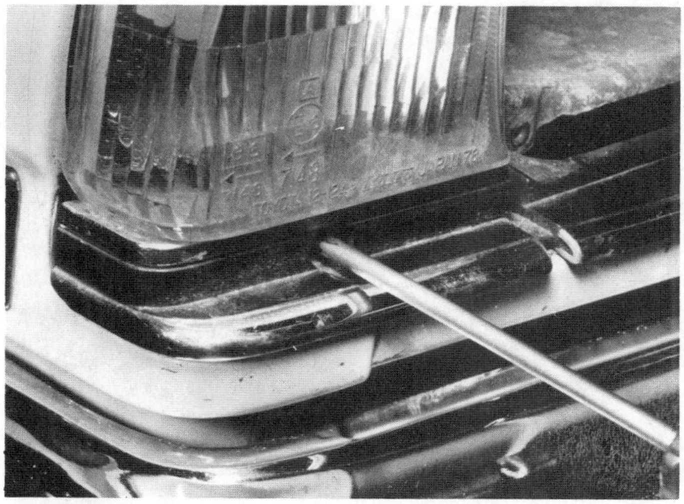

19.1d Front side light: remove unit screws ...

19.1e ... withdraw unit ...

19.1f ... and remove bulb and holder from rear

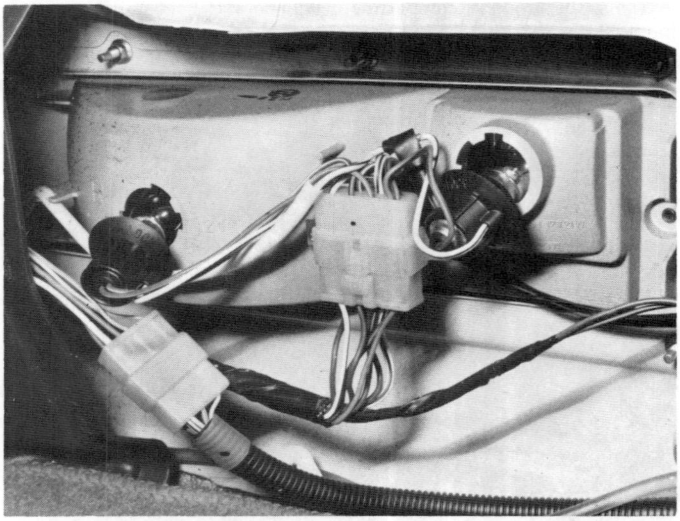

19.3 Rear combination light bulbs and holders on Coupe and Liftback models are removed from within luggage compartment

19.4a Rear licence plate removal from bumper: remove lens cover ...

19.4b ... lift lens away for access to bulb

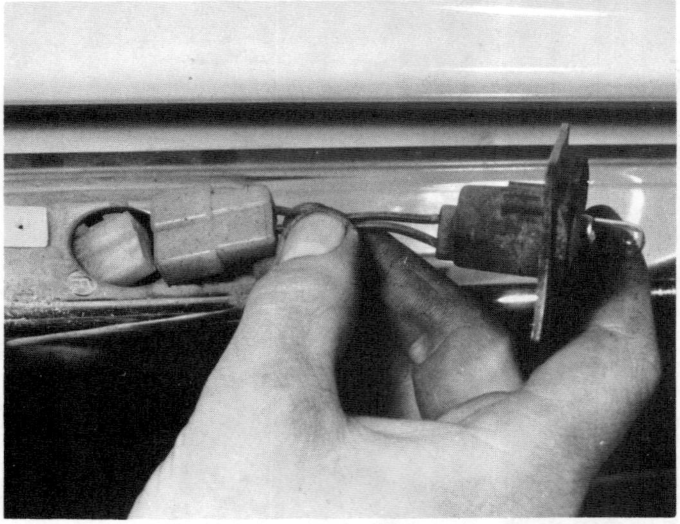

19.4c To remove bulb and holder, pull through and detach wiring connector

19.5 Foglight: remove lens and extract bulb

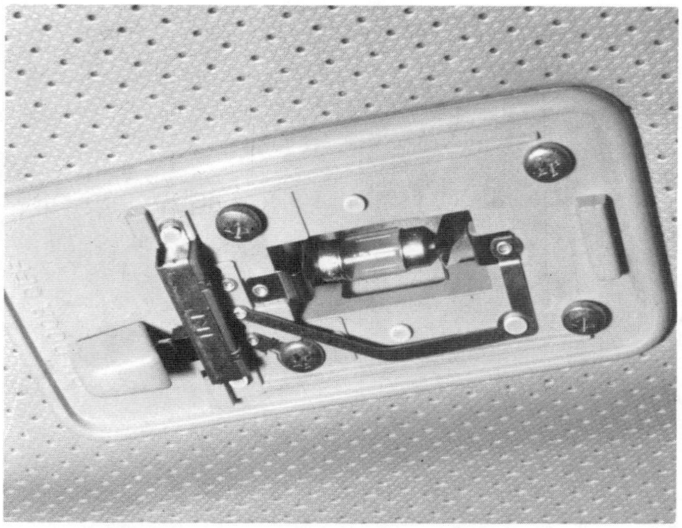

19.6a Interior roof light showing festoon bulb (lens removed)

19.6b Luggage compartment light: remove lens ...

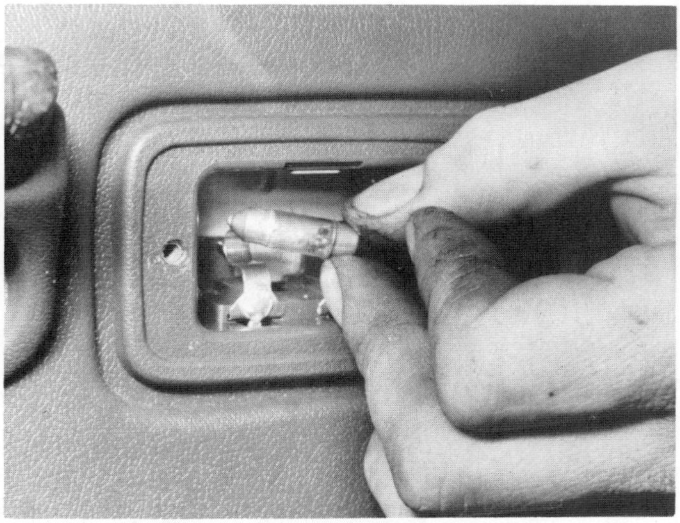

19.6c ... and withdraw festoon bulb (Liftback shown)

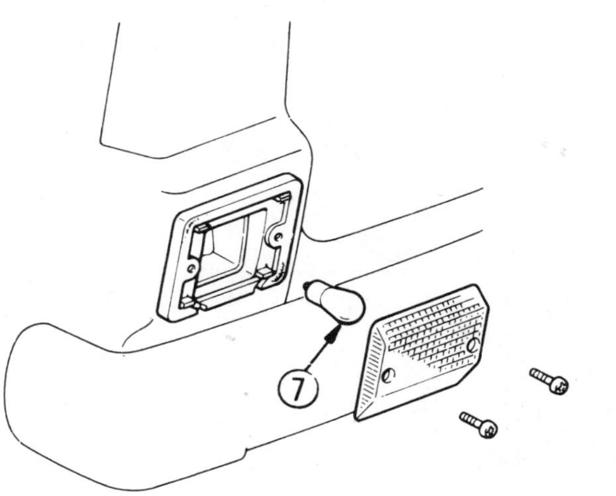

Fig. 10.76 Reverse (back-up) light assembly – Estate (Sec 19)

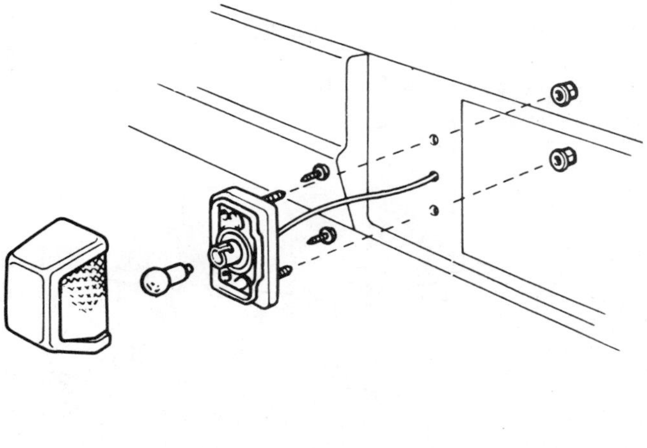

Fig. 10.77 License plate light assembly – Saloon, Coupe and Liftback models fitted with Urethane bumper (Sec 19)

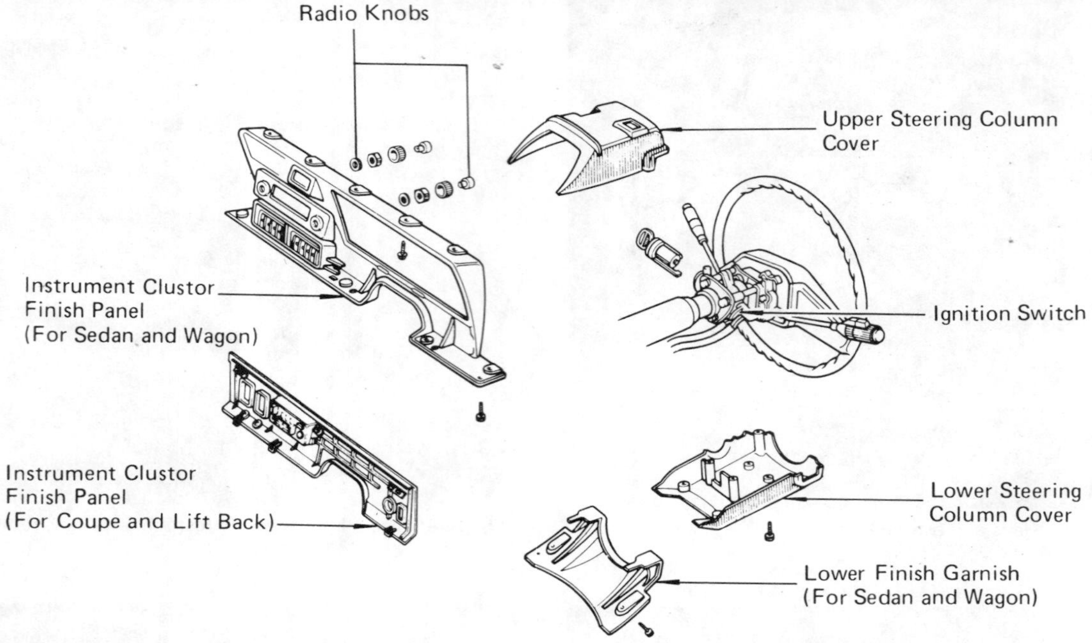

Fig. 10.78 Remove items shown according to model – left-hand drive shown (Sec 20)

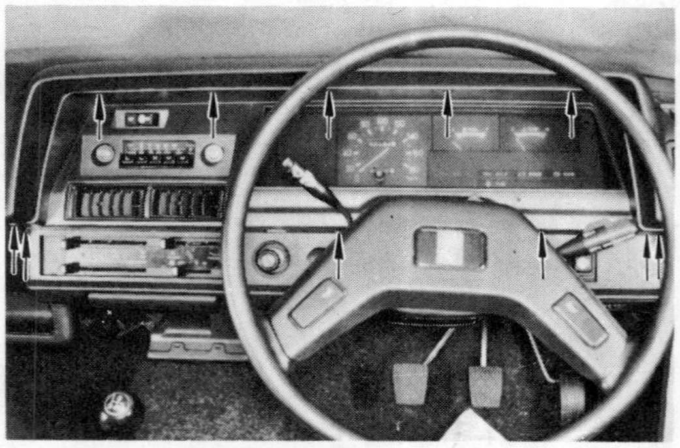

Fig. 10.79 Instrument panel facia screw locations (Saloon and Estate) (Sec 20)

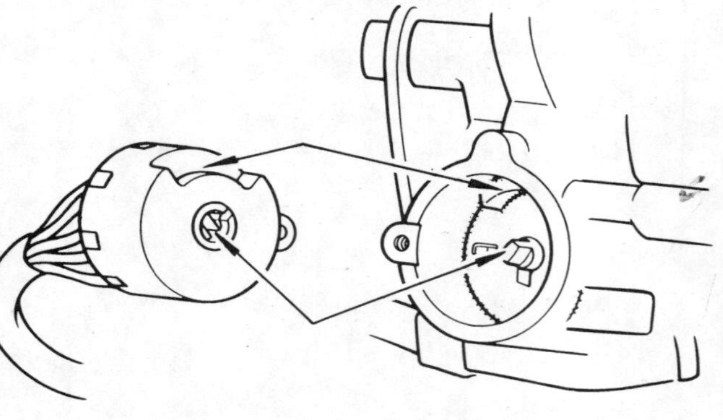

Fig. 10.80 Align ignition with recess and bracket tab as indicated when reassembling (Sec 20)

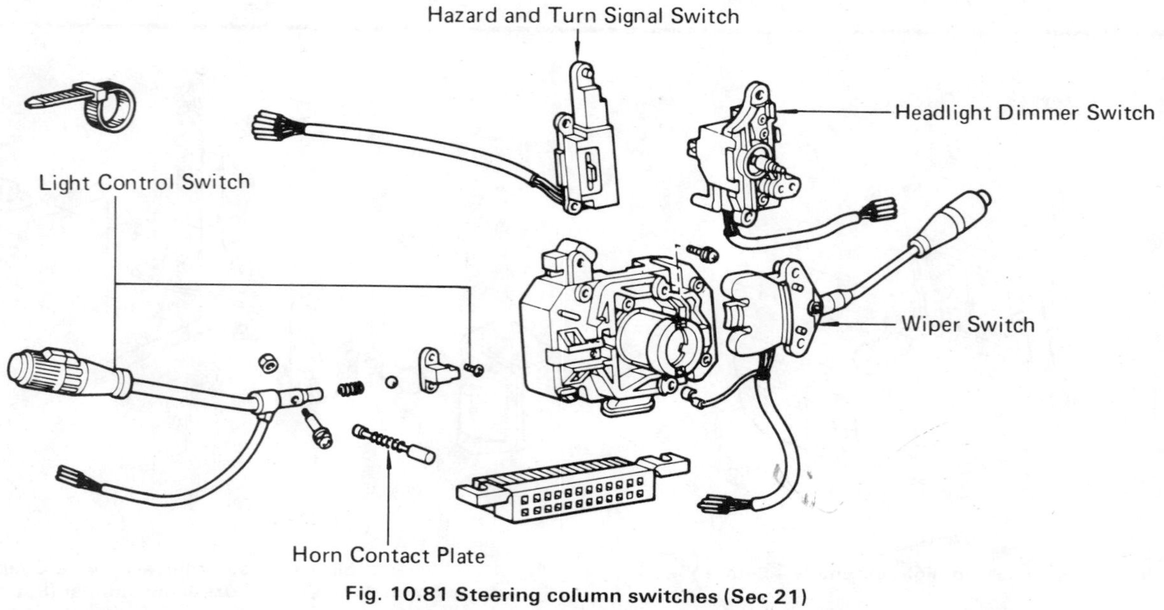

Fig. 10.81 Steering column switches (Sec 21)

7 Indicator and warning light bulbs can be renewed if the instrument panel is withdrawn as described in Section 29. The bulbholders are twisted out of the rear of the panel and the capless bulbs removed.

20 Ignition switch and lock cylinder – removal and refitting

1 Disconnect the battery earth lead.
2 Remove the instrument panel cluster facia. On the Coupe and Liftback models this panel is clipped into position and is detached by pulling the upper edge outwards (Fig. 10.78).
3 On other models you will have to pull free the radio control knobs and unscrew the radio retaining nuts from the control shafts. Now remove the eleven screws securing the panel in position, the locations of the various screws being shown in Fig. 10.79. With all the screws removed, insert the blade of a screwdriver between the safety pad and the facia panel and lever it free along its top edge.
4 On Saloon and Estate models remove the retaining screws and detach the lower finish panel.
5 Remove the steering column covers.
6 Turn the ignition key to the ALL position, then holding down the securing pin with a suitable piece of stiff wire withdraw the cylinder by pulling on the key.
7 Disconnect the wiring harness plug from its position near the switch.
8 Unscrew and remove the ignition switch securing screw and withdraw the switch (photo).
9 Refitting is a reversal of removal, but on completion check the operation of the various column switches and lock cylinder.

21 Steering column switches – removal and refitting

1 Disconnect the battery earth (ground) lead.
2 Prise free and remove the centre pad from the steering wheel and unscrew the steering wheel retaining nut. Mark the relative positions of the shaft and wheel, then pull the wheel free. It should withdraw from the shaft using arm pressure (photo).
3 Remove the instrument panel cluster facia as described in the previous Section in paragraphs 2 or 3 as applicable.
4 Remove the retaining screws and detach the lower finish panel (Saloon and Estate only), and the lower steering column cover (all models) (photo).
5 Remove the upper column cover (photo).
6 Detach the respective lead wires from the column switches at the multi-connector, then the four switch to column fastenings and withdraw the switch from the column (photo).
7 The light switch stalk can be removed from the main switch by removing the retaining screws and clamps, but take care not to lose the spring and ball as the stalk is removed.
8 The dimmer, wiper and indicator switches can all be removed as required from the switch unit being located by screws (Fig. 10.81).
9 Refitting is a reversal of the removal procedure. Tighten the steering wheel nut to the specified torque setting. On completion check the various switch functions for satisfactory operation.

22 Horns – removal and refitting

1 If a horn works badly or fails completely, first check the wiring leading to it for short circuits, blown fuse or loose connections. Also check that the horn is firmly secured and there is nothing lying on the horn body.
2 The horns are located each side at the front end behind the front grille panel. Access for removal or to check the wiring connections can be made by reaching up from underneath between the bumper and lower body section (photo).
3 Each horn is attached to the body by a single fixing bolt. Unscrew and remove the bolt and withdraw the horn sufficiently to detach the wiring connections. The horn(s) can then be removed.
4 Refit in the reverse order of removal. Check operation of horns on completion.

20.8 Ignition switch showing securing screw (arrowed)

21.2 Remove steering wheel nut and mark relative positions of wheel and column before withdrawing the wheel

21.4 Removing the column lower cover retaining screws

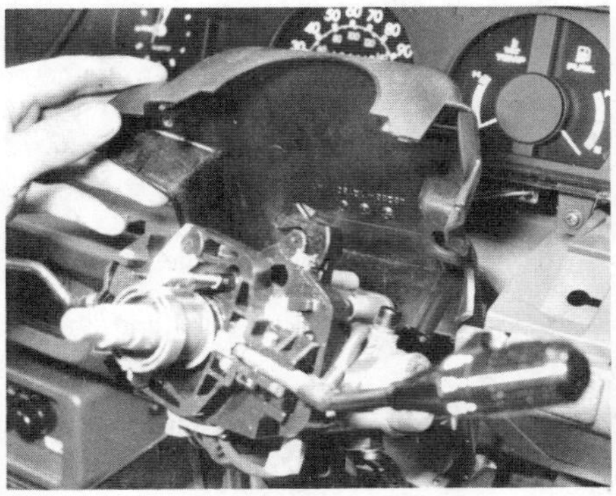
21.5 Removing the column upper cover

21.6 Steering column switches and retaining screws on end face

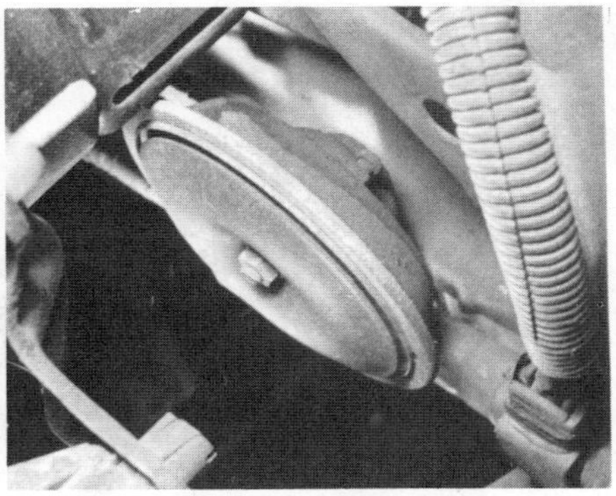
22.2 Horn – view from above

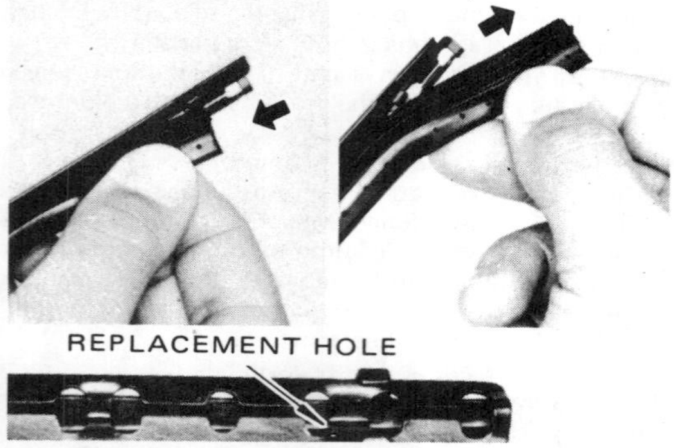

Fig. 10.82 Wiper blade removal (conventional type) (Sec 23)

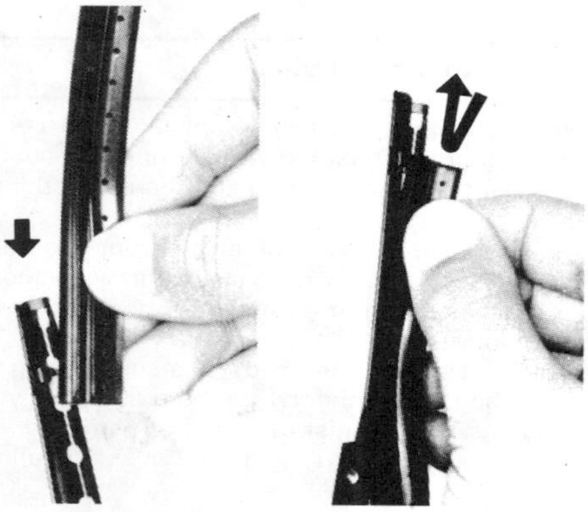

Fig. 10.83 Wiper blade refitting (conventional type) (Sec 23)

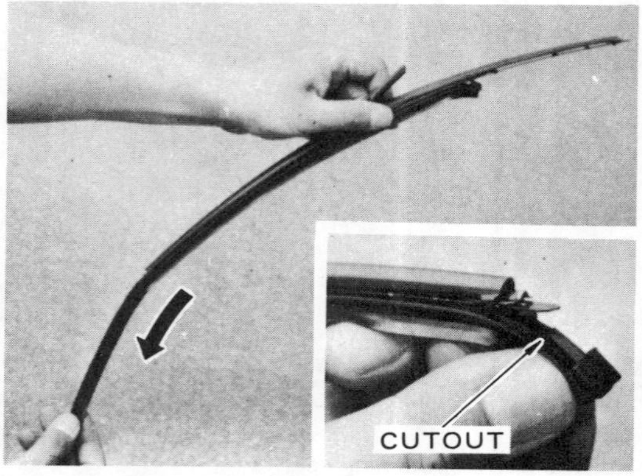

Fig. 10.84 Hook type wiper blade removal (Sec 23)

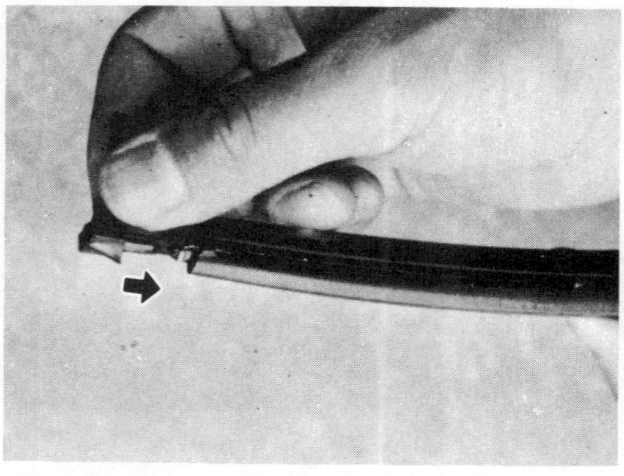

Fig. 10.85 Hook type wiper blade refitting (Sec 23)

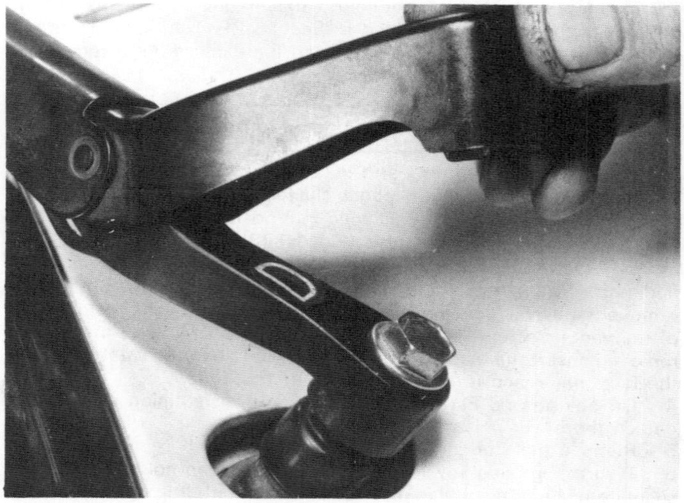

23.4 Pivot back the cover for access to the wiper arm bolt

23 Windscreen wiper blades and arms – removal and refitting

1 If the windscreen wiper blades are in need of renewal owing to wear or cracking they can be removed from the arm for replacement. To do this, pull the rubber, at the outer end, away from the arm so that the blade disengages from the end slot. Then pull the rubber along the line of the blade to withdraw it (Fig. 10.82).

2 To insert the new blade, slide it along the blade in reverse engaging in the slot as it is fitted. It will then expand into the engagement hole in the end (Fig. 10.83).

3 An alternative 'hook type' blade is sometimes fitted. With this type, pull the end of the blade out and away from the cut-out in the arm. Then pull and slide the blade out along the line of the arm to remove it from the opposite end of the frame (Fig. 10.84). When inserting the new blade, use the cut-out and feed the blade through the location slot in the frame. When in position the blade tip at each end should be fully engaged with the frame (Fig. 10.85).

4 The wiper arm assembly can be removed by prising back the pivot nut cover and unscrewing the nut. Mark or note the relative position of the arm and pivot shaft and pull free the arm (photo).

5 Refit in reverse order to removal and check operation on completion. Check the wiping arc of the wiper blades on a wet screen and adjust the position of the arms if necessary by removing them and moving one or more splines in the appropriate direction.

24 Windscreen wiper motor and linkage – removal and refitting

1 Disconnect the battery earth (ground) lead.

2 Remove the wiper arms and blades as described in the previous Section.

3 The cowl ventilator louvre panel in front of the windscreen must now be removed. To do this use a screwdriver or other suitable tool as a lever and prise free the retaining clips, but take care not to damage the body paintwork (Fig. 10.86). When all of the retaining clips are prised free, the panel can be lifted away (Fig. 10.87).

4 Prise free the clips and remove the hole cover.

5 Detach the wiring connectors to the wiper motor unit.

6 Detach the linkage from the wiper motor crank arm. Use a screwdriver or similar tool to lever between the arm and the link to separate them.

7 Unscrew and remove the four motor retaining bolts and lift the motor out.

8 To remove the wiper linkage, prise the link and pivot arms apart and remove the pivot arm retaining screws. Lift the linkage assembly clear.

9 Refitting is a reversal of the removal procedure. Lubricate the linkage pivots before assembly. When fitting the wiper motor, position it as shown in Fig. 10.88 so that the link arm is at the angle indicated from the horizontal.

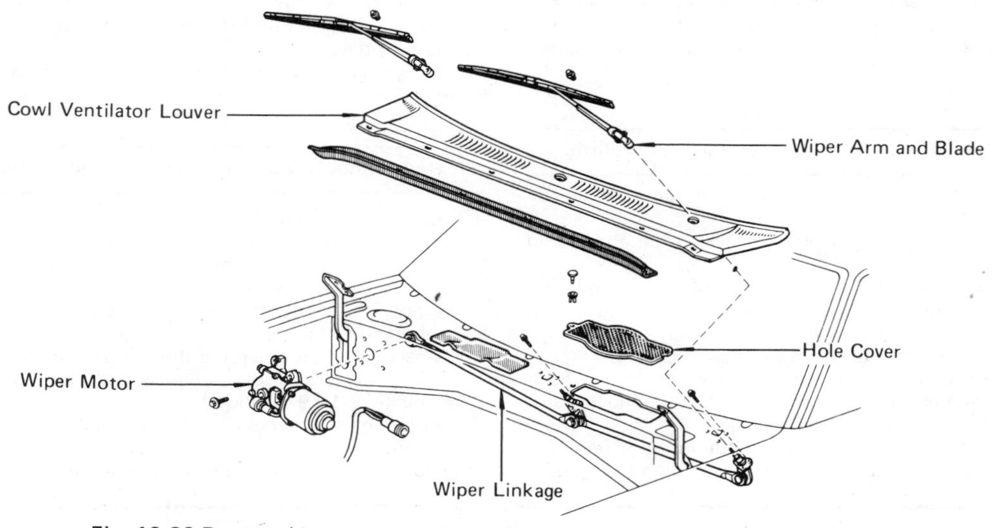

Fig. 10.86 Remove/detach items shown for access to wiper motor unit (Sec 24)

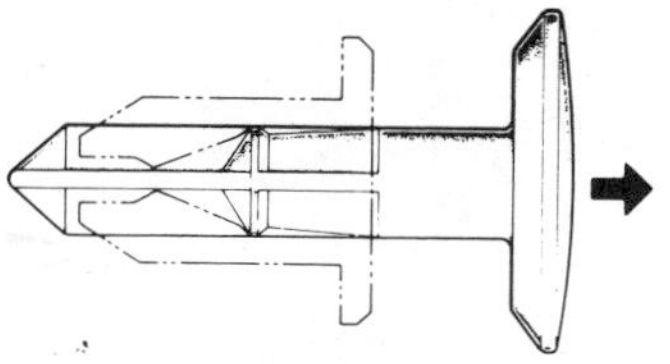
Fig. 10.87 Louver panel retaining clip (Sec 24)

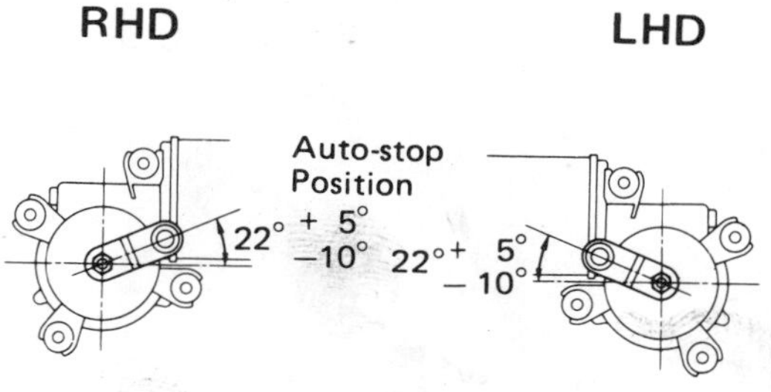

Fig. 10.88 Correct refitting link arm angle (Sec 24)

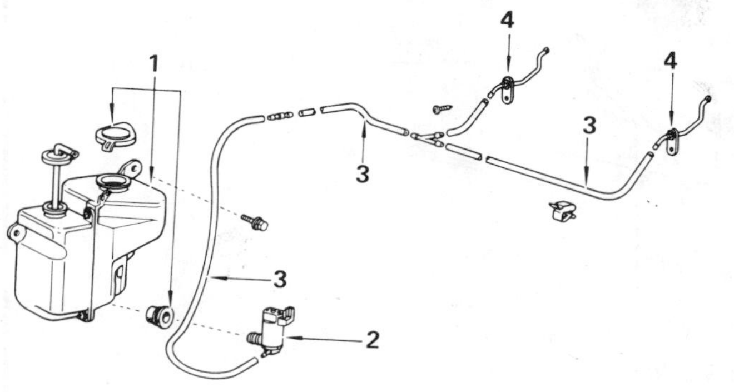

Fig. 10.89 Windscreen washer assembly components (Sec 25)

1 *Reservoir*
2 *Motor and pump*
3 *Hose*
4 *Nozzles*

10 When the wires are reconnected, turn the ignition on and set the wiper switch to the AUTO-STOP position, then the OFF position to ensure that the link arm angle is correct.

11 When refitting is complete check the wiping arc of the wiper blades on a wet screen to ensure that the sweep is correct and the PARK position is satisfactory.

25 Windscreen washer – general

1 The windscreen washer reservoir is located in the engine compartment on the inner wing panel just to the rear of the engine coolant expansion tank reservoir.

2 The washer reservoir, pump motor and associated components are shown in Fig. 10.89.

3 The interconnecting hoses are a push fit onto the various connections.

4 The pump/motor unit can be removed by emptying the reservoir and detaching the supply hose and the wiring connection. The pump can then be detached from the unit (photo).

5 Refit in reverse order to removal. Top up the reservoir and check for satisfactory operation and any signs of leakage from the pump and hose connections.

6 Always keep the fluid reservoir filled and do not operate the electric pump with a dry reservoir. In any case, operation of the washer pump should be limited to periods not exceeding 20 seconds.

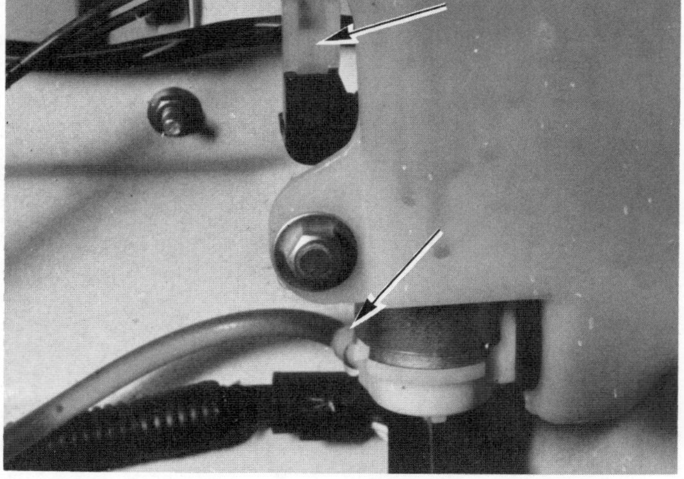
25.4 Windscreen washer reservoir pump hose and wiring connections

7 It is recommended that a proprietary screen cleaning solvent is used in the reservoir and during very cold weather add some methylated spirit *but never engine anti-freeze,* as this will damage the vehicle paintwork.

26 Rear wiper (Coupe/Liftback/Estate) – removal and refitting

1 The wiper motor is mounted at the base of the glass within the tailgate.
2 To remove the wiper motor assembly, unscrew the nut and withdraw the wiper arm.
3 Lift away the rubber cover and unscrew the retaining nut (photo).
4 Carefully prise free the rear cover panel retaining studs and remove the panel.
5 Detach the wiring connector to the wiper motor (photo).
6 Unscrew the wiper motor securing nuts, detach the motor from the operating link arm and remove the motor (Fig. 10.90). The link arm is detached by prising free with a screwdriver.
7 Refit in the reverse order of removal. When the motor is bolted in position, reconnect the wiring and link arm, and then with the ignition switched ON, set the wiper to the AUTO-STOP position. The wiper arm can then be refitted in the parked position on the pivot and the ignition switched off.
8 Refit the inner panel and on completion, check the operation of the wiper.

27 Rear window washer – removal and refitting

Coupe and Liftback

1 The reservoir and pump unit are located in the tailgate cavity. For access, first remove the trim panel from the tailgate by carefully prising free the retaining studs.
2 Empty the contents of the reservoir and then detach the wiring connector to the pump unit and the feed hose.
3 Unscrew and remove the three retaining nuts/bolts and withdraw the unit. If necessary the pump unit can now be detached from the reservoir (Fig. 10.91) (photo).
4 Refitting is a reversal of the removal procedure. Check that the wiring and hose connections are securely made and then top up the reservoir and check for satisfactory operation.

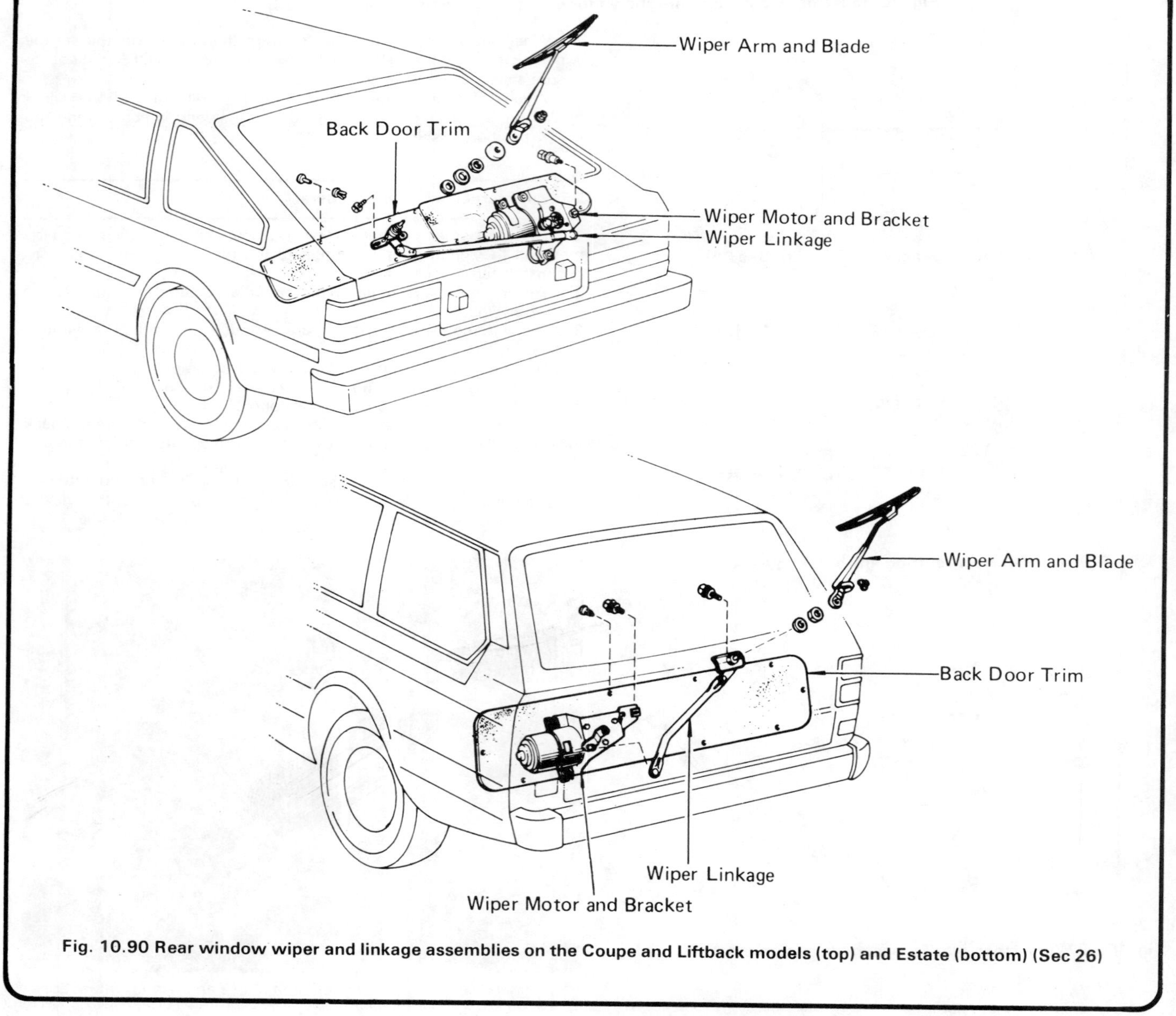

Fig. 10.90 Rear window wiper and linkage assemblies on the Coupe and Liftback models (top) and Estate (bottom) (Sec 26)

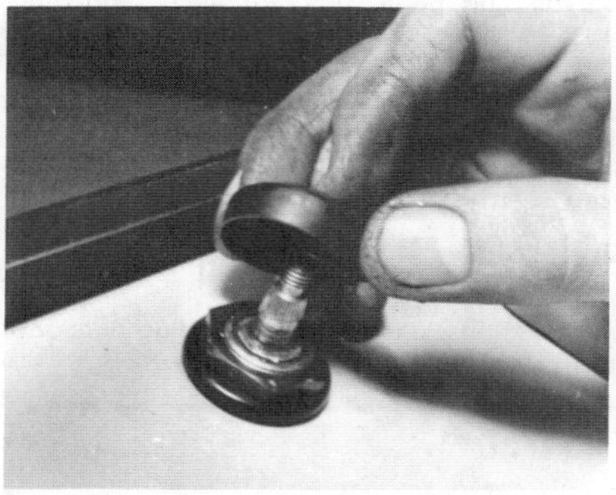

26.3 Rear wiper retaining nut and rubber cover – wiper arm removed

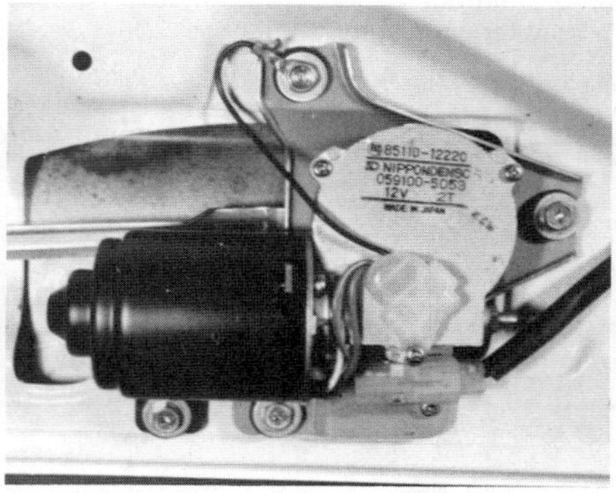

26.5 The rear screen wiper motor showing retaining bolts and wiring connections

27.3 Rear screen washer reservoir – Coupe and Liftback models

Estate

5 The procedures for removing and refitting the rear washer and pump unit are the same as those given in paragraphs 1 to 4 above except that the washer/pump unit is located in the side panel at the rear (Fig. 10.92).

Washer hose and nozzle

6 The rear washer hose is run from the washer reservoir/pump unit through the inner body channels to the nozzle.

7 Renewal of the hose will therefore necessitate the partial removal of the headlining rear trim and the rear of the headlining itself. As this is not a task recommended for the home mechanic, it is suggested that the hose removal and refitting is entrusted to your Toyota dealer. The nozzle can be removed by prising free as shown (Fig. 10.93) but take care not to damage the surrounding paintwork (lever on a piece of cardboard to protect the panel). Pull the hose through sufficiently to disconnect the nozzle, but take care not to let the hose drop back into the bodywork whilst the nozzle is removed. When the hose is

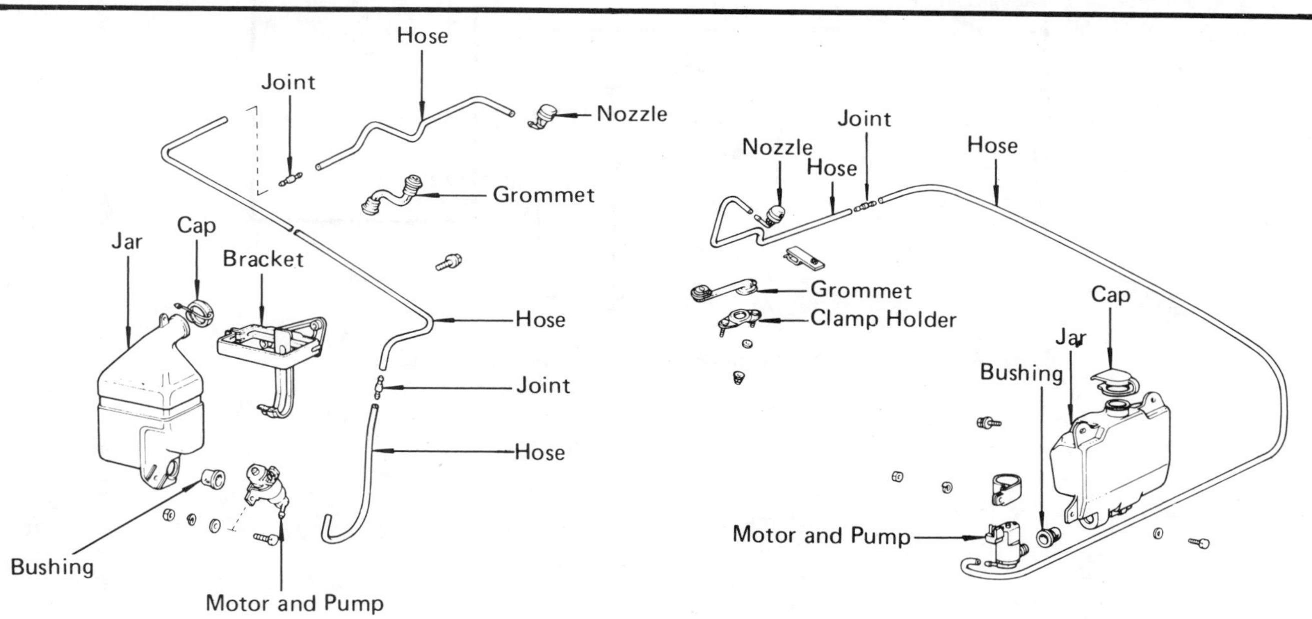

Fig. 10.91 Rear window washer components for Estate (left) and Coupe and Liftback (right) (Sec 27)

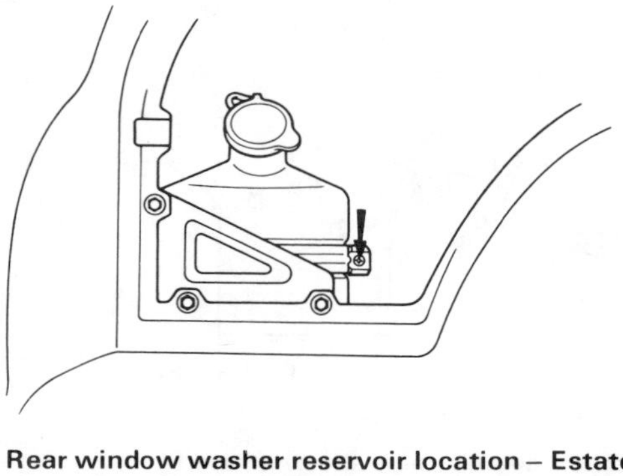

Fig. 10.92 Rear window washer reservoir location – Estate (Sec 27)

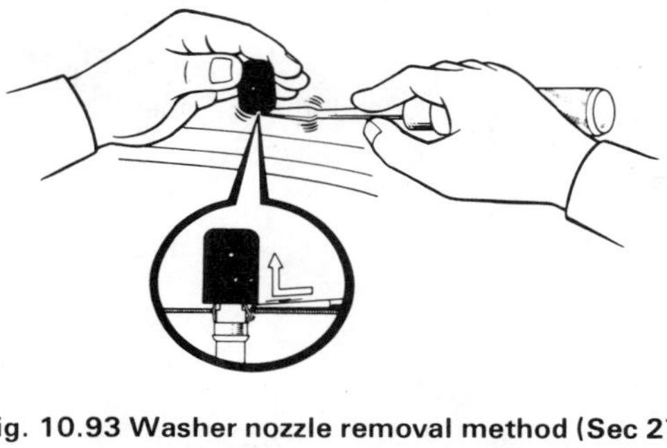

Fig. 10.93 Washer nozzle removal method (Sec 27)

reconnected to the nozzle, press the nozzle into position in the body. Then check its operation and jet alignment which may require slight adjustment.

28 Headlight cleaner – general

1 Only fitted to some models, the circuitry of the system is shown in Fig. 10.94.
2 Should the reservoir fluid level empty at any time, do not operate the cleaner pump.
3 Use only windscreen washer fluid not engine anti-freeze.
4 Removal of the reservoir and pump unit are as described in Section 27.

29 Instrument panel – removal and refitting

1 Disconnect the battery earth (ground) lead, then proceed as follows.

Saloon and Estate

2 Pull free the radio control knobs, unscrew the retaining nuts and remove with the washers (Fig. 10.95).

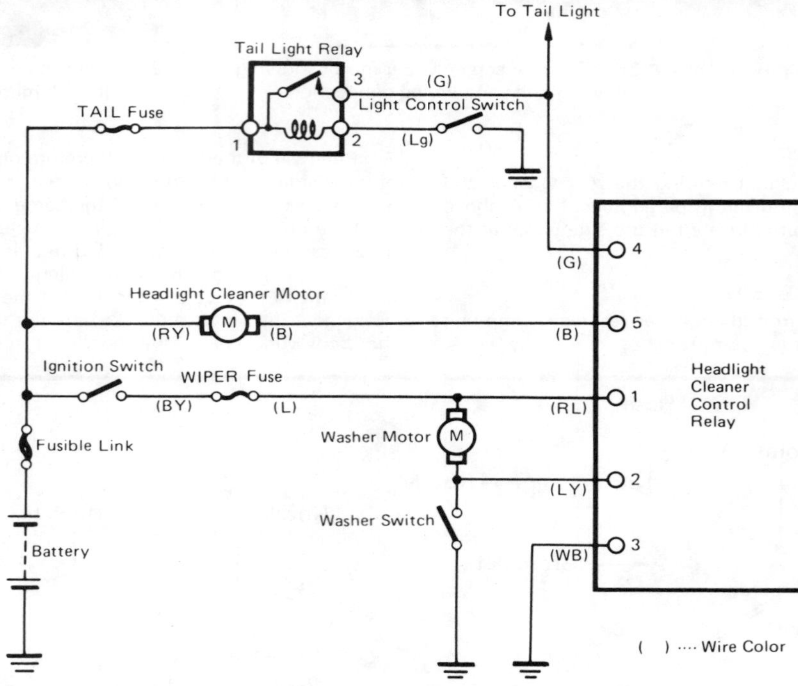

Fig. 10.94 The headlight cleaner circuit (Sec 28)

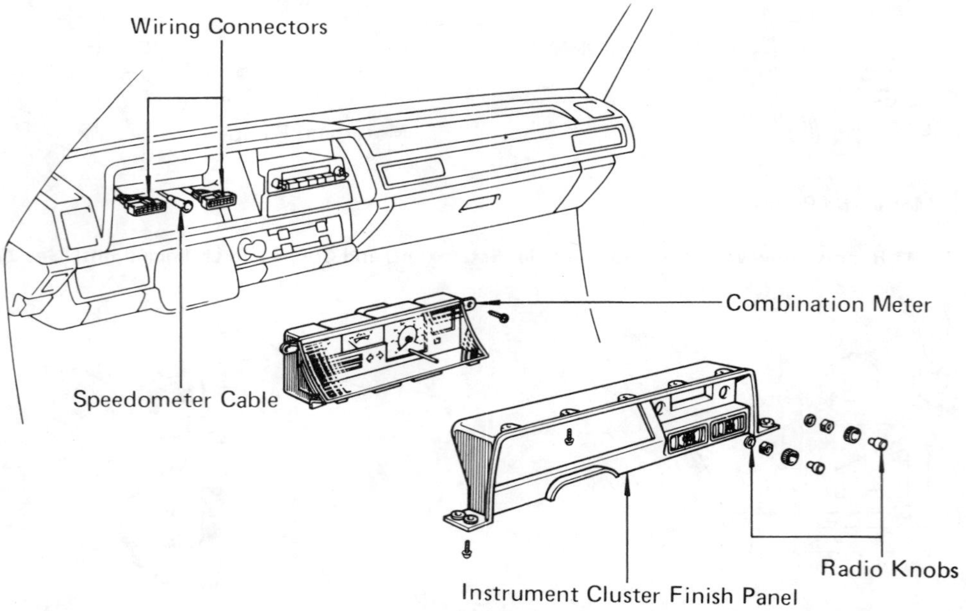

Fig. 10.95 Instrument panel removal (Saloon and Estate) – detach items shown (Sec 29)

3 Unscrew and remove the instrument cluster finish panel retaining screws and withdraw the panel.
4 Reach up underneath and behind the instrument panel and disconnect the speedometer cable from the speedometer (Fig. 10.96).

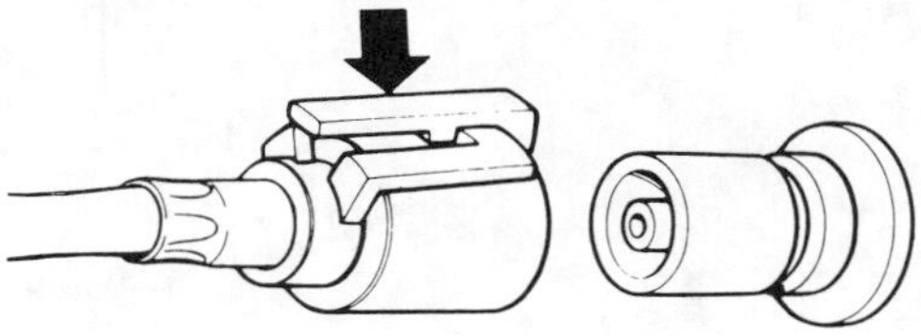

Fig. 10.96 Cable detachment from speedometer (Sec 29)

5 Unscrew and remove the instrument panel retaining screws and then withdraw the panel to the point where the wiring connectors can be detached. The panel can then be withdrawn completely.
6 Refitting is a reversal of the removal procedure. Ensure that the wiring connections are secure and on completion check the operations of the instruments.

Coupe and Liftback
7 Prise free the instrument cluster finish panel by pulling it free at the top, pivot it on its lower edge and lift it clear. Take care not to damage the lower retaining pawls (photos).
8 Unscrew and remove the screws securing the cluster finish upper panel.
9 Reach up underneath and behind the instrument panel and disconnect the speedometer cable and the panel wiring connectors.

29.7a Prise away the cluster finish panel on the top edge ...

29.7b ... and lift the panel clear (Coupe and Liftback)

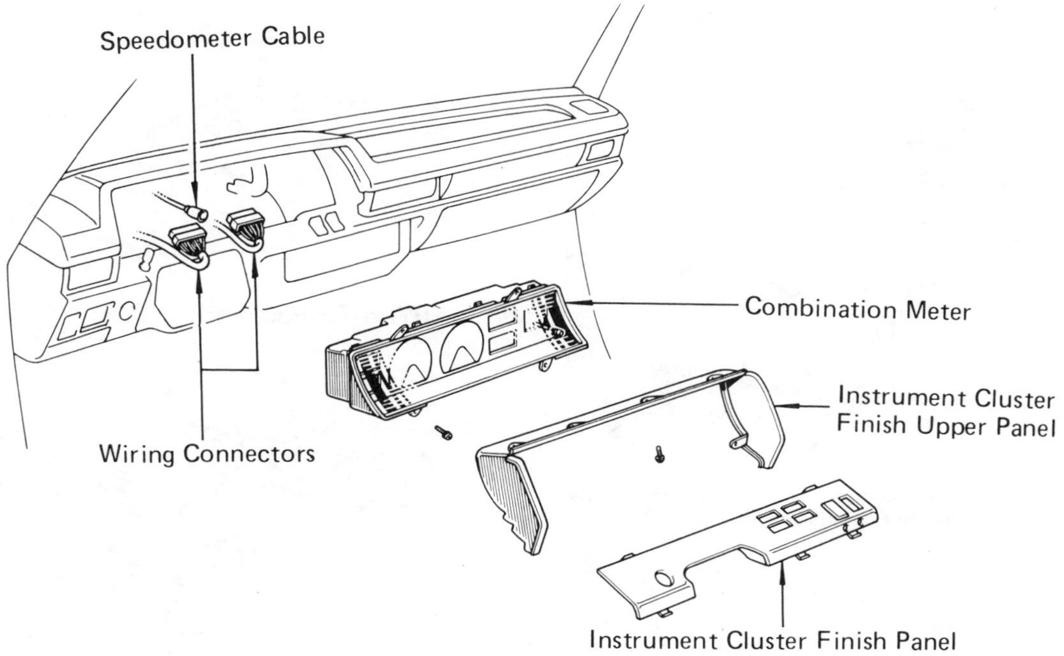

Fig. 10.97 Instrument panel removal (Coupe and Liftback) – detach items shown (Sec 29)

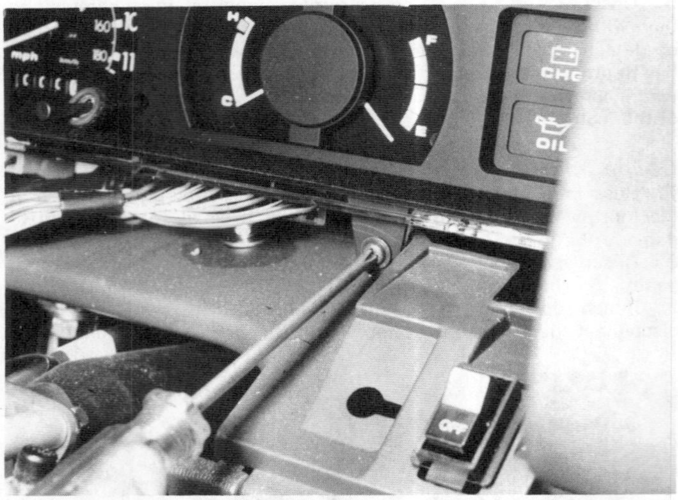

29.10a Remove the instrument panel retaining screws ...

29.10b ... and withdraw the panel (Coupe and Liftback)

10 Unscrew and remove the instrument panel retaining screws then withdraw the panel (photos).
11 Refitting is a reversal of the removal details. Ensure that the wiring connections are secure and on completion check the operations of the instruments.

30 Instruments – removal and refitting

1 The instruments are only accessible for inspection or renewal with the instrument panel withdrawn from the facia as described in the previous Section. This also applies to the instrument panel bulbs.
2 The various instrument panel types and layouts are shown in the accompanying exploded diagrams (Fig. 10.98 and 10.99).
3 When dismantling or refitting any components from the instrument panel, take care not to damage the printed circuits exposed on its rear face (photo).
4 To renew any of the panel bulbs simply twist and withdraw the bulbholder concerned (photo). The bulb can then be extracted from its holder and renewed.
5 The lens is secured to the combination instrument panel by screws and clips. With this removed any of the instruments can be withdrawn forwards having first released their retaining screws or nuts on the rear face. When removing an instrument take particular care to handle it carefully (photo).
6 Repair (if possible) of instruments should be entrusted to your

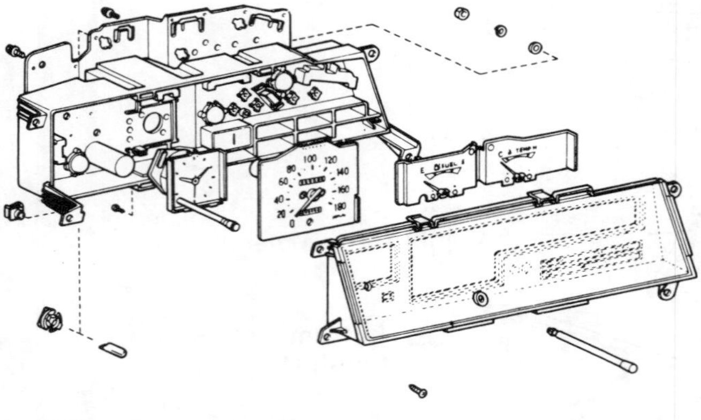

Fig. 10.98 Instrument panel (combination meter) components – (Saloon and Estate) (Sec 30)

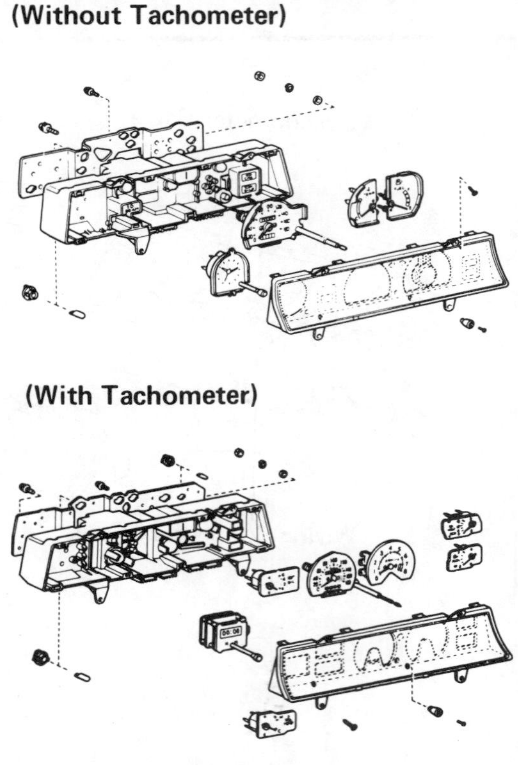

Fig. 10.99 Instrument panel (combination meter) components – (Coupe and Liftback models) (Sec 30)

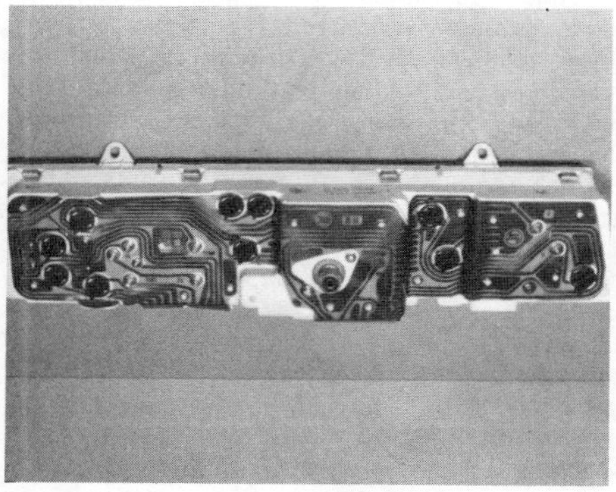

30.3 Instrument panel rear face (Liftback shown), showing printed circuits and bulbholder locations

30.4 Bulb removal from instrument panel

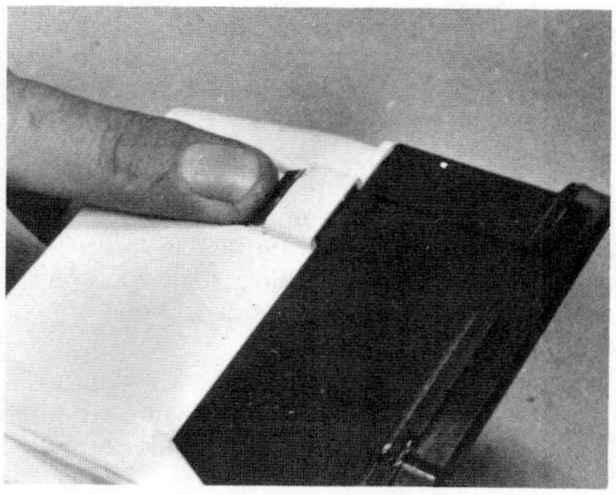

30.5 Lens cover to instrument panel securing clips

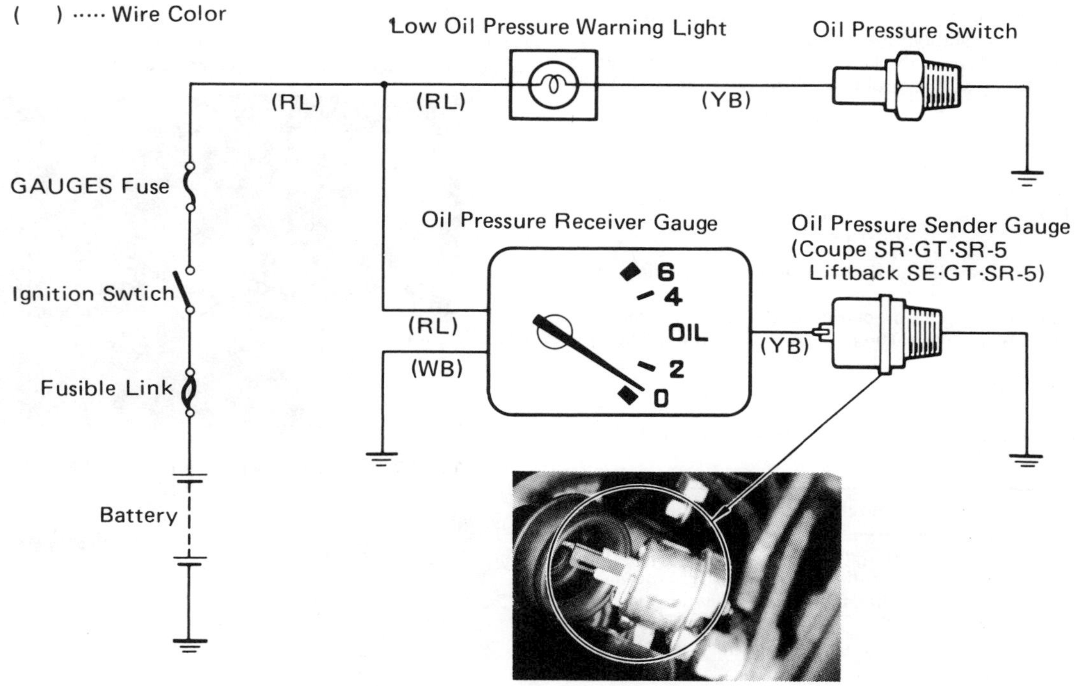

Fig. 10.100 Oil pressure gauge/warning light circuit (Sec 31)

Toyota dealer or an instrument repair specialist.

7 Refit in the reverse order of removal and check instruments for satisfactory operation on completion.

31 Instruments – testing

Oil pressure warning light

1 If an oil pressure warning light is fitted, if the light fails to illuminate when the ignition key is first turned 'ON', check the bulb and the electrical connections (Fig 10.100).

2 If the light comes on when the engine is running or fails to go out once the engine has started, immediately switch off and trace the cause. The sender switch which is screwed into the outlet port of the oil filter is designed to operate at an oil pressure of between 2.8 and 5.7 lbf/in^2 (0.2 and 0.4 kgf/cm^2). At this pressure, the circuit is broken by the switch contacts and the warning lamp should be out.

3 Provided the engine is in good condition, renew the sender switch and test again by starting the engine. If the light still remains on, the engine oil level may be low, the oil pump worn or drive sheared or the oil filter clogged.

Oil pressure gauge

4 If an oil pressure gauge is fitted and a low or very high reading is observed and yet the engine is known to be in good condition, pull the lead from the terminal on the back of the gauge and earth the terminal using a piece of cable with a 3.4W bulb incorporated in it. Turn the ignition switch 'ON' when the bulb should light and the gauge needle should deflect. If this does not happen, renew the gauge (Fig. 10.101).

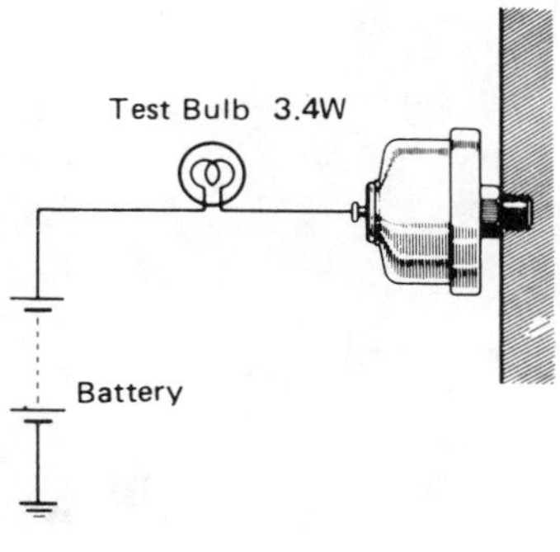

Fig. 10.101 Oil pressure switch test (Sec 31)

5 To check the oil pressure sender unit, pull off the lead from it and connect battery (+) voltage to it but passing it through a 3.4W bulb. With the engine stationary, the test bulb should be out, with the engine running, the bulb should flash and the number of flashes increase with the engine speed. Renew the sender unit if it does not behave in this way.

6 If the oil pressure gauge and sender unit are proved to be satisfactory, then if the engine is generally in good condition, the cause of very low reading will be due to low oil level or the oil pump drive sheared. Exceptionally high readings may be caused by a seized pressure relief valve or clogged filter.

Water temperature gauge

7 Should a fault occur in the water temperature indicated reading, first check that the cooling system is correctly filled and then check the security of all connecting leads.

8 Reach up behind the temperature gauge (or withdraw the panel) and pull off the lead from the back of the gauge. Earth its terminal having a 12v, 3.4W bulb in the lead.

9 Turn the ignition ON when the bulb should light up. After a few seconds, the bulb should start to flash and the gauge needle deflect.

10 If this test proves satisfactory, then check the sender unit by measuring the resistance between the sender unit terminal and earth using a circuit tester. The results should be in accordance with the following table.

Temperature	*Resistance*
140°F (60°C)	*104 ohms*
176°F (80°C)	*51.9 ohms*
230°F (110°C)	*21.1 ohms*
266°F (130°C)	*12.4 ohms*

11 Renewal of the gauge can be carried out after withdrawing the instrument panel.

12 Renewal of the sender unit can be carried out after unscrewing it from its thermostat housing location. The cooling system will of course have to be drained first.

Fuel gauge

13 If a fault occurs in the fuel gauge refer to Chapter 3, Section 7.

32 Instrument panel switches – removal and refitting

1 The position and type of instrument panel and facia panel switches is dependent on the model and operating territory. To generalize information given, the switch type rather than each individual switch removal and refitting detail is given.

2 Before removing any switch unit, first disconnect the battery earth (ground) lead.

Rocker switches

3 Rocker switches are secured in position by compression 'tag' clips which are integral with their outer body. The switch removal method will vary according to its location. Where access to the rear of the switch is possible, reach behind it and disconnect the wiring connector. Then compress the tag clips each side of the switch body by gripping with the thumb and index finger and simultaneously push the switch outwards through its location aperture.

4 On some switches where access from the rear is not possible, the switch is prised free by inserting a screwdriver, or similar suitable, tool under the switch surround flange and levering against the mounting panel. The switch is eased out and then when sufficiently clear, the wiring disconnected for switch removal (Fig. 10.102).

5 On Coupe and Liftback models the rocker switches, located in the instrument cluster lower finish panel, can only be removed by first removing the panel itself. To remove this panel, prise it free along its top edge and pivot it back to release it from its lower edge clips. The rocker switch can then be prised out of its location aperture (photo).

6 Where a rocker switch houses an integral warning bulb, the bulb can be extracted by twisting and pulling free its holder and the bulb then removed from the holder (photos).

7 To refit the rocker switches, whichever type, reconnect the wiring and simply push the switch back into position in its panel aperture. Check its operation on completion.

De-fogger switch (Coupe and Liftback – USA and Canada)

8 Use a small electrical screwdriver as shown and insert it into the slot on the underside of the switch knob at the rear (Fig. 10.103). Push

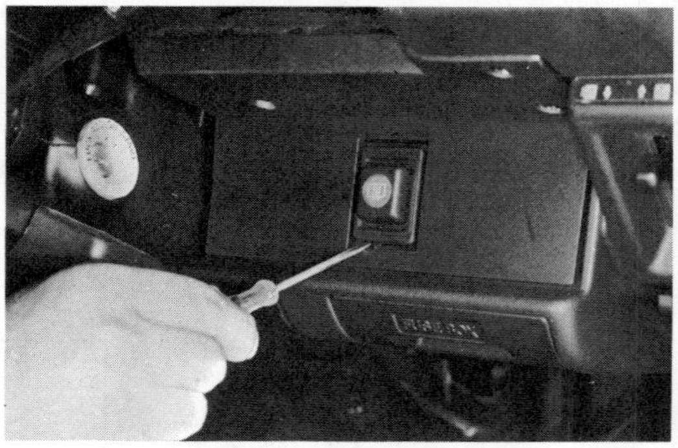

Fig. 10.102 De-fogger switch removal – (Saloon and Estate) (Sec 32)

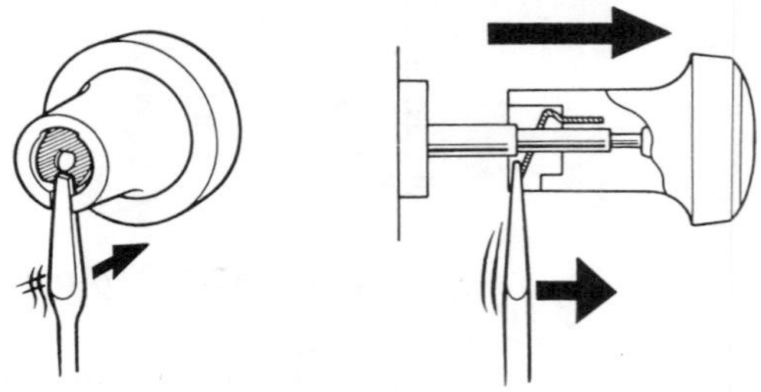

Fig. 10.103 De-fogger switch removal – (Coupe and Liftback – USA and Canada) (Sec 32)

32.5 Typical rocker switch installation – this is the rear fog light switch on a Liftback model with cluster panel removed

32.6a Rocker switch with integral warning light ...

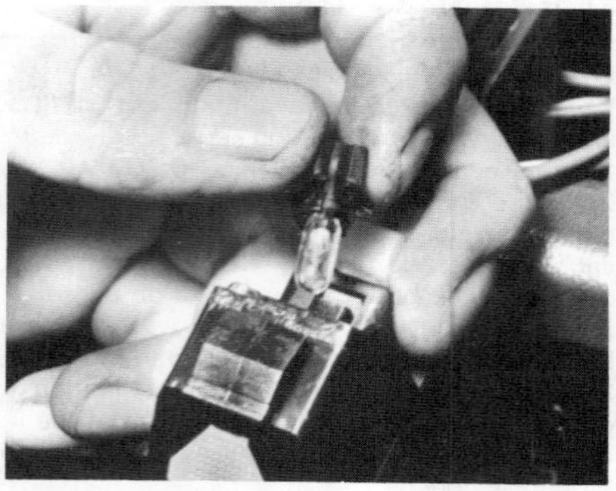

32.6b Twist and pull bulbholder to remove bulb. Pull bulb from holder

on the retainer and pull the knob free from the switch shaft. Unscrew the switch locknut and remove the switch through the panel aperture. Disconnect the wires to remove the switch completely. Refit in reverse order to removal. Simply push the knob onto the shaft to locate it.

De-fogger switch (Estate, USA and Canada)

9 First remove the instrument cluster finish panel and then use a screwdriver as shown to lever the switch from its location aperture (Fig. 10.104).

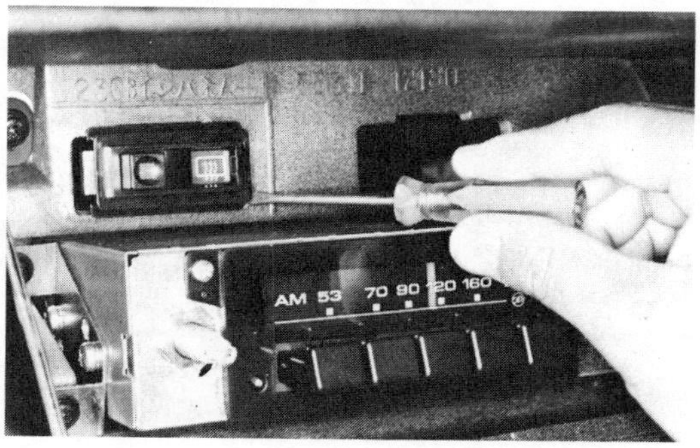

Fig. 10.104 De-fogger switch removal (Estate – USA) (Sec 32)

10 The switch can be withdrawn and the wires disconnected.
11 Refit in reverse order of removal and check operation on completion.

33 Heater control panel – removal and refitting

1 Disconnect the battery earth lead.
2 Reach under the facia and detach the four heater control cables from their clamps.
3 On the Saloon and Estate models, carefully remove the instrument cluster finish panel, pull free the control knobs and remove the heater control lens. When removing the lens care must be taken not to bend the end clips. Remove the three retaining screws and withdraw the lower central panel (Fig. 10.105). Detach the wire connector from the blower unit switch, withdraw the control unit and then remove the blower switch from the control. Detach and remove the control cables.
4 On Coupes and Liftback models pull free the heater control knobs and then remove the three control panel retaining screws and withdraw the panel (photos). Remove the ashtray and its holder, then reach through and detach the blower switch wire. Withdraw the heater control unit. The blower switch and control cables can now be disconnected.

Fig. 10.105 Cluster lower finish panel retaining screws – (Saloon and Estate) (Sec 33)

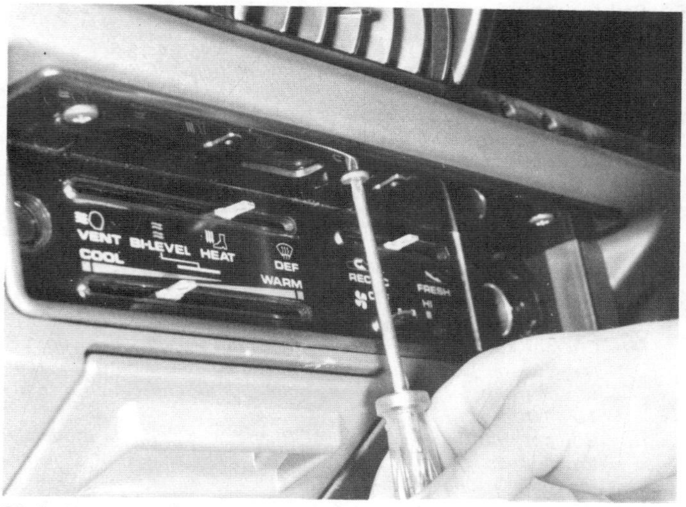

33.4a Heater control panel removal (Coupe and Liftback models): remove retaining screws ...

33.4b ... withdraw the panel ...

33.4c ... for access to the control retaining screws

5 Refitting is a reversal of the removal procedure but note the following control settings:

(a) *Heater control lever setting: Fit with all levers pointing towards the panel outer edges (Fig. 10.106).*
(b) *Air inlet damper: Blower lever must be set against the stopper as shown in Fig. 10.107.*
(c) *Mode select damper – standard type: Pivot the lever in the direction of the arrow to make contact with the stopper. Connect the cable and then push the upper control lever (vent) so that it contacts its stopper and fit the cable (Fig. 10.108).*
(d) *Mode select damper – air mix type: Pivot the rotary damper lever in direction of arrow to contact its stopper then connect the cable (Fig. 10.109).*
(e) *Coolant control valve (4K engine models): Set valve control lever to the COOL position and attach cable with pin at the top of the hole. Pull on the cable slightly and clamp it (Fig. 10.110).*
(f) *Coolant control valve (2T, 2T-B and 3T-C engine models): Proceed as given in (e), but push the valve control lever forwards as shown in Fig. 10.111.*

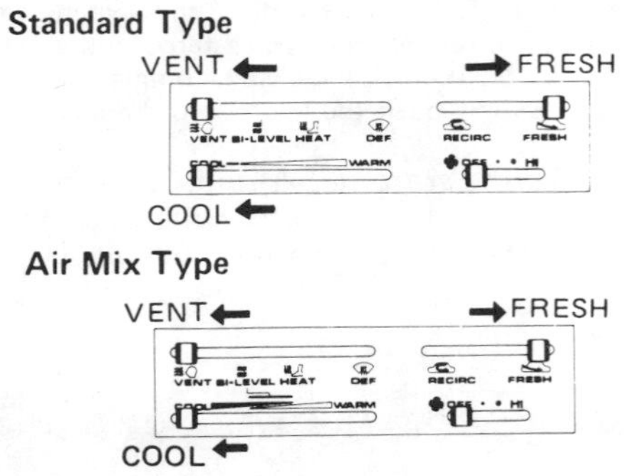

Fig. 10.106 Set heater controls as shown when refitting (Sec 33)

(g) *Air mix damper: Push damper control to COOL position, locate and clamp the cable (Fig. 10.112).*

6 On completion check the operation of each control to ensure that the cables do not bind and the levers fully open and close.

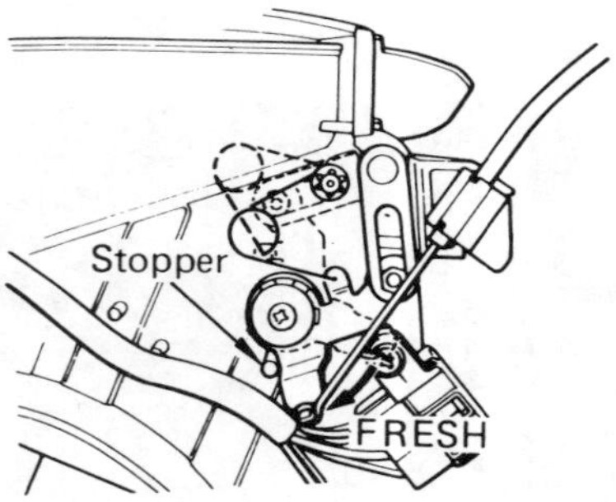

Fig. 10.107 Set blower lever against stopper (air inlet damper) (Sec 33)

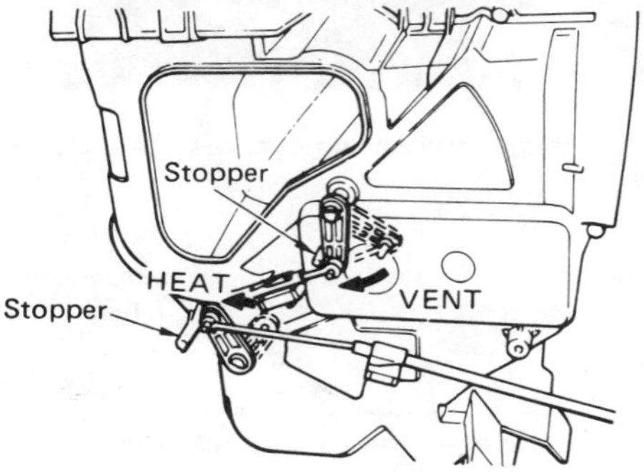

Fig. 10.108 Mode select damper cable refitting (Sec 33)

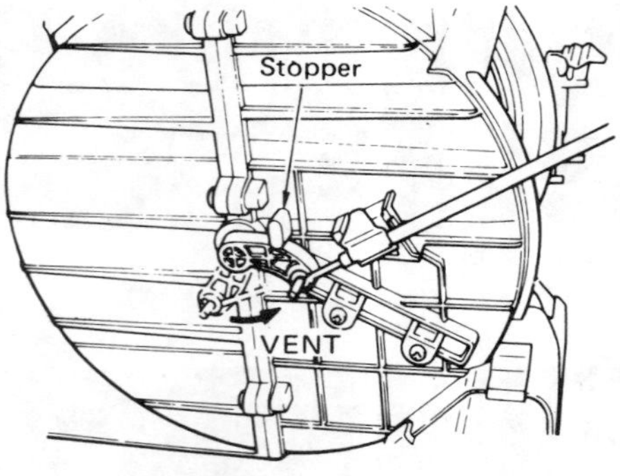

Fig. 10.109 Air mix cable refitting (Sec 33)

Fig. 10.110 Coolant control valve cable connection – 4K engine models (Sec 33)

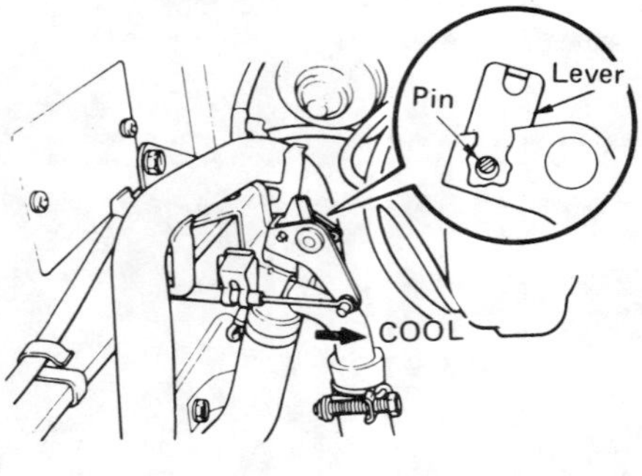

Fig. 10.111 Coolant control valve cable connection – 2T, 2T-B and 3T-C engine models (Sec 33)

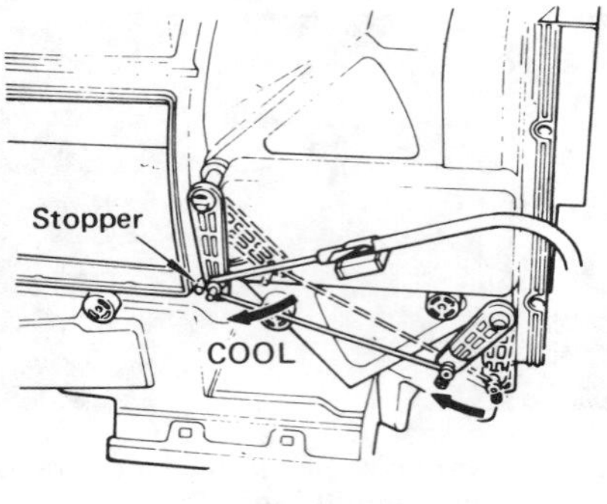

Fig. 10.112 Air mix damper cable connection (Sec 33)

34 Heater unit – removal and refitting

All models

1 Disconnect the battery earth lead.
2 Drain the cooling system with the heater coolant control valve set in its hot position. Refer to Chapter 2 if necessary.
3 Unbolt and remove the front seats.
4 Remove the console box which is secured by four screws, (Fig. 10.113).
5 Remove the retaining screws and lift clear the door scuff plates each side and fold back the carpet at the front.
6 Where fitted remove the retaining screws and bolts and detach the rear heater ducting each side.
7 If fitted, remove the undertray which is secured by two screws.
8 Remove the glove compartment also secured by screws.
9 Detach and remove the blower duct.
10 Unbolt and remove the instrument brace.

Saloon and Estate

11 Remove the heater control panel as described in Section 33, and the instrument panel as described in Section 29.
12 Remove the ashtray and its holder.
13 Disconnect and remove the radio (Section 37).

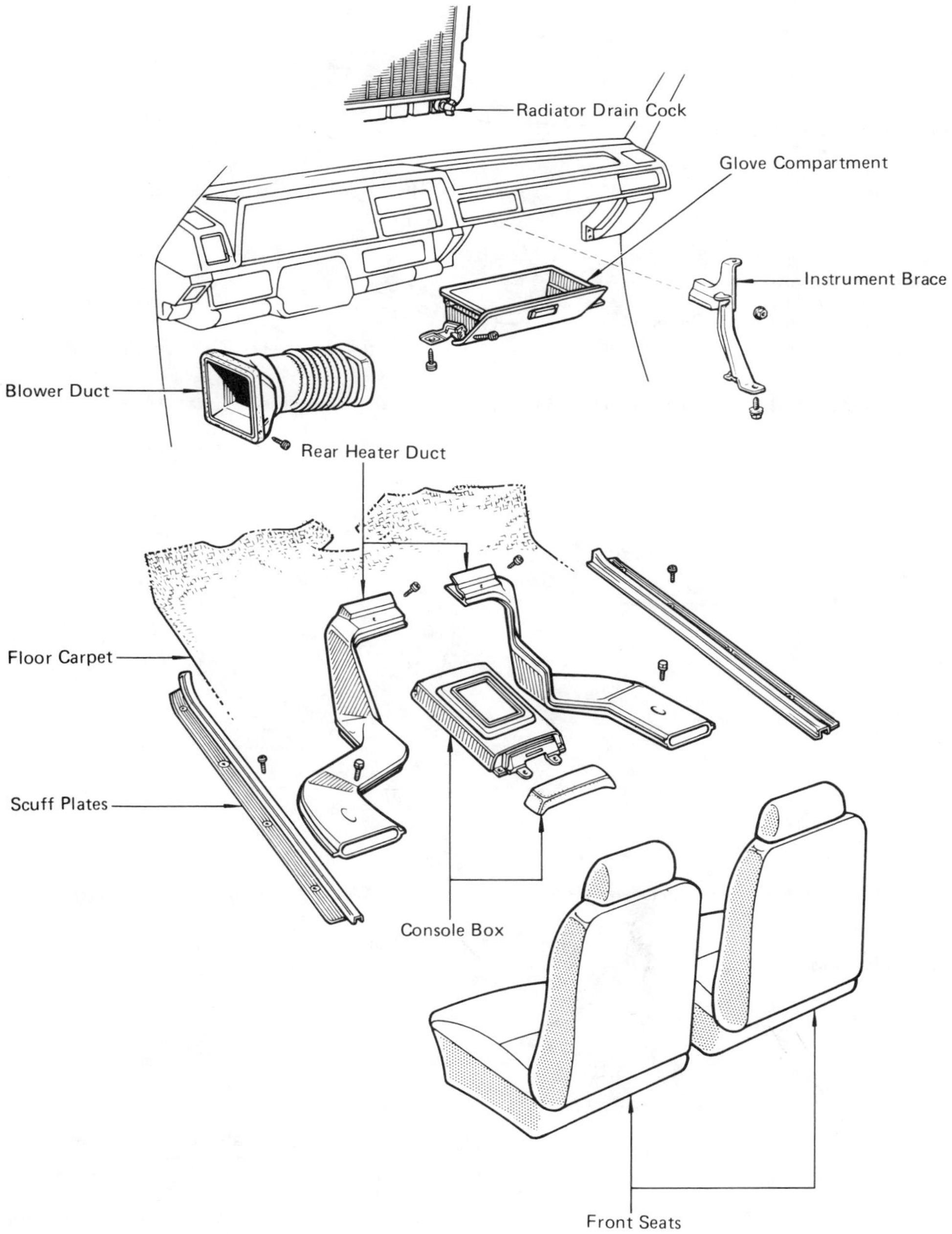

Fig. 10.113 Console box and associated components to be detached for heater unit removal – (all models) (Sec 34)

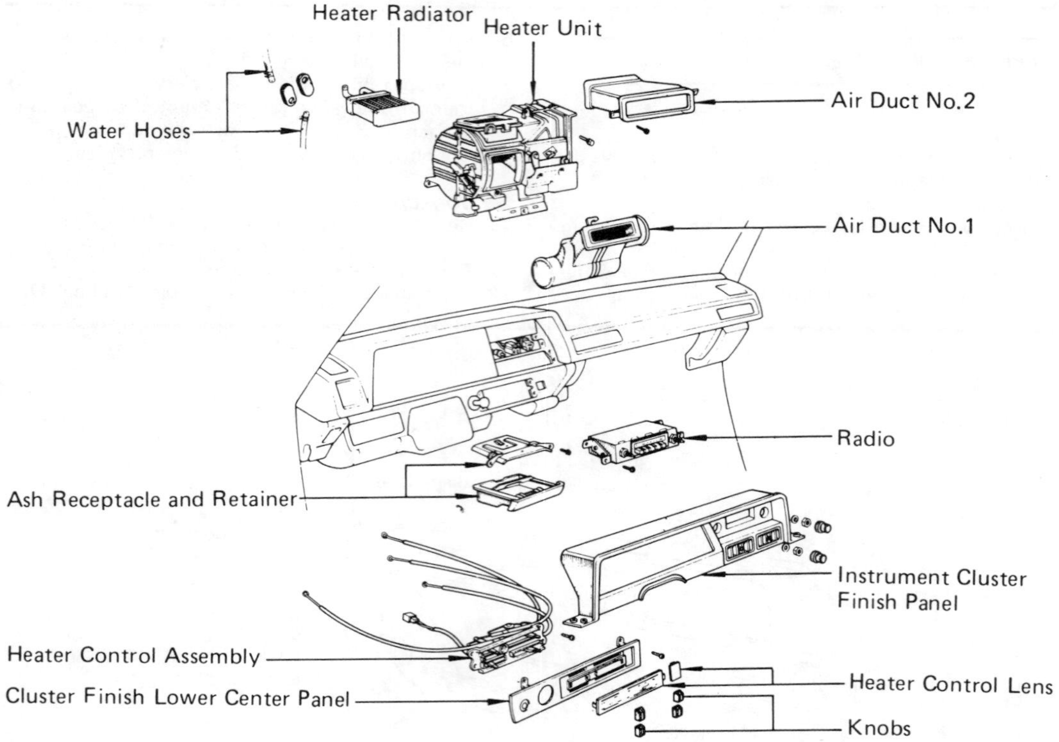

Fig. 10.114 Detach items shown for heater removal – (Saloon and Estate) (Sec 34)

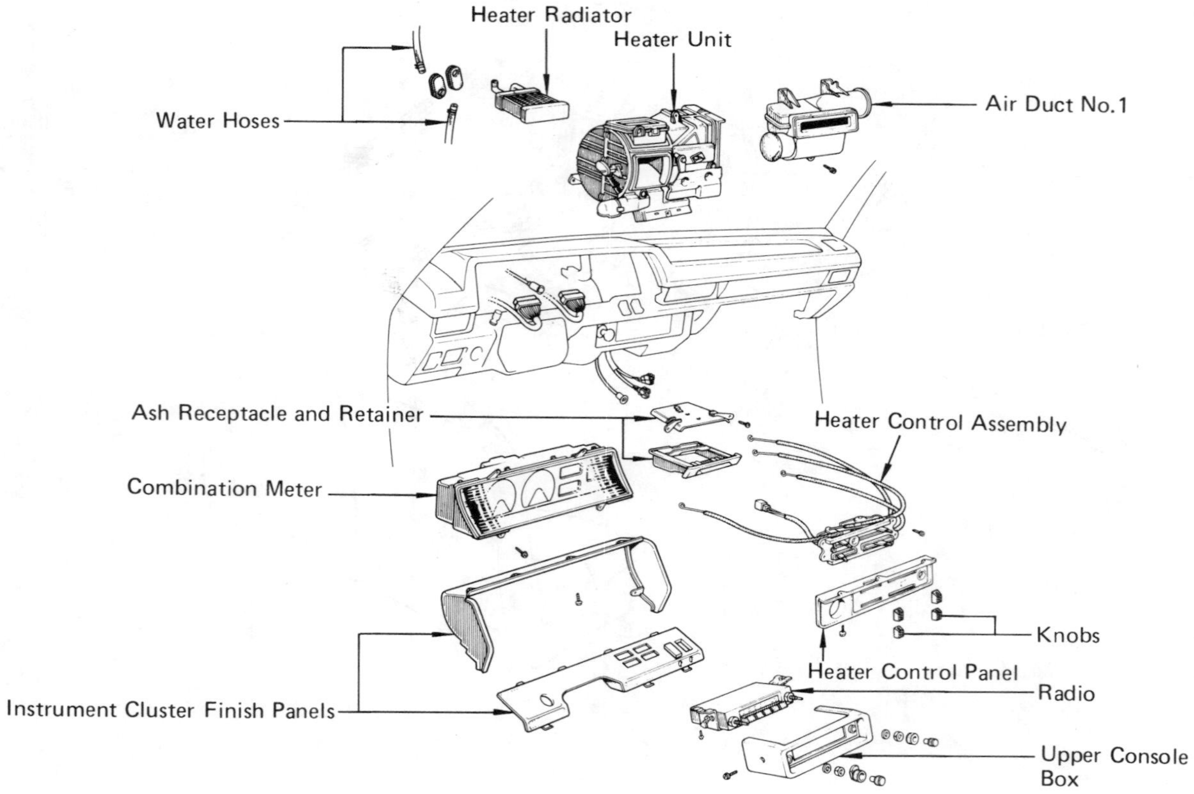

Fig. 10.115 Detach items shown for heater removal – (Coupe and Liftback) (Sec 34)

14 Remove the number 2 and number 1 air ducts in that order.
15 Disconnect the heater hoses and grommets (Fig. 10.114).
16 The heater unit can now be unbolted and removed. Also remove the heater radiator.

Coupe and Liftback

17 Remove the instrument panel as given in Section 29.
18 Remove the radio as given in Section 37.
19 Remove the ashtray and its retainer.
20 Remove the heater control panel as given in Section 33.
21 Detach and remove the air ducting unit to the right of the heater unit. Prise free from heater with a screwdriver.
22 Disconnect the heater hoses and grommets.
23 The heater unit can now be unbolted and removed. Also remove the heater radiator.

Refitting – all models

24 The refitting procedure for the heater unit on all models is a reversal of the removal procedure.
25 Take care to refit the heater unit the correct way up. The radiator unit must be fitted from the passenger side (Fig. 10.116).
26 Check that the supply and return hose connections are securely made and on completion check for any signs of leaks when the engine is at its normal operating temperature with the heater full on.

Fig. 10.116 Heater unit radiator refitting (Sec 34)

35 Heater blower motor – removal and refitting

1 If the heater motor is to be removed, owing to a malfunction in its operation, it is advisable to first remove the heater motor relay and resistor for checking. These are attached to the body of the heater unit and are removed by first detaching their wires (disconnect the battery earth first) and then unscrewing their fixing screw. Have the relay unit and resistor checked by your Toyota dealer and if found to be defective renew as necessary. The heater circuit diagram is shown in Fig. 10.117.
2 If the blower motor has to be removed, start by first removing the undertray (where fitted) which is secured by two screws.
3 Remove the glovebox which is secured by four screws.
4 The blower motor unit is now accessible and the ducting can be prised free using a suitable screwdriver.
5 The blower motor unit can now be unbolted and removed.

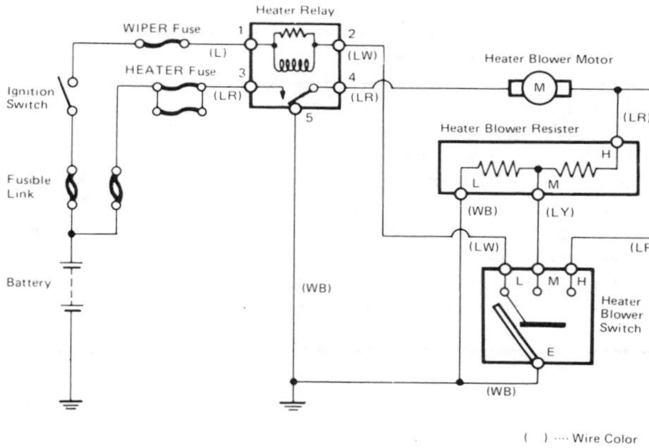

Fig. 10.117 Heater unit circuit diagram (Sec 35)

6 To remove the blower motor from the main housing, unscrew and remove the three retaining screws and withdraw the motor and fan assembly. Try not to damage the gasket as the motor is withdrawn.

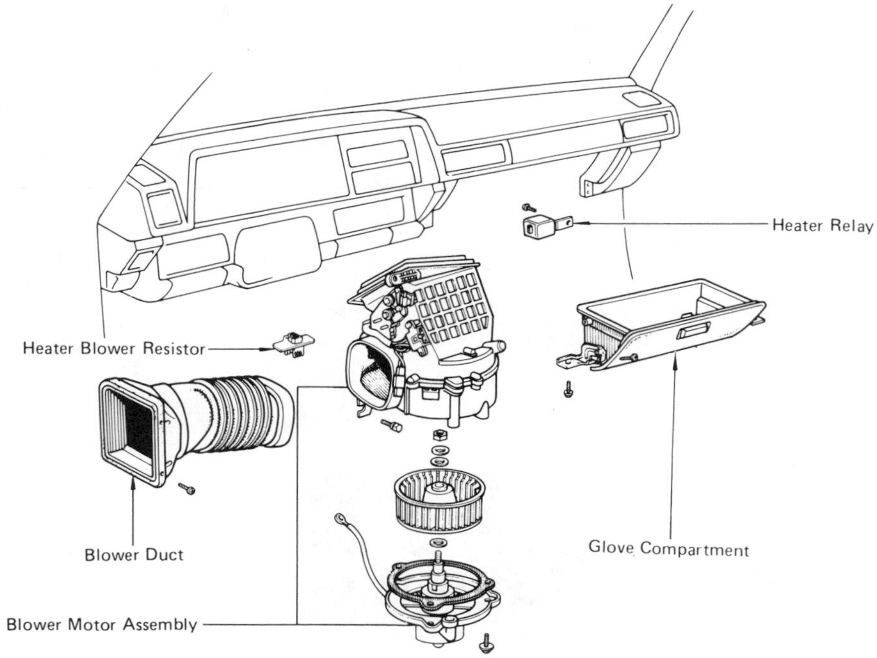

Fig. 10.118 Heater blower motor showing associated components to be detached for its removal (Sec 35)

7 Have the motor tested by your Toyota dealer and if defective have it repaired or renewed.
8 Refitting is a reversal of the removal procedure. Check the operation of the motor before refitting the glovebox.

36 Seat belt warning light and buzzer – removal and refitting

1 The seat belt warning light and buzzer system is, at the time of writing, fitted to USA and Canada market models only.
2 The circuitry in the system is shown in Fig. 10.119.
3 The two main components are the warning switch, located on the steering column and the buzzer unit. They are shown in Fig. 10.120 and 10.121.
4 If either unit is to be removed, first disconnect the battery, then the wiring connections to the unit concerned and then detach the unit from its fastening position.
5 Refit in reverse and check operation.

37 Radio – removal and refitting

1 Disconnect the battery earth terminal lead.
2 Pull free the radio tuner and volume control knobs, then unscrew and remove the retaining nuts.
3 On Saloon and Estate models, withdraw the radio and instrument cluster panel (Section 29).
4 On Coupe and Liftback models, remove the retaining screws each side and withdraw the upper console box.
5 Unscrew and remove the radio attachment screws and partially withdraw the radio to allow the antenna lead and power/earth supply lead connections to be detached. Then remove the radio completely.
6 Refitting is a reversal of the removal procedure. Check operation on completion. You may need to make a fine adjustment of the antenna trimmer for improved reception. To do this check that the antenna is fully raised, position the tuner to about 1400 kHz and turn the volume up. Now use a suitable screwdriver and turn the antenna trimmer of the radio to give the maximum clarity. You may need to remove the cluster panel from the front of the radio to allow access to the trimmer screw depending on the design of the radio (Fig. 10.123).

38 Radio antenna – removal and refitting

1 Remove the front wing (fender) liner panel on the side concerned, which is secured by bolts and clips (Fig. 10.124).
2 From the antenna itself, unscrew and remove the set nut (Fig. 10.125).
3 From within the wing underside, unscrew and remove the antenna retaining bracket bolt, then withdraw the antenna downwards.
4 Detach the lead from the radio and pull it through the grommet in the body panel to allow its removal together with the antenna.
5 Refit in the reverse order of removal.

39 Radio speaker – removal and refitting

1 Carefully prise free the trim panel in which the speaker is set to allow access to the rear of the speaker (Fig. 10.126).
2 Detach the wires at the speaker connections then disconnect the speaker unit from the trim panel.
3 Refit in reverse order of removal.

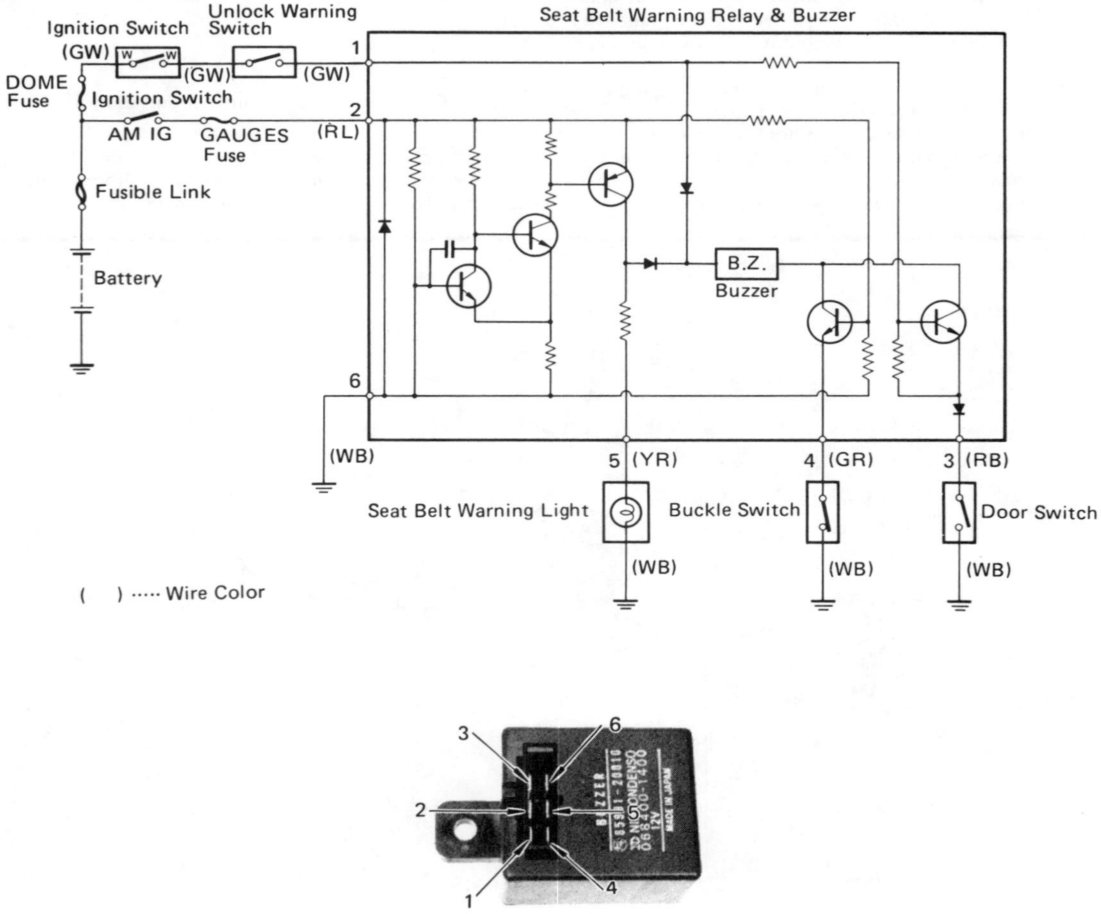

Fig. 10.119 Seat belt warning light and buzzer circuit (Sec 36)

Fig. 10.120 The seat belt warning buzzer (Sec 36)

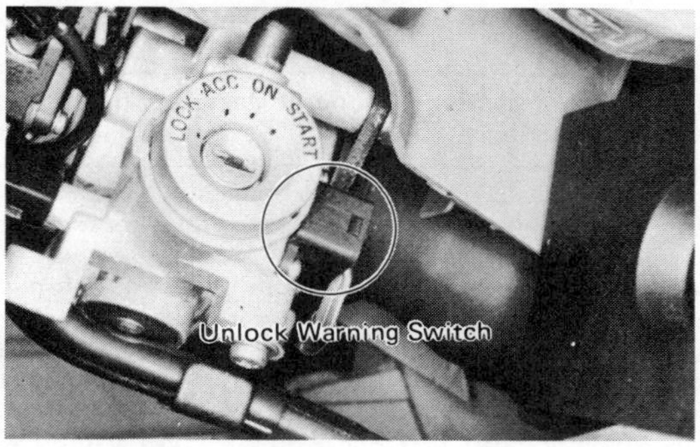

Fig. 10.121 The seat belt warning switch (Sec 36)

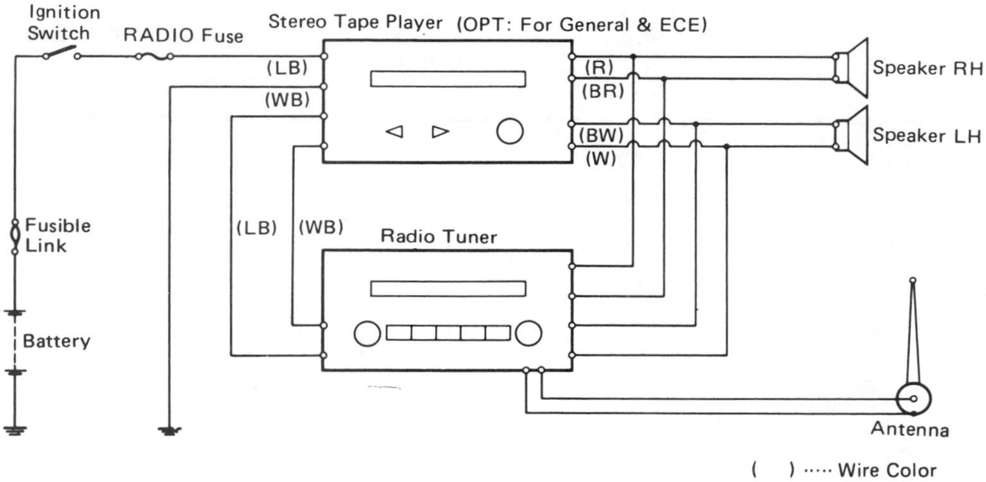

Fig. 10.22 The radio, speaker and antenna circuits (Sec 37)

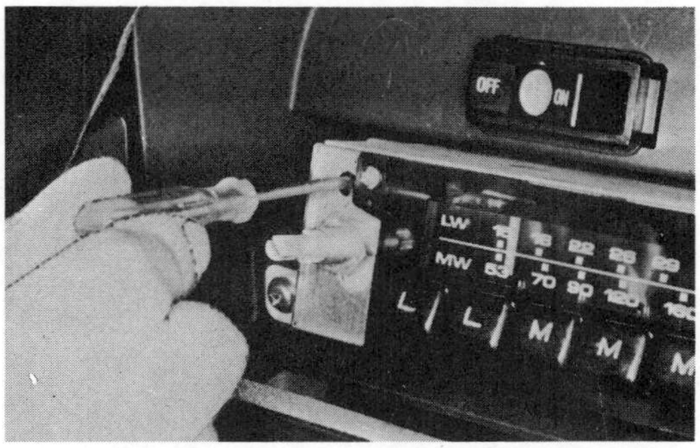

Fig. 10.123 Adjusting the antenna trimmer to improve reception (Sec 37)

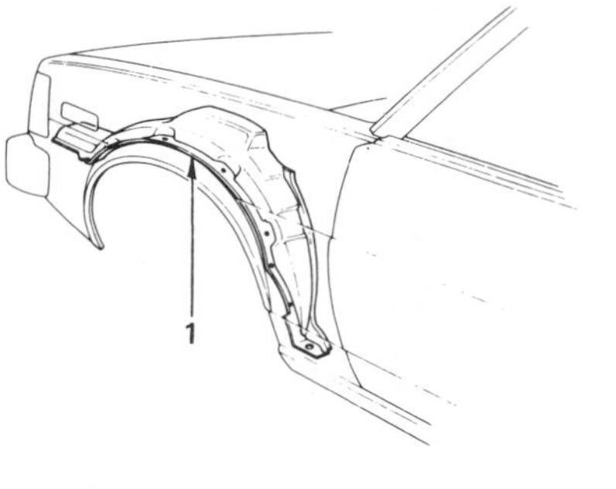

Fig. 10.124 Front wing liner panel (Sec 38)

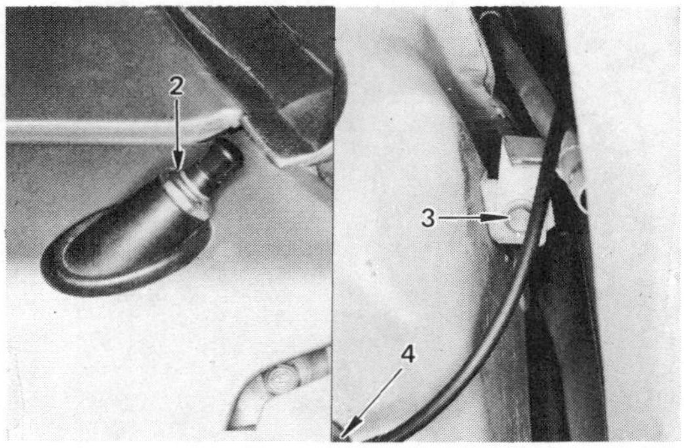

Fig. 10.125 Remove antenna set nut (2) and bolt (3). Pull through the grommet (4) (Sec 38)

Fig. 10.126 Speaker unit location in trim panel (Sec 39)

40 Air conditioning system – general description and maintenance

1 The optionally specified system comprises a heater and cooling unit, a belt driven compressor, a condenser and a receiver, together with the necessary temperature controls.
2 The oil filled compressor is driven from the crankshaft pulley and incorporates a magnetic type clutch.
3 Servicing of the system is outside the scope of the home mechanic as special equipment is needed to purge or recharge the system with refrigerant gas, and dismantling of any part of the system must not be undertaken, in the interest of safety, without first having discharged the system pressure.
4 To maintain optimum performance of the system, the owner should limit his operations to the following:

(a) Checking the tension of the compression driving belt. (See Chapter 2).
(b) Checking the security of all hoses and unions.
(c) Always keeping the ignition timing correctly set.
(d) Checking the security of the electrical connections.
(e) Regularly cleaning the air intake filter.

5 Use a soft brush to remove accumulations of dust and flies from the condenser fins.
6 During the winter months, operate the air conditioning system for a few minutes each week to lubricate the interior of the compressor pump, as lack of use may cause deterioration in the moving parts.

41 Neutral starter switch (automatic transmission) – removal, refitting and adjustment

A20 transmission switch removal and refitting

1 Disconnect the battery earth lead.
2 Referring to Fig. 10.129 remove the console box unit which is secured in position by a screw each side at the front and two screws along its rear edge. Prise free the cover for access to the rear screws.

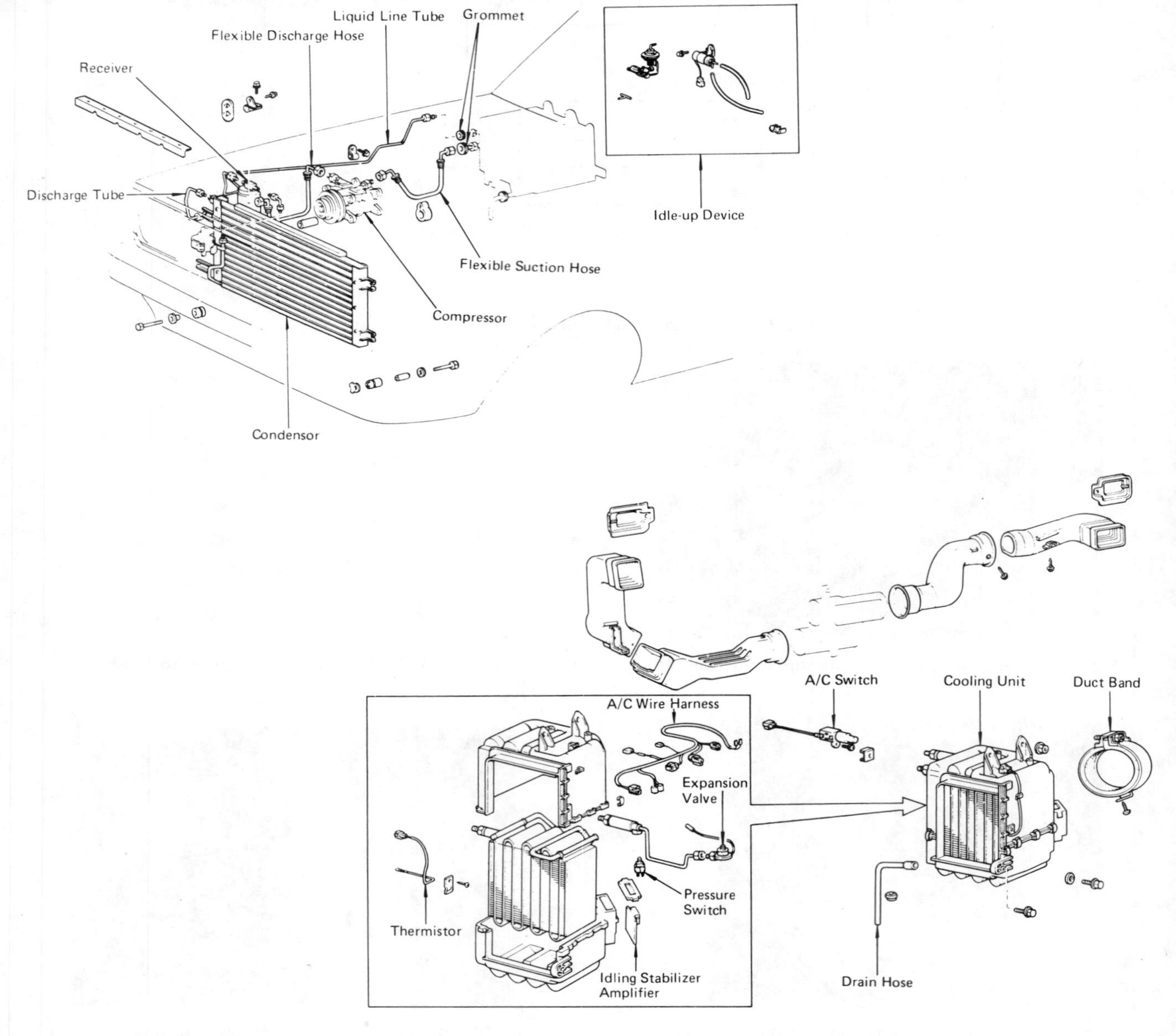

Fig. 10.127 Air conditioning system components and locations (Sec 40)

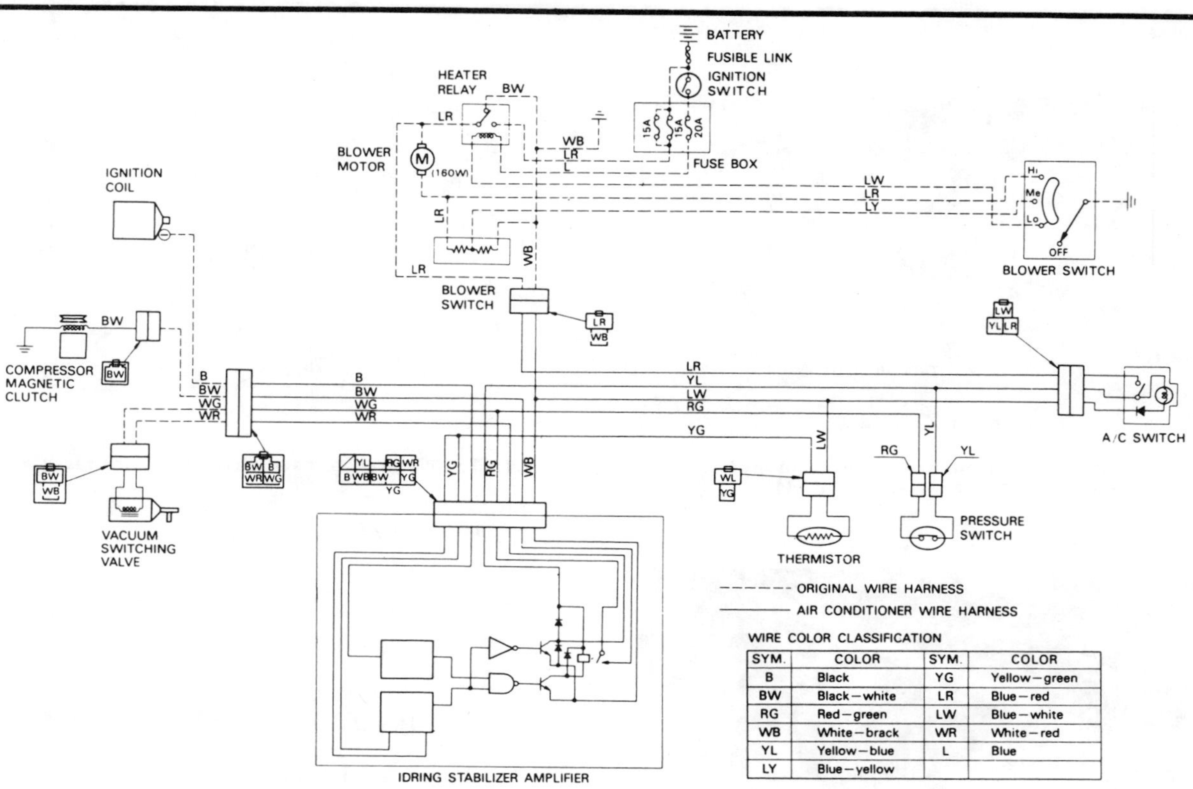

SYM.	COLOR	SYM.	COLOR
B	Black	YG	Yellow–green
BW	Black–white	LR	Blue–red
RG	Red–green	LW	Blue–white
WB	White–brack	WR	White–red
YL	Yellow–blue	L	Blue
LY	Blue–yellow		

Fig. 10.128 Air conditioning system wiring diagram (Sec 40)

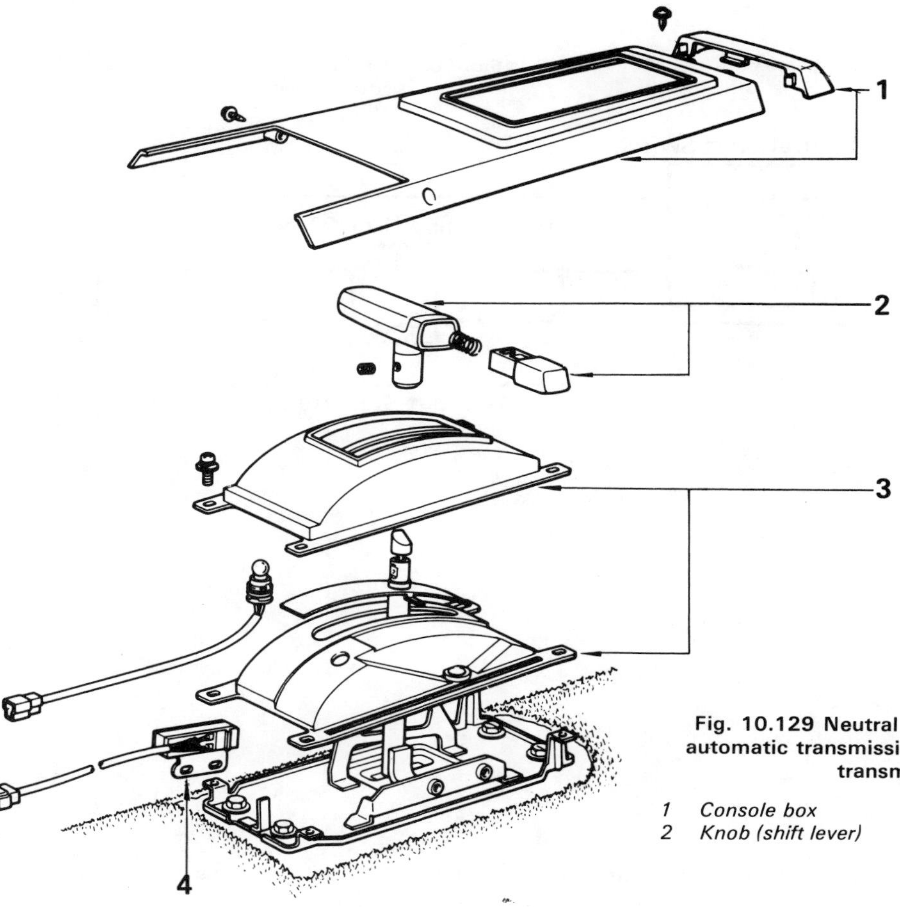

Fig. 10.129 Neutral starter switch and associated automatic transmission selector components – A20 transmission (Sec 41)

1 Console box
2 Knob (shift lever)
3 Housing and position indicator
4 Neutral starter switch

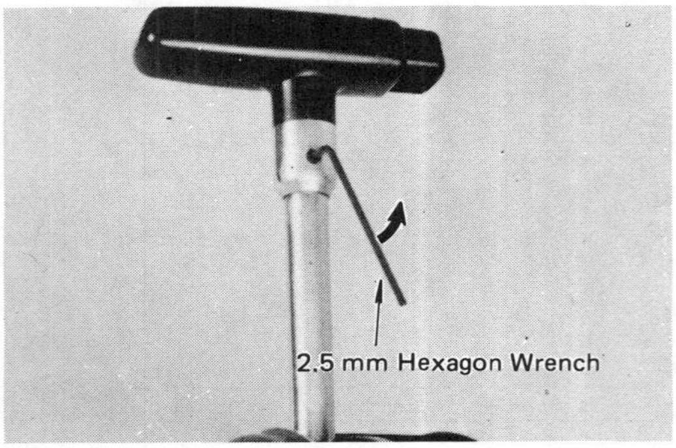

Fig. 10.130 Remove the grub screw and lift knob clear – A20 transmission (Sec 41)

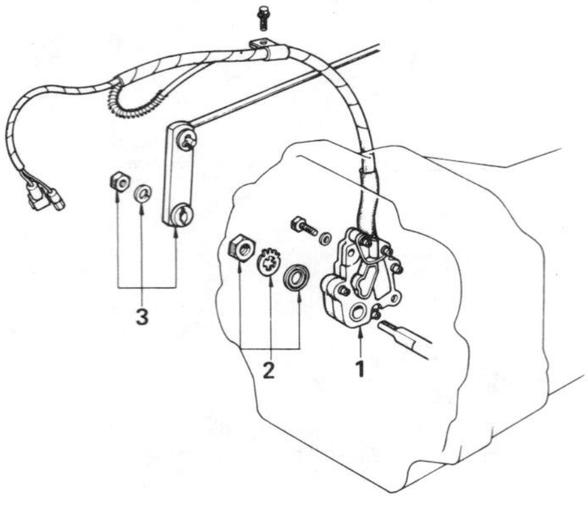

Fig. 10.131 Neutral start switch on A40 transmission (Sec 41)

1 Switch
2 Nut and nut stopper grommet
3 Control shaft lever

Fig. 10.132 Align the match markings – A40 transmission (Sec 41)

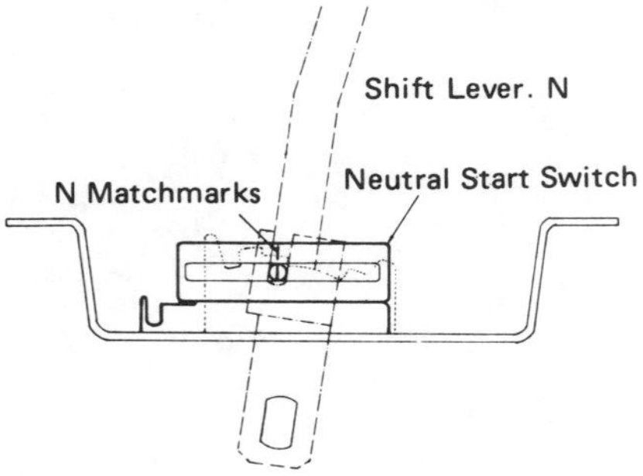

Fig. 10.133 Align the match markings – A20 transmission (Sec 41)

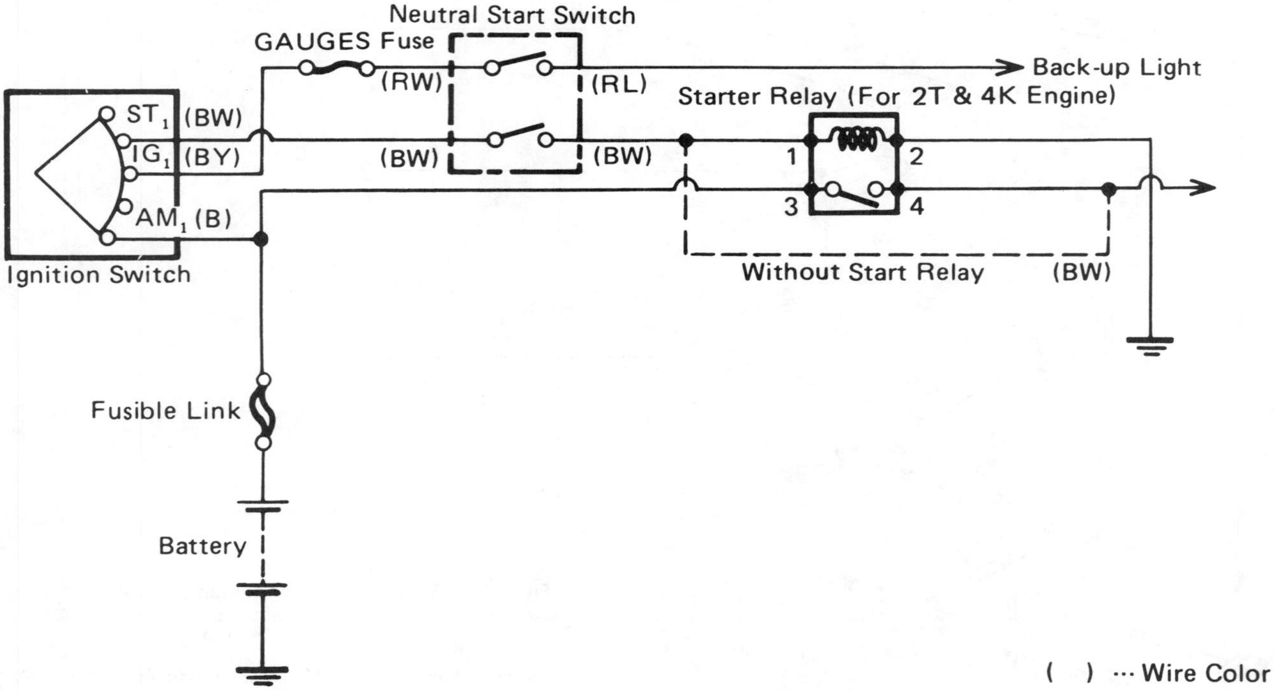

Fig. 10.134 The automatic transmission neutral start switch wiring diagram – A20 and A40 transmissions (Sec 41)

3 Remove the grub screw using a 2.5 mm Allen key and lift the shift lever knob assembly from the lever (Fig. 10.130).
4 Remove the retaining screws and lift clear the upper and lower housing covers, disconnecting the control illumination light and the neutral start switch wire connectors. The neutral start switch should have positional match marks on it.
5 Refit in the reverse order of removal and check adjustment of the starter switch on completion (see paragraph 14).

A40 transmission switch removal and refitting

6 Disconnect the battery earth lead.
7 You will need to work underneath the vehicle so raise and support it on axle stands.
8 Referring to Fig. 10.131 unscrew and remove the nut and washer securing the control shaft lever to the switch shaft.
9 Detach the lever from the switch shaft then peen back the tags of the lockwasher and remove the inner nut and the washer and grommet.
10 Withdraw the switch and disconnect the lead wire connections.
11 Refit in the reverse order of removal. When the inner nut is secure bend over the tag of the lockwasher to secure it. Ensure that the grommet is fitted with its cavity side facing the transmission.
12 When fitting the lever align the switch slot with the neutral base line as shown (Fig. 10.132). Check that the wiring connections are securely made and not compressed.
13 On completion check the operation and adjustment of the switch as follows.

A20 and A40 transmissions

14 Move the shift lever through the various function positions and check for correct operation as follows:

(a) In positions N or P only – engine should start. The engine should not start with the lever in any other position.
(b) Reversing lights should come on when lever is moved to R position.

15 If the above checks showed a malfunction in the selection, then adjust the neutral starter switch as follows according to type with the engine off.

(a) A20 transmission: Loosen off the neutral starter switch location screw, set the lever to the N range and move the switch to align the match marks then retighten the screw. Recheck switch operation (Fig. 10.133).
(b) A40 transmission: Loosen off the switch nut and align the switch slot with the neutral base line as shown in Fig. 10.132.

16 The wiring diagram for the neutral starter switch is shown in Fig. 10.134. If the neutral starter switch is known to be operational and correctly adjusted, but trouble persists, check the circuit connections and associated components.

42 Fault diagnosis – electrical system

Symptom	Reason(s)
Starter motor fails to turn engine	
No electricity at starter motor	Battery discharged. Battery defective internally. Battery terminal leads loose or earth lead not securely attached to body. Loose or broken connections in starter motor circuit. Starter motor switch or solenoid faulty.
Electricity at starter motor: faulty motor	Starter brushes badly worn, sticking or brush wires loose. Commutator dirty, worn or burnt. Starter motor armature faulty. Field coils earthed.
Starter motor turns engine very slowly	
Electrical defects	Battery in discharged condition. Starter brushes badly worn, sticking or brush wires loose. Loose wires in starter motor circuit.
Starter motor operates without turning engine	
Mechanical damage	Pinion or flywheel gear teeth broken or worn.
Starter motor noisy or excessively rough engagement	
Lack of attention or mechanical damage	Pinion or flywheel gear teeth broken or worn. Starter motor retaining bolts loose.
Battery will not hold charge for more than a few days	
Wear or damage	Battery defective internally. Electrolyte level too low or electrolyte too weak due to leakage. Plate separators no longer fully effective. Battery plates severely sulphated.
Insufficient current flow to keep battery charged	Battery plates severely sulphated. Drivebelt slipping. Battery terminal connections loose or corroded. Alternator not charging. Short in lighting circuit causing continual battery drain. Regulator unit not working correctly.
Ignition light fails to go out, battery runs flat in a few days	
Alternator not charging	Drivebelt loose and slipping or broken. Brushes worn, sticking, broken or dirty. Brush springs weak or broken.
Regulator fails to work correctly	Regulator incorrectly set. Open circuit in wiring of regulator unit.

Symptom	Reason(s)

Failure of individual electrical equipment to function correctly is dealt with alphabetically, item-by-item, under the headings list below:

Symptom	Reason(s)
Horn	
Horn operates all the time	Horn push either earthed or stuck down. Horn cable to horn push earthed.
Horn fails to operate	Blown fuse. Cable or cable connection loose, broken or disconnected. Horn has an internal fault.
Horn emits intermittent or unsatisfactory noise	Cable connections loose. Horn incorrectly adjusted.
Lights	
Lights do not come on	If engine not running, battery discharged. Light bulb filament burnt out or bulbs broken. Wire connections loose, disconnected or broken. Light switch shorting or otherwise faulty.
Lights come on but fade out	If engine not running battery discharged. Light bulb filament burnt out or bulbs or sealed beam units broken. Wire connections loose, disconnected or broken. Light switch shorting or otherwise faulty.
Lights give very poor illumination	Lamp glasses dirty. Lamps badly out of adjustment. Incorrect bulb with too low wattage fitted. Existing bulbs old and badly discoloured.
Lights work erratically - flashing on and off, especially over bumps	Battery terminals or earth connection loose. Lights not earthing properly. Contacts in light switch faulty.
Wipers	
Wiper motor fails to work	Blown fuse. Wire connections loose, disconnected, or broken. Brushes badly worn. Armature worn or faulty. Field coils faulty.
Wiper motor works very slowly and takes excessive current	Commutator dirty, greasy or burnt. Armature bearings dirty or unaligned. Armature badly worn or faulty. Armature thrust adjuster screw overtightened.
Wiper motor works slowly and takes little current	Brushes badly worn. Commutator dirty, greasy or burnt. Armature badly worn or faulty.

Colour code

B	*Black*
Br	*Brown*
G	*Green*
Gr	*Grey*
L	*Light blue*
LG	*Light green*
O	*Orange*
R	*Red*
W	*White*
Y	*Yellow*

The first letter indicates the basic colour and subsequent letters indicate the spiral trace colour

Key to colour codes used in the wiring diagrams

Key to wiring diagram Fig. 10.135 for 1981 Toyota Corolla Saloon and Estate models

Note: *Some of the items listed are not applicable to UK models*

Component number	Grid location	Components
001	C2	A/C amplifier
004	D1	Alternator
010	D1	Battery
013	B8	Cigarette lighter
017	C8	Clock
022	D2	Condenser
027	A3	Diode
028	B2	Distributor
040	B2	Fuel cut solenoid
041	B3	Fuel gauge
042	B3	Fuel level sender
047	A2	Fuse box
048	C1	Fusible link
051	C2	Heater choke coil
052	B2	Heater resistor
055	C5	Horn (LH)
057	C5	Horn (RH)
061	B2	Ignition coil
063	D2	Magnet clutch
073	B8	Radio
075	B4	Rear window defogger
076	D2	Regulator
087	B8	Speaker (RH)
088	B8	Speaker (LH)
093	B8	Stereo
095	D2	Thermistor
106	D2	VSV
112	B2	VSV
109	B3	Water temperature gauge
110	D3	Water thermo sender
203	C8	Ashtray light
204	B8	A/T indicator light
205	D4	Back-up light (RH)
206	D3	Back-up light (LH)
207	C3	Brake warning light
208	A3	Charge warning light
210	C8	Cigarette lighter light
211	C7	Clearance light (RH)
212	B7	Clearance light (LH)
213	C8	Clock light
214	B8	Combination meter light
224	B3	Fuel level warning light
227	C4	Hazard red indicator light
228	B6	Headlight (RH)
228	B7	Headlight (RH)
229	B6	Headlight (LH)
231	B8	Heater control light
232	C6	High beam indicator light
235	C8	Interior light
238	B7	License plate light (RH)
239	C7	License plate light (LH)
242	B3	Oil warning light
243	C8	Open door warning light
245	B3	PKB light
250	C7	Rear fog light
257	D4	Stop light (RH)
258	D4	Stop light (LH)
259	C7	Tail light (RH)
260	B7	Tail light (LH)

Component number	Grid location	Components
263	D5	Turn signal light, front (RH)
264	D4	Turn signal light, left (LH)
265	D5	Turn signal indicator light (RH)
266	D4	Turn signal indicator light (LH)
267	C5	Turn signal light, rear (RH)
268	C4	Turn signal light, rear (LH)
269	C5	Turn signal light, side (RH)
270	C4	Turn signal light, side (LH)
405	C2	Electric fan motor
406	B5	Headlight cleaner motor
407	B2	Headlight blower motor
415	C1	Starter motor
417	C5	Washer motor, rear (Estate)
418	B5	Windshield washer motor
419	B5	Windshield wiper motor
420	C5	Wiper motor, rear
604	D3	Bulb check relay
611	B6	Dimmer relay
616	B2	Electric fan relay
617	B4	Flasher relay
621	C4	Hazard red indicator light relay
622	A6	Headlight relay
623	B5	Headlight cleaner relay
625	B2	Heater relay
634	B1	Main relay
637	D7	Rear fog light relay
641	B1	Starter relay (2-A/T)
644	A7	Tail light relay
650	B5	Intermittent wiper relay
801	B3	A/C switch
806	A3	Back-up light switch
807	C3	Brake fluid level switch
811	A4	Defogger switch
813	B6	Dimmer switch
815	D8	Door courtesy switch, front (RH)
816	D8	Door coutesy switch, front (LH)
817	D8	Door courtesy switch, rear (RH)
818	D8	Door courtesy switch, rear (LH)
823	D7	Rear fog light switch
824	B3	Fuel level warning switch
826	A4	Hazard switch
827	C3	Heater blower switch
828	C5	Horn switch
829	A1	Ignition switch
831	C8	Interior light switch
834	C7	Light control switch
835	D3	Low pressure cut switch
840	B1	Neutral start switch
844	B3	Oil pressure switch
846	C3	PKB switch
865	A4	Stop light switch
867	C2	Thermo switch
870	B2	TOP switch
874	B4	Turn signal switch
880	C5	Washer switch, rear (Estate)
882	A5	Windshield washer switch
883	A5	Windshield wiper switch
884	C5	Wiper switch, rear (Estate)

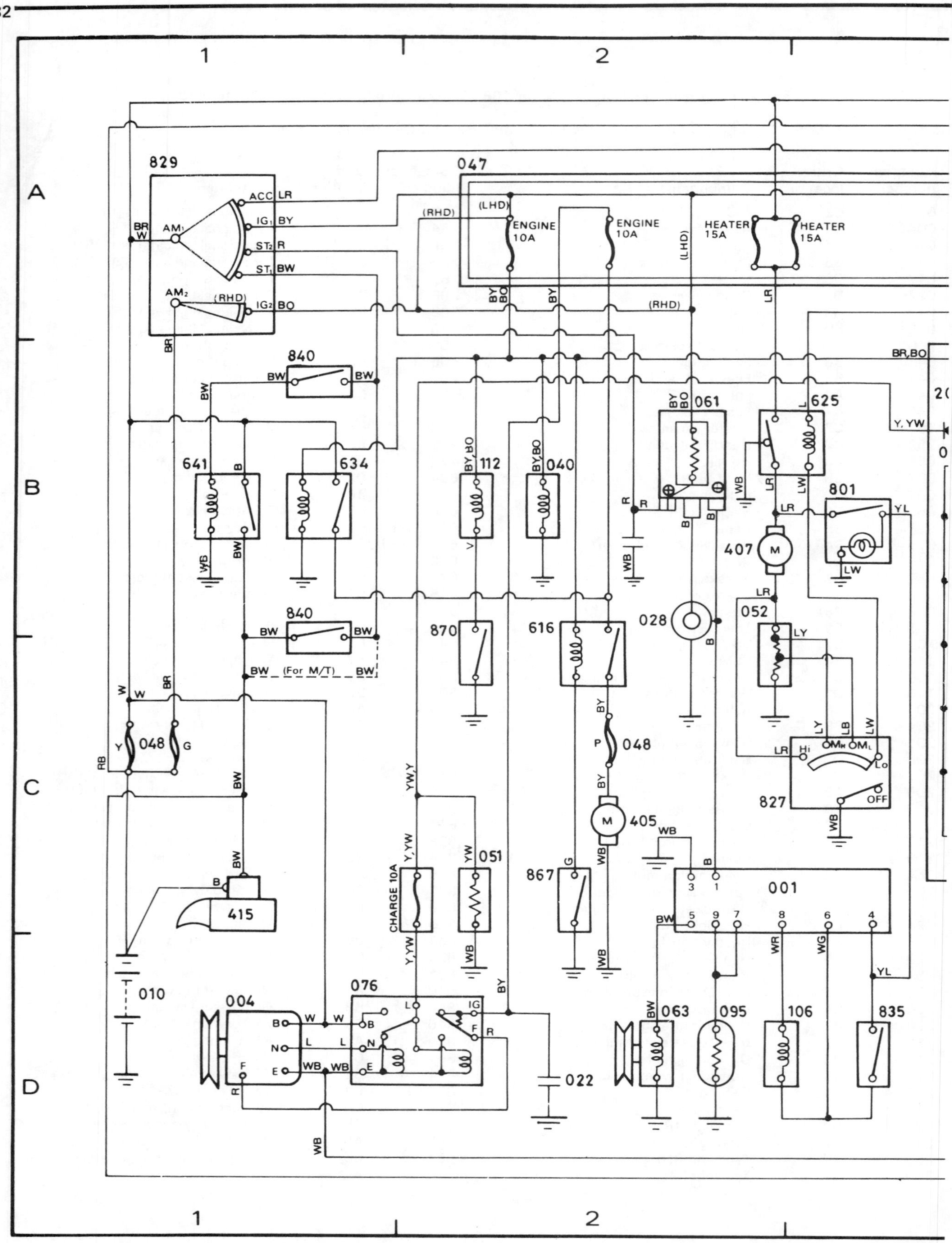

Fig. 10.135 Wiring diagram for 1981 Saloon and Estate models

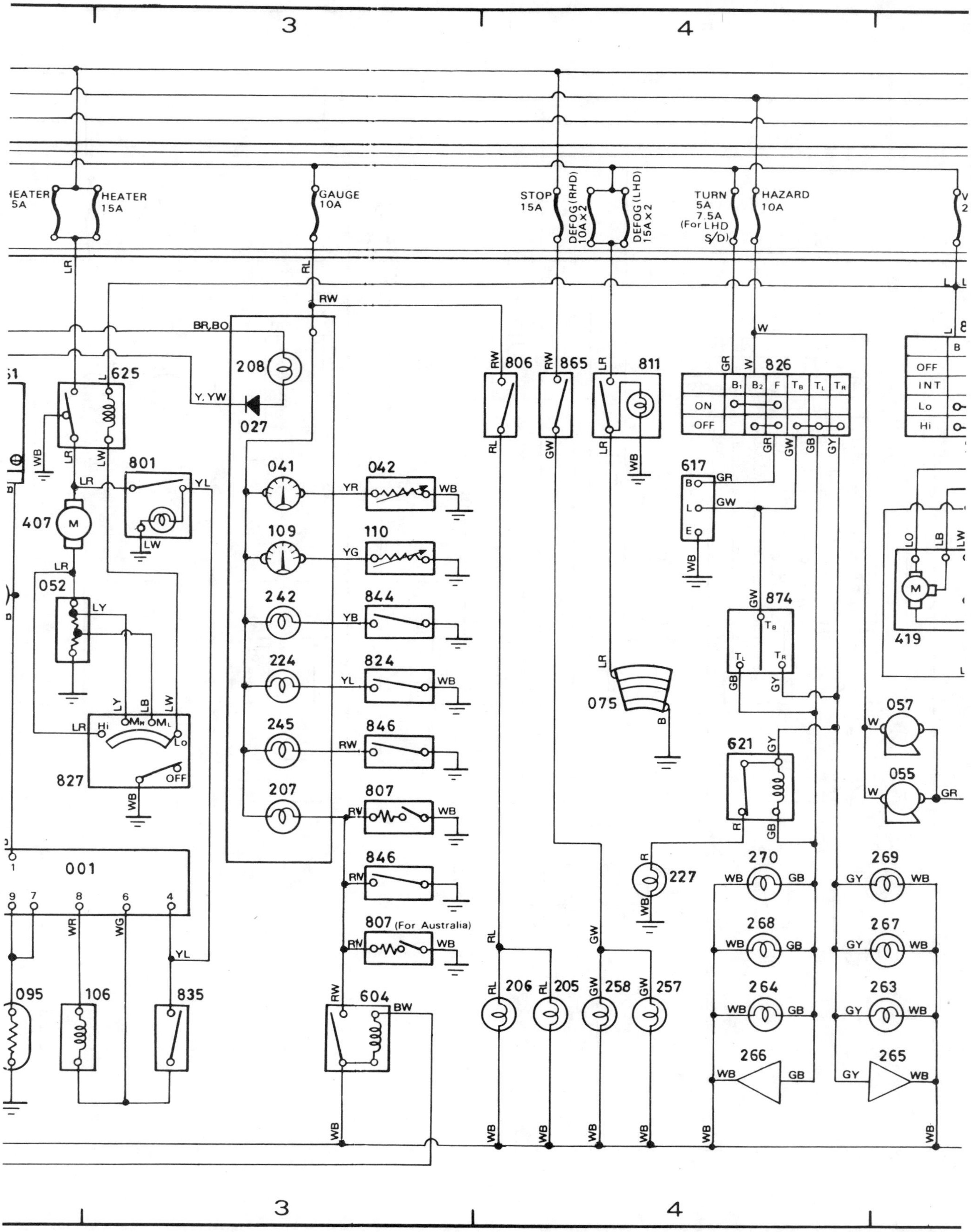

Fig. 10.135 Wiring diagram for 1981 Saloon and Estate models (continued)

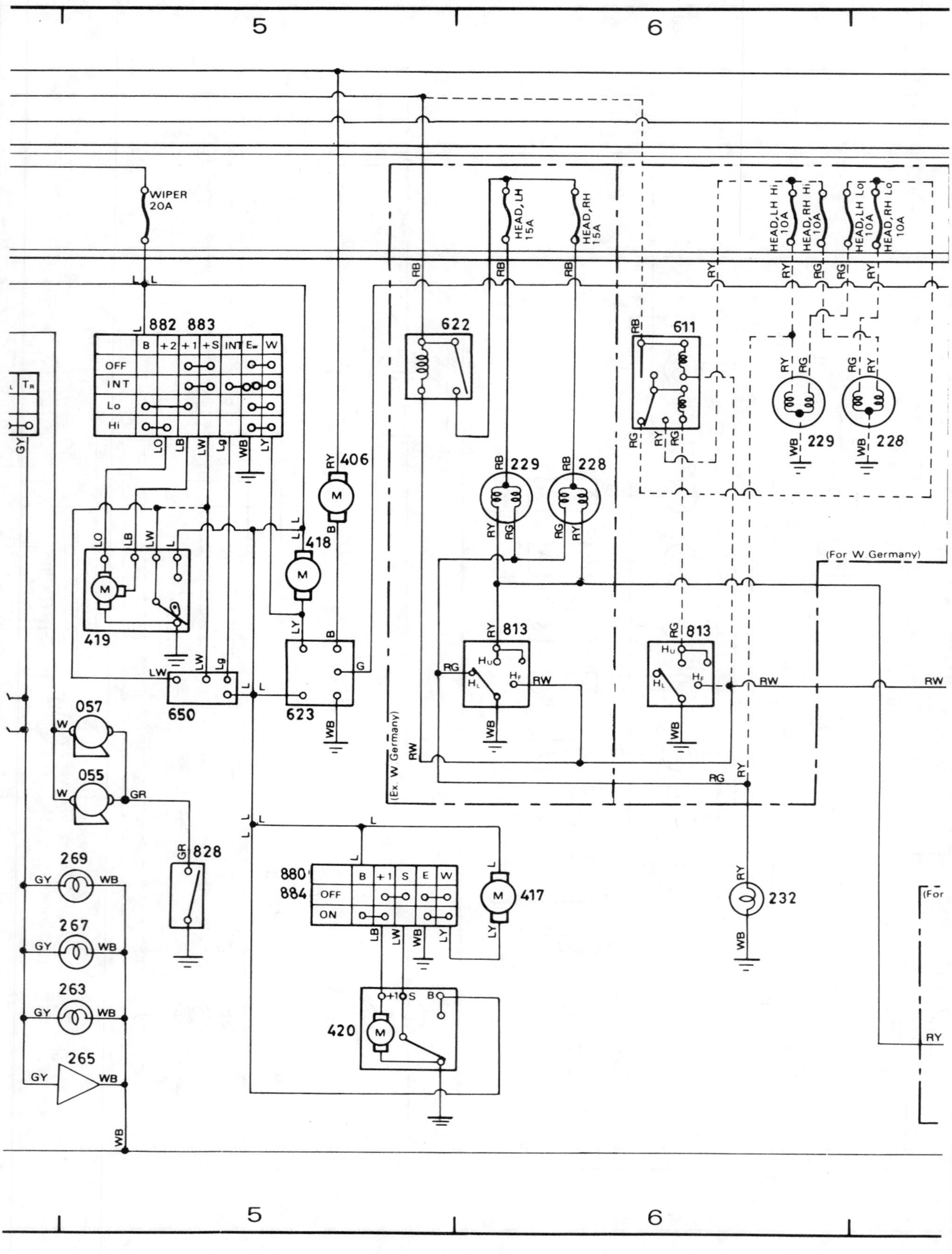

Fig. 10.135 Wiring diagram for 1981 Saloon and Estate models (continued)

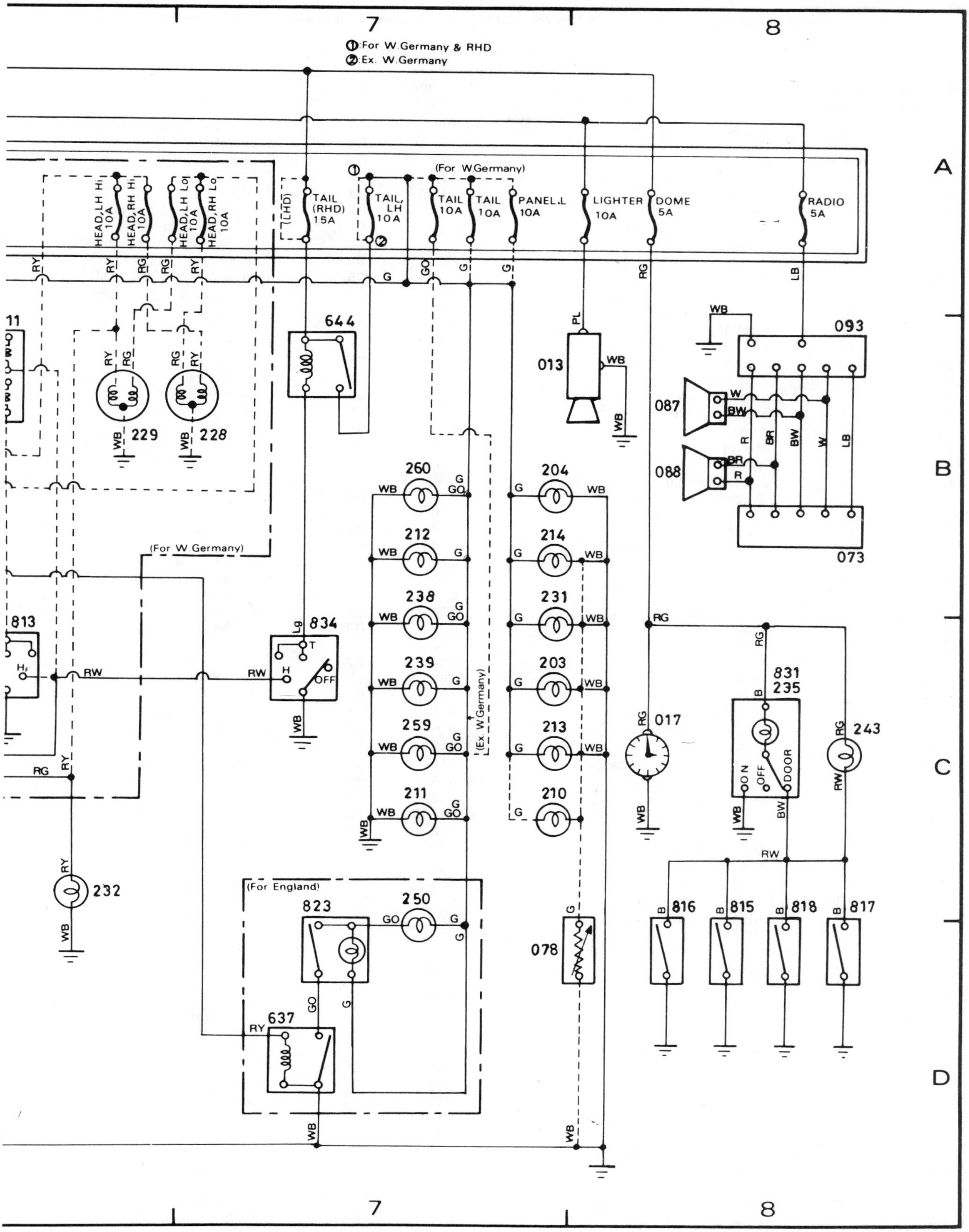

Fig. 10.135 Wiring diagram for 1981 Saloon and Estate models (continued)

Key to wiring diagram Fig. 10.136 for 1981 Toyota Corolla Liftback and Coupe models

Note: *Some of the items listed are not applicable to UK models*

Component number	Grid location	Components
001	C2	A/C amplifier
004	D1	Alternator
010	C1	Battery
013	B8	Cigarette lighter
017	C8	Clock
018	B8	Clock (digital)
020	C3	Combination meter (+B)
021	C3	Combination meter (Ground)
022	B2/D1	Condenser
028	B2	Distributor
039	D2	Emission control computer
040	B2	Fuel cut solenoid
041	D3	Fuel gauge
042	D3	Fuel lever sender
047	A2	Fuse box
048	C1	Fusible link
051	C1	Heater choke coil
052	B2	Heater resistor
055	C5	Horn (LH)
057	C5	Horn (RH)
061	B2	Ignition coil
063	D2	Magnet clutch
069	B3	Oil pressure gauge
070	B3	Oil pressure sender
073	D8	Radio
075	B4	Rear window defogger
076	D1	Regulator
078	C8	Rheostat
087	D8	Speaker (RH)
088	D8	Speaker (LH)
091	D2	Speed sensor
093	D8	Stereo
094	C3	Tachometer
095	D2	Thermistor
103	C3	Voltmeter
106	D2	VSV (for A/C)
112	C2	VSV (for emission control system)
112	B2	VSV
109	D3	Water temperature gauge
110	D3	Water thermo sensor
203	C8	Ashtray light
204	B8	A/T indicator light
205	D4	Back-up light (RH)
206	D4	Back-up light (LH)
207	C3	Brake warning light
208	A3	Charge warning light
209	B3	Choke warning light
210	C8	Cigarette lighter light (RHD and Coupe)
211	C7	Clearance light (RH)
212	B7	Clearance light (LH)
213	C8	Clock light
214	B8	Combination meter light
215	B8	Deck room light
224	B3	Fuel level warning light
227	C4	Hazard red indicator light
228	B6	Headlight (RH)
229	B6	Headlight (LH)
231	B8	Heater control light
232	C6	High beam indicator light
235	C8	Interior light
238	B7	License plate light (RH)
239	C7	License plate light (LH)
242	B3	Oil warning light
243	C8	Open door warning light
245	B3	PKB light
250	C7	Rear fog light
251	D7	Rear fog indicator light
257	D4	Stop light (RH)
258	D4	Stop light (LH)
259	C7	Tail light (RH)
260	B7	Tail light (LH)
263	D5	Turn signal light, front (RH)
264	D4	Turn signal light, left (LH)
265	D5	Turn signal indicator light (RH)
266	D4	Turn signal indicator light (LH)
267	C5	Turn signal light, rear (RH)
268	C4	Turn signal light, rear (LH)
269	C5	Turn signal light, side (RH)
270	C4	Turn signal light, side (LH)
405	C2	Electric fan motor
406	B5	Headlight cleaner motor
407	B2	Headlight blower motor
415	C1	Starter motor
417	C6	Washer motor, rear
418	B5	Windshield washer motor
419	B5	Windshield wiper motor
420	D5	Wiper motor, rear
604	D3	Bulb check relay
611	B6	Dimmer relay
616	C2	Electric fan relay
617	B4	Flasher relay
621	C4	Hazard red indicator light relay
622	B6	Headlight relay
623	B5	Headlight cleaner relay
625	B3	Heater relay
634	B1	Main relay
637	D7	Rear fog light relay
641	B1	Starter relay
644	B7	Tail light relay
650	C5	Intermittent wiper relay
801	B3	A/C switch
806	B4	Back-up light switch
807	C3	Brake fluid level switch
809	B3	Choke warning switch
810	B8	Deck room light switch
811	B4	Defogger switch
813	C6	Dimmer switch
815	C8	Door courtesy switch, front (RH)
816	C8	Door courtesy switch, front (LH)
823	D7	Rear fog light switch
824	B3	Fuel level warning switch
826	B4	Hazard switch
827	C2	Heater blower switch
828	C5	Horn switch
829	A1	Ignition switch
831	C8	Interior light switch
834	C7	Light control switch
835	D3	Low pressure cut switch
840	B1	Neutral start switch
844	B3	Oil pressure switch
846	C3	PKB switch
846	B3	PKB switch
865	B4	Stop light switch
867	D2	Thermo switch (electric fan)
867	B2	Thermo switch
870	C2	TOP switch
870	B2	TOP switch
874	B4	Turn signal switch
876	C2	Vacuum switch
880	C5	Washer switch, rear
882	B5	Windshield washer switch
883	B5	Windshield wiper switch
884	C5	Wiper switch, rear

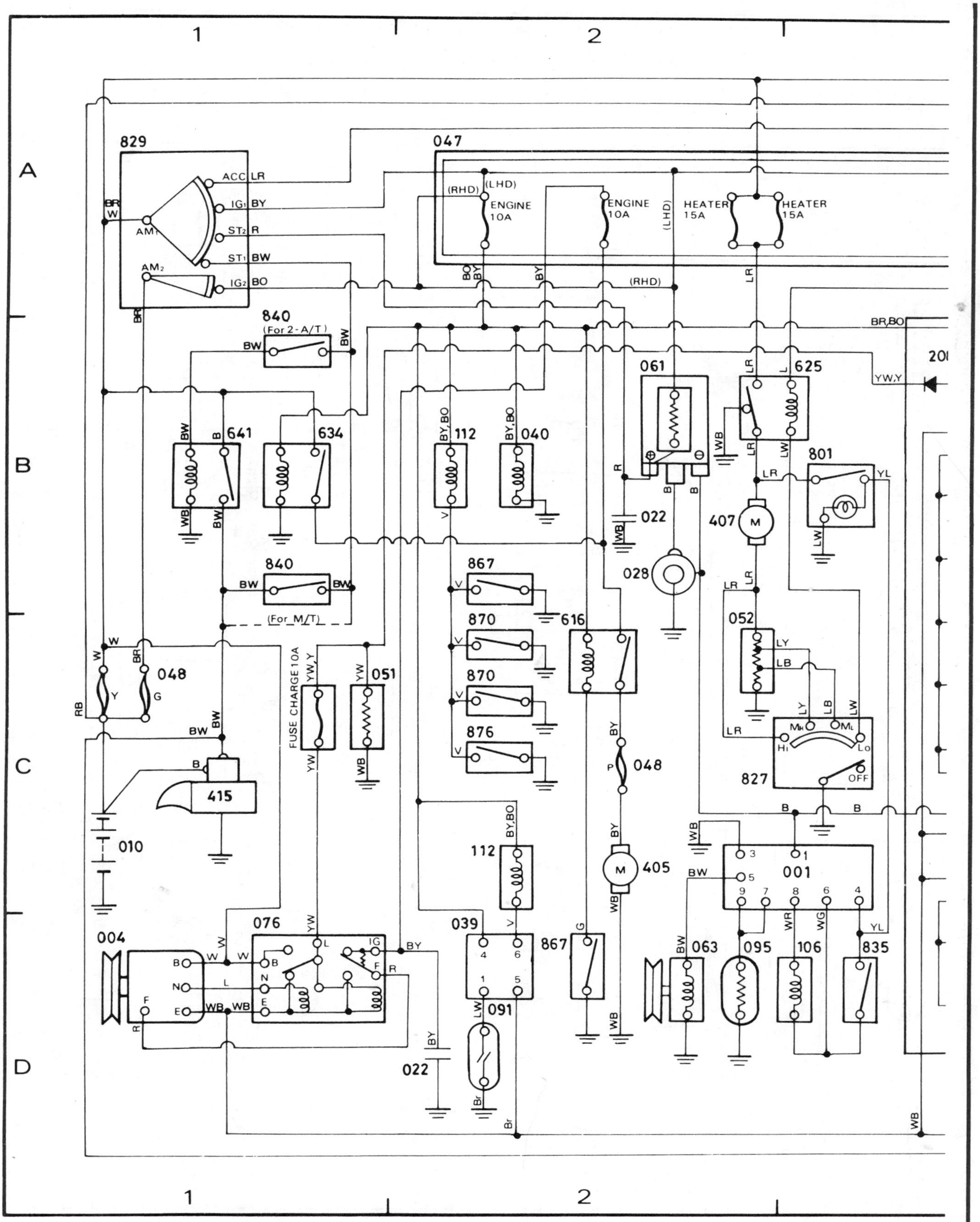

Fig. 10.136 Wiring diagram for 1981 Liftback and Coupe models

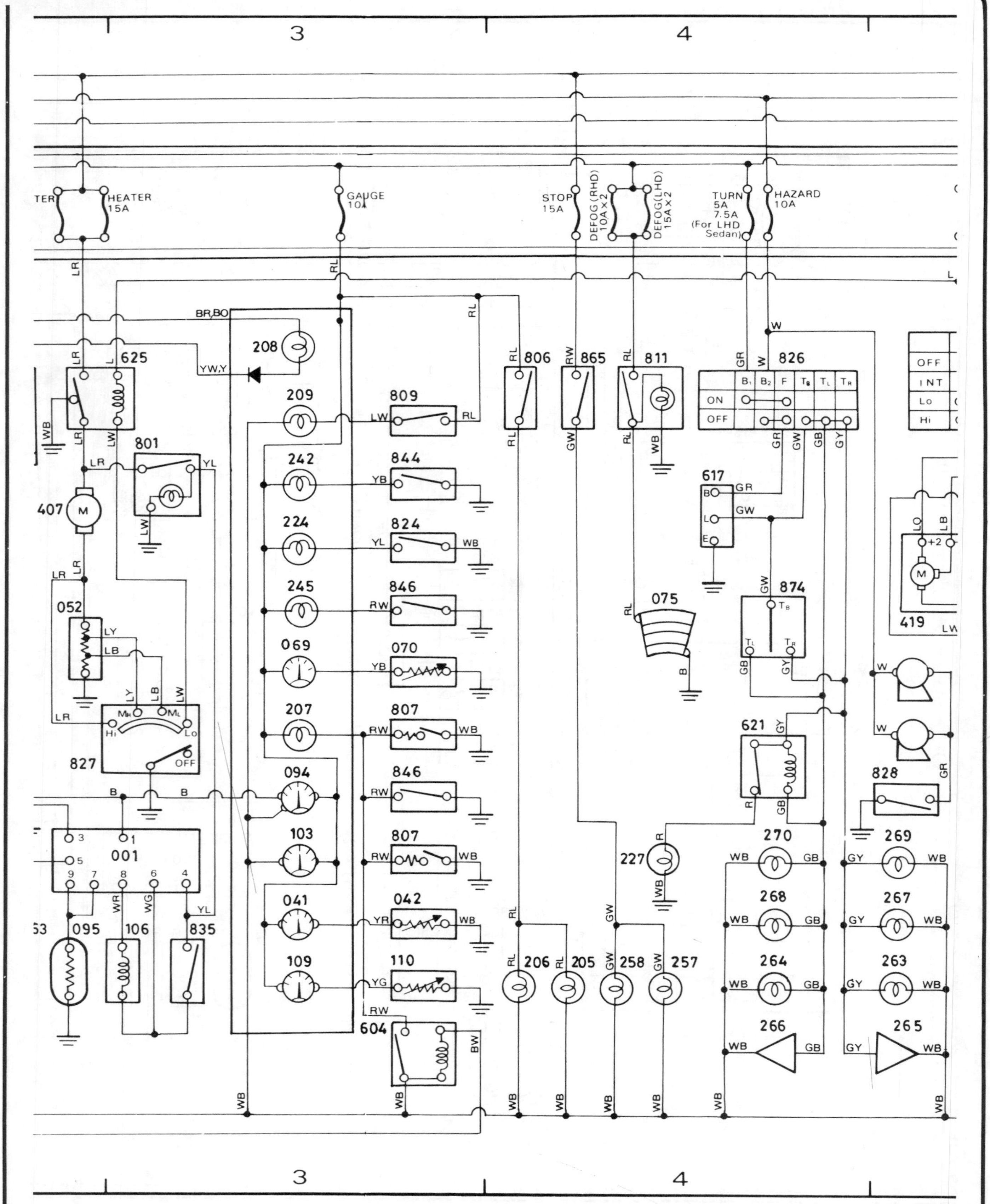

Fig. 10.136 Wiring diagram for 1981 Liftback and Coupe models (continued)

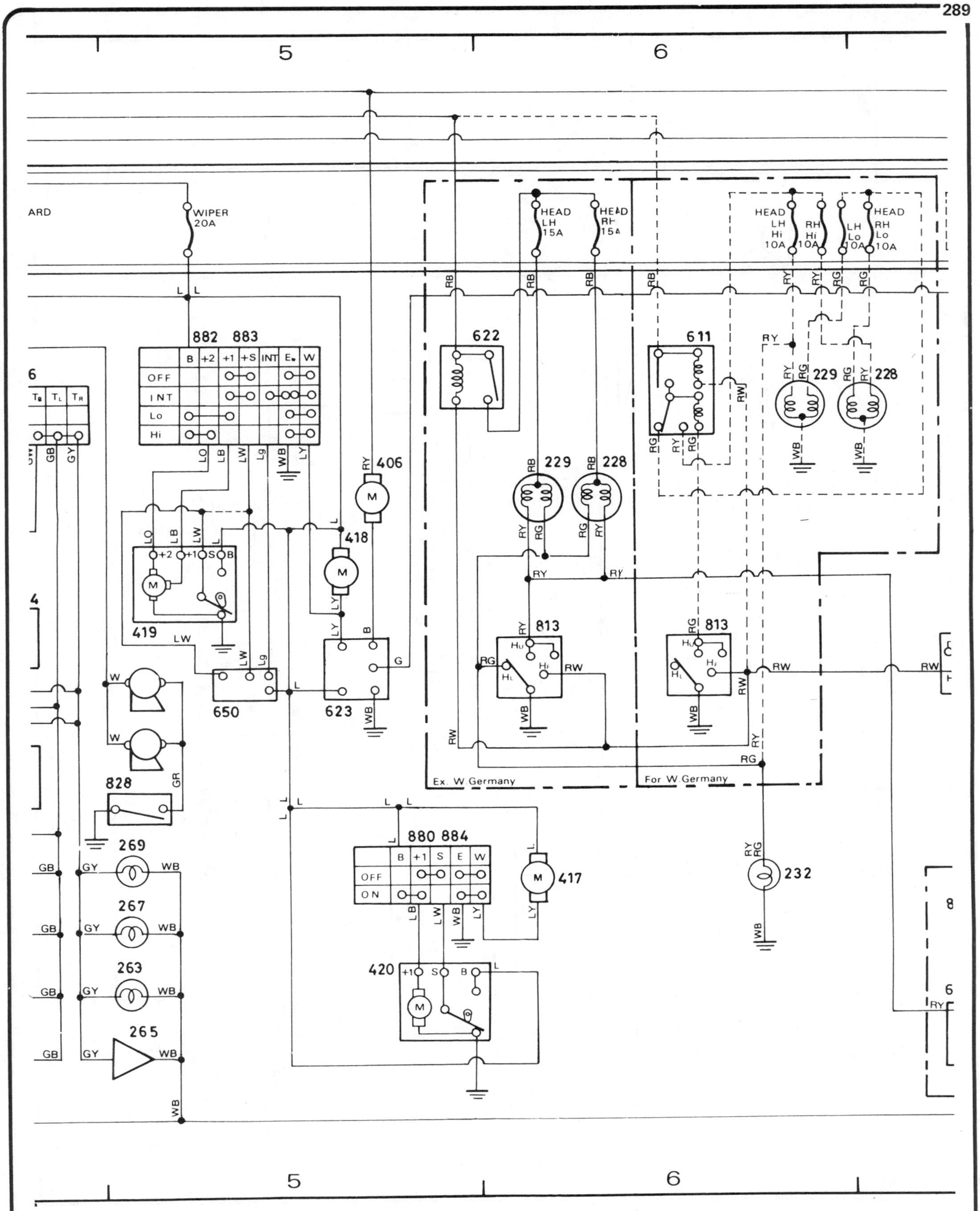

Fig. 10.136 Wiring diagram for 1981 Liftback and Coupe models (continued)

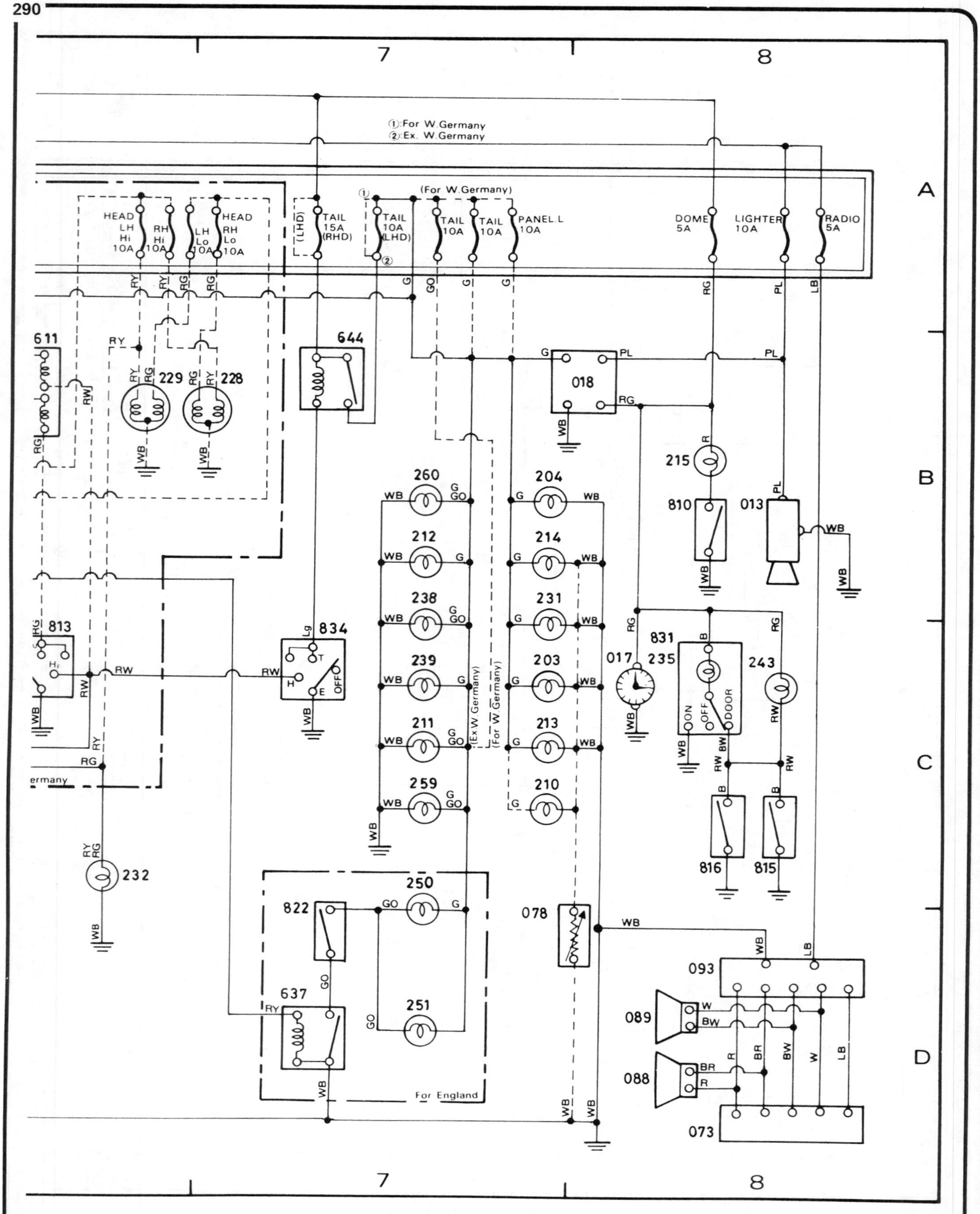

Fig. 10.136 Wiring diagram for 1981 Liftback and Coupe models (continued)

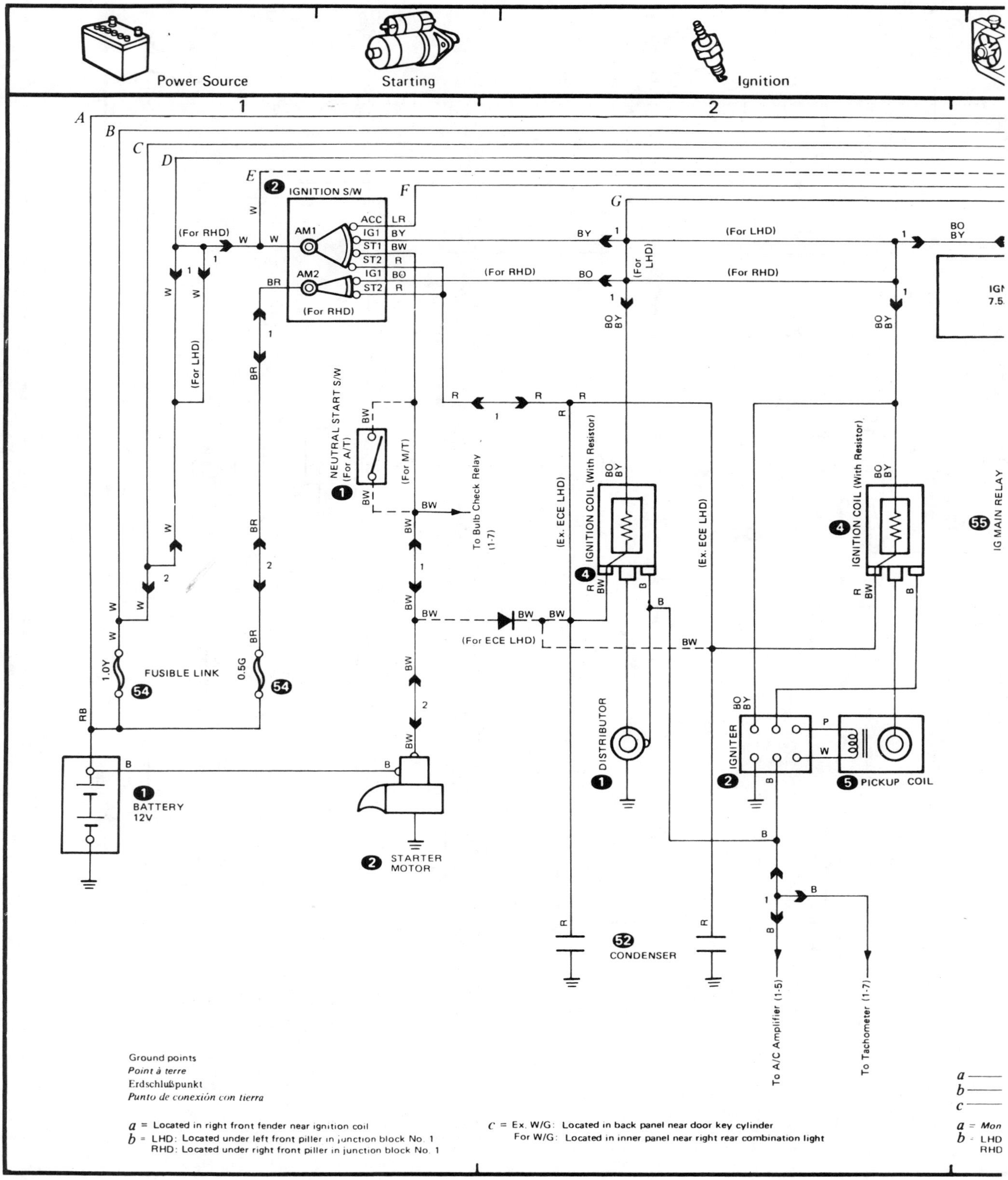

Fig. 10.137 Wiring diagram for 1982 Corolla models

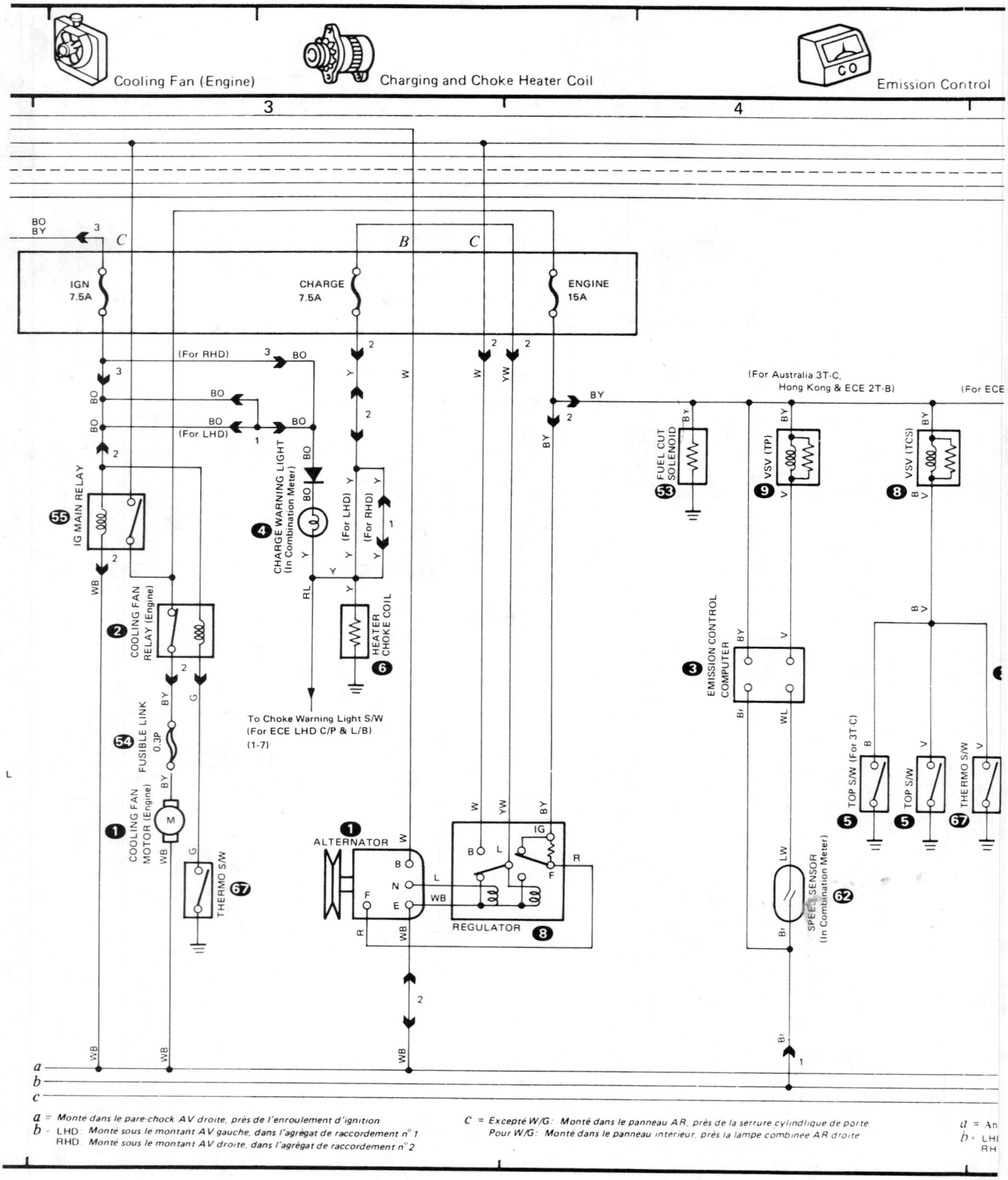

Fig. 10.137 Wiring diagram for 1982 Corolla models (continued)

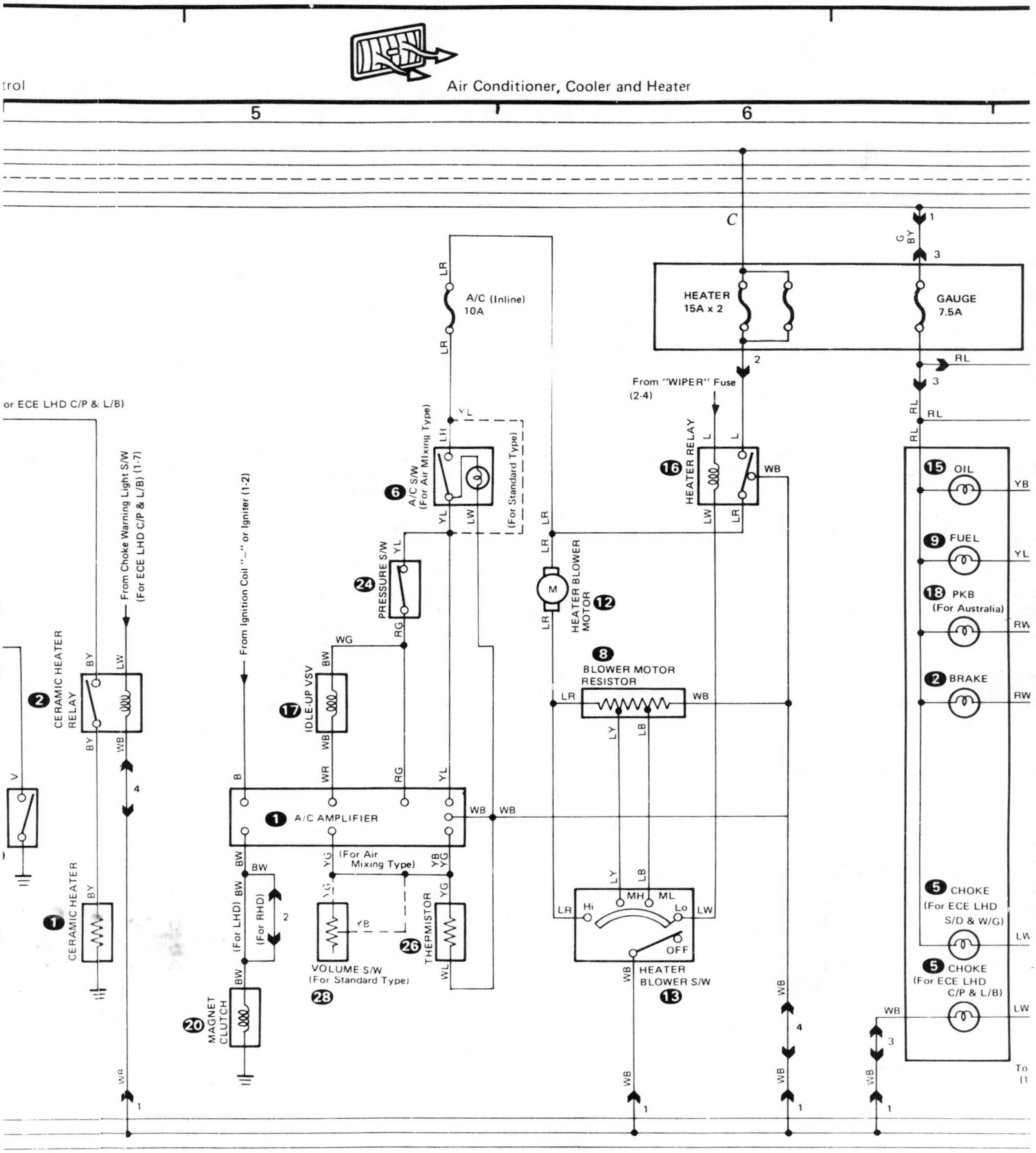

l = Angebracht im rechten Vorderpuffer, in der Nähe von Abreißzundung
) LHD Angebracht hinter der linken Vordersäule in der Anschlußdose Nr. 1
RHD Angebracht hinter der rechten Vordersäule in der Anschlußdose Nr. 2

C = Ausgenommen W/G: Angebracht in der Hintertafel, in der Nähe von Zylinderschlß der Tür
Zu W/G: Angebracht in der Innentafel, in der Nähe von richten Rückenkombinationslampe

a =
b

Fig. 10.137 Wiring diagram for 1982 Corolla models (continued)

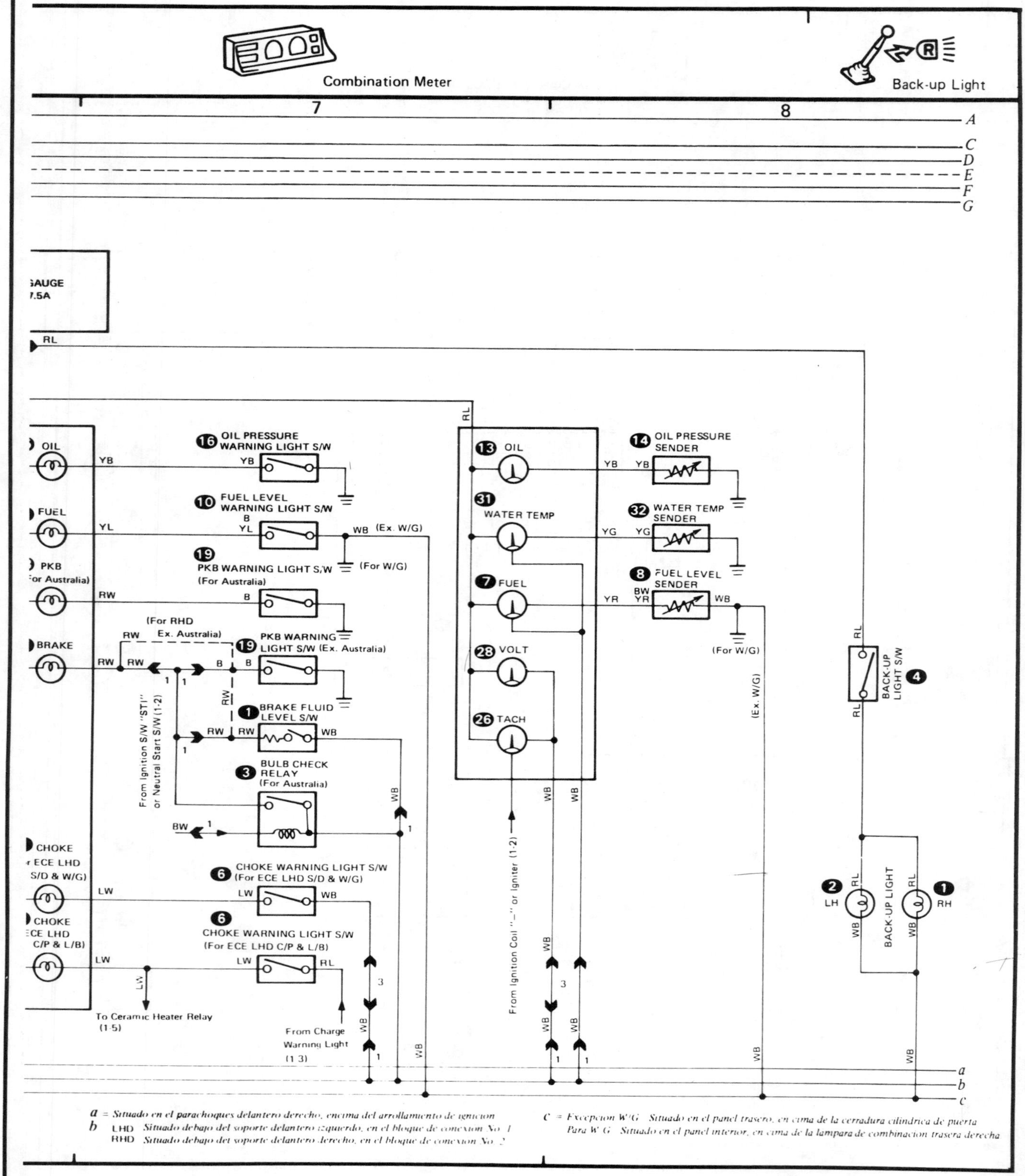

Fig. 10.137 Wiring diagram for 1982 Corolla models (continued)

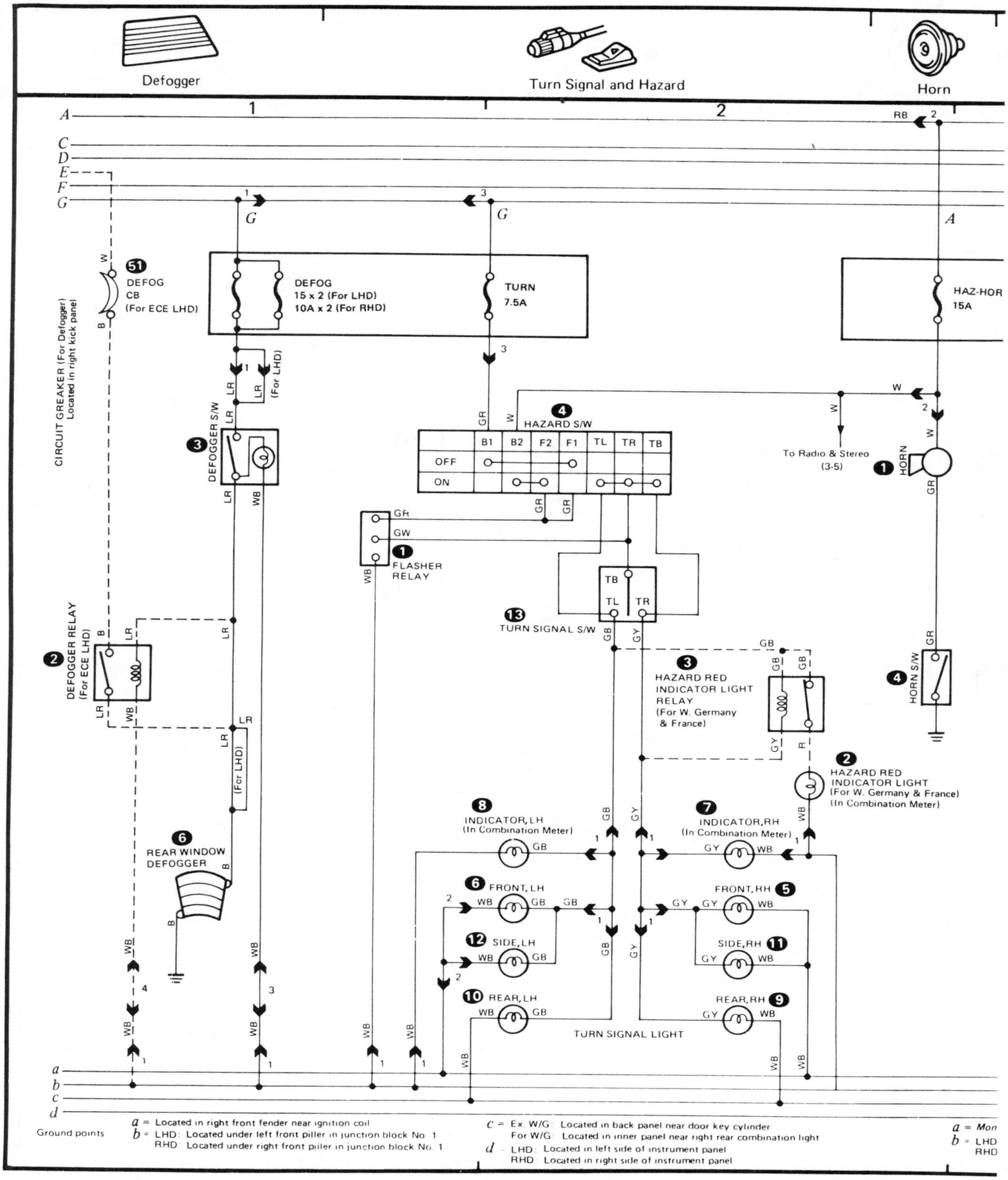

Fig. 10.137 Wiring diagram for 1982 Corolla models (continued)

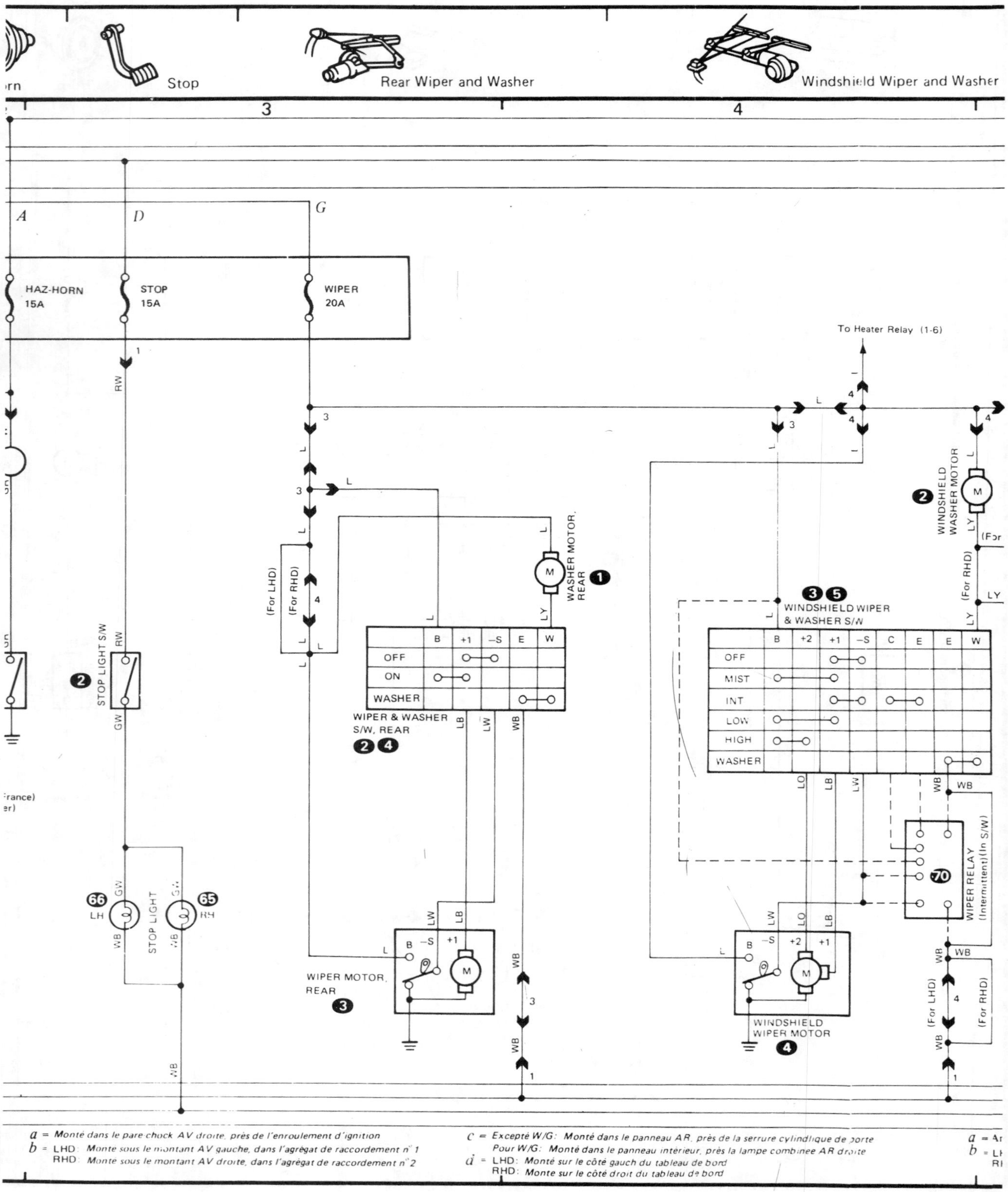

Fig. 10.137 Wiring diagram for 1982 Corolla models (continued)

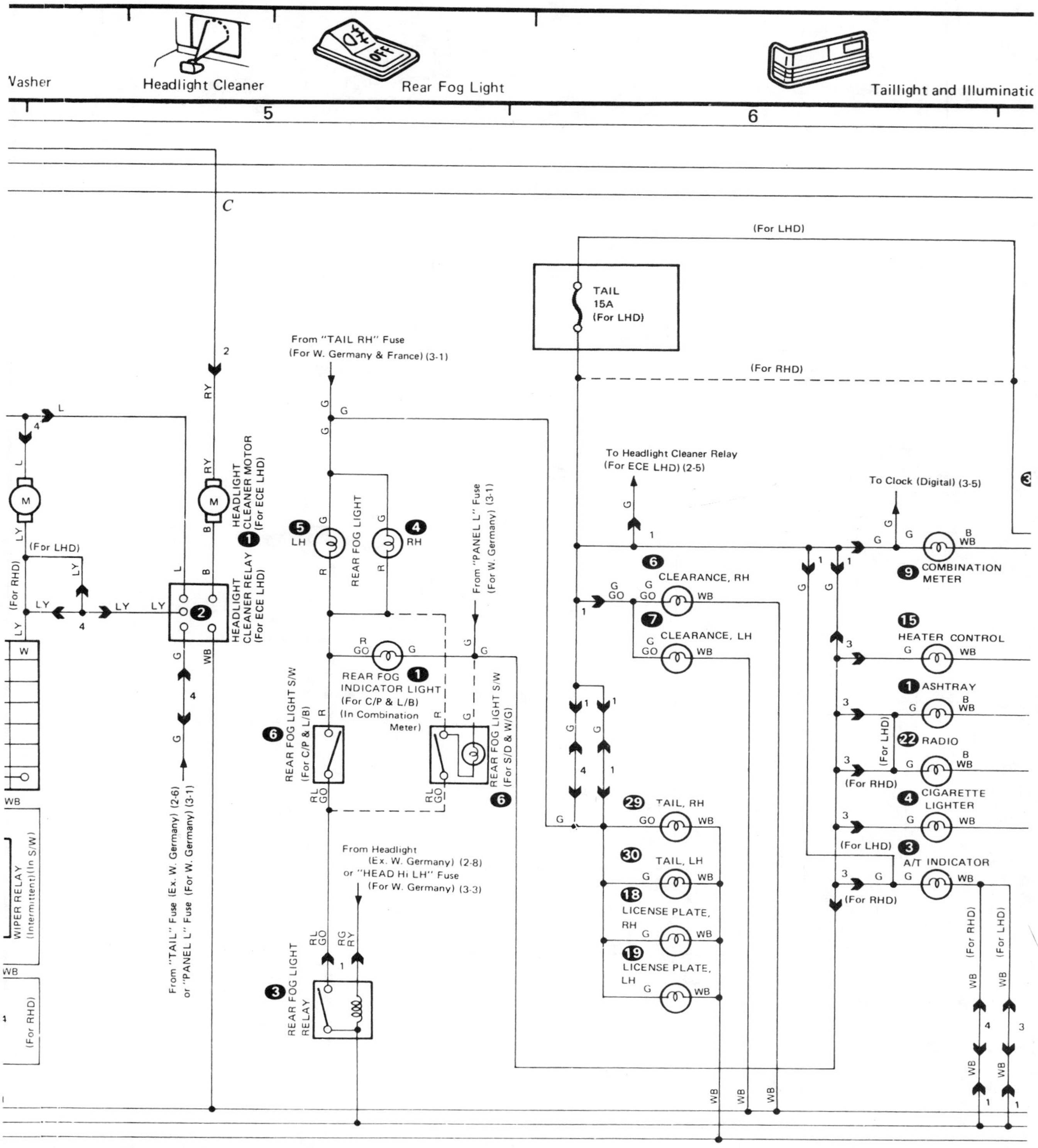

a = Angebracht im richten Vorderpuffer, in der Nahe von Abreißzundung
b LHD: Angebracht hinter der linken Vordersäule in der Anschlußdose Nr. 1
RHD: Angebracht hinter der rechten Vordersäule in der Anschlußdose Nr. 2

C = Ausgenommen W/G: Angebracht in der Hintertafel, in der Nahe von Zylinderschlß der Tur
Zu W/G: Angebracht in der Innentafel, in der Nahe von richten Ruckenkombinationslampe
d LHD: Angebracht an der linken Seite des Instrumentenbretts
RHD: Angebracht an der richten Seite des Instrumentenbretts

a = Si
b = Li
R

Fig. 10.137 Wiring diagram for 1982 Corolla models (continued)

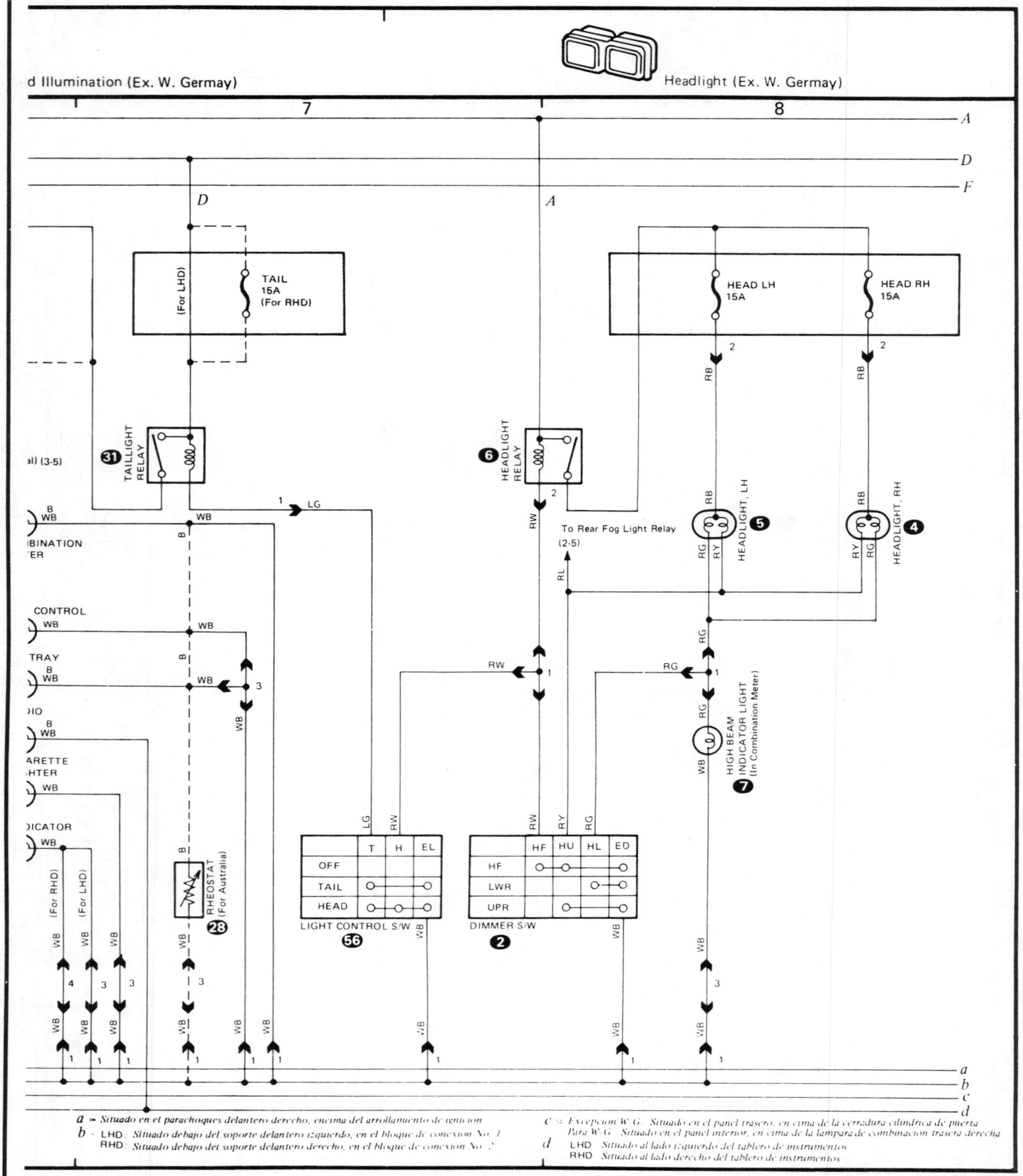

Fig. 10.137 Wiring diagram for 1982 Corolla models (continued)

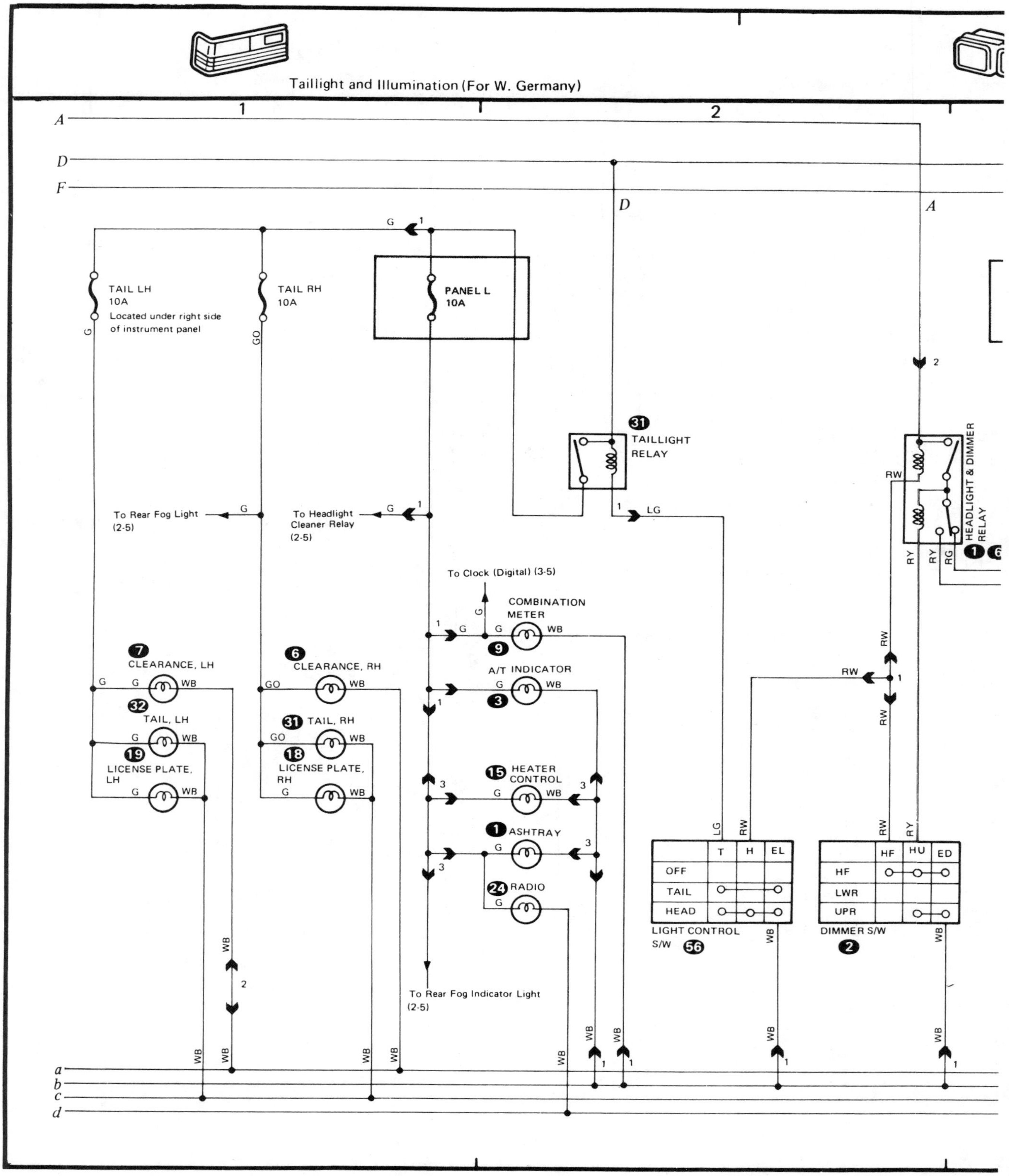

Fig. 10.137 Wiring diagram for 1982 Corolla models (continued)

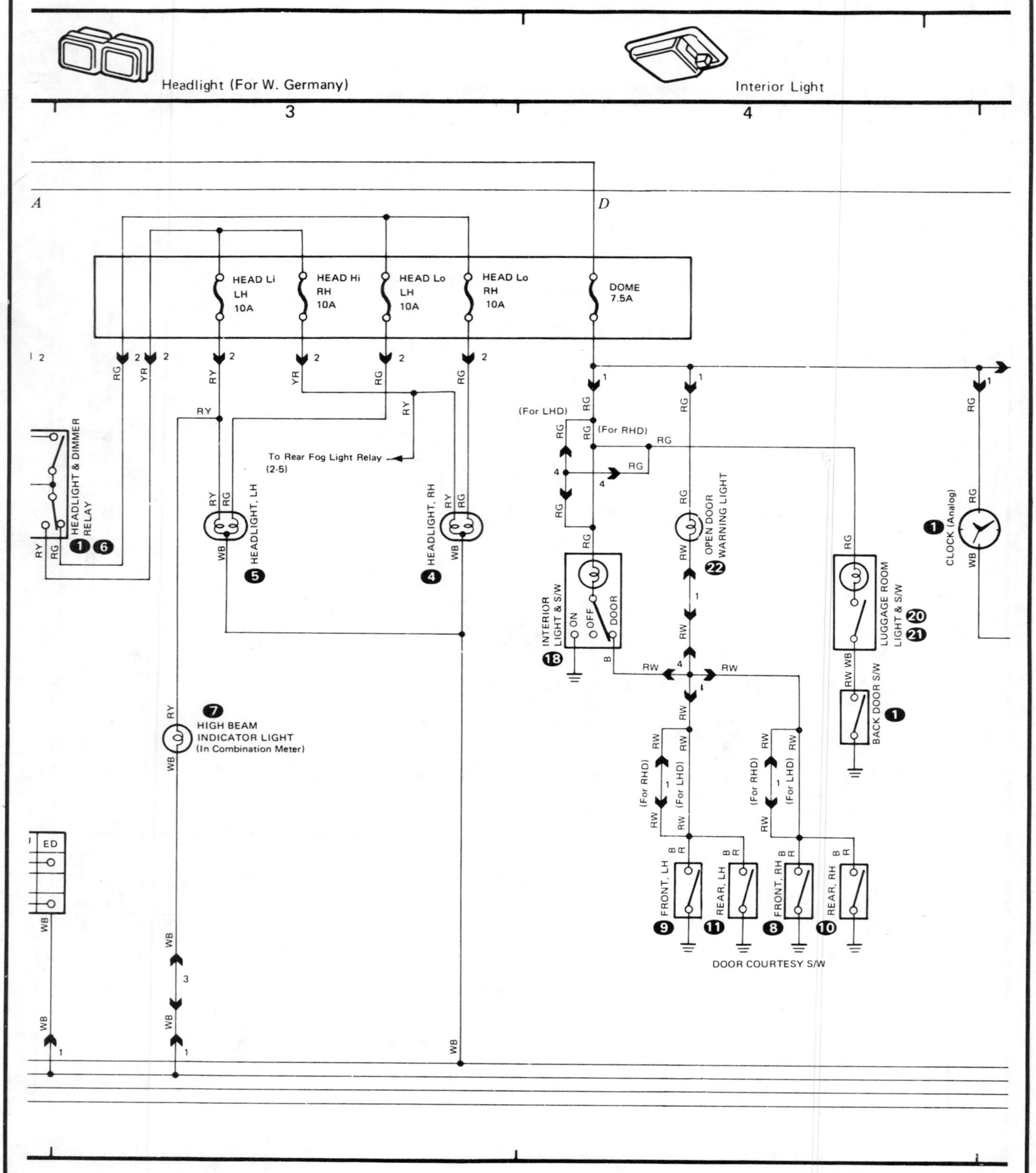

Fig. 10.137 Wiring diagram for 1982 Corolla models (continued)

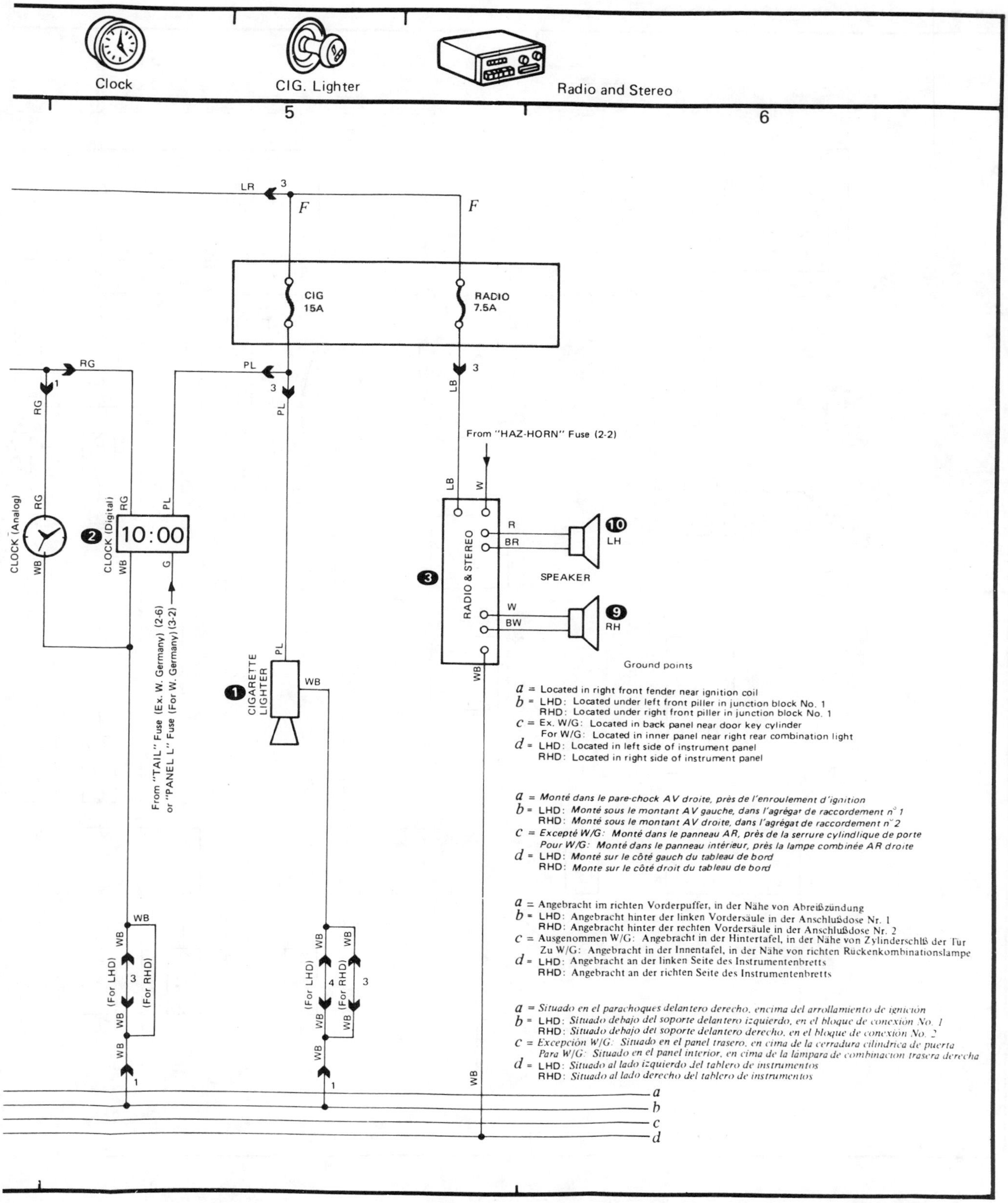

Fig. 10.137 Wiring diagram for 1982 Corolla models (continued)

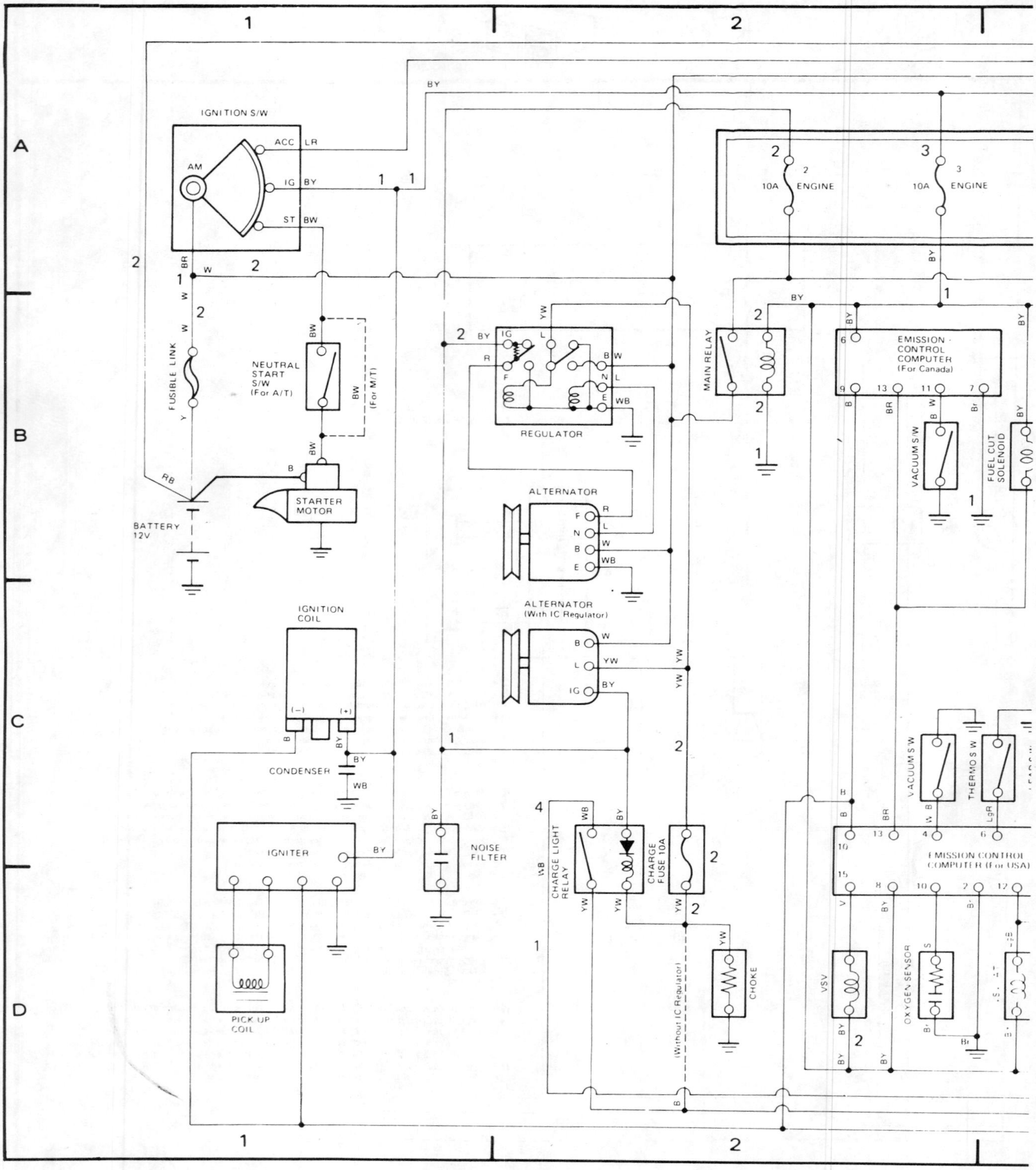

Fig. 10.138 Wiring diagram for 1981 USA and Canadian Saloon and Estate models

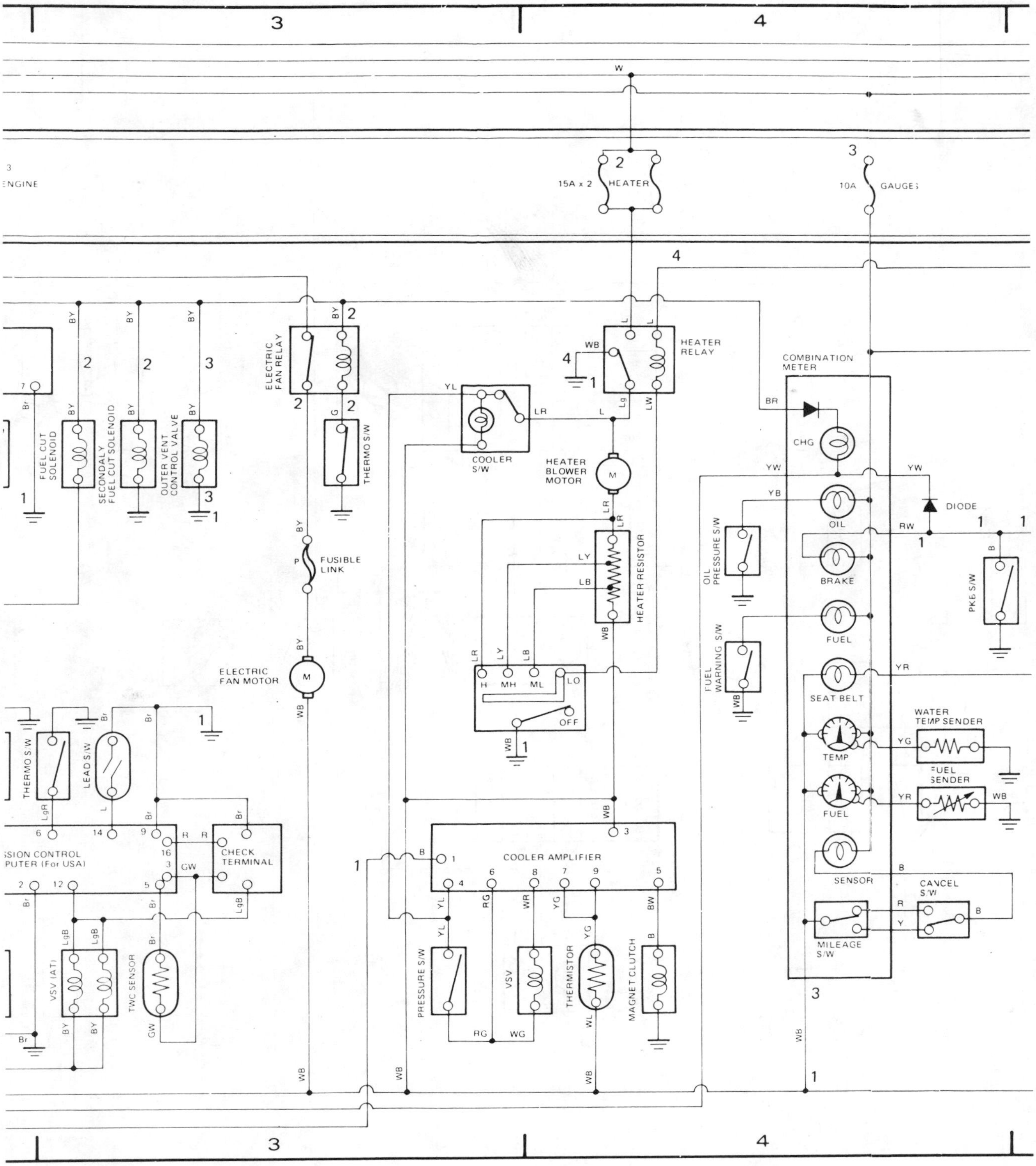

Fig. 10.138 Wiring diagram for 1981 USA and Canadian Saloon and Estate models (continued)

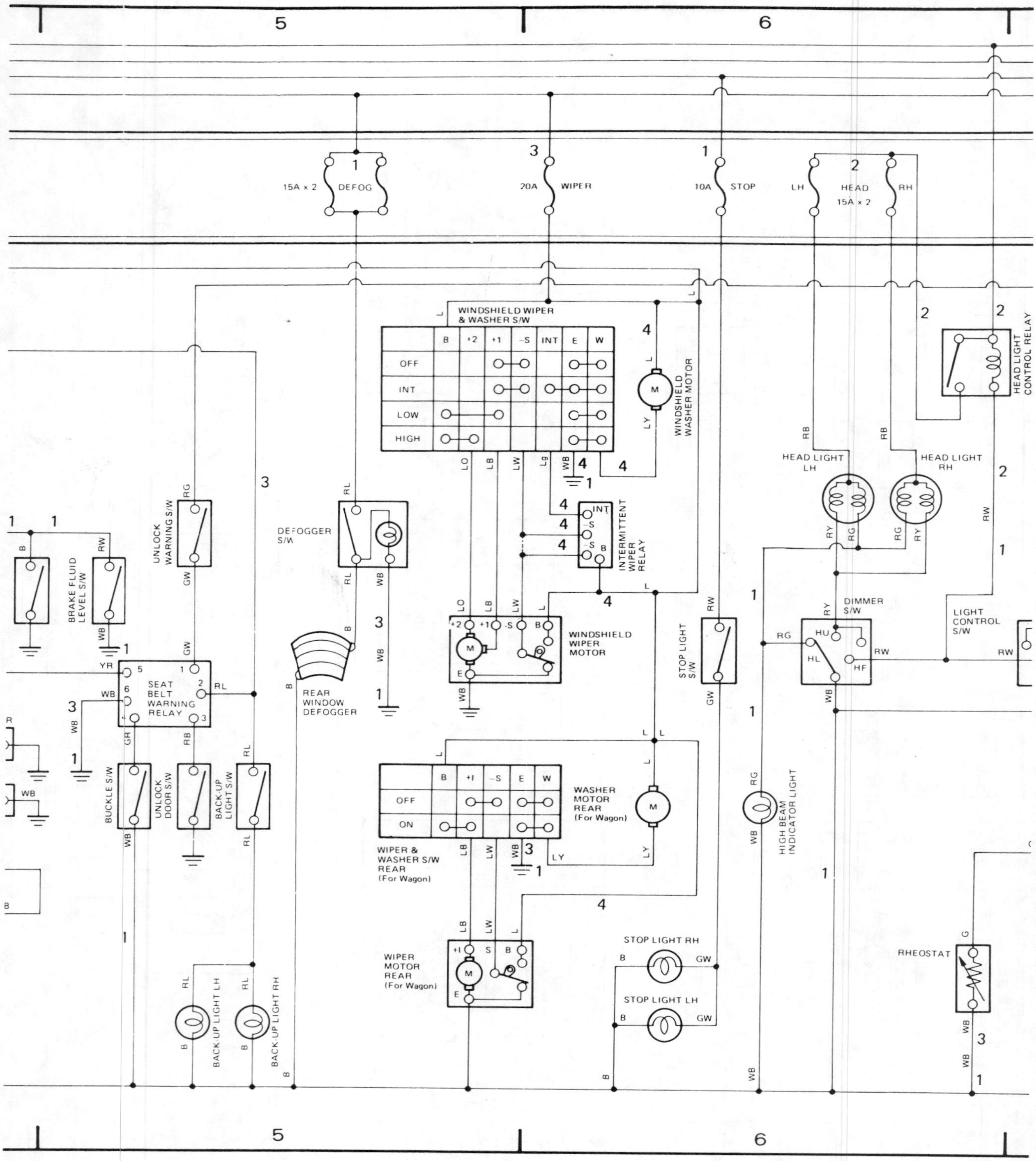

Fig. 10.138 Wiring diagram for 1981 USA and Canadian Saloon and Estate models (continued)

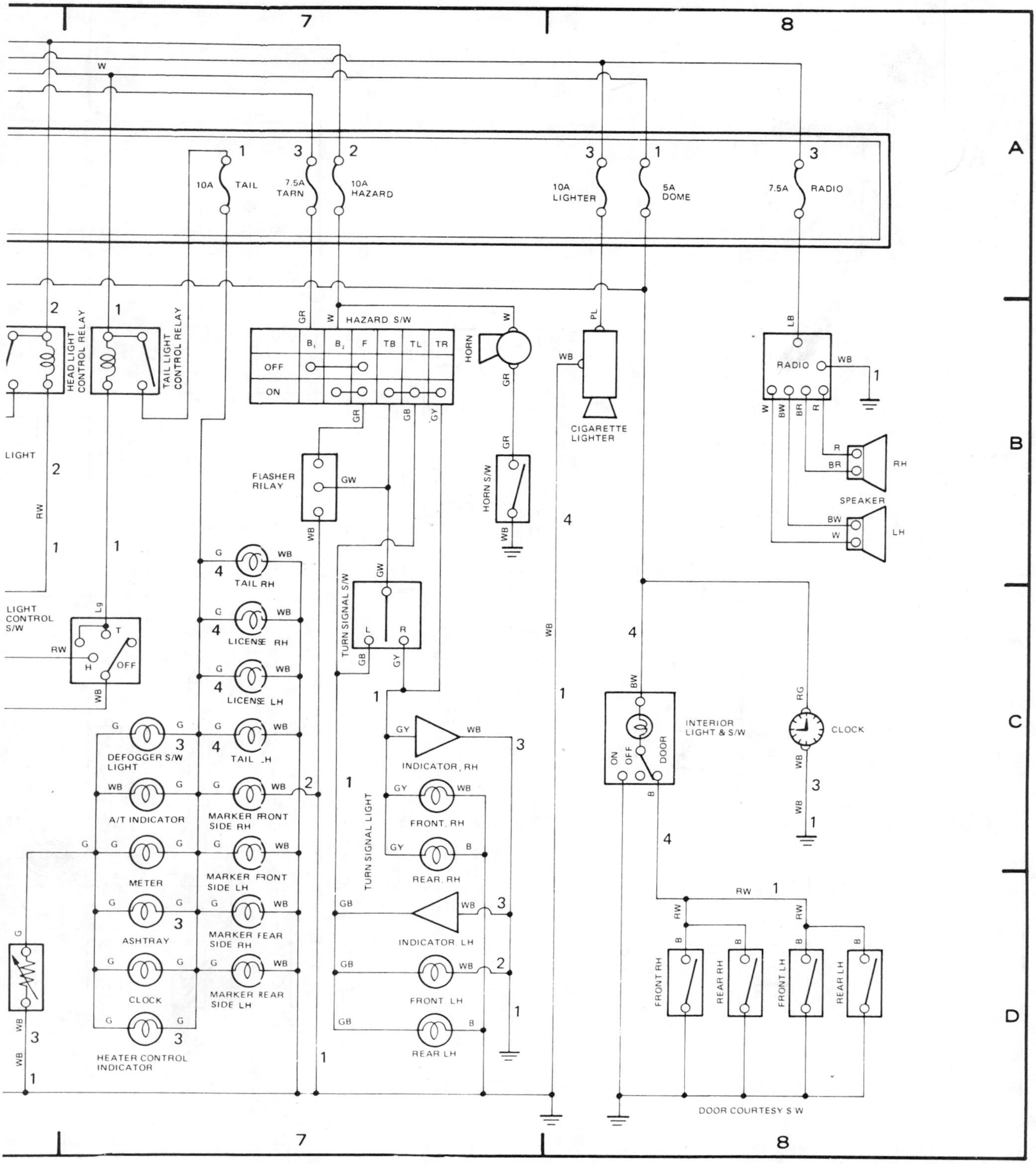

Fig. 10.138 Wiring diagram for 1981 USA and Canadian Saloon and Estate models (continued)

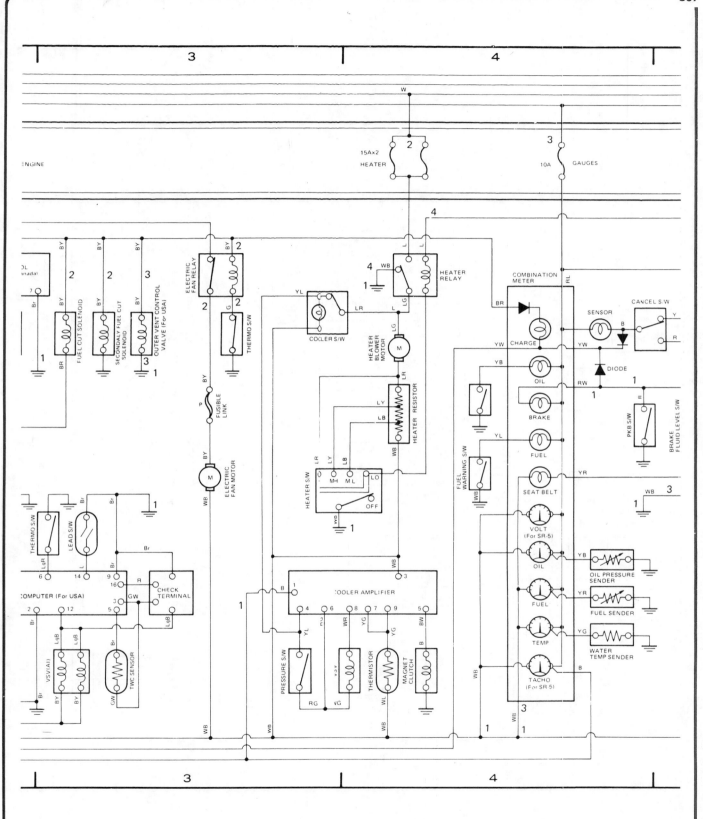

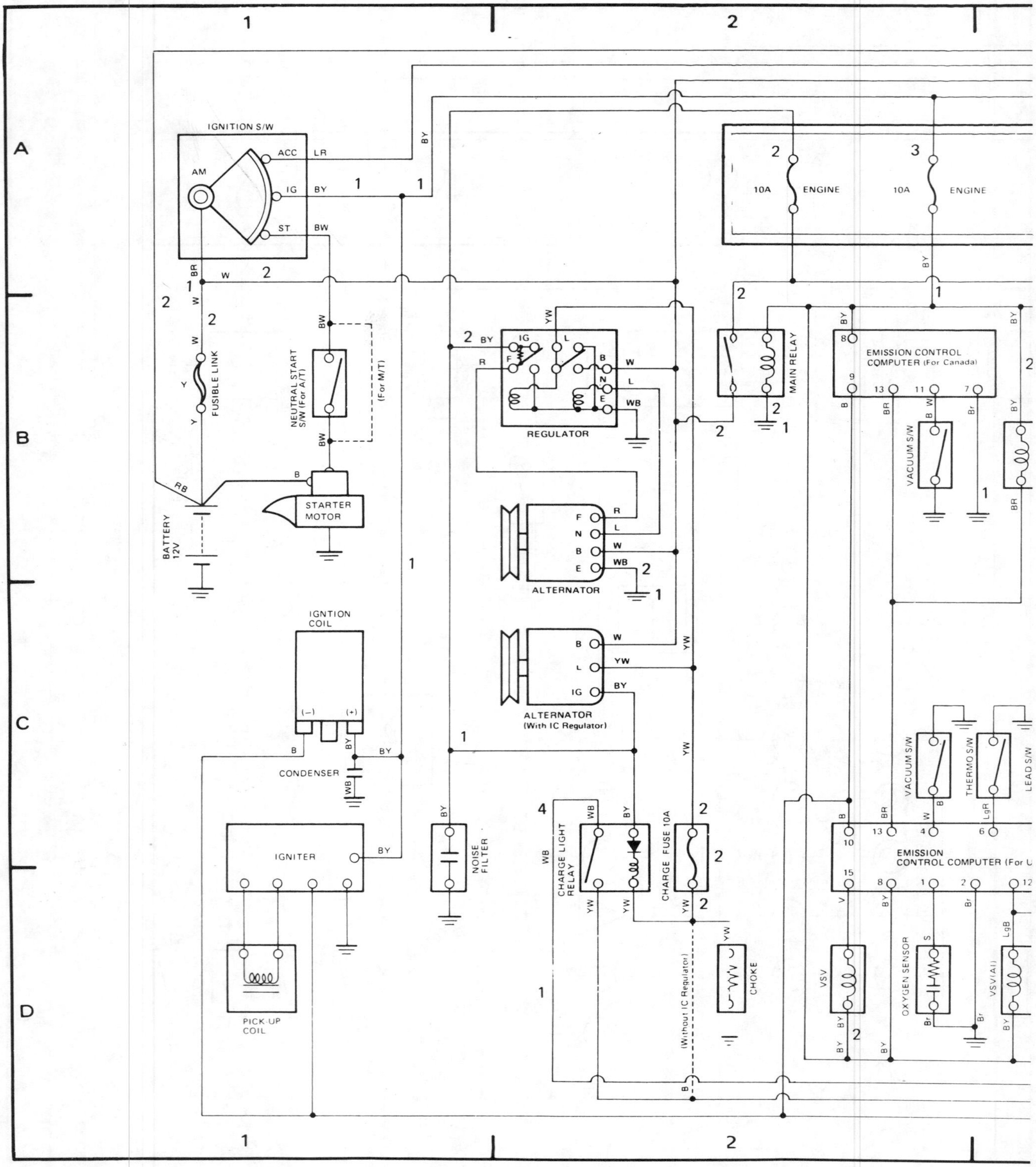

Fig. 10.139 Wiring diagram for 1981 USA and Canadian Coupe and Liftback models

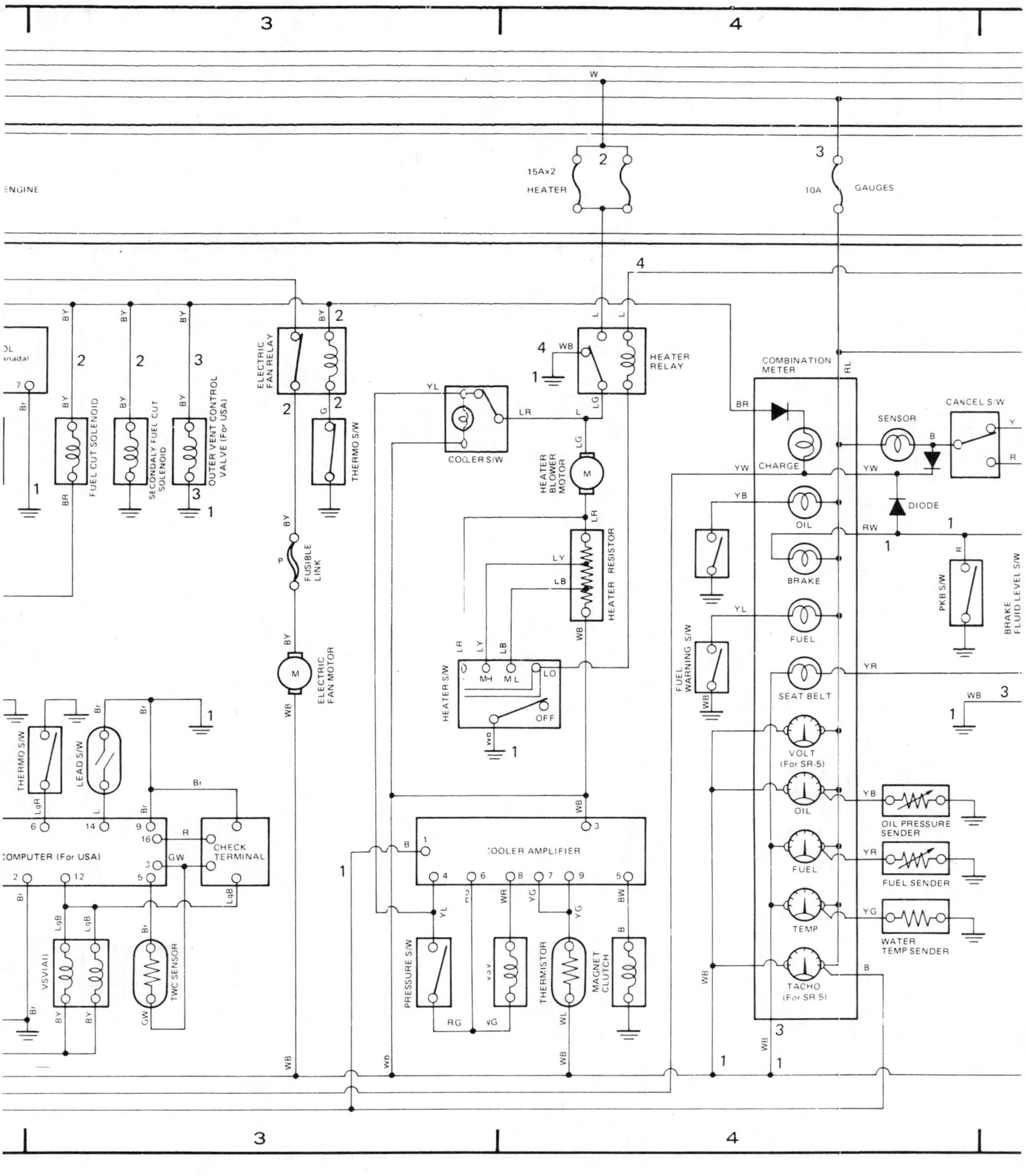

Fig. 10.139 Wiring diagram for 1981 USA and Canadian Coupe and Liftback models (continued)

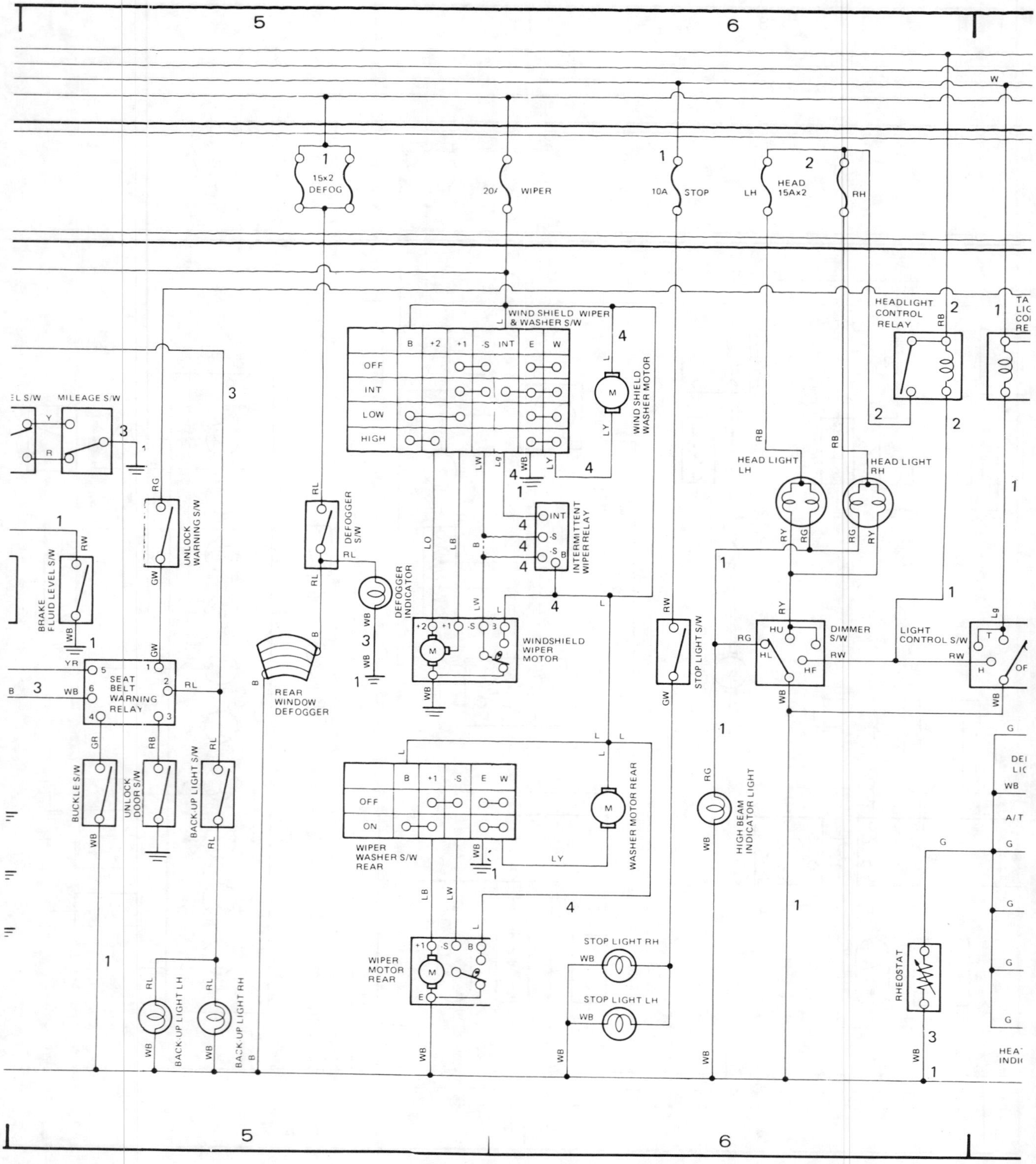

Fig. 10.139 Wiring diagram for 1981 USA and Canadian Coupe and Liftback models (continued)

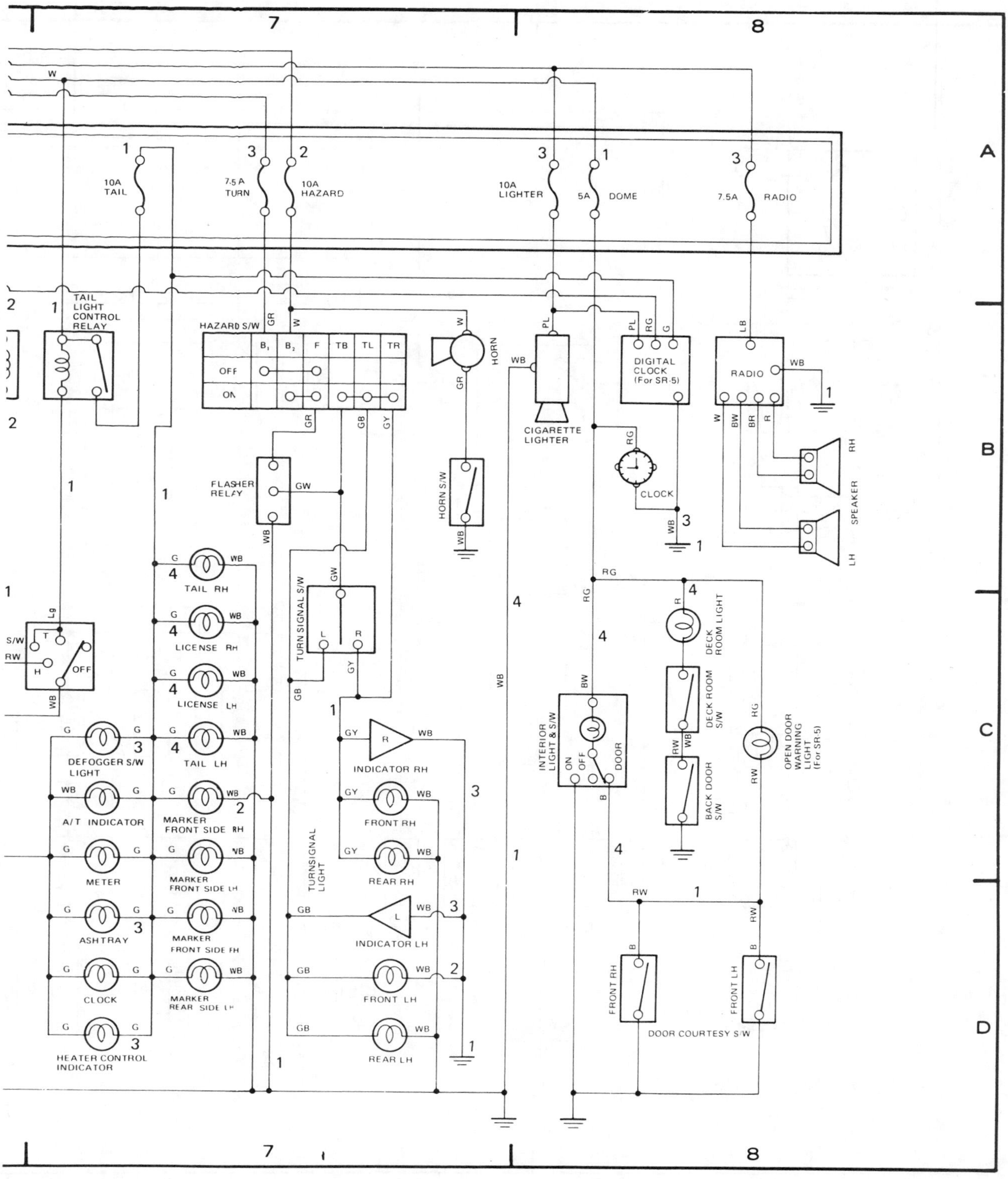

Fig. 10.139 Wiring diagram for 1981 USA and Canadian Coupe and Liftback models (continued)

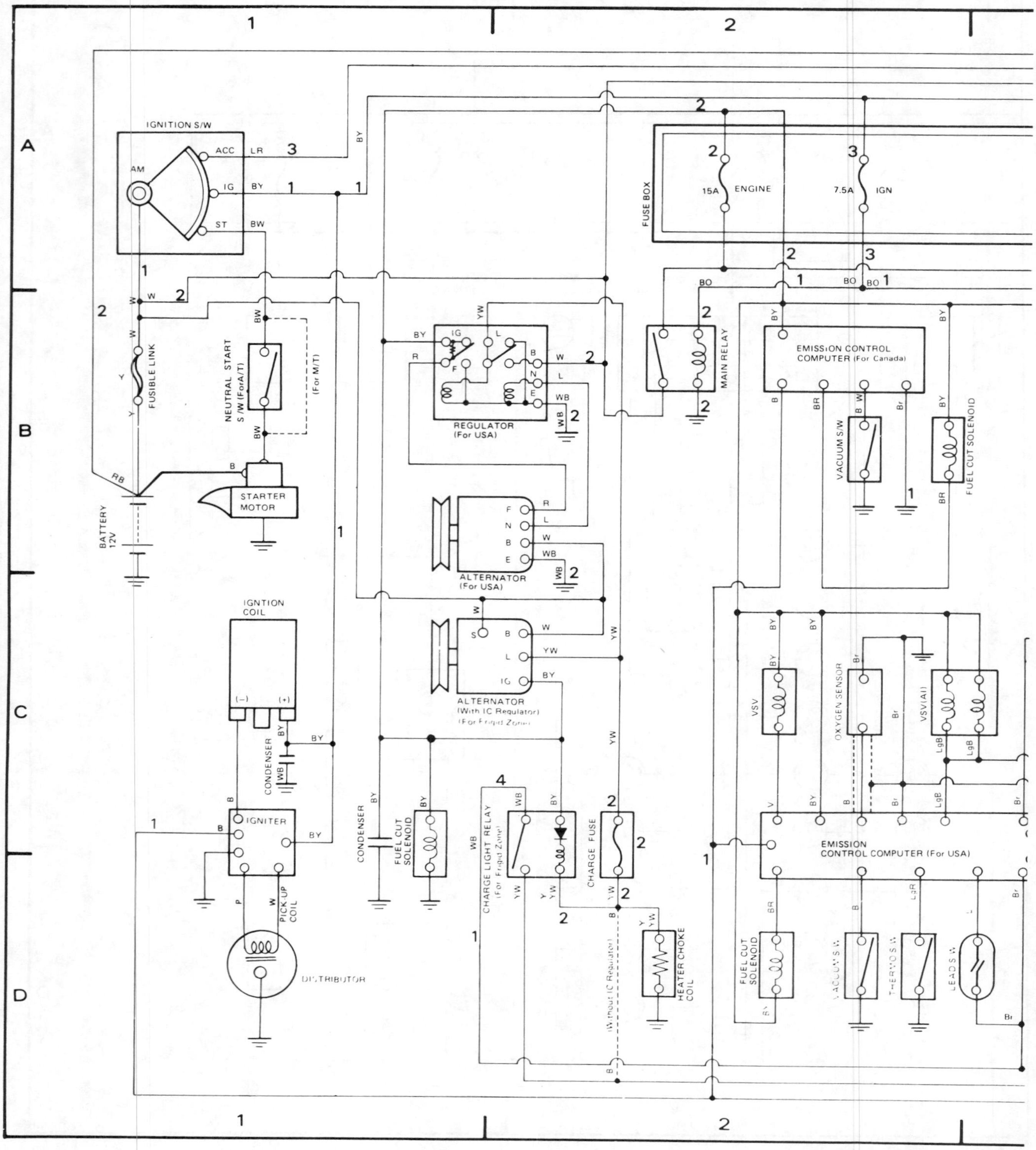

Fig. 10.140 Wiring diagram for 1982 USA and Canadian Corolla models

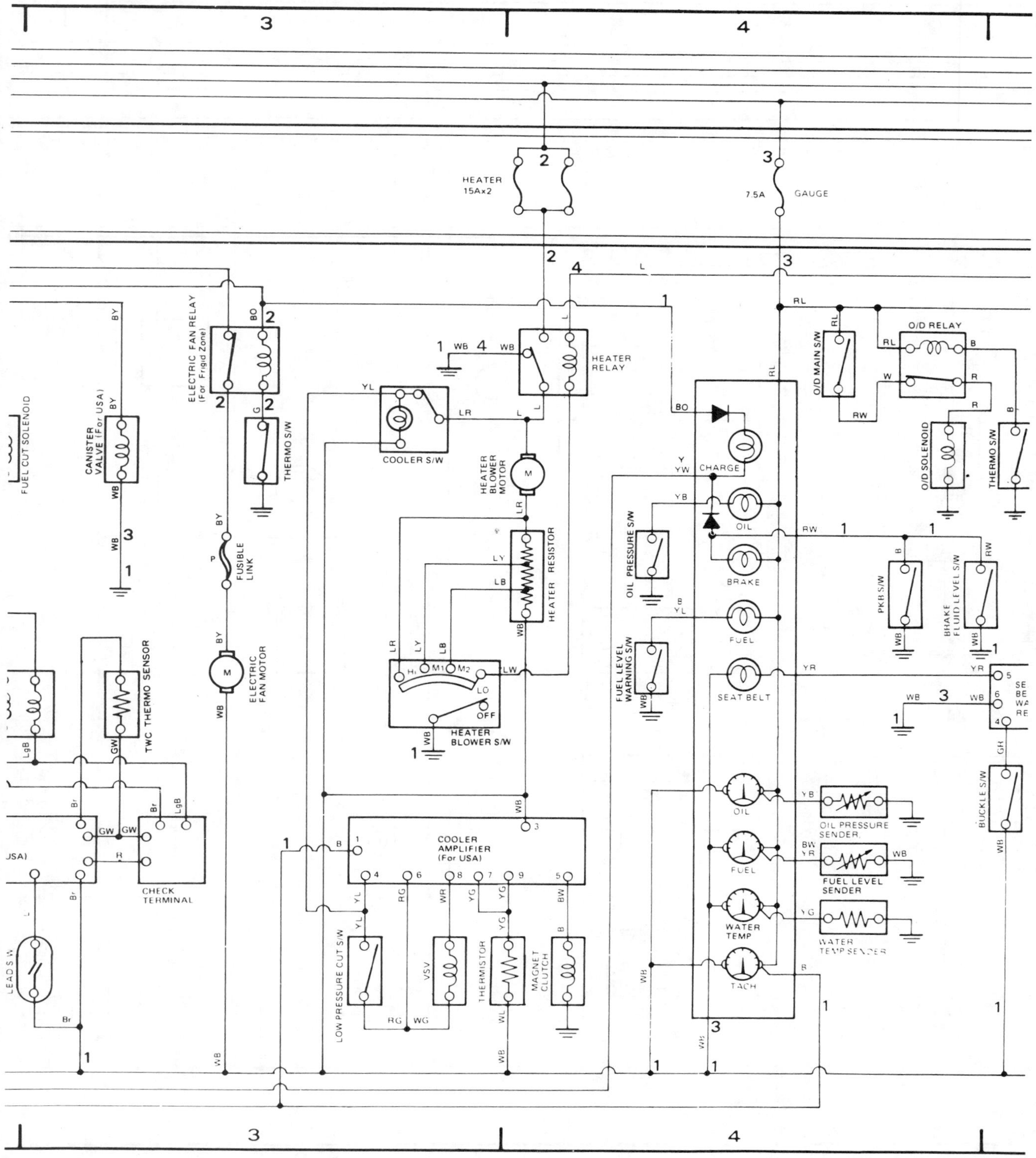

Fig. 10.140 Wiring diagram for 1982 USA and Canadian Corolla models (continued)

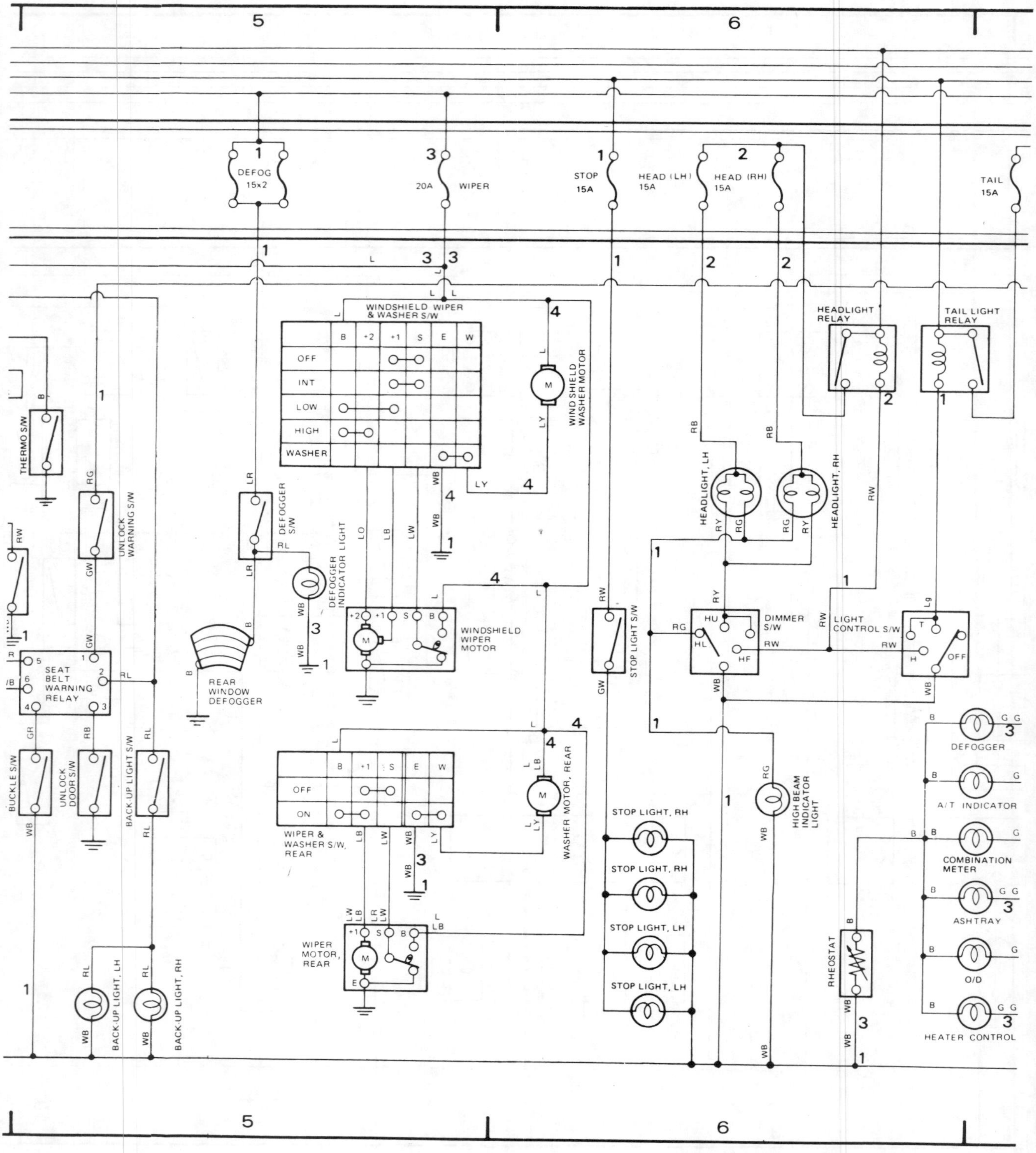

Fig. 10.140 Wiring diagram for 1982 USA and Canadian Corolla models (continued)

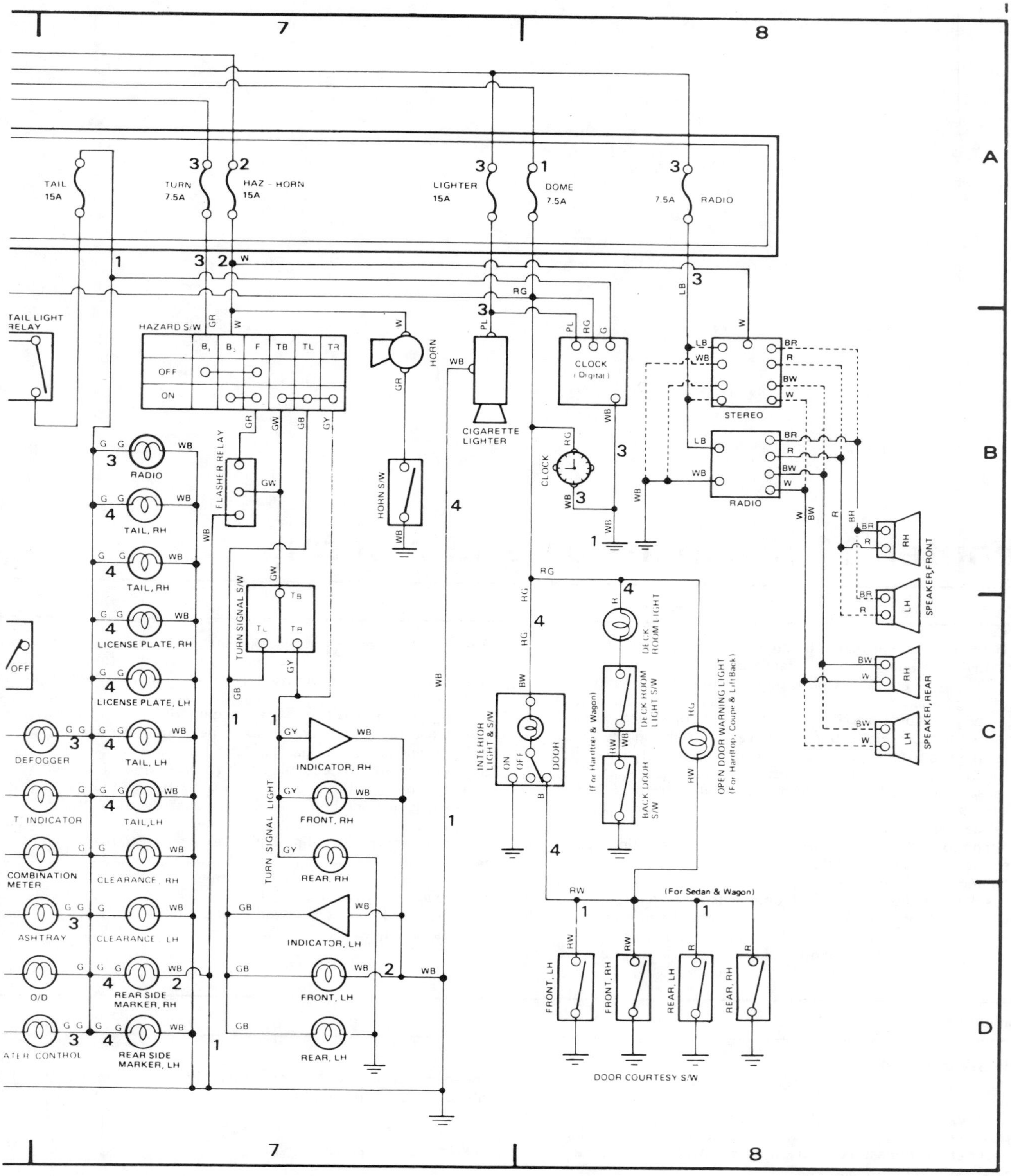

Fig. 10.140 Wiring diagram for 1982 USA and Canadian Corolla models (continued)

Chapter 11 Suspension and steering

Contents

Specifications

Front suspension

Type	Independent by MacPherson struts with coil spring, integral shock absorbers and anti-roll bar
Front hub bearing preload:	
Initial setting	Tighten to 19 to 23 lbf ft (2.6 to 3.2 kgf m)
Final setting (measured with spring balance)	0.7 to 1.5 lbf (0.3 to 0.7 kgf)
Balljoint maximum vertical play:	
4K engine models	Zero
2T, 2T-B and 3T-C engine models	0.098 in (2.5 mm)

Rear suspension

Type:	
All models except Estate	Live axle with four link location, coil springs and telescopic shock absorbers
Estate models	Live axle with semi-elliptic leaf springs and telescopic shock absorbers

Steering

Type:	
Saloon and Estate models	Rack and pinion
Coupe and Liftback models	Recirculating ball (power steering optional on certain models)
Rack and pinion steering:	
Steering wheel free play	0 to 1.18 in (0 to 30 mm)
Maximum steering rack run-out	0.012 in (0.3 mm)
Pinion oil seal drive in depth	0.020 in (0.5 mm)
Pinion bearing preload (turning)	1.3 to 2.2 lbf in (1.5 to 2.5 kgf cm)
Rack guide spring cap installation:	
Step 1 – tighten to	1.8 lbf ft (2.5 kgf m)
Step 2 – slacken by	12°
Total turning preload (rack installed)	6.5 to 8.2 lbf in (7.5 to 9.5 kgf cm)
Recirculating ball steering:	
Steering wheel free play	0 to 1.18 in (0 to 30 mm)
Sector shaft endfloat	0 to 0.002 in (0 to 0.05 mm)
Wormshaft bearing starting preload:	
Without sector shaft	1.7 to 3.5 lbf in (2 to 4 kgf cm)
With sector shaft installed	4.3 to 7.0 lbf in (5 to 8 kgf cm)
Steering gearbox oil capacity	230 to 250 cc
Steering gearbox oil level	Less than 0.98 in (25 mm) below filler plug orifice
Power steering:	
Power piston ball clearance:	
Standard	0.0008 to 0.0024 in (0.02 to 0.06 mm)
Limit	0.0059 in (0.15 mm)
Cross-shaft adjuster screw endfloat	0.0012 to 0.0020 in (0.03 to 0.05 mm)
Wormshaft bearing starting preload:	
Without cross-shaft	3.5 to 5.6 lbf in (4.0 to 6.5 kgf cm)
With cross-shaft installed	5.2 to 8.2 lbf in (6.0 to 9.5 kgf cm)
Drivebelt tension:	
Approximate deflection under 22 lbf (10 kgf m) load	0.3 to 0.5 in (8.0 to 12.0 mm)
Approximate deflection using Burroughs tension gauge BT-33-73F	60 to 100 lbf (27 to 45 kgf)

Steering angles

Toe-in:	
UK models:	
Bias tyre	0.12 ± 0.04 in (3.0 ± 1.0 mm)
Radial tyre	0.04 ± 0.04 in (1.0 ± 1.0 mm)
USA and Canada models up to 1982:	
Bias tyre	0.12 ± 0.04 in (3.0 ± 1.0 mm)
Radial tyre	0.04 ± 0.04 in (1.0 ± 1.0 mm)
USA and Canada models, 1982 onwards	0.04 ± 0.04 in (1.0 ± 1.0 mm)
Camber:	
4K engine models:	
All models except Estate	1° 09′ ± 30′
Estate models	0° 49′ ± 30′
2T and 2T-B engine models	1° 22′ ± 30′
3T-C engine models	1° 05′ ± 30′
Maximum allowable difference side-to-side	0° 30′
Castor:	
4K engine models:	
All models except Estate	1° 50′ ± 30′
Estate models	1° 19′ ± 30′
2T and 2T-B engine models	1° 49′ ± 30′
3T-C engine models:	
All models except Estate	1° 45′ ± 30′
Estate models	1° 35′ ± 30′
Maximum allowable difference side-to-side	0° 30′
Steering axis inclination:	
4K engine models:	
All models except Estate	8° 06′
Estate models	8° 33′
2T and 2T-B engine models	8° 6′
3T-C engine models:	
All models except Estate	8° 25′ ± 30′
Estate models	8° 20′ ± 30′

Roadwheels and tyres

Wheels:	
Type	Pressed steel or aluminium alloy
Size:	
All models except Coupe	4.5J
Coupe models	5.0J

Tyres:		
Tyre size:		
Saloon and Estate models	155 SR 13 Radial ply	
Liftback models	165 SR 13 Radial ply	
Coupe models	185/70 HR 13 Radial ply	
Tyre pressures (cold)*	**Front**	**Rear**
Saloon models	24 lbf/in² (1.7 kgf/cm²)	27 lbf/in² (1.9 kgf/cm²)
Estate models	24 lbf/in² (1.7 kgf/cm²)	28 lbf/in² (2.0 kgf/cm²)
Liftback models	24 lbf/in² (1.7 kgf/cm²)	27 lbf/in² (1.9 kgf/cm²)
Coupe models	24 lbf/in² (1.7 kgf/cm²)	26 lbf/in² (1.8 kgf/cm²)

**Refer also to vehicle handbook and tyre pressure decal affixed to bodywork for variations on the above pressures*

Torque wrench settings	**lbf ft**	**kgf m**
Front axle/suspension		
Wheel nut	66 to 86	9.0 to 12.0
Crossmember to body	76 to 97	10.5 to 13.5
Lower arm to crossmember	51 to 65	7.0 to 9.0
Balljoint to knuckle arm	51 to 65	7.0 to 9.0
Strut bar to strut bar bracket	55 to 79	7.5 to 11.0
Stabilizer cushion	10 to 15	1.4 to 2.2
Stabilizer bracket to strut bar bracket	8 to 11	1.0 to 1.6
Strut bar bracket to body	29 to 32	4.0 to 4.5
Strut bar to lower arm	29 to 32	4.0 to 4.5
Knuckle arm to shock absorber	51 to 65	7.0 to 9.0
Suspension support to apron	11 to 15	1.5 to 2.2
Suspension support to shock absorber	29 to 39	4.0 to 5.5
Shock absorber to ring nut	73 to 108	10.0 to 15.0
Rack and pinion steering		
Idler arm to relay rod	37 to 51	5.0 to 7.0
Relay rod to tie-rod	37 to 51	5.0 to 7.0
Knuckle arm to tie-rod	37 to 51	5.0 to 7.0
Tie-rod to tie-rod tube	11 to 14	1.5 to 2.0
Column tube to hole cover	8 to 11	1.0 to 1.6
Column tube to mainshaft stopper retainer	11 to 28	1.6 to 4.0
Column bracket to instrument panel	22 to 32	3.0 to 4.5
Steering wheel to shaft nut	22 to 29	3.0 to 4.0
Intermediate to pinion steering mainshaft	27 to 34	3.8 to 4.8
Pinion bearing adjuster screw locknut	58 to 75	8.0 to 10.5
Rack guide spring cap locknut to rack housing	37 to 47	5.0 to 6.5
Rack end to rack	47 to 65	6.5 to 9.0
Tie-rod to rach end	11 to 14	1.5 to 2.0
Rack housing bracket to body	22 to 32	3.0 to 4.5
Tie-rod to knuckle arm	37 to 51	5.0 to 7.0
Recirculating ball type steering		
Mainshaft to flexible coupling	15 to 22	2.0 to 3.0
Steering wheel to shift nut	22 to 29	3.0 to 4.0
Column bracket to instrument panel	22 to 32	3.0 to 4.5
Worm bearing adjuster nut to screw locknut	95 to 122	13.0 to 17.0
Sector shaft adjuster screw locknut	14 to 22	1.9 to 3.1
Steering gear housing to body	26 to 37	3.5 to 5.0
Pitman arm to steering relay rod	37 to 51	5.0 to 7.0
Pitman arm to sector shaft	73 to 101	10.0 to 14.0
Sector shaft cover	11 to 15	1.5 to 2.2
Power steering		
Rear housing to tank	8 to 11	1.0 to 1.6
Rear to front housing	29 to 39	4.0 to 5.5
Rotor shaft to pump pulley	32 to 39	4.5 to 5.5
Gear housing to valve housing	29 to 39	4.0 to 5.5
Cross-shaft adjuster screw locknut	29 to 39	4.0 to 5.5
End cover to gear housing	29 to 39	4.0 to 5.5
Gear housing to body	26 to 37	3.5 to 5.0
Pitman arm to relay rod	37 to 51	5.0 to 7.0
Pitman arm to cross-shaft	73 to 101	10.0 to 14.0
Mainshaft to flexible coupling	15 to 22	2.0 to 3.0
Pressure hose union nut	29 to 37	4.0 to 5.0
Return pipe	24 to 30	3.2 to 4.2
Wormshaft adjuster locknut	32 to 39	4.5 to 5.5

Rear suspension

	lbf ft	kgf m
Axleshaft bearing retainer	22 to 53	3.0 to 7.4
Shock absorber to axle	22 to 32	3.0 to 4.5
Shock absorber to body	14 to 22	1.9 to 3.1
Lateral control rod to axle	37 to 57	5.0 to 8.0
Lateral control rod to body	55 to 75	7.5 to 10.5
Upper control arm to axle	55 to 75	7.5 to 10.5
Upper control arm to body	55 to 75	7.5 to 10.5
Lower control arm to axle	55 to 75	7.5 to 10.5
Lower control arm to body	55 to 75	7.5 to 10.5
Leaf spring central bolt	11 to 15	1.5 to 2.2
Leaf sprign U-bolt nuts	22 to 32	3.0 to 4.5
Spring bracket – outer	29 to 39	4.0 to 5.5
Spring bracket – inner	8 to 11	1.0 to 1.6
Spring shackle	37 to 51	5.0 to 7.0
Roadwheel nut	66 to 86	9.0 to 12.0

1 General description

The front suspension fitted to all models is of MacPherson strut type. The struts are secured at their upper ends to reinforced areas under the wings and attached at their lower ends to balljoints at the outer ends of the track control arms.

A drag strut (radius rod) is fitted between the track control arm and the bodyframe to positively locate the suspension track control arm. A stabiliser bar is fitted.

The rear suspension on all models except the Estate (Wagon) is of four-link type with coil springs and double-acting shock absorbers. Longitudinal movement of the rear axle is controlled by the lower control arm, and side to side movement by the upper arms. The telescopic shock absorbers are attached to brackets on the axle tube at their lower ends, and to the body underframe at their upper ends.

On Estate models, the rear suspension is of semi-elliptic leaf spring type secured with U-bolts below the rear axle casing. Telescopic shock absorbers are fitted.

The steering is of either rack and pinion type or recirculating ball type depending on model. Power steering is available and fitted to some models (with recirculating ball steering only).

2 Maintenance and inspection

1 Refer to 'Routine Maintenance' Section at the front of the manual and carry out the checks and lubrication operations at the specified mileage intervals.

2 The most important job is inspection of all the steering and suspension components at regular intervals.

3 First check the condition of the dust excluding gaiters on the front

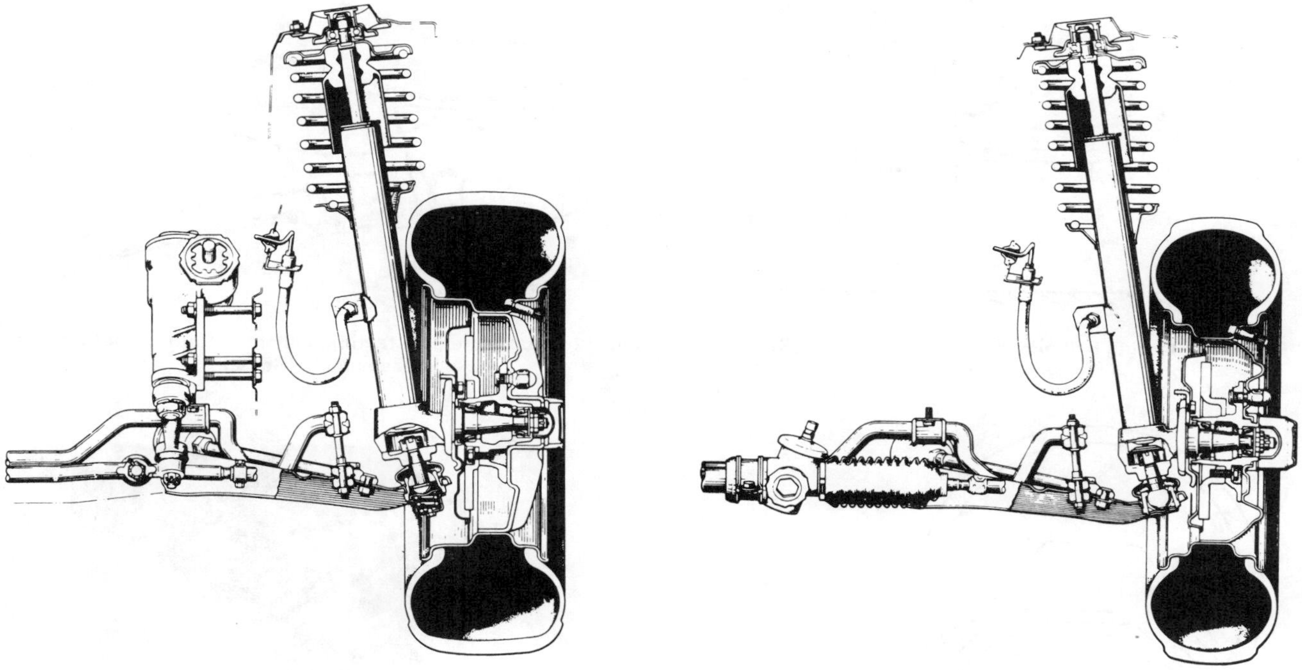

Fig. 11.1 Sectional views of the front axle and suspension shown with rack and pinion steering (right) and recirculating ball type steering (left) – LH drive shown for both (Sec 1)

suspension struts, and rack gaiters (rack and pinion models).
4 Inspect the condition of the balljoints dust excluding boots. If these are split, they must be renewed.
5 At the specified intervals, check all the steering and suspension nuts and bolts and tighten if necessary to the specified torque wrench settings. Also check the wheel nuts for security.
6 Check the steering balljoints by jacking up the front of the vehicle and positioning a 7.5 inch thick block under the roadwheel. Lower the jack to give a half loading on the front coil springs. Fit safety stands as shown and then use a lever to move the lower arm up and down whilst checking the balljoint for excessive wear. Measure the amount of play and compare it with the specified maximum amount allowable. The joints will have to be renewed if worn beyond the specified figure.
7 Lubricate the steering balljoints at the specified routine maintenance intervals by removing the plug at the base of the joint and pump some molybdenum disulphide grease into the joint.
8 With the vehicle jacked up at the front end and the roadwheels clear of the ground, grip the roadwheels top and bottom and attempt to rock them. Any movement may indicate incorrectly adjusted hub bearings, worn bearings or worn track control arm bushes. Lubricate the front wheel bearings at the specified intervals as given in Section 3.
9 Check the steering linkages for security and excessive wear and the steering box for signs of fluid leakage. Check the steering wheel free play which should not exceed the specified amount. To adjust the steering box free play, the front wheels must be clear of the ground and facing forwards. Loosen off the locknut on the steering box and turn the adjuster screw in small increments to achieve the correct adjustment. Turn the screw clockwise to decrease the play. Tighten the locknut on completion then turn the steering wheel fully in each

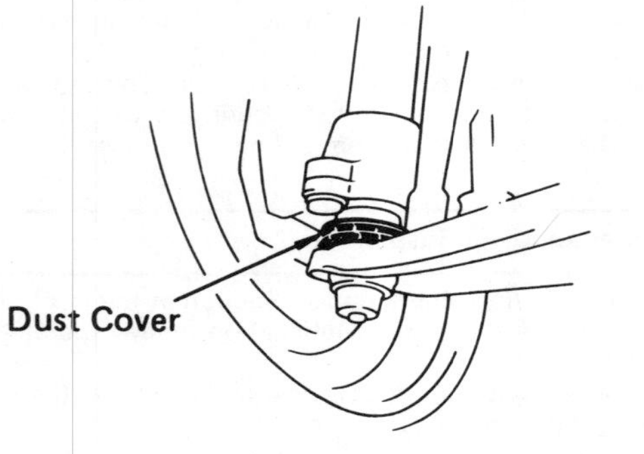

Fig. 11.2 Check condition of dust covers on suspension strut (Sec 2)

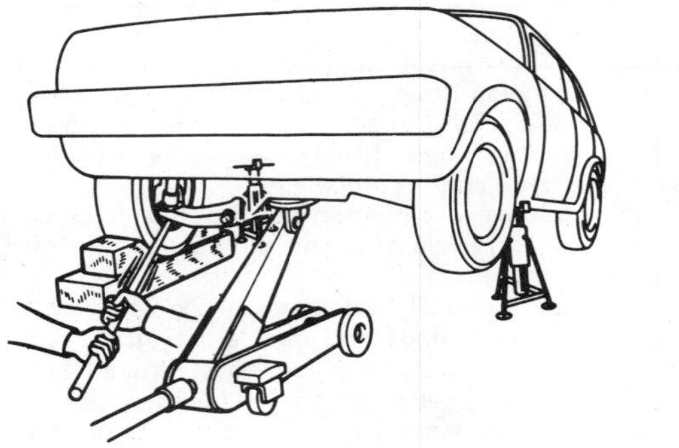

Fig. 11.3 Steering balljoint vertical play check method (Sec 2)

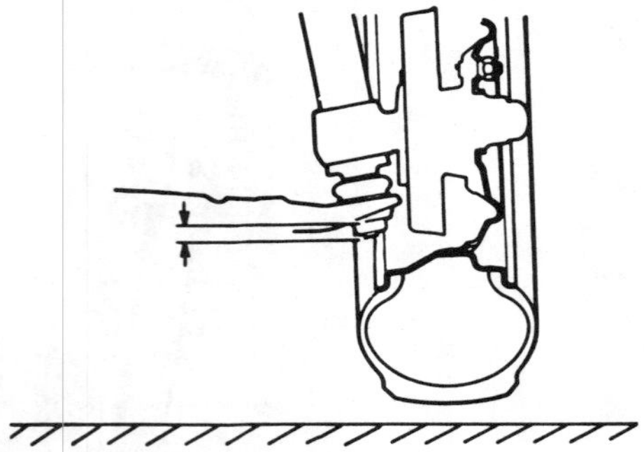

Fig. 11.4 Steering balljoint end play check point (Sec 2)

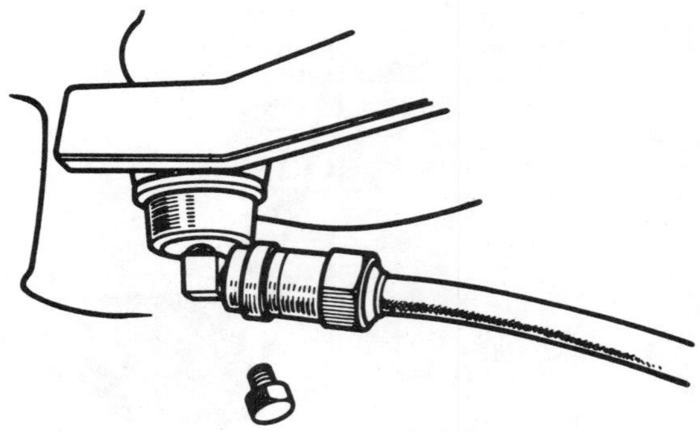

Fig. 11.5 Lubricate the steering balljoints. Remove bolt, insert grease nipple (Sec 2)

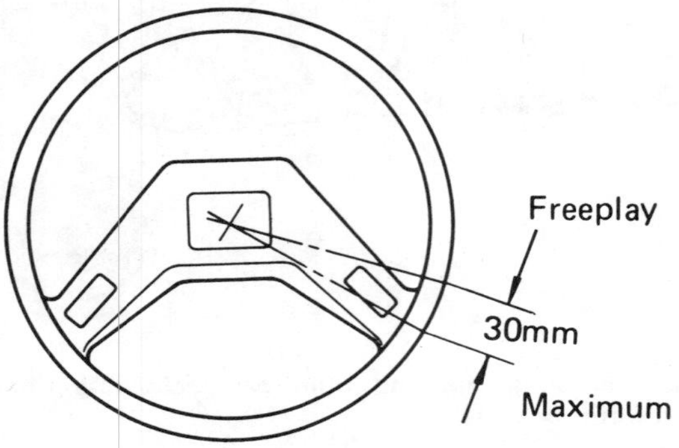

Fig. 11.6 Check the steering wheel free play (Sec 2)

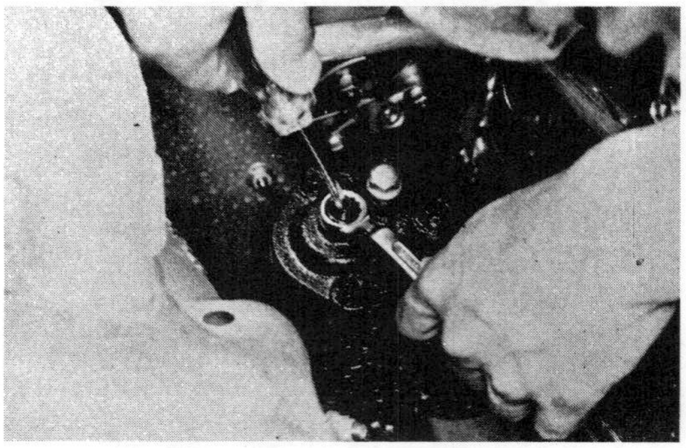

Fig. 11.7 Adjusting the steering box to take up play – recirculating ball type (Sec 2)

direction to ensure its action is free, not binding and without tight spots. This adjustment is only possible on the recirculating ball type steering box.
10 With the recirculating ball steering box the oil level should be maintained at the correct level as shown.
11 On models fitted with power steering, periodic checks must be made to ensure that the fluid level in the reservoir is correct and that the pump drivebelt tension is adjusted to the specified figure.
12 Periodic checks must be made to ensure that the rear suspension components are in good condition, in particular the lateral, upper and lower control rod bushes and fixings (four-link suspension) or leaf spring bushes and U-bolt fixings on Estate models.

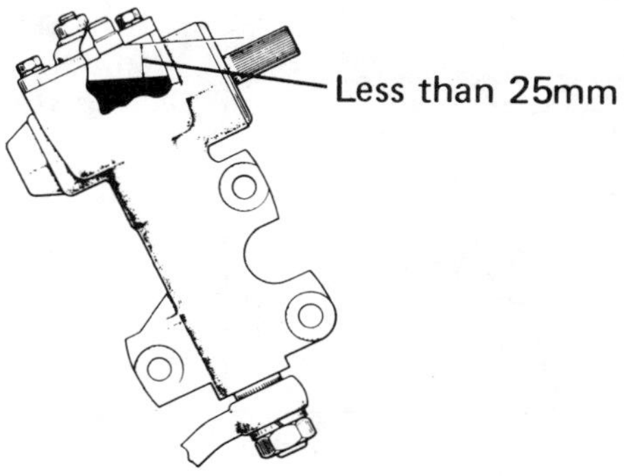

Fig. 11.8 Steering box oil level – recirculating ball type (Sec 2)

3 Front hubs – removal, servicing, refitting and adjustment

1 At the intervals specified in the Routine Maintenance Section at the beginning of this manual, jack-up the front of the vehicle and remove the roadwheels.
2 Remove the brake caliper unit as described in Chapter 9. There is no need to disconnect the hydraulic hose but simply tie the caliper assembly to the front suspension strut using a piece of wire.
3 Prise off the grease cap and extract the split pin.
4 Remove the nut retainer and unscrew and remove the nut and thrust washer.
5 Pull the hub assembly from the stub axle, complete with brake disc.
6 Extract the outer bearing race from the hub.
7 Extract the oil seal, which must be renewed, and then extract the inner bearing race.
8 Wash out all old grease from the bearings and hub using petrol or a suitable grease solvent. Check the bearings and their tracks for wear, damage or scoring.
9 If they are found to be in a serviceable condition, repack the inside of the hub with grease.
10 If either the inner or outer bearings require renewal, drive out the old tracks with a brass drift and then press in the new bearing tracks, ensuring that they are housed correctly.
11 Where both front hubs are being serviced at the same time, do not mix the bearing components as the races and tracks are matched in production.
12 The disc should not be removed from the hub unless it is to be refaced or renewed.
13 Reassembly is a reversal of the removal procedure. Drive the new oil seal carefully into position and smear it with grease.
14 Relocate the hub/disc unit onto the stub axle, refit the outer bearing race with thrust washer and then adjust the bearings for preload as follows.
15 Fit and tighten the hub nut to the specified initial torque setting whilst rotating the hub. Now loosen off the nut so that it is hand tight only and then check the bearing preload.
16 To do this attach a spring balance to one of the roadwheel studs and observe the pull effort which is required to rotate the hub. This should be as given in the Specifications.
17 Tighten or loosen the nut to adjust as necessary then when the adjustment is correct, refit the adjuster cap and insert a new split pin to secure in the set position.
18 Fill the grease cap about 1/3rd full with grease and knock it into position.
19 Refit the brake caliper (Chapter 9), refit the roadwheels and lower the car.

4 Front coil springs and shock absorbers – removal, inspection and refitting

1 Loosen the front roadwheel nuts on the side concerned and then raise the front of the vehicle and support on safety stands. Remove the roadwheel.
2 The front shock absorbers are removed as a unit together with the coil spring and stub axle assembly.
3 Disconnect the front brake flexible hose to rigid hose connection at the mounting bracket on the wing inner panel. To prevent excess fluid leakage from the brake line when disconnected, seal off the reservoir filler neck with a sheet of clean polythene stretched across the filler neck and secured with an elastic band. Plug the exposed pipe ends when separated to prevent the ingress of dirt.

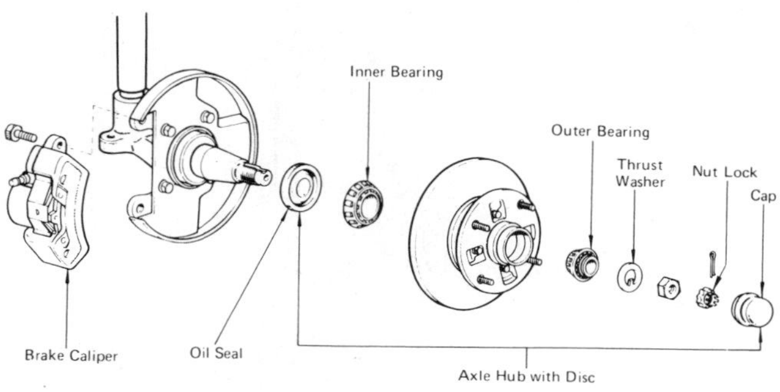

Fig. 11.9 Front wheel hub and associated components (Sec 3)

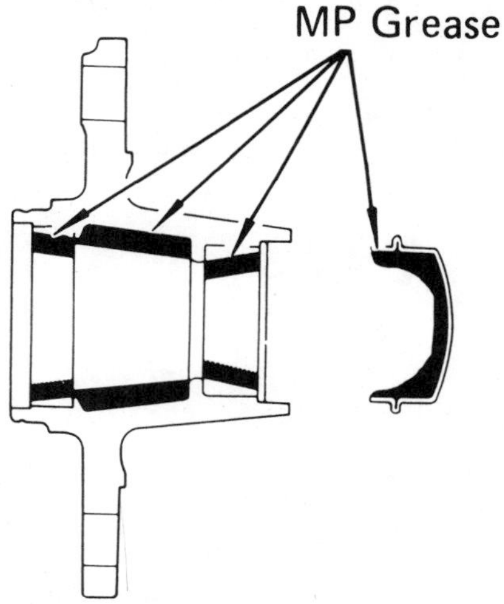

Fig. 11.10 Front hub lubrication points (Sec 3)

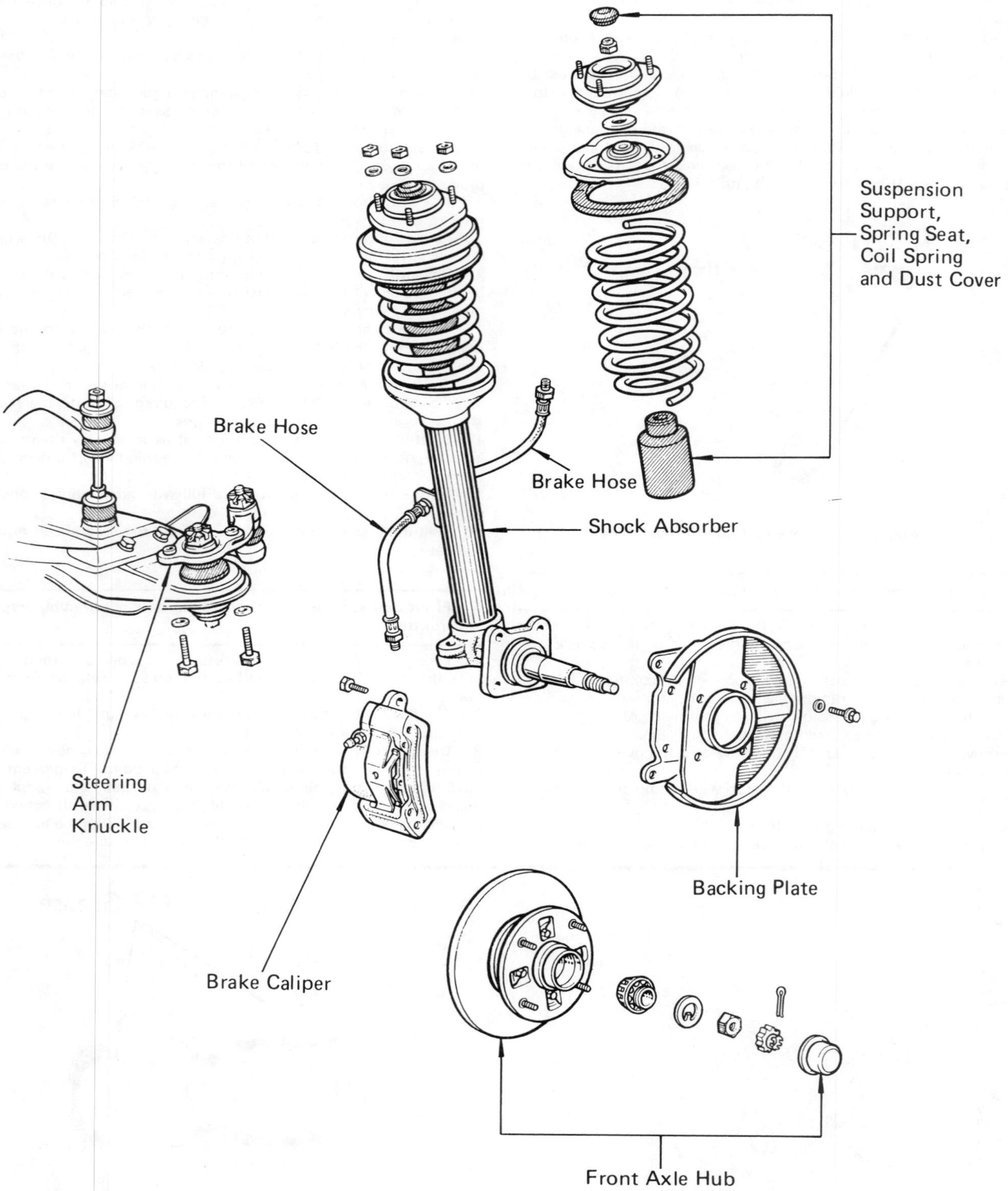

Fig. 11.11 Front coil spring and shock absorber and associated components (Sec 4)

4.4 Front shock absorber top end securing nuts

4 Unscrew and remove the three securing nuts at the top of the shock absorber at the wing mounting within the engine compartment (photo).

5 Unscrew and remove the two bolts securing the shock absorber to the steering knuckle arm.

6 The front shock absorber, axle hub and brake caliper unit can now be withdrawn. Push downwards on the suspension lower arm so that the shock absorber clears the collars, which protrude from the knuckle bolt holes, by 0.20 in (5 mm) as shown.

7 To remove the coil spring from the strut assembly you will need a suitable coil spring compressor to retain the spring tension during subsequent dismantling operations, and also for reassembly. Do not proceed further unless you have such a tool.

8 Locate the spring compressor into position and check that it is fully engaged on the spring.

9 Prise free the rubber bung from the top of the unit to expose the nut and bearing. Unscrew the nut whilst gripping the spring seat to prevent it rotating, (if available, use the special Toyota service tool number 09729-22021).

10 With the nut removed withdraw the suspension support, release the spring compressor and remove the coil spring with seat and dust cover noting how each is located.

11 Clean and inspect the components for signs of excessive wear or damage.

12 Check the spring for signs of deformity and if possible check its length against a new one. If necessary renew it, and also the opposing front suspension coil spring. To renew one spring only could cause adverse handling characteristics.

13 Check the bearing in the spring seat, and the seat itself, for signs of wear or damage and renew as necessary. The bearing inner race should rotate freely.

14 Renew the spring bumper, dust seal and also the bearing dust cover if decayed or damaged.

15 Check the operation of the shock absorber by withdrawing and then pushing the piston rod back into the cylinder. Its action should be smooth whilst offering some resistance. If the shock absorber has been leaking it will have to be dismantled for inspection and the oil seal renewed. This is a test best entrusted to your Toyota dealer who will dismantle the unit and check its serviceability.

16 If the shock absorber is to be renewed or possibly, dismantled you will need to remove the wheel hub and disc assembly, as described in Section 3. The backplate must also be removed.

17 To reassemble the strut unit, recompress the coil spring sufficiently to allow refitting of the various components.

18 Reassemble in the reverse order to removal, fitting the spring bumper, the spring and seat, which should be aligned with the piston rod. Align the coil spring lower end with the seat dent as shown.

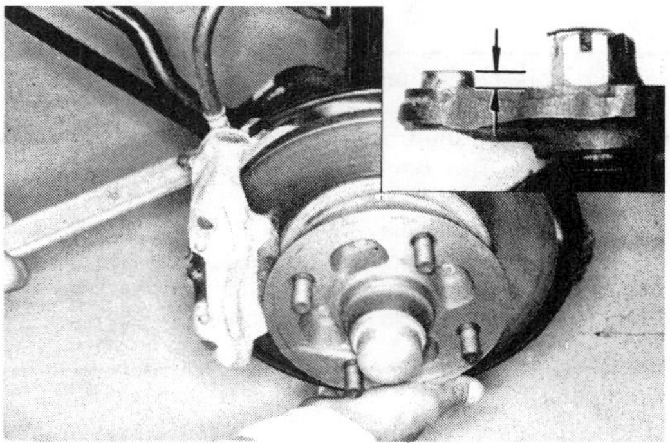

Fig. 11.12 Lever suspension arm downwards so that shock absorber clears the protruding collars (Sec 4)

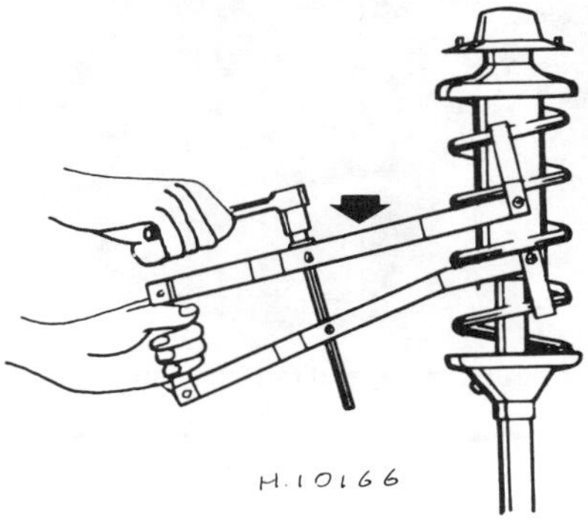

Fig. 11.13 Using a spring compressor (arrow) on the front coil spring (Sec 4)

Fig. 11.14 Correctly align the spring and seat (Sec 4)

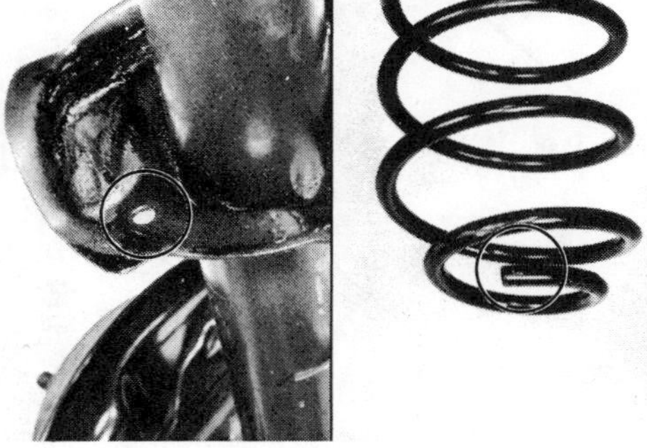

Fig. 11.15 Engage the lower end of spring into the seat dent (Sec 4)

19 The upper side of the dust seal must be lubricated with grease.
20 Relocate the top support and fit a new nut to secure it. Tighten the nut to the specified torque wrench setting whilst simultaneously gripping the support to prevent it from rotating.
21 Pack the support bearing and cavity with grease and refit the rubber bung. Remove the spring compressor.
22 Relocate the strut assembly into position and temporarily tighten the three upper mounting nuts.
23 Relocate the lower end of the shock absorber strut with the suspension lower arm, levering it down over the alignment collars. Refit the attachment bolts and tighten them to the specified torque setting. Grease bearing and refit the cap (photo).
24 Now fully tighten the three upper mounting nuts to the specified torque setting.
25 If applicable, reassemble the backplate, wheel hub and disc assembly as given in Section 3.
26 Reconnect the brake hydraulic lines. Top up and bleed the brakes as described in Chapter 9.
27 Refit the roadwheel and on completion have the front wheel alignment checked by your Toyota dealer. A provisional alignment check can be made as given in Section 10.

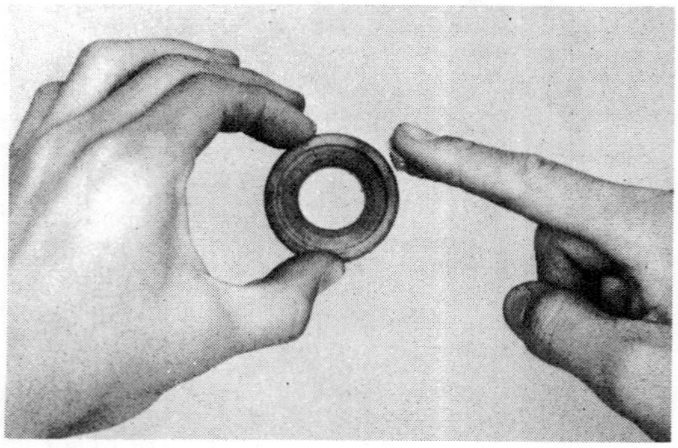

Fig. 11.16 Lubricate seal upper face with grease (Sec 4)

4.23 Grease the strut bearing and refit the cap

5 Front suspension stabiliser bar – removal and refitting

1 Jack-up the front of the vehicle and support it on axle stands.
2 Remove the engine under shield.
3 Unscrew and remove the bolts which secure the ends of the stabiliser bar to the track control arm. Note the arrangement of rubber bushes, retainers and spacers.
4 Unbolt the stabiliser brackets from the bodyframe.
5 Now unbolt both ends of one of the strut bars (unbolt the bracket from the bodyframe at one end) and remove the strut bar complete with bracket still attached to it at one end. Do not disturb the strut bar to bracket setting.
6 The stabilizer bar can now be withdrawn through the strut bar bracket hole.
7 Clean and inspect the stabilizer bar, bushes, and through bolts. Renew any damaged or worn components.
8 Refitting is a reversal of removal but tighten all nuts and bolts to the specified torque wrench settings.

6 Strut bar – removal and refitting

1 To remove this component, raise the front of the vehicle and remove the roadwheel.
2 Unbolt the bar from the track control arm and from the bodyframe attachment bracket. The backing nut at the bracket is staked in position and should not be removed so that refitting is not complicated. However, where a new bar is to be fitted, tighten the nuts at the bracket end in accordance with the appropriate diagram to the specified torque settings, and then stake the new backing nut (photo).
3 Refit the roadwheel and lower the vehicle.

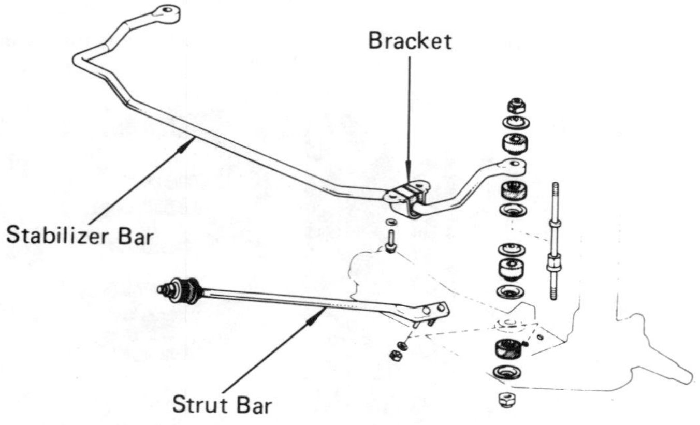

Fig. 11.17 Front stabilizer bar and strut bar components (Sec 5)

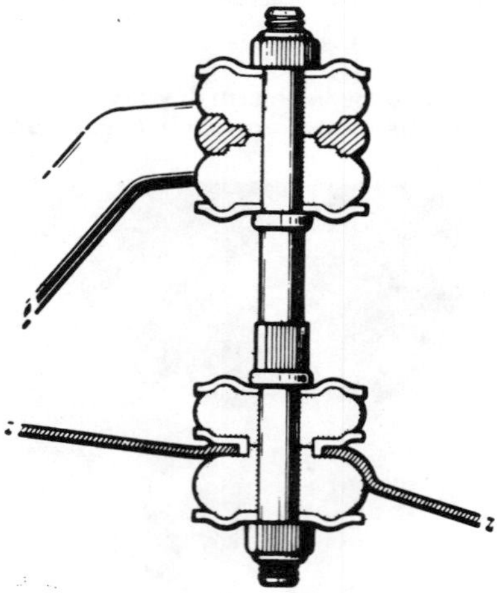

Fig. 11.18 Stabilizer bushes, retainers and spacers to be assembled in order shown (Sec 5)

6.2 Strut bar to track control arm location

7 Front suspension track control arm balljoint dust excluder – renewal

1 To renew one of the track control arm balljoint flexible dust excluders, raise the front of the vehicle and support it on axle stands.
2 Remove the roadwheel.
3 Extract the bolts which secure the base of the suspension strut to the steering arm. Depress the track control arm to release it from the suspension strut hollow positioning dowels.
4 Disconnect the trackrod end from the eye in the steering arm. Use a balljoint separator for this or forked wedges. Although a balljoint can be released by unscrewing the nut from its taper pin and striking both sides of the eye into which the taper pin engages with two large hammers simultaneously, this is not to be recommended due to the possibility of damaging adjacent components.
5 Extract the split pin and unscrew the castellated nut from the balljoint taper pin at the end of the track control arm.
6 Using a suitable extractor, press the balljoint taper pin out of the steering arm.
7 There is now sufficient working room to be able to prise off the dust cover and retaining ring from the balljoint.
8 Fit the new dust cover and always use a new retaining ring. Apply

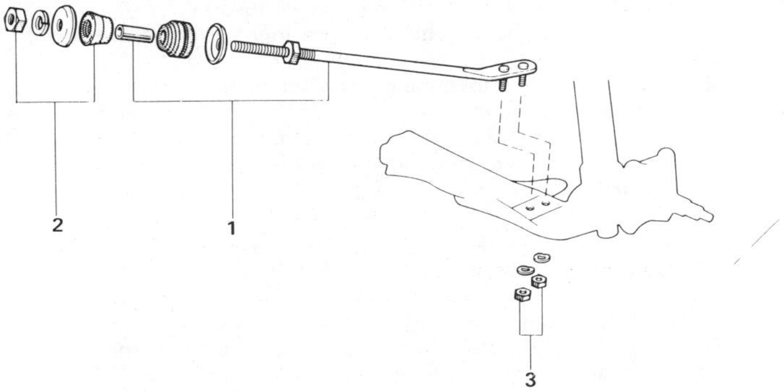

Fig. 11.19 Strut bar assembly components (Sec 6)

1 Strut bar, retainer, bush and collar
2 Strut bar bush and retainer
3 Nut

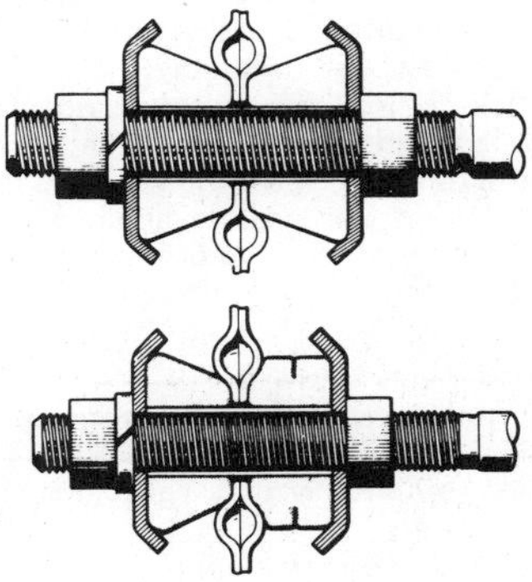

Fig. 11.20 Strut bar showing bush types and orientation (Sec 6)

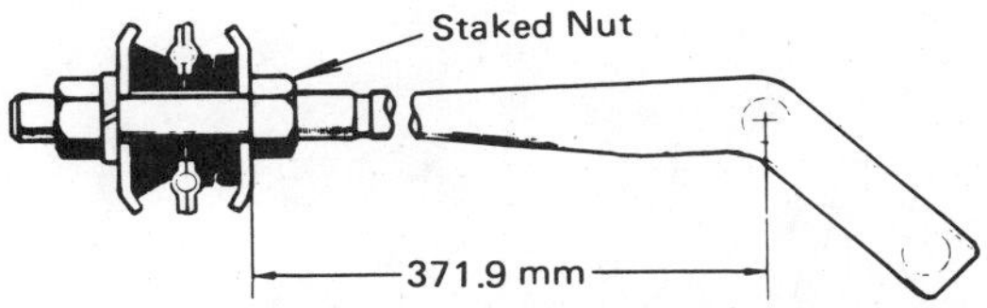

Fig. 11.21 Strut bar bolt hole to nut distance to be as shown (Sec 6)

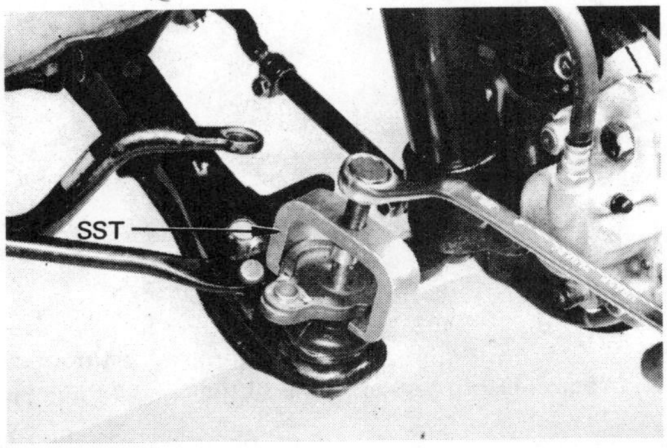

Fig. 11.22 Separating steering arm from balljoint taper pin (Sec 7)

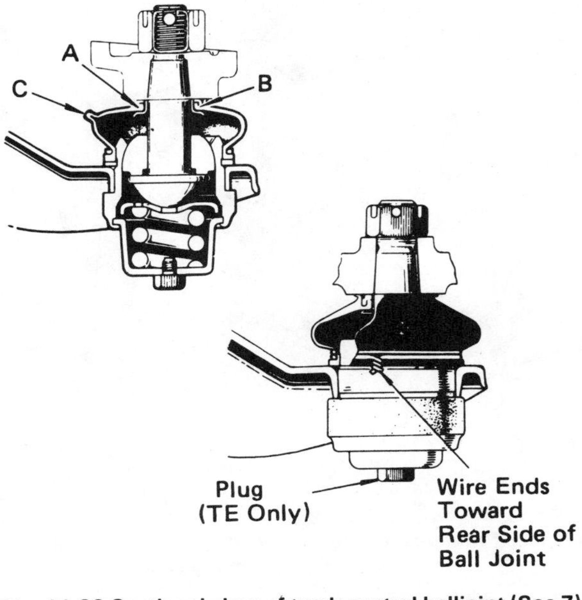

Fig. 11.23 Sectional view of track control balljoint (Sec 7)

Grease sections A and B
Vent C must face to rear when fitted

grease to the parts of the cover A and B and ensure that the vent in the cover is towards the rear of the vehicle.
9 Unscrew the plug from the balljoint and substitute a grease nipple. Inject grease and then refit the plug.
10 Reconnect the balljoint to the steering arm and tighten the nut to the specified torque wrench setting. Insert a new split pin.
11 Reconnect the steering arm to the base of the suspension strut.
12 Reconnect the trackrod end balljoint to the steering arm eye.
13 Refit the roadwheel and lower the vehicle.
14 It should be noted that if the track control arm balljoint is worn, it can only be renewed complete with the control arm as an assembly, (see Section 8).

8 Front suspension track control arm – removal, renovation and refitting

1 Repeat the operations described in paragraphs 2, 3 and 4 of the preceding Section.
2 Disconnect the strut bar and the stabiliser bar from the track control arm.
3 Unscrew and remove the pivot bolt which secures the inner end of the track control arm to the bodyframe crossmember.
4 The track control arm can now be withdrawn from the vehicle.
5 If the bushes are worn at the inner end of the arm, they can be removed and new ones fitted either using a press or a long bolt, nuts, washers and distance pieces of suitable diameter.
6 If the track control arm balljoint is worn, it can only be renewed as part of a complete new arm assembly.
7 Refit the track control arm by reversing the removal operations. Tighten all nuts and bolts to the specified torque wrench settings **except** the control arm inner pivot bolt. Screw this up only finger tight until the vehicle is on the ground again with the jacks removed. Bounce the body up and down two or three times and then tighten the bolt to the specified torque wrench setting.

9 Front bodyframe crossmember – removal and refitting

1 This operation is normally only called for in exceptional cases of damage or severe corrosion.
2 Remove the engine undershield.
3 Support the weight of the engine either by attaching a hoist to it

Fig. 11.24 Pressing new bushes into the control arm eye using suitable diameter tubing (Sec 8)

or by supporting it on a jack and a block of wood placed under the sump.
4 Disconnect the engine mountings from the crossmember brackets.
5 On vehicles fitted with rack and pinion steering unbolt and remove the steering link assembly (see Section 13) and the stay rod.
6 Where fitted, disconnect the engine absorber.
7 Remove the pivot bolts from the inner ends of the lower track control arms.
8 Unscrew and remove the bolts which hold the crossmember to the bodyframe side members. Do not attempt to move the vehicle while the track control arms are disconnected.
9 Refit the new crossmember by reversing the removal operations. Tighten all bolts to specified torque.

10 Steering angles and front wheel alignment

1 Accurate front wheel alignment is essential for slow tyre wear and good steering. Before checking or adjusting the alignment, ensure that the tyres are correctly inflated, the front hub bearings are correctly adjusted, the front wheels are balanced and not buckled, the strut shock absorbers are serviceable, and that the track-rod ends are not worn.

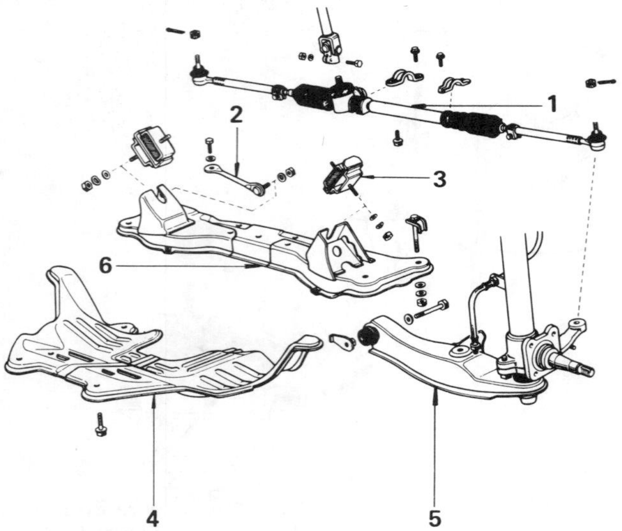

Fig. 11.25 Front bodyframe crossmember and rack and pinion associated components (Sec 9)

1 Steering link assembly
2 Stay rod
3 Engine mounting
4 Engine under cover
5 Track control arm
6 Crossmember

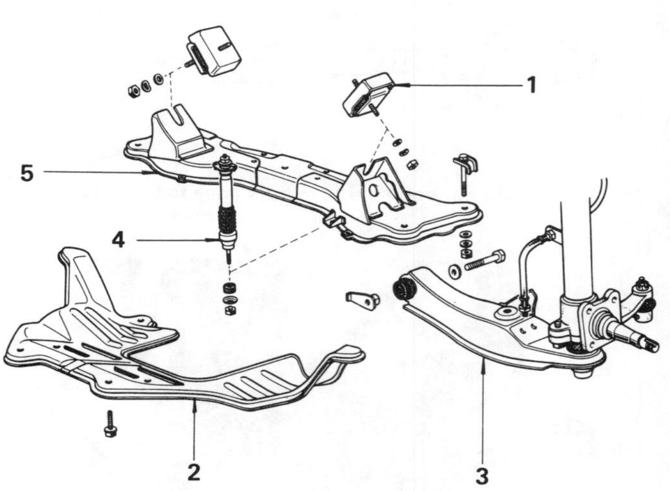

Fig. 11.26 Front bodyframe crossmember components recirculating ball steering models (Sec 9)

1 Engine mounting
2 Engine under cover
3 Track control arm
4 Engine absorber (for ECE)
5 Crossmember

2 Wheel alignment consists of four main factors:

(a) *Camber, the angle at which the front wheels are set from the vertical when viewed from the front of the car*
(b) *Castor, the angle at which the steering axis is set from the vertical when viewed from the side of the car*
(c) *Steering axis inclination, the angle at which the steering axis is set from the vertical when viewed from the front of the car*
(d) *Toe-in, the amount by which the distance between the front edges of the roadwheels (measured at hub height) is less than the corresponding distance between the rear edges of the front roadwheels*

3 Camber and steering axis inclination are not adjustable. Castor can be adjusted by altering the length of the strut bar. Toe-in can be adjusted by repositioning the track-rod ends on the rack ends.
4 Accurate checking of steering angles and wheel alignment is only possible with expensive equipment and is therefore best entrusted to your Toyota dealer. However, reasonable adjustment of toe-in is possible by using a home made adjustable trammel bar.
5 Drive the car onto level ground and adjust the trammel bar between the centres of the tyre tread on the rear of the front tyres. Mark the tyres with a small dot at the point where the trammel bar touches the tyres.
6 Move the car forwards so that the marks are now at hub height on the front of the tyres (wheel turned through 180°). Move the trammel bar to the front of the car without altering the adjustment. The distance between the two dots should now be less than the first distance by the specified amount of toe-in.
7 To adjust rack and pinion steering models, loosen the track (tie) rod pinch-bolts and remove the steering gear bellows outer clips. Turn each rack end by equal amounts until the toe-in is correct (hold the track-rods quite still with a pair of grips), then tighten the pinch-bolts and refit the bellows clips.
8 To adjust recirculating ball steering models, loosen off the track (tie) rod clamps and rotate the tube on each side equal amounts as required. Retighten the clamps and check that the rod end angles are at 90° to each other.

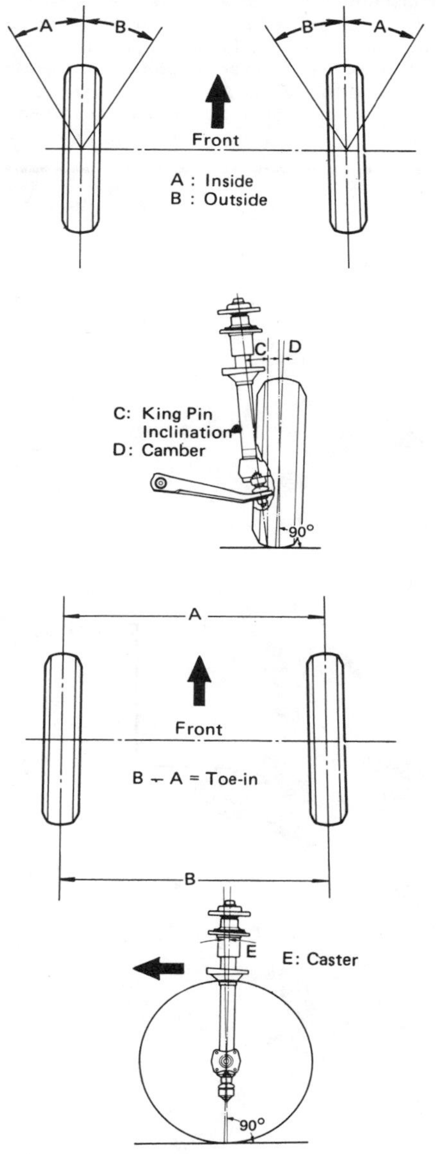

Fig. 11.27 Diagram to show various wheel alignment angles and checks (Sec 10)

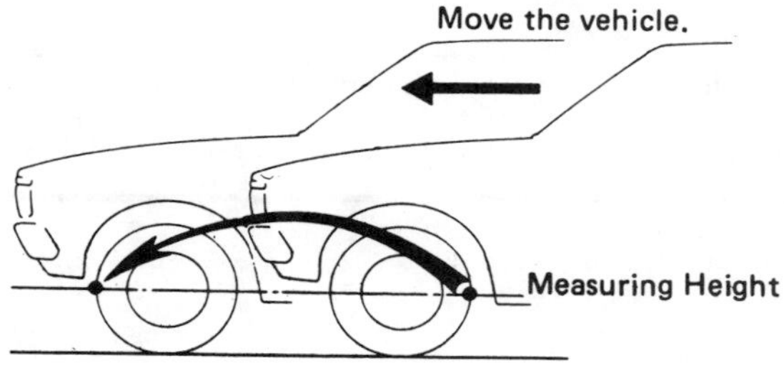

Fig. 11.28 Measuring height on wheel for toe-in adjustment check (Sec 10)

Fig. 11.29 Position trammel bar as shown to check toe-in (Sec 10)

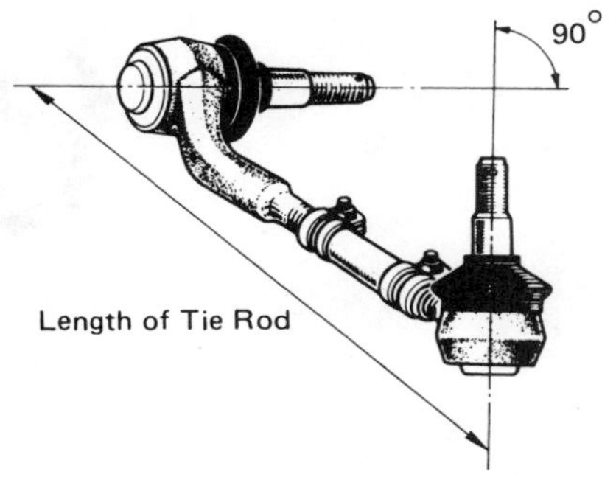

Fig. 11.30 Check rod angle is as shown after making adjustment of toe-in. The toe rod length each side must be kept equal – recirculating ball steering type shown (Sec 10)

11 Steering wheel – removal and refitting

1 Set the front roadwheels in the straight-ahead position. Disconnect the battery negative terminal.
2 With a screwdriver, prise the pad from the centre of the steering wheel.
3 Unscrew and remove the steering wheel retaining nut with a socket or box spanner.
4 Mark the relative position of the wheel to the steering shaft by dot punching the end faces.
5 Pull the steering wheel from the shaft splines; do not attempt to jar it off as this may damage the shaft shear pins. If it is very tight, a puller will have to be used.
6 Refitting is a reversal of removal, but make sure that the steering wheel engages the direction indicator cancelling cam and that the previously made marks are aligned. Tighten the retaining nut to the specified torque.

12 Steering column (rack and pinion type) – removal, overhaul and refitting

1 Remove the steering wheel as described in Section 11.
2 Unscrew the universal joint clamp bolts, pull the intermediate steering shaft from the steering gear, then withdraw the shaft from the main steering shaft universal joint.
3 Remove the steering column switches as described in Chapter 10.
4 Disconnect the ignition switch wiring plug.
5 Unscrew the bolts securing the hole cover to the bulkhead.
6 Unscrew the upper column mounting bolts and nut, remove the earth lead and wedge, and withdraw the column from inside the car. Recover the hole cover spacer.
7 Remove the ignition key cylinder as described in Chapter 10.
8 Unscrew the securing bolts and withdraw the retainer plate from the main steering shaft.
9 Using circlip pliers extract the circlip, then unbolt the upper bearing bracket from the steering column.
10 Withdraw the upper bearing bracket and upper tube from the steering shaft. On some models it will be necessary to remove the steering lock set bolt by drilling a 3 or 4 mm diameter hole in it and unscrewing it with an extractor.
11 Unbolt and detach the hole cover, ring and plate from the column lower end.
12 Unbolt and remove the mainshaft stopper retainer.
13 Withdraw the column tube then remove the snap-ring and bearing from the mainshaft.
14 Clean all components and wipe them dry for inspection.
15 Check the universal joint for signs of excessive wear, also the upper bracket bearing and lower column bearing. Examine the shear pin for damage and the mainshaft for deformity. Check the tube and other associated components and renew any defective items as necessary.

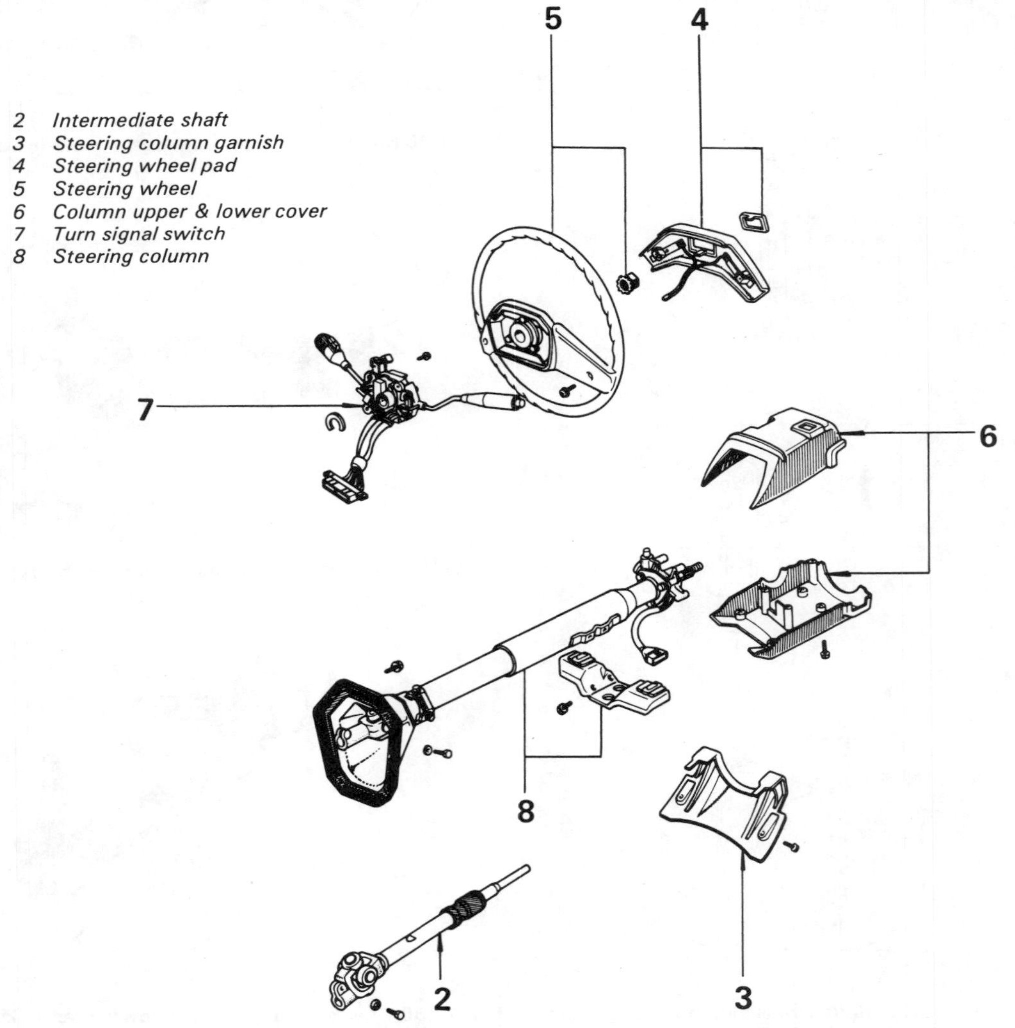

Fig. 11.31 Rack and pinion steering column associated components (Sec 12)

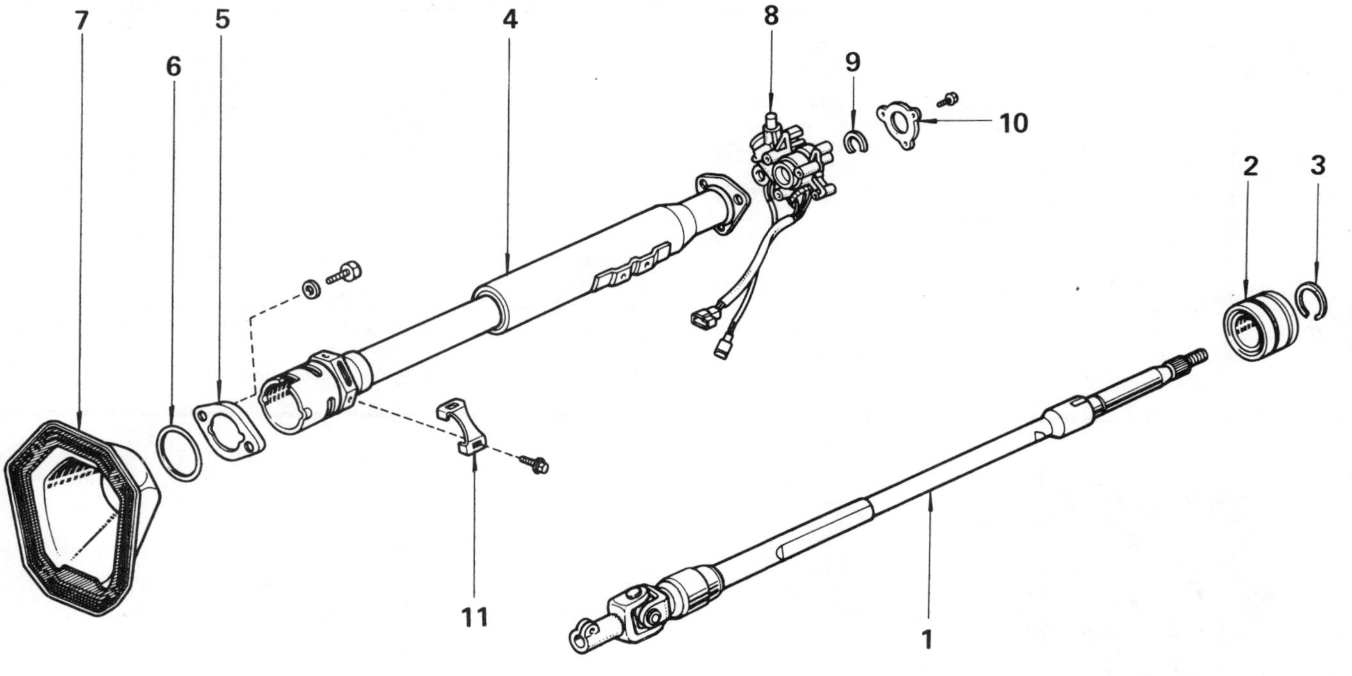

Fig. 11.32 Steering column components (rack and pinion type) (Sec 12)

1 *Mainshaft*
2 *Bearing*
3 *Snap ring*
4 *Column tube*
5 *Plate*
6 *Ring*
7 *Hole cover*
8 *Upper bracket*
9 *Snap ring*
10 *Retainer*
11 *Stopper retainer*

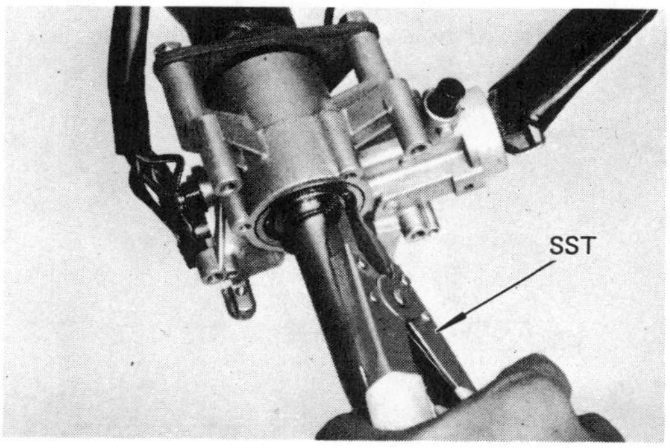

Fig. 11.33 Remove circlip from the upper bracket housing (Sec 12)

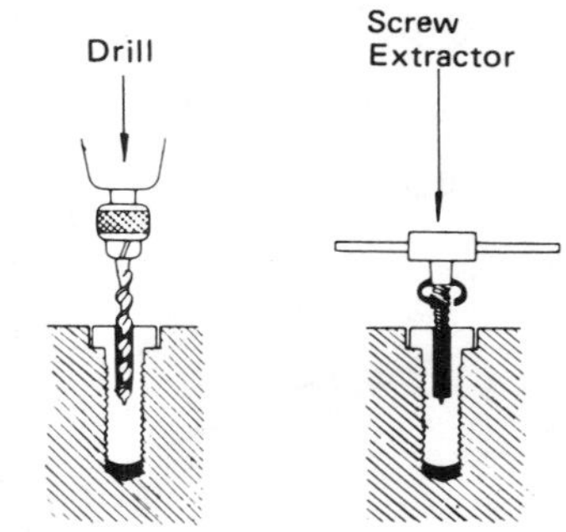

Fig. 11.34 Drill out and extract the steering lock set bolt (Sec 12)

Fig. 11.35 Mainshaft stopper bolt removal (Sec 12)

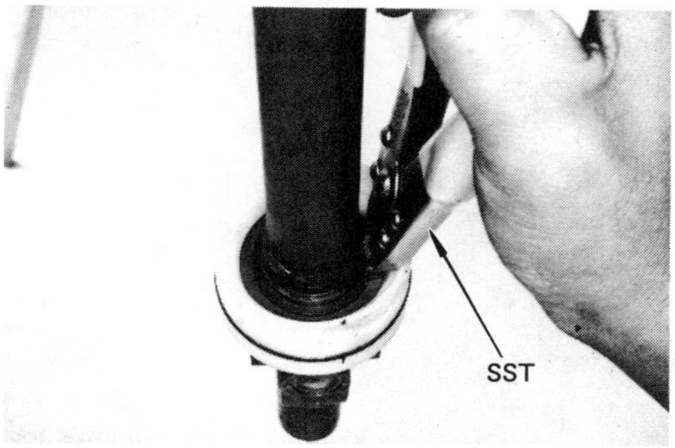

Fig. 11.36 Extract the snap-ring to remove bearing from mainshaft (Sec 12)

16 Reassembly and refitting procedures are a reversal of dismantling and removal, but the following additional points should be noted:

(a) *The mainshaft must not receive an impact during assembly and refitting of the column. Lubricate bearings with grease.*
(b) *When assembling the cover pawl to the column tube align it as shown.*
(c) *Where applicable, fit a new steering lock set bolt and tighten it to the point where the head shears off.*
(d) *Release the steering lock when reassembling the upper column and bracket and tube to the mainshaft.*
(e) *Use new circlips and tighten all fastenings to their specified torque wrench settings.*
(f) *The wedge must be located between the upper column and bulkhead so that the tube of the upper column is concentric with the steering shaft.*
(g) *Fit the intermediate shaft with the steering wheel and roadwheels in the straight-ahead position.*
(h) *When refitting the steering wheel align the indicator cancel cam claw with the hole in the wheel.*
(i) *On completion check the operation of the various switch controls and the steering lock. Check the steering wheel play and the action of the steering for satisfactory operation.*

13 Steering gear (rack and pinion) – removal, overhaul and refitting

1 Jack-up the front of the car and support it on stands. Remove the roadwheels.

2 Unscrew and remove the intermediate steering shaft clamp bolts.

Fig. 11.37 Cover pawl to align with column tube (Sec 12)

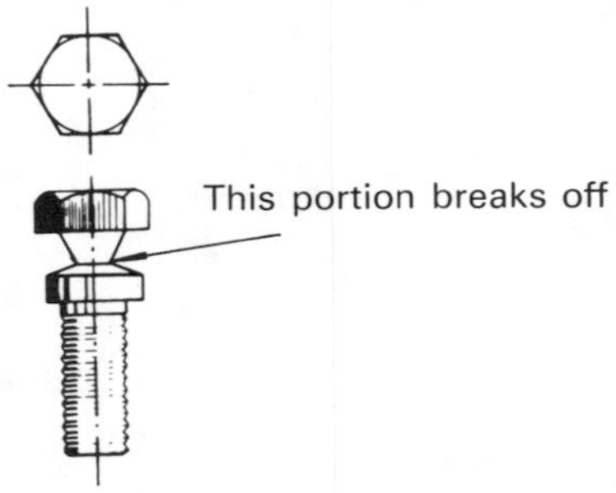

Fig. 11.38 Steering lock set bolt (Sec 12)

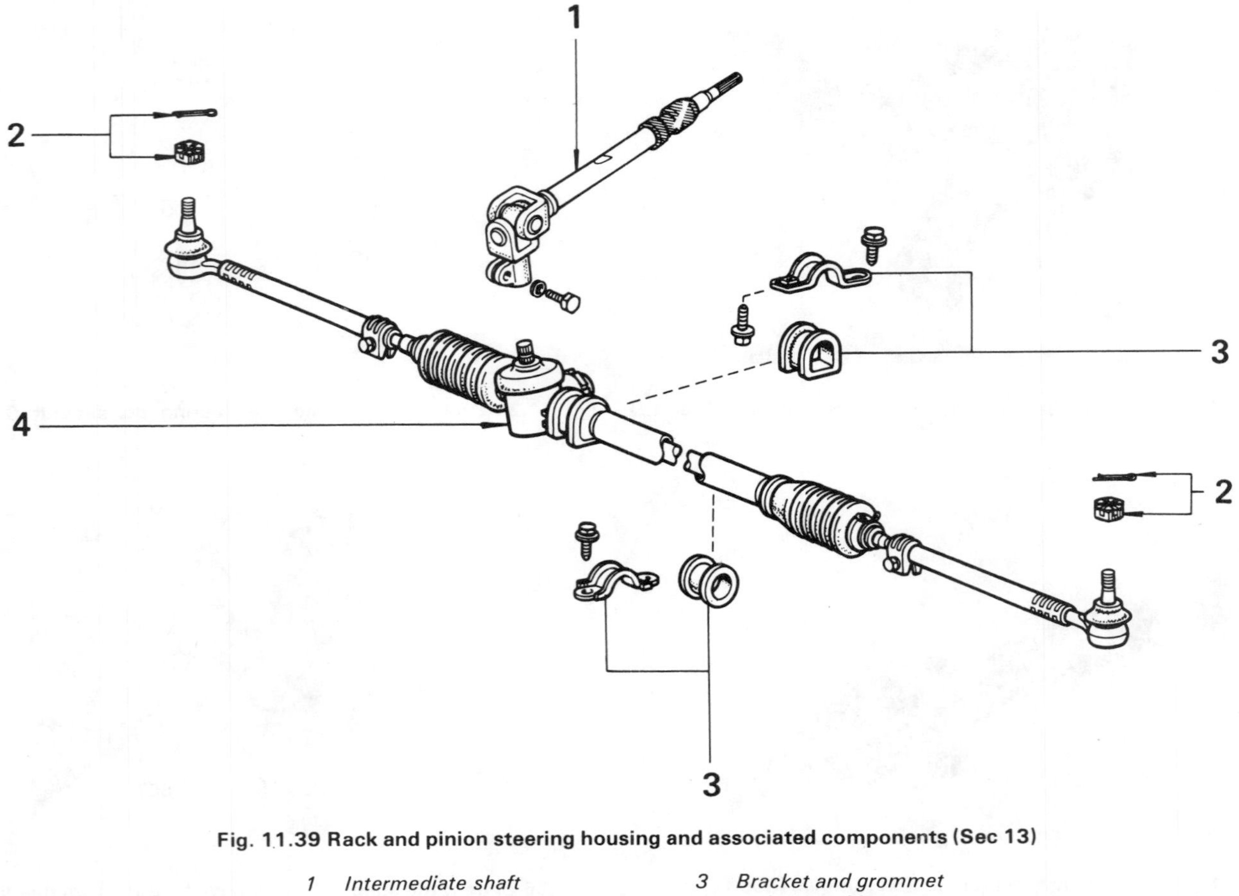

Fig. 11.39 Rack and pinion steering housing and associated components (Sec 13)

1 *Intermediate shaft*
2 *Cotter pin and nut*
3 *Bracket and grommet*
4 *Link assembly*

Pull the shaft from the steering gear and withdraw it from the main steering shaft universal joint.
3 Extract the split pins and unscrew the track-rod end nuts. Disconnect the track-rod ends from the steering knuckle arms using a suitable separator.
4 Unscrew and remove the steering gear mounting clamp bolts and remove the clamps.
5 Lift the steering gear from the front crossmember and withdraw it from beneath the car. Take care not to damage the rubber rack boots.
6 Clean the exterior of the steering gear and grip it in a soft-jawed vice around the grooved mounting.
7 Mark the position of the track-rod ends on the rack ends, and also mark each track-rod end for location. Loosen the pinch-bolts and unscrew the track-rod ends.
8 Remove the spring and hose clips from the rubber bellows.

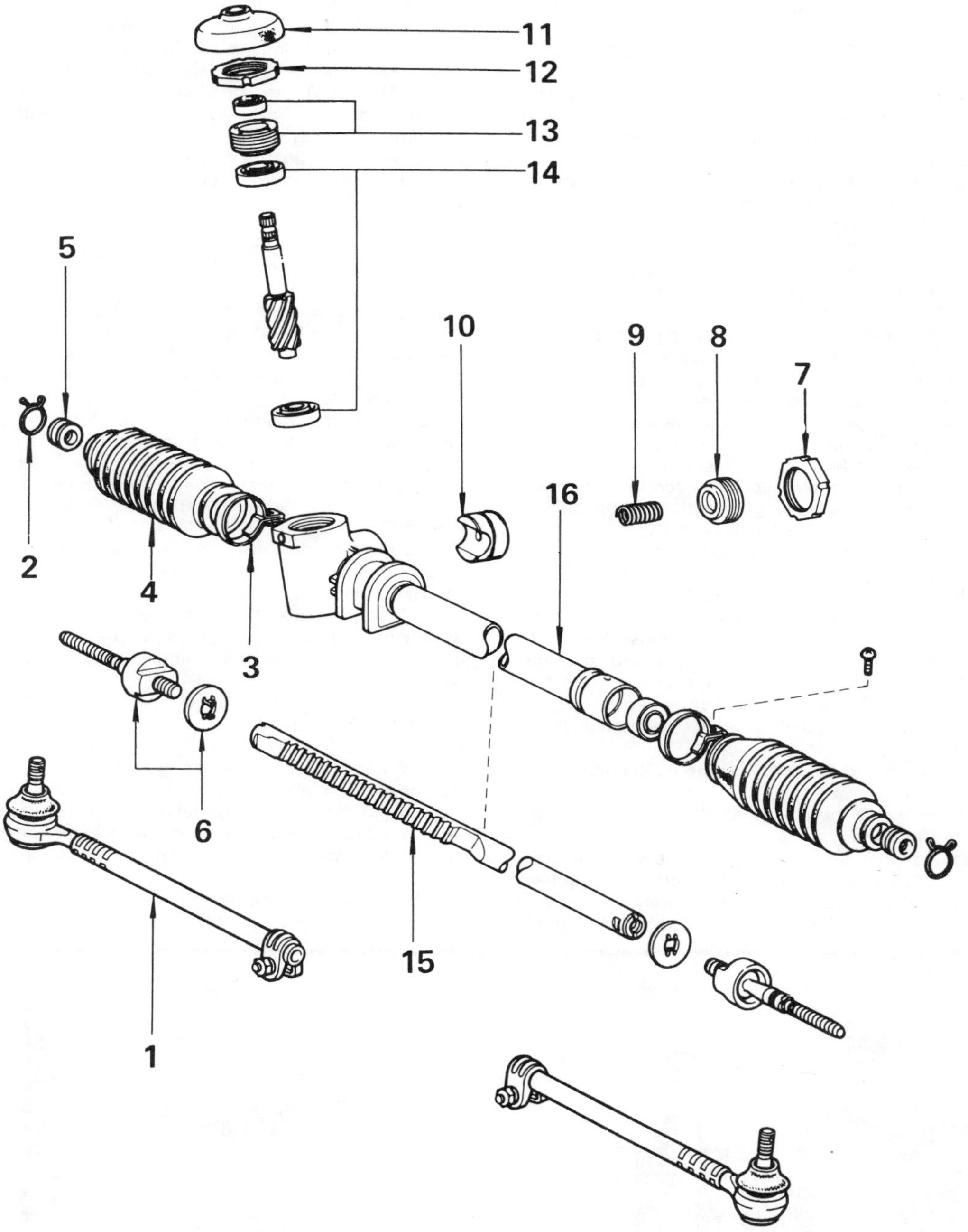

Fig. 11.40 Rack and pinion unit components (Sec 13)

1 Track rod end
2 Clip
3 Clamp
4 Rack boot
5 Rack end dust seal
6 Rack end & claw washer
7 Lock nut
8 Rack guide spring cap
9 Spring
10 Rack guide
11 Dust cover
12 Lock nut
13 Pinion bearing adjusting screw & pinion oil seal
14 Pinion & pinion bearing
15 Rack
16 Rack housing

Withdraw the bellows and dust seals from the rack ends and mark the bellows left-hand and right-hand sides as they are different.
9 Bend up the tab washers and mark the rack ends left-hand and right-hand sides.
10 Hold the rack steady, then unscrew and remove the rack ends and tab washers. Take care not to damage the surface of the rack when supporting with spanner. Mark each rack end right- and left-hand for identification.
11 Unscrew and remove the rack guide thrust bearing locknut and the spring cap, using a hexagon key for the latter.
12 Extract the spring and rack guide and urethane spacer (1981 models on).
13 Prise the dust cover from the pinion and unscrew the adjusting screw locknut.
14 Unscrew the pinion bearing adjusting screw, using the special tool available or a suitable pin wrench. The tool incorporates two pegs for locating in the screw, and if necessary one can easily be made out of flat steel and two bolts of suitable diameter.
15 Pull the rack from the pinion end of the steering gear until the pinion is located in the recess and is not in mesh with the teeth.
16 Extract the pinion and bearing using a pair of pliers and a hammer as shown. Take care not to damage the splines.
17 Withdraw the rack from the pinion end of the steering gear.
18 Using a screwdriver, lever the oil seal from the pinion bearing adjusting screw.
19 Using a suitable puller, remove the upper bearing from the pinion. Alternatively support the bearing in a vice and drive the pinion through it. Recover the spacer and note its location for correct reassembly.
20 Heat the pinion end of the steering gear in boiling water, then tap it on a piece of wood to release the lower pinion bearing.
21 Wash all components in paraffin and wipe them dry with lint-free cloth. Examine the components for wear and deterioration and renew them as necessary. If the bush in the end of the steering gear housing requires renewal, it can be driven out using a length of metal rod. Fully drive in the new bush using a suitable tubular drift.
22 Commence reassembly by fitting the pinion lower bearing into the housing after having heated the housing in boiling water. Make sure that the bearing is located the correct way round.
23 Wipe away any traces of water, then pack the pinion lower bearing and housing with a lithium based grease. Smear grease also on the housing bush. The housing should be approximately half full of grease.
24 Grease the rack teeth and insert it into the pinion end of the housing until the recess is in line with the pinion aperture.
25 Using suitable tubing drive the pinion bearing into position with its seal face downwards.
26 Grease the pinion teeth and bearing. Tap the pinion and bearing into the housing.
27 Drive the new oil seal into the pinion adjusting screw, leaving it protruding by 0.02 in (0.5 mm).
28 Grease the oil seal lip, then insert and tighten the adjusting screw until the pinion turning torque is 3.2 lbf in (3.7 kgf cm) measured with a torque wrench. A special adaptor will be required to check the torque. Now loosen the screw until the preload is 2.0 to 2.9 lbf in (2.3 to 3.3 kgf cm).
29 Smear some liquid sealer on the base of the locknut, then tighten it onto the adjusting screw to the specified torque, holding the adjusting screw with the pin wrench. Check that the pinion turning torque is now reduced to within the specified limits.
30 Push the rack into its normal central position and at the same time mesh it with the pinion.
31 Lubricate the rack guide and rack guide ridge with grease and insert it through the housing. On 1981 models onwards a urethane spacer is fitted to the rack guide and this is shown in the figure.
32 On pre 1981 models (without the urethane spacer), refit the spring and cap and initially tighten the cap to a torque of 18 lbf ft (2.5 kgf m). From this position loosen the cap 12° and check the pinion turning torque (preload) using a suitable torque wrench. It should be as given in the Specifications. On 1981 models onwards fitted with the urethane spacer, refit the spring and cap and tighten it down three or four times to the specified initial tightening torque given above. From this position loosen the cap about 90° and then adjust the pinion preload by rotating the spring cap to give the following preload settings:

Maximum preload 8.7 to 11.3 lbf in (10 to 13 kgf cm)
Minimum preload 5.2 lbf in (6.0 kgf cm)

Check preload settings through complete rack stroke.
33 Smear some liquid sealer on the base of the spring cap locknut, then tighten it onto the cap to the specified torque.
34 Check that the pinion turning torque is now within the specified limits (rack fitted).
35 Fit the rubber dust cover.
36 Grease the rack end balljoints, locate the tab washers, and screw the rack ends into the rack. With the tab washers located in the rack grooves, tighten the rack ends to the specified torque and bend over the tab washers. A special adaptor will be needed for the torque wrench.
37 Fit the rack end dust seals and check that the pressure transfer holes in the housing are unobstructed.
38 Refit the rubber bellows (rack boots) taking care not to twist them when fitting and also ensure that each is fitted to its correct side.
39 Fit the bellow clamps and tighten as shown.
40 Locate the rack boot securing clips as shown with the ends facing out.
41 Turn the pinion and check the length of the rack stroke which should be as specified.
42 Refit the steering gear to the front crossmember, locate the clamps, and tighten the retaining bolts.
43 Insert the track-rod ends into the steering knuckle arms. Tighten the nuts to the specified torque and fit the split-pins.
44 With the steering wheels in the straight-ahead position, refit the intermediate steering shaft and tighten the clamp bolts to the specified torque.
45 Refit the roadwheels and lower the car to the ground.
46 Adjust the front wheel alignment as described in Section 10.

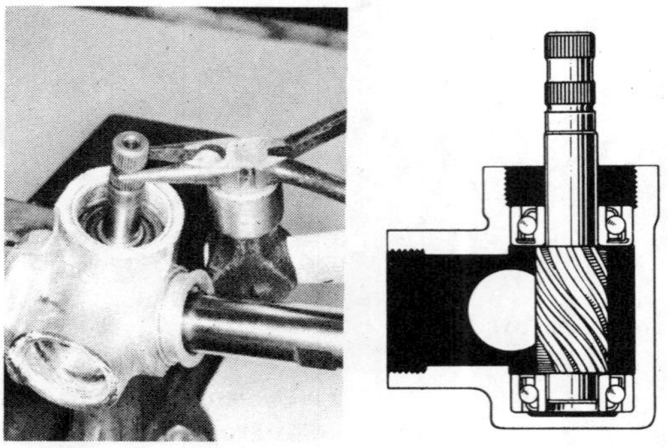

Fig. 11.41 Pinion and upper bearing removal (Sec 13)

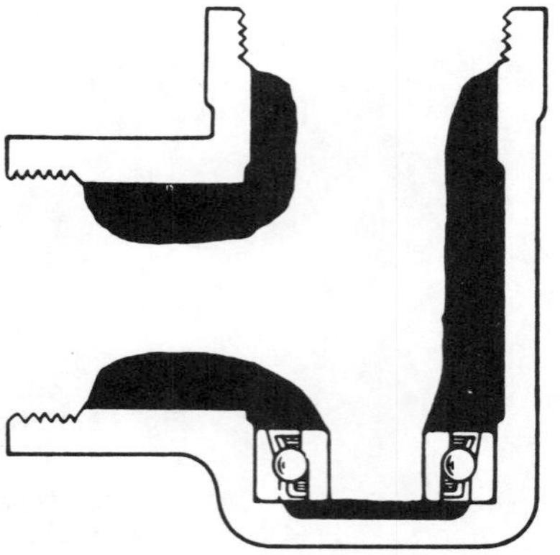

Fig. 11.42 Lubricate the rack housing with grease. Note bearing orientation (Sec 13)

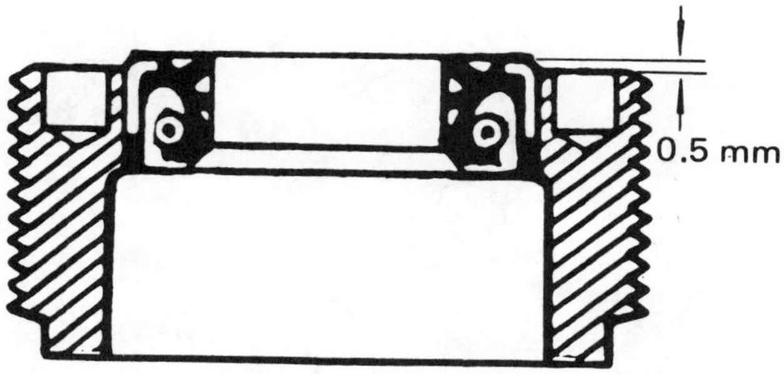

Fig. 11.43 Fitted depth of pinion oil seal to be as shown (Sec 13)

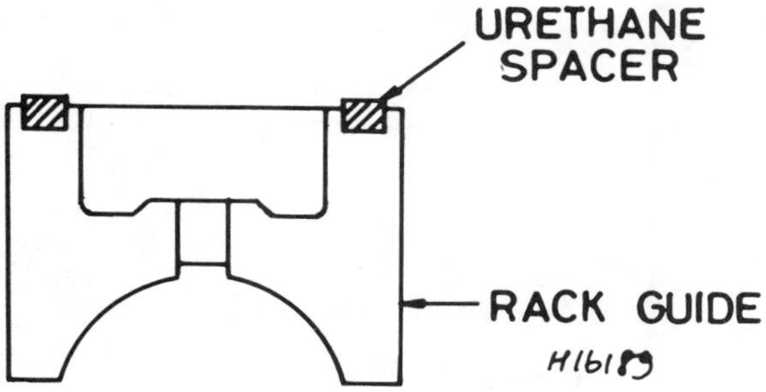

Fig. 11.44 Urethane spacer location on the rack guide fitted to 1981 models onwards (Sec 13)

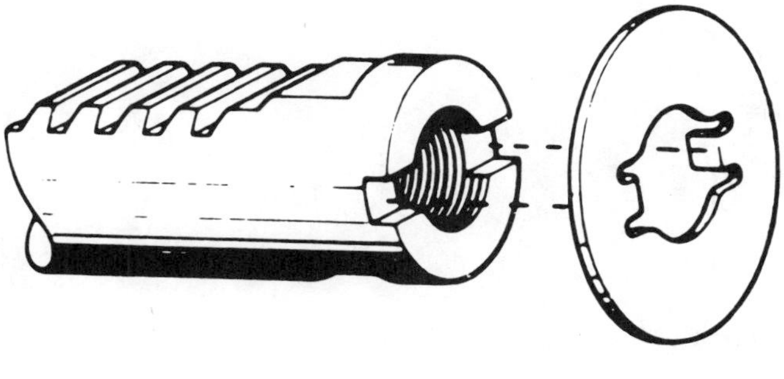

Fig. 11.45 Align tab washers with rack and grooves (Sec 13)

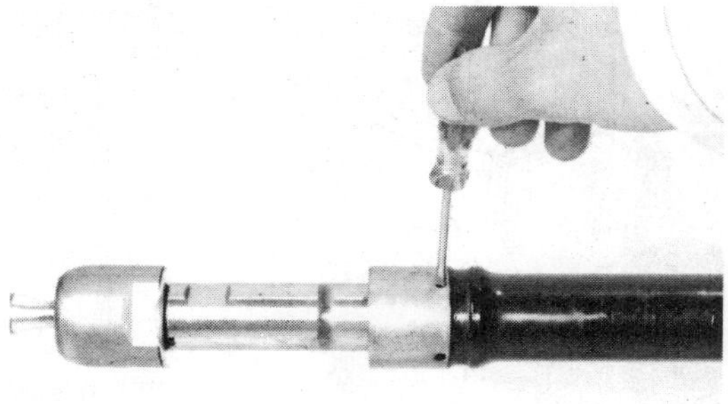

Fig. 11.46 Check that the transfer holes are clear (Sec 13)

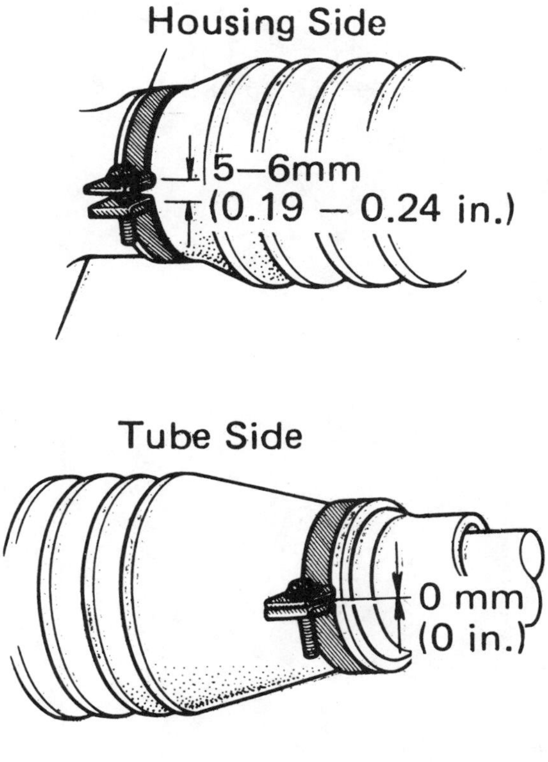

Fig. 11.47 Rack boot identification – left at top, right-hand at bottom (Sec 13)

Fig. 11.48 Rack boot clamp positions (Sec 13)

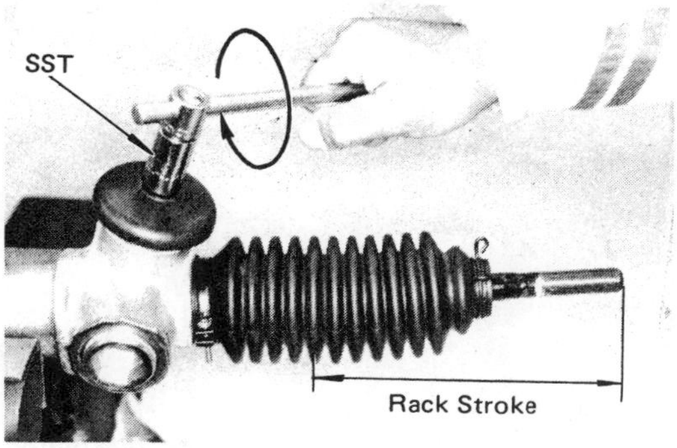

Fig. 11.49 Rack stroke check method (Sec 13)

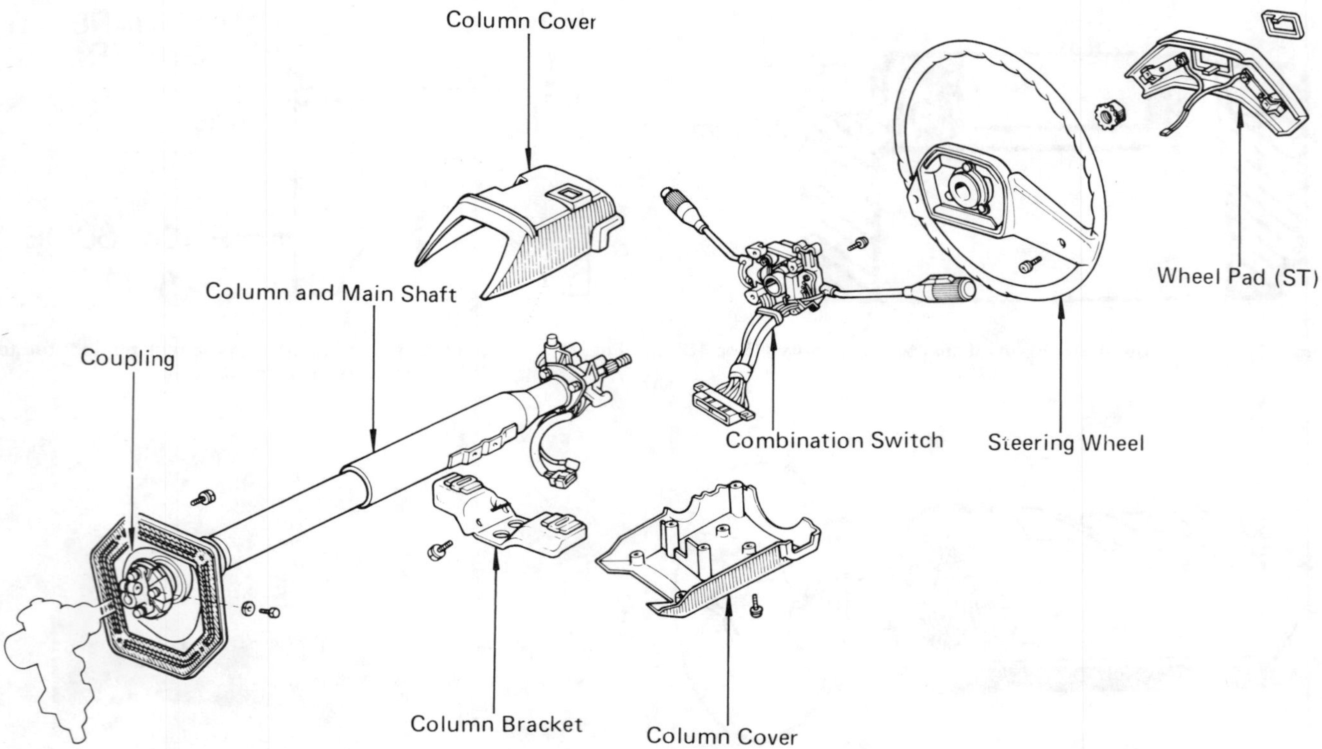

Fig. 11.50 Steering column and associated components – recirculating ball steering (Sec 14)

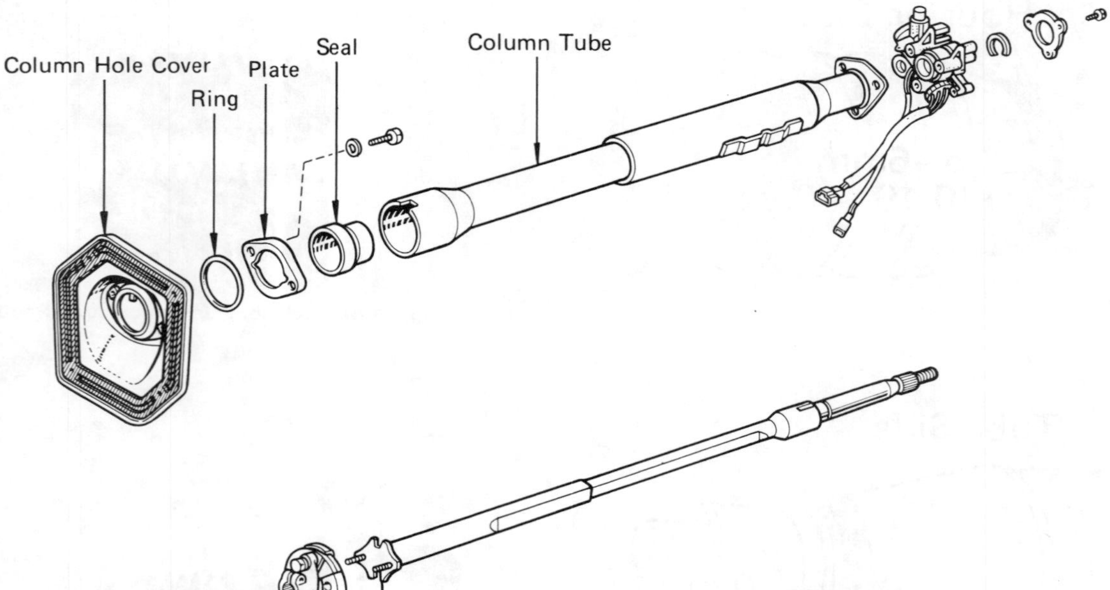

Fig. 11.51 Steering column components – recirculating ball type (Sec 14)

14 Steering column (recirculating ball type) – removal, overhaul and refitting

1 The steering column and the associated components to be detached for this removal are shown in the figure. The steering column and mainshaft components are also illustrated.
2 The column removal, overhaul and refitting details are similar to those given for the rack and pinion type column given in Section 12.
3 Ignore those items in that Section which do not apply, but note the following details which are applicable to the recirculating ball type column:

(a) *The lower column dust seal is prised out of the tube using a suitable screwdriver as a lever. When inserting the new seal, smear its outer surfaces with a sealant before fitting it into position.*
(b) *Smear the mainshaft with grease when refitting.*
(c) *When the column is being refitted into position, locate and finger tighten the upper column bracket retaining nuts, then fit the steering column hole cover and tighten its retaining bolts to the specified torque wrench setting. The upper column bracket retaining bolts can then be tightened to their specified torque wrench settings (photos).*
(d) *After the column is secured, tighten the coupling set bolts to the specified torque wrench setting.*

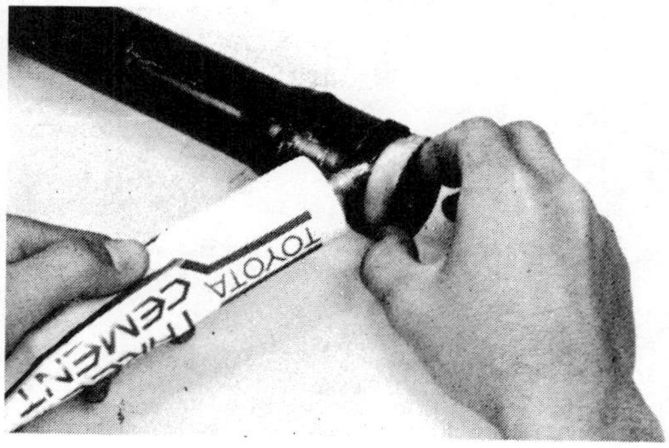

Fig. 11.52 Smear seal with sealant when fitting (Sec 14)

15 Steering gear (recirculating ball type) – removal, overhaul and refitting

1 Working within the engine compartment, mark the alignment of the flexible coupling yoke to the pinion shaft of the steering gear and then unscrew the coupling pinch bolt and remove it. It is best to have the front roadwheels in the straight ahead position before carrying out this work (photo).

14.3a Steering column to bulkhead hole cover (inside)

14.3b Upper steering column mounting bolts

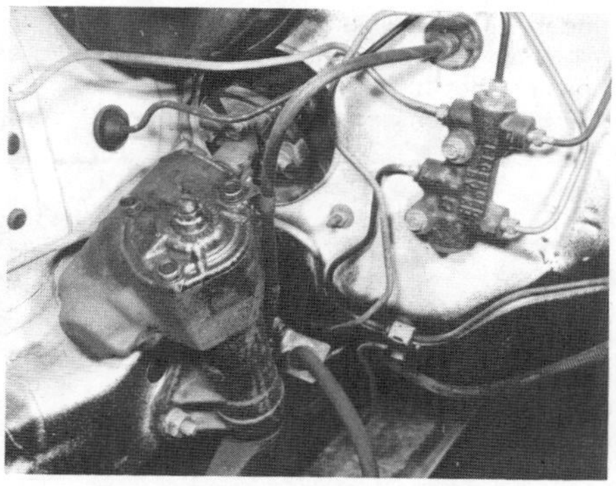

15.1 General view showing the recirculating ball steering box assembly location in engine compartment. The flexible coupling and mounting bolts can also be seen

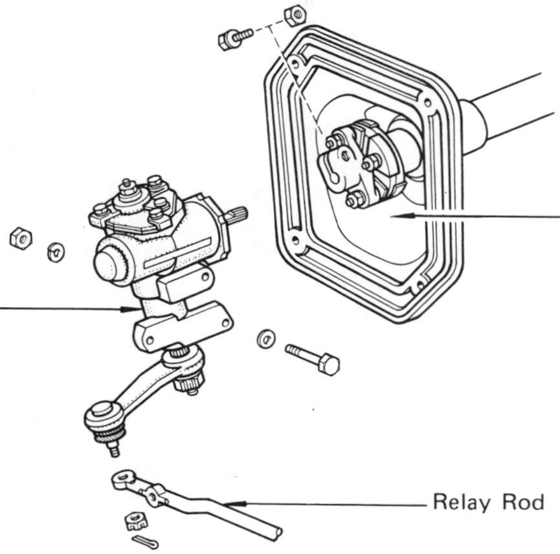

Fig. 11.53 Recirculating ball steering box and associated components (Sec 15)

2 Disconnect the steering relay rod balljoint from the steering Pitman arm using a suitable extractor or forked wedges (photo).
3 Unbolt the steering gear from the bodyframe and remove it downwards from the vehicle.
4 Using a substantial puller, draw off the steering Pitman arm, having first removed the retaining nut and made relative alignment marks across the shaft and arm.
5 Drain the oil from the gear housing.
6 Release and remove the sector shaft adjuster screw locknut, remove the sector shaft end cover bolts and remove the cover by winding the adjuster screw out of it with a screwdriver.
7 Withdraw the sector shaft.
8 Release the worm bearing adjuster locknut and then using a pin wrench, unscrew and remove the bearing adjuster from the gear housing.
9 Withdraw the worm assembly complete with the bearing races.
10 Do not dismantle the ball shaft but if defective, renew the complete worm/nut assembly.
11 On some models, needle roller type bearings are used for the sector shaft. In this case, any wear must be rectified by renewal of the bearings, gear case and sector shaft as a matched assembly.
12 On vehicles with bushes in which the sector shaft runs, have your dealer renew them if they are worn as they will require reaming after fitting and a new matching sector shaft to go with them.
13 Check the gap between the end face of the sector shaft adjuster screw and the recess in the shaft. This should not exceed 0.0020 in (0.05 mm). Adjustment can be made if necessary by fitting a thrust washer from the six different thicknesses available and locating it under the head of the adjuster screw.
14 New worm bearing outer tracks should be **pressed** into the gear housing, not drifted into position.
15 Before reassembly, check that all components are clean and during reassembly lubricate the respective bearings and seals with grease.
16 Commence reassembly by fitting the wormshaft into the housing then locate the adjuster screw and locknut. Tighten the adjuster screw down to seat the bearings, loosen off and then retighten the screw so that it is a 'snug' fit.

15.2 Underside view of recirculating ball steering box showing Pitman arm attachments (arrowed)

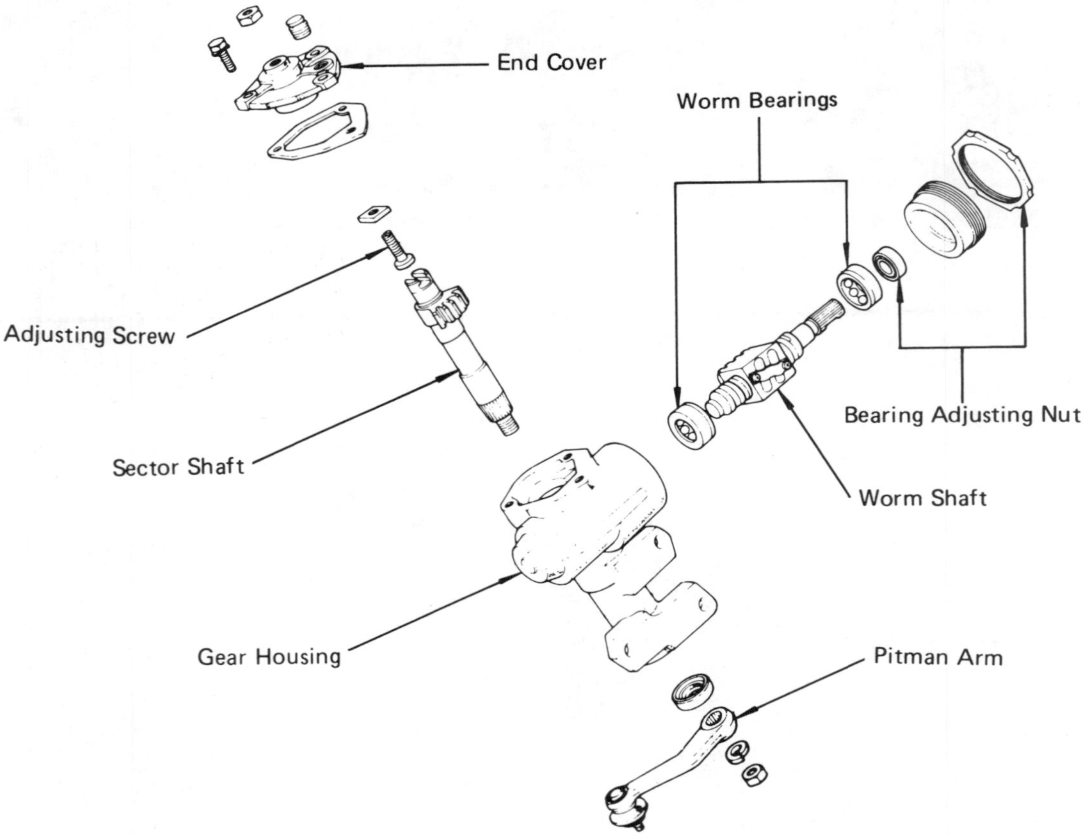

Fig. 11.54 Recirculating ball steering box components (Sec 15)

17 Wind a cord round the splines of the pinion shaft and attach it to a spring balance. The pinion shaft should start to turn when the spring balance records a pull in accordance with the following preload (starting):

1.7 to 3.5 lbf in (2 to 4 kgf cm)

Check the preload in both directions.
18 Adjust by means of the bearing adjuster and then tighten the locknut and recheck the preload.
19 Move the ball nut to the centre position on the worm and insert the sector shaft so that its centre tooth meshes with the centre groove of the ball nut.
20 Fit the sector shaft adjuster screw, thrust washer and end cover. Locate and hand tighten the end cover bolts and fully slacken the adjuster screw. Now tighten the three cover bolts to the specified torque wrench setting.
21 Set the wormshaft in the neutral position by halving the total shaft rotations then make an alignment mark between the shaft and housing.
22 Again wind a cord round the splined end of the pinion shaft and adjust the starting torque (preload) using the spring balance method and the sector shaft at its centre position. Turn the adjuster screw until the pinion shaft starts to turn when the reading on the spring balance is in accordance with the following:

Worm bearing preload plus 2.6 to 3.5 lbf in (3 to 4 kgf cm)

On achieving the correct preload setting, tighten the locknut to the specified torque whilst holding the adjuster screw in position with a screwdriver to prevent it turning from the set position. Recheck the preload setting on completion.
23 Refit the Pitman arm aligning the arm and shaft marks to ensure correct positioning.

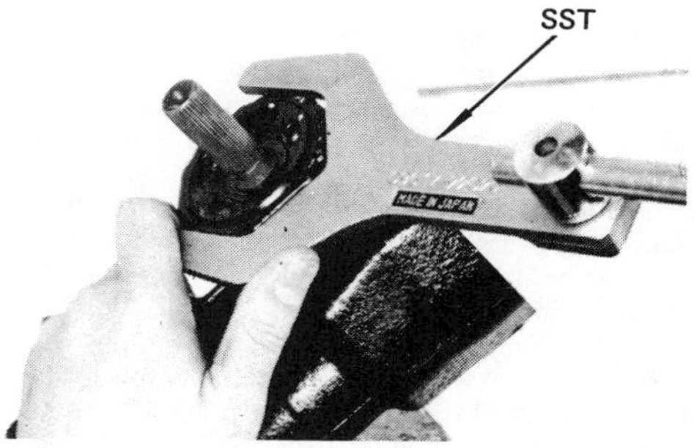

Fig. 11.55 Removing worm adjuster locknut (Sec 15)

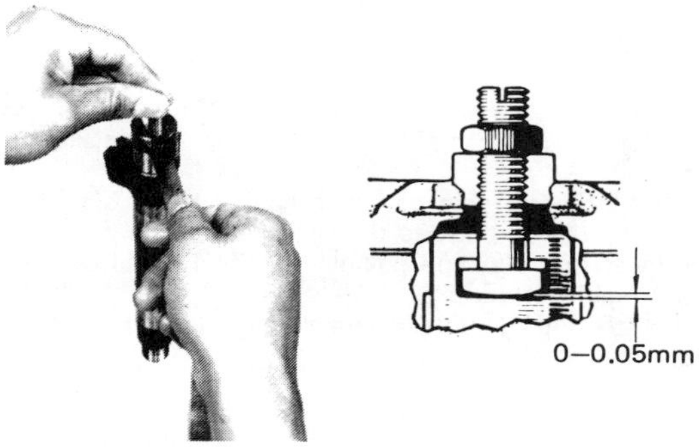

Fig. 11.56 Check the sector shaft thrust clearance with feeler gauges clearance limit as shown (Sec 15)

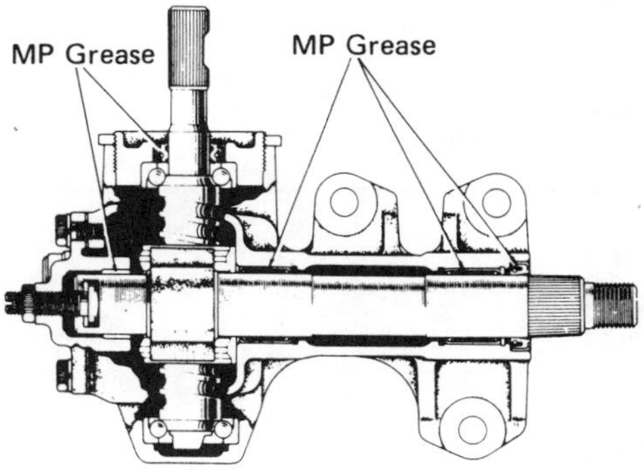

Fig. 11.57 Lubricate points indicated when reassembling (Sec 15)

Fig. 11.58 Ball nut and sector shaft to be centrally meshed (Sec 15)

Fig. 11.59 Make alignment marks between wormshaft and housing (Sec 15)

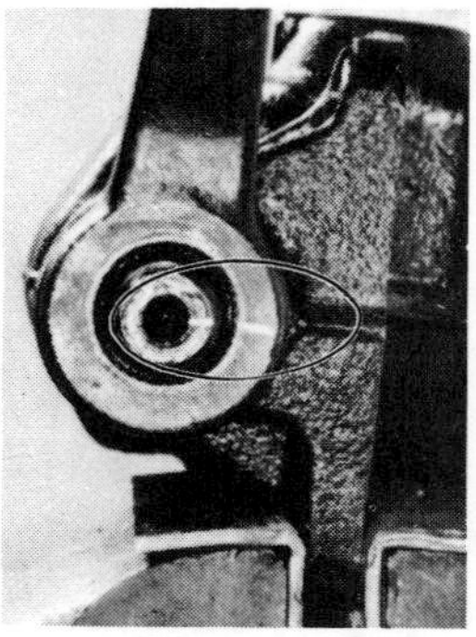

Fig. 11.60 Align Pitman arm and shaft marks (Sec 15)

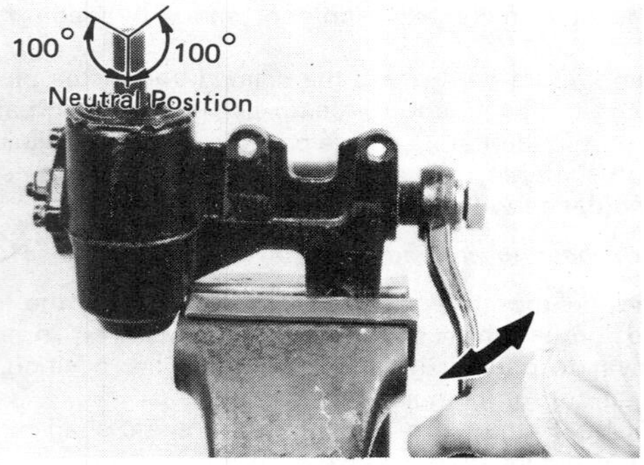

Fig. 11.61 Check sector shaft for backlash (Sec 15)

24 Check the sector shaft for backlash within its arc of travel 100° from the neutral position. There should be no backlash in either direction.
25 Refit the steering gear to the vehicle by reversing the removal operations, tighten all bolts to the specified torque.
26 Reconnect the relay rod balljoint to the Pitman arm and fit and tighten the taper pin nut.
27 Fill the steering box to the level of the filler plug with the correct specified grade of oil.

16 Power steering gear housing – removal, overhaul and refitting

1 Unscrew the coupling bolt nut and withdraw the bolt from the coupling.
2 Disconnect the pressure and return hydraulic line hoses from the steering box. Allow for fluid spillage and on detachment, plug the hoses to prevent the ingress of dirt.
3 Disconnect the steering relay rod balljoint from the Pitman arm. Use a suitable extractor, puller or fork wedges to separate the arm from the joint.
4 Unscrew and remove the four steering gear housing securing bolts and then withdraw the steering housing unit.
5 Drain the oil from the gear housing and wipe clean its exterior prior to dismantling.
6 Make an alignment mark on the Pitman arm and the shaft, then unscrew the securing nut and withdraw the arm from the shaft using a suitable puller.
7 Remove the four end cover bolts and also the adjuster screw locknut and washer. Turn the cross-shaft adjuster screw clockwise and remove the cover.
8 The cross (sector) shaft can now be driven out of the housing in the direction shown.
9 Unscrew and remove the four worm gear valve body retaining screws, then jam your thumb against the power piston nut (through the cam-shaft and cover aperture) and rotate the worm shaft anti clockwise. Carefully withdraw the valve body and the power piston unit ensuring that the power piston nut does not become disengaged from the wormshaft.
10 With the various components dismantled, clean them for inspection.
11 Examine the gear housing for signs of damage.
12 Check the power piston ball clearance by mounting the body in a vice (with soft jaws) as shown and, using a dial indicator, measure the ball clearance by moving the worm gear up and down. The clearance should not exceed 0.0059 in (0.15 mm). Excessive clearance will necessitate renewal of the power control valve unit.
13 Examine the gears and the end cover and bearings for signs of excessive wear or damage and renew as necessary. The O-ring seal should be renewed anyway.
14 Measure the cross-shaft adjuster screw endplay by supporting the shaft in a soft jaw vice and using a dial indicator as shown check that the endfloat is within the specified limits of 0.0012 to 0.0020 in (0.03 to 0.05 mm). If adjustment is necessary, relieve the locknut stake with a chisel and loosen off the locknut. The screw can now be adjusted to provide the specified endplay. Retighten and stake-lock the locknut.
15 If the needle roller bearings are to be renewed, extract the oilseal and then remove the snap-ring, metal spacer, teflon seal and the O-ring. The bearings can then be driven out using a suitable drift, but take care not to damage the housing.
16 Refit the upper bearing in reverse, but ensure that it is fitted with the long edge on the outer race outwards. Align the bearing top end with the housing end face.

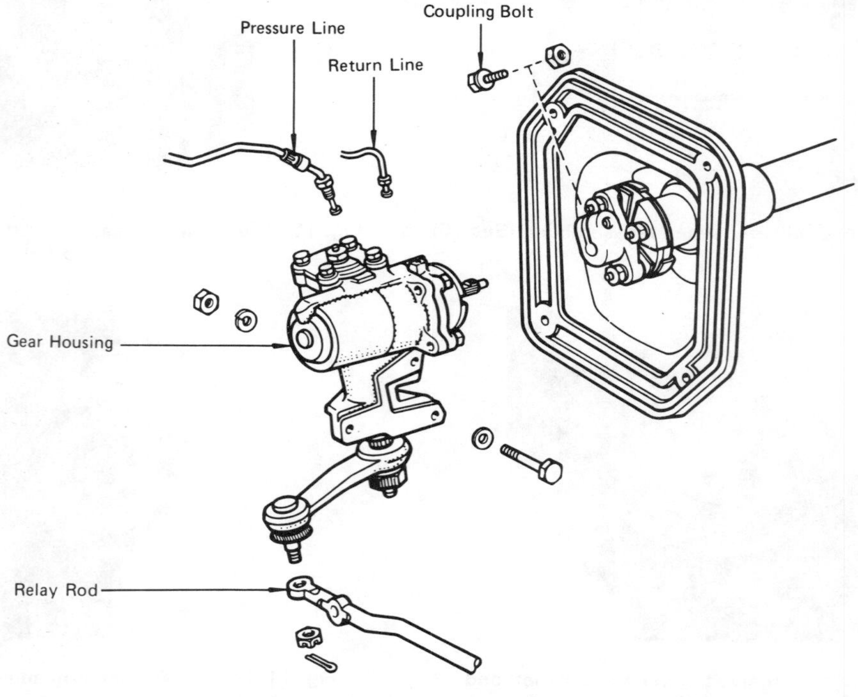

Fig. 11.62 Power steering gearbox and associated components (Sec 16)

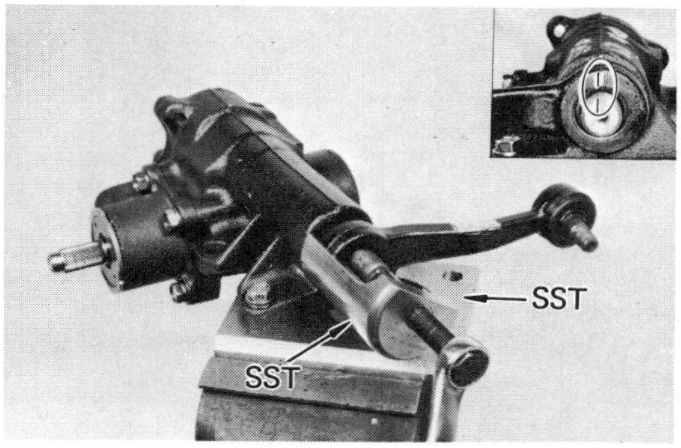

Fig. 11.63 Withdraw Pitman arm using suitable puller having made alignment marks across arm and shaft (inset) (Sec 16)

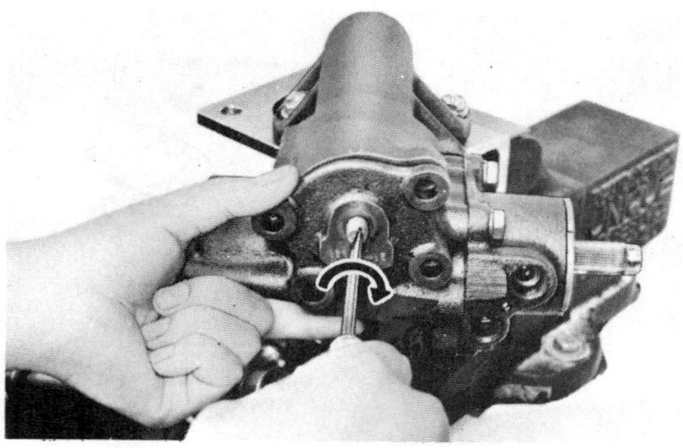

Fig. 11.64 Turn adjuster screw clockwise to remove cover (Sec 16)

Fig. 11.65 Remove cross-shaft in direction indicated (Sec 16)

Fig. 11.66 Valve body removal with thumb holding power piston (Sec 16)

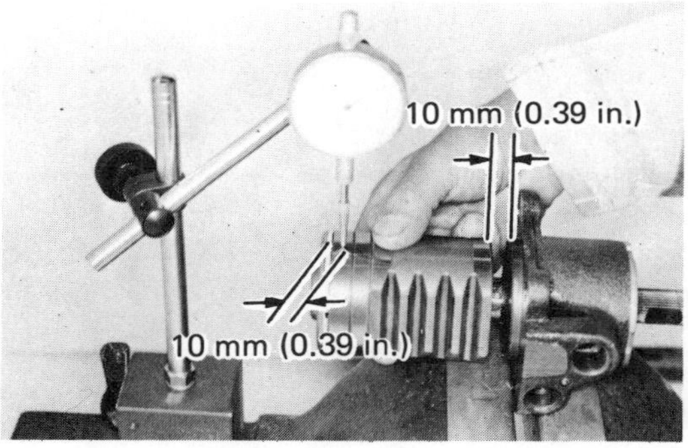

Fig. 11.67 Power piston ball clearance check (Sec 16)

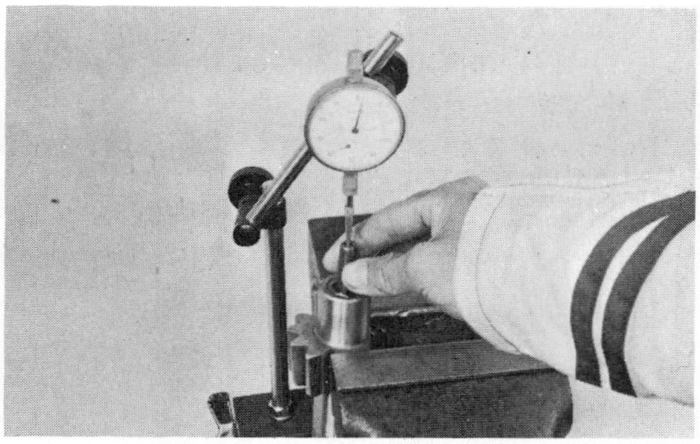

Fig. 11.68 Checking cross-shaft adjuster screw end play (Sec 16)

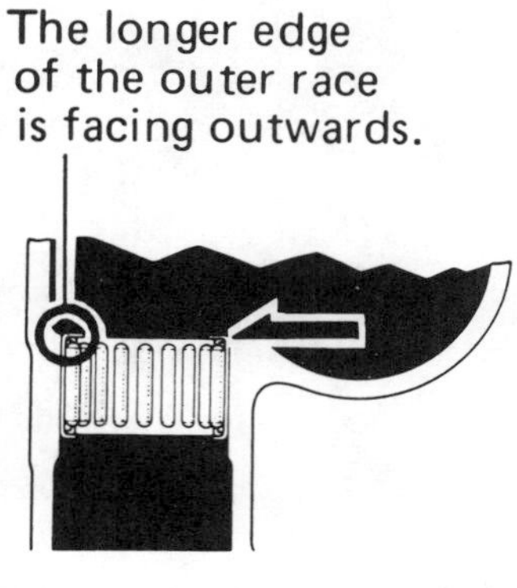

The longer edge of the outer race is facing outwards.

Fig. 11.69 Upper roller bearing orientation (Sec 16)

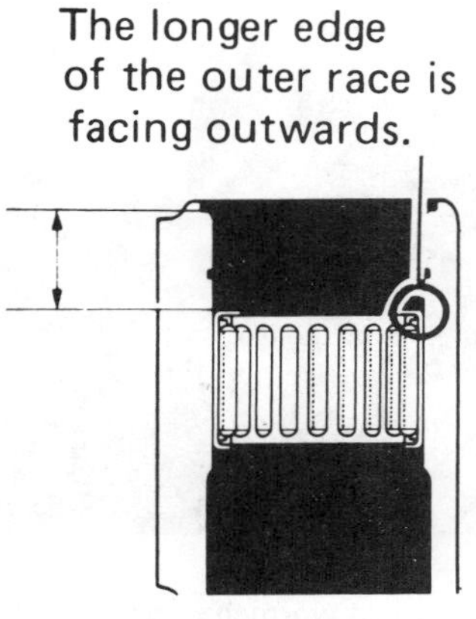

The longer edge of the outer race is facing outwards.

Fig. 11.70 Lower roller bearing orientation (Sec 16)

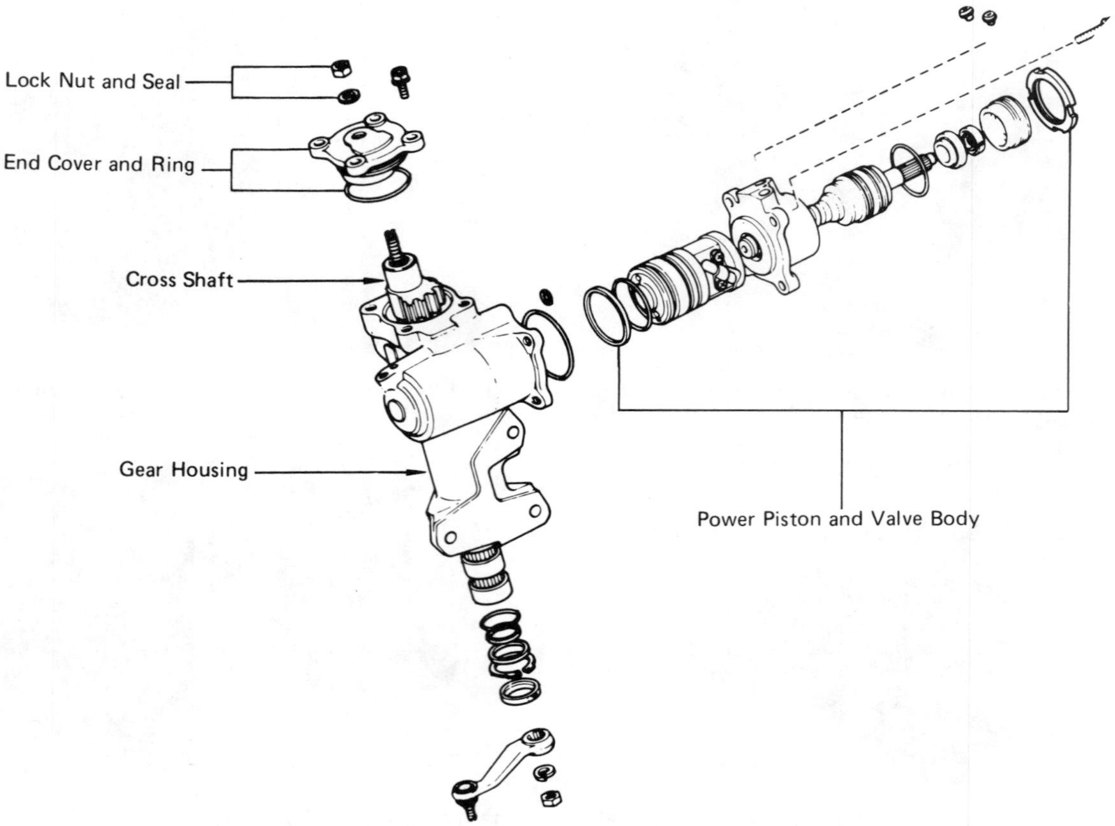

Fig. 11.71 Power steering gearbox components (Sec 16)

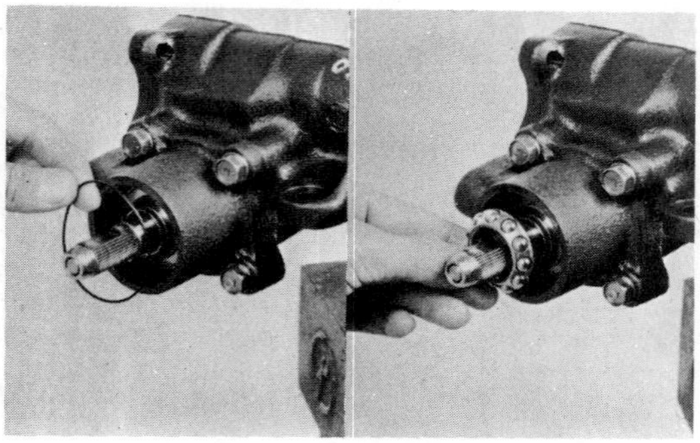

Fig. 11.72 Locate new O-ring and fit bearing (Sec 16)

Fig. 11.73 Check/adjust wormshaft preload setting (Sec 16)

Fig. 11.74 Stake locknut to secure (Sec 16)

17 Refit the lower bearing so that it is located 0.764 in (19.4 mm) from the housing inner end face.
18 Reassemble the O-ring, teflon ring and spacer and secure by inserting a new snap-ring.
19 Reassemble the gear housing by inserting two new O-rings and then fit the valve body into the housing. Retighten the cap screws in a progressive and diagonal sequence to their specified torque wrench setting.
20 If the old worm shaft bearing is being refitted, use a C-spanner or similar suitable tool and unscrew the worm bearing locknut. Then extract the bearing and the O-ring.
21 If damaged or worn, the bearing must be renewed.
22 Prise free the old oil seal from the cap and drive a new one into position. Locate a new O-ring and then insert the bearing and cap.
23 Tighten the bearing cap to provide the correct worm bearing preload. To check this wind a cord round the splines of the wormshaft and attach the cord to a spring balance. The shaft should start to turn when the correct preloading is applied and this is between 3.5 to 5.6 lbf in (4.0 to 6.5 kgf cm). Prevent the power piston nut from turning during this check.
24 With the correct preload adjustment made retighten the lock nut whilst preventing the bearing nut from turning. Recheck the preload on completion.
25 Insert the cross-shaft and fit the end cover with a new O-ring. The adjuster screw should be fully loosened off when fitting the cover and the worm gear centrally adjusted in the housing. Push the cover and cross-shaft into the housing so that the central teeth engage. Then fit the cap screws and tighten in a diagonal manner to the specified torque setting.
26 Now rotate the wormshaft onto full lock in each direction and note the central position. Centre the wormshaft and then rotate the adjuster screw to provide the wormshaft preload setting of 5.2 to 8.2 lbf in (6.0 to 9.5 kgf cm). Measure the preload in a similar manner to that given in paragraph 23 whilst simultaneously turning the adjuster screw.
27 On setting the preload, fit a new washer and locknut and tighten to the specified torque setting whilst preventing the screw from turning from the set position. Check the preload setting on completion.
28 Refit the Pitman arm onto the shaft aligning the marks made on removal and tighten the nut to the specified torque.
29 Using a suitable centre punch, stake lock the worm setting locknut at three interspaced intervals as shown.
30 Refit the gear housing to the car in a reverse order of the removal procedure. Tighten the respective fastenings to their specified torque settings.
31 Top up the reservoir fluid level on completion and bleed the system as given in Section 17.

17 Power steering – fluid level check and system bleeding

1 This check must be made with the vehicle on level ground, the engine idling and at the normal operating temperature and ideally after a run so that the fluid temperature is between 104° to 176°F (40° to 80°C).
2 Turn the steering wheel from lock to lock a few times then make the level check by removing the reservoir cap to which a dipstick is attached. If the fluid level is below the specified minimum level mark on the dipstick top up the fluid level with some ATF Dexron fluid, then refit the cap, and switch off the engine.
3 To bleed the power steering system check that the fluid level is up to the mark, then jack up the car at the front and support with axle stands.
4 Turn the steering wheel through full lock in each direction a few times and then recheck the reservoir fluid level. Top up if necessary.
5 Start and run the engine at 1000 rpm or less and turn the steering wheel from lock to lock a few times then return it to its central position.
6 Check the condition of the fluid in the reservoir which should not be cloudy or foaming. The fluid should not be above the maximum level mark with the engine stopped. When the engine is stopped the fluid level may rise initially by a maximum permissible amount of 0.20 in (5 mm). Any rise above that is not permissible and a fault probably exists in the vane pump which should be repaired as necessary.

18 Power steering pump and drivebelt – removal and refitting

1 Unscrew and remove the pump drivebelt pulley nut whilst pushing the belt to increase its tension and prevent the pulley from turning.
2 Detach the coolant pipe clamp from the pump bracket.
3 Detach the hydraulic return line hose at the pump, then detach the supply hose, but have a container ready underneath it in which to catch the fluid when the line is disconnected.
4 Slacken off the idler pulley unit and adjuster bolt, release the belt tension and remove the belt.
5 Now remove the pulley and pump unit, which is secured by three mounting bolts.
6 Refit in the reverse order to removal, tightening the fastenings to the specified torque settings where applicable. Adjust the drivebelt tension to that specified. When fitting a new drivebelt recheck the tension after an initial mileage and take up any possible stretch which may have occurred.
7 Top up the fluid level in the reservoir and bleed the system as given in Section 17. Check for fluid leaks from the hose connections on completion.

19 Track-rod end balljoints – testing and renewal

1 The track-rod end balljoints should be examined for deterioration and wear at the intervals specified in Routine Maintenance.
2 Grip the track-rod near the balljoint and attempt to move it back and forth in a horizontal plane. Renew the track-rod end if any movement is evident.

Fig. 11.75 Check power steering reservoir fluid level (Sec 17)

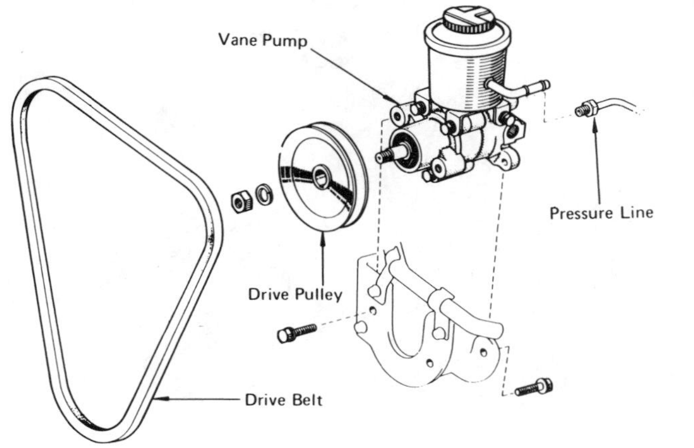

Fig. 11.76 Power steering vane pump and associated components (Sec 18)

3 Jack-up the front of the car and support it on axle stands. Remove the roadwheel.
4 Extract the split-pin and unscrew the nut but do not fully remove it at this stage. Use a balljoint separator and free the track-rod end from the steering knuckle arm, then remove the nut and separator. Separate the control arm from the knuckle arm.
5 Mark the position of the track-rod end on the rack end threads. Loosen the pinch-bolt and unscrew the track-rod end while holding the rack end or Pitman arm end stationary.
6 Refitting is a reversal of removal, but it will be necessary to check and adjust the front wheel alignment as described in Section 10.
7 When refitted check that the rod length each side is equal and the joint angles are adjusted as described in Section 10.

20 Rear shock absorber – removal, testing and refitting

1 Jack-up the rear of the car and support it with axle stands placed under the axle tube. Remove the roadwheel.
2 On leaf spring rear suspension models unscrew the upper shock

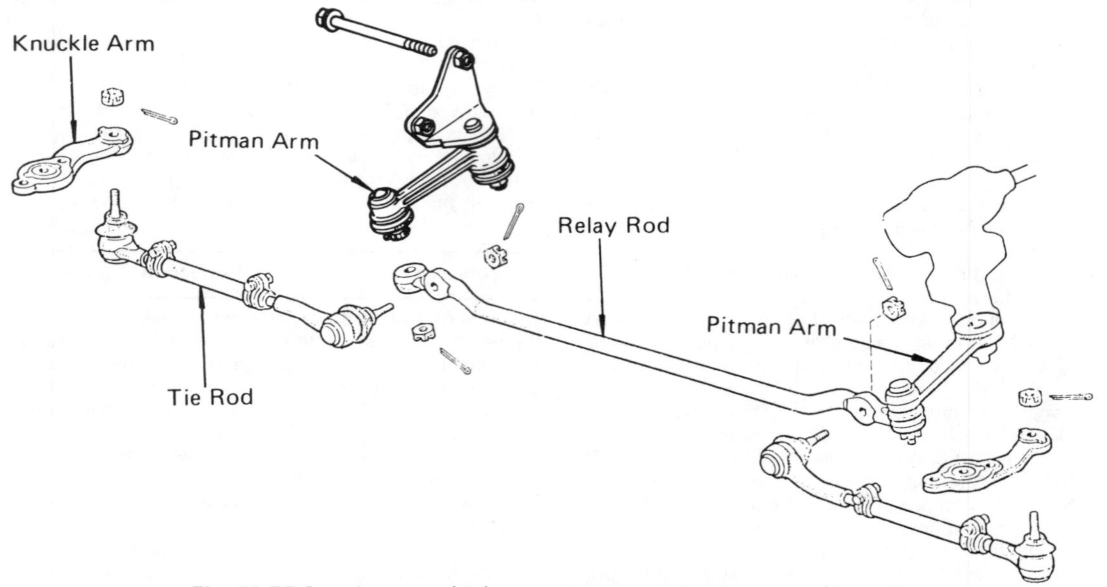

Fig. 11.77 Steering track (tie) rod and associated components (Sec 19)

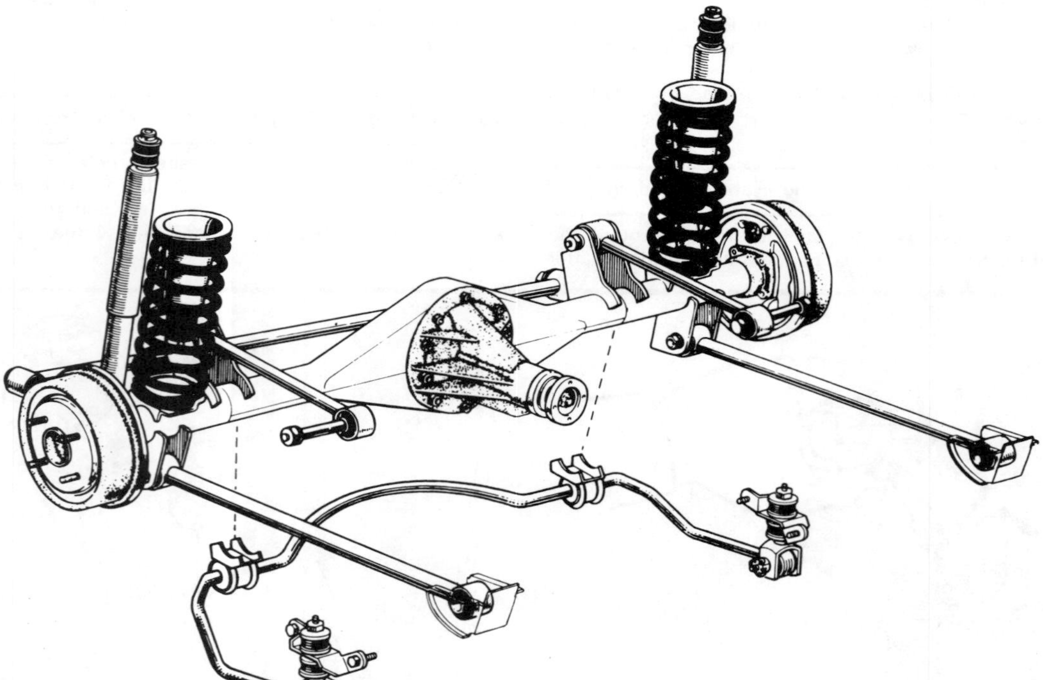

Fig. 11.78 Rear suspension assembly – four-link type (Sec 20)

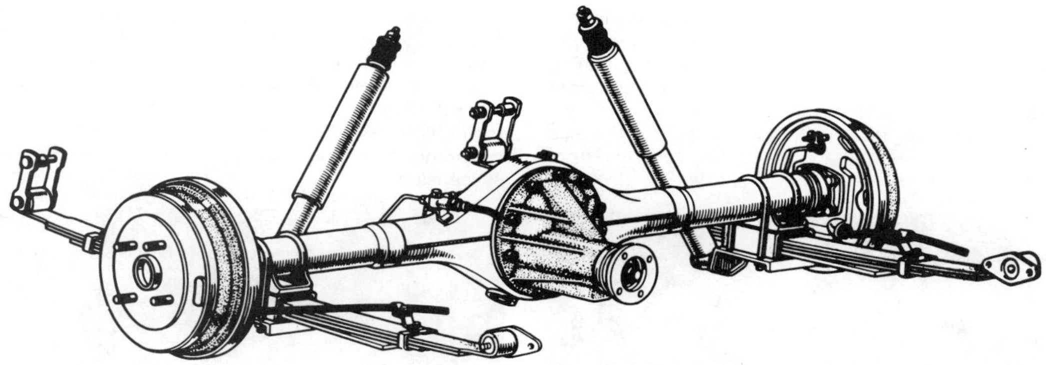

Fig. 11.79 Rear suspension assembly – leaf spring type (Sec 20)

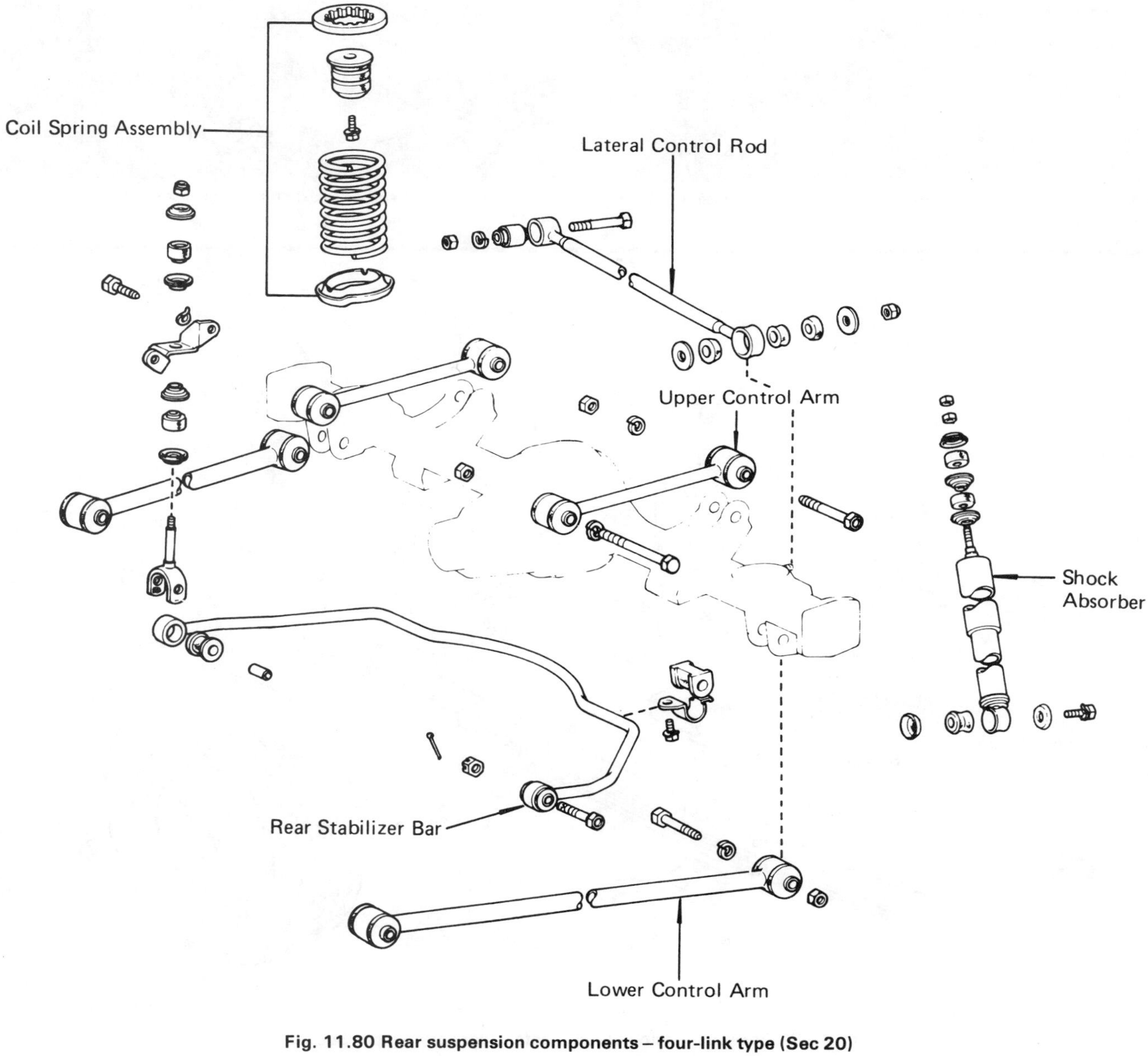

Fig. 11.80 Rear suspension components – four-link type (Sec 20)

absorber/frame mounting nuts. On the four-link suspension models, work inside the vehicle to remove any trim panel concealing the upper shock absorber mounting. Unscrew and remove the locknut, retaining nut and mounting components from the top of the shock absorber (photo). Note the order of removal to ensure correct refitting.
3 Unscrew the shock absorber lower mounting bolt from the axle tube, recover the spacers, and withdraw the shock absorber from beneath the car (photo).
4 Grip the lower shock absorber mounting in a vice with the shock absorber vertical, then fully extend and retract the unit ten or twelve times. The resistance should be smooth in both directions without any squelching noises. Renew the unit if it is proved unserviceable.
5 Refitting is a reversal of removal, but check that the upper mounting is assembled as shown in Fig. 11.80 and only tighten the mounting nuts and bolt with the full weight of the car on the suspension.

20.2 Remove trim cover for access to shock absorber upper retaining nut (four-link suspension type)

20.3 Rear shock absorber to axle tube (four-link suspension type)

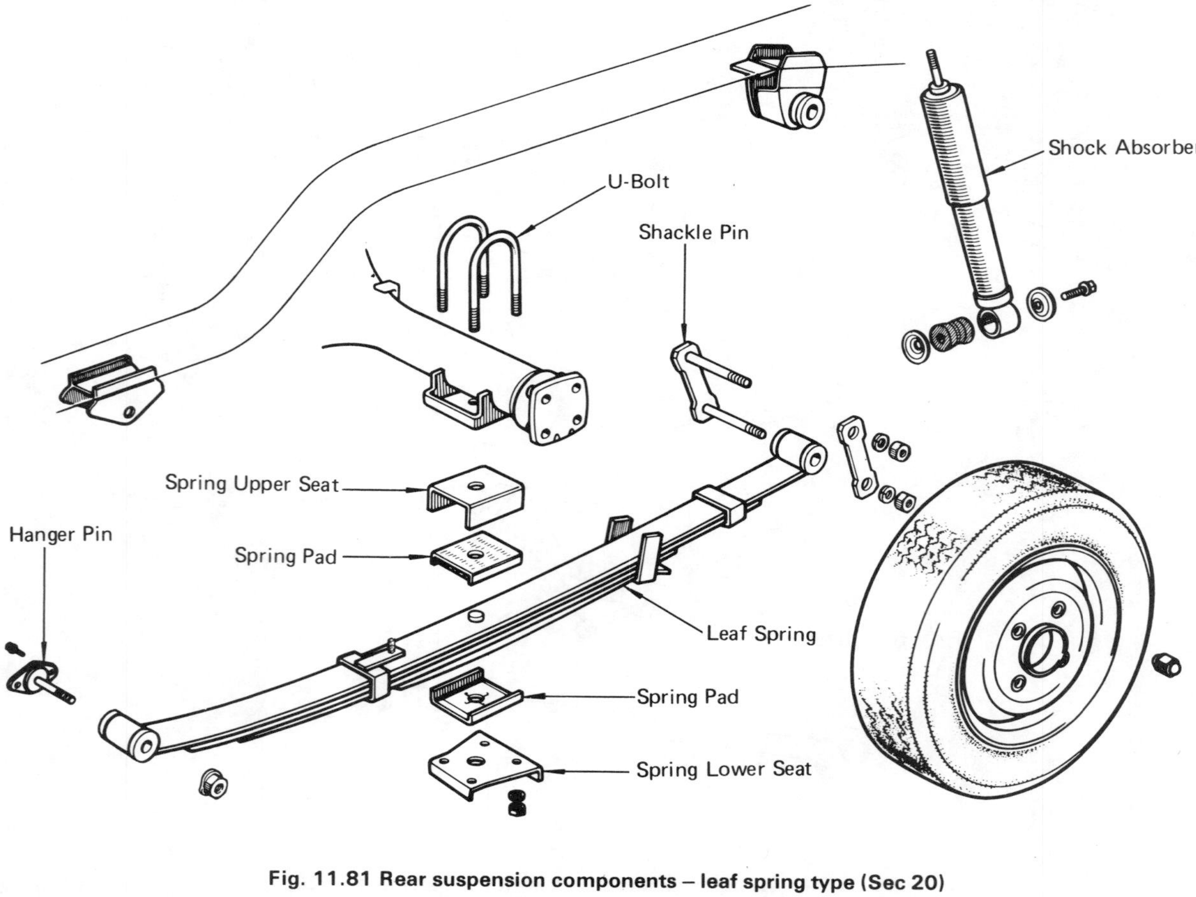

Fig. 11.81 Rear suspension components – leaf spring type (Sec 20)

21 Rear coil spring – removal and refitting

1 Jack-up the rear of the car and support it with axle stands placed beneath the underframe.
2 Support the axle tube with a trolley jack and remove the shock absorber as described in Section 20.
3 Unscrew and remove the bolt securing the shock absorber to the axle housing and detach the shock absorber.
4 Unscrew the retaining nut and detach the lateral control rod from the axle housing.
5 Lower the axle tube until the coil spring and seats can be lifted out. Remove the spring bumper where fitted. Take care when lowering the axle not to put under tension the hydraulic brake lines (and the handbrake cable).
6 Refitting is a reversal of the removal procedure. Make sure that the insulators are correctly fitted and the spring is fully engaged in its seats. Refer to the previous Section for notes on the shock absorber refitting procedure.

22 Lateral control rod (four-link type) – removal and refitting

1 Position a jack under the axle housing, raise the rear of the vehicle and then locate safety stands each side at the rear to further support the vehicle.
2 Unscrew the lateral control rod to axle housing mounting nut (photo).
3 Unscrew the lateral control rod to bodyfame bracket mounting nut. Remove the rod and bushes.
4 If the old bushes are worn or decayed they must be removed by pressing out and new bushes pressed in. If the rod is damaged it must be renewed.
5 Refit in reverse order of removal and tighten retaining nuts to the specified torque wrench setting.

22.2 Lateral control rod axle fixing

Fig. 11.82 Locate coil spring lower insulator (Sec 21)

Fig. 11.83 Fit the upper insulator onto the spring (Sec 21)

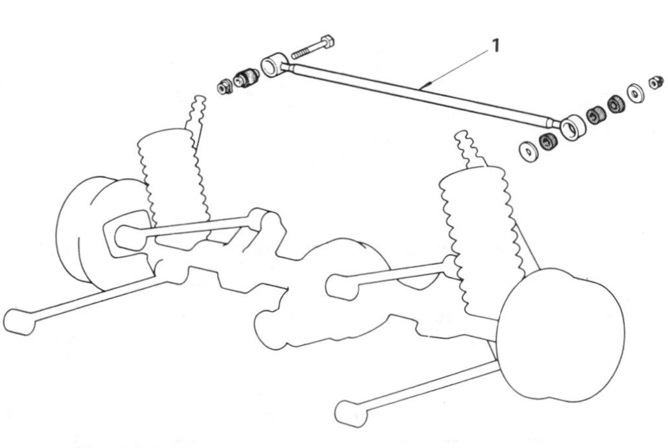

Fig. 11.84 Lateral control rod and bushes (Sec 22)

1 Lateral control rod

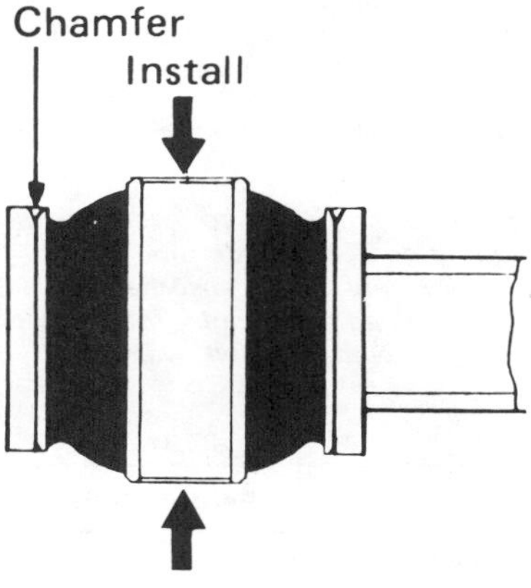

Fig. 11.85 Lateral control rod bushes orientation (Sec 22)

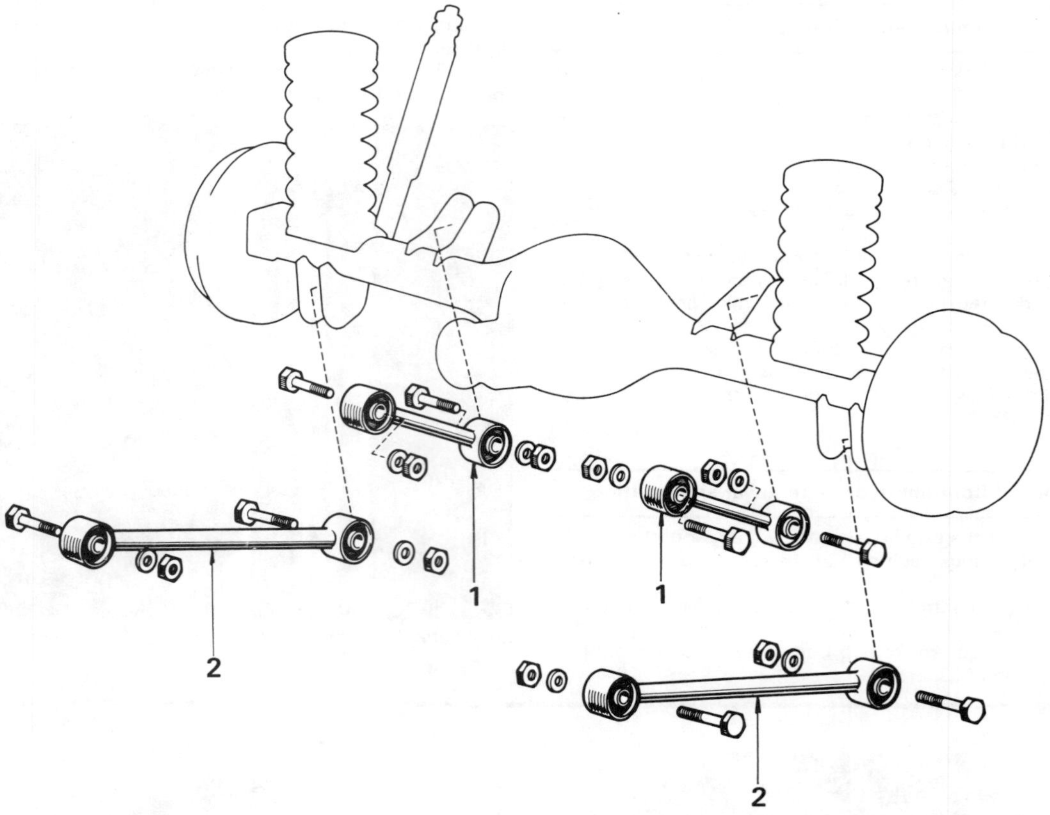

Fig. 11.86 Upper and lower control arm assemblies (Sec 23)

1 Upper control arm *2 Lower control arm*

23 Rear upper and lower control arms (four-link type) – removal and refitting

1 Jack-up the rear of the car and support it with axle stands placed beneath the axle tube. Support the front of the differential casing with a trolley jack. Remove the roadwheel.
2 Unscrew and remove the mounting bolts from the control arm. When removing the lower control arm, it will be necessary to detach the shock absorber lower mounting and handbrake cable support.
3 Remove the control arm and examine it for damage and deterioration. If the bushes in the lower control arm need renewing, they can be removed and refitted in a vice using suitable tubing. Note that a chamfer is cut on one side of the control arm to facilitate fitting. No lubricant should be used.
4 Refitting is a reversal of removal, but the following additional points should be noted:

(a) *The lower control arm must be located with the handbrake cable mounting nearer the axle tube*
(b) *The control arm and shock absorber mounting bolts must initially be assembled finger tight, then fully tightened to the specified torque with the full weight of the car on the suspension*

24 Rear stabilizer bar (four-link type) – removal and refitting

1 Position the car over an inspection pit, onto ramps at the rear or jack up and support with safety stands.
2 Unbolt and detach the two stabilizer bar location brackets.
3 Unbolt and detach the stabilizer bar at each end mounting and withdraw it from under the car.
4 Renew any worn or defective bushes or associated components.
5 Refit in the reverse order to removal. When reassembling the bracket to the underbody refer to Figure 11.87 for correct fitting. Tighten all fastenings to their specified torque wrench settings.

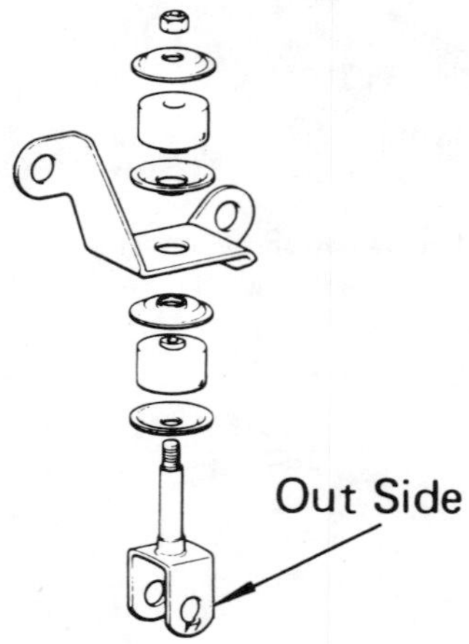

Fig. 11.87 Rear stabilizer bracket to body orientation (Sec 24)

25 Leaf spring – removal and refitting

1 Jack up the rear of the vehicle by positioning the jack under the differential housing. Support the bodyframe with safety stands and remove the rear roadwheels.
2 Detach the handbrake cable from the location clamp on the spring.

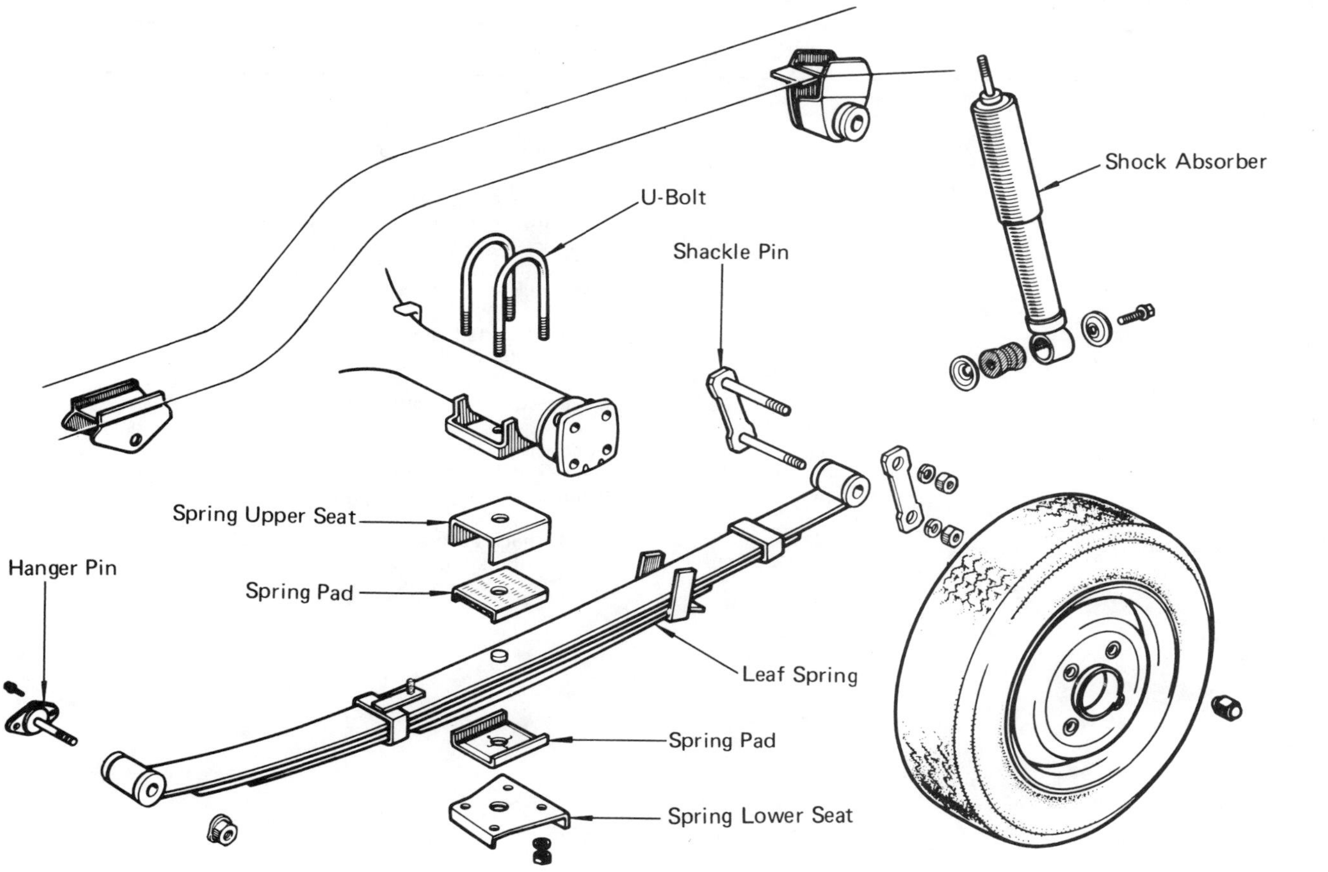

Fig. 11.88 Rear leaf spring and associated components (Sec 25)

3 Lower the jack so that the spring tension is free.
4 Unbolt and detach the shock absorber from the spring seat.
5 Unscrew and remove the spring U-bolt to axle mounting nuts. Remove the spring seat and U-bolts.
6 Unscrew and remove the hanger pin nut at the front of the spring and the shackle pin nuts at the rear end of the spring. Withdraw the hanger pin and shackle pin assembly and remove the spring.
7 Note that whilst the roadsprings are removed, the axle must be retained in its supported position to avoid stretching the brake hoses, and the handbrake cable.
8 The springs should be cleaned off using a wire brush and examined for any signs of fractures or distortion. If damage is evident the spring assembly must be renewed as a unit or dismantled and overhauled/reset by a competent spring specialist.
9 Renew the spring bushes if they are worn or damaged.
10 Refitting is a reversal of the removal procedure. Do not fully tighten the hanger pin nut(s) or shackle pin nuts until the vehicle is free standing. Bounce the rear end of the vehicle up and down a few times to seat the spring bushes and then tighten the pin nuts to their specified torque wrench settings.

26 Wheels and tyres

1 The roadwheels are of either pressed steel type or aluminium.
2 Periodically remove the wheels, clean dirt and mud from the inside and outside surfaces and examine for signs of rusting/corrosion or rim damage and rectify as necessary.
3 Apply a smear of light grease to the wheel studs before screwing on the nuts and finally tighten them to specified torque.
4 The tyres fitted may be of crossply, bias belt or radial construction. Never mix tyres of different construction. The tyres must be checked regularly for signs of excessive or uneven wear and their pressures maintained according to type as given in the Specifications. A damaged tyre must be renewed or if possible repaired by a competent tyre specialist. Where the depth of the tyre tread has worn to 1 mm or less the tyre must be renewed. Many tyres have tread wear indicators at various points around the circumference.

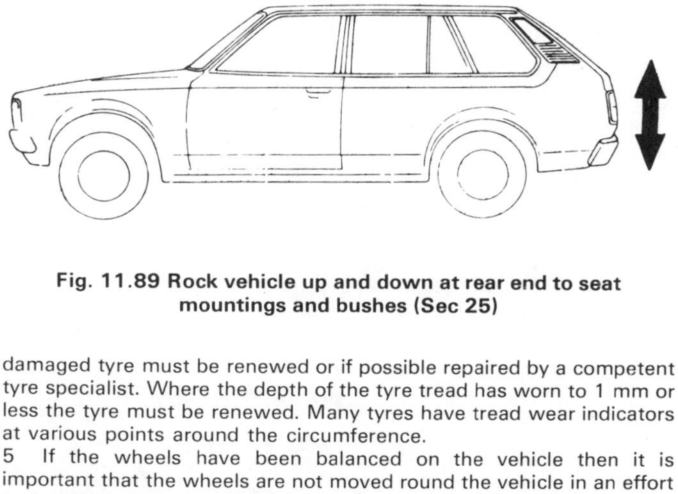

Fig. 11.89 Rock vehicle up and down at rear end to seat mountings and bushes (Sec 25)

5 If the wheels have been balanced on the vehicle then it is important that the wheels are not moved round the vehicle in an effort to equalize tread wear. If a wheel is removed, then the relationship of the wheel studs to the holes in the wheel should be marked to ensure exact replacement, otherwise the balance of wheel, hub and tyre will be upset.
6 Where the wheels have been balanced off the vehicle, then they may be moved round to equalize wear. Include the spare wheel in any rotational pattern. If radial tyres are fitted, do not move the wheels from side to side but only interchange the front and rear wheels on the same side.
7 Balancing the wheels is an essential factor in good steering and road holding. When the tyres have been in use for about half their useful life the wheels should be rebalanced to compensate for the lost tread rubber due to wear.

27 Fault diagnosis – suspension and steering

Symptom	Reason(s)
Lost motion at steering wheel	Worn rack and pinion or steering box Worn track-rod end balljoints Worn suspension arm balljoints
Steering wander	Worn steering gear Worn track-rod end or suspension arm balljoints Incorrect front wheel alignment Incorrectly adjusted front hub bearings Tyre pressures incorrect
Heavy or stiff steering	Dry or distorted steering rack Incorrect front wheel alignment Incorrect tyre pressures Seized suspension strut upper bearing
Wheel wobble and vibration	Roadwheels out of balance or buckled Weak shock absorbers Worn track-rod end or suspension arm balljoints
Excessive pitching or rolling	Weak shock absorbers Weak or broken coil spring

Chapter 12 Bodywork and underframe

Contents

1 General description

1 The body and underframe is of a unitary, all steel welded construction.

2 The four main body styles produced are outlined in the accompanying illustrations.

3 In the interest of economy of repair, the front wings are detachable, otherwise, the body panels are not renewable without cutting and welding.

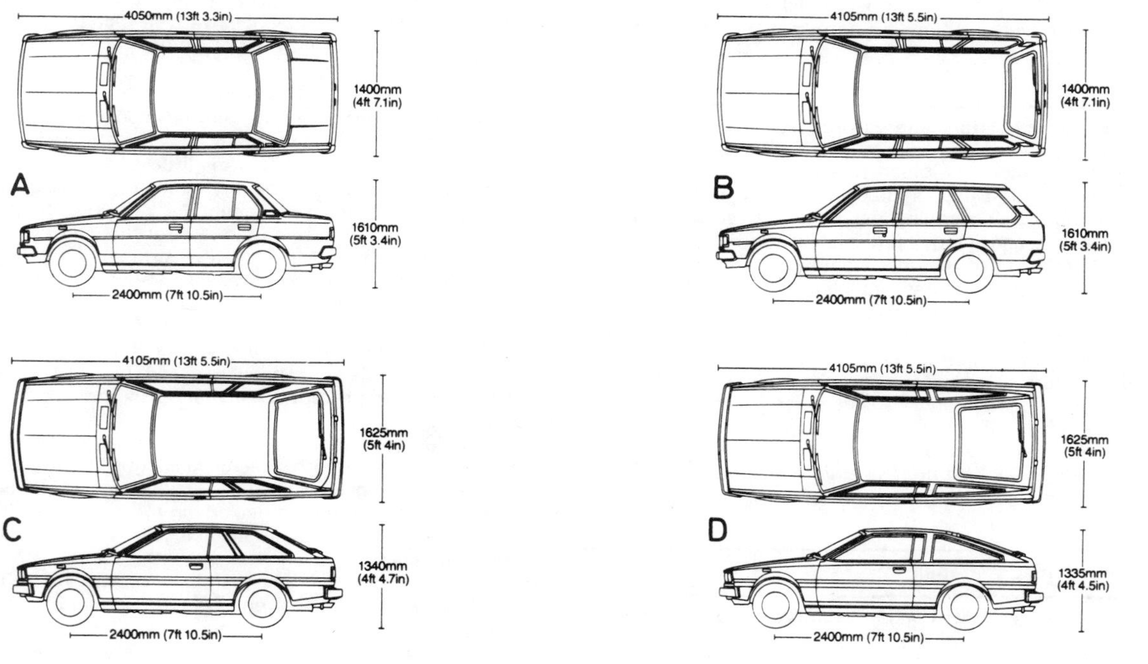

Fig. 12.1 Profiles and overall dimensions of the Corolla body types available – typical dimensions only (Sec 1)

A Saloon (Sedan) *B Estate (Wagon)* *C Liftback* *D Coupe*

2 Maintenance – bodywork and underframe

1 The general condition of a vehicle's bodywork is the one thing that significantly affects its value. Maintenance is easy but needs to be regular. Neglect, particularly after minor damage, can lead quickly to further deterioration and costly repair bills. It is important also to keep watch on those parts of the vehicle not immediately visible, for instance the underside, inside all the wheel arches and the lower part of the engine compartment.
2 The basic maintenance routine for the bodywork is washing – preferably with a lot of water, from a hose. This will remove all the loose solids which may have stuck to the vehicle. It is important to flush these off in such a way as to prevent grit from scratching the finish. The wheel arches and underframe need washing in the same way to remove any accumulated mud which will retain moisture and tend to encourage rust. Paradoxically enough, the best time to clean the underframe and wheel arches is in wet weather when the mud is thoroughly wet and soft. In very wet weather the underframe is usually cleaned of large accumulations automatically and this is a good time for inspection.
3 Periodically, it is a good idea to have the whole of the underframe of the vehicle steam cleaned, engine compartment included, so that a thorough inspection can be carried out to see what minor repairs and renovations are necessary. Steam cleaning is available at many garages and is necessary for removal of the accumulation of oily grime which sometimes is allowed to become thick in certain areas. If steam cleaning facilities are not available, there are one or two excellent grease solvents available which can be brush applied. The dirt can then be simply hosed off.
4 After washing paintwork, wipe off with a chamois leather to give an unspotted clear finish. A coat of clear protective wax polish will give added protection against chemical pollutants in the air. If the paintwork sheen has dulled or oxidised, use a cleaner/polisher combination to restore the brilliance of the shine. This requires a little effort, but such dulling is usually caused because regular washing has been neglected. Always check that the door and ventilator opening drain holes and pipes are completely clear so that water can be drained out. Bright work should be treated in the same way as paintwork. Windscreens and windows can be kept clear of the smeary film which often appears, by adding a little ammonia to the water. If they are scratched, a good rub with a proprietary metal polish will often clear them. Never use any form of wax or other body or chromium polish on glass.

3 Maintenance – upholstery and carpets

1 Mats and carpets should be brushed or vacuum cleaned regularly to keep them free of grit. If they are badly stained remove them from the vehicle for scrubbing or sponging and make quite sure they are dry before refitting. Seats and interior trim panels can be kept clean by wiping with a damp cloth. If they do become stained (which can be more apparent on light coloured upholstery) use a little liquid detergent and a soft nail brush to scour the grime out of the grain of the material. Do not forget to keep the headlining clean in the same way as the upholstery. When using liquid cleaners inside the vehicle do not over-wet the surfaces being cleaned. Excessive damp could get into the seams and padded interior causing stains, offensive odours or even rot. If the inside of the vehicle gets wet accidentally it is worthwhile taking some trouble to dry it out properly, particularly where carpets are involved. *Do not leave oil or electric heaters inside the vehicle for this purpose.*

4 Minor body damage – repair

The photographic sequences on pages 350 and 351 illustrate the operations detailed in the following sub-sections.

Repair of minor scratches in bodywork

If the scratch is very superficial, and does not penetrate to the metal of the bodywork, repair is very simple. Lightly rub the area of the scratch with a paintwork renovator, or a very fine cutting paste, to remove loose paint from the scratch and to clear the surrounding bodywork of wax polish. Rinse the area with clean water.

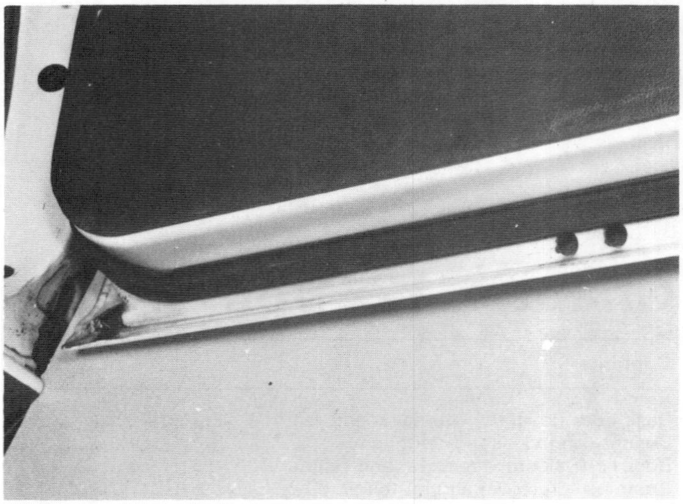

2.4 Keep drain channels in bottom edge of doors clear

Apply touch-up paint to the scratch using a fine paint brush; continue to apply fine layers of paint until the surface of the paint in the scratch is level with the surrounding paintwork. Allow the new paint at least two weeks to harden: then blend it into the surrounding paintwork by rubbing the scratch area with a paintwork renovator or a very fine cutting paste. Finally, apply wax polish.

Where the scratch has penetrated right through to the metal of the bodywork, causing the metal to rust, a different repair technique is required. Remove any loose rust from the bottom of the scratch with a penknife, then apply rust inhibiting paint to prevent the formation of rust in the future. Using a rubber or nylon applicator fill the scratch with bodystopper paste. If required, this paste can be mixed with cellulose thinners to provide a very thin paste which is ideal for filling narrow scratches. Before the stopper-paste in the scratch hardens, wrap a piece of smooth cotton rag around the top of a finger. Dip the finger in cellulose thinners and then quickly sweep it across the surface of the stopper-paste in the scratch; this will ensure that the surface of the stopper-paste is slightly hollowed. The scratch can now be painted over as described earlier in this Section.

Repair of dents in bodywork

When deep denting of the vehicle's bodywork has taken place, the first task is to pull the dent out, until the affected bodywork almost attains its original shape. There is little point in trying to restore the original shape completely, as the metal in the damaged area will have stretched on impact and cannot be reshaped fully to its original contour. It is better to bring the level of the dent up to a point which is about $\frac{1}{8}$ in (3 mm) below the level of the surrounding bodywork. In cases where the dent is very shallow anyway, it is not worth trying to pull it out at all. If the underside of the dent is accessible, it can be hammered out gently from behind, using a mallet with a wooden or plastic head. Whilst doing this, hold a suitable block of wood firmly against the outside of the panel to absorb the impact from the hammer blows and thus prevent a large area of the bodywork from being 'belled-out'.

Should the dent be in a section of the bodywork which has a double skin or some other factor making it inaccessible from behind, a different technique is called for. Drill several small holes through the metal inside the area – particularly in the deeper section. Then screw long self-tapping screws into the holes just sufficiently for them to gain a good purchase in the metal. Now the dent can be pulled out by pulling on the protruding heads of the screws with a pair of pliers.

The next stage of the repair is the removal of the paint from the damaged area, and from an inch or so of the surrounding 'sound' bodywork. This is accomplished most easily by using a wire brush or abrasive pad on a power drill, although it can be done just as effectively by hand using sheets of abrasive paper. To complete the preparation for filling, score the surface of the bare metal with a screwdriver or the tang of a file, or alternatively, drill small holes in the affected area. This will provide a really good 'key' for the filler paste.

To complete the repair see the Section on filling and re-spraying.

Repair of rust holes or gashes in bodywork

Remove all paint from the affected area and from an inch or so of the surrounding 'sound' bodywork, using an abrasive pad or a wire brush on a power drill. If these are not available a few sheets of abrasive paper will do the job just as effectively. With the paint removed you will be able to gauge the severity of the corrosion and therefore decide whether to renew the whole panel (if this is possible) or to repair the affected area. New body panels are not as expensive as most people think and it is often quicker and more satisfactory to fit a new panel than to attempt to repair large areas of corrosion.

Remove all fittings from the affected area except those which will act as a guide to the original shape of the damaged bodywork (eg headlamp shells etc). Then, using tin snips or a hacksaw blade, remove all loose metal and any other metal badly affected by corrosion. Hammer the edges of the hole inwards in order to create a slight depression for the filler paste.

Wire brush the affected area to remove the powdery rust from the surface of the remaining metal. Paint the affected area with rust inhibiting paint; if the back of the rusted area is accessible treat this also.

Before filling can take place it will be necessary to block the hole in some way. This can be achieved by the use of zinc gauze or aluminium tape.

Zinc gauze is probably the best material to use for a large hole. Cut a piece to the approximate size and shape of the hole to be filled, then position it in the hole so that its edges are below the level of the surrounding bodywork. It can be retained in position by several blobs of filler paste around its periphery.

Aluminium tape should be used for small or very narrow holes. Pull a piece off the roll and trim it to the approximate size and shape required, then pull off the backing paper (if used) and stick the tape over the hole; it can be overlapped if the thickness of one piece is insufficient. Burnish down the edges of the tape with the handle of a screwdriver or similar, to ensure that the tape is securely attached to the metal underneath.

Bodywork repairs – filling and re-spraying

Before using this Section, see the Sections on dent, deep scratch, rust holes and gash repairs.

Many types of bodyfiller are available, but generally speaking those proprietary kits which contain a tin of filler paste and a tube of resin hardener are best for this type of repair. A wide, flexible plastic or nylon applicator will be found invaluable for imparting a smooth and well contoured finish to the surface of the filler.

Mix up a little filler on a clean piece of card or board – measure the hardener carefully (follow the maker's instructions on the pack) otherwise the filler will set too rapidly or too slowly.

Using the applicator apply the filler paste to the prepared area; draw the applicator across the surface of the filler to achieve the correct contour and to level the filler surface. As soon as a contour that approximates to the correct one is achieved, stop working the paste – if you carry on too long the paste will become sticky and begin to 'pick up' on the applicator. Continue to add thin layers of filler paste at twenty-minute intervals until the level of the filler is just proud of the surrounding bodywork.

Once the filler has hardened, excess can be removed using a metal plane or file. From then on, progressively finer grades of abrasive paper should be used, starting with a 40 grade production paper and finishing with 400 grade wet-and-dry paper. Always wrap the abrasive paper around a flat rubber, cork, or wooden block – otherwise the surface of the filler will not be completely flat. During the smoothing of the filler surface the wet-and-dry paper should be periodically rinsed in water. This will ensure that a very smooth finish is imparted to the filler at the final stage.

At this stage the 'dent' should be surrounded by a ring of bare metal, which in turn should be encircled by the finely 'feathered' edge of the good paintwork. Rinse the repair area with clean water, until all of the dust produced by the rubbing-down operation has gone.

Spray the whole repair area with a light coat of primer – this will show up any imperfections in the surface of the filler. Repair these imperfections with fresh filler paste or bodystopper, and once more smooth the surface with abrasive paper. If bodystopper is used, it can be mixed with cellulose thinners to form a really thin paste which is ideal for filling small holes. Repeat this spray and repair procedure until you are satisfied that the surface of the filler, and the feathered edge of the paintwork are perfect. Clean the repair area with clean water and allow to dry fully.

The repair area is now ready for final spraying. Paint spraying must be carried out in a warm, dry, windless and dust free atmosphere. This condition can be created artificially if you have access to a large indoor working area, but if you are forced to work in the open, you will have to pick your day very carefully. If you are working indoors, dousing the floor in the work area with water will help to settle the dust which would otherwise be in the atmosphere. If the repair area is confined to one body panel, mask off the surrounding panels; this will help to minimise the effects of a slight mis-match in paint colours. Bodywork fittings (eg chrome strips, door handles etc) will also need to be masked off. Use genuine masking tape and several thicknesses of newspaper for the masking operations.

Before commencing to spray, agitate the aerosol can thoroughly, then spray a test area (an old tin, or similar) until the technique is mastered. Cover the repair area with a thick coat of primer; the thickness should be built up using several thin layers of paint rather than one thick one. Using 400 grade wet-and-dry paper, rub down the surface of the primer until it is really smooth. While doing this, the work area should be thoroughly doused with water, and the wet-and-dry paper periodically rinsed in water. Allow to dry before spraying on more paint.

Spray on the top coat, again building up the thickness by using several thin layers of paint. Start spraying in the centre of the repair area and then, using a circular motion, work outwards until the whole repair area and about 2 inches of the surrounding original paintwork is covered. Remove all masking material 10 to 15 minutes after spraying on the final coat of paint.

Allow the new paint at least two weeks to harden, then, using a paintwork renovator or a very fine cutting paste, blend the edges of the paint into the existing paintwork. Finally, apply wax polish.

5 Major body damage – repair

Where serious damage has occurred or large areas of the body need renewal due to rusting it means certainly that complete new sections or panels will need welding in and this is best left to the professionals. If the damage is due to impact it will also be necessary to completely check the alignment of the body shell structure. Due to the principle of construction the strength and shape of the whole car can be affected by damage to a relatively small area. In such instances the services of a Toyota garage with specialist jigs are essential. If a body is left misaligned it is first of all dangerous as the car will not handle properly, and secondly, uneven stresses will be imposed on the steering, engine and transmission, causing abnormal wear or complete failure. Tyre wear may also be excessive.

6 Maintenance – hinges, door catches and locks

1 Oil the hinges of the bonnet, boot and doors with a drop or two of light oil periodically. A good time is after the car has been washed.

2 Oil the bonnet safety catch thrust pin periodically.

3 Do not over-lubricate door latches and strikers. Normally one or two drops regularly applied is better than a lot at one go.

7 Doors – tracing of rattles and their rectification

1 Check first that the door is not loose at the hinges and that the latch is holding the door firmly in position. Check also that the door lines up with the aperture in the body.

2 If the hinges are loose or the door is out of alignment it will be necessary to reset the hinge position as described in Section 8.

3 If the latch is holding the door properly it should hold the door tightly when fully latched and the door should line up with the body. If it is out of alignment it needs adjustment as described in Section 9. If loose some part of the mechanism must be worn out and requiring renewal.

4 Other rattles from the door would be closed by wear or looseness in the window winder, the glass channels and sill strips or the door buttons and interior latch release mechanism. All these are dealt with in subsequent Sections.

This sequence of photographs deals with the repair of the dent and paintwork damage shown in this photo. The procedure will be similar for the repair of a hole. It should be noted that the procedures given here are simplified – more explicit instructions will be found in the text

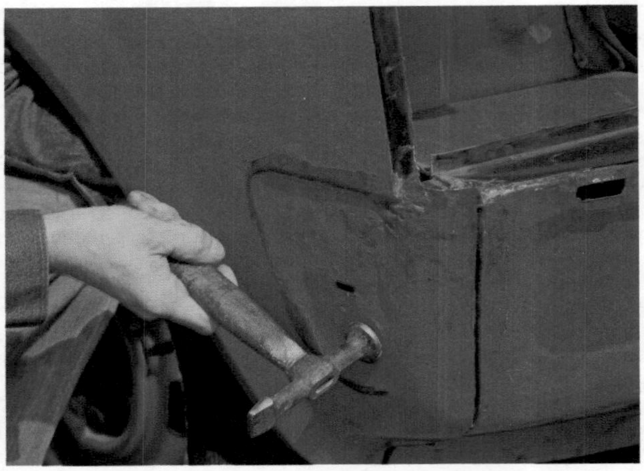

In the case of a dent the first job – after removing surrounding trim – is to hammer out the dent where access is possible. This will minimise filling. Here, the large dent having been hammered out, the damaged area is being made slightly concave

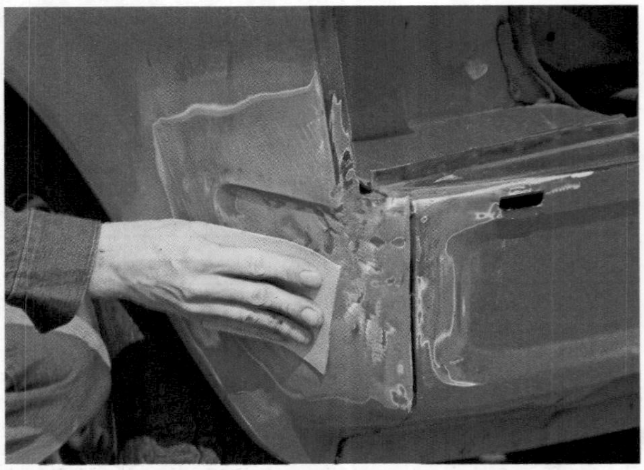

Now all paint must be removed from the damaged area, by rubbing with coarse abrasive paper. Alternatively, a wire brush or abrasive pad can be used in a power drill. Where the repair area meets good paintwork, the edge of the paintwork should be 'feathered', using a finer grade of abrasive paper

In the case of a hole caused by rusting, all damaged sheet-metal should be cut away before proceeding to this stage. Here, the damaged area is being treated with rust remover and inhibitor before being filled

Mix the body filler according to its manufacturer's instructions. In the case of corrosion damage, it will be necessary to block off any large holes before filling – this can be done with aluminium or plastic mesh, or aluminium tape. Make sure the area is absolutely clean before ...

... applying the filler. Filler should be applied with a flexible applicator, as shown, for best results; the wooden spatula being used for confined areas. Apply thin layers of filler at 20-minute intervals, until the surface of the filler is slightly proud of the surrounding bodywork

Initial shaping can be done with a Surform plane or Dreadnought file. Then, using progressively finer grades of wet-and-dry paper, wrapped around a sanding block, and copious amounts of clean water, rub down the filler until really smooth and flat. Again, feather the edges of adjoining paintwork

The whole repair area can now be sprayed or brush-painted with primer. If spraying, ensure adjoining areas are protected from over-spray. Note that at least one inch of the surrounding sound paintwork should be coated with primer. Primer has a 'thick' consistency, so will find small imperfections

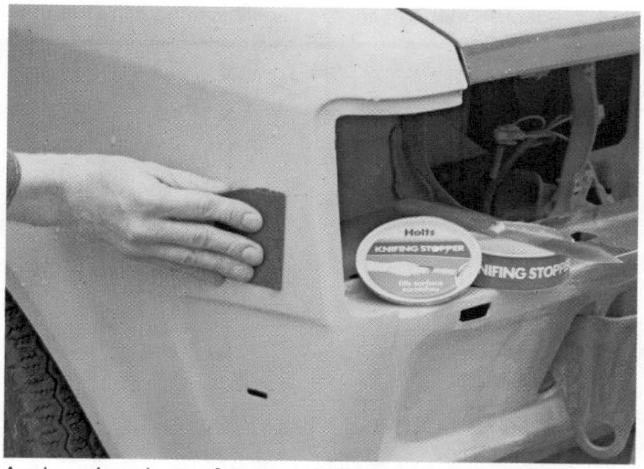

Again, using plenty of water, rub down the primer with a fine grade wet-and-dry paper (400 grade is probably best) until it is really smooth and well blended into the surrounding paintwork. Any remaining imperfections can now be filled by carefully applied knifing stopper paste

When the stopper has hardened, rub down the repair area again before applying the final coat of primer. Before rubbing down this last coat of primer, ensure the repair area is blemish-free – use more stopper if necessary. To ensure that the surface of the primer is really smooth use some finishing compound

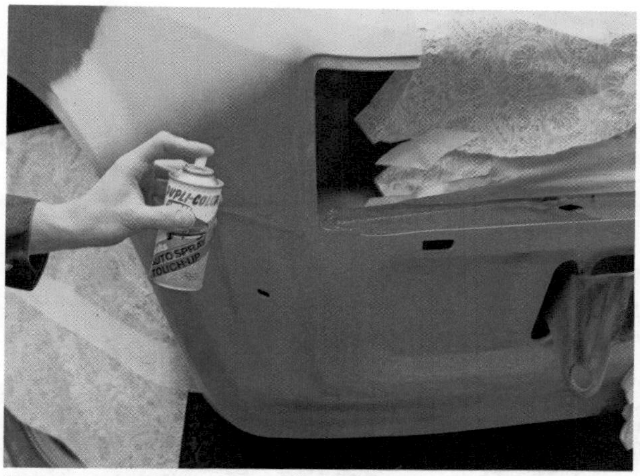

The top coat can now be applied. When working out of doors, pick a dry, warm and wind-free day. Ensure surrounding areas are protected from over-spray. Agitate the aerosol thoroughly, then spray the centre of the repair area, working outwards with a circular motion. Apply the paint as several thin coats

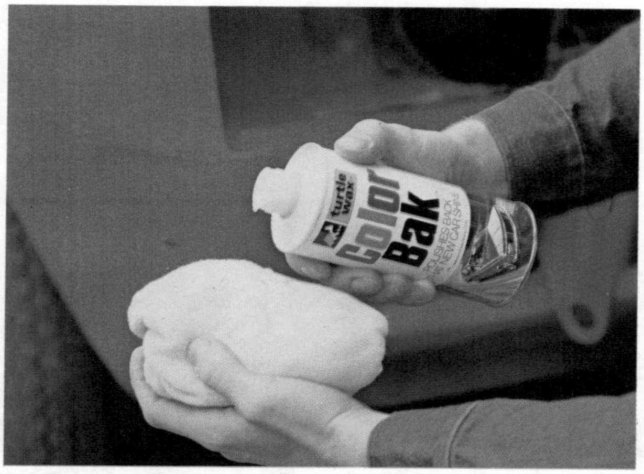

After a period of about two weeks, which the paint needs to harden fully, the surface of the repaired area can be 'cut' with a mild cutting compound prior to wax polishing. When carrying out bodywork repairs, remember that the quality of the finished job is proportional to the time and effort expended

8 Door alignment – hinge adjustment

1 The hinges are adjustable both on the door and pillar mountings. Access to some of the bolts will require removal of trim and the use of a spanner.
2 When re-aligning is necessary first slacken the bolts holding the hinge to the door and reposition the door as required and make sure the bolts are thoroughly tightened up again. If the amount of movement on the door half of the hinge is insufficient it may be adjusted at the door pillar.
3 If the hinges themselves are worn at the hinge pin the door should be detached from the hinges, the hinges removed and new ones fitted.

9 Door latch striker – alignment

1 Assuming that the door hinges are correctly aligned but the trailing edge of the door is not flush with the body when the door is fully latched, then the striker plate needs adjusting.
2 Slacken the two crosshead screws holding the striker plate to the door pillar just enough to hold the striker plate in position and then push the plate to the inner limit of its position. Try and shut the door, moving the striker plate outwards until the latch is able to engage fully (photo).
3 Without pulling on the release handle but working inside the car push the door outwards until it is flush with the bodywork. This will move the striker plate along with the latch.
4 Release the latch very carefully so as not to disturb the striker plate and open the door. Tighten down the striker plate securing screws.

10 Door lock components – removal and refitting

1 The operations are similar on all models but reference should be made to the appropriate illustrations for exact details of individual components.
2 Unscrew the armrest securing screws and remove the armrest. On some models the screws are covered by a clip-on cover which can be carefully prised free (photos).
3 To remove the window regulator handle insert a clean piece of rag as shown between the handle and panel, then spring free the retaining clip. The clip will literally spring free so be prepared to catch it if removed with the door open. Withdraw the regulator handle and nylon protector washer (photo).
4 Unscrew and remove the door inside handle/lock bezel retaining screw and remove the bezel (photos).
5 Insert the fingers or a blade between the edge of the trim panel and the door frame and jerk the panel securing clips from their holes.

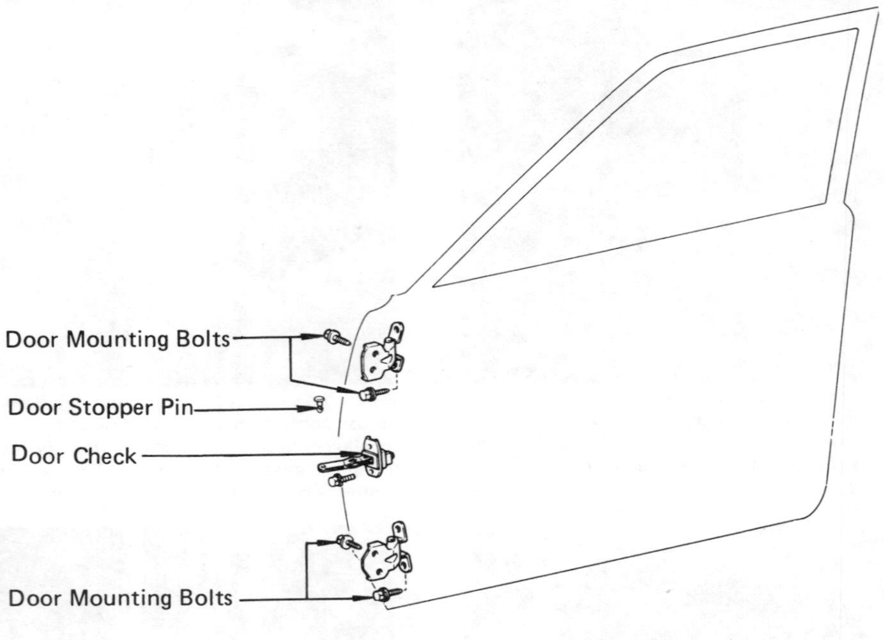

Fig. 12.2 Front door hinge and check strap assemblies (Sec 8)

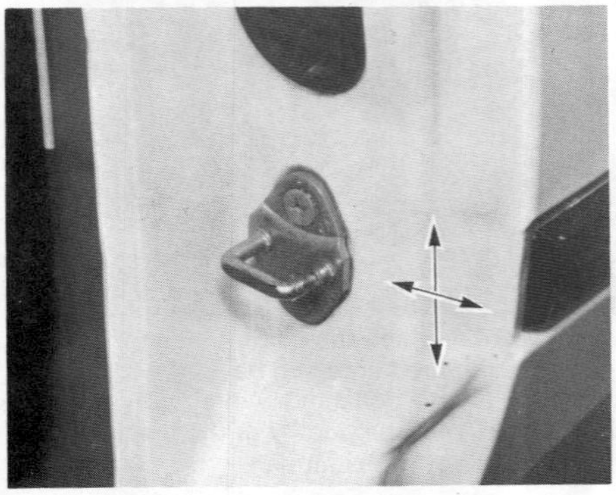

9.2 Door striker alignment adjustment

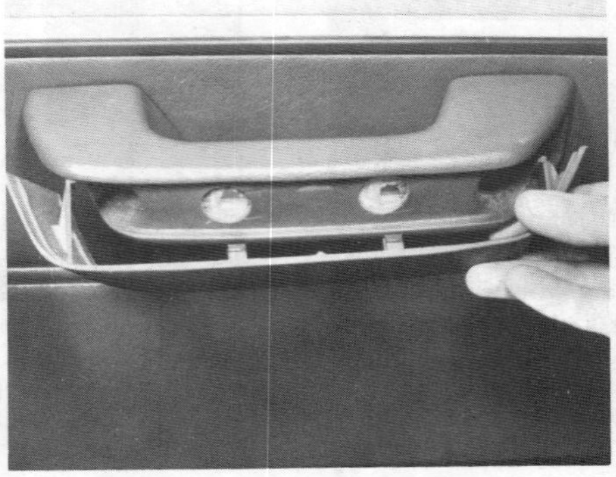

10.2a Remove cover from armrest ...

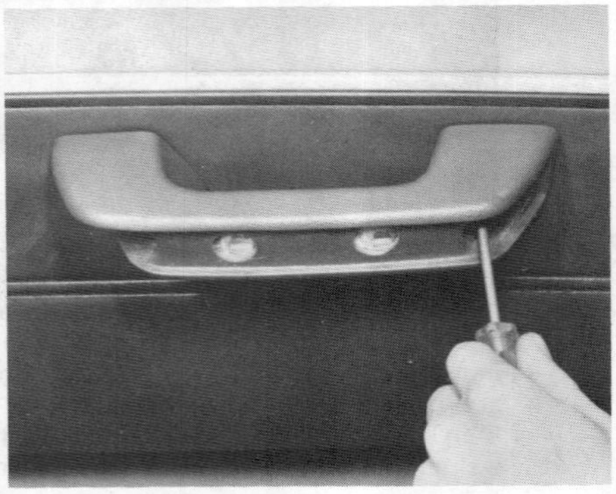

10.2b ... for access to retaining screws

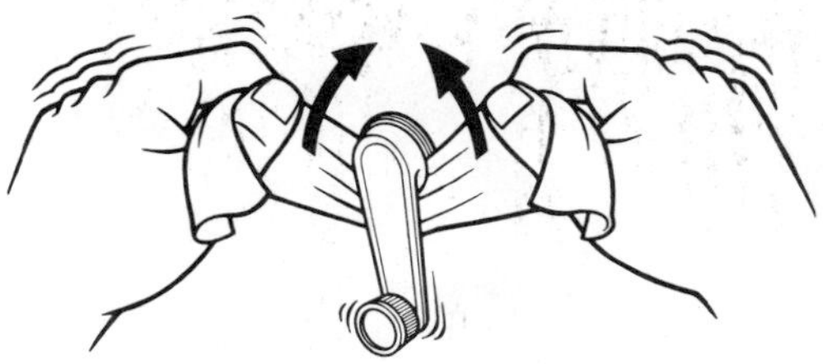

Fig. 12.3 Method for extracting the window regulator retaining clip (Sec 10)

Work around the edge of the panel until it can be removed from the door (photo).

6 Carefully peel away the waterproof sheeting (service cover) from the door and place it to one side.

7 To remove the lock assembly, temporarily refit the window regulator handle and raise the glass fully.

8 Disconnect the door opening control link and the outside control link rods from the lock.

9 Disconnect the lock cylinder link and lock control link rods.

10.3 Remove regulator and nylon washer

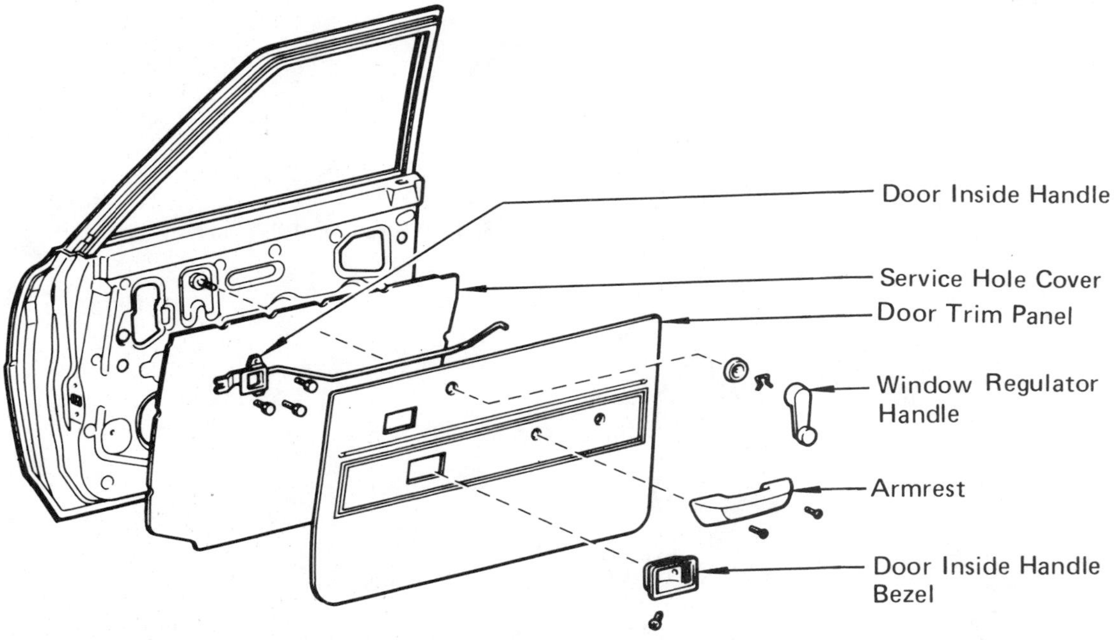

Fig. 12.4 Front door and interior trim components (Sec 10)

10.4a Remove retaining screw and ...

10.4b ... withdraw the bezel

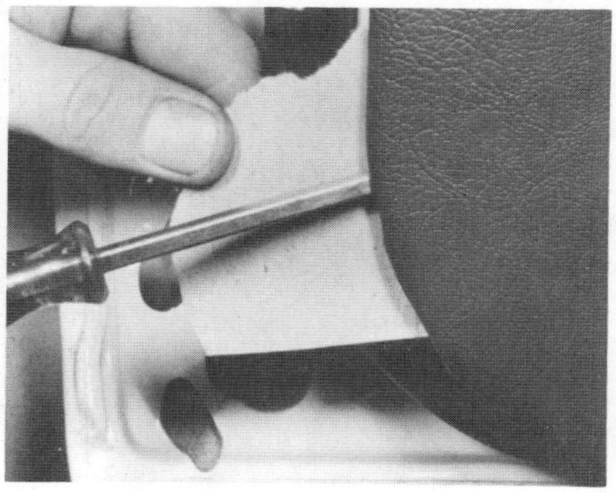

10.5 Prise free the trim panel – note cardboard to protect bodywork

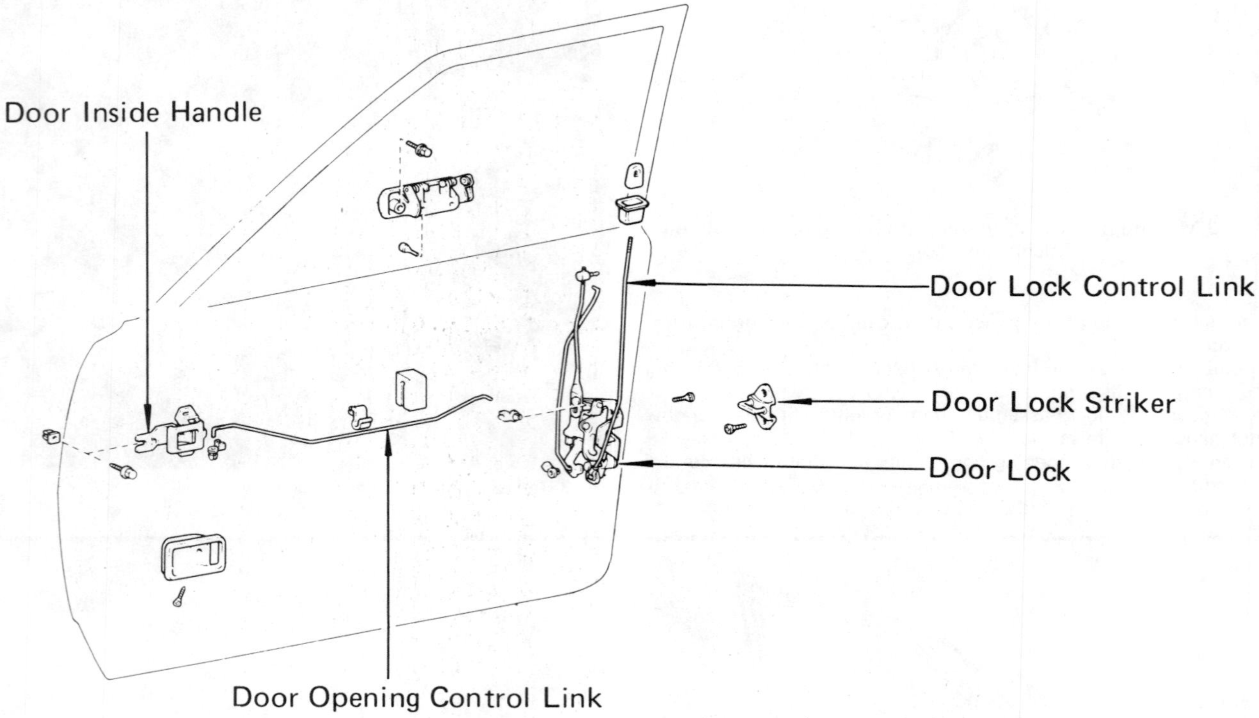

Fig. 12.5 Typical front door locks and linkages (Sec 10)

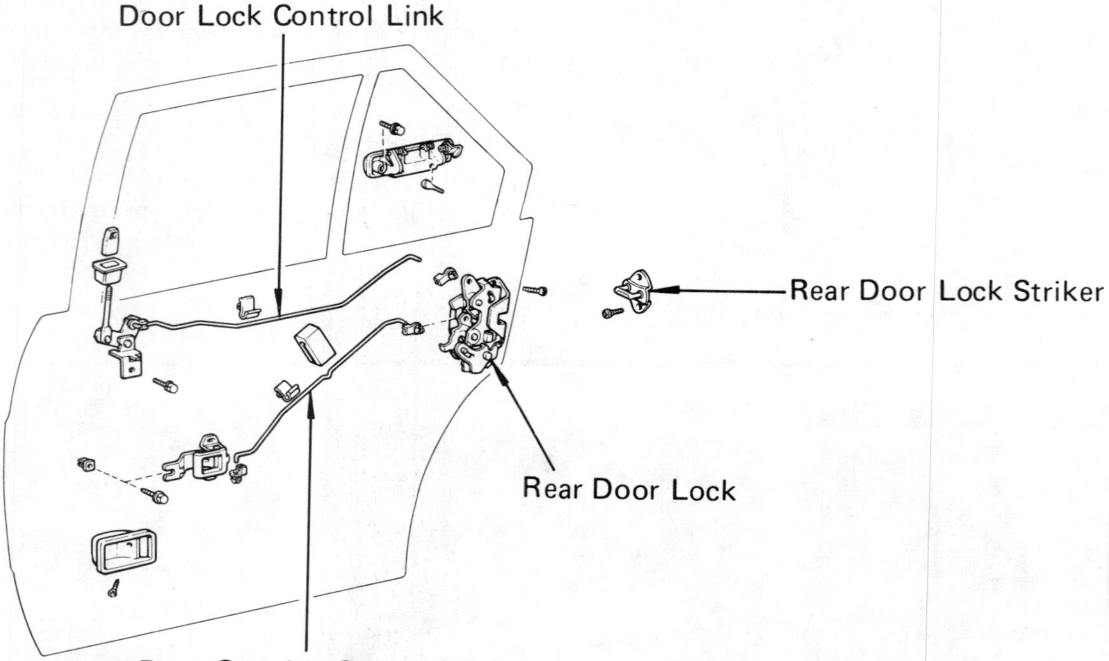

Fig. 12.6 Typical rear door locks and linkages (Sec 10)

10 Unscrew and remove the three lock unit retaining screws (photo).
11 The exterior handle can be removed after disconnecting the control link at the securing bolts. The latter are accessible from inside the door.
12 The key-operated lock cylinder can be removed once its securing circlip and clamp have been extracted.
13 The interior remote control handle can be removed if the link rod is detached and the handle mounting screws extracted (photo).
14 Refitting is a reversal of removal but the following adjustments must be carried out.
15 When refitting the interior lock control handle, insert the securing screws finger tight initially and push the control (with link rod attached) towards the front of the vehicle until resistance is felt and then move it back between 0.02 and 0.04 in (0.5 and 1.0 mm).
16 The exterior handle link rod should be adjusted so that there is clearance of between 0.02 and 0.04 in (0.5 and 1.0 mm) before the handle actuates the lock mechanism.

11 Door window regulator – removal and refitting

1 Remove the door interior trim as previously described and lower the glass fully (Section 10).
2 On Coupe and Liftback models unbolt and detach the door glass front guide.
3 Unscrew the regulator retaining bolts and tilt the unit accordingly

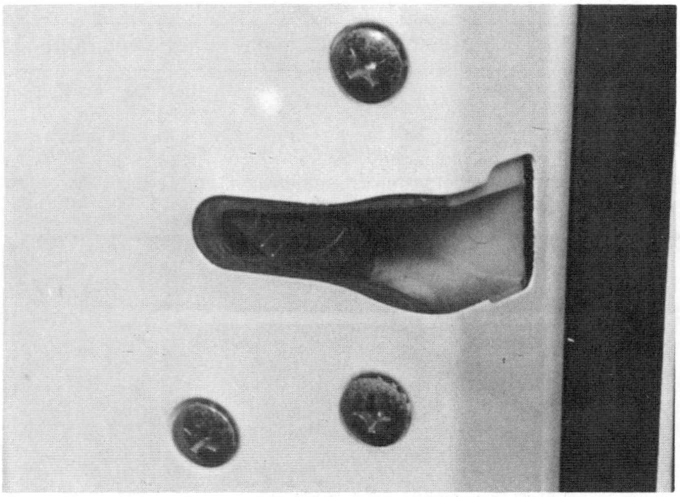

10.10 Lock retaining screws in door trailing edge

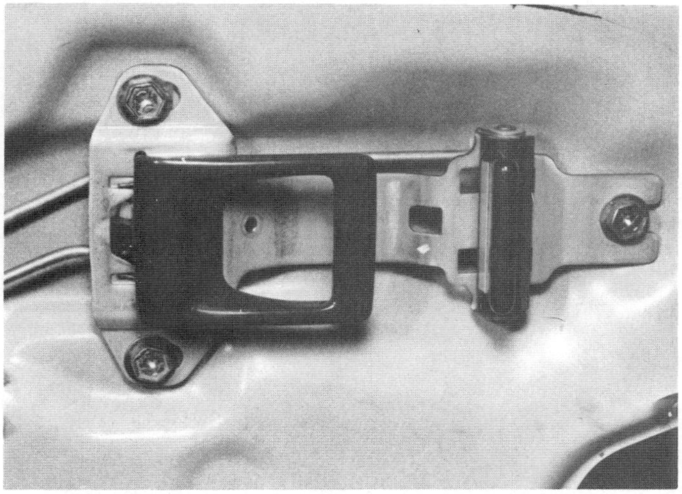

10.13 Interior remote control handle unit showing the three securing bolts

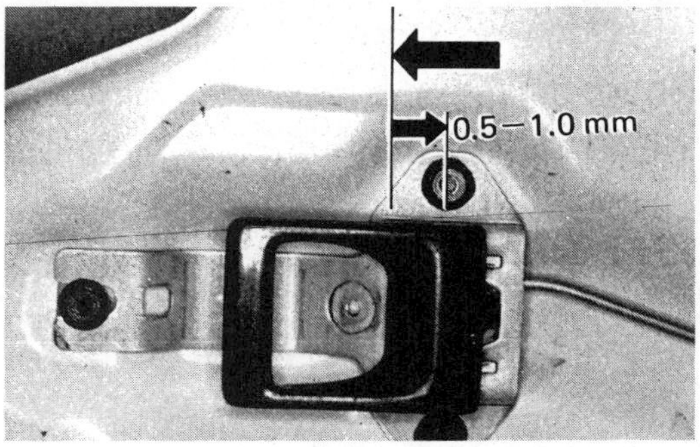

Fig. 12.7 Adjust remote control handle as shown (front and rear) (Sec 10)

Fig. 12.8 Front door external handle adjustment – detach control link (1) and raise handle amount shown. Turn adjuster (2) to locate pin into hole (Sec 10)

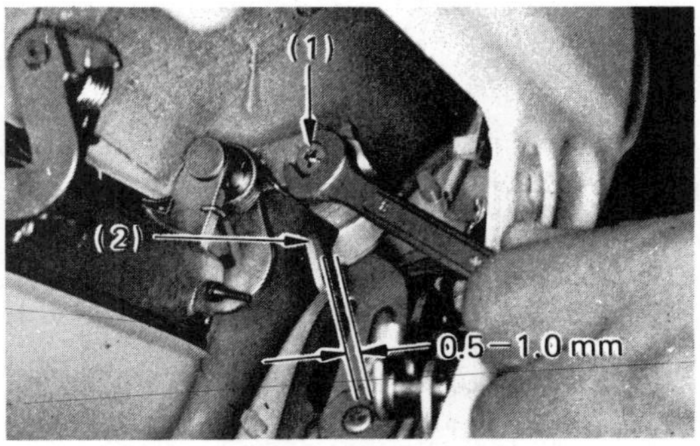

Fig. 12.9 Rear door external handle adjustment: Loosen screw (1), adjust handle and lever (2) to adjustment shown (Sec 10)

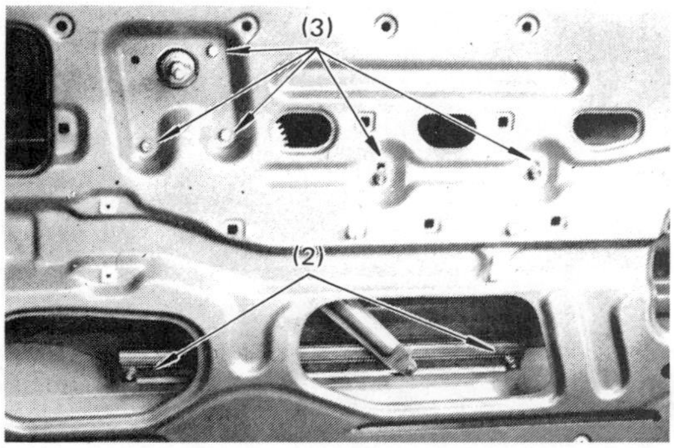

Fig. 12.10 Window regulator bolts (3) and channel bolts (2) (Saloon and Estate) (Sec 11)

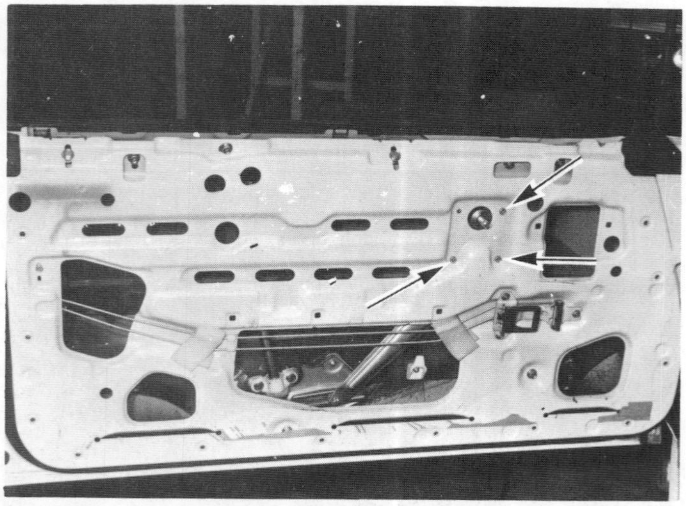

11.3 Window regulator bolt positions (Coupe and Liftback)

to disengage it from the glass channel then withdraw the regulator from the door cavity. On some models, the regulator arm is retained in the glass channel by two bolts which should be removed (photo).

4 Refitting is a reversal of removal but apply grease to all moving parts of the regulator and to the glass channel slides.

5 Refit the regulator in the reverse order to removal. On Saloon and Estate models the glass should be adjusted to ensure that the top edge of the glass is parallel with the top edge of the door. Adjust the equalizer accordingly then retighten the equalizer retaining bolts (encircled).

6 Check window actuation on completion before refitting the trim assembly. For window adjustment on Coupe and Liftback models refer to Section 13.

12 Front door glass (Saloon and Estate) – removal and refitting

1 Remove the door interior trim as previously described in Section 10.

2 Lower the glass fully and extract the two bolts which secure the regulator arm to the glass channel.

3 Remove the weatherstrip (belt moulding) from the top edge of the door waistline.

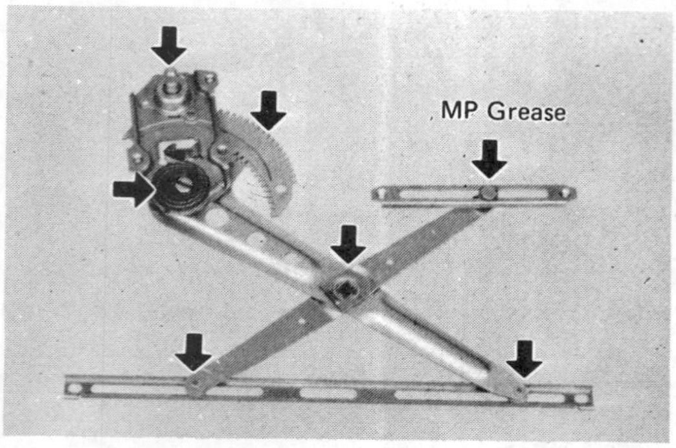

Fig. 12.11 Lubricate regulator at points indicated before refitting (Sec 11)

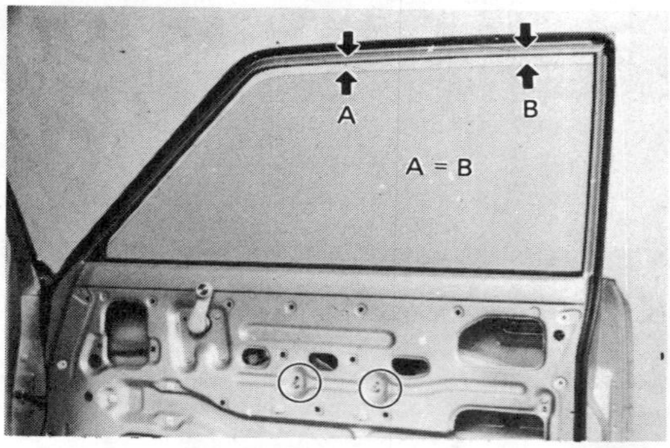

Fig. 12.12 Window alignment adjustment is by equalizer bolts (encircled) on Saloon and Estate models (Sec 11)

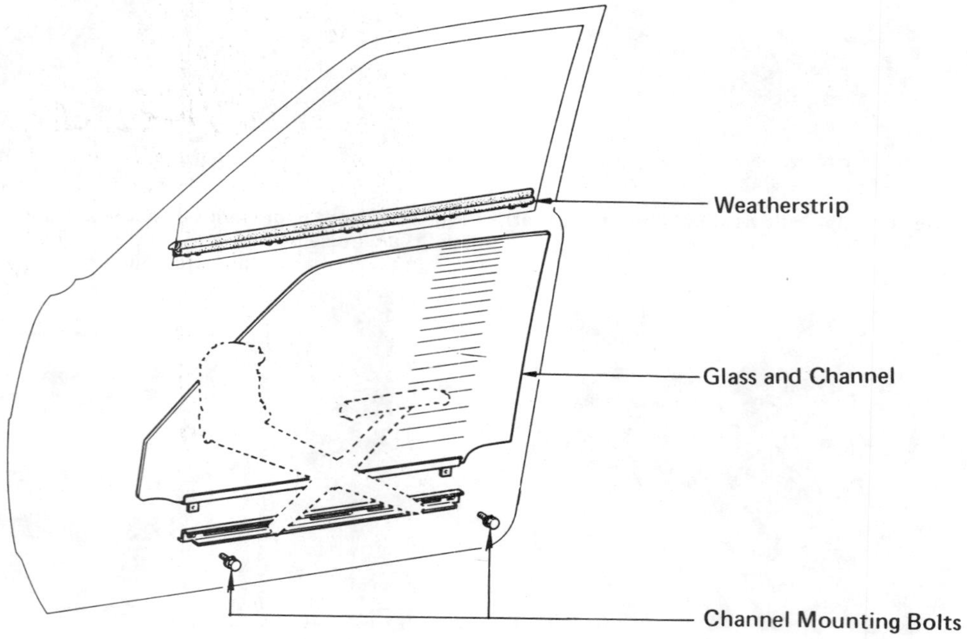

Fig. 12.13 Front door glass (Saloon and Estate) (Sec 12)

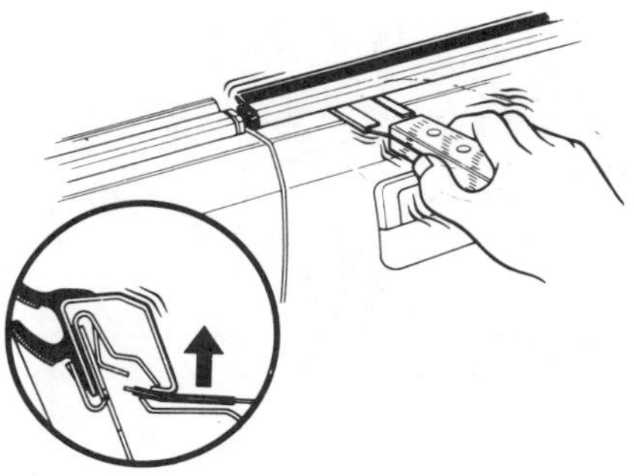

Fig. 12.14 Use flat lever as shown to prise the weatherstrip free from the door (Sec 12)

4 Withdraw the glass with channel attached.
5 The channel can be removed from the glass if necessary by tapping it off with a hammer and thin piece of hardwood.
6 When fitting the glass channel to the glass, set it as shown in the diagram. Tap the channel into position using a soft faced hammer and apply soapy water to the rubber to ease its installation.
7 Refitting is a reversal of removal but adjust the glass side guides to give smooth operation.

13 Front door glass (Coupe and Liftback) – removal and refitting

1 Remove the door interior trim as described in Section 10.
2 Remove the weatherstrip from the door rear edge. This is secured at the top by a screw on the inside. Lower the window.
3 Detach the belt moulding from the top edge of the door. This is secured in place by a screw at each end and clip retainers which are prised free.
4 Unscrew and remove the glass front guide rail retaining nut (top) and bolt (bottom).
5 Detach the trim support and the door glass upper stoppers.
6 Now raise the window about 1.5 in (40 mm) and remove the guide setting bolts.
7 Pull free the regulator lift arm bracket from the glass and then temporarily position the base of the lower guide bracket onto the service aperture edge.

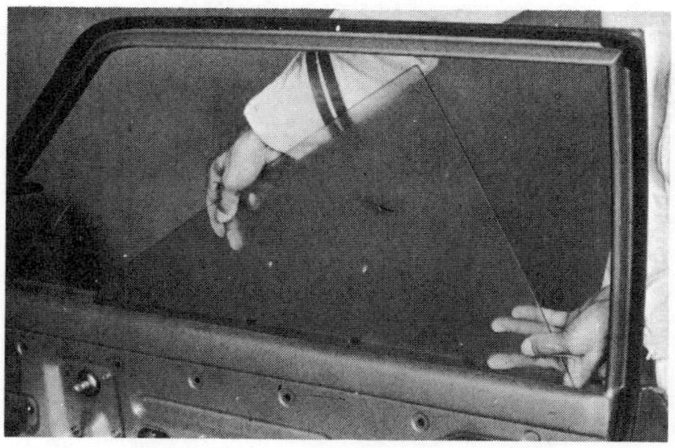

Fig. 12.15 Door glass removal (Saloon and Estate) (Sec 12)

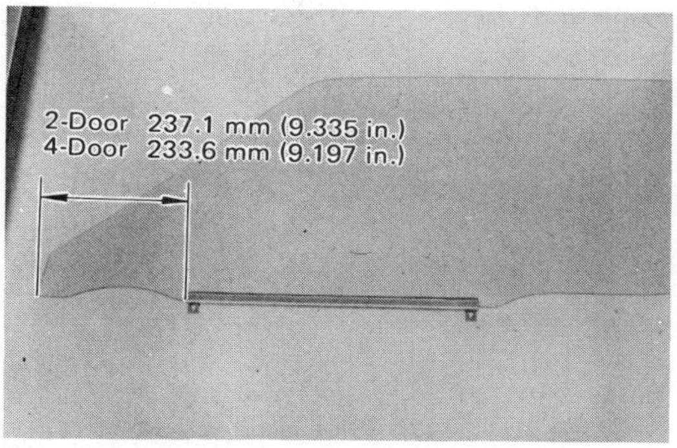

Fig. 12.16 Locate the window channel as indicated according to body type (Sec 12)

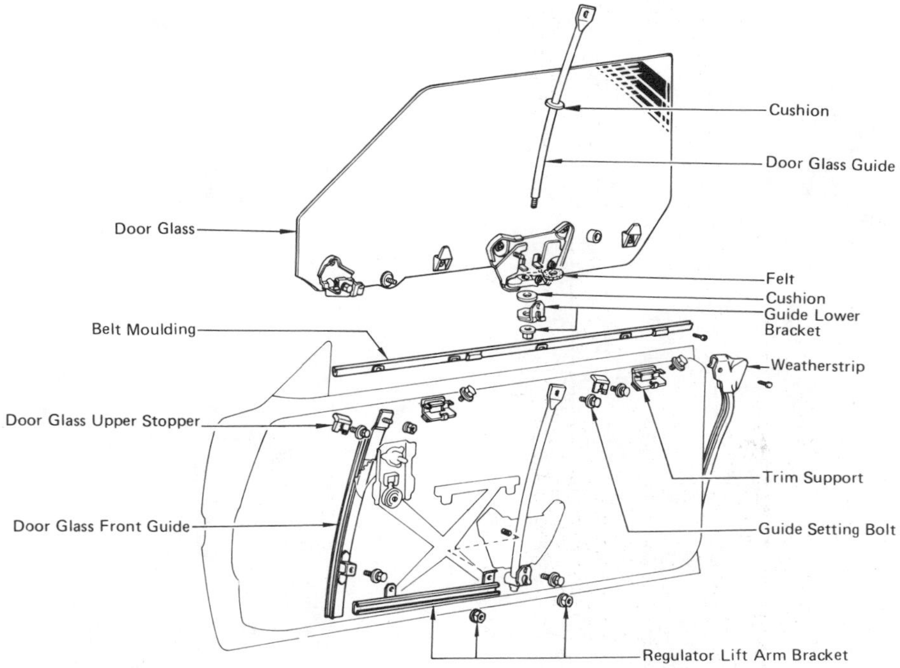

Fig. 12.17 Door glass and associated components (Coupe and Liftback) (Sec 13)

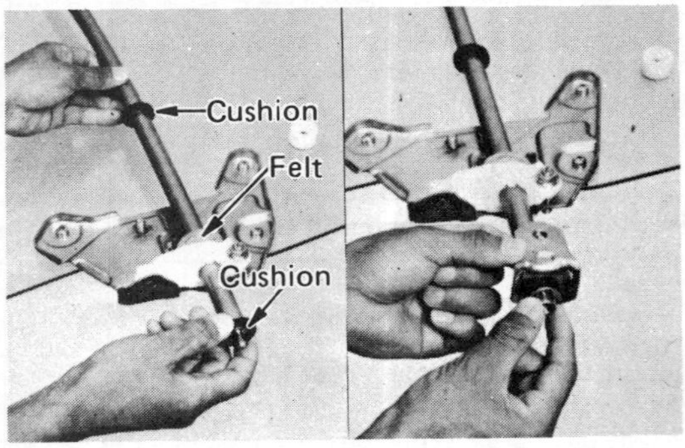

Fig. 12.18 Reassemble the glass guide to bracket (Sec 13)

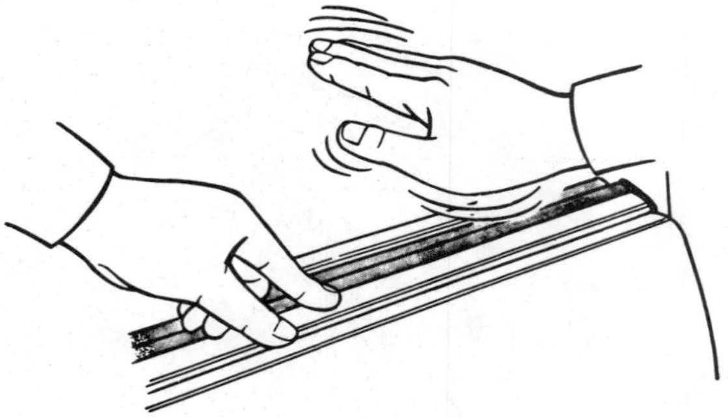

Fig. 12.19 Belt moulding refitting method (Sec 13)

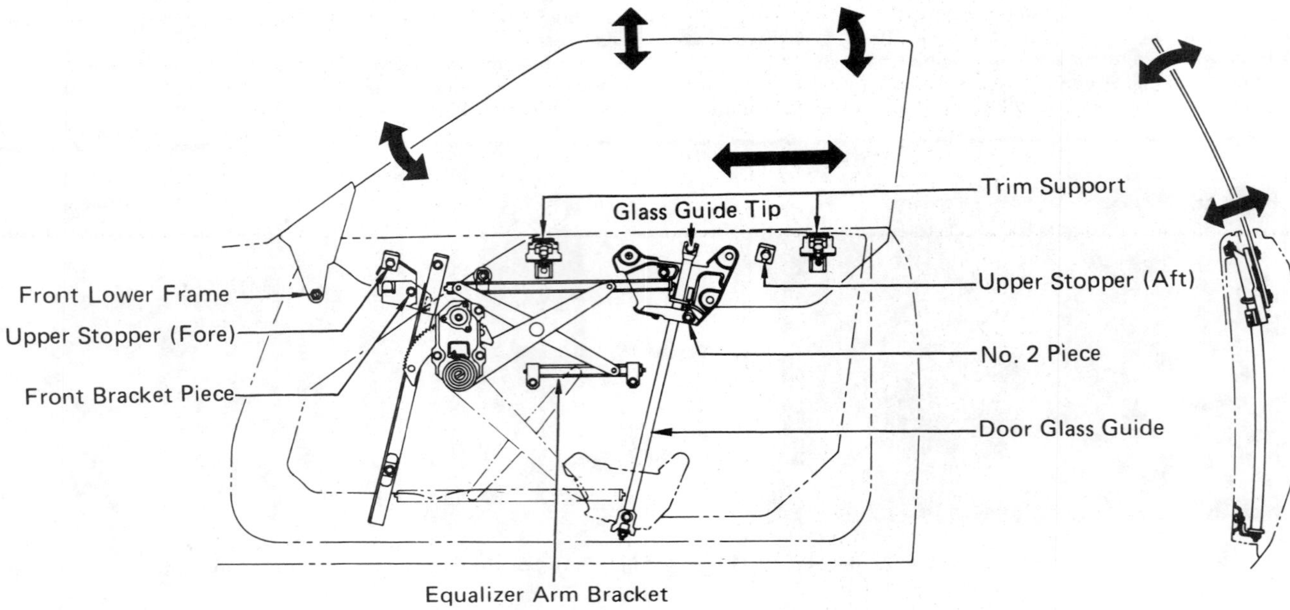

Fig. 12.20 Door glass to be adjusted by items indicated (Coupe and Liftback) (Sec 13)

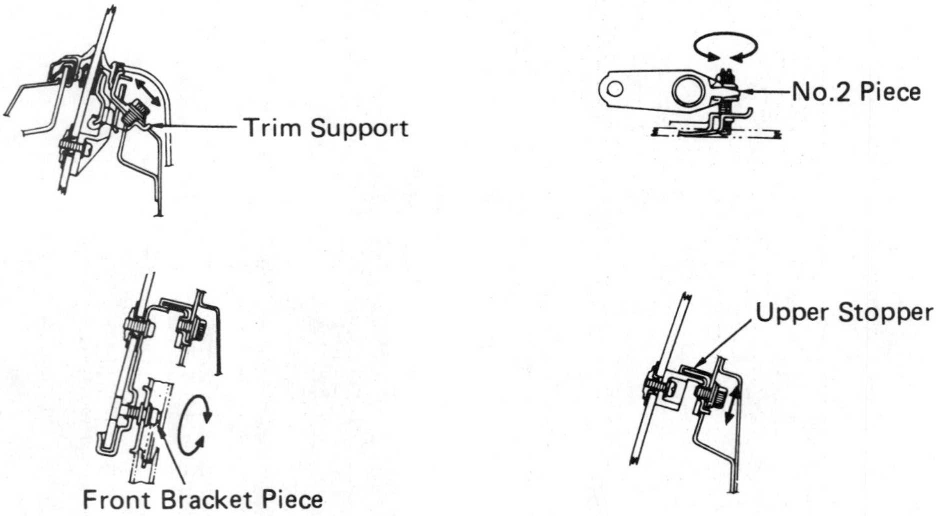

Fig. 12.21 Door glass adjusters and functions (Coupe and Liftback) (Sec 13)

Trim support – glass to belt moulding adjustment
Front bracket and No 2 piece – upper glass contact adjustment
Upper stopper – glass upper positional adjustment

8 Tilt the glass towards the inner door panel edge and lift it out through the top of the door. The four stoppers and the bracket can then be removed from the glass.
9 To refit the glass first locate the cushions and felt onto the guide and fit the glass guide lower bracket. Tighten the setting nut temporarily.
10 Reinsert the glass into the door together with the guide assembly, tilting the glass as it is fitted.
11 Reattach the regulator lift arm to the glass, then insert the glass guide.
12 Refit the upper stoppers and the trim supports.
13 Reconnect the front guide to the guide bracket.
14 Refit the rear edge weatherstrip and then the belt moulding. Tap the moulding into position by hand.
15 The glass must now be checked for adjustment. The door to body fitting must be correct before making any glass adjustment.
16 Refer to the figure and first adjust the trim support with the glass and moulding so that they are in contact.
17 Adjust the position of the upper glass guide lip by sliding the glass backwards and forwards.
18 Tilt the equalizer to adjust the alignment of the glass, then adjust the glass fitting at the top by moving the 'fore' and 'aft' stoppers accordingly.
19 With the above adjustments made the glass to front pillar adjustment can be made by altering the position of the front lower frame.
20 Check that the window regulation is satisfactory then refit the trim panel and associated components.

14 Rear door glass (Saloon and Estate) – removal and refitting

1 Remove the door inner trim panel as described in Section 10.
2 Lower the door glass and then detach the inner and outer weatherstrip.
3 Partially remove the weatherstrip from the door outer edge at the top. Also partially remove the glass run.
4 Remove the division bar which is secured by a screw at the top and two bolts down the inside.
5 Disengage the glass regulator from the glass regulator roller channel, working through the inner inspection aperture in the door. Now pull and manoeuvre the glass upwards and remove it from the door.
6 If the glass is to be removed from its location channel, tap the channel free using a hammer and thin piece of hardboard.
7 When refitting the glass to the channel, set it as shown in the figure. Tap the channel in position using a soft-faced hammer and apply soapy water to the channel to ease assembly.
8 To remove the rear door quarter window pull it forwards together with its weatherstrip.
9 Refitting is the reversal of the removal procedure. Check the operation of the regulator before refitting the inner trim panel.

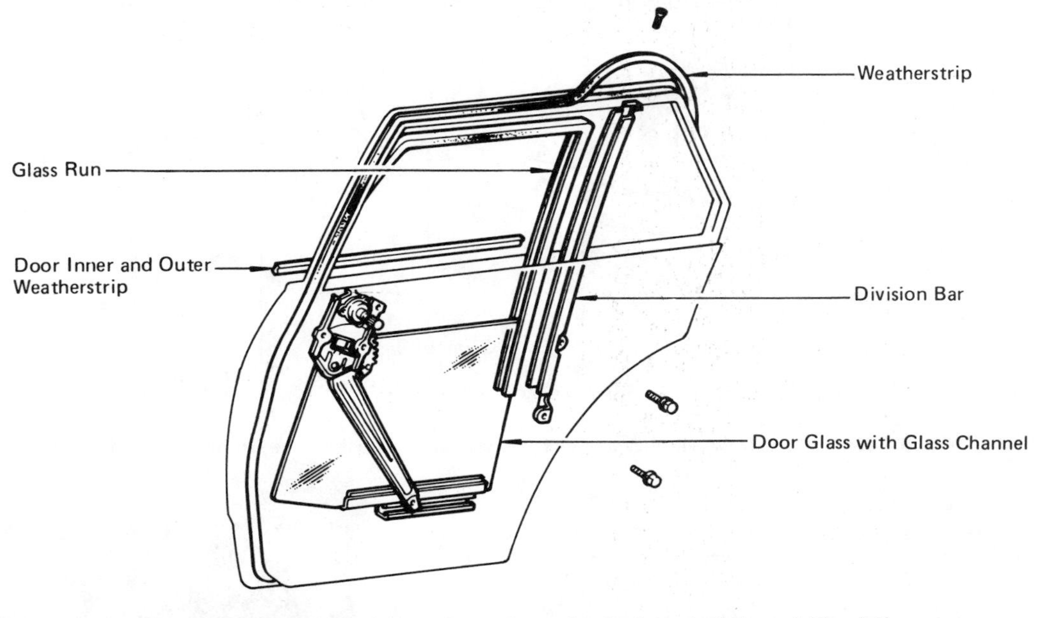

Fig. 12.22 Rear door glass and weatherstrips (Saloon and Estate) (Sec 14)

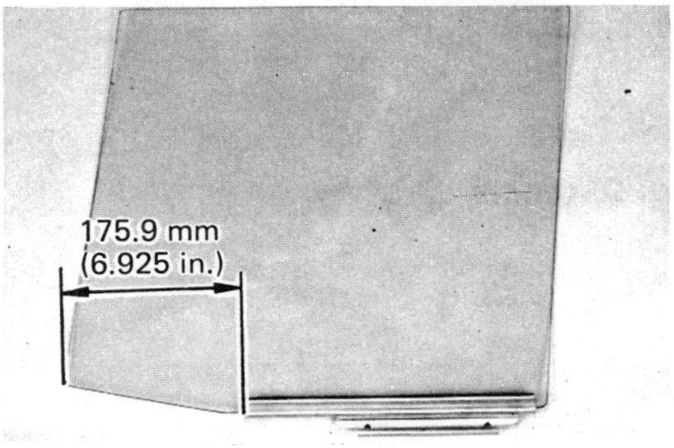

Fig. 12.23 Rear door glass to window channel fitting position (Saloon and Estate) (Sec 14)

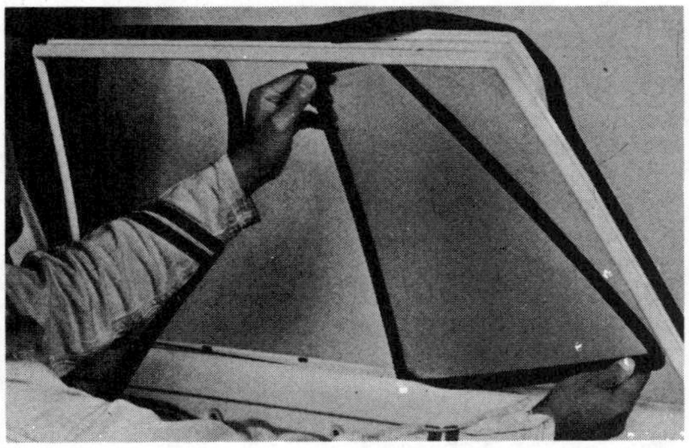

Fig. 12.24 Remove rear door quarter window with weatherstrip (Saloon and Estate) (Sec 14)

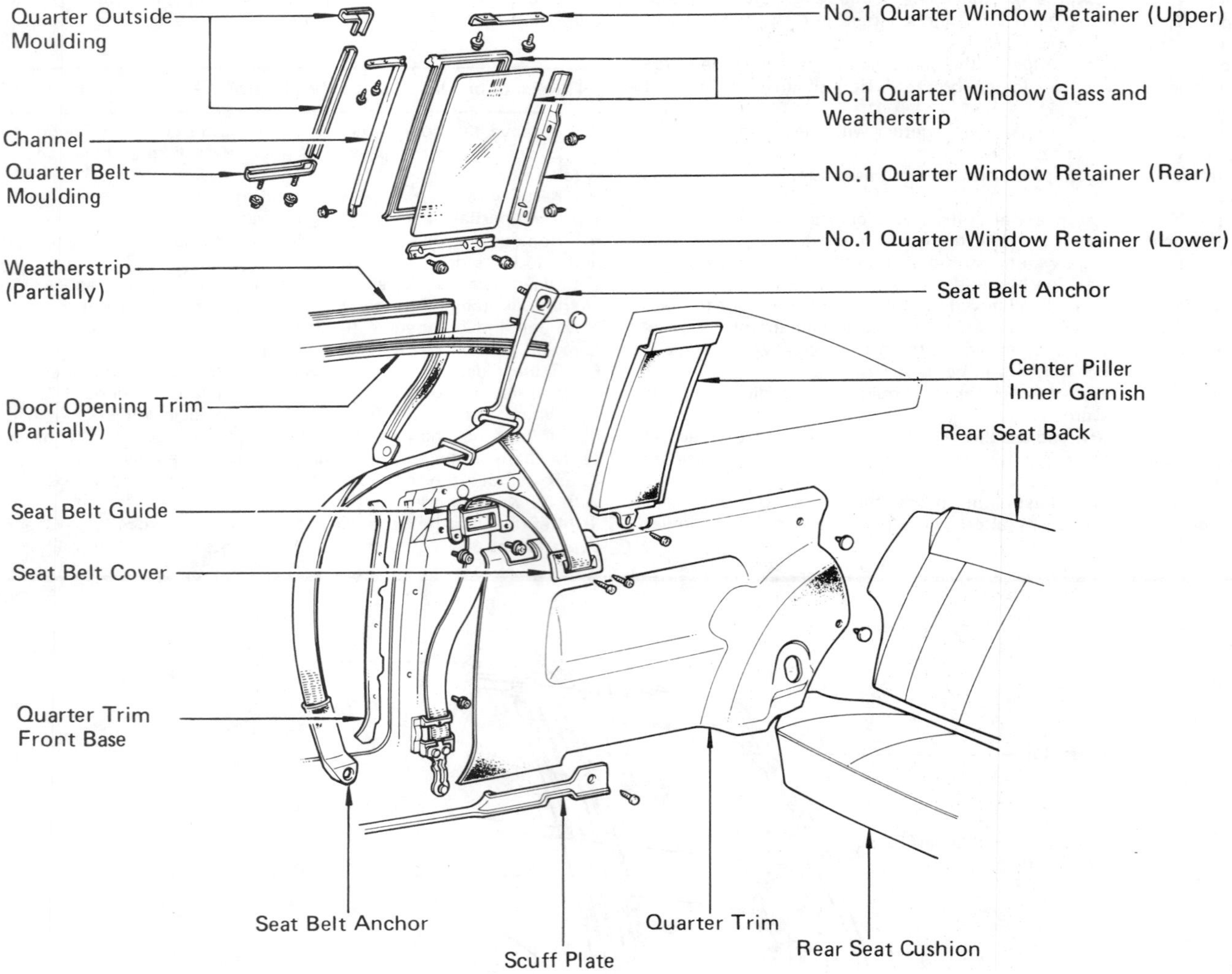

Fig. 12.25 Rear No 1 quarter window and associated components on the Coupe model (Sec 15)

15 Number 1 quarter window (Coupe) – removal and refitting

1 Remove the rear seat and backrest.
2 Unscrew the retaining screws and lift clear the floor scuff plate.
3 Unscrew and remove the screws securing the seat belt cover.
4 The quarter trim panel is now removed. Insert a screwdriver between the plastic retainers and the panel and prise free.
5 Now detach the upper and lower seat belt anchors and belt guide.
6 Detach and remove the quarter trim front base, then partially prise back the weatherstrip and the door opening trim.
7 Remove the channel setting screws and then withdraw the channel.
8 Detach the quarter belt moulding and then remove the front outer moulding followed by the lower, upper and rear number 1 quarter window retainers.
9 The quarter window glass and weatherstrip can now be removed. Prise the weatherstrip free using a screwdriver.
10 Before refitting clean any old adhesive sealant from the weatherstrip (if it is to be reused).
11 Refit the glass and weatherstrip. A 0.20 in (5 mm) strip of Butyl tape must be applied to the groove in the weatherstrip, but no tape must be allowed into the channel.
12 Refit the respective window retainers (renewing any damaged clips).
13 The remainder of the reassembly details are a reversal of the removal procedures.

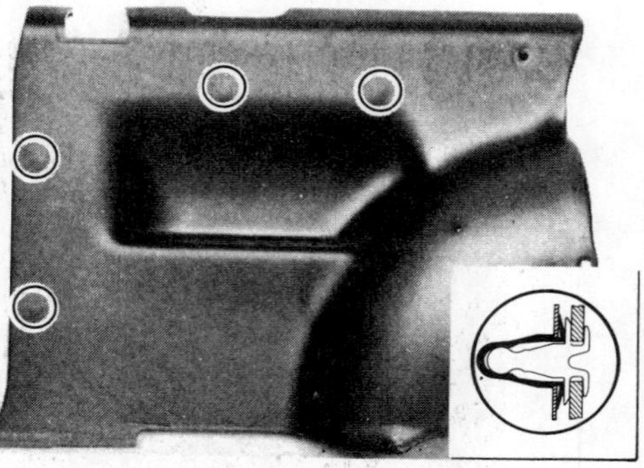

Fig. 12.26 Rear quarter trim retainer positions on the Coupe (Sec 15)

16 Number 1 quarter window – (Liftback) – removal and refitting

1 Remove the rear seat and backrest.
2 Remove the scuff plate from the floor which is secured by screws (photo).
3 Remove the weatherstrip which is secured by a single screw (photo).

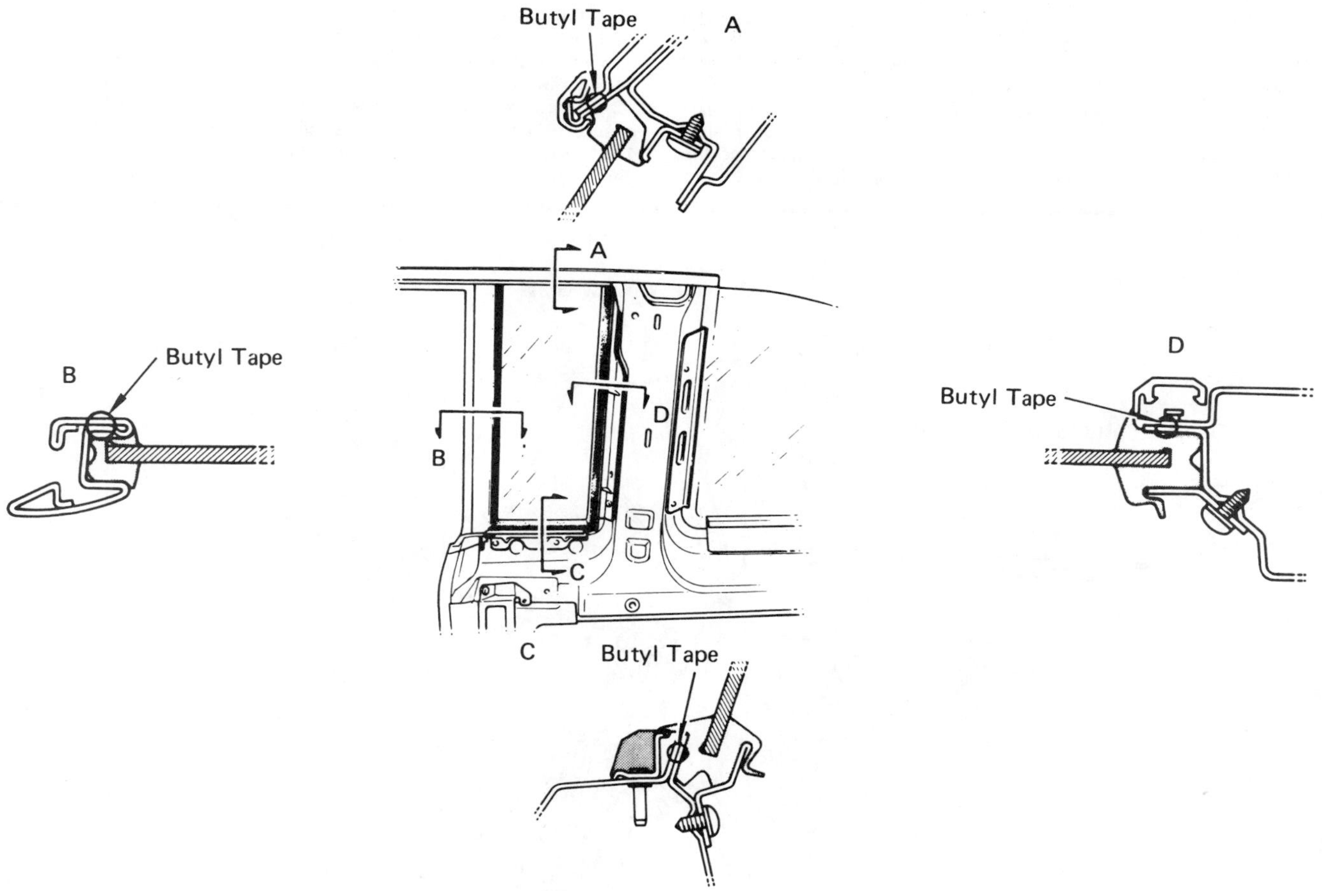

Fig. 12.27 Apply Butyl tape to points indicated (Sec 15)

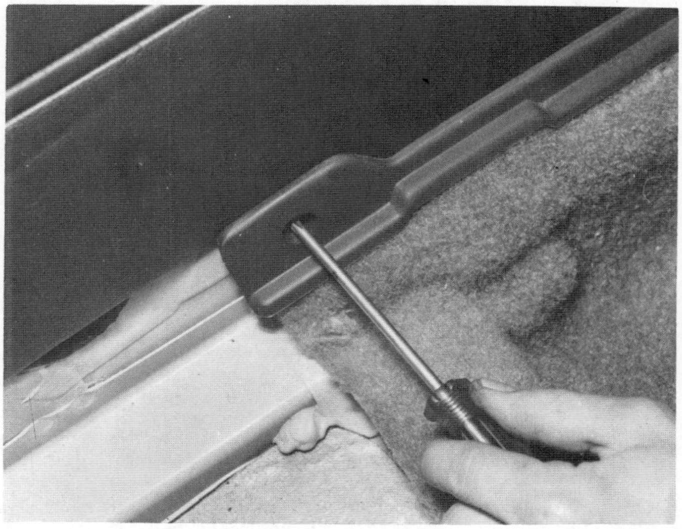

16.2 Remove the scuff plate ...

16.3 ... and the weatherstrip (Liftback)

4 Remove the window regulator handle in the manner described in Section 10 for the door window regulator.
5 Remove the seat belt cover which is secured by screws (photo).
6 Prise free the retainers using a screwdriver and detach the trim panel. Take care not to damage the retainers or panel.
7 Now detach the quarter trim front base, the seat belt anchor, seat belt guide and the plastic cover from the service hole (photo).
8 Detach the quarter belt moulding and the quarter window upper stoppers.
9 Wind down the window to its halfway point then extract the channel setting pin using a pair of long nose pliers (photo).
10 Loosen off the upper stud bolt locking nuts then press in the stud bolts and move the guide outwards.
11 Loosen off the lower stud bolt locknut and remove the stud bolt from the guide.
12 The quarter window glass can now be removed by pulling upwards and tilting it forwards, but take care not to damage the panel during removal.
13 Before refitting the quarter window lubricate the sliding parts and ensure that the guide and roller sliding action is satisfactory.
14 Insert the glass into position and reverse the procedures given in paragraphs 8 to 11 inclusive, but do not fully tighten the upper and

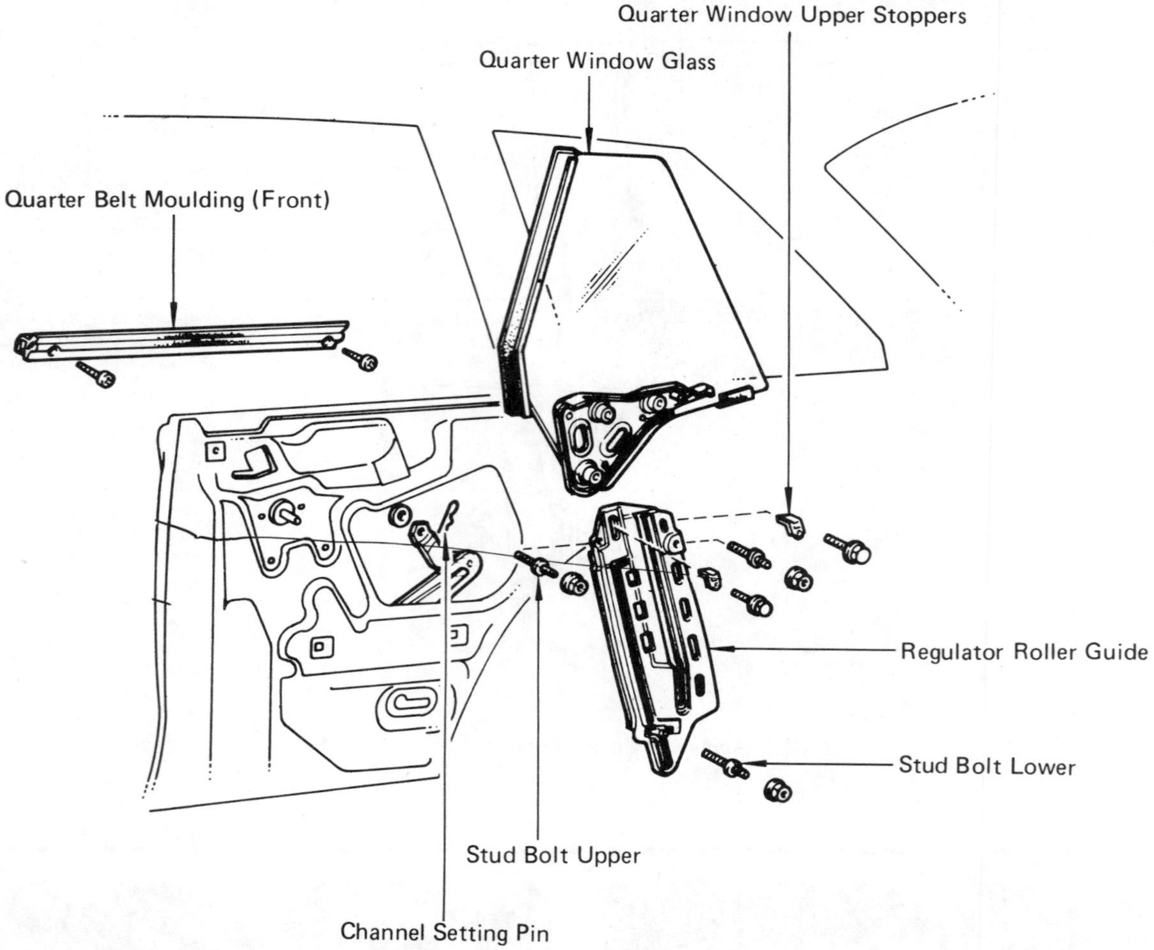

Fig. 12.28 No 1 quarter window and associated components (Liftback) (Sec 16)

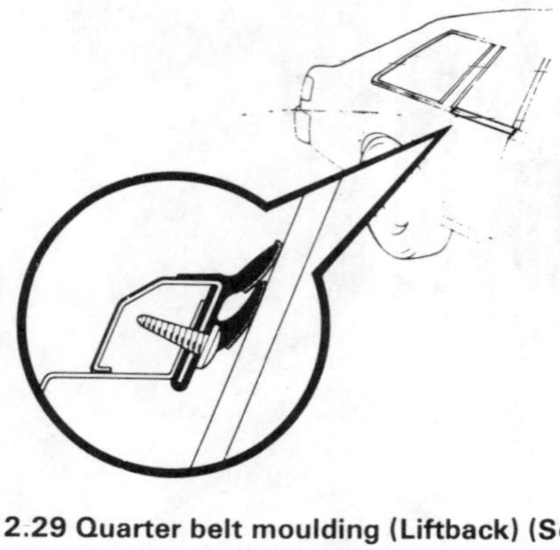

Fig. 12.29 Quarter belt moulding (Liftback) (Sec 16)

Fig. 12.30 Loosen the upper stud bolt locknuts (Liftback) (Sec 16)

16.5 Seat belt cover removal (Liftback)

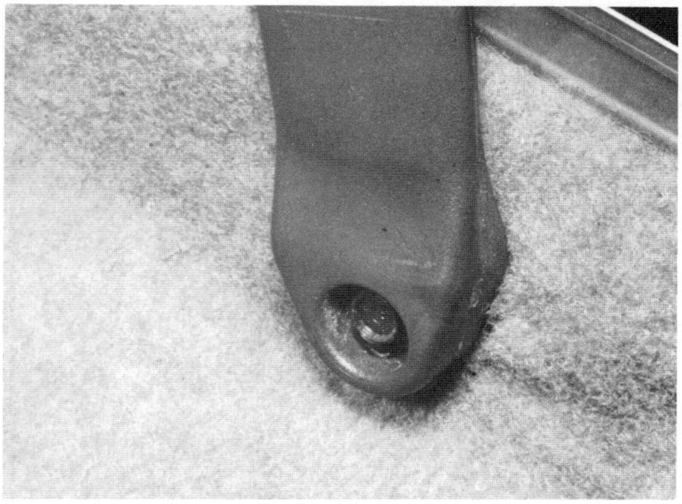

16.7 Detach the seat belt anchor (Liftback)

lower stud bolt locknuts until the window is adjusted for correct positioning when raised. Adjust by turning the stud bolts or sliding them along in the direction required. If the glass is too low raise the position of the upper stopper bolts as necessary, but ensure that the window touches both the front and rear stopper when set.

15 Having adjusted the window position reverse the removal procedure given in paragraphs 1 to 7.

17 Number 1 quarter window regulator (Liftback) – removal and refitting

1 Proceed as given in the previous Section to remove the quarter trim panel and the quarter window glass.

2 To remove the regulator unscrew and remove the three retaining bolts (photo) and then withdraw the regulator through the service aperture in the inner panel.

3 If the regulator is worn or damaged renew it as a unit.

4 Before refitting the regulator lubricate the sliding parts with grease.

5 Refit in the reverse order of removal.

18 Rear quarter window glass (Coupe and Liftback) – removal and refitting

Should it be necessary to remove and refit this window at any time, it is recommended that it be entrusted to your Toyota dealer or a competent automotive body repair shop. This is because it entails certain specialised procedures.

19 Windscreen – removal and refitting

1 Windscreen refitting is no light task. Leave this to a specialist if possible. Instructions are given below for the more ambitious.

2 Remove the windscreen wiper arms and blades and the cowl ventilator louvre.

3 Inside the vehicle remove the rear view mirror and the windscreen pillar side trim on each side.

4 If the screen is of non-laminated type and has already shattered and been knocked out, use a vacuum cleaner to pick up as much as possible of the glass crystals.

5 Switch on the heater boost motor and adjust the controls to 'Screen Defrost' but watch out for flying pieces of glass which might be blown out of the ducting.

6 If the screen is unbroken or is of the laminated type, carefully ease out the windscreen mouldings from the weatherstrip.

16.9 Channel setting pin (Liftback)

17.2 Window regulator bolts (No 1 quarter window – Liftback)

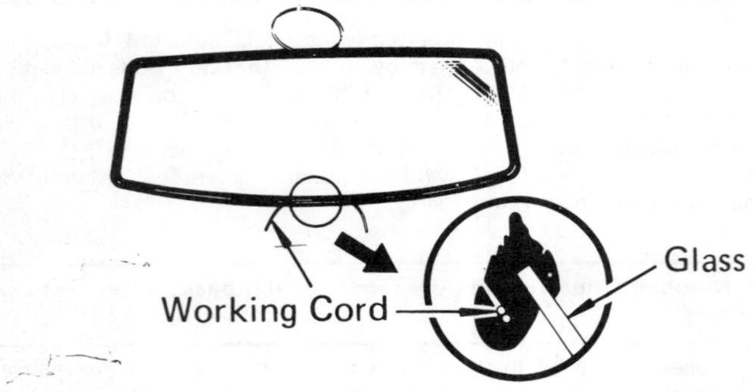

Fig. 12.31 Cord fitting diagram for windscreen fitting (Sec 19)

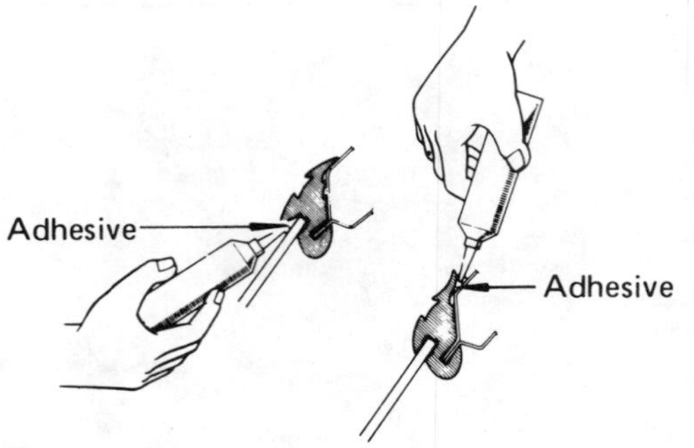

Fig. 12.32 Adhesive cement application points (Sec 19)

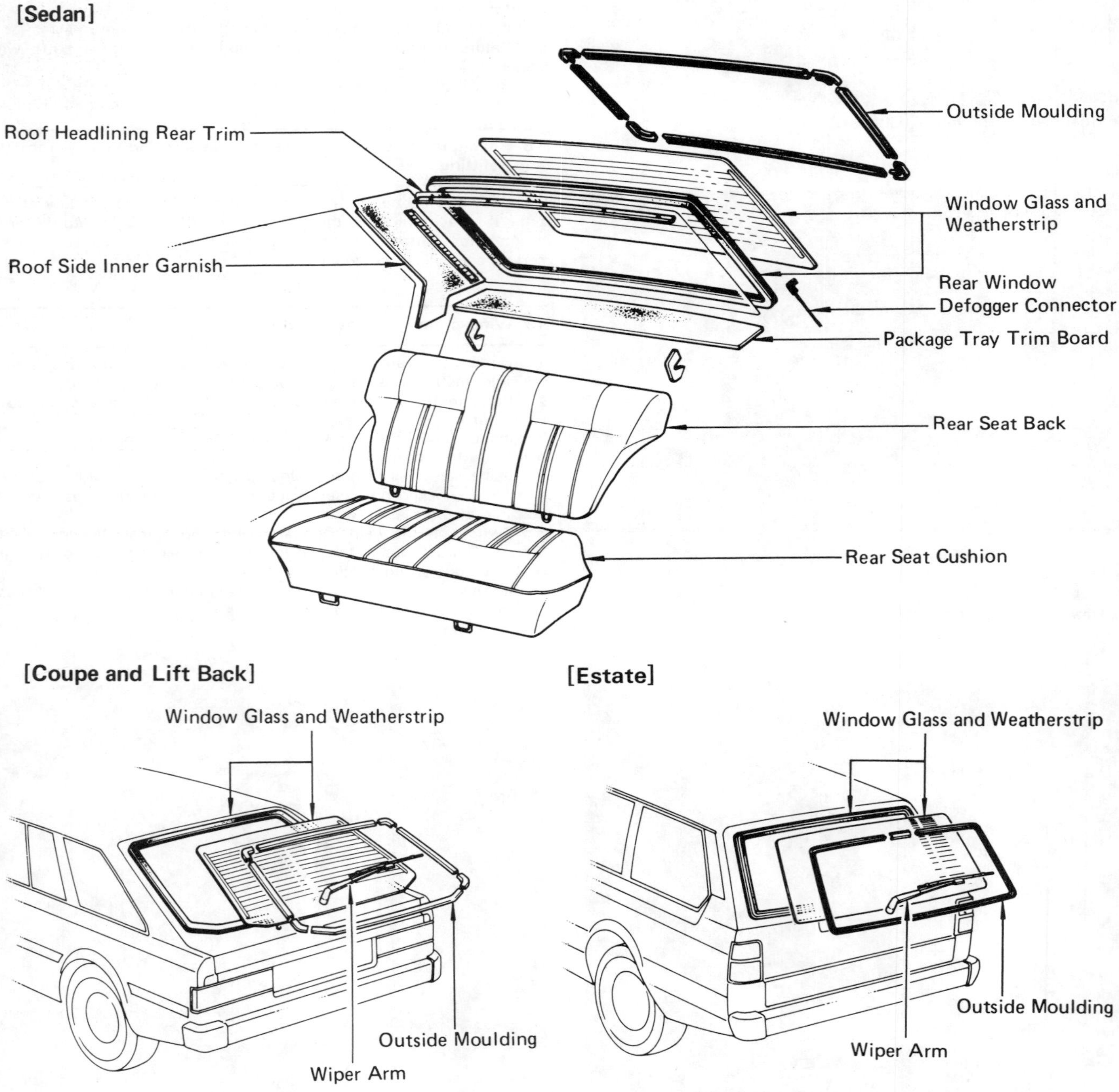

Fig. 12.33 Rear window and weatherstrip components (Sec 20)

7 The assistance of a second person should now be enlisted, ready to catch the glass when it is released from its aperture.
8 Using a screwdriver break the seal between the weatherstrip and the aperture taking care not to scratch the paintwork.
9 Working from inside the car, commencing at one top corner, press the glass and ease it and the rubber weatherstrip from the aperture lip.
10 Remove the rubber weatherstrip from the glass.
11 Now is the time to remove all pieces of glass if the screen has shattered (toughened type glass).
12 Carefully inspect the rubber weatherstrip for signs of splitting or other deterioration. Clean all traces of sealing compound from the weatherstrip and windscreen aperture flange.
13 To refit the glass first place the rubber weatherstrip onto the glass edge.
14 Place a piece of cord onto the body flange groove of the weatherstrip and cross the ends at the top centre of the weatherstrip.
15 Offer up the glass and weather strip to the aperture and using the cord pull the rubber lip over the body flange. Whilst this is being done a person outside the car must apply firm pressure to the glass to ensure that the weatherstrip seats correctly onto the body flange.
16 If the weatherstrip is new, or stiff, lubricate the aperture and weatherstrip flanges with a little concentrated soap and water solution or washing-up liquid.
17 Apply some adhesive cement between the weatherstrip and the body and also between the weatherstrip and the glass.
18 Carefully refit the weatherstrip moulding using a screwdriver or special fitting tool and finally refit the interior mirror, the wiper arms and cowl ventilator louvre.

20 Rear window – removal and refitting

The operations are almost identical with those described for the windscreen, except that the leads to the heater element should be disconnected before removal of the glass.

On Liftback, Estate and Coupe models you will also need to remove the rear window wiper arm and blade.

21 Doors – removal and refitting

1 Open the door to its fullest extent and support its lower edge on jacks or blocks covered with rag to prevent damage to the paintwork.

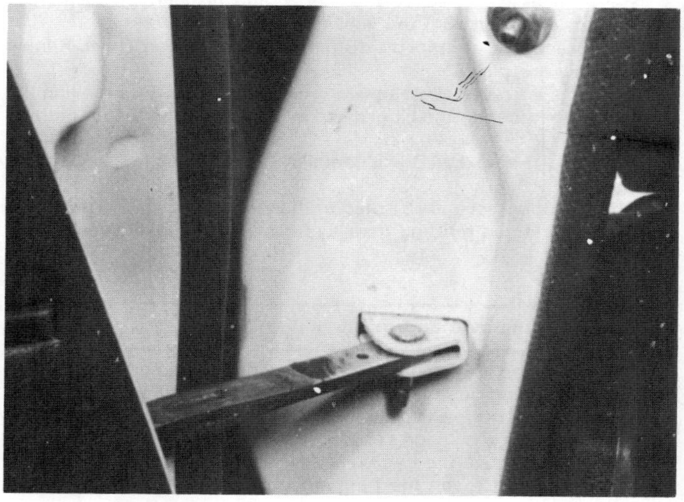

21.3 Check strap and stopper pin

2 Mark the position of the hinge plates on the edges of the doors.
3 Using a pair of needle nose pliers, push in on the claw underneath the check strap retainer and pull the stopper pin up to remove it (photo). Leave the claw in raised position.
4 Have an assistant support the door in the vertical position and unscrew and remove the hinge bolts from the door side.
5 Lift the door away.
6 If the hinges must be removed from the door pillars, again mark their position before unbolting them.
7 Refit the door by reversing the removal operations, adjust if necessary after reference to Section 8.

22 Back door (tailgate) – removal and refitting

1 Open the door fully and disconnect the leads from the heating element, wiper motor and the tubing from the washer jet.
2 Disconnect the stays.

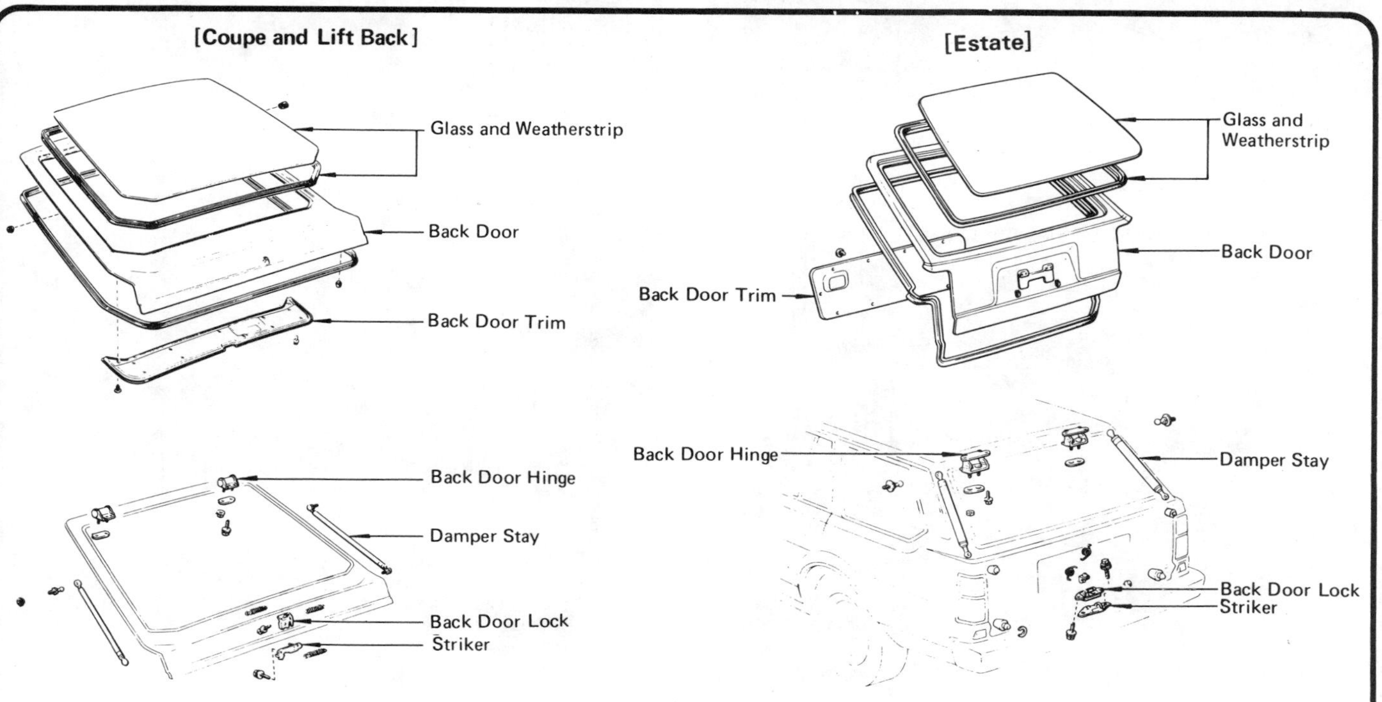

Fig. 12.34 Rear door/tailgate components (Sec 22)

3 Have an assistant support the door and disconnect the hinges from it. Lift the door from the vehicle (photo).
4 On no account attempt to dismantle the gas-filled stays. Renew them if they are faulty.
5 Refitting is a reversal of removal, adjust if necessary by moving the position of the door on the hinges and by adjustment of the lock striker (photo).
6 Refer to Chapter 10 for details of the washer and wiper mechanism.
7 The back door lock is attached to the tailgate by two bolts (photo) and its removal and refitting details are similar to those given for the boot lid lock.

23 Bonnet – removal and refitting

1 With the bonnet open, use a soft pencil and mark the outline position of both hinges on the bonnet to act as a guide to refitting.
2 With the help of an assistant to support the front of the bonnet undo and remove the hinge securing bolt.
3 Undo and remove the two bolts and washers securing the bonnet to each hinge. Lift away the bonnet from over the front of the car (photo).
4 Reassembly and refitting is the reverse sequence to removal. Several adjustments are necessary and should be carried out as follows:
5 Adjustment of the bonnet in the aperture is effected by slackening the bonnet to hinge securing bolts and repositioning the bonnet in the aperture. To lift the rear edge of the bonnet, the hinge can be raised once the securing bolts to the body have been slackened. To lift the front edge of the bonnet slacken the bonnet lock dowel securing nut and screw out the dowel by the required amount. Tighten the locknut. The bump stops at the front of the engine compartment should also be adjusted to be compatible with the new setting of the lock dowel. The lock mechanism which is attached to the crossmember above the radiator is adjustable for position to ensure positive closure of the bonnet. Simply loosen off the attachment bolts and move the lock accordingly to the right, left or either direction vertically, then retighten the bolts and check its operation. Further adjustment may be necessary.

24 Boot lid (Saloon) – removal and refitting

1 With the boot lid open, mark the fitted position of the hinge relative to the boot lid.
2 An assistant should now support the weight of the boot lid and

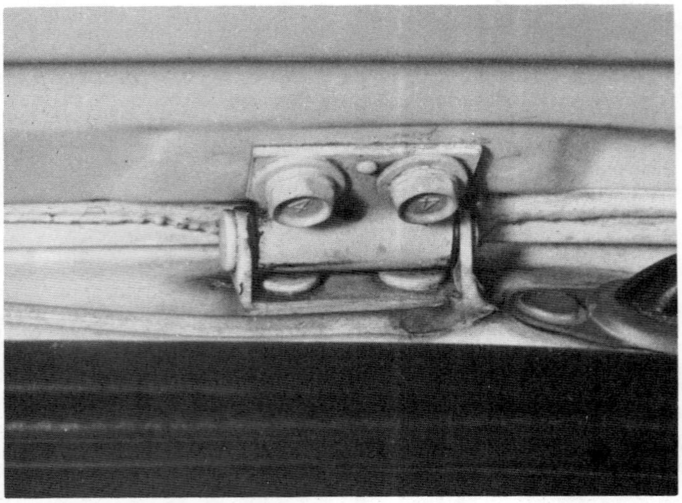

22.3 Back door hinges (Liftback)

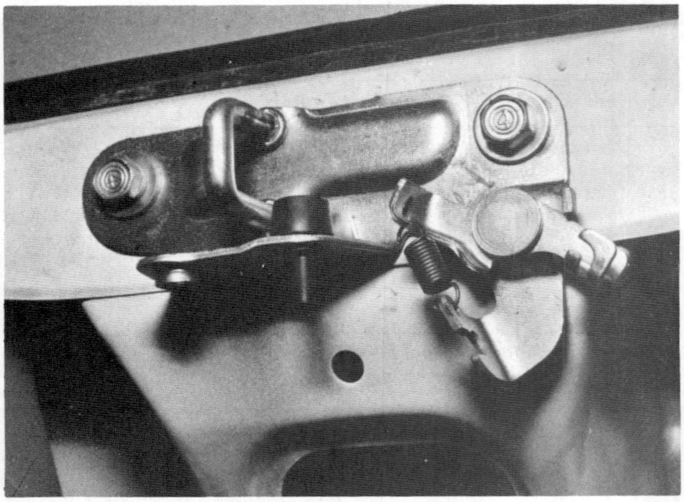

22.5 Back door lock striker (Liftback)

22.7 Back door lock (Liftback)

23.3 Bonnet hinges and securing bolts

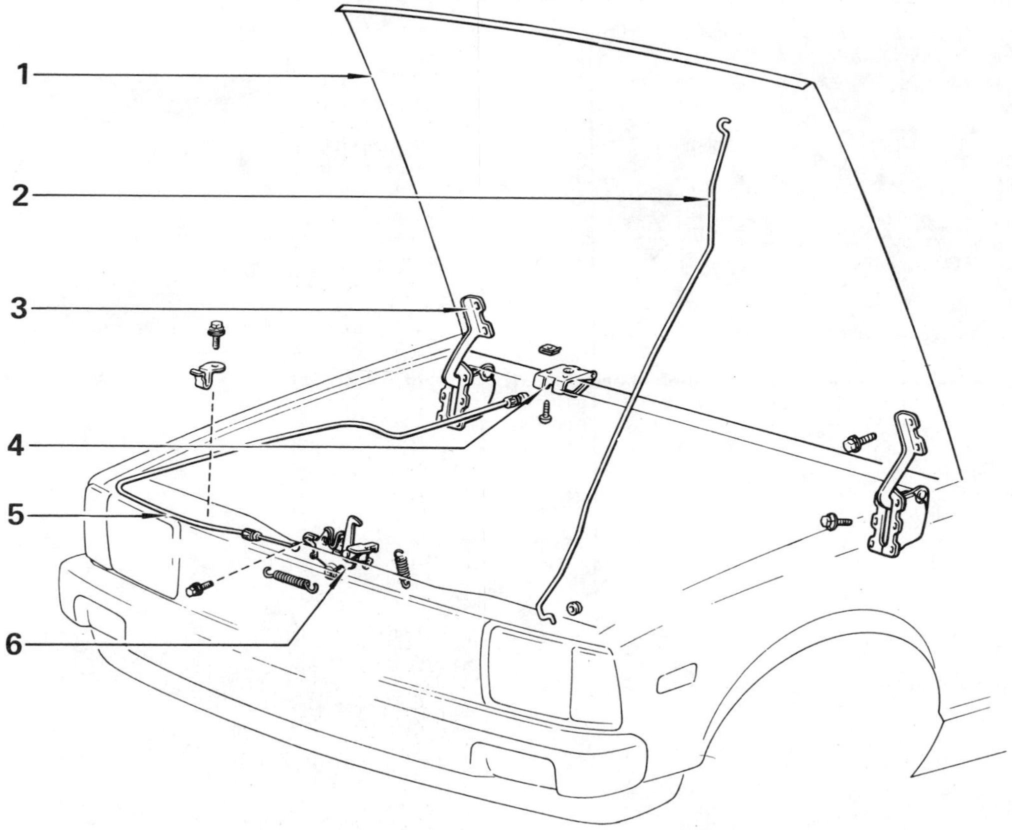

Fig. 12.35 Bonnet and associated components (Sec 23)

1	*Bonnet*	*3*	*Hinge*	*5*	*Control cable*
2	*Support*	*4*	*Lock release lever*	*6*	*Bonnet lock*

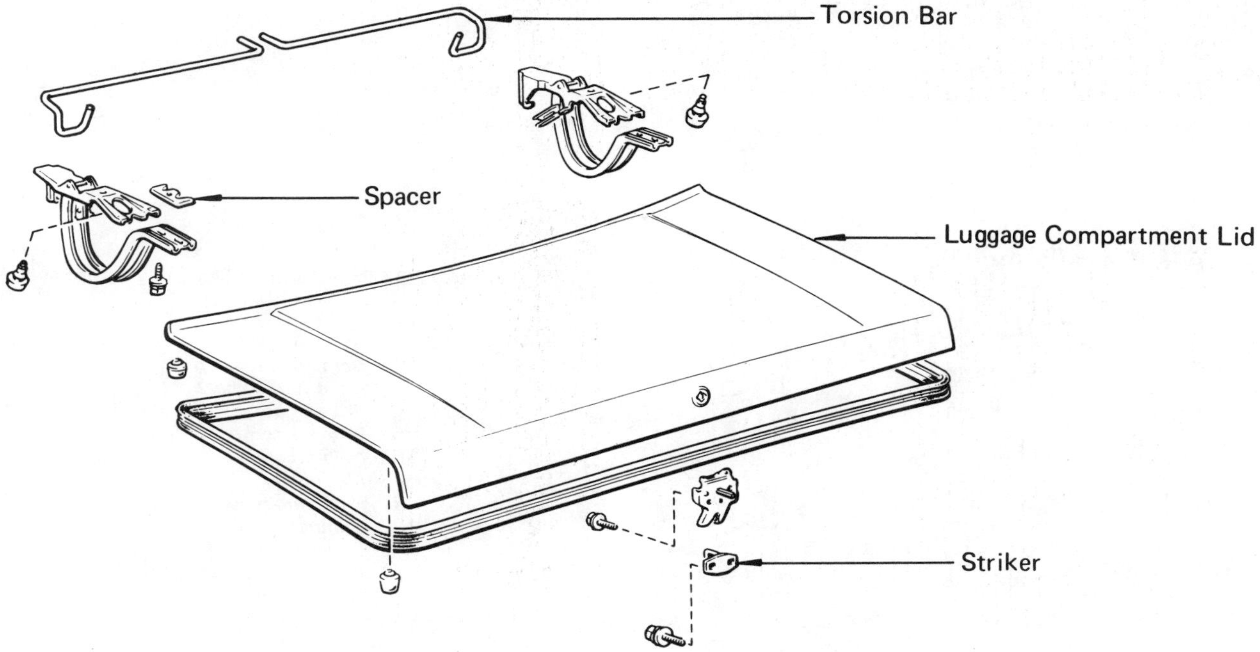

Fig. 12.36 Boot lid and associated components (Saloon) (Sec 24)

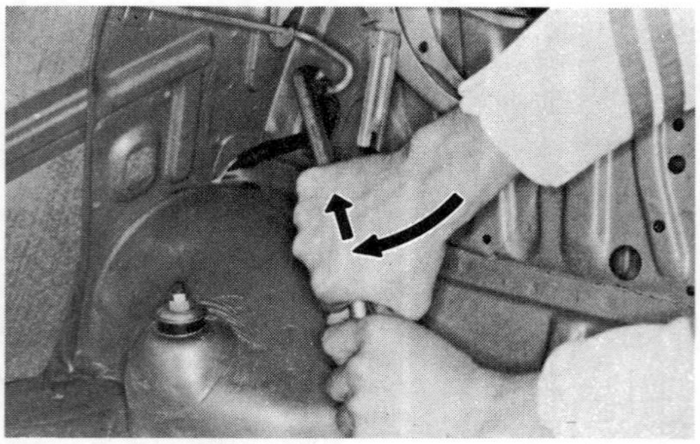

Fig. 12.37 Boot lid torsion bar removal using hooked bar (Sec 24)

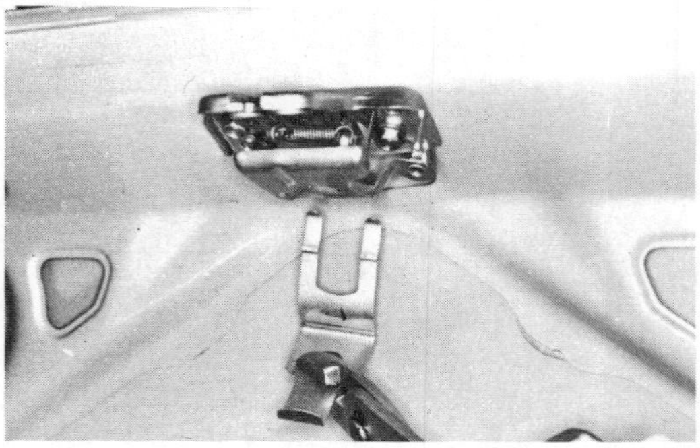

Fig. 12.38 Boot lid lock cylinder retainer removal (Sec 24)

UK models

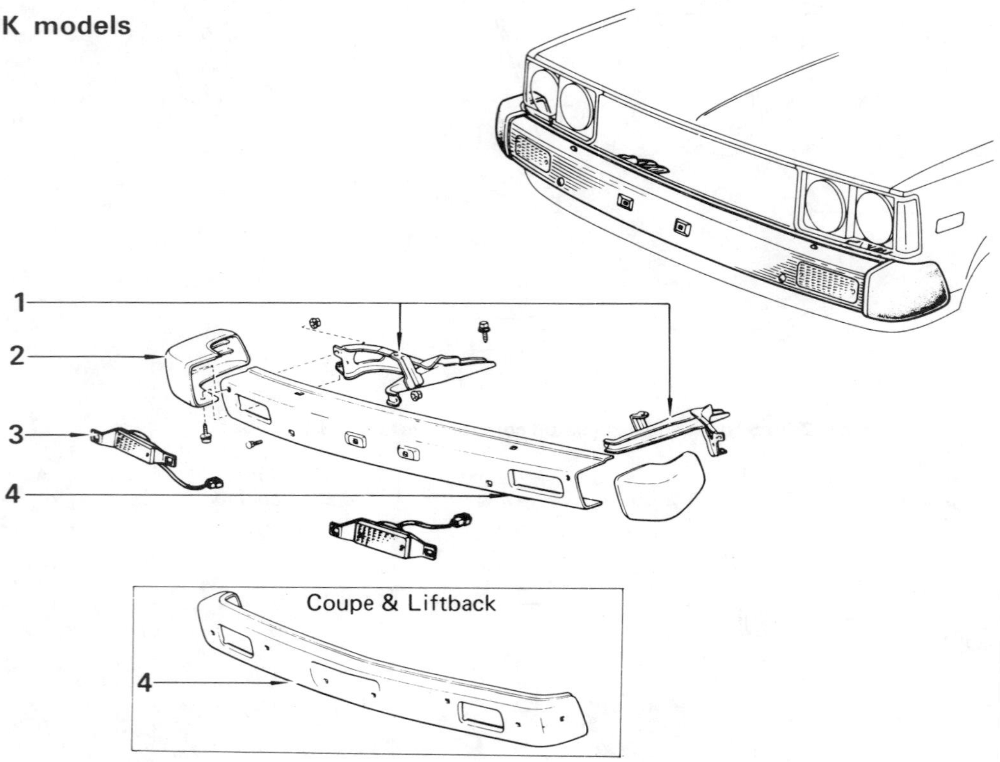

USA & Canada models

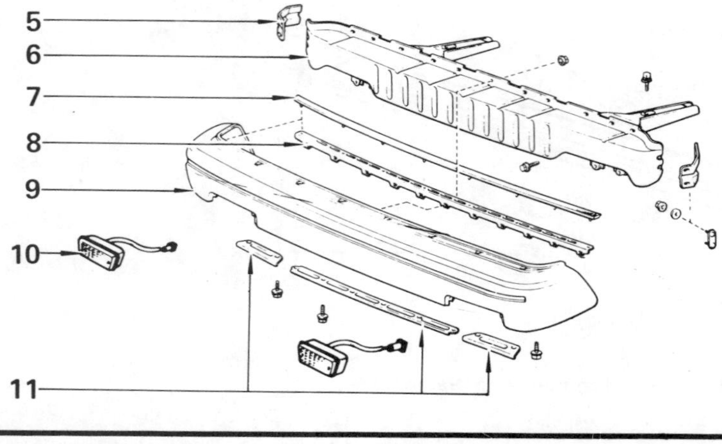

Fig. 12.39 Front bumper assembly components (Sec 25)

1 *Bumper stay*
2 *Bumper extension*
3 *Front turn signal light*
4 *Bumper bar*
5 *Bumper corner reinforcement*
6 *Reinforcement*
7 *Moulding*
8 *Moulding mounting plate*
9 *Bumper absorber*
10 *Front turn signal light*
11 *Bumper lower retainer*

then undo and remove the four bolts and washers securing the boot lid to the hinges.
3 Lift away the boot lid and recover the hinge spacers.
4 If necessary the torsion bar may be removed by detaching at one end to release the tension and then lifting away.
5 To remove the lock cylinder release the spring retainer with a pair of pliers, detach the pull rod and lift away the lock cylinder.
6 To remove the lock from the boot lid undo and remove the securing bolts and washers.
7 Reassembly and refitting of the boot lid, lock and hinges is the reverse sequence to removal.
8 The following adjustments may be required if the hinge to body bolts have been disturbed or new components fitted.
9 Adjustment of the boot lid in the aperture is effected by slackening the boot lid to hinge securing bolts and repositioning the boot lid in the aperture.
10 To lift or lower the hinge end of the boot lid fit or remove hinge spacers as necessary.
11 To adjust the lock slacken the lock striker securing bolts and move the striker as necessary. Tighten the securing bolts.

25 Bumpers – removal and refitting

1 Disconnect the battery earth lead.
2 Bumper removal is dependent on model and market but all types are mounted by means of support stay brackets to the main body. USA and Canada models have impact absorbing type bumper assemblies

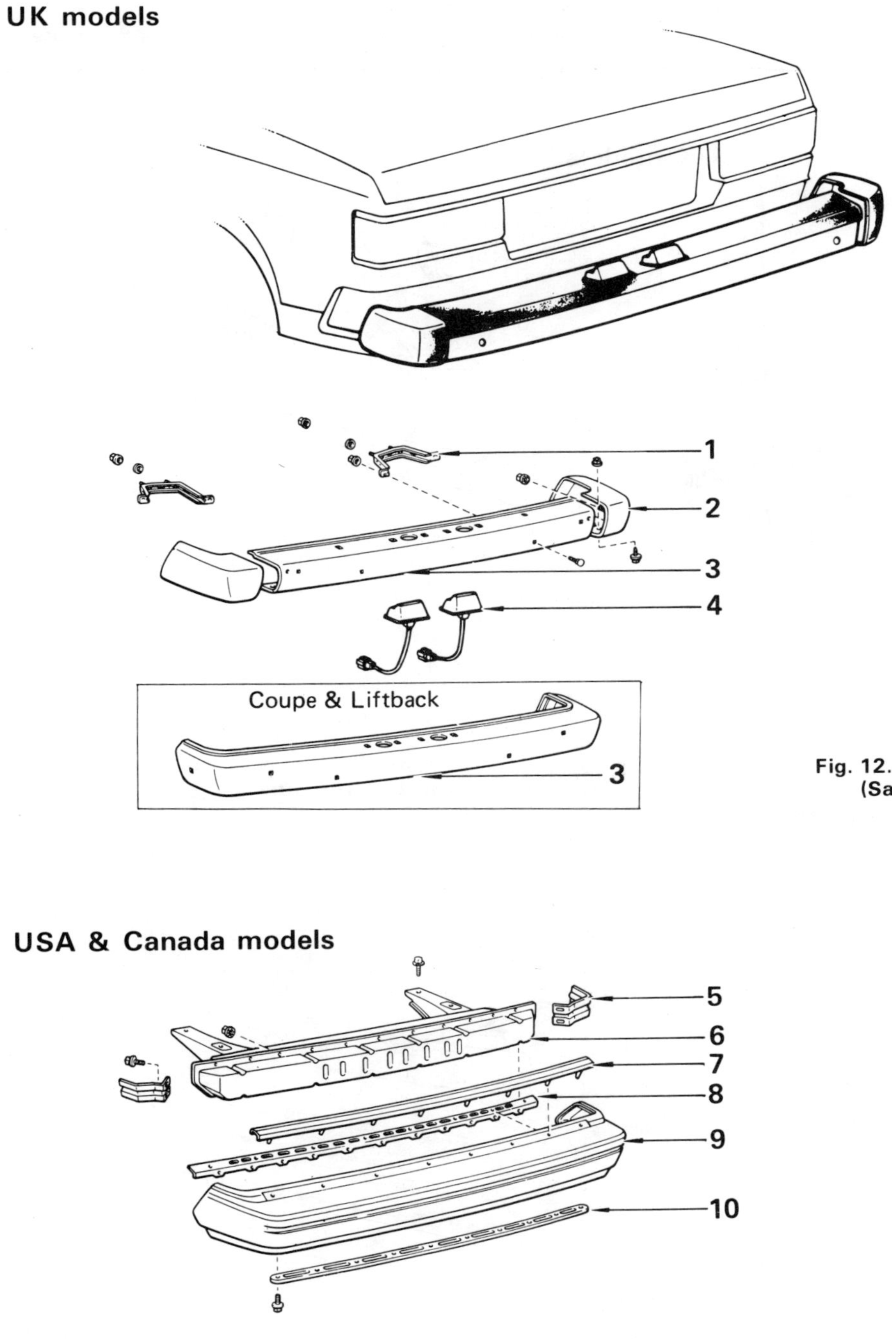

Fig. 12.40 Rear bumper assembly components (Saloon, Coupe and Liftback) (Sec 25)

1 Stay bracket
2 Extension
3 Bumper bar
4 Licence plate light
5 Corner reinforcement
6 Reinforcement
7 Moulding
8 Moulding mounting plate
9 Bumper absorber
10 Lower retainer

fitted to the front and rear.

3 Before unbolting the bumpers, detach the turn signal (indicator) light leads at the front or the license plate light leads at the rear on all models except the Estate (Wagon) variants.

4 The bumpers can be removed by unbolting them from the stay brackets or by unbolting the stay brackets from the bodyframe, and withdrawing the complete assembly.

5 If dismantling the impact absorbing type bumper assemblies the multi-component construction of the bumper unit should be noted.

6 Refitting is a reversal of the removal procedure. Check the bumper for alignment before fully tightening the retaining bolts.

7 On completion check the operation of the turn signal (front) and/or license plate lights (rear).

26 Front wing (fender) – removal and refitting

1 Disconnect the battery earth leads and remove the battery and its carrier.

2 Remove the windscreen wiper arm assemblies and then the cowl ventilator louvre located at the base of the windscreen.

3 Detach and remove the front bumper as described in the previous Section.

4 Detach and remove the rocker (sill) panel moulding.

5 From underneath the wing remove the liner and clips and disconnect the side marker light lead (where applicable).

6 Remove the retaining screws and withdraw the headlight surround panel, disconnecting the sidelight lead as it is removed.

7 Unbolt and remove the wing mirror.

8 Remove the antenna from the wing (as described in Chapter 10).

9 The respective wing panel retaining bolts can now be unscrewed and removed, and the wing panel withdrawn.

10 Refitting the front wing is a reversal of the removal process. Do not fully tighten the wing securing bolts until the wing panel has been correctly aligned with the adjacent body components. A new wing packing strip should be used if the old one has deteriorated or was damaged during the wing removal.

11 Check operation of all lights on completion of the reassembly.

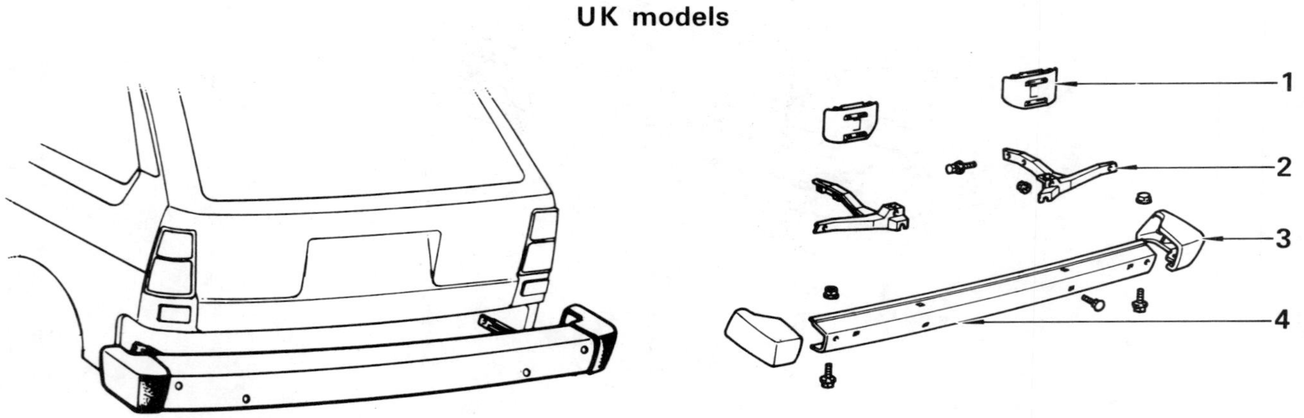

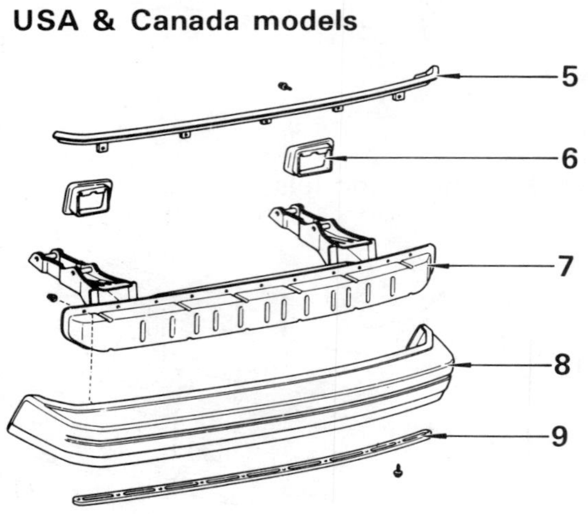

Fig. 12.41 Rear bumper assembly components (Estate) (Sec 25)

1 *Stay seal*
2 *Stay bracket*
3 *Extension*
4 *Bumper bar*
5 *Bumper filler*
6 *Stay seal*
7 *Reinforcement*
8 *Bumper absorber*
9 *Lower retainer*

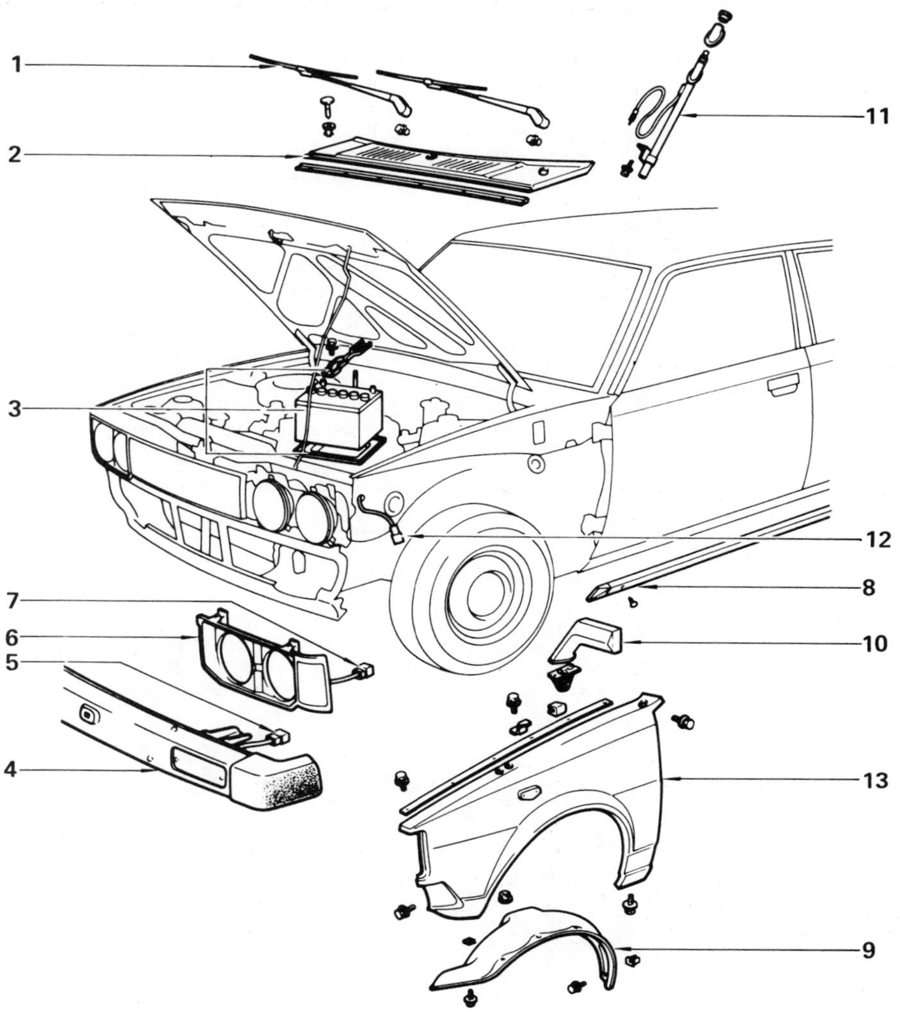

Fig. 12.42 Front wing panel and associated components (Sec 26)

1 Wiper arm
2 Cowl ventilator louver
3 Battery & battery carrier
4 Front bumper
5 Front turn signal light connector
6 Headlight door
7 Clearance light connector
8 Rocker panel moulding
9 Liner
10 Mirror
11 Antenna
12 Side turn signal light connector
13 Front wing

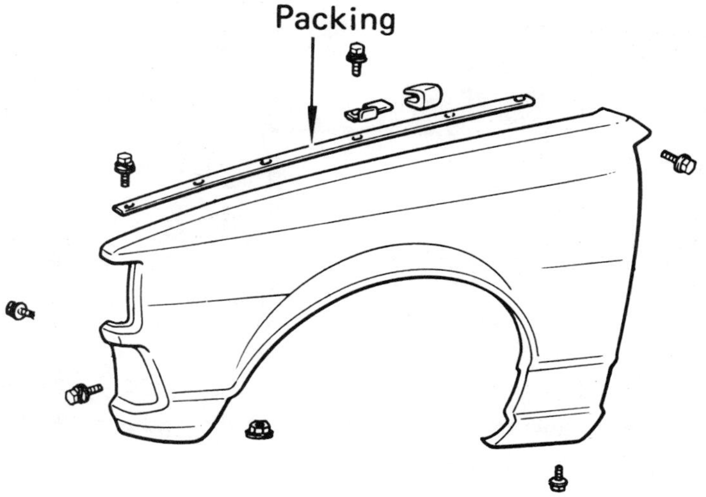

Fig. 12.43 Fit new packing strip and don't forget to locate the bonnet cushions when refitting the wing panel (Sec 26)

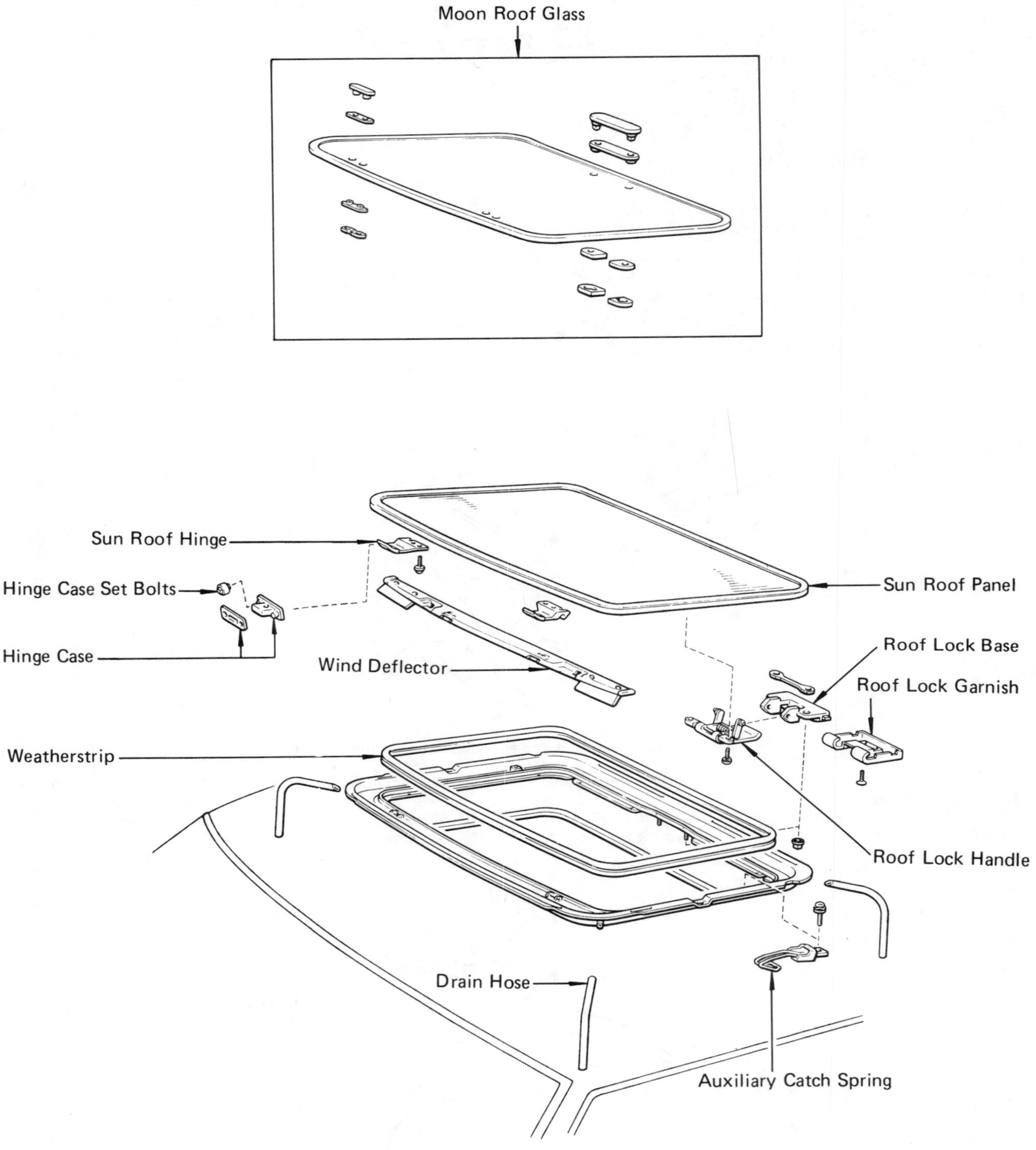

Fig. 12.44 Sunroof and moonroof and associated components (Sec 27)

Fig. 12.45 Detach panel clip from lifter link then lever up the deflector for removal (Sec 27)

27 Sunroof and moonroof components

1 The sunroof, moonroof and their associated components are shown in the figure. Apart from the panels the removal and refitting of their associated components is as follows.

Wind deflector

2 To remove the wind deflector first remove the roof panel. Then using a suitable screwdriver as a lever, detach the panel clip from the lifter link. The guide clip and deflector can then in turn be levered up and removed.
3 Refit in reverse order to removal, pressing the clip into the guide bracket.

Hinge case

4 Removal of the roof panel hinge case necessitates the detachment and removal of the roof headlining. This task should be entrusted to your Toyota dealer.
5 With the headlining removed, detach the wind deflector then unscrew and remove the hinge case retaining bolts and withdraw the case.
6 Refit in reverse getting your Toyota dealer to refit the headlining.

Sunroof headlining

7 This can be removed by lifting the panel out, then detaching the lock handle. The headlining is secured to the panel by press clips which can be prised free using a suitable flat lever or screwdriver, but take care not to damage the panel.
8 Refit in reverse order, pressing the headlining clips into position.

Conversion factors

Length (distance)

Inches (in)	X	25.4	= Millimetres (mm)	X	0.0394	= Inches (in)
Feet (ft)	X	0.305	= Metres (m)	X	3.281	= Feet (ft)
Miles	X	1.609	= Kilometres (km)	X	0.621	= Miles

Volume (capacity)

Cubic inches (cu in; in^3)	X	16.387	= Cubic centimetres (cc; cm^3)	X	0.061	= Cubic inches (cu in; in^3)
Imperial pints (Imp pt)	X	0.568	= Litres (l)	X	1.76	= Imperial pints (Imp pt)
Imperial quarts (Imp qt)	X	1.137	= Litres (l)	X	0.88	= Imperial quarts (Imp qt)
Imperial quarts (Imp qt)	X	1.201	= US quarts (US qt)	X	0.833	= Imperial quarts (Imp qt)
US quarts (US qt)	X	0.946	= Litres (l)	X	1.057	= US quarts (US qt)
Imperial gallons (Imp gal)	X	4.546	= Litres (l)	X	0.22	= Imperial gallons (Imp gal)
Imperial gallons (Imp gal)	X	1.201	= US gallons (US gal)	X	0.833	= Imperial gallons (Imp gal)
US gallons (US gal)	X	3.785	= Litres (l)	X	0.264	= US gallons (US gal)

Mass (weight)

Ounces (oz)	X	28.35	= Grams (g)	X	0.035	= Ounces (oz)
Pounds (lb)	X	0.454	= Kilograms (kg)	X	2.205	= Pounds (lb)

Force

Ounces-force (ozf; oz)	X	0.278	= Newtons (N)	X	3.6	= Ounces-force (ozf; oz)
Pounds-force (lbf; lb)	X	4.448	= Newtons (N)	X	0.225	= Pounds-force (lbf; lb)
Newtons (N)	X	0.1	= Kilograms-force (kgf; kg)	X	9.81	= Newtons (N)

Pressure

Pounds-force per square inch (psi; lbf/in^2; lb/in^2)	X	0.070	= Kilograms-force per square centimetre (kgf/cm^2; kg/cm^2)	X	14.223	= Pounds-force per square inch (psi; lbf/in^2; lb/in^2)
Pounds-force per square inch (psi; lbf/in^2; lb/in^2)	X	0.068	= Atmospheres (atm)	X	14.696	= Pounds-force per square inch (psi; lbf/in^2; lb/in^2)
Pounds-force per square inch (psi; lbf/in^2; lb/in^2)	X	0.069	= Bars	X	14.5	= Pounds-force per square inch (psi; lbf/in^2; lb/in^2)
Pounds-force per square inch (psi; lbf/in^2; lb/in^2)	X	6.895	= Kilopascals (kPa)	X	0.145	= Pounds-force per square inch (psi; lbf/in^2; lb/in^2)
Kilopascals (kPa)	X	0.01	= Kilograms-force per square centimetre (kgf/cm^2; kg/cm^2)	X	98.1	= Kilopascals (kPa)

Torque (moment of force)

Pounds-force inches (lbf in; lb in)	X	1.152	= Kilograms-force centimetre (kgf cm; kg cm)	X	0.868	= Pounds-force inches (lbf in; lb in)
Pounds-force inches (lbf in; lb in)	X	0.113	= Newton metres (Nm)	X	8.85	= Pounds-force inches (lbf in; lb in)
Pounds-force inches (lbf in; lb in)	X	0.083	= Pounds-force feet (lbf ft; lb ft)	X	12	= Pounds-force inches (lbf in; lb in)
Pounds-force feet (lbf ft; lb ft)	X	0.138	= Kilograms-force metres (kgf m; kg m)	X	7.233	= Pounds-force feet (lbf ft; lb ft)
Pounds-force feet (lbf ft; lb ft)	X	1.356	= Newton metres (Nm)	X	0.738	= Pounds-force feet (lbf ft; lb ft)
Newton metres (Nm)	X	0.102	= Kilograms-force metres (kgf m; kg m)	X	9.804	= Newton metres (Nm)

Power

Horsepower (hp)	X	745.7	= Watts (W)	X	0.0013	= Horsepower (hp)

Velocity (speed)

Miles per hour (miles/hr; mph)	X	1.609	= Kilometres per hour (km/hr; kph)	X	0.621	= Miles per hour (miles/hr; mph)

*Fuel consumption**

Miles per gallon, Imperial (mpg)	X	0.354	= Kilometres per litre (km/l)	X	2.825	= Miles per gallon, Imperial (mpg)
Miles per gallon, US (mpg)	X	0.425	= Kilometres per litre (km/l)	X	2.352	= Miles per gallon, US (mpg)

Temperature

Degrees Fahrenheit = (°C x 1.8) + 32

Degrees Celsius (Degrees Centigrade; °C) = (°F - 32) x 0.56

**It is common practice to convert from miles per gallon (mpg) to litres/100 kilometres (l/100km), where mpg (Imperial) x l/100 km = 282 and mpg (US) x l/100 km = 235*

General repair procedures

Whenever servicing, repair or overhaul work is carried out on the car or its components, it is necessary to observe the following procedures and instructions. This will assist in carrying out the operation efficiently and to a professional standard of workmanship.

Joint mating faces and gaskets

Where a gasket is used between the mating faces of two components, ensure that it is renewed on reassembly, and fit it dry unless otherwise stated in the repair procedure. Make sure that the mating faces are clean and dry with all traces of old gasket removed. When cleaning a joint face, use a tool which is not likely to score or damage the face, and remove any burrs or nicks with an oilstone or fine file.

Make sure that tapped holes are cleaned with a pipe cleaner, and keep them free of jointing compound if this is being used unless specifically instructed otherwise.

Ensure that all orifices, channels or pipes are clear and blow through them, preferably using compressed air.

Oil seals

Whenever an oil seal is removed from its working location, either individually or as part of an assembly, it should be renewed.

The very fine sealing lip of the seal is easily damaged and will not seal if the surface it contacts is not completely clean and free from scratches, nicks or grooves. If the original sealing surface of the component cannot be restored, the component should be renewed.

Protect the lips of the seal from any surface which may damage them in the course of fitting. Use tape or a conical sleeve where possible. Lubricate the seal lips with oil before fitting and, on dual lipped seals, fill the space between the lips with grease.

Unless otherwise stated, oil seals must be fitted with their sealing lips toward the lubricant to be sealed.

Use a tubular drift or block of wood of the appropriate size to install the seal and, if the seal housing is shouldered, drive the seal down to the shoulder. If the seal housing is unshouldered, the seal should be fitted with its face flush with the housing top face.

Screw threads and fastenings

Always ensure that a blind tapped hole is completely free from oil, grease, water or other fluid before installing the bolt or stud. Failure to do this could cause the housing to crack due to the hydraulic action of the bolt or stud as it is screwed in.

When tightening a castellated nut to accept a split pin, tighten the nut to the specified torque, where applicable, and then tighten further to the next split pin hole. Never slacken the nut to align a split pin hole unless stated in the repair procedure.

When checking or retightening a nut or bolt to a specified torque setting, slacken the nut or bolt by a quarter of a turn, and then retighten to the specified setting.

Locknuts, locktabs and washers

Any fastening which will rotate against a component or housing in the course of tightening should always have a washer between it and the relevant component or housing.

Spring or split washers should always be renewed when they are used to lock a critical component such as a big-end bearing retaining nut or bolt.

Locktabs which are folded over to retain a nut or bolt should always be renewed.

Self-locking nuts can be reused in non-critical areas, providing resistance can be felt when the locking portion passes over the bolt or stud thread.

Split pins must always be replaced with new ones of the correct size for the hole.

Special tools

Some repair procedures in this manual entail the use of special tools such as a press, two or three-legged pullers, spring compressors etc. Wherever possible, suitable readily available alternatives to the manufacturer's special tools are described, and are shown in use. In some instances, where no alternative is possible, it has been necessary to resort to the use of a manufacturer's tool and this has been done for reasons of safety as well as the efficient completion of the repair operation. Unless you are highly skilled and have a thorough understanding of the procedure described, never attempt to bypass the use of any special tool when the procedure described specifies its use. Not only is there a very great risk of personal injury, but expensive damage could be caused to the components involved.

Index

Printed by
J H Haynes & Co Ltd
Sparkford Nr Yeovil
Somerset BA22 7JJ England